Battle Cry of Freedom

"McPherson handles all . . . with a beautifully organized, compelling narrative and prose whose occasional leap into modern ebullience SHOULD CAPTIVATE A NEW GENERATION OF CIVIL WAR READERS." *Chicago Tribune*

"THIS IS AN EPIC STORY TOLD IN EPIC STYLE, written in clear, luminous prose. . . . a zesty, meaty intellectual feast that will nourish and satisfy the reader." *The Houston Post*

"Exhaustively researched, written with skill and assurance. . . . THIS BOOK MAY NOT BE SUPERSEDED IN OUR TIME." *Newsday*

"ONE OF THE BEST BOOKS ON [THE] SUBJECT. . . . McPherson combines fine scholarship with a clear writing style and a sense for dramatic narrative." *The Grand Rapids Press*

"BREATHES NEW LIFE INTO WHAT IT ALL MEANS. . . . McPherson weaves together a story that makes the legends and the ideologies seem like fresh material, worthy of fresh thinking." *Richmond Times-Dispatch*

Other books by James M. McPherson

The Struggle for Equality: Abolitionists and the Negro in the Civil War and Reconstruction

The Negro's Civil War

Marching Toward Freedom: The Negro in the Civil War

Blacks in America: Bibliographical Essays (with others)

The Abolitionist Legacy: From Reconstruction to the NAACP

Region, Race, and Reconstruction: Essays in Honor of C. Vann Woodward (coeditor)

Ordeal by Fire: The Civil War and Reconstruction

BATTLE CRY OF FREEDOM

The Civil War Era

JAMES M. McPHERSON

OXFORD
UNIVERSITY PRESS

OXFORD
UNIVERSITY PRESS

Oxford   New York
Auckland   Bangkok   Buenos Aires
Cape Town   Chennai   Dar es Salaam   Delhi   Hong Kong   Istanbul
Karachi   Kolkata   Kuala Lumpur   Madrid   Melbourne   Mexico City   Mumbai
Nairobi   São Paulo   Shanghai   Taipei   Tokyo   Toronto

Copyright © 1988 by Oxford University Press

First published by Oxford University Press, Inc., 1988
First issued as an Oxford University Press paperback, 2003
198 Madison Avenue, New York, New York 10016

www.oup.com

Oxford is a registered trademark of Oxford University Press

Library of Congress Cataloging-in-Publication Data
McPherson, James M.
Battle cry freedom.
(The Oxford history of the United States; v. 6)
Bibliography: p. Includes index
ISBN-13:   / 978-0-19-516895-2 pbk
ISBN-10: 0-19-503863-0 / 0-19-516895-X (pbk)
1. United States—History—Civil War, 1861–1865—Campaigns.
2. United States—History—Civil War, 1861–1865.
I. Title.
II. Series.
E173.094 vol. 6 [E470]
973.7'3 87-11045

7 9 8 6
Printed in the United States of America

BATTLE CRY OF FREEDOM

The original words and music of this sprightly song were written in the summer of 1862 by George F. Root, one of the North's leading Civil War composers. So catchy was the tune that southern composer H. L. Schreiner and lyricist W. H. Barnes adapted it for the Confederacy. The different versions became popular on both sides of the Mason-Dixon line. Reproduced here are Verse 3 and the Chorus of each version.

Preface

Both sides in the American Civil War professed to be fighting for freedom. The South, said Jefferson Davis in 1863, was "forced to take up arms to vindicate the political rights, the freedom, equality, and State sovereignty which were the heritage purchased by the blood of our revolutionary sires." But if the Confederacy succeeded in this endeavor, insisted Abraham Lincoln, it would destroy the Union "conceived in Liberty" by those revolutionary sires as "the last, best hope" for the preservation of republican freedoms in the world. "We must settle this question now," said Lincoln in 1861, "whether in a free government the minority have the right to break up the government whenever they choose."

Northern publicists ridiculed the Confederacy's claim to fight for freedom. "Their motto," declared poet and editor William Cullen Bryant, "is not liberty, but slavery." But the North did not at first fight to free the slaves. "I have no purpose, directly or indirectly, to interfere with slavery in the States where it exists," said Lincoln early in the conflict. The Union Congress overwhelmingly endorsed this position in July 1861. Within a year, however, both Lincoln and Congress decided to make emancipation of slaves in Confederate states a Union war policy. By the time of the Gettysburg Address, in November 1863, the North was fighting for a "new birth of freedom" to transform the Constitution written by the founding fathers, under which the United States had become the world's largest slaveholding country, into a charter of emancipation for a republic where, as the northern version of "The Battle Cry of Freedom" put it, "Not a man shall be a slave."

The multiple meanings of slavery and freedom, and how they dissolved and re-formed into new patterns in the crucible of war, constitute a central theme of this book. That same crucible fused the several states bound loosely in a federal *Union* under a weak central government into a new *Nation* forged by the fires of a war in which more Americans lost their lives than in all of the country's other wars combined.

Americans of the Civil War generation lived through an experience in which time and consciousness took on new dimensions. "These are fearfully critical, anxious days, in which the destinies of the continent for centuries will be decided," wrote one contemporary in a sentence typical of countless others that occur in Civil War diaries and letters. "The excitement of the war, & interest in its incidents, have absorbed everything else. We think and talk of nothing else," wrote Virginia's fire-eater Edmund Ruffin in August 1861, a remark echoed three days later by the Yankee sage Ralph Waldo Emerson: "The war . . . has assumed such huge proportions that it threatens to engulf us all—no preoccupation can exclude it, & no hermitage hide us." The conflict "crowded into a few years the emotions of a lifetime," wrote a northern civilian in 1865. After Gettysburg, General George Meade told his wife that during the past ten days "I have lived as much as in the last thirty years." From faraway London, where he served his father as a private secretary at the American legation, young Henry Adams wondered "whether any of us will ever be able to live contented in times of peace and laziness. Our generation has been stirred up from its lowest layers and there is that in its history which will stamp every member of it until we are all in our graves. We cannot be commonplace. . . . One does every day and without a second thought, what at another time would be the event of a year, perhaps of a life." In 1882 Samuel Clemens found that the Civil War remained at the center of southern consciousness: it was "what A.D. is elsewhere; they date from it." This was scarcely surprising, wrote Twain, for the war had "uprooted institutions that were centuries old . . . transformed the social life of half the country, and wrought so profoundly upon the entire national character that the influence cannot be measured short of two or three generations."

Five generations have passed, and that war is still with us. Hundreds of Civil War Round Tables and Lincoln Associations flourish today. Every year thousands of Americans dress up in blue or gray uniforms

and take up their replica Springfield muskets to re-enact Civil War battles. A half-dozen popular and professional history magazines continue
to chronicle every conceivable aspect of the war. Hundreds of books
about the conflict pour off the presses every year, adding to the more
than 50,000 titles on the subject that make the Civil War by a large
margin the most written-about event in American history. Some of these
books—especially multi-volume series on the Civil War era—have
achieved the status of classics: James Ford Rhodes's seven-volume *History of the United States* from the Compromise of 1850 to the Compromise of 1877; Allan Nevins's four-volume *Ordeal of the Union* from
1847 to 1861, and four more on *The War for the Union*; David M.
Potter's 600-page study *The Impending Crisis 1848–1861*; Bruce Catton's three volumes on the Army of the Potomac (*Mr. Lincoln's Army;
Glory Road*; and *A Stillness at Appomattox*), his three additional volumes, *The Centennial History of the Civil War*, plus two volumes on
Ulysses S. Grant's Civil War career; Douglas Southall Freeman's magnificent four-volume biography *R.E. Lee* and his additional three-vol-
ume *Lee's Lieutenants*; and Shelby Foote's *The Civil War*, three en-
grossing volumes totaling nearly three thousand pages.

Alongside these monumental studies the present effort to compress
the war and its causes into a single volume seems modest indeed.
Nevertheless, I have tried to integrate the political and military events
of this era with important social and economic developments to form a
seamless web synthesizing up-to-date scholarship with my own research
and interpretations. Except for Chapter 1, which traces the contours of
American society and economy in the middle decades of the nineteenth
century, I have chosen a narrative framework to tell my story and point
its moral. This choice proceeds not only from the overall design of the
Oxford History but also from my own convictions about how best to
write the history of these years of successive crises, rapid changes, dramatic events, and dynamic transformations. A topical or thematic approach could not do justice to this dynamism, this complex relationship
of cause and effect, this intensity of experience, especially during the
four years of war when developments in several spheres occurred almost
simultaneously and impinged on each other so powerfully and immediately as to give participants the sense of living a lifetime in a year.

As an example: the simultaneous Confederate invasions of Maryland
and Kentucky in the late summer of 1862 occurred in the context of
intense diplomatic activity leading toward possible European intervention in the war, of Lincoln's decision to issue an emancipation procla-

mation, of anti-black and anti-draft riots and martial law in the North, and of hopes by Peace Democrats to capture control of the Union Congress in the fall elections. Each of these events directly affected the others; none can be understood apart from the whole. A topical or thematic approach that treated military events, diplomacy, slavery and emancipation, anti-war dissent and civil liberties, and northern politics in separate chapters, instead of weaving them together as I have attempted to do here, would leave the reader uninformed about how and why the battle of Antietam was so crucial to the outcome of all these other developments.

The importance of Antietam and of several other battles in deciding "the destinies of the continent for centuries" also justifies the space given to military campaigns in this book. Most of the things that we consider important in this era of American history—the fate of slavery, the structure of society in both North and South, the direction of the American economy, the destiny of competing nationalisms in North and South, the definition of freedom, the very survival of the United States—rested on the shoulders of those weary men in blue and gray who fought it out during four years of ferocity unmatched in the Western world between the Napoleonic Wars and World War I.

The most pleasant task in writing a book is the expression of gratitude to people and institutions that have helped the author. The resources of the Firestone Library at Princeton University and of the Henry E. Huntington Library in San Marino, California, provided most of the research material on which this book is based. A year at the Center for Advanced Study in the Behavioral Sciences at Stanford, where part of this book was written, supplemented an earlier sabbatical year at the Huntington to give me the time and opportunity for reading, research, and writing about the Civil War era. These two rich and rewarding years in California were financed in part by Princeton University, in part by fellowships funded by the National Endowment for the Humanities, and in part by the Huntington Library and the Behavioral Sciences Center. To all of them I am especially indebted for the support that made the writing of *Battle Cry of Freedom* possible. To Gardner Lindzey, Margaret Amara, and the staff of the Behavioral Sciences Center who helped me gain access to the riches of the Stanford and Berkeley libraries I also express my appreciation. The staff of the Manuscripts Collection of the Library of Congress, and Richard Sommers as Archivist-Historian at the U.S. Army Military History Institute at Carlisle, Pennsylvania, extended me every courtesy and assistance during research visits to these superb repositories. I also thank the staffs of the photographs and prints divisions at the libraries where I obtained photographs for the illustrations in this book. To Armstead Robinson I express belated thanks for permission to quote material from the manuscript of his forthcoming book *Bitter Fruits of Bondage*.

George Fredrickson read an early draft of this book and offered valuable suggestions for improvement, as did my colleague Allan Kulikoff who kindly read Chapters 1 and 20. Sheldon Meyer, Senior Vice President of Oxford University Press, has been in on the project from the beginning and has shepherded it through to conclusion with an expert helping hand. Managing Editor Leona Capeless at Oxford refined the manuscript with her careful editing and cheerful encouragement. To Vann Woodward I owe more than I can express. Teacher, friend, scholar, editor, he has guided my growth as an historian for nearly thirty years, offered the highest example of craftmanship, and done more than anyone else to bring this book to fruition. To Willie Lee Rose also I owe much as a friend and fellow graduate student at Johns Hopkins who did more than anyone else except Vann to introduce me to the mysteries of the guild.

Without the love and companionship of my wife Patricia this volume could never have come into existence. Not only did she help with some of the research and read early drafts with a sharp eye for confused or overblown rhetoric; she also joined me in the tiresome but essential task of correcting proofs, and suggested the title. Finally to Jenny, and to Dahlia and her friends, I express warm appreciation for helping me understand the potential as well as problems of Civil War cavalry.

Princeton   J. M. M.
June 1987

Contents

Illustrations appear following pages 332 and 684

Maps

MAPS

Editor's Introduction

No period of American history makes greater demands on the historian than that of the Civil War. To meet this extraordinary challenge all the classic accounts have resorted to multivolume solutions. The one by Allan Nevins, for example, required eight large volumes, and another has used that many without attempting to be comprehensive. One of the remarkable aspects of the present achievement is that the author has been able to cover the period so completely and admirably within the covers of one volume. It is a large volume, to be sure, and will probably be the longest of the ten in *The Oxford History of the United States*. That it should, despite its size, cover the shortest period assigned calls for some comment on the part of the editor.

First, a look at the disparity between the length of the book and the brevity of the period. Precious little correlation exists between the importance, complexity, and abundance of historical events and the length of the time it takes for them to occur. Some history of momentous consequence requires centuries to unfold, while history of comparable importance can take place with staggering speed. Here we are clearly dealing with history of the latter type. In his Preface to this volume, James McPherson has spoken of the Civil War generation as having "lived through an experience in which time and consciousness took on new dimensions." These new dimensions have to be reckoned with by the historians recording the experience. If participants in that era had the experience of "living a lifetime in a year," historians can reasonably demand more pages and chapters to do justice to such years. That also helps to explain why far more has been written about these particular years than any others in American history. The more written, the more disclosed, and the more questions and controversies to be coped with by latter-day historians.

Given the latitude granted in the matter of pages, is it not reasonable to expect a more complete treatment of all aspects and themes of the period? Normally so, yes. But again, this is hardly a normal period. What normality can be claimed for it consists largely of the continuation of familiar themes of American history: westward expansion and settlement, Indian removal and resistance, economic growth and development, the tides of European immigration, the back-and-forth of diplomatic exchange. None of these classic themes are missing from the Civil War period, and all get some attention in these pages, but they are necessarily subordinated to the dominant theme or integrated with it. It is hard to imagine a historian in his right mind pausing between the roar of Gettysburg and the fall of Vicksburg for a topical chapter on internal improvements or the westward movement. Like other historians engaged in writing the *Oxford History*, McPherson has made agreements with the authors of the previous and following volumes regarding responsibility for full treatment of overlapping themes.

Of the ten periods covered in this series there is not one when Americans were not involved in some war or other. Two of them are called world wars—three counting one in the eighteenth century. What then is to be said to justify the exceptional attention and space allotted to this particular war? There are numerous criteria at hand for rating the comparative magnitude of wars. Among them are the numbers of troops or ships committed, the years the conflict lasted, the amount of treasure spent, the numbers of objectives gained or lost, and so on. One simple and eloquent measurement is the numbers of casualties sustained. After describing the scene at nightfall on September 17, 1862, following the battle called Antietam in the North and Sharpsburg in the South, McPherson writes:

> The casualties at Antietam numbered four times the total suffered by American soldiers at the Normandy beaches on June 6, 1944. More than twice as many Americans lost their lives in one day at Sharpsburg as fell in combat in the War of 1812, the Mexican War, and the Spanish-American War *combined*.

And in the final reckoning, American lives lost in the Civil War exceed the total of those lost in all the other wars the country has fought added together, world wars included. Questions raised about the proportion of space devoted to military events of this period might be considered in the light of these facts.

C. Vann Woodward

Battle Cry of Freedom

Prologue
From the Halls of Montezuma

On the morning of September 14, 1847, brilliant sunshine burned off the haze in Mexico City. A mild breeze sprang up to blow away the smell of gunpowder lingering from the bloody battle of Chapultepec. Unshaven, mud-stained soldiers of the United States army in threadbare uniforms marched into the Plaza de Armas, formed a ragged line, and stood at weary attention as a shot-torn American flag rose over the ancient capital of the Aztecs. Civilians looked on in disappointed wonder. Were these tattered gringoes the men who had vanquished the splendid hosts of Santa Anna?

Martial music suddenly blared from a street entering the plaza. Jaunty dragoons with drawn sabers cantered into the square escorting a magnificent bay charger ridden by a tall general resplendent in full-dress uniform with gold epaulets and white-plumed chapeau. The Mexicans broke into involuntary applause. If they must endure the humiliation of conquest, they preferred their conquerors to look the part. As the band played *Yankee Doodle* and *Hail to the Chief*, General Winfield Scott dismounted and accepted formal surrender of the city. Cross-belted U.S. marines soon patrolled the Halls of Montezuma while at nearby Guadalupe Hidalgo the American envoy Nicholas Trist negotiated a treaty that enlarged the territory of the United States by nearly one-quarter and reduced that of Mexico by half. During the sixteen previous months, American forces under Generals Scott and Zachary Taylor had won ten major battles, most of them against larger Mexican armies defending

3

fortified positions. The Duke of Wellington had pronounced Scott's campaign against Mexico City the most brilliant in modern warfare.

But ironies and squabbles marred the triumphs. The war had been started by a Democratic president in the interest of territorial expansion and opposed by Whigs whose antiwar position helped them wrest control of the House in the congressional elections of 1846. Yet the two commanding generals in this victorious war were Whigs. Democratic President James K. Polk relieved Whig General Scott of command after Scott had ordered the court-martial of two Democratic generals who had inspired newspaper articles claiming credit for American victories. The president recalled his own envoy for appearing to be too soft toward the Mexicans; Trist ignored the recall and negotiated a treaty which obtained all of Mexico that Polk had hoped for originally but less than he now wanted. Polk nevertheless sent the treaty to the Senate, where a combination of Whigs who wanted no Mexican territory and Democrats who wanted more came within four votes of defeating it. The antiwar party nominated war hero Zachary Taylor for president in 1848 and won; the same party nominated war hero Winfield Scott for president four years later and lost. Congressmen from northern states tried to enact a proviso banning slavery from the territories acquired by a war in which two-thirds of the volunteer soldiers had come from slave states. General Taylor was a slaveholder but opposed the expansion of slavery when he became president. The discord generated by the Mexican War erupted fifteen years later in a far larger conflict whose foremost hero was elected president two decades after he, as Lieutenant Sam Grant, had helped win the decisive battle of Chapultepec in a war that he considered "one of the most unjust ever waged by a stronger against a weaker nation."[1]

The bickering Americans won the Mexican War because their adversaries were even more riven by faction. They won also because of the marksmanship and élan of their mixed divisions of regulars and volunteers and above all because of the professionalism and courage of their junior officers. Yet the competence of these men foreshadowed the ultimate irony of the Mexican War, for many of the best of them would fight against each other in the next war. Serving together on Scott's staff were two bright lieutenants, Pierre G. T. Beauregard and George B. McClellan. Captain Robert E. Lee's daring reconnaissances behind Mexican lines prepared the way for two crucial American victories. In

1. *Personal Memoirs of U. S. Grant*, 2 vols. (New York, 1885), I, 53.

one of his reports Captain Lee commended Lieutenant Grant. The latter received official thanks for his role in the attack on Mexico City; these thanks were conveyed to him by Lieutenant John Pemberton, who sixteen years later would surrender to Grant at Vicksburg. Lieutenants James Longstreet and Winfield Scott Hancock fought side by side in the battle of Churubusco; sixteen years later Longstreet commanded the attack against Hancock's corps at Cemetery Ridge, an attack led by George Pickett, who doubtless recalled the day that he picked up the colors of the 8th Infantry in its assault on Chapultepec when Lieutenant Longstreet fell wounded while carrying these colors. Albert Sidney Johnston and Joseph Hooker fought together at Monterrey; Colonel Jefferson Davis's Mississippi volunteers broke a Mexican charge at Buena Vista while artillery officers George H. Thomas and Braxton Bragg fought alongside each other in this battle with the same spirit they would fight against each other as army commanders at a ridge a thousand miles away in Tennessee. Lee, Joseph E. Johnston, and George Gordon Meade served as Scott's engineer officers at the siege of Vera Cruz, while offshore in the American fleet Lieutenant Raphael Semmes shared a cabin with Lieutenant John Winslow, whose U.S.S. *Kearsarge* would sink Semmes's C.S.S. *Alabama* seventeen years later and five thousand miles away.

The Mexican War fulfilled for the United States its self-proclaimed manifest destiny to bestride the continent from sea to shining sea. But by midcentury the growing pains of this adolescent republic threatened to tear the country apart before it reached maturity.

1

The United States at Midcentury

I

The hallmark of the United States has been growth. Americans have typically defined this process in quantitative terms. Never was that more true than in the first half of the nineteenth century, when an unparalleled rate of growth took place in three dimensions: population, territory, and economy. In 1850, Zachary Taylor—the last president born before the Constitution—could look back on vast changes during his adult life. The population of the United States had doubled and then doubled again. Pushing relentlessly westward and southward, Americans had similarly quadrupled the size of their country by settling, conquering, annexing, or purchasing territory that had been occupied for millennia by Indians and claimed by France, Spain, Britain, and Mexico. During the same half-century the gross national product increased sevenfold. No other nation in that era could match even a single component of this explosive growth. The combination of all three made America the *Wunderkind* nation of the nineteenth century.

Regarded as "progress" by most Americans, this unrestrained growth had negative as well as positive consequences. For Indians it was a story of contraction rather than expansion, of decline from a vital culture toward dependence and apathy. The one-seventh of the population that was black also bore much of the burden of progress while reaping few of its benefits. Slave-grown crops sustained part of the era's economic growth and much of its territorial expansion. The cascade of cotton

6

from the American South dominated the world market, paced the industrial revolution in England and New England, and fastened the shackles of slavery more securely than ever on Afro-Americans.

Even for white Americans, economic growth did not necessarily mean unalloyed progress. Although per capita income doubled during the half-century, not all sectors of society shared equally in this abundance. While both rich and poor enjoyed rising incomes, their inequality of wealth widened significantly. As the population began to move from farm to city, farmers increasingly specialized in the production of crops for the market rather than for home consumption. The manufacture of cloth, clothing, leather goods, tools, and other products shifted from home to shop and from shop to factory. In the process many women experienced a change in roles from producers to consumers with a consequent transition in status. Some craftsmen suffered debasement of their skills as the division of labor and power-driven machinery eroded the traditional handicraft methods of production and transformed them from self-employed artisans to wage laborers. The resulting potential for class conflict threatened the social fabric of this brave new republic.

More dangerous was the specter of ethnic conflict. Except for a sprinkling of German farmers in Pennsylvania and in the valleys of the Appalachian piedmont, the American white population before 1830 was overwhelmingly British and Protestant in heritage. Cheap, abundant land and the need for labor in a growing economy, coupled with the pressure of population against limited resources in northern Europe, impelled first a trickle and then a flood of German and Irish immigrants to the United States in the generation after 1830. Most of these new Americans worshipped in Roman Catholic churches. Their growing presence filled some Protestant Americans with alarm. Numerous nativist organizations sprang up as the first line of resistance in what became a long and painful retreat toward acceptance of cultural pluralism.

The greatest danger to American survival at midcentury, however, was neither class tension nor ethnic division. Rather it was sectional conflict between North and South over the future of slavery. To many Americans, human bondage seemed incompatible with the founding ideals of the republic. If all men were created equal and endowed by the creator with certain inalienable rights including liberty and the pursuit of happiness, what could justify the enslavement of several millions of these men (and women)? The generation that fought the Revolution abolished slavery in states north of the Mason-Dixon line; the new states north of the Ohio River came into the Union without bondage. South of those boundaries, however, slavery became essential to the region's economy and culture.

Meanwhile, a wave of Protestant revivals known as the Second Great Awakening swept the country during the first third of the nineteenth century. In New England, upstate New York, and those portions of the Old Northwest above the 41st parallel populated by the descendants of New England Yankees, this evangelical enthusiasm generated a host of moral and cultural reforms. The most dynamic and divisive of them was abolitionism. Heirs of the Puritan notion of collective accountability that made every man his brother's keeper, these Yankee reformers repudiated Calvinist predestination, preached the availability of redemption to anyone who truly sought it, urged converts to abjure sin, and worked for the elimination of sins from society. The most heinous social sin was slavery. All people were equal in God's sight; the souls of black folks were as valuable as those of whites; for one of God's children to enslave another was a violation of the Higher Law, even if it was sanctioned by the Constitution.

By midcentury this antislavery movement had gone into politics and had begun to polarize the country. Slaveholders did not consider themselves egregious sinners. And they managed to convince most non-slaveholding whites in the South (two-thirds of the white population there) that emancipation would produce economic ruin, social chaos, and racial war. Slavery was not the evil that Yankee fanatics portrayed; it was a positive good, the basis of prosperity, peace, and white supremacy, a necessity to prevent blacks from degenerating into barbarism, crime, and poverty.

The slavery issue would probably have caused an eventual showdown between North and South in any circumstances. But it was the country's sprawling growth that made the issue so explosive. Was the manifest destiny of those two million square miles west of the Mississippi River to be free or slave? Like King Solomon, Congress had tried in 1820 to solve that problem for the Louisiana Purchase by splitting it at the latitude of 36° 30′ (with slavery allowed in Missouri as an exception north of that line). But this only postponed the crisis. In 1850 Congress postponed it again with another compromise. By 1860 it could no longer be deferred. The country's territorial growth might have created a danger of dismemberment by centrifugal force in any event. But slavery brought this danger to a head at midcentury.

II

At the time of the Louisiana Purchase in 1803 the United States was an insignificant nation on the European periphery. Its population was about the same as Ireland's. Thomas Jefferson thought that the empire for liberty he had bought from Napoleon was sufficient to absorb a hundred generations of America's population growth. By 1850, two generations later, Americans were not only filling up this empire but were spilling over into a new one on the Pacific coast. A few years after 1850 the United States surpassed Britain to become the most populous nation in the Western world save Russia and France. By 1860 the country contained nearly thirty-two million people, four million of them slaves. During the previous half-century the American population had grown four times faster than Europe's and six times the world average.[1]

Three factors explained this phenomenon: a birth rate half again as high as Europe's; a death rate slightly lower; and immigration. All three were linked to the relative abundance of the American economy. The ratio of land to people was much greater than in Europe, making food supply more plentiful and enabling couples to marry earlier and to have more children. Though epidemics frequently ravaged North America, they took a lesser toll in its largely rural environment than among Europe's denser population. The land/people ratio in the United States raised wages and offered opportunities that attracted five million immigrants during that half-century.

Although the United States remained predominantly rural in this period, the urban population (defined as those living in towns or cities with 2,500 or more people) grew three times faster than the rural population from 1810 to 1860, going from 6 percent to 20 percent of the total. This was the highest *rate* of urbanization in American history. During those same decades the percentage of the labor force engaged in non-agricultural pursuits grew from 21 to 45 percent.[2] Meanwhile the rate of natural increase of the American population, while remaining higher than Europe's, began to slow as parents, desiring to provide their children with more nurture and education, decided to have fewer of them. From 1800 to 1850 the American birth rate declined by 23 per-

1. Peter D. McClelland and Richard J. Zeckhauser, *Demographic Dimensions of the New Republic* (Cambridge, Mass., 1982), 87.
2. Stanley Lebergott, "Labor Force and Employment, 1800–1960," in Dorothy Brady, ed., *Output, Employment and Productivity in the U.S. after 1800*, Studies in Income and Wealth (Princeton, 1966), 119.

cent. The death rate also declined slightly—but probably no more than 5 percent.[3] Yet the population continued to grow at the same pace through the whole period—about 35 percent each decade—because rising immigration offset the decline of the birth rate. For the half-century as a whole, the margin of births over deaths caused three-quarters of the population increase while immigration accounted for the rest.[4]

Economic growth fueled these demographic changes. The population doubled every twenty-three years; the gross national product doubled every fifteen. Economic historians do not agree when this "intensive" rate of growth began, for the data to measure it are fragmentary before 1840. What remains clear is that until the early nineteenth century economic growth was "extensive"—virtually the same as population growth. At some point after the War of 1812—probably following recovery from the depression of 1819–23—the economy began to grow faster than the population, producing an estimated *per capita* increase of national output and income averaging 1.7 percent annually from 1820 to 1860.[5] The fastest rates of growth occurred in the 1830s and 1850s, interrupted by a major depression from 1837 to 1843 and a lesser one in 1857–58.

Although most Americans benefited from this rise of income, those at the top benefited more than those at the bottom. While average income rose 102 percent, real wages for workers increased by somewhere between 40 and 65 percent.[6] This widening disparity between rich and

3. An improved diet and standard of living, which should have lowered the death rate more than this, were partly offset by urbanization and immigration. Mortality rates were always higher in cities before the twentieth century, and many immigrants suffered an initially higher death rate as they entered a new disease environment. Large numbers of Irish immigrants arrived with lowered resistance because of malnutrition; they also crowded into the poorest districts of cities.

4. McClelland and Zeckhauser, *Demographic Dimensions*, 101, 108–9; Robert V. Wells, *Revolutions in Americans' Lives: A Demographic Perspective on the History of Americans, Their Families, and Their Society* (Westport, Conn., 1982), 92–104.

5. For a summary of recent research on this question, see Susan Lee and Peter Passell, *A New Economic View of American History* (New York, 1979), 52–62; Robert E. Gallman, "Economic Growth," in Glenn Porter, ed., *Encyclopedia of American Economic History*, 3 vols. (New York, 1980), 133–50; and Stanley L. Engerman and Robert E. Gallman, "U.S. Economic Growth, 1783–1860," *Research in Economic History*, 8 (1983), 1–46.

6. This is the range of estimates contained in three studies of the subject, all of them based on fragmentary data: Alvin H. Hansen, "Factors Affecting the Trend of Real Wages," *American Economic Review*, 15 (1925), 27–41; Donald R. Adams, Jr.,

poor appears to have characterized most capitalist economies during their early decades of intensive growth and industrialization. American workers probably fared better in this respect than those of most European countries. Indeed, a debate still rages over whether British workers suffered an *absolute decline* of real wages during the first half-century of the industrial revolution.[7]

Improved transportation was a prerequisite of economic development in a country as large as the United States. Before 1815 the only cost-efficient means of carrying freight long distances were sailing ships and downriver flatboats. Most American roads were rutted dirt paths all but impassable in wet weather. The cost of transporting a ton of goods thirty miles inland from an American port equalled the cost of carrying the same goods across the Atlantic. To travel from Cincinnati to New York took a minimum of three weeks; the only feasible way to ship freight between the same two cities was down the Ohio and Mississippi rivers to New Orleans and then by salt water along the Gulf and Atlantic coasts—a trip of at least seven weeks. It is not surprising, therefore, that America's transatlantic trade exceeded internal commerce, that most manufactured goods purchased in the United States came from Britain, that artisans sold mainly custom goods in local markets, that farmers living more than a short distance from navigable water consumed most of what they raised—and that the economy grew little if any faster than population.

All this changed after 1815 as a result of what historians, without exaggeration, have called a transportation revolution. Private companies, states, even the national government financed the construction of all-weather macadamized roads. More important, New York state pioneered the canal era by building the Erie Canal from Albany to Buffalo, linking New York City to the Northwest by water and setting off a frenzy of construction that produced 3,700 miles of canals by 1850.

"Prices and Wages," in Porter, ed., *Encyclopedia of American Economic History*, 229–46, which summarizes all relevant research up to the time of its writing; and Donald R. Adams, Jr., "The Standard of Living During American Industrialization: Evidence from the Brandywine Region, 1800–1860," *Journal of Economic History*, 42 (1982), 903–17.

7. For a summary of that debate for Britain and other countries, see John Komlos, "Stature and Nutrition in the Habsburg Monarchy: The Standard of Living and Economic Development in the Eighteenth Century," *AHR*, 90 (1985), 1149–51. See also Donald R. Adams, Jr., "Some Evidence on English and American Wage Rates, 1790–1830," *Journal of Economic History*, 30 (1970), 499–520.

During those same years, steamboats made Robert Fulton's dream come true by churning their way along every navigable river from Bangor to St. Joseph. The romance and economic importance of steamboats were eclipsed in both respects by the iron horse in the 1850s. The 9,000 miles of rail in the United States by 1850 led the world, but paled in comparison with the 21,000 additional miles laid during the next decade, which gave to the United States in 1860 a larger rail network than in the rest of the world combined. Iron ribbons breached the Appalachians and bridged the Mississippi. An even newer invention, the telegraph, sent instant messages along copper wires and leaped beyond the railheads to span the continent by 1861.

These marvels profoundly altered American life. They halved overland transport costs by road to 15 cents a ton-mile. But roads soon became unimportant except for short hauls and local travel. Canal rates dropped to less than one cent a ton-mile, river rates even lower, and rail charges to less than three cents by 1860. Despite higher rates, the railroad's greater speed and dependability (most canals froze in winter; rivers became unnavigable in low water or floods) gave it an edge. Towns bypassed by the tracks shriveled; those located on the iron boomed, especially if they also enjoyed water transport. Springing from the prairie shores of Lake Michigan, Chicago became the terminus for fifteen rail lines by 1860, its population having grown by 375 percent during the previous decade. Racing at breakneck speeds of thirty miles an hour, the iron horse cut travel time between New York and Chicago from three weeks to two days. Train wrecks soon exceeded steamboat explosions as a prime cause of accidental death. But together these modes of transport reduced the shipment time of freight between, for example, Cincinnati and New York from fifty days to five. Cincinnati became the meatpacking capital of the United States. The difference between the wholesale price of western pork in Cincinnati and New York declined from $9.53 to $1.18 a barrel; the difference in the wholesale price of western flour between the same two cities dropped from $2.48 to 28 cents.

The telegraph provided instant quotations on these and other price changes all over the country. Along with the railroad and with technological innovations in printing and paper-making, the telegraph vastly increased the influence of newspapers, the country's principal medium of communication. The price of a single issue dropped from six cents in 1830 to one or two cents by 1850. Circulation increased twice as fast as population. The "latest news" became hours rather than days old.

Fast trains carried weekly editions of metropolitan newspapers (like Horace Greeley's *New York Tribune*) to farmers a thousand miles away, where they shaped political sentiments. In 1848 several major newspapers pooled resources to form the Associated Press for the handling of telegraphic dispatches.[8]

The transportation revolution refashioned the economy. As late as 1815, Americans produced on their farms or in their homes most of the things they consumed, used, or wore. Most clothing was sewn by mothers and daughters, made from cloth that in many cases they had spun and woven themselves by the light of candles they had dipped or by natural light coming through windows in houses built of local materials from a nearby sawmill or brickyard by local carpenters or masons or by the male members of the household. Shoes were made by members of the family or by the village cordwainer from leather cured at a local tannery. Blacksmiths forged the tools and farm implements used in the community. Even firearms were built with handicraft skill and pride by a nearby craftsman. In larger towns and cities, master tailors or shoemakers or cabinetmakers or wheelwrights presided over small shops where they worked with a few journeymen and an apprentice or two who turned out fine custom or "bespoke" goods for wealthier purchasers. In an age of slow and expensive overland transport, few of these items were sold more than twenty miles from where they were made.

This pre-industrial world could not survive the transportation revolution, which made possible a division of labor and specialization of production for ever larger and more distant markets. More and more farmers specialized in crops for which their soil and climate were most suitable. With the cash from sale of these crops they bought food and clothing and hardware previously made locally or by themselves but now grown, processed, or manufactured elsewhere and shipped in by canal or rail. To sow and reap these specialized crops, farmers bought newly invented seed drills, cultivators, mowers, and reapers that a burgeoning farm machinery industry turned out in ever-increasing numbers.

In towns and cities, entrepreneurs who became known as "merchant capitalists" or "industrialists" reorganized and standardized the production of a variety of goods for large-volume sale in regional and eventually national markets. Some of these new entrepreneurs came from the

8. An enormous literature has grown up to describe and analyze these changes in transportation and communications; perhaps the most vivid account remains George Rogers Taylor, *The Transportation Revolution, 1815–1860* (New York, 1951).

ranks of master craftsmen who now planned and directed the work of employees to whom they paid wages by the day or by the piece instead of sharing with them the work of fabricating a product and the proceeds of its sale. Other merchant capitalists and industrialists had little or no prior connection with the "trade" (shoemaking, tailoring, etc.). They were businessmen who provided capital and organizing skills to restructure an enterprise in a more efficient manner. This restructuring took various forms, but had one dominant feature in common: the process of making a product (shoes or furniture, for example), which had previously been performed by one or a few skilled craftsmen, was broken down into numerous steps each requiring limited skills and performed by a separate worker. Sometimes the worker did his task with hand tools, but increasingly with the aid of power-driven machinery.

Highly mechanized industries like textiles went early to the factory system, where all operations were housed under one roof with a single source of power (usually water, sometimes steam) to drive the machines. This system enabled the New England textile industry to increase its annual output of cotton cloth from 4 million yards in 1817 to 308 million in 1837. In less mechanized enterprises like garment-sewing, operations took place in smaller shops with part of the process being "put out" to semiskilled workers—often women and children—in their homes and returned to the shop for finishing. This remained true even after the invention in the 1840s of the sewing machine, which could be operated in the home as well as in a factory.

Whatever the precise mixture of power machinery and hand tools, of central shop and putting out, the main characteristics of this new mode of production were division and specialization of labor, standardization of product, greater discipline of the labor force, improved efficiency, higher volume, and lower costs. These factors reduced wholesale commodity prices by 45 percent from 1815 to 1860. During the same years consumer prices declined even more, by an estimated 50 percent.[9]

By 1860 the nascent outline of the modern American economy of mass consumption, mass production, and capital-intensive agriculture

9. Adams, "Prices and Wages," in Porter, ed., *Encyclopedia of American Economic History*, 234. The choice of 1815 as a base year for measurement distorts the picture somewhat, for prices in that year were still inflated from the War of 1812. Even if one chooses the depression year of 1819, however, the decline of wholesale and consumer prices over the next 40 years was an impressive 24 and 41 percent respectively.

was visible. Its development had been uneven across different regions and industries. It was far from complete even in the most advanced sections of the country like New England, where many village black-smiths and old-time shoemakers could still be found. On the frontier west of the Mississippi and on many internal frontiers in the older sections where the transportation revolution had not yet penetrated—the upland and piney woods regions of the South, for example, or the forests of Maine and the Adirondacks—it had scarcely begun. Many Americans still lived in a nearly self-sufficient handicraft, premarket economy not much different from what their grandparents had known. But the more advanced sectors of the economy had already given the United States the world's highest standard of living and the second-highest industrial output, closing in fast on their British cousins despite the latter's half-century head start in the industrial revolution.[10]

Those cousins had begun to sit up and take notice. The victory of *America* over fourteen British yachts in the 1851 race of the Royal Yacht Squadron shocked the world's leading maritime power. The race occurred during the international industrial exhibition at the Crystal Palace in London, where the products of American industry evoked great curiosity. It was not so much the quality of American muskets, reapers, locks, and revolvers that impressed Britons, but the way in which they had been produced by machine-made interchangeable parts. The concept of interchangeability was not new in 1851. Nor was it exclusively American. The French arms industry had pioneered interchangeable parts for muskets as early as the 1780s. But most of those parts had been fashioned by skilled craftsmen working with hand tools. Their interchangeability was at best approximate. What was new to European observers in 1851 was the American technique of making each part by a special-purpose machine, which could reproduce an endless number of similar parts within finer tolerances than the most skilled of craftsmen could achieve. The British named this process "the American system of manufactures," and so it has been known ever since.[11]

The interchangeability of parts fabricated by this "system" was often

10. Edgar Winfield Martin, *The Standard of Living in 1860: American Consumption on the Eve of the Civil War* (Chicago, 1942), 400–401.
11. The best studies of the origins of the American system of manufacturers are Nathan Rosenberg, ed., *The American System of Manufactures* (Edinburgh, 1969); David A. Hounshell, *From the American System to Mass Production 1800–1932* (Baltimore, 1984); and Otto Mayr and Robert C. Post, eds., *Yankee Enterprise: The Rise of the American System of Manufactures* (Washington, 1981).

less than advertised. Hand-filing was sometimes necessary to attain an exact fit. Precision machines and gauges with tolerances within a thousandth of an inch came a generation or two later. Nevertheless, a test of ten randomly selected muskets each made in a separate year from 1844 to 1853 at the Springfield (Massachusetts) armory convinced British skeptics. A workman disassembled the parts, jumbled them in a box, and reassembled ten muskets flawlessly.

It was no coincidence that interchangeability was first perfected in small-arms manufacture. In wartime an army needs a large number of weapons in a hurry and must be able to replace damaged parts in an equal hurry. The U.S. government armories at Springfield and Harper's Ferry had gradually developed the process during the generation before 1850. The British imported American machinery to establish the Enfield Armoury during the Crimean War. Samuel Colt also set up a revolver factory in London stocked with machinery from Connecticut. These events symbolized a transfer of world leadership in the machine-tool industry from Britain to the United States.

During the 1850s, delegations of British industrialists visiting America sent back reports on a wide variety of products manufactured by special-purpose machines: clocks and watches, furniture and a host of other wood products, nails and screws, nuts and bolts, railroad spikes, locks, plows, and so on. "There is nothing that cannot be produced by machinery," Samuel Colt told a committee of Parliament in 1854—and by then the British were ready to believe him.[12]

The principles of mass production in America extended to what seemed unlikely practices: for example, the building of houses. This was the era in which "balloon-frame" construction was invented. Today at least three-quarters of American houses are built this way. Before the 1830s, however, houses were generally built in one of three ways: of logs rough-hewn by axes; of brick or stone; or of heavy timbers shaped by carpenters and joined by mortoise and tenon fastened with wooden pegs. The first was cheap but drafty and hardly satisfactory for a growing middle class of rising affluence; the latter two were solid but expensive and slow to build, requiring skilled masons or carpenters who were in short supply in overnight cities, like Chicago, that required a great deal of housing in a hurry. To meet these needs the first balloon-frame buildings appeared during the 1830s in Chicago and in Rochester, a boom town on

12. Eugene S. Ferguson, "Technology as Knowledge," in Edwin T. Layton, Jr., ed., *Technology and Social Change in America* (New York, 1973), 23.

the Erie Canal. These houses were constructed with the now familiar combination of machine-sawed boards fastened together with factory-produced nails to form the skeleton of a frame house. Machine-sawed siding and shingles and factory-made doors and window parts filled in the frame. Skeptics scoffed that these "balloon frames" would blow away in the first high wind. But in fact they were remarkably strong, for the boards were nailed together in such a way that every strain went against the grain of the wood. These houses could be put up in a fraction of the time and at a fraction of the cost of houses built by traditional methods. So successful was this "Chicago construction" that it spread quickly to every part of the country.[13]

Balloon-frame houses illustrated four of the factors cited then and later to explain the emergence of the American system of manufactures. The first was what economists call demand and what social historians might call a democracy of consumption: the need or desire of a growing and mobile population for a variety of ready-made consumer goods at reasonable prices. Considering themselves members of the "middling classes," most Americans in the 1850s were willing and able to buy ready-made shoes, furniture, men's clothing, watches, rifles, even houses. If these products lacked the quality, finish, distinction, and durability of fine items made by craftsmen, they were nevertheless functional and affordable. A new institution, the "department store," sprang up to market the wares of mass production to a mass public. European visitors who commented (not always favorably) on the relationship between a political system of universal (white) manhood suffrage and a socioeconomic system of standardized consumption were right on the mark. Grinding poverty and luxurious wealth were by no means absent from the United States, but what impressed most observers was the broad middle.

Another factor that gave rise to the American system was the shortage and consequent high cost of labor. A deficiency of skilled carpenters, for example, spawned the balloon-frame house. "The labouring classes are comparatively few," reported a British industrial commission that visited the United States in 1854, "and to this very want . . . may be attributed the extraordinary ingenuity displayed in many of these labour-saving machines, whose automatic action so completely supplies the place of the more abundant hand labour of the older manufacturing

13. Daniel J. Boorstin, *The Americans: The National Experience* (New York, 1965), 148–52.

countries." Europeans found surprisingly little opposition to mechanization among American workers. With labor scarce in the first place, new machines instead of displacing workers, as they often did elsewhere, tended rather to multiply each worker's productivity. American "workmen hail with satisfaction all mechanical improvements," reported a British industrialist (with exaggeration), "the importance and value of which, as releasing them from the drudgery of unskilled labour, they are enabled by education to understand and appreciate."[14]

While not rejecting this labor-scarcity thesis, some historians emphasize a third reason for the capital-intensive nature of the American system—the high resource endowment of the United States. Resources are a form of capital; three outstanding examples in this period were land, wood, and abundant water-power sites especially in New England. The high ratio of land to people encouraged a form of agriculture that would have been wasteful elsewhere but made economic sense in the United States, where the use of machinery achieved a modest yield per acre but a high yield per man-hour of labor. Wood was as plentiful in America as it was scarce in Europe; consequently it had a myriad uses in the new world—fuel for steamboats and locomotives, lumber for houses, frames and parts for machines, and so on. American machine tools were developed first in woodworking industries, where they shaped almost anything made of wood: furniture, musket stocks, axe handles, wheel spokes, doors, and hundreds of other items. Machined products were far more wasteful of wood than handcrafted items, but economically rational where wood was cheap and labor expensive. The American lead in woodworking machines laid the groundwork for an emerging superiority in metalworking machines after 1850. Fast-flowing streams provided a cheap source of energy for American mills that enabled water to retain its status as the principal source of industrial power in the United States until 1870.[15]

A fourth reason offered by British observers to explain American economic efficiency was an educational system that had produced wide-

14. Quotations from H. J. Habbakuk, *American and British Technology in the Nineteenth Century* (Cambridge, 1967), 6–7, and Douglass C. North, *The Economic Growth of the United States 1790–1860* (Englewood Cliffs, 1961), 173.

15. Paul A. David, *Technical Choice, Innovation and Economic Growth: Essays on American and British Experience in the Nineteenth Century* (Cambridge, 1975), 87–90; Rosenbereg, ed., *American System*, 58–59; Dolores Greenberg, "Reassessing the Power Patterns of the Industrial Revolution: An Anglo-American Comparison," *AHR*, 87 (1982), 1237–61.

spread literacy and "adaptative versatility" among American workers. By contrast a British workman trained by long apprenticeship "in the trade" rather than in schools lacked "the ductility of mind and the readiness of apprehension for a new thing" and was "unwilling to change the methods which he has been used to," according to an English manufacturer. The craft apprenticeship system was breaking down in the United States, where most children in the Northeast went to school until age fourteen or fifteen. "Educated up to a far higher standard than those of a much superior social grade in the Old World . . . every [American] workman seems to be continually devising some new thing to assist him in his work, and there is a strong desire . . . to be 'posted up' in every new improvement."[16]

This was perhaps putting it a bit strongly. But many American technological innovations were indeed contributed by workers themselves. Elias Howe, a journeyman machinist in Boston who invented a sewing machine, was one of many examples. This was what contemporaries meant when they spoke of Yankee ingenuity. They used "Yankee" in all three senses of the word: Americans; residents of northern states in particular; and New Englanders especially. Of 143 important inventions patented in the United States from 1790 to 1860, 93 percent came out of the free states and nearly half from New England alone—more than twice that region's proportion of the free population. Much of the machine-tool industry and most of the factories with the most advanced forms of the American system of manufactures were located in New England. An Argentine visitor to the United States in 1847 reported that New England migrants to other regions had carried "to the rest of the Union the . . . moral and intellectual aptitude [and] . . . manual aptitude which makes an American a walking workshop. . . . The great colonial and railroad enterprises, the banks, and the corporations are founded and developed by them."[17]

The connection made by British observers between Yankee "adaptative versatility" and education was accurate. New England led the world in educational facilities and literacy at midcentury. More than 95 per-

16. Rosenberg, ed., *American System*, 203; John E. Sawyer, "The Social Basis of the American System of Manufacturing," *Journal of Economic History*, 14 (1954), 377–78.
17. Roger Burlingame, *March of the Iron Men: A Social History of Union Through Invention* (New York, 1938), 469–76; Domingo Faustino Sarmiento, *Sarmiento's Travels in the United States in 1847*, trans. Michael A. Rockland (Princeton, 1970), 198.

cent of its adults could read and write; three-fourths of the children aged five to nineteen were enrolled in school, which they attended for an average of six months a year. The rest of the North was not far behind. The South lagged with only 80 percent of its white population literate and one-third of the white children enrolled in school for an average of three months a year. The slaves, of course, did not attend school and only about one-tenth of them could read and write. Even counting the slaves, nearly four-fifths of the American population was literate in the 1850s, compared with two-thirds in Britain and northwest Europe and one-fourth in southern and eastern Europe. Counting only the free population, the literacy rate of 90 percent in the United States was equaled only by Sweden and Denmark.[18]

The rise of schooling in these countries since the seventeenth century had grown out of the Protestant Reformation. The priesthood of all believers needed to know how to read and understand God's word. In the nineteenth century, religion continued to play an important role in American education. Most colleges and many secondary schools were supported by church denominations. Even the public schools still reflected their Protestant auspices. Since 1830 a rapid expansion and rationalization of the public school system had spread westward and southward from New England—though it had not yet penetrated very far below the Ohio. As secretary of the Massachusetts State Board of Education and a tireless publicist, Horace Mann presided over reforms which included the establishment of normal schools to train teachers, the introduction of standardized graded curricula, the evolution of various kinds of rural district schools and urban charity schools into a public school *system*, and extension of public education to the secondary level.

An important purpose of these schools remained the inculcation of Protestant ethic values "of regularity, punctuality, constancy and industry" by "moral and religious instruction daily given," according to the Massachusetts superintendent of schools in 1857. These values, along

18. Albert Fishlow, "The Common School Revival: Fact or Fancy?" in Henry Rosovsky, ed., *Industrialization in Two Systems* (New York, 1966), 40–67; *A Compendium of the Seventh Census of the United States* (Washington, 1854), 141–51; Carlo M. Cippolla, *Literacy and Development in the West* (Harmondsworth, Eng., 1969); Carl F. Kaestle, *Pillars of the Republic: Common Schooling and American Society, 1780–1860* (New York, 1983), 13–74; Lee Soltow and Edward Stevens, *The Rise of Literacy and the Common School in the United States: A Socioeconomic Analysis to 1870* (Chicago, 1981), 89–142.

with cognitive skills and knowledge, also served the needs of a growing capitalist economy. Schools were "the grand agent for the development or augmentation of national resources," wrote Horace Mann in 1848, "more powerful in the production and gainful employment of the total wealth of a country than all the other things mentioned in the books of the political economists."[19] Textile magnate Abbott Lawrence advised a Virginia friend who wanted his state to emulate New England's industrial progress that "you cannot expect to develop your resources without a general system of popular education; it is the lever to all permanent improvement." "Intelligent laborers," added another Yankee businessman in 1853 as if in echo of British visitors, "can add much more to the capital employed in a business than those who are ignorant."[20]

III

Recent scholarship has challenged the observations quoted earlier that American workers readily embraced the new industrial order.[21] Skilled artisans in particular appear to have resisted certain features of capitalist development. They formed trade unions and workingmen's parties which attained considerable strength in the 1830s, when tensions caused by the transition from a localized craft economy to an expanding capitalism were most acute. Disputes about wages and control of the work process

19. Michael B. Katz, *The Irony of Early School Reform: Educational Innovation in Mid-Nineteenth Century Massachusetts* (Cambridge, Mass., 1968), 43; Horace Mann, "Annual Report of 1848," in *The Life and Works of Horace Mann*, 5 vols. (Boston, 1891), IV, 245–51.
20. Abbott Lawrence, *Letters to William C. Rives of Virginia* (Boston, 1846), 6; Arthur A. Ekirch, *The Idea of Progress in America, 1815–1860* (New York, 1944), 197.
21. This and the following paragraphs have drawn on some of the numerous studies of the antebellum working class that have appeared in recent years, including Alan Dawley, *Class and Community: The Industrial Revolution in Lynn* (Cambridge, Mass., 1976); Anthony F. C. Wallace, *Rockdale: The Growth of an American Village in the Early Industrial Revolution* (New York, 1978); Thomas Dublin, *Women at Work: The Transformation of Work and Community in Lowell, Massachusetts, 1826–1860* (New York, 1979); Jonathan Prude, *The Coming of Industrial Order: Town and Factory Life in Rural Massachusetts, 1810–1860* (Cambridge, 1983); Sean Wilentz, *Chants Democratic: New York City and the Rise of the American Working Class, 1788–1850* (New York, 1984); Walter Licht, *Working for the Railroad: The Organization of Work in the Nineteenth Century* (Princeton, 1983); Steven J. Ross, *Workers on the Edge: Work, Leisure, and Politics in Industrializing Cincinnati, 1788–1890* (New York, 1985); Christine Stansell, *City of Women: Sex and Class in New York, 1789–1860* (New York, 1986).

provoked strikes and other forms of conflict. Worker activism declined after 1837 as the depression generated unemployment which drew the fangs of militancy. After recovery from the depression, vastly increased immigration intensified ethnic and religious divisions within the working class. Nativism, temperance, and the growing sectional conflict took precedence over the economic issues that had prevailed in the 1830s. Nevertheless, frictions persisted in the workplace and occasionally erupted, as in the Massachusetts shoemakers' strike of 1860.

Technological innovation was not the main cause of worker unrest. To be sure, machines displaced some craftsmen or downgraded their skills. But most machines during this era executed simple repetitive motions previously performed by unskilled or semiskilled workers. And even when more complex machine tools replaced some artisans, they expanded other categories of highly skilled workers—machinists, tool-and-die makers, millwrights, civil and mechanical engineers—whose numbers doubled during the 1850s.[22] The transportation and communications revolutions created whole new occupations, some of them skilled and well paid—steamboat pilots, railroad men, telegraphers. The latter two categories increased fivefold in the 1850s. The rapid westward expansion of the urban frontier, the extraordinary mobility of the American population, and regional differentials in the pace of technological development meant that skilled workers who were displaced by new technology in one part of the country could go west and find a job. European observers who contrasted workers' resistance to innovation in their own countries with workers' receptivity toward change in the United States were not off the mark.

Nor was declining income the principal cause of worker unrest in the United States. Despite bursts of inflation in the mid-1830s and mid-1850s, and periods of unemployment caused by depressions, the long-term trend of real wages was upward. Of course people live in the short run, and the average worker trying to make ends meet during economic downturns in, say, 1841 or 1857 lacked the mollifying perspective of an historian. Moreover, the wages of male artisans in certain occupations suffered erosion when the introduction of new methods or new machines enabled employers to hire "green hands" or "slop workers," often women and children, to perform separate parts of a sequential process previously done entirely by skilled workers. It was no coincidence that

22. Calculated from the occupational lists in the 1850 and 1860 censuses.

much of the unrest occurred in specific trades experiencing this de-skilling process: shoemakers, tailors, weavers, cabinetmakers, printers.

Then, too, despite the generally rising trend of real wages, workers at the bottom of the scale, especially women, children, and recent immigrants, labored long hours in sweatshops or airless factories for a pittance. They could make a living only if other members of their families also worked. For some of these laborers, however, the pennies they earned as domestic servants or factory hands or stevedores or seamstresses or hod-carriers or construction workers represented an improvement over the famine conditions they had left in Ireland. Nevertheless, poverty was widespread and becoming more so among laborers in large cities with a substantial immigrant population. New York packed an immense populace of the poor into noisome tenements, giving the city a death rate nearly twice as high as London.[23]

Although the working poor of New York would explode into the worst riot of American history in 1863, these people did not provide the cutting edge of labor protest in the antebellum era. It was not so much the level of wages as the very concept of wages itself that fueled much of this protest. Wage labor was a form of dependency that seemed to contradict the republican principles on which the country had been founded. The core of republicanism was liberty, a precious but precarious birthright constantly threatened by corrupt manipulations of power. The philosopher of republicanism, Thomas Jefferson, had defined the essence of liberty as independence, which required the ownership of productive property. A man dependent on others for a living could never be truly free, nor could a dependent class constitute the basis of a republican government. Women, children, and slaves were dependent; that defined them *out* of the polity of republican freemen. Wage laborers were also dependent; that was why Jefferson feared the development of industrial capitalism with its need for wage laborers. Jefferson envisaged an ideal America of farmers and artisan producers who owned their means of production and depended on no man for a living.

But the American economy did not develop that way. Instead, skilled craftsmen who owned their tools and sold the products of their labor for a "just price" found themselves gradually drawn into a relationship where they sold their labor. Instead of working for themselves, they worked for someone else. Instead of earning a just price for their skill, they earned

23. Martin, *Standard of living in 1860,* 174.

wages whose amount was determined not by the intrinsic value of their labor but by what an increasingly distant "market" would bear. No longer were "master" and "journeyman" bound together by the commonality of their trade and by the journeyman's expectation of becoming a master himself. More and more they were separated into "employer" and "employee," with different and sometimes conflicting interests. The employer wanted to maximize profits, which meant improving the efficiency and controlling the costs of production, including wages. The employee became dependent on the "boss" not only for wages but also for the means of production—machines that the worker himself could no longer hope to own. The emergence of industrial capitalism from 1815 to 1860 thus began to forge a new system of class relations between capitalists who owned the means of production and workers who owned only their labor power. Journeymen artisans who experienced this process did not like it. They and their spokesmen offered a sharp critique of emerging capitalism.

Capitalism was incompatible with republicanism, they insisted. Dependence on wages robbed a man of his independence and therefore of his liberty. Wage labor was no better than slave labor—hence "wage slavery." The boss was like a slaveowner. He determined the hours of toil, the pace of work, the division of labor, the level of wages; he could hire and fire at will. The pre-industrial artisan had been accustomed to laboring as much or as little as he pleased. He worked by the job, not by the clock. If he felt like taking time off for a drink or two with friends, he did so. But in the new regimen all laborers worked in lockstep; the system turned them into machines; they became slaves to the clock. Manufacturers encouraged the temperance movement that gathered force after 1830 because its Protestant ethic virtues of sobriety, punctuality, reliability, and thrift were precisely the values needed by disciplined workers in the new order. Some employers banned drinking on the job and tried even to forbid their workers to drink *off* the job. For men who considered their thrice-daily tipple a right, this was another mark of slavery.

In the eyes of labor reformers, capitalism also violated other tenets of republicanism: virtue, commonweal, and equality. Virtue required individuals to put the community's interest above their own; capitalism glorified the pursuit of self-interest in the quest for profits. Commonweal specified that a republic must benefit all the people, not just favored classes. But by granting charters and appropriating money to establish banks, create corporations, dig canals, build railroads, dam streams, and undertake other projects for economic development, state and local governments had favored certain classes at the expense of others. They had created *monopolies*, concentrations of power that endangered liberty. They had also fostered a growing inequality of wealth (defined as ownership of real and personal property). In the largest American cities by the 1840s, the wealthiest 5 percent of the population owned about 70 percent of the taxable property, while the poorest half owned almost nothing. Although wealth was less unequal in the countryside, in the nation as a whole by 1860 the top 5 percent of free adult males owned 53 percent of the wealth and the bottom half owned only 1 percent. Age as well as class accounted for this disparity—most twenty-one-year-olds owned little or nothing while most sixty-year-olds owned something, and the average man could expect to increase his wealth fivefold during the passage from youth to maturity. Nevertheless, ownership of property was becoming an elusive goal for Americans at the lower end of the economic scale.[24]

Denunciations of this state of affairs rang with republican rhetoric. Wage labor was "drawing the chains of slavery, and riveting them closer and closer around the limbs of free labor," declared one orator. The factory bound its workers "hand and foot by a system of petty despotism as galling as ever oppressed the subjects of tyranny in the old world."[25] A versifier drew the parallel between America's fight for liberty in 1776 and the workers' struggle a half-century later:

> For liberty our fathers fought
> Which with their blood they dearly bought,
> The Fact'ry system sets at nought. . . .
> Great Britain's curse is now our own,
> Enough to damn a King and Throne.[26]

To counter the power of this new tyranny a worker had only the right to withdraw his labor—to quit and go elsewhere, or to strike. This was more power than chattel slaves had, but whether it was sufficient to

24. Edward Pessen, *Riches, Class and Power Before the Civil War* (Lexington, Mass., 1973), esp. chap. 3; Lee Soltow, *Men and Wealth in the United States 1850–1870* (New Haven, 1975), 99, 180, 183; Ross, *Workers on the Edge*, 75; Jeffrey G. Williamson and Peter H. Lindert, *American Inequality: A Macroeconomic History* (New York, 1980), 36–39.
25. Dawley, *Class and Community*, 82; John Ashworth, *"Agrarians & Aristocrats": Party Political Ideology in the United States, 1837–1846* (London, 1983), 31.
26. Prude, *The Coming of Industrial Order*, 120.

redress the balance with capital was endlessly debated then and ever since. Radicals did not think so. They proposed a variety of schemes to equalize wealth and property or to circumvent the wage system by producers' cooperatives. There was also a proliferation of communitarian experiments in the 1830s and 1840s, ranging from the Transcendentalists' rather tame venture at Brook Farm to John Humphrey Noyes's notorious Oneida Community, where marital partners as well as property were held in common.

But these were pinpricks on the periphery of capitalism. Closer to the center was an antimonopoly crusade that channeled itself through the Jacksonian Democratic party. This movement united trade unions and labor spokesmen with yeoman farmers, especially those in the upland South and lower Northwest who stood on the edge of the market revolution apprehensive of being drawn into it. These groups evinced a producers' consciousness based on the labor theory of value: all genuine wealth is derived from the labor that produced it and the proceeds of that wealth should go to those who created it. These "producing classes" did not include bankers, lawyers, merchants, speculators, and other "capitalists" who were "bloodsuckers" or "parasites" that "manipulated 'associated wealth' " and "have grown fat upon the earnings of the toil worn laborer."[27] Of all the "leeches" sucking the lifeblood of farmers and workers, bankers were the worst. Banks in general and the Second Bank of the United States in particular became the chief symbol of capitalist development during the 1830s and the chief scapegoat for its perceived ills.

Part of the capital for the American industrial revolution came from state and local governments, which financed roads, canals, and education. Part came from foreign investors who sought higher yields in the fast-growing American economy than they could get at home. Part came from retained earnings of American companies. But state-chartered banks were a growing source of capital. Their numbers tripled while their assets increased fivefold from 1820 to 1840. After standing still during the depression of the 1840s, the number and assets of banks doubled again from 1849 to 1860. Their notes constituted the principal form of money in the antebellum era.[28]

Important as banks were to economic development, they were even

27. *Ibid.*, 218; Dawley, *Class and Community*, 44.
28. Bureau of the Census, *Historical Statistics of the United States* (Washington, 1960), 623–25.

more significant as a political issue. A two-party system of Democrats and Whigs formed around Andrew Jackson's veto of the recharter of the Second Bank of the United States in 1832. For a dozen years or more after the Panic of 1837 the banking question remained the most polarizing issue in state politics, pitting pro-banking Whigs against anti-banking Democrats. The latter portrayed the concentration of wealth in banks as the gravest threat to liberty since George III. "Banks have been the known enemies of our republican government from the beginning," they proclaimed, "the engine of a new form of oppression . . . a legacy that the aristocratic tendencies of a bygone age has left, as a means to fill the place of baronial usurpation and feudal exactions." Banks caused "the artificial inequality of wealth, much pauperism and crime, the low state of public morals, and many of the other evils of society. . . . In justice to equal rights let us have no banks."[29]

In reply, supporters of banks ridiculed such sentiments as puerile and reactionary. The "credit system," they declared, was "the offspring of free institutions," an agency of economic growth that had brought unprecedented prosperity to all Americans. "Our want is capital," said an Ohio Whig in 1843. "We want, through the facilities of well-regulated . . . banks, to be able to develop the great resources of our State." The man "who should at this day recommend an entire abandonment of our credit system" was no less antediluvian than "he who should attempt to substitute a Pennsylvania wagon for a locomotive or a canal packet, or should endeavor to stem the restless current of the Mississippi in a flatboat."[30]

Northern Whigs and their Republican successors after 1854 elaborated a free-labor rationale for their vision of capitalist development. To the artisan argument that the system of wages and division of labor alienated workers from employers, Whigs replied that greater efficiency benefited both alike by raising wages as well as profits. "The interests of the capitalist and the laborer are . . . in perfect harmony with each other," wrote Whig economist Henry Carey of Philadelphia. "Each derives advantage from every measure that tends to facilitate . . . growth."[31]

29. James Roger Sharp, *The Jacksonians versus the Banks: Politics in the States after the Panic of 1837* (New York, 1970), 313; William G. Shade, *Banks or No Banks: The Money Issue in Western Politics, 1832–1865* (Detroit, 1972), 157, 117, 124.
30. Sharp, *Jacksonians versus the Banks*, 198; Ashworth, "Agrarians & Aristocrats," 82.
31. Eric Foner, *Free Soil, Free Labor, Free Men: The Ideology of the Republican Party before the Civil War* (New York, 1970), 19.

To the claim that all wealth was created by labor, Whigs replied that the banker who mobilized capital, the entrepreneur who put it to work, and the merchant who organized markets were "laborers" that created wealth just as surely as did the farmer or craftsman who worked with his hands. To the proposition that wages turned the worker into a slave, the free-labor ideology replied that wage dependency need be only temporary; that in an economy of rapid growth and a society of equal opportunity and free public education, a young man who practiced the virtues of hard work, self-discipline, self-improvement, thrift, and sobriety could pull himself up by his own bootstraps and become self-employed or a successful employer himself.

Americans in the mid-nineteenth century could point to plenty of examples, real as well as mythical, of self-made men who by dint of "industry, prudence, perseverance, and good economy" had risen "to competence, and then to affluence."[32] With the election of Abraham Lincoln they could point to one who had risen from a log cabin to the White House. "I am not ashamed to confess that twenty five years ago I was a hired laborer, mauling rails, at work on a flat-boat—just what might happen to any poor man's son!" Lincoln told an audience at New Haven in 1860. But in the free states a man knows that "he can better his condition . . . there is no such thing as a freeman being fatally fixed for life, in the condition of a hired laborer." "Wage slave" was a contradiction in terms, said Lincoln. "The man who labored for another last year, this year labors for himself, and next year he will hire others to labor for him." If a man "continue through life in the condition of the hired laborer, it is not the fault of the system, but because of either a dependent nature which prefers it, or improvidence, folly, or singular misfortune." The "*free* labor system," concluded Lincoln, "opens the way for all—gives hope to all, and energy, and progress, and improvement of condition to all." It was precisely the lack of this hope, energy, and progress in the slave South that made the United States a House Divided.[33]

However idealized Lincoln's version of the American Dream may have been,[34] this ideology of upward mobility mitigated class conscious-

32. Ashworth, "*Agrarians & Aristocrats*," 66–67.
33. CWL, II, 364, III, 478, 479, IV, 24.
34. Stephan Thernstrom, *The Other Bostonians: Poverty and Progress in the American*

ness and conflict in the United States. "There is not a working boy of average ability in the New England States, at least," observed a visiting British industrialist in 1854, "who has not an idea of some mechanical invention or improvement in manufactures, by which, in good time, he hopes to better his position, or rise to fortune and social distinction." A Cincinnati newspaper reported in 1860 that "of all the multitude of young men engaged in various employments of this city, there is not one who does not desire, and even confidently expect, to become rich."[35] The Gospel of Success produced an outpouring of self-improvement literature advising young men how to get ahead. This imparted a dynamism to American life, but also a frenetic pace and acquisitive materialism that repelled some Europeans and troubled many Americans.

Whigs and Republicans supported all kinds of "improvements" to promote economic growth and upward mobility—"internal improvements" in the form of roads, canals, railroads, and the like; tariffs to protect American industry and labor from low-wage foreign competition; a centralized, rationalized banking system. Many of them endorsed the temperance crusade, which sobered up the American population to the extent of reducing the per capita adult consumption of liquor from the equivalent of seven gallons of 200-proof alcohol annually in the 1820s to less than two gallons by the 1850s. During the same years the per capita consumption of coffee and tea doubled. Whigs also supported public schools as the great lever of upward mobility. Common schools, said New York's Whig Governor William H. Seward, were "the great levelling institutions of the age . . . not by levelling all to the condition of the base, but by elevating all to the association of the wise and good." Horace Mann believed that education "does better than to disarm

Metropolis, 1880–1970 (Cambridge, Mass., 1973), 220–61, surveys the findings of various studies of occupational mobility in the United States. They indicate that in the nineteenth century about one-third of Americans moved from lower to higher occupational status during their lives (and one-tenth moved the other way), while a larger percentage of their sons moved up. This was not the same as moving from wage labor to self-employment, of course, since a worker moving from an unskilled to a skilled job or to white-collar status probably remained a wage-earner. These studies trace the career patterns of only that half of the population who remained in the same area from one census to the next. The extraordinary geographical mobility of Americans may indicate an even higher level of upward social mobility, for people tend to move in order to better themselves.

35. Rosenberg, ed., American System, 204; Foner, Free Soil, 14.

the poor of their hostility toward the rich; it prevents their being poor."[36]

People who subscribed to these Whig-Republican principles tended to be those who had succeeded in the market economy, or aspired to. Numerous studies of antebellum voting patterns have shown that Whigs and Republicans did best among upwardly mobile Protestants in white-collar and skilled occupations and among farmers who lived near transportation networks that drew them into the market economy. These were "insiders" who welcomed the capitalist transformation of the nineteenth century and for the most part benefited from it. Although some Democrats, especially in the South, were also insiders, the greatest Democratic support came from "outsiders": workers who resented the de-skilling of artisan occupations and the dependency of wage labor; Catholic immigrants at the bottom of the status and occupational ladder who took umbrage at Yankee Protestant efforts to reform their drinking habits or force their children into public schools; heirs of the Jefferson-Jackson distrust of banks, corporations, or other concentrations of wealth that threatened republican liberty; yeoman farmers in the upcountry or backcountry who disliked city slickers, merchants, banks, Yankees, or anybody else who might interfere with their freedom to live as they pleased.[37]

Given the illogicality of American politics, these generalizations are subject to numerous qualifications. Despite their marginality, the tiny number of black men who lived in the half-dozen northern states that allowed them to vote formed a solid Whig bloc. The Democratic party's professed egalitarianism was for whites only. Its commitment to slavery and racism was blatant in the North as well as the South, while Whig-

---

36. Ashworth, "Agrarians & Aristocrats," 165; Mann, "Annual Report of 1848," in Life and Works of Horace Mann, IV, 251.

37. The studies on which this paragraph is based are too numerous for full citation here: among the most recent and enlightening are Foner, Free Soil; Ashworth, "Agrarians & Aristocrats"; Wilentz, Chants Democratic; Daniel Walker Howe, The Political Culture of the American Whigs (Chicago, 1979); Ronald P. Formisano, The Transformation of Political Culture: Massachusetts Parties 1790's–1840's (New York, 1982); Donald B. Cole, Jacksonian Democracy in New Hampshire, 1800–1851 (Cambridge, Mass., 1970); J. Mills Thornton III, Politics and Power in a Slave Society: Alabama, 1800–1860 (Baton Rouge, 1978); Steven Hahn, The Roots of Southern Populism: Yeoman Farmers and the Transformation of the Georgia Upcountry, 1850–1890 (New York, 1983); and Harry L. Watson, Jacksonian Politics and Community Conflict: The Emergence of the Second American Party System in Cumberland County, North Carolina (Baton Rouge, 1981).

gery grew in part from the same evangelical reformism that had generated the abolitionist movement. At the other end of the social scale, Democratic leaders in New York included many bankers and merchants who had nothing in common with the Irish-American masses in the tenements except their allegiance to the same party. The generalizations in the preceding paragraph, therefore, describe a tendency, not an axiom.

That tendency was perhaps most visible in the older states of the Northwest—Ohio, Indiana, and Illinois. Most of the initial settlers there had come from the upper South and Pennsylvania. They populated the southern part of the region and evolved a corn-hog-whiskey economy, selling their small surplus in markets accessible by the Ohio-Mississippi river network. They were called Buckeyes, Hoosiers, Suckers; they dressed in homsepun clothes dyed with the oil of walnut or butternut trees, and hence acquired the generic name Butternuts. They remained rural, southern, and localist in their orientation, hostile toward "Yankees" of New England heritage who settled the northern portions of these states made accessible by the Erie Canal after 1825. These Yankees established a wheat-cattle-sheep-dairy farming economy linked to eastern markets by the burgeoning rail network after 1850. The railroads and the rapidly multiplying banks, industries, towns and cities owned or controlled by the "Yankees" caused these parts of the states to grow faster than the Butternut sections. A quantitative analysis of socioeconomic and cultural variables in Illinois in 1850 found the Yankee areas positively correlated with the production of wheat, cheese, and wool, with farm value per acre and the percentage of improved land, the value of farm machinery, banks and pro-bank sentiment, urbanization, population growth, schools, literacy, Congregational and Presbyterian churches, and temperance and antislavery societies. The Butternut areas were positively correlated with the production of corn, sweet potatoes, and whiskey, with anti-bank and anti-black sentiments, illiteracy, and Baptist churches. Needless to say the Butternut districts were overwhelmingly Democratic while the Yankee counties voted Whig and after 1854 Republican.[38]

Another Democratic voting bloc were literal outsiders—the immi-

38. Shade, *Banks or No Banks*, 136–37. See also Henry B. Hubbart, *The Older Middle West, 1840–1880* (New York, 1936), and Richard Lyle Power, *Planting Corn Belt Culture: The Impress of the Upland Southerner and Yankee in the Old Northwest* (Indianapolis, 1953).

grants. During the first forty years of the republic, immigrants had not come in large numbers. Even in the 1820s arrivals averaged fewer than 13,000 each year. In the next decade, however, this figure quadrupled. The pressure of a growing population on limited resources in Britain, Ireland, and western Germany squeezed thousands into ships bound for higher wages or cheap land in the new world. Despite economic depression in America during the early 1840s, the annual number of immigrants jumped 40 percent over the boom years of the thirties. Recovery from the depression in the United States coincided with the potato-famine years in Ireland and political unrest on the Continent associated with the revolutions of 1848. These push-pull forces impelled three million immigrants across the Atlantic in the decade after 1845. This was the largest proportionate influx of foreign-born in American history.

Before 1840 three-quarters of the immigrants were Protestants, mainly from Britain. Half of all newcomers who joined the labor force went into skilled or white-collar occupations and another third became farmers. But as immigration increased sixfold during the next two decades, its religious and occupational mix changed dramatically. Two-thirds of the new immigrants were Catholics from Ireland and Germany. And while the proportion of farmers (mostly German) held up, the percentage of every other category declined except unskilled and semiskilled laborers, mainly Irish, who jumped to nearly half of the total.[39]

The poverty, religion, and cultural alienation of the Irish made them triple outsiders. Anti-Catholic and ethnic riots occurred in several northeastern cities during the 1830s and 1840s. The worst erupted in 1844 at Philadelphia, where a pair of three-way battles between Protestants, Irish Catholics, and the militia left at least sixteen dead, scores wounded, two churches and dozens of other buildings destroyed. "Nativist" political parties sprang up in various cities with the goals of lengthening the period of naturalization before immigrants could become citizens and voters, and of restricting officeholding to natives. These parties managed to elect a mayor of New York and three congressmen

39. Douglass C. North, "Capital Formation in the United States during the Early Period of Industrialization: A Reexamination of the Issues," in Robert W. Fogel and Stanley L. Engerman, eds., *The Reinterpretation of American Economic History* (New York, 1971), 279; North, *Growth of the American Economy*, 98; William F. Adams, *Ireland and Irish Emigration to the New World from 1815 to the Famine* (New Haven, 1932); Robert Joseph Murphy, "The Catholic Church in the United States During the Civil War Period," *Records of the American Catholic Historical Society*, 39 (1928), 293–94.

from Philadelphia. This nativism was actually more anti-Catholic than anti-immigrant. Indeed, Protestant immigrants (especially from northern Ireland) were among the most violent "nativists." Although the movement drew on middle-class leaders, it recruited a large following among skilled Protestant workers. Their ethnic hostility toward fellow laborers did much to abort the Jacksonian birth of worker solidarity. But because of the Whiggish overtones of nativism, it cemented the Democratic allegiance of Catholic immigrants more firmly than ever. Political nativism would explode even more destructively in the 1850s, when it contributed to the breakdown of the two-party system that preceded the Civil War.[40]

The economic transformation had an ambiguous impact on another group of political outsiders—women. The shift of manufacturing from household to shop or factory altered the function of many families from units of production to units of consumption. The transition of agriculture from subsistence to cash crops had a similar though less pronounced effect on farm families. These changes modified the primary economic role of most free women from producers to consumers. (Slave women, of course, continued to work in the fields as they had always done.) Instead of spinning yarn, weaving cloth, making soap and candles and the like at home, women increasingly bought these things at the store.

To be sure, some women took jobs in textile mills or did outwork as seamstresses, milliners, shoe binders, and so on. Though few if any women (except slaves) were counted in the labor force of agriculture (though farm women certainly worked hard), construction, mining, or transportation, many continued to work as domestic servants and laundresses. At midcentury one-fourth of the employees in manufacturing were women, while in the textile industry women and girls constituted nearly two-thirds of the wage workers. Nevertheless, only 25 percent of white women worked outside the home before marriage and fewer than 5 percent did so while married. Many young single women—like the famous Lowell girls who worked in the textile mills of that city—were

40. Michael Feldberg, *The Turbulent Era: Riot and Disorder in Jacksonian America* (New York, 1980), 9–32; Ray Allen Billington, *The Protestant Crusade 1800–1860: A Study of the Origins of American Nativism* (New York, 1938), 193–237; David Montgomery, "The Shuttle and the Cross: Weavers and Artisans in the Kensington Riots of 1844," *Journal of Social History*, 5 (1972), 411–46; Wilentz, *Chants Democratic*, 315–25.

part of the labor force for only two or three years while they built a dowry for marriage. The middle-class ideal for women was home and motherhood. And the enormous popularity of women's magazines (more than a hundred existed during this era, led by the renowned *Godey's Lady's Book*) diffused this ideal through society.

The economic transformation took men as producers *out* of the home into office or factory. This separation of job from home evoked a notion of separate "spheres" for men and women. Man's sphere was the bustling, competitive, dynamic world of business, politics, affairs of state. Woman's world was the home and family; her role was to bear and nurture children and to make the home a haven to which the husband returned from work each day to find love and warmth at the hearth. To the extent that this "cult of domesticity" removed women from the "real world" and confined them to an inferior sphere, it was a setback to any quest for equal rights and status.[41]

But did domesticity constitute a real setback? Historians have begun to qualify this interpretation. The economic transformation coincided with—and in part caused—a change in the quality of family life as well as the quantity of children. As the family became less an economic unit it ripened into a covenant of love and nurturance of children. The ideal of romantic love increasingly governed the choice of a marriage partner, a choice made more and more by young people themselves rather than by their parents. And if wives now had a lesser economic role, they enjoyed a larger familial one. Patriarchal domination of wife and children eroded in urban areas as fathers went away from home for most waking hours and mothers assumed responsibility for socializing and

41. A stimulating and growing literature on the history of women and the family in the nineteenth century has made this an exciting field of study. The list of important books is too long for citation here; my account has been influenced by the following works, among others: Catherine Clinton, *The Other Civil War: American Women in the Nineteenth Century* (New York, 1984); Nancy F. Cott, *The Bonds of Womanhood: "Woman's Sphere" in New England, 1780–1835* (New Haven, 1977); Kathryn Kish Sklar, *Catharine Beecher: A Study in American Domesticity* (New Haven, 1973); Mary P. Ryan, *Cradle of the Middle Class: The Family in Oneida County, New York, 1790–1865* (Cambridge, 1981); Carl N. Degler, *At Odds: Women and the Family in America from the Revolution to the Present* (New York, 1980); Ellen Carol DuBois, *Feminism and Suffrage: The Emergence of an Independent Women's Movement in America 1848–1869* (Ithaca, 1978); Suzanne Lebsock, *The Free Women of Petersburg: Status and Culture in a Southern Town, 1784–1860* (New York, 1984); and Catherine Clinton, *The Plantation Mistress: Woman's World in the Old South* (New York, 1982).

educating the children. Affection and encouragement of self-discipline replaced repression and corporal punishment as the preferred means of socialization in middle-class families. These families became more child-centered—a phenomenon much noted by European visitors. Childhood emerged as a separate stage of life. And as parents lavished more love on their children, they had fewer of them and devoted more resources to their education by sending them to school in greater numbers for longer periods of time.

This helps explain the simultaneous decline of the birth rate and the rise of education in the nineteenth century. Women played a crucial part in these developments and derived significant benefits from them. Middle-class marriages became more of an equal partnership than ever before. In some respects women attained a superior position in the partnership. If men ruled outside the home, women tended to rule within it. The decision to have fewer children was a mutual one but probably most often initiated by women. It required some sacrifice of traditional male sexual prerogatives. The principal means of contraception—continence and *coitus interruptus*—placed the responsibility of restraint on males. Fewer children meant that middle-class women in 1850 were less continuously burdened by pregnancy, childbirth, and nursing than their mothers and grandmothers had been. This not only enabled them to give each child more affection; it also freed them for activities outside the home.

For, in an apparent paradox, the concept of a woman's sphere *within* the family became a springboard for extension of that sphere beyond the hearth. If women were becoming the guardians of manners and morals, the custodians of piety and child-training, why should they not expand their demesne of religion and education outside the home? And so they did. Women had long constituted a majority of church members; during the Second Great Awakening they increased their prevalence in that realm. This evangelical revival also produced a "benevolent empire" of Bible societies, moral reform organizations, and social uplift associations of all kinds—most notably the temperance and abolitionist movements. Women were active in all of these efforts, first in separate female societies but increasingly in "mixed" associations after women abolitionists made this breakthrough in the 1830s.

Women's advances in education were even more impressive. Before the nineteenth century girls in America, as everywhere else, received much less formal education than boys, and a considerably higher proportion of women than men were illiterate. By 1850 that had changed in the United States, where girls went to elementary school and achieved literacy in virtually the same proportions as boys—the only country where that was yet true. Higher education was still a male domain, but several female "seminaries" for advanced secondary schooling were founded during the second quarter of the nineteenth century. Oberlin College admitted both women and men soon after its founding in 1833. Even more important, perhaps, was the feminization of the teaching profession. Like most other social and economic changes, this process began in New England and spread gradually westward and southward. By 1850 nearly three-quarters of the public school teachers in Massachusetts were women.

Another educating profession was opening to women during this era—writing for publication. The new emphasis on home and family created a huge audience for articles and books on homemaking, child-rearing, cooking, and related subjects. Women's magazines proliferated to meet the need. A paying profession arose for female writers. The expanded literacy and leisure of women, combined with the romanticism and sentimentalism of Victorian culture, also spawned a lucrative market for fiction which focused on the tribulations of love, marriage, home, family, and death. A bevy of authors turned out scores of sentimental best sellers—"that damned mob of scribbling women," Nathaniel Hawthorne called them, perhaps in envy of their royalty checks.

Therefore while the notion of a domestic sphere closed the front door to women's exit from the home into the real world, it opened the back door to an expanding world of religion, reform, education, and writing. Inevitably, women who could write or speak or teach or edit magazines began to ask why they should not be paid as much as men for these services and why they could not also preach, practice law or medicine, hold property independently of their husbands—and vote. Thus "domestic feminism"—as some historians label it—led by an indirect route to a more radical feminism that demanded equal rights in all spheres. In 1848 a convention in the upstate New York village of Seneca Falls launched the modern woman's rights movement. Its Declaration of Sentiments, modeled on the Declaration of Independence, proclaimed "that all men and women are created equal" and deserved their "inalienable rights" including the elective franchise. The convention met in a church; one of its two foremost organizers, Elizabeth Cady Stanton, had been educated in the first women's seminary, at Troy, New York; the other, Lucretia Mott, had started her adult life as a schoolteacher; both had been active in the abolitionist movement. These activities constituted part of the back door of domestic feminism which in 1848 nudged open the front door a tiny crack.[42]

IV

The evolution of the child-centered nurturing family during this era helped inspire abolitionists to focus on the greatest perceived sin of American slavery: the tragic irony that caused the institution simultaneously to encourage the slave family and to threaten it with destruction.

Slave marriages had no legal basis in the United States. More than half of the bondsmen in 1850 lived on farms or plantations with fewer than twenty slaves where they had difficulty finding marital partners in the same quarters. But slaves nevertheless married and raised large families. Most slaveowners encouraged this process, in part because abolition of the African slave trade after 1807 made them dependent on natural increase to meet the labor demands of an expanding cotton kingdom. In contrast to the United States, slave economies in most other parts of the western hemisphere reached their peak development while the African slave trade flourished. Thus they relied mainly on imports to keep up their labor supply. They also imported twice as many males as females and discouraged their slaves from forming families. In consequence, while the slave population of the United States doubled by natural reproduction every twenty-six years, slaves in other new world societies experienced a net natural *decrease*.[43]

But North American slavery undermined the same family structure that it simultaneously encouraged. Responsible masters did their best to avoid breaking up slave families by sale or removal. Not all masters felt such a responsibility, however, and in any case they could not reach beyond the grave to prevent sales to satisfy creditors in settlement of an

42. In addition to DuBois, *Feminism and Suffrage*, and Lebsock, *Free Women of Petersburg*, 195–236, see Keith Melder, "Ladies Bountiful: Organized Women's Benevolence in early 19th-Century America," *New York History*, 48 (1967), 231–54; Mary Kelley, *Private Woman, Public State: Literary Domesticity in Nineteenth Century America* (New York, 1984); and Barbara Epstein, *The Politics of Domesticity: Women, Evangelism, and Temperance in Nineteenth-Century America* (Middletown, Conn., 1981).
43. Philip D. Curtin, *The Atlantic Slave Trade: A Census* (Madison, 1969); C. Vann Woodward, "Southern Slaves in the World of Thomas Malthus," in Woodward, *American Counterpoint: Slavery and Racism in the North-South Dialogue* (Boston, 1971), 78–106.

estate. The continual expansion of the plantation economy to new frontiers uprooted many slaves who left behind family members as they trekked
westward. Recent studies of slave marriages have found that about one-
fourth of them were broken by owners or heirs who sold or moved
husband or wife apart from the other.[44] The sale of young children
apart from parents, while not the normal pattern, also occurred with
alarming frequency.

This breakup of families was the largest chink in the armor of slavery's defenders. Abolitionists thrust their swords through the chink. One
of the most powerful moral attacks on the institution was Theodore
Weld's *American Slavery as It Is*, first published in 1839 and reprinted
several times. Made up principally of excerpts from advertisements and
articles in southern newspapers, the book condemned slavery out of the
slaveowners' own mouths. Among hundreds of similar items in the book
were reward notices for runaway slaves containing such statements as
"it is probable he will aim for Savannah, as he said he had children in
that vicinity," or advertisements like the following from a New Orleans
newspaper: "NEGROES FOR SALE.—A negro woman 24 years of age, and
two children, one eight and the other three years. Said negroes will be
sold separately or together as desired."[45]

Harriet Beecher Stowe used Weld's book as a source for scenes in the
most influential indictment of slavery of all time, *Uncle Tom's Cabin*
(of which more later). Written in the sentimental style made popular by
best-selling women novelists, *Uncle Tom's Cabin* homed in on the
breakup of families as the theme most likely to pluck the heartstrings of
middle-class readers who cherished children and spouses of their own.
Eliza fleeing across the ice-choked Ohio River to save her son from the
slave-trader and Tom weeping for children left behind in Kentucky when

44. The following studies have found a marriage breakup rate by action of owners
    ranging from one-fifth to one-third: John W. Blassingame, *The Slave Community*
    (New York, 1972), 89–92; Herbert Gutman and Richard Sutch, "The Slave Fam-
    ily: Protected Agent of Capitalist Masters or Victim of Slave Trade?" in Paul A.
    David et al., *Reckoning with Slavery* (New York, 1976), 127–29; Herbert Gutman,
    The Black Family in Slavery and Freedom (New York, 1976), 146–47; Paul D.
    Escott, *Slavery Remembered: A Record of the Twentieth-Century Slave Narratives*
    (Chapel Hill, 1979), 46–48; and C. Peter Ripley, "The Black Family in Transi-
    tion: Louisiana, 1860–1865," *JSH*, 41 (1975), 377–78.
45. Weld, *American Slavery as It Is: Testimony of a Thousand Witnesses* (New York,
    1839), 165, 168.

he was sold South are among the most unforgettable scenes in American letters.

Although many northern readers shed tears at Tom's fate, the political and economic manifestations of slavery generated more contention than moral and humanitarian indictments. Bondage seemed an increasingly peculiar institution in a democratic republic experiencing a rapid transition to free-labor industrial capitalism. In the eyes of a growing number of Yankees, slavery degraded labor, inhibited economic development, discouraged education, and engendered a domineering master class determined to rule the country in the interests of its backward institution. Slavery undermined "intelligence, vigor, and energy," asserted New York's antislavery Whig leader William Henry Seward in the 1840s. It had produced in the South "an exhausted soil, old and decaying towns, wretchedly-neglected roads . . . an absence of enterprise and improvement." The institution was "incompatible with all . . . the elements of the security, welfare, and greatness of nations." Slavery and free labor, said Seward in his most famous speech, were "antagonistic systems" between which raged an "irrepressible conflict" that must result in the destruction of slavery.[46]

But whether or not slavery was backward and inefficient, as Seward maintained, it was extraordinarily productive. The yield of raw cotton doubled each decade after 1800, the greatest increase for any agricultural commodity. Cotton from the American South grown mostly by slave labor furnished three-fourths of the world's supply. Southern staples provided three-fifths of all American exports, earning foreign exchange that played an important part in American economic growth. And while slavery certainly made the Old South "different" from the North, the question whether differences outweighed similarities and generated an irrepressible conflict remains a matter of interpretation. North and South, after all, shared the same language, the same Constitution, the same legal system, the same commitment to republican institutions, the same predominantly Protestant religion and British ethnic heritage, the same history, the same memories of a common struggle for nationhood.

Yet by the 1850s Americans on both sides of the line separating freedom from slavery came to emphasize more their differences than simi-

46. Foner, *Free Soil*, 41, 51; George E. Baker, ed., *The Works of William H. Seward*, 5 vols. (New York, 1853–84), IV, 289–92.

larities. Yankees and Southrons spoke the same language, to be sure, but they increasingly used these words to revile each other. The legal system also became an instrument of division, not unity: northern states passed personal liberty laws to defy a national fugitive slave law supported by the South; a southern-dominated Supreme Court denied the right of Congress to exclude slavery from the territories, a ruling that most northerners considered infamous. As for a shared commitment to Protestantism, this too had become divisive rather than unifying. The two largest denominations—Methodist and Baptist—had split into hostile northern and southern churches over the question of slavery, and the third largest—Presbyterian—split partly along sectional lines and partly on the issue of slavery. The ideology of republicanism had also become more divisive than unifying, for most northerners interpreted it in a free-labor mode while most southerners insisted that one of the most cherished tenets of republican liberty was the right to property—including property in slaves.

People on both sides began pointing with pride or alarm to certain quantitative differences between North and South. From 1800 to 1860 the proportion of the northern labor force in agriculture had dropped from 70 to 40 percent while the southern proportion had remained constant at 80 percent. Only one-tenth of southerners lived in what the census classified as urban areas, compared with one-fourth of northerners. Seven-eighths of the immigrants settled in free states. Among antebellum men prominent enough to be later chronicled in the *Dictionary of American Biography*, the military profession claimed twice the percentage of southerners as northerners, while the ratio was reversed for men distinguished in literature, art, medicine, and education. In business the proportion of Yankees was three times as great, and among engineers and inventors it was six times as large.[47] Nearly twice the percentage of northern youth attended school. Almost half of the southern people (including slaves) were illiterate, compared to 6 percent of residents of free states.

Many conservative southerners scoffed at the Yankee faith in education. The *Southern Review* asked: "Is this the way to produce producers? To make every child in the state a literary character would not be a good qualification for those who must live by manual labor." The South, replied Massachusetts clergyman Theodore Parker in 1854, was "the foe

47. Rupert B. Vance, "The Geography of Distinction: The Nation and Its Regions, 1790–1927," *Social Forces*, 18 (1939), 175–76.

to Northern Industry—to our mines, our manufactures, and our commerce . . . to our democratic politics in the State, our democratic culture in the school, our democratic work in the community." Yankees and Southrons could no more mix than oil and water, agreed Savannah lawyer and planter Charles C. Jones, Jr. They "have been so entirely separated by climate, by morals, by religion, and by estimates so totally opposite of all that constitutes honor, truth, and manliness, that they cannot longer exist under the same government."[48]

Underlying all of these differences was the peculiar institution. "On the subject of slavery," declared the *Charleston Mercury* in 1858, "the North and South . . . are not only two Peoples, but they are rival, hostile Peoples."[49] This rivalry concerned the future of the republic. To nineteenth-century Americans the West represented the future. Expansion had been the country's lifeblood. So long as the slavery controversy focused on the morality of the institution where it already existed, the two-party system managed to contain the passions it aroused. But when in the 1840s the controversy began to focus on the expansion of slavery into new territories it became irrepressible.

"Westward the course of empire takes its way," Bishop George Berkeley had written of the New World in the 1720s. Westward looked Thomas Jefferson to secure an empire of liberty for future generations of American farmers. Even President Timothy Dwight of Yale University, who as a New England Federalist belonged to the region and group least enthusiastic about westward expansion, waxed eloquent in a poem of 1794:

> All hail, thou western world! by heaven design'd
> Th' example bright, to renovate mankind.
> Soon shall thy sons across the mainland roam;
> And claim, on far Pacific shores, their home;
> Their rule, religion, manners, arts, convey,
> And spread their freedom to the Asian sea.

A half-century later another Yankee who had never been to the West also found its attractions irresistible. "Eastward I go only by force," wrote

48. *Southern Review* quoted in Kaestle, *Pillars of the Republic*, 207; Parker quoted in John L. Thomas, ed., *Slavery Attacked: The Abolitionist Crusade* (Englewood Cliffs, 1965), 149; Jones in Robert Manson Myers, ed., *The Children of Pride: A True Story of Georgia and the Civil War* (New York, 1972), 648.
49. John McCardell, *The Idea of a Southern Nation: Southern Nationalists and Southern Nationalism, 1830–1860* (New York, 1979), 270–71.

Henry David Thoreau, "but westward I go free. Mankind progresses from East to West." [50]

"Go West, young man," advised Horace Greeley during the depression of the 1840s. And westward did they go, by millions in the first half of the nineteenth century, in obedience to an impulse that has never ceased. "The West is our object, there is no other hope left for us," wrote a departing migrant. "There is nothing like a new country for poor folks." "Old America seems to be breaking up, and moving westward," wrote one pioneer on his way to Illinois in 1817. "We are seldom out of sight, as we travel on this grand track towards the Ohio, of family groups behind, and before us." [51] From 1815 to 1850 the population of the region west of the Appalachians grew nearly three times as fast as the original thirteen states. During that era a new state entered the Union on the average of every three years. By the 1840s the states between the Appalachians and the Mississippi had passed the frontier stage. It had been a frontier of rivers, mainly the Ohio-Mississippi-Missouri network with their tributaries, which had carried settlers to their new homes and provided their initial links with the rest of the world.

After pushing into the first tier of states beyond the Mississippi, the frontier in the 1840s leapfrogged more than a thousand miles over the semi-arid Great Plains and awesome mountain ranges to the Pacific Coast. This was first a frontier of overland trails and of sailing routes around the horn; of trade in beaver skins from the mountains, silver from Santa Fe, and cattle hides from California. By the 1840s it had also become a farming frontier as thousands of Americans sold their property at depression prices, hitched their oxen to Conestoga wagons, and headed west over the Oregon, California, and Mormon trails to a new future—on land that belonged to Mexico or was claimed by Britain. That was a small matter, however, because most Americans considered it their "manifest destiny" to absorb these regions into the United States. Boundless prospects awaited settlers who would turn "those wild

50. Henry Nash Smith, *Virgin Land: The American West as Symbol and Myth* (Vintage Books ed., New York, 1957), 11; Loren Baritz, "The Idea of the West," *AHR*, 66 (1961), 639.
51. Lewis O. Saum, *The Popular Mood of Pre-Civil War America* (Westport, Conn., 1980), 205; Malcolm J. Rohrbough, *The Trans-Appalachian Frontier: People, Societies, and Institutions 1775–1850* (New York, 1978), 163.

forests, trackless plains, untrodden valleys" into "one grand scene of continuous improvements, universal enterprise, and unparalleled commerce," proclaimed the author of an emigrants' guide to Oregon and California. "Those fertile valleys shall groan under the immense weight of their abundant products; those numerous rivers shall teem with countless steamboats . . . the entire country will be everywhere intersected with turnpike roads, railroads, and canals." [52]

By all odds the most remarkable westward migration before the California gold rush of 1849 was the Mormon hegira to the Great Salt Lake basin. The first indigenous American religion, Mormonism sprang from the spiritual enthusiasm aroused by the Second Great Awakening among second-generation New England Yankees in the "burned-over district" of upstate New York. Founder and Prophet Joseph Smith built not only a church but also a utopian community, which like dozens of others in that era experimented with collective ownership of property and unorthodox marital arrangements. Unlike most other utopias, Mormonism survived and flourished.

But the road to survival was filled with obstacles. The Mormons' theocratic structure was both a strength and a weakness. Claiming direct communication with God, Smith ruled his band with iron discipline. Marshaled into phalanxes of tireless workers, true believers created prosperous communities wherever they settled. But Smith's messiah complex, his claim that Mormonism was the only true religion and would inherit the earth, his insistence on absolute obedience, spawned schisms within the movement and resentment without. Harried from New York and Ohio, the Mormons migrated west to create their Zion in Missouri. But Missourians had no use for these Yankee Saints who received revelations from God and were suspected of abolitionist purposes. Mobs massacred several Mormons in 1838–39 and drove the remainder across the Mississippi to Illinois. There the faithful prospered for several years despite the economic depression. Peripatetic missionaries converted thousands to the faith. They built the river town of Nauvoo into a thriving New England city of 15,000 souls. But Gentile neighbors envied the Saints' prosperity and feared their private army, the Nauvoo Legion. When yet another schismatic offshoot disclosed Smith's latest revelation sanctioning polygamy, the Prophet ordered the dissenters'

52. Lansford Hastings, *Emigrants' Guide to Oregon and California* (1845), quoted in Kevin Starr, *Americans and the California Dream* (New York, 1973), 15.

printing press destroyed. Illinois officials arrested Smith and his brother; in June 1844 a mob broke into the jail and murdered them.[53]

Smith's successor Brigham Young recognized that the Saints could not build their Zion among hostile unbelievers. Thus he led an exodus in 1846–47 to the basin of the Great Salt Lake in Mexican territory, a region apparently so inhospitable that no other white men wanted it. There the only neighbors would be Indians, who according to Mormon theology were descendants of one of Israel's lost tribes whom it was their duty to convert.

Brigham Young proved to be one of the nineteenth century's most efficient organizers. Like Joseph Smith, he had been born in Vermont. What Young lacked in the way of Smith's charisma he more than compensated for with an iron will and extraordinary administrative ability. He organized the Mormon migration down to the last detail. Under his theocratic rule, centralized planning and collective irrigation from mountain streams enabled Mormons to survive their starving time during the first two winters at Salt Lake and to make the desert literally bloom—not as a rose, but with grain and vegetables. As thousands of new converts arrived each year from Europe as well as the United States, the Great Basin Zion attained a population of 40,000 by 1860. Young even managed to prevent the faithful from joining the various gold rushes to California in 1849 and to the Virginia City and Denver regions in 1859. The Mormons earned more from trade with prospectors on their way to the gold fields than most of the miners did after they got there.

The greatest threat to the Saints was conflict with the United States government, which acquired the Great Basin from Mexico just as the Mormons were founding their Zion at Salt Lake. In 1850, Young persuaded Washington to name him governor of the new territory of Utah. This united church and state at the top and preserved peace for a time. But Gentile territorial judges and other officials complained that their authority existed in name only; the people obeyed laws handed down and interpreted by the church hierarchy. Tensions between Mormons and Gentiles sometimes escalated to violent confrontations. American

53. These and subsequent paragraphs are based on Wallace Stegner, *The Gathering of Zion: The Story of the Mormon Trail* (New York, 1964); Leonard J. Arrington, *Great Basin Kingdom* (Cambridge, Mass., 1958); Arrington, *Brigham Young: American Moses* (New York, 1985); Newell G. Bringhurst, *Brigham Young and the Expanding Frontier* (Boston, 1985); and Norman F. Furniss, *The Mormon Conflict, 1850–1859* (New Haven, 1960).

opinion turned sharply against the Saints in 1852 when the church openly embraced plural marriage as divinely ordained (Brigham Young himself took a total of 55 wives). In 1856 the first national platform of the Republican party branded polygamy a "barbarism" equal to slavery. In 1857 President James Buchanan declared the Mormons to be in rebellion and sent troops to force their submission to a new governor. During the Saints' guerrilla warfare against these soldiers in the fall of 1857, a group of Mormon fanatics massacred 120 California-bound emigrants at Mountain Meadows. This prompted the government to send more troops. A realist, Young accepted the inevitable, surrendered his civil authority, restrained his followers, and made an uneasy peace with the United States. When the next president, Abraham Lincoln, was asked what he intended to do about the Mormons, he replied that since they were the least of his problems "I propose to let them alone."

Like so much of American history, the westward movement seems to be a story of growth and success. But for the original Americans—the Indians—it was a bitter tale of contraction and defeat. By 1850 the white man's diseases and wars had reduced the Indian population north of the Rio Grande to half of the estimated one million who had lived there two centuries earlier. In the United States all but a few thousand Indians had been pushed west of the Mississippi. Democratic administrations in the 1830s had carried out a forced removal of 85,000 Indians of the five "civilized nations"—Cherokee, Choctaw, Creek, Chickasaw, and Seminole—from the southeastern states to an Indian territory set aside for them just west of Arkansas. Also in the 1830s a ruthless repression of Black Hawk's attempt to reclaim ancestral homelands in Illinois and the final suppression of Seminole resistance in Florida brought more than two centuries of Indian warfare east of the Mississippi to an end.

By then the government had decided to establish a "permanent Indian frontier" along roughly the 95th meridian (the western borders of Arkansas and Missouri). Beyond this line, Indians could roam freely in what explorer Zebulon Pike had labeled The Great American Desert. But the idea of a permanent Indian frontier lasted scarcely a decade. The overland westward migrations, the conquest of Mexican territory, and the discovery of gold in California opened this vast region to the manifest destiny of white Americans. So the government revived the burlesque of negotiations with Indian chiefs for cessions of huge chunks of territory in return for annuity payments that were soon soaked up by purchases of firewater and other white man's goods from wily traders. Since there was no more western frontier beyond which to push the

Indians of the Pacific coast, a policy evolved to place them on "reservations" where they could learn the white man's ways or perish. Most reservations were located on poor land, and a good many Indians had little inclination to learn the white man's ways. So they perished—in California alone disease, malnutrition, firewater, and homicide reduced the Indian population from an estimated 150,000 in 1845 to 35,000 by 1860. Although the Great Plains and the desert Southwest remained as yet uncoveted by white settlers, the reservation policy foretokened the fate of the proud warriors of these regions a decade or two later.[54]

The manifest destiny that represented hope for white Americans thus spelled doom for red Americans. And it also lit a slow fuse to a powder keg that blew the United States apart in 1861.

54. Robert M. Utley, *The Indian Frontier of the American West 1846–1890* (Albuquerque, 1984), 31–64.

2

Mexico Will Poison Us

I

James K. Polk presided over the acquisition of more territory than any other president in American history. During his one-term administration the country expanded by two-thirds with the annexation of Texas, the settlement of the Oregon boundary, and the seizure of all Mexican provinces north of 31°. Having been elected in 1844 on a platform demanding Oregon to a northern boundary of 54° 40′ and Texas to a southern boundary of the Rio Grande River, Polk compromised with Britain on 49° but went to war against Mexico for Texas—with California and New Mexico thrown in for good measure. And thereby hung a tale of sectional conflict that erupted into civil war a decade and a half later.[1]

"Mr. Polk's War" evoked opposition from Whigs in Congress, who voted against the resolution affirming a state of war with Mexico in May 1846. After the Democratic majority passed this resolution, however, most Whigs supported appropriations for the armies confronting enemy forces. Having witnessed the disappearance of the Federalist party after it opposed the War of 1812, a Whig congressman said sardonically that he now favored "war, pestilence, and famine." Nevertheless, Whigs continued to accuse Polk of having provoked the conflict by sending

1. Polk's motives and actions are laid out in detail by Charles G. Sellers, *James K. Polk, Continentalist 1843–1846* (Princeton, 1966).

American troops into territory claimed by Mexico. They sniped at the administration's conduct of the war and opposed territorial acquisition as a result of it. Encouraged by the elections of 1846 and 1847, in which they picked up 38 seats and gained control of the House, Whigs intensified their attacks on Polk. One of these new Whig congressmen, a lanky, craggy Illinoisian with gray eyes, disheveled black hair, and ill-fitting clothes introduced resolutions calling for information about the exact spot where Mexicans had shed American blood to start the war. Though the House tabled Abraham Lincoln's resolutions, it did pass one sponsored by another Whig declaring that the war had been "unnecessarily and unconstitutionally begun by the President."[2]

Like the war, Manifest Destiny was mainly a Democratic doctrine. Since the day when Thomas Jefferson overcame Federalist opposition to the purchase of Louisiana, Democrats had pressed for the expansion of American institutions across the whole of North America whether the residents—Indians, Spaniards, Mexicans, Canadians—wanted them or not. When God crowned American arms with success in the Revolution, vouchsafed a Democratic congressman in 1845, He had not "designed that the original States should be the only abode of liberty on earth. On the contrary, He only designed them as the great center from which civilization, religion, and liberty should radiate and radiate until the whole continent shall bask in their blessing." "Yes, more, more, more!" echoed John L. O'Sullivan, inventor of the phrase Manifest Destiny. "More . . . till our national destiny is fulfilled and . . . the whole boundless continent is ours."[3]

Whigs were not averse to extending the blessings of American liberty, even to Mexicans and Indians. But they looked askance at doing so by force. Befitting the evangelical origins of much Whig ideology, they placed their faith in mission more than in annexation. " 'As a city set upon a hill,' " the United States should inculcate the ideas of "true republicanism" by example rather than conquest, insisted many Whigs.

2. CG, 30 Cong., 1 Sess., 64, 95, and Appendix, 93–95. The best study of opposition to the war is John H. Schroeder, *Mr. Polk's War: American Opposition and Dissent, 1846–1848* (Madison, 1973). But see also Robert W. Johannsen, *To the Halls of the Montezumas: The War with Mexico in the American Imagination* (New York, 1985), which shows how popular the war was with the public outside of New England and a few other areas along the Atlantic seaboard.

3. John Wentworth of Illinois and O'Sullivan quoted in Frederick Merk, *Manifest Destiny and Mission in American History: A Reinterpretation* (New York, 1963), 28, 52.

Although it would "be a gain to mankind if we could spread over Mexico the Idea of America—that all men are born free and equal in rights," said antislavery clergyman Theodore Parker in 1846, "we must first make real those ideas at home." While the Democratic notion of progress envisioned the spread of existing institutions over *space*, the Whig idea envisaged the improvement of those institutions over *time*. "Opposed to the instinct of boundless acquisition stands that of Internal Improvement," said Horace Greeley. "A nation cannot simultaneously devote its energies to the absorption of others' territories and the improvement of its own."[4]

Acquisition of Mexican territory was Polk's principal war aim. The desire of American settlers in Oregon and California for annexation to the United States had precipitated the dual crises with Britain and Mexico in 1846. Praising these emigrants as "already engaged in establishing the blessings of self-government in the valleys of which the rivers flow to the Pacific," Polk had pledged to extend American law to "the distant regions which they have selected for their homes."[5] A treaty with Britain secured Oregon north to the 49th parallel. But efforts to persuade Mexico to sell California and New Mexico had failed. So Polk decided to use force. Soon after becoming president he ordered the Pacific fleet to stand ready to seize California's ports in the event of war with Mexico. In the fall of 1845 Polk instructed the U.S. consul at Monterey to encourage annexation sentiment among American settlers and disaffected Mexicans.

Americans in California needed little encouragement, especially when they had among them a glory-hunting captain of the army topographical corps, John C. Frémont. Famous for his explorations of the West, Frémont was also the son-in-law of Missouri's powerful Senator Thomas Hart Benton. When rumors of war with Mexico reached the Sacramento valley, Frémont took it upon himself to assist settlers in an uprising that proclaimed an independent California. This "bear flag republic" (its flag bore the image of a grizzly bear) enjoyed a brief existence before its citizens celebrated official news of the war that ensured their annexation by the United States.

---

4. Schroeder, *Mr. Polk's War*, 75–76; Parker, "A Sermon of War," in Robert E. Collins, ed., *Theodore Parker: American Transcendentalist* (Metuchen, N.J., 1973), 252; Greeley quoted in Daniel Walker Howe, *The Political Culture of the American Whigs* (Chicago, 1979), 21.
5. Sellers, *Polk*, 210.

While these proceedings unfolded, Missouri volunteers and a regiment of regulars were marching over the Santa Fe trail to seize the capital of New Mexico. Commanded by Stephen Watts Kearny, these tough dragoons occupied Santa Fe on August 18, 1846, without firing a shot. After raising the American flag, Kearny left behind a garrison and pushed across the desert to California with a hundred men who joined a few hundred sailors, marines, and volunteers to subdue Mexican resistance there by January 1847. During the next several months a string of stunning American victories south of the Rio Grande culminating in the capture of Mexico City ensured the permanence of these American conquests. The only remaining question was how much territory to take.

Polk's appetite was originally sated by New Mexico and California. In April 1847 he sent Nicholas Trist to Mexico as a commissioner to negotiate a treaty for these provinces. But the ease of American conquest made Polk suddenly hungry for more territory. By the fall of 1847 a Democratic movement to annex "all Mexico"—or at least several additional provinces—was in full cry. The whipsaw cuts and rasps of all-Mexico Democrats and no-territory Whigs left Trist on a precarious limb three thousand miles away in Mexico City where the proud Santa Anna proved reluctant to yield up half his country. Polk sided with the hard-liners in Washington and recalled Trist in October 1847. But a breakthrough in negotiations appeared possible just as Trist received the recall dispatch, so he disobeyed orders and signed a treaty that fulfilled Polk's original instructions. In return for a payment by the United States of $15 million plus the assumption of Mexican debts to American citizens, Mexico recognized the Rio Grande boundary of Texas and ceded New Mexico and upper California to the United States.[6] When this Treaty of Guadalupe Hidalgo reached Washington in February 1848, Polk initially spurned it. On second thought, however, he submitted it to the Senate, where the Whigs would have enough votes to defeat any treaty that sliced off more Mexican territory but might approve one that avoided the appearance of conquest by paying Mexico for California and New Mexico. The strategy worked; the Senate ratified the treaty by a vote of 38-14, with five of the opposition votes coming from Democrats

6. This cession included the present states of California, Nevada, and Utah, most of New Mexico and Arizona, and parts of Oklahoma, Colorado, and Wyoming as well as one-third of Texas.

who wanted more territory and seven from Whigs who wanted none.[7]

This triumph of Manifest Destiny may have reminded some Americans of Ralph Waldo Emerson's prophecy that "the United States will conquer Mexico, but it will be as the man swallows the arsenic, which brings him down in turn. Mexico will poison us."[8] He was right. The poison was slavery. Jefferson's Empire for Liberty had become mostly an empire for slavery. Territorial acquisitions since the Revolution had added the slave states of Louisiana, Missouri, Arkansas, Florida, and Texas to the republic, while only Iowa, just admitted in 1846, had increased the ranks of free states. Many northerners feared a similar future for this new southwestern empire. They condemned the war as part of a "slave power conspiracy" to expand the peculiar institution. Was not President Polk a slaveholder? Had he not been elected on a platform of enlarging slave territory by annexing Texas? Were not proslavery southerners among the most aggressive proponents of Manifest Destiny? Did not most of the territory (including Texas) wrested from Mexico lie south of the old Missouri Compromise line of 36° 30'—a traditional demarcation between freedom and slavery? The Massachusetts legislature indicted this "unconstitutional" war with its "triple object of extending slavery, of strengthening the slave power, and of obtaining control of the free states." James Russell Lowell's rustic Yankee philosopher Hosea Biglow fretted that

> They just want this Californy
> So's to lug new slave-states in
> To abuse ye, an' to scorn ye,
> An' to plunder ye like sin.[9]

Polk could not understand what the fuss was about. "In connection with the Mexican War," he wrote in his diary, slavery was "an abstract question. There is no probability that any territory will ever be acquired from Mexico in which slavery would ever exist." Agitation was thus "not only mischievous but wicked." But a good many congressmen—

---

7. *Senate Executive Docs.*, 30 Cong., 1 Sess., no. 52, p. 36. The other two opposition votes came from Democrats who disliked the treaty for other reasons.
8. Edward W. Emerson and Waldo E. Forbes, eds., *Journals of Ralph Waldo Emerson*, 10 vols. (Boston, 1909–14), VII, 206.
9. H. V. Ames, ed., *State Documents on Federal Relations* (Philadelphia, 1906), 241–42; *The Works of James Russell Lowell*, Standard Library ed., 11 vols. (Boston, 1890), VIII, 46–47.

even some in Polk's own party—did not share the president's conviction. They believed agitation of the question necessary. This issue overshadowed all others from 1846 to 1850. Hundreds of congressmen felt moved to speak on the matter. Some of them agreed with Polk that it was an "abstract" issue because "natural conditions" would exclude slavery from these lands. "The right to carry slaves to New Mexico or California is no very great matter," said John J. Crittenden of Kentucky, because "no sensible man would carry his slaves there if he could."[10] But numerous southerners disagreed. They noted that cotton was already grown in river valleys of New Mexico. Slaves had labored in mines for centuries and would prove ideal mineworkers in these territories. "California is peculiarly adapted for slave labor," resolved a southern convention. "The right to have [slave] property protected in the territory is not a mere abstraction." A Georgia newspaper heightened abolitionist suspicions of a slave-power conspiracy by professing a broader purpose in opening these territories to slavery: it would "secure to the South the balance of power in the Confederacy, and, for all coming time . . . give to her the control in the operations of the Government."[11]

Of the congressmen who spoke on this matter, more than half expressed confidence (if southern) or fear (if northern) that slavery would go into the new territories if allowed to do so.[12] Many of them conceded that the institution was unlikely to put down deep roots in a region presumed to be covered with deserts and mountains. But to make sure, northern congressmen voted for a resolution to exclude slavery therefrom. This was the fateful Wilmot Proviso. As Congress neared adjournment on the sultry Saturday night of August 8, 1846, Pennsylvania's first-term Representative David Wilmot rose during the debate on an appropriations bill for the Mexican War and moved an amendment: "that, as an express and fundamental condition of the acquisition of any territory from the Republic of Mexico . . . neither slavery nor involuntary servitude shall ever exist in any part of said territory."[13]

10. Milo Milton Quaife, ed., *The Diary of James K. Polk during His Presidency, 1845 to 1849,* 4 vols. (Chicago, 1910), II, 308; Michael F. Holt, *The Political Crisis of the 1850s* (New York, 1978), 77.

11. Robert S. Starobin, *Industrial Slavery in the Old South* (New York, 1970), 18–20; *Milledgeville Federal Union,* Nov. 10, 1846, quoted in Schroeder, *Mr. Polk's War,* 55.

12. Desmond D. Hart, "The Natural Limits of Slavery Expansion: The Mexican Territories as a Test Case," *Mid-America,* 52 (1970), 119–31.

13. CG, 29 Cong., 1 Sess., 1217.

More lay behind this maneuver than met the eye. Antislavery conviction motivated Wilmot and his allies, but so did a desire to settle old political scores. Wilmot acted for a group of northern Democrats who were vexed with Polk and fed up with southern domination of the party. Their grievances went back to 1844 when southerners had denied Martin Van Buren the presidential nomination because he refused to endorse the annexation of Texas. The Polk administration had given the patronage in New York to anti-Van Buren "Hunkers." Rate reductions in the Walker Tariff of 1846 embittered Pennsylvania Democrats who thought they had secured a pledge for higher duties on certain items. Polk's veto of a rivers and harbors bill angered Democrats from Great Lakes and western river districts. The administration's compromise on the 49th parallel for the Oregon boundary incensed the many Democrats who had chanted the slogan "Fifty-four forty or fight!" Having voted for the annexation of Texas with its disputed Rio Grande border at risk of war with Mexico, they felt betrayed by Polk's refusal to risk war with Britain for all of Oregon. "Our rights to Oregon have been shamefully compromised," declared an Ohio Democrat. "The administration is Southern, Southern, Southern! . . . Since the South have fixed boundaries for free territory, let the North fix boundaries for slave territories." "The time has come," agreed Connecticut Congressman Gideon Welles, "when the Northern democracy should make a stand. Every thing has taken a Southern shape and been controlled by Southern caprice for years." We must, Welles concluded "satisfy the northern people . . . that we are not to extend the institution of slavery as a result of this war."[14]

When Wilmot introduced his proviso, therefore, he released the pent-up ire of northern Democrats, many of whom cared less about slavery in new territories than about their power within the party. Northern Whigs, who had a more consistent antislavery record, were delighted to support the proviso. This bipartisan northern coalition in the House passed it over the united opposition of southern Democrats and Whigs. This was a dire omen. The normal pattern of division in Congress had

14. *Cleveland Plain Dealer*, June 22, Aug. 5, 1846, quoted in Stephen E. Maizlish, *The Triumph of Sectionalism: The Transformation of Ohio Politics 1844–1856* (Kent, 1983), 56, 60–61; Welles to Martin Van Buren, July 28, 1846, June 30, 1848, quoted in Richard H. Sewell, *Ballots for Freedom: Antislavery Politics in the United States 1837–1860* (New York, 1976), 143; speech by Welles in the House, Jan. 7, 1847, in CG, 29 Cong., 2 Sess., 136. See also Eric Foner, "The Wilmot Proviso Revisited," *JAH*, 56 (1969), 262–79.

occurred along party lines on issues such as the tariff, the Bank, federal aid to internal improvements, and the like. The Wilmot Proviso wrenched this division by parties into a conflict of sections. The political landscape would never again be the same. "As if by magic," commented the *Boston Whig*, "it brought to a head the great question that is about to divide the American people."[15]

The full impact of the proviso did not become apparent immediately, for Congress adjourned in 1846 before the Senate could vote on it. But northern Democrats reintroduced it at the next session, prompting an anguished lament from the president, who began to comprehend the whirlwind he was reaping as the result of his war. "The slavery question is assuming a fearful . . . aspect," wrote Polk in his diary. It "cannot fail to destroy the Democratic party, if it does not ultimately threaten the Union itself."[16] The House again passed Wilmot's amendment by a sectional vote. But the South's greater power in the Senate (15 slave states and 14 free states composed the Union in 1847) enabled it to block the proviso there. Arm-twisting by the administration eventually compelled enough northern Democrats in the House to change their votes to pass the appropriations bill without the proviso. But the crisis had not been resolved—only postponed.

Free-soil sentiment in 1847 can be visualized in three concentric circles. At the center was a core of abolitionists who considered slavery a sinful violation of human rights that should be immediately expiated. Surrounding and drawing ideological nourishment from them was a larger circle of antislavery people who looked upon bondage as an evil—by which they meant that it was socially repressive, economically backward, and politically harmful to the interests of free states.[17] This circle comprised mainly Whigs (and some Democrats) from the Yankee belt of states and regions north of the 41st parallel who regarded this issue

15. Aug. 15, 1846, quoted in Potter, *Impending Crisis*, 23.
16. Quaife, ed., *Diary of Polk*, II, 305.
17. Three-fifths of the slaves were counted as part of the population on which representation in the House was based. This gave southern voters relatively greater influence in national politics than northern voters. Because the average population of the slave states was less than that of free states, the equal representation of each state by two senators gave the South disproportionate power in the Senate as well. And since each state's electoral vote equaled its combined number of senators and representatives, the South also enjoyed disparate power in presidential elections. With 30 percent of the voting population in 1848, the slave states cast 42 percent of the electoral votes.

as more important than any other in American politics. The outer circle contained all those who had voted for the Wilmot Proviso but did not necessarily consider it the most crucial matter facing the country and were open to compromise. This outer circle included such Whigs as Abraham Lincoln, who believed slavery "an unqualified evil to the negro, the white man, and the State" which "deprives our republican example of its just influence in the world—enables the enemies of free institutions, with plausibility, to taunt us as hypocrites," but who also believed that "the promulgation of abolition doctrines tends rather to increase than to abate its evils" by uniting the South in defense of the institution.[18] The outer circle also included Democrats, like Martin Van Buren, who cared little about the consequences of slavery for the slaves and had been allied with the "slave power" until it had blocked Van Buren's nomination in 1844.

All free soilers—except perhaps some of the Van Burenites—concurred with the following set of propositions: free labor was more efficient than slave labor because it was motivated by the inducement of wages and the ambition for upward mobility rather than by the coercion of the lash; slavery undermined the dignity of manual work by associating it with servility and thereby degraded white labor wherever bondage existed; slavery inhibited education and social improvements and kept poor whites as well as slaves in ignorance; the institution therefore mired all southerners except the slaveowning gentry in poverty and repressed the development of a diversified economy; slavery must be kept out of all new territories so that free labor could flourish there.

For some members of the two outer circles these propositions did not spring from a "squeamish sensitiveness . . . nor morbid sympathy for the slave," as David Wilmot put it. "The negro race already occupy enough of this fair continent. . . . I would preserve for free white labor a fair country . . . where the sons of toil, of my own race and own color, can live without the disgrace which association with negro slavery brings upon free labor." If slavery goes into the new territories, wrote free-soil editor and poet William Cullen Bryant, "the free labor of all the states will not." But if slavery is kept out, "the free labor of the states [will go] there . . . and in a few years the country will teem with an active and energetic population."[19]

18. CWL, I, 74–75; II, 255; III, 92.
19. CG, 29 Cong., 2 Sess., Appendix, 314–17; New York Evening Post, Nov. 10, 1847.

Southerners bristled at these attacks on their social system. At one time a good many of them had shared the conviction that slavery was an evil—albeit a "'necessary" one for the time being because of the explosive racial consequences of emancipation. But the sense of evil had faded by 1830 as the growing world demand for cotton fastened the tentacles of a booming plantation economy on the South. Abolitionist attacks on slavery placed southerners on the defensive and goaded them into angry counterattacks. By 1840 slavery was no longer a necessary evil; it was "a great moral, social, and political blessing—a blessing to the slave, and a blessing to the master." It had civilized African savages and provided them with cradle-to-grave security that contrasted favorably with the miserable poverty of "free" labor in Britain and the North. By releasing whites from menial tasks it elevated white labor and protected it from degrading competition with free Negroes. Slavery eliminated the specter of class conflict that would eventually destroy free-labor societies, for it "promotes equality among the free by dispensing with grades and castes among them, and thereby preserves republican institutions."[20] It also established the foundation for an upper class of gentlemen to cultivate the arts, literature, hospitality, and public service. It created a far superior society to that of the "vulgar, contemptible, counter-jumping" Yankees. Indeed, said Senator Robert M. T. Hunter of Virginia, "there is not a respectable system of civilization known to history whose foundations were not laid in the institution of domestic slavery." "Instead of an evil," said John C. Calhoun in summing up the southern position, slavery was "a positive good . . . the most safe and stable basis for free institutions in the world."[21]

Proponents of slavery naturally wished to offer the blessings of this institution to the new territories. Even those who did not expect bondage to flourish there resented the northern effort to exclude it as an insult to southern honor. The Wilmot Proviso pronounced "a degrading inequality" on the South, declared a Virginian. It "says in effect to the Southern man, Avaunt! you are not my equal, and hence are to be

---

20. Senator Albert Gallatin Brown of Mississippi quoted in David Donald, *Charles Sumner and the Coming of the Civil War* (New York, 1960), 348; resolution of a Southern Rights convention in Montgomery, March 1852, quoted in J. Mills Thornton III, *Politics and Power in a Slave Society: Alabama, 1800–1860* (Baton Rouge, 1978), 206–7.

21. Hunter quoted in Donald, *Sumner and the Coming of the Civil War*, 349; Calhoun in CG, 25 Cong., 2 Sess., Appendix, 61–62.

excluded as carrying a moral taint." Having furnished most of the soldiers who conquered Mexican territory, the South was particularly outraged by the proposal to shut them out of its benefits. "When the war-
worn soldier returns to his home," asked an Alabamian, "is he to be
told that he cannot carry his property to the country won by his blood?"[22]
"No true Southron," said scores of them, would submit to such "social
and sectional degradation. . . . Death is preferable to acknowledged
inferiority."[23]

In addition to their sacred honor, slaveholders had "the lives and
fortunes of ourselves and families" at stake. Enactment of the Wilmot
Proviso would yield ten new free states, warned James Hammond of
South Carolina. The North would then "ride over us rough shod" in
Congress, "proclaim freedom or something equivalent to it to our slaves
and reduce us to the condition of Hayti. . . . Our only safety is in
equality of POWER. If we do not act now, we deliberately consign our
children, not our posterity, but our *children* to the flames."[24]

Southerners challenged the constitutionality of the Wilmot Proviso.
Admittedly, precedent seemed to sanction congressional exclusion of
slavery from territories. The first Congress under the Constitution had
reaffirmed the Northwest Ordinance of 1787 banning the institution
from the Northwest Territory. Subsequent Congresses re-enacted the
ordinance for each territory carved out of the region. The Compromise
of 1820 prohibited slavery north of 36° 30' in the Louisiana Purchase.
Southern congressmen had voted for these laws. But in February 1847
Senator John C. Calhoun introduced resolutions denying the right of
Congress to exclude slave property from the territories. "Tall, careworn,
with fevered brow, haggard cheek and eye, intensely gazing," as Henry
Clay described him, Calhoun insisted that territories were the "common
property" of sovereign states. Acting as the "joint agents" of these states,
Congress could no more prevent a slaveowner from taking his human
property to the territories than it could prevent him from taking his
horses or hogs there. If the North insisted on ramming through the

22. Both quotations from Chaplain W. Morrison, *Democratic Politics and Sectional-
    ism: The Wilmot Proviso Controversy* (Chapel Hill, 1967), 65.
23. *Ibid.*; Don E. Fehrenbacher, *The South and Three Sectional Crises* (Baton Rouge,
    1980), 26; William J. Cooper, Jr., *The South and the Politics of Slavery 1828–
    1856* (Baton Rouge, 1978), 239.
24. William L. Barney, *The Road to Secession: A New Perspective on the Old South*
    (New York, 1972), 105–6.

Wilmot Proviso, warned Calhoun in sepulchral tones, the result would be "political revolution, anarchy, civil war."[25]

The Senate did not pass the Calhoun resolutions. As the presidential election of 1848 neared, both major parties sought to heal the sectional rifts within their ranks. One possible solution, hallowed by tradition, was to extend the Missouri Compromise line through the middle of the new territories to the Pacific. Polk and his cabinet endorsed this policy. Ailing and prematurely aged, the president did not seek renomination. Secretary of State James Buchanan made 36° 30' the centerpiece of his drive for the nomination. Several times in 1847–48 the Senate passed a version of this proposal, with the backing of most southern senators, who yielded the principle of slavery in all the territories for the sake of securing its legality in some. But the northern majority in the House voted it down.

Another idea emerged from the maelstrom of presidential politics. This one came to be known as popular sovereignty It was identified in 1848 mainly with Michigan's Senator Lewis Cass, Buchanan's main rival for the Democratic presidential nomination. Maintaining that settlers in territories were as capable of self-government as citizens of states, Cass proposed that they should decide for themselves whether to have slavery. This idea had the political charm of ambiguity, for Cass did not specify *when* voters might choose for or against slavery—during the territorial stage or only when adopting a state constitution. Most contemporaries presumed the former—including Calhoun, who therefore opposed popular sovereignty because it could violate the property rights of southern settlers. But enough southerners saw merit in the approach to enable Cass to win the nomination—though significantly the platform did not endorse popular sovereignty. It did reject the Wilmot Proviso and the Calhoun resolutions, however. The Democratic party continued the tradition of trying to preserve intersectional unity by avoiding a firm position on slavery.

So did the Whigs. Indeed they adopted no platform at all, and nominated the hero of a war that most of them had opposed. Nothing illustrated better the strange-bedfellow nature of American politics than Zachary Taylor's candidacy. A thick-set man with stubby legs and heavy brows contracted into a perpetual frown, careless in dress, a career army officer (but not a West Pointer) with no discernible political opinions,

25. CG, 29 Cong., 2 Sess., 453–55. Clay's description of Calhoun is quoted in Nevins, *Ordeal*, I, 24.

Taylor seemed unlikely presidential timber. The handsome, imposing General-in-Chief Winfield Scott, a dedicated professional with a fondness for dress uniforms, and an articulate Whig, looked like a better choice if the anti-war party felt compelled to mend its image by nominating a military candidate. But Scott had the defects of his virtues. His critics considered him pompous. He had a penchant for writing foot-in-mouth public letters which made him vulnerable to ridicule. His nickname—Old Fuss and Feathers—conveys the nature of his political liabilities. And Taylor had the virtues of his defects, as the image conveyed by *his* sobriquet of Rough and Ready illustrates. Many voters in this new age of (white) manhood suffrage seemed to prefer their candidates rough-hewn. As a war hero Taylor claimed first priority on public affection. Although Scott had planned and led the campaign of 1847 that captured Mexico City, Taylor's victories of 1846 along the Rio Grande and his extraordinary triumph against odds of three to one at Buena Vista in February 1847 had made his reputation before Scott got started.

Buena Vista launched a Taylor bandwagon that proved unstoppable. Rough and Ready's main rival for the nomination (besides Scott) was Henry Clay. Urbane, witty, popular, the seventy-year-old Clay was Mr. Whig—a founder of the party and architect of its "American System" to promote economic growth by a protective tariff, a national bank, and federal aid to internal improvements. As a three-time loser in presidential contests, however, Clay carried the liabilities as well as assets of a long political career. Like a majority of his party he had opposed the annexation of Texas and the Mexican War.[26] But the Whigs could not hope to win the election without carrying some states where annexation and the war had been popular. Taylor seemed to be the answer.

The general was also a godsend to southern Whigs, who faced an erosion of strength at home because of the persistent support of northern Whigs for the Wilmot Proviso. (Most northern Democrats had abandoned Wilmot's Proviso for Cass's formula of popular sovereignty.) Southern Whig leaders, especially Senator John J. Crittenden of Kentucky and Congressman Alexander Stephens of Georgia, maneuvered the Taylor boom into a southern movement. Taylor's ownership of Louisiana and Mississippi plantations with more than a hundred slaves seemed to assure his safety on the issue of most importance to southern-

26. In a sad irony, one of Clay's sons was killed at Buena Vista. Another prominent Whig and opponent of the Mexican adventure, Daniel Webster, also lost a son in the war.

ers. "The truth is," declared Robert Toombs of Georgia, Clay "has sold himself body and soul to the Northern Anti-Slavery Whigs." Taylor, on the other hand, was a "Southern man, a slaveholder, a cotton planter" identified "from birth, association, and conviction . . . with the South."[27]Southern delegates to the Whig convention provided the votes to deny Clay the nomination on the first ballot and then to award it to Taylor on the fourth.

Taylor's candidacy brought to a head a long-festering schism in northern Whiggery. "Of course, we cannot & will not under any circumstances support General Taylor," wrote Charles Sumner of Massachusetts. "We cannot support any body who is not known to be against the extension of Slavery." Sumner spoke for a faction of the party known as "Conscience Whigs." They challenged a more conservative group labeled "Cotton Whigs" because of the prominence of textile magnates in their ranks. The Cotton faction had opposed the Mexican War and favored the Wilmot Proviso. But their position on these issues seemed lukewarm, and in 1848 they wished to join hands with southern Whigs in behalf of Taylor and victory. Unable to sanction this alliance of "lords of the loom" with "lords of the lash," Conscience Whigs bolted the party. Their purpose, in Sumner's words, was no less than "a new crystallization of parties, in which there shall be one grand Northern party of Freedom."[28]

The time appeared ripe for such a movement. In New York the Van Buren faction of Democrats was ready for revolt. Dubbed "Barnburners" (after the legendary Dutch farmer who burned his barn to rid it of rats), this faction sent a separate delegation to the national Democratic convention. When the convention voted to seat both New York delegations, the Barnburners stomped out and held their own conclave to nominate Van Buren on a Wilmot Proviso platform. Antislavery Democrats and Whigs from other northern states cheered. The Barnburner

---

27. Toombs to James Thomas, April 16, 1848, in Ulrich B. Phillips, ed., *The Correspondence of Robert Toombs, Alexander H. Stephens, and Howell Cobb*, Annual Report of the American Historical Association, 1911, vol. 2 (Washington, 1913), 103–4; *New Orleans Bee* and *Charleston Mercury* quoted in Joseph G. Rayback, *Free Soil: The Election of 1848* (Lexington, Ky., 1970), 42, 43.

28. Sumner to Salmon P. Chase, Feb. 7, 1848, Dec. 12, 1846, Chase Papers, Library of Congress. For the development of this split within the Whig party of Massachusetts, see Kinley J. Brauer, *Cotton versus Conscience: Massachusetts Whig Politics and Southwestern Expansion, 1843–1848* (Lexington, Ky., 1967).

convention provided the spark for an antislavery political blaze; the Liberty party offered itself as kindling.

Founded in 1839 by simon-pure abolitionists, the Liberty party had thus far managed to win only 3 percent of the northern votes for its presidential candidate, in 1844. Since that election, party leaders had been debating future strategy. A radical faction wanted to proclaim a new doctrine that the Constitution empowered the government to abolish slavery *in the states*. But a more pragmatic majority under the leadership of Salmon P. Chase wanted to move in the other direction—toward a coalition with antislavery Whigs and Democrats. An astute lawyer who had defended fugitive slaves, Chase combined religious conviction and humorlessness with unquenchable ambition and shrewd political insight. Although Liberty men must continue to proclaim the goal of ending slavery everywhere, said Chase, they could best take the first step toward that goal by joining with those who believed in keeping it out of the territories—whatever else they believed. If such a coalition gained enough leverage in Ohio to elect Chase to the U. S. Senate, so much the better. Chase planted feelers with Conscience Whigs and Barnburner Democrats in the spring of 1848. These ripened into a Free Soil convention in August, after the major-party nominations of Cass and Taylor had propelled antislavery men out of their old allegiances.

The Free Soil convention at Buffalo resembled nothing so much as a camp meeting. Fifteen thousand fervent "delegates" thronged into the sweltering city. Gathered under a huge canopy erected in the park, they cheered endless oratory damning the slave power while an executive committee of 465 met in the church to do the real work. This committee accomplished something of a miracle by fusing factions from three parties that held clashing opinions on banking, tariffs, and other economic issues. These questions, the staples of American politics for two decades, must give way to a more important one, said veteran Whig Congressman Joshua Giddings of Ohio: "Our political conflicts must be in future between slavery and freedom."[29] The committee created its new fusion party by nominating a Barnburner for president and a Conscience Whig for vice president on a Liberty platform drafted mainly by Chase. The "mass convention" in the park roared its approval of the committee's work.

Acceptance of Martin Van Buren as presidential nominee was not

29. Maizlish, *Triumph of Sectionalism*, 89.

easy for Liberty men and Conscience Whigs. As a proslavery Jacksonian, the Little Magician had earned the apparent undying enmity of
abolitionists and Whigs in the 1830s. But a new age dawned in 1848.
Van Buren now endorsed exclusion of slavery from the territories and
abolition of slavery in the District of Columbia. His Barnburner backers
proclaimed bondage "a great moral, social, and political evil—a relic of
barbarism which must necessarily be swept away in the progress of
Christian civilization." Speaking to fellow Whigs, Sumner said that "it
is not for the Van Buren of 1838 that we are to vote, but the Van Buren
of *to-day*."[30] With Charles Francis Adams as vice-presidential nominee, the ticket strengthened its Conscience image. Charles Francis inherited the antislavery mantle from his father John Quincy, who had
died earlier in the year. Joshua Leavitt, a founder of the Liberty party
and a co-worker with John Quincy Adams against the congressional gag
rule on antislavery petitions, brought tears to many eyes at the Buffalo
convention with an emotional speech recounting the courage of pioneer
abolitionists. Leavitt then offered his blessing to the new Free Soil coalition. "The Liberty Party is not dead," he declaimed, "but *translated*."
Vowing to "fight on, and fight ever" for "Free Soil, Free Speech, Free
Labor, and Free Men," the delegates returned home to battle for the
Lord.[31]

Free Soilers made slavery the campaign's central issue. Both major
parties had to abandon their strategy of ignoring the question. Instead,
they tried to win support in each section by obfuscating it. Democrats
circulated different campaign biographies of Cass in North and South.
In the North they emphasized popular sovereignty as the best way to
keep slavery out of the territories. In the South Democrats cited Cass's
pledge to veto the Wilmot Proviso and pointed with pride to the party's
success (over Whig opposition) in acquiring territory into which slavery
might expand.

Having no platform to explain and a candidate with no political record to defend, Whigs had an easier time appearing to be all things to

---

30. Both quotations from Rayback, *Free Soil*, 211, 247.
31. This account of the Free Soil convention is drawn from Rayback, 201–30; Morrison, *Democratic Politics and Sectionalism*, 145–55; Frederick J. Blue, *The Free
Soilers: Third Party Politics 1848–1854* (Urbana, 1973); Brauer, *Cotton vs. Conscience*, 229–45; Sewell, *Ballots for Freedom*, 142–58; and John Mayfield, *Rehearsal for Republicanism: Free Soil and the Politics of Antislavery* (Port Washington, N.Y., 1980), 111–19.

all men. In the North they pointed to Taylor's pledge *not* to veto whatever Congress decided to do about slavery in the territories. Those antislavery Whigs who supported Taylor in the belief that he would take
their side—William H. Seward and Abraham Lincoln, for example—
turned out to be right. Southerners should have paid more attention to
a speech by Seward at Cleveland. Affable, artful, sagacious, an instinc-
tive politician but also a principled opponent of slavery, Seward would
soon emerge as one of Taylor's main advisers. "Freedom and slavery are
two antagonistic elements of society," he told a Cleveland audience.
"Slavery can be limited to its present bounds"; eventually "it *can* and
must be abolished."[32] But in the South, Taylor's repute as the hero of
Buena Vista and his status as a large slaveholder dazzled many eyes.
"We prefer Old Zack with his sugar and cotton plantations and four
hundred negroes," proclaimed the *Richmond Whig*. "Will the people of
[the South] vote for a Southern President or a Northern one?" asked a
Georgia newspaper.[33]

Most of them voted for a southern one. Taylor carried eight of the
fifteen slave states with a majority of 52 percent. He also carried seven
of fifteen free states, though the Whig popular vote in the North dropped
to 46 percent because of Free-Soil inroads. But while they won 14 percent of the northern vote and supplanted Democrats as the second party
in Vermont, Massachusetts, and New York, the Free Soilers did not
carry a single state. Nor did they affect the election's outcome: though
Van Buren carried enough Democratic votes in New York to give the
state to Taylor, Free Soilers neutralized this effect by attracting enough
Whig voters in Ohio to put that state in Cass's column. Despite stresses
produced by the slavery issue, the centripetal forces of party overcame
the centrifugal forces of section.[34]

Nevertheless, those stresses had wrenched the system almost to the
breaking point. Free Soilers hoping to realign American politics into a
struggle between freedom and slavery professed satisfaction with the
election. "The public mind has been stirred on the subject of slavery to
depths never reached before," wrote Sumner. "The late election," agreed
one of his confreres, "is only the Bunker Hill of the moral & political

32. Nevins, *Ordeal*, I, 212; James Ford Rhodes, *History of the United States from the
    Compromise of 1850 . . .* 7 vols. (New York, 1893–1906), I, 162.
33. Quoted in Cooper, *The South and the Politics of Slavery*, 265, 262.
34. For detailed election data and an analysis, see Rayback, *Free Soil*, 279–302.

revolution which can terminate only in success to the side of freedom."[35]

II

Almost unnoticed in the East during the presidential campaign, another dramatic event of 1848 presaged further strains on the two-party system. Workers constructing a sawmill for John Sutter near Sacramento in January discovered flecks of gold in the river bed. Despite Sutter's attempt to keep the news quiet, word spread to San Francisco. Gold fever turned the port into a ghost town by June as the population headed for the Sierra foothills. In August the news reached the Atlantic coast, where it encountered skepticism from a public surfeited with fabulous tales from the West. But in December the whole country took notice when Polk's last annual message to Congress included a reference to the "extraordinary" finds in California. As if on cue, a special agent from the gold fields arrived in Washington two days later with a tea caddy containing 320 ounces of pure gold. Doubt disappeared; everyone became a true believer; many dreamed of striking it rich; and a hundred thousand of them headed West. The trickle of migrants to California during the previous decade became a flood in the great gold rush of '49, soon chronicled in song and story and ultimately transmuted into miles of Hollywood celluloid. Some eighty thousand of these Forty-niners actually reached California during that first year. Thousands of others died on the way, many from a cholera epidemic. A few of the Forty-niners struck it rich; but toil, hardship, and disappointment became the lot of most. Yet still they came, until by the census year of 1850 California had a larger population than Delaware or Florida. The territory's quest to become the thirty-first state sparked a renewed sectional crisis back East.

What the hell-roaring mining camps needed most was law and order. At first each camp elected its own officials and enforced a rough justice. But this was scarcely adequate for a large region with a mostly male population "from every hole and corner of the world" quick to violate or defend personal rights with revolver or hangman's rope. A few companies of the army provided the only semblance of national authority in

35. Sumner to Salmon P. Chase, Nov. 16, 1848, Chase Papers, Library of Congress; Preston King to Sumner, Dec. 25, 1848, Sumner Papers, Houghton Library, Harvard University.

California. But the soldiers proved to be a weak reed, for the lure of gold caused many of them to desert. California needed a territorial government. So did New Mexico with its substantial Hispanic and Indian population and its growing Mormon settlement next to the Great Salt Lake. In December 1848, President Polk urged the lame-duck Congress to create territorial governments for California and New Mexico. To resolve the vexing slavery question, Polk recommended extension of the 36° 30' line to the Pacific.[36]

But Congress would have none of that. During the short session that expired on March 4 fistfights flared in both Houses, southern members shouted threats of secession, and no territorial legislation could command a majority. In the House, northern congressmen reaffirmed the Wilmot Proviso, drafted a territorial bill for California that excluded slavery, passed a resolution calling for abolition of the slave trade within the District of Columbia, and even considered a bill to abolish slavery itself in the capital. These actions enraged southerners, who used their power in the Senate to quash them all.

A southern caucus asked Calhoun to draft an "Address" setting forth the section's position on these iniquities. The South Carolinian readily complied, sensing a renewed opportunity to create the Southern Rights party he had long hoped for. Rehearsing a long list of northern "aggressions"—including the Northwest Ordinance, the Missouri Compromise, state personal liberty laws that blocked recovery of fugitive slaves, and the Wilmot Proviso—the Address reiterated Calhoun's doctrine of the constitutional right to take slaves into all territories, reminded southerners that their "property, prosperity, equality, liberty, and safety" were at stake, and warned that the South might secede if her rights were not protected.[37]

But Calhoun's heavy artillery misfired. Although forty-six of the seventy-three southern Democrats in Congress signed his Address, only two of forty-eight Whigs did so. Having just won the presidency, southern Whigs did not want to undercut their party before Taylor even took office. "We do not expect an administration which we have brought into power [to]

---

36. The quotation is from Ray Allen Billington, *The Far Western Frontier 1830–1860* (New York, 1956). This book contains a fine account of the California gold rush and related matters.

37. Richard Cralle, ed., *The Works of John C. Calhoun*, 6 vols. (New York, 1854–55), VI, 285–313.

do any act or permit any act to be done [against] our safety," explained Robert Toombs. "We feel *secure* under General Taylor," added Alexander Stephens.[38]

So much greater the shock, then, when they discovered Taylor to be a free-soil wolf in the clothing of a state's rights sheep. Like a good military commander, Taylor planned to break the slavery stalemate by a flank attack to bypass the territorial stage and admit California and New Mexico directly as states. But this would produce two more free states. Under Mexican law, slavery had been illegal in these regions. Southern newspapers reprinted an editorial from the *San Francisco Star* which stated that 99 of 100 settlers considered slavery "an unnecessary moral, social, and political curse upon themselves and posterity." California and New Mexico would tip the Senate balance against the South, perhaps irrevocably. "For the first time," said Senator Jefferson Davis of Missisippi, "we are about permanently to destroy the balance of power between the sections." This was nothing less than a "plan of concealing the Wilmot Proviso under a so-called state constitution."[39] It raised "a point of honor," according to other southern Democrats, who vowed never to "consent to be thus degraded and enslaved" by such a "monstrous trick and injustice."[40]

But Taylor went right ahead. He sent agents to Monterey and Santa Fe to urge settlers to adopt state constitutions and apply for admission. Californians had begun this process even before Taylor's emissary arrived. In October 1849 they approved a free-state constitution and in November elected a governor and legislature that petitioned Congress for statehood. New Mexico was slower to act. Few English-speaking citizens lived in this huge region except the Latter-day Saints at Salt Lake—and their relations with the government were tense. Moreover, Texas claimed half of the present-day state of New Mexico and part of Colorado. This border dispute would have to be settled before statehood for New Mexico could be considered.

A free California might not have raised southern hackles so much

---

38. Toombs to John J. Crittenden, Jan. 22, 1849, Stephens to Crittenden, Jan. 17, 1849, quoted in Cooper, *The South and the Politics of Slavery*, 271.

39. Nevins, *Ordeal*, I, 22; *CG*, 31 Cong., 1 Sess., Appendix, 1533; Davis to W. R. Cannon, Jan. 8, 1850, Civil War Collection, Henry E. Huntington Library.

40. Quotations from Robert W. Johannsen, *Stephen A. Douglas* (New York, 1973), 245; Fehrenbacher, *The South and Three Sectional Crises*, 40; Cooper, *The South and the Politics of Slavery*, 278.

had not other developments caused southerners to view Taylor as a traitor to his class. Forty years in the army had given old Rough and Ready a national rather than sectional perspective. He hoped to strengthen the Whig party by winning Free Soilers back into its ranks. In August 1849 the president told a Pennsylvania audience that "the people of the North need have no apprehension of the further extension of slavery."[41] Having pledged not to veto legislation on this subject, Taylor informed an appalled Robert Toombs that he meant what he said even if Congress saw fit to pass the Wilmot Proviso. Worst of all, Senator Seward became a presidential friend and adviser. Publicity about all of this buffeted southern Whigs, who took a beating in off-year state elections during 1849. "The slavery question," wrote a Georgian, "is the only question which in the least affects the results of the elections." Having "utterly abandoned the South" and "estranged the whole Whig party" there, Taylor's actions dangerously shortened southern tempers.[42]

Tension thickened when Congress met in December 1849. Taylor's coattails had not been long enough to carry Whigs into control of either House.[43] Twelve Free Soilers held the balance between 112 Democrats and 105 Whigs in the lower House. The Democratic candidate for speaker was Howell Cobb, a genial moderate from Georgia. The Whig candidate was Robert Winthrop of Massachusetts, a Cotton Whig who had served as speaker in the previous Congress. Several Democrats refused to support Cobb, while Free Soilers of Whig background would not vote for Winthrop despite his earlier support of the Wilmot Proviso. More ominously, a half-dozen southern Whigs led by Stephens and Toombs opposed Winthrop *because* of that action and also because the Whig caucus refused to reject the Proviso. "I [shall] hold no connection with a party that did not disconnect itself from those aggressive abolition movements," declared Stephens. To resist "the dictation of Northern

41. Potter, *Impending Crisis*, 87.
42. Nevins, *Ordeal*, I, 241–42; Cooper, *The South and the Politics of Slavery*, 280, 286.
43. Democrats retained a majority of eight in the Senate, where Salmon P. Chase joined John P. Hale of New Hampshire as the second Free Soil senator. Chase had been elected by a coalition of Democrats and Free Soilers in the Ohio legislature as part of a bargain by which Free Soilers enabled Democrats to control the legislature in return for Democratic support of Chase for senator and for repeal of Ohio's "black laws" which had restricted black access to schools, courts, and other public agencies.

hordes of Goths and Vandals," the South must make "the necessary preparations of men and money, arms and munitions, etc., to meet the emergency."[44]

Through three weeks and sixty-two ballots the House failed to elect a speaker. Threats of disunion became a byword during this crisis. "If, by your legislation, you seek to drive us from the territories of California and New Mexico," thundered Toombs, *I am for disunion*." "We have calculated the value of the Union," warned Albert Gallatin Brown of Mississippi. "We ask you to give us our rights" in California; "if you refuse, I am for taking them by armed occupation." The South's liberty was at stake as much now as in 1776, for "it is clear," according to an Alabama congressman, "that the power to dictate what sort of property the State may allow a citizen to own and work—whether oxen, horses, or negroes . . . is alike despotic and tyrannical."[45] Several fistfights broke out between southerners and northerners in the House. The Senate caught the same fever. Jefferson Davis reportedly challenged an Illinois congressman to a duel, and Senator Henry S. Foote (also of Mississippi) drew a loaded revolver during a heated debate. Finally, in desperation the House adopted a special rule allowing election of a speaker by a plurality and named Cobb to the post on the sixty-third ballot. It was an inauspicious start for the 1850s.

Was the Union in serious danger? Did southerners really intend to secede, or were they bluffing to force concessions? Free Soilers believed they were bluffing. Chase shrugged off "the stale cry of disunion." Joshua Giddings dismissed it as "gasconade" to "frighten dough-faces into a compliance with their measures." Seward observed that "the malcontents of the South . . . expect to compel compromise. I think the President is willing to try conclusions with them as General Jackson was with the nullifiers."[46]

Taylor did indeed intend to call the southern bluff, if bluff it was. His message to Congress in January 1850 urged admission of California as a state immediately and of New Mexico when it was ready. Taylor never receded from this position. When Toombs and Stephens appealed

44. Cooper, *The South and the Politics of Slavery*, 282; Fehrenbacher, *The South and Three Sectional Crises*, 40.
45. CG, 31 Cong., 1 Sess., 27–28, 257–61; Thornton, *Politics and Power in a Slave Society*, 213.
46. Rhodes, *History of the U.S.*, I, 131–33. In the political lexicon of the time a doughface was "a northern man with southern principles."

to him as a southerner, warning him that the South would not "submit" to these insults, Taylor lost his temper. In unpresidential language he told them that he would personally lead an army to enforce the laws and hang any traitors he caught—including Toombs and Stephens—with as little compunction as he had hanged spies and deserters in Mexico. Taylor afterward commented to an associate that he had previously regarded Yankees as the aggressors in sectional disputes, but his experience since taking office had convinced him that southerners were "intolerant and revolutionary" and that his former son-in-law Jefferson Davis was their "chief conspirator."[47]

Presidential threats did nothing to pacify the South. "There is a bad state of things here," reported an Illinois congressman. "I fear this Union is in danger."[48] Calhoun himself found southern congressmen "more determined and bold than I ever saw them. Many avow themselves disunionists, and a still greater number admit, that there is little hope of any remedy short of it." Calhoun may have overstated the case. Those who avowed themselves disunionists per se—who scorned Yankees, believed that irreconcilable differences existed between North and South, and earned the label "fire-eaters" because of their passionate avowal of southern nationalism—were still a minority, even in South Carolina. A larger number, including Calhoun himself, preserved at least a "little hope" of a remedy short of secession. In Calhoun's case it was mighty little, to be sure. "As things now stand," he wrote privately on February 16, 1850, the South "cannot with safety remain in the Union . . . and there is little or no prospect of any change for the better." Nevertheless, Calhoun and other southerners continued to press for "some timely and effective measure" of concession by the North to avert secession.[49]

Hanging over the head of Congress like a sword of Damocles was a scheduled convention of slave-state delegates "to devise and adopt some mode of resistance to northern aggression." Thus had Calhoun's long-ripening project for southern unity come to fruition. Suffering the onset of consumption that would send him to his grave within five months, the South Carolinian remained in the background and let Mississippi

47. *Ibid.*, 134; Thelma Jennings, *The Nashville Convention: Southern Movement for Unity, 1848–1851* (Memphis, 1980), 49.
48. Potter, *Impending Crisis*, 89.
49. J. Franklin Jameson, ed., *Correspondence of John C. Calhoun*, in Annual Report of the American Historical Association, 1899, vol. II (Washington, 1900), 780–82; Jennings, *Nashville Convention*, 50.

take the lead. A bipartisan meeting at Jackson in October 1849 issued a call for a convention at Nashville the following June. Few could doubt the purpose of this enterprise: it would form an "unbroken front" of southern states "to present . . . to the North the alternative of dissolving the partnership" if Yankees did not cease violating southern rights. The lower-South cotton states plus Virginia elected delegations during the winter. While Whigs in the upper South held back, the movement generated enough momentum to alarm many Americans.[50]

In this crisis Henry Clay strode once more on stage and offered a plan to buy off southern threats, as he had done twice before in 1820 and 1833. The ensuing debates of 1850 became the most famous in the history of Congress. Sharing the footlights with Clay were Calhoun and Daniel Webster, the other two members of the great Senate triumvirate that had dominated American statesmanship for decades. All three had been born during the Revolution. They had devoted their careers to preserving the heritage of the Fathers—Clay and Webster as nationalists, and Calhoun as a sectionalist who warned that Union could survive only if the North and South shared equal power within it. All three had known repeated frustration in their quest for the presidency. All were playing in their final show, Clay and Webster as composers of compromise, Calhoun as a brooding presence warning of disaster even after his death at the end of the first act. Some of the rising stars of the next generation also played prominent roles in this great drama: Senators Stephen A. Douglas, William H. Seward, Jefferson Davis, and Salmon P. Chase.

On January 29, 1850, Clay presented eight resolutions to the Senate. He grouped the first six in pairs, each offering a concession to both sections. The first pair would admit California as a state and organize the remainder of the Mexican cession without "any restriction or condition on the subject of slavery." The second pair of resolutions settled the boundary dispute between Texas and New Mexico in favor of the latter and compensated Texas by federal assumption of debts contracted during its existence as an independent republic. This would reduce the potential for carving an additional slave state out of Texas but would put the state's finances on sound footing.[51] Many holders of Texas bonds

50. Jennings, *Nashville Convention*, 3–79; quotations from 7, 24–25.
51. The terms of Texas's annexation had authorized its division into as many as four additional states. This authority was never exercised, but in 1850 some southerners

were southerners; the head of a powerful lobby for this part of the Compromise of 1850 was a South Carolinian. Clay's third pair of resolutions called for abolition of the slave trade in the District of Columbia but a guarantee of slavery itself in the District. If these six proposals yielded slightly more to the North than to the South, Clay's final pair of resolutions tipped the balance southward by denying congressional power over the interstate slave trade and calling for a stronger law to enable slaveholders to recover their property when it fled to free states.[52]

The eventual Compromise of 1850 closely resembled Clay's proposals. But seven months of oratory, debate, and exhausting cloakroom bargaining lay ahead. And the "Compromise" that finally emerged was not really a compromise in which all parties conceded part of what they wanted, but a series of separately enacted measures each of which became law with a majority of congressmen from one section voting against a majority of those from the other. The Compromise of 1850 undoubtedly averted a grave crisis. But hindsight makes clear that it only postponed the trauma.

Generations of schoolchildren recited the famous Senate speeches of the Compromise debate. "I wish to speak to-day, not as a Massachusetts man, nor as a Northern man, but as an American," said Daniel Webster as he began his Seventh of March Address that would cause former antislavery admirers to repudiate him. "I speak to-day for the preservation of the Union. Hear me for my cause." Having opposed the Mexican War and supported the Wilmot Proviso, Webster now urged northerners to bury the passions of the past. Do not "taunt or reproach" the South with the Proviso. Nature would exclude slavery from New Mexico. "I would not take pains uselessly to reaffirm an ordinance of nature, nor to re-enact the will of God." As for disunion, Webster warned fire-eaters that it could no more take place "without convulsion" than "the heavenly bodies [could] rush from their spheres, and jostle each other in the realms of space, without causing the wreck of the universe!"[53]

Webster's speech appealed to a broad range of Americans who by March 1850 were rallying in support of compromise. But it contrasted

---

hoped for at least one additional state to be cloned from Texas, especially if its claims to part of New Mexico were upheld.

52. Southerners had already introduced a stringent fugitive slave bill at this session. For more on the fugitive slave issue see the chapter following.

53. CG, 31 Cong., 1 Sess., Appendix, 269–76.

sharply with addresses by senators speaking for citizens outside that middle range. Three days before Webster's speech, the dying Calhoun gave his valedictory to the nation. Too weak to speak for himself, the gaunt Carolinian sat wrapped in flannels while James Mason of Virginia read his speech to the Senate. Calhoun's prophecies of doom were reflected in the piercing eyes that stared from deep sockets within the shroud. "The great and primary cause" of danger "is that the equilibrium between the two sections has been destroyed." The North had grown faster than the South in population, wealth, and power. This had happened because of discriminatory legislation favoring the North: the Northwest Ordinance and the Compromise of 1820 which excluded southern property from a vast domain; tariffs and federal aid to internal improvements (Calhoun neglected to mention that he had once supported these measures) to foster northern enterprises at southern expense. Yankees had wantonly attacked southern institutions until one by one the bonds of Union had snapped: the Methodist and Baptist denominations had separated into northern and southern churches; voluntary associations were dividing over slavery; political parties themselves were splitting in the same way; soon "nothing will be left to hold the States together except force." What could be done to forestall this fate? Because the North had always been the aggressor, it must cease criticizing slavery, return fugitive slaves, give the South equal rights in the territories, and consent to a constitutional amendment "which will restore to the South, in substance, the power she possessed of protecting herself before the equilibrium between the two sections was destroyed." [54] California was the test case. Admission of this free state would serve notice of a purpose to "destroy irretrievably the equilibrium between the two sections." In such circumstances southern states could not "remain in the Union consistently with their honor and safety." [55]

William H. Seward spoke for Americans at the opposite pole from Calhoun. In a speech on March 11, Seward condemned "any such compromise" as Clay had proposed. Slavery was an unjust, backward, dying institution, said the New York senator. Its days were numbered.

---

54. Calhoun probably had in mind his posthumously published proposal, in *Disquisition on Government*, for a "concurrent majority" in which the country would have a northern and a southern president each with a veto power over congressional legislation.
55. CG, 31 Cong., 1 Sess., Appendix, 451–55.

"You cannot roll back the tide of social progress." Not only did the Constitution sanction the power of Congress to exclude slavery from the territories, but also "there is a higher law than the Constitution," the law of God in whose sight all persons are equal. The present crisis "embraces the fearful issue whether the Union shall stand, and slavery, under the steady, peaceful action of moral, social, and political causes, be removed by gradual voluntary effort, and with compensation; or whether the Union shall be dissolved and civil war ensue, bringing on violent but complete and immediate emancipation."[56]

Seward's Higher Law speech caused a sensation. Southerners branded it "monstrous and diabolical"; Clay pronounced it "wild, reckless, and abominable." Even Taylor condemned it. "This is a nice mess Governor Seward has got us into," the president observed to a pro-administration editor. "The speech must be disclaimed at once."[57] Disclaimed or not, Seward's sentiments represented opinion in the upper North as accurately as Calhoun's expressed that of the lower South. Nevertheless, men from the upper South and lower North continued to work feverishly for a settlement between the two extremes. While oratory continued before crowded galleries, committees sought a compromise that could command a majority.

A special Senate committee of thirteen with Clay as chairman reported a bill that combined several measures in one package: admission of California; organization of two territories (New Mexico and Utah) without restrictions on slavery; and settlement of the Texas boundary dispute in favor of New Mexico with compensation to Texas of $10 million to fund her pre-statehood debt. Derisively labeled an "Omnibus Bill" by President Taylor, this package was designed to attract a majority from both sections by inducing each to accept the parts it did not like in order to get the parts it wanted. The approach seemed promising enough to defuse the fire-eaters at the Nashville Convention which met on June 3. Disunion fever had abated since late winter. No delegates came from six slave states and only a few unofficial delegates from two others. Whigs in particular were conspicuous by their absence. Recognizing that it had no mandate for radical action, the convention adopted a wait-and-see attitude. Delegates passed a resolution favoring extension

56. Ibid., 260–69.
57. Nevins, Ordeal, I, 301–2. Seward carried the title "Governor" because he had served as governor of New York.

of the 36° 30' line to the Pacific and adjourned to reconvene again after Congress acted.[58]

But as the legislators labored through the heat of a Washington summer it became obvious that the omnibus strategy was backfiring. A pro-compromise bloc of upper-South Whigs and lower-North Democrats emerged in support of the strategy. But they numbered fewer than one-third of each house. Most other congressmen signified their intention to vote against the package in order to defeat the parts they opposed. A three-way split among the Whigs grew increasingly bitter. Taylor and most northern Whigs insisted on their California-only policy, believing that acquiescence in (potential) slavery in New Mexico and Utah would wreck the party in the North. Lower-South Whigs adamantly opposed a free California. Clay's pro-compromise Whigs endured the slings and arrows of both sides. The hostility of Taylor toward Clay and Webster became especially caustic.

Into this volatile atmosphere came a new crisis in late June. A handful of civilians and soldiers had convened a convention in Santa Fe to write a free-state constitution. It was ratified by an electorate casting fewer than eight thousand votes. Taylor urged the admission of New Mexico along with that of California, thereby doubling the insult to southern honor. Meanwhile the governor of Texas threatened to uphold with force his state's claim to Santa Fe and all the rest of New Mexico east of the Rio Grande. A clash between Texans and the U. S. army seemed imminent. As July 4 approached, southerners bristled with threats to fight for Texas. "Freemen from the Delaware to the Rio Grande [will] rally to the rescue," squeaked Alexander Stephens with all the bellicosity his ninety pounds could muster. And "when the 'Rubicon' is passed, the days of this Republic will be numbered."[59] Taylor did not flinch. After preparing orders for the Santa Fe garrison to stand firm, he spent a hot Fourth of July listening to speeches at the unfinished Washington Monument. Assuaging his hunger and thirst with large quantities of raw vegetables, cherries, and iced milk, the president fell ill next day and died on July 9 of acute gastroenteritis.

Whether for weal or woe, Taylor's death marked a turning point in the crisis. The new president, Millard Fillmore, was a New York Whig hostile to the Seward faction in his own state. Sympathetic to the Com-

58. Jennings, *Nashville Convention*, 135–66.
59. Holman Hamilton, *Prologue to Conflict: The Crisis and Compromise of 1850* (Lexington, Ky., 1964), 105.

promise, this northern president tilted almost as far South as the southern President Taylor had tilted North. Fillmore shelved New Mexico's application for statehood and gave his support to the omnibus. Nevertheless, the Senate spent a month passing a bewildering series of amendments and rescindments of amendments before sending Clay's measure down to defeat on July 31. Exhausted and disillusioned, the once-redoubtable Kentuckian left Washington to recuperate at Newport. His younger colleagues remained in the caldron on Capitol Hill to pick up the pieces.

And it was by pieces that the "Compromise" finally passed. Representing the new generation, Stephen A. Douglas came on stage to star in the third act. A man whose capacity for liquor was exceeded only by his capacity for work (the combination would kill him eleven years later at the age of 48), Douglas earned the sobriquet Little Giant for his great political prowess contained in a frame five feet four inches tall. Never a believer in the omnibus strategy, Douglas stripped the vehicle down to its component parts and put together a majority for each of those parts. Northerners of both parties and border-state Whigs supplied the votes for admission of California, prohibition of the slave trade in the District, and payment of $10 million to Texas (quickly accepted) to settle the border dispute with New Mexico. Many northern Democrats joined southerners of both parties to enact a stronger fugitive slave law and organize Utah and New Mexico as territories without restrictions on slavery. Fillmore helped the cause by persuading enough northern Whigs to abstain from the votes on the fugitive slave and territorial bills to allow their passage. On all these measures the divisions occurred mainly along sectional rather than party lines, another sign that the existing two-party system was crumbling under the weight of slavery.[60]

Nevertheless, Douglas's achievement seemed to have broken the deadlock that had paralyzed government and threatened the republic since 1846. It lanced the boil of tension that had festered in Congress during one of its longest and most contentious sessions in history. Most of the country gave a sigh of relief. Champagne and whiskey flowed freely in the capital. Tipsy crowds shouting "The Union is saved!" serenaded the politicians who had saved it. "Every face I meet is happy," wrote one observer. "The successful are rejoicing, the neutrals have all joined the winning side, and the defeated are silent." President Fillmore

60. The roll-call votes in both houses are conveniently presented in Hamilton, *Prologue to Conflict*, 191–200.

christened the Compromise "a final settlement" of all sectional problems, and this phrase soon became the hallmark of political orthodoxy.
Only Calhounites and Free Soilers challenged its finality.[61]

But these curmudgeons of the right and left were temporarily isolated.
When the Nashville Convention met again in November only half of
the delegates—from seven states—showed up. Even these true believers
seemed to recognize the futility of their proceedings. They passed resolutions denouncing the Compromise and affirming the right of secession. But their only concrete proposal was a call for another Southern
Rights convention—somewhere, sometime. South Carolina fire-eaters
came away from Nashville determined that next time they would not
dawdle in cooperative action with other states, which only sicklied o'er
the native hue of resolution with the pale cast of thought. They would
act alone in the expectation that other states would follow.[62]

Free Soilers also condemned "the consummation of the iniquities of
this most disgraceful session of Congress"—as Charles Francis Adams
expressed it. Salmon P. Chase believed that "the question of slavery in
the territories has been avoided. It has not been settled."[63] He was right.
In its final form the legislation organizing Utah and New Mexico specified that when admitted as states "they shall be received into the Union,
with or without slavery, as their constitution may prescribe at the time
of their admission." This said nothing about slavery *during the territorial stage*. The omission was deliberate. Congress passed the buck by
expediting the appeal of territorial laws to the Supreme Court. As it
happened, no slavery case came up from these territories. Several slaveholders carried their property to Utah, where Governor Brigham Young
and his legislature obliged them by legalizing the institution in 1852
(the same year that the Saints openly endorsed polygamy). New Mexico
also enacted a slave code in 1859. But neither territory was likely to
strengthen the South in Congress. The census of 1860 counted twenty-
nine slaves in Utah and none in New Mexico; in any event, statehood
for either was distant. California furnished an irony that may have settled Calhoun more comfortably in his grave. Court decisions in that
state permitted the "sojourn" (sometimes for several years) of slaveowners with their property. For a time in the 1850s California probably had

61. Nevins, *Ordeal*, I, 343, 345–46.
62. Jennings, *Nashville Convention*, 187–211.
63. Adams quoted in Hamilton, *Prologue to Conflict*, 167; Chase quoted in Potter,
    Impending Crisis, 116.

more slaves than Utah and New Mexico combined. And this new free state did not tip the Senate balance against the South, for its senators were Democrats of a decidedly doughface cast.[64]

"I think the settlement of the last session and the firm course of the Administration in the execution of the fugitive slave law have given a new lease to slavery," wrote a North Carolina Whig at the beginning of 1851. "Property of that kind has not been so secure for the last twenty-five years."[65] He was wrong—and precisely because of the administration's "firm course" in enforcing the fugitive slave law. Although one of the least-debated parts of the Compromise, this measure turned out to be the most divisive legacy of the "final settlement."

64. Hamilton, *Prologue to Conflict*, 174–77, 203–4; William E. Franklin, "The Archy Case: The California Supreme Court Refuses to Free a Slave," *Pacific Historical Review*, 32 (1963), 137–54; Paul Finkelman, "The Law of Slavery and Freedom in California 1848–1860," *California Western Law Review*, 17 (1981), 437–64.
65. William A. Graham to his brother, Jan. 6, 1851, in Nevins, *Ordeal*, I, 349.

3

An Empire for Slavery

I

On all issues but one, antebellum southerners stood for state's rights and a weak federal government. The exception was the fugitive slave law of 1850, which gave the national government more power than any other law yet passed by Congress. This irony resulted from the Supreme Court's decision in *Prigg v. Pennsylvania* (1842).

In the typical oblique language of the Constitution on slavery, Article IV, Section 2, stipulated that any "person held to service or labor in one state" who escaped to another "shall be delivered up on claim of the party to whom such service or labor shall be due." The Constitution did not specify how this provision should be enforced. A federal law of 1793 authorized slaveowners to cross state lines to recapture their property and bring it before any local magistrate or federal court to prove ownership. This law provided the fugitive with no protection of habeas corpus, no right to a jury trial, no right to testify in his own behalf. Some northerners believed that the law amounted to an invitation for kidnappers to seize free blacks. And indeed, professional slave catchers did not always take pains to make sure they had captured the right man nor did every judge go out of his way to ensure that a supposed fugitive matched the description on the affidavit. A good many slave catchers did not bother to take their captured prey before a court but simply spirited it south by the quickest route.

To remedy such abuses, several northern states enacted personal liberty laws. These measures variously gave fugitives the rights of testimony, habeas corpus, and trial by jury, or they imposed criminal penalties for kidnapping. In the hands of antislavery officials, some of these laws could be used to inhibit the capture of fugitives. In 1837, Pennsylvania convicted Edward Prigg of kidnapping after he had seized a slave woman and her children and returned them to their Maryland owner. Prigg's lawyers appealed the case to the U. S. Supreme Court, which in 1842 rendered a complex decision. Declaring the Pennsylvania anti-kidnapping law of 1826 unconstitutional, the Court upheld the fugitive slave law of 1793 and affirmed that a slaveholder's right to his property overrode any contrary state legislation. At the same time, however, the Court ruled that enforcement of the fugitive slave clause of the Constitution was a federal responsibility and that states need not cooperate in any way. This opened the floodgates for a new series of personal liberty laws (nine between 1842 and 1850) that prohibited the use of state facilities in the recapture of fugitives.[1]

In some areas of the North, owners could not reclaim their escaped property without the help of federal marshals. Black leaders and sympathetic whites in numerous communities formed vigilance committees to organize resistance to such efforts. These committees cooperated with the legendary underground railroad which carried fugitives north toward freedom. Magnified by southerners into an enormous Yankee network of lawbreakers who stole thousands of slaves each year, the underground railroad was also mythologized by its northern conductors who related their heroic deeds to grandchildren. The true number of runaway slaves is impossible to determine. Perhaps several hundred each year made it to the North or to Canada. Few of these fugitives had escaped from the lower South, the region that clamored loudest for a stronger fugitive slave law—less for practical advantage than as a matter of principle. Like a free California, northern aid to escaping slaves was an insult to southern honor. "Although the loss of property is felt," said Senator James Mason of Virginia, "the loss of honor is felt still more." The fugitive slave law, commented another politician, was "the only mea-

---

1. *Prigg v. Pennsylvania*, 16 Peters 539 (1842). For details and analyses of early personal liberty laws, see Thomas D. Morris, *Free Men All: The Personal Liberty Laws of the North 1780–1861* (Baltimore, 1974), 1–106; Stanley W. Campbell, *The Slave Catchers: Enforcement of the Fugitive Slave Law 1850–1860* (Chapel Hill, 1970), 3–14; and Don E. Fehrenbacher, *The Dred Scott Case: Its Significance in American Law and Politics* (New York, 1978), 40–47.

sure of the Compromise [of 1850] calculated to secure the rights of the South."[2]

To secure these rights the law seemed to ride roughshod over the prerogatives of northern states. Yankee senators had tried in vain to attach amendments to the bill guaranteeing alleged fugitives the rights to testify, to habeas corpus, and to a jury trial. Southerners indignantly rejected the idea that these American birthrights applied to slaves. The fugitive slave law of 1850 put the burden of proof on captured blacks but gave them no legal power to prove their freedom. Instead, a claimant could bring an alleged fugitive before a federal commissioner (a new office created by the law) to prove ownership by an affidavit from a slave-state court or by the testimony of white witnesses. If the commissioner decided against the claimant he would receive a fee of five dollars; if in favor, ten dollars. This provision, supposedly justified by the paper work needed to remand a fugitive to the South, became notorious among abolitionists as a bribe to commissioners. The 1850 law also required U. S. marshals and deputies to help slaveowners capture their property and fined them $1000 if they refused. It empowered marshals to deputize citizens on the spot to aid in seizing a fugitive, and imposed stiff criminal penalties on anyone who harbored a fugitive or obstructed his capture. The expenses of capturing and returning a slave were to be borne by the federal treasury.[3]

The operation of this law confirmed the impression that it was rigged in favor of claimants. In the first fifteen months after its passage, eighty-four fugitives were returned to slavery and only five released. During the full decade of the 1850s, 332 were returned and only eleven declared free.[4] Nor did the law contain a statute of limitations. Some of the first fugitives returned to slavery had been longtime residents of the North. In September 1850, federal marshals arrested a black porter who had lived in New York City for three years and took him before a commissioner who refused to record the man's insistence that his mother was a free Negro, and remanded him to his claimant owner in Balti-

2. Quotations from Nevins, Emergence, II, 489; and Nevins, Ordeal, I, 385. For a scholarly analysis of the underground railroad and the realities of the fugitive question, see Larry Gara, The Liberty Line: The Legend of the Underground Railroad (Lexington, Ky., 1961).

3. The law is conveniently printed in Holman Hamilton, Prologue to Conflict: The Crisis and Compromise of 1850 (Lexington, Ky., 1964), 204–8, and its provisions are summarized in Campbell, Slave Catchers, 23–25.

4. Campbell, Slave Catchers, 207.

more. Several months later slave catchers seized a prosperous black tailor who had resided in Poughkeepsie for many years and carried him back to South Carolina. In February 1851 agents arrested a black man in southern Indiana, while his horrified wife and children looked on, and returned him to an owner who claimed him as a slave who had run away nineteen years earlier. A Maryland man asserted ownership of a Philadelphia woman who he said had run away twenty-two years previously. For good measure he also claimed her six children born in Philadelphia. In this case the commissioner found for the woman's freedom. And in the cases of the Poughkeepsie tailor and the New York porter, black and white friends raised money to buy their freedom. But most fugitives who were carried south stayed there.[5]

Antislavery lawyers challenged the fugitive slave law, but in 1859 the U. S. Supreme Court upheld it.[6] Long before this, however, blacks and their white allies had done everything they could to nullify the law by flight and resistance. The quick seizures of blacks who had long lived in the North sent a wave of panic through northern Negro communities. Many black people fled to Canada—an estimated three thousand in the last three months of 1850 alone. During the 1850s the Negro population of Ontario doubled to eleven thousand.

Some dramatic flights took place almost literally under the noses of slave catchers. In Boston lived a young couple, William and Ellen Craft, whose initial escape from slavery in Georgia two years earlier had become celebrated in the antislavery press. Light-skinned enough to pass for white, Ellen had cut her hair short, dressed in male attire, and impersonated a sickly white gentleman going north for medical treatment accompanied by "his" servant (William). They had thus traveled to freedom on real above-ground railroads. A skilled cabinetmaker, William Craft found work in Boston. He and his wife joined the church of Theodore Parker, head of the local vigilance committee, whose congregation included several other fugitive slaves. The publicity surrounding the Crafts naturally attracted their owner's attention. As soon as the fugitive slave bill became law he sent two agents to recapture them. This was like throwing a rubber ball against a brick wall. Boston was the communications center of abolitionism. Under the "higher law"

5. *Ibid.*, 199–206; Potter, *Impending Crisis*, 131–32; Philip S. Foner, *History of Black Americans from the Compromise of 1850 to the End of the Civil War* (Westport, Conn., 1983), 33–36; Nevins, *Ordeal*, I, 385–86.
6. *Ableman v. Booth*, 21 Howard 506.

doctrine, blacks and whites there had vowed to resist the fugitive slave law. "We must trample this law under our feet," said Wendell Phillips. It "is to be denounced, resisted, disobeyed," declared the local antislavery society. "As moral and religious men, [we] cannot obey an immoral and irreligious statute." When the slave catchers arrived in Boston on October 25, 1850, they vowed to get the Crafts "if [we] have to stay here to all eternity, and if there are not men enough in Massachusetts to take them, [we] will bring them some from the South." As things turned out, they stayed five days and brought no one. Parker hid Ellen Craft in his house, where he kept a loaded revolver on his desk. William went to ground in the house of a black abolitionist who kept two kegs of gunpowder on his front porch and a veritable arsenal in the kitchen. Members of the vigilance committee put up posters around town describing the "man-stealers," harassed them in the streets, and warned them on October 30 that their safety could not be assured if they remained any longer. They left on the afternoon train.[7]

President Fillmore denounced the Bostonians, threatened to send in federal troops, and assured the Crafts' owner that if he wanted to try again the government would help him "with all the means which the Constitution and Congress have placed at his disposal." But the vigilance committee put the Crafts on a ship to England. Parker sent a defiant missive to Fillmore by way of a parting shot. "I would rather lie all my life in jail, and starve there, than refuse to protect one of these parishioners of mine," the pastor told the president. "I must reverence the laws of God, come of that what will come. . . . You cannot think that I am to stand by and see my own church carried off to slavery and do nothing."[8]

Boston remained the cockpit of this new revolution. In February 1851 a black waiter, who had taken the name of Shadrach when he escaped from Virginia a year earlier, was seized in a Boston coffeehouse by agents to whom he was serving coffee. They rushed him to the federal courthouse while an angry crowd gathered outside. Denied the use of state facilities by the personal liberty law, a handful of deputy federal marshals tried to guard Shadrach. Suddenly a group of black men broke

---

7. Quotations from Foner, *History of Black Americans*, 19; and Lawrence Lader, *The Bold Brahmins: New England's War Against Slavery 1831–1863* (New York, 1961), 141.

8. Foner, *History of Black Americans*, 37; Lader, *Bold Brahmins*, 143.

into the courtroom, overwhelmed the marshals, and snatched Shadrach away to put him on the underground railroad to Canada. While Shadrach settled in Montreal, where he opened a restaurant, an uproar ensued behind him in the states. Abolitionists exulted. "This Shadrach is delivered out of his burning, fiery furnace," wrote Theodore Parker. "I think it is the most noble deed done in Boston since the destruction of the tea in 1773." But conservative Boston papers branded the rescue "an outrage . . . the triumph of mob law." In Washington, Daniel Webster called it treason, and Henry Clay demanded an investigation to find out "whether we shall have a government of white men or black men in the cities of this country." Determined to snuff out resistance to the fugitive slave law, President Fillmore ordered the district attorney to prosecute all "aiders and abettors of this flagitious offense." A grand jury indicted four blacks and four whites, but juries refused to convict them. "Massachusetts Safe Yet! The Higher Law Still Respected," proclaimed an antislavery newspaper. But a Savannah editor expressed a more common opinion—perhaps in the North as well as in the South—when he denounced Boston as "a black speck on the map—disgraced by the lowest, the meanest, the BLACKEST kind of NULLIFICATION."[9]

The federal government soon got a chance to flex its muscles in Boston. A seventeen-year-old slave named Thomas Sims escaped from Georgia in February 1851 and stowed away on a ship to Boston, where he too found work as a waiter. When his owner traced him, the mayor of Boston decided to allow the police to be deputized by federal marshals to cooperate in Sims's arrest. This time officials sealed the courthouse with a heavy chain (which abolitionists publicized as a symbol of the slave power's reach into the North) and guarded it with police and soldiers. For nine days in April 1851 vigilance committee lawyers vainly sought writs of habeas corpus and tried other legal maneuvers to free Sims. When the federal commissioner found for his owner, 300 armed deputies and soldiers removed him from the courthouse at 4:00 a.m. and marched him to the navy yard, where 250 U. S. soldiers waited to place him on a ship going south to slavery.[10]

9. Details and quotations are drawn from James Ford Rhodes, *History of the United States from the Compromise of 1850 . . .* 7 vols. (New York, 1893–1906), I, 210; Campbell, *Slave Catchers*, 148–51; Lader, *Bold Brahmins*, 161–67; and Foner, *History of Black Americans*, 37–39.
10. Sims's owner subsequently sold him at the slave auction in Charleston. He was

Boston's mercantile elite had vindicated law and order. And for the next three years no more fugitive cases arose in Boston—if only because several score of vulnerable black people fled the city. The scene of resistance shifted elsewhere for a time. So far this resistance had produced no casualties except a few cuts and bruises. Most abolitionists had traditionally counseled nonviolence. Some of them, like William Lloyd Garrison, were pacifists. But the fugitive slave law eroded the commitment to nonviolence. "The only way to make the Fugitive Slave Law a dead letter," said black leader Frederick Douglass in October 1850, "is to make half a dozen or more dead kidnappers." Newspapers in several communities reported that "the colored people are arming." In Pittsburgh, "revolvers, bowie knives, and other deadly weapons found a ready sale." In Springfield, Massachusetts, a white wool merchant named John Brown with the glint of a Biblical warrior in his eye organized a black self-defense group which he named the Gileadites.[11]

It seemed only a matter of time before real blood would be shed. When the time came the place was Christiana, a Pennsylvania village near the Maryland border, about halfway between Philadelphia and another village named Gettysburg. A Quaker community that had extended a welcome to fugitives, Christiana was anything but peaceable or friendly on September 11, 1851. That morning a Maryland slaveowner accompanied by several relatives and three deputy marshals came seeking two fugitives who had escaped two years earlier and were reported to be hiding in the house of another black man. They found the fugitives, along with two dozen armed black men vowing to resist capture. Two Quakers appeared and advised the slave hunters to retreat for their own good. The owner refused, declaring that "I will have my property, or go to hell." Shooting broke out. When it was over the slaveowner lay dead and his son seriously wounded (two other whites

---

taken to New Orleans and sold to a brickmason in Vicksburg, Mississippi, where Sims was living when Union troops besieged the city in 1863. He escaped into federal lines and obtained a special pass from General Ulysses S. Grant to return to Boston, where he arrived in time to watch the presentation of colors to the 54th Massachusetts Infantry, the first black regiment recruited in the North. A dozen years after the Civil War, Sims became a clerk and messenger in the office of the U. S. attorney general, under whose auspices he had been remanded to slavery a generation earlier. Campbell, *Slave Catchers*, 117–21; Lader, *Bold Brahmins*, 174–80; Foner, *History of Black Americans*, 39–42.

11. Philip S. Foner, *The Life and Writings of Frederick Douglass*, 4 vols. (New York, 1950–55), II, 207; Foner, *History of Black Americans*, 29–30.

and two blacks were lightly wounded). The blacks disappeared into the countryside; their three leaders sped on the underground railroad to Canada.[12]

The "Battle of Christiana" became a national event. "Civil War— The First Blow Struck," proclaimed a Lancaster, Pennsylvania, newspaper. The *New York Tribune* pronounced the verdict of many Yankees: "But for slavery such things would not be; but for the Fugitive Slave Law they would not be in the free States." The conservative press took a different view of this "act of insurrection" that "never would have taken place but for the instigations which have been applied to the ignorant and deluded blacks by the fanatics of the 'higher law' creed." Southerners announced that "unless the Christiana rioters are hung . . . WE LEAVE YOU! . . . If you fail in this simple act of justice, THE BONDS WILL BE DISSOLVED."[13]

This time Fillmore called out the marines. Together with federal marshals they scoured the countryside and arrested more than thirty black men and a half-dozen whites. The government sought extradition of the three fugitives who had escaped to Ontario, but Canadian officials refused. To show that it meant business, the administration prosecuted alleged participants not merely for resisting the fugitive slave law but for treason. A federal grand jury so indicted thirty-six blacks and five whites. The government's case quickly degenerated into farce. A defense attorney's ridicule made the point: "Sir—did you hear it? That three harmless non-resisting Quakers and eight-and-thirty wretched, miserable, penniless negroes, armed with corn cutters, clubs, and a few muskets, and headed by a miller, in a felt hat, without arms and mounted on a sorrel nag, levied war against the United States." The government's efforts to discredit resistance produced increased sympathy for abolitionists, one of whom reported that "the cause is in a very promising position just now. . . . These Treason Trials have been a great windfall." After the jury acquitted the first defendant, one of the Quakers, the government dropped the remaining indictments and decided not to press other charges.[14]

12. The fullest account is Jonathan Katz, *Resistance at Christiana: The Fugitive Slave Rebellion, Christiana, Pennsylvania, September 11, 1851* (New York, 1974); quotation from 96.
13. Foner, *History of Black Americans*, 54, 57; Rhodes, *History of the United States*, I, 223; Campbell, *Slave Catchers*, 152; Katz, *Resistance at Christiana*, 138.
14. Katz, *Resistance at Christiana*, 156–243; quotations from Foner, *History of Black*

While this was going on, another dramatic rescue took place in Syracuse, New York. In that upstate city lived a black cooper named William McHenry, popularly known as Jerry, who had escaped from slavery in Missouri. His owner's agent made the mistake of having Jerry arrested when an antislavery convention was meeting in Syracuse and the town was also crowded with visitors to the county fair. Two of the North's most prominent abolitionists, Gerrit Smith and Samuel J. May, organized a plan to rescue Jerry from the police station. May, a Unitarian clergyman, told his congregation that God's law took precedence over the fugitive slave law, which "we must trample . . . under foot, be the consequences what they may." A large group of blacks and whites broke into the police station on October 1, grabbed Jerry, sped him away in a carriage, and smuggled him across Lake Ontario to Canada. A grand jury indicted twelve whites and twelve blacks (this time for riot, not treason), but nine of the blacks had already escaped to Canada. Of those who stood trial only one was convicted—a black man who died before he could appeal the verdict.[15]

Northern resistance to the fugitive slave law fed the resentment of fire-eaters still seething over the admission of California. "We cannot stay in the Union any longer," said one, "with such dishonor attached to the terms of our remaining." South Carolina, Georgia, and Mississippi held conventions in 1851 to calculate the value of the Union. The fire-eater William L. Yancey toured Alabama stirring up demands for similar action. The governor of South Carolina assumed that "there is now not the slightest doubt but that . . . the state will secede."[16]

But already a reaction was setting in. The highest cotton prices in a decade and the largest cotton crop ever caused many a planter to think twice about secession. Whig unionism reasserted itself under the leadership of Toombs and Stephens. Old party lines temporarily dissolved as a minority of Democrats in Georgia, Alabama, and Mississippi joined Whigs to form Constitutional Union parties to confront Southern Rights Democrats. Unionists won a majority of delegates to the state conventions, where they advocated "cooperation" with other states rather than secession by individual states. As the Nashville convention had dem-

Americans, 62, and from J. Miller McKim to William Lloyd Garrison, Dec. 31, 1851, Garrison Papers, Boston Public Library.

15. Campbell, _Slave Catchers_, 154–57; Foner, _History of Black Americans_, 42–46.

16. Avery O. Craven, _The Growth of Southern Nationalism 1848–1861_ (Baton Rouge, 1953), 103; Potter, _Impending Crisis_, 128.

onstrated, cooperation was another word for inaction. Unionists won the governorships of Georgia and Mississippi (where Jefferson Davis ran as the Southern Rights candidate), the legislatures of Georgia and Alabama, and elected fourteen of the nineteen congressmen from these three states. Even in South Carolina the separatists suffered a setback. This denouement of two years of disunion rhetoric confirmed the belief of many northerners that secession threats had been mere "gasconade" to frighten the government into making concessions.[17]

But a closer analysis would have qualified this conclusion. Unionists proclaimed themselves no less ardent for "the safety . . . rights and honor of the slave holding states" than Southern Rights Democrats. In several states unionists adopted the "Georgia Platform" which declared that while the South did "not wholly approve" of the Compromise of 1850 she would "abide by it as a permanent adjustment of this sectional controversy"—so long as the North similarly abided. BUT—any action by Congress against slavery in the District of Columbia, any refusal to admit a new slave state or to recognize slavery in the new territories would cause Georgia (and other states) to resist, with secession "as a last resort." Above all, "upon a faithful execution of the *Fugitive Slave Law* . . . depends the preservation of our much beloved Union."[18]

Southern unionism, in other words, was a perishable commodity. It would last only so long as the North remained on good behavior. This truth did much to neutralize the apparent triumph of southern Whiggery in these 1851 elections. For while Whigs provided the bulk of unionist votes, the Democratic tail of this coalition wagged the Whig dog. The Georgia platform held northern Whigs hostage to support of the fugitive slave law and slavery in the territories. With Fillmore in the White House, the situation seemed stabilized for the time being. But northern Whigs were restless. Most of them were having a hard time swallowing the fugitive slave law. The party was sending a growing number of radical antislavery men to Congress: Thaddeus Stevens of Pennsylvania and George W. Julian entered the House in 1849; Benjamin Wade of Ohio came to the Senate in 1851. If such men as these gained con-

---

17. Potter, *Impending Crisis*, 122–30; William J. Cooper, Jr., *The South and the Politics of Slavery 1828–1856* (Baton Rouge, 1978), 304–10; Craven, *Growth of Southern Nationalism*, 103–15; Nevins, *Ordeal*, I, 354–79; J. Mills Thornton III, *Politics and Power in a Slave Society: Alabama, 1800–1860* (Baton Rouge, 1978), 188–200; John Barnwell, *Love of Order: South Carolina's First Secession Crisis* (Chapel Hill, 1982), 123–90.
18. Potter, *Impending Crisis*, 128.

trol of the party it would splinter along North-South lines. Southern Whigs had barely survived Taylor's apostasy; another such shock would shatter them.

After the rescue of the fugitive Jerry in Syracuse, furor over the fugitive slave law declined. Perhaps this happened because the legions of law and order finally prevailed. Or perhaps nearly all the eligible fugitives had decamped to Canada. In any event, fewer than one-third as many blacks were returned from the North to slavery in 1852 as in the first year of the law's operation.[19] Democrats, conservative Whigs, mercantile associations, and other forces of moderation organized public meetings throughout the North to affirm support of the Compromise including the fugitive slave law.

These same forces, aided by the Negrophobia that characterized much of the northern population, went further than this. In 1851 Indiana and Iowa and in 1853 Illinois enacted legislation barring the immigration of *any* black persons, free or slave. Three-fifths of the nation's border between free and slave states ran along the southern boundaries of these states. Intended in part to reassure the South by denying sanctuary to fugitive slaves, the exclusion laws also reflected the racist sentiments of many whites, especially Butternuts. Although Ohio had repealed its Negro exclusion law in 1849, many residents of the southern tier of Ohio counties wanted no part of black people and were more likely to aid the slave catcher than the fugitive.[20]

Nevertheless, resentment of the fugitive slave law continued to simmer among many Yankees. Even the heart of an occasional law-and-order man could be melted by the vision of a runaway manacled for return to bondage. Among evangelical Protestants who had been swept into the antislavery movement by the Second Great Awakening, such a vision generated outrage and activism. This was what gave *Uncle Tom's Cabin* such astounding success. As the daughter, sister, and wife of Congregational clergymen, Harriet Beecher Stowe had breathed the doctrinal air of sin, guilt, atonement, and salvation since childhood. She could clothe these themes in prose that throbbed with pathos as well as bathos. After running serially in an antislavery newspaper for nine months, *Uncle Tom's Cabin* came out as a book in the spring of 1852. Within a year it sold 300,000 copies in the United States alone—

19. Campbell, *Slave Catchers*, 207.
20. *Ibid.*, 49–62; Leon F. Litwack, *North of Slavery: The Negro in the Free States 1790–1860* (Chicago, 1961), 64–74.

comparable to at least three million today. The novel enjoyed equal popularity in Britain and was translated into several foreign languages. Within a decade it had sold more than two million copies in the United States, making it the best seller of all time in proportion to population.

Although Stowe said that God inspired the book, the fugitive slave law served as His mundane instrument. "Hattie, if I could use a pen as you can, I would write something that will make this whole nation feel what an accursed thing slavery is," said her sister-in-law after Congress passed the law. "I will if I live," vowed Harriet. And she did, writing by candlelight in the kitchen after putting her six children to bed and finishing the household chores. Unforgettable characters came alive in these pages despite a contrived plot and episodic structure that threatened to run away with the author. "That triumphant work," wrote Henry James, who had been moved by it in his youth, was "much less a book than a state of vision."[21] Drawing on her observance of bondage in Kentucky and her experiences with runaway slaves during a residence of eighteen years in Cincinnati, this New England woman made the image of Eliza running across the Ohio River on ice floes or Tom enduring the beatings of Simon Legree in Louisiana more real than life for millions of readers. Nor was the book simply an indictment of the South. Some of its more winsome characters were southerners, and its most loathsome villain, Simon Legree, was a transplanted Yankee. Mrs. Stowe (or perhaps God) rebuked the whole nation for the sin of slavery. She aimed the novel at the evangelical conscience of the North. And she hit her mark.

It is not possible to measure precisely the political influence of *Uncle Tom's Cabin*. One can quantify its sales but cannot point to votes that it changed or laws that it inspired. Yet few contemporaries doubted its power. "Never was there such a literary *coup-de-main* as this," said Henry Wadsworth Longfellow. In England, Lord Palmerston, who as prime minister a decade later would face a decision whether to intervene on behalf of the South in the Civil War, read *Uncle Tom's Cabin* three times and admired it not so much for the story as "for the statesmanship of it." As Abraham Lincoln was grappling with the problem of slavery in the summer of 1862, he borrowed from the Library of Congress *A Key to Uncle Tom's Cabin*, a subsequent volume by Stowe containing documentation on which she had based the novel. When Lincoln met

21. Charles H. Foster, *The Rungless Ladder: Harriet Beecher Stowe and New England Puritanism* (Durham, N.C., 1954), 12, 28–29.

the author later that year, he reportedly greeted her with the words: "So you're the little woman who wrote the book that made this great war."[22]

Uncle Tom's Cabin struck a raw nerve in the South. Despite efforts to ban it, copies sold so fast in Charleston and elsewhere that booksellers could not keep up with the demand. The vehemence of southern denunciations of Mrs. Stowe's "falsehoods" and "distortions" was perhaps the best gauge of how close they hit home. "There never before was anything so detestable or so monstrous among women as this," declared the *New Orleans Crescent*. The editor of the *Southern Literary Messenger* instructed his book reviewer: "I would have the review as hot as hellfire, blasting and searing the reputation of the vile wretch in petticoats who could write such a volume." Within two years proslavery writers had answered *Uncle Tom's Cabin* with at least fifteen novels whose thesis that slaves were better off than free workers in the North was capsulized by the title of one of them: *Uncle Robin in His Cabin in Virginia and Tom Without One in Boston.*[23] A decade later during the Civil War a South Carolina diarist with doubts of her own about slavery reflected the obsession of southerners with *Uncle Tom's Cabin* by using it as a constant benchmark to measure the realities of life in the South.[24]

In a later age "Uncle Tom" became an epithet for a black person who behaved with fawning servility toward white oppressors. This was partly a product of the ubiquitous Tom shows that paraded across the stage for generations and transmuted the novel into comic or grotesque melodrama. But an obsequious Tom was not the Uncle Tom of Stowe's pages. That Tom was one of the few true Christians in a novel intended to stir the emotions of a Christian public. Indeed, Tom was a Christ

22. Longfellow quoted in Thomas F. Gossett, *Uncle Tom's Cabin and American Literature* (Dallas, 1985), 166; Palmerston quoted in Edmund Wilson, *Patriotic Gore: Studies in the Literature of the American Civil War* (New York, 1962), 8; Earl Schenck Miers, ed., *Lincoln Day by Day: A Chronology 1809–1865*, 3 vols. (Washington, 1960), III, 121; Herbert Mitgang, ed., *Abraham Lincoln: A Press Portrait* (Chicago, 1971), 373. Dramatized versions of *Uncle Tom's Cabin* quickly reached the stage. At first these plays expressed the novel's themes and augmented its antislavery message. As time went on, however, "Tom Shows" lost much of their antislavery content and became minstrel-show parodies.

23. Gossett, *Uncle Tom's Cabin and American Culture*, 185–211; Craven, *Growth of Southern Nationalism*, 153–57.

24. See the frequent references to Mrs. Stowe and her book in C. Vann Woodward, ed., *Mary Chesnut's Civil War* (New Haven, 1981).

figure. Like Jesus he suffered agony inflicted by evil secular power. Like Jesus he died for the sins of humankind in order to save the oppressors as well as his own people. Stowe's readers lived in an age that understood this message better than ours. They were part of a generation that experienced not embarrassment but inspiration when they sang the words penned a decade later by another Yankee woman after she watched soldiers march off to war:

> As he died to make men holy,
> Let us die to make men free.

II

The South's defensive-aggressive temper in the 1850s stemmed in part from a sense of economic subordination to the North. In a nation that equated growth with progress, the census of 1850 alarmed many southerners. During the previous decade, population growth had been 20 percent greater in the free states than in the slave states. Lack of economic opportunity seemed to account for this ominous fact. Three times as many people born in slave states had migrated to free states as vice versa, while seven-eighths of the immigrants from abroad settled in the North, where jobs were available and competition with slave labor nonexistent. The North appeared to be racing ahead of the South in crucial indices of economic development. In 1850 only 14 percent of the canal mileage ran through slave states. In 1840 the South had possessed 44 percent of the country's railroad mileage, but by 1850 the more rapid pace of northern construction had dropped the southern share to 26 percent.[25] Worse still were data on industrial production. With 42 percent of the population, slave states possessed only 18 percent of the country's manufacturing capacity, a decline from the 20 percent of 1840. More alarming, nearly half of this industrial capital was located in the four border states whose commitment to southern rights was shaky.

The one bright spot in the southern economy was staple agriculture. By 1850 the price of cotton had climbed back to nearly double its low of 5.5 cents a pound in the mid-1840s. But this silver lining belonged to a dark cloud. The states that grew cotton kept less than 5 percent of it at home for manufacture into cloth. They exported 70 percent of it

25. It should be noted, however, that the principal cities and staple-producing areas of the South were located on or near navigable rivers, which made canals and railroads less important than in the North.

abroad and the remainder to northern mills, where the value added by manufacture equaled the price that raw cotton brought the South, which in turn imported two-thirds of its clothing and other manufactured goods from the North or abroad. But even this did not fully measure the drain of dollars from the South's export-import economy. Some 15 or 20 percent of the price of raw cotton went to "factors" who arranged credit, insurance, warehousing, and shipping for planters. Most of these factors represented northern or British firms. Nearly all the ships that carried cotton from southern ports and returned with manufactured goods were built and owned by northern or British companies. On their return voyages from Europe they usually put in at northern ports because of the greater volume of trade there, trans-shipping part of their cargoes for coastwise or overland transport southward, thereby increasing freight charges on imported goods to the South.[26]

Southern self-condemnation of this "degrading vassalage" to Yankees became almost a litany during the sectional crisis from 1846 to 1851. "Our whole commerce except a small fraction is in the hands of Northern men," complained a prominent Alabamian in 1847. "Take Mobile as an example—⅞ of our Bank Stock is owned by Northern men. . . . Our wholesale and retail business—everything in short worth mentioning is in the hands of men who invest their profits at the North. . . . Financially we are more enslaved than our negroes."[27] Yankees "abuse and denounce slavery and slaveholders," declared a southern newspaper four years later, yet "we purchase all our luxuries and necessaries from the North. . . . Our slaves are clothed with Northern manufactured goods [and] work with Northern hoes, ploughs, and other implements.

26. The data in these paragraphs have been compiled mainly from various schedules of the U. S. census reports for 1840 and 1850. Some of this material is conveniently summarized in tables in Lewis C. Gray, *History of Agriculture in the Southern United States to 1860*, 2 vols. (Washington, 1933), II, 1043; Arthur M. Schlesinger, Jr., ed., *History of American Presidential Elections 1789–1968*, 4 vols. (New York, 1971), II, 1128–52; and in *Twelfth Census of the United States Taken in the Year 1900*, *Manufactures*, Part II (Vol. 8), 982–89. Tables on canal and railroad mileage and on American foreign trade can be found in George Rogers Taylor, *The Transportation Revolution, 1815–1860* (New York, 1951), 71, 451. Harold Woodman, *King Cotton and His Retainers* (Lexington, Ky., 1968), and Douglass C. North, *The Economic Growth of the United States 1790–1860* (New York, 1961), document the colonial economic status of the South as an exporter of raw materials and an importer of capital and manufactured goods.

27. Joseph W. Lesesne to John C. Calhoun, Sept. 12, 1847, in J. Franklin Jameson, ed., *Correspondence of John C. Calhoun* (Washington, 1900), 1134–35.

. . . The slaveholder dresses in Northern goods, rides in a Northern saddle . . . reads Northern books. . . . In Northern vessels his products are carried to market . . . and on Northern-made paper, with a Northern pen, with Northern ink, he resolves and re-resolves in regard to his rights." How could the South expect to preserve its power, asked the young southern champion of economic diversification James B. D. De Bow, when "the North grows rich and powerful whilst we at best are stationary?"[28]

In 1846 De Bow had established a magazine in New Orleans with the title *Commercial Review of the South and West* (popularly known as *De Bow's Review*) and a hopeful slogan on its cover, "Commerce is King." The amount "lost to us annually by our vassalage to the North," said De Bow in 1852, was "one hundred million dollars. Great God! Does Ireland sustain a more degrading relation to Great Britain? Will we not throw off this humiliating dependence?" De Bow demanded "action! ACTION!! *ACTION!!!*—not in the rhetoric of Congress, but in the busy hum of mechanism, and in the thrifty operations of the hammer and anvil."[29] Plenty of southerners cheered De Bow's words, but they got more rhetoric than action.

De Bow was inspired to found his journal by the vision of a southern commercial empire evoked at a convention in Memphis in 1845. This meeting renewed a tradition of southern conclaves that had begun in the 1830s with a vow "to throw off the degrading shackles of our commercial dependence."[30] The dominant theme in these early conventions was the establishment of southern-owned shipping lines for direct trade with Europe. The Memphis convention, the first to meet after a six-year hiatus, focused on the need for railroad connections between the lower Mississippi valley and the south Atlantic coast. No such railroads nor any southern shipping lines had materialized by 1852, but De Bow prodded the commercial convention movement into life again that year with a meeting at New Orleans. Thereafter a similar gathering met at least once a year through 1859 in various southern cities.

These conventions were prolific in oratory and resolutions. In addi-

28. Alabama newspaper quoted in Robert Royal Russel, *Economic Aspects of Southern Sectionalism, 1840–1861* (Urbana, 1923), 48; *De Bow's Review*, 12 (1851), 557.
29. De Bow's speech to a southern commercial convention in New Orleans, January 1852, quoted in Herbert Wender, *Southern Commercial Conventions 1837–1859* (Baltimore, 1930), 85; *De Bow's Review*, 13 (1852), 571; 9 (1850), 120.
30. Resolution adopted by the first southern commercial convention in Augusta, Georgia, October 1837, quoted in Wender, *Southern Commercial Conventions*, 18.

tion to the call for direct trade with Europe in southern ships, they urged river and harbor improvements, railroad construction, and a southern route for a railroad to the Pacific. They pressed southerners to emulate Yankees in the building of factories. The delegates also devoted some attention to cultural matters. Noting with shame that most books and magazines read by southerners came from northern authors and presses, that the South sent many of its brightest sons to northern colleges, and that a shocking number of southern college presidents, professors, schoolteachers, and even newspaper editors were natives of Yankeedom, the conventions called for the establishment and patronage of southern publishers, magazines, authors, professors, and colleges.

Of all these enterprises, the industrial gospel aroused the most enthusiasm. "Give us factories, machine shops, work shops," declared southern journalists, and "we shall be able ere long to assert our rights." Textiles seemed the South's most logical route to industrialization. "Bring the spindles to the cotton," became a rallying cry of southern promoters. "South Carolina and Georgia possess advantages, which only need to be fostered to lead to success in cotton manufacturing," declared William Gregg, who had proven his credentials by establishing a large textile mill at Graniteville in the South Carolina piedmont. "Have we not the raw material on the spot, thus saving the freight of a double transportation? Is not labor cheaper with us than with our northern brethren?" Next to industry as the South's salvation stood railroads. "This railroad business is the *dispensation* of the present era," wrote one of South Carolina's few Whigs in 1853. "There have been two great dispensations of Civilization, the Greek & Christian and now comes the railroad."[31]

The South did take significant strides in the 1850s. The slave states more than quadrupled their railroad mileage, outstripping the northern pace which merely tripled mileage in that section. Capital invested in southern manufacturing rose 77 percent, exceeding the rate of population growth so that the amount invested per capita increased 39 percent.

31. *Huntsville Advocate* and *Richmond Republican*, editorials in August 1850, quoted in Arthur C. Cole, *The Whig Party in the South* (Washington, 1913), 208; Herbert Collins, "The Southern Industrial Gospel before 1860," *JSH*, 12 (1946), 391; William C. Preston to Waddy Thompson, Sept. 7, 1853, in Robert S. Tinkler, "Against the Grain: Unionists and Whigs in Calhoun's South Carolina," Senior Thesis, Princeton University, 1984, p. 92.

The value of southern-produced textiles increased 44 percent. But like Alice in Wonderland, the faster the South ran, the farther behind it seemed to fall. While the slave states' proportion of national railroad mileage increased to 35 percent in 1860, this was less than the 44 percent of 1840. By an index of railroad mileage per capita and per thousand square miles, the North remained more than twice as well supplied with rail transportation in 1860. And the amount of capital invested per mile in trackage and rolling stock was 30 percent greater in the free than in the slave states. While per capita investment in manufacturing increased no faster in the North than in the South during the 1850s, the population of free states grew more than that of slave states (40 percent to 27 percent) so that the southern share of national manufacturing capacity dropped from 18 to 16 percent. The effort to bring the spindles to the cotton failed: in 1860 the value of cotton textiles manufactured in the slave states was only 10 percent of the American total.[32] Nearly half of the southern spindles were in states that grew virtually no cotton. The city of Lowell, Massachusetts, operated more spindles in 1860 than all eleven of the soon-to-be Confederate states combined.[33] Two-fifths of all southern manufacturing capital in 1860 was in the four border states. Northern banks, mercantile firms, factors, and shipping lines continued to monopolize the southern carrying trade.[34]

32. These data are for the value of textile products reported in the manufactures section of the census. They do not include household manufactures, which were apparently greater in the South than the North, proportionately, judging from the amount of raw cotton consumed in the slave states, which amounted to an estimated 19 percent of the American total during the 1850s.

33. Stephen J. Goldfarb, "A Note on Limits to the Growth of the Cotton-Textile Industry in the Old South," *JSH*, 48 (1982), 545.

34. Two econometric historians have argued that by world standards the southern economy in 1860 did not lag significantly in commercial and industrial development. Using three per-capita indices—railroad mileage, cotton textile production, and pig iron production, Robert Fogel and Stanley Engerman found that the South ranked just behind the North in railroads but ahead of every other country. In textile production the South ranked sixth and in pig iron eighth. But the railroad index they used is specious, for railroads connect *places* as well as people. By an index that combines population and square miles of territory the South's railroad capacity was not only less than half of the North's but also considerably less than that of several European countries in 1860. Combining the two measures of industrial capacity used by Fogel and Engerman, the South produced only one-nineteenth as much per capita as Britain, one-seventh as much as Belgium, one-

Proponents of industrial development below the Potomac confessed frustration. Southerners were "destitute of every feature which characterizes an industrious people," mourned textile manufacturer William Gregg. Southern industries had "fagged, sickened, and died" because "there is a canker-worm at work" that had "undermine[d] the best efforts at success" and "blighted the fairest hopes of the Southern manufacturer."[35]

Contemporaries and historians have advanced several explanations for this "failure of industrialization in the slave economy," as the subtitle of a recent study has termed it. Following the lead of Adam Smith, classical economists considered free labor more efficient than slave labor because the free worker is stimulated by the fear of want and the desire for betterment. A slave, wrote Smith, "can have no other interest but to eat as much, and to labour as little as possible." Yankee opponents of slavery agreed. "Enslave a man," declared Horace Greeley, "and you destroy his ambition, his enterprise, his capacity. In the constitution of human nature, the desire of bettering one's condition is the mainspring of effort."[36] The northern journalist and landscape architect Frederick Law Olmsted made three extensive trips through the South in the 1850s which resulted in three books that portrayed a shiftless, indolent, rundown society as the fruit of bondage. The subsistence level at which slaves and many "poor whites" lived discouraged the development of a market for consumer goods that could have stimulated southern manufacturing.[37]

---

fifth as much as the North, and one-fourth as much as Sweden—rather significant differences which tend to undermine the point they are trying to make. See Robert William Fogel and Stanley L. Engerman, *Time on the Cross: The Economics of American Negro Slavery* (Boston, 1974), 254–56.

35. William Gregg, "Domestic Industry—Manufactures at the South," *De Bow's Review*, 8 (1850), 134–36, and "Southern Patronage to Southern Imports and Domestic Industry," *ibid.*, 29 (1860), 77–83.

36. Smith quoted in David Brion Davis, *The Problem of Slavery in the Age of Revolution 1770–1823* (Ithaca, 1975), 352; Greeley quoted in Eric Foner, *Free Soil, Free Labor, Free Men: The Ideology of the Republican Party before the Civil War* (New York, 1970), 46.

37. Olmsted's three books were titled *A Journey in the Seaboard Slave States* (1856), *A Journey Through Texas* (1857), and *A Journey in the Back Country* (1860). In 1861 Olmsted abridged the three volumes into one with the title *The Cotton Kingdom*. For the question of a southern consumer market, see Eugene D. Genovese, *The Political Economy of Slavery* (New York, 1965), esp. chaps. 7 and 8.

These explanations for southern "backwardness" have some merit. Yet they are not entirely convincing. The successful employment of slaves as well as white workers in southern textile mills, in iron foundries like the Tredegar Works in Richmond, and in other industries demonstrated a potential for industrialization on a greater scale. As for the lack of a home market, southern consumers generated a significant demand for *northern*-made shoes, clothing, locomotives, steamboats, farm implements—to name just a few products—that encouraged such promoters as Gregg and De Bow to believe that a market for southern manufactures existed if it could only be exploited.

Other accounts of southern industrialization have focused not on deficiencies of labor or of demand but on a lack of capital. Capital was abundant in the South, to be sure: in 1860, according to the census measure of wealth (real and personal property), the average southern white male was nearly twice as wealthy as the average northern white man.[38] The problem was that most of this wealth was invested in land and slaves. A British visitor to Georgia in 1846 was "struck with the difficulty experienced in raising money here by small shares for the building of mills. 'Why,' say they, 'should all our cotton make so long a journey to the North, to be manufactured there, and come back to us at so high a price? It is because all spare cash is sunk here in purchasing negroes.' " A northerner described the investment cycle of the southern economy: "To sell cotton in order to buy negroes—to make more cotton to buy more negroes, 'ad infinitum,' is the aim and direct tendency of all the operations of the thorough going cotton planter."[39]

Was this preference for reinvestment in slaves economically rational? No, answered an earlier generation of historians following the lead of Ulrich B. Phillips, who found plantation agriculture a decreasingly profitable enterprise that southern whites preserved for cultural rather than economic reasons.[40] Yes, answered a more recent generation of historians, who have analyzed bushels of data and concluded that slave ag-

38. Lee Soltow, *Men and Wealth in the United States 1850–1870* (New Haven, 1975), 65.

39. Sir Charles Lyell, *Second Visit to the United States*, 2 vols. (London, 1846), II, 35; Joseph Holt Ingraham, *The Southwest, by a Yankee*, 2 vols. (New York, 1835), II, 91.

40. See especially Ulrich B. Phillips, *American Negro Slavery* (New York, 1918) and *Life and Labor in the Old South* (Boston, 1929); and Genovese, *Political Economy of Slavery*.

riculture yielded as great a return on capital as potential alternative investments.[41] Maybe, is the answer of still another group of economic historians, who suggest that investments in railroads and mills might have yielded higher returns than agriculture, that cotton was living on the borrowed time of an almost saturated market, and that whatever the rationality of individual planter reinvestment in agriculture the collective result inhibited the economic development of the South as a whole.[42]

Some evidence points to the South's agrarian value system as an important reason for lack of industrialization. Although the light of Jeffersonian egalitarianism may have dimmed by 1850, the torch of agrarianism still glowed. "Those who labor in the earth are the chosen people of God . . . whose breasts He has made His peculiar deposit for substantial and genuine virtue," the husbandman of Monticello had written. The proportion of urban workingmen to farmers in any society "is the proportion of its unsound to its healthy parts" and adds "just so much to the support of pure government, as sores do to the strength of the human body."[43] The durability of this conviction in the South created a cultural climate unfriendly to industrialization. "In cities and factories, the vices of our nature are more fully displayed," declared James Hammond of South Carolina in 1829, while rural life "promotes a generous hospitality, a high and perfect courtesy, a lofty spirit of independence . . . and all the nobler virtues and heroic traits." An Englishman traveling through the South in 1842 found a widespread feeling "that the labours of the people should be confined to agriculture, leaving manufactures to Europe or to the States of the North."[44]

Defenders of slavery contrasted the bondsman's comfortable lot with the misery of wage slaves so often that they began to believe it. Beware

41. Kenneth M. Stampp, *The Peculiar Institution: Slavery in the Ante-Bellum South* (New York, 1956); Alfred H. Conrad and John R. Meyer, "The Economics of Slavery in the Ante Bellum South," *Journal of Political Economy*, 66 (1958), 95–130; Fogel and Engerman, *Time on the Cross*.

42. Alfred H. Conrad et al., "Slavery as an Obstacle to Economic Growth in the United States: A Panel Discussion," *Journal of Economic History*, 27 (1967), 518–60; Gavin Wright, *The Political Economy of the Cotton South* (New York, 1978); Fred Bateman and Thomas Weiss, *A Deplorable Scarcity: The Failure of Industrialization in the Slave Economy* (Chapel Hill, 1981).

43. *Notes on the State of Virginia*, ed. William Peden (Chapel Hill, 1955), 164–65.

44. Hammond quoted in Orville Vernon Burton, *In My Father's House Are Many Mansions: Family and Community in Edgefield, South Carolina* (Chapel Hill, 1985), 37; James S. Buckingham, *The Slave States of America*, 2 vols. (London, 1842), II, 112.

of the "endeavor to imitate . . . Northern civilization" with its "filthy, crowded, licentious factories," warned a planter in 1854. "Let the North enjoy their hireling labor with all its . . . pauperism, rowdyism, mobism and anti-rentism," said the collector of customs in Charleston. "We do not want it. We are satisfied with our slave labor. . . . We like old things—old wine, old books, old friends, old and fixed relations between employer and employed."[45]

By the later 1850s southern agrarians had mounted a counterattack against the gospel of industrialization. The social prestige of planters pulled other occupations into their orbit rather than vice versa. "A large plantation and Negroes are the *ultima Thule* of every Southern gentleman's ambition," wrote a frustrated Mississippi industrial promoter in 1860. "For this the lawyer pores over his dusty tomes, the merchant measures his tape . . . the editor drives his quill, and the mechanic his plane—all, all who dare to aspire at all, look to this as the goal of their ambition." After all, trade was a lowly calling fit for *Yankees*, not for gentlemen. "That the North does our trading and manufacturing mostly is true," wrote an Alabamian in 1858, "and we are willing that they should. Ours is an agricultural people, and God grant that we may continue so. It is the freest, happiest, most independent, and with us, the most powerful condition on earth."[46]

Many planters did invest in railroads and factories, of course, and these enterprises expanded during the 1850s. But the trend seemed to be toward even greater concentration in land and slaves. While per capita southern wealth rose 62 percent from 1850 to 1860, the average price of slaves increased 70 percent and the value per acre of agricultural land appreciated 72 percent, while per capita southern investment in manufacturing increased only 39 percent. In other words, southerners had a larger portion of their capital invested in land and slaves in 1860 than in 1850.[47]

45. "The Prospects and Policy of the South, as They Appear to the Eyes of a Planter," *Southern Quarterly Review*, 26 (1854), 431–32; William J. Grayson, *Letters of Curtius* (Charleston, 1852), 8.

46. *Vicksburg Sun*, April 9, 1860; Alabamian quoted in Russel, *Economic Aspects of Southern Sectionalism*, 207.

47. During the same period the per capita wealth of northerners increased 26 percent and per capita northern investment in industry rose 38 percent. Data on per capita wealth are from Soltow, *Men and Wealth*, 67; data on the price of slaves are from Phillips, *American Negro Slavery*, 371; all other data cited here have been compiled from the published census returns of 1850 and 1860.

Although the persistence of Jeffersonian agrarianism may help explain this phenomenon, the historian can discover pragmatic reasons as well. The 1850s were boom years for cotton and for other southern staples. Low cotton prices in the 1840s had spurred the crusade for economic diversification. But during the next decade the price of cotton jumped more than 50 percent to an average of 11.5 cents a pound. The cotton crop consequently doubled to four million bales annually by the late 1850s. Sugar and tobacco prices and production similarly increased. The apparent insatiable demand for southern staples caused planters to put every available acre into these crops. The per capita output of the principal southern food crops actually declined in the 1850s, and this agricultural society headed toward the status of a food-deficit region.[48]

Although these trends alarmed some southerners, most expressed rapture over the dizzying prosperity brought by the cotton boom. The advocates of King Commerce faded; King Cotton reigned supreme. "Our Cotton is the most wonderful talisman in the world," declared a planter in 1853. "By its power we are transmuting whatever we choose into whatever we want." Southerners were "unquestionably the most prosperous people on earth, realizing ten to twenty per cent on their capital with every prospect of doing as well for a long time to come," boasted James Hammond. "The slaveholding South is now the controlling power of the world," he told the Senate in 1858. "Cotton, rice, tobacco, and naval stores command the world. . . . No power on earth dares . . . to make war on cotton. Cotton is king."[49]

By the later 1850s southern commercial conventions had reached the same conclusion. The merger of this commercial convention movement with a parallel series of planters' conventions in 1854 reflected the

48. The production of corn, sweet potatoes, and hogs in the slave states decreased on a per capita basis by 3, 15, and 22 percent respectively from 1850 to 1860. The possibility that southerners were becoming a beef-eating people does not seem a satisfactory explanation for the per capita decrease of hogs. The number of cattle per capita in the South increased only 3 percent during the decade, and according to Robert R. Russel virtually all of this increase was in dairy cows, not beef cattle. Russel, *Economic Aspects of Southern Sectionalism*, 203. The data in this paragraph, compiled mainly from the published census returns of 1850 and 1860, are conveniently available in tabular form in Schlesinger, ed., *History of American Presidential Elections*, II, 1128 ff.

49. Planter quoted in John McCardell, *The Idea of a Southern Nation: Southern Nationalists and Southern Nationalism, 1830–1860* (New York, 1979), 134; Hammond to William Gilmore Simms, April 22, 1859, quoted in Nevins, *Emergence*, I, 5; CG, 35 Cong., 1 Sess., 961–62.

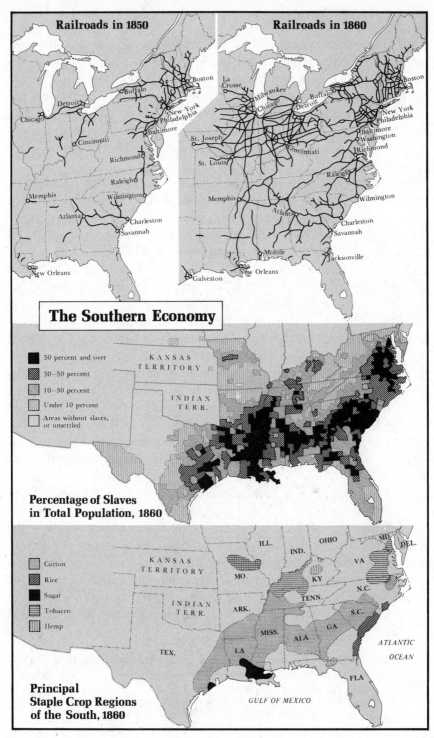

Railroads in 1850

La Crosse · Boston · Buffalo · Detroit · Chicago · New York · Philadelphia · Baltimore · Cincinnati · Richmond · Raleigh · Memphis · Wilmington · Atlanta · Charleston · Savannah · New Orleans

Railroads in 1860

La Crosse · Milwaukee · Chicago · Detroit · Buffalo · Boston · New York · Philadelphia · St. Joseph · St. Louis · Cincinnati · Baltimore · Washington · Richmond · Raleigh · Memphis · Wilmington · Atlanta · Charleston · Savannah · Mobile · New Orleans · Galveston · Jacksonville

The Southern Economy

Percentage of Slaves in Total Population, 1860

KANSAS TERRITORY
INDIAN TERR.

- 50 percent and over
- 30–50 percent
- 10–30 percent
- Under 10 percent
- Areas without slaves, or unsettled

Principal Staple Crop Regions of the South, 1860

ILL. · IND. · OHIO · MD. · DEL. · KANSAS TERRITORY · MO. · VA · KY. · N.C. · TENN. · INDIAN TERR. · ARK. · S.C. · MISS. · ALA · GA · LA · TEX. · FLA · ATLANTIC OCEAN · GULF OF MEXICO

- Cotton
- Rice
- Sugar
- Tobacco
- Hemp

trend. Thereafter slave agriculture and its defense became the dominant theme of the conventions. Even *De Bow's Review* moved in this direction. Though De Bow continued to give lip service to industrialization, his *Review* devoted more and more space to agriculture, proslavery polemics, and southern nationalism. By 1857 the politicians had pretty well taken over these "commercial" conventions. And the main form of commerce they now advocated was a reopening of the African slave trade.[50]

Federal law had banned this trade since the end of 1807. Smuggling continued on a small scale after that date; in the 1850s the rising price of slaves produced an increase in this illicit traffic and built up pressure for a repeal of the ban. Political motives also actuated proponents of repeal. Agitation of the question, said one, would give "a sort of spite to the North and defiance of their opinions." A delegate to the 1856 commercial convention insisted that "we are entitled to demand the opening of this trade from an industrial, political, and constitutional consideration. . . . With cheap negroes we could set the hostile legislation of Congress at defiance. The slave population after supplying the states would overflow into the territories, and nothing could control its natural expansion." For some defenders of slavery, logical consistency required a defense of the slave trade as well. "Slavery is right," said a delegate to the 1858 convention, "and being right there can be no wrong in the natural means of its formation." Or as William L. Yancey put it: "If it is right to buy slaves in Virginia and carry them to New Orleans, why is it not right to buy them in Africa and carry them there?"[51]

Why not indeed? But most southerners failed to see the logic of this argument. In addition to moral repugnance toward the horrors of the "middle passage" of slaves across the Atlantic, many slaveowners in the upper South had economic reasons to oppose reopening of the African trade. Their own prosperity benefitted from the rising demand for slaves; a growing stream of bondsmen flowed from the upper South to the cotton states. Nevertheless, the commercial convention at Vicksburg in 1859 (attended by delegates from only the lower South) called for repeal

50. McCardell, *Idea of a Southern Nation*, 129–40; Otis Clark Skipper, *J. D. B. De Bow: Magazinist of the Old South* (Athens, Ga., 1958), 81–97; Wender, *Southern Commercial Conventions*, 207,225.

51. Potter, *Impending Crisis*, 398–99; Wender, *Southern Commercial Conventions*, 178, 213.

of the ban on slave imports. Proponents knew that they had no chance of success in Congress. But they cared little, for most of them were secessionists who favored a southern nation that could pass its own laws. In the meantime they could try to circumvent federal law by bringing in "apprentices" from Africa. De Bow became president of an African Labor Supply Association formed for that purpose. In 1858 the lower house of the Louisiana legislature authorized the importation of such apprentices. But the senate defeated the measure.[52]

Frustrated in their attempts to change the law, fire-eaters turned their efforts to breaking it. The most famous example of the illicit slave trade in the 1850s was the schooner *Wanderer*, owned by Charles A. L. Lamar, member of a famous and powerful southern family. Lamar organized a syndicate that sent several ships to Africa for slaves. One of these was the *Wanderer*, a fast yacht that took on a cargo of five hundred Africans in 1858. The four hundred survivors of the voyage to Georgia earned Lamar a large profit. But federal officials had got wind of the affair and arrested Lamar along with several crew members. Savannah juries acquitted all of them. The grand jurors who had indicted Lamar suffered so much vilification from the local press as dupes of Yankee agitators that they published a bizarre recantation of their action and advocated repeal of the 1807 law prohibiting the slave trade. "Longer to yield to a sickly sentiment of pretended philanthropy and diseased mental aberration of 'higher law' fanatics," said the jurors in reference to opponents of the trade, "is weak and unwise." When northerners criticized the acquittal of Lamar, a southern newspaper denounced Yankee hypocrisy: "What is the difference between a Yankee violating the fugitive slave law in the North, and a Southern man violating . . . the law against the African slave trade in the South?" Lamar repurchased the *Wanderer* at public auction and went on with his slave-trading ventures until the Civil War, in which he was killed at the head of his regiment.[53]

III

Those who wanted to import more slaves also wanted to acquire more slave territory. For this purpose a good many southerners looked not to

52. For a study of the movement to reopen the African slave trade, see Ronald T. Takaki, *A Pro-Slavery Crusade: The Agitation to Reopen the African Slave Trade* (New York, 1971).

53. Quotations from Nevins, *Emergence*, I, 436; and Takaki, *Pro-Slavery Crusade*, 220. See also Tom Henderson Wells, *The Slave Ship* Wanderer (Athens, Ga., 1967).

the rather unpromising regions already part of the United States but to lands south of the border. At the 1856 commercial convention a delegate from Texas proposed a toast that was drunk with enthusiasm: "To the Southern republic bounded on the north by the Mason and Dixon line and on the south by the Isthmus of Tehuantepec, including Cuba and all other lands on our southern shore."[54]

This version of Manifest Destiny was not new in 1856. Eight years earlier, just after the Senate had approved the treaty acquiring California and New Mexico, President Polk had outlined his next goal: "I am decidedly in favour of purchasing Cuba & making it one of the States of [the] Union."[55] This idea appealed particularly to southerners as a way to expand their political power. "The Pearl of the West Indies," proclaimed one annexationist pamphlet, "with her thirteen or fifteen representatives in Congress, would be a powerful auxiliary to the South." Believing that the Gulf of Mexico was "a basin of water belonging to the United States," Senator Jefferson Davis declared in 1848 that "Cuba must be ours" in order to "increase the number of slaveholding constituencies."[56]

Polk authorized his minister to Spain to offer $100 million for the island. But this effort died stillborn. The American minister's clumsy efforts both amused and angered Spanish officials. A North Carolina politician with the implausible name of Romulus M. Saunders, the minister knew no language but English "& even this he sometimes murders," commented Secretary of State Buchanan. The Spanish foreign minister informed Saunders that sooner than sell Cuba, Spain "would prefer seeing it sunk in the ocean." In any case it was unlikely that Congress, with its Whig and Wilmot Proviso majority in the House, would have appropriated funds to buy a territory containing nearly half a million slaves. Whig victory in the 1848 presidential election ended official efforts to acquire Cuba—for the time being.[57]

Annexationists were not surprised by this failure. After all Texas, California, and New Mexico had been won only by revolution and war; they were willing to apply the same methods in Cuba. Their champion

54. Wender, Southern Commercial Conventions, 168.
55. Milo Milton Quaife, ed., The Diary of James K. Polk during His Presidency, 1845 to 1849, 4 vols. (Chicago, 1910), III, 446.
56. Basil Rauch, American Interest in Cuba: 1848–1855 (New York, 1948), 111; CG, 30 Cong., 1 Sess., Appendix, 599; Robert E. May, The Southern Dream of a Caribbean Empire 1854–1861 (Baton Rouge, 1973), 11.
57. Rauch, American Interest in Cuba, 48–100; quotations from 97–98.

was a handsome, charismatic Cuban soldier of fortune named Narciso Lopez who had fled to New York in 1848 after Spanish officials foiled his attempt to foment an uprising of Cuban planters. Lopez recruited an army of several hundred adventurers, Mexican War veterans, and Cuban exiles for an invasion of the island. He asked Jefferson Davis to lead the expedition. The senator demurred and recommended his friend Robert E. Lee, who considered it but politely declined. Lopez thereupon took command himself, but the Taylor administration got wind of the enterprise and sent a naval force to seize Lopez's ships and block his departure in September 1849.

Undaunted, Lopez began to organize a new expedition of "filibusters" (from the Spanish filibustero, meaning freebooter or pirate). Believing northerners too "timid and dilatory" for this venture, Lopez left New York for New Orleans, where he planned to "rest his hopes on the men of the bold West and chivalric South."[58] On the way he stopped in Mississippi to ask Governor John Quitman to command the invasion force. Quitman was a veteran of the Mexican War, in which he had risen to major general and commanded the assault that took Mexico City. A fire-eater who scattered threats of secession during the crisis of 1850, Quitman was tempted by the offer but turned it down because he felt compelled to remain at his post in Mississippi. He did help Lopez recruit men and raise money to buy weapons. Lopez obtained arms and volunteers from similar sources in Louisiana. In May 1850 his army of six hundred men sailed from New Orleans to the accompaniment of cheering crowds and the "winking encouragement" of public officials. Lopez landed on the northwest coast of Cuba, captured the town of Cardenas, and burned the governor's mansion. But the expected uprising of Cuban revolutionaries failed to materialize. When Spanish troops closed in on Cardenas the filibusters retreated to their ship, which barely outraced a pursuing Spanish warship to Key West, where the expeditionary force ingloriously dissolved.[59]

Nevertheless, Lopez received a hero's welcome in the lower South. Dozens of towns and organizations offered him salutes, parades, toasts,

---

58. Quoted in John Hope Franklin, *The Militant South 1800–1861* (Cambridge, Mass., 1956), 105.

59. Chester Stanley Urban, "New Orleans and the Cuban Question during the Lopez Expeditions of 1849–1851: A Local Study in 'Manifest Destiny,' " *Louisiana Historical Quarterly*, 22 (1939), 1125; Robert E. May, *John A. Quitman: Old South Crusader* (Baton Rouge, 1985), 236–39.

and banquets. Southern senators demanded American action to punish Spain. "I want Cuba, and I know that sooner or later we must have it," declared Jefferson Davis's fellow senator from Mississippi, Albert Gallatin Brown. But Brown would not stop there. "I want Tamaulipas, Potosi, and one or two other Mexican States; and I want them all for the same reason—for the planting and spreading of slavery." The *Southern Standard* had an even larger vision. "With Cuba and St. Domingo, we could control the productions of the tropics, and, with them, the commerce of the world, and with that, the power of the world." Indeed, pronounced *De Bow's Review*, "we have a destiny to perform, 'a manifest destiny' over all Mexico, over South America, over the West Indies."[60]

Zachary Taylor's administration, then trying to bring in California and New Mexico as free states, was unmoved by this rhetoric. The government indicted Lopez, Quitman, and several other southerners for violation of the neutrality laws. Quitman threatened to use the Mississippi militia to defend the state's sovereignty against federal marshals. But he finally calmed down, resigned the governorship, and agreed to be arrested. Three trials in New Orleans of one defendant (a Mississippi planter) ended in hung juries, whereupon the federal government dropped the remaining indictments. Wild celebrations marked this denouement. "If the evidence against Lopez were a thousand fold stronger," commented a New Orleans newspaper, "no jury could be impaneled to convict him because public opinion makes a law."[61]

Thus vindicated, the filibusters tried again in 1851. William J. Crittenden of Kentucky, nephew of the attorney general, commanded a "regiment" of southern volunteers in the invasion force of 420 men. Once again port officials in New Orleans colluded with the filibusters to allow their departure on August 3, 1851, in a ship loaded to the gunwales. But this time Spanish troops were ready and waiting. They had already suppressed a premature local uprising intended to cooperate with the invaders. In several engagements the Spaniards killed two hundred of the filibusters and captured the rest. Cuban officials sent 160 of the prisoners to Spain, garroted Lopez in front of a large crowd

60. May, *Southern Dream of a Caribbean Empire*, 9; Jesse T. Carpenter, *The South as a Conscious Minority, 1789–1861* (New York, 1930), 179; *De Bow's Review*, 9 (1850), 167.
61. *Orleanian*, June 8, 1850, quoted in Urban, "New Orleans and the Cuban Question," *loc. cit.*, 1132. See also May, *Quitman*, 240–52.

in Havana, and lined up fifty American prisoners including Crittenden in the public square and executed them by firing squad.[62]

When this news reached New Orleans, mobs rioted out of control. They destroyed the Spanish consulate and sacked shops owned by Spaniards. "Blood for Blood!" blazoned the New Orleans Courier. "Our brethren must be avenged! Cuba must be seized!"[63] But the Fillmore administration, embarrassed by its negligent failure to stop the filibusters before they reached Cuba, confined its activities to a successful diplomatic effort to release the remaining American prisoners from Spain.

Filibustering died down for a time while expansionists concentrated on winning a friendly administration in the election of 1852. The spread-eagle nationalism of the "Young America" element in the Democratic party made Cuba an important issue in this election.[64] The Young Americans were by no means all southerners. Stephen Douglas of Illinois was their foremost champion. But expansion remained preeminently a southern priority. "The desire that Cuba should be acquired as a Southern conquest, is almost unanimous among Southern men," commented one observer. "The safety of the South is to be found only in the extension of its peculiar institutions," said another. The election of Franklin Pierce as president caused Young Americans to celebrate with bonfires and torchlight parades brandishing such banners as "The Fruits of the Late Democratic Victory—Pierce and Cuba."[65]

Pierce's first actions pleased these partisans. "The policy of my Administration will not be controlled by any timid forebodings of evil from expansion," the new president promised in his inaugural address. "Our position on the globe, render[s] the acquisition of certain possessions . . . eminently important for our protection. . . . [The] future is boundless."[66] Pierce filled his cabinet and the diplomatic corps with votaries of Manifest Destiny. Of all these appointments, that of Pierre Soulé as minister to Spain offered the clearest signal of the administration's intentions. A native of France whose republicanism had forced

62. Rauch, American Interest in Cuba, 151–63; Charles H. Brown, Agents of Manifest Destiny: The Lives and Times of the Filibusters (Chapel Hill, 1980), 67–88.
63. Urban, "New Orleans and the Cuban Question," loc. cit., 1159.
64. For a fuller treatment of this election, see the chapter following.
65. Quotations from McCardell, Idea of a Southern Nation, 258–59, and Brown, Agents of Manifest Destiny, 105.
66. James D. Richardson, comp., Messages and Papers of the Presidents, 20 vols. (Washington, 1897–1917), VII, 2731–32.

him to emigrate to Louisiana in 1825, the firebrand Soulé hailed the European revolutions of 1848 to free the Continent from monarchy even as he supported filibusters to Cuba to bring that island into the Union as a slave state. Within a year of his arrival at Madrid, Soulé denounced the monarchy, wounded the French ambassador in a duel, presented a forty-eight hour ultimatum (which Spain ignored) over an incident involving an American ship at Havana, and began intriguing with Spanish revolutionaries.

Despite all this, the only expansionist achievement of the Pierce administration was the Gadsden Purchase. And even that came to less than southerners had hoped. A railroad promoter from South Carolina, James Gadsden became minister to Mexico with the purpose of buying additional territory for a railroad route from New Orleans to the Pacific. Antislavery Yankees suspected that he had another purpose in mind as well: to acquire territory suitable for future admission as slave states. They may have been right. Gadsden initially offered Santa Anna up to $50 million for nearly 250,000 square miles of northern Mexico. The canny Mexican leader needed the money, as always, but could not see his way clear to selling off almost one-third of what was left of his country. Santa Anna finally made a $15 million deal with Gadsden to sell 55,000 square miles, but northern senators cut out 9,000 of these before enough northern Democrats joined southern senators to approve the treaty in 1854.[67]

Gadsden's efforts were crowded out of the limelight by Cuba. Determined to acquire the island one way or another, Pierce knew that Spain was no more willing to sell in 1853 than five years earlier. Surviving evidence indicates that the administration therefore hoped to foster a Texas-style revolution in Cuba supported by another filibuster invasion. The secretary of state's instructions to Soulé in Madrid stated that, while a renewed effort to purchase Cuba was "inopportune," the United States expected the island to "release itself or be released from its present Colonial subjection."[68] Pierce apparently met with John Quitman in July 1853 and encouraged him to go ahead with a filibuster expedition, this time with more men backed by more money than Lopez's ill-fated invasions. Quitman needed little encouragement. "We have been swindled . . . out of the public domain," he declared. "Even a portion

67. Paul Neff Garber, The Gadsden Treaty (Philadelphia, 1923).
68. William R. Manning, ed., Diplomatic Correspondence of the United States: Inter-American Affairs, 1831–1860, 12 vols. (Washington, 1932–39), XI, 160–66.

of Texas, supposed to be secured as slaveholding, has been wrested from us [by settlement of the boundary dispute in favor of New Mexico]. . . . The golden shore of the Pacific . . . is denied to Southern labor. . . . We are now hemmed in on the west as well as the north." Thus it was time "to strike with effect" in Cuba "after the fashion of Texas."[69]

Prominent southerners endorsed Quitman's project. The governor of Alabama actively supported it. Numerous political leaders in Texas helped organize the expedition which was scheduled, like the others, to depart from New Orleans. "Now is the time to act," wrote Alexander Stephens from Georgia, "while England and France have their hands full" with the Crimean War and could not interfere.[70] By the spring of 1854 Quitman had recruited several thousand volunteers. Cuban exiles made contacts with revolutionary groups on the island to coordinate yet another uprising. Senator John Slidell of Louisiana, backed by other southern senators, introduced a resolution to suspend the neutrality law. The foreign relations committee was about to report this resolution favorably when, with apparent suddenness in May 1854, the administration turned negative and reined in Quitman.[71]

What had happened? Apparently the administration, which had spent all of its political capital in obtaining passage of the Kansas-Nebraska Act, decided to back off from a second proslavery enterprise that might wreck the northern half of the party.[72] "The Nebraska question has sadly shattered our party in all the free states," wrote Secretary of State William M. Marcy, "and deprived it of the strength which was needed & could have been much more profitably used for the acquisition of Cuba." On May 31, the day after he signed the Kansas-Nebraska Act, Pierce issued a proclamation enjoining filibustering at pain of suffering the full penalties of the neutrality law.[73]

But this did not end efforts to acquire Cuba. Deciding in 1854 to

69. Rauch, *American Interest in Cuba*, 200–201; McCardell, *Idea of a Southern Nation*, 256.
70. May, *Southern Dream of a Caribbean Empire*, 39.
71. This paragraph has drawn upon the accounts in Rauch, *American Interest in Cuba*, 262–86; Potter, *Impending Crisis*, 183–88; May, *Southern Dream of a Caribbean Empire*, 46–60; and Brown, *Agents of Manifest Destiny*, 109–23.
72. For the Kansas-Nebraska Act and its consequences, see the chapter following.
73. May, *Quitman*, 270–95; May, *Southern Dream of a Caribbean Empire*, 60–67; Brown, *Agents of Manifest Destiny*, 124–44; quotation from May, *Southern Dream*, 60.

exploit the sorry financial plight of the Spanish government, Pierce authorized Soulé to offer as much as $130 million for the island. If Spain turned this down, Soulé was then to direct his effort "to the next desirable object, which is to detach that island from the Spanish dominion." Whatever this cryptic instruction may have meant, if the administration expected Soulé to operate through the quiet channels of diplomacy they had mistaken their man. In October 1854 he met at Ostend in Belgium with his fellow ministers to Britain and France, James Buchanan and John Mason. The volatile Louisianian somehow persuaded the normally cautious Buchanan as well as the naive Mason to sign a memorandum that became known as the Ostend Manifesto. "Cuba is as necessary to the North American republic as any of its present . . . family of states," proclaimed this document. If the United States decided that its security required possession of the island, and Spain persisted in refusing to sell, then "by every law, human and Divine, we shall be justified in wresting it from Spain."[74]

In his usual fashion, Soulé had failed to keep the Ostend meeting secret from the European press. An American newspaper also picked up details of the "Manifesto" and broke the story in November 1854. Antislavery newspapers denounced the "shame and dishonor" of this "Manifesto of the Brigands," this "highwayman's plea" to "grasp, to rob, to murder, to grow rich on the spoils of provinces and toils of slaves."[75] The House subpoenaed the diplomatic correspondence and published it. Already reeling from a Kansas-Nebraska backlash that had cost the Democrats sixty-six of their ninety-one northern congressmen in the 1854 elections, the shell-shocked administration forced Soulé's resignation and abandoned all schemes to obtain Cuba. Quitman nevertheless renewed plans for a filibustering expedition in the spring of 1855. Pierce finally persuaded him to desist—a task made easier when Spanish troops in January 1855 arrested and executed several Cuban revolutionaries, an unpleasant reminder of what might be in store for leaders of another invasion.

Meanwhile, public attention shifted a few hundred miles west by south of Havana where the most remarkable and successful filibuster leader was tracing his meteoric career. Born in Nashville in 1824, William Walker bore few outward signs of the ambition for power that burned within him. Shy and taciturn, ascetic, sandy-haired and freckled, five

74. Manning, ed., *Diplomatic Correspondence*, XI, 175–78, 193–94.
75. Potter, *Impending Crisis*, 192; Nevins, *Ordeal*, II, 362.

feet five inches tall and weighing less than 120 pounds, his only distinctive feature was a pair of luminous, transfixing, grey-green eyes. After graduating *summa cum laude* from the University of Nashville at the age of fourteen, this restless prodigy studied medicine in Europe, earned a medical degree from the University of Pennsylvania at the age of nineteen, but practiced for only a short time before moving to New Orleans to study law. After a brief career as a lawyer, Walker turned to journalism and became an editor of the *New Orleans Crescent*.[76]

In 1849 Walker joined the stream of humanity moving to California. But his restive soul found no repose in that golden state. As a journalist he attacked crime and helped inspire the vigilante movement in San Francisco. He fought three duels and was twice wounded. In 1853 Walker finally found his avocation. With forty-five heavily armed men he sailed from San Francisco to "colonize" Baja California and Sonora. His professed intent was to subdue the Apaches, bring the blessings of American civilization and Anglo-Saxon energy to these benighted Mexican provinces, and incidentally to exploit Sonora's gold and silver deposits.

This was neither the first nor last of many American filibustering expeditions south of the border during the unquiet years following the Mexican War. The chronic instability and frequent overthrows of the government in Mexico City created power vacuums filled by bandit chieftains and gringo invaders who kept the border in a constant state of upheaval. Walker's expedition enjoyed more initial success than most such enterprises. His filibusters captured La Paz, the sleepy capital of Baja California. Walker proclaimed himself president of this new republic and proceeded to annex Sonora without having set foot in that richer province. This bold action attracted more recruits from California. Walker's army of footloose Forty-niners, with few supplies and less military experience, marched through rugged mountains, rafted across the Colorado River, and invaded Sonora. Exhausted, starving, and mutinous, fifty of Walker's men deserted and the rest retreated in the face of a superior force that killed several of them. With thirty-four survivors Walker fled across the border and surrendered to American authorities

76. This and following paragraphs on Walker's career are drawn mainly from William O. Scroggs, *Filibusters and Financiers: The Story of William Walker and His Associates* (New York, 1916); Albert Z. Carr, *The World and William Walker* (New York, 1963); Frederic Rosengarten, Jr., *Freebooters Must Die! The Life and Death of William Walker* (Wayne, Pa., 1976); and Brown, *Agents of Manifest Destiny*, 174 ff.

at San Diego in May 1854. Hailed as a hero by many San Franciscans, Walker stood trial for violating the neutrality law and was acquitted by a jury that took eight minutes to reach its verdict.

This Sonoran exercise was merely a warm-up for the real game. American attention in the early 1850s focused on the Central American isthmus as a land bridge between the Atlantic and Pacific oceans. A canal through these jungles would shorten the passage between California and the rest of the United States by weeks. Nicaragua seemed to offer the best route for such a canal, but the difficulty and cost of construction would be great. Meanwhile the New York transportation tycoon Cornelius Vanderbilt established the Accessory Transit Company to carry passengers and freight between New York and San Francisco via Nicaragua. Attracted by the tropical climate with its potential for the production of fruit, cotton, sugar, and coffee, other American investors began casting covetous eyes on the region. But the political climate discouraged investment; Nicaragua seemed in a constant state of revolution, having suffered through fifteen presidents in the six years before 1855. The temptation for filibustering there was almost irresistible; William Walker proved unable to resist it.

In 1854 Walker signed a contract with the rebels in Nicaragua's current civil war and in May 1855 sailed from San Francisco with the first contingent of fifty-seven men to support this cause. Because Britain was backing the other side and American-British tensions had escalated in recent years, U. S. officials looked the other way when Walker departed. With financial support from Vanderbilt's transit company, Walker's filibusters and their rebel allies defeated the "Legitimists" and gained control of the government. Walker appointed himself commander in chief of the Nicaraguan army as Americans continued to pour into the country—two thousand by the spring of 1856. President Pierce granted diplomatic recognition to Walker's government in May.

Although Walker himself and half of his filibusters were southerners, the enterprise thus far did not have a particularly pro-southern flavor. By mid-1856, however, that was changing. While much of the northern press condemned Walker as a pirate, southern newspapers praised him as engaged in a "noble cause. . . . It is our cause at bottom." In 1856 the Democratic national convention adopted a plank written by none other than Pierre Soulé endorsing U. S. "ascendancy in the Gulf of Mexico."[77] Proponents of slavery expansion recognized the opportuni-

77. New Orleans Daily Delta, April 18, 1856, quoted in Franklin, Militant South, 120; Schlesinger, ed., History of American Presidential Elections, II, 1039.

ties there for plantation agriculture. Indeed, Central America offered even more intriguing possibilities than Cuba, for its sparse mixed-blood population and weak, unstable governments seemed to make it an easy prey.[78] Of course the Central American republics had abolished slavery a generation earlier. But this was all the better, for it would allow southerners to establish slave plantations without competition from local planters. "A barbarous people can never become civilized without the salutary apprenticeship which slavery secured," declared a New Orleans newspaper that urged southern emigration to Walker's Nicaragua. "It is the duty and decreed prerogative of the wise to guide and govern the ignorant . . . through slavery, and the sooner civilized men learn their duty and their right the sooner will the real progress of civilization be rescued."[79]

During 1856 hundreds of would-be planters took up land grants in Nicaragua. In August, Pierre Soulé himself arrived in Walker's capital and negotiated a loan for him from New Orleans bankers. The "grey-eyed man of destiny," as the press now described Walker, needed this kind of help. His revolution was in trouble. The other Central American countries had formed an alliance to overthrow him. They were backed by Cornelius Vanderbilt, whom Walker had angered by siding with an anti-Vanderbilt faction in the Accessory Transit Company. The president of Nicaragua defected to the enemy, whereupon Walker installed himself as president in July 1856. The Pierce administration withdrew its diplomatic recognition. Realizing that southern backing now represented his only hope, Walker decided "to bind the Southern States to Nicaragua as if she were one of themselves," as he later put it. On September 22, 1856, he revoked Nicaragua's 1824 emancipation edict and legalized slavery again.[80]

This bold gamble succeeded in winning southern support. "No movement on the earth" was as important to the South as Walker's, proclaimed one newspaper. "In the name of the white race," said another, he "now offers Nicaragua to you and your slaves, at a time when you have not a friend on the face of the earth." The commercial convention meeting at Savannah expressed enthusiasm for the "efforts being made to introduce civilization in the States of Central America, and to

78. In the 1850s the population of Nicaragua, for example, was about one-twelfth of its present total.
79. *Louisiana Courier*, Nov. 12, 1857, quoted in Chester Stanley Urban, "The Ideology of Southern Imperialism," *Louisiana Historical Quarterly*, 39 (1956), 66.
80. William Walker, *The War in Nicaragua* (New York, 1860), 263.

develop these rich and productive regions by the introduction of slave labor."[81] Several shiploads of new recruits arrived from New Orleans and San Francisco during the winter of 1856–57 to fight for Walker. But they were not enough. Some of them reached Nicaragua just in time to succumb to a cholera epidemic that ravaged Walker's army even as the Central American alliance overwhelmed it in battle. On May 1, 1857, Walker surrendered his survivors to a United States naval commander whose ship carried them back to New Orleans. They left behind a thousand Americans dead of disease and combat.

This did not end the matter. Indeed, in the South it had barely begun. A wild celebration greeted Walker's return. Citizens opened their hearts and purses to the "grey-eyed man of destiny" as he traveled through the South raising men and money for another try. In November 1857 Walker sailed from Mobile on his second expedition to Nicaragua. But the navy caught up with him and carried his army back to the states. Southern newspapers erupted in denunciation of this naval "usurpation of power." Alexander Stephens urged the court-martial of the commodore who had detained Walker. Two dozen southern senators and congressmen echoed this sentiment in an extraordinary congressional debate. "A heavier blow was never struck at southern rights," said a Tennessee representative, "than when Commodore Paulding perpetrated upon our people his high-handed outrage." The government's action proved that President Buchanan was just like other Yankees in wanting to "crush out the expansion of slavery to the South." In May 1858 a hung jury in New Orleans voted 10-2 to acquit Walker of violating the neutrality law.[82]

This outpouring of southern sympathy swept Walker into a campaign to organize yet another invasion of Nicaragua. A second tour of the lower South evoked an almost pathological frenzy among people who believed themselves locked in mortal combat with Yankee oppressors. At one town Walker appealed "to the mothers of Mississippi to bid their sons buckle on the armor of war, and battle for the institutions, for the honor of the Sunny South."[83] The sons of Mississippi responded. Walk-

81. May, *Southern Dream of a Caribbean Empire*, 108–9; Russel, *Economic Aspects of Southern Sectionalism*, 140.
82. *CG*, 35 Cong., 1 Sess., 562; May, *Southern Dream of a Caribbean Empire*, 113–26.
83. *Aberdeen [Miss.] Prairie News*, July 1, 1858, quoted in Percy Lee Rainwater, "Economic Benefits of Secession: Opinions in Mississippi in the 1850's," *JSH*, 1 (1935), 462.

er's third expedition sailed from Mobile in December 1858, but their ship hit a reef and sank sixty miles from the Central American coast. Despite the humiliation of returning to Mobile in the British ship that rescued them, the filibusters received their customary tumultuous welcome.

But Walker's act was growing stale. When he set out again to recruit support for a fourth try, the crowds were smaller. Walker wrote a book about his Nicaraguan experiences, appealing to "the hearts of Southern youth" to "answer the call of honor."[84] A few southern youths answered the call. Ninety-seven filibusters traveled in small groups to a rendezvous in Honduras where they hoped to find backing for a new invasion of Nicaragua. Instead they found hostility and defeat. Walker surrendered to a British navy captain, expecting as usual to be returned to the United States. Instead the captain turned him over to local authorities. On September 12, 1860, the grey-eyed man met his destiny before a Honduran firing squad.

His legacy lived on, not only in Central American feelings about gringoes but also in North American feelings about the sectional conflict that was tearing apart the United States. When Senator John J. Crittenden proposed to resolve the secession crisis in 1861 by reinstating the 36° 30' line between slavery and freedom in all territories "now held, or hereafter acquired," Abraham Lincoln and his party rejected the proposal on the ground that it "would amount to a perpetual covenant of war against every people, tribe, and State owning a foot of land between here and Tierra del Fuego."[85]

This was only a slight exaggeration. Having begun the decade of the 1850s with a drive to defend southern rights by economic diversification, many southerners ended it with a different vision of southern enterprise—the expansion of slavery into a tropical empire controlled by the South. This was the theme of a book published in 1859 by Edward A. Pollard, a Virginia journalist and future participant-historian of the Confederacy. "The path of our destiny on this continent," wrote Pollard,

> lies in . . . tropical America [where] we may see an empire as powerful and gorgeous as ever was pictured in our dreams of history . . .
> an empire . . . representing the noble peculiarities of Southern civi-

84. Walker, *The War in Nicaragua*, 278.
85. CG, 36 Cong., 2 Sess., 651.

lization . . . having control of the two dominant staples of the world's commerce—cotton and sugar. . . . The destiny of Southern civilization is to be consummated in a glory brighter even than that of old.[86]

Another Virginian, George Bickley, put this fantasy on an organized basis with his Knights of the Golden Circle, founded in the mid-1850s to promote a "golden circle" of slave states from the American South through Mexico and Central America to the rim of South America, curving northward again through the West Indies to close the circle at Key West. "With this addition to either our *system,* the *Union,* or to a Southern Confederacy," wrote Bickley in 1860, "we shall have in our hands the Cotton, Tobacco, Sugar, Coffee, Rice, Corn, and Tea lands of the continent, and the world's great storehouse of mineral wealth."[87]

Thus had Thomas Jefferson's Empire for Liberty become transmuted by 1860 into Mississippi Congressman L. Q. C. Lamar's desire to "plant American liberty with southern institutions upon every inch of American soil."[88] But the furor over this effort to plant the southern version of liberty as slavery along the Gulf of Mexico took a back seat to the controversy sparked by the effort to plant it in Kansas.

86. Pollard, *Black Diamonds* (New York, 1859), 52–53, 108–9.
87. May, *Southern Dream of a Caribbean Empire,* 150.
88. CG, 35 Cong., 1 Sess., 279.

4

Slavery, Rum, and Romanism

I

The year 1852 turned out to be the last one in which the Whig party contested a presidential election. Millard Fillmore's efforts to enforce the fugitive slave law won him the support of southern Whigs for re-nomination. But the president had alienated antislavery Whigs, espe-cially the Seward faction in Fillmore's own state of New York. Seward favored the nomination of Winfield Scott, a Virginian (but not a slave-holder). The Whig convention presented the curious spectacle of most southern delegates favoring a northern candidate, and vice versa, while many anti-war Whigs of four years earlier once again backed a general who had led American troops to victory in the war these Whigs had opposed. Maneuvers at the convention heightened the impression of Whig stultification. Southerners obtained enough support from north-ern moderates to adopt a plan pledging to "acquiesce in" the Compro-mise of 1850 "as a settlement in principle and substance" of the "dan-gerous and exciting" slavery question. All votes against this plank came from those northern Whigs who provided half of Scott's delegate sup-port. Balloting for a presidential nominee ground through 52 roll calls as Yankee delegates furnished 95 percent of Scott's vote and southern delegates cast 85 percent of Fillmore's. On the fifty-third ballot a dozen southern moderates switched to Scott and put him over the top.[1]

1. Potter, *Impending Crisis*, 232–33; Roy and Jeannette Nichols, "Election of 1852,"

This denouement dismayed many southern Whigs. Suspecting that Seward had engineered the outcome, they feared a reprise of the Taylor debacle. When Scott's acceptance letter included only a lukewarm endorsement of the platform, they were sure of it. "If we support him," wrote a North Carolinian, "we must expect to constitute a tail to the army of abolitionists in front." Nine southern Whig congressmen led by Alexander Stephens and Robert Toombs announced their refusal to back Scott. As the campaign proceeded, defections of southern Whigs became a stampede. On election day Scott won 35 percent of the popular vote in the lower South (compared with Taylor's 50 percent four years earlier) and carried only Kentucky and Tennessee among the fifteen slave states. In the eleven future Confederate states the Whigs in 1852–53 elected no governors and merely fourteen of sixty-five congressmen while maintaining control of only the Tennessee legislature. Alexander Stephens's pronouncement that "the Whig party is dead" seemed no exaggeration in the lower South.[2]

The transmigration of southern Whigs into Democrats was made easier by the increasing friendliness of northern Democrats toward the South. Even the return of Barnburners to the Democratic fold seemed not to hinder this process. The Democratic national convention adopted no fewer than three planks pledging fidelity to the Compromise of 1850, and affirmed that "Congress has no power . . . to interfere with questions of slavery"—except of course to help masters recover fugitives.[3] Because of the party rule requiring a two-thirds majority to nominate a president, southern delegates were able to block the candidacies of Lewis Cass and Stephen Douglas, whose notions about popular sovereignty made them suspect. But the southerners could not nominate their own candidate, the pliable James Buchanan. Through forty-eight ballots the party remained apparently as deadlocked as the Whigs. On the forty-ninth they nominated dark horse Franklin Pierce of New Hampshire, a former senator and a Mexican War veteran, who was acceptable to all factions and safe on slavery despite his Yankee background. Albert G. Brown of Mississippi considered Pierce "as reliable as Calhoun himself," while a South Carolina fire-eater mused that "a nomination so

in Arthur M. Schlesinger, Jr., ed., *History of American Presidential Elections 1789–1968*, 4 vols. (New York, 1971), II, 943–44.

2. William J. Cooper, Jr., *The South and the Politics of Slavery 1828–1856* (Baton Rouge, 1978), 330, 343.

3. Schlesinger, ed., *History of Presidential Elections*, II, 952.

favorable to the South had not been anticipated." Going into the cam-paign more united than in any election since Jackson's day, the Dem-ocrats won by a landslide.[4]

Pierce fulfilled southern expectations. Although his efforts to acquire Cuba failed, the administration enforced the fugitive slave law vigor-ously and opened the remainder of the Louisiana Purchase north of 36° 30' to slavery. But it did so at great cost to domestic tranquility, to the structure of the Democratic party, and ultimately to the Union itself.

In March 1854, Anthony Burns escaped from slavery in Virginia and stowed away on a ship to Boston. There he found a job in a clothing store. But the literate Burns made the mistake of writing to his brother, still a slave. Intercepting the letter, their owner learned of Burns's whereabouts and headed north to reclaim his property. A deputy mar-shal arrested Burns on May 24 and placed him under heavy guard in the federal courthouse. The vigilance committee went into action, sponsoring a Faneuil Hall meeting which resolved that "resistance to tyrants is obedience to God." Suiting action to words, a biracial group of abolitionists led by thirty-year-old Unitarian clergyman Thomas Wentworth Higginson tried to rescue Burns in an attack on the court-house with axes, revolvers, and a battering ram. Higginson and a black man broke through the door but were clubbed back outside by deputy marshals as a shot rang out and one of the deputies fell dead.

Appealed to for help, President Pierce ordered several companies of marines, cavalry, and artillery to Boston, where they joined state militia and local police to keep the peace while a federal commissioner deter-mined Burns's fate. "Incur any expense," Pierce wired the district attor-ney in Boston, "to insure the execution of the law." The president also ordered a revenue cutter to stand by to carry Burns back to Virginia. Knowing that it was futile, vigilance committee lawyers nevertheless tried every legal maneuver they could think of while Bostonians raised money to purchase Burns's freedom. His owner seemed willing to sell, but the U. S. attorney refused to sanction this solution. To vindicate the law

4. Quotations from Cooper, *The South and the Politics of Slavery*, 334. In addition to carrying all but two slave states, Pierce won every northern state except Vermont and Massachusetts, though he would have lost also Ohio and Connecticut had not the Free Soil party attracted antislavery Whigs away from Scott. With the return of Barnburners to the Democratic party, the Free Soil share of the northern popular vote dropped to 6 percent. Pierce received 51 percent of the national popular vote to Scott's 44 percent. Democrats won control of Congress by more than a two-thirds majority in the House and a nearly two-thirds margin in the Senate.

he pushed the case to a successful conclusion. On June 2 the troops marched Burns to the wharf through streets lined with sullen Yankees standing in front of buildings draped in black with the American flag hanging upside down and church bells tolling a dirge to liberty in the cradle of the American Revolution. At the cost of $100,000 (equal to perhaps two million 1987 dollars) the Pierce administration had upheld the majesty of the law.[5]

The fallout from this affair radiated widely. "When it was all over, and I was left alone in my office," wrote a heretofore conservative Whig, "I put my face in my hands and wept. I could do nothing less." The textile magnate Amos A. Lawrence said that "we went to bed one night old fashioned, conservative, Compromise Union Whigs & waked up stark mad Abolitionists."[6] A federal grand jury indicted Higginson, Theodore Parker, Wendell Phillips, and four other white and black abolitionists for riot and inciting to riot. After a district judge quashed the first indictment on a technicality, the government dropped the charges because it recognized the impossibility of winning a jury trial in Massachusetts. William Lloyd Garrison publicly burned a copy of the Constitution on the Fourth of July while thousands breathed Amen to his denunciation of this document as a covenant with death. The New England states passed new personal liberty laws that collided in various ways with federal law.[7]

Ohio, Michigan, and Wisconsin also passed stronger personal liberty laws after fugitive slave controversies in those states. The most poignant of these cases involved Margaret Garner, who in January 1856 escaped with her husband and four children from Kentucky to Ohio. When a posse was about to capture them, Margaret seized a kitchen knife, slit

5. Jane H. Pease and William H. Pease, *The Fugitive Slave Law and Anthony Burns* (Philadelphia, 1975); Stanley W. Campbell, *The Slave Catchers: Enforcement of the Fugitive Slave Law 1850–1860* (New York, 1970), 124–32; Philip S. Foner, *History of Black Americans from the Compromise of 1850 to the End of the Civil War* (Westport, Conn., 1983), 69–77; Tilden G. Edelstein, *Strange Enthusiasm: A Life of Thomas Wentworth Higginson* (New Haven, 1968), 155–61. A year later a committee in Boston did finally purchase Burns's freedom. He attended Oberlin College for a time before emigrating to Canada, where he died in 1862.
6. George S. Hilliard to Francis Lieber, June 1, 1854, Francis Lieber Papers, Henry E. Huntington Library; Amos Lawrence to Giles Richards, June 1, 1854, quoted in Pease and Pease, *The Fugitive Slave Law and Anthony Burns*, 43.
7. Thomas D. Morris, *Free Men All: The Personal Liberty Laws of the North 1780–1861* (Baltimore, 1974), 219–20; Campbell, *The Slave Catchers*, 202–6.

the throat of one daughter, and tried to kill her other children rather than see them returned to slavery. The state of Ohio requested jurisdiction over Garner to try her for manslaughter, but a federal judge overruled state officials and ordered the Garners returned to their owner. That worthy gentleman promptly sold them down the river to New Orleans. On the way there one of Margaret's other children achieved the emancipation she had sought for him, by drowning after a steamboat collision.[8]

Even more important than the fugitive slave issue in arousing northern militancy was the Kansas-Nebraska Act passed by Congress in May 1854. Coming at the same time as the Anthony Burns case, this law may have been the most important single event pushing the nation toward civil war. Kansas-Nebraska finished off the Whig party and gave birth to a new, entirely northern Republican party.

The genesis of Kansas-Nebraska lay in the same impulse that had propelled Americans westward from the beginning. Restless settlers and land speculators had begun to cast covetous eyes on the fertile soil of the Kansas and Platte river valleys. By 1852, also, the idea of a transcontinental railroad through the region had become the dream of entrepreneurs, politicians, and frontiersmen alike. But until the government extracted land cessions from the Indians and organized the area as a territory, the region could not be surveyed and farmers could not settle there. Everyone talked about a railroad to California, growled a Missouri congressman, but "in the name of God, how is the railroad to be made if you will never let people live on the lands through which the road passes?"[9] Southerners were in no hurry to organize this territory, for it lay north of 36° 30' where slavery was excluded by the Missouri Compromise. Besides, they preferred a southern route for a Pacific railroad through the already organized territory of New Mexico, with New Orleans as its eastern terminus.

It so happened that two Illinois Democrats—William A. Richardson and Stephen A. Douglas—were chairmen respectively of the House and Senate committees on territories. Both were champions of Young America's manifest destiny to expand ever westward. A large investor in Chicago real estate, Douglas had enhanced the value of his property by securing a federal land grant for a railroad from that city to Mobile. Perhaps hoping to repeat the scenario from Chicago to San Francisco,

8. Foner, *History of Black Americans*, 87–91; Campbell, *The Slave Catchers*, 144–47.
9. *CG*, 32 Cong., 2 Sess., 560.

Douglas and Richardson in 1853 reported bills to organize Nebraska territory embracing most of the remaining portion of the Louisiana Purchase north of 36° 30'. The House quickly passed the measure, but opposition from southern senators tabled it in March 1853. To get his bill enacted, Douglas needed the support of at least a half-dozen southern senators. And they let him know exactly what it was going to cost.[10]

The most powerful Senate bloc was a quartet of southerners who boarded together at a house on F Street. This "F Street Mess," as they called themselves, consisted of James M. Mason and Robert M. T. Hunter of Virginia, Andrew P. Butler of South Carolina, and David R. Atchison of Missouri—chairmen respectively of the foreign relations, finance, and judiciary committees, and president pro tem. In this last capacity Atchison was next in line for the presidency because Pierce's vice president had died during his second month in office. Intemperate, profane, and bellicose, Atchison was the most outspoken defender of southern rights in the Senate. His slaveholding constituents opposed the organization of Nebraska territory, for Missouri would thenceforth "be surrounded by free territory. . . . With the emissaries of abolitionists around us . . . this species of property would become insecure." Atchison announced that he would see Nebraska "sink in hell" before voting to organize it as free soil. We must "extend the institutions of Missouri over the territory," pledged a meeting addressed by Atchison, "at whatever sacrifice of blood or treasure." From the F Street Mess the word came to Douglas: if he wanted Nebraska he must repeal the ban on bondage there and place "slaveholder and non-slaveholder upon terms of equality."[11]

Douglas knew that such action would "raise a hell of a storm" in the North. So he first tried to outflank the Missouri Compromise instead of

10. The literature on the origins of the Kansas-Nebraska Act is large and contentious. For a useful summary of much of it, see Roy F. Nichols, "The Kansas-Nebraska Act: A Century of Historiography," MVHR, 43 (1956), 187–212. The most lucid account of the origins of this legislation is Potter, Impending Crisis, 145–76. My account has also drawn upon Nevins, Ordeal, II, 88–121; Harry V. Jaffa, Crisis of the House Divided: An Interpretation of the Lincoln-Douglas Debates (Garden City, N.Y., 1959), 104–80; Robert W. Johannsen, Stephen A. Douglas (New York, 1973), 374–434; Roy F. Nichols, Franklin Pierce (Philadelphia, 1958), 319–24; James A. Rawley, Race and Politics: "Bleeding Kansas" and the Coming of the Civil War (Philadelphia, 1969), 21–57; and Don E. Fehrenbacher, The Dred Scott Case: Its Significance in American Law and Politics (New York, 1978), 178–87.
11. Quotations from Nevins, Ordeal, II, 92–93; and Rawley, Race and Politics, 28.

repealing it. His initial version of the Nebraska bill in January 1854 reproduced the language of the Utah and New Mexico legislation four years earlier, providing that Nebraska, when admitted as a state or states, would come in "with or without slavery, as their constitutions may prescribe."[12] But for southerners this did not meet the case. If the Missouri Compromise prevailed during the territorial stage, slavery could never gain a foothold. Atchison turned the screws, whereupon Douglas discovered that a "clerical error" had omitted a section of the bill stating that "all questions pertaining to slavery in the Territories . . . are to be left to the people residing therein."[13] But this was not yet good enough, for the Missouri Compromise still lived despite the implicit circumvention of it by the clerical-error clause. So Douglas took the fateful step. He added an explicit repeal of the ban on slavery north of 36° 30'. More than that, his new version of the bill organized two territories—Nebraska west of Iowa, and Kansas west of Missouri. This looked like a device to reserve Kansas for slavery and Nebraska for freedom, especially since the climate and soil of eastern Kansas were similar to those of the Missouri River basin in Missouri, where most of the slaves in that state were concentrated.

This did indeed provoke a hell of a storm that made the debates of 1850 look like a gentle shower. The first clouds blew up from the Pierce administration itself. The president feared the political consequences of repudiating a covenant sanctified by thirty-four years of national life. Except for Secretary of War Jefferson Davis and Secretary of the Navy James Dobbin of North Carolina, the cabinet opposed the repeal clause. The administration drafted a vague alternative that would have referred the whole question of slavery in the territories to the Supreme Court. But this did not satisfy the F Street Mess. With Davis and Douglas they pried their way into the White House on Sunday, January 22 (Pierce disliked doing business on the Sabbath), and confronted the president with an ultimatum: endorse repeal or lose the South. Pierce surrendered. Moreover, he agreed to make the revised Kansas-Nebraska bill "a test of party orthodoxy."[14]

Northern Democrats and Whigs were stunned by Douglas's bill. But Free Soilers were not surprised. It was just what they had expected from the "Slave Power." And they were ready with a response to rally the

12. CG, 33 Cong., 2 Sess., 115.
13. Potter, *Impending Crisis*, 159.
14. Rawley, *Race and Politics*, 35.

North against this "gross violation of a sacred pledge," this "atrocious plot" to convert free territory into a "dreary region of depotism, inhabited by masters and slaves." These phrases came from the collaborative pens of Salmon P. Chase, Charles Sumner, Joshua Giddings, and three other free-soil congressmen who published an "Appeal of the Independent Democrats" in the *National Era*—the same paper that had serialized *Uncle Tom's Cabin*.[15]

This Appeal set the keynote for an outpouring of angry speeches, sermons, and editorials in Congress and across the North. The moderate *New York Times* predicted that the northern backlash could "create a deep-seated, intense, and ineradicable hatred of the institution [slavery] which will crush its political power, at all hazards, and at any cost." Hundreds of "anti-Nebraska" meetings sent resolutions and petitions to Congress. "This crime shall not be consummated," declared a typical resolution. "Despite corruption, bribery, and treachery, Nebraska, the heart of our continent, shall forever continue free." Of ten northern state legislatures in session during the first months of 1854, the five controlled by Whigs denounced the bill and four of the five controlled by Democrats refused to endorse it. Only the Illinois legislature, under pressure from Douglas, approved the measure. In Congress northern Whigs unanimously opposed it. The newly elected Whig senator from Maine, William Pitt Fessenden, considered Douglas's bill "a terrible outrage. . . . The more I look at it the more enraged I become. It needs but little to make me an out & out abolitionist."[16]

Douglas insisted that repeal of the ban on slavery north of 36° 30' was nothing new. The Compromise of 1850, he declared, had superseded that restriction by allowing popular sovereignty in former Mexican territory north as well as south of that line. Northern senators exposed the speciousness of this argument. The Compromise of 1850 applied only to the Mexican cession, not to the Louisiana Purchase, and no one at the time—Douglas included—had thought otherwise. The supersedence theory emerged as a rationalization for a policy forced on Douglas

15. *National Era*, Jan. 24, 1854. Why these six antislavery leaders designated themselves Independent Democrats is not clear. Nearly all of them had been Whigs before becoming Free Soilers. The name may have been a legacy from the 1852 election, when the Free Soilers had called their party the Free Democracy.
16. *New York Times*, Jan. 24, 1854; resolution quoted in Nevins, *Ordeal*, II, 127; William P. Fessenden to Ellen Fessenden, Feb. 26, 1854, quoted in Richard H. Sewell, *Ballots for Freedom: Antislavery Politics in the United States 1837–1860* (New York, 1976), 259.

by southern pressure. Nevertheless, Democratic party discipline and Douglas's parliamentary legerdemain pushed the bill through the Senate in March by a vote of 41 to 17 with only five of the twenty free-state Democrats joining northern Whigs and Free Soilers in opposition.[17]

Northern Democrats in the House who had to face elections in the fall proved more resistant to administration pressure. Nevertheless Alexander Stephens, floor manager of the bill, applied "whip and spur" and drove it to passage on May 22 by a vote of 115 to 104. "I feel as if the *Mission* of my life was performed," wrote an exultant Stephens.[18] Perhaps so, but only by giving the *coup de grâce* to the intersectional two-party system. Every northern Whig in the two houses voted against the bill, while 25 of 34 southern Whigs voted or were paired for it. Of 75 southern Democrats, 72 voted or were paired for the measure while 49 of 108 northern Democrats voted or were paired against it. Many of the latter knew that an affirmative vote meant defeat for reelection, while a negative vote meant an end to influence in the party establishment. Only seven of the northern representatives who voted Aye won reelection, while several who voted Nay left the Democratic party never to return. For northern and southern Whigs the bitter divisions caused a final parting of the ways. "The Whig party has been killed off effectually by that miserable Nebraska business," wrote Truman Smith of Connecticut, who resigned in disgust from the Senate. "We Whigs of the North are unalterably determined never to have even the slightest political correspondence or connexion" with southern Whigs.[19] That was fine with southerners. "We will have no party association . . . with Northern Whigs," they declared, "until they shall give unmistakable evidence of repentance [of] the impulses of a wild fanaticism."[20]

17. These figures include senators who were paired or declared for and against the bill. The actual roll-call vote was 37 to 14. In addition to the northern senators who voted against the bill, two Whigs and one Democrat from slave states also voted No, mainly because they feared a northern backlash that might harm the South. See Robert P. Russel, "The Issues in the Congressional Struggle Over the Kansas-Nebraska Bill, 1854," *JSH* 29 (1963), 208–9.

18. Nevins, *Ordeal*, II, 156; Rawley, *Race and Politics*, 55. The vote totals here include those paired or declared for and against the bill. The actual vote was 113 to 100.

19. Quoted in William E. Gienapp, "The Origins of the Republican Party, 1852–1856," Ph.D. dissertation, University of California at Berkeley, 1980, p. 323. The published version of this study, with the same title (New York, 1987), appeared too late to be cited here.

20. This is a composite quotation from the *Richmond Whig*, *Florida Sentinel*, and

Adding insult to injury, southern senators killed a bill passed by a predominantly northern vote in the House to provide settlers with a 160-acre homestead grant on public lands. Such a law, explained one southerner, "would prove a most efficient ally for Abolition by encouraging and stimulating the settlement of free farms with Yankees and foreigners pre-committed to resist the participancy of slaveholders in the public domain."[21]

The question was, who would pick up the pieces of the smashed political parties? In the lower South, Democrats would soon sweep most of the remaining shards of Whiggery into their own dustbin. In the upper South, Whigs clung to a precarious existence—under different names—for a few more years. In the North, matters were more complicated. Some antislavery Whigs like William H. Seward hoped to rejuvenate the party for the 1854 state and congressional elections by absorbing Free Soilers and anti-Nebraska Democrats. But the latter groups declined to be absorbed. Instead, along with many Whigs they proposed to abandon "mere party names, and rally as one man for the reestablishment of liberty and the overthrow of the Slave Power."[22] New antislavery coalitions thus formed throughout the North to contest the fall elections. These coalitions called themselves by various names—Anti-Nebraska, Fusion, People's, Independent—but the one name that emerged most prominently was Republican. An anti-Nebraska rally at a church in Ripon, Wisconsin, seems to have been the first to adopt this label. A meeting of thirty congressmen in Washington endorsed the name on May 9. The new party in Michigan officially designated itself Republican in July. Conventions in numerous congressional districts, especially in the Old Northwest, chose this name that resonated with the struggle of 1776. "In view of the necessity of battling for the first principles of republican government," resolved the Michigan convention, "and against the schemes of aristocracy the most revolting and oppressive with which the earth was ever cursed, or man debased, we will co-operate and be known as Republicans."[23]

The campaigns in the North were intense and bitter, nowhere more

---

Southern Recorder, all quoted in Cooper, The South and the Politics of Slavery, 358.

21. Jabez L. M. Curry to Clement C. Clay, July ?, 1854, quoted in Nevins, Ordeal, II, 335.

22. National Era, May 22, 1854.

23. Quoted in Michael F. Holt, The Political Crisis of the 1850s (New York, 1978), 154.

than in Douglas's own state of Illinois. Douglas opened the canvass with a speech on September 1 in Chicago, where a hostile crowd shouted him down for two hours until he strode angrily off the platform and headed for friendlier districts downstate. Meanwhile, Abraham Lincoln was "aroused . . . as he had never been before" by the Kansas-Nebraska Act.[24] Still calling himself a Whig, Lincoln took the stump in behalf of anti-Nebraska candidates for the legislature, hoping that victory would forge a legislative majority to elect him to the U. S. Senate. Lincoln and Douglas confronted each other on the same platform in speeches at Springfield and Peoria during October. In these addresses Lincoln set forth the themes that he would carry into the presidency six years later.

The founding fathers, said Lincoln, had opposed slavery. They adopted a Declaration of Independence that pronounced all men created equal. They enacted the Northwest Ordinance of 1787 banning slavery from the vast Northwest Territory. To be sure, many of the founders owned slaves. But they asserted their hostility to slavery in principle while tolerating it temporarily (as they hoped) in practice. That was why they did not mention the words "slave" or "slavery" in the Constitution, but referred only to "persons held to service." "Thus, the thing is hid away, in the constitution," said Lincoln, "just as an afflicted man hides away a wen or a cancer, which he dares not cut out at once, lest he bleed to death; with the promise, nevertheless, that the cutting may begin at the end of a given time." The first step was to prevent the spread of this cancer, which the fathers took with the Northwest Ordinance, the prohibition of the African slave trade in 1807, and the Missouri Compromise restriction of 1820. The second was to begin a process of gradual emancipation, which the generation of the fathers had accomplished in the states north of Maryland.

Lincoln denied "that there CAN be MORAL RIGHT in the enslaving of one man by another." But he did not want to pass judgment on southern people. When they "tell us they are no more responsible for the origin of slavery, than we, I acknowledge the fact. . . . They are just what we would be in their situation. . . . When it is said that the institution exists, and that it is very difficult to get rid of it," Lincoln acknowledged that fact also. "I surely will not blame them for not doing what I should not know how to do myself. If all earthly power were given me, I should not know what to do, as to the existing institution. My first impulse would be to free all the slaves, and send them to Lib-

24. *CWL*, IV, 67.

eria." But a moment's reflection convinced him of the impossibility of that. "What then, free them and keep them among us as underlings? Is it quite certain that this betters their condition? . . . What next? Free them, and make them politically and socially, our equals?" Even if Lincoln's own feelings would accept this, "we well know that those of the great mass of white people will not. . . . A universal feeling, whether well or ill-founded, cannot be safely disregarded."

In any case, the Constitution protected slavery where it already existed. But that "furnishes no more excuse for permitting slavery to go into our own free territory, than it would for reviving the African slave trade." The great "moral wrong and injustice" of the Kansas-Nebraska Act was that it opened territory previously closed to slavery, thus putting the institution "on the high road to extension and perpetuity" instead of restricting it in order gradually to end it. Popular sovereignty was false in principle and pernicious in practice, said Lincoln. Its assumption that the question of slavery in a territory concerned only the people who lived there was wrong. It affected the future of the whole nation. "Is not Nebraska, while a territory, a part of us? Do we not own the country? And if we surrender the control of it, do we not surrender the right of self-government?" I "can not but hate" this *declared* indifference, but as I must think, covert *real* zeal for the spread of . . . the monstrous injustice of slavery." Douglas's assertion that natural conditions would prevent bondage from taking root in Kansas was a "LULLABY argument." Temperature, rainfall, and soil in eastern Kansas were the same as in Missouri and Kentucky. Five slave states already existed north of the 36° 30' line. "Climate will not . . . keep slavery out of these territories . . . nothing in *nature* will." Lincoln knew that Missourians had already taken slaves to Kansas. The only way to stop them was for Congress to vote slavery out.

But such action, Douglas had protested, would be contrary to the settlers' "sacred right of self-government." Nonsense, replied Lincoln. *Slavery* was contrary to that right. "When the white man governs himself that is self-government; but when he governs himself, and also governs another man . . . that is despotism. . . . The negro is a *man*. . . . There can be no moral right in connection with one man's making a slave of another," "Let no one be deceived," concluded Lincoln:

> The spirit of seventy-six and the spirit of Nebraska, are utter antagonisms. . . . Little by little . . . we have been giving up the old for the new faith. Near eighty years ago we began by declaring that all men are created equal; but now from that beginning we have run

down to the other declaration, that for some men to enslave others is a "sacred right of self-government." These principles cannot stand together. . . . Our republican robe is soiled, and trailed in the dust. Let us repurify it. . . . Let us re-adopt the Declaration of Independence, and with it, the practices, and policy, which harmonize with it. . . . If we do this, we shall not only have saved the Union; but we shall have so saved it, as to make, and to keep it, forever worthy of the saving.[25]

This eloquent speech expressed the platform of the new Republican party. Lincoln did not formally become a Republican for another year or more, after the Whig party had crumbled beyond salvation. Nor did he go as far as many other Republicans who called for abolition of slavery in the District of Columbia and repeal of the fugitive slave law. But Lincoln's affirmation of moral opposition to slavery, his belief that the national government had a right and duty to exclude it from the territories, and his conviction that this "cancer" must eventually be cut out, became hallmarks of the Republican party. The historical basis of Lincoln's argument, of course, had some holes in it, and Douglas lost no time in driving his own oratory through the largest of them. The same supposedly antislavery fathers who had excluded slavery from the Northwest Territory had allowed it to expand into southwest territories, laying the groundwork for seven new slave states and the great cotton kingdom of the lower South. But free soilers brushed this problem aside; if the republicans of the Jeffersonian era had fallen short of the mark in some things, the new Republicans of the 1850s would not repeat the same mistake. Slavery must not expand; the party that had passed the Kansas-Nebraska Act must be repudiated.

A majority of northern voters in 1854 seemed to agree. The elections were a stunning rebuke to the Democrats. After carrying all but two northern states in 1852, they lost control of all but two free-state legislatures in 1854. The number of northern Democrats in the House would drop from 93 to 23, who would be far outnumbered by their 58 southern Democratic colleagues. Perhaps one-quarter of northern Democratic voters deserted their party in this election.[26]

Having elected 150 congressmen under various labels, opponents of

25. *Ibid.*, II, 247–83. These quotations are from Lincoln's famous speech in Peoria on Oct. 16, 1854.
26. These election results are calculated from the *Whig Almanac* (published by the *New York Tribune*) for 1854 and 1855.

the Democrats would control the next House—if they could come to-gether under the same political umbrella. But that was a big if. The difficulty of doing so was illustrated by Lincoln's fortunes in Illinois, where the anti-Nebraska coalition had a substantial majority on a joint ballot of the legislature. Lincoln's fellow Whigs constituted about three-quarters of this coalition. But a half-dozen anti-Nebraska Democrats refused to vote for a Whig for U. S. senator, causing Lincoln to fall short of a majority in ballot after ballot. Finally, to prevent the election of a Douglas Democrat, Lincoln threw his support to an anti-Nebraska Democrat, Lyman Trumbull, who thereby won on the tenth ballot.[27]

The muddy waters in Illinois were quite translucent compared with the murky depths of northern politics elsewhere. Up from the great deep came a tidal wave of nativism that seemed to swamp even the anti-Nebraska movement in some areas, especially in states east of Ohio. "Nearly everybody appears to have gone altogether deranged on Nativism," yelped a Pennsylvania Democrat in 1854. "The 'Know Nothing' fever is epidemic here," wrote a Pennsylvanian from another part of the state. A Connecticut politician lamented that nativists "are making havoc with the Democratic party here," while a Whig leader in upstate New York warned that his district was "very badly infected with Knowno-thingism." Variously described as a "tornado," a "hurricane," a "freak of political insanity," these "Know Nothings" swept the state elections of 1854 in Massachusetts and Delaware, polled an estimated 40 and 25 percent of the vote in Pennsylvania and New York, and made impressive showings in other parts of the Northeast and the border states.[28] Who were these mysterious Know Nothings, where did they come from, and what did they stand for?

II

The nativist parties that had flared up in the early 1840s died back to embers after the elections of 1844. Recovery from the depression mitigated the tensions between native and foreign-born workers which had sparked the riots of that year. Even as the volume of immigration quadrupled following the European potato blight of the mid-forties, the ac-

---

27. Don E. Fehrenbacher, *Prelude to Greatness: Lincoln in the 1850's* (New York, 1962), 37–39. This balloting was not for Douglas's seat in the Senate. Having been reelected in 1852, Douglas would come up again in 1858 when he faced Lincoln in a more famous contest.
28. Holt, *Political Crisis of the 1850s*, 157–58.

celerating American economy seemed able to absorb all who came. The Mexican War and the ensuing controversy over slavery focused political energy on those issues. War against a Catholic nation might have been expected to fan anti-Roman sentiments—except that the Democratic war party was also the party of immigrants, while the Whigs, who had earlier dallied with nativism, opposed the war.

In the 1852 presidential election the Whigs, led by anti-nativist William H. Seward, tried to appeal for the Irish and Catholic vote. General Scott, Whig presidential candidate, was a high-church Episcopalian who had educated his daughters in a convent. As commander of American forces in Mexico he had protected Church property. In 1852 the Whigs planted friendly Irish questioners in audiences addressed by Scott, giving the candidate a chance to declare how much he "loved to hear that rich Irish brogue."[29] But this clumsy effort backfired, for while Irish Americans as usual voted Democratic, many Whigs were offended by the appeal to "paddies" and stayed home on election day. As the slavery issue knocked southern Whigs loose from their party, a renewal of ethnic hostilities did the same in a number of northern states.

Several causes contributed to this revival of nativism. Immigration during the first five years of the 1850s reached a level five times greater than a decade earlier. Most of the new arrivals were poor Catholic peasants or laborers from Ireland and Germany who crowded into the tenements of large cities. Crime and welfare costs soared. Cincinnati's crime rate, for example, tripled between 1846 and 1853 and its murder rate increased sevenfold. Boston's expenditures for poor relief rose threefold during the same period.[30] Native-born Americans attributed these increases to immigrants, especially the Irish, whose arrest rate and share of relief funds were several times their percentage of the population. Natives were not necessarily the most nativist. Earlier Protestant immigrants from England, Scotland, and especially Ulster had brought their anti-Catholic sentiments with them and often formed the vanguard of anti-Irish rioters and voters in the United States. Radicals and agnostics among the Forty-eighters who had fled Germany after suppression of the 1848 revolutions carried to America a bitter enmity toward the Catholic Church which had sided with the forces of counterrevolution.

29. Potter, *Impending Crisis*, 245.
30. Jed Dannenbaum, "Immigrants and Temperance: Ethnocultural Conflict in Cincinnati, 1845–1860," *Ohio History*, 87 (1978), 127–28; Oscar Handlin, *Boston's Immigrants: A Study in Acculturation* (Cambridge, Mass., 1941), 240.

Indeed, the Church entered a period of reaction during the papacy of Pius IX (1846–78). The 1848–49 revolutions and wars of unification in Italy made Pius "a violent enemy of liberalism and social reform." He subsequently proclaimed the doctrine of papal infallibility and issued his Syllabus of Errors condemning socialism, public education, rationalism, and other such iniquities. "It is an error," declared the Pope, "to believe that the Roman Pontiff can and ought to reconcile himself to, and agree with, progress, liberalism, and modern civilization." The American Catholic hierarchy took its cue from the Pope. Archbishop John Hughes of New York attacked abolitionists, Free Soilers, and various Protestant reform movements as kin to the "Red Republicanism" of Europe.[31]

Immigration had caused Catholic church membership to grow three times faster than Protestant membership in the 1840s. Pointing with pride to this fact (which Protestants viewed with alarm), Archbishop Hughes in 1850 delivered a well-publicized address *The Decline of Protestantism and Its Causes*. "The object we hope to accomplish," said Hughes, "is to convert all Pagan nations, and all Protestant nations. . . . There is no secrecy in all this. . . . Our mission [is] to convert the world—including the inhabitants of the United States—the people of the cities, and the people of the country . . . the Legislatures, the Senate, the Cabinet, the President, and all!" The archbishopric's newspaper proclaimed that "Protestantism is effete, powerless, dying out . . . and conscious that its last moment is come when it is fairly set, face to face, with Catholic truth."[32]

Such words fanned the embers of anti-Catholicism. Folk memories of Bloody Mary, the Spanish Armada, the Gunpowder Plot, the Glorious Revolution of 1688, and Foxe's *Book of Martyrs* were part of the Anglo-American Protestant consciousness. The Puritan war against popery had gone on for two and one-half centuries and was not over yet. In 1852 the first Plenary Council of American bishops, meeting in Baltimore, attacked the godlessness of public education and decided to seek

31. Quotations from Robert Kelley, *The Transatlantic Persuasion: The Liberal-Democratic Mind in the Age of Gladstone* (New York, 1969), 106; Eric Hobsbawm, *The Age of Capital, 1848–1875* (New York, 1976), 106; Walter G. Sharrow, "Northern Catholic Intellectuals and the Coming of the Civil War," *New-York Historical Society Quarterly*, 58 (1974), 45.
32. Hughes's address is quoted in Ray Allen Billington, *The Protestant Crusade 1800–1860* (New York, 1938), 291; *Freeman's Journal*, March 4, 1848, quoted in *ibid.*, 290.

tax support for Catholic schools or tax relief for parents who sent their children to such schools. During 1852–53 this effort set off bitter campaigns in a dozen northern cities and states (including Maryland). "Free School" tickets drawn from both major parties, but especially from the Whigs, won several elections on the platform of defending public schools as the nursery of republicanism against the "bold effort" of this "despotic faith" to "unite . . . the Church and the State," to "uproot the tree of Liberty" and "substitute the mitre for our liberty cap." Archbishop Hughes replied in kind, branding public schools as wellsprings of "Socialism, Red Republicanism, Universalism, Infidelity, Deism, Atheism, and Pantheism."[33]

In the midst of these school campaigns, Hughes threw the hierarchy into another emotional struggle, this one over control of church property. Catholic churches in many areas were owned by a lay board of trustees representing the congregation. This accorded with Protestant practice but defied Catholic tradition. Attempts by the clergy to gain control of church property reached into several state legislatures, which refused after acrimonious debates to sanction clerical control—and indeed, in some cases tried to mandate lay control. In July 1853 Monsignor Gaetano Bedini arrived in the United States as a papal nuncio to adjudicate the property dispute in certain dioceses. After doing so in favor of the clergy, Bedini toured the country to bestow the papal blessing on American Catholics. Much of the Protestant and nativist press erupted in frenzy. "He is here," exclaimed one journal, "to find the best way to rivet Italian chains upon us which will bind us as slaves to the throne of the most fierce tyranny the world knows." The Church's role in suppressing Italian nationalist uprisings in 1848–49 also aroused radical expatriates from several Catholic countries against Bedini, whom they labeled the "Butcher of Bologna." As Bedini's tour continued, riots broke out in several cities that he visited, and upon his departure for Italy in February 1854 he had to be smuggled aboard a ship in the New York harbor to escape a mob.[34]

The temperance movement also exacerbated ethnic tensions. Before 1850 this movement had been primarily one of self-denial and moral

---

33. Dannenbaum, "Immigrants and Temperance," loc. cit., 129; Holt, Political Crisis of the 1850s, 162; Vincent P. Lannie, "Alienation in America: The Immigrant Catholic and Public Education in Pre-Civil War America," Review of Politics, 32 (1970), 515.
34. Billington, Protestant Crusade, 300–303.

suasion aimed at persuading the Protestant middle and working classes to cast out demon rum and become sober, hard-working, upward-striving citizens. As such it had enjoyed an astonishing success. But conspicuous holdouts against this dry crusade were Irish and German immigrants, for whom taverns and beer gardens were centers of social and political life. A perceived rise of drunkenness, brawling, and crime especially among the Irish population helped turn temperance reform into a coercive movement aimed at this recalcitrant element. Believing that liquor was a cause of social disorder, prohibitionists sought passage of state laws to ban the manufacture and sale of alcoholic beverages. They achieved their first major victory in Maine in 1851. This success set off a wave of "Maine law" debates in other legislatures. The Democratic party generally opposed temperance laws while the Whigs were divided. Fearful of alienating "wet" voters, Whigs refused to take a stand and thereby estranged the large temperance component in their ranks. Coalitions of drys from all parties captured control of enough legislatures from 1852 to 1855 to enact Maine laws in a dozen additional states including all of New England, New York and Delaware, and several midwestern states.[35]

These laws, like Prohibition in a later generation, were frequently honored in the breach. Nonenforcement was widespread; legislatures or courts in several states subsequently repealed the laws or restricted their scope. Those who wanted to drink could continue to do so; those who did not had stopped doing so under the influence of the earlier moral-suasion phase of the crusade. By 1861 only three of the thirteen states that had legislated prohibition were still dry. The larger significance of the prohibition movement in the 1850s was not the laws it enacted but the impetus it gave to nativism. A Catholic newspaper classified prohibition with "State Education Systems, Infidelity, Pantheism," abolitionism, socialism, women's rights, and "European Red Republicanism" as "parts of a great whole, at war with God." Temperance advocates replied in kind. "It is liquor which fills so many Catholic (as well as other)

35. There are a number of good studies of drinking and the temperance movement in this era: see especially Ian R. Tyrrell, *Sobering Up: From Temperance to Prohibition in Antebellum America, 1800–1860* (Westport, Conn., 1979); W. J. Rorabaugh, *The Alcoholic Republic: An American Tradition* (New York, 1976); Jed Dannenbaum, *Drink and Disorder: Temperance Reform in Cincinnati from the Washingtonian Revival to the WCTU* (Urbana, 1984); and Norman H. Clark, *Deliver Us from Evil: An Interpretation of American Prohibition* (New York, 1976), chaps. 2–4.

homes with discord and violence . . . fills our prisons with Irish culprits, and makes the gallows hideous with so many Catholic murderers," declared Horace Greeley's *New York Tribune*. "The fact that the
Catholics of this country keep a great many more grog shops and sell
more liquor in proportion to their number than any other denomina-
tion, creates and keeps alive a strong prejudice against them."[36]

Buffeted by the winds of anti-Nebraska, anti-liquor, anti-Catholic,
and anti-immigrant, the two-party system in the North was ready for
collapse by 1854. And it was not only the antislavery Republicans who
picked up the pieces. In several states a new and powerful nativist party
seemed to glean even more from the wreckage. A number of secret
fraternal societies restricted in membership to native-born Protestants
had sprung up by the 1850s. Two of them in New York, the Order of
United Americans and the Order of the Star Spangled Banner, had
merged in 1852 under the leadership of James Barker. Against the background of Protestant-Catholic clashes over public schools, the Bedini
visit, and temperance campaigns, the dynamic Barker organized hundreds
of lodges all over the country with an estimated membership ranging up
to a million or more. Members were pledged to vote for no one except
native-born Protestants for public office. In secret councils the Order
endorsed certain candidates or nominated its own. When asked by outsiders about the Order, members were to respond "I know nothing."
Because of their secrecy and tight-knit organization, these "Know Nothings" became a potentially powerful voting bloc.[37]

They drew their membership mainly from young men in white-collar
and skilled blue-collar occupations. A good many of them were new
voters. One analysis showed that men in their twenties were twice as
likely to vote Know Nothing as men over thirty. Their leaders were also
"new men" in politics who reflected the social backgrounds of their

36. *Cincinnati Catholic Telegraph*, March 19, July 9, 1853, quoted in Dannenbaum,
    "Immigrants and Temperance," *loc. cit.*, 134; *New York Tribune*, quoted in Nev-
    ins, *Ordeal*, II, 329.
37. General treatments of the Know Nothings include Billington, *Protestant Crusade*,
    especially chaps. 11–26; Ira M. Leonard and Robert D. Parmet, *American Nativ-
    ism, 1830–1860* (New York, 1971); and Carleton Beals, *Brass-Knuckle Crusade:
    The Great Know-Nothing Conspiracy, 1820–1860* (New York, 1960), a sensa-
    tionalized and untrustworthy account. In addition to several state studies of the
    Know Nothings, there is one regional monograph: W. Darrell Overdyke, *The
    Know-Nothing Party in the South* (Baton Rouge, 1950). For the Catholic response,
    see Robert Francis Hueston, *The Catholic Press and Nativism 1840–1860* (New
    York, 1976).

constituency. In Pittsburgh more than half of the Know-Nothing leaders were under thirty-five and nearly half were artisans and clerks. Know Nothings elected to the Massachusetts legislature in 1854 consisted mainly of skilled workers, rural clergymen, and clerks in various enterprises. Maryland's leaders were younger and less affluent than their Democratic counterparts.[38]

As a political movement, the Know Nothings had a platform as well as prejudices. They generally favored temperance and always opposed tax support for parochial schools. Their main goal was to reduce the power of foreign-born voters in politics. Under federal law, immigrants could become naturalized citizens after five years in the United States. In a few large cities Democratic judges obligingly issued naturalization papers almost as soon as immigrants got off the boat. Most states limited the vote to citizens, though several allowed immigrants to vote within a year of establishing residence. By the early 1850s the heavy wave of immigration that had begun in 1846 was showing up in voting rolls. Since immigrants were preponderantly young adults, the number of foreign-born voters grew faster than their proportion of the population. In Boston, for example, immigrant voters increased by 195 percent from 1850 to 1855 while the native-born vote rose only 14 percent. Because this "foreign" vote was mainly Democratic, Catholic, and wet, its rapid growth had alarming implications to Whigs, Protestants, and temperance reformers—and even to some native-born Democrats of the working class who found themselves competing with foreign-born laborers willing to work for lower wages. Rural residents also resented the growing power of the immigrant vote in the cities. The Know Nothings called for an increase of the waiting period for naturalization to twenty-one years. In some states they wished to restrict officeholding to native-born citizens and to impose a waiting period of several years after naturalization before immigrants could vote. They did not propose limits on immigration per se, though some Know Nothings probably hoped that by making citizenship and political rights more difficult to obtain they might discourage immigrants from coming to the United States.

Most Know Nothings in northern states also opposed the Kansas-

38. Holt, *Political Crisis of the 1850s*, 186–89; Gienapp, "Origins of the Republican Party," 348–49; Jean H. Baker, *Ambivalent Americans: The Know-Nothing Party in Maryland* (Baltimore, 1977), 63–68; Robert D. Parmet, "Connecticut's Know-Nothings: A Profile," *The Connecticut Historical Society Bulletin*, 31 (July 1966), 84–90; Dale Baum, *The Civil War Party System: The Case of Massachusetts, 1848–1876* (Chapel Hill, 1984), 27–28.

Nebraska Act. In some areas they joined anti-Nebraska coalitions in 1854. This raised the complex question of the relationship between Know Nothings and the new Republican party. The antislavery movement grew from the same cultural soil of evangelical Protestanism as temperance and nativism. Some free soilers viewed slavery and Catholicism alike as repressive institutions. Both were "founded and supported on the basis of ignorance and tyranny," resolved a Know-Nothing lodge in Massachusetts, and thus "there can exist no real hostility to Roman Catholicism which does not embrace slavery, its natural co-worker in opposition to freedom and republican institutions."[39] The support of immigrant Catholic voters for the proslavery "Hunker" wing of the Democratic party cemented this perceived identity of slavery and Catholicism. So did frequent editorials in the Catholic press branding the free-soil movement as "wild, lawless, destructive fanaticism." Competing with free blacks at the bottom of the social order, Irish Americans were intensely anti-Negro and frequently rioted against black people in northern cities. In 1846 a solid Irish vote had helped defeat a referendum to grant equal voting rights to blacks in New York state. "No other class of our citizens was so zealous, so unanimous in its hostility to Equal Suffrage without regard to color," commented the *New York Tribune* bitterly. " 'Would you have your daughter marry a naygur?' was their standing flout at the champions of democracy irrespective of race and color." In 1854 a Massachusetts free soiler summarized the issues in the forthcoming elections as "freedom, temperance, and Protestantism against slavery, rum, and Romanism."[40]

On the other hand, many antislavery leaders recognized the incongruity of nativism with their own ideology. "I do not perceive," wrote Abraham Lincoln, "how any one professing to be sensitive to the wrongs of the negroes, can join in a league to degrade a class of white men." William H. Seward had battled the nativists in his state for more than a decade. The New York Republican platform in 1855 declared that "we repudiate and condemn the proscriptive and anti-republican doctrines of the order of Know-Nothings."[41] An "anti-slavery man," said George W. Julian, founder of the Republican party in Indiana, "is, of

39. Billington, *Protestant Crusade*, 425. For a fuller treatment of this question, see William E. Gienapp, "Nativism and the Creation of a Republican Majority in the North before the Civil War," *JAH*, 72 (1985), 529–59.
40. Hueston, *The Catholic Press and Nativism*, 211; *New York Tribune*, Aug. 26, 1854; *Boston Advertiser*, quoted in Gienapp, "Origins of the Republican Party," 500.
41. CWL, II, 316; Gienapp, "Nativism and the Creation of a Republican Majority," *loc. cit.*, 537.

necessity, the enemy of [this] organized scheme of bigotry and proscription, which can only be remembered as the crowning and indelible shame of our politics." Since "we are against Black Slavery, because the slaves are deprived of human rights," declared other Republicans, "we are also against . . . [this] system of Northern Slavery to be created by disfranchising the Irish and Germans."[42]

Genuine free soilers also deplored the Know-Nothing craze as a red herring that diverted attention from "the real question of the age," slavery. "Neither the Pope nor the foreigners ever can govern the country or endanger its liberties," wrote Charles A. Dana, managing editor of Greeley's New York Tribune, "but the slavebreeders and slavetraders do govern it." Dana vowed in 1854 never to mention the Know Nothings in the Tribune "except to give 'em a devil of a whale."[43] George Julian even suspected that this "distracting crusade against the Pope and foreigners" was a "cunning" scheme of proslavery interests "to divide the people of the free states upon trifles and side issues, while the South remained a unit in defense of its great interest."[44]

Nevertheless, as a matter of political expediency, free-soil leaders in several states formed alliances with the Know Nothings in 1854 and 1855. In some cases they did so with the intention of taking over the movement in order to channel it in an antislavery direction. Massachusetts provided the clearest example of this. In that state the issues of the Mexican War and Wilmot Proviso had reshuffled political alignments so that a coalition of Free Soilers (including Conscience Whigs) and Democrats had gained control of the legislature from 1850 to 1852. The coalition elected Charles Sumner to the Senate and proposed or passed a number of reforms: a mechanic's lien law, a ten-hour law for laborers, general banking and incorporation laws, prohibition legislation, and reapportionment of the legislature to shift some power from Boston (with its Cotton Whigs and its large Irish vote) to central and western Massachusetts. The conservative Whig and Boston vote narrowly defeated reapportionment in a referendum in 1853. This provided the main spark for the Know-Nothing fire of 1854 that swept out of western Massachu-

42. Gienapp, "Origins of the Republican Party," 641; Hans L. Trefousse, The Radical Republicans: Lincoln's Vanguard for Racial Justice (New York, 1969), 86; Sewell, Ballots for Freedom, 269; Holt, Political Crisis of the 1850s, 171.

43. Liberator, Nov. 10, 1854; Dana quoted in Eric Foner, Free Soil, Free Labor, Free Men: The Ideology of the Republican Party before the Civil War (New York, 1970), 234, and in Trefousse, The Radical Republicans, 85.

44. Quoted in Foner, Free Soil, Free Labor, Free Men, 233, and in Sewell, Ballots for Freedom, 267.

setts and kindled the whole state, electing the governor, an over-whelming majority of the legislature, and all of the congressmen. The Whig establishment was traumatized by this conflagration. "I no more suspected the impending result," wrote a Whig journalist, "than I looked for an earthquake which would level the State House and reduce Faneuil Hall to a heap of ruins."[45]

Free Soil/Republican leaders like Charles Francis Adams and Charles Sumner were taken equally by surprise. But that was not true of all free soilers. Indeed one of them, Henry Wilson, had much to do with the outcome. Like many of the younger Know-Nothing voters, Wilson had been an apprentice and journeyman shoemaker in his youth. The "Natick Cobbler," as he was called, became a shoe manufacturer, went into politics as a Whig, and in 1848 helped found the Free Soil party. In 1854 the new Republican party nominated Wilson for governor. Whigs, Democrats, and Know Nothings also nominated candidates. Shrewdly perceiving that the nativist frenzy would overwhelm the other parties, Wilson joined the Know-Nothing movement in the hope of controlling it. Some free soilers expressed disgust with this strategy. "When the freedom of an empire is at issue," wrote one of them, "Wilson runs off to chase a paddy!"[46] Wilson remained on the ticket as Republican candidate but came in a distant fourth, having persuaded most of his free-soil followers to vote Know Nothing.

There was method in Wilson's apparent madness, as a choleric Cotton Whig recognized. The Know Nothings, he wrote, "have been controlled by the most desperate sort of Free Soil adventurers. Henry Wilson and Anson Burlingame have ruled the hour. . . . Our members of Congress are one and all of the ultra-agitation Anti-Slavery Stamp."[47] The Know-Nothing legislature elected Wilson to the Senate, where he did nothing for nativism but much for the antislavery cause. The only nativist laws passed by this legislature were a literacy qualification for voting and a measure disbanding several Irish militia companies—and the latter was in part an antislavery gesture, since these companies had provided much of the manpower that returned Anthony Burns to bondage.[48] The legislature also enacted a new personal liberty law and a

---

45. Gienapp, "Origins of the Republican Party," 493.
46. Edward L. Pierce to Horace Mann, Jan. 18, 1855, quoted in *ibid.*, 592.
47. Robert C. Winthrop to John P. Kennedy, Jan. 3, 1855, quoted in Nevins, *Ordeal*, II, 343.
48. The legislatures of Connecticut and Rhode Island also enacted literacy qualifications for voting. Only some 4 or 5 percent of adults in these states were illiterate—

bill forbidding racial segregation in public schools—the first such law ever passed. In addition, these Know-Nothing lawmakers passed a series of reform measures that earned them an ironic reputation as one of the most progressive legislatures in the state's history: abolition of imprisonment for debt, a married women's property act, creation of an insurance commission, compulsory vaccination of school children, expansion of the power of juries, and homestead exemption from seizure for debt.[49]

Republicans and Know-Nothings had succeeded in breaking down the Whigs and weakening the Democrats in most parts of the North. But in 1855 it remained uncertain which of these two new parties would emerge as the principal alternative to the Democrats. In about half of the states, Republicans had become the second major party. In the other half the American party, as the Know Nothings now named their political arm, seemed to prevail. But a development of great significance occurred in 1855. The center of nativist gravity began to shift southward. While the Know Nothings added Connecticut, Rhode Island, New Hampshire, and California to the state governments they controlled, they also won elections in Maryland and Kentucky, gained control of the Tennessee legislature, polled at least 45 percent of the votes in five other southern states, and did better in the South as a whole than the Whigs had done since 1848.

In much of the South the American party was essentially the Whig party under a new name. To be sure, a tradition of nativism existed in the South despite the relatively small number of immigrants and Catholics there. This nativism undergirded the American party in Maryland, Louisiana, Missouri, and to some degree in Kentucky—states that contained cities with large immigrant populations. "Citizens of New Orleans!!" proclaimed a political handbill of 1854. "You have an important duty to perform tomorrow in the election of a District Attorney. . . .

---

but most of them were Irish immigrants. Know Nothings with Republican support subsequently passed a law requiring naturalized citizens in Massachusetts to wait two years after naturalization before they could vote. This requirement was repealed during the Civil War. In 1850 Republican legislatures in New York and Michigan passed voter registration laws designed to curb illegal voting, measures aimed in part at practices attributed to big-city Democratic machines and Irish voters. Joel H. Silbey, *The Partisan Imperative: The Dynamics of American Politics Before the Civil War* (New York, 1985), 141–54; Ronald P. Formisano, *The Birth of Mass Political Parties: Michigan, 1827–1861* (Princeton, 1971), 285–87.

49. Baum, *The Civil War Party System*, 27–31.

Father Mullen and the Jesuits can no longer rule this city. . . . The Irish are . . . making our elections scenes of violence and fraud. . . . Americans! Shall we be ruled by Irish and Germans?"[50] Nativist riots and election-day violence figured more prominently in southern cities than in the North. In Baltimore various gangs such as the Plug Uglies and Blood Tubs became notorious enforcers of Know-Nothing dominance at the ballot box. Ethnic political riots killed four people in New Orleans, ten in St. Louis, seventeen in Baltimore, and at least twenty-two in Louisville during the mid-1850s. In some areas of the upper South, especially Maryland, the American party appealed equally to Democrats and Whigs. But elsewhere in the South it drew mainly from former Whigs who preferred the political company of nativists to that of Democrats. And the Know Nothings' nationalism became a unionist counterweight to the increasingly sectionalist Democrats.[51]

The slavery issue soon split the Know Nothings along sectional lines. At the first national council of the American party, in June 1855 at Philadelphia, Henry Wilson led a bolt of most northern delegates when southerners and northern conservatives passed a plank endorsing the Kansas-Nebraska Act. From this time forth the party wasted away in the North while it grew stronger in the South. The logical place for antislavery Know Nothings to go was into the Republican party, which stood ready to receive them if it could do so without sanctioning nativism. Abraham Lincoln voiced the Republican dilemma in this matter. "Of their principles," Lincoln said of the Know Nothings, "I think little better than I do of the slavery extensionists. . . . Our progress in degeneracy appears to me to be pretty rapid. As a nation, we began by declaring that 'all men are created equal.' We now practically read it 'all men are created equal, except negroes.' When the Know-Nothings get control, it will read 'all men are created equal, except negroes, and foreigners, and catholics.' When it comes to this I should prefer emigrating to some country where they make no pretence of loving liberty—to Russia, for instance, where despotism can be taken pure, and without the base alloy of hypocrisy." Nevertheless, in central Illinois the Know Nothings "are mostly my old political and personal friends." Without them "there is not sufficient materials to combat the Nebraska

50. Overdyke, The Know-Nothing Party in the South, 21–22, 24.
51. Ibid., passim; Baker, Ambivalent Americans, passim; James H. Broussard, "Some Determinants of Know-Nothing Electoral Strength in the South," Louisiana History, 7 (1966), 5–20.

democracy." Lincoln was willing "to 'fuse' with anybody I can fuse on ground which I think is right." The only hope of carrying Illinois was to "get the elements of this organization" on our own terms after "Know-Nothingism has . . . entirely tumbled to pieces."[52]

In Ohio, Salmon P. Chase showed how this might be done. After winning all of the congressional districts in 1854, the Ohio anti-Nebraska coalition looked forward to electing Chase governor in the state elections of 1855. But could they do it without Know-Nothing support? Militant free soilers like Joshua Giddings thought so. The nativists, he said, were "unjust, illiberal, and un-American. We will never unite with such a party, in any compact whatever." Chase seemed to agree. "I cannot proscribe men on account of their birth," he wrote. "I cannot make religious faith a political test." He therefore recognized in January 1855 that the strength of "the Know-Knothing movement . . . may make the election of a man in my position impossible."[53]

But Chase's ambition soon caused him to waffle. He privately expressed a willingness to work with antislavery Know Nothings if he could do so without "sacrificing principle." "It seems to me you have said enough against the Kns, and had better hold up," he told a journalistic ally in February 1855. "My idea is to fight nobody who does not fight us." We might acknowledge "that there was some ground for the uprising of the people against papal influences & organized foreignism" so long as we insist on "the importance of keeping the anti-slavery idea paramount."[54] In effect, Chase wanted Republicans to spurn nativist *policies* while recognizing nativism as a cultural impulse. In particular, he was willing to make a gesture toward anti-Catholicism but not to alienate Protestant immigrants, especially the large German vote, whose support Republicans wanted and needed. This shading toward anti-Romanism but away from a generalized nativism became a way for Re-

52. Lincoln to Owen Lovejoy, Aug. 11, 1855, Lincoln to Joshua F. Speed, Aug. 24, 1855, CWL, II, 316, 323.
53. Giddings quoted in William E. Gienapp, "Salmon P. Chase, Nativism, and the Formation of the Republican Party in Ohio," Ohio History, 93 (1984), 11; Chase quoted in Trefousse, Radical Republicans, 84, and in Stephen E. Maizlish, The Triumph of Sectionalism: The Transformation of Ohio Politics, 1844–1856 (Kent, Ohio, 1983), 207.
54. Chase to E. S. Hamlin, Nov. 21, 1854, Feb. 9, Jan. 22, 1855, quoted in Maizlish, Triumph of Sectionalism, 206, 208, and in Gienapp, "Salmon P. Chase, Nativism," 10.

publicans to absorb some Know Nothings without feeling that they were "sacrificing principle."

Chase managed to walk this tightrope without falling. The conservative Know Nothings nominated a separate ticket in Ohio. Radical free soilers threatened to do the same if Chase made any concessions to the nativists. The Republican state convention nominated Chase on an antislavery platform that, in the candidate's words, did not "contain a squint toward Knism." The nominees for other state offices, however, were men of Know-Nothing background—though Chase considered them "honest men . . . sincerely opposed to slavery" who "adhere but slightly to their order." Proclaiming that "there is nothing before the people but the vital issue of slavery," Chase privately predicted that Know Nothingism would "gracefully give itself up to die."[55]

Perhaps. In any case, the main ethnocultural issue in the campaign was anti-black racism injected by the Democrats, who rapidly perfected the technique of tarring "Black Republicans" with the brush of Negro equality. Labeling the Chase candidacy "Sambo's State Ticket," Ohio Democrats proclaimed that Republicans intended to sacrifice "the interests of more than twenty millions of people . . . to those of three millions of blacks." The Republican policy of limiting the expansion of slavery would inevitably become a program of emancipation, which would let loose "three to five millions of uncivilized, degraded, and savage men . . . to roam the country" and take bread from the mouths of white laboring men.[56]

Chase survived these onslaughts and won the governorship with 49 percent of the vote to 43 percent for the Democrats and 8 percent for the separate American ticket. Though they could not have won without Know-Nothing support, Republicans came to power in Ohio committed to an antislavery platform and not bound by promises to nativists. They demonstrated this political legerdemain once again in the prolonged battle over the speakership of the national House of Representatives that convened in December 1855.

The chaos of parties at the opening of this Congress reflected the devastation wrought by the 1854–55 elections. Most estimates counted somewhere in the neighborhood of 105 Republican congressmen, 80 Democrats, and 50 Americans. Of the last, thirty-one came from slave

55. Gienapp, "Chase, Nativism," 22, 24, 26.
56. Maizlish, *Triumph of Sectionalism*, 220.

states and a half-dozen of the rest were conservatives on the slavery question. Of the Democrats, only twenty-three came from free states and a few of these were uncomfortable in the traces with southern colleagues. Of the Republicans (not all of whom yet acknowledged that label), perhaps two-thirds had at least a nominal connection with Know-Nothingism, though half or more of these placed a higher priority on antislavery than on nativism. One of the latter was Nathaniel P. Banks of Massachusetts, a onetime Democrat and then a Know Nothing who like his colleague Henry Wilson in the Senate now wanted to harness the Know-Nothing cart to the Republican horse. The Republicans nominated Banks for speaker, but in ballot after ballot during two increasingly tense months Banks fell short of the 118 votes needed for election. The process, however, crystallized his supporters as Republicans, and when the House on February 2, 1856, finally changed the rules to allow a plurality to prevail, Banks won the speakership with 103 votes on the 133rd ballot. If any one moment marked the birth of the Republican party, this was it.

What made possible this remarkable eclipse of Know Nothings and surge of Republicans to become the North's majority party within less than two years? Part of the answer lay in a dramatic decline of immigration, which during the years after 1854 fell to less than half of the level it had attained in the first half of the decade. But the main reason could be expressed in two words: Bleeding Kansas. Events in that far-off territory convinced most northerners that the slave power was after all a much greater threat to republican liberty than the Pope was.

5

The Crime Against Kansas

I

Having lost the battle in Congress for a free Kansas, antislavery men determined to wage the war on the prairie itself. "Since there is no escaping your challenge," William H. Seward told southern senators on May 25, 1854, "I accept it in behalf of the cause of freedom. We will engage in competition for the virgin soil of Kansas, and God give the victory to the side which is stronger in numbers as it is in right."[1] In Massachusetts the erstwhile conservative Amos Lawrence was chief financial backer of the New England Emigrant Aid Company, formed in the summer of 1854 to promote free-soil settlement of Kansas. Few New Englanders actually went there, but the company did provide aid to farmers from midwestern states who began to trickle into Kansas. Lawrence's role was reflected in the name of the town that became headquarters of the free-state forces in the territory.

At the outset, however, Missourians from just across the border were stronger in numbers than the free soilers and at least equal in determination. "We are playing for a mighty stake," Senator David Atchison of Missouri assured Virginia's Robert M. T. Hunter. "The game must be played boldly. . . . If we win we carry slavery to the Pacific Ocean, if we fail we lose Missouri Arkansas Texas and all the territories." Fifteen years earlier Missourians had harried and burned the Mormons out of

1. CG, 33 Cong., 1 Sess., Appendix, 769.

145

the state; Atchison was confident of their ability to give free soilers the same treatment in Kansas. "We are organizing," he told Jefferson Davis. "We will be compelled to shoot, burn & hang, but the thing will soon be over. We intend to 'Mormonize' the Abolitionists."[2]

Atchison did his best to fulfill this promise. When Andrew Reeder, a Pennsylvania Democrat, arrived in Kansas as territorial governor in the fall of 1854 he called an election for a delegate to Congress. This became the first of many Kansas elections in which the normal rowdiness of frontier politics was magnified a hundredfold by the contest over slavery. In November 1854, Atchison and other prominent Missourians led an invasion of "border ruffians" into Kansas to swell the vote for the proslavery candidate. Derided as "Pukes" by northern-born settlers, many of these lank, unshaven, unwashed, hard-drinking Missourians had little material interest in slavery but even less love for "those long-faced, sanctimonious Yankees" devoted to "sickly sycophantic love for the nigger."[3] The border ruffians won the first round. Casting more than 1,700 ballots that a subsequent congressional committee found to be fraudulent, they elected a proslavery delegate to Congress.

They probably could have won in a fair election. Governor Reeder took a census in preparation for the next election (of a territorial legislature) in March 1855. Of 8,501 *bona fide* residents (including 242 slaves), 2,905 were legal voters, of whom three-fifths had come from Missouri and other slave states. Nevertheless Atchison wanted to make sure of victory. "Mark every scoundrel among you that is the least tainted with free-soilism, or abolitionism, and exterminate him," the senator's lieutenant in Missouri exhorted a crowd at St. Joseph. "To those having qualms of conscience . . . the time has come when such impositions must be disregarded, as your lives and property are in danger. . . . Enter every election district in Kansas . . . and vote at the point of a

2. Atchison to Hunter, quoted in James A. Rawley, *Race and Politics: "Bleeding Kansas" and the Coming of the Civil War* (Philadelphia, 1969), 81; Atchison to Davis, Sept. 24, 1854, quoted in William E. Gienapp, "The Origins of the Republican Party, 1852–1856," Ph.D. dissertation, University of California at Berkeley, 1980, pp. 570–71.
3. The stereotypes of each other held by Yankees and Pukes are analyzed in Michael Fellman, "Rehearsal for the Civil War: Antislavery and Proslavery at the Fighting Point in Kansas, 1854–1856," in Lewis Perry and Michael Fellman, eds., *Antislavery Reconsidered: New Perspectives on the Abolitionists* (Baton Rouge, 1979), 287–307; quotation from p. 300. The phrase "border ruffians" was coined by Horace Greeley but proudly adopted by the Missourians.

Bowie knife or revolver!" Taking a leave from the Senate, Atchison again led a band of border ruffians into Kansas. "There are eleven hundred men coming over from Platte County to vote," he told his followers, "and if that ain't enough we can send five thousand—enough to kill every God-damned abolitionist in the Territory."[4] Five thousand was about the number that came—4,908 according to a congressional investigation—and cast illegal ballots to elect a territorial legislature composed of thirty-six proslavery men and three free soilers. "Missourians have nobly defended *our* rights," stated an Alabama newspaper. "All hail!" declared the proslavery *Leavenworth Herald.* "Come on, Southern men! Bring your slaves and fill up the Territory. Kansas is saved."[5]

Governor Reeder was appalled by these proceedings. He had come to Kansas sympathetic toward slavery, but the Missourians' threats against his life if he interfered with their activities converted him to the other side. He ordered new elections in one-third of the districts. Free-soil candidates won most of them, but when the legislature met in July 1855 it contemptuously seated the original proslavery victors. Reeder had meanwhile gone to Washington, where he pleaded with Pierce to repudiate this burlesque. But the president was swayed by arguments of Atchison, Douglas, and other Democrats that the Emigrant Aid Company had provoked the problem and Republican newspapers had blown it out of proportion. Atchison also persuaded Pierce to replace Reeder with someone more pliable, who turned out to be Wilson Shannon from Ohio. One of Shannon's first responsibilities was to enforce a slave code enacted by the legislature that imposed a fine and imprisonment for expressing opinions against slavery, authorized the death penalty for encouraging slave revolts or helping slaves to escape, required all voters to take an oath to uphold these laws, and retroactively legalized the border ruffian ballots by requiring no prior residence in Kansas in order to vote.[6]

Free-soil Kansans—who by the fall of 1855 outnumbered bona fide

4. John Stringfellow quoted by Alice Nichols, *Bleeding Kansas* (New York, 1954), 26, from a report of his speech in the proslavery *Leavenworth Herald;* Atchison's words reported in testimony before a congressional committee by Dr. G. A. Butler, a settler from Tennessee, quoted in Nevins, *Ordeal,* II, 385.
5. *Jacksonville (Ala.) Republican,* quoted in Rawley, *Race and Politics,* 89; *Leavenworth Herald,* quoted in Nichols, *Bleeding Kansas,* 29.
6. Nevins, *Ordeal,* II, 384–90; Jay Monaghan, *Civil War on the Western Border, 1854– 1865* (New York, 1955), 17–30; Roy F. Nichols, *Franklin Pierce* (2nd ed., Philadelphia, 1958), 407–18.

proslavery settlers—had no intention of obeying these laws or of recognizing the "bogus legislature" that had passed them. Northern settlers armed themselves with new Sharps breechloading rifles sent from New England. Free soilers organized politically and called a convention to meet at Topeka in October. They drew up a free-state constitution and called elections for a new legislature and governor. Proslavery voters of course boycotted these elections. By January 1856 Kansas had two territorial governments: the official one at Lecompton and an unofficial one at Topeka representing a majority of actual residents.

Partisans of both sides in the territory were walking arsenals; it was only a matter of time until a shooting war broke out. The murder of a free-soil settler by a proslavery man in November 1855 set off a series of incidents that seemed likely to start the war. Some 1,500 Missourians crossed the border to march on the free-soil stronghold of Lawrence, where 1,000 men waited to receive them with Sharps rifles and a howitzer. Federal troops stood by idly because they had received no orders from the inert Pierce administration. Governor Shannon went to Lawrence and persuaded both sides to disband their forces. With Atchison's help he managed to prod the reluctant Missourians homeward. "If you attack Lawrence now," Atchison told them, "you attack as a mob, and what would be the result? You could cause the election of an abolition President, and the ruin of the Democratic party. Wait a little. You cannot now destroy these people without losing more than you would gain."[7]

This reasoning hardly encouraged prospects for a permanent peace. A severe winter did more than anything else to keep things quiet for the next few months. But violence sprouted with the dandelions in the spring of 1856. The annual migration of settlers promised to increase the free-state majority. The proslavery response called for bravado. "Blood for Blood!" blazoned the *Atchison Squatter Sovereign*. "Let us purge ourselves of all abolition emissaries . . . and give distinct notice that all who do not leave immediately for the East, will leave for eternity!"[8] Proslavery Judge Samuel Lecompte instructed a grand jury to indict members of the free-state government for treason. Since many of these men lived in Lawrence, the attempt to arrest them provided another opportunity for Missourians, now deputized as a posse, to attack this bastion of Yankee abolitionists. Dragging along five cannon, they laid

7. Nevins, *Ordeal*, II, 411.
8. *Ibid.*, 433.

siege to the town on May 21. Not wishing to place themselves in further contempt of law, free-state leaders decided against resistance. The "posse" of some 800 men thereupon poured into Lawrence, demolished its two newspaper offices, burned the hotel and the home of the elected free-soil governor, and plundered shops and houses.

All of this occurred against the backdrop of a national debate about Kansas. Both Republicans and Democrats in Congress introduced bills for the admission of Kansas as a state—the former under the Topeka free-state constitution, the latter after an election of a new constitutional convention to be administered by the Lecompton territorial government. Southerners viewed this matter as crucial to their future. "The admission of Kansas into the Union as a slave state is now a point of honor," wrote Congressman Preston Brooks of South Carolina in March 1856. "The fate of the South is to be decided with the Kansas issue. If Kansas becomes a hireling [i.e. free] State, slave property will decline to half its present value in Missouri . . . [and] abolitionism will become the prevailing sentiment. So with Arkansas; so with upper Texas."[9]

Since Republicans controlled the House, and Democrats the Senate, neither party's Kansas bill could become law. Both parties focused on the propaganda value of the issue looking toward the presidential election. Republicans gained more from this strategy because Democratic support of proslavery excesses in Kansas offered a ready-made opportunity to dramatize yet another slave-power attack on northern rights. Blessed with an able corps of young antislavery reporters on the scene in Kansas, whose zeal sometimes exceeded their accuracy, the burgeoning galaxy of Republican newspapers exploited Bleeding Kansas for all it was worth.

Southerners continued to give them plenty to exploit. Hard on the heels of the "Sack of Lawrence" came shocking news from the U. S. Capitol itself. All spring Charles Sumner had been storing up wrath toward what he considered "The Crime Against Kansas"—the title of a two-day address he delivered to crowded Senate galleries May 19–20. "I shall make the most thorough and complete speech of my life," Sumner informed Salmon P. Chase a few days before the address. "My soul is wrung by this outrage, & I shall pour it forth." So he did, with more passion than good taste. "Murderous robbers from Missouri," Sumner declared, "hirelings picked from the drunken spew and vomit of an uneasy civilization" had committed a "rape of a virgin territory, compelling it to the hateful embrace of slavery." Sumner singled out members

9. *Ibid.*, 427.

of the F Street Mess for specific attack, including South Carolina's Andrew P. Butler, who had "discharged the loose expectoration of his speech"
in demanding the disarming of free-state men in Kansas. Butler's home
state with "its shameful imbecility from Slavery" had sent to the Senate
in his person a "Don Quixote who had chosen a mistress to whom he
has made his vows, and who . . . though polluted in the sight of the
world, is chaste in his sight—I mean the harlot, Slavery."[10]

Sumner's speech produced an uproar—in the Senate, where several
Democrats rebuked him, and in the press, where even Republican praise
was tempered by reservations about the rhetoric. The only thing that
prevented some southerner from challenging Sumner to a duel was the
knowledge that he would refuse. Besides, dueling was for social equals;
someone as low as this Yankee blackguard deserved a horsewhipping—
or a caning. So felt Congressman Preston Brooks, a cousin of Andrew
Butler. Two days after the speech Brooks walked into the nearly empty
Senate chamber after adjournment and approached the desk where
Sumner was writing letters. Your speech, he told the senator, "is a libel
on South Carolina, and Mr. Butler, who is a relative of mine." As
Sumner started to rise, the frenzied Brooks beat him over the head thirty
times or more with a gold-headed cane as Sumner, his legs trapped
under the bolted-down desk, finally wrenched it loose from the floor
and collapsed with his head covered by blood.[11]

This incident incensed even those Yankees who had little use for
Sumner. "Bleeding Sumner" joined Bleeding Kansas as a symbol of the
slave power's iniquities. The South, declared one newspaper, "cannot
tolerate free speech anywhere, and would stifle it in Washington with
the bludgeon and the bowie-knife, as they are now trying to stifle it in
Kansas by massacre, rapine, and murder." "Has it come to this," asked
William Cullen Bryant of the New York Evening Post, "that we must
speak with bated breath in the presence of our Southern masters? . . .
Are we to be chastised as they chastise their slaves? Are we too, slaves,
slaves for life, a target for their brutal blows, when we do not comport
ourselves to please them?"[12]

10. Sumner to Chase, May 15, 1856, Chase Papers, Library of Congress; The Works
   of Charles Sumner, 12 vols. (Boston, 1873), IV, 125–48.
11. David Donald, Charles Sumner and the Coming of the Civil War (New York,
   1960), 289–97.
12. Cincinnati Gazette, May 24, 1856; New York Evening Post, May 23, 1856, quoted

Adding insult to injury, the South lionized Brooks as a hero. Although some southerners regretted the affair for its galvanizing effect on the North, public approval of Brooks's act far outweighed qualms. Newspapers in his own state expressed pride that Brooks had "stood forth so nobly in defense of . . . the honor of South Carolinians." The *Richmond Enquirer* pronounced "the act good in conception, better in execution, and best of all in consequence. The vulgar Abolitionists in the Senate are getting above themselves. . . . They have grown saucy, and dare to be impudent to gentlemen! . . . The truth is, they have been suffered to run too long without collars. They must be lashed into submission."[13] A Louisiana planter and former army officer, Braxton Bragg, wrote that the House should pass a vote of thanks to Brooks. "You can reach the sensibilities of such dogs" as Sumner, wrote Bragg, "only through their heads and a big stick." Brooks himself boasted that "every Southern man sustains me. The fragments of the stick are begged for as *sacred relicts*." When the House voted 121 to 95 to expel him, southern opposition prevented the necessary two-thirds majority. Brooks resigned anyway and returned home to seek vindication by reelection. South Carolinians fêted him and sent him back to Washington with triumphant unanimity. From all over the South, Brooks received dozens of new canes, some inscribed with such mottoes as "Hit Him Again" and "Use Knock-Down Arguments."[14]

This southern response outraged northern moderates even more than the caning had done. "It was not the attack itself (horrible as that was) that excited me," wrote an old-line Whig who thereafter voted Republican, "but the tone of the Southern Press, & the approbation, apparently, of the whole Southern People." A Boston conservative who had previously defended the South now "must in sorrow concede a lower civilization than I would ever before believe, tho' [Theodore] Parker, & those called extreme, have often & calmly insisted upon this very fact, while I have warmly denied it." Republican organizers reported that

in William E. Gienapp, "The Crime Against Sumner: The Caning of Charles Sumner and the Rise of the Republican Party," *CWH*, 25 (1979), 230, 232.

13. *Charleston Courier*, Aug. 29, 1856, quoted in Avery O. Craven, *The Growth of Southern Nationalism 1848–1861* (Baton Rouge, 1953), 233; *Richmond Enquirer*, June 9, 1856, quoted in Gienapp, "The Crime Against Sumner," 222.

14. Bragg quoted in Donald, *Sumner*, 305; Brooks quoted in Gienapp, "The Crime Against Sumner," 221; the mottoes on the canes quoted in John Hope Franklin, *The Militant South 1800–1861* (Cambridge, Mass., 1956), 54–55.

they had "never before seen anything at all like the present state of deep, determined, & desperate feelings of hatred, & hostility to the further extension of slavery, & its political power."[15]

Brooks's only punishment was a $300 fine levied by a district court. Sumner's injuries, complicated by a post-traumatic syndrome that turned psychogenic neurosis into physical debility, kept him away from the Senate most of the time for the next four years.[16] During that time the Massachusetts legislature reelected him as a symbolic rebuke to the "barbarism of slavery." A good many Yankees wanted to go beyond such passive protest. "If the South appeal to the rod of the slave for argument with the North," wrote a New York clergyman in his diary, "no way is left for the North, but to strike back, or be slaves."[17] Out in Kansas lived a fifty-six-year-old abolitionist who also believed in this Old Testament injunction of an eye for an eye. Indeed, John Brown looked much like the Biblical warrior who slew his enemies with the jawbone of an ass—though Brown favored more up-to-date weapons like rifles, and, on one infamous occasion, broadswords.

The father of twenty children, Brown had enjoyed little success over the years in his various business and farming enterprises. In 1855 he joined six of his sons and a son-in-law who had taken up claims in Kansas. A zealot on the subject of slavery with an almost mesmeric influence over many of his associates, Brown enlisted in a free-state military company (which included his sons) for service in the guerrilla conflict that was spreading during the spring of 1856. On their way to help defend Lawrence against the Missourians in May, this company learned that the unresisting town had been pillaged. The news threw Brown into a rage at the proslavery forces and contempt for the failure of Lawrence men to fight. That was no way to make Kansas free, he told his men. We must "fight fire with fire," must "strike terror in the hearts of the proslavery people." When further word reached Brown's party of the caning of Sumner in Washington, Brown "went crazy— crazy," according to witnesses. "Something must be done to show these barbarians that we, too, have rights," Brown declared. He reckoned that proslavery men had murdered at least five free-soilers in Kansas since the troubles began. Brown conceived of a "radical, retaliatory measure" against "the slave hounds" of his own neighborhood near Pottawatomie

15. All quotations from Gienapp, "The Crime Against Sumner," 231, 234, 235.
16. See the thorough and persuasive analysis in Donald, *Sumner*, 312–47.
17. Henry Dana Ward quoted in Gienapp, "The Crime Against Sumner," 232.

Creek—none of whom had anything to do with those murders. With four of his sons and three other men, Brown abducted five proslavery settlers from their cabins on the night of May 24–25 and coolly split open their skulls with broadswords. An eye for an eye.[18]

This shocking massacre went unpunished by legal process. Federal officials did manage to arrest two of Brown's sons who had *not* taken part in the affair, while proslavery bands burned the Brown homesteads. The twin traumas of Lawrence and Pottawatomie escalated the bushwhacking war in Kansas. One of Brown's sons was among some two hundred men killed in this conflict. Considering themselves soldiers in a holy war, Brown and his other sons somehow evaded capture and were never indicted for the Pottawatomie killings. And despite strenuous efforts by the U.S. army to contain this violence, the troops were too few to keep up with the hit and run raids that characterized the fighting.

As news of the Pottawatomie massacre traveled eastward, a legend grew among antislavery people that Brown was not involved or that if he was he had acted in self-defense.[19] Not surprisingly, Republican newspapers preferred to dwell on the "barbarism" of border ruffians and Preston Brooks rather than on the barbarism of a free-state fighter. In any event, the Pottawatomie massacre was soon eclipsed by stories of other "battles" under headlines in many newspapers featuring "The Civil War in Kansas." More than anything else, that civil war shaped the context for the presidential election of 1856.

II

It was by no means certain when the year opened that the Republicans would become the North's second major party. The American party

18. Stephen B. Oates, *To Purge This Land with Blood: A Biography of John Brown* (New York, 1970), 126–37; quotations from 128–29, 133, based on later testimony by men in Brown's military company. A substantial part of the huge historical literature on John Brown focuses on the Pottawatomie massacre. Although some contemporaries denied Brown's role in the affair, historians accept it while disagreeing about motives and details. The account here is based on that in Oates's biography, the most recent and reasonable analysis of the massacre. Fuller details with a different slant on many matters can be found in James C. Malin, *John Brown and the Legend of Fifty-six* (Philadelphia, 1942), a frustrating book because of its sprawling, structureless format, but based on an astonishing amount of research in Kansas history.

19. Malin, *John Brown and the Legend of Fifty-six*, contains an exhaustive account of the various filters through which contemporaries and later historians viewed and distorted the Pottawatomie massacre.

held a national convention in February with hopes of healing its sectional breach of the previous year. Some of the northern delegates who had walked out in June 1855 returned. But once more an alliance of southerners with New York and Pennsylvania conservatives defeated a resolution calling for repeal of the Kansas-Nebraska Act. Seventy Yankee delegates thereupon exited to organize a "North American" party. The remaining delegates nominated Millard Fillmore as the American party candidate for president.

The North Americans called a convention to meet a few days before the Republican gathering in June. Their intent was to nominate an antislavery nativist whom the Republicans would be compelled to endorse in order to avoid splitting the antislavery vote. But the outcome demonstrated the impossibility of the nativist tail wagging the antislavery dog. Once again Nathaniel Banks, who had just consolidated Republican control of the House by his election as speaker, served as a stalking horse for Republican absorption of North Americans. Still in good standing among nativists, Banks allowed his name to be put in nomination as the North American presidential candidate. After the Republicans nominated their candidate, Banks would withdraw in his favor, leaving the North Americans little choice but to endorse the Republican nominee. Several delegates to the North American convention were privy to this plot. It worked just as planned. Banks received the nomination, whereupon all eyes turned to Philadelphia, where the Republicans convened their first national convention.

Republican leaders like ex-Whig Thurlow Weed of New York and ex-Democrat Francis Preston Blair of Maryland were shrewd men. Recognizing that old loyalties would inhibit some political veterans from attending a "Republican" conclave, they did not use that label in the call for a convention. Instead they invited delegates "without regard to past political differences or divisions, who are opposed to the repeal of the Missouri Compromise [and] to the policy of the present Administration." The platform and candidate would have to be carefully crafted to attract as many and alienate as few voters as possible. Especially delicate was the task of winning both nativists and immigrants (at least Protestant immigrants). Almost as difficult was the fusion of former Whigs and Democrats. The platform pursued these goals by concentrating on issues that united disparate elements and ignoring or equivocating on those that might divide them. Four-fifths of the platform dealt with slavery; it damned the administration's policy in Kansas, asserted the right of Congress to ban slavery in the territories, called for admission of Kansas as a free state, denounced the Ostend Manifesto, and quoted the Declaration of Independence as authority for free-soil principles. Two brief planks echoed the ancient Whig program of government financing for internal improvements by endorsing such aid for a transcontinental railroad and for rivers and harbors improvements—projects that would also attract Democratic support in areas benefitting from them (Pierce had vetoed three rivers and harbors bills). The final plank, relating to nativism, was a masterpiece of ambiguity. By opposing all legislation that might restrict "liberty of conscience and equality of rights among citizens," the platform seemed to rebuke nativism. But by specifying "citizens" it apparently did not preclude the Know-Nothing plan (which Republicans had no real intention of carrying out) to lengthen the waiting period for naturalization to twenty-one years. And "liberty of conscience" was also a code phrase for Protestants who resented Catholic attempts to ban the reading of the King James Bible in public schools.[20]

Because the Republican party was new, its platform was more important than usual in American politics. But of course the candidate would do even more to shape the party's image. Seward and Chase were the most prominent possibilities. But each had made enemies among groups that Republicans needed to attract: nativists, antislavery Democrats, or conservative Whigs. Besides, Seward and his adviser Thurlow Weed doubted the chances for Republican victory in 1856 and preferred to wait for better odds in 1860. The most "available" man, precisely because he had almost no political experience and therefore no record to defend, was John C. Frémont. The dashing image of this "Pathfinder" of the West was a political asset. Frémont would win votes, predicted one Republican strategist, "from the romance of his life and position."[21] His marriage to the headstrong Jessie Benton, daughter of the legendary Jacksonian Thomas Hart Benton, who was an enemy of the Atchison faction in Missouri, provided Frémont with important connections among ex-Democrats. His role in promoting a free California in 1849 and his endorsement of a free Kansas in 1856 gave him good antislavery credentials. Frémont thus won the nomination on the first

20. The call for the convention is quoted in Gienapp, "Origins of the Republican Party," 864; the platform is reprinted in Arthur M. Schlesinger, Jr., ed., *History of American Presidential Elections 1789–1968*, 4 vols. (New York, 1971), II, 1039–41.
21. Richard H. Sewell, *Ballots for Freedom: Antislavery Politics in the United States 1837–1860* (New York, 1976), 283.

ballot. Ex-Whigs received a sop with the selection of New Jersey's William Dayton for vice president.

Dayton's nomination threatened to upset the delicate scheme to secure North American endorsement of the Republican candidates. Banks declined the North American nomination as planned, but in return for backing Frémont the nativists expected Republican endorsement of their vice-presidential nominee. When the Republicans refused, North Americans made angry noises for a time but finally accepted Dayton. Their endorsement of the Republican ticket required them to swallow an extra-large slice of humble pie, for Frémont's father had been a Catholic and the Pathfinder had been married by a priest. False rumors circulated during the campaign that Frémont himself was a secret Catholic. Some embittered North Americans, especially in Pennsylvania, vowed to support Fillmore, but that candidate offered them cold comfort because he was only a nominal Know Nothing and his main backing came from southern ex-Whigs who could not bring themselves to affiliate with Democrats.

As an organized political movement, nativism went into a long eclipse after 1856. Hostility to Romanism (as well as Rum) remained a subterranean current within Republicanism. But for mainstream Republicans the Slave Power, not Catholicism, was the danger that threatened American liberties. "You are here today," the party chairman had told delegates to the Republican convention, "to give direction to a movement which is to decide whether the people of the United States are to be hereafter and forever chained to the present national policy of the extension of slavery." [22]

In all respects the Democratic candidate was Frémont's opposite. The Pathfinder at forty-three was the youngest presidential nominee thus far; James Buchanan at sixty-five was one of the oldest. While the colorful Frémont and his ambitious wife had made numerous enemies as well as friends over the years, the dour Presbyterian bachelor Buchanan seemed colorless and safe. While Frémont had served in public office only three months as senator from California, Buchanan had held so many offices that he was known as "Old Public Functionary"—congressman for a decade, senator for another decade, five years in the diplomatic service

22. Nevins, *Ordeal*, II, 460. For an account of nativism in the 1856 election that emphasizes Republican ambivalence, see William E. Gienapp, "Nativism and the Creation of a Republican Majority in the North before the Civil War," *JAH*, 72 (1985), 541–48.

as minister to Russia and to Britain, and four years as secretary of state. But Buchanan shared one political attribute with Frémont—availability. He had been out of the country as minister to Britain during the Kansas-Nebraska furor. Unlike Pierce and Douglas, the other candidates for the nomination, he carried no taint of responsibility for the mess in Kansas. Buchanan also came from Pennsylvania, which was shaping up as the crucial battleground of the election.

At the Democratic national convention Pierce and Douglas drew much of their support from southern delegates grateful for their role in repealing the Missouri Compromise. Most of Buchanan's votes came from the North—an irony, for Buchanan would turn out to be more pro-southern than either of his rivals. As the balloting went on through more than a dozen roll calls, Pierce and then Douglas withdrew for the sake of harmony, enabling Buchanan to win on the seventeenth ballot. Reversing the proportions of the Republican platform, the Democratic document devoted little more than a fifth of its verbiage to the slavery issue. It endorsed popular sovereignty and condemned the Republicans as a "sectional party" inciting "treason and armed resistance to law in the Territories." Other planks in the platform reasserted old Jacksonian chestnuts: state's rights; a government of limited powers; no federal aid to internal improvements; no national bank so "dangerous to our republican institutions and the liberties of the people."[23]

The campaign evolved into two separate contests: Buchanan vs. Fillmore in the South and Buchanan vs. Frémont in the North. Electioneering was lackluster in most parts of the South because the outcome was a foregone conclusion. Though Fillmore won 44 percent of the popular vote in slave states, he carried only Maryland. Frémont won all of the upper North—New England plus Michigan and Wisconsin— with a lopsided margin of 60 percent of the popular vote to 36 percent for Buchanan and 4 percent for Fillmore. Large Republican majorities in the Yankee regions of upstate New York, northern Ohio, and northern Iowa ensured a Frémont victory in those states as well. The vital struggle took place in the lower-North states of Pennsylvania, Indiana, Illinois, and New Jersey. Pennsylvania and any of the others, or all of them except Pennsylvania, when added to the almost solid South would give Buchanan the presidency.

Democrats concentrated their efforts on the lower North, where they presented an image of Union-saving conservatism as an alternative to

Republican extremism. The old issues of banks, internal improvements, and the tariff seemed of little interest in this election. Even the newer ones of temperance and nativism affected only regional pockets. Democrats of course went through the motions of branding Republicans as neo-Whig promoters of banks and protective tariffs or as bigoted heirs of the Know Nothings. But the salient issues were slavery, race, and above all Union. On these matters northern Democrats could take their stand not necessarily as defenders of slavery but as protectors of the Union and the white race against the disunionist Black Republicans.

These Yankee fanatics were a sectional party, charged Democrats. That was quite true. In only four slave states (all in the upper South) did Frémont tickets appear, and the Republicans won considerably less than one percent of the vote in these states. If Frémont won the presidency by carrying a solid North, warned Democrats, the Union would crumble. As Buchanan himself put it, "the Black Republicans must be . . . boldly assailed as disunionists, and this charge must be re-iterated again and again."[24] Southerners helped along the cause by threatening to secede if the Republicans won. "The election of Frémont," declared Robert Toombs, "would be the end of the Union, and ought to be." When the September state elections in Maine went overwhelmingly Republican, Governor Henry Wise of Virginia put his militia on alert and wrote privately: "If Frémont is elected there will be a revolution." Senator James Mason of Virginia added that the South "should not pause but proceed at once to 'immediate, absolute and eternal separation.' "[25]

These warnings proved effective. Many old-line Whigs—including the sons of Henry Clay and Daniel Webster—announced their support for Buchanan as the only way to preserve the Union. Even Frémont's father-in-law Thomas Hart Benton, despite his hatred of the Democratic leadership, urged his followers to vote for Buchanan. Other Whig conservatives in crucial states like New York, Pennsylvania, and Illinois voted for Fillmore (whose campaign the Democrats secretly helped to finance), thereby dividing the anti-Democratic vote and helping place the latter two states in the Democratic column.

Not only would a Republican victory destroy the Union, said Democrats, but by disturbing slavery and race relations it would also menace

24. Buchanan quoted in Roy F. Nichols and Philip S. Klein, "Election of 1856," in Schlesinger, ed., *History of Presidential Elections*, II, 1028.
25. Toombs quoted in Potter, *Impending Crisis*, 262; Wise and Mason quoted in Roy F. Nichols, *The Disruption of American Democracy* (New York, 1948), 44.

white supremacy in both North and South. "Black Republicans," an Ohio Democratic newspaper told voters, intended to "turn loose . . . millions of negroes, to elbow you in the workshops, and compete with you in the fields of honest labor." Democrats in Pittsburgh pronounced the main issue to be "the white race or the negro race" because "the one aim of the party that supports Frémont" was "to elevate the African race in this country to complete equality of political and economic condition with the white man." Indiana Democrats organized a parade which included young girls in white dresses carrying banners inscribed "Fathers, save us from nigger husbands!"[26]

These charges of disunionism and racial equality placed Republicans on the defensive. In vain did they respond that the real disunionists were the southerners threatening to secede. In vain also did Republicans insist that they had no intention to "elevate the African race to complete equality with the white man." On the contrary, said a good many Republicans, the main purpose of excluding slavery from the territories was to protect white settlers from degrading competition with black labor. To refute the charge of egalitarian abolitionism, the free-state "constitution" of Kansas contained a provision excluding free blacks as well as slaves. "It is not so much in reference to the welfare of the Negro that we are here," Lyman Trumbull told the Republican convention, but "for the protection of the laboring whites, for the protection of ourselves and our liberties." Abolitionists like Lewis Tappan and William Lloyd Garrison denounced the Republican party precisely because it "had no room for the slave or the free man of color. . . . Its morality . . . is 'bounded by 36 deg. 30 min. . . . It is a complexional party, exclusively for white men, not for all men."[27]

But Republican denials failed to convince thousands of voters in the lower North that the party was not, after all, a "Black Republican" communion ruled by "a wild and fanatical sentimentality toward the black race."[28] Democrats could point to many Republicans who had spoken in behalf of equal rights for blacks. They noted that most men now calling themselves Republicans had voted recently for the enfranchise-

---

26. Quotations from Stephen E. Maizlish, *The Triumph of Sectionalism: The Transformation of Ohio Politics, 1844–1856* (Kent, Ohio, 1983), 232; Michael F. Holt, *The Political Crisis of the 1850s* (New York, 1978), 187; Rawley, *Race and Politics*, 167.

27. Quotations from Rawley, *Race and Politics*, 151.

28. *Frémont: His Supporters and Their Record*, a Democratic campaign pamphlet reprinted in Schlesinger, ed., *History of Presidential Elections*, II, 1071.

ment of blacks in New York, Wisconsin, and elsewhere, and that the Massachusetts legislators who had ended school segregation now backed Frémont. Democrats could also point to endorsements of Republicans by prominent black men like Frederick Douglass, who declared that Frémont's election "will prevent the establishment of Slavery in Kansas, overthrow Slave Rule in the Republic . . . and [put] the mark of national condemnation on Slavery."[29] Next to the taint of disunion, the tarbrush of black equality was the biggest obstacle to Republican success in large parts of the North.

Republicans knew that to win they must attack, not defend. They perceived the Achilles heel of the opposition to be subservience to the slave power. "The slave drivers," declared an Ohio Republican, "seek to make our country a great slave empire: to make slave breeding, slave selling, slave labor, slave extension, slave policy, and slave dominion, FOREVER THE CONTROLLING ELEMENTS OF OUR GOVERNMENT." A Republican victory, predicted a meeting in Buffalo, would ensure "for our country a government of the people, instead of a government by an oligarchy; a government maintaining before the world the rights of men rather than the privileges of masters."[30]

The precise point of Republican attack was Kansas. Shall I speak of "the tariff, National Bank, and internal improvements, and the controversies of the Whigs and Democrats?" asked Seward rhetorically in a campaign speech. "No," he answered, "they are past and gone. What then, of Kansas? . . . Ah yes, that is the theme . . . and nothing else." A lifelong Democrat who decided to vote Republican explained that "had the Slave Power been less *insolently aggressive,* I would have been content to see it extend . . . but when it seeks to extend its sway by fire & sword [in Kansas] I am ready to say hold, enough!" He told a Democratic friend who tried to persuade him to return to the party: "Reserve no place for me. I shall not come back."[31]

The campaign generated a fervor unprecedented in American politics. Young Republicans marched in huge torchlight parades chanting

29. Philip S. Foner, *The Life and Writings of Frederick Douglass,* 4 vols. (New York, 1950–55), II, 401.
30. Quotations from Maizlish, *Triumph of Sectionalism,* 230; Holt, *Political Crisis of 1850s,* 197.
31. Rawley, *Race and Politics,* 160–61; Gienapp, "Origins of the Republican Party," 1069–70.

a hypnotic slogan: "Free Soil, Free Speech, Free Men, Frémont!" Henry Wadsworth Longfellow found it "difficult to sit still with so much excitement in the air." A veteran politician in Indiana marveled: "Men, Women & Children all seemed to be out, with a kind of fervor, I have never witnessed before in six Pres. Elections in which I have taken an active part. . . . In '40, all was jubilant—Now there is little effervescence—but a solemn earnestness that is almost painful."[32] The turnout of eligible voters in the North was an extraordinary 83 percent. The northern people seemed to be "on the tiptoe of Revolution," wrote one awestruck politician, while a journalist confirmed that "the process now going on in the politics of the United States is a *Revolution*."[33]

While this passion mobilized a large Republican vote, it deepened the foreboding that drove many ex-Whigs to vote for Buchanan or Fillmore. The Pierce administration also took steps to defuse the Kansas time bomb. Overwhelmed by his inability to control the violence there, territorial Governor Wilson Shannon resigned in August. Pierce replaced him with John W. Geary, whose six-foot five frame and fearless manner made him a commanding figure. Only thirty-six years old, Geary had pursued several careers with success: attorney, civil engineer, Mexican War officer who had led an assault at Chapultepec, and the first mayor of San Francisco, where he had subdued outlaws in that wide-open city. If anyone could pacify Kansas in time to save the Democrats, Geary was the man. He reportedly said that he went to Kansas "carrying a Presidential candidate on his shoulders."[34] By facing down guerilla bands from both sides and using federal troops (whose numbers in Kansas reached 1,300) with boldness and skill, Geary suppressed nearly all of the violence by October. Kansas ceased to bleed—temporarily at least.

The dawn of peace in Kansas brought some disaffected northern Democrats back into the fold. As they took stock of the greater number of northern than southern settlers in the territory, they saw that popular sovereignty might make Kansas a free state after all. While 20 percent or more of traditional Democrats in the upper North appear to have

32. Gienapp, "Origins of the Republican Party," 1042; Nevins, *Ordeal*, II, 487.
33. Hendrick Booraem V, *The Formation of the Republican Party in New York: Politics and Conscience in the Antebellum North* (New York, 1983), 190; Nichols and Klein, "Election of 1856," in Schlesinger, ed., *History of Presidential Elections*, II, 1031.
34. Nevins, *Ordeal*, II, 484n.

voted Republican in 1856, the figure in the lower North was probably 10 percent or less.[35] This partial resurgence from the disaster of 1854 enabled the party to recoup some of its earlier losses. From only 25 seats in the House, northern Democrats rebounded to 53, though they were still outnumbered by 75 southern Democrats and 92 Republicans.[36] Most important, while Frémont carried eleven northern states with 114 electoral votes, Buchanan carried the remaining five (Pennsylvania, New Jersey, Indiana, and Illinois along with California) with 62, which added to his 112 from the South gave him a comfortable margin. Buchanan was a minority president in the popular vote, however, having won 45 percent of that vote nationally—56 percent in the South and 41 percent in the North.[37]

Southerners did not intend to let Buchanan forget that he owed his election mostly to them. "Mr. Buchanan and the Northern Democracy are dependent on the South," noted a Virginia judge after the election as he outlined his idea of a southern program for the next four years. "If we can succeed in Kansas, keep down the Tariff, shake off our Commercial dependence on the North and add a little more slave territory, we may yet live free men under the Stars and Stripes."[38]

III

Success in Kansas would require a bold strategy to overcome the estimated two-to-one majority of free-soil settlers. The proslavery legislature, elected by border ruffians in 1855 and still the official lawmaking body, was equal to the occasion. Meeting in January 1857, it ignored Governor Geary's request to modify the draconian slave code that prescribed the death penalty for certain antislavery acts. Instead, the legislature enacted a bill for what amounted to a rigged constitutional con-

35. Joel H. Silbey, *The Partisan Imperative: The Dynamics of American Politics Before the Civil War* (New York, 1985), 96; Thomas B. Alexander, "The Dimensions of Voter Partisan Constancy in Presidential Elections from 1840 to 1860," in Stephen E. Maizlish and John J. Kushma, eds., *Essays on American Antebellum Politics, 1840–1860* (College Station, Texas, 1982), 75.
36. Fourteen Americans were elected to the House. In the Senate 25 of the 37 Democrats were southerners. Twenty Republicans and five Whig-Americans (four from the upper South and one from Texas) completed the Senate roster.
37. Frémont's share of the national popular vote was 33 percent, virtually all from the North where he won 55 percent of the total. Fillmore's share was 22 percent, consisting of 44 percent of the southern vote and 13 percent of the northern.
38. Rawley, *Race and Politics*, 172.

vention. Specifying the election of delegates in June, the measure entrusted country sheriffs (all proslavery) with the registration of voters, and designated county commissioners (also proslavery) to choose judges of election. Given the record of previous elections in Kansas, little acumen was needed to discern the purpose of these provisions. To top them off, the bill specified that the new constitution drawn up by the convention would go into effect without a referendum.

Geary was appalled. He had come to Kansas as a Democrat who "heartily despised" the "pernicious" doctrines of abolition. But he soon became convinced of the "criminal complicity of public officials" in trying to make Kansas a slave state "at all hazards." This started him on the path to free soil and a career as a fighting general in the Civil War and Republican governor of Pennsylvania afterwards. In 1857 he vetoed the convention bill. The legislature promptly passed it over his veto. At loggerheads with territorial officials, his life threatened almost daily, without support from the lame-duck Pierce administration, Geary resigned on March 4, 1857. After leaving Kansas he gave an interview in which he condemned its "felon legislature." Geary had put down lawless elements in the nation's toughest town, San Francisco, but Kansas proved too much for him.[39]

Faced during his first days in office with the same Kansas problem that had wrecked the Pierce administration, Buchanan was determined that it should not ruin his. He prevailed upon Robert J. Walker, a Mississippian who had served with Buchanan in Polk's cabinet, to go to Kansas as territorial governor and give it a state constitution drafted by orderly process and approved by a referendum. More than a foot shorter than Geary in height, Walker was his equal in courage. But he too found Kansas more than he could handle. Though a southerner, he acknowledged that the free-state men had a majority in any fair election. The problem was that the election of delegates scheduled for June would not be fair. Arriving in Kansas at the end of May—too late to change the electoral procedures—Walker urged free-state men to participate anyway. Not wishing to sanction the legitimacy of this election, they refused. With only 2,200 of 9,250 registered voters participating, proslavery delegates won all the seats to the convention scheduled to meet at Lecompton in September.

These farcical proceedings got Walker's governorship off on the wrong foot. His sharpest critics were fellow southerners. They opposed a ref-

39. *Ibid.*, 176–79; quotations from 176–77, 179.

erendum on the forthcoming constitution; Walker favored one. From the moment he arrived in the territory, therefore, he had to endure hostility from southerners on the ground and back East. When word came from Washington that Buchanan backed the governor's insistence on a referendum, southern Democrats rose in righteous indignation. *"We are betrayed,"* they cried, "by an administration that went into power on [southern] votes." All four southern members of the cabinet turned against Walker. Several state legislatures and Democratic state conventions censured him. From Mississippi, Jefferson Davis denounced Walker's "treachery." Several southerners dragged out the time-honored threat to secede unless the administration fired Walker and backed down on the referendum issue.[40]

This pressure caused Buchanan to cave in. The South won yet another of its Pyrrhic victories. Before this happened, however, Kansans went to the polls yet again, to elect a new territorial legislature. Walker persuaded free soilers to vote this time by promising to enforce strict fairness. But lo and behold, the initial returns seemed to indicate an astonishing proslavery victory. Closer investigation uncovered the curious phenomenon of two remote districts with 130 legal voters having reported almost 2,900 ballots. In one case some 1,600 names had been copied onto the voting rolls from an old Cincinnati city directory. Throwing out the fraudulent returns, Walker certified a free-state majority in the next territorial legislature. This action provoked more bitter outcries from southerners against "tampering" with the returns.

While this furor continued, the constitutional convention completed its work at Lecompton. The document that emerged was in most respects conventional. But it declared that "the right of property is before and higher than any constitutional sanction, and the right of the owner of a slave to such slave and its increase is the same and as inviolable as the right of the owner of any property whatever." No amendment to the constitution could be made for seven years, and even after that time "no alteration shall be made to affect the rights of property in the ownership of slaves."[41] Here was the solution of a problem of urgent na-

---

40. Thomas W. Thomas to Alexander Stephens, June 15, 1857; *New Orleans Crescent*, July 17, 1857; both quoted in Craven, *Growth of Southern Nationalism*, 284; Davis quoted in George Fort Milton, *The Eve of Conflict: Stephen A. Douglas and the Needless War* (Boston, 1934), 267.

41. The Lecompton constitution is printed in Daniel W. Wilder, *The Annals of Kansas* (Topeka, 1875), 134–47; the quoted clauses on slavery are from 140 and 146.

tional interest, offered by a convention representing one-fifth of the potential voters in Kansas. And to make sure that those voters did not reject its handiwork, the convention decided to send the constitution and a petition for statehood to Congress without a referendum—in defiance of all pledges by Walker and Buchanan.

With Democratic control of Congress, and southern control of the Democratic party, proslavery forces believed that this desperate gambit would succeed. But it was too barefaced for most Democrats, including some southerners, who sought a way to preserve the form of a referendum without its substance. On November 7 the convention modified its position. It now mandated a referendum, not on the whole constitution, but only on two alternative slavery clauses designated as the "Constitution with Slavery" or the "Constitution with no Slavery." This seemed fair enough—except that the constitution with no slavery specified that, while "Slavery shall no longer exist" in Kansas, "the right of property in slaves now in this Territory shall in no manner be interfered with." In effect, the constitution with no slavery merely prohibited the future importation of slaves into Kansas. Free soilers saw this choice as a Heads you win, Tails I lose proposition. They therefore denounced it as "The Great Swindle." Much of the northern Democratic press joined their Republican rivals in expressing outrage at this "dirty piece of work."[42] Even if free-state men voted for the constitution with no slavery, they asked, what would stop slaveowners from smuggling human property across the 200-mile border with Missouri? Once in Kansas this property would be as "inviolable" as any other. Several southern states banned the importation of slaves, but such laws had proved meaningless. And in any case, the chances of defeating the constitution *with* slavery were problematical, because the convention put the polling machinery for the referendum in the hands of the same officials who had shown so much previous skill in rigging elections.

Governor Walker denounced the outcome at Lecompton as "a vile fraud, a bare counterfeit." It was "impossible" that Buchanan would accept it, said Walker, for as recently as October 22 the president had reiterated his support for a fair referendum. But proslavery men who smiled and said that Buchanan had changed his mind were right. To one northern Democrat who bitterly protested the president's reversal, Buchanan said he had no choice: if he did not accept the results of the Lecompton convention, southern states would either "secede from the

42. Nevins, *Emergence*, I, 236–37.

Union or take up arms against him."[43] Walker left Kansas never to return—the fourth governor in three years to be ground between the millstones of slavery and free soil.

On December 3, 1857, Walker's friend Stephen A. Douglas stormed into the White House to confront Buchanan on the "trickery and juggling" of this Lecompton constitution. To give Kansas statehood under such a travesty of popular sovereignty, Douglas warned the president, would destroy the Democratic party in the North. If Buchanan insisted on going through with it, Douglas swore to oppose him in Congress. "Mr. Douglas," replied Buchanan, "I desire you to remember that no Democrat ever yet differed from an administration of his own choice without being crushed. . . . Beware of the fate of Tallmadge and Rives," two senators who had gone into political oblivion after crossing Andrew Jackson. Douglas riposted: "Mr. President, I wish you to remember that General Jackson is dead, sir."[44] The gage was down for a duel that would split the Democratic party and ensure the election of a Republican president in 1860.

The "fraudulent submission" (Douglas's words) of the Lecompton constitution to Kansas voters occurred on December 21. Free soilers refused to participate in this referendum, which thereby approved the constitution "with slavery" by a vote of 6,226 to 569. (As usual, an investigation found 2,720 of the majority votes to have been fraudulent.) Meanwhile the new free-soil territorial legislature scheduled its own referendum for January 4, 1858. Voters this time would have an opportunity to accept or reject the whole constitution. Proslavery voters boycotted this referendum, which resulted in a poll of 138 for the constitution "with slavery," 24 for it "with no slavery," and 10,226 against the constitution.

Congress now had two referenda to choose from. Fire-eaters below the Potomac heated up their rhetoric to ensure the correct choice. Yancey in Alabama talked of forming committees of public safety to "fire the Southern heart" and "precipitate the cotton states into a revolution." Governors and legislatures stood by to call conventions to consider secession if Congress refused to admit Kansas under the "duly ratified" Lecompton constitution. "If Kansas is *driven out of the Union for being a Slave State*," asked South Carolina's Senator James Hammond, "can any Slave State remain in it with honor?" The southern people, de-

43. Milton, *Eve of Conflict*, 270–71.
44. Robert W. Johannsen, *Stephen A. Douglas* (New York, 1973), 581–86.

clared a Georgia congressman, intended "to have equality in this Union or independence out of it."[45] These threats stiffened Buchanan's backbone. On February 2, 1858, he sent the Lecompton constitution to Congress with a message recommending admission of a sixteenth slave state. Kansas, proclaimed the president, "is at this moment as much a slave state as Georgia or South Carolina."[46]

The Lecompton issue gripped Congress for several months. It evoked more passion than even the initial Kansas-Nebraska Act four years earlier. The lineup was the same now as then—with two significant differences: this time Douglas led the opposition; and the new Republican party dominated northern representation in the House. Douglas's political future hung in the balance. If he had supported Lecompton, southern backing for his presidential nomination in 1860 would have been assured. But in those circumstances the nomination would have been worth little. The millstone of Lecompton would sink Democratic chances of carrying any northern state. Douglas did not hesitate in his choice. He could never vote, he told the Senate, to "force this constitution down the throats of the people of Kansas, in opposition to their wishes and in violation of our pledges."[47] Telegrams and letters by the bushel poured into Washington praising Douglas's stand. "You have adopted the only course that could save the Northern Democracy from annihilation at the next election," ran a typical letter.[48] Douglas even had the novel experience of seeing himself lionized by such members of the opposition as Horace Greeley, who wanted to adopt him as a good Republican.

From the South, however, came little but eternal damnation. Southerners professed "astonishment" that the Illinoisian had turned against them. "Douglas was with us until the time of trial came," said a Georgian, "then he deceived and betrayed us." A South Carolinian lamented that "this defection of Douglas has done more than all else to shake my confidence in Northern men on the slavery issue, for I have long regarded him as one of our safest and most reliable friends." As the con-

---

45. Yancey quoted in Craven, *Growth of Southern Nationalism*, 289; Hammond in Johannsen, *Douglas*, 600; Georgia congressman in Don E. Fehrenbacher, *The South and Three Sectional Crises* (Baton Rouge, 1980), 54.
46. James D. Richardson, ed., *Compilation of the Messages and Papers of the Presidents*, 20 vols. (Washington, 1897), VII, 3010.
47. *CG*, 35 Cong., 1 Sess., 14–19.
48. Don E. Fehrenbacher, *The Dred Scott Case: Its Significance in American Law and Politics* (New York, 1978), 466.

troversy sharpened, southern rhetoric toward Douglas became more heated: he was "at the head of the Black column . . . stained with the dishonor of treachery without a parallel . . . patent double dealing . . . detestable heresies . . . filth of his defiant recreancy . . . a *Dead Cock in the Pit* . . . away with him to the tomb which he is digging for his political corpse."[49]

With its southern-dominated Democratic majority, the Senate approved admission of Kansas as a slave state on March 23, 1858. In the House the administration could count on at least half of the northern Democrats, as in 1854. But this time that was not enough to win the battle. "Battle" was not too strong a word for events in the House. On one occasion during an all-night session Republican Galusha Grow of Pennsylvania walked over to the Democratic side to confer with a few northern Democrats. Lawrence Keitt of South Carolina shouted at him: "Go back to your side of the House, you Black Republican puppy!" Replying with a sneering remark about slave drivers, Grow grappled with Keitt and knocked him down. Congressmen from both sides rushed into the melee. "There were some fifty middle-aged and elderly gentlemen pitching into each other like so many Tipperary savages," wrote a reporter describing this 2:00 a.m. free-for-all, "most of them incapable, from want of wind and muscle, of doing each other any serious harm." But Alexander Stephens believed that "if any weapons had been on hand it would probably have been a bloody one. All things here are tending my mind to the conclusion that the Union cannot and will not last long."[50] On April 1, in a dramatic roll call, 22 (of 53) northern Democrats joined the Republicans and a handful of Americans to defeat Lecompton by a vote of 120 to 112. "The agony is over," wrote a Douglas Democrat, "and thank God, the right has triumphed!"[51]

To save face, the administration supported a compromise by which Kansans would vote again on acceptance or rejection of Lecompton under the guise of a referendum on an adjustment in the size of the customary land grant to be received upon admission to statehood. Rejection of the land grant would defer statehood for at least two years.

---

49. Alexander H. Stephens to —— Pritchard, Dec. 9, 1857, Stephens Papers, Louis A. Warren Lincoln Library and Museum; Fehrenbacher, *Dred Scott Case*, 466, 468, 483; Johannsen, *Douglas*, 599.
50. *New York Weekly Tribune*, Feb. 13, 1859, quoted in Nevins, *Emergence*, I, 288; Stephens quoted in Rawley, *Race and Politics*, 239–40.
51. Johannsen, *Douglas*, 610.

Spurning this subterfuge as a bribe, Kansans defeated it on August 2 by a vote of 11,300 to 1,788. During this time Kansas had resumed bleeding from a number of wounds. Jayhawkers and border ruffians raided and ambushed each other with considerable ferocity. In May 1858, almost on the second anniversary of the Pottawatomie massacre, a proslavery band evened the score by seizing nine free-state settlers from their cabins and shooting them by firing squad (four survived their wounds). John Brown himself reappeared in the territory. His band invaded Missouri, killed a slaveholder, and liberated eleven slaves and a good many horses and took them to Canada.

Free-state Kansans organized a Republican party and elected two-thirds of the delegates to a new constitutional convention in 1859. Kansas finally came in as a free state in January 1861, joining California, Minnesota, and Oregon, whose entry since the Mexican War had given the North a four-state edge over the South. Kansas also became one of the most Republican states in the Union. Though most of the free-state settlers had originally been Democrats, the struggle with the slave power pushed them into the Republican party, which regularly rolled up two- or three-to-one majorities during the early years of statehood.

With enemies like the Democrats, Republicans scarcely needed friends. As if Kansas were not enough, the Buchanan administration, the Supreme Court, and southern Democrats ventured several other actions seemingly designed to assure Republican victory in the presidential election of 1860.

6

Mudsills and Greasy Mechanics
for A. Lincoln

I

Dred Scott lived all but two of his sixty-odd years in obscurity. The fame he achieved late in life was not for himself but for what he represented. Scott had been a slave of army surgeon John Emerson, who had taken him from Missouri to posts in Illinois and at Fort Snelling in the northern part of the Louisiana Purchase (now Minnesota) for several years in the 1830s. At Fort Snelling, Scott married a slave also owned by Emerson. She gave birth to a daughter in territory made free by the Missouri Compromise while Emerson was returning the Scotts to Missouri. After Emerson died and his widow inherited the Scotts, white friends of Dred Scott in St. Louis advised him in 1846 to sue for freedom on grounds of prolonged residence in a free state and a free territory. Scott did so. Thus began an eleven-year saga that started as a simple freedom suit and escalated into the most notorious *cause célèbre* in American constitutional history.

Scott first lost his suit but then won it on re-trial in St. Louis county court in 1850. On appeal the Missouri supreme court overturned this decision in 1852 and remanded the Scotts to slavery. The case was beginning to acquire political significance. Missouri courts had previously granted freedom to slaves in cases similar to Scott's. In overturning those precedents and asserting that Missouri law prevailed despite Scott's residence in free territory, the state supreme court was reacting to proslavery pressures. Scott's lawyers, who now included a Vermont-born resident of St. Louis, thought they could win the case if they could get it before a federal court. Scott's owner having moved to New York, the lawyers appealed to federal circuit court under the diverse-citizenship clause of the Constitution which gives federal courts jurisdiction over cases involving citizens of different states. In 1854 the circuit court for Missouri accepted the case (thereby affirming Scott's status as a citizen) but upheld the Missouri court's denial of his suit for freedom. Scott's lawyers appealed to the U.S. Supreme Court. Proslavery elements welcomed this move. The potential of the case for resolving crucial constitutional issues had become clear. And the Supreme Court had a southern majority.

The justices first heard arguments on the case in 1856 and held it over for reargument in the 1856–57 session—perhaps to avoid rendering a decision before the presidential election. Three main questions were before the Court: 1) As a black man, was Scott a citizen with a right to sue in federal courts? 2) Had prolonged residence (two years in each place) in a free state and territory made Scott free? 3) Was Fort Snelling actually free territory—that is, did Congress in 1820 have the right to ban slavery in the Louisiana Purchase north of 36° 30'? The Court could have ducked questions one and three by merely reaffirming the decisions of the Missouri supreme court and the federal circuit court that Missouri law governed Scott's status. Precedents existed for doing so; the Supreme Court itself in *Strader v. Graham* (1851) had refused to accept an appeal from the Kentucky supreme court which had ruled that slaves from Kentucky taken temporarily to Ohio remained slaves under Kentucky law. And indeed, for a time it appeared that the Court would take this way out. On February 14, 1857, a majority of justices voted to reaffirm the *Strader* principle and let it go at that. Justice Samuel Nelson of New York began to write the decision. But a few days later the majority reversed itself and decided to issue a comprehensive ruling covering all aspects of the case.

Why did the Court take this fateful step? Answers to this question have been uncertain and partisan. Only fragmentary accounts of the justices' confidential discussions leaked out, some of them years later. One interpretation of this evidence maintains that the two non-Democrats on the Court, John McLean of Ohio and Benjamin Curtis of Massachusets, stated their intention to dissent from the narrow decision prepared by Nelson. Their dissent would not only uphold Scott's freedom but would also affirm black citizenship and endorse the right of Congress to prohibit slavery in the territories. Not wishing these dissents to stand as the Court's only statement on such contentious issues, the southern majority reconsidered its decision to ignore them and voted to have Chief Justice Roger B. Taney write a comprehensive ruling. Thus, according to this interpretation, McLean and Curtis were responsible for provoking the vexatious Dred Scott decision that superseded Nelson's innocuous opinion.[1]

But the truth appears to be more complex. For a decade the question of slavery in the territories had threatened the Union. Politicians had been trying to pass the buck to the courts since the Compromise of 1850, which had provided for expedited appeal to the Supreme Court of any suit concerning slave property in the territories of Utah and New Mexico—a provision repeated verbatim in the Kansas-Nebraska Act of 1854. The problem was that because these territories did not prohibit slavery, no such suit materialized. But here, conveniently, came a suit from another part of the Louisiana Purchase. The yearning for settlement of this question by "judicial statesmanship" was widespread in Washington during the winter of 1856–57, especially among southerners. Alexander Stephens, a friend of Justice James M. Wayne of Georgia and a distant cousin of Justice Robert Grier of Pennsylvania, wrote privately in December 1856: "I have been urging all the influence I could bring to bear upon the Sup. Ct. to get them no longer to postpone the case on the Mo. Restriction. . . . I have reason to believe they will [decide] that the restriction was unconstitutional." Other southerners exerted similar pressures on the Court. They seemed to be succeeding. Two weeks later Stephens reported that "from what I hear *sub rosa* [the decision] will be according to my own opinions upon every point. . . . The restriction of 1820 will be held to be unconstitutional. The Judges are all writing out their opinions I believe *seriatim*. The Chief Justice will give an elaborate one."[2]

The five southern justices did want to rule against Congress's right to ban slavery from the territories. Some of them had indeed begun writing opinions to that effect. But the difficulty was in getting the two northern Democratic justices, Grier and Nelson, to go along with them. This was why the southerners had reluctantly decided to sidestep the issue

1. This was long the standard interpretation; its foremost exponent was Frank H. Hodder, "Some Phases of the Dred Scott Case," MVHR, 41 (1929), 3–22.
2. Alexander Stephens to Linton Stephens, Dec. 15, 1856, in Richard M. Johnston and William H. Browne, *Life of Alexander H. Stephens*, rev. ed. (Philadelphia, 1883), 326; letter from Stephens dated Jan. 1, 1857, quoted in Nevins, *Emergence*, I, 108.

with Nelson's narrow ruling. Word that McLean and Curtis would raise the broader questions in their dissents gave southern justices the pretext they needed to change their minds. They approved a motion by Wayne that Taney should prepare a decision covering all aspects of the case.[3]

There still remained the problem of cajoling a concurrence from at least one northern justice to avoid the appearance of a purely sectional ruling. Nelson could not be persuaded—he had already written his opinion and was probably miffed by his colleagues' intent to bypass it. But Grier was pliable. He was also from Buchanan's home state. The president-elect was anxious to have the territorial question resolved. In response to a suggestion from Justice John Catron of Tennessee, Buchanan brought highly improper but efficacious influence to bear on Grier, who succumbed. Taney had his northern justice and could proceed with his ruling.[4]

It was an opinion he had long wanted to write. Eighty years old, the chief justice was frail and ill. The death of his wife and daughter two years earlier in a yellow fever epidemic had left him heart-stricken. Yet he clung to life determined to defend his beloved South from the malign forces of Black Republicanism. In his younger days Taney had been a Jacksonian committed to liberating American enterprise from the shackles of special privilege. As Jackson's secretary of the treasury he had helped destroy the Second Bank of the United States. His early decisions as chief justice had undermined special corporate charters. But the main theme of his twenty-eight year tenure on the Court was the defense of slavery. Taney had no great love of the institution for its own sake, having freed his own slaves. But he did have a passionate commitment "to southern life and values, which seemed organically linked to the peculiar institution and unpreservable without it."[5] In private letters Taney expressed growing anger toward "northern aggres-

3. This analysis is based on the accounts in Don E. Fehrenbacher, *The Dred Scott Case: Its Significance in American Law and Politics* (New York, 1978), 305–11; James A. Rawley, *Race and Politics: "Bleeding Kansas" and the Coming of the Civil War* (Philadelphia, 1969), 275–81; and Nevins, *Emergence*, I, 107–10, II, 473–77.

4. The correspondence between Buchanan, Catron, and Grier in February 1857 was discovered in the Buchanan papers by his biographer Philip Auchampaugh, who presented the evidence in "James Buchanan, the Court and the Dred Scott Case," *Tennessee Historical Magazine*, 9 (1926), 231–40. See also Fehrenbacher, *Dred Scott Case*, 311–13.

5. These are the words of Don E. Fehrenbacher, in *Dred Scott Case*, 559. See also Fehrenbacher, "Roger B. Taney and the Sectional Crisis," *JSH*, 43 (Nov. 1977), 555–66.

sion." "Our own southern countrymen" were in great danger, he wrote; "the knife of the assassin is at their throats."[6] Taney's southern colleagues on the Court shared this apprehension, according to historian Don Fehrenbacher; Justice Peter Daniel of Virginia was "a brooding proslavery fanatic" and the other three were "unreserved defenders of slavery." Because of this "emotional commitment so intense that it made perception and logic utterly subservient," the Dred Scott decision was "essentially visceral in origin . . . a work of unmitigated partisanship, polemical in spirit [with an] extraordinary cumulation of error, inconsistency, and misrepresentation."[7]

Taney's opinion took up first the question whether Dred Scott, as a black man, was a citizen with the right to sue in federal courts. Taney devoted more space to this matter than to anything else. Why he did so is puzzling, for in the public mind this was the least important issue in the case. But southern whites viewed free blacks as an anomaly and a threat to the stability of slavery; Taney's own state of Maryland contained the largest free Negro population of any state. The chief justice's apparent purpose in negating U.S. citizenship for blacks, wrote Fehrenbacher, was "to launch a sweeping counterattack on the antislavery movement and . . . to meet every threat to southern stability by separating the Negro race absolutely from the federal Constitution and all the rights that it bestowed." To do so, however, he had to juggle history, law, and logic in "a gross perversion of the facts."[8] Negroes had not been part of the "sovereign people" who made the Constitution, Taney ruled; they were not included in the "all men" whom the Declaration of Independence proclaimed "created equal." After all, the author of that Declaration and many of the signers owned slaves, and for them to have regarded members of the enslaved race as potential citizens would have been "utterly and flagrantly inconsistent with the principles they asserted." For that matter, wrote Taney, at the time the Constitution was adopted Negroes "had for more than a century before been regarded as beings of an inferior order . . . so far inferior, that they had no rights which a white man was bound to respect."[9]

6. From letters written by Taney in 1856 and 1860, quoted in Fehrenbacher, "Taney and the Sectional Crisis," *loc. cit.*, 561, 556.
7. Fehrenbacher, *Dred Scott Case*, 234, 3, 559.
8. *Ibid.*, 341, 349.
9. The question of Negro citizenship occupies pp. 403–27 of Taney's opinion in *Dred Scott v. Sandford* 19 Howard 393.

This was false, as Curtis and McLean pointed out in their dissents. Free blacks in 1788 and later had many legal rights (to hold and bequeath property, make contracts, seek redress in courts, among others). In five of the thirteen states that ratified the Constitution black men were legal voters and participated in the ratification process. No matter, said Taney, these were rights of state citizenship and the question at issue was United States citizenship. A person might "have all of the rights and privileges of the citizen of a State," opined the chief justice, and "yet not be entitled to the rights and privileges of a citizen in any other State"—a piece of judicial legerdemain that contradicted Article IV, Section 2 of the Constitution: "The citizens of each state shall be entitled to all privileges and immunities of citizens in the several states."

Having established to his satisfaction that blacks were not citizens,[10] Taney could have stopped there and refused jurisdiction because the case was not properly before the Court. That he did not do so rendered the remainder of his decision, in the opinion of many contemporaries and the earliest generations of historians, *obiter dictum*—a statement in passing on matters not formally before the Court and therefore without force of law. But Taney insisted that because the circuit court had considered all aspects of the case and decided them "on their merits," the whole case including the constitutionality of the Missouri Compromise restriction on which Scott based part of his suit for freedom *was* properly before the Court. Modern scholars agree. Whatever else Taney's ruling was, it was not *obiter dictum*.

Taney and six other justices (with only Curtis and McLean dissenting) concurred that Scott's "sojourn" for two years in Illinois and for a similar period at Fort Snelling, *even if the latter was free territory*, did not make him free once he returned to Missouri.[11] To this matter Taney devoted only one of the 55 pages of his opinion. The constitutionality of the Missouri Compromise received 21 pages of labored prose arguing that Congress never had the right to prohibit slavery in a territory. That the Constitution (Article IV, Section 3) gave Congress the power to "make all needful rules and regulations" for the territories was

---

10. Two justices explicitly concurred with Taney's opinion on this matter, while Curtis and McLean dissented. Because the other four justices did not discuss this issue in their concurring opinions, their silence was an implicit acceptance of Taney's opinion as the ruling of the Court. See Fehrenbacher, *Dred Scott Case*, 324–30, for an analysis of this matter.

11. Ten weeks after the decision Scott's owner manumitted him. Scott died a year later.

not relevant, said the chief justice in a typical example of hair-splitting, because rules and regulations were not laws. The Fifth Amendment protected persons from being deprived of life, liberty, or property without due process; slavery was no different from other property, and a ban on slavery was therefore an unconstitutional deprivation of property. "And if Congress itself cannot do this," continued Taney in what he intended as a blow against popular sovereignty, "it could not authorize a territorial government to exercise" such a power. This clearly was *obiter dictum*, since the question of the power of a territorial government over slavery was not part of the case.

Republicans adopted the dissents by Curtis and McLean as their official position on the case. Not only was Scott a free man by virtue of his prolonged residence in free territory, said the dissenters, but he was also a citizen under the Constitution. And that Constitution did empower Congress to prohibit slavery in the territories. "*All* needful rules and regulations" meant precisely what it said. The first Congress under the Constitution had reaffirmed the Northwest Ordinance of 1787 banning slavery in the Northwest Territory. Subsequent Congresses down through 1820 excluded slavery from specific territories on four additional occasions. Many framers of the Constitution were alive during this period, and none objected to these acts. Indeed, several framers served in Congress and voted for them or, as presidents of the United States, signed them into law! If the exclusion of slavery from a territory violated due process, asked Curtis, what of the 1807 law ending importation of slaves from Africa? Indeed, what of laws in *free states* banning slavery? In any case, to prevent a slaveowner from taking his slaves into a territory did not deprive him of that property.[12]

Instead of removing the issue of slavery in the territories from politics, the Court's ruling became itself a political issue. Northern Democrats gloated that Taney's opinion was "the funeral sermon of Black Republicanism . . . crushing and annihilating . . . the anti-slavery platform . . . at a single blow." Southerners congratulated themselves that "Southern opinion upon the subject of Southern slavery . . . is now the supreme law of the land." The decision "crushes the life out of that miserable . . . Black Republican organization."[13] But the Republican

---

12. Curtis's dissent was fuller and more powerful than McLean's. It can be found on pp. 564–633 of 19 Howard.
13. *Cincinnati Enquirer*, March 8, 1857, quoted in Stanley I. Kutler, ed., *The Dred Scott Decision: Law or Politics?* (Boston, 1967), 54–55; *Philadelphia Pennsylvan-*

party declined to die. Its press condemned this "jesuitical decision" based on "gross historical falsehoods" and a "willful perversion" of the Constitution. If this ruling "shall stand for law," wrote William Cullen Bryant, slavery was no longer the "peculiar institution" of fifteen states but "a Federal institution, the common patrimony and shame of all the States. . . . Hereafter, wherever our . . . flag floats, it is the flag of slavery. . . . Are we to accept, without question . . . that hereafter it shall be a slaveholders' instead of the freemen's Constitution? Never! Never!" In this spirit several Republican state legislatures passed resolutions asserting that the ruling was "not binding in law and conscience."[14]

The *New York Tribune* declared contemptuously that this decision by "five slaveholders and two doughfaces"[15] was a "*dictum* . . . entitled to just as much moral weight as would be the judgment of a majority of those congregated in any Washington bar-room." The *dictum* theory justified Republican refusal to recognize the ruling as a binding precedent. They proclaimed an intent to "reconstitute" the Court after winning the presidency in 1860 and to overturn the "inhuman dicta" of *Dred Scott*. "The remedy," said the *Chicago Tribune*, was "the ballot box. . . . Let the next President be Republican, and 1860 will mark an era kindred with that of 1776."[16]

It soon dawned on northern Democrats that Taney had aimed to discomfit them as well as the Republicans. Although the question of popular sovereignty had not been directly before the Court, the principle of *Dred Scott* was not merely that Congress had no power to exclude slavery from a territory, but that slave property *could not be excluded*. Douglas grasped this nettle fearlessly. Yes, he said in a speech at Springfield, Illinois, in June 1857, the Dred Scott decision was law and all good citizens must obey it. A master's right to take slaves into any territory was irrevocable. BUT—citizens of a territory could still control this matter. How? The right of property in slaves "necessarily remains a

ian, March 10, 1857, *New York Herald*, March 8, 1857, *Augusta Constitutionalist*, March 15, 1857, *New Orleans Picayune*, March 20, 1857, all quoted in Fehrenbacher, *Dred Scott Case*, 418–19.

14. The Republican press quoted in Charles Warren, *The Supreme Court In United States History*, rev. ed., 2 vols. (Boston, 1926), II, 302–9; Bryant quoted in Nevins, *Emergence*, I, 96; action of legislatures described in Fehrenbacher, *Dred Scott Case*, 431–35.

15. All five southern justices had been slaveowners, though only three of them still owned slaves in 1857.

16. *New York Tribune*, March 7, 1857; *Chicago Tribune*, March 12, 19, 1857.

barren and worthless right," said Douglas, "unless sustained, protected and enforced by appropriate police regulations and local legislation" which depended on "the will and the wishes of the people of the Territory."[17]

This anticipated the famous Freeport doctrine enunciated by Douglas more than a year later in his debates with Lincoln. It was an ingenious attempt to enable both northern and southern Democrats to have their cake and eat it. It might have worked had not Lecompton crumbled Democratic unity. When that happened, southern Democrats insisted on another dessert. They agreed with Douglas that the Dred Scott decision would not enforce itself. "The Senator from Illinois is right," conceded Senator Albert G. Brown of Mississippi. "By non-action, by unfriendly action . . . the Territorial Legislature can exclude slavery." But that would amount to a denial of the "right of protection for our slave property in the Territories. The Constitution as expounded by the Supreme Court, awards it. We demand it; we mean to have it." Congress must pass a federal slave code for the territories, said Brown, and enforce it with the United States army if necessary. If pirates seized ships owned by citizens of Massachusetts, senators of that state would demand naval protection. "Have I, sir, less right to demand protection for my slave property in the Territories?" If you of the North "deny to us rights guarantied by the Constitution . . . then, sir . . . the Union is a despotism [and] I am prepared to retire from the concern."[18]

Thus instead of crippling the Republican party as Taney had hoped, the Dred Scott decision strengthened it by widening the sectional schism among Democrats. Republicans moved quickly to exploit their advantage by depicting the decision as the consequence of a slave-power conspiracy. Seward and Lincoln were two of the foremost advocates of a conspiracy theory. Citing "whisperings" between Taney and Buchanan at the inaugural ceremony plus other unnamed evidence, Seward charged collusion between the president-elect and the chief justice. One day after the inauguration and one day before announcing the decision, said Seward, "the judges, without even exchanging their silken robes for courtiers' gowns, paid their salutations to the President, in the Executive palace. Doubtlessly the President received them as graciously as Charles I did the judges who had, at his instance, subverted the statutes of English liberty." Seward's accusations provoked an uproar. Some historians have echoed Democratic opinion that they were "venomous" and "slan-

17. Fehrenbacher, *Dred Scott Case*, 455–56.
18. *CG*, 35 Cong., 2 Sess., 1242–43.

derous."[19] But in fact Seward hit uncomfortably close to the mark. He might almost have read the letter from Buchanan to Grier urging the Pennsylvania justice to go along with the southern majority.

Seward's insinuations enraged Taney. The chief justice said later that if the New Yorker had won the presidency in 1860 he would have refused to administer the oath. Ironically, Taney did administer the oath to a man who had made a similar accusation. In a speech after his nomination for senator from Illinois in 1858, Abraham Lincoln reviewed the process by which Democrats had repealed the Missouri Compromise in 1854 and then declared it unconstitutional in 1857. We cannot *know* that all of this was part of a conspiracy to expand slavery, conceded Lincoln. "But when we see a lot of framed timbers . . . which we know have been gotten out at different times and places by different workmen—Stephen, Franklin, Roger and James, for instance—and when we see these timbers joined together, and see they exactly make the frame of a house . . . we find it impossible to not *believe* that Stephen and Franklin and Roger and James . . . all worked upon a common *plan*."[20]

The same speech included a more famous house metaphor. " 'A house divided against itself cannot stand,' " said Lincoln quoting Jesus. "I believe this government cannot endure, permanently half *slave* and half *free*." The opponents of slavery hoped to stop the spread of the institution and "place it where the public mind shall rest in the belief that it is in the course of ultimate extinction." But advocates of slavery—including those conspiring carpenters—were trying to "push it forward, till it shall become lawful in *all* the States . . . *North* as well as *South*." How could they do this? "Simply [by] the next Dred Scott decision. It is merely for the Supreme Court to decide that no State under the Constitution can exclude it, just as they have already decided that . . . neither Congress nor the Territorial Legislature can do it." Article VI of the Constitution affirms that the Constitution and laws of the United States "shall be the supreme law of the land . . . anything in the Constitution or laws of any State to the contrary notwithstanding." If, therefore, the U.S. Constitution protected "the right of property in a slave," noted Lincoln, then "nothing in the Constitution or laws of any State

19. Warren, *Supreme Court*, II, 326. The quotation from Seward is in CG, 35 Cong., 1 Sess., 941.
20. CWL, II, 465–66. The discerning reader will recognize the four carpenters as Stephen Douglas, Franklin Pierce, Roger Taney, and James Buchanan.

can destroy the right of property in a slave." Lincoln himself believed that "the right of property in a slave is *not* distinctly and expressly affirmed in the Constitution." But Democrats including Douglas believed that it was. If they had their way, Lincoln told Illinois Republicans in June 1858, "we shall *lie down* pleasantly dreaming that the people of *Missouri* are on the verge of making their State *free*; and we shall *awake* to the *reality*, instead, that the *Supreme* Court has made *Illinois* a *slave* State."[21]

Did Lincoln and other Republicans really believe that the Dred Scott decision was part of a conspiracy to expand slavery into free *states?* Or were they creating a bugaboo to frighten northern voters? Stephen Douglas presumed the latter. "A school boy knows" that the Court would never make "so ridiculous a decision," said Douglas. "It is an insult to men's understanding, and a gross calumny on the Court." A good many historians have echoed Douglas's words.[22] But was the Republican claim ridiculous? In November 1857 the *Washington Union*, organ of the Buchanan administration, carried an article asserting that the abolition of slavery in northern states had been an unconstitutional attack on property. In private correspondence and in other contexts not conducive to propaganda, Republicans expressed genuine alarm at the implications of *Dred Scott.* "The Constitution of the United States is the paramount law of every State," Senator James Doolittle of Wisconsin pointed out, "and if that recognizes slaves as property, as horses are property, no State constitution or State law can abolish it." Noting that Scott had lived as a slave in Illinois for two years, the New York legislature denounced the doctrine that "a master may take his slave into a Free State without dissolving the relation of master and slave. . . . [This] will bring slavery within our borders, against our will, with all its unhallowed, demoralizing, and blighting influences."[23]

The legislature's concern was not abstract. Pending in the New York courts was a case concerning a slaveholder's right to retain ownership of his slaves while in transit through a free state. *Lemmon v. The People* had originated in 1852 when a New York judge upheld the freedom of

---

21. *Ibid.*, II, 461–62, 467, III, 27, 230–31.
22. Douglas in *ibid.*, III, 53, 267–68. For historians' comments see especially Nevins, *Emergence*, I, 362, and James G. Randall, *Lincoln the President*, 4 vols. (New York, 1945–55), I, 116.
23. *Washington Union*, Nov. 17, 1857; CG, 35 Cong., 1 Sess., 385; Nevins, *Emergence*, I, 86; *New York Assembly Documents*, 80th Session (1857), no. 201.

eight slaves who had left their Virginia owner while in New York City on their way to Texas. Most northern states had earlier granted slave-owners the right of transit or temporary sojourn with their slaves. But by the 1850s all except New Jersey and Illinois had laws on the books offering freedom to any slave brought by a master within their borders. The Dred Scott decision challenged the principle of these laws. Virginia therefore decided to take the Lemmon case to the highest New York court (which upheld the state law in 1860) and would undoubtedly have appealed it to Taney's Supreme Court had not secession intervened. The Lemmon case might well have become Lincoln's "next Dred Scott decision." Recent scholarship sustains Lincoln's apprehension that the Taney Court would have sanctioned "some form of slavery in the North."[24] Even the right of transit or temporary sojourn was, from the antislavery point of view, an ominous foot in the door. "If a man can hold a slave one day in a free state," asked a Republican newspaper, "why not one month, why not one year? Why could not his 'transit' be indefinitely lengthened, his 'visit' a practical permanency?"[25]

II

Thus in the context of *Dred Scott*, Lincoln's "warning that slavery might become lawful everywhere was . . . far from absurd." His attempt to identify Douglas with this proslavery conspiracy ("Stephen and Franklin and Roger and James") was part of Lincoln's campaign for the Senate in 1858.[26] During the Lecompton debate Douglas had said that he cared not whether slavery was voted down or up in Kansas—his concern was that Kansas have a fair vote. This "care not" policy, said Lincoln, had been prolific of evil, for it enabled the proponents of slavery to push forward their program of expansion without effective opposition. The only way to stop them was to elect Republicans "whose hearts are in the work—who *do care* for the result," who "consider slavery a moral,

24. Paul Finkelman, *An Imperfect Union: Slavery, Federalism, and Comity* (Chapel Hill, 1981), 323. This fine study provides a thorough analysis of the Lemmon case and its context. See also Fehrenbacher, *Dred Scott*, 444–45.
25. *Springfield Republican*, Oct. 12, 1857, quoted in Fehrenbacher, *Dred Scott*, 314.
26. Quotation from Don E. Fehrenbacher, *Prelude to Greatness: Lincoln in the 1850's* (Stanford, 1962), 123. Technically neither Lincoln nor Douglas was a "candidate" in this election, for state legislatures chose senators, and the Illinois election in 1858 was for members of the legislature. But given Douglas's national importance, and the Republican party's "nomination" of Lincoln for senator, the main focus of the legislative election was the senatorship.

social, and political wrong," who "will oppose . . . the modern Democratic idea that slavery is as good as freedom, and ought to have room for expansion all over the continent."[27]

This was the message that Lincoln carried to Illinois voters in dozens of speeches during that summer of '58. Douglas traversed the same territory branding Lincoln a Black Republican whose abolition doctrines would destroy the Union and flood Illinois with thousands of thick-lipped, bullet-headed, degenerate blacks. Lincoln "believes that the Almighty made the Negro equal to the white man," said Douglas at Springfield in July. "He thinks that the Negro is his brother. I do not think the Negro is any kin of mine at all. . . . This government . . . was made by white men, for the benefit of white men and their posterity, to be executed and managed by white men."[28]

Desiring to confront Douglas directly, Lincoln proposed a series of debates. Douglas agreed to seven confrontations in various parts of the state. These debates are deservedly the most famous in American history. They matched two powerful logicians and hard-hitting speakers, one of them nationally eminent and the other little known outside his region. To the seven prairie towns came thousands of farmers, workers, clerks, lawyers, and people from all walks of life to sit or stand outdoors for hours in sunshine or rain, heat or cold, dust or mud. The crowds participated in the debates by shouted questions, pointed comments, cheers, and groans. The stakes were higher than a senatorial election, higher even than the looming presidential contest of 1860, for the theme of the debates was nothing less than the future of slavery and the Union. Tariffs, banks, internal improvements, corruption, and other staples of American politics received not a word in these debates—the sole topic was slavery.[29]

27. CWL, II, 468, III, 92.
28. Paul M. Angle, ed., *Created Equal? The Complete Lincoln-Douglas Debates of 1858* (Chicago, 1958), 62, 60.
29. In each debate the opening speaker talked for one hour, his opponent responded for an hour and a half, and the first speaker closed for half an hour. Douglas and Lincoln alternated as opening speaker, Douglas opening and closing four of the seven debates. Because of the importance of the debates, they received wide coverage in the press. Stenographers (then called "phonographers") from one Republican and one Democratic newspaper recorded every word including crowd reactions. A verbatim publication of the debates in book form first appeared in 1860. There are three modern annotated editions of the debates: CWL, III, 1–325; Angle,

In the fashion of debaters, Douglas and Lincoln opened with slashing attacks designed to force the other man to spend his time defending vulnerable positions. A Republican journalist phrased this strategy in a letter of advice to one of Lincoln's associates: "When you see Abe at Freeport, for God's sake tell him to 'Charge Chester! charge!' . . . We must not be parrying all the while. We want the deadliest thrusts. Let us see blood follow any time he closes a sentence."[30] Lincoln's main thrust was the accusation that Douglas had departed from the position of the founding fathers, while the Republicans were upholding that position. Like the fathers, Republicans "insist that [slavery] should as far as may be, be treated as a wrong, and one of the methods of treating it as a wrong is to make provision that *it shall grow no larger*." Lincoln reiterated that the country could not exist forever half slave and half free; it had existed in that condition so far only because until 1854 most Americans shared the founders' faith that restricting slavery's growth would put it on the path to ultimate extinction. But Douglas not only "*looks to no end of the institution of slavery*," he looks to its "*perpetuity and nationalization*." He is thus "eradicating the light of reason and the love of liberty in this American people."[31]

In one respect Lincoln's celebrated Freeport question was a departure from this strategy of linking Douglas to the slave power. Was there any lawful way, Lincoln asked at Freeport, that the people of a territory could exclude slavery if they wished to do so? The point of the question, of course, was to nail the contradiction between *Dred Scott* and popular sovereignty. Folklore history has portrayed this question as the stone that slew Goliath. If Douglas answered No, he alienated Illinois voters and jeopardized his re-election to the Senate. If he answered Yes, he alienated the South and lost their support for the presidency in 1860. The problem with this thesis is that Douglas had already confronted the issue many times. Lincoln knew how he would answer the question: "He will instantly take ground that slavery can not actually exist in the territories, unless the people desire it, and so give it protective territorial legislation. If this offends the South he will let it offend them; as at all events he

ed., *Created Equal*; and Robert W. Johannsen, ed., *The Lincoln-Douglas Debates of 1858* (New York, 1965).

30. Charles H. Ray to Elihu B. Washburne, Aug. 23, 1858, quoted in Fehrenbacher, *Prelude to Greatness*, 123.

31. CWL, III, 313, 18, 29.

means to hold on to his chances in Illinois. . . . He cares nothing for the South—he knows he is already dead there" because of his opposition to Lecompton.[32] Lincoln asked the question anyway; Douglas answered as expected. His answer became famous in retrospect as the Freeport doctrine. It did play a role in prompting the southern demand for a territorial slave code—an issue that split the Democratic party in 1860. But this would have happened anyway. Lincoln did not press the question in subsequent debates, for its tendency to highlight Douglas's differences from southern Democrats ran counter to Lincoln's effort to highlight their similarities.[33]

Douglas's counterattack smote Lincoln's house-divided metaphor. Why cannot the country continue to "exist divided into free and slave States?" asked Douglas. Whatever their personal sentiments toward slavery, the founding fathers "left each State perfectly free to do as it pleased on the subject." If the nation "cannot endure thus divided, then [Lincoln] must strive to make them all free or all slave, which will inevitably bring about a dissolution of the Union." To talk about ultimate extinction of slavery "is revolutionary and destructive of the existence of this Government." If it means anything, it means "warfare between the North and the South, to be carried on with ruthless vengeance, until the one section or the other shall be driven to the wall and become the victim of the rapacity of the other." No, said Douglas, "I would not endanger the perpetuity of this Union. I would not blot out the great inalienable rights of the white men for all the negroes that ever existed."[34]

Lincoln's inclusion of blacks among those "created equal" was a "monstrous heresy," said Douglas. "The signers of the Declaration had no reference to the negro . . . or any other inferior and degraded race, when they spoke of the equality of men." Did Thomas Jefferson "intend to say in that Declaration that his negro slaves, which he held and treated as property, were created his equals by Divine law, and that he was violating the law of God every day of his life by holding them as slaves? ('No, no.')"[35]

Douglas hit his stride in exploitation of the race issue. He considered it a sure winner in southern and central Illinois. The Negro "must al-

32. Lincoln to Henry Asbury, July 31, 1858, in CWL, II, 530.
33. For a good analysis of the Freeport question, see Fehrenbacher, Prelude to Greatness, 121–42.
34. CWL, III, 8, 35, 111, 322.
35. Ibid., 113, 216.

ways occupy an inferior position," shouted Douglas to cheering partisans. "Are you in favor of conferring upon the negro the rights and privileges of citizenship? ('No, no.') Do you desire to strike out of our State Constitution that clause which keeps slaves and free negroes out of the State . . . in order that when Missouri abolishes slavery she can send one hundred thousand emancipated slaves into Illinois, to become citizens and voters on an equality with yourselves? ('Never,' 'no.') . . . If you desire to allow them to come into the State and settle with the white man, if you desire them to vote . . . then support Mr. Lincoln and the Black Republican party, who are in favor of the citizenship of the negro. ('Never, never.')"[36]

How did Douglas know that Lincoln favored these things? Black speakers were campaigning for him in the Yankee districts of northern Illinois, showing "how much interest our colored brethren [feel] in the success of their brother Abe. (Renewed laughter.)" Why, in Freeport Douglas saw a handsome carriage drive up to a Lincoln meeting. "A beautiful young lady was sitting on the box seat, whilst Fred. Douglass and her mother reclined inside, and the owner of the carriage acted as driver. . . . If you, Black Republicans, think that the negro ought to be on a social equality with your wives and daughters, whilst you drive the team, you have a perfect right to do so. . . . Those of you who believe that the negro is your equal . . . of course will vote for Mr. Lincoln. ('Down with the negro,' no, no, &c.)"[37]

Douglas's harping on this theme exasperated Lincoln. "Negro equality! Fudge!!" he wrote privately. "How long . . . shall there continue knaves to vend, and fools to gulp, so low a piece of demagougeism?" But try as he might, Lincoln could not ignore the issue. As he emerged from his hotel for the fourth debate at Charleston in southern Illinois, a man asked him if he was "really in favor of producing a perfect equality between negroes and white people." Placed on the defensive, Lincoln responded defensively. "Anything that argues me into his idea of a perfect social and political equality," complained Lincoln of Douglas's innuendoes, "is but a specious and fantastic arrangement of words, by

36. *Ibid.*, 9.
37. *Ibid.*, 171, 55–56. Douglas managed to win back the confidence of some southerners with his racist rhetoric. After reading Douglas's speeches, a friend of Alexander Stephens wrote that "Douglas, with all his past objectionable conduct . . . is *sound on niggers.* . . . I prefer him . . . to a crazy fanatic [Lincoln], who openly proclaims the equality of the white and black races." J. Henly Smith to Alexander Stephens, Aug. 3, 1858, quoted in Fehrenbacher, *Dred Scott Case,* 497.

which a man can prove a horse chestnut to be a chestnut horse." Lincoln admitted that he believed black people "entitled to all the natural rights enumerated in the Declaration of Independence, the right to life, liberty, and the pursuit of happiness." But "I do not understand that because I do not want a negro woman for a slave I must necessarily have her for a wife. (Cheers and laughter)" So that his horse chestnut should no longer be mistaken for a chestnut horse, Lincoln spelled out his position with clarity: "I am not, nor ever have been in favor of bringing about in any way the social and political equality of the white and black races, (applause)—that I am not nor ever have been in favor of making voters or jurors of negroes, nor of qualifying them to hold office, nor to intermarry with white people; and I will say in addition to this that there is a physical difference between the races which I believe will for ever forbid the two races living together on terms of social and political equality."[38]

So far Lincoln would go in concession to the prejudices of most Illinois voters. But no farther. "Let us discard all this quibbling about this man and the other man—this race and that race and the other race being inferior," he said in Chicago. Instead let us "unite as one people throughout this land, until we shall once more stand up declaring that all men are created equal." Whether or not the black man was equal to the white man in mental or moral endowment, "in the right to eat the bread, without leave of anybody else, which his own hand earns, *he is my equal and the equal of Judge Douglas, and the equal of every living man*. (Great applause.)" As for political rights, racial intermarriage, and the like, these were matters for the state legislature, "and as Judge Douglas seems to be in constant horror that some such danger is rapidly approaching, I propose as the best means to prevent it that the Judge be kept at home and placed in the State Legislature where he can fight the measures. (Uproarious laughter and applause.)"[39]

Despite Lincoln's wit, Douglas scored points on this issue. The Little Giant also backed Lincoln into a corner on the matter of slavery's "ultimate extinction." More than once Lincoln had said: "I have no purpose directly or indirectly to interfere with the institution of slavery in the States where it exists." "Well, if he is not in favor of that," asked Douglas, "how does he expect to bring slavery in a course of ultimate extinction? ('Hit him again.')" With such obfuscatory rhetoric, charged

38. *CWL*, III, 399, 16, 145–46.
39. *Ibid.*, II, 501, III, 16, 146.

Douglas, the Black Republicans tried to conceal their purpose to attack slavery and break up the Union. Lincoln replied that when he spoke of *ultimate* extinction, he meant just that. "I do not mean . . . it will be in a day, nor in a year, nor in two years. I do not suppose that in the most peaceful way ultimate extinction would occur in less than a hundred years at the least; but that it will occur in the best way for both races in God's good time, I have no doubt. (Applause.)" Like the abolitionists, Lincoln refused to be drawn into discussion of a "plan" for ending slavery. He hoped that southerners would once again come to regard bondage as an evil, just as Washington, Jefferson, and the other founders had regarded it. And just as they had limited its expansion as a first step toward ending the evil, "I have no doubt that it *would* become extinct, for all time to come, if we but re-adopted the policy of the fathers."[40]

In any case the questions of "a perfect social and political equality . . . upon which Judge Douglas has tried to force the controversy . . . are false issues," said Lincoln in the concluding debate. The true issue was the morality and future of slavery. "That is the issue that will continue in this country when these poor tongues of Judge Douglas and myself shall be silent. It is the eternal struggle between these two principles—right and wrong—throughout the world . . . from the beginning of time. . . . The one is the common right of humanity and the other the divine right of kings. . . . No matter in what shape it comes, whether from a king who seeks to bestride the people of his own nation and live by the fruit of their labor, or from one race of men as an apology for enslaving another race, it is the same tyrannical principle."[41]

In the judgment of history—or at least of most historians—Lincoln "won" the debates. The judgment of Illinois voters in 1858 is more difficult to discover. Republican and Democratic candidates for the legislature won virtually the same number of votes statewide—125,000 for each party.[42] Democrats carried all but three of the fifty-four southern counties and Republicans all but six of the forty-eight northern counties. Because the legislature had not been reapportioned to reflect the faster growth of northern counties in the 1850s, and because eight of

40. *Ibid.*, III, 16, 165, 323, 181, 117.
41. *Ibid.*, 312, 315.
42. Republican candidates won about 125,000 votes, Douglas Democrats 121,000, and anti-Douglas Buchanan Democrats 5,000. *Tribune Almanac*, 1859, pp. 60–61.

the thirteen holdover senators not up for election were Democrats, that party had a majority of fifty-four to forty-six in the next legislature and elected Douglas. It was a significant triumph for the Little Giant. He confirmed his standing as leader of his party in the North and its strongest candidate for the next presidential nomination. For Lincoln the election was a victory in defeat. He had battled the famous Douglas on at least even terms, clarified the issues between Republicans and northern Democrats more sharply than ever, and emerged as a Republican spokesman of national stature.[43]

Democrats also carried five of the nine congressional districts in Illinois. That made the state one of the few northern bright spots for the party in 1858. Elsewhere Democrats suffered almost as great a debacle as in 1854. In the next House of Representatives the number of northern Democrats would drop from fifty-three to thirty-two. In the four lower-North states carried by Buchanan in 1856 (Pennsylvania, Indiana, Illinois, and New Jersey) the party balance shifted in 1858 from twenty-nine Democratic and twenty-one Republican congressmen to sixteen Democrats and thirty-four Republicans. The Republican share of the vote in these four states jumped from 35 percent in 1856 (when the American party was in the field) to 52 percent in 1858. Buchanan had invited a few friends to an elegant White House dinner on election night. As telegrams bearing tidings of the returns from Pennsylvania came in, "we had a merry time of it," wrote the president next day, "laughing among other things over our crushing defeat. It is so great that it is almost absurd."[44]

Lecompton and *Dred Scott* accounted for much of this Republican gain. Once again, victories by the "slave power" had produced a backlash that strengthened its deadliest enemies in the North. Other issues also worked in favor of the Republicans. The disappearance of the American party in the North pushed most of the remaining nativists into Republican ranks because they continued to perceive Democrats as the party of Romanism. In manufacturing regions the Democratic tariff policy and the depression following the Panic of 1857 intensified voter backlash. Republicans also benefited from continued southern opposi-

---

43. The best analysis of the election is in Fehrenbacher, *Prelude to Greatness*, 114–20.
44. *Tribune Almanac*, 1860, p. 18; Fehrenbacher, *Dred Scott Case*, 563–64; Buchanan to Harriet Lane, Oct. 15, 1858, quoted in Nevins, *Emergence*, I, 400.

tion to homestead legislation and to federal aid for construction of a transcontinental railroad.

III

A dozen years of growth and prosperity came to a jolting halt in 1857–58.[45] The Panic of 1857 had both foreign and domestic roots. The Crimean War (1854–56) had cut off Russian grain from the European market. American exports mushroomed to meet the need. This intensified a surge of speculation in western lands. The decade-long expansion of all economic indices had also produced rapid rises in the prices of stocks and bonds. From 1848 to 1856 the number of banks increased 50 percent and their notes, loans, and deposits doubled. Railroad mileage and capital grew threefold from 1850 to 1857. Textile mills, foundries, and factories ran at full tilt to meet an apparently insatiable demand. California gold continued to pump millions of dollars monthly into the economy. By 1856, however, pessimists began to discern some cracks in this economic structure. Much of the capital invested in American railroads, insurance companies, and banks came from Europe, especially Britain. The Crimean War plus simultaneous British and French colonial ventures in the Far East drained specie from the banks of those countries. This brought a doubling and even tripling of interest rates in Britain and France, causing European investors to sell lower-yielding American securities to reinvest at home. The resulting decline in the prices of some American stocks and bonds in 1856–57 in turn reduced the assets of American banks holding these securities. Meanwhile British banks increased the ratio of reserves to liabilities, causing some American banks to do the same. And a buildup of unsold inventories caused several American textile mills to shut down temporarily.[46]

By the summer of 1857 the combination of speculative fever in some parts of the economy and ominous cutbacks in others created a climate of nervous apprehension. "What can be the end of all this but another

---

45. There had been a Wall Street panic and a brief recession in the winter of 1854–55.

46. This analysis of the background of the Panic of 1857 is based on George W. Van Vleck, *The Panic of 1857: An Analytical Study* (New York, 1943); Nevins, *Emergence*, I, 176–97; and Peter Temin, "The Panic of 1857," *Intermountain Economic Review*, 6 (Spring 1975), 1–12.

general collapse like that of 1837?" asked the financial writer of the *New York Herald*. "The same premonitory symptoms that prevailed in 1835–36 prevail in 1857 in a tenfold degree . . . paper bubbles of all descriptions, a general scramble for western lands and town and city sites, millions of dollars, made or borrowed, expended in fine houses and gaudy furniture. . . . That a storm is brewing on the commercial horizon there can be no doubt."[47]

Given this mood, any financial tremor was likely to become an earthquake through the mechanism of self-fulfilling prophecy. On August 24 came the tremor: the New York branch of an Ohio investment house suspended payments because the cashier had embezzled its funds. The crisis of confidence set off by this event reverberated through the economy. Financial markets in most parts of the country were now connected by telegraph; the novelty of instant communication charged these markets with a volatility that caused a rumor in one region to become a crisis somewhere else. Depositors made runs on banks, which had to call in loans to obtain specie. This caused over-extended speculators and entrepreneurs to go under. A wave of panic selling hit Wall Street. As the ripple of these failures began to spread through the country in September, a ship carrying $2 million in gold from California went to the bottom in a storm. By mid-October all but a handful of the nation's banks had suspended specie payments. Factories shut down; business failures multiplied; railroads went bankrupt; construction halted; crop prices plummeted; the intricate structure of land speculation collapsed like a house of cards; immigration dropped in 1858 to its lowest level in thirteen years; imports fell off; and the federal treasury (whose revenues came mainly from tariffs and land sales) ran a deficit for the first time in a decade. Men and women by hundreds of thousands lost their jobs and others went on short time or took wage cuts as the winter of 1857–58 came on.

Remembering that some of the European revolutions in 1848 (which had been preceded by a financial downturn) had taken a radical turn toward class warfare, Americans wondered if they would experience similar events. Unemployed workers in several cities marched in demonstrations carrying banners demanding work or bread. In New York a large crowd broke into the shops of flour merchants. On November 10 a mob gathered in Wall Street and threatened forced entry into the U.S. cus-

47. *New York Herald*, June 27, July 18, 1857, quoted in Van Vleck, *Panic of 1857*, 60, 63.

toms house and subtreasury whose vaults contained $20 million. Soldiers and marines dispersed them, but unrest persisted through the winter, causing more than one anxious citizen to apprehend that "a nightmare broods over society."[48]

Though often militant in rhetoric, however, these demonstrations generated little violence. No one was killed and few were injured—in sharp contrast to the Know-Nothing riots a few years earlier and the ongoing guerrilla warfare in Kansas. Relief and public works in northern cities helped alleviate hardships over the winter. One of the most striking consequences of the depression was a religious revival that brought people of all occupations together in prayer meetings at which they contemplated God's punishment for the sins of greed and high living that had caused the crash.[49]

Perhaps the Lord took pity. The depression of 1857–58 turned out to be milder and shorter than expected. California gold came east in large quantities during the fall and winter. Banks in New York resumed specie payments by December 1857, and those elsewhere followed suit during the next few months. The stock market rebounded in the spring of 1858. Factories reopened, railroad construction resumed its rapid pace, and unemployment declined. By early 1859 recovery was almost complete. Trade unions, which had all but disappeared under impact of the depression, revived in 1859 and began a series of strikes to recoup pre-depression wages. In February 1860 the shoemakers of Lynn, Massachusetts, went out in what became the largest strike in American history to that time, eventually involving 20,000 workers in the New England shoe industry.

The political effects of the depression may have equaled its economic consequences. It took time, however, for political crosscurrents to settle into a pattern that benefited Republicans. The initial tendency to blame banks for the panic seemed to give Democrats an opportunity to capitalize on their traditional anti-bank posture. They did reap some political profits in the Old Northwest. But elsewhere the issue had lost much of its old partisan salience because Democrats had become almost as pro-bank as the opposition. Republicans of Whig origin pointed the finger of blame at the absence of a national bank to ride herd over

48. Quoted in James L. Huston, "A Political Response to Industrialism: The Republican Embrace of Protectionist Labor Doctrine," *JAH*, 70 (1983), 49.
49. Timothy L. Smith, *Revivalism and Social Reform: American Protestantism on the Eve of the Civil War* (New York, 1957), ch. 4.

irresponsible practices of state banks. Several Republicans called for revival of something like the Second Bank of the United States from the
grave in which Andrew Jackson had buried it two decades earlier. Democratic tariff policies also came under indictment from Whiggish Republicans.

Although no modern historian has attributed the depression of 1857–
58 to low tariffs, Horace Greeley and his fellow protectionists did so.
The Walker Tariff enacted by Democrats in 1846 had remained in effect until 1857. It had been mildly protectionist with average duties of
about 20 percent, the lowest since 1824. Another Democratic tariff passed
in March 1857 lowered duties still further and enlarged the free list.
The depression began a few months later. Greeley not surprisingly saw
a causal connection. "No truth of mathematics," intoned the *New York
Tribune*, "is more clearly demonstrable than that the ruin about us is
fundamentally attributable to the destruction of the Protective Tariff."[50]

Republicans made tariff revision one of their priorities, especially in
Pennsylvania, where recovery of the iron industry lagged behind other
sectors. The argument that the lower 1857 duties had enabled British
industry to undersell American railroad iron carried great weight among
workers as well as ironmasters. Indeed, Republicans pitched their strongest
tariff appeals to labor, which had more votes than management. "We
demand that American laborers shall be protected against the pauper
labor of Europe," they declared. A higher tariff would "give employment to thousands of mechanics, artisans, laborers, who have languished for months in unwilling idleness." Such arguments seemed to
work, for in the 1858 elections Republicans scored large gains in Pennsylvania industrial districts.[51]

The tariff issue provides an illustration of how political fallout from
the depression exacerbated sectional tensions. In each of three congressional sessions between the Panic and the election of 1860, a coalition
of Republicans and protectionist Democrats tried to adjust the 1857 duties slightly upward. Every time an almost solid South combined with
half or more of the northern Democrats to defeat them. With an econ-

50. *New York Tribune*, Oct. 22, 1857, quoted in Philip S. Foner, *Business and Slavery: The New York Merchants and the Irrepressible Conflict* (Chapel Hill, 1941),
142n.
51. *Lebanon* (Pa.) *Courier*, quoted in Huston, "A Political Response to Industrialism,"
loc. cit., 53; *New York Tribune*, quoted in Van Vleck, *Panic of 1857*, 104; *Tribune
Almanac*, 1859, pp. 52–53.

omy based on the export of raw materials and the import of manufactured goods, southerners had little interest in raising the prices of what
they bought in order to subsidize profits and wages in the North. Thus
Congress remained, in the view of one bitter Republican, "shamelessly
prostituted, in a base subserviency to the Slave Power." A Pennsylvanian discerned a logical connection between the South's support for the
Lecompton constitution and its opposition to tariff adjustment: "popular
rights disregarded in Kansas; free industry destroyed in the States."[52]

Sectional alignments were even more clear on three land-grant measures of the 1850s: a homestead act, a Pacific railroad act, and grants to
states for the establishment of agricultural and mechanical colleges. The
idea of using the federal government's vast patrimony of land for these
purposes had been around for a decade or more. All three measures
took on added impetus from the depression of 1857–58. Free land would
help farmers ruined by the Panic get a new start. According to the theories of labor reformer George Henry Evans, homesteads would also
give unemployed workingmen an opportunity to begin new lives as independent landowners and raise the wages of laborers who remained
behind. Construction of a transcontinental railroad would tap the wealth
of the West, bind the country together, provide employment, and increase the prosperity of all regions. Agricultural and mechanical colleges
would make higher education available to farmers and skilled workingmen. All three measures reflected the Whig ideology of a harmony of
interests between capital and labor, which would benefit mutually from
economic growth and improved education. Along with a tariff to protect
American workers and entrepreneurs, these land-grant measures became
the new Republican free-labor version of Henry Clay's venerable American System. Republicans could count on more northern Democratic
support for the land bills than for the tariff, especially from Douglas
Democrats in the Old Northwest.

But most southerners opposed these measures. The homestead act
would fill up the West with Yankee settlers hostile to slavery. "Better
for us," thundered a Mississippian, "that these territories should remain
a waste, a howling wilderness, trod only by red hunters than be so settled."[53] Southerners also had little interest in using the public lands to

52. Foner, *Business and Slavery*, 141; Huston, "A Political Response to Industrialism,"
    loc. cit., 53.
53. *Columbus* (Miss.) *Democrat*, quoted in Avery O. Craven, *An Historian and the
    Civil War* (Chicago, 1964), 38.

establish schools most of whose students would be Yankees. Nor did they have much stake in the construction of a Pacific railroad with an expected eastern terminus at St. Louis or Chicago. Southern senators provided most of the votes in 1858 to postpone consideration of all three bills. At the next session of Congress a series of amendments to the railroad bill whittled it down to a meaningless provision for preliminary bids. In February 1859 Republicans and two-thirds of the northern Democrats in the House passed a homestead act. Vice-President Breck-inridge of Kentucky broke a tie vote in the Senate to defeat it. But enough northern Democrats joined Republicans in both Senate and House to pass the land-grant college act. Buchanan paid his debts to southern Democrats by vetoing it.

A somewhat different path led to a similar outcome in the first session of the 36th Congress (1859–60), elected in 1858 and containing more Republicans than its predecessor. Disagreement over a northern *vs.* a southern route once again killed the Pacific railroad bill. The South also continued to block passage of a land-grant college act over Buchanan's veto. But a homestead act reached the president's desk. The House had passed it by a vote in which 114 of the 115 Ayes came from northern members and 64 of the 65 Nays from southern members. After much parliamentary maneuvering the Senate passed a modified version of the bill. A conference committee worked out a compromise, but Buchanan vetoed it as expected. Southern opposition in the Senate blocked an attempt to pass it over his veto.[54]

The southern checkmate of tariff, homestead, Pacific railroad, and land-grant college acts provided the Republicans with vote-winning issues for 1860. During the effort to pass the homestead bill in 1859, Republicans tangled with Democrats over another measure that would also become an issue in 1860—the annexation of Cuba. Manifest Destiny was a cause that united most Democrats across sectional lines. Whatever they thought of slavery in Kansas, they agreed on the desirability of annexing Cuba with its 400,000 slaves. Both Douglas and Buchanan spoke in glowing terms of Cuba; the signs seemed to point to a rapprochement of warring Democratic factions, with Cuba as the glue to piece them together. In his December 1858 message to Congress,

54. This account of the fate of these three measures in the 35th and the 36th Congress has been drawn mainly from Roy F. Nichols, *The Disruption of American Democracy* (New York, 1948), 192, 231–33; and from Nevins, *Emergence*, I, 444–55, II, 188–95.

Buchanan called for new negotiations with Spain to purchase Cuba. Senator John Slidell of Louisiana introduced a bill to appropriate $30 million for a down payment. The foreign relations committee approved it in February 1859. For the next two weeks the $30 million bill was the main topic of Senate debate. Republicans rang all the changes of the slave power conspiracy, prompting southerners to reply in kind while northern Democrats kept a low profile. Republican strategy was to delay the bill until adjournment on March 4, 1859. At the same time they hoped to bring the homestead bill, already passed by the House, to a vote. Democrats refused to allow this unless Republicans permitted a vote on Cuba. The question, said the irreverent Ben Wade of Ohio, was "shall we give niggers to the niggerless, or land to the landless?"[55] In the end the Senate did neither, so each party prepared to take the issues to the voters in 1860.

Meanwhile a clash between Douglas and southern Democrats over the issue of a federal slave code for territories had reopened the party's Lecompton wounds. The Senate Democratic caucus fired the first round by removing Douglas from his chairmanship of the committee on territories. Then on February 23, 1859, southern senators lashed out at Douglas in language usually reserved for Black Republicans. The Little Giant's sin was an assertion that he would never vote for a slave code to enforce bondage in a territory against the will of a majority living there. Popular sovereignty, said Jefferson Davis, who led the attack on Douglas, was "full of heresy." A refusal to override it would make Congress "faithless to the trust they hold at the hands of the people of the States." "We are not . . . to be cheated," the Mississippian declared, by men who "seek to build up a political reputation by catering to the prejudice of a majority to exclude the property of a minority." For such men, said Davis as he looked Douglas in the eye, the South had nothing but "scorn and indignation."[56]

This debate registered the rise in rhetorical temperature during the late 1850s. Southern aggressiveness was bolstered by self-confidence growing out of the Panic of 1857. The depression fell lightly on the South. Cotton and tobacco prices dipped only briefly before returning to their high pre-Panic levels. The South's export economy seemed insulated from domestic downturns. This produced a good deal of boasting below the Potomac, along with expressions of mock solicitude for

55. CG, 35 Cong., 2 Sess., 1354.
56. Ibid., 1247, 1248, 1255, 1257.

the suffering of unemployed wage slaves in the North. "Who can doubt, that has looked at recent events, that cotton is supreme?" asked James Hammond of South Carolina in his celebrated King Cotton speech to the Senate on March 4, 1858. "When the abuse of credit had destroyed credit and annihilated confidence; when thousands of the strongest commercial houses in the world were coming down . . . when you came to a dead lock, and revolutions were threatened, what brought you up? . . . We have poured in upon you one million six hundred thousand bales of cotton just at the moment to save you from destruction. . . . We have sold it for $65,000,000, and saved you." Slavery demonstrated the superiority of southern civilization, continued Hammond. "In all social systems there must be a class to do the menial duties, to perform the drudgery of life. . . . It constitutes the very mud-sill of society. . . . Such a class you must have, or you would not have that other class which leads progress, civilization, and refinement. . . . Your whole hireling class of manual laborers and 'operatives,' as you call them, are essentially slaves. The difference between us is, that our slaves are hired for life and well compensated . . . yours are hired by the day, not cared for, and scantily compensated."[57]

This mudsill theme was becoming increasingly visible in southern propaganda. The most extreme expression of it occurred in the writings of George Fitzhugh. A frayed-at-the-elbows scion of a Virginia First Family, Fitzhugh wrote prolifically about "the failure of free society." In 1854 and 1857 he gathered his essays into books entitled *Sociology for the South* and *Cannibals All!* The latter was published a few weeks before the Panic of 1857 and seemed almost to predict it. Free labor under capitalism was a war of each against all, wrote Fitzhugh, a sort of social cannibalism. "Slavery is the natural and normal condition of society," he maintained. "The situation of the North is abnormal and anomalous." To bestow "upon men equality of rights, is but giving license to the strong to oppress the weak" because "capital exercises a more perfect compulsion over free laborers than human masters over slaves; for free laborers must at all times work or starve, and slaves are supported whether they work or not." Therefore "we slaveholders say you must recur to domestic slavery, the oldest, the best, the most common form of Socialism" as well as "the natural and normal condition of the laboring men, white or black."[58]

57. *Selections from the Letters and Speeches of the Hon. James H. Hammond, of South Carolina* (New York, 1866), 317–19.
58. Fitzhugh, *Cannibals All! or, Slaves Without Masters*, ed. C. Vann Woodward

Fitzhugh's ideas flowed a bit outside the mainstream of the proslavery argument, which distinguished sharply between free whites and slave blacks and assigned an infinite superiority to the former *because* they were white. But while Fitzhugh's notions were eccentric they were not unique. Some proslavery proponents drew a distinction between southern yeomen and northern workers or farmers. Southerners were superior because they lived in a slave society. Yankees *were* perhaps fit only to be slaves. To explain this, southerners invented a genealogy that portrayed Yankees as descendants of the medieval Anglo-Saxons and southerners as descendants of their Norman conquerors. These divergent bloodlines had coursed through the veins of the Puritans who settled New England and the Cavaliers who colonized Virginia. "The Southern people," concluded an article in the *Southern Literary Messenger*, "come of that race . . . recognized as Cavaliers . . . directly descended from the Norman Barons of William the Conqueror, a race distinguished in its earliest history for its warlike and fearless character, a race in all times since renowned for its gallantry, chivalry, honor, gentleness, and intellect."[59] If matters came to a fight, therefore, one Norman southerner could doubtless lick ten of those menial Saxon Yankees.

Whether or not southern superiority resulted from "the difference of race between the Northern people and the Southern people," as the *Southern Literary Messenger* would have it, the vaunted virtues of a free-labor society were a sham. "The great evil of Northern *free* society," insisted a South Carolina journal, "is that it is burdened with a *servile class of mechanics and laborers*, unfit for self-government, yet clothed with the attributes and powers of citizens." A Georgia newspaper was even more emphatic in its distaste. "Free Society! we sicken at the name. What is it but a conglomeration of greasy mechanics, filthy operatives, small-fisted farmers, and moon-struck theorists? . . . The prevailing class one meets with [in the North] is that of mechanics struggling to be genteel, and small farmers who do their own drudgery, and yet are hardly fit for association with a Southern gentleman's body servant."[60]

(Cambridge, Mass., 1960), 40, 32, 31; Fitzhugh, *Sociology for the South*, in Eric L. McKitrick, ed., *Slavery Defended: The View of the Old South* (Englewood Cliffs, N.J., 1963), 38; article by Fitzhugh in *Richmond Enquirer*, and extract from *Sociology for the South*, in Harvey Wish, ed., *Ante-Bellum: Writings of George Fitzhugh and Hinton Rowan Helper on Slavery* (New York, 1960), 9, 85.

59. *Southern Literary Messenger*, 30 (June 1860), 401-9.
60. South Carolina newspaper quoted in Nevins, *Ordeal*, II, 498; *Muscogee Herald*, quoted in *New York Tribune*, Sept. 10, 1856.

Northern newspapers picked up and reprinted such articles. Yankees did not seem to appreciate southern sociology. Sometimes the response was good-humored, as demonstrated by a banner at one of the Lincoln-Douglas debates: "SMALL-FISTED FARMERS, MUD SILLS OF SOCIETY, GREASY MECHANICS, FOR A. LINCOLN." Other reactions were angrier and some-times unprintable. No doubt some of the soldiers who marched through Georgia and South Carolina with Sherman a few years later had read these descriptions of themselves as greasy mechanics and servile farmers.

In any event, northerners gave as good as they got in this warfare of barbs and insults. In a famous campaign speech of 1858, William H. Seward derided the southern doctrine that "labor in every society, by whomsoever performed, is necessarily unintellectual, groveling, and base." The idea had produced the backwardness of the South, said Seward, the illiteracy of its masses, the dependent colonial status of its economy. In contrast "the free-labor system educates all alike, and by opening all the fields of industrial employment to . . . all classes of men . . . brings into the highest possible activity all the physical, moral and social energies of the whole State." A collision between these two systems impended, "an irrepressible conflict between opposing and enduring forces, and it means that the United States must and will . . . become either entirely a slave-holding nation, or entirely a free-labor nation."[61]

Southerners claimed that free labor was prone to unrest and strikes. Of course it was, said Abraham Lincoln during a speaking tour of New England in March 1860 that coincided with the shoemakers' strike. "*I am glad to see that a system prevails in New England under which laborers* CAN *strike* when they want to (Cheers). . . . I *like* the system which lets a man quit when he wants to, and wish it might prevail everywhere. (Tremendous applause.)" The glory of free labor, said Lincoln, lay in its open competition for upward mobility, a competition in which most Americans finished ahead of where they started in life. "I want every man to have the chance—and I believe a black man is en-titled to it—in which he *can* better his condition." That was the signif-icance of the irrepressible conflict and of the house divided, concluded Lincoln, for if the South got its way "free labor that *can* strike will give way to slave labor that cannot!"[62]

The harshest indictment of the South's social system came from the

61. George E. Baker, ed., *The Works of William H. Seward*, 5 vols. (New York, 1853–84), IV, 289–92.
62. CWL, IV, 24, 8.

pen of a white southerner, Hinton Rowan Helper. A self-appointed spokesman for nonslaveholding whites, Helper was almost as eccentric in his own way as George Fitzhugh. Of North Carolina yeoman stock, he had gone to California in the gold rush to make his fortune but returned home disillusioned. Brooding on the conditions he perceived in the Carolina upcountry, Helper decided that "slavery lies at the root of all the shame, poverty, ignorance, tyranny and imbecility of the South." Echoing the free-soil argument, Helper maintained that slavery degraded all labor to the level of bond labor. Planters looked down their noses at nonslaveholders and refused to tax themselves to provide a decent school system. "Slavery is hostile to general education," Helper declared in his 1857 book *The Impending Crisis.* "Its very life, is in the ignorance and stolidity of the masses." Data from the 1850 census— which had alarmed the southern elite itself a few years earlier—furnished Helper information that, used selectively, enabled him to "prove" the superior productivity of a free-labor economy. The hay crop of the North alone, he claimed, was worth more than the boasted value of King Cotton and all other southern staples combined. Helper urged nonslaveholding whites to use their votes—three-fourths of the southern total—to overthrow "this entire system of oligarchical despotism" that had caused the South to "welter in the cesspool of ignorance and degradation. . . . Now is the time for them to assert their rights and liberties . . . [and] strike for Freedom in the South."[63]

If Helper had published this book in North Carolina or in Baltimore, where he was living when he completed it, *The Impending Crisis* might have languished in obscurity. Endless recitals of statistics dulled its cutting edge of criticism. But no southern publisher would touch it. So Helper lugged his manuscript to New York, where it was published in the summer of 1857. The *New York Tribune* recognized its value to Republicans and printed an eight-column review. This caused readers both North and South to take notice. Helper had probably overstated the disaffection of nonslaveholders from the southern social system. Outside the Appalachian highlands many of them were linked to the ruling class by ties of kinship, aspirations for slave ownership, or mutual dislike of Yankees and other outsiders. A caste system as well as a form of labor, slavery elevated all whites to the ruling caste and thereby reduced the potential for class conflict. However poor and illiterate some

63. From Helper, *Impending Crisis of the South,* as reprinted in Wish, ed., *Ante-Bellum,* 201, 253, 187, 181, 202.

whites may have been, they were still white. If the fear of "nigger equality" caused most of the northern working class to abhor Republicans even where blacks constituted only 2 or 3 percent of the population, this fear operated at much higher intensity where the proportion of blacks was tenfold greater. But while Helper exaggerated yeoman alienation in the South, so also did many slaveholders who felt a secret foreboding that nonslaveowners in regions like Helper's Carolina upcountry might turn against their regime. Several southern states therefore made it a crime to circulate *The Impending Crisis*. This of course only attracted more attention to the book. A Republican committee raised funds to subsidize an abridged edition in 1859 to be scattered far and wide as a campaign document. The abridgers ensured a spirited southern reaction by adding such captions as "The Stupid Masses of the South" and "Revolution—Peacefully if we can, Violently if we must."[64] Sixty-eight Republican congressmen endorsed a circular advertising the book.

One of them was John Sherman of Ohio, a moderate ex-Whig who later confessed that he had signed the endorsement without reading the book. Sherman's signature caused another donnybrook over the election of a speaker of the House when the 36th Congress convened in December 1859. Though Republicans outnumbered Democrats 113 to 101 in the House, upper-South Americans held the balance of power. Republicans nominated Sherman for speaker because he seemed temperate enough to attract a few votes from these former Whigs. But discovery of his endorsement of Helper's book set off an uproar that inhibited slave-state congressmen from voting for him. Through two months and forty-four ballots the House remained deadlocked on the edge of violence. Southerners denounced Helper, his book, and anyone connected with either as "a traitor, a renegade, an apostate . . . infamous . . . abominable . . . mendacious . . . incendiary, insurrectionary."[65] Most congressmen came armed to the sessions; the sole exception seemed to be a former New England clergyman who finally gave in and bought a pistol for self-defense. Partisans in the galleries also carried weapons. One southerner reported that a good many slave-state congressmen expected and wanted a shootout on the House floor: they "are willing to fight the question out, and to settle it right there. . . . I can't help

---

64. Potter, *Impending Crisis*, 387.
65. *Ibid.*; Avery O. Craven, *The Growth of Southern Nationalism 1848–1861* (Baton Rouge, 1953), 251; Edward Channing, *A History of the United States*, 6 vols. (New York, 1905–25), VI, 208n.

wishing the Union were dissolved and we had a Southern confederacy."
The governor of South Carolina informed one of his state's congressmen on December 20, 1859: "If . . . you upon consultation decide to
make the issue of force in Washington, write or telegraph me, and I
will have a regiment in or near Washington in the shortest possible
time."[66]

Through all this the Republicans supported Sherman, who consistently fell a few votes short of a majority. Democrats and Americans
tried several combinations; a Douglas Democrat could have been elected
with American support had not lower-South Democrats refused to support him. Southerners also rejected the precedent of suspending the
rules to allow a plurality to elect a speaker. Having organized the Senate
with sixteen of the twenty-two committees headed by southern chairmen, they were quite ready to keep the House unorganized until they
got their way. "Better the wheels of government should stop [and the
Union] demonstrate itself to be a failure and find an end," wrote southerners privately to each other, "than our principles, our honor be in-
fringed upon."[67] To prevent this outcome, Sherman finally withdrew,
and the Republicans nominated lackluster William Pennington of New
Jersey, who because of his support of the fugitive slave law a decade
earlier picked up enough border-state support to win the speakership.

Nothing yet had so dramatized the parting bonds of Union as this
struggle in the House. The hair-trigger temper of southerners is easier
to understand if one keeps in mind that the contest opened just three
days after John Brown was hanged in Virginia for trying to incite a slave
insurrection. Brown's raid at Harper's Ferry was an ominous beginning
to the fateful twelve months that culminated in the presidential election
of 1860.

66. Quotations from Nevins, *Emergence*, II, 121–22.
67. E. W. Marshall to William Porcher Miles, Jan. 20, 1860, in Steven A. Channing,
    Crisis of Fear: Secession in South Carolina (New York, 1970), 109; Edward C.
    Bullock to Clement C. Clay, Dec. 30, 1859, in J. Mills Thornton III, *Politics and
    Power in a Slave Society: Alabama, 1800–1860* (Baton Rouge, 1978), 390.

7

The Revolution of 1860

Like Dred Scott, John Brown lived the first fifty-odd years of his life in obscurity. Unlike Scott, he attained notoriety not through the law but by lawlessness. Except for a brief reappearance in the Kansas wars, however, Brown's activities for three years after 1856 were more mysterious than notorious. He made several trips east to raise money for the freedom fight in Kansas. As he shuttled back and forth, Brown evolved a plan to strike against slavery in its heartland. Like the Old Testament warriors he admired and resembled, he yearned to carry the war into Babylon. He studied books on guerrilla warfare and on slave revolts. Fascinated by the ability of small bands to hold off larger forces in mountainous terrain, Brown conceived the idea of a raid into the Appalachian foothills of Virginia. From there he would move southward along the mountains attracting slaves to his banner. In May 1858 Brown journeyed with eleven white followers to a community of former slaves in Chatham, Canada. Thirty-four blacks met secretly with Brown's group to adopt a "provisional constitution" for the republic of liberated slaves to be established in the mountains. The delegates elected Brown commander in chief of the army of this new nation.[1]

John Brown had never shared the commitment of most abolitionists

---

1. Stephen B. Oates, *To Purge This Land with Blood: A Biography of John Brown* (New York, 1970), 243–47.

to nonviolence. Not for him was the Christ-like martyrdom of Uncle Tom. Brown's God was the Jehovah who drowned Pharoah's mercenaries in the Red Sea; his Jesus was the angry man who drove money-changers from the temple. "Without shedding of blood there is no remission of sin," was his favorite New Testament passage (Hebrews 9:22). Bondage was "a most barbarous, unprovoked, and unjustifiable war" of masters against slaves, declared the preamble of Brown's Chatham constitution. Victory over these "thieves and murderers" could be won only by a revolution. "Talk! talk! talk!" exclaimed Brown in disgust after attending a meeting of the New England Anti-Slavery Society. "That will never free the slaves. What is needed is action—action." [2]

Events during the 1850s had converted some abolitionists to Brown's view. Violence had won the Southwest from Mexico; threats of violence by southerners in Congress had opened most of it to slavery. Armed filibusters tried to win Cuba and Central America for slavery. Closer to home, the fugitive slave law did more than anything else to discredit nonviolence. Before 1850 Frederick Douglass had been a pacifist. "Were I asked the question whether I would have my emancipation by the shedding of one single drop of blood," he said in the 1840s, "my answer would be in the negative. . . . The only well grounded hope of the slave for emancipation is the operation of moral force." But a month after enactment of the fugitive slave law he changed his tune and advocated "forcible resistance" to the law. "Slave-holders . . . tyrants and despots have no right to live," said Douglass now. "The only way to make the fugitive slave law a dead letter is to make half a dozen or more dead kidnappers." [3] One of Douglass's favorite sayings became, "who would be free must himself strike the blow." Like Frantz Fanon and other philosophers of anticolonial revolution a century later, Douglass came to believe that only through violence could the oppressed earn self-respect and the respect of their oppressors.

Many free soilers in Kansas also concluded that as the slave power had lived by the sword, it must die by the sword. In 1855 a New England Garrisonian, Charles Stearns, went to Lawrence, Kansas, to open a store. Having once served a term in jail rather than serve in the militia, Stearns retained his pacifist principles during his first months in the territory. But eventually he succumbed, as he explained in a letter

2. Ibid., 234, 271–72.
3. Carleton Mabee, *Black Freedom: The Nonviolent Abolitionists from 1830 through the Civil War* (New York, 1970), 291–95.

to his former mentor Garrison: "The cold-blooded murder, last night, of one of our best citizens, has decided me. I am sorry to deny the principles of Jesus Christ, after contending for them so long, but it is not for myself that I am going to fight. It is for God and the slaves." Another convert was Gerrit Smith, wealthy landowner and philanthropist of upstate New York. A vice president of the American Peace Society, Smith declared in 1856 that "hitherto I have opposed the bloody abolition of slavery." But when the slave power "begins to march its conquering bands into [Kansas] . . . I and ten thousand other peace men are not only ready to have it repulsed with violence, but pursued even unto death with violence."[4]

Smith became a member of the "Secret Six" who backed John Brown's scheme to invade the South. Like Smith, the other five were men of means and standing: Thomas Wentworth Higginson, Transcendental clergyman and writer; Theodore Parker, leading intellectual light of Unitarianism; Samuel Gridley Howe, a physician of international repute for his work with the blind and the deaf; George L. Stearns, a prosperous manufacturer; and Franklin B. Sanborn, a young educator and protégé of Emerson. The cause that bonded these men was their support for the free-state activists in Kansas. Most of them had also participated in resistance to the fugitive slave law. Parker headed the vigilance committee in Boston, while Higginson had led the abortive attack to free Anthony Burns in 1854. Several of the Secret Six had stood by in impotent rage while the police, militia, army, and marines had marched Burns back to slavery.

This scene burned in their memories. Their work for Kansas fanned the flames. It also brought them into contact with John Brown. They were ready for his message of action. Like Frederick Douglass, they had come to believe that the slaves could achieve manhood and liberation only by striking a blow themselves. Slavery "is destined, as it began in blood, so to end," wrote Higginson in 1858. "Never in history was there an oppressed people who were set free by others." Perhaps unconscious of the irony, the Secret Six (all white men) considered John Brown (also white) the ideal leader of the slaves in their strike for freedom. This grim, hatchet-faced old warrior impressed these descendants of Puritans as "a high-minded unselfish, belated Covenanter," a "Cromwellian Ironside introduced in the nineteenth century for a special purpose."[5]

4. Ibid., 319, 318.
5. Liberator, May 28, 1858; Oates, To Purge This Land, 237.

In 1858 Brown revealed to the Secret Six his plans for an invasion of the southern Appalachians. With varying degrees of enthusiasm or skepticism they agreed to support him. Stearns diverted funds intended for Kansas to the purchase of guns and pikes to arm the slaves that Brown expected to flock to his standard. Under an assumed name Brown rented a farm in Maryland across the Potomac River from Harper's Ferry, Virginia. He planned to seize the U. S. armory and arsenal there and distribute its arms to the slaves as they joined up with him. Brown's shock troops for this purpose ultimately consisted of five black men and seventeen whites, including three of his sons. This was a pitifully small "army" to invade slave territory and attack U.S. property.

Brown did try to attract more black recruits. In particular he urged his old friend Frederick Douglass to join him as a sort of liaison officer to the slaves. Brown met Douglass secretly in an old quarry near Chambersburg, Pennsylvania, in August 1859. "Come with me, Douglass," he said. "I want you for a special purpose. When I strike, the bees will begin to swarm, and I shall want you to help hive them." But Douglass refused. He was convinced that Brown had embarked on a suicidal mission, "an attack on the federal government" that "would array the whole country against us." Harper's Ferry was a "perfect steel-trap," said Douglass. Situated on a peninsula formed by the confluence of the Potomac and Shenandoah rivers, surrounded on all sides by commanding heights, it was indefensible against a counterattack. You will "never get out alive," Douglass warned Brown. The old warrior could not conceal his disappointment at Douglass's refusal. Other black recruits on whom Brown had relied also failed to show up. One of them wrote apologetically from Cleveland: "I am disgusted with myself and the whole Negro set, *God dam em!*"[6]

As summer turned to fall and additional recruits did not arrive, Brown decided to go with what he had. A sort of fatalism stole over him. He wrote a "Vindication of the Invasion" in the past tense as if it had already failed. When he finally moved, in mid-October, he did so without previous notice to the slaves he expected to join him, without rations, without having scouted any escape routes from Harper's Ferry, with no apparent idea of what to do after capturing the armory buildings. It was almost as if he knew that failure with its ensuing martyrdom

6. *Life and Times of Frederick Douglass, Written by Himself* (Collier Books ed., New York, 1962), 317–20; Benjamin Quarles, *Allies for Freedom: Blacks and John Brown* (New York, 1974), 80.

would do more to achieve his ultimate goal than any "success" could have done. In any event, that was how matters turned out.

Leaving three men to guard his base, Brown led the other eighteen into Harper's Ferry after dark on October 16. They quickly captured the armory complex defended by a single watchman. Brown sent a patrol into the countryside to pass the word among slaves and bring in several hostages, including a great grandnephew of George Washington. Having done this much, Brown sat down to wait—presumably for those black bees to swarm. But the only slaves to come in were a few brought by the patrol. Ironically, the first casualty was a free Negro baggage-master at the railroad station who was killed by Brown's bridge guard in the dark when he walked out on the trestle looking for the night watchman. Brown stopped the eastbound midnight train and held it for several hours, but then unaccountably let it proceed—to spread the alarm.

By midmorning on October 17, residents of Harper's Ferry were sniping at Brown's men while Virginia and Maryland militia converged on the town. During the afternoon eight of Brown's men (including two of his sons) and three townsmen were killed while seven of the raiders escaped (two of them were later captured). Brown retreated with his survivors and prisoners to the thick-walled fire-engine house, where he made a stand. During the night a company of U. S. marines arrived, commanded by two cavalry officers, Colonel Robert E. Lee and Lieutenant J. E. B. Stuart. After the militia had declined the honor of storming the engine house, Lee sent in the marines. They attacked with battering ram and bayonets, not firing a shot in order to avoid risk to the hostages. With the loss of one man the marines killed two raiders and captured the others including Brown, who was wounded by an officer's dress sword. Less than thirty-six hours after it started, John Brown's strange effort to free the slaves was over.

But the repercussions resounded for years. Passions ran high in Virginia, where mobs clamored for Brown's blood. To forestall a lynching the state of Virginia hastily indicted, tried, and convicted Brown of treason, murder, and fomenting insurrection. The judge sentenced him to hang one month later, on December 2. The other six captured raiders also received swift trials; four of them (including two blacks) were hanged on December 16 and the remaining two on March 16, 1860. The matter of Brown's northern supporters provoked great interest. Brown had left behind at the Maryland farmhouse a carpetbag full of documents and letters, some of them revealing his relationship with the Secret Six. Of those gentlemen, Parker was in Europe dying of tuberculosis, and

Higginson stood firm in Massachusetts, making no apology for his role and defying anyone to arrest him. But the other four beat an abject retreat. Stearns, Howe, and Sanborn fled to Canada, while Gerrit Smith suffered a breakdown and was confined for several weeks in the Utica insane asylum.

The Canadian exiles returned after Brown was hanged, but when the Senate established an investigating committee chaired by James Mason of Virginia, Sanborn again headed north to avoid testifying. From Canada he wrote Higginson imploring him "in case you are summoned . . . do not tell what you know to the enemies of the cause." Higginson expressed contempt toward such behavior. "Sanborn, is there no such thing as *honor* among confederates? . . . Can your clear moral sense . . . justify holding one's tongue . . . to save ourselves from all share in even the reprobation of society when the nobler man whom we have provoked on into danger is the scapegoat of that reprobation—& the gallows too?"[7]

Sanborn refused a summons from the Mason committee and resisted an attempt by the sergeant at arms of the Senate to arrest him. Massachusetts Chief Justice Lemuel Shaw voided the arrest warrant on a technicality. Howe and Stearns did go to Washington and faced the Mason committee. For some reason the committee never called Higginson— probably because by February 1860 Mason's resolve to uncover a northern conspiracy had weakened, and he did not want to give Higginson a national platform to proclaim his sentiments. Perhaps for the same reason, Howe and Stearns found the committee's questions "so unskillfully framed that they could, without literal falsehood," deny prior knowledge of Brown's plan to attack Harper's Ferry. A historian reading their testimony, however, will be convinced that they told several falsehoods. In any event, the Mason committee found no conspiracy, and no one except the men actually present with Brown at Harper's Ferry was ever indicted.[8]

Reaction in the South to Brown's raid brought to the surface a paradox that lay near the heart of slavery. On the one hand, many whites

7. Tilden G. Edelstein, *Strange Enthusiasm: A Life of Thomas Wentworth Higginson* (New Haven, 1968), 232, 226.
8. C. Vann Woodward, "John Brown's Private War," in Woodward, *The Burden of Southern History* (Baton Rouge, 1960), 51–52; Jeffrey S. Rossbach, *Ambivalent Conspirators: John Brown, the Secret Six, and a Theory of Slave Violence* (Philadelphia, 1982), 236–66.

lived in fear of slave insurrections. On the other, southern whites insisted that slaves were well treated and cheerful in their bondage. The news of Harper's Ferry sent an initial wave of shock and rage through the South, especially when newspapers reported that among the papers found in Brown's carpetbag were maps of seven southern states designating additional targets. For several weeks wild rumors circulated of black uprisings and of armed abolitionists marching from the North to aid them. By the time of Brown's execution, however, many in the South uttered a sigh of relief. Not only had the rumors proved false, but southerners also gradually realized that not a single slave had voluntarily joined Brown. The South's professed belief in the slaves' tranquility was right after all! It was only Yankee fanatics who wanted to stir up trouble.

The problem of those Yankee fanatics would soon cause southern opinion to evolve into a third phase of unreasoning fury, but not until the antislavery reaction to Harper's Ferry had itself gone through two phases. The first northern response was a kind of baffled reproach. The *Worcester Spy*, an antislavery paper in Higginson's home town, characterized the raid as "one of the rashest and maddest enterprises ever." To William Lloyd Garrison the raid, "though disinterested and well intended," seemed "misguided, wild, and apparently insane."[9] But such opinions soon changed into a perception of Brown as a martyr to a noble cause. His behavior during and after his trial had much to do with this transformation. In testimony, letters, interviews, and above all in his closing speech to the court he exhibited a dignity and fortitude that impressed even Virginia's Governor Henry Wise and the fire-eater Edmund Ruffin. Throughout the trial Brown insisted that his object had not been to incite insurrection but only to free slaves and arm them in self-defense. This was disingenuous, to say the least. In southern eyes it was also a distinction without a difference. In his closing speech prior to sentencing, Brown rose to a surpassing eloquence that has echoed down the years:

> I deny everything but what I have all along admitted: of a design on my part to free slaves. . . . Had I interfered in the manner which I admit . . . in behalf of the rich, the powerful, the intelligent, the so-called great . . . every man in this Court would have deemed it an act worthy of reward rather than punishment.

9. *Worcester Spy*, Oct. 20, 27, 1859, quoted in Edelstein, *Strange Enthusiasm*, 222; *Liberator*, Oct. 21, 1859.

This Court acknowledges, too, as I suppose, the validity of the law of God. I see a book kissed, which I suppose to be the Bible, or at least the New Testament, which teaches me that all things whatsoever I would that men should do to me, I should do even so to them. It teaches me, further, to remember them that are in bonds as bound with them. I endeavored to act up to that instruction. . . . Now, if it is deemed necessary that I should forfeit my life for the furtherance of the ends of justice, and mingle my blood further with the blood of my children and with the blood of millions in this slave country whose rights are disregarded by wicked, cruel, and unjust enactments, I say, let it be done.[10]

These words moved Theodore Parker to pronounce Brown "not only a martyr . . . but also a SAINT." They inspired Ralph Waldo Emerson to prophesy that the old warrior would "make the gallows as glorious as the cross."[11] Brown understood his martyr role, and cultivated it. "I have been *whipped* as the saying is," he wrote his wife, "but am sure I can recover all the lost capital occasioned by that disaster; by only hanging a few moments by the neck; and I feel quite determined to make the utmost possible out of a defeat." Like Christ, to whom Brown unabashedly compared himself, he would accomplish in death the salvation of the poor he had failed while living to save. Brown spurned all schemes to cheat the hangman's rope by rescue or by pleading insanity. "I am worth inconceivably more to hang," he told his brother, "than for any other purpose."[12]

Extraordinary events took place in many northern communities on the day of Brown's execution. Church bells tolled; minute guns fired solemn salutes; ministers preached sermons of commemoration; thousands bowed in silent reverence for the martyr to liberty. "I have seen nothing like it," wrote Charles Eliot Norton of Harvard. More than a thousand miles away in Lawrence, Kansas, the editor of the *Republican* wrote that "the death of no man in America has ever produced so profound a sensation. A feeling of deep and sorrowful indignation seems to possess the masses."[13] A clergyman in Roxbury, Massachusetts, de-

---

10. From the report of Brown's speech in the *New York Herald*, Nov. 3, 1859, printed in Oswald Garrison Villard, *John Brown, 1800–1859: A Biography Fifty Years After* (Boston, 1910), 498–99.
11. Woodward, "John Brown's Private War," 54.
12. Robert Penn Warren, *John Brown, The Making of a Martyr* (New York, 1929), 428–29; Oates, *To Purge This Land*, 335.
13. Nevins, *Emergence*, II, 99; Oates, *To Purge This Land*, 356.

clared that Brown had made the word Treason "holy in the American language"; young William Dean Howells said that "Brown has become an idea, a thousand times purer and better and loftier than the Republican idea"; Henry David Thoreau pronounced Brown "a crucified hero."[14]

What can explain this near-canonization of Brown? Some Yankees professed to admire Brown for daring to strike the slave power that was accustomed to pushing the North around with impunity. "This will be a great day in our history," wrote Henry Wadsworth Longfellow in his diary on the day of Brown's execution, "the date of a new Revolution,— quite as much needed as the old one." When the Virginians hanged Brown they were "sowing the wind to reap the whirlwind, which will come soon." This was the spirit that two years later made "John Brown's Body" the favorite marching song of the Union army. But there was more to it than that. Perhaps the words of Lafayette quoted at a commemoration meeting in Boston got to the crux of the matter: "I never would have drawn my sword in the cause of America if I could have conceived that thereby I was helping to found a nation of slaves."[15] John Brown had drawn *his* sword in an attempt to cut out this cancer of shame that tainted the promise of America. No matter that his method was misguided and doomed to failure. "History, forgetting the errors of his judgment in the contemplation of his unfaltering course . . . and of the nobleness of his aims," said William Cullen Bryant, "will record his name among those of its martyrs and heroes." Most of Brown's eulogists similarly distinguished between his "errors of judgment" and "the nobleness of his aims." Though "Harper's Ferry was insane," stated the religious weekly *The Independent*, "the controlling motive of his demonstration was sublime." It was "the work of a madman," conceded Horace Greeley even as he praised the "grandeur and nobility" of Brown and his men.[16]

The distinction between act and motive was lost on southern whites. They saw only that millions of Yankees seemed to approve of a murderer who had tried to set the slaves at their throats. This perception provoked a paroxysm of anger more intense than the original reaction to the raid. The North "has sanctioned and applauded theft, murder,

14. Woodward, "John Brown's Private War," 58; Nevins, *Emergence*, II, 99; Oates, *To Purge This Land*, 354.
15. Warren, *John Brown*, 437; Villard, *John Brown*, 560.
16. Nevins, *Emergence*, II, 99; Woodward, "John Brown's Private War," 48–49.

treason," cried *De Bow's Review*. Could the South afford any longer "to live under a government, the majority of whose subjects or citizens regard John Brown as a martyr and a Christian hero?" asked a Baltimore newspaper.[17] No! echoed from every corner of the South. "The Harper's Ferry invasion has advanced the cause of disunion more than any event that has happened since the formation of the government," agreed two rival Richmond newspapers. It had "wrought almost a ·complete revolution in the sentiments . . . of the oldest and steadiest conservatives. . . . Thousands of men . . . who, a month ago, scoffed at the idea of a dissolution of the Union . . . now hold the opinion that its days are numbered." A North Carolinian confirmed this observation. "I have always been a fervid Union man," he wrote privately in December 1859, "but I confess the endorsement of the Harper's Ferry outrage . . . has shaken my fidelity and . . . I am willing to take the chances of every possible evil that may arise from disunion, sooner than submit any longer to Northern insolence."[18]

To reassure the South that sympathy for Brown was confined to a noisy minority, northern conservatives organized large anti-Brown meetings. They condemned "the recent outrage at Harper's Ferry" as a crime "not only against the State of Virginia, but against the Union itself. . . . [We] are ready to go as far as any Southern men in putting down all attempts of Northern fanatics to interfere with the constitutional rights of the South."[19] Democrats saw an opportunity to rebuild their bridges to the South and to discredit Republicans by linking them to Brown. Harper's Ferry, said Stephen Douglas, was the "natural, logical, inevitable result of the doctrines and teachings of the Republican party." Democrats singled out Seward for special attack, for they expected him to win the Republican presidential nomination. Seward was the "arch agitator who is responsible for this insurrection," they asserted. His "bloody and brutal" irrepressible conflict speech had inspired Brown's bloody and brutal act.[20]

17. Oates, *To Purge This Land*, 323; Villard, *John Brown*, 568.
18. *Richmond Enquirer* and *Richmond Whig*, quoted in Henry T. Shanks, *The Secession Movement in Virginia, 1847–1861* (Richmond, 1934),·90; William A. Walsh to L. O'B. Branch, Dec. 8, 1859, in Avery O. Craven, *The Growth of Southern Nationalism 1848–1861* (Baton Rouge, 1953), 311.
19. Villard, *John Brown*, 563; Philip S. Foner, *Business and Slavery: The New York Merchants and the Irrepressible Conflict* (Chapel Hill, 1941), 161–62.
20. Oates, *To Purge This Land*, 310; Villard, *John Brown*, 472; Nevins, *Emergence*, II, 104.

Fearing political damage, Republican leaders hastened to disavow Brown. Seward condemned the old man's "sedition and treason" and pronounced his execution "necessary and just." Even though Brown "agreed with us in thinking slavery wrong," said Lincoln, "that cannot excuse violence, bloodshed, and treason." Governor Samuel Kirkwood of Iowa decried Brown's "act of war" as "a greater crime" than even "the filibuster invaders of Cuba and Nicaragua were guilty of," though "in the minds of many" Brown's raid was "relieved to some extent of its guilt [because] the blow was struck for freedom, and not for slavery."[21]

Southerners did not like this comparison of Brown with the filibusters. They also detected a sting in the tail of Lincoln's and Kirkwood's remarks ("agreed with us in thinking slavery wrong . . . blow was struck for freedom"). To southern people the line separating Lincoln's moral convictions from Brown's butchery was meaningless. "We regard every man," declared an Atlanta newspaper, "who does not boldly declare that he believes African slavery to be a social, moral, and political blessing" as "an enemy to the institutions of the South." As for the supportive resolutions of northern conservatives, they were so much "gas and vaporing." "Why have not the conservative men at the North frowned down the infamous black-republican party?" asked De Bow's Review. "They have foreborne to crush it, till now it overrides almost everything at the North." On the Senate floor Robert Toombs warned that the South would "never permit this Federal government to pass into the traitorous hands of the Black Republican party." "Defend yourselves!" Toombs thundered to the southern people. "The enemy is at your door, wait not to meet him at your hearthstone, meet him at the doorsill, and drive him from the temple of liberty, or pull down its pillars and involve him in a common ruin."[22]

John Brown's ghost stalked the South as the election year of 1860 opened. Several historians have compared the region's mood to the "Great Fear" that seized the French countryside in the summer of 1789 when peasants believed that the "King's brigands are coming" to slaughter them.[23] Keyed up to the highest pitch of tension, many slaveholders

21. Seward and Kirkwood quoted in Villard, John Brown, 564–68; CWL, III, 502.
22. Atlanta Confederacy, quoted in Nevins, Emergence, II, 108n; DeBow's Review, 29 (July 1860), reprinted in Paul F. Paskoff and Daniel J. Wilson, eds., The Cause of the South: Selections from DeBow's Review 1846–1867 (Baton Rouge, 1982), 219–20; CG, 36 Cong., 1 Sess., Appendix, 93.
23. Ollinger Crenshaw, The Slave States in the Presidential Election of 1860 (Balti-

and yeomen alike were ready for war to defend hearth and home against those Black Republican brigands. Thousands joined military companies; state legislatures appropriated funds for the purchase of arms. Every barn or cotton gin that burned down sparked new rumors of slave insurrections and abolitionist invaders. Every Yankee in the South became *persona non grata*. Some of them received a coat of tar and feathers and a ride out of town on a rail. A few were lynched. The citizens of Boggy Swamp, South Carolina, ran two northern tutors out of the district. "Nothing definite is known of their abolitionist or insurrectionary sentiments," commented a local newspaper, "but being from the North, and, therefore, necessarily imbued with doctrines hostile to our institutions, their presence in this section has been obnoxious." The northern-born president of an Alabama college had to flee for his life. In Kentucky a mob drove thirty-nine people associated with an antislavery church and school at Berea out of the state. Thirty-two representatives in the South of New York and Boston firms arrived in Washington reporting "indignation so great against Northerners that they were compelled to return and abandon their business."[24] In this climate of fear and hostility, Democrats prepared for their national convention at Charleston in April 1860.

II

Most southern Democrats went to Charleston with one overriding goal: to destroy Douglas. In this they were joined by a scattering of administration Democrats from the North. Memories of Lecompton and the Freeport doctrine thwarted all efforts to heal the breach. This "Demagogue of Illinois," explained an Alabama editor, "deserves to perish upon the gibbet of Democratic condemnation, and his loathsome carcass to be cast at the gate of the Federal City."[25] Some lower-South Democrats even preferred a Republican president to Douglas in order to make the alternatives facing the South starkly clear: submission or secession. And they ensured this result by proceeding to cleave the Democratic party in two.

---

more, 1945), chap. 5; Woodward, "John Brown's Private War," 67–68; Oates, *To Purge This Land*, 322–23.

24. Woodward, "John Brown's Private War," 62–66; Nevins, *Emergence*, II, 108n.

25. *Opelika Weekly Southern Era*, April 18, 1860, quoted in Donald E. Reynolds, *Editors Make War: Southern Newspapers in the Secession Crisis* (Nashville, 1970), 35.

The Alabama Democratic convention took the first step in January 1860 by instructing its delegates to walk out of the national convention if the party refused to adopt a platform pledging a federal slave code for the territories. Other lower-South Democratic organizations followed suit. In February, Jefferson Davis presented the substance of southern demands to the Senate in resolutions affirming that neither Congress nor a territorial legislature could "impair the constitutional right of any citizen of the United States to take his slave property into the common territories. . . . It is the duty of the federal government there to afford, for that as for other species of property, the needful protection."[26] The Senate Democratic caucus, dominated by southerners, endorsed the resolutions and thereby threw down the gauntlet to Douglas at Charleston.

In the fevered atmosphere of 1860, Charleston was the worst possible place for the convention.[27] Douglas delegates felt like aliens in a hostile land. Fire-eating orators held forth outdoors each evening. Inside the convention hall, northerners had a three-fifths majority because delegates were apportioned in the same way as electoral votes rather than by party strength. Douglas's supporters were as determined to block a slave-code plank as southerners were to adopt one. There was thus an "irrepressible conflict" in the party, wrote the brilliant young journalist from Cincinnati Murat Halstead, whose reports provide the best account of the convention. "The South will not yield a jot of its position. . . . The Northern Democracy . . . are unwilling to submit themselves to assassination or to commit suicide."[28]

The crisis came with the report of the platform committee, in which each state had one vote. California and Oregon joined the slave states to provide a majority of 17 to 16 for a slave-code plank similar to the Jefferson Davis resolutions. The minority report reaffirmed the 1856 platform endorsing popular sovereignty and added a pledge to obey a Supreme Court decision on the powers of a territorial legislature. This was not good enough for southerners. They accepted the axiom of the Freeport doctrine that a Court decision would not enforce itself. Slave property needed federal protection, said the committee chairman, a North

26. CG, 36 Cong., 1 Sess., 658.
27. Charleston had been selected as the site by a special Democratic committee chaired by a New Yorker who hoped that the choice of a southern city would promote party harmony!
28. William B. Hesseltine, ed., *Three Against Lincoln: Murat Halstead Reports the Caucuses of 1860* (Baton Rouge, 1960), 35, 44.

Carolinian, so that when the United States acquired Cuba, Mexico, and Central America any slaveholder could take his property there with perfect security. The foremost orator for southern rights, William Lowndes Yancey, gave a rousing speech in favor of the majority report. The galleries rang with cheers as Yancey launched into his peroration: "We are in a position to ask you to yield," he said to northern delegates. "What right of yours, gentlemen of the North, have we of the South ever invaded? . . . Ours are the institutions which are at stake; ours is the property that is to be destroyed; ours is the honor at stake."[29]

After this eloquence the replies of northern delegates sounded futile, indeed almost funereal. "We cannot recede from [popular sovereignty] without personal dishonor," said a Douglas Democrat from Ohio, "*never, never, never,* so help us God." And they did not. After two days of bitter parliamentary wrangling, Douglas men pushed through their platform by a vote of 165 to 138 (free states 154 to 30, slave states 11 to 108). Fifty delegates from the lower South thereupon walked out. Everything that followed was anticlimax. Douglas could not muster the two-thirds majority required for nomination. Nor could the convention agree on anyone else during fifty-seven acrimonious ballots. Exhausted and heartsick, the delegates adjourned to try again six weeks later in the more hospitable clime of Baltimore. Yancey gave them a ringing farewell. Speaking in Charleston's moonlit courthouse square, he inspired a huge crowd to give three deafening cheers "for an Independent Southern Republic" with his concluding words: "Perhaps even now, the pen of the historian is nibbed to write the story of a new revolution."[30]

Attempts to reunite the party seemed hopeless. Delegates from the Northwest went home angry toward their southern brethren. "I never heard Abolitionists talk more uncharitably and rancorously of the people of the South than the Douglas men," wrote a reporter. "They say they do not care a d—n where the South goes. . . . 'She may go out of the Convention into hell,' for all they care." But most southern bolters aimed to seek readmission at Baltimore. Their strategy was "to rule or ruin," wrote Alexander Stephens, who had moved toward moderation during the past year and was now supporting Douglas.[31] If readmitted, the bol-

29. *Speech of William L. Yancey of Alabama, Delivered in the National Democratic Convention* (Charleston, 1860).

30. Nevins, *Emergence*, II, 215; Robert W. Johannsen, *Stephen A. Douglas* (New York, 1973), 754; Hesseltine, ed., *Three Against Lincoln*, 86.

31. Hesseltine, ed., *Three Against Lincoln*, 101; Stephens quoted in George Fort Mil-

ters intended to insist again on a slave-code platform and if defeated to walk out again, this time with the promise of most upper-South delegates to join them. If they were denied admission, the same upper-South delegates would bolt and help their cotton-state compatriots form a new party.

But Douglas's supporters in several lower-South states organized rival delegations to Baltimore. The fate of the Democratic party hung on the credentials fight there. After sober second thoughts about their willingness to let the bolters go to hell, most northern delegates were willing to compromise by seating some of the bolters and some of the challengers. But anti-Douglas southerners wanted all or nothing. They walked out once more, followed by most delegates from the upper South and a handful of proslavery northerners—more than one-third of the total. The bolters quickly organized their own convention and nominated John C. Breckinridge of Kentucky (the current vice president) for president on a slave-code platform. The dispirited loyalists nominated Douglas and returned home with renewed bitterness in their hearts toward the rebels who had all but ensured the election of a Black Republican president.[32]

Republicans helped along that cause by adroit action at their national convention in Chicago. The basic problem confronting the party was the need to carry nearly all of the free states in order to win. Expecting to lose California, Oregon, and perhaps New Jersey, they must capture Pennsylvania and either Indiana or Illinois among the states they had lost in 1856 to achieve an electoral majority. William H. Seward's weakness in these lower-North states formed a growing cloud on the horizon of his anticipated nomination. To carry these states, a Republican had to attract support from many of the Fillmore votes of 1856. Seward's long record of hostility to nativism would undercut this effort. More important, his higher-law and irrepressible-conflict speeches had given him a radical reputation that daunted old Whig conservatives. Despite Seward's repudiation of John Brown and his ideals, some Harper's Ferry mud clung to his coattails. In addition, years of internecine Whig warfare in New York had earned Seward numerous enemies, among

        ton, *The Eve of Conflict: Stephen A. Douglas and the Needless War* (Boston, 1934), 468.

32. Nevins, *Emergence*, II, 262–72; Roy F. Nichols, *The Disruption of American Democracy* (New York, 1948), 309–20; Milton, *Eve of Conflict*, 450–79; Johannsen, *Douglas*, 759–73; Hesseltine, ed., *Three Against Lincoln*, 178–278.

them Horace Greeley. A Seward nomination might also rob Republicans of the issue of corruption that scandals in the Buchanan administration had given them the opportunity to exploit. The bad smell of recent franchise grants by the New York legislature that could be traced to Seward's political manager Thurlow Weed tainted his candidate's repute. The rowdy, hard-drinking claque of gallery supporters that the Seward delegation brought to Chicago did nothing to improve the New Yorker's image.[33]

Coming into the convention with a large lead based on strength in upper-North states, Seward hoped for a first-ballot nomination. But Republicans were sure to win those states no matter whom they nominated. Pragmatists from all regions and politicians from the doubtful states combined in a stop-Seward movement. They had plenty of potential candidates: favorite sons from Vermont and New Jersey, and four men with state or regional backing whose aspirations went beyond favorite-son status: Salmon P. Chase of Ohio, Simon Cameron of Pennsylvania, Edward Bates of Missouri, and Abraham Lincoln of Illinois. But Chase shared Seward's handicap of a radical reputation and did not command unanimous support from even his own state. Cameron's notoriety as a spoilsman who had been in turn a Democrat, a Know-Nothing, and had flirted with Whiggery, militated against his candidacy among delegates concerned that the party should appear to be as pure as Caesar's wife. Bates seemed for a time Seward's strongest challenger because Greeley and the influential Blair family backed him in the hope that he might carry even a few border states as well as the lower North. But the colorless sixty-seven-year-old Missourian had been a slaveholder, a Know-Nothing, and in 1856 he had supported Fillmore. He therefore alienated too many constituencies whose support was essential—especially German Protestants. The belief that a Republican might carry a border state was fanciful, and Bates wound up with delegate support mainly from marginal states where Republican prospects were bleak or hopeless: Missouri, Maryland, Delaware, and Oregon.

This left Lincoln. By the time the convention's opening gavel came down on May 16, Lincoln had emerged from a position as the darkest of horses to that of Seward's main rival. Party leaders gradually recognized that the Illinoisian had most of the strengths and few of the weaknesses of an ideal candidate. He was a former antislavery Whig in a

---

33. Mark W. Summers, " 'A Band of Brigands': Albany Lawmakers and Republican National Politics, 1860," CWH, 30 (1984), 101–19.

party made up mostly of former antislavery Whigs. But despite his house-divided speech, he had a reputation as a moderate. Many former Democrats in the party could not stomach Seward, but they remembered with appreciation Lincoln's gesture in stepping aside to permit the election of antislavery Democrat Lyman Trumbull to the Senate in 1855. Lincoln had opposed the Know Nothings, which would help him with the German vote, but not so conspicuously as to drive away former American voters who would refuse to support Seward. Already known popularly as Honest Abe, Lincoln had a reputation for integrity that compared favorably with the dubious image of Thurlow Weed's New York machine. Of humble origins, Lincoln personified the free-labor ideology of equal opportunity and upward mobility. He *had* been born in a log cabin. In a stroke of political genius, one of Lincoln's managers exhibited at the Illinois state convention a pair of weatherbeaten fence rails that Lincoln had supposedly split thirty years earlier. From then on, Lincoln the railsplitter became the symbol of frontier, farm, opportunity, hard work, rags to riches, and other components of the American dream embodied in the Republican self-image. Finally, Lincoln was from a state and region crucial to Republican chances, particularly if Douglas as expected became the nominee of northern Democrats. Except for William Henry Harrison, who died after a month in office, no president had been elected from the Old Northwest. The fastest-growing part of the country, this region believed that its turn had come. The selection of Chicago as the convention site incalculably strengthened Lincoln's candidacy. Huge, enthusiastic crowds composed mostly of Illinoisians turned up at the large hall built for the convention and nicknamed the "wigwam." Counterfeit tickets enabled thousands of leather-lunged Lincoln men to pack the galleries.

Lincoln was not an unknown factor in national politics before 1860. His contest with Douglas had won wide attention; the publication of the debates early in 1860 enhanced his reputation. In 1859 Lincoln had given political speeches in a half-dozen midwestern states. In February 1860 he addressed a large audience in New York's Cooper Institute and went on to New England where he gave eleven speeches. This first appearance of Lincoln in the Northeast was a triumph, enabling his supporters back in Illinois to crow that "no man has ever before risen so rapidly to political eminence in the United States."[34] Partly on the

---

34. William E. Baringer, *Lincoln's Rise to Power* (Boston, 1937), 41 for quotation, and chaps. 1–4 for the emergence of Lincoln as Seward's main rival.

basis of these speeches Lincoln picked up delegate support in New England, winning nineteen votes from this Seward stronghold on the first ballot at Chicago.

Yet so obscure was Lincoln in certain circles before his nomination that some pundits had not included his name on their lists of seven or a dozen or even twenty-one potential candidates. Several newspapers spelled his first name Abram. But not for long. The turning point came when Indiana decided to join Illinois to give Lincoln solid first-ballot support from two of the most important lower-North states. This gave Lincoln's managers, a little known but brilliant group of Illinoisians, the chance to win a pledge from Pennsylvania to cast most of its second-ballot votes for Lincoln after the first-ballot gesture to Cameron. All through the feverish night of May 17–18 the Illinois politicos worked to line up other scattered second-ballot support for Lincoln. Despite the latter's injunction from Springfield to *"make no contracts that will bind me,"* his lieutenants in Chicago probably promised cabinet posts and other patronage plums to Indianians, to Cameron of Pennsylvania, and perhaps to the Blairs of Maryland and Missouri. How important these pledges were in winning votes is debatable—after all, Weed could make similar promises on Seward's behalf. The belief that Lincoln could carry the lower North and Seward could not was the most powerful Lincoln weapon. And delegates from other states were influenced by the action of Indiana and Pennsylvania because they knew that the party must capture them to win.[35]

The first ballot revealed Seward's weakness and Lincoln's surprising strength. With 233 votes needed to nominate, Seward fell sixty short at 173½ while Lincoln polled 102. The direction of the wind became

35. For Lincoln's injunction, see *CWL*, IV, 50. Historians have long debated whether Lincoln's lieutenants pledged cabinet posts to Cameron and others. Evidence for such commitments is mostly second-hand or circumstantial. For an argument that binding pledges played a vital role, see Barringer, *Lincoln's Rise*, 214, 266–67, 277, 334; for an opposing argument that no binding deals were made, see Willard L. King, *Lincoln's Manager: David Davis* (Cambridge, Mass., 1960), 137–38, 141, 162–64. For an assertion that pledges were made but were only one of several factors in securing Indiana and Pennsylvania for Lincoln, see Nevins, *Emergence*, II, 256–57. For a balanced judgment that even if pledges were made they were less important than the conviction that Seward could not carry the lower North, see Don E. Fehrenbacher, *Prelude to Greatness: Lincoln in the 1850's* (Stanford, 1962), 159. Whether or not there were any firm promises, there does seem to have been an "understanding" that Cameron and Caleb Smith of Indiana would get cabinet posts—and so they did.

clear on the second ballot as Seward gained fewer than a dozen votes while Vermont, Pennsylvania, and scattered votes from other states including some of Ohio's switched to Lincoln, bringing him almost even with Seward at 181 votes. During these ballots the wigwam was electric with an excitement unprecedented in American politics. Ten thousand spectators, most of them for Lincoln, jammed the galleries and made so much noise that a reporter exhausted his store of similes to describe it: "Imagine all the hogs ever slaughtered in Cincinnati giving their death squeals together, a score of big steam whistles going. . . . A herd of buffaloes or lions could not have made a more tremendous roaring." The crowd communicated a palpable impulse to delegates, reinforcing the dramatic growth of Lincoln's second-ballot total to convey an impression of irresistible momentum. As the third ballot began, suspense stretched nerves almost to the breaking point. Six more New England votes switched to Lincoln, along with eight from New Jersey, nine from Maryland, four more from his native Kentucky. When another fifteen Chase votes from Ohio went to Lincoln, the rafters literally shook with reverberation. Scores of pencils added the total before the clerk announced it: Lincoln had 231½ votes. Amid a sudden silence the Ohio chairman leaped onto his chair and announced the change of four more votes to Lincoln. With this "there was the rush of a great wind in the van of a storm—and in another breath, the storm was there . . . thousands cheering with the energy of insanity." [36]

None of the forty thousand people in and around the wigwam ever forgot that moment. All except the diehard Seward delegates were convinced that they had selected the strongest candidate. Few could know that they had also chosen the best man for the grim task that lay ahead. To balance the ticket the convention nominated for vice president Hannibal Hamlin of Maine, a former Democrat and one of Lincoln's earliest supporters in New England but also a friend of Seward. The Republican platform was one of the most effective documents of its kind in American history. While abating none of the antislavery convictions expressed in the 1856 platform, it softened the language slightly and denounced John Brown's raid as "the gravest of crimes." Gladly accepting the issues handed to Republicans by the opposition, the platform pledged support for a homestead act, rivers and harbors improvements, and federal aid for construction of a transcontinental railroad. For Pennsylvania, and for the Whiggish elements of the party in general,

36. Hesseltine, ed., *Three Against Lincoln*, 165, 158, 171.

the platform contained a tariff plank that called for an "adjustment" of rates "to encourage the development of the industrial interests of the whole country" and "secure to the workingmen liberal wages." Another plank tilted the party away from nativism by declaring opposition to "any change in our naturalization laws or any state legislation by which the rights of citizens . . . from foreign lands shall be abridged or impaired." To southern disunionists the platform issued a warning against "contemplated treason, which it is the imperative duty of an indignant people sternly to rebuke and forever silence."[37]

III

The excitement and optimism at Chicago carried over into the Republican campaign. This young party exuded the ebullience of youth. First-time voters flocked to the Republican standard. Thousands of them enrolled in "Wide-Awake" clubs and marched in huge parades carrying torches mounted on the ubiquitous fence rails that became a symbol of this campaign. Political songbooks rolled off the presses, and party faithful sang their theme song, "Ain't you glad you joined the Republicans?"

One advantage the Republicans enjoyed over their opponents was party unity. The disappointed Sewardites followed their leader's example and stumped with enthusiasm for Lincoln. Only a handful of abolitionists on the left and a rather larger number of Whig-Americans on the right showed signs of alienation. The latter represented the main obstacle to Republican hopes of sweeping the North. Like the mythical phoenix, the Whig party kept rising from its own ashes. In 1860 it did so in the guise of the Constitutional Union party, which had held its convention a week before the Republicans. These conservatives decided that the best way to avoid the calamity of disunion was to take no stand at all on the issues that divided North and South. Instead of a platform, therefore, they adopted a pious resolution pledging "to recognize no political principle other than *the Constitution . . . the Union . . . and the Enforcement of the Laws.*" The convention nominated wealthy slaveholder John Bell of Tennessee for president and venerable Cotton Whig Edward Everett of Massachusetts for vice president. Few delegates were under sixty years of age; this "Old Gentlemen's Party" became a butt of gentle ridicule by Republicans, who described the Bell-Everett ticket as

37. The platform is printed in Arthur M. Schlesinger, Jr., ed., *History of American Presidential Elections*, 4 vols. (New York, 1971), II, 1124–27.

"worthy to be printed on gilt-edged satin paper, laid away in a box of musk, and kept there." At the same time, southern Democrats accused Constitutional Unionists of "insulting the intelligence of the American people" by trying to organize a "party which shall ignore the slavery question. That issue must be met and settled."[38]

Constitutional Unionists did not expect to win the election. The best they could hope for was to carry several upper-South states and weaken Lincoln sufficiently in the lower North to deny him an electoral majority. This would throw the election of a president into the House, where each state had one vote but no party controlled a majority of states. Democrats might then combine with Whig-American-Unionists to elect Breckinridge, a Kentuckian who could perhaps be weaned away from his extremist southern-rights backers. Or the Constitutional Unionists might have enough leverage to elect Bell. Or if the House failed to name a president by March 4, 1861, the vice president elected by the Democratic Senate would become acting president. That worthy individual would be either Breckinridge's running mate Joseph Lane of Oregon, a proslavery native of North Carolina, or the Constitutional Unionists' own Edward Everett.[39]

But this spoiling strategy backfired. In several southern states the Constitutional Unionists felt compelled to prove themselves just as faithful to southern rights as the Democrats by embracing a federal slave code for the territories. This provoked many conservative ex-Whigs in the North to vote for Lincoln as the lesser of evils. "I will vote the Republican ticket next Tuesday," wrote a New Yorker who had initially intended to vote for Bell. "The only alternative is everlasting submission to the South. . . . I want to be able to remember that I voted right at this grave crisis. The North must assert its rights, now, and take the consequences."[40] The Bell-Everett ticket won less than 3 percent of the northern vote and took no states out of the Lincoln column.

38. *Springfield Republican*, quoted in Dale Baum, *The Civil War Party System: The Case of Massachusetts, 1848–1876* (Chapel Hill, 1984), 50; [Lexington] *Kentucky Statesman*, May 8, 1860, in Dwight Lowell Dumond, ed., *Southern Editorials on Secession* (New York, 1931), 76.

39. Crenshaw, *Slave States in the Presidential Election of 1860*, 59–73; Thomas B. Alexander, "The Civil War as Institutional Fulfillment," *JSH*, 47 (1981), 11–13, 16, 20.

40. *The Diary of George Templeton Strong: The Civil War 1860–1865*, ed. Allan Nevins and Milton Halsey Thomas (New York, 1952), 56–57. For an analysis of the attempt by southern Constitutional Unionists to compete with Breckinridge Dem-

The election of 1860 was unique in the history of American politics. The campaign resolved itself into two separate contests: Lincoln *vs.* Douglas in the North; Breckinridge *vs.* Bell in the South. Republicans did not even have a ticket in ten southern states, where their speakers would have been greeted with a coat of tar and feathers—or worse—if they had dared to appear. In the remaining five slave states—all in the upper South—Lincoln received 4 percent of the popular votes, mostly from antislavery Germans in St. Louis and vicinity. Breckinridge fared a little better in the North, where he won 5 percent of the popular votes, enough to deny California and Oregon to Douglas. Lincoln carried these states by a plurality and all other free states except New Jersey by a majority of the popular vote.

This was accomplished only by hard work. Though repudiated by the South and by the Buchanan administration, Douglas remained a formidable opponent. At the outset of the campaign he appeared to have a chance of winning eight northern and one or two border states with some 140 of the 303 electoral votes. To prevent this, Republicans mounted a campaign unprecedented in energy and oratory. Lincoln himself observed the customary silence of presidential candidates, but all other party leaders great and small took to the stump and delivered an estimated 50,000 speeches. Republicans made a special effort headed by Carl Schurz to reduce the normal Democratic majority among German-Americans. They achieved some success among German Protestants—enough, perhaps, to make a difference in the close states of Illinois and Indiana—though the lingering perceptions of Republican dalliance with nativism and temperance kept the Catholic vote overwhelmingly Democratic.[41]

In a bold break with tradition, Douglas campaigned for himself. In ill health, his voice hoarse, he nevertheless ranged through the whole

---

ocrats in "Southernness," see John V. Mering, "The Slave-State Constitutional Unionists and the Politics of Consensus," *JSH*, 43 (1977), 395–410.

41. For conflicting interpretations of the unresolved question of the German vote in 1860, see the essays in Frederick C. Luebke, ed., *Ethnic Voters and the Election of Lincoln* (Lincoln, Neb., 1971). The latest estimates of the German vote are contained in William E. Gienapp, "Who Voted for Lincoln?" John L. Thomas, ed., *Abraham Lincoln and the American Political Tradition* (Amherst, 1986), 50–97, which finds that while the proportion of German Americans voting Republican in 1860 was less than half, the increase from 1856 was dramatic and may have helped provide the margin of Republican victory in Pennsylvania as well as Indiana and Illinois.

country (except the west coast) from July to November in an exhausting tour that undoubtedly did much to bring on his death a year later. It was a courageous effort, but a futile one. Douglas carried the message to both North and South that he was the only *national* candidate, the only leader who could save the country from disunion. But in reality, Douglas Democrats were scarcely more a national party than the Republicans. Most southern Democrats painted Douglas nearly as black as Lincoln, and a traitor to boot. Douglas wound up with only 12 percent of the southern popular vote.

If the Democratic charge of sectionalism against Republicans lacked credibility this time, the old standby of branding them racial egalitarians retained its potency. Republicans had increased their vulnerability on this issue by placing a constitutional amendment to enfranchise blacks on the ballot in New York state.[42] If you want to vote "cheek by jowl with a large 'buck nigger,' " chanted Democratic orators and editors, if you want to support "a party that says *'a nigger is better than an Irishman,' "* if you are "ready to divide your patrimony with the negro . . . vote for the Republican candidate."[43] A Democratic float in a New York parade carried life-size effigies of Horace Greeley and a "good looking nigger wench, whom he caressed with all the affection of a true Republican." A banner proclaimed that "free love and free niggers will certainly elect Old Abe." The *New York Herald*, largest Democratic newspaper in the country, predicted that if Lincoln was elected "hundreds of thousands" of fugitive slaves would "emigrate to their friends—the Republicans—North, and be placed by them side by side in competition with white men. . . . African amalgamation with the fair daughters of the Anglo Saxon, Celtic, and Teutonic races will soon be their portion under the millennium of Republican rule."[44]

This onslaught wilted a good many Republicans. Although most party newspapers in New York endorsed the equal suffrage amendment, few

42. Negroes in New York state could vote only if they met a $250 property qualification. No such restriction applied to whites. The constitutional amendment would have removed the restriction on black voters.

43. *Albany Argus*, Sept. 7, 1860, *Ovid Bee*, Nov. 7, 1860, quoted in Phyllis F. Field, *The Politics of Race in New York: The Struggle for Black Suffrage in the Civil War Era* (Ithaca, 1982), 116, 118; *New York Herald*, Nov. 5, 1860; Albon Man, Jr., "Labor Competition and the New York Draft Riots of 1863," *Journal of Negro History*, 36 (1951), 379.

44. *New York Herald*, Oct. 24, Nov. 5, 6, 1860, quoted in Field, *Politics of Race*, 117, and in Man, "Labor Competition and the New York Draft Riots," 378–79.

speakers mentioned it, and the party made little effort in its behalf. Nearly one-third of the Republican voters joined virtually all Democrats in voting against it, sending the measure to a resounding defeat, even though Lincoln carried New York.[45] And in the lower North generally, Republicans played down the moral issue of slavery while emphasizing other matters of regional concern. In Pennsylvania and New Jersey they talked about the tariff; from Ohio to California the Republicans portrayed themselves as a homestead party, an internal improvements party, a Pacific railroad party. This left Democrats with less opportunity to exploit the race issue. "The Republicans, in their speeches, say nothing of the nigger question," complained a Pennsylvania Democrat, "but all is made to turn on the Tariff." Of course the Republican position on these issues constituted a flank attack on the slave power. After Buchanan had vetoed the homestead act, even a Democratic paper in Iowa denounced the president as an "old sinner" and his northern associates as "pimps and hirelings" of "the Slave Propagandists."[46]

The Buchanan administration handed Republicans another issue: corruption. Americans had always viewed malfeasance and abuse of power as the gravest dangers to republican liberty. Not only was Buchanan, in Republican eyes, the pliant tool of the slave power but his administration also, in the words of historian Michael Holt, "was undoubtedly the most corrupt before the Civil War and one of the most corrupt in American history."[47] An exposure of frauds filled a large volume compiled by a House investigating committee. The committee's report came off the presses in June 1860, just in time for an abridged edition to be distributed as a Republican campaign document.

This report topped off a series of previous investigations that disclosed a sorry record of graft and bribery in government contracts, the civil service, and Congress itself. The War and Navy departments had awarded contracts without competitive bidding to firms that made contributions to the Democratic party. Postmasters in New York and Chicago under both Pierce and Buchanan had siphoned public funds into party coffers for years. Democrats had used some of this money in congressional

45. The vote in favor of the amendment was 37 percent. Lincoln won 54 percent of the vote in New York.
46. ——— Helfenstein to Stephen A. Douglas, July 31, 1860, in Reinhard H. Luthin, *The First Lincoln Campaign* (Cambridge, Mass., 1944), 208; *Dubuque Herald*, quoted in *ibid.*, 179.
47. Michael F. Holt, *The Political Crisis of the 1850s* (New York, 1978), 214.

contests in 1858. They had also bribed judges to naturalize immigrants prematurely so they could vote in the crucial states of Pennsylvania and Indiana in 1856, and had "colonized" Irish railroad construction work- ers in Indiana to help swing that state to Buchanan. The New York postmaster fled the country in 1860 when auditors found his accounts $155,000 short. The House committee also dug up evidence that the administration had bribed congressmen to vote for admission of Kansas under the Lecompton constitution. Government printing contracts, long a lucrative source of patronage, became a greater scandal than ever un- der Buchanan. Kickbacks from payments exceeding by several times the printing cost found their way into the party treasury.

Secretary of War John Floyd presented the biggest target to graft hunters. He had sold government property for much less than its real value to a consortium headed by cronies. He had also signed padded bills pre- sented to the War Department by a contractor in financial difficulties who then used these signed bills as collateral for bank loans and for negotiable bonds from an Interior Department Indian trust fund. Al- though partially revealed before the election, Floyd's full complicity in this matter did not come out until December 1860, when Buchanan allowed him to resign without punishment. A Virginian, Floyd pro- nounced himself a secessionist and returned home, where he was fêted by like-minded compatriots who praised one of his final acts in office— an order (subsequently countermanded) to transfer 125 cannon from Pittsburgh to arsenals in Mississippi and Texas.[48]

Republicans made big capital out of these scandals. To be sure, Buchanan was not running for re-election, and most northern Demo- crats had already repudiated his administration. But some Douglas Democrats had also been caught with their hands in the till, and the whole party was tarnished by the image of corruption. The "plunder of the public treasury," declared the Republican platform, "shows that an entire change of administration is imperatively demanded." Republican campaigners combined this crusade to "throw the rascals out" with de- nunciations of the slave power. The revelations of malfeasance, said Charles Francis Adams, had shown how "the slaveholding interest has

48. Michael F. Holt, "James Buchanan, 1857–1861," in C. Vann Woodward, ed., *Responses of the Presidents to Charges of Misconduct* (New York, 1974), 86–96; David E. Meerse, "Buchanan, Corruption and the Election of 1860," CWH, 12 (1966), 116–31; Nichols, *Disruption of American Democracy*, 284–87, 328–31; Nevins, *Emergence*, II, 196–200, 372–75.

been driven to the expedient of attempting to bribe the people of the Free States with their own money in order to maintain itself in control of the government." Horace Greeley spoke of "not one merely but two Irrepressible Conflicts—the first between . . . Free Labor . . . and aggressive, all-grasping Slavery propagandism . . . [the second] between honest administration on one side, and wholesale executive corruption, legislative bribery, and speculative jobbery on the other; and we recognize in Honest Abe Lincoln the right man to lead us in both."[49] The future would reveal that a good many Republican politicians were none too honest themselves. But in 1860 the party carried an unsullied banner of reform and freedom against the tired old corrupt proslavery Democrats.

To some members of their constituency, however, the Republican message seemed sour. When party orators discussed slavery, especially in the lower North, they often took pains to describe Republicanism as the true "White Man's Party." Exclusion of slavery from the territories, they insisted, meant exclusion of black competition with white settlers. This caused several abolitionists to denounce the Republicans as no better than Douglas Democrats. William Lloyd Garrison believed that "the Republican party means to do nothing, can do nothing, for the abolition of slavery in the slave states." Wendell Phillips even went so far as to call Lincoln "the Slave Hound of Illinois" because he refused to advocate repeal of the fugitive slave law.[50]

But some Republicans came almost up to the abolitionist standard. In the upper North the old evangelical fervor against bondage infused their rhetoric. After the Republican convention Seward rediscovered the irrepressible conflict. Even in Missouri he boldly proclaimed that freedom "is bound to go through. As it has already gone through eighteen of the states of the Union, so it is bound to go through all of the other fifteen . . . for the simple reason that it is going through all the world."[51]

Gubernatorial candidates John Andrew of Massachusetts and Austin Blair of Michigan, Senators Charles Sumner, Salmon P. Chase, and Benjamin Wade, Congressmen George W. Julian and Thaddeus Ste-

49. Meerse, "Buchanan, Corruption and the Election of 1860," loc. cit., 125, 124.
50. These and similar quotations can be found in James M. McPherson, The Struggle for Equality: Abolitionists and the Negro in the Civil War and Reconstruction (Princeton, 1964), 11–18, and in McPherson, The Negro's Civil War (New York, 1965), 3–10.
51. Emerson D. Fite, The Presidential Campaign of 1860 (New York, 1911), 192.

vens, nearly the whole Republican party of Vermont, and a host of other party leaders were abolitionists in all but name. Many of them *did* favor repeal of the fugitive slave law, along with the abolition of slavery in the District of Columbia and the prohibition of the interstate slave trade.

Believing that these men embodied the progressive spirit and future thrust of the Republican party, many abolitionists supported it in 1860. "Lincoln's election will indicate growth in the right direction," wrote one, while Frederick Douglass acknowledged that a Republican victory "must and will be hailed as an anti-slavery triumph."[52] Southerners thought so too. Democrats below the Potomac considered Lincoln "a relentless, dogged, free-soil border ruffian . . . a vulgar mobocrat and a Southern hater . . . an illiterate partisan . . . possessed only of his inveterate hatred of slavery and his openly avowed predilections of negro equality." As the election neared, the increasing likelihood that a solid North would make Lincoln president brewed a volatile mixture of hysteria, despondency, and elation in the South. Whites feared the coming of new John Browns encouraged by triumphant Black Republicans; unionists despaired of the future; secessionists relished the prospect of southern independence. Even the weather during that summer of 1860 became part of the political climate: a severe drought and prolonged heat wave withered southern crops and drove nerves beyond the point of endurance.[53]

Stories of slave uprisings that followed the visits of mysterious Yankee strangers, reports of arson and rapes and poisonings by slaves crowded the southern press. Somehow these horrors never seemed to happen in one's own neighborhood. Many of them, in fact, were reported from faraway Texas. And curiously, only those newspapers backing Breckinridge for president seemed to carry such stories. Bell and Douglas newspapers even had the effrontery to accuse Breckinridge Democrats of getting up "false-hoods and sensation tales" to "arouse the passions of the people and drive them into the Southern Disunion movement."[54]

But this accusation must have been wrong. No less a personage than

52. McPherson, *Struggle for Equality*, 16; McPherson, *Negro's Civil War*, 8.
53. *Charleston Mercury*, Oct. 15, 1860, and *Richmond Enquirer*, May 21, 1860, quoted in Craven, *Growth of Southern Nationalism*, 346. William L. Barney, *The Secessionist Impulse: Alabama and Mississippi in 1860* (Princeton, 1974), 153–63, contains a perceptive analysis of the impact of the drought on southern political behavior.
54. Crenshaw, *Slave States in the Presidential Election of 1860*, 97 and 97n.

R. S. Holt, a wealthy Mississippi planter and brother of the U.S. post-master general, reported that "we have constantly a foretaste of what Northern brother-hood means, in almost daily conflagrations & in dis-covery of poison, knives & pistols distributed among our slaves by em-issaries sent out for that purpose. . . . There cannot be found in all the planting States a territory ten miles square in which the foot prints of one or more of these miscreants have not been discovered." Fortu-nately, Holt added, "Miracles & Providence" had prevented the accom-plishment of their "hellish" designs. But Congressman Lawrence M. Keitt of South Carolina was not willing to trust to Providence. "I see poison in the wells in Texas—and fire for the houses in Alabama," he wrote. "How can we stand it? . . . *It is enough to risk disunion on.*"[55]

In vain, then, did a southern conservative point out that most of these atrocity stories "turned out, on examination, to be totally false, and *all of them* grossly exaggerated."[56] On the eve of the election a Mississip-pian observed that "the minds of the people are aroused to a pitch of excitement probably unparalleled in the history of our country." A writer in a Texas Methodist weekly was sure that "the designs of the abolition-ists are . . . poison [and] fire" to "deluge [the South] in blood and flame . . . and force their fair daughters into the embrace of buck ne-groes for wives." However irrational these fears, the response was real— vigilante lynch law that made the John Brown scare of the previous winter look like a Sunday School picnic. "It is better for us to hang ninety-nine innocent (suspicious) men than to let one guilty one pass," wrote a Texan, "for the guilty one endangers the peace of society."[57]

This mass hysteria caused even southern unionists to warn Yankees that a Republican victory meant disunion. "The Election of Lincoln is Sufficient Cause for Secession," a Bell supporter in Alabama entitled his speech. The moderate Benjamin H. Hill of Georgia insisted that "this Government and Black Republicanism cannot live together. . . . At no period of the world's history have four thousand millions of prop-erty debated whether it ought to submit to the rule of an enemy." Not to be outdone in southern patriotism, the leading Douglas newspaper

55. R. S. Holt to Joseph Holt, Nov. 9, 1860, Lawrence Keitt to James H. Hammond, Sept. 10, Oct. 23, 1860, in *ibid.*, 105–6, 108.
56. William L. Barney, *The Road to Secession: A New Perspective on the Old South* (New York, 1972), 149.
57. *Natchez Free Trader*, Nov. 2, 1860, and *Texas Christian Advocate* quoted in Cren-shaw, *Slave States in the Presidential Election of 1860*, 111, 95–96; Texan quoted in Reynolds, *Editors Make War*, 103–4.

in Georgia thundered: "Let the consequences be what they may—whether the Potomac is crimsoned in human gore, and Pennsylvania Avenue is paved ten fathoms deep with mangled bodies . . . the South will never submit to such humiliation and degradation as the inauguration of Abraham Lincoln."[58]

The fever spread to the border states. A unionist editor in Louisville professed to have received hundreds of letters "all informing us of a settled and widely-extended purpose to break up the Union" if Lincoln was elected. "We admit that the conspirators are mad, but such madness 'rules the hour.' " John J. Crittenden, Kentucky's elder statesman of unionism, heir of Henry Clay's mantle of nationalism, gave a speech just before the election in which he denounced the "profound fanaticism" of Republicans who "think it their duty to destroy . . . the white man, in order that the black might be free. . . . [The South] has come to the conclusion that in case Lincoln should be elected . . . she could not submit to the consequences, and therefore, to avoid her fate, will secede from the Union."[59]

Republicans refused to take these warnings to heart. They had heard them before, a dozen times or more. In 1856 Democrats had used such threats to frighten northerners into voting Democratic. Republicans believed that the same thing was happening in 1860. It was "the old game of scaring and bullying the North into submission to Southern demands," said the Republican mayor of Chicago. In a speech at St. Paul, Seward ridiculed this new southern effort "to terrify or alarm" the North. "Who's afraid? (Laughter and cries of 'no one.') Nobody's afraid; nobody can be bought." Nor did Lincoln expect "any formidable effort to break up the Union. The people of the South have too much sense," he thought, "to attempt the ruin of the government."[60]

Hindsight was to reveal that southerners meant what they said. Two sagacious historians have maintained that Republican failure to take these warnings seriously was a "cardinal error."[61] Yet it is hard to see what Republicans could have done to allay southern anxieties short of dis-

58. John V. Mering, "The Constitutional Union Campaign of 1860: An Example of the Paranoid Style," *Mid-America*, 60 (1978), 101; Dwight L. Dumond, *The Secession Movement 1860–1861* (New York, 1931), 106, 104.

59. *Louisville Daily Journal*, Aug. 13, 1860, in Dumond, ed., *Southern Editorials on Secession*, 159; Mering, "The Constitutional Union Campaign of 1860," 99.

60. *New York Herald*, Aug. 1, Oct. 18, 1860; CWL, IV, 95.

61. Nevins, *Emergence*, II, 305; Potter, *Impending Crisis*, 433.

solving their party and proclaiming slavery a positive good. As a committee of the Virginia legislature put it, "the very existence of such a party is an offense to the whole South." A New Orleans editor regarded every northern vote cast for Lincoln as "*a deliberate, cold-blooded insult and outrage*" to southern honor. It was not so much what Republicans might do as what they stood for that angered southerners. "No other 'overt act' can so imperatively demand resistance on our part," said a North Carolina congressman, "as the simple election of their candidate."[62]

Lincoln rejected pleas from conservatives that he issue a statement to mollify the South. "What is it I could say which would quiet alarm?" he asked in October. "Is it that no interference by the government, with slaves or slavery within the states, is intended? I have said this so often already, that a repetition of it is but mockery, bearing an appearance of weakness." Lincoln would have been willing to repeat these statements "if there were no danger of encouraging bold bad men . . . who are eager for something new upon which to base new misrepresentations—men who would like to frighten me, or, at least, to fix upon me the character of timidity and cowardice. They would seize upon almost any letter I could write, as being an '*awful coming down.*' "[63]

Douglas did speak out. On his first foray into the South he told crowds in North Carolina that he would "hang every man higher than Haman who would attempt . . . to break up the Union by resistance to its laws." Campaigning in Iowa when he learned that Republicans had swept the October state elections in Pennsylvania, Ohio, and Indiana,[64] Douglas said to his private secretary: "Mr. Lincoln is the next President. We must try to save the Union. I will go South." Go he did, to Tennessee, Georgia, and Alabama, at some risk to his deteriorating health and even to his life. Douglas courageously repeated his warnings against secession. The whole North would rise up to prevent it, he said pointedly. "I hold that the election of any man on earth by the American

62. *New Orleans Crescent*, Nov. 9, 1860, quoted in Craven, *Growth of Southern Nationalism*, 358; Virginia legislative committee quoted in Villard, *John Brown*, 567; CG, 36 Cong., 1 Sess., 455.
63. Lincoln to George T. M. Davis, Oct. 17, 1860, Lincoln to George D. Prentice, Oct. 19, 1860, in CWL, IV, 132–33, 135.
64. Several states held state elections on a different date from the presidential election, which then as now took place on the first Tuesday after the first Monday in November.

people, according to the Constitution, is no justification for breaking up this government." Southerners listened to him, but they did not hear.[65]

The only shred of hope for Democrats was a "fusion" of the three opposition parties in key northern states to deny Lincoln their electoral votes and throw the election into the House. But the legacy of warfare between Douglas and Buchanan thwarted cooperation, while the Know-Nothing ancestry of the Constitutional Unionists bred distrust among foreign-born Democrats. After many meetings in smoke-filled rooms, fusion arrangements among all three parties emerged in New York and Rhode Island. Three of New Jersey's seven electors ran on fusion tickets; in Pennsylvania the Breckinridge and Douglas electors managed to fuse, but a rebellious group of Douglas Democrats refused to support the ticket. All of this effort was in vain. Lincoln won majorities over the combined opposition in New York, Pennsylvania, and Rhode Island; the three fusion electors in New Jersey gave Douglas his only northern electoral votes. He also carried Missouri, while Bell won Virginia, Kentucky, and his native Tennessee. Breckinridge carried the rest of the South, winning 45 percent of the section's popular votes to Bell's 39 percent.[66] Though Lincoln won only 40 percent of the national popular vote (54 percent in the North), his 180 electoral votes gave him a comfortable cushion over the necessary minimum of 152. Even if the opposition had combined against him in every free state he would have lost only New Jersey, California, and Oregon, and still would have won the presidency with 169 electoral votes.

To southerners the election's most ominous feature was the magnitude of Republican victory north of the 41st parallel. Lincoln won more than 60 percent of the vote in that region, losing scarcely two dozen counties. Three-quarters of the Republican congressmen and senators in the next Congress would represent this "Yankee" and antislavery portion of the free states. These facts were "full of portentous significance," declared the *New Orleans Crescent*. "The idle canvass prattle about Northern conservatism may now be dismissed," agreed the *Richmond Examiner*. "A party founded on the single sentiment . . . of hatred of African slavery, is now the controlling power." No one could any longer "be deluded . . . that the Black Republican party is a moderate" party,

---

65. Johannsen, *Douglas*, 788–803.
66. In South Carolina, presidential electors were still chosen by the legislature. Breckinridge would have carried the state overwhelmingly in a popular vote.

pronounced the *New Orleans Delta*. "It is, in fact, essentially a revolutionary party."[67]

Whether or not the party was revolutionary, antislavery men concurred that a revolution had taken place. "We live in revolutionary times," wrote an Illinois free soiler, "& I say God bless the revolution." Charles Francis Adams, whose grandfather and father had been defeated for reelection to the presidency by slaveowners, wrote in his diary the day after Lincoln's victory: "The great revolution has actually taken place. . . . The country has once and for all thrown off the domination of the Slaveholders."[68]

67. *New Orleans Daily Crescent*, Nov. 13, 1860, and *Richmond Semi-Weekly Examiner*, Nov. 9, 1860, in Dumond, ed., *Southern Editorials on Secession*, 237, 223; *New Orleans Daily Delta*, Nov. 3, 1860, quoted in Peyton McCrary, *Abraham Lincoln and Reconstruction: The Louisiana Experiment* (Princeton, 1978), 52.
68. Horace White to Lyman Trumbull, Dec. 30, 1860, in William E. Baringer, *A House Dividing: Lincoln as President Elect* (Springfield, Ill., 1945), 236; Adams quoted in Eric Foner, *Free Soil, Free Labor, Free Men: The Ideology of the Republican Party before the Civil War* (New York, 1970), 223.

8

The Counterrevolution of 1861

I

The second Continental Congress had deliberated fourteen months before declaring American independence in 1776. To produce the United States Constitution and put the new government into operation required nearly two years. In contrast, the Confederate States of America organized itself, drafted a constitution, and set up shop in Montgomery, Alabama, within three months of Lincoln's election.

The South moved so swiftly because, in seeming paradox, secession proceeded on a state-by-state basis rather than by collective action. Remembering the lesson of 1850, when the Nashville Convention had turned into a forum of caution and delay, fire-eaters determined this time to eschew a convention of states until the secession of several of them had become a *fait accompli*. And because the ground had long since been plowed and planted, the harvest of disunion came quickly after the thunderstorm of Lincoln's election.

Not surprisingly, South Carolina acted first. "There is nothing in all the dark caves of human passion so cruel and deadly as the hatred the South Carolinians profess for the Yankees," wrote the correspondent of the London *Times* from Charleston. The enmity of Greek for Turk was child's play "compared to the animosity evinced by the 'gentry' of South Carolina for the 'rabble of the North.' . . . 'The State of South Carolina was,' I am told, 'founded by gentlemen. . . . Nothing on earth shall ever induce us to submit to any union with the brutal, bigoted blackguards of the New England States!' "[1] In this mood the South Carolina legislature called a convention to consider secession. Amid extraordinary scenes of marching bands, fireworks displays, militia calling themselves Minute Men, and huge rallies of citizens waving palmetto flags and shouting slogans of southern rights, the convention by a vote of 169–0 enacted on December 20 an "ordinance" dissolving "the union now subsisting between South Carolina and other States."[2]

As fire-eaters had hoped, this bold step triggered a chain reaction by conventions in other lower-South states. After the Christmas holidays—celebrated this year with a certain ambivalence toward the teachings of the Prince of Peace—Mississippi adopted a similar ordinance on January 9, 1861, followed by Florida on January 10, Alabama on January 11, Georgia on January 19, Louisiana on January 26, and Texas on February 1. Although none of these conventions exhibited the unity of South Carolina's, their average vote in favor of secession was 80 percent. This figure was probably a fair reflection of white opinion in those six states. Except in Texas, the conventions did not submit their ordinances to the voters for ratification. This led to charges that a disunion conspiracy acted against the will of the people. But in fact the main reason for non-submission was a desire to avoid delay. The voters had just elected delegates who had made their positions clear in public statements; another election seemed superfluous. The Constitution of 1787 had been ratified by state conventions, not by popular vote; withdrawal of that ratification by similar conventions satisfied a wish for legality and symmetry. In Texas the voters endorsed secession by a margin of three to one; there is little reason to believe that the result would have been different in any of the other six states.[3]

Divisions in the lower South occurred mainly over tactics and timing, not goals. A majority favored the domino tactics of individual state secession followed by a convention of independent states to form a new confederacy. But a significant minority, especially in Alabama, Georgia, and Louisiana, desired some sort of cooperative action *preceding*

1. Frank Moore, ed., *The Rebellion Record*, I (New York, 1861), "Documents," 315.
2. Steven A. Channing, *Crisis of Fear: Secession in South Carolina* (New York, 1970), 282–85.
3. For good summaries of the historiography of the question of popular support for secession, see Ralph A. Wooster, "The Secession of the Lower South: An Examination of Changing Interpretations, *CWH*, 7 (1961), 117–27, and William J. Donnelly, "Conspiracy or Popular Movement: The Historiography of Southern Support for Secession," *North Carolina Historical Review*, 42 (1965), 70–84.

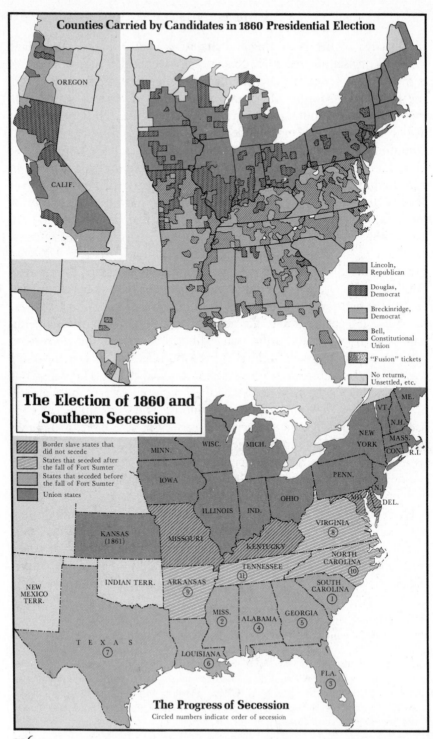

Counties Carried by Candidates in 1860 Presidential Election

OREGON

CALIF.

Lincoln,
Republican

Douglas,
Democrat

Breckinridge,
Democrat

Bell,
Constitutional
Union

"Fusion" tickets

No returns,
Unsettled, etc.

The Election of 1860 and Southern Secession

Border slave states that
did not secede

States that seceded after
the fall of Fort Sumter

States that seceded before
the fall of Fort Sumter

Union states

MINN.

WISC.   MICH.

ME.

VT.

N.H.

NEW
YORK

MASS.

CONN.   R.I.

IOWA

PENN.

ILLINOIS   IND.

OHIO

N.J.

MD.   DEL.

KANSAS
(1861)

MISSOURI

KENTUCKY

VIRGINIA
⑧

NORTH
CAROLINA
⑩

NEW
MEXICO
TERR.

INDIAN TERR.

ARKANSAS
⑨

TENNESSEE
⑪

SOUTH
CAROLINA
①

MISS.
②

ALABAMA
④

GEORGIA
⑤

T E X A S
⑦

LOUISIANA
⑥

FLA.
③

The Progress of Secession
Circled numbers indicate order of secession

236

secession to ensure unity among at least the cotton-South states. These "cooperationists," however, did not fully agree among themselves. At the radical end of their spectrum were cooperative secessionists, who professed as much ardor for southern independence as immediate secessionists but argued that a united South could present a stronger front than could a few independent states. But they were undercut by the swiftness of events, which produced a league of a half-dozen seceded states within six weeks of South Carolina's secession. As a Georgia cooperationist admitted ruefully in mid-January, four states "*have* already seceded. . . . In order to *act* with them, we must secede with them."[4]

At the center of the cooperationist spectrum stood a group that might be labeled "ultimatumists." They urged a convention of southern states to draw up a list of demands for presentation to the incoming Lincoln administration—including enforcement of the fugitive slave law, repeal of personal liberty laws, guarantees against interference with slavery in the District of Columbia or with the interstate slave trade, and protection of slavery in the territories, at least those south of 36° 30'. If Republicans refused this ultimatum, then a united South would go out. Since Republicans seemed unlikely to promise all of these concessions and most southerners would not trust them even if they did, the ultimatumists commanded little support in secession conventions.

The third and most conservative group of cooperationists were conditional unionists, who asked fellow southerners to give Lincoln a chance to prove his moderate intentions. Only if Republicans committed some "overt act" against southern rights should the South resort to the drastic step of secession. But while the ranks of conditional unionists contained influential men like Alexander Stephens, they too were swept along by the pace of events. "The prudent and conservative men South," wrote Senator Judah P. Benjamin of Louisiana, who counted himself one of them, were not "able to stem the wild torrent of passion which is carrying everything before it. . . . It is a revolution . . . of the most intense character . . . and it can no more be checked by human effort, for the time, than a prairie fire by a gardener's watering pot."[5]

Other southerners used similar metaphors to describe the phenomenon. "It is a complete landsturm. . . . People are wild. . . . You might

---

4. *Rome Weekly Courier*, Jan. 17, 1861, quoted in Michael P. Johnson, *Toward a Patriarchal Republic: The Secession of Georgia* (Baton Rouge, 1977), 111.
5. Benjamin to Samuel L. M. Barlow, Dec. 9, 1860, Barlow Papers, Henry E. Huntington Library.

as well attempt to control a tornado as to attempt to stop them."[6] Secession was an unequivocal act which relieved the unbearable tension that had been building for years. It was a catharsis for pent-up fears and hostilities. It was a *joyful* act that caused people literally to dance in the streets. Their fierce gaiety anticipated the celebratory crowds that gathered along the Champs-Élysées and the Unter den Linden and at Picadilly Circus in that similarly innocent world of August 1914. Not that the flag-waving, singing crowds in Charleston and Savannah and New Orleans wanted or expected war; on the contrary, they believed that "the Yankees were cowards and would not fight"—or said they did, to assure the timid that there was no danger. "So far as civil war is concerned," remarked an Atlanta newspaper blithely in January 1861, "we have no fears of that in Atlanta." A rural editor thought that women and children armed with popguns firing "Connecticut wooden nutmegs" could deal with every Yankee likely to appear in Georgia. Senator James Chesnut of South Carolina offered to drink all the blood shed as a consequence of secession. It became a common saying in the South during the secession winter that "a lady's thimble will hold all the blood that will be shed."[7]

Cooperationists were not so sure about this. "War I look for as almost certain," wrote Alexander Stephens, who also warned that "revolutions are much easier started than controlled, and the men who begin them [often] . . . themselves become the victims."[8] But Stephens's prescient warning was lost in the wind, and he joined the revolution himself when his state went out. Before that happened, however, the cooperationists had demonstrated considerable strength in each state except South Carolina and Texas. In elections for convention delegates, candidates representing some kind of cooperationist position polled at least 40 percent of the vote in those five states. Many eligible voters had not gone to the polls in these elections, leading to a belief that the potential cooperationist electorate was even larger. In Alabama and Georgia, 39 and 30 percent respectively of the delegates voted against the final res-

6. Channing, *Crisis of Fear*, 251; Nevins, *Emergence*, II, 321.
7. Donald E. Reynolds, *Editors Make War: Southern Newspapers in the Secession Crisis* (Nashville, 1970), 174; E. Merton Coulter, *The Confederate States of America 1861–1865* (Baton Rouge, 1950), 15.
8. Stephens to _____, Nov. 25, 1860, in Ulrich B. Phillips, ed., *The Correspondence of Robert Toombs, Alexander H. Stephens, and Howell Cobb*, in *Annual Report* of the American Historical Association, 1911, vol. II (Washington, 1913), 504–5.

olution of secession despite the enormous pressures brought on them to go along with the majority.

This caused many northerners and some historians to exaggerate the strength of unionism in the lower South. As late as July 1861, Lincoln expressed doubt "whether there is, to-day, a majority of the legally qualified voters of any State, except perhaps South Carolina, in favor of disunion." A century later several historians echoed this faith in a silent majority of southern unionists. "It can hardly be said that a majority of the South's white people deliberately chose to dissolve the Union in 1861," wrote one. "Secession was not basically desired even by a majority in the lower South," concluded another, "and the secessionists succeeded less because of the intrinsic popularity of their program than because of the extreme skill with which they utilized an emergency psychology."[9]

Though an emergency psychology certainly existed, the belief in a repressed unionist majority rests on a misunderstanding of southern unionism. As a Mississippi "unionist" explained after Lincoln's election, he was no longer "a Union man in the sense in which the North is Union." His unionism was conditional; the North had violated the condition by electing Lincoln. Cooperationists in Alabama who voted against secession cautioned outsiders not to "misconstrue" their action. "We scorn the Black Republicans," they declared. "The State of Alabama cannot and will not submit to the Administration of Lincoln. . . . We intend to resist . . . but our resistance is based upon . . . unity of action, with the other slave states." Or as a Mississippi cooperationist put it: "Cooperation before secession was the first object of my desire. Failing this I am willing to take the next best, subsequent cooperation or cooperation after secession."[10] This was the position of most delegates who initially opposed immediate secession. It was a weak foundation on which to build a faith in southern unionism.

Was secession constitutional? Or was it an act of revolution? The

9. CWL, IV, 437; Charles Grier Sellers, "The Travail of Slavery," in Sellers, ed., The Southerner as American (Chapel Hill, 1960), 70; David M. Potter, Lincoln and His Party in the Secession Crisis (New Haven, 1942, reissued 1962 with new preface), 208.

10. Percy Lee Rainwater, Mississippi: Storm Center of Secession 1856–1861 (Baton Rouge, 1938), 173; J. Mills Thornton III, Politics and Power in a Slave Society: Alabama, 1800–1860 (Baton Rouge, 1978), 416–17; Dwight L. Dumond, The Secession Movement 1860–1861 (New York, 1931), 200–202.

Constitution is silent on this question. But most secessionists believed in the legality of their action. State sovereignty, they insisted, had preceded national sovereignty. When they had ratified the Constitution, states delegated some of the functions of sovereignty to a federal government but did not yield its fundamental attributes. Having ratified the Constitution by a convention, a state could reassert total sovereignty in the same manner. This theory presented a slight problem for states (five of the seven) that had come into the Union after 1789. But they, too, despite the appearance of being creatures rather than creators of the Union, could assert the prior sovereignty of their states, for each had formed a state constitution (or in the case of Texas, a national constitution) *before* petitioning Congress for admission to the Union.

Those southerners (mostly conditional unionists) who found this theory a bit hard to swallow could fall back on the right of revolution. Senator Alfred Iverson of Georgia conceded that while no state had a constitutional right to secede "each State has the right of revolution. . . . The secession of a State is an act of revolution." The mayor of Vicksburg described secession as "a mighty political revolution which [will] result in placing the Confederate States among the Independent nations of the earth."[11] A Confederate army officer declared that he had "never believed the Constitution recognized the right of secession. I took up arms, sir, upon a broader ground—the right of revolution. We were wronged. Our properties and liberties were about to be taken from us. It was a sacred duty to rebel."[12]

Sporting blue cockades (the symbol of secession), some of these enthusiastic revolutionaries even sang "The Southern Marseillaise" in the streets of Charleston and New Orleans.[13] Ex-Governor Henry Wise of Virginia, who urged the formation of committees of public safety, glo-

---

11. CG, 36 Cong., 2 Sess., 10–11; Peter F. Walker, *Vicksburg: A People at War* (Chapel Hill, 1960), 43.
12. George Ward Nichols, *The Story of the Great March* (New York, 1865), 302.
13. Part of the lyrics went like this:

Sons of the South, awake to glory!
Hark! hark! what myriads bid you rise.
Your children, wives, and grandsires hoary,
Behold their tears and hear their cries.

. . .

To arms! to arms! ye brave,
Th' avenging sword unsheath! (Reynolds, *Editors Make War*, 184).

ried in his reputation as the "Danton of the Secession Movement in Virginia." Carried away by an excess of Robespierrian zeal, a Georgia disunionist warned cooperationists that "we will go for revolution, and if you . . . oppose us . . . we will brand you as traitors, and chop off your heads."[14]

But the American Revolution, not the French, was the preferred model for secessionists. *Liberté* they sought, but not *égalité* or *fraternité*. Were not "the men of 1776 . . . Secessionists?" asked an Alabamian. If we remain in the Union, said a Florida slaveholder, "we will be deprived of that right for which our fathers fought in the battles of the revolution." From "the high and solemn motive of defending and protecting the rights . . . which our fathers bequeathed to us," declared Jefferson Davis, let us "renew such sacrifices as our fathers made to the holy cause of constitutional liberty."[15]

What were these rights and liberties for which Confederates contended? The right to own slaves; the liberty to take this property into the territories; freedom from the coercive powers of a centralized government. Black Republican rule in Washington threatened republican freedoms as the South understood them. The ideology for which the fathers had fought in 1776 posited an eternal struggle between liberty and power. Because the Union after March 4, 1861, would no longer be controlled by southerners, the South could protect its liberty from the assaults of hostile power only by going out of the Union. "On the 4th of March, 1861," declared a Georgia secessionist, "we are either *slaves in the Union or freemen out of it*." The question, agreed Jefferson Davis and a fellow Mississippian, was " 'Will you be slaves or will be independent?' . . . Will you consent to be robbed of your property" or will you "strike bravely for liberty, property, honor and life?"[16] Submission to Black Republicans would mean "the loss of liberty, property, home, country—everything that makes life worth having," proclaimed a South Carolinian. "I am engaged in the glorious cause of liberty and justice,"

14. Emory M. Thomas, *The Confederacy as a Revolutionary Experience* (Englewood Cliffs, N.J., 1971), 31; Johnson, *Patriarchal Republic*, 39.

15. Alabamian and Floridian quoted in James Oakes, *The Ruling Race: A History of American Slaveholders* (New York, 1982), 240, 239; Rowland, *Davis*, V, 43, 202.

16. Johnson, *Patriarchal Republic*, 36; Moore, ed., *Rebellion Record*, VI, "Documents," 299; William L. Barney, *The Secessionist Impulse: Alabama and Mississippi in 1860* (Princeton, 1974), 192.

wrote a Confederate soldier, "fighting for the rights of man—fighting for all that we of the South hold dear." [17]

What stake did nonslaveholding whites have in this crusade for the freedom of planters to own slaves? Some secessionists worried a great deal about this question. What if Hinton Rowan Helper was right? What if nonslaveowners were potential Black Republicans? "The great lever by which the abolitionists hope to extirpate slavery in the States is the aid of non-slaveholding citizens in the South," fretted a Kentucky editor. How would they ply this lever? By using the patronage to build up a cadre of Republican officeholders among nonslaveowners—first in the border states and upcountry where slavery was most vulnerable, and then in the heart of the cotton kingdom itself. Governor Joseph E. Brown of Georgia feared that some whites would be "bribed into treachery to their own section, by the allurements of office." When Republicans organized their "Abolition party . . . of Southern men," echoed the *Charleston Mercury*, "the contest for slavery will no longer be one between the North and the South. It will be in the South, between the people of the South." [18]

The elections of delegates to secession conventions seemed to confirm this fear. Many upcountry districts with few slaves sent cooperationist delegates. In the conventions, delegates supporting delay or cooperation owned, on the average, less wealth and fewer slaves than immediate secessionists. The implications of these data should not be pushed too far. A good many low-slaveholding Democratic counties voted for immediate secession, while numerous high-slaveholding Whig counties backed cooperation. And of course cooperationism did not necessarily mean unionism. Nevertheless, the partial correlation of cooperationism with low slaveholding caused concern among secessionists. [19]

17. *Charleston Mercury*, Oct. 11, 1860, in Dwight L. Dumond, ed., *Southern Editorials on Secession* (New York, 1931), 181; Michael Barton, "Did the Confederacy Change Southern Soldiers?" in Harry P. Owens and James J. Cooke, eds., *The Old South in the Crucible of War* (Jackson, 1983), 71.

18. *Kentucky Statesman*, Oct. 5, 1860, in Dumond, *The Secession Movement*, 117n.; Allen D. Candler, ed., *The Confederate Records of the State of Georgia*, 5 vols. (Atlanta, 1909–11), I, 47; *Charleston Mercury*, Oct. 11, 1860, in Dumond, ed., *Southern Editorials*, 179.

19. Seymour Martin Lipset, "The Emergence of the One-Party South—The Election of 1860," in Lipset, *Political Man: The Social Bases of Politics* (Anchor Books ed., New York, 1963), 372–84; Potter, *Impending Crisis*, 503–4; Johnson, *Patriarchal Republic*, 63–78; Peyton McCrary, Clark Miller, and Dale Baum, "Class and Party

So they undertook a campaign to convince nonslaveholders that they too had a stake in disunion. The stake was white supremacy. In this view, the Black Republican program of abolition was the first step toward racial equality and amalgamation. Georgia's Governor Brown carried this message to his native uplands of north Georgia whose voters idolized him. Slavery "is the poor man's best Government," said Brown. "Among us the poor white laborer . . . does not belong to the menial class. The negro is in no sense his equal. . . . He belongs to the only true aristocracy, the race of *white men*." Thus yeoman farmers "will never consent to submit to abolition rule," for they "know that in the event of the abolition of slavery, they would be greater sufferers than the rich, who would be able to protect themselves. . . . When it becomes necessary to defend our rights against so foul a domination, I would call upon the mountain boys as well as the people of the lowlands, and they would come down like an avalanche and swarm around the flag of Georgia."[20]

Much secessionist rhetoric played variations on this theme. The election of Lincoln, declared an Alabama newspaper, "shows that the North [intends] to free the negroes and force amalgamation between them and the children of the poor men of the South." "Do you love your mother, your wife, your sister, your daughter?" a Georgia secessionist asked nonslaveholders. If Georgia remained in a Union "ruled by Lincoln and his crew . . . in TEN years or less our CHILDREN will be the *slaves* of negroes."[21] "If you are tame enough to submit," declaimed South Carolina's Baptist clergyman James Furman, "Abolition preachers will be at hand to consummate the marriage of your daughters to black husbands." No! No! came an answering shout from Alabama. "Submit to have our wives and daughters choose between death and gratifying the hellish lust of the negro!! . . . Better ten thousand deaths than submission to Black Republicanism."[22]

To defend their wives and daughters, presumably, yeoman whites therefore joined planters in "rallying to the standard of Liberty and

in the Secession Crisis: Voting Behavior in the Deep South," *Journal of Interdisciplinary History*, 8 (1978), 429–57; and Ralph Wooster, *The Secession Conventions of the South* (Princeton, 1962), passim, esp. 259–66.

20. Johnson, *Patriarchal Republic*, 48; Steven Hahn, *The Roots of Southern Populism: Yeoman Farmers and the Transformation of the Georgia Upcountry*, 1850–1890 (New York, 1983), 86–87.

21. Reynolds, *Editors Make War*, 125–26; Johnson, *Patriarchal Republic*, 47–48.

22. Channing, *Crisis of Fear*, 287; Barney, *Secessionist Impulse*, 228.

Equality for white men" against "our Abolition enemies who are pledged to prostrate the white freemen of the South down to equality with negroes." Most southern whites could agree that "democratic liberty exists solely because we have black slaves" whose presence "promotes equality among the free." Hence "freedom is not possible without slavery."[23]

This Orwellian definition of liberty as slavery provoked ridicule north of the Potomac. For disunionists to compare themselves to the Revolutionary fathers "is a libel upon the whole character and conduct of the men of '76," declared William Cullen Bryant's *New York Evening Post*. The founders fought "to establish the rights of man . . . and principles of universal liberty." The South was rebelling "not in the interest of general humanity, but of a domestic despotism. . . . Their motto is not liberty, but slavery." Thomas Jefferson's Declaration of Independence spoke for "Natural Rights against Established Institutions," added the *New York Tribune*, while "Mr. Jeff. Davis's caricature thereof is made in the interest of an unjust, outgrown, decaying Institution against the apprehended encroachments of Natural Human Rights." It was, in short, not a revolution for liberty but a counterrevolution "reversing the wheels of progress . . . to hurl everything backward into deepest darkness . . . despotism and oppression."[24]

Without assenting to the rhetoric of this analysis, a good many disunionists in effect endorsed its substance. The signers of the Declaration of Independence were wrong if they meant to include Negroes among "all men," said Alexander Stephens after he had become vice president of the Confederacy. "Our new government is founded upon exactly the opposite idea; its foundations are laid, its cornerstone rests, upon the great truth that the negro is not equal to the white man; that slavery . . . is his natural and normal condition. This, our new government, is the first in the history of the world based upon this great physical, philosophical, and moral truth." Black Republicans were the real revolutionaries. They subscribed to "tenets as radical and revolutionary" as those of the abolitionists, declared a New Orleans newspaper. These "revolutionary dogmas," echoed numerous southerners, were "active and

23. *LINCOLN ELECTED!* Broadside from Bell County, Texas, Nov. 8, 1860, McLellan Lincoln Collection, John Hay Library, Brown University; Thornton, *Politics and Power in a Slave Society*, 321, 206–7; *Richmond Enquirer*, April 15, 1856, quoted in Oakes, *The Ruling Race*, 141.
24. *New York Evening Post*, Feb. 18, 1861; *New York Tribune*, March 27, 1861, May 21, 1862.

bristling with terrible designs and as ready for bloody and forcible realities as ever characterized the ideas of the French revolution."[25] Therefore it was "an abuse of language" to call secession a revolution, said
Jefferson Davis. We left the Union "to save ourselves from a revolution"
that threatened to make "property in slaves so insecure as to be comparatively worthless." In 1861 the Confederate secretary of state advised
foreign governments that southern states had formed a new nation "to
preserve their old institutions" from "a revolution [that] threatened to
destroy their social system."[26]

This is the language of counterrevolution. But in one respect the
Confederacy departed from the classic pattern of the genre. Most coun-
terrevolutions seek to restore the *ancien régime*. The counterrevolution-
aries of 1861 made their move before the revolutionaries had done anything—indeed, several months before Lincoln even took office. In this
regard, secession fit the model of "pre-emptive counterrevolution" developed by historian Arno Mayer. Rather than trying to restore the old
order, a pre-emptive counterrevolution strikes first to protect the status
quo before the revolutionary threat can materialize. "Conjuring up the
dangers of leaving revolutionaries the time to prepare their forces and
plans for an assault on *their* terms," writes Mayer, "counterrevolution-
ary leaders urge a preventive thrust." To mobilize support for it, they
"intentionally exaggerate the magnitude and imminence of the revolutionary threat."[27]

Though Mayer was writing about Europe in the twentieth century,
his words also describe the immediate secessionists of 1860. They exaggerated the Republican threat and urged pre-emptive action to forestall the dangers they conjured up. The South could not afford to wait
for an "overt act" by Lincoln against southern rights, they insisted. "If
I find a coiled rattlesnake in my path," asked an Alabama editor, "do I
wait for his 'overt act' or do I smite him in his coil?" When conditional
unionists tell us "that it will be several years before Lincoln will have
control of the sword and the purse through the instrumentality of Congress," observed a Mississippian, that only "furnishes additional argu-

25. *Augusta Daily Constitutionalist*, March 30, 1861; *New Orleans Bee*, June 25, 1860,
    quoted in Reynolds, *Editors Make War*, 23; Thornton, *Politics and Power in a
    Slave Society*, 416; *Columbia Daily South Carolinian*, Aug. 3, 1860, in Dumond,
    ed., *Southern Editorials*, 154.
26. Rowland, *Davis*, V, 50, 72, IV, 357; O.R. *Navy*, Ser. 2, Vol. 3, pp. 257–58.
27. *The Dynamics of Counterrevolution in Europe, 1870–1956: An Analytic Frame-
    work* (New York, 1971), 86.

ment for action NOW. Let us rally . . . before the enemy can make good his promise to overwhelm us. . . . Delay is dangerous. Now is the time to strike."[28]

II

Seldom in history has a counterrevolution so quickly provoked the very revolution it sought to pre-empt. This happened because most northerners refused to condone disunion. On that matter, if on little else, the outgoing and incoming presidents of the United States agreed.

In his final message to Congress, on December 3, 1860, James Buchanan surprised some of his southern allies with a firm denial of the right of secession. The Union was not "a mere voluntary association of States, to be dissolved at pleasure by any one of the contracting parties," said Buchanan. "We the People" had adopted the Constitution to form "a *more* perfect Union" than the one existing under the Articles of Confederation, which had stated that "the Union shall be perpetual." The framers of the national government "never intended to implant in its bosom the seeds of its own destruction, nor were they guilty of the absurdity of providing for its own dissolution." State sovereignty was *not* superior to national sovereignty, Buchanan insisted. The Constitution bestowed the highest attributes of sovereignty exclusively on the federal government: national defense; foreign policy; regulation of foreign and interstate commerce; coinage of money. "This Constitution," stated that document, "and the laws of the United States . . . shall be the supreme law of the land . . . any thing in the constitution or laws of any State to the contrary notwithstanding." If secession was legitimate, warned the president, the Union became "a rope of sand" and "our thirty-three States may resolve themselves into as many petty, jarring, and hostile republics. . . . By such a dread catastrophe the hopes of the friends of freedom throughout the world would be destroyed. . . . Our example for more than eighty years would not only be lost, but it would be quoted as a conclusive proof that man is unfit for self-government."[29]

Thousands of northern editorials and speeches echoed these themes. Fears of a domino effect were especially pervasive. "A successful rebel-

---

28. *Wetumpka Enquirer*, Nov. ?, 1860, quoted in Reynolds, *Editors Make War*, 142; *Jackson Mississippian*, Nov. 14, 1860, quoted in Rainwater, *Mississippi, Storm Center of Secession*, 163.

29. James D. Richardson, comp., *Compilation of the Messages and Papers of the Presidents, 1789–1897*, 10 vols. (Washington, 1897), V, 628–37.

lion by a few States now," ran an editorial typical of hundreds, "will be followed by a new rebellion or secession a few years hence." This was not mere alarmism. Some Americans were already speculating about a division of the country into three or four "confederacies" with an independent Pacific coast republic thrown in for good measure. Several New York merchants and Democrats with ties to the South were talking of setting up as a free city. A prominent New York lawyer secretly informed railroad president George B. McClellan in December 1860 that "when secession is fairly inaugurated at the South, we mean to do a little of the same business here & cut loose from the fanactics of New England & of the North generally, including most of our own State." In January 1861 Mayor Fernando Wood brought this matter into the open with a message to the aldermen advocating the secession of New York City. The project went nowhere, but it did plant seeds of copperheadism that germinated a couple of years later.[30]

"The doctrine of secession is anarchy," declared a Cincinnati newspaper. "If any minority have the right to break up the Government at pleasure, because they have not had their way, there is an end of all government." Lincoln too considered secession the "essence of anarchy." He branded state sovereignty a "sophism." "The Union is older than any of the States," Lincoln asserted, "and, in fact, it created them as States." The Declaration of Independence transformed the "United Colonies" into the United States; without this union then, there would never have been any "free and independent States." "Having never been States, either in substance, or in name, *outside* the Union," asked Lincoln, "whence this magical omnipotence of 'State rights,' asserting a claim of power to lawfully destroy the Union itself?" Perpetuity was "the fundamental law of all national governments." No government "ever had provision in its organic law for its own termination. . . . No State, upon its own mere motion, can lawfully get out of the Union. . . . They can only do so against law, and by revolution."[31]

Neither Lincoln nor any other northerner denied the right of revolution. After all, Yankees shared the legacy of 1776. But there was no

30. *Providence Daily Post*, Nov. 19, 1860, in Howard C. Perkins, ed., *Northern Editorials on Secession* (New York, 1942), 183; Samuel L. M. Barlow to McClellan, Dec. 6, 1860, Barlow Papers, Henry E. Huntington Library; William C. Wright, *The Secession Movement in the Middle Atlantic States* (Rutherford, N.J., 1973), 176–79.

31. *Cincinnati Daily Commercial*, May 6, 1861, in Perkins, ed., *Northern Editorials*, 828; CWL, IV, 264–65, 268, 433–37.

"right of revolution at *pleasure*," declared a Philadelphia newspaper. Revolution was "a moral right, when exercised for a morally justifiable cause," wrote Lincoln. But "when exercised without such a cause revolution is no right, but simply a wicked exercise of physical power." The South had no just cause. The event that precipitated secession was the election of a president by a constitutional majority. The "central idea" of the Union cause, said Lincoln, "is the necessity of proving that popular government is not an absurdity. We must settle this question now, whether in a free government the minority have the right to break up the government whenever they choose."[32]

But how was it to be settled? This problem was compounded by the lame-duck syndrome in the American constitutional system. During the four-month interval between Lincoln's election and inauguration, Buchanan had the executive power but felt little responsibility for the crisis, while Lincoln had responsibility but little power. The Congress elected in 1860 would not meet in regular session for thirteen months, while the Congress that did meet in December 1860 experienced an erosion of authority as members from the lower South resigned when their states seceded. Buchanan's forceful denial of the legality of disunion ended with a lame confession of impotence to do anything about it. Although the Constitution gave no state the right to withdraw, said the president, it also gave the national government no power "to coerce a State into submission which is attempting to withdraw."[33]

Republicans ridiculed this reasoning. Buchanan had demonstrated that "no state has the right to secede unless it wishes to," jibed Seward, and that "it is the President's duty to enforce the laws, unless somebody opposes him."[34] But Republicans seemed unable to come up with any better alternative. Several options presented themselves: coercion, compromise, or allowing "the erring sisters to depart in peace." Although various Republican leaders sanctioned each of these approaches at one time or another, none of the options commanded a majority before April 1861. Instead, a rather vague fourth alternative emerged—described as "masterly inactivity" or a "Fabian policy"—a position of watchful waiting, of making no major concessions but at the same time

32. *Philadelphia Ledger*, Dec. 28, 1860, quoted in Kenneth M. Stampp, *And the War Came: The North and the Secession Crisis, 1860–61* (Baton Rouge, 1950), 34; CWL, IV, 434n.; Dennett, *Lincoln/Hay*, 19.
33. Richardson, *Messages and Papers*, V, 634–36.
34. Stampp, *And the War Came*, 56.

avoiding needless provocation, in the hope that the disunion fever would run its course and the presumed legions of southern unionists would bring the South back to its senses.

When Congress convened in December several Republicans, especially from the Old Northwest, "swore by everything in the Heavens above and the Earth beneath that they would convert the rebel States into a wilderness." "Without a little blood-letting," wrote Michigan's radical, coarse-grained Senator Zachariah Chandler, "this Union will not . . . be worth a rush." The danger of losing access to the lower Mississippi valley may have accounted for the bellicosity of many mid-westerners. The people of the Northwest, said the *Chicago Tribune*, would never negotiate for free navigation of the river. "It is *their right*, and they will assert it to the extremity of blotting Louisiana out of the map."[35]

And how would customs duties be collected at southern ports? Whose customhouses were they—American or Confederate? In the nullification crisis of 1832, Andrew Jackson had vowed to use force to collect duties in South Carolina and to hang the nullification leaders. "Oh, for one hour of Jackson!" exclaimed many Yankee Republicans who developed a sudden retrospective affection for this Tennessee Democrat. If letters received by Republican congressmen were any indication, their constituents stood ready to "coerce" the rebels. "We elected Lincoln," wrote an Illinoisian, "and are just as willing, if necessity requires, to fight for him. . . . Little Boone [County] can be relied on for 500 Wide Awakes, well armed and equipped." Lincoln "must *enforce the laws of the U. States against all rebellion*," added an Ohioan, "no matter what the consequences."[36]

Lincoln seemed to agree. In December 1860 he told his private secretary that the very existence of government "implies the legal power, right, and duty . . . of a President to execute the laws and maintain the existing government." Lincoln quietly passed word to General-in-

35. Henry Adams, "The Great Secession Winter of 1860–61," in Adams, *The Great Secession Winter of 1860–61 and Other Essays*, ed. George Hochfield (New York, 1958), 4; Chandler to Austin Blair, Feb. 11, 1861, in Nevins, *Emergence*, II, 411–12; *Chicago Tribune*, Feb. 25, 1861, in Perkins, ed., *Northern Editorials*, 558.

36. *Springfield (Mass.) Republican*, Dec. 17, 1860; A. W. Metcalf to Lyman Trumbull, Dec. 12, 1860, in William E. Baringer, *A House Dividing: Lincoln as President Elect* (Springfield, Ill., 1945), 237; J. W. Whiting to Trumbull, Nov. 19, 1860, E. D. Mansfield to Salmon P. Chase, Nov. 26, 1860, in Stampp, *And the War Came*, 27.

Chief Winfield Scott to make ready to collect the customs and defend federal forts in seceded states, or to retake them if they had been given up before his inauguration. In Springfield the *Illinois State Journal*, quasi-official spokesman for Lincoln during this period, warned that "disunion by armed force is treason, and treason must and will be put down at all hazards. . . . The laws of the United States must be executed—the President has no discretionary power on the subject—his duty is emphatically pronounced in the Constitution."[37]

Republicans preferred to distinguish between "coercion"—which had a harsh ring—and enforcement of the laws. "It is not making war upon a State to execute the laws," insisted the *Boston Advertiser*. But to southerners this was a distinction without a difference. To "execute the laws" in a foreign country—the Confederacy—would mean war. "Why, sir," asked Louis Wigfall of Texas, "if the President of the United States were to send a fleet to Liverpool, and attempt there . . . to collect the revenue . . . would anybody say that the British Government was responsible for the bloodshed that might follow?"[38]

In any event the whole question was hypothetical until March 4, for Buchanan intended no "coercion." And even if he had, the resources were pitifully inadequate. Most of the tiny 16,000-man army was scattered over two thousand miles of frontier, while most of the navy's ships were patrolling distant waters or laid up for repair. The strongest armed forces during the winter of 1860–61 were the militias of seceding states. Moreover, upper-South unionists who had managed to keep fire-eaters in their states at bay made an impression on Republicans with warnings that anything which smacked of coercion would tip the balance toward secession. For a time, therefore, Republican opinion drifted uncertainly while other groups sought to fashion a compromise.

Buchanan's message to Congress set the agenda for these efforts. He first blamed the North in general and Republicans in particular for "the incessant and violent agitation of the slavery question" which had now "produced its natural effects" by provoking disunion. Because of Republicans, said the president, "many a matron throughout the South retires at night in dread of what may befall herself and children before morn-

---

37. John G. Nicolay and John Hay, *Abraham Lincoln: A History*, 10 vols. (New York, 1890), III, 248; Lincoln to Francis P. Blair, Dec. 21, 1860, Lincoln to Elihu B. Washburne, Dec. 22, 1860, in *CWL*, IV, 157, 159; *Illinois State Journal*, Nov. 14, Dec. 20, 1860, in Nevins, *Emergence*, II, 356–57.
38. Both quotations from Stampp, *And the War Came*, 39, 44.

ing." Buchanan stopped short of asking the Republican party to dissolve; instead he asked northerners to stop criticizing slavery, repeal their "unconstitutional and obnoxious" personal liberty laws, obey the fugitive slave law, and join with the South to adopt a constitutional amendment protecting slavery in all territories. Unless Yankees proved willing to do these things, said Buchanan, the South would after all "be justified in revolutionary resistance to the Government." As an additional sign of northern good will, Buchanan also advised support for his long-standing effort to acquire Cuba, which would further placate southern fears by adding a large new slave state to the Union.[39]

Republican responses to these suggestions may be readily imagined. The printable comments included: "Pharasaical old hypocrite . . . bristling with the spirit of a rabid slaveocracy . . . wretched drivel . . . truckling subserviency to the Cotton Lords . . . gross perversion of facts . . . brazen lies." After the voters had just rejected the Breckinridge platform by a margin of 4,000,000 to 670,000 in the presidential election, Buchanan "proposes an unconditional surrender . . . of six-sevenths of the people to one-seventh . . . by *making the Breckinridge platform a part of the Constitution!*"[40]

Although few of the compromise proposals introduced in Congress went so far as Buchanan's, they all shared the same feature: Republicans would have to make all the concessions. Republicans refused to succumb to what they considered blackmail. Indeed, the possibility that a coalition of Democrats and Constitutional Unionists might patch together a "shameful surrender" and call it compromise caused some Republicans to prefer the alternative of letting the cotton states "go in peace." Having long regarded the Union as a "covenant with death," Garrisonian abolitionists were glad that slaveholders had broken the covenant. Even non-Garrisonians agreed, in Frederick Douglass's words, that "if the Union can only be maintained by new concessions to the slaveholders [and] a new drain on the negro's blood, then . . . let the Union perish." Several radical Republicans initially took a similar position. If South Carolina wanted to leave, said the *Chicago Tribune* in October 1860, "let her go, and like a limb lopped from a healthy trunk, wilt and rot where she falls." Horace Greeley's *New York Tribune* prominently advocated the go-in-peace approach. "If the Cotton States shall

---

39. Richardson, *Messages and Papers*, V, 626–27, 630, 638, 642.
40. Various Republican editorials quoted in Perkins, ed., *Northern Editorials*, 154, 127; 137, 152, 146, 138, 147.

become satisfied that they can do better out of the Union than in it, we insist on letting them go," wrote Greeley in a famous editorial three days after Lincoln's election. "We hope never to live in a republic whereof one section is pinned to the residue by bayonets."[41]

A genuine desire to avoid war accounted in part for this attitude. But other motives were probably more important, for all of these Republicans subsequently endorsed war to preserve the Union. Greeley's go-in-peace editorials represented a dual gambit, one part aimed at the North and the other at the South. Like most Republicans, Greeley believed at first that southern states did not really intend to secede; "they simply mean to bully the Free States into concessions." Even after South Carolina went out, Greeley wrote to Lincoln that "I fear nothing . . . but another disgraceful backdown of the free States. . . . Another nasty compromise, whereby everything is conceded and nothing secured, will so thoroughly disgrace and humiliate us that we can never again raise our heads."[42] To advise the North to let the disunionists go, therefore, became a way of deflecting compromise. Toward the South, Greeley expected his gambit to operate like the strategy of parents who tell an obstreperous adolescent son, after his repeated threats to run away from home, "There's the door—go!" By avoiding talk of coercion it might also allow passions to cool and give unionists breathing room to mobilize their presumed silent majority below the Potomac.[43]

Go-in-peace sentiment faded as it became clear that the dreaded alternative of compromise would not come to pass. To sift all the compromise proposals introduced in Congress, each house set up a special committee. The Senate "Committee of Thirteen" included powerful men: William H. Seward, Benjamin Wade, Stephen Douglas, Robert Toombs, Jefferson Davis, and John J. Crittenden. It was Crittenden who cobbled together a plan which he proposed as a series of amendments to the Constitution. In their final form these amendments would

41. *Douglass' Monthly*, Jan. 1861; *Chicago Tribune*, Oct. 11, 1860, quoted in Stampp, *And the War Came*, 22; *New York Tribune*, Nov. 9, 1860.
42. *New York Tribune*, Nov. 20, 1860; Greeley to Lincoln, Dec. 22, 1860, Abraham Lincoln Papers, Library of Congress.
43. This analysis of Greeley's motives has been much influenced by David M. Potter's perceptive writings on the subject, especially "Horace Greeley and Peaceable Secession," and "Postscript," in Potter, *The South and the Sectional Conflict* (Baton Rouge, 1968), 219–42, and Potter, *Lincoln and His Party*, 51–57. For a slightly different interpretation see Bernard A. Weisberger, "Horace Greeley: Reformer as Republican," *CWH*, 23 (1977), 5–25.

have guaranteed slavery in the states against future interference by the national government; prohibited slavery in territories north of 36° 30′ and protected it south of that line in all territories "now held, *or hereafter acquired*" (italics added); forbidden Congress to abolish slavery on any federal property within slave states (forts, arsenals, naval bases, etc.); forbidden Congress to abolish slavery in the District of Columbia without the consent of its inhabitants *and* unless it had first been abolished by both Virginia and Maryland; denied Congress any power to interfere with the interstate slave trade; and compensated slaveholders who were prevented from recovering fugitives in northern states. These constitutional amendments were to be valid for all time; no future amendment could override them.[44]

Despite the one-sided nature of this "compromise," some Republican businessmen who feared that a secession panic on Wall Street might deepen into another depression urged party leaders to accept it. Thurlow Weed—and by implication Seward—gave signs in December of a willingness to do so. But from Springfield came word to stand firm. "Entertain no proposition for a compromise in regard to the *extension* of slavery," Lincoln wrote to key senators and congressmen. "The tug has to come, & better now, than any time hereafter." Crittenden's compromise, Lincoln told Weed and Seward, "would lose us everything we gained by the election. . . . Filibustering for all South of us, and making slave states would follow . . . to put us again on the high-road to a slave empire." The very notion of a territorial compromise, Lincoln pointed out, "acknowledges that slavery has equal rights with liberty, and surrenders all we have contended for. . . . We have just carried an election on principles fairly stated to the people. Now we are told in advance, the government shall be broken up, unless we surrender to those we have beaten. . . . If we surrender, it is the end of us. They will repeat the experiment upon us *ad libitum*. A year will not pass, till we shall have to take Cuba as a condition upon which they will stay in the Union."[45]

Following Lincoln's advice, all five Republicans on the Senate Com-

---

44. *CG*, 36 Cong., 2 Sess., 114. The Constitution contained a precedent for these "unamendable" amendments: Article V, which prohibits any change in the equal representation of each state in the Senate.

45. Lincoln to Lyman Trumbull, Dec. 10, 1860, to William Kellogg, Dec. 11, to Elihu B. Washburne, Dec. 13, to Thurlow Weed, Dec. 17, to William H. Seward, Feb. 1, 1861, to John D. DeFrees, Dec. 18, 1860, to James T. Hale, Jan. 11, 1861, in *CWL*, IV, 149–51, 154, 183, 155, 172.

mittee of Thirteen voted against the Crittenden compromise. On the grounds that any compromise would be worthless if opposed by the Republicans, Toombs and Davis also voted No, sending the measure down to defeat 7–6. Crittenden then took his proposal to the Senate floor, where on January 16 it was rejected by a vote of 25–23, with all 25 negative votes cast by Republicans. Fourteen senators from states that had seceded or were about to secede did not vote. Although Crittenden's compromise resurfaced again later, Republican opposition and lower-South indifference continued to doom it.[46]

Did this mean that Republicans killed the last, best hope to avert disunion? Probably not. Neither Crittenden's nor any other compromise could have stopped secession in the lower South. No compromise could undo the event that triggered disunion: Lincoln's election by a solid North. "We spit upon every plan to compromise," wrote one secessionist. "No human power can save the Union, all the cotton states will go," said Jefferson Davis, while Judah Benjamin agreed that "a settlement [is] totally out of our power to accomplish."[47] On December 13, before any compromises had been debated—indeed, before any states had actually seceded—more than two-thirds of the senators and representatives from seven southern states signed an address to their constituents: "The argument is exhausted. All hope of relief in the Union, through the agency of committees, Congressional legislation, or constitutional amendments, is extinguished. . . . The honor, safety, and independence of the Southern people are to be found in a Southern Confederacy."[48] Delegates from seven states who met in Montgomery on February 4, 1861, to organize a new nation paid no attention to the compromise efforts in Washington.

But it was significant that only seven slave states were represented at Montgomery. By February 1861 the main goal of compromise maneuvers was to keep the other eight from going out. The legislatures of five of these states had enacted provisions for the calling of conventions.[49]

46. Nevins, *Emergence*, II, 390–98; CG, 36 Cong., 2 Sess., 409.
47. Reynolds, *Editors Make War*, 169; Davis quoted in Samuel C. Buttersworth to Samuel L. M. Barlow, Dec. 3, 1860, Benjamin to Barlow, Dec. 9, 1860, Barlow Papers, Henry E. Huntington Library.
48. Edward McPherson, *The Political History of the United States of America during the Great Rebellion*, 2nd ed. (Washington, 1865), 37.
49. The legislatures of Kentucky and Delaware refused to provide for conventions and the governor of Maryland did not call his legislature into session.

But thereafter the resemblance to events below the 35th parallel ceased. Voters in Virginia, Arkansas, and Missouri elected a majority of unionists to their conventions. Voters in North Carolina and Tennessee, given the choice of voting for or against the holding of a convention, voted against doing so. Although the Confederate states sent commissioners to the upper-South conventions with appeals to join their southern sisters, the Missouri and Arkansas conventions rejected secession in March (Arkansas by a narrow margin) and Virginia did the same by a two-to-one margin on April 4. The main reason for this outcome was the lesser salience of slavery in the upper South. Slaves constituted 47 percent of the population in the Confederate states but only 24 percent in the upper South; 37 percent of the white families in Confederate states owned slaves compared with 20 percent of the families in the upper South.[50]

This failure of secession in the upper South seemed to confirm the Republican belief in the region's basic unionism. But much of that unionism was highly conditional. The condition was northern forbearance from any attempt to "coerce" Confederate states. The Tennessee legislature resolved that its citizens "will as one man, resist [any] invasion of the soil of the South at any hazard and to the last extremity." To put teeth into a similar admonition by the Virginia legislature, the convention of that commonwealth remained in session to watch developments after initially voting down secession. Moderate Republicans heeded these warnings and trod softly during the first three months of 1861. This was the time of "masterly inactivity," of limited concessions to strengthen that silent majority of lower-South unionists so they could begin a "voluntary reconstruction" of their states. Seward in particular had abandoned the irrepressible conflict to become chief of the conciliationists. "Every thought that we think," he wrote to Lincoln on January 27, "ought to be conciliatory, forbearing and patient, and so open the way for the rising of a Union Party in the seceding States which will bring them back into the Union." Although less optimistic than Seward, Lincoln approved of this approach so long as it involved "no compromise which *assists* or *permits* the extension" of slavery.[51]

Republicans on the special House Committee of Thirty-Three (one

50. Calculated from the census of 1860.
51. Mary E. R. Campbell, *The Attitude of Tennesseans toward the Union* (New York, 1961), 161–62; Seward to Lincoln, Jan. 27, 1861, Lincoln to Seward, Feb. 1, 1861, CWL, IV, 183.

for each state)[52] had first demonstrated the possibilities of such a "Fabian policy." Charles Francis Adams sponsored a proposal to admit New Mexico (which included present-day Arizona) as a state. This maneuver had a deep purpose: to divide the upper and lower South and cement the former to the Union by the appearance of concession on the territorial question. New Mexico had a slave code and a few slaves. But everyone recognized that the institution would not take root there; as Crittenden noted, the ultimate consequence of New Mexico's admission would be to give the North another free state. Lower-South members of the committee scorned the proposal while several upper-South members approved it, thereby accomplishing Adams's intention. He persuaded nine of the fifteen Republicans on the committee to endorse this apparent violation of the party's platform. The measure therefore obtained committee approval on December 29. When it finally reached a floor vote two months later, however, a three-to-one negative Republican margin defeated it. Nevertheless, during those two months the New Mexico scheme had played a part in keeping the upper South in the Union.[53]

Two other recommendations from the Committee of Thirty-Three helped along this cause. Both received Seward's active and Lincoln's passive endorsement. The first was a resolution calling for faithful obedience to the fugitive slave law and repeal of personal liberty laws in conflict with it. This passed the House on February 27 with the support of about half the Republican representatives. Next day the House adopted a proposed Thirteenth Amendment to the Constitution guaranteeing slavery in the states against any future interference by the federal government. This was too much for three-fifths of the Republicans to swallow, but the two-fifths who did vote for it in both House and Senate gave this Amendment the bare two-thirds majority needed to send it to the states for ratification. Before that process got anywhere, however, other matters intervened to produce four years later a Thirteenth Amendment that abolished slavery.

Seward's conciliation policy also bore fruit in the form of a "peace convention" that assembled in Washington on February 4, the same day that the Confederate constitutional convention met in Montgomery. Called by the Virginia legislature, the peace convention further

---

52. Members from two of the seven seceding states refused to participate in any of the committee's sessions, and members from four others boycotted several of them.
53. Potter, *Lincoln and His Party*, 290–302.

divided the upper and lower South. The seceded states plus Arkansas refused to send delegates. Five northern states also failed to participate— California and Oregon because of distance; Michigan, Wisconsin, and Minnesota because their Republican leaders distrusted the enterprise. Many Republicans in other states shared this distrust, but Seward persuaded them to support the project as a gesture of good will. Taking the Crittenden compromise as a starting point, this "Old Gentlemen's Convention" accomplished little except to mark time. Many of the delegates belonged to a past era, typified by the chairman, seventy-one-year-old ex-President John Tyler of Virginia. Debates were aimless or acrimonious; Republican participation was perfunctory or hostile. After three weeks of labor, the convention brought forth the Crittenden compromise modified to make it slightly more palatable to the North. Extension of the 36° 30' line would apply only to "present territory" and a majority vote of senators from both the free and slave states would be required to obtain any new territory.[54] When this recommendation went before Congress, it suffered an unceremonious defeat, mainly by Republican votes.

Six hundred miles distant the Confederate convention appeared by contrast to be a triumph of efficiency. In six days the delegates at Montgomery drafted a temporary constitution, turned themselves into a provisional Congress for the new government, elected a provisional president and vice president, and then spent a more leisurely month fashioning a permanent constitution and setting the machinery of government in motion. Elections for a bicameral Congress and for a president and vice president to serve the single six-year term prescribed by the Constitution were to be held in November 1861.

Although Barnwell Rhett and a few other fire-eaters came to Montgomery as delegates, they took a back seat at a convention that did its best to project a moderate image to the upper South. Befitting the new Confederacy's claim to represent the true principles of the U. S. Constitution which the North had trampled upon, most of the provisional

---

54. The key vote in the convention was 9-8 in favor of this territorial provision, as follows:

Free states: 5 yes, 6 no, 3 abstentions
Slave states: 4 yes, 2 no, 1 abstention.

For detailed accounts of the convention, see Robert G. Gunderson, *Old Gentlemen's Convention: The Washington Peace Conference of 1861* (Madison, 1961), and Jesse L. Keene, *The Peace Convention of 1861* (Tuscaloosa, 1961).

constitution was copied verbatim from that venerable document. The same was true of the permanent Confederate Constitution, adopted a month later, though some of its departures from the original were significant. The preamble omitted the general welfare clause and the phrase "a more perfect Union," and added a clause after We the People: "each State acting in its sovereign and independent character." Instead of the U. S. Constitution's evasions on slavery ("persons held to service or labor"), the Confederate version called a slave a slave. It guaranteed the protection of bondage in any new territory the Confederacy might acquire. The Constitution did forbid the importation of slaves from abroad, to avoid alienating Britain and especially the upper South, whose economy benefitted from its monopoly on export of slaves to the lower South. The Constitution permitted a tariff for revenue but not for protection of domestic industries, though what this distinction meant was unclear since the clause did not define it. Another clause forbade government aid for internal improvements. The Constitution also nurtured state's rights by empowering legislatures to impeach Confederate officials whose duties lay wholly within a state. After weakening the executive by limiting the president to a single six-year term, the Constitution strengthened that branch by giving the president a line-item veto of appropriations and granting cabinet officers a potential non-voting seat on the floor of Congress (this was never put into effect).[55]

Most interest at Montgomery focused on the choice of a provisional president. There was no shortage of aspirants, but the final nod went to a West Point graduate who would have preferred to become commander of the Confederacy's army. As the most prominent of the original secessionists, Rhett and Yancey had a strong claim for preference. But conditional unionists north of the 35th parallel, especially in Virginia, regarded them as no less responsible than the blackest of Republicans for the tragic division of the country that was forcing them to choose sides. Since the new Confederacy—containing scarcely 10 percent of the country's white population and 5 percent of its industrial capacity— desperately needed the allegiance of the upper South, Yancey and Rhett were ruled out. Toombs, Stephens, and Howell Cobb, all from Georgia, seemed to fit the bill better. But the Georgia delegation could not unite on one of them. Moreover, as a conditional unionist until the last minute, Stephens was suspect in the eyes of original secessionists, while

55. The Constitution is conveniently printed in Emory M. Thomas, *The Confederate Nation 1861–1865* (New York, 1979), 307–22.

Toombs, a former Whig, suffered a similar handicap among the long-time Democrats who predominated at Montgomery. Toombs's heavy drinking—he appeared at a party falling-down drunk two nights before the balloting for president—also hurt his chances. Word from Richmond that Virginia's pro-secession senators Mason and Hunter favored Jefferson Davis proved decisive. Austere, able, experienced in government as a senator and former secretary of war, a Democrat and a secessionist but no fire-eater, Davis was the ideal candidate. Though he had not sought the job and did not really want it, the delegates elected him unanimously on February 9. His sense of duty—and destiny—bid him accept. To console Georgia and strengthen the Confederacy's moderate image, one-time Whig and more recently Douglas Democrat Alexander Stephens received the vice presidency. To satisfy geographical balance, Davis apportioned the six cabinet posts among each state of the Confederacy except his own Mississippi, with the top position of secretary of state going to the sulking Toombs.[56]

"The man and the hour have met!" So said a genial William L. Yancey as he introduced Jefferson Davis to a cheering crowd in Montgomery on February 16. It was on this occasion that "Dixie" began its career as the unofficial Confederate anthem. Perhaps inspired by the music, Davis made a brief, bellicose speech. "The time for compromise has now passed," he said. "The South is determined to maintain her position, and make all who oppose her smell Southern powder and feel Southern steel." His inaugural address two days later was more pacific. He assured everyone that the Confederacy wished to live in peace and extended a warm invitation to any states that "may seek to unite their fortunes to ours."[57] Davis then settled down to the heavy responsibilities of organizing a new nation—and of enlarging its borders.

Abraham Lincoln's chief concern was to prevent that enlargement. And part of the energy expended in building *his* cabinet was directed to that end. Putting together a cabinet gave Lincoln no end of trouble. The infant Republican party was still a loose coalition of several previous parties, of down-east Yankees and frontiersmen, radicals and conservatives, ideologues and pragmatists, of upper North and lower North and

56. *Ibid.*, 37–66; E. Merton Coulter, *The Confederate States of America* (Baton Rouge, 1950), 19–32.
57. Bruce Catton, *The Coming Fury* (Garden City, N.Y., 1961), 214–15; Rowland, *Davis*, V, 47–53.

border-state tycoons like the Blairs of Maryland, of strong leaders several of whom still considered themselves better qualified for the presidency than the man who won it. Lincoln had to satisfy all of these interests with his seven cabinet appointments, which would also indicate the direction of his policy toward the South.[58]

With an aplomb unparalleled in American political history, the president-elect appointed his four main rivals for the nomination to cabinet posts. Lincoln did not hesitate in his choices of Seward for secretary of state and Bates for attorney general. Cameron represented a more formidable problem. The Pennsylvanian believed that he had a commitment from Lincoln's convention managers. In any case, to leave him out would cause disaffection. But putting him in provoked an outcry when word leaked that Lincoln had offered Cameron the treasury. Many Republicans considered the "Winnebago Chief"—a derisive nickname Cameron had acquired years earlier when he had allegedly cheated an Indian tribe in a supply contract—to be "a man destitute of honor and integrity." Taken aback, Lincoln withdrew the offer, whereupon Cameron's friends mobilized a campaign in his behalf that distracted the party as the inauguration neared. Lincoln finally settled the matter— but not the controversy—by giving Cameron the war department. The treasury went to Chase, who had become a leader of the "iron-back" Republicans opposed to any hint of concession to the South. Chase's appointment so offended Seward that he withdrew his acceptance as secretary of state—an obvious attempt to make Lincoln dump Chase. This was the first test of Seward's ambition to be "premier" of the administration. "I can't afford to let Seward take the first trick," Lincoln told his private secretary. The president-elect persuaded Seward to back down and remain in the cabinet with Chase—though one more confrontation lay ahead before Seward was convinced that Lincoln intended to be his own premier.[59]

Paying a debt to Indiana for early support of his nomination, Lincoln named Caleb Smith secretary of the interior. The fussy, bewigged Connecticut Yankee Gideon Welles received the navy department. Lincoln

---

58. This and the following paragraphs on Lincoln's purposes and problems in putting together a cabinet are drawn from James G. Randall, *Lincoln the President*, 4 vols. (New York, 1946–55), I, 256–72; Nevins, *Emergence*, II, 436–55; Nicolay and Hay, *Lincoln*, III, 347–72; and Baringer, *A House Dividing*, passim.
59. Quotations from Nevins, *Emergence*, II, 441, and Nicolay and Hay, *Lincoln*, III, 371.

wanted to appoint a non-Republican from the upper South as a gesture of good will to hold this region in the Union. He offered a portfolio to Congressman John Gilmer of North Carolina. But to join a Black Republican administration was too much of a political risk, so Gilmer turned down the offer on grounds that Lincoln's refusal to compromise on slavery in the territories made it impossible for him to accept. Lincoln thereupon rounded out his cabinet with Montgomery Blair as postmaster general. Though a resident of Maryland, Blair was a Republican and an "iron-back."[60]

Even more important than the cabinet as a sign of future policy would be Lincoln's inaugural address. Knowing that the fate of the upper South, and of hopes for voluntary reconstruction of the lower South, might rest on what he said on March 4, Lincoln devoted great care to every phrase of the address. It went through several drafts after consultation with various Republican leaders, especially Seward. This process began in Springfield two months before the inauguration and continued through Lincoln's twelve-day roundabout trip by rail to Washington, during which he made dozens of speeches to trackside crowds and official receptions. The president-elect felt an obligation to greet the multitudes who lined his route to catch a glimpse of their new leader. In effect, Lincoln was making a whistle-stop tour *after* his election, even to the point of climbing down from the train to kiss the eleven-year-old girl in upstate New York who had suggested that he grow the beard which was now filling out on his face.

This tour may have been a mistake in two respects. Not wishing by a careless remark or slip of the tongue to inflame the crisis further, Lincoln often indulged in platitudes and trivia in his attempts to say nothing controversial. This produced an unfavorable impression on those who were already disposed to regard the ungainly president-elect as a commonplace prairie lawyer. Second, Lincoln's mail and the national press had for weeks been full of threats and rumors of assassination. A public journey of this sort with all stops announced in advance greatly increased the risk of violence. Two days before he was scheduled to travel through Baltimore, a city rife with secession sympathizers and notorious for political riots, Lincoln's party got wind of a plot to assassinate him as he changed trains there. Indeed, warnings came from two independent sources—a Pinkerton detective force employed by the rail-

60. Daniel W. Crofts, "A Reluctant Unionist: John A. Gilmer and Lincoln's Cabinet," *CWH*, 24 (1978), 225–49.

road and an agent of the war department—both of which had infiltrated Baltimore's political gangs. Lincoln reluctantly consented to a change in his schedule which took him secretly through Baltimore in the middle of the night. An assassination plot probably did exist; the danger was real. But Lincoln thereafter regretted the decision to creep into Washington "like a thief in the night." It embarrassed many of his supporters and enabled opposition cartoonists to ridicule him. The whole affair started his administration off on the wrong foot at a time when it needed the appearance of firmness and command.[61]

Lincoln put the finishing touches on his inaugural address during these first days in Washington. While he had been composing it, seven states were not only seceding but were also seizing federal property within their borders—customshouses, arsenals, mints, and forts. The first draft of the inaugural therefore had one theme and two variations. The theme was Lincoln's determination to preserve an undivided Union. The variations contrapuntally offered a sword and an olive branch. The sword was an intention to use "all the powers at my disposal" to "reclaim the public property and places which have fallen; to hold, occupy, and possess these, and all other property and places belonging to the government, and to collect the duties on imports." The olive branch was a reiteration of his oft-repeated pledge not "to interfere with the institution of slavery where it exists" and to enforce the constitutional injunction for the return of fugitive slaves. Lincoln also promised the South that "the government will not assail *you*, unless you *first* assail *it*."[62]

Seward and Lincoln's Illinois confidant Orville Browning found the sword too prominent in this draft. The upper South, not to mention the Confederate government, was sure to regard any attempt to "reclaim" forts and other property as "coercion." And even the promise not to assail these states unless they first assailed the government contained a veiled threat. Seward persuaded Lincoln to delete "unless you *first* assail *it*" and to soften a few other phrases. He also drafted a peroration appealing to the historic patriotism of southern people. The president-elect added a passage assuring southerners that whenever "in any interior locality" the hostility to the United States was "so great and so universal, as to prevent competent resident citizens from holding the Federal offices," he would suspend government activities "for the time."

61. Randall, *Lincoln the President*, I, 288–91; Norma B. Cuthbert, ed., *Lincoln and the Baltimore Plot* (San Marino, Cal., 1949).

62. CWL, IV, 254, 250–52, 261.

Most significantly, perhaps, Browning prevailed on Lincoln to drop his threat to *reclaim* federal property, so that the final version of the address vowed only to "hold, occupy, and possess" such property and to "collect duties and imposts."[63]

These phrases were ambiguous. How would the duties be collected? By naval vessels stationed offshore? Would this be coercion? How could the government "hold, occupy and possess" property that was under control of Confederate forces? The only remaining property in Union hands were two obscure forts in the Florida Keys along with Fort Pickens on an island at the mouth of Pensacola Bay and Fort Sumter on an island in Charleston harbor. Fort Sumter had become a commanding symbol of national sovereignty in the very cradle of secession, a symbol that the Confederate government could not tolerate if it wished its own sovereignty to be recognized by the world. Would Lincoln use force to defend Sumter? The ambiguity was intentional. Hoping to avoid provocation, Lincoln and Seward did not wish to reveal whether the velvet glove enclosed an iron fist.

There was no ambiguity about the peroration, revised and much improved from Seward's draft. "I am loth to close," said Lincoln. "We are not enemies, but friends. We must not be enemies. Though passion may have strained, it must not break our bonds of affection. The mystic chords of memory, stretching from every battle-field, and patriot grave, to every living heart and hearthstone, all over this broad land, will yet swell the chorus of the Union, when again touched, as surely they will be, by the better angels of our nature."

Contemporaries read into the inaugural address what they wished or expected to see. Republicans were generally satisfied with its "firmness" and "moderation." Confederates and their sympathizers branded it a "Declaration of War." Douglas Democrats in the North and conditional unionists in the south formed the constituencies that Lincoln most wanted and needed to reach. From these quarters the verdict was mixed but encouraging. "I am with him," said Douglas. Influential Tennesseans commended the "temperance and conservatism" of the address. And John Gilmer of North Carolina, though he had been unwilling to join Lincoln's cabinet, approved the president's first act in office. "What more does any reasonable Southern man expect or desire?" Gilmer asked.[64]

---

63. The final version of the address is in *ibid.*, 249–71.

64. Douglas quoted in *Providence Daily Post*, Mar. 8, 1861, in Perkins, ed., *Northern*

Lincoln had hoped to cool passions and buy time with his inaugural address—time to organize his administration, to prove his pacific intent, to allow the seeds of voluntary reconstruction to sprout. But when the new president went to his office for the first time on the morning after the inauguration, he received a jolt. On his desk lay a dispatch from Major Robert Anderson, commander of the Union garrison at Fort Sumter. Anderson reported that his supplies would last only a few more weeks. Time was running out.

III

Fort Sumter stood on a man-made granite island four miles from downtown Charleston at the entrance to the bay. With brick walls forty feet high and eight to twelve feet thick, designed to mount 146 big guns, this new fort when fully manned by 650 soldiers could stop anything trying to enter or leave the harbor. But at the beginning of December 1860 Fort Sumter was untenanted except by workmen completing the construction of its interior. Most of the eighty-odd soldiers of the U. S. garrison at Charleston occupied Fort Moultrie, an obsolete work a mile across the bay from Sumter on an island easily accessible from the mainland and exposed to capture from the rear. The Carolinians had expected to get Moultrie along with Sumter and all other United States property in Charleston for the asking. Even before seceding, South Carolina officials began pressing the Buchanan administration on this matter. After declaring its independence, the republic of South Carolina sent commissioners to Washington to negotiate for the forts and the arsenal. Their quest was backed by hundreds of militiamen in Charleston who vowed to drive the Yankees out if they did not leave voluntarily.

The garrison at Fort Moultrie was not commanded by a Yankee, however. Major Robert Anderson was a Kentuckian, a former slave-owner who sympathized with the South but remained loyal to the flag he had served for thirty-five years. A man haunted by a tragic vision, Anderson wanted above all to avert a war that would divide his own family as well as his state and nation. Yet he knew that if war came, it was likely to start on the spot where he stood. Carolina hotspurs were straining at the leash; if they attacked, honor and his orders would re-

Editorials, 645; Tennesseans quoted in Reynolds, _Editors Make War_, 192; Gilmer quoted in Randall, _Lincoln the President_, I, 308–9.

quire him to resist. Once the flag was fired upon and blood shed, there would be no stopping the momentum of war.

Like Anderson, President Buchanan keenly desired to prevent such a calamity—at least until he left office on March 4. One way to forestall a clash, of course, was to withdraw the garrison. Though urged to do so by three southern members of his cabinet, Buchanan refused to go this far. He did promise South Carolina congressmen on December 10 not to send the reinforcements Anderson had requested. In return, South Carolina pledged not to attack Anderson while negotiations for transfer of the forts were going on. The Carolinians also understood Buchanan to have agreed not to change the military status quo at Charleston in any way.[65]

While Buchanan dithered, Anderson acted. Interpreting ambiguous orders from the War Department as giving him authority to move his command from weak Fort Moultrie to powerful Fort Sumter if necessary to deter an attack, Anderson did so with stealth and skill after dark on the evening of December 26. Having made this move to preserve the peace, Anderson awoke next morning to find himself a hero in the North for thumbing his nose at the arrogant Carolinians and a villain to angry southerners who branded the occupation of Sumter as a violation of Buchanan's pledge. "You are today the most popular man in the nation," wrote a Chicagoan to Anderson. Leverett Saltonstall of Boston praised Anderson as the *one true man* in the country. "While you hold Fort Sumter, I shall not despair of our noble, our glorious Union." But the *Charleston Mercury* charged that Anderson's "gross breach of faith" had inaugurated civil war, while Jefferson Davis rushed to the White House to berate a "dishonored" president.[66]

The harried Buchanan almost succumbed to southern insistence that he must order the garrison back to Moultrie. But he knew that if he did so, he and his party would lose their last shred of respect in the North. A prominent Democrat in New York reported that "Anderson's course is universally approved and if he is recalled or if Sumter is surrendered . . . Northern sentiment will be unanimous in favor of hanging Buchanan. . . . I am not joking—Never have I known the *entire people*

65. Nevins, *Emergence*, II, 347–50, 357–58; Catton, *Coming Fury*, 145–46; Elbert B. Smith, *The Presidency of James Buchanan* (Lawrence, Kansas, 1975), 169–70.
66. Northern statements and *Charleston Mercury* quoted in William A. Swanberg, *First Blood: The Story of Fort Sumter* (New York, 1957), 136, 108; Davis quoted in Smith, *Buchanan*, 179.

more unanimous on any question. We are ruined if Anderson is disgraced or if Sumter is given up."[67] A cabinet reshuffle also stiffened Buchanan's backbone. The southern members and one infirm Yankee resigned during December and early January. Into their places stepped staunch unionists, especially Secretary of War Joseph Holt (a Kentuckian), Attorney General Edwin M. Stanton, and Secretary of State Jeremiah Black. Stanton and Black drafted for Buchanan a reply to the South Carolina commissioners rejecting their demand for Sumter. Buoyed by this new experience of firmness, Buchanan went further—he approved a proposal by General-in-Chief Scott to reinforce Anderson.

In an effort to minimize publicity and provocation, Scott sent the reinforcements (200 soldiers) and supplies on the unarmed merchant vessel *Star of the West*. Bungling marred the whole enterprise, however. Word of the mission leaked to the press, while the War Department failed to get notice of it to Anderson, so that the garrison at Sumter was about the only interested party that lacked advance knowledge of the *Star of the West*'s arrival at the harbor entrance January 9. South Carolina artillery fired on the ship and scored one hit before her civilian captain, discretion eclipsing valor, turned around and headed out to sea. These could have been the opening shots of a civil war. But they were not—because Anderson did not fire back. Lacking information and orders, he did not want to start a war on his own responsibility. So the guns of Sumter remained silent.[68]

Wrath in both North and South rose almost to the bursting point. But it did not burst. Despite mutual charges of aggression, neither side wanted war. Secessionists from other states quietly warned South Carolinians to cool down lest they provoke a conflict before the new Confederacy was organized and ready. A tacit truce emerged whereby the Carolinians left the Sumter garrison alone so long as the government did not try again to reinforce it. A similar (and explicit) arrangement prevailed at Fort Pickens—where, in contrast to Sumter, the navy could have landed reinforcements on the island at any time well out of range of southern guns.

Fort Pickens, however, remained something of a sideshow. The spotlight of history focused on Charleston and Fort Sumter. Anderson and

---

67. Samuel L. M. Barlow to William M. Browne, Dec. 29, 1860, Barlow Papers. See also Stampp, *And the War Came*, 70–79.
68. The best accounts of this incident are Catton, *Coming Fury*, 176–81, and Swanberg, *First Blood*, 144–49.

his men became in northern eyes the defenders of a modern Thermo-pylae. James Buchanan and Governor Francis Pickens of South Caro-lina handed the fate of these men over to Abraham Lincoln and Jeffer-son Davis. The new Confederate president sent another trio of commissioners to Washington to negotiate for the transfer of Forts Sum-ter and Pickens to his government. He also sent newly commissioned General Pierre G. T. Beauregard, a Louisianian, to take command of the thousands of militia and several dozen big seacoast guns and mortars ringing Charleston harbor and pointing at the lonely soldiers inside Fort Sumter.

This was the situation when Lincoln learned on March 5 that the garrison was running short of supplies. The new president faced some hard choices. He could scrape together every available warship and sol-dier to shoot their way into the bay with supplies and reinforcements. But this would burden him with the onus of starting a war. It would divide the North and unite the South including most of the not-yet-seceded states. Or Lincoln could prolong peace and perhaps keep the upper South in the Union by withdrawing the garrison and yielding Sumter. But this too would divide the North, demoralize much of the Republican party, perhaps fatally wreck his administration, constitute an implicit acknowledgment of the Confederacy's independence, and send a signal to foreign governments whose diplomatic recognition the Confederacy was earnestly seeking. Or Lincoln could play for time, hoping to come up with some solution to preserve this vital symbol of sover-eignty without provoking a war that would divide his friends and unite his enemies. Lincoln had six weeks at the outside to find a solution, for by then Anderson's men would be starved out of Sumter. These pres-sures sent the untried president to a sleepless bed with a sick headache more than once during those six weeks.[69]

Lincoln's dilemma was made worse by conflicting counsels and cross purposes within his government. General Scott said that reinforcement was now impossible without a large fleet and 25,000 soldiers. The gov-ernment had neither the ships nor the men. Scott's advice to pull out

69. This and the following paragraphs on Lincoln and Fort Sumter—one of the most thoroughly studied questions in American history—are based on a variety of sources including Catton, *Coming Fury*, 271–325; Swanberg, *First Blood*, 219–332; Rich-ard N. Current, *Lincoln and the First Shot* (Philadelphia, 1963); Kenneth M. Stampp, "Lincoln and the Strategy of Defense in 1861," *JSH*, 11 (1945), 297–323; Nevins, *War*, I, 30–74; Potter, *Impending Crisis*, 570–83; Randall, *Lincoln the President*, I, 311–50; and Nicolay and Hay, *Lincoln*, III, 375–449, IV, 1–63.

swayed the secretaries of war and navy. Seward also concurred. He wanted
to give up Sumter for political as well as military reasons. Such a gesture of peace and good will, he told Lincoln, would reassure the upper
South and strengthen unionists in Confederate states. Seward was playing a deep and devious game. In line with his aspirations to be premier
of this administration, he established independent contact through an
intermediary with the Confederate commissioners. On his own authority, and without Lincoln's knowledge, Seward passed the word to these
commissioners that Sumter would be yielded. He also leaked this news
to the press. Within a week of Lincoln's inauguration, northern papers
carried "authoritative" stories that Anderson's men would be pulled out.

Lincoln had made no such decision—though the nearly unanimous
advice of those who were paid to advise him nearly persuaded him to
do so. But what then would become of his inaugural pledge to "hold,
occupy, and possess" federal property? At the very least he could reinforce Fort Pickens; on March 12, General Scott issued orders for that
purpose.[70] When Lincoln polled his cabinet on March 15 concerning
Sumter, however, five of the seven secretaries recommended evacuation. A sixth, Chase, advised resupplying the garrison only if it could
be done without risking war. Montgomery Blair alone wanted to hold
on to the fort whatever the risk. He believed that instead of encouraging
southern unionists, surrender would discourage them. Only "measures
which will inspire respect for the power of the Government and the
firmness of those who administer it" could sustain them, said Blair. To
give up the fort meant giving up the Union.[71]

Lincoln was inclined to think so, too. And Blair offered the president
more than supportive advice. He introduced Lincoln to his brother-in-
law Gustavus V. Fox, a thirty-nine-year-old Massachusetts businessman
and former navy lieutenant. Fox was the first of many such men who
would surge into prominence during the next four years: daring, able,
fertile with ideas for doing things that the creaking old military estab-

70. Like so much else in the crisis of the forts, the first attempt to reinforce Pickens
    was also bungled. The naval captain on the Pickens station refused to carry out the
    order, which had been sent to the army officer commanding the troops on ship-
    board, because the order was not signed by the secretary of the navy. The captain
    cited his previous orders not to reinforce so long as the Confederates refrained from
    attacking Pickens. When Lincoln learned on April 6 of this foul-up, it may have
    influenced his final decision to send supplies to Fort Sumter.
71. Excerpts from the written opinions of the seven secretaries are printed in CWL,
    IV, 285.

lishment said could not be done. Fox proposed to send a troop transport escorted by warships to the bar outside Charleston harbor. Men and supplies could there be transferred to tugs or small boats which could cross the bar after dark for a dash to Sumter. Warships and the Sumter garrison would stand by to suppress attempts by Confederate artillery to interfere.

It might just work; in any case, Lincoln was willing to think about it. For he was now hearing from the constituency that had elected him. Many Republicans were outraged by reports that Sumter was to be surrendered. "HAVE WE A GOVERNMENT?" shouted newspaper headlines. "The bird of our country is a debilitated chicken, disguised in eagle feathers," commented a disgusted New York lawyer. "Reinforce Fort Sumter at all hazards!" ran a typical letter from a northern citizen. "If Fort Sumter is evacuated, the new administration is done forever," declared another.[72] Even Democrats called for reinforcement of the "gallant band who are defending their country's honor and its flag in the midst of a hostile and traitorous foe." The prolonged uncertainty was stretching nerves to the breaking point. "The Administration *must have a policy of action*," proclaimed the *New York Times*. "Better almost anything than additional suspense," echoed other northern papers. "The people want *something* to be decided on [to] serve as a rallying point for the abundant but discouraged loyalty of the American heart."[73]

These signs of northern opinion hardened Lincoln's resolve. Meanwhile, however, Seward continued to tell Confederate commissioners that Sumter would be given up. One of the three emissaries that Lincoln sent to Charleston to appraise matters, his old friend Ward H. Lamon, seems to have told Carolinians and Anderson himself that evacuation was imminent. Hawks and doves within the administration were clearly on a collision course. The crash came on March 28. That day Lincoln learned that General Scott wanted to evacuate *both* Forts Pickens and Sumter. His grounds for urging this were political rather than military: "The evacuation of both the forts," wrote the general, "would instantly soothe and give confidence to the eight remaining slave-holding States, and render their cordial adherence to this Union perpetual."

72. Perkins, ed., *Northern Editorials*, 652; Strong, *Diary*, 109; Current, *Lincoln and the First Shot*, 118; Stampp, *And the War Came*, 266.
73. *New York Times*, April 3, 1861; *New York Morning Express*, April 5, 1861, quoted in Stampp, *And the War Came*, 268.

Lincoln called his cabinet into emergency session after a state dinner that evening. "Blank amazement" registered on most faces as an obviously nettled president read to them Scott's memorandum. The general (a Virginian) was advising unconditional surrender to the Confederacy. Whether or not influenced by Seward (as most cabinet members assumed), Scott's politically motivated recommendation rendered suspect his initial opinion that reinforcement of Sumter was impossible. The cabinet reversed its vote of two weeks earlier. Four of the six members (Caleb Smith still went along with Seward; Cameron was absent) now favored resupply of Sumter. All six supported additional reinforcement of Pickens. Lincoln issued orders for a secret expedition to carry out the latter task. More momentously, he also instructed Fox to ready ships and men for an attempt to reinforce Sumter.[74]

This backed Seward into a corner. His assurances to southern commissioners, his peace policy of voluntary reconstruction, his ambitions to be premier—all appeared about to collapse. To recoup his position Seward acted boldly—and egregiously. He intervened in the Fort Pickens reinforcement and managed to divert the strongest available warship from the Sumter expedition, with unfortunate consequences. Then on April 1 he sent an extraordinary proposal to Lincoln. In mystifying fashion, Seward suggested that to abandon Sumter and hold Pickens would change the issue from slavery to Union. Beyond that, the secretary of state would "demand explanations" from Spain and France for their meddling in Santo Domingo and Mexico, and declare war if their explanations were unsatisfactory. Presumably this would reunite the country against a foreign foe. "Whatever policy we adopt," Seward pointed out, "it must be somebody's business to pursue and direct it incessantly." He left little doubt whom he had in mind.

Lincoln's astonishment when he read this note can well be imagined. Not wanting to humiliate Seward or lose his services, however, the president mentioned the matter to no one and wrote a polite but firm reply the same day. He had pledged to hold, occupy and possess federal property, Lincoln reminded his secretary of state, and he could not see how holding Sumter was any more a matter of slavery or less a matter of Union than holding Pickens. Ignoring Seward's idea of an ultimatum

74. Nicolay and Hay, *Lincoln*, III, 394–95, 429–34; Current, *Lincoln and the First Shot*, 75–81. Rumors had already reached Washington that Lincoln's first order to reinforce Pickens had not been carried out.

to Spain or France, Lincoln told him that whatever policy was decided upon, "*I must do it.*"[75] A chastened Seward said nothing more about this and served as one of Lincoln's most loyal advisers during the next four years.

Seward recognized that he would have to endure accusations of deceit from southerners when his assurances of Sumter's evacuation turned out to be wrong. He made one last effort to salvage the situation. The Virginia convention, still in session, would undoubtedly vote to secede if a clash of arms occurred. Seward persuaded Lincoln to meet with a Virginia unionist in Washington on April 4. The purpose was to see if a bargain could be struck: evacuation of Sumter in return for adjournment of the convention without secession. Just before his inauguration Lincoln had expressed interest in this idea. Whether he explicitly offered such a deal in his private conversation with John Baldwin in April 4 has long been a matter of controversy.[76] In any event nothing came of this meeting, from which Lincoln emerged with a soured view of Virginia unionism. That very day he gave the go-ahead for the Sumter expedition.[77]

The nature of that enterprise had changed subtly but significantly from Fox's first proposal. Instead of trying to shoot its way into the harbor, the task force would first attempt only to carry supplies to Anderson. Warships and soldiers would stand by for action but if Confederate batteries did not fire on the supply boats they would not fire back, and the reinforcements would remain on shipboard. Lincoln would notify Governor Pickens in advance of the government's peaceful intention to send in provisions only. If Confederates opened fire on the unarmed boats carrying "food for hungry men," the South would stand convicted of an aggressive act. On its shoulders would rest the blame for starting a war. This would unite the North and, perhaps, keep the South divided. If southerners allowed the supplies to go through, peace and the status quo at Sumter could be preserved and the Union government would have won an important symbolic victory. Lincoln's new conception of the resupply undertaking was a stroke of genius. In effect he was

75. CWL, IV, 316–18, for Seward's memorandum and Lincoln's reply.
76. Historians have analyzed the meager evidence on this matter in varying ways; for a summary of the evidence, with citations to relevant works, see William C. Harris, "The Southern Unionist Critique of the Civil War," CWH, 31 (1985), 50–51.
77. Current, *Lincoln and the First Shot*, 96.

telling Jefferson Davis, "Heads I win, Tails you lose." It was the first sign of the mastery that would mark Lincoln's presidency.[78]

On April 6, Lincoln sent a special messenger to Charleston to inform Governor Pickens that "an attempt will be made to supply Fort-Sumter with provisions only; and that, if such attempt be not resisted, no effort to throw in men, arms, or ammunition, will be made, without further notice, [except] in case of an attack on the Fort."[79] This put the ball in Jefferson Davis's court. The Confederate president was also under great pressure to "do something." Seward's dream of voluntary reconstruction was Davis's nightmare. "The spirit and even the patriotism of the people is oozing out under this do-nothing policy," complained a Mobile newspaper. "If something is not done pretty soon . . . the whole country will become so disgusted with the sham of southern independence that the first chance the people get at a popular election they will turn the whole movement topsy-turvy." Other Alabamians agreed that war

78. Contemporaries and historians have long debated Lincoln's motives and purposes in this Sumter resupply plan. Three main positions emerged in the debate: 1) Lincoln knew that he could save his administration and party only by war, so he deliberately manipulated the Confederacy into firing the first shot so that he could have his war at maximum political advantage. The two principal historians who advanced this interpretation, both of them southerners, were Charles W. Ramsdell, "Lincoln and Fort Sumter," *JSH*, 3 (1937), 259–88; and J. S. Tilley, *Lincoln Takes Command* (Chapel Hill, 1941). 2) Lincoln wanted to preserve the status quo to give the policy of voluntary reconstruction a new lease on life, but he feared that giving up Sumter would discredit the government and bolster the Confederacy in the eyes of the world. Hoping to preserve peace but willing to risk war, he devised the resupply scheme in such a way as to give Confederates the choice of peace or war. This interpretation has been advanced mainly by James G. Randall, *Lincoln the Liberal Statesman* (New York, 1947), 88–117, and David M. Potter, "Why the Republicans Rejected Both Compromise and Secession," in George Harmon Knoles, ed., *The Crisis of the Union, 1860–1861* (Baton Rouge, 1965), 90–106. 3) Lincoln would have been happy to preserve the peace but probably expected the Confederates to open fire; either way he won. Numerous historians have offered this interpretation; it is most prominently identified with Kenneth M. Stampp, "Lincoln and the Strategy of Defense in the Crisis of 1861," *loc. cit.*, and Current, *Lincoln and the First Shot*, 182–208. The differences between interpretations 2 and 3 are subtle, and hinge on efforts to read Lincoln's mind to guess what he wanted or expected the Confederates to do. Although he never said explicitly what he expected them to do, Lincoln had become rather disillusioned with the prospects for voluntary reconstruction and he had plenty of reason to believe that the Confederates would open fire on a peaceful resupply effort. Therefore interpretation 3 seems most plausible.

79. *CWL*, IV, 323.

was the best way "of avoiding the calamity of reconstruction. . . . South Carolina has the power of putting us beyond the reach of reconstruction by taking Fort Sumter at any cost. . . . Sir, unless you sprinkle blood in the face of the people of Alabama, they will be back in the old Union in less than ten days!"[80]

Even if the seven lower-South states held together, the Confederacy's future was precarious without the upper South. After talking with Virginia secessionists, the fire-eater Louis Wigfall urged a prompt attack on Sumter to bring that commonwealth into the fold. The hot-blooded Edmund Ruffin and Roger Pryor, vexed by the lingering unionism in their native state of Virginia, echoed this exhortation. "The shedding of blood," wrote Ruffin, "will serve to change many voters in the hesitating states, from the submission or procrastinating ranks, to the zealous for immediate secession." If you want us to join you, Pryor told Charlestonians, "*strike a blow!*" The *Charleston Mercury* was willing. "Border southern States will never join us until we have indicated our power to free ourselves—until we have proven that a garrison of seventy men cannot hold the portal of our commerce," declared the *Mercury*. "Let us be ready for war. . . . The fate of the Southern Confederacy hangs by the ensign halliards of Fort Sumter."[81]

Therefore to Abraham Lincoln's challenge, Shall it be Peace or War? Jefferson Davis replied, War. A fateful cabinet meeting in Montgomery on April 9 endorsed Davis's order to Beauregard: reduce the fort *before* the relief fleet arrived, if possible. Anderson rejected Beauregard's ritual summons to surrender, but remarked in passing that he would be starved out in a few days if help did not arrive. The Confederates knew that help was about to arrive, so they opened fire on April 12 at 4:30 a.m. Fox's fleet, scattered by a gale and prevented by high seas from launching the supply boats, was helpless to intervene.[82] After thirty-three hours of bombardment by four thousand shot and shells which destroyed part

---

80. Mobile newspaper quoted in Current, *Lincoln and the First Shot*, 134; J. L. Pugh to William Porcher Miles, Jan. 24, 1861, in Richard N. Current, "The Confederates and the First Shot," *CWH*, 7 (1961), 365; J. G. Gilchrist quoted in Nevins, *War*, I, 68.

81. Current, *Lincoln and the First Shot*, 151, 139; William K. Scarborough, ed., *The Diary of Edmund Ruffin*, Vol. I: *Toward Independence*, October 1856–April 1861 (Baton Rouge, 1972), 542; *Charleston Mercury*, Jan. 24, 1861.

82. Fox was also handicapped by the absence of *U.S.S. Powhatan*, the navy's strongest available warship. A tragicomic confusion of orders for which both Seward and Lincoln were responsible had diverted the *Powhatan* to the Fort Pickens expedition.

of the fort and set the interior on fire, Anderson's exhausted garrison surrendered. Able to man only a few of Sumter's forty-eight mounted guns, they had fired a thousand rounds in reply—without much effect. On April 14 the American flag came down and the Confederate stars and bars rose over Sumter.

This news galvanized the North. On April 15 Lincoln issued a proclamation calling 75,000 militiamen into national service for ninety days to put down an insurrection "too powerful to be suppressed by the ordinary course of judicial proceedings." The response from free states was overwhelming. War meetings in every city and village cheered the flag and vowed vengence on traitors. "The heather is on fire," wrote a Harvard professor who had been born during George Washington's presidency. "I never knew what a popular excitement can be. . . . The whole population, men, women, and children, seem to be in the streets with Union favors and flags." From Ohio and the West came "one great Eagle-scream" for the flag. "The people have gone stark mad!"[83] In New York City, previously a nursery of pro-southern sentiment, a quarter of a million people turned out for a Union rally. "The change in public sentiment here is wonderful—almost miraculous," wrote a New York merchant on April 18. "I look with awe on the national movement here in New York and all through the Free States," added a lawyer. "After our late discords, it seems supernatural." The "time before Sumter" was like another century, wrote a New York woman. "It seems as if we never were alive till now; never had a country till now."[84]

Democrats joined in the eagle-scream of patriotic fury. Stephen Douglas paid a well-publicized national unity call to the White House and then traveled home to Chicago, where he told a huge crowd: "There are only two sides to the question. Every man must be for the United States or against it. There can be no neutrals in this war, *only patriots—or traitors.*" A month later Douglas was dead—a victim probably of cirrhosis of the liver—but for a year or more his war spirit lived on among most Democrats. "Let our enemies perish by the sword," was the theme of

83. CWL, IV, 331–32; *Life, Letters, and Journals of George Ticknor,* 2 vols. (Boston, 1876), II, 433–34; Jane Stuart Woolsey to a friend, May 10, 1861, in Henry Steele Commager, ed., *The Blue and the Gray,* 2 vols. (rev. and abridged ed., New York, 1973), I, 48; Jacob D. Cox, "War Preparations in the North," in *Battles and Leaders,* I, 86.

84. Philip S. Foner, *Business and Slavery: The New York Merchants and the Irrepressible Conflict* (Chapel Hill, 1941), 207; Strong, *Diary,* 136; Commager, ed., *Blue and Gray,* I, 47.

Democratic editorials in the spring of 1861. "All squeamish sentimentality should be discarded, and bloody vengeance wreaked upon the heads of the contemptible traitors who have provoked it by their dastardly impertinence and rebellious acts."[85]

To the War Department from northern governors came pleas to increase their states' quotas of troops. Lincoln had called on Indiana for six regiments; the governor offered twelve. Having raised the requisitioned thirteen regiments, Ohio's governor wired Washington that "without seriously repressing the ardor of the people, I can hardly stop short of twenty." From Governor John Andrew of Massachusetts came a terse telegram two days after Lincoln's call for troops: "Two of our regiments will start this afternoon—one for Washington, the other for Fort Monroe; a third will be dispatched tomorrow, and the fourth before the end of the week."[86] It began to appear that something larger than a lady's thimble might be needed to hold the blood shed in this war.

85. Robert W. Johannsen, *Stephen A. Douglas* (New York, 1973), 868; *Wisconsin Daily Patriot*, April 24, 1861, *Columbus Daily Capital City Fact*, April 13, 1861, in Perkins, ed., *Northern Editorials*, 750, 727.

86. Robert E. Sterling, "Civil War Draft Resistance in the Middle West," Ph.D. dissertation, Northern Illinois University, 1974, pp. 15–16; O.R., Ser. 3, Vol. 1, p. 79.

9

Facing Both Ways:
The Upper South's Dilemma

I

The outbreak of war at Fort Sumter confronted the upper South with a crisis of decision. Its choice could decide the fate of the Confederacy. These eight states contained most of the South's resources for waging war: more than half of its population, two-thirds of its white population, three-quarters of its industrial capacity, half of its horses and mules, three-fifths of its livestock and food crops. In addition, men of high potential as military leaders hailed from these states: Robert E. Lee, Thomas J. Jackson, Joseph E. Johnston, James E. B. Stuart, and Ambrose Powell Hill of Virginia; Daniel H. Hill of North Carolina; Albert Sidney Johnston and John Bell Hood of Kentucky; Nathan Bedford Forrest of Tennessee.

The upper South's response to Lincoln's April 15 militia requisition seemed to promise well for the Confederacy. Kentucky "will furnish no troops for the wicked purpose of subduing her sister Southern States," the governor wired Washington. Tennessee "will not furnish a single man for the purpose of coercion," proclaimed her governor, "but fifty thousand if necessary for the defense of our rights and those of our Southern brothers." The secessionist governor of Missouri hurled the gage at the president's feet: "Your requisition is illegal, unconstitutional, revolutionary, inhuman. . . . Not one man will the State of Missouri furnish to carry on any such unholy crusade." The governors of Virginia, North Carolina, and Arkansas sent similar replies, while the governors of Maryland and Delaware remained ominously silent.[1]

These references to "our rights" and "southern brothers" suggest the motives that impelled four of the eight states into the Confederacy and left three others with large secessionist minorities. "We must either identify ourselves with the North or the South," wrote a Virginian, while two former North Carolina unionists expressed the view of most of their fellows: "The division must be made on the line of slavery. The South must go with the South. . . . Blood is thicker than Water."[2] Newspapers in Tennessee and Arkansas proclaimed that "the identity of object and the community of interest existing in all the slaveholding States must and will unite them." Faced with a choice between "subjugation" and defense of "honor . . . liberty . . . rights," the decision was "as certain as the laws of gravity."[3]

In the eyes of southern unionists, this tragic war was mainly Lincoln's fault. What the president described in his proclamation of April 15 calling out the militia as a necessary measure to "maintain the honor, the integrity, and the existence of our National Union" was transmuted south of the Potomac into an unconstitutional coercion of sovereign states. "In North Carolina the Union sentiment was largely in the ascendant and gaining strength until Lincoln prostrated us," wrote a bitter unionist. "He could have adopted no policy so effectual to destroy the Union. . . . I am left no other alternative but to fight for or against my section. . . . Lincoln has made us a unit to resist until we repel our invaders or die." John Bell, the 1860 presidential candidate of the Constitutional Union party from whom many moderates in the upper South took their cue, announced in Nashville on April 23 his support for a "united South" in "the unnecessary, aggressive, cruel, unjust wanton war which is being forced upon us" by Lincoln's mobilization of militia.[4]

---

1. O.R., Series III, Vol. I, pp. 70, 72, 76, 81, 83.
2. *Staunton Vindicator*, March 22, 1861, quoted in Donald E. Reynolds, *Editors Make War: Southern Newspapers in the Secession Crisis* (Nashville, 1970), 196; *Wilmington Journal*, March 4, 1861, quoted in W. Buck Yearns and John G. Barrett, eds., *North Carolina Civil War Documentary* (Chapel Hill, 1980), 21; *Raleigh Register*, May 10, 1861.
3. *Nashville Patriot*, April 24, 1861, *Nashville Republican Banner*, May 9, 1861, in Dwight L. Dumond, ed., *Southern Editorials on Secession* (Washington, 1931), 511, 514; *Fort Smith Daily Times and Herald*, April 5, 1861, quoted in Reynolds, *Editors Make War*, 195–96.
4. James G. de.R. Hamilton, ed., *The Correspondence of Jonathan Worth*, 2 vols. (Ra-

Such explanations for conversion to secession were undoubtedly sincere. But their censure of Lincoln had a certain self-serving quality. The claim that his call for troops was the cause of the upper South's decision to secede is misleading. As the telegraph chattered reports of the attack on Sumter April 12 and its surrender next day, huge crowds poured into the streets of Richmond, Raleigh, Nashville, and other upper South cities to celebrate this victory over the Yankees. These crowds waved Confederate flags and cheered the glorious cause of southern independence. They demanded that their own states join the cause. Scores of such demonstrations took place from April 12 to 14, *before* Lincoln issued his call for troops. Many conditional unionists were swept along by this powerful tide of southern nationalism; others were cowed into silence.

News of Sumter's fall reached Richmond on the evening of April 13. A jubilant procession marched on the state capitol where a battery fired a hundred-gun salute "in honor of the victory." The crowd lowered the American flag from the capitol building and ran up the Confederate stars and bars. Everyone "seemed to be perfectly frantic with delight, I never in all my life witnessed such excitement," wrote a participant. "Everyone is in favor of secession." Citizens of Wilmington, North Carolina, reacted to the news of Sumter with "the wildest excitement," flew Confederate flags from public buildings, and fired salutes to them. In Goldsboro, North Carolina, the correspondent of the *Times* of London watched "an excited mob" with "flushed faces, wild eyes, screaming mouths, hurrahing for 'Jeff Davis' and 'the Southern Confederacy,' so that the yells overpowered the discordant bands which were busy with 'Dixie's Land.' " These outbursts were not merely a defensive response to northern aggression. Rather they took on the character of a celebration, a joyous bonding with southern brothers who had scored a triumph over the Black Republican Yankees.[5]

The Virginia convention moved quickly to adopt an ordinance of

leigh, 1909), I, 143, 150–51; J. Milton Henry, "Revolution in Tennessee, February 1861 to June 1861," *Tennessee Historical Quarterly*, 18 (1959), 115; Mary E. R. Campbell, *The Attitude of Tennesseeans toward the Union, 1847–1861* (New York, 1961), 194.

5. Letter from J. H. Baughman of Richmond, April 14, 1861, quoted in Henry T. Shanks, *The Secession Movement in Virginia, 1847–1861* (Richmond, 1934), 268n.; J. Carlyle Sitterson, *The Secession Movement in North Carolina* (Chapel Hill, 1939), 239; William Howard Russell, *My Diary North and South*, ed. Fletcher Pratt (New York, 1954), 52.

secession, but not quickly enough for an *ad hoc* assembly in another Richmond hall that called itself the "Spontaneous Southern Rights Convention." Passions ran high on the streets and in both convention halls. Mobs threatened violence against unionist delegates from west of the Alleghenies. On April 17 ex-Governor Henry Wise electrified the official convention with a fiery speech. He announced that Virginia militia were *at that instant* seizing the federal armory at Harper's Ferry and preparing to seize the Gosport navy yard near Norfolk. At such a moment no true Virginian could hesitate; the convention passed an ordinance of secession by a vote of 88 to 55.[6]

Although Wise's announcement was slightly premature, he knew whereof he spoke: he had planned the Harper's Ferry expedition himself. A hard-bitten secessionist whose long white hair and wrinkled face made him look older than his fifty-four years, Wise had been governor when John Brown attacked Harper's Ferry. Perhaps this experience turned Wise's mind to the importance of the rifle works there, one of the two armories owned by the United States government (the other was at Springfield, Massachusetts). Without consulting Virginia's current Governor John Letcher, whom he considered lukewarm on secession, Wise met with militia officers on April 16 to set their regiments in motion for Harper's Ferry and Norfolk. Letcher belatedly approved these moves. On April 18, one day after passage of the secession ordinance, several companies of militia closed in on Harper's Ferry, defended by 47 U.S. army regulars. To prevent capture of the valuable rifle machinery, the soldiers set fire to the works and fled. The Virginians moved in and saved most of the machinery, which they shipped to Richmond, where it soon began turning out guns for the Confederacy.

An even greater prize was the Gosport navy yard, the country's premier naval base and the largest shipbuilding and repair facility in the South. Of the twelve hundred cannon and ten ships there in April 1861, many of the guns and four of the warships were modern and serviceable, including the powerful forty-gun steam frigate *Merrimack*. Most of the civilian workers and naval officers at the yard were southerners; a majority of the officers would soon resign to join the Confederacy. Commanding the eight hundred sailors and marines stationed at the yard was Commodore Charles McCauley, a bibulous sixty-eight-year-old veteran who had gone to sea before Abraham Lincoln and Jefferson

---

6. Several delegates who voted No or were absent subsequently voted Aye, making the final tally 103 to 46.

Davis were born. McCauley proved unequal to the crisis posed by several thousand Virginia militia reported to be heading for the navy yard. He refused to allow the *Merrimack* and the other three ships to escape when they had a chance to do so on April 18. The next day, just before reinforcements arrived aboard two warships from Washington, McCauley ordered all facilities at the yard burned, the cannon spiked, the ships scuttled. Even these unnecessary actions were bungled; the dry dock, ordnance building, and several other structures failed to burn; most of the cannon remained salvageable and were soon on their way to forts throughout the South; the hull of the *Merrimack* survived intact and ready for its subsequent conversion into the famous ironclad *C.S.S. Virginia*.

These events occurred before Virginia officially seceded, because the ordinance would not become final until ratified in a referendum on May 23. But the mood of the people predestined the outcome. For all practical purposes Virginia joined the Confederacy on April 17. A week later Governor Letcher and the convention concluded an alliance with the Confederacy that allowed southern troops to enter the state and placed Virginia regiments under Confederate control. On April 27 the convention invited the Confederate government to make Richmond its permanent capital. The southern Congress, tired of the inadequate, overcrowded facilities in Montgomery and eager to cement Virginia's allegiance, accepted the invitation on May 21. When Virginians went to the polls on May 23 they ratified a *fait accompli* by a vote of 128,884 to 32,134.

Virginia brought crucial resources to the Confederacy. Her population was the South's largest. Her industrial capacity was nearly as great as that of the seven original Confederate states combined. The Tredegar Iron Works in Richmond was the only plant in the South capable of manufacturing heavy ordnance. Virginia's heritage from the generation of Washington, Jefferson, and Madison gave her immense prestige that was expected to attract the rest of the upper South to the Confederacy. And as events turned out, perhaps the greatest asset that Virginia brought to the cause of southern independence was Robert E. Lee.

Lee was fifty-four years old in 1861, the son of a Revolutionary War hero, scion of the First Families of Virginia, a gentleman in every sense of the word, without discernible fault unless a restraint that rarely allowed emotion to break through the crust of dignity is counted a fault. He had spent his entire career in the U.S. army since graduating second in his West Point class of 1829. Lee's outstanding record in the Mexican War, his experience as an engineer officer, as a cavalry officer, and as superintendent of West Point had earned him promotion to full colonel on March 16, 1861. General-in-Chief Winfield Scott considered Lee the best officer in the army. In April, Scott urged Lincoln to offer Lee field command of the newly levied Union army. As a fellow Virginian Scott hoped that Lee, like himself, would remain loyal to the service to which he had devoted his life. Lee had made clear his dislike of slavery, which he described in 1856 as "a moral and political evil." Until the day Virginia left the Union he had also spoken against secession. "The framers of our Constitution never exhausted so much labor, wisdom, and forbearance in its formation," he wrote in January 1861, "if it was intended to be broken up by every member of the [Union] at will. . . . It is idle to talk of secession."[7]

But with Virginia's decision, everything changed. "I must side either with or against my section," Lee told a northern friend. His choice was foreordained by birth and blood: "I cannot raise my hand against my birthplace, my home, my children." On the very day he learned of Virginia's secession, April 18, Lee also received the offer of Union command. He told his friend General Scott regretfully that he must not only decline, but must also resign from the army. "Save in defense of my native State," said Lee, "I never desire again to draw my sword." Scott replied sadly: "You have made the greatest mistake of your life, but I feared it would be so." Five days later Lee accepted appointment as commander in chief of Virginia's military forces; three weeks after that he became a brigadier general in the Confederate army. Most officers from the upper South made a similar decision to go with their states, some without hesitation, others with the same bodeful presentiments that Lee expressed on May 5: "I foresee that the country will have to pass through a terrible ordeal, a necessary expiation perhaps for our national sins."[8]

Scores of southern officers, however, like Scott remained loyal to nation rather than section. Some of them played key roles in the eventual triumph of nation over section: Virginian George H. Thomas, who saved the Union Army of the Cumberland at Chickamauga and destroyed the Confederate Army of Tennessee at Nashville; Tennessean David G.

---

7. James Ford Rhodes, *History of the United States from the Compromise of 1850* . . . 7 vols. (New York, 1893–1906), III, 299; Nevins, *War*, I, 109.
8. Nevins, *War*, I, 107; Douglas Southall Freeman, *R. E. Lee: A Biography*, 4 vols. (New York, 1934–35), I, 437, 441.

Farragut, who captured New Orleans and damned the torpedoes at Mobile Bay; North Carolinian John Gibbon, who became one of the best division commanders in the Army of the Potomac while three of his brothers fought for the South. At the same time a few northern-born officers who had married southern women chose to go with their wives' section rather than with their own, and rose to high positions in the Confederacy: New Jersey's Samuel Cooper, who married a Virginian and became adjutant general in the Confederate army; Pennsylvanian John Pemberton, who also married a Virginia woman and rose to command of the Army of Mississippi, which he surrendered to Grant at Vicksburg; and Josiah Gorgas, also of Pennsylvania, who married the daughter of an Alabama governor, became chief of ordnance for the Confederacy, where he created miracles of improvisation and instant industrialization to keep Confederate armies supplied with arms and ammunition.

II

The example of Virginia—and of Robert E. Lee—exerted a powerful influence on the rest of the upper South. Arkansas was the next state to go. Its convention had adjourned in March without taking action, subject to recall in case of emergency. Lincoln's call for troops supplied the emergency; the convention reassembled on May 6. Even before the delegates arrived in Little Rock, however, pro-secession Governor Henry Rector aligned his state with the Confederacy by seizing federal arsenals at Fort Smith and Little Rock and by allowing Confederate forces to place artillery to command the Mississippi at Helena. The convention met in an atmosphere of high emotion, the galleries packed with spectators waving Confederate flags. Within minutes an ordinance of secession came to the floor. A motion to submit this ordinance to a referendum—a test vote of unionist strength at the convention—was defeated 55 to 15. Most of the fifteen minority delegates came from the Ozark Plateau of northwest Arkansas, where few slaves lived. After defeat of this motion, the convention passed the ordinance of secession by a vote of 65 to 5.[9]

North Carolina and Tennessee also went out during May. Even before calling the legislature into special session, the governor of North Carolina ordered the militia to seize three federal forts on the coast and

---

9. Four unionist delegates later changed their votes, making the final tally 69 to 1.

the arsenal in Fayetteville. The legislature met on May 1 and authorized an election on May 13 for a convention to meet on May 20. During these weeks everyone in the state, even in the previously unionist mountain counties, seemed to favor secession. "This furor, this moral epidemic, swept over the country like a tempest, before which the entire population seemed to succumb," wrote a participant.[10] After a test vote on a procedural matter showed that the moderates were a minority, the delegates on May 20 unanimously enacted an ordinance of secession. Meanwhile the Tennessee legislature short-circuited the convention process by adopting a "Declaration of Independence" and submitting it to a referendum scheduled for June 8. Tennessee imitated the action of Virginia by concluding a military alliance with the Confederacy and allowing Confederate troops to enter the state several weeks before the referendum. That election recorded 104,913 for secession and 47,238 against. Significantly, however, the voters of mountainous east Tennessee cast 70 percent of their ballots against secession.

Although speeches and editorials in the upper South bristled with references to rights, liberty, state sovereignty, honor, resistance to coercion, and identity with southern brothers, such rhetoric could not conceal the fundamental issue of slavery. The following table shows the correlation between slaveholding and support for secession in the Virginia and Tennessee conventions.[11]

	Median no. of slaves owned by delegates		Delegates from counties with fewer than 25% slaves		Delegates from counties with more than 25% slaves	
	Va.	Tenn.	Va.	Tenn.	Va.	Tenn.
Voting for Secession	11.5	6.5	34	30	53	23
Voting against Secession	4	2	39	20	13	2

The popular vote in secession referendums illustrated the point even more graphically. The voters in 35 Virginia counties with a slave population of only 2.5 percent opposed secession by a margin of three to one, while voters in the remainder of the state, where slaves constituted

10. Sitterson, *Secession Movement in North Carolina*, 241.
11. The data in this table were compiled from Ralph A. Wooster, *The Secession Conventions of the South* (Princeton, 1962), 151, 153, 183, 185.

36 percent of the population, supported secession by more than ten to one. The thirty counties of east Tennessee that rejected secession by more than two to one contained a slave population of only 8 percent, while the rest of the state, with a slave population of 30 percent, voted for secession by a margin of seven to one. Similar though less dramatic correlations existed in Arkansas and North Carolina, where moderate delegates had a median slaveholding about half that of the all-out secessionists.[12]

The *Nashville Patriot* of April 24, 1861, was conscious of no irony when it cited the "community of interest existing in all the slaveholding States" as the reason why these states must unite to defend "justice and liberty."[13] The upper South, like the lower, went to war to defend the freedom of white men to own slaves and to take them into the territories as they saw fit, lest these white men be enslaved by Black Republicans who threatened to deprive them of these liberties.

III

In the four border states the proportion of slaves and slaveowners was less than half what it was in the eleven states that seceded. But the triumph of unionism in these states was not easy and the outcome (except in Delaware) by no means certain. Maryland, Kentucky, and Missouri contained large and resolute secessionist minorities. A slight twist in the chain of events might have enabled this faction to prevail in any of these states. Much was at stake in this contest. The three states would have added 45 percent to the white population and military manpower of the Confederacy, 80 percent to its manufacturing capacity, and nearly 40 percent to its supply of horses and mules. For almost five hundred miles the Ohio river flows along the northern border of Kentucky, providing a defensive barrier or an avenue of invasion, depending on which side could control and fortify it. Two of the Ohio's navigable tributaries, the Cumberland and Tennessee rivers, penetrate through Kentucky into the heart of Tennessee and northern Alabama. Little wonder that Lincoln was reported to have said that while he hoped to have God on his side, he must have Kentucky.

Control of Maryland was even more immediately crucial, for the state enclosed Washington on three sides (with Virginia on the fourth) and

12. *Ibid.*, 200, 265.
13. Dumond, ed., *Southern Editorials on Secession*, 510–11.

its allegiance could determine the capital's fate at the outset of the war. Like the lower South, Maryland had voted for Breckinridge in the presidential election. Southern-Rights Democrats controlled the legislature; only the stubborn refusal of unionist Governor Thomas Hicks to call the legislature into session forestalled action by that body. The tobacco counties of southern Maryland and the eastern shore of the Chesapeake Bay were secessionist. The grain-growing counties of northern and western Maryland, containing few slaves, were safe for the Union. But the loyalty of Baltimore, with a third of the state's population, was suspect. The mayor's unionism was barely tepid, and the police chief sympathized with the South. Confederate flags appeared on many city homes and buildings during the tense days after Sumter. The traditional role of mobs in Baltimore politics created a volatile situation. Only a spark was needed to ignite the state's secessionists; such a spark hit the streets of Baltimore on April 19.

On that day the 6th Massachusetts Regiment—the first fully equipped unit to respond to Lincoln's call for troops—entered Baltimore on its way to Washington. No rail line passed through Baltimore, so the troops had to detrain at the east-side station and cross the city to board a train to the capital. A mob gathered in the path of the soldiers and grew increasingly violent. Rioters attacked the rear companies of the regiment with bricks, paving stones, and pistols. Angry and afraid, a few soldiers opened fire. That unleashed the mob. By the time the Massachusetts men had fought their way to the station and entrained for Washington, four soldiers and twelve Baltimoreans lay dead and several score groaned with wounds. They were the first of more than 700,000 combat casualties during the next four years.

Maryland flamed with passion. Here was coercion in deadly earnest. Worst of all, the soldiers who had killed Baltimore citizens were from the blackest of Black Republican states. To prevent more northern regiments from entering Baltimore, the mayor and the chief of police, with the reluctant approval of Governor Hicks, ordered the destruction of bridges on the railroads from Philadelphia and Harrisburg. Secessionists also tore down telegraph lines from Washington through Maryland. The national capital was cut off from the North. For several days, rumors were the only form of information reaching Washington. They grew to alarming proportions. Virginia regiments and armed Maryland secessionists were said to be converging on the capital. Washington was gripped by a siege mentality. Citizens' groups and government clerks formed themselves into volunteer companies. At General Scott's orders, these units sandbagged and barricaded public buildings and prepared the imposing Treasury edifice for a last-stand defense.

Reports filtered through of an aroused North and of more regiments determined to force their way through Maryland at any cost. But the rumors of an impending attack by Virginians seemed more real than the hope of rescue from the North. Lincoln looked wistfully out of the northern windows of the White House and murmured, "Why don't they come?" On April 24 he visited the officers and wounded men of the 6th Massachusetts. "I don't believe there is any North," Lincoln gloomily told the soldiers. "The [New York] Seventh Regiment is a myth. Rhode Island is not known in our geography any longer. You are the only Northern realities."[14]

But next day a troop train carrying the crack New York 7th puffed into Washington, followed by more trains bearing additional regiments from northeastern states. They had arrived over a circuitous route via Annapolis under the command of Benjamin F. Butler, who thereby achieved one of the few military successes of his contentious career. A clever lawyer and shrewd politician whose paunchy physique, balding head, drooping mustache, and cocked left eye gave him a shifty appearance that matched his personality, Butler was a Massachusetts Democrat soon to become a Republican. From Governor Andrew he had wrested an appointment as brigadier general of the militia that Andrew had mobilized upon Lincoln's call for troops. The 6th Massachusetts had been the first regiment of this brigade to leave for Washington. When Butler, following with the 8th Massachusetts, learned of the riot in Baltimore and the burning of railroad bridges, he detrained the 8th at the head of Chesapeake Bay, commandeered a steamboat, and landed the regiment at Annapolis. The 8th Massachusetts contained several railwaymen and mechanics in its ranks. Finding that secessionists had ripped up tracks and destroyed rolling stock on the line from Annapolis to Washington, Butler called for volunteers to repair the rusting derelict of a locomotive he found in the Annapolis yards. A private stepped forward: "That engine was made in our shop; I guess I can fit her up and run her."[15] Setting a pattern for the feats of railroad construction that helped the North win the war, Butler's troops and the 7th New York reopened the line over which thousands of northern soldiers poured into Washington.

14. Dennett, Lincoln/Hay, 11.
15. Nevins, War, I, 85.

Although Baltimore remained tense, the buildup of Union military strength along Maryland's railroads and a declaration of martial law in the city on May 13 dampened secession activities. Nevertheless, Governor Hicks succumbed to pressures to call the legislature into session. Lincoln considered sending troops to arrest disunionist legislators, but thought better of it. To the president's surprise, the legislature turned out to be all bark and no bite. The lower house denounced the war which "the Federal Government had declared on the Confederate States" and proclaimed Maryland's "resolute determination to have no part or lot, directly or indirectly, in its prosecution." At the same time, however, the legislature refused to consider an ordinance of secession or to call a convention to do so. In effect, the legislators accepted Governor Hicks's recommendation of "a neutral position between our brethren of the North and of the South."[16]

As a means of avoiding a difficult choice, "neutrality" was a popular stance in the border states during the first weeks after Sumter. But given Maryland's strategic location and the thousands of northern soldiers stationed in the state or passing through it, neutrality soon became an impossible dream. Indigenous Maryland unionism began to assert itself. The state's economic health was based on rail and water connections with the North. President John W. Garrett of the Baltimore and Ohio Railroad was a firm unionist and offered the railroad's facilities to carry troops and supplies from the West. Unionist candidates won all six seats in a special congressional election on June 13. By that time the state had also organized four Union regiments. Marylanders who wanted to fight for the Confederacy had to depart for Virginia to organize Maryland regiments on Confederate soil.

Union officials nonetheless continued to worry about underground Confederate activities in Baltimore. Army officers overreacted by arresting a number of suspected secessionists and imprisoning them in Fort McHenry. One of those arrested was a grandson of Francis Scott Key, who had written "The Star Spangled Banner" when the fort was under British fire a half-century earlier. Another was John Merryman, a wealthy landowner and lieutenant in a secessionist cavalry unit that had burned bridges and torn down telegraph wires during the April troubles. Merryman's lawyer petitioned the federal circuit court in Baltimore for a

16. Lincoln to Winfield Scott, April 25, 1861, in CWL, IV, 344; Dean Sprague, *Freedom under Lincoln* (Boston, 1965), 31–32; Rhodes, *History of the U.S.*, III, 275–76.

writ of habeas corpus. The senior judge of this court was none other than Roger B. Taney,[17] who on May 26 issued a writ ordering the commanding officer at Fort McHenry to bring Merryman before the court to show cause for his arrest. The officer refused, citing Lincoln's April 27 suspension of the writ of habeas corpus in portions of Maryland.

This confrontation became the first of several celebrated civil liberties cases during the war. Article I, Section 9, of the Constitution stipulates that the privilege of the writ of habeas corpus "shall not be suspended, unless when in cases of rebellion or invasion the public safety may require it." In a circuit court ruling on May 28, Taney denied the president's right to suspend the writ. The provision authorizing the suspension, he pointed out, appears in the article of the Constitution specifying the powers of Congress; therefore only Congress can exercise the power. Moreover, Taney continued, the Constitution does not authorize the arrest of civilians by army officers without the sanction of civil courts, nor does it permit a citizen to be held in prison indefinitely without trial.[18]

The Republican press denounced Taney's opinion as a new species of proslavery sophistry. Lincoln refused to obey it. Several prominent constitutional lawyers rushed into print to uphold the legality of Lincoln's position. The particular location of the habeas corpus clause in the Constitution was irrelevant, they maintained; suspension was an emergency power to be exercised in case of rebellion; the president was the only person who could act quickly enough in an emergency, especially when Congress was not in session. The whole purpose of suspending the writ, said these legal scholars, was to enable army officers to arrest and detain without trial suspected traitors when civil authorities and courts were potentially sympathetic with treason, as in Baltimore.[19]

In his message to the special session of Congress on July 4, 1861, Lincoln took note of the Merryman case. The president considered his primary duty to be the suppression of rebellion so that the laws of the

17. Under the organization of the federal court system at that time, the Supreme Court Justice from each of the nine circuits served also as the presiding judge of the circuit court.
18. *Ex parte Merryman*, 17 *Fed. Cas.* 144.
19. "Opinion of Attorney General Bates, July 5, 1861," in O.R., Ser. II, Vol. 2, pp. 20–30; Reverdy Johnson, *Power of the President to Suspend the Habeas Corpus Writ* (New York, 1861); Horace Binney, *The Privilege of the Writ of Habeas Corpus under the Constitution* (Philadelphia, 1862).

United States could be executed in the South. Suspension of the writ was a vital weapon against rebellion. "Are all the laws, *but one* [the right of habeas corpus], to go unexecuted," asked the president rhetorically, "and the government itself go to pieces, lest that one be violated?"[20] Whatever the respective merits of Taney's and Lincoln's positions, Taney commanded no troops and could not enforce his opinion, while Lincoln did and could. Merryman was released after seven weeks at Fort McHenry and indicted in the U. S. circuit court, but his case never came to trial because the government knew that a Maryland jury would not convict him.

While lawyers continued to argue, the army arrested the Baltimore police chief, four police commissioners, and several prominent citizens for their roles in the April 19 riot and their alleged continuing subversive activities. More was yet to come. After Confederate victory in the battle of Manassas on July 21, secessionists in Maryland became bold again. A special session of the legislature in August rang with rhetoric denouncing the "gross usurpation, unjust, tyrannical acts of the President of the United States."[21] By the time another extra session was scheduled to meet on September 17, the administration was alarmed by reports of a plot for a simultaneous Confederate invasion of Maryland, insurrection in Baltimore, and enactment of secession by the legislature. Lincoln decided to take drastic action. Union troops sealed off Frederick (where the legislature was meeting) and arrested thirty-one secessionist members along with numerous other suspected accessories to the plot, including Mayor George Brown of Baltimore. All were imprisoned for at least two months, until after the election of a new legislature in November.

Not surprisingly, this balloting resulted in a smashing victory for the Union party. After the election, prisoners regarded as least dangerous were released upon taking an oath of allegiance to the United States. Most of the rest were released on similar conditions in February 1862. A few hard cases remained in prison until all Maryland political prisoners were freed in December 1862. Although Lincoln justified the prolonged detention of these men on grounds of "tangible and unmistakable evidence" of their "substantial and unmistakable complicity with those in armed rebellion," the government never revealed the evidence

20. *CWL*, IV, 430.
21. Jean H. Baker, *The Politics of Continuity: Maryland Political Parties from 1858 to 1870* (Baltimore, 1973), 58.

or brought any of the prisoners to trial. Some of them, probably including Mayor Brown, were guilty of little more than southern sympathies
or lukewarm unionism. They were victims of the obsessive quest for
security that arises in time of war, especially civil war.[22]

A thousand miles to the west of Maryland, events equally dramatic
and more violent marked the struggle to keep Missouri in the Union.
Dynamic personalities polarized this struggle even more than the situation warranted. On one extreme stood Governor Claiborne Fox Jackson, a proslavery Democrat and onetime leader of the border ruffians.
On the other stood Congressman Francis P. Blair, Jr., whose connections in Washington included a brother as postmaster general and a
father as an adviser of Lincoln. Blair had used his influence to secure
the appointment of Captain Nathaniel Lyon as commander of the soldiers stationed at the U. S. arsenal in St. Louis—the largest arsenal in
the slave states, with 60,000 muskets and other arms in storage. A Connecticut Yankee and a twenty-year veteran of the army, Lyon was a free
soiler whose intense blue eyes, red beard, and commanding voice offered better clues than his small stature to the zeal and courage that
made him an extraordinary leader of men. Lyon had served in Kansas
when Claiborne Fox Jackson had led proslavery invaders from Missouri.
In 1861 the Lyon and the Fox once again faced each other in a confrontation of greater than Aesopian proportions.

In his inaugural address as governor on January 5, 1861, Jackson had
told Missourians: "Common origin, pursuits, tastes, manners and customs . . . bind together in one brotherhood the States of the South.
. . . [Missouri should make] a timely declaration of her determination
to stand by her sister slave-holding States."[23] The lieutenant governor,
speaker of the house, and a majority of the controlling Democratic party
in the legislature took the same position. The unionism of the state
convention elected to consider secession had frustrated their hopes. In
the aftermath of Sumter, however, Jackson moved quickly to propel
Missouri into the Confederacy. He took control of the St. Louis police
and mobilized units of the pro-southern state militia, which seized the
small U. S. arsenal at Liberty, near Kansas City. On April 17, the same

22. *CWL*, IV, 523; Sprague, *Freedom under Lincoln*, chaps. 16–18; Charles B. Clark,
"Suppression and Control of Maryland, 1861–1865," *Maryland Magazine of History*, 54 (1959), 241–71.
23. William E. Parrish, *Turbulent Partnership: Missouri and the Union, 1861–1865*
(Columbia, Mo., 1963), 6–7.

day that the governor spurned Lincoln's call for troops, he wrote to Jefferson Davis asking for artillery to assist in the capture of the St. Louis arsenal. On May 8 several large crates labeled "marble" but containing four cannons and ammunition arrived in St. Louis from Baton Rouge—where earlier they had been seized from the federal arsenal in that city. The artillery soon appeared in a grove on the edge of St. Louis, "Camp Jackson," where the southern militia was drilling.

Blair and Lyon matched Jackson's every move. Lyon mustered into federal service several regiments organized by the German American population, the hard core of unionism in St. Louis. To reduce the danger of secessionist capture of surplus arms in the arsenal, Lyon and Blair arranged for the secret transfer of 21,000 muskets across the river to Illinois. Word of the plan leaked out, and an excited crowd gathered at the wharf on the evening of April 25. Lyon decoyed them by sending a few boxes of ancient flintlock muskets to a docked steamboat where an Illinois militia captain pretended to wait for them. The mob seized the boxes and triumphantly bore them away. At midnight the 21,000 modern muskets crossed the Mississippi on another steamboat.

Lyon was not content to remain on the defensive and allow passions to cool, as conditional unionists advised. He decided to capture the 700 militiamen and their artillery at Camp Jackson. On May 9 he made a personal reconnaissance by carriage through the camp disguised in a dress and shawl as Frank Blair's mother-in-law. The next day he surrounded Camp Jackson with four regiments of German Americans and two companies of regulars. The militia surrendered without firing a shot. The shooting started later. As Lyon marched the prisoners through the city, a raucous crowd lined the road and grew to dangerous size. Shouting "Damn the Dutch" and "Hurrah for Jeff Davis," the mob threw brickbats and rocks at the German soldiers. When someone shot an officer, the soldiers began firing back. Before they could be stopped, twenty-eight civilians and two soldiers lay dead or dying, with uncounted scores wounded. That night mobs roamed the streets and murdered several lone German Americans. Next day another clash took the lives of two soldiers and four civilians.

Panic reigned in St. Louis, while anger ruled the state capital at Jefferson City, where the legislature quickly passed Governor Jackson's bills to place the state on a war footing. The events in St. Louis pushed many conditional unionists into the ranks of secessionists. The most prominent convert was Sterling Price, a Mexican War general and former governor, whom Jackson appointed as commander of the pro-southern militia. Missouri appeared headed for a civil war within its own borders. Moderates made one last effort to avert fighting by arranging a June 11 conference between Jackson and Price on one side and Blair and Lyon (now a brigadier general) on the other. Jackson and Price offered to disband their regiments and prevent Confederate troops from entering Missouri if Blair and Lyon would do the same with respect to Union regiments. After four hours of argument about these terms, Lyon rose angrily and declaimed: "Rather than concede to the State of Missouri for one single instant the right to dictate to my Government in any matter . . . I would see you . . . and every man, woman, and child in the State, dead and buried. *This means war.*"[24]

Lyon was as good as his word. Four days after this conference he occupied Jefferson City. Price's militia and the legislature abandoned the capital without resistance. They withdrew fifty miles up the Missouri River to Boonville, where Lyon relentlessly pursued and drove them from the town on June 17 after a skirmish with few casualties. Price's defeated forces retreated all the way to the southwest corner of Missouri by early July, with the unionists close on their heels. Lyon became the North's first war hero. With little outside help he had organized, equipped, and trained an army, won the first significant Union victories of the war, and gained control of most of Missouri.

But he had stirred up a hornets' nest. Although guerrilla bands would have infested Missouri in any case, the polarization of the state by Lyon's and Blair's actions helped turn large areas into a no-man's land of hit-and-run raids, arson, ambush, and murder. Confederate guerrilla chieftains William Quantrill, "Bloody Bill" Anderson, and George Todd became notorious bushwhackers. Their followers Jesse and Frank James and Cole and Jim Younger became even more famous—or infamous— after the war. Unionist "Jayhawker" counterinsurgency forces, especially the Kansans led by James Lane, Charles Jennison, and James Montgomery, matched the rebel bushwhackers in freebooting tactics. More than any other state, Missouri suffered the horrors of internecine warfare and the resulting hatreds which persisted for decades after Appomattox.

None of this fighting dislodged Union political control of most of the state. This control was exercised in a unique manner. The governor and most of the legislature had decamped. The only unionist body with some claim to sovereignty was the state convention that had adjourned

---

24. Thomas L. Snead, *The Fight for Missouri from the Election of Lincoln to the Death of Lyon* (New York, 1886), 199–200.

in March after rejecting secession. On July 22, therefore, a quorum of the convention reassembled, constituted itself the provisional government of Missouri, declared the state offices vacant and the legislature nonexistent, and elected a new governor and other state officials. Known as the "Long Convention" (to establish the analogy with the Long Parliament of the English Civil War), the convention ruled Missouri until January 1865, when a government elected under a new free-state constitution took over.

Meanwhile Claiborne Jackson called the pro-southern legislature into session at Neosho near the Arkansas border. Less than a quorum showed up, but on November 3, 1861, this body enacted an ordinance of secession. The Congress in Richmond admitted Missouri as the twelfth Confederate state on November 28. Although Missouri sent senators and representatives to Richmond, its Confederate state government was driven out of Missouri shortly after seceding and existed as a government in exile for the rest of the war.

Nearly three-quarters of the white men in Missouri and two-thirds of those in Maryland who fought in the Civil War did so on the side of the Union. Kentucky was more evenly divided between North and South; at least two-fifths of her white fighting men wore gray. Kentucky was the birthplace of both Abraham Lincoln and Jefferson Davis. Heir to the nationalism of Henry Clay, Kentucky was also drawn to the South by ties of kinship and culture. Three slave states and three free states touched its borders. Precisely because Kentucky was so evenly divided in sentiment and geography, its people were loath to choose sides. A month after Lincoln's call for troops, the legislature resolved that "this state and the citizens thereof shall take no part in the Civil War now being waged [but will] occupy a position of strict neutrality."[25]

Kentuckians took pride in their traditional role as mediator between North and South. Three times Henry Clay had devised historic sectional compromises: in 1820, 1833, and 1850. In 1861 Clay's successor John J. Crittenden had tried to devise a fourth. Even as late as May 1861, Kentucky unionists still believed that Crittenden's compromise offered the best hope to save the Union. Governor Beriah Magoffin appealed to the governors of the three midwestern states on Kentucky's northern border for a conference to propose mediation between the warring parties. He sent emissaries to Tennessee and Missouri for the same purpose. If all six states formed a united front, thought Magoffin, they

25. Lowell Harrison, *The Civil War and Kentucky* (Lexington, 1975), 9.

could compel North and South to make peace. But the Republican midwestern governors, busy mobilizing their states for war, refused to have anything to do with the idea, while Tennessee soon made its commitment to the Confederacy. A border states conference held in Frankfort on June 8 attracted delegates from only Kentucky and Missouri. They adjourned in futility after passing unnoticed resolutions.

In theory, neutrality was little different from secession. "Neutrality!!" exclaimed a Kentucky unionist in May 1861. "Why, Sir, this is a declaration of State Sovereignty, and is the very principle which impelled South Carolina and other States to secede." Lincoln agreed—in theory. But he, like other pragmatic unionists, recognized that neutrality was the best they could expect for the time being. The alternative was actual secession. For several weeks after the surrender of Fort Sumter, Breckinridge Democrats filled the state with rhetoric about southern rights, solidarity with sister states, and the like. Thousands of Kentuckians began filtering into Tennessee to join Confederate units. Although Governor Magoffin formally rejected Jefferson Davis's call for troops as he had rejected Lincoln's, Magoffin sympathized with the South and secretly permitted Confederate recruiting agents to enter the state. Even some Kentucky unionists declared that if northern soldiers tried to coerce the South, "Kentucky should promptly unsheath her sword in behalf of what will then have become her common cause." Sensitive to the delicate balance of opinion in his native state, Lincoln assured Kentucky unionist Garrett Davis on April 26 that while "he had the unquestioned right at all times to march the United States troops into and over any and every State," he had no present intention of doing so in Kentucky. If the state "made no demonstration of force against the United States, he would not molest her."[26]

Lincoln carried this promise to the extreme of allowing an immense trade through the state to the Confederacy. Horses, mules, food, leather, salt, and other military supplies, even munitions, entered Tennessee via Kentucky. Many Yankees denounced this trade (even as others quietly counted their profits from it). Midwestern governors and the army soon halted most river shipments by placing armed steamboats and artillery along the Ohio River. But the Louisville and Nashville Railroad continued to haul trainloads of provisions from Kentucky to Confederate supply centers in Tennessee. Even though Lincoln had declared a blockade

26. E. Merton Coulter, *The Civil War and Readjustment in Kentucky* (Chapel Hill, 1926), 92, 44; CG, 37 Cong., 2 Sess., Appendix, 82–83.

of Confederate ports, he hesitated to impose a land blockade against Kentucky lest he violate her "neutrality." Not until August 16, after state elections had shown that unionists were in firm control of Kentucky, did Lincoln issue a proclamation banning all trade with the Confederacy. Even this did not entirely halt the trade, but at least it made such commerce illegal and drove it underground.[27]

Lincoln's forbearance toward Kentucky paid off. Unionists became more outspoken, and fence-sitters jumped down onto the Union side. The legacy of Henry Clay began to assert itself. Unionist "home guard" regiments sprang up to counter the pro-southern "state guard" militia organized by Governor Magoffin. Union agents clandestinely ferried 5,000 muskets across the river from Cincinnati to arm the home guards. Kentuckian Robert Anderson, of Fort Sumter fame, established Union recruiting camps for Kentucky volunteers on the Ohio side of the river to match the Confederate camps just across the Tennessee line. At a special election on June 20, unionists won more than 70 percent of the votes and gained control of five of Kentucky's six congressional seats.[28] This balloting understated pro-Confederate sentiment, for many southern-rights voters refused to participate in an election held under the auspices of a government they rejected. Nevertheless, the regular election of the state legislature on August 5 resulted in an even more conclusive Union victory: the next legislature would have a Union majority of 76 to 24 in the House and 27 to 11 in the Senate.

This legislative election marked the beginning of the end of neutrality in Kentucky. Military activities along the state's borders soon forced the new legislature to declare its allegiance. Several northern regiments were stationed in Cairo, Illinois, at the confluence of the Ohio and Mississippi rivers. An equally large Confederate force occupied northwest Tennessee, fewer than fifty miles away. Key to the control of the Mis-

27. Coulter, *Civil War and Readjustment in Kentucky*, 73; CWL, IV, 486–87. Lincoln's proclamation was an implementation of legislation enacted July 13, 1861, forbidding trade with the Confederate states.

28. Most states held their congressional elections in the fall of even-numbered years, as they do today. But because a congressman so elected would not take his seat until thirteen months later, some states, including Maryland and Kentucky, held congressional elections in the odd-numbered year in which that Congress was scheduled to meet. Because Lincoln had called the 37th Congress into special session on July 4, 1861, Maryland and Kentucky had to hold special elections in June, a fortuitous circumstance that gave unionists in both states a chance to demonstrate their majorities and consolidate their control.

sissippi between these two forces was the high bluff at the rail terminal of Columbus, Kentucky. Both rival commanders cast covetous eyes on Columbus, and each feared—correctly—that the other intended to seize and fortify the heights there.

The Confederate commander was Leonidas Polk, tall and soldier-like in appearance, member of a distinguished southern family, a West Point graduate near the top of his class who had left the army in 1827 to enter the ministry and rise to a bishopric of the Episcopal church. When war came in 1861, he doffed his clerical robes and donned a major general's uniform. An officer of high reputation, Polk never measured up to his early military promise and did not survive the war. The opposing Union commander was Ulysses S. Grant, slouchy and unsoldier-like in appearance, of undistinguished family, a West Point graduate from the lower half of his class who had resigned from the army in disgrace for drunkenness in 1854 and had failed in several civilian occupations before volunteering his services to the Union in 1861. "I feel myself competent to command a regiment," Grant had diffidently informed the adjutant general in a letter of May 24, 1861—to which he received no reply.[29] Grant's commission as colonel and his promotion to brigadier general came via the congressman of his district and the governor of Illinois, who were scraping the barrel for officers to organize the unwieldly mass of Illinois volunteers. A man of no reputation and little promise, Grant would rise to the rank of lieutenant general commanding all the Union armies and become president of the United States.

Polk moved first to grasp the prize of Columbus. On September 3, troops from his command entered Kentucky and occupied the town. Grant responded by occupying Paducah and Smithland at the mouths of the strategically crucial Tennessee and Cumberland rivers. Both sides had invaded Kentucky, but by moving first the Confederates earned the stigma of aggressor. This converted the legislature from lukewarm to warlike unionism. On September 18 the American flag rose over the capitol and legislators resolved by a three to one margin that Kentucky having been "invaded by the forces of the so-called Confederate States . . . the invaders must be expelled."[30] Governor Magoffin and Senator Breckinridge resigned to cast their lot with the Confederacy. Other Kentuckians followed them. On November 18 a convention of two hundred delegates passed an ordinance of secession and formed a provisional gov-

29. *Personal Memoirs of U. S. Grant*, 2 vols. (New York, 1885), I, 239.
30. Edward Conrad Smith, *The Borderland in the Civil War* (New York, 1927), 301.

ernment, which the Congress in Richmond admitted as the thirteenth Confederate state on December 10. By the end of the year 35,000 Confederate troops occupied the southwest quarter of Kentucky, facing more than 50,000 Federals who controlled the rest of the state.

War had finally come to Kentucky. And here more than anywhere else it was literally a brothers' war. Four grandsons of Henry Clay fought for the Confederacy and three others for the Union. One of Senator John J. Crittenden's sons became a general in the Union army and the other a general in the Confederate army. The Kentucky-born wife of the president of the United States had four brothers and three brothers-in-law fighting for the South—one of them a captain killed at Baton Rouge and another a general killed at Chickamauga. Kentucky regiments fought each other on several battlefields; in the battle of Atlanta, a Kentucky Breckinridge fighting for the Yankees captured his rebel brother.

IV

The unionism of the fourth border state, tiny Delaware, was never in doubt. For all practical purposes Delaware was a free state. Less than 2 percent of its people were slaves, and more than 90 percent of its black population was free. In January 1861 the legislature had expressed "unqualified disapproval" of secession, and never again considered the question. The state's few slaveholders and Confederate sympathizers lived mainly in the southern counties, bordering Maryland's eastern shore.[31]

Each of the four upper South states that seceded contained a large area with little more commitment to slavery and the Confederacy than Delaware—western Virginia, western North Carolina, eastern Tennessee, and northern Arkansas. The economy and society of two of these upland regions were so distinct from the remainder of their states as to produce wartime movements for separate statehood. West Virginia managed to secede from the Confederacy and rejoin the Union. A similar effort in east Tennessee failed, leaving a legacy of bitterness that persisted long after the war.

The thirty-five counties of Virginia west of the Shenandoah Valley and north of the Kanawha River contained a quarter of Virginia's white population in 1860. Slaves and slaveowners were rare among these narrow valleys and steep mountainsides. The region's culture and economy

31. Harold Hancock, "Civil War Comes to Delaware," CWH, 2 (1956), 29–56.

were oriented to nearby Ohio and Pennsylvania rather than to the faraway lowlands of Virginia. The largest city, Wheeling, was only sixty miles from Pittsburgh but 330 miles from Richmond. For decades the plebeian mountaineers, underrepresented in a legislature dominated by slaveholders, had nursed grievances against the "tidewater aristocrats" who governed the state. Slaves were taxed at less than a third of their market value while other property was taxed at full value. The lion's share of state internal improvements went to the eastern counties, while the northwest cried out in vain for more roads and railroads. "Western Virginia," declared a Clarksburg newspaper during the secession winter of 1860–61, "has suffered more from . . . her eastern brethren than ever the Cotton States all put together have suffered from the North."[32]

The events of 1861 brought to a head the longstanding western sentiment for separate statehood. Only five of the thirty-one delegates from northwest Virginia voted for the secession ordinance on April 17. Voters in this region rejected ratification by a three to one margin. Mass meetings of unionists all over the northwest coalesced into a convention at Wheeling on June 11. The main issue confronting this convention was immediate versus delayed steps toward separate statehood for western Virginia. The stumbling block to immediate action was Article IV, Section 3, of the U. S. Constitution, which requires the consent of the legislature to form a new state from the territory of an existing one. The Confederate legislature of Virginia would not consent to a separate state, of course, so the Wheeling convention formed its own "restored government" of Virginia. Branding the Confederate legislature in Richmond illegal, the convention declared all state offices vacant and on June 20 appointed new state officials, headed by Francis Pierpoint as governor. Lincoln recognized the Pierpoint administration as the de jure government of Virginia. A rump legislature, theoretically representing the whole state but in practice representing only the northwestern counties, thereupon elected two U. S. senators from Virginia, who were seated by the Senate on July 13, 1861. Three congressmen from western Virginia also took their seats in the House.

When the Wheeling convention reconvened, in August 1861, a prolonged debate took place between separatists and conservatives. The latter found it difficult to swallow the idea that a legislature representing only one-fifth of Virginia's counties could act for the whole state. But the convention finally adopted an "ordinance of dismemberment" on

32. Smith, *Borderland in the Civil War*, 105.

August 20, subject to ratification by a referendum on October 24, 1861, at which the voters would also elect delegates to a constitutional convention for the new state of "Kanawha." All of these proceedings occurred against the backdrop of military operations in which a Union army invaded western Virginia and defeated a smaller Confederate army. This achievement was crucial to the success of the new-state movement; without the presence of victorious northern troops, the state of West Virginia could not have been born.

Union forces moved into western Virginia for strategic as well as political reasons. The Baltimore and Ohio Railroad and the Ohio River ran through this region and along its border for two hundred miles. The most direct rail link between Washington and the Midwest, the B & O would play an important role in Civil War logistics. In May 1861 the Confederates at Harper's Ferry had already cut the railroad while rebel militia in northwest Virginia occupied the line at Grafton and burned bridges west of there. Western Virginia unionists pleaded with Washington for troops; preoccupied with defense of the capital, General Scott could offer little help. But across the Ohio River, Governor William Dennison of Ohio came to the rescue. Like many other states, Ohio raised more regiments than called for in Lincoln's April 15 proclamation. Dennison was particularly fortunate to have the assistance of George B. McClellan, William S. Rosecrans, and Jacob D. Cox, all of them destined for prominent Civil War commands. McClellan and Rosecrans had graduated near the top of their West Point classes and had gone on to successful civilian careers in business and engineering after resigning from successful careers in the army. Cox was an Oberlin graduate, an outstanding lawyer, a founder of the Republican party in Ohio, and a brigadier general of Ohio militia. These three men organized the regiments raised by Governor Dennison and his equally energetic neighbor, Governor Oliver P. Morton of Indiana. Taking command of these troops, McClellan sent a vanguard across the Ohio River on May 26 to link up with two unionist Virginia regiments.

Their initial objective was the B & O junction at Grafton, sixty miles south of Wheeling. The colonel commanding the Confederate detachment at Grafton withdrew his outnumbered forces to Philippi, fifteen miles farther south. Three thousand Union soldiers, in service only five weeks, pursued with forced night marches through the rain over wretched roads at a pace that would have done credit to veteran troops. Although a planned pincers attack on the 1,500 Confederates at Philippi miscarried on June 3, the rebels fled twenty-five miles southward to Beverly with such haste that northern newspapers derisively labeled the affair "The Philippi Races."

On June 21, McClellan arrived at Grafton to take personal command of the campaign. Thirty-four years old, possessing charm, culture, great ability and an even greater ego, McClellan exhibited in West Virginia a nascent Napoleonic complex that manifested itself in the writing of dispatches and proclamations, though not in the handling of troops in battle. "Soldiers!" he declaimed in an address to his troops at Grafton. "I have heard that there was danger here. I have come to place myself at your head and to share it with you. I fear now but one thing—that you will not find foemen worthy of your steel."[33]

Robert E. Lee also hoped that McClellan's soldiers would meet worthy foemen. But Lee, functioning in Richmond as a sort of commander in chief of Virginia's armed forces, had few men and less steel to spare for faraway western Virginia. He scraped together a few thousand reinforcements and sent them to Beverly under the command of Robert S. Garnett. With 4,500 men "in a most miserable condition as to arms, clothing, equipment, and discipline," Garnett fortified the passes through which ran the main roads from the Shenandoah Valley to Wheeling and Parkersburg.[34]

By the end of June, McClellan had 20,000 men in trans-Allegheny Virginia. Five or six thousand of them guarded the B & O, which had been reopened to Washington. McClellan sent another 2,500 men under Jacob Cox to move up the Kanawha River to Charleston. With the remaining twelve thousand, McClellan planned to encircle and trap Garnett's little army. Leaving four thousand men to make a feint against Laurel Mountain, McClellan took three brigades to launch the main attack at Rich Mountain eight miles to the south. Rather than assault the Confederate trenches head-on, McClellan accepted Rosecrans's plan for a flank attack by one brigade while McClellan with two others stood ready to exploit whatever successes Rosecrans achieved. Guided by a local unionist over a narrow mountain track, Rosecrans's Ohio and Indiana regiments rolled up the rebel flank on July 11 and killed, wounded, or captured 170 of the 1,300 Confederates at a cost of about sixty casualties to themselves. Misinterpreting the sounds of battle through the woods and laurel thickets, McClellan feared that Rosecrans was losing; he therefore failed to launch the follow-up attack, and allowed most of

33. O.R., Ser. I. Vol. 2, p. 197.
34. Ibid., 236.

the rebels to escape. Jacob Cox, writing later as a historian of the campaign, pointed out that McClellan in West Virginia "showed the same characteristics which became well known later. There was the same overestimate of the enemy, the same tendency to interpret unfavorably the sights and sounds in front, the same hesitancy to throw in his whole force when he knew that his subordinate was engaged."[35]

Despite McClellan's timidity, Rosecrans's attack sent the Confederates into a pell-mell retreat. Five hundred of them were subsequently captured, while Garnett's main force of three thousand at Laurel Mountain, with the Federals now in their rear, fled over bad roads to the north and east. Union brigades pursued and on July 13 attacked Garnett's rear guard at Corrick's Ford, where Garnett lost his life—the first Civil War general killed in action. Although most of the rebels got away, the campaign cleared northwest Virginia of organized southern forces. Northern newspapers hailed this as a stunning success. McClellan did not hesitate to take the credit. On July 16 he issued another proclamation that read well in the press, which had begun to call him "The Young Napoleon": "Soldiers of the Army of the West! . . . You have annihilated two armies. . . . You have taken five guns, twelve colors, fifteen hundred stand of arms, one thousand prisoners . . . Soldiers! I have confidence in you, and I trust you have learned to confide in me."[36]

McClellan's victories enabled the reconvened Wheeling convention to enact the separate statehood ordinance in August. Before the referendum on October 24 took place, however, the Confederates made a determined effort to recapture western Virginia. By August they had managed to get 20,000 troops into the trans-Allegheny region, outnumbering the Federals there for the only time in the war. But most of these men were untrained, many were armed with unreliable old smoothbore muskets or even with squirrel rifles and shotguns, and one-third of them were on the sick list—mostly with measles and mumps which struck down farm boys who had never before been exposed to these childhood diseases. Sick or well, five thousand of the Confederate troops served in two independent commands headed by John B. Floyd and Henry A. Wise, former governors of Virginia and eager secessionists who now thirsted after military glory. In July, Jacob Cox's Ohioans had maneuvered Wise's brigade all the way up the Kanawha River to White Sul-

35. Cox, "McClellan in West Virginia," *Battles and Leaders*, I, 137.
36. O.R., Ser. I, Vol. 2, p. 236.

phur Springs, a hundred miles east of Charleston. Floyd's brigades reinforced Wise, but the two men cordially hated each other and spent more time feuding than planning a counterattack against Cox.[37]

Meanwhile the government in Richmond sent Robert E. Lee to take overall command of Confederate forces in western Virginia. Lee went personally to Huntersville, where 10,000 wet, sick, hungry Confederate soldiers confronted 3,000 Union troops dug in on the high ground of Cheat Mountain, a few miles south of the Rich Mountain pass from which Rosecrans had driven the rebels in July. The southern people expected great things of Lee. But this time he disappointed them. His complicated plan for a convergence of five separate columns against two Union positions was frustrated by the difficult terrain, the inexperience of his officers, the fatigue and sickness of his men—and by the weather. Rain had been falling during most of the forty-five days before Lee's troops moved out on September 10. Mud slowed their movements to a crawl. After some skirmishing that cost each side fewer than a hundred casualties had eliminated all chance of surprise, Lee gave up and called off the operation on September 15. The Federals remained in control of the Allegheny passes. Supply problems prevented further Confederate operations in this area. With the typical tall-tale humor of soldiers, the men told stories of mules that died of exhaustion hauling wagons over muddy roads and sank into the mire until only their ears were showing. About this time Lee began to grow a beard, which came in gray.

Lee took most of his troops south to the Kanawha Valley to reinforce Floyd and Wise, whose advance had been checked by Rosecrans at Carnifex Ferry on September 10. Jefferson Davis finally resolved the disputes between these two political generals by recalling Wise to Richmond. When Lee arrived in the Kanawha region his troops outnumbered the Federals, but once again rain, sickness, and terrain—plus Rosecrans's effective generalship—foiled a Confederate attempt to trap the enemy. Rosecrans pulled his forces back to a more defensible position on October 6. Seeing no chance to attack them successfully, Lee returned to Richmond at the end of October. He soon went to South Carolina to shore up Confederate coastal defenses, leaving behind a damaged reputation. In August, Richmond newspapers had predicted that he would drive the Yankees back to Ohio; in October they mocked him as "Granny Lee" and "Evacuating Lee." The acerbic *Richmond*

37. John B. Floyd to Jefferson Davis, Aug. 16, 1861, Civil War Collection, Henry E. Huntington Library.

Examiner pronounced Lee "outwitted, outmaneuvered, and outgeneraled." [38]

During the first half of November, Rosecrans resumed his offensive. With much maneuvering but little fighting, he forced Floyd to withdraw entirely from what is today West Virginia. The Kanawha Valley as well as northwest Virginia thereafter remained under Union military control—except for periodic rebel raids and constant guerrilla warfare. Most of the Kanawha Valley had voted for secession in the May 23 referendum; Confederate sentiment persisted there even after this region became part of the new state of West Virginia. Like Missouri and other parts of the border South, West Virginia suffered from a savage war within the larger war—neighbor against neighbor, bushwhacker against bushwhacker. Rebel guerrillas tied down thousands of Union troops, whose counterinsurgency efforts enjoyed little more success than similar efforts in recent wars. As the exasperated Union infantry commander Robert H. Milroy put it in October 1862: "We have now over 40,000 men in the service of the U. S. in Western Va. . . . [but] our large armies are useless here. They cannot catch guerrillas in the mountains any more than a cow can catch fleas. We must inaugurate a system of Union guerrillas to put down the rebel guerrillas." [39] Milroy suited action to words. He carried out such ruthless counter-guerrilla warfare that the Confederates put a price on his head.

Union military control of western Virginia was firm enough to permit the statehood referendum to take place as scheduled on October 24, 1861. The voters overwhelmingly endorsed a new state, but the turnout was small. Pro-Confederate voters in more than a dozen counties boycotted the election. Nevertheless, the constitutional convention in January 1862 established boundaries that included fifty counties, and the "restored state legislature of Virginia" sanctioned the creation of the new state of West Virginia on May 23, 1862. About 4 percent of the people in the proposed new state were slaves. Recognizing that a Republican Congress was unlikely to admit another slave state, the constitutional convention came within one vote of enacting gradual emancipation. Congress did indeed require emancipation as a condition of West Vir-

38. Quoted in William M. Lamers, *The Edge of Glory: A Biography of General William S. Rosecrans* (New York, 1961), 42.
39. Milroy to Francis Pierpont, Oct. 27, 1862, quoted in Richard O. Curry, *A House Divided: A Study of Statehood Politics and the Copperhead Movement in West Virginia* (Pittsburgh, 1964), 75.

ginia's statehood in a bill passed by the Senate in July 1862 and by the House in December. West Virginians accepted this condition. The new state came into the Union on June 20, 1863, with a constitution freeing the slaves born after July 4, 1863, and all others on their twenty-fifth birthday.

Republicans in 1861 viewed events in western Virginia as a model for the reconstruction of Union governments in other parts of the upper South. East Tennessee seemed the most promising locale for this effort. Unionists there held two conventions in 1861, at Knoxville on May 30–31 and at Greeneville on June 17–20. Former Whigs and Democrats cooperated warily in this effort against the greater enemy. Their leaders were Andrew Johnson, a lifelong Democrat, and William G. Brownlow, a former Methodist clergyman turned fighting editor of the *Knoxville Whig* whose profane language toward secessionists belied his nickname of "Parson" Brownlow. Johnson was the only U.S. senator from a seceding state who remained loyal to the Union. Brownlow stayed at the helm of his newspaper, flew the American flag over his home, and vowed to "fight the Secession leaders till Hell freezes over, and then fight them on the ice." Of plebeian origins, Johnson and Brownlow expressed the resentments of their nonslaveholding constituents against the secessionist gentry. "A cheap purse-proud set they are," said Johnson, "not half as good as the man who earns his bread by the sweat of his brow." Brownlow insisted that east Tennessee yeomen "can never live in a Southern Confederacy and be made hewers of wood and drawers of water for a set of aristocrats and overbearing tyrants."[40]

Unionists in east Tennessee could accomplish little without northern military support. Lincoln continually pressed his generals for action in this theater. But distance, logistical difficulties, and Kentucky stood in the way. So long as Lincoln was nursing unionism in Kentucky by respecting her neutrality, no northern troops could cross the state to reach east Tennessee. Even after Union forces moved into Kentucky in September 1861, the forbidding terrain and lack of transport facilities over the Cumberland Mountains made military operations difficult, especially in winter. While two railroads, a navigable river, and a macadamized turnpike carried troops and supplies from Ohio to the main

---

40. Brownlow quoted in Foote, *Civil War*, I, 51; Johnson quoted in Eric L. McKitrick, *Andrew Johnson and Reconstruction* (Chicago, 1960), 87; Brownlow in Knoxville Whig, Jan. 13, 1861, quoted in James W. Patton, *Unionism and Reconstruction in Tennessee, 1860–1869* (Chapel Hill, 1934), 57.

theaters of operations in western Virginia, no such routes ran from Union bases in eastern Kentucky 150 miles over the mountains to Knoxville.

In November, however, word of a northern invasion reached Union partisans in east Tennessee. With arms smuggled to them by northern agents they went into action, burning five railroad bridges and ambushing Confederate outposts. But the Yankees did not come. The reason was William Tecumseh Sherman. Commander of Union forces in Kentucky, the volatile, red-haired Sherman had not yet developed the *sang-froid* he displayed later in the war. Apprehensive about a buildup of Confederate forces in central Kentucky, Sherman called off the planned invasion of east Tennessee by a small army under General George H. Thomas, who had approached within forty miles of the Tennessee border. Sherman's inflated estimates of Confederate strength and his waspish comments to reporters caused hostile newspapers to call him insane. The administration relieved him of command and transferred him to an obscure post in Missouri. Sherman's career, like Robert E. Lee's, was almost eclipsed by failure before the war was seven months old.

Sherman's successor, Don Carlos Buell, reluctantly yielded to administration pressure and ordered Thomas to renew his advance. A Union-loyal Virginian, large and imposing in appearance, methodical and deliberate in his movements, Thomas led his 4,000-man army over almost nonexistent mountain roads in winter rains and sleet. On January 19, 1862, a Confederate army of equal size attacked Thomas at Logan's Cross Roads near Mill Springs, Kentucky, but was repulsed and then routed by a Union counterattack. Despite his victory, Thomas could advance no farther in the harsh mountain winter. By spring, Union advances in western and central Tennessee would divert all efforts to that quarter. Ironically, while northern armies "liberated" the Confederate portion of Tennessee they left the unionist portion to fend for itself—to Lincoln's chagrin.

Without northern help, east Tennessee unionists suffered grievously for their loyalty. Confederate troops cracked down after the bridge burnings in November. They declared martial law, executed five bridge-burners, arrested Brownlow and turned his printing office into an arms factory, and imprisoned hundreds of unionists—a much more thorough suppression of dissent than northern forces had carried out in Maryland. Brownlow's genius for self-dramatization turned him into a martyr and an embarrassment to the Confederates, who therefore released and escorted him to Union lines in March 1862.

Many other east Tennesseans made individual and group escapes to join the Union army. Even though that army did not occupy east Tennessee until September 1863, more than halfway through the war, 30,000 white Tennesseeans fought for the North—more than from any other Confederate state.

V

The actions of the eight upper South states in 1861 had an important but equivocal impact on the outcome of the war. One can begin to measure that impact by noting the possible consequences of what did *not* happen. If all eight states (or all but Delaware) had seceded, the South might well have won its independence. If all eight had remained in the Union, the Confederacy surely could not have survived as long as it did. As it was, the balance of military manpower from these states favored the South. The estimated 425,000 soldiers they furnished to southern armies comprised half of the total who fought for the Confederacy. These same states furnished some 235,000 white soldiers and eventually 85,000 blacks to the Union armies—together amounting to only 15 percent of the men who fought for the Union.[41] Nevertheless,

41. Data on the number of men who served in the Civil War armies can be no better than estimates. Few reliable records of Confederate enlistments survived the destruction and loss of Confederate archives at the end of the war. Estimates of the number of men who fought for the Confederacy are therefore based on fragmentary evidence. These estimates range from a low of 600,000 men to a high of 1,400,000. The fullest discussion of this matter can be found in Thomas L. Livermore, *Numbers and Losses in the Civil War in America 1861–1865* (Boston, 1901), 1–63. After extraordinarily complex calculations, Livermore estimated the number of Confederate soldiers at something over one million. But Livermore was a Union army veteran, with a tendency to overstate the numbers of the enemy he had faced, and some of the assumptions on which he based his calculations are dubious. Perhaps the most balanced discussion of the matter is Edward Channing, *A History of the United States*, Vol. 6, *The War for Southern Independence* (New York, 1925), 430–44. Channing estimated that 800,000 men fought for the Confederacy. Another respected Civil War scholar, E. B. Long, has offered an estimate of 750,000 (Long, *The Civil War Day by Day: An Almanac*, Garden City, N.Y., 1971, p. 705). Perhaps the firmest evidence on this question is the number of surviving veterans of the Union and Confederate armies counted by the census of 1890. The number of Confederate veterans at that date totaled 42 percent of the number of living Union veterans. Applying this ratio to the generally accepted estimate of 2,100,000 Union soldiers and sailors gives a total of 882,000 Confederate soldiers and sailors. Since a higher proportion of southerners were killed in the war, the actual total may have been higher. In any case, it seems safe to estimate that somewhere in the neighborhood of 850,000 to 900,000 men fought for the Con-

the ability of the North to mobilize this much manpower from slave states gave an important impetus to the Union war effort. And the strategic importance of the rivers, railroads, and mountains of the border states (including West Virginia) can hardly be exaggerated. On the other hand, guerrilla warfare and the problems of administering sizable regions with populations of doubtful loyalty tied down large numbers of Union troops in the border states.

The divided allegiance of the upper South complicated the efforts by both sides to define their war aims and to find a strategy for achieving these aims. For while the Union and Confederate governments were contending for the upper South, they were also mobilizing their armed forces and deciding how to use them.

---

federacy. The proportion of these from the upper South was derived from a variety of primary and secondary sources for those states, and on extrapolation from the number of white men of military age in these states counted by the 1860 census.

Data for the number of Union soldiers cited in this paragraph and elsewhere in this book are based on the full records for each state maintained by the War Department. Nevertheless, the figures for white Union soldiers must also be estimates. The War Department kept records of *enlistments*, which must be adjusted downward to avoid double (sometimes even triple) counting of men who re-enlisted. This adjustment is not necessary for black soldiers, who were not permitted to enlist before late 1862, so their three-year terms did not expire before the end of the war.

10

Amateurs Go to War

I

War fever during the months after Sumter overrode sober reflections on the purpose of the fighting. Most people on both sides took for granted the purpose and justice of their cause. Yankees believed that they battled for flag and country. "We must fight now, not because we want to subjugate the South . . . but because we *must*," declared a Republican newspaper in Indianapolis. "The Nation has been defied. The National Government has been assailed. If either can be done with impunity . . . we are not a Nation, and our Government is a sham." The *Chicago Journal* proclaimed that the South had "outraged the Constitution, set at defiance all law, and trampled under foot that flag which has been the glorious and consecrated symbol of American Liberty." Nor did northern Democratic editors fall behind their Republican rivals in patriotism. "We were born and bred under the stars and stripes," wrote a Pittsburgh Democrat. Although the South may have had just grievances against Republicans, "when the South becomes an enemy to the American system of government . . . and fires upon the flag . . . our influence goes for that flag, no matter whether a Republican or a Democrat holds it."[1]

1. *Indianapolis Daily Journal*, April 27, 1861, *Chicago Daily Journal*, April 17, 1861, *Pittsburgh Post*, April 15, 1861, all quoted from Howard C. Perkins, ed., *Northern Editorials on Secession*, 2 vols. (New York, 1942), 814, 808, 739.

Scholars who have examined thousands of letters and diaries written by Union soldiers found them expressing similar motives; "fighting to maintain the best government on earth" was a common phrase. It was a "grate strugle for the Union, Constitution, and law," wrote a New Jersey soldier. "Our glorious institutions are likely to be destroyed. . . . We will be held responsible before God if we don't do our part in helping to transmit this boon of civil & religious liberty down to succeeding generations." A midwestern recruit enlisted as "a duty I owe to my country and to my children to do what I can to preserve this government as I shudder to think what is ahead for them if this government should be overthrown." Americans of 1861 felt responsible to their forebears as well as to God and posterity. "I know . . . how great a debt we owe to those who went before us through the blood and sufferings of the Revolution," wrote a New England private to his wife on the eve of the first battle of Bull Run (Manassas). "I am willing—perfectly willing—to lay down all my joys in this life, to help maintain this government, and to pay that debt."[2]

One of Lincoln's qualities of greatness as president was his ability to articulate these war aims in pithy prose. "Our popular government has often been called an experiment," Lincoln told Congress on July 4, 1861. "Two points in it, our people have already settled—the successful *establishing*, and the successful *administering* of it. One still remains—its successful maintenance against a formidable internal attempt to overthrow it. . . . This issue embraces more than the fate of these United States. It presents to the whole family of man, the question, whether a constitutional republic, or a democracy . . . can or cannot, maintain its territorial integrity, against its own domestic foes."[3]

The flag, the Union, the Constitution, and democracy—all were symbols or abstractions, but nonetheless powerful enough to evoke a willingness to fight and die for them. Southerners also fought for ab-

2. Wiley, *Billy Yank,* 40; New Jersey and midwestern soldiers quoted in Randall Clair Jimerson, "A People Divided: The Civil War Interpreted by Participants," Ph.D. dissertation, University of Michigan, 1977, pp. 38–39; New England soldier quoted in William C. Davis, *Battle at Bull Run* (Garden City, 1977), 91–92. Two other studies contain numerous quotations from soldiers' letters making the same point: Reid Mitchell, "The Civil War Soldier: Ideology and Experience," Ph.D. dissertation, University of California at Berkeley, 1985; and Earl J. Hess, "Liberty and Self-Control: Republican Values in the Civil War North," Ph.D. dissertation, Purdue University, 1986.

3. *CWL,* IV, 439, 426.

stractions—state sovereignty, the right of secession, the Constitution as *they* interpreted it, the concept of a southern "nation" different from the American nation whose values had been corrupted by Yankees. "Thank God! we have a country at last," said Mississippian L. Q. C. Lamar in June 1861, a country "to live for, to pray for, to fight for, and if necessary, to die for." "Submission to the yoke of depotism," agreed army recruits from North Carolina and Georgia, would mean "servile subjugation and ruin." Another North Carolinian was "willing to give up my life in defence of my Home and Kindred. I had rather be dead than see the Yanks rule this country." He got his wish—at Gettysburg.[4]

Although southerners later bridled at the official northern name for the conflict—"The War of the Rebellion"—many of them proudly wore the label of rebel during the war itself. A New Orleans poet wrote these words a month after Sumter:

> Yes, call them rebels! 'tis the name
>   Their patriot fathers bore,
> And by such deeds they'll hallow it,
>   As they have done before.

Jefferson Davis said repeatedly that the South was fighting for the same "sacred right of self-government" that the revolutionary fathers had fought for. In his first message to Congress after the fall of Sumter, Davis proclaimed that the Confederacy would "seek no conquest, no aggrandizement, no concession of any kind from the States with which we were lately confederated; all we ask is to be let alone."[5]

Both sides believed they were fighting to preserve the heritage of republican liberty; but Davis's last phrase ("all we ask is to be let alone") specified the most immediate, tangible Confederate war aim: defense against invasion. Regarding Union soldiers as vandals bent on plundering the South and liberating the slaves, many southerners literally believed they were fighting to defend home, hearth, wives, and sisters. "Our men *must* prevail in combat, or lose their property, country, freedom, everything," wrote a southern diarist. "On the other hand, the enemy, in yielding the contest, may retire into their own country, and possess everything they enjoyed before the war began." A young English immigrant to Arkansas enlisted in the army after he was swept off his

4. Lamar quoted in E. Merton Coulter, *The Confederate States of America 1861–1865* (Baton Rouge, 1950), 57; soldiers quoted in Jimerson, "A People Divided," 20, 23.
5. Coulter, *Confederate States*, 60; Rowland, *Davis*, V, 84.

feet by a recruitment meeting. He later wrote that his southern friends "said they would welcome a bloody grave rather than survive to see the proud foe violating their altars and their hearths." Southern women brought irresistible pressure on men to enlist. "If every man did not hasten to battle, they vowed they would themselves rush out and meet the Yankee vandals. In a land where women are worshipped by the men, such language made them war-mad."[6] A Virginian was avid "to be in the front rank of the first brigade that marches against the invading foe who now pollute the sacred soil of my beloved native state with their unholy tread." A Confederate soldier captured early in the war put it more simply. His tattered homespun uniform and even more homespun speech made it clear that he was not a member of the planter class. His captors asked why he, a nonslaveholder, was fighting to uphold slavery. He replied: "I'm fighting because you're down here."[7]

For this soldier, as for many other southerners, the war was not about slavery. But without slavery there would have been no Black Republicans to threaten the South's way of life, no special southern civilization to defend against Yankee invasion. This paradox plagued southern efforts to define their war aims. In particular, slavery handicapped Confederate foreign policy. The first southern commissioners to Britain reported in May 1861 that "the public mind here is entirely opposed to the Government of the Confederate States of America on the question of slavery. . . . The sincerity and universality of this feeling embarrass the Government in dealing with the question of our recognition."[8] In their explanations of war aims, therefore, Confederates rarely mentioned slavery except obliquely in reference to northern violations of southern rights. Rather, they portrayed the South as fighting for liberty and self-government—blithely unmindful of Samuel Johnson's piquant question about an earlier generation of American rebels: "How is it that we hear the loudest *yelps* for liberty among the drivers of negroes?"

For reasons of their own most northerners initially agreed that the war had nothing to do with slavery. In his message to the special session

6. Jones, *War Clerk's Diary* (Miers), 181; *The Autobiography of Sir Henry M. Stanley*, ed. Dorothy Stanley (Boston and London, 1909), 165.

7. Thomas B. Webber to his mother, June 15, 1861, Civil War Times Illustrated Collection, United States Military History Institute, Carlisle, Pa.; Foote, *Civil War*, I, 65.

8. William L. Yancey and A. Dudley Mann to Robert Toombs, May 21, 1861, in James D. Richardson, comp., *A Compilation of the Messages and Papers of the Confederacy*, 2 vols. (Nashville, 1906), II, 37.

of Congress on July 4, 1861, Lincoln reaffirmed that he had "no purpose, directly or indirectly, to interfere with slavery in the States where it exists." The Constitution protected slavery in those states; the Lincoln administration fought the war on the theory that secession was unconstitutional and therefore the southern states still lived under the Constitution. Congress concurred. On July 22 and 25 the House and Senate passed similar resolutions sponsored by John J. Crittenden of Kentucky and Andrew Johnson of Tennessee affirming that the United States fought with no intention "of overthrowing or interfering with the rights or established institutions of [the seceded] States" but only "to defend and maintain the supremacy of the Constitution and to preserve the Union with all the dignity, equality, and rights of the several States unimpaired."[9]

Republicans would soon change their minds about this. But in July 1861 even radicals who hoped that the war *would* destroy slavery voted for the Crittenden-Johnson resolutions (though three radicals voted No and two dozen abstained). Most abolitionists at first also refrained from open criticism of the government's neutral course toward slavery. Assuming that the "death-grapple with the Southern slave oligarchy" must eventually destroy slavery itself, William Lloyd Garrison advised fellow abolitionists in April 1861 to " 'stand still, and see the salvation of God' rather than attempt to add anything to the general commotion."[10]

A concern for northern unity underlay this decision to keep a low profile on the slavery issue. Lincoln had won less than half of the popular vote in the Union states (including the border states) in 1860. Some of those who had voted for him, as well as all who had voted for his opponents, would have refused to countenance an antislavery war in 1861. By the same token, an explicit avowal that the defense of slavery was a primary Confederate war aim might have proven more divisive than unifying in the South. Both sides, therefore, shoved slavery under the rug as they concentrated their energies on mobilizing eager citizen soldiers and devising strategies to use them.

II

The United States has usually prepared for its wars after getting into them. Never was this more true than in the Civil War. The country

---

9. CWL, IV, 263, 438–39; CG, 37 Cong., 1 Sess., 222-23, 258-62.
10. Garrison to Oliver Johnson, April 19, 1861, William Lloyd Garrison Papers, Boston Public Library.

was less ready for what proved to be its biggest war than for any other war in its history. In early 1861 most of the tiny 16,000-man army was scattered in seventy-nine frontier outposts west of the Mississippi. Nearly a third of its officers were resigning to go with the South. The War Department slumbered in ancient bureaucratic routine. Most of its clerks, as well as the four previous secretaries of war, had come from the South. All but one of the heads of the eight army bureaus had been in service since the War of 1812. General-in-Chief Winfield Scott, seventy-four years old, suffered from dropsy and vertigo, and sometimes fell asleep during conferences. Many able young officers, frustrated by drab routine and cramped opportunities, had left the army for civilian careers. The "Winnebago Chief" reputation of Secretary of War Cameron did not augur well for his capacity to administer with efficiency and honesty the huge new war contracts in the offing.

The army had nothing resembling a general staff, no strategic plans, no program for mobilization. Although the army did have a Bureau of Topographical Engineers, it possessed few accurate maps of the South. When General Henry W. Halleck, commanding the Western Department in early 1862, wanted maps he had to buy them from a St. Louis bookstore. Only two officers had commanded as much as a brigade in combat, and both were over seventy. Most of the arms in government arsenals (including the 159,000 muskets seized by Confederate states) were old smoothbores, many of them flintlocks of antique vintage.

The navy was little better prepared for war. Of the forty-two ships in commission when Lincoln became president, most were patrolling waters thousands of miles from the United States. Fewer than a dozen warships were available for immediate service along the American coast. But there were some bright spots in the naval outlook. Although 373 of the navy's 1,554 officers and a few of its 7,600 seamen left to go with the South, the large merchant marine from which an expanded navy would draw experienced officers and sailors was overwhelmingly northern. Nearly all of the country's shipbuilding capacity was in the North. And the Navy Department, unlike the War Department, was blessed with outstanding leadership. Gideon Welles, whose long gray beard and stern countenance led Lincoln to call him Father Neptune, proved to be a capable administrator. But the real dynamism in the Navy Department came from Assistant Secretary Gustavus V. Fox, architect of the Fort Sumter expedition. Within weeks of Lincoln's proclamation of a blockade against Confederate ports on April 19, the Union navy had bought or chartered scores of merchant ships, armed them, and dispatched them to blockade duty. By the end of 1861 more than 260 warships were on duty and 100 more (including three experimental ironclads) were under construction.

The northern naval outlook appeared especially bright in contrast to the southern. The Confederacy began life with no navy and few facilities for building one. The South possessed no adequate shipyards except the captured naval yard at Norfolk, and not a single machine shop capable of building an engine large enough to power a respectable warship. While lacking material resources, however, the Confederate navy possessed striking human resources, especially Secretary of the Navy Stephen R. Mallory and Commanders Raphael Semmes and James D. Bulloch.

Mallory was a former U.S. senator from Florida with experience as chairman of the Senate naval affairs committee. Although snubbed by high Richmond society because of his penchant for women of questionable virtue, Mallory proved equal to the task of creating a navy from scratch. He bought tugboats, revenue cutters, and river steamboats to be converted into gunboats for harbor patrol. Recognizing that he could never challenge the Union navy on its own terms, Mallory decided to concentrate on a few specialized tasks that would utilize the South's limited assets to maximum advantage. He authorized the development of "torpedoes" (mines) to be planted at the mouths of harbors and rivers; by the end of the war such "infernal devices" had sunk or damaged forty-three Union warships. He encouraged the construction of "torpedo boats," small half-submerged cigar-shaped vessels carrying a contact mine on a bow-spar for attacking blockade ships. It was only one step from this concept to that of a fully submerged torpedo boat. The Confederacy sent into action the world's first combat submarine, the *C.S.S. Hunley*, which sank three times in trials, drowning the crew each time (including its inventor Horace Hunley) before sinking a blockade ship off Charleston in 1864 while going down itself for the fourth and last time.

Mallory knew of British and French experiments with ironclad warships. He believed that the South's best chance to break the blockade was to build and buy several of these revolutionary vessels, equip them with iron rams, and send them out to sink the wooden blockade ships. In June 1861 Mallory authorized the rebuilding of the half-destroyed *U.S.S. Merrimack* as the Confederacy's first ironclad, rechristened the *C.S.S. Virginia*. Although work proceeded slowly because of shortages, the South invested much hope in this secret weapon (which was no secret to the Federals, whose intelligence agents penetrated loose southern security). The Confederacy began converting other vessels into iron-clads, but its main source for these and other large warships was expected to be British shipyards. For the sensitive task of exploiting this source, Mallory selected James D. Bulloch of Georgia.

With fourteen years' experience in the U.S. navy and eight years in commercial shipping, Bulloch knew ships as well as anyone in the South. He also possessed the tact, social graces, and business acumen needed for the job of getting warships built in a country whose neutrality laws threw up a thicket of obstacles. Arriving at Liverpool in June 1861, Bulloch quickly signed contracts for two steam/sail cruisers that eventually became the famed commerce raiders *Florida* and *Alabama*. In the fall of 1861 he bought a fast steamer, loaded it with 11,000 Enfield rifles, 400 barrels of gunpowder, several cannons, and large quantities of ammunition, took command of her himself, and ran the ship through the blockade into Savannah. The steamer was then converted into the ironclad ram *C.S.S. Atlanta*. Bulloch returned to England, where he continued his undercover efforts to build and buy warships. His activities prompted one enthusiastic historian to evaluate Bulloch's contributions to the Confederacy as next only to those of Robert E. Lee.[11]

The commerce raiders built in Britain represented an important part of Confederate naval strategy. In any war, the enemy's merchant shipping becomes fair game. The Confederates sent armed raiders to roam the oceans in search of northern vessels. At first the South depended on privateers for this activity. An ancient form of wartime piracy, privateering had been practiced with great success by Americans in the Revolution and the War of 1812. In 1861, Jefferson Davis proposed to turn this weapon against the Yankees. On April 17, Davis offered letters of marque to any southern shipowner who wished to turn privateer. About twenty such craft were soon cruising the sea lanes off the Atlantic coast, and by July they had captured two dozen prizes.

Panic seized northern merchants, whose cries forced the Union navy to divert ships from blockade duty to hunt down the "pirates." They enjoyed some success, but in doing so caused a crisis in the legal definition of the war. Refusing to recognize the Confederacy as a legitimate government, Lincoln on April 19, 1861, issued a proclamation threatening to treat captured privateer crews as pirates. By midsummer a number of such crews languished in northern jails awaiting trial. Jefferson Davis

11. Philip Van Doren Stern, *When the Guns Roared: World Aspects of the American Civil War* (Garden City, N.Y., 1965), 249–50.

declared that for every privateer hanged for piracy he would have a Union prisoner of war executed. The showdown came when Philadelphia courts convicted several privateer officers in the fall of 1861. Davis had lots drawn among Union prisoners of war, and the losers—including a grandson of Paul Revere—were readied for retaliatory hanging. The country was spared this eye-for-an-eye bloodbath when the Lincoln administration backed down. Its legal position was untenable, for in the same proclamation that had branded the privateers as pirates Lincoln had also imposed a blockade against the Confederacy. This had implicitly recognized the conflict as a war rather than merely a domestic insurrection. The Union government's decision on February 3, 1862, to treat captured privateer crews as prisoners of war was another step in the same direction.

By this time, Confederate privateers as such had disappeared from the seas. Their success had been short-lived, for the Union blockade made it difficult to bring prizes into southern ports, and neutral nations closed their ports to prizes. The Confederacy henceforth turned to commerce raiders—warships manned by naval personnel and designed to sink rather than to capture enemy shipping. The transition from privateering to commerce raiding began in June 1861, when the five-gun steam sloop *C.S.S. Sumter* evaded the blockade at the mouth of the Mississippi and headed toward the Atlantic. Her captain was Raphael Semmes of Alabama, a thirty-year veteran of the U.S. navy who now launched his career as the chief nemesis of that navy and terror of the American merchant marine. During the next six months the *Sumter* captured or burned eighteen vessels before Union warships finally bottled her up in the harbor at Gibraltar in January 1862. Semmes sold the *Sumter* to the British and made his way across Europe to England, where he took command of the *C.S.S. Alabama* and went on to bigger achievements.

Despite ingenuity and innovations, however, the Confederate navy could never overcome Union supremacy on the high seas or along the coasts and rivers of the South. The Confederacy's main hopes rode with its army. A people proud of their martial prowess, southerners felt confident of their ability to whip the Yankees in a fair fight—or even an unfair one. The idea that one Southron could lick ten Yankees—or at least three—really did exist in 1861. "Just throw three or four shells among those blue-bellied Yankees," said a North Carolinian in May 1861, "and they'll scatter like sheep." In southern eyes the North was a nation of shopkeepers. It mattered not that the Union's industrial capacity was many times greater than the Confederacy's. "It was not the improved *arm*, but the improved *man*, which would win the day," said Henry Wise of Virginia. "Let brave men advance with flint locks and old-fashioned bayonets, on the popinjays of Northern cities . . . and he would answer for it with his life, that the Yankees would break and run."[12]

Expecting a short and glorious war, southern boys rushed to join the colors before the fun was over. Even though the Confederacy had to organize a War Department and an army from the ground up, the South got an earlier start on mobilization than the North. As each state seceded, it took steps to consolidate and expand militia companies into active regiments. In theory the militia formed a ready reserve of trained citizen soldiers. But reality had never matched theory, and in recent decades the militia of most states had fallen into decay. By the 1850s the old idea of militia service as an obligation of all males had given way to the volunteer concept. Volunteer military companies with distinctive names—Tallapoosa Grays, Jasper Greens, Floyd Rifles, Lexington Wild Cats, Palmetto Guards, Fire Zouaves—sprang up in towns and cities across the country. In states that retained a militia framework, these companies were incorporated into the framework and became, in effect, the militia. The training, discipline, and equipment of these units varied widely. Many of them spent more time drinking than drilling. Even those that made a pretense of practicing military maneuvers sometimes resembled drum and bugle corps more than fighting outfits. Nevertheless, it was these volunteer companies that first answered the call for troops in both South and North.

By early spring 1861 South Carolina had five thousand men under arms, most of them besieging Fort Sumter. Other southern states were not far behind. The Confederate Congress in February created a War Department, and President Davis appointed Leroy P. Walker of Alabama as Secretary of War. Though a politician like his Union counterpart Simon Cameron, Walker had a better reputation for honesty and efficiency. More important, perhaps, Jefferson Davis himself was a West Point graduate, a combat veteran of the Mexican War, and a former secretary of war in the U.S. government. Although Davis's fussy supervision of Confederate military matters eventually led to conflict with some army officers, the president's martial expertise helped speed southern mobilization in 1861.

12. North Carolinian quoted in Nevins, *War*, I, 96; Wise quoted in Jones, *War Clerk's Diary* (Miers), 3.

On March 6 the Confederate Congress authorized an army of 100,000 volunteers for twelve months. Most of the militia regiments already organized were sworn into the Confederate army, while newly formed units scrambled for arms and equipment. At first the states, localities, and individuals rather than the Confederate government equipped these regiments. Although the South selected cadet gray as its official uniform color, each regiment initially supplied its own uniforms, so that Confederate armies were garbed in a confusing variety of clothing that defied the concept of "uniform." Cavalrymen and artillery batteries provided their own horses. Some volunteers brought their own weapons, ranging from bowie knives and Colt revolvers to shotguns and hunting rifles. Many recruits from planter families brought their slaves to wash clothes and cook for them. Volunteer companies, following the venerable militia tradition, elected their own officers (captain and lieutenants). State governors officially appointed regimental officers (colonel, lieutenant colonel, and major), but in many regiments these officers were actually elected either by the men of the whole regiment or by the officers of all the companies. In practice, the election of officers was often a *pro forma* ratification of the role that a prominent planter, lawyer, or other individual had taken in recruiting a company or a regiment. Sometimes a wealthy man also paid for the uniforms and equipment of a unit he had recruited. Wade Hampton of South Carolina, reputed to be the richest planter in the South, enlisted a "legion" (a regiment-size combination of infantry, cavalry, and artillery) that he armed and equipped at his own expense—and of which, not coincidentally, he became colonel.

By the time Lincoln called for 75,000 men after the fall of Sumter, the South's do-it-yourself mobilization had already enrolled 60,000 men. But these soldiers were beginning to experience the problems of logistics and supply that would plague the southern war effort to the end. Even after the accession of four upper-South states, the Confederacy had only one-ninth the industrial capacity of the Union. Northern states had manufactured 97 percent of the country's firearms in 1860, 94 percent of its cloth, 93 percent of its pig iron, and more than 90 percent of its boots and shoes. The Union had more than twice the density of railroads per square mile as the Confederacy, and several times the mileage of canals and macadamized roads. The South could produce enough food to feed itself, but the transport network, adequate at the beginning of the war to distribute this food, soon began to deteriorate because of a lack of replacement capacity. Nearly all of the rails had come from the North or from Britain; of 470 locomotives built in the United States during 1860, only nineteen had been made in the South.

The Confederate army's support services labored heroically to overcome these deficiencies. But with the exception of the Ordnance Bureau, their efforts always seemed too little and too late. The South experienced a hothouse industrialization during the war, but the resulting plant was shallow-rooted and poor in yield. Quartermaster General Abraham Myers could never supply the army with enough tents, uniforms, blankets, shoes, or horses and wagons. Consequently Johnny Reb often had to sleep in the open under a captured blanket, to wear a tattered homespun butternut uniform, and to march and fight barefoot unless he could liberate shoes from a dead or captured Yankee.

Confederate soldiers groused about this in the time-honored manner of all armies. They complained even more about food—or rather the lack of it—for which they held Commissary-General Lucius B. Northrop responsible. Civilians also damned Northrop for the shortages of food at the front, the rising prices at home, and the transportation nightmares that left produce rotting in warehouses while the army starved. Perhaps because of his peevish, opinionated manner, Northrop became "the most cussed and vilified man in the Confederacy."[13] Nevertheless, Jefferson Davis kept him in office until almost the end of the war, a consequence, it was whispered, of cronyism stemming from their friendship as cadets at West Point. Northrop's unpopularity besmudged Davis when the war began to go badly for the South.

The Ordnance Bureau was the one bright spot of Confederate supply. When Josiah Gorgas accepted appointment as chief of ordnance in April 1861 he faced an apparently more hopeless task than did Myers or Northrop. The South already grew plenty of food, and the capacity to produce wagons, harness, shoes, and clothing seemed easier to develop than the industrial base to manufacture gunpowder, cannon, and rifles. No foundry in the South except the Tredegar Iron Works had the capability to manufacture heavy ordnance. There were no rifle works except small arsenals at Richmond and at Fayetteville, North Carolina, along with the captured machinery from the U.S. Armory at Harper's Ferry, which was transferred to Richmond. The du Pont plants in Delaware produced most of the country's gunpowder; the South had manufactured almost none, and this heavy, bulky product would be difficult

13. Woodward, *Chesnut's Civil War*, 124.

to smuggle through the tightening blockade. The principal ingredient of gunpowder, saltpeter (potassium nitrate, or "niter"), was also imported.

But Gorgas proved to be a genius at organization and improvisation. He almost literally turned plowshares into swords.[14] He sent Caleb Huse to Europe to purchase all available arms and ammunition. Huse was as good at this job as James Bulloch was at his task of building Confederate warships in England. The arms and other supplies Huse sent back through the blockade were crucial to Confederate survival during the war's first year. Meanwhile Gorgas began to establish armories and foundries in several states to manufacture small arms and artillery. He created a Mining and Niter Bureau headed by Isaac M. St. John, who located limestone caves containing saltpeter in the southern Appalachians, and appealed to southern women to save the contents of chamber pots to be leached for niter. The Ordnance Bureau also built a huge gunpowder mill at Augusta, Georgia, which under the superintendency of George W. Rains began production in 1862. Ordnance officers roamed the South buying or seizing stills for their copper to make rifle percussion caps; they melted down church and plantation bells for bronze to build cannon; they gleaned southern battlefields for lead to remold into bullets and for damaged weapons to repair.

Gorgas, St. John, and Rains were unsung heroes of the Confederate war effort.[15] The South suffered from deficiencies of everything else, but after the summer of 1862 it did not suffer seriously for want of ordnance—though the quality of Confederate artillery and shells was always a problem. Gorgas could write proudly in his diary on the third anniversary of his appointment: "Where three years ago we were not making a gun, a pistol nor a sabre, no shot nor shell (except at the Tredegar Works)—a pound of powder—we now make all these in quantities to meet the demands of our large armies."[16]

14. See Frank E. Vandiver, *Ploughshares into Swords: Josiah Gorgas and Confederate Ordnance* (Austin, Texas, 1952). An excellent study of the Confederacy's chief ordnance plant, the Tredegar Iron Works, is Charles B. Dew, *Ironmaker to the Confederacy: Joseph R. Anderson and the Tredegar Iron Works* (New Haven, 1966).

15. Unsung, because while other men were winning glory and promotion on the battlefield, these officers—without whom the battles could not have been fought—languished in lower ranks. Gorgas was not promoted to brigadier general until November 10, 1864, St. John not until February 16, 1865, and Rains ended the war as a colonel.

16. Frank E. Vandiver, ed., *The Civil War Diary of General Josiah Gorgas* (University, Ala., 1947), 91.

But in 1861 these achievements still lay in the future. Shortages and administrative chaos seemed to characterize the Ordnance Bureau as much as any other department of the army. In a typical report, a southern staff officer in the Shenandoah Valley wrote on May 19 that the men were "unprovided, unequipped, unsupplied with ammunition and provisions. . . . The utter confusion and ignorance presiding in the councils of the authorities . . . is without a parallel." Despite the inability to equip men already in the army, the Confederate Congress in May 1861 authorized the enlistment of up to 400,000 additional volunteers for three-year terms. Recruits came forward in such numbers that the War Department, by its own admission, had to turn away 200,000 for lack of arms and equipment. One reason for this shortage of arms was the hoarding by state governors of muskets seized from federal arsenals when the states seceded. Several governors insisted on retaining these weapons to arm regiments they kept at home (instead of sending them to the main fronts in Virginia or Tennessee) to defend state borders and guard against potential slave uprisings. This was an early manifestation of state's-rights sentiment that handicapped centralized efforts. As such it was hardly the Richmond government's fault, but soldiers in front-line armies wanted to blame somebody, and Secretary of War Walker was a natural scapegoat. "The opinion prevails throughout the army," wrote General Beauregard's aide-de-camp at Manassas on June 22, "that there is great imbecility and shameful neglect in the War Department."[17] Although Beauregard's army won the battle of Manassas a month later, criticism of Walker rose to a crescendo. Many southerners believed that the only thing preventing the Confederates from going on to capture Washington after the victory was the lack of supplies and transportation for which the War Department was responsible. Harassed by criticism and overwork, Walker resigned in September and was replaced by Judah P. Benjamin, the second of the five men who eventually served in the revolving-door office of war secretary.

III

Walker—like his successors—was a victim of circumstances more than of his own ineptitude. The same could not be said of his counterpart in Washington. Although Simon Cameron was also swamped by the rapid

17. Nevins, War, I, 115; O.R., Ser. IV, Vol. 1, p. 497; James C. Chesnut to Mary Boykin Chesnut, June 22, in Woodward, Chesnut's Civil War, 90.

buildup of an army that exceeded the capacity of the bureaucracy to equip it, he was more deserving of personal censure than Walker.

The North started later than the South to raise an army. The Union had more than 3.5 times as many white men of military age as the Confederacy. But when adjustments are made for the disloyal, the unavailable (most men from the western territories and Pacific coast states), and for the release of white workers for the Confederate army by the existence of slavery in the South, the actual Union manpower superiority was about 2.5 to 1. From 1862 onward the Union army enjoyed approximately this superiority in numbers. But because of its earlier start in creating an army, the Confederacy in June 1861 came closer to matching the Union in mobilized manpower than at any other time in the war.

Lincoln's appeal for 75,000 ninety-day militiamen had been based on a law of 1795 providing for calling state militia into federal service. The government soon recognized that the war was likely to last more than three months and to require more than 75,000 men. On May 3, Lincoln called for 42,000 three-year army volunteers and 18,000 sailors, besides expanding the regular army by an additional 23,000 men. The president did this without congressional authorization, citing his constitutional power as commander in chief. When Congress met in July it not only retroactively sanctioned Lincoln's actions but also authorized another one million three-year volunteers. In the meantime some states had enrolled *two-year* volunteers (about 30,000 men), which the War Department reluctantly accepted. By early 1862 more than 700,000 men had joined the Union army. Some 90,000 of them had enlisted in the ninety-day regiments whose time had expired. But many of these men had re-enlisted in three-year regiments, and several ninety-day regiments had converted themselves into three-year units.

These varying enlistments confused contemporaries as much as they have confused historians. Indeed, the Union recruitment process, like the Confederate, was marked by enterprise and vigor at the local and state levels degenerating into confusion at the national level. Secretary of War Cameron's slipshod administrative procedures frustrated the brisk, businesslike governors. "Twenty-four hundred men in camp and less than half of them armed," Indiana's Governor Morton wrote to Cameron early in the war. "Why has there been such delay in sending arms? . . . No officer here yet to muster troops into service. Not a pound of powder or a single ball sent us, or any sort of equipment. Allow me to ask what is the cause of all this?" A few months later Ulysses S. Grant, commanding the Union base at Cairo, Illinois, voiced a typical plaint: "There is great deficiency in transportation. I have no ambulances. The clothing received has been almost universally of an inferior quality and deficient in quantity. The arms in the hands of the men are mostly the old flint-lock repaired. . . . The Quartermaster's Department has been carried on with so little funds that Government credit has become exhausted." By the end of June, Cameron was turning away offers of regiments. As Lincoln ruefully admitted in his July 4 message to Congress, "one of the greatest perplexities of the government, is to avoid receiving troops faster than it can provide for them." [18]

Staters, cities, and individuals took up the slack left by the national government. Most governors convened their legislatures, which appropriated funds to equip and supply regiments at state expense until the army could absorb them. Governors sent purchasing agents to Europe, where they competed with each other and with Confederate agents to bid up the price of the Old World's surplus arms to supply the armies of the New. The states contracted with textile mills and shoe factories for uniforms and shoes. Municipalities raised money to organize and supply "their" regiments. Voluntary associations such as the Union Defense Committee of New York sprang into existence to recruit regiments, equip them, and charter ships or trains to transport them to Washington. A group of northern physicians and women formed the United States Sanitary Commission to supplement the inadequate and outdated facilities of the Army Medical Bureau.

The earliest northern regiments, like the southern, were clad in a colorful variety of uniforms: blue from Massachusetts and Pennsylvania; gray from Wisconsin and Iowa; gray with emerald trim from Vermont; black trousers and red flannel shirts from Minnesota; and gaudy "Zouave" outfits from New York with their baggy red breeches, purple blouses, and red fezzes. The Union forces gathering in Washington looked like a circus on parade. The variety of uniforms in both Union and Confederate armies, and the similarity of some uniforms on opposite sides, caused tragic mixups in early battles when regiments mistook friends for enemies or enemies for friends. As fast as possible the northern government overcame this situation by clothing its soldiers in the standard light blue trousers and dark blue blouse of the regular army.

By the latter part of 1861 the War Department had taken over from the states the responsibility for feeding, clothing, and arming Union

18. O.R., Ser. III, Vol. 1, p. 89; Ser. I, Vol. 7, p. 442; CWL, IV, 432.

soldiers. But this process was marred by inefficiency, profiteering, and corruption. To fill contracts for hundreds of thousands of uniforms, textile manufacturers compressed the fibers of recycled woolen goods into a material called "shoddy." This noun soon became an adjective to describe uniforms that ripped after a few weeks of wear, shoes that fell apart, blankets that disintegrated, and poor workmanship in general on items necessary to equip an army of half a million men and to create its support services within a few short months. Railroads overcharged the government; some contractors sold muskets back to the army for $20 each that they had earlier bought as surplus arms at $3.50; sharp horse traders sold spavined animals to the army at outrageous prices. Simon Cameron became the target of just as well as unjust criticism of such transactions. He signed lucrative contracts without competitive bidding and gave a suspiciously large number of contracts to firms in his home state of Pennsylvania. The War Department routed a great deal of military traffic over the Northern Central Railroad and the Pennsylvania Railroad in which Cameron and Assistant Secretary of War Thomas Scott had direct financial interests.

The House created an investigatory committee on contracts that issued a report in mid-1862 condemning Cameron's management. By then Lincoln had long since gotten rid of Cameron by sending him to St. Petersburg as minister to Russia. The new secretary of war was Edwin M. Stanton, a hard-working, gimlet-eyed lawyer from Ohio who had served briefly as attorney general in the Buchanan administration. A former Democrat with a low opinion of Lincoln, Stanton radically revised both his politics and his opinion after taking over the war office in January 1862. He also became famous for his incorruptible efficiency and brusque rudeness toward war contractors—and toward everyone else as well.

Even before Stanton swept into the War Department with a new broom, the headlong, helter-skelter, seat-of-the pants mobilization of 1861 was just about over. The army's logistical apparatus had survived its shakedown trials and had even achieved a modicum of efficiency. The northern economy had geared up for war production on a scale that would make the Union army the best fed, most lavishly supplied army that had ever existed. Much of the credit for this belonged to Montgomery Meigs, who became quartermaster general of the army in June 1861. Meigs had graduated near the top of his West Point class and had achieved an outstanding record in the corps of engineers. He supervised a number of large projects including the building of the new Capitol dome and construction of the Potomac Aqueduct to bring water to Washington. His experience in dealing with contractors enabled him to impose some order and honesty on the chaos and corruption of early war contracts. Meigs insisted on competitive bidding whenever possible, instead of the cost-plus system favored by manufacturers who liked to inflate profits by padding costs.

Nearly everything needed by an army except weapons and food was supplied by the Quartermaster Bureau: uniforms, overcoats, shoes, knapsacks, haversacks, canteens, mess gear, blankets, tents, camp equipage, barracks, horses, mules, forage, harnesses, horseshoes and portable blacksmith shops, supply wagons, ships when the army could be supplied by water, coal or wood to fuel them, and supply depots for storage and distribution. The logistical demands of the Union army were much greater than those of its enemy. Most of the war was fought in the South where Confederate forces operated close to the source of many of their supplies. Invading northern armies, by contrast, had to maintain long supply lines of wagon trains, railroads, and port facilities. A Union army operating in enemy territory averaged one wagon for every forty men and one horse or mule (including cavalry and artillery horses) for every two or three men. A campaigning army of 100,000 men therefore required 2,500 supply wagons and at least 35,000 animals, and consumed 600 tons of supplies each day. Although in a few noted cases—Grant in the Vicksburg campaign, Sherman in his march through Georgia and the Carolinas—Union armies cut loose from their bases and lived off the country, such campaigns were the exception.

Meigs furnished these requirements in a style that made him the unsung hero of northern victory. He oversaw the spending of $1.5 billion, almost half of the direct cost of the Union war effort. He compelled field armies to abandon the large, heavy Sibley and Adams tents in favor of portable shelter tents known to Yankee soldiers as "dog tents"—and to their descendants as pup tents. The Quartermaster Bureau furnished clothing manufacturers with a series of graduated standard measurements for uniforms. This introduced a concept of "sizes" that was applied to men's civilian clothing after the war. The army's voracious demand for shoes prompted the widespread introduction of the new Blake-McKay machine for sewing uppers to soles. In these and many other ways, Meigs and his Bureau left a permanent mark on American society.

IV

In the North as in the South, volunteer regiments retained close ties to their states. Enlisted men elected many of their officers and governors appointed the rest. Companies and even whole regiments often consisted of recruits from a single township, city, or county. Companies from neighboring towns combined to form a regiment, which received a numerical designation in chronological order of organization: the 15th Massachusetts Infantry, the 2nd Pennsylvania Cavalry, the 4th Volunteer Battery of Ohio Artillery, and so on. Ethnic affinity also formed the basis of some companies and regiments: the 69th New York was one of many Irish regiments; the 79th New York were Highland Scots complete with kilted dress uniforms; numerous regiments contained mostly men of German extraction. Sometimes brothers, cousins, or fathers and sons belonged to the same company or regiment. Localities and ethnic groups retained a strong sense of identity with "their" regiments. This helped to boost morale on both the home and fighting fronts, but it could mean sudden calamity for family or neighborhood if a regiment suffered 50 percent or more casualties in a single battle, as many did.

The normal complement of a regiment in both the Union and Confederate armies was a thousand men formed in ten companies. Within a few months, however, deaths and discharges because of sickness significantly reduced this number. Medical examinations of recruits were often superficial. A subsequent investigation of Union enlistment procedures in 1861 estimated that 25 percent of the recruits should have been rejected for medical reasons. Many of these men soon had to be invalided out of the army. Within a year of its organization a typical regiment was reduced to half or less of its original number by sickness, battle casualties, and desertions. Instead of recruiting old regiments up to strength, states preferred to organize new ones with new opportunities for patronage in the form of officers' commissions and pride in the number of regiments sent by the state. Of 421,000 new three-year volunteers entering the Union army in 1862, only 50,000 joined existing regiments. Professional soldiers criticized this practice as inefficient and wasteful. It kept regiments far below strength and prevented the leavening of raw recruits by seasoned veterans. In 1862 and 1863, many old regiments went into combat with only two or three hundred men while new regiments suffered unnecessary casualties because of inexperience.

Professional soldiers also deplored the practice of electing officers in volunteer regiments. If one assumes that an army is a nonpolitical institution based on rigorous training, discipline, and unquestioning obedience to orders, the election of officers indeed made little sense. In the American tradition, however, citizen soldiers remained citizens even when they became soldiers. They voted for congressmen and governors; why should they not vote for captains and colonels? During the early stages of the do-it-yourself mobilization in 1861, would-be officers assumed that military skills could be quickly learned. Hard experience soon began to erode this notion. Many officers who obtained commissions by political influence proved all too obviously incompetent. A soldier in a Pennsylvania regiment complained in the summer of 1861: "Col. Roberts has showed himself to be ignorant of the most simple company movements. There is a total lack of system about our regiment. . . . Nothing is attended to at the proper time, nobody looks ahead to the morrow. . . . We can only justly be called a mob & one not fit to face the enemy." Officers who panicked at Bull Run and left their men to fend for themselves were blamed for the rout of several Union regiments. "Better offend a thousand ambitious candidates for military rank," commented *Harper's Weekly*, "than have another flight led by colonels, majors, and captains."[19]

On July 22, the day after the defeat at Bull Run, the Union Congress authorized the creation of military boards to examine officers and remove those found to be unqualified. Over the next few months hundreds of officers were discharged or resigned voluntarily rather than face an examining board. This did not end the practice of electing officers, nor of their appointment by governors for political reasons, but it went part way toward establishing minimum standards of competence for those appointed. As the war lengthened, promotion to officer's rank on the basis of merit became increasingly the rule in veteran regiments. By 1863 the Union army had pretty well ended the practice of electing officers.

This practice persisted longer in the Confederacy. Nor did the South establish examining boards for officers until October 1862. Yet Confederate officers, at least in the Virginia theater, probably did a better job than their Union counterparts during the first year or two of the war. Two factors help to explain this. First, Union General-in-Chief Winfield Scott decided to keep the small regular army together in 1861 rather than to disperse its units among the volunteer army. Hundreds of officers and non-coms in the regular army could have provided drill instructors and tactical leadership to the volunteer regiments. But Scott

19. Wiley, *Billy Yank*, 26; *Harper's Weekly*, V (Aug. 10, 1861), 449.

kept them with the regulars, sometimes far away on the frontier, while raw volunteers bled and died under incompetent officers in Virginia. The South, by contrast, had no regular army. The 313 officers who resigned from the U.S. army to join the Confederacy contributed a crucial leaven of initial leadership to the southern armies.

Second, the South's military schools had turned out a large number of graduates who provided the Confederacy with a nucleus of trained officers. In 1860 of the eight military "colleges" in the entire country seven were in the slave states. Virginia Military Institute in Lexington and The Citadel in Charleston were justly proud of the part their alumni played in the war. One-third of the field officers of Virginia regiments in 1861 were V.M.I. alumni. Of the 1,902 men who had ever attended V.M.I., 1,781 fought for the South. When Confederate regiments elected officers, they usually chose men with some military training. Most northern officers from civilian life had to learn their craft by experience, with its cost in defeat and casualties.

Political criteria played a role in the appointment of generals as well as lesser officers. In both North and South the president commissioned generals, subject to Senate confirmation. Lincoln and Davis found it necessary to consider factors of party, faction, and state as carefully in appointing generals as in naming cabinet officers or postmasters. Many politicians coveted a brigadier's star for themselves or their friends. Lincoln was particularly concerned to nurture Democratic support for the war, so he commissioned a large number of prominent Democrats as generals—among them Benjamin F. Butler, Daniel E. Sickles, John A. McClernand, and John A. Logan. To augment the loyalty of the North's large foreign-born population, Lincoln also rewarded ethnic leaders with generalships—Carl Schurz, Franz Sigel, Thomas Meagher, and numerous others. Davis had to satisfy the aspirations for military glory of powerful state politicians; hence he named such men as Robert A. Toombs of Georgia and John B. Floyd and Henry A. Wise of Virginia as generals.

These appointments made political sense but sometimes produced military calamity. "It seems but little better than murder to give important commands to such men as Banks, Butler, McClernand, Sigel, and Lew Wallace," wrote the West Point professional Henry W. Halleck, "yet it seems impossible to prevent it."[20] "Political general" became almost a synonym for incompetency, especially in the North. But this

20. O.R., Ser. I, Vol. 34, pt. 3, pp. 332–33.

was often unfair. Some men appointed for political reasons became first-class Union corps commanders—Frank Blair and John Logan, for example. West Pointers Ulysses S. Grant and William T. Sherman received their initial commissions through the political influence of Congressman Elihu Washburne of Illinois and Senator John Sherman (William's brother) of Ohio. And in any case, West Point professionals held most of the top commands in both North and South—and some of them made a worse showing than the political generals. Generals appointed from civilian life sometimes complained bitterly that the "West Point clique" ran the armies as closed corporations, controlling promotions and reserving the best commands for themselves.

The appointment of political generals, like the election of company officers, was an essential part of the process by which a highly politicized society mobilized for war. Democracy often characterized the state of discipline in Civil War armies as well. As late as 1864 the inspector-general of the Army of Northern Virginia complained of "the difficulty of having orders properly and promptly executed. There is not that spirit of respect for and obedience to general orders which should pervade a military organization." Just because their neighbors from down the road back home now wore shoulder straps, Johnny Reb and Billy Yank could see no reason why their orders should be obeyed unless the orders seemed reasonable. "We have tite Rools over us, the order was Red out in dress parade the other day that we all have to pull off our hats when we go to the coln or genrel," wrote a Georgia private. "You know that is one thing I wont do. I would rather see him in hell before I will pull off my hat to any man and tha Jest as well shoot me at the start." About the same time a Massachessetts private wrote that "drill & saluting officers & guard duty is played out."[21]

Many officers did little to inspire respect. Some had a penchant for drinking and carousing—which of course set a fine example for their men. In the summer of 1861 the 75th New York camped near Baltimore on its way to Washington. "Tonight not 200 men are in camp," wrote a diary-keeping member of the regiment despairingly. "Capt. Catlin, Capt. Hurburt, Lt. Cooper and one or two other officers are under arrest. A hundred men are drunk, a hundred more at houses of ill fame. . . . Col. Alford is very drunk all the time now." In 1862 a North

21. Ibid., Ser. I, Vol. 42, pt. 2, p. 1276; Steven H. Hahn, The Roots of Southern Populism: Yeoman Farmers and the Transformation of the Georgia Upcountry, 1850–1890 (New York, 1983), 118; Wiley, Billy Yank, 220.

Carolina private wrote of his captain: "He put . . . [me] in the gard house one time & he got drunk again from Wilmington to Goldsboro on the train & we put him in the Sh-t House So we are even."[22]

Such officers were in the minority, however, and over time a number of them were weeded out by resignation or by examining boards. The best officers from civilian life took seriously their new profession. Many of them burned the midnight oil studying manuals on drill and tactics. They avoided giving petty or unreasonable orders and compelled obedience to reasonable ones by dint of personality and intellect rather than by threats. They led by example, not prescript. And in combat they led from the front, not the rear. In both armies the proportion of officers killed in action was about 15 percent higher than the proportion of enlisted men killed. Generals suffered the highest combat casualties; their chances of being killed in battle were 50 percent greater than the privates'.

Civil War regiments learned on the battlefield to fight, not in the training camp. In keeping with the initial lack of professionalism, the training of recruits was superficial. It consisted mainly of the manual of arms (but little target practice), company and regimental drill in basic maneuvers, and sometimes brigade drill and skirmishing tactics. Rarely did soldiers engage in division drill or mock combat. Indeed, brigades were not combined into divisions until July 1861 or later, nor divisions into corps until the spring and summer of 1862.[23] Regiments sometimes

22. Bruce Catton, *Mr. Lincoln's Army* (Garden City, N.Y., 1956), 64–65; Wiley, *Johnny Reb*, 242.

23. Both the Union and Confederate armies were organized in similar fashion. Four infantry regiments (later in the war sometimes five or six) formed a brigade, commanded by a brigadier general. Three (sometimes four) brigades comprised a division, commanded by a brigadier or major general. Two or more divisions (usually three) constituted an army corps, commanded by a major general in the Union army and by a major or lieutenant general in the Confederacy. A small army might consist of a single corps; the principal armies consisted of two or more. In theory the full strength of an infantry regiment was 1,000 men; of a brigade, 4,000; of a division, 12,000 ; and of a corps, 24,000 or more. In practice the average size of each unit was a third to a half of the above numbers in the Union army. Confederate divisions and corps tended to be larger than their Union counterparts because a southern division often contained four brigades and a corps four divisions. Cavalry regiments often had twelve rather than ten companies (called "troops" in the cavalry). Cavalry regiments, brigades, or divisions were attached to divisions, corps, or armies as the tactical situation required. By 1863 Confederate cavalry divisions sometimes operated as a semi-independent corps, and by 1864 the Union cavalry

went into combat only three weeks after they had been organized, with predictable results. General Helmuth von Moltke, chief of the Prussian general staff, denied having said that the American armies of 1861 were nothing but armed mobs chasing each other around the countryside— but whether he said it or not, he and many other European professionals had reason to believe it. By 1862 or 1863, however, the school of experience had made rebel and Yankee veterans into tough, combat-wise soldiers whose powers of endurance and willingness to absorb punishment astonished many Europeans who had considered Americans all bluster and no grit. A British observer who visited the Antietam battlefield ten days after the fighting wrote that "in about seven or eight acres of wood there is not a tree which is not full of bullets and bits of shell. It is impossible to understand how anyone could live in such a fire as there must have been here." [24]

V

Amateurism and confusion characterized the development of strategies as well as the mobilization of armies. Most officers had learned little of strategic theory. The curriculum at West Point slighted strategic studies in favor of engineering, mathematics, fortification, army administration, and a smattering of tactics. The assignment of most officers to garrison and Indian-fighting duty on the frontier did little to encourage the study of strategy. Few if any Civil War generals had read Karl von Clausewitz, the foremost nineteenth-century writer on the art of war. A number of officers had read the writings of Antoine Henry Jomini, a Swiss-born member of Napoleon's staff who became the foremost interpreter of the great Corsican's campaigns. All West Point graduates had absorbed Jominian principles from the courses of Dennis Hart Mahan, who taught at the military academy for nearly half a century. Henry W. Halleck's *Elements of Military Art and Science* (1846), essentially a translation of Jomini, was used as a textbook at West Point. But Jomini's

---

followed suit, carrying such independent operations to an even higher level of development. Field artillery batteries (a battery consisted of four or six guns) were attached to brigades, divisions, or corps as the situation required. About 80 percent of the fighting men in the Union army were infantry, 14 percent cavalry, and 6 percent artillery. The Confederates had about the same proportion of artillery but a somewhat higher proportion of cavalry (nearly 20 percent).

24. Quoted in Jay Luvaas, *The Military Legacy of the Civil War: The European Inheritance* (Chicago, 1959), 18–19.

influence on Civil War strategy should not be exaggerated, as some historians have done.[25] Many Jominian "principles" were common-sense ideas hardly original with Jomini: concentrate the mass of your own force against fractions of the enemy's; menace the enemy's communications while protecting your own; attack the enemy's weak point with your own strength; and so on. There is little evidence that Jomini's writings influenced Civil War strategy in a direct or tangible way; the most successful strategist of the war, Grant, confessed to having never read Jomini.

The trial and error of experience played a larger role than theory in shaping Civil War strategy. The experience of the Mexican War governed the thinking of most officers in 1861. But that easy victory against a weak foe in an era of smoothbore muskets taught some wrong lessons to Civil War commanders who faced a determined enemy armed (after 1861) largely with rifled muskets. The experience necessary to fight the Civil War had to be gained in the Civil War itself. As generals and civilian leaders learned from their mistakes, as war aims changed from limited to total war, as political demands and civilian morale fluctuated, military strategy evolved and adjusted. The Civil War was pre-eminently a *political* war, a war of peoples rather than of professional armies. Therefore political leadership and public opinion weighed heavily in the formation of strategy.

In 1861 many Americans had a romantic, glamorous idea of war. "I am absent in a glorious cause," wrote a southern soldier to his homefolk in June 1861, "and glory in being in that cause." Many Confederate recruits echoed the Mississippian who said he had joined up "to fight the Yankees—all fun and frolic." A civilian traveling with the Confederate government from Montgomery to Richmond in May 1861 wrote that the trains "were crowded with troops, and all as jubilant, as if they were going to a frolic, instead of a fight."[26] A New York volunteer wrote home soon after enlisting that "I and the rest of the boys are in fine spirits . . . feeling like larks." Regiments departing for the front paraded before cheering, flag-waving crowds, with bands playing martial airs and visions of glory dancing in their heads. "The war is making us all tend-

---

25. For a perceptive critique of the "Jominian school," see Grady McWhiney and Perry D. Jamieson, *Attack and Die: Civil War Military Tactics and the Southern Heritage* (University, Ala., 1982), 146–53.

26. Davis, *Battle at Bull Run*, 57; Wiley, *Johnny Reb*, 27; Hudson Strode, *Jefferson Davis: Confederate President* (New York, 1959), 89.

Stephen A. Douglas

Louis A. Warren Lincoln Library and Museum

William H. Seward

Library of Congress

Free-state men ready to defend Lawrence, Kansas, in 1856

The Kansas State Historical Society

Stockpile of rails in the U.S. Military Rail Roads yards at Alexandria

U.S. Army Military History Institute

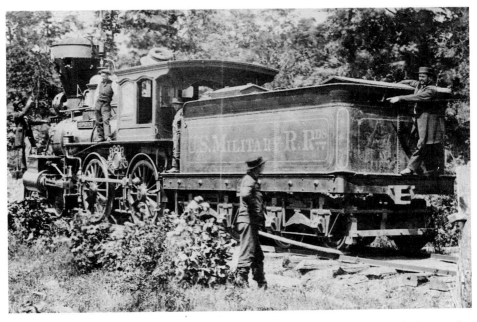

U.S. Military Rail Roads locomotive with crew members pointing at holes in the smokestack and tender caused by rebel shells

U.S. Army Military History Institute

B & O trains carrying troops and supplies meeting at Harper's Ferry

U.S. Military Academy Library

Railroad bridge built by Union army construction crew in Tennessee after rebel raiders
burned the original bridge

Minnesota Historical Society

Blockade-runner *Robert E. Lee,* which ran the blockade fourteen times before being captured on the fifteenth attempt

Library of Congress

U.S.S. Minnesota, 47-gun steam frigate, flagship of the Union blockade fleet that captured the *Robert E. Lee*

Minnesota Historical Society

Above: Abraham Lincoln

Louis A. Warren Lincoln Library and Museum

Right: George B. McClellan

Louis A. Warren Lincoln Library and Museum

Below: U.S.S. Cairo, one of "Pook's turtles," which fought on the Tennessee and Mississippi rivers until sunk by a Confederate "torpedo" in the Yazoo River near Vicksburg in December 1862

U.S. Army Military History Institute

Jefferson Davis

Library of Congress

Robert E. Lee

Library of Congress

Thomas J. "Stonewall" Jackson

Library of Congress

James E. B. "Jeb" Stuart

Library of Congress

Clara Barton
Library of Congress

Mary Anne "Mother" Bickerdyke
U.S. Army Military History Institute

Wounded soldiers and nurse at Union army hospital in Fredericksburg
Library of Congress

"Before" and "after" photographs of a young contraband who became
a Union drummer boy

U.S. Army Military History Institute

Black soldiers seated with white officers and freedmen's teachers standing behind them

Library of Congress

erly sentimental," wrote southern diarist Mary Boykin Chesnut in June 1861. So far it was "all parade, fife, and fine feathers."[27]

Many people on both sides believed that the war would be short— one or two battles and the cowardly Yankees or slovenly rebels would give up. An Alabama soldier wrote in 1861 that the next year would bring peace "because we are going to kill the last Yankey before that time if there is any fight in them still. I believe that J. D. Walker's Brigade can whip 25,000 Yankees. I think I can whip 25 myself." Northerners were equally confident; as James Russell Lowell's fictional Yankee philosopher Hosea Biglow ruefully recalled:

> I hoped, las' Spring, jest arter Sumter's shame
> When every flagstaff flapped its tethered flame,
> An' all the people, startled from their doubt,
> Come musterin' to the flag with sech a shout,—
> I hoped to see things settled 'fore this fall,
> The Rebbles licked, Jeff Davis hanged, an' all.[28]

With such confidence in quick success, thoughts of strategy seemed superfluous. Responsible leaders on both sides did not share the popular faith in a short war. Yet even they could not foresee the kind of conflict this war would become—a total war, requiring total mobilization of men and resources, destroying these men and resources on a massive scale, and ending only with unconditional surrender. In the spring of 1861 most northern leaders thought in terms of a limited war. Their purpose was not to conquer the South but to suppress insurrection and win back the latent loyalty of the southern people. The faith in southern unionism lingered long.

A war for limited goals required a strategy of limited means. General-in-Chief Winfield Scott devised such a strategy. As a Virginia unionist, Scott deprecated a war of conquest which even if successful would produce "fifteen devastated provinces! [i.e., the slave states] not to be brought into harmony with their conquerors, but to be held for generations, by heavy garrisons, at an expense quadruple the net duties or taxes which it would be possible to extort from them." Instead of invading the South, Scott proposed to "envelop" it with a blockade by sea and a fleet of gunboats supported by soldiers along the Mississippi. Thus sealed off

27. Wiley, *Billy Yank*, 27; Woodward, *Chesnut's Civil War*, 69.
28. Alabamian quoted in McWhiney and Jamieson, *Attack and Die*, 170; Biglow in Nevins, *War*, I, 75.

from the world, the rebels would suffocate and the government "could bring them to terms with less bloodshed than by any other plan."[29]

Scott's method would take time—time for the navy to acquire enough ships to make the blockade effective, time to build the gunboats and train the men for the expedition down the Mississippi. Scott recognized the chief drawback of his plan—"the impatience of our patriotic and loyal Union friends. They will urge instant and vigorous action, regardless, I fear, of the consequences."[30] Indeed they did. Northern public opinion demanded an invasion to "crush" the rebel army covering Manassas, a rail junction in northern Virginia linking the main lines to the Shenandoah Valley and the deep South. Newspapers scorned Scott's strategy as the "Anaconda Plan." The Confederate government having accepted Virginia's invitation to make Richmond its capital, the southern Congress scheduled its next session to begin there on July 20. Thereupon Horace Greeley's *New York Tribune* blazoned forth with a standing headline:

FORWARD TO RICHMOND! FORWARD TO RICHMOND!

The Rebel Congress Must Not be
Allowed to Meet There on the
20th of July

BY THAT DATE THE PLACE MUST BE HELD
BY THE NATIONAL ARMY

Other newspapers picked up the cry of On to Richmond. Some hinted that Scott's Anaconda Plan signified a traitorous reluctance to invade his native state. Many northerners could not understand why a general who with fewer than 11,000 men had invaded a country of eight million people, marched 175 miles, defeated larger enemy armies, and captured their capital, would shy away from invading Virginia and fighting the enemy twenty-five miles from the United States capital. The stunning achievements of an offensive strategy in Mexico tended to make both Union and Confederate commanders offensive-minded in the early phases of the Civil War. The success of Lyon in Missouri and of

---

29. Charles Winslow Elliott, *Winfield Scott: The Soldier and the Man* (New York, 1937), 698; O.R., Ser. I, Vol. 51, pt. 1, pp. 369–70.
30. O.R., Ser. I, Vol. 51, pt. 1, p. 387.

McClellan in western Virginia seemed to confirm the value of striking first and striking fast.

Scott remained unconvinced. He considered the ninety-day regiments raw and useless; the three-year regiments would need several months' training before they were ready for a campaign. But Scott was out of step with the political imperatives of 1861. Public pressure made it almost impossible for the government to delay military action on the main Virginia front. Scott's recommended blockade of southern seaports had begun, and his proposed move down the Mississippi became part of Union strategy in 1862. But events ultimately demonstrated that the North could win the war only by destroying the South's armies in the field. In that respect the popular clamor for "smashing" the rebels was based on sound if oversanguine instinct. Lincoln thought that an attack on the enemy at Manassas was worth a try. Such an attack came within his conception of limited war aims. If successful it might discredit the secessionists; it might lead to the capture of Richmond; but it would not destroy the social and economic system of the South; it would not scorch southern earth.

By July 1861 about 35,000 Union troops had gathered in the Washington area. Their commander was General Irvin McDowell, a former officer on Scott's staff with no previous experience in field command. A teetotaler who compensated by consuming huge amounts of food, McDowell did not lack intelligence or energy—but he turned out to be a hard-luck general for whom nothing went right. In response to a directive from Lincoln, McDowell drew up a plan for a flank attack on the 20,000 Confederates defending Manassas Junction. An essential part of the plan required the 15,000 Federals near Harper's Ferry under the command of Robert Patterson, a sixty-nine-year-old veteran of the War of 1812, to prevent the 11,000 Confederates confronting him from reinforcing Manassas.

McDowell's plan was a good one—for veteran troops with experienced officers. But McDowell lacked both. At a White House strategy conference on June 29, he pleaded for postponement of the offensive until he could train the new three-year men. Scott once again urged his Anaconda Plan. But Quartermaster-General Meigs, when asked for his opinion, said that "I did not think we would ever end the war without beating the rebels. . . . It was better to whip them here than to go far into an unhealthy country to fight them [in Scott's proposed expedition down the Mississippi]. . . . To make the fight in Virginia was cheaper and better as the case now stood."[31] Lincoln agreed. As for the rawness of McDowell's troops, Lincoln seemed to have read the mind of a rebel officer in Virginia who reported his men to be so deficient in "discipline and instruction" that it would be "difficult to use them in the field. . . . I would not give one company of regulars for the whole regiment." The president ordered McDowell to begin his offensive. "You are green, it is true," he said, "but they are green, also; you are all green alike."[32]

The southern commander at Manassas was Pierre G. T. Beauregard, the dapper, voluble hero of Fort Sumter, Napoleonic in manner and aspiration. Heading the rebel forces in the Shenandoah Valley was Joseph E. Johnston, a small, impeccably attired, ambitious but cautious man with a piercing gaze and an outsized sense of dignity. In their contrasting offensive- and defensive-mindedness, Beauregard and Johnston represented the polarities of southern strategic thinking. The basic war aim of the Confederacy, like that of the United States in the Revolution, was to defend a new nation from conquest. Confederates looked for inspiration to the heroes of 1776, who had triumphed over greater odds than southerners faced in 1861. The South could "win" the war by not losing; the North could win only by winning. The large territory of the Confederacy—750,000 square miles, as large as Russia west of Moscow, twice the size of the thirteen original United States—would make Lincoln's task as difficult as Napoleon's in 1812 or George III's in 1776. The military analyst of the *Times* of London offered the following comments early in the war:

> It is one thing to drive the rebels from the south bank of the Potomac, or even to occupy Richmond, but another to reduce and hold in permanent subjection a tract of country nearly as large as Russia in Europe. . . . No war of independence ever terminated unsuccessfully except where the disparity of force was far greater than it is in this case. . . . Just as England during the revolution had to give up conquering the colonies so the North will have to give up conquering the South.[33]

31. Russell F. Weigley, *Quartermaster General of the Union Army: A Biography of M. C. Meigs* (New York, 1959), 172.
32. Douglas Southall Freeman, *Lee's Lieutenants: A Study in Command*, 3 vols. (New York, 1943–44), I, 13; T. Harry Williams, *Lincoln and His Generals* (New York, 1952), 21.
33. London *Times*, July 18, 1861, Aug. 29, 1862.

Jefferson Davis agreed; early in the war he seems to have envisaged a strategy like that of George Washington in the Revolution. Washington traded space for time; he retreated when necessary in the face of a stronger enemy; he counterattacked against isolated British outposts or detachments when such an attack promised success; above all, he tried to avoid full-scale battles that would have risked annihilation of his army and defeat of his cause. This has been called a strategy of attrition—a strategy of winning by not losing, of wearing out a better equipped foe and compelling him to give up by prolonging the war and making it too costly.[34]

But two main factors prevented Davis from carrying out such a strategy except in a limited, sporadic fashion. Both factors stemmed from political as well as military realities. The first was a demand by governors, congressmen, and the public for troops to defend every portion of the Confederacy from penetration by "Lincoln's abolition hordes." Thus in 1861, small armies were dispersed around the Confederate perimeter along the Arkansas-Missouri border, at several points on the Gulf and Atlantic coasts, along the Tennessee-Kentucky border, and in the Shenandoah Valley and western Virginia as well as at Manassas. Historians have criticized this "cordon defense" for dispersing manpower so thinly that Union forces were certain to break through somewhere, as they did at several points in 1862.[35]

The second factor inhibiting a Washingtonian strategy of attrition was the temperament of the southern people. Believing that they could whip any number of Yankees, many southerners scorned the notion of "sitting down and waiting" for the Federals to attack. "The idea of waiting for blows, instead of inflicting them, is altogether unsuited to the genius of our people," declared the *Richmond Examiner*. "The aggressive policy is the truly defensive one. A column pushed forward into Ohio or Pennsylvania is worth more to us, as a defensive measure, than a whole tier of seacoast batteries from Norfolk to the Rio Grande."[36] The southern press clamored for an advance against Washington in the same tone that northern newspapers cried On to Richmond. Beauregard devised

---

34. See especially Russell F. Weigley, *The American Way of War: A History of United States Military Strategy and Policy* (Bloomington, 1973), 3–17, 96.

35. T. Harry Williams, "The Military Leadership of North and South," and David M. Potter, "Jefferson Davis and the Political Factors in Confederate Defeat," in David Donald, ed., *Why the North Won the Civil War* (New York, 1960), 45–46, 108–10.

36. *Richmond Examiner*, Sept. 27, 1861.

several bold plans for an offensive against McDowell. But the question became moot when Beauregard learned of McDowell's offensive against him.

The Confederates eventually synthesized these various strands of strategic theory and political reality into what Davis called an "offensive-defensive" strategy. This consisted of defending the Confederate homeland by using interior lines of communication (a Jominian but also common-sense concept) to concentrate dispersed forces against an invading army and, if opportunity offered, to go over to the offensive, even to the extent of invading the North. No one ever defined this strategy in a systematic, comprehensive fashion. Rather, it emerged from a series of major campaigns in the Virginia-Maryland and Tennessee-Kentucky theaters during 1862, and culminated at Gettysburg in 1863. It almost emerged, in embryonic form, from the first battle of Manassas (Bull Run) in July 1861, a small battle by later Civil War standards but one that would have important psychological consequences in both the North and the South.

11

Farewell to the Ninety Days' War

I

General McDowell had good reason for his reluctance to march green troops "Forward to Richmond" in July 1861. Circumstances beyond his control plagued the campaign from its outset. Scheduled to begin July 8, the movement of McDowell's 30,000 men was delayed by shortages of supply wagons and by the necessity to organize late-arriving regiments into brigades and divisions. When the army finally began to move out on July 16, the terms of several ninety-day men were about to expire. Indeed, an infantry regiment and artillery battery went home on the eve of the ensuing battle. The longer enlistments of Confederate soldiers gave them a psychological advantage, for the recruit whose time was almost up seemed less motivated to fight.

Out in the Shenandoah Valley, General Robert Patterson likewise feared that the ninety-day recruits in his army of 15,000 would not stand fast in a real battle against Joseph E. Johnston's 11,000 Confederates. This was one of several reasons why Patterson failed in his task of pinning down Johnston in the Valley while McDowell attacked Beauregard at Manassas. Patterson was also confused by orders from Washington that left it unclear whether he should attack or merely maneuver against Johnston. Wrongly believing himself outnumbered by the enemy, Patterson chose the safer course of maneuver. Unfortunately, he maneuvered himself right out of the campaign. On July 18 and 19, Johnston's army gave him the slip, marched from Winchester to the railroad at Piedmont, and entrained for Manassas. With their arrival the Confederate forces at Manassas became equal in size to McDowell's invading army.

Beauregard had been forewarned of McDowell's advance by his espionage network in Washington, headed by Rose O'Neal Greenhow, a friend of several northern politicians but also a Confederate spy. In the best romantic tradition, coded messages carried by southern belles riding fast steeds brought word of Union plans. Even with this advance knowledge, Johnston could not have reinforced Beauregard in time if McDowell's army had moved faster than a snail's pace. At this stage of the war, soldiers without marching experience carrying fifty pounds of equipment took three days to cover a distance that road-wise veterans later slogged in one day. At every turn in the road, troops halted to clear away trees felled by rebel axemen or to seek cover from rumored "masked batteries." Halts at the head of a column undulated accordion-like back to the rear, where men got tired of standing for hours in the July sun and wandered off to look for water or to pick blackberries. When the Yankees finally reached Centreville, three miles from the Confederate defenses behind Bull Run, they had eaten all their food and had to delay another day while more rations were brought up. Lacking trained cavalry, McDowell personally scouted enemy lines and discovered that rugged terrain and strong defenses on the Confederate right ruled out his original plan to turn that flank. Another day went by as he planned an attack on the left flank and scouted the roads in that direction. While this was going on, the overworked railroad was bringing Johnston's troops to Manassas. By the time McDowell launched his assault on the morning of July 21, three Valley brigades had arrived and the fourth was on its way.

Despite all the delays, McDowell's attack came within an ace of success. Beauregard had distributed his troops along the south bank of Bull Run, a sluggish, tree-choked river a few miles north of Manassas. Confederate regiments guarded the railroad bridge on the right, the Warrenton turnpike bridge six miles upstream on the left, and a half-dozen fords between the bridges. Expecting McDowell to attack toward the railroad, Beauregard placed nine of his ten and one-half brigades on that flank, from which he planned to anticipate the Yankees by launching his own surprise assault on the morning of July 21. Instead, the roar of artillery and crack of musketry several miles upstream shortly after sunrise indicated that McDowell had sprung his surprise first.

The Union attacking column, 10,000 strong, had roused itself at 2:00

a.m. and stumbled through the underbrush and ruts of a cart track on a six-mile flanking march while other regiments made a feint at the turnpike bridge. The flanking column forded Bull Run two miles upriver from the bridge, where no Confederates expected them. The commander of rebel forces at the bridge was Colonel Nathan "Shanks" Evans (so-called because of his spindly legs), a hard-bitten, hard-drinking South Carolinian. Recognizing the Union shelling of the bridge as a feint and seeing the dust cloud from the flanking column to his left, Evans took most of his troops to meet the first Yankee brigade pouring across the fields. Evans slowed the Union attack long enough for two brigades of Confederate reinforcements to come up.

For two hours 4,500 rebels gave ground grudgingly to 10,000 Yankees north of the turnpike. Never before under fire, the men on both sides fought surprisingly well. But lack of experience prevented northern officers from coordinating simultaneous assaults by different regiments. Nevertheless, the weight of numbers finally pushed the Confederates across the turnpike and up the slopes of Henry House Hill. Several southern regiments broke and fled to the rear; McDowell appeared to be on the verge of a smashing success. A multitude of northern reporters, congressmen, and other civilians had driven out from Washington to watch the battle. They could see little but smoke from their vantage point two miles from the fighting. But they cheered reports of Union victory, while telegrams to Washington raised high hopes in the White House.

The reports were premature. Johnston and Beauregard had sent additional reinforcements to the Confederate left and had arrived personally on the fighting front, where they helped rally broken Confederate units. For several hours during the afternoon, fierce but uncoordinated attacks and counterattacks surged back and forth across Henry House Hill (named for the home of Judith Henry, a bedridden widow who insisted on remaining in her house and was killed by a shell). Men whom the war would make famous were in the thick of the fighting: on the Union side Ambrose E. Burnside, William Tecumseh Sherman, and Oliver O. Howard, each of whom commanded a brigade and would command an army before the war was over; on the Confederate side Beauregard and Johnston, the former in field command and the latter in overall command; along with James E. B. ("Jeb") Stuart, the dashing, romantic, bearded, plumed, and deadly efficient colonel of a cavalry regiment that broke one Union infantry attack with a headlong charge; Wade Hampton, whose South Carolina legion suffered heavy casualties; and Thomas J. Jackson, a former professor at V.M.I. now commanding a brigade of Virginians from the Shenandoah Valley. Humorless, secretive, eccentric, a stern disciplinarian without tolerance for human weaknesses, a devout Presbyterian who ascribed Confederate successes to the Lord and likened Yankees to the devil, Jackson became one of the war's best generals, a legend in his own time.

The legend began there on Henry House Hill. As the Confederate regiments that had fought in the morning retreated across the hill at noon, Jackson brought his fresh troops into line just behind the crest. General Barnard Bee of South Carolina, trying to rally his broken brigade, pointed to Jackson's men and shouted something like: "There is Jackson standing like a stone wall! Rally behind the Virginians!" But at least one observer placed a different construction on Bee's remark, claiming that the South Carolinian gestured angrily at Jackson's troops standing immobile behind the crest, and said: "Look at Jackson standing there like a damned stone wall!" Whatever Bee said—he could not settle the question by his own testimony, for a bullet killed him soon afterward—Jackson's brigade stopped the Union assault and suffered more casualties than any other southern brigade this day. Ever after, Jackson was known as "Stonewall" and his men who had stood fast at Manassas became the Stonewall Brigade.[1]

Much confusion of uniforms occurred during the battle. On numerous occasions regiments withheld their fire for fear of hitting friends, or fired on friends by mistake. The same problem arose with the national flags carried by each regiment. With eleven stars on a blue field set in the corner of a flag with two red and one white horizontal bars, the Confederate "stars and bars" could be mistaken for the stars and stripes in the smoke and haze of battle. Afterwards Beauregard designed a new battle flag, with white stars embedded in a blue St. Andrew's Cross on a red field, which became the familiar banner of the Confederacy.[2]

One mixup in uniforms affected the outcome of the battle. At the height of the fighting for Henry House Hill, two Union artillery batteries were blasting gaps in the Confederate line. Suddenly a blue-clad

1. For a discussion of the controversy over what Bee really said, see Douglas Southall Freeman, *Lee's Lieutenants: A Study in Command*, 3 vols. (New York, 1943–44), I, 733–34.
2. With the admission of Missouri and Kentucky to the Confederacy in late 1861, the Confederate flags acquired thirteen stars—which by coincidence evoked memories of the first American war for independence.

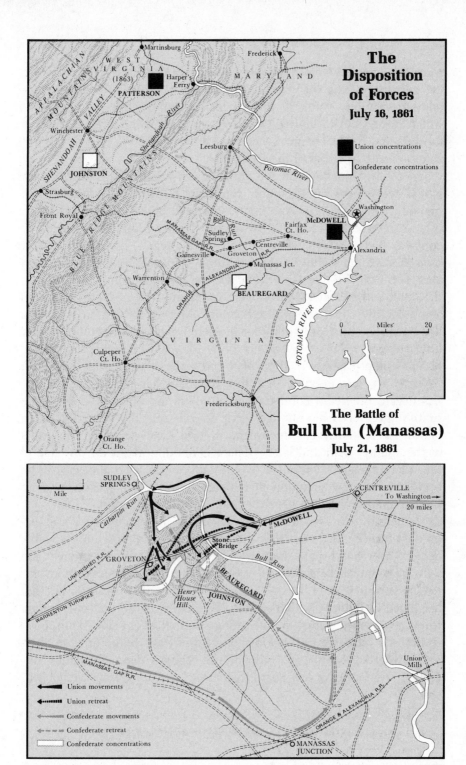

The Disposition
of Forces
July 16, 1861

■ Union concentrations

□ Confederate concentrations

West Virginia (1863)

Martinsburg

Frederick

MARYLAND

Harper's Ferry

PATTERSON

Shenandoah River

Winchester

Leesburg

Potomac River

Washington

JOHNSTON

Shenandoah Valley

Strasburg

Fairfax Ct. Ho.

McDOWELL

Front Royal

Bull Run

Sudley Springs

Manassas Gap R.R.

Centreville

Alexandria

Gainesville

Groteon

R.R.

Manassas Jct.

Blue Ridge Mountains

Warrenton

Orange & Alexandria

BEAUREGARD

POTOMAC RIVER

Appalachian Mountains

0   Miles   20

VIRGINIA

Culpeper Ct. Ho.

Fredericksburg

Orange Ct. Ho.

The Battle of
Bull Run (Manassas)
July 21, 1861

SUDLEY SPRINGS

0   Mile   1

CENTREVILLE

To Washington →

20 miles

Catharpin Run

McDOWELL

Stone Bridge

GROVETON

Bull Run

Unfinished R.R.

BEAUREGARD

Henry House Hill

JOHNSTON

Warrenton Turnpike

Manassas Gap R.R.

Union Mills

→ Union movements

⇢ Union retreat

→ Confederate movements

⇠ Confederate retreat

▭ Confederate concentrations

Orange & Alexandria R.R.

MANASSAS JUNCTION

343

regiment emerged from the woods seventy yards to the right of two of the guns. Thinking the regiment might be its requested infantry support, the artillery withheld fire for fatal minutes while the regiment, which turned out to be the 33rd Virginia of Jackson's brigade, leveled muskets and fired. The guns were wiped out and the Union attack lost cohesion in that sector of the battlefield.

Indeed, by midafternoon the northern army lost what little cohesion it had everywhere, as regiments continued to fight in a disconnected manner, stragglers began melting to the rear, and McDowell failed to get two reserve brigades into the action. Johnston and Beauregard, by contrast, had brought up every unit within reach, including the last brigade from the Valley, just off the train and marching onto the field abut 4:00 p.m. By that time the rebels had an equal number of men in the battle zone (about 18,000 were eventually engaged on each side) and a decisive superiority in fresh troops. Most of the Union regiments had been marching or fighting for the better part of fourteen hours with little food or water on a brutally hot, sultry day. Seeing Confederate reinforcements appear in front of them, some northern soldiers asked: "Where are *our* reserves?" At this moment, sensing his advantage, Beauregard ordered a counterattack all along the line. As Confederate units surged forward a strange, eerie scream rent the air. Soon to be known as the rebel yell, this unearthly wail struck fear into the hearts of the enemy, then and later. "There is nothing like it on this side of the infernal region," recalled a northern veteran after the war. "The peculiar corkscrew sensation that it sends down your backbone under these circumstances can never be told. You have to feel it."[3]

Startled by this screaming counterattack the discouraged and exhausted Yankee soldiers, their three-month term almost up, suddenly decided they had fought enough. They began to fall back, slowly and with scattered resistance at first, but with increasing panic as their officers lost control, men became separated from their companies, and the last shred of discipline disappeared. The retreat became a rout as men threw away guns, packs, and anything else that might slow them down in the wild scramble for the crossings of Bull Run. Some units of Sherman's brigade and several companies of regulars maintained their discipline and formed a rear guard that slowed the disorganized rebel pursuit.[4]

---

3. Bruce Catton, *Glory Road: The Bloody Route from Fredericksburg to Gettysburg* (Garden City, N.Y., 1952), 57.
4. Sherman's brigade suffered more casualties (including the death of Colonel James

Fleeing Union soldiers became entangled with panic-stricken civilians. Some congressmen tried in vain to stop wild-eyed soldiers, now miles from the battlefield, who had no intention of stopping short of the far side of the Potomac. "The further they ran, the more frightened they grew," stated one of the congressmen.

> We called to them, tried to tell them there was no danger, called them to stop, implored them to stand. We called them cowards, denounced them in the most offensive terms, put out our heavy revolvers, and threatened to shoot them, but all in vain; a cruel, crazy, mad, hopeless panic possessed them, and communicated to everybody about in front and rear. The heat was awful, although now about six; the men were exhausted—their mouths gaped, their lips cracked and blackened with the powder of the cartridges they had bitten off in the battle, their eyes starting in frenzy; no mortal ever saw such a mass of ghastly wretches.[5]

Back on the other side of Bull Run, jubilant rebels celebrated their victory and rounded up hundreds of Union prisoners. Jefferson Davis himself had turned up at the moment of victory. A warrior at heart, Davis could not sit still in Richmond while the battle raged eighty miles away. He chartered a special train, obtained a horse near Manassas, and rode with an aide toward the fighting in mid-afternoon through a swelling stream of wounded and stragglers who cried out "Go back! We are whipped!" Though Davis knew that the rear areas of a battlefield always presented a scene of disorder and defeat no matter what was going on at the front, he rode on with a sinking heart. Was this to be the fate of his Confederacy? As he neared Johnston's headquarters, however, the sounds of battle rolled away to the north. Johnston came forward with the news of southern triumph. Elated, Davis urged vigorous pursuit of the beaten enemy. Although some Confederate units had gone a mile or two beyond Bull Run, Johnston and Beauregard believed that no full-scale pursuit was possible. In Johnston's words, "our army was more disorganized by victory than that of the United States by defeat."[6]

When the magnitude of Confederate victory sank in during the fol-

---

Cameron, brother of the secretary of war) and probably fought better than any other Union brigade. Sherman was rewarded by promotion to command of Union forces in Kentucky, where he underwent an attack of nerves and a demotion, as narrated in Chapter 9, above.

5. Albert Riddle, quoted in Samuel S. Cox, *Three Decades of Federal Legislation, 1855–1885* (Providence, 1885), 158.

6. Johnston, "Responsibilities of the First Bull Run," *Battles and Leaders*, I, 252.

lowing weeks, southern newspapers began to seek scapegoats for the failure to "follow up the victory and take Washington." An unseemly row
burst out in which the partisans of each of the principals—Davis, Johnston, Beauregard—blamed one of the others for this "failure." Postwar
memoirs by the three men continued the controversy. But the prospect
of "taking" Washington in July 1861 was an illusion, as all three recognized at the time. McDowell formed a defensive line of unbloodied
reserves at Centreville on the night of July 21. Early next morning a
heavy rain began to turn the roads into soup. Confederate logistics were
inadequate for a sustained advance even in good weather. The army
depots at Manassas were almost bare of food. Despite a mood of panic
in Washington, the rebels were not coming—and could not have
come.

In July 1861 the controversy about failure to pursue lay in the future.
The South erupted in joy over a victory that seemed to prove that one
Southron could indeed lick any number of Yankees. It was easy to forget that the numbers engaged were equal, that Confederate troops had
fought on the defensive for most of the battle (easier than attacking,
especially for green troops), and that the Yankees had come close to
winning. In any case the battle of Manassas (or Bull Run, as the North
named it[7]) was one of the most decisive tactical victories of the war.
Although its strategic results came to seem barren to many in the South,

---

7. The Union and Confederacy gave different names to several Civil War battles:

Union name	Confederate name	Date
Bull Run	Manassas	July 21, 1861
Logan's Cross Roads	Mill Springs	Jan. 19, 1862
Pittsburg Landing	Shiloh	April 6–7, 1862
2nd Bull Run	2nd Manassas	Aug. 29–30, 1862
Antietam	Sharpsburg	Sept. 17, 1862
Chaplin Hills	Perryville	Oct. 8, 1862
Stone's River	Murfreesboro	Dec. 30, 1862–Jan. 2, 1863
Opequon Creek	Winchester	Sept. 19, 1864

In each case but one (Shiloh) the Confederates named the battle after the town that
served as their base, while the Union forces chose the landmark nearest to the fighting or to their own lines, usually a river or stream. In the case of Shiloh (Pittsburg
Landing), the South named the battle after a small church near the spot of their
initial attack; the North named it after the river landing they fought to defend. In
the cases of Shiloh, Perryville, and Winchester the North eventually accepted the
Confederate name for the battle, and those names are used in this book. For each
of the other battles, neither name has any intrinsic superiority over the other, so the
names are used interchangeably.

the battle did postpone for eight months any further Union efforts to invade Virginia's heartland. And the price in casualties was small compared with later battles. About 400 Confederates were killed and 1,600 wounded, of whom some 225 would die of their wounds. The Union forces also lost about 625 killed and mortally wounded, 950 non-mortally wounded, and more than 1,200 captured.[8]

Perhaps the most profound consequences of the battle were psychological. But these consequences were full of paradox. The South's gleeful celebration generated a cockiness heedless of the Biblical injunction that pride goeth before a fall. Manassas was *one of the decisive battles of the world,*" wrote political leader Thomas R. R. Cobb of Georgia. It *"has* secured our independence." Edmund Ruffin considered "this hard-fought battle virtually the close of the war." He thought Beauregard's next step should be "a dash upon Philadelphia, & the laying it in ashes . . . as full settlement & acquittance for the past northern outrages."[9] The *Mobile Register* predicted that the Union army would "never again advance beyond cannon shot of Washington." The *Richmond Whig* went even further: "The breakdown of the Yankee race, their unfitness for empire, forces dominion on the South. We are compelled to take the sceptre of power. We must adapt ourselves to our new destiny."[10]

Immediately after the battle the shame and despair of many northerners almost caused them to agree with these southern assessments. "Today will be known as *BLACK MONDAY,*" wrote a New Yorker when he heard the news. "We are utterly and disgracefully routed, beaten, whipped." Horace Greeley, whose *New York Tribune* had done so much to prod the government into premature action, endured a week of self-reproachful, sleepless nights before writing a despondent letter to Lincoln: "On every brow sits sullen, scorching, black despair. . . . If it is best for the country and for mankind that we make peace with the rebels, and on their own terms, do not shrink even from that."[11]

---

8. Civil War casualties cannot be known with exactitude because of incomplete or faulty reports. The figures cited here represent the best approximation from available evidence. Some of the Union captured were wounded. In Civil War battles about 15 percent of the wounded subsequently died of their wounds.

9. E. Merton Coulter, *The Confederate States of America 1861–1865* (Baton Rouge, 1950), 345; *The Diary of Edmund Ruffin,* Vol. II, *The Years of Hope April 1861– June 1863,* ed. William K. Scarborough (Baton Rouge, 1976), 96, 98.

10. *Mobile Register* quoted in J. Cutler Andrews, *The South Reports the Civil War* (Princeton, 1970), 92; *Richmond Whig* quoted in Nevins, *War,* I, 221.

11. Strong, *Diary,* 169; Greeley to Lincoln, July 29, 1861, Lincoln Papers, Library of Congress.

Yet the deep, long-lasting impact of Bull Run on the North was not defeatism, but renewed determination. The London *Times* correspondent predicted such a result the day after the battle: "This prick in the great Northern balloon will let out a quantity of poisonous gas, and rouse the people to a sense of the nature of the conflict on which they have entered." In a sermon on a text from Proverbs—"adversity kills only where there is a weakness to be killed"—one of the North's leading clergymen expressed this new mood of grim resolution. It was echoed by a soldier in the ranks: "I shall see the thing played out, or die in the attempt." Even as Greeley was writing despairingly to Lincoln, an editorial in the *Tribune* by another hand maintained that "it is not characteristic of Americans to sit down despondently after a defeat. . . . Reverses, though stunning at first, by their recoil stimulate and quicken to unwonted exertion. . . . Let us go to work, then, with a will."[12]

Lincoln agreed with this editorial rather than with Greeley's letter. Though shaken by the news of Bull Run, the president and General Scott did not panic. They worked through the night to salvage some order from the chaos of defeat. "The fat is in the fire now," wrote Lincoln's private secretary, "and we shall have to crow small until we can retrieve the disgrace somehow. The preparations for the war will be continued with increased vigor by the Government." The day after Bull Run, Lincoln signed a bill for the enlistment of 500,000 three-year men. Three days later he signed a second bill authorizing another 500,000.[13] Volunteers thronged recruiting offices during the next few weeks; offers of new regiments poured in from northern governors; and soon the regiments themselves began to crowd into the training camps surrounding Washington, where they found a dynamic, magnetic general to command them: George B. McClellan.

At 2:00 a.m. on the morning after Bull Run, a telegram summoned McClellan to take command of this new army of three-year volunteers, soon to be named the Army of the Potomac. When McClellan arrived in Washington on July 26 he found "no army to command—only a

12. William Howard Russell, *My Diary North and South*, ed. Fletcher Pratt (New York, 1954), 234; sermon by Horace Bushnell cited in Bruce Catton, *The Coming Fury* (New York, 1961), 468; soldier quoted in William C. Davis, *Battle at Bull Run* (Garden City, N.Y., 1977), 255; *New York Tribune*, July 30, 1861.

13. John Nicolay to his wife, July 23, 1861, quoted in Catton, *Coming Fury*, 469. The two enlistment laws are printed in O.R., Ser. III, Vol. 1, pp. 380–83.

mere collection of regiments cowering on the banks of the Potomac, some perfectly raw, others dispirited by the recent defeat."[14] Whatever self-serving overtones one might detect in these words, McClellan did accomplish all that was expected of him in his first two months of command. His military police rounded up stragglers and combed their officers out of Washington barrooms. His examining boards weeded incompetent officers out of the army. McClellan was a superb organizer and administrator. He was a professional with regard to training. He turned recruits into soldiers. He instilled discipline and pride in his men, who repaid him with an admiration they felt toward no other general. McClellan forged the Army of the Potomac into a fighting machine second to none—this was his important contribution to ultimate Union victory—but he proved unable to run this machine at peak efficiency in the crisis of battle.

Not all southerners shared the post-Manassas conviction of Confederate invincibility. Mary Boykin Chesnut perceived that the victory "lulls us into a fool's paradise of conceit" while it "will wake every inch of [northern] manhood." A diary-keeping clerk in the Confederate War Department fumed a month after the battle: "We are resting on our oars, while the enemy is drilling and equipping 500,000 or 600,000 men." With the benefit of hindsight, participants on both sides agreed after the war that the one-sided southern triumph in the first big battle "proved the greatest misfortune that would have befallen the Confederacy." Such an interpretation has become orthodoxy in Civil War historiography.[15]

This orthodoxy contains much truth, but perhaps not the whole truth. The confidence gained by the men who won at Manassas imbued them with an *esprit de corps* that was reinforced by more victories in the next two years. At the same time the Union defeat instilled a gnawing, half-acknowledged sense of martial inferiority among northern officers in the Virginia theater. Thus the battle of Manassas, and more importantly the collective southern and northern memories of it, became an important part of the psychology of war in the eastern theater. This psychology helps explain why McClellan, having created a powerful army, was

14. Quoted in Kenneth P. Williams, *Lincoln Finds a General*, 5 vols. (New York, 1949–59), I, 113.
15. Woodward, *Chesnut's Civil War*, 111; Jones, *War Clerk's Diary* (Miers), 43; Edward A. Pollard, *The Lost Cause: A New Southern History of the War of the Confederacy* (New York, 1866), 152.

reluctant to commit it to all-out battle. He always feared, deep down, that the enemy was more powerful than he. And the Confederates, armed with the morale of victory, enjoyed an edge that went far toward evening the material odds against them in Virginia.[16] Hence the paradox of Bull Run: its legacy of confidence both hurt and helped the South; the humiliation and renewed determination both hurt and helped the North.

II

Two days after Bull Run, Lincoln penned a memorandum on future Union strategy. Efforts to make the blockade effective were to be pushed forward; Maryland was to be held "with a gentle [!], but firm, and certain hand"; Union troops in Virginia were to be reinforced, thoroughly trained, and prepared for a new invasion; the inept Patterson was to be replaced by a new commander of the army at Harper's Ferry (Nathaniel P. Banks); Union armies in the western theaters were to take the offensive, "giving rather special attention to Missouri."[17]

Lincoln had high expectations of his newly appointed commander of the Western Department (mainly Missouri), John C. Frémont. Famed as the Pathfinder of the West, Frémont's eleven years' experience in the army's topographical corps gave him a military reputation unmatched by most other political generals. But the formidable difficulties of a Missouri command—a divided population, guerrilla warfare, political intrigue, war contract profiteering, impending Confederate invasions from Arkansas and Tennessee—quickly brought out the weaknesses in Frémont's character. He was showy rather than solid. His naiveté and his ambition to build quickly a large army and navy for a grand sweep down the Mississippi made him easy prey for contractors whose swollen profits produced a new crop of scandals. Frémont could have survived all this if he had produced victories. But instead, soon after he arrived in St. Louis on July 25, Union forces in Missouri suffered reverses that came as aftershocks to the earthquake at Bull Run.

Frémont's appointment brought Nathaniel Lyon under his command. After chasing Sterling Price's militia to the southwest corner of the state, Lyon's small army of 5,500 men occupied Springfield at the

16. For an astute development of this thesis, see Michael C. C. Adams, *Our Masters the Rebels: A Speculation on Union Military Failure in the East, 1861–1865* (Cambridge, Mass., 1978).

17. CWL, IV, 457–58.

end of a precarious supply line nearly 200 miles from St. Louis. Lyon faced a motley southern force composed of Price's 8,000 Missourians and 5,000 other Confederate troops under General Ben McCulloch, a rough-hewn frontiersman who had won his spurs as an Indian fighter, Mexican War officer, and Texas Ranger. Price was eager to redeem Missouri from the Yankee and "Dutch" troops under Lyon. McCulloch distrusted the reliability of Price's Missourians, two or three thousand of whom lacked weapons while the rest carried an indiscriminate variety of hunting rifles, shotguns, and ancient muskets. McCulloch finally yielded, with great reluctance, to Price's entreaties for an offensive.

In the meantime, Lyon learned that Frémont could send him no reinforcements. All Union troops seemed to be needed elsewhere to cope with guerrillas and to counter a rebel incursion into southeast Missouri that threatened the Union base at Cairo, Illinois. Outnumbered by more than two to one, with the ninety-day enlistments of half his men about to expire, Lyon's only choice seemed to be retreat. But the fiery red-haired general could not bear to yield southwest Missouri without a fight. He decided to attack McCulloch and Price before they could attack him.

Disregarding the maxims of military textbooks (just as Robert E. Lee later did to win his greatest victories), Lyon divided his small army in the face of a larger enemy and sent a flanking column of 1,200 men under Franz Sigel on a night march around to the south of the Confederate camp along Wilson's Creek, ten miles south of Springfield. While Sigel came up on the Confederate rear, Lyon would attack from the front with the main Union force. The Federals carried out this difficult maneuver successfully, achieving surprise in a two-pronged attack at sunrise on August 10. But McCulloch and Price kept their poise and rallied their men for a stand-up, seesaw firefight at short range along the banks of Wilson's Creek and on the slopes of a nearby hill.

The battle was marked by two turning points that finally enabled the rebels to prevail. First, after initially driving back the Confederates on the southern flank, Sigel's attack came to a halt after another incident of mistaken identity. A Louisiana regiment clad in uniforms similar to the militia gray of Lyon's 1st Iowa approached close enough to Sigel's vanguard to pour in a murderous volley before the unionists recognized them as enemies. Sigel's attack disintegrated; a Confederate artillery barrage and infantry counterattack soon scattered his demoralized brigade to the four winds. The Louisianians and Arkansans in this part of the field then joined the Missourians fighting Lyon's main force, whom they now outnumbered by three to one. In the thick of the fighting, Lyon was twice wounded slightly and his horse was shot from under him before a bullet found his heart. This demoralized the unionists, who in addition had almost run out of ammunition. Slowly they pulled back, yielding the battlefield to the enemy and withdrawing to Springfield unpursued by the equally battered southerners.

Each side in this bloody battle suffered about 1,300 casualties, a considerably higher proportion of losses than at Bull Run. Although the Confederates' tactical victory at Wilson's Creek was much less decisive than at Manassas and its impact on public opinion outside Missouri was small, its strategic consequences at first seemed greater. The Union forces retreated all the way to Rolla, 100 miles north of Springfield. Having gained confidence and prestige, Price marched northward to the Missouri River, gathering recruits on the way. With 18,000 troops he surrounded the 3,500-man garrison at Lexington, the largest city between St. Louis and Kansas City. Frémont scraped together a small force to reinforce the garrison, but it could not break through Price's ring. After three days of resistance, Lexington surrendered on September 20.

Price's reputation soared, while Frémont's plummeted. In two months of command he appeared to have lost half of Missouri. Confederate guerrillas stepped up their activities. The Blair family, once Frémont's sponsors, turned against him and began intriguing for his removal. And a bold step that Frémont had taken to reverse the decline of his fortunes backfired and helped to seal his fate.

On August 30 Frémont issued a startling proclamation. As commanding general he took over "the administrative powers of the State," declared martial law, announced the death penalty for guerrillas caught behind Union lines, confiscated the property and freed the slaves of all Confederate activists in Missouri.[18] Two motives seem to have impelled this rash action: first, the felt need for draconian measures to suppress guerrillas and to intimidate rebel sympathizers; second, a desire to win favor with antislavery Republicans. Frémont accomplished his second goal, but at the cost of alienating Lincoln, who was engaged in sensitive efforts to keep Kentucky in the Union. The president wrote privately to Frémont ordering him to shoot no guerrillas "without first having my approbation," for if he were to execute captured guerrillas indiscriminately, "the Confederates would very certainly shoot our best men in

18. O.R., Ser. I, Vol. 3, pp. 466–67.

their hands, in retaliation; and so, man for man, indefinitely."[19] Second, Lincoln warned Frémont that freeing the slaves of rebels would "alarm our Southern Union friends, and turn them against us—perhaps ruin our rather fair prospect for Kentucky." The president asked (not ordered) Frémont to modify this part of his proclamation to conform with an act passed by Congress on August 6, which confiscated only the property (including slaves) used directly in the Confederate war effort.[20]

A wiser man would have treated Lincoln's request as an order. But with a kind of proconsular arrogance that did not sit well with Lincoln, Frémont refused to modify his proclamation without a public order to do so. He also sent his high-spirited wife (daughter of the legendary Thomas Hart Benton) to Washington to persuade Lincoln of his error. Jessie Frémont offended the president by hinting at her husband's superior wisdom and greater prestige. She did Frémont's cause considerable harm. Even as she spoke, letters from border-state unionists were arriving at the White House expressing alarm and disaffection. "We could stand several defeats like that at Bulls Run, better than we can this proclamation if endorsed by the Administration," wrote Kentuckian Joshua Speed, Lincoln's oldest and best friend. "Do not allow us by the foolish action of a military popinjay to be driven from our present active loyalty." On the day after Jessie Benton Frémont's visit, Lincoln publicly ordered her husband to modify his emancipation edict.[21]

After this, Frémont's days as commander in Missouri were numbered. Knowing that he could save himself only by a military victory, he pulled together an army of 38,000 men and set forth to destroy Price's militia. Since capturing Lexington, Price had learned the difference between an invasion and a raid. He lacked the manpower and logistical capacity to turn his raid into a successful occupation of captured territory. More than half of his troops melted away to harvest crops or to go off bushwhacking on their own. Price retreated again to the southwest

19. Even as Lincoln wrote these words, the rebel guerrilla chieftain M. Jeff Thompson in southeast Missouri issued a proclamation promising that for every man executed under Frémont's edict, he would "HANG, DRAW AND QUARTER a minion of said Abraham Lincoln." Jay Monaghan, *Civil War on the Western Border 1854–1865* (Boston, 1955), 185.
20. CWL, IV, 506.
21. Speed to Lincoln, Sept. 7, 1861, Lincoln Papers, Library of Congress; CWL, IV, 517–18.

corner of the state. Before the Federals caught up with him, Lincoln removed Frémont from command. Union forces would eventually defeat and scatter Price's army, but when that happened Frémont would be far away in western Virginia about to embark on another failure.

III

Lincoln's revocation of Frémont's emancipation order and his removal of the general from command stirred up a controversy. The issue was slavery. During the weeks after congressional passage in July of the Crittenden-Johnson resolutions disavowing antislavery war aims, many Republicans began to change their minds. Abolitionists who had earlier remained silent began to speak out. An important catalyst of this change was the Union defeat at Bull Run. "The result of the battle was a fearful blow," wrote an abolitionist, but "I think it may prove the means of rousing this stupid country to the extent & difficulty of the work it has to do." A rebellion sustained *by* slavery in defense *of* slavery could be suppressed only by moving *against* slavery. As Frederick Douglass expressed this conviction: "To fight against slaveholders, without fighting against slavery, is but a half-hearted business, and paralyzes the hands engaged in it. . . . Fire must be met with water. . . . War for the destruction of liberty must be met with war for the destruction of slavery."[22]

Recognizing that racism or constitutionalism would prevent many northerners from accepting moral arguments for emancipation as a war aim, antislavery spokesmen developed the argument of "military necessity." Southerners boasted that slavery was "a tower of strength to the Confederacy" because it enabled the South "to place in the field a force so much larger in proportion to her population than the North." Precisely, agreed emancipationists. Slaves constituted more than half of the South's labor force. They raised food and built fortifications and hauled supplies for rebel armies. They worked in mines and munitions plants. Slave labor was so important to the southern war effort that the government impressed slaves into service before it began drafting white men as soldiers. "The very stomach of this rebellion is the negro in the form of a slave," said Douglass. "Arrest that hoe in the hands of the negro, and you smite the rebellion in the very seat of its life."[23]

22. Moncure D. Conway to Ellen Conway, July 23, 1861, Moncure D. Conway Papers, Columbia University Library; *Douglass' Monthly*, Sept., May, 1861.
23. *Montgomery Advertiser*, Nov. 6, 1861; *Douglass' Monthly*, July 1861.

How could this be done under the Constitution, which protected slavery? Rebels had forfeited their constitutional rights, answered emancipationists. Their property was liable to confiscation as a punishment for treason. Moreover, while in theory the South was engaged in domestic insurrection, in practice it was waging a war. The Lincoln administration had already recognized this by proclaiming a blockade and by treating captured rebel soldiers as prisoners of war. Having thus conceded belligerent status to the Confederacy, the Union could also confiscate enemy property as a legitimate act of war.[24]

Benjamin Butler was the first prominent figure to act on these arguments. Back in May, three slaves who had been working on southern fortifications escaped to Butler's lines at Fortress Monroe, Virginia. Their owner—a Confederate colonel—appeared next day under flag of truce and, citing the fugitive slave law, demanded the return of his property. Butler replied that since Virginia claimed to be out of the Union, the fugitive slave law did not apply. He labeled the escaped slaves "contraband of war" and put them to work in his camp. Northern newspapers picked up the contraband of war phrase and thereafter the slaves who came into Union lines were known as contrabands.

The administration, after some hesitation, approved Butler's policy. By July nearly a thousand contrabands had rejoined the Union at Fortress Monroe. Their legal status was ambiguous. Butler decided to clarify it by addressing pointed questions to the War Department. In a letter of July 30 which soon appeared in the newspapers, he asked Secretary of War Cameron: "Are these men, women, and children, slaves? Are they free? . . . What has been the effect of the rebellion and a state of war upon [their] status? . . . If property, do they not become the property of the salvors? But we, their salvors, do not need and will not hold such property . . . has not, therefore, all proprietary relation ceased?"[25]

Hard questions, these, and explosive ones. While Butler wrote, Congress was wrestling with the same questions in debate on a bill to confiscate property used in aid of the rebellion. John J. Crittenden of Ken-

24. For a lucid discussion of these questions, see James G. Randall, *Constitutional Problems under Lincoln*, rev. ed. (Urbana, 1951), chaps. 12–16.

25. Jessie A. Marshall, ed., *Private and Official Correspondence of General Benjamin F. Butler during the Period of the Civil War*, 5 vols. (Norwood, Mass., 1917), I, 185–87. Other relevant correspondence between Butler and the War Department is conveniently reprinted in Ira Berlin et al., eds., *The Destruction of Slavery*, Vol. I of *Freedom: A Documentary History of Emancipation 1861–1867* (Cambridge, 1985), 70–75.

tucky insisted that Congress had no more right to legislate against slavery in the states during wartime than in peacetime. True, agreed Republicans, but Congress *can* punish treason by confiscation of property, a penalty that operated against the individual but not the institution. In this tentative, limited fashion the Republicans enacted a confiscation act on August 6. Butler had his answer, such as it was. The contrabands were no longer slaves if—and only if—they had been employed directly by the Confederate armed services. But were they then free? The law did not say. This was hardly the ringing endorsement of emancipation that abolitionists had begun to call for. But it went too far for Democratic and border-state congressmen. All but three of them voted against the bill while all but six Republicans voted for it. This was the first breach in bipartisan support for Union war measures. It was a signal that if the conflict became an antislavery war it would thereby become a Republican war.

Such a prospect worried Lincoln in 1861. That was why he had revoked Frémont's emancipation edict, which went well beyond the confiscation act by applying to *all* slaves owned by rebels and by declaring those slaves *free*.[26] The president's action was unpopular with most Republicans. "It is said we must consult the border states," commented an influential Connecticut Republican. "Permit me to say *damn* the border states. . . . A thousand Lincolns cannot stop the people from fighting slavery." Even Orville Browning, conservative senator from Illinois and Lincoln's close friend, criticized the revocation of Frémont's edict. Stung by this response, Lincoln chose to reply in a private letter to Browning. Frémont's action, he said, was "not within the range of *military* law, or necessity." He could have confiscated enemy property including slaves as Butler had done, "but it is not for him to fix their permanent future condition [by declaring them free]. That must be settled according to laws made by law-makers, and not by military proclamations." Browning had endorsed Frémont's policy as "the only means of saving the government." On the contrary, said Lincoln, "it is itself the surrender of government." When a company of Union soldiers from Kentucky heard about Frémont's edict, said Lincoln, they "threw down their arms

26. It should be noted that Butler's contraband policy also went beyond the confiscation act. Butler retained the wives and children of contrabands, even though they had not worked directly for the Confederate armed forces. For that matter, many of the male slaves who had entered Union lines did not legitimately come under the specific terms of the act either.

and disbanded." If the order had not been modified, "the very arms we had furnished Kentucky would be turned against us. I think to lose Kentucky is nearly the same as to lose the whole game. Kentucky gone, we can not hold Missouri, nor, as I think, Maryland. These all against us, and the job on our hands is too large for us. We would as well consent to separation at once, including the surrender of this capitol." And in any case, "can it be pretended that it is any longer [a] . . . government of Constitution and laws, wherein a General, or a President, may make permanent rules of property by proclamation?"[27]

One wonders if Lincoln remembered these words when a year later he did endeavor to make a permanent rule of property with his Emancipation Proclamation declaring the slaves "forever free." But a lifetime of change had been compressed into that one year. The slavery issue just would not fade away. The slaves themselves would not let it fade away. By ones and twos, dozens and scores, they continued to convert themselves to "contrabands" by coming into Union lines. It proved extremely difficult for their owners to pry them out again, even in the unionist border states. Many northern regiments gave refuge to fugitives and refused to yield them up despite orders to do so.[28]

Radical Republicans countenanced such action. And by October 1861 some radicals were urging not only freeing the contrabands but also arming them to fight for the Union. Secretary of War Cameron endorsed such action in his annual report: "Those who make war against the Government justly forfeit all rights of property. . . . It is as clearly a right of the Government to arm slaves, when it may become necessary, as it is to use gun-powder taken from the enemy."[29] Cameron released his report to the press on December 1 without prior approval from the president. When an astonished Lincoln read these words he ordered Cameron to recall the report and delete this paragraph. But some newspapers had already published it. Cameron's precipitate ac-

27. Joseph R. Hawley to Gideon Welles, Sept. 17, 1861, quoted in James G. Randall, *Lincoln the President*, 4 vols. (New York, 1946–54), II, 21; Lincoln to Browning, Sept. 22, 1861, CWL, IV, 531–32.
28. For rich detail on the continuing escapes of contrabands into Union lines and on the relationship between the army and the slaveholders who tried to retrieve their property, see Berlin et al., eds., *The Destruction of Slavery*, and Barbara J. Fields, *Slavery and Freedom on the Middle Ground: Maryland during the Nineteenth Century* (New Haven, 1985).
29. John G. Nicolay and John Hay, *Abraham Lincoln: A History*, 10 vols. (New York, 1890), V, 125–26.

tion, like Frémont's, contributed to a widening rift between Lincoln and the radical wing of his party. Soon Cameron, like Frémont, lost his job. In both cases the main reason for removal was inefficiency, not abolitionism, but few radicals believed that the slavery issue had nothing to do with it.

In his annual message on December 3, 1861, Lincoln said: "I have been anxious and careful" that the war "shall not degenerate into a violent and remorseless revolutionary struggle." But abolitionists and some Republicans were already viewing it as a revolutionary conflict between two social systems. "WE ARE THE REVOLUTIONISTS!" wrote Virginia-born, New England-educated Moncure Conway in 1861. Although the Confederates "justify themselves under the right of revolution," Conway continued, their cause "is not a revolution but a rebellion against the noblest of revolutions." The North, wrote another abolitionist, must proclaim freedom as a war aim and thereby accomplish *the glorious second American Revolution.*[30] Thaddeus Stevens, the grim-visaged Cromwellian leader of radical Republicans in the House, called for precisely the kind of violent, remorseless struggle Lincoln hoped to avoid: "Free every slave—slay every traitor—burn every rebel mansion, if these things be necessary to preserve this temple of freedom." We must "treat this [war] as a radical revolution," said Stevens, "and remodel our institutions." Stevens's colleagues were not prepared to go quite this far, but by December 1861 they had moved a long way beyond their position of a few months earlier. On December 4, by a solid Republican vote, the House refused to reaffirm the Crittenden resolution disavowing an antislavery purpose in the war.[31]

IV

The slavery issue played a part in a growing Republican disenchantment with McClellan. But more important than slavery were McClellan's defects of character and generalship.

"McClellan is to me one of the mysteries of the war," said Ulysses S. Grant a dozen years after the conflict. Historians are still trying to solve

---

30. CWL, V, 48–49; Moncure D. Conway, *The Rejected Stone: or, Insurrection vs. Resurrection in America* (Boston, 1861), 75–80, 110; *Principia*, May 4, 1861.
31. Stevens quoted in T. Harry Williams, *Lincoln and the Radicals* (Madison, 1941), 12, and Margaret Shortreed, "The Anti-Slavery Radicals, 1840–1868," *Past and Present*, no. 16 (1959), 77; House action in CG, 37 Cong., 2 Sess., 15.

that mystery.[32] Life seemed to have prepared McClellan for greatness. His birth into a well-to-do Philadelphia family and his education at the best private schools prepared him for admission to West Point by special permission when he was two years under the minimum age. After graduating second in his class, McClellan won renown at the age of twenty for engineering achievements in the Mexican War. His subsequent army career included assignment as an American observer of the Crimean War. In 1857 he resigned his commission to become chief engineer and vice president of a railroad at the age of thirty and president of another railroad two years later. In May 1861, at the age of thirty-four, he became the second-ranking general in the U. S. army and in July he took command of the North's principal field army. McClellan came to Washington, in the words of the London *Times* correspondent, as "the man on horseback" to save the Union; the press lionized him; a sober-minded contemporary wrote that "there is an indefinable *air of success* about him and something of the 'man of destiny.' "[33]

But perhaps McClellan's career had been too successful. He had never known, as Grant had, the despair of defeat or the humiliation of failure. He had never learned the lessons of adversity and humility. The adulation he experienced during the early weeks in Washington went to his head. McClellan's letters to his wife revealed the beginnings of a messiah complex. "I find myself in a strange position here: President, Cabinet, Genl. Scott & all deferring to me," he wrote the day after arriving in Washington. "By some strange operation of magic I seem to have become *the* power of the land." Three days later he visited Capitol Hill and was "quite overwhelmed by the congratulations I received and the respect with which I was treated." Congress seemed willing "to give me my way in everything." The next week McClellan reported that he had received "letter after letter—have conversation after conversation calling on me to save the nation—alluding to the Presidency, Dictatorship, etc." McClellan said he wanted no part of such powers, but he did revel in the cheers of his soldiers as he rode along their lines—cheers that reinforced his Napoleonic self-image. "You have no idea how the men

32. Quotation from Warren W. Hassler, Jr., *General George B. McClellan: Shield of the Union* (Baton Rouge, 1957), xv. For a good summary of writings on McClellan, see Joseph L. Harsh, "On the McClellan-Go-Round," in John T. Hubbell, ed., *Battles Lost and Won: Essays from Civil War History* (Westport, Conn., 1975), 55–72.
33. Russell, *My Diary North and South*, 240; Nevins, *War*, I, 269.

brighten up now when I go among them. I can see every eye glisten.
. . . You never heard such yelling. . . . I believe they love me. . . .
God has placed a great work in my hands. . . . I was called to it; my
previous life seems to have been unwittingly directed to this great end."[34]

The first victim of McClellan's vainglory was General-in-Chief Scott.
More than twice McClellan's age, Scott was America's foremost living
soldier, a hero of two wars, second only to George Washington in military reputation. But Scott's fame belonged to past wars. McClellan aspired to be the hero of this one. A rivalry with the "old general," as
McClellan privately called Scott, soon developed. In truth, there could
be only one head of the post-Bull Run military buildup. McClellan set
about this task with great energy. He put in eighteen-hour days that
achieved quick and visible results. McClellan communicated directly
with the president, bypassing Scott. The latter, whose age and infirmi-
ties prevented him from doing more than a few hours of daily paper-
work, grew piqued at being left out of things. McClellan complained
that Scott was frustrating his plans to expand and prepare the army for
an early offensive. "I am leaving nothing undone to increase our force,"
McClellan wrote to his wife in early August, "but that confounded old
Gen'l always comes in my way. He is a perfect incubus. He understands
nothing, appreciates nothing. . . . I do not know whether he is a *do-
tard* or a *traitor*. . . . If he *cannot* be taken out of my path, I . . .
will resign and let the admin[istration] take care of itself. . . . The
people call upon me to save the country—I *must* save it and cannot
respect anything that is in the way."[35] Lincoln tried to mediate between
the two generals, but only succeeded in delaying the inevitable. The
president finally succumbed to pressure from Republican senators and
allowed Scott to retire on November 1 "for reasons of health." Mc-
Clellan succeeded him as general in chief. Lincoln cautioned Mc-
Clellan that the dual jobs of general in chief and commander of the
Army of the Potomac "will entail a vast labor upon you." Replied
McClellan: "I can do it all."[36]

34. McClellan to Ellen Marcy McClellan, July 27, 30, Aug. 9, Oct. 31, 1861, Mc-
    Clellan Papers, Library of Congress. These letters to his wife consist of extracts
    from the originals, copied by McClellan himself sometime after the war. There is
    no way of knowing whether he edited these copies in any substantive way, for the
    originals no longer exist. The extracts are in Series C, Container 7 of the Mc-
    Clellan Papers. Edited versions of some of these letters were published in W. C.
    Prime, ed., *McClellan's Own Story* (New York, 1887).
35. McClellan to Ellen Marcy McClellan, Aug. 8, 9, 1861, McClellan Papers.
36. Dennett, *Lincoln/Hay*, 33.

The senators helped force Scott's retirement because McClellan convinced them that the "old general" was mainly responsible for the army's inactivity. When McClellan had first arrived in Washington he expressed an intent to "carry this thing 'en grand' & crush the rebels in one campaign."[37] Republicans thought this had the right ring. But McClellan soon began to express fears that Beauregard was about to march forward with a huge army to crush *him*. A curious lack of confidence began to creep into McClellan's words and deeds, even as he continued to think of himself as God's chosen instrument to save the republic. The first signs appeared of a chronic tendency to overestimate enemy strength and to use this estimate as an excuse to remain on the defensive. In October, McClellan had 120,000 men while Beauregard and Johnston had only 45,000 in and near Manassas. But McClellan professed to believe that the enemy numbered 150,000 and was preparing to attack him.[38]

The Confederates had pushed their picket posts within sight of Washington. They had also established batteries on the lower Potomac to interdict river traffic to the capital. In late September the southerners withdrew from one exposed position on Munson's Hill a few miles southwest of Washington. When the Federals moved in, instead of the large cannon they had expected they found a log shaped and painted to

37. McClellan to Ellen Marcy McClellan, Aug. 2, 1861, McClellan Papers.
38. The head of McClellan's secret service, Allan Pinkerton, has long been notorious for providing the inflated estimates of Confederate troop numbers on which McClellan based his calculations. Pinkerton deserves some but perhaps not all of this notoriety. His activities embraced two spheres: espionage behind enemy lines and counter-espionage behind Union lines. As founder of the famous Pinkerton detective agency, he naturally employed numerous agents who had been trained as detectives. These men did a good job of ferreting out and arresting Confederate agents, for their previous experience fitted them for such work. As espionage agents they were less successful. They tended to accept too readily the rumors and gossip about rebel units and movements they picked up in Richmond and elsewhere. But even when they did acquire accurate information, their figures on Confederate numbers usually included *all* troops in a given theater (for example, all of Virginia east of the Blue Ridge Mountains). By the time these figures reached McClellan and he had digested them, they had become transmuted into the number of men *in Johnston's army alone*. It is not clear whether McClellan or Pinkerton was primarily responsible for this error. In any case McClellan believed what he wanted to believe—that the enemy outnumbered him and he therefore could not undertake an offensive until he outnumbered the enemy—something that, given McClellan's psychology, was never likely to happen. For a good discussion of this question, see Edwin C. Fishel, "The Mythology of Civil War Intelligence," in Hubbell, ed., *Battles Lost and Won*, 83–106.

resemble a cannon. This "Quaker gun" embarrassed McClellan and called into question his reports of superior Confederate forces. The patience of northern people with the lack of action against the saucy rebels had begun to wear thin. The Quaker gun incident further dissipated the once-enormous reservoir of support and adulation for McClellan. As the fine, dry days of October wore away and the Army of the Potomac still made no advance, some Republicans began to suspect McClellan's competence and even his loyalty. The daily telegraphic bulletin, "All quiet along the Potomac," which had reassured northerners just after Bull Run, now became a phrase of derision aimed at McClellan. " 'Young Napoleon' is going down as fast as he went up," wrote an Indiana Republican after testing the pulse of public opinion. Lyman Trumbull said in November that if McClellan's army went into winter quarters without fighting a battle "I very much fear the result would be recognition of the Confederacy by foreign governments [and] the demoralization of our own people. . . . Action, action is what we want and must have."[39]

Action did temporarily break the quiet along the Potomac on October 21, but not the kind the North was hoping for. The rebels held the town of Leesburg, Virginia, forty miles upriver from Washington. Hoping to dislodge them, McClellan ordered General Charles P. Stone to make a "slight demonstration" from the Maryland side of the river while other Union regiments marched upriver on the Virginia side to threaten the Confederate flank. Stone assigned the mission to Colonel Edward Baker, a former Illinois politician and old friend of Lincoln, who had named his second son after him. Baker sent most of his brigade across the river, where it ran into a Confederate brigade posted in the woods at the top of a hundred-foot bank called Ball's Bluff. With no previous combat experience, Baker and his men took poorly chosen positions. After some lively skirmishing, in which Baker was killed, the Confederates drove the Yankees in disorder down the bank and into the river, where some of those who escaped bullets were drowned. More than half of Baker's 1,700 men were killed, wounded, or captured.

This humiliating disaster evoked from Lincoln tears of grief for Baker's death and provoked among Republicans an angry search for a scapegoat. When Congress met in December it established a Joint Committee on the Conduct of the War to investigate the causes for defeat at Ball's Bluff and Bull Run. Benjamin Wade chaired the committee and radical Republicans dominated it. Damned by its critics as a "Jacobin"

39. Nevins, *War*, I, 300; Williams, *Lincoln and the Radicals*, 45.

conspiracy to guillotine Democratic generals and praised by its defenders as a foe of inefficiency and corruption in the army, the committee was a bit of both.[40] In its early months it did function something like a star chamber court in its quest for scapegoats. The committee's first victim was General Stone. This officer had acquired a proslavery reputation because of a bitter exchange of letters with Governor Andrew of Massachusetts concerning the return to slavery of contrabands who had sought refuge with Massachusetts regiments under Stone's command. Several witnesses before the committee vaguely described alleged contacts between Stone and Confederate officers. Even though this testimony built a case of treason against Stone, whom the committee suspected of sending his men into a trap, the general was given no opportunity to confront his accusers or even to read their testimony. While McClellan tried for a time to protect his subordinate, he soon realized that Stone was a surrogate for the committee's real target—himself. When additional dubious evidence of Stone's supposed dealings with the enemy came to McClellan, he turned it over to Secretary of War Stanton, who ordered Stone's arrest. For six months this luckless—and probably innocent—general was imprisoned at Fort Lafayette. No formal charges were ever ever brought against him. He was finally released and restored to minor commands, but his career was ruined.[41]

Whether or not McClellan threw Stone to the wolves to protect himself,[42] he had clearly gotten into deep political waters by the end of 1861. McClellan was a Democrat. Some of his closest army comrades in prewar days had been southerners, including Joseph Johnston whose army at Manassas McClellan seemed reluctant to attack. Although no admirer of slavery, McClellan liked abolitionists even less. He had po-

---

40. For criticism of the committee, see especially William W. Pierson, Jr., "The Committee on the Conduct of the Civil War," AHR, 23 (1918), 550–76; T. Harry Williams, "The Committee on the Conduct of the War," Journal of the American Military History Institute, 3 (1939), 139–56. For a defense of the committee, see Hans L. Trefousse, "The Joint Committee on the Conduct of the War: A Reassessment," CWH, 10 (1964), 5–19; and Howard C. Westwood, "The Joint Committee on the Conduct of the War—A Look at the Record," Lincoln Herald, 80 (1978), 3–15.

41. Committee on the Conduct of the War, Reports, 1863 (Washington, 1863), Vol. II; R. B. Irwin, "Ball's Bluff and the Arrest of General Stone," Battles and Leaders, II, 123–34; Williams, Lincoln and the Radicals, 94–104.

42. Stone himself came to believe this, and T. Harry Williams strongly suggests such an interpretation in Lincoln and the Radicals, 101, 104.

litical ties with New York Democrats who had begun to mention him as the party's next presidential candidate. To one of these Democrats, McClellan wrote in November: "Help me to dodge the nigger—we want nothing to do with him. *I* am fighting to preserve the integrity of the Union. . . . To gain that end we cannot afford to mix up the negro question."[43]

Lincoln at this time would have agreed with McClellan's expression of war aims. The president also did his best to shield McClellan from the growing criticism of the army's inactivity. "I intend to be careful and do as well as possible," McClellan told Lincoln during one of their early discussions. "Just don't let them hurry me, is all I ask." Lincoln replied: "You shall have your own way in the matter." The president borrowed books on military science from the Library of Congress and sat up late trying to master the elements of strategy. As an amateur he was willing to defer to McClellan the professional. At the same time, as a professional in his own field the president tried to educate the general in the realities of politics—especially the danger of ignoring political pressures in a people's war. At one of their frequent meetings, Lincoln tried to make McClellan see that the demands of Republican leaders for action were "a reality, and must be taken into account."[44]

McClellan not only resisted such realities; in private he also expressed his contempt for all Republican politicians—including Lincoln. In letters to his wife he wrote that "I can't tell you how disgusted I am becoming with these wretched politicians—they are a most despicable set of men. . . . I am becoming daily more disgusted with this imbecile administration." The cabinet contained "some of the greatest geese I have ever seen. . . . Seward is the meanest of them all—a meddlesome, officious, incompetent little puppy. . . . Welles is a garrulous old woman . . . Bates an old fool. . . . The presdt. is nothing more than a well meaning baboon . . . 'the original gorilla.' . . . It is sickening in the extreme . . . [to] see the weakness and unfitness of the poor beings who control the destinies of this great country."[45]

One evening in November, Lincoln and Seward called on McClellan at home. He was out at a wedding party; when he returned an hour

43. McClellan to Samuel L. M. Barlow, Nov. 8, 1861, S. L. M. Barlow Papers, Henry E. Huntington Library.
44. Foote, *The Civil War*, I, 142; Williams, *Lincoln and the Radicals*, 45.
45. McClellan to Ellen Marcy McClellan, Oct. 2, 7, 10, Nov. 2, 17, 1861, McClellan Papers.

later and learned of his visitors, McClellan ignored them and went up-stairs. Half an hour later a servant informed the president and secretary of state that the general had gone to bed. Lincoln's private secretary was furious, but the president reportedly said: "I will hold McClellan's horse if he will only bring us success."[46]

But that was the rub. Military success could be achieved only by taking risks; McClellan seemed to shrink from the prospect. He lacked the mental and moral courage required of great generals—the will to *act*, to confront the terrible moment of truth on the battlefield. Having experienced nothing but success in his career, he was afraid to risk fail-ure. He also suffered from what might be termed the "Bull Run syn-drome"—a paralysis that prevented any movement against the Confed-erates until the army was thoroughly prepared. McClellan excelled at preparation, but it was never quite complete. The army was perpetually *almost* ready to move—but the enemy was always larger and better pre-pared.

To cover his fears, McClellan tried to shift the blame to others. "I am here in a terrible place," he had written in August. "The enemy have from 3 to 4 times my force [in fact, McClellan then had twice the enemy's force]—the Presdt. is an idiot, the old General is in his dot-age—they cannot or will not see the true state of affairs." In November, when McClellan had nearly three times the number of men and more than three times the weight of artillery as the Confederates in his front, he complained: "I cannot move without more means. . . . I have left nothing undone to make this army what it ought to be. . . . I am thwarted and deceived by these incapables at every turn. . . . It now begins to look as if we are condemned to a winter of inactivity. If it is so the fault will not be mine; there will be that consolation for my conscience, even if the world at large never knows it."[47]

V

Jefferson Davis was also having problems with the *amour propre* of his generals. On August 31 the Confederate president named five men to the rank of full general.[48] Joseph E. Johnston and Pierre G. T. Beau-regard were fourth and fifth on the list, below Adjutant General Samuel

46. Dennett, *Lincoln/Hay*, 34–35; Foote, *The Civil War*, I, 143.
47. McClellan to Ellen Marcy McClellan, Aug. 16, Nov. 2, 1861, McClellan Papers.
48. No Union officer at this time held a higher rank than major general, two grades below full general.

Cooper, Albert Sidney Johnston, and Robert E. Lee. When Joseph Johnston learned of this, he erupted in outrage. Not only was this ranking illegal, he informed Davis in a hotly worded letter, it was also an insult to his honor. He had outranked all of these men in the United States army, and by the terms of the law creating the Confederate grade of full general he still outranked them. Moreover, Cooper was a desk general (and a Yankee to boot, having been born and raised in New Jersey); A. S. Johnston had just arrived in the Confederacy after a slow trip from California and had not yet heard a shot fired in anger; Lee had won no battles and was even then floundering in West Virginia; while he, Joe Johnston, had won the battle of Manassas. Davis had committed a "violation of my rights as an officer," Johnston told the president, "tarnished my fair fame as a soldier and a man," and "degraded one who has served laboriously from the commencement of the war . . . and borne a prominent part in the one great event of the war, for the benefit of persons [none] of whom has yet struck a blow for the Confederacy."[49]

Insulted by the tone of Johnston's letter, Davis sent an icy reply: "Sir, I have just received and read your letter of the 12th instant. Its language is, as you say, unusual; its arguments and statements utterly one sided, and its insinuations as unfounded as they are unbecoming."[50] Not until later did Davis explain that he had ranked Johnston below Lee and A. S. Johnston because the latter two had held higher line commissions in the U. S. army than Joseph Johnston, whose rank as general had been a staff commission—a dubious rationale, which in any case did not apply to Cooper, who had also held a staff appointment in the old army.

The main effect of this graceless dispute was to plant a seed of hostility between Davis and Johnston that was to bear bitter fruit for the Confederacy. It also demonstrated an important difference between Davis and Lincoln as war leaders. A proud man sensitive of his honor, Davis could never forget a slight or forgive the man who committed it. Not for him was Lincoln's willingness to hold the horse of a haughty general if he would only win victories.

Davis also quarreled with Beauregard. The jaunty Louisianian's report on the battle of Manassas became public in October. It implied that Davis had delayed Johnston's reinforcement of Beauregard almost

49. Johnston to Davis, Sept. 12, 1861, O.R., Ser. IV, Vol. 1, pp. 605–8.
50. Davis to Johnston, Sept. 14, 1861, ibid., 611.

to the point of disaster. It noted Davis's rejection of Beauregard's grandiose plan for an offensive *before* the battle in a manner that caused the press to confuse this issue with the then-raging controversy over responsibility for failing to follow up the victory by capturing Washington. Throughout the report Beauregard's flamboyant prose tended to magnify his own role. Miffed, Davis reprimanded the general for writing an account that "seemed to be an attempt to exalt yourself at my expense."[51] One way to deal with Beauregard, who had grown restless in his role as second in command to Johnston in Virginia, was to send him as far away from Richmond as possible. In January 1862, Davis transferred Beauregard to the Tennessee-Kentucky theater, where he could try to help the other Johnston—Albert Sidney—cope with the buildup of Union forces in Kentucky.

Despite quarrels with his generals, Davis faced the New Year with more confidence than Lincoln. Since mid-July the Confederacy had won most of the important land battles in the war: Manassas, Wilson's Creek, Lexington (Mo.), Ball's Bluff. Although the Union navy had achieved some significant victories, these had not yet led anywhere. One of the apparent naval triumphs—the capture of southern commissioners James Mason and John Slidell from the British ship *Trent*—had even produced a Yankee backdown in the face of British threats. Northern banks had suspended specie payments and the government faced a financial crisis.[52] Northern morale was at its lowest ebb since the days after Bull Run. The London *Times* correspondent in Washington reported that every foreign diplomat but one agreed that "the Union is broken for ever, and the independence of the South virtually established."[53] The Army of the Potomac went into winter quarters having done nothing to dislodge enemy outposts within sight of that river; worse still, McClellan fell ill with typhoid fever in mid-December, leaving the army without a functioning commander for nearly a month. Lincoln had assigned two promising generals, Henry W. Halleck and Don Carlos Buell, to command of the Missouri and Kentucky theaters, but in January both reported an early advance impossible. "It is exceedingly discouraging," wrote Lincoln on a copy of Halleck's letter to him. "As

51. *Ibid.*, Ser. I, Vol. 2, pp. 484–504; Davis to Beauregard, Oct. 30, 1861, in Rowland, *Davis*, V, 156–57.
52. Naval affairs, the *Trent* crisis, and financial developments will be discussed in subsequent chapters.
53. Russell, *My Diary North and South*, 259.

everywhere else, nothing can be done." On the day he wrote these words, January 10, 1862, the president dropped into Quartermaster General Meigs's office. "General, what shall I do?" he asked despondently. "The people are impatient; Chase has no money; . . . the General of the Army has typhoid fever. The bottom is out of the tub. What shall I do?" [54]

But January 1862 proved to be the darkness before dawn for the Union cause. Although other dark nights would follow, the four months after January turned out to be one of the brightest periods of the war for the North.

54. CWL, V, 95; "General M. C. Meigs on the Conduct of the Civil War," AHR, 26 (1921), 292.

12

Blockade and Beachhead:
The Salt-Water War, 1861–1862

I

The navy achieved some of the Union's most important military successes in 1861. The primary naval task was the blockade. It was no easy task. The Confederacy's 3,500 miles of coastline included ten major ports and another 180 inlets, bays, and river mouths navigable by smaller vessels. By June 1861 three dozen blockade ships were patrolling this coastline. Additional blockaders were commissioned or chartered every week—some of them old sailing brigs, others converted sidewheeler ferryboats—which joined the modern steam frigates and sloops of war in the ceaseless, tedious cruising off southern ports.[1]

At first these ships were too few to apprehend more than one out of every dozen merchant vessels running the blockade. Even as the blockaders gained in numbers and effectiveness, another difficulty became obvious. The navy had only two bases in the South: Hampton Roads at the mouth of the James River opposite Confederate-held Norfolk; and Key West, Florida. Some ships spent nearly as much time going to and from these bases for supplies and repairs as they did on blockade duty. To remedy the problem, the navy decided to seize additional southern

---

1. A frigate was a three-masted warship mounting thirty to fifty guns; a sloop, also generally three-masted, carried ten to twenty-four guns. Using its steam-powered screw propeller for maneuvering and fighting, a steam warship could switch to sails for long-distance cruising.

harbors to serve as bases. While plans for the first such operation went forward, the navy scored its initial victory of the war at Hatteras Inlet in North Carolina.

For 200 miles along the North Carolina coast runs a series of barrier islands penetrated by a half-dozen inlets, of which Hatteras Inlet was the only one navigable by large ships. Behind this barrier lay the Albemarle and Pamlico sounds, inland seas with rail and canal connections to the interior. This transport network served as Richmond's back door to the Atlantic, the front door being closed by Union control of Hampton Roads. Numerous blockade runners passed through Hatteras Inlet during the war's early months. The North Carolina sounds also served as a haven for privateers that dashed through the inlets to capture unwary merchant vessels. What the privateers failed to snatch, the frequent storms off Cape Hatteras sometimes wrecked, for the rebels had dismantled the lighthouse and removed all navigation buoys from this treacherous coast.

No self-respecting navy could tolerate this "nest of pirates." Commodore Silas Stringham of the Atlantic blockading squadron put together a flotilla of seven ships carrying 141 guns to wipe it out. Two transports carrying 900 soldiers and marines under Benjamin Butler's command accompanied the task force. The soldiers' job was to assault the rear of the two forts guarding Hatteras Inlet after the ships had shelled them from the sea. Naval doctrine held that ships alone could not destroy well-armed forts. Perhaps this would have proved true if the half-finished forts had been well armed. As it turned out, however, the flotilla's rifled cannon battered them into submission on August 28–29 while cruising just out of range of their nineteen smoothbore guns. On August 29 the 670 men in the forts surrendered without Butler's troops having fired a shot. When news of this victory reached the North it took some of the sting out of Bull Run and Wilson's Creek. In North Carolina panic reigned along the tidewater as Tarheels expected Yankee hordes to descend on all their coastal towns. But the bluejackets were not ready to follow up their victory—yet.

The next naval success required scarcely any effort at all. Off the coast of Mississippi halfway between New Orleans and Mobile lies Ship Island. In September 1861 the Confederates obligingly abandoned its half-completed fortifications after a token shelling by the U. S. S. Massachusetts. The Federals occupied the island and built up a base for the Gulf blockade squadron and for a campaign to capture New Orleans.

Meanwhile a formidable fleet was heading down the Atlantic coast toward Port Royal, South Carolina. This task force consisted of seventeen warships, twenty-five colliers, and thirty-three transports carrying 12,000 infantry, 600 marines, and their supplies. A gale off Cape Hatteras on November 1 scattered the fleet and foundered several transports carrying much of the army's ammunition and most of its landing boats. This mishap canceled the original plan for troops to land and assault the two forts guarding the entrance to Port Royal Bay. Once again the navy would have to do the job alone.

This was not a pleasant prospect for Flag Officer Samuel du Pont, nephew of the founder of the du Pont gunpowder company and a veteran of forty-six years in the navy. The traditional belief that one gun on shore was equal to four on shipboard seemed to give the forty-three guns in the forts a better than even chance against 157 in the fleet. But du Pont was about to overturn the tradition. Using tactics made possible by steam power, he ordered his ships to steam back and forth past the forts in an oval pattern, pounding them with heavy broadsides while presenting moving targets in return. On November 7 the Union fleet carried out this plan with deadly precision, knocking out both forts after only four hours of firing. The Confederate defenders and white civilians fled the coastal sea islands connected by waterways radiating out from Port Royal Bay. Union forces occupied this region of rich long-staple cotton plantations. Left behind by their owners were some ten thousand contrabands who soon became part of an abolitionist experiment in freedmen's education and cotton planting with free labor.

At the cost of thirty-one casualties, the Union navy secured the finest natural harbor on the south Atlantic coast. More than that, the navy acquired a reputation of invincibility that depressed morale along the South's salt-water perimeter. The day after the capture of Port Royal, Robert E. Lee arrived in Savannah as the newly appointed commander of the south Atlantic coastal defenses. He regarded this assignment as "another forlorn hope expedition—worse than West Virginia." Lee recognized that sea power gave Yankees the option of striking when and where they pleased. "There are so many points to attack, and so little means to meet them on water," he sighed, "that there is but little rest."[2] Lee had little choice but to concentrate Confederate defenses at strategic points, yielding most of the coastline to the enemy. During the next

2. Lee to Mildred Lee (his daughter), Nov. 15, 1861, in Robert E. Lee, Jr., *Recollections and Letters of Robert E. Lee* (New York, 1904), 55; James M. Merrill, *The Rebel Shore: The Story of Union Sea Power in the Civil War* (Boston, 1957), 44.

few months, bluejackets seized several other harbors and ports as far south as St. Augustine, Florida. In April 1862, siege guns planted on an island at the mouth of the Savannah River battered down Fort Pulaski, giving the Federals control of the entrance to Savannah.

Another joint army-navy expedition—in which the army for once did most of the fighting—sealed off all harbors in North Carolina except Wilmington. This expedition launched the checkered career of Ambrose E. Burnside, a handsome, florid, personable Rhode Islander whose imposing muttonchop whiskers would contribute a new word to the language with an anagram (sideburns) of his name. After leading a brigade at Bull Run, Burnside had gone home to organize a division of soldiers accustomed to working around water and boats. They would need such skills, for their objective was to follow up the capture of Hatteras Inlet by gaining control of the North Carolina sounds. The Yankees' toughest foe in this enterprise turned out not to be the rebels, but the weather. Burnside's flotilla of makeshift gunboats, coal scows, and passenger steamboats carrying his 12,000 troops was scattered by a gale off Hatteras on January 13 that wrecked three of his vessels. Two more weeks of gale-force winds forced the expeditionary force to hunker down in misery just inside Hatteras Inlet. When the weather finally moderated, seasick soldiers welcomed the prospect of combat as a lesser evil.

Their first target was Roanoke Island, a swampy piece of land ten miles long, two miles wide, and rich in legend—a land where the memory of Virginia Dare and the inscrutable word "Croatan" marked the mysterious fate of England's first North American colony. Controlling the passage between Pamlico Sound and Albemarle Sound, Roanoke Island was the key to Richmond's back door. Commander of the 3,000 Confederate soldiers, four batteries with thirty-two guns, and seven one-gun gunboats defending the island was Henry A. Wise, the political general transferred here from his feuds with fellow Virginian John Floyd in West Virginia. Wise had learned enough about war to recognize the inadequacy of his "mosquito-fleet" gunboats, badly sited batteries, and poorly trained, outnumbered troops. He pleaded with Richmond for more men and more guns, but Richmond seemed strangely indifferent.

This indifference cost them dearly, for the Yankees were coming with power. On February 7–8, Burnside's sixteen gunboats mounting sixty-four guns drove off the mosquito fleet and neutralized the Confederate shore batteries while steamers towed landing boats through the surf and 7,500 soldiers waded ashore on Roanoke Island. There they plunged through "impenetrable" knee-deep swamps and smashed through rebel entrenchments, suffering only 264 casualties. For this price they captured the island's 2,675 defenders. General Wise escaped but his son, an infantry captain, was killed in the fighting. Next day Union gunboats destroyed the mosquito fleet and seized Elizabeth City on the mainland. During the next several weeks, Yankees captured all the North Carolina ports on the sounds, including New Berne and Beaufort with their rail connections to the interior and Beaufort's fine harbor, which became another base for the blockade fleet.

Here was amphibious warfare with style. It won a promotion to major general for Burnside. It raised northern morale and dampened southern spirits. The Confederate Congress set up a committee to investigate the Roanoke Island disaster. The hue and cry forced Judah Benjamin to resign as secretary of war (though Davis, who liked Benjamin, promptly appointed him secretary of state). By April 1862 every Atlantic coast harbor of importance except Charleston and Wilmington (N.C.) was in Union hands or closed to blockade runners. Because of this, and because of the increasing number of Union warships, the blockade tightened considerably during the first half of 1862. Moreover, southern hopes to breach the blockade with their (not so) secret weapon—the ironclad C. S. S. *Virginia*—had been dashed by the *U. S. S. Monitor*.

Having no traditions and few old-navy prejudices to overcome, the rebels got a head start into the new era of ironclad warships. In July 1861 they began grafting an armor-plated casemate onto the salvaged hull of the frigate *Merrimack*. Work began in July. The capacity of the Tredegar Iron Works was stretched to the limit to construct two layers of two-inch iron plate sufficient to protect a superstructure 178 feet long and 24 feet high above the waterline and one-inch plate covering the 264-foot hull down to three feet below the waterline. The superstructure sloped at an angle of 36° to give added protection by causing enemy shots to ricochet. The strange appearance of this craft, rechristened the *Virginia*, reminded observers of a barn floating with only its roof above water. The *Virginia* was armed with ten guns, four on each broadside plus fore and aft seven-inch pivot rifles. Attached to her prow was an iron ram to stave in the hulls of wooden warships. The principal defects of this otherwise formidable vessel were its unreliable engines and deep draft. Unable to build new engines of adequate horsepower, the rebels reconditioned the two old *Merrimack* engines that had been condemned by the prewar navy and slated for replacement. The weight of the *Virginia*'s armor gave her a draft of twenty-two feet. This prevented operations in shallow water while her unseaworthiness prevented her from venturing into the open sea. The weak engines and ungainly design limited her speed to four or five knots and made her so unmaneuverable that a 180-degree turn took half an hour. Some of these problems would not become apparent until the *Virginia* was launched; in the meantime she inspired hope in the South and fear in the North.

This fear was the main factor in overcoming northern inertia on the ironclad question. With a conventional navy superior to anything the Confederates could construct, and preoccupied with the need to build up the blockade fleet, Secretary of the Navy Welles did not at first want to experiment with newfangled notions. But rumors of rebel activities caused Congress to force his hand with a law of August 3, 1861, directing the construction of three prototype ironclads. Welles set up a naval board to assess the dozens of proposals submitted by shipbuilders. The board accepted two, which resulted in the building of the *Galena* and the *New Ironsides*, ships of conventional design overlaid by iron plating.

No bid came from John Ericsson, the irascible genius of marine engineering who had contributed the screw propeller and several other innovations to ship design. Bitter about earlier feuds with the navy, Ericsson sulked in his New York office until a shipbuilder persuaded him to submit his radical design to the Navy Department. Ericsson's proposal incorporated several novel features. A wooden hull sheathed with thin iron plate would be overlaid by a flat deck 172 feet long with perpendicular sides extending below the waterline and protected by 4.5 inch armor plating. The propeller, anchor, and all vital machinery would be protected by this shell, which was designed to float with less than two feet of freeboard, giving the craft the appearance of a raft—and also presenting a small target to enemy fire. Sitting on the deck was Ericsson's most important innovation: a revolving turret encased in eight inches of armor and containing two eleven-inch guns. This turret, along with the shallow draft (11 feet), light displacement (1,200 tons, about one-fourth of the *Virginia*'s displacement), and eight-knot speed would give Ericsson's ship maneuverability and versatility. She could almost literally dance around a heavier enemy and fire in any direction.

Lincoln and Welles were impressed by Ericsson's design. But would it float? More specifically, would it stay afloat in a heavy sea? Some members of the naval board were skeptical. They had never seen anything like this cheesebox on a raft. Ericsson appeared before the board and overcame their doubts with a bravura performance. They awarded him a contract, but ridicule of "Ericsson's folly" by senior navy officers caused Welles to hedge his bet: the ship must prove a "complete success" (whatever that meant) or its builders must refund every penny of the $275,000 the government agreed to pay for it. Ericsson was not concerned; he had confidence in his creation. He subcontracted the work to several firms to save time, and supervised almost every detail personally. Starting three months later than the South, northern industry launched Ericsson's ironclad on January 30, 1862, two weeks before the Confederates launched the *Virginia*. Doubters present at each launching predicted that these crazy craft would never float, but cheered the disproof of their predictions. Several more weeks were required to finish the fittings of both ships. Ericsson named his vessel *Monitor* (one who admonishes and corrects wrongdoers). There was no time for test runs to determine whether she fulfilled the terms of the contract; the *Monitor*'s test would be trial by combat.

On March 8 the *Virginia* steamed out from Norfolk on what her crew assumed was a test run. But this too was to be the real thing. Five Union ships mounting a total of 219 guns guarded the mouth of the James River at Hampton Roads: the *Minnesota, Roanoke, St. Lawrence, Congress,* and *Cumberland*. The last three were sailing ships—pride of the navy in the 1840s but already made obsolescent by steam. The first two were steam frigates (the *Roanoke* was disabled by a broken shaft), pride of the navy in 1862. But the fighting this day would make them obsolescent as well. Rumors that the *Merrimack* (as the Federals continued to call the *Virginia*) was coming out had circulated for weeks. Today she came, heading first for the twenty-four-gun *Cumberland*, sending several shells into her side before ramming and tearing a seven-foot hole in her hull that sent her to the bottom. While this was happening, the *Cumberland* and *Congress* fired numerous broadsides at the *Virginia*, which "struck and glanced off," in the words of a northern observer, "having no more effect than peas from a pop-gun."[3] This was not quite accurate; before the day was over two of the *Virginia*'s guns were knocked out, every fitting on deck and part of her smokestack were shot away, her ram was wrenched off by the collision with the *Cumberland*, two of her crew were killed and several were wounded. But none of the ninety-eight shots that struck her penetrated the armor or did any disabling damage.

After sinking the *Cumberland*, the *Virginia* went after the fifty-gun *Congress*, raking the helpless vessel with broadsides which started fires that eventually reached the powder magazine and blew her up. The

3. William C. Davis, *Duel between the First Ironclads* (Garden City, N.Y., 1975), 89.

Minnesota having run aground in an effort to help her sister ships, the *Virginia* turned her attention to this flagship of the fleet that had captured Hatteras Inlet the previous August. But the *Virginia*'s deep draft prevented her from closing with the *Minnesota* as night came on. The rebels left the *Minnesota* and the other ships for the morrow, and called it a day.

And what a day—the worst in the eighty-six-year history of the U. S. navy. The *Virginia* sank two proud ships within a few hours—a feat no other enemy would accomplish until 1941. At least 240 bluejackets had been killed, including the captain of the *Congress*—more than the navy suffered on any other day of the war. The whole Union fleet at Hampton Roads—still the main blockade base—was threatened with destruction. A taste of panic flavored the telegrams to Washington that night. The cabinet met in emergency session next morning. Secretary of the Navy Welles tried to calm Secretary of War Stanton's nerves with news that the *Monitor* was on its way from Brooklyn to Hampton Roads to confront the *Virginia*. But would she get there in time? And even if she did, was this two-gun "tin can on a shingle" any match for the rebel monster?

She did, and she was. The *Monitor* had arrived alongside the *Minnesota* the night before, her crew exhausted from fighting a storm that had almost sunk them on the way from Brooklyn. The prospect of fighting the *Virginia*, however, started their adrenalin pulsing again. When the Confederate ship steamed out on the morning of March 9 to finish off the Federal fleet, her crew spied a strange craft next to the *Minnesota*. "We thought at first it was a raft on which one of the *Minnesota*'s boilers was being taken to shore for repairs," said a *Virginia* midshipman. But the boiler ran out a gun and fired. A *Monitor* crewman described the *Virginia*'s response: "You can see surprise in a ship just as you can see it in a man, and there was surprise all over the Merrimac." The rebels turned their attention from the stranded *Minnesota* to this strange vessel that began circling the sluggish *Virginia* "like a fice dog" and hurling 175-pound shot from her eleven-inch guns. For two hours the ironclads slugged it out. Neither could punch through the other's armor, though the *Monitor*'s heavy shot cracked the *Virginia*'s outside plate at several places. At one point the southern ship grounded. As the shallower-draft *Monitor* closed in, many aboard the *Virginia* thought they were finished. But she broke loose and continued the fight, trying without success to ram the *Monitor*. By this time the *Virginia*'s wheezy engines were barely functioning, and one of her lieutenants found her "as unwieldly as Noah's Ark." The *Monitor* in turn tried to ram the *Virginia*'s stern to disable her rudder or propeller, but just missed. Soon after this a shell from the *Virginia* struck the *Monitor*'s pilot house, wounding her captain. The Union ship stopped fighting briefly; the *Virginia*, in danger of running aground again, steamed back toward Norfolk. Each crew thought they had won the battle, but in truth it was a draw. The exhausted men on both sides ceased fighting—almost, it seemed, by mutual consent.[4]

This day saw the completion of a revolution in naval warfare begun a generation earlier by the application of steam power to warships. Doomed were the graceful frigates and powerful line-of-battle ships with their towering masts and sturdy oak timbers. When the news of the *Monitor-Virginia* duel reached England, the London *Times* commented: "Whereas we had available for immediate purposes one hundred and forty-nine first-class warships, we have now two, these two being the *Warrior* and her sister *Ironside* [Britain's experimental ironclads]. There is not now a ship in the English navy apart from these two that it would not be madness to trust to an engagement with that little *Monitor*."[5]

Of more immediate interest in Washington, the Union fleet at Hampton Roads was saved. For the next two months the *Monitor* and *Virginia* eyed each other warily but did not fight. With no ironclads in reserve, neither side could risk losing its indispensable weapon. When McClellan's army invaded the Virginia peninsula and forced the Confederates back toward Richmond in May 1862, Norfolk fell to the Federals and the *Virginia* was stranded. Too unseaworthy to fight her way into open water and too deep-drafted to retreat up the James River, the plucky ironclad was blown up by her crew on May 11, less than three months after she had been launched. The *Monitor* also failed to live until her first birthday. On the last day of 1862 she sank in a gale off Cape Hatteras while being towed south for a blockade assignment.

Despite their defects, the *Virginia* and *Monitor* were prototypes for the subsequent ironclads built or begun by both sides during the war: 21 by the Confederacy and 58 by the Union. Many of these never saw action; all were designed for bay and river fighting; none achieved the fame of their progenitors. The existence of rebel ironclads lurking in

4. Foote, *The Civil War*, I, 260; Davis, *Duel between the First Ironclads*, 120–21, 127.
5. Quoted in John Taylor Wood, "The First Fight of Iron-Clads," *Battles and Leaders*, I, 692.

southern rivers provoked a state of anxiety in the Union navy known as "ram fever," but had little effect on the course of the war. Steam/sail warships built of wood remained the mainstay of the Union's deep-water navy. But in the last third of the nineteenth century the world's navies converted to iron and steel, incorporating the principal features of Ericsson's folly: low profiles, speed and maneuverability, revolving gun turrets, and a few guns of heavy caliber rather than multiple-gun broadsides.

II

Blockade duty in the Union navy offered few opportunities for glory. The main enemy was boredom. About 500 ships took part in the blockade during the war, with perhaps an average of 150 on patrol at a given time over the four years of fighting. These ships captured or destroyed about 1,500 blockade runners. Assuming that for every runner captured, a blockade ship sighted or chased a dozen, this meant that the average blockader sighted a runner once every three or four weeks and participated in one or two captures a year. "Day after day, day after day, we lay inactive, roll, roll," was the description of blockade service by one officer. Another wrote to his mother that she could get an idea of what blockade duty was like if she were to "go to the roof on a hot summer day, talk to a half-dozen degenerates, descend to the basement, drink tepid water full of iron rust, climb to the roof again, and repeat the process at intervals until [you are] fagged out, then go to bed with everything shut tight."[6]

Only the chance to strike it rich kept blockade sailors sane and alert. The crew shared half and half with the government the proceeds from every prize they captured. This amounted to about 7 percent of the prize's value for the captain, a lesser portion for each officer, and 16 percent shared among the seamen. The dream of hitting the jackpot in this system sometimes came true: within nine days in the fall of 1864 the little gunboat *Aeolus* captured two runners unassisted, earning $40,000 for her captain, $8,000 to $20,000 for each of her officers, and $3,000 for each seaman.

Potential profits as well as actual excitement were greater for the crews of blockade runners. "Nothing I have ever experienced can compare

6. Richard S. West, Jr., *Mr. Lincoln's Navy* (New York, 1957), 60; Merrill, *Rebel Shore*, 69.

with it," wrote a British officer on a runner. "Hunting, pig-sticking, steeple-chasing, big-game hunting, polo—I have done a little of each— all have their thrilling moments, but none can approach running a blockade."[7] But such a comment did not apply to the first year of the war. The blockade then resembled a sieve more than a cordon; the small risk of running it raised cargo prices and insurance rates but offered few thrills. By the summer of 1862, though, things were different. With most of the South's ports sealed off or occupied, the blockade fleet could concentrate on the few ports remaining open. Experience had taught northern captains to station smaller ships inshore as picket boats to send up rocket signals when a runner approached the harbor entrance attempting to enter or leave. All warships within sight would then converge on the runner. Several miles out a second cordon of Union ships patrolled a wider area, giving chase to outward-bound runners spotted by the picket boats or inward-bound ships spotted by themselves.

This system worked reasonably well against slow or large blockade runners in conditions of good visibility. But such craft trying to run the blockade in these conditions soon disappeared from southern shores. In their place came sleek, fast, shallow-drafted vessels built (mostly in Britain) for the purpose, painted gray for low visibility, burning smokeless anthracite, with low freeboard, telescoping smokestacks, and underwater steam-escape valves. With pilots on board who knew every inch of the coast, these ships chose moonless, foggy, or stormy nights to make their dash into or out of a channel from which all navigation markers had been removed except coded shore lights to guide the pilots. Under such circumstances, a runner might pass within 200 yards of a warship without being detected. Some runners carried signal rockets identical to those used by the Union navy, which they fired in a wrong direction to confuse pursuit.

Nassau, Bermuda, and Havana became the principal bases for blockade runners. There they took on cargoes of guns, ammunition, shoes, army blankets, medicines, salt, tea, liquor, hoop skirts, and corset stays. When the Union navy acquired enough ships it established a third cordon of blockaders patrolling these ports (despite British and Spanish protests) to intercept runners hundreds of miles from southern shores. The blockade runners usually escaped these patrols, however, and made the run to Wilmington, Charleston, Mobile, or some other port where they picked up cotton for the return run.

7. Robert Carse, *Blockade: The Civil War at Sea* (New York, 1958), 41.

Wilmington and Nassau became wartime boom towns—rowdy, violent, bawdy, awash with wealth and greed.[8] The chance of profits from a successful voyage outweighed the one chance in three (by 1864) of capture. Owners could make back their investment in one or two round trips, clearing pure profit with every subsequent voyage. Cotton prices in European markets soared to six, eight, ten times their prewar levels, enabling speculators who bought cotton in the South and shipped it out to earn a return of several hundred percent. By 1864 captains of blockade runners received $5,000 or more in gold for a round trip, other officers from $750 to $3,500, and common seamen $250. In addition, captains reserved part of the cargo space for their own cotton (outgoing) or high-value goods (incoming) which they sold at auction. Many of the owners, captains, and crews were British, including some former royal navy officers who had resigned to pursue this more lucrative career. Although patriotism actuated the numerous southerners who also owned and operated blockade runners, the profit motive was not entirely absent. The North treated captured southern crews as prisoners of war but could not risk the diplomatic consequences of imprisoning foreign crew members, so let them go. The crowding out of war matériel by high-value consumer goods on incoming runners became so notorious that in early 1864 the Confederate government enacted (much evaded) regulations banning luxury goods and requiring all runners to allot at least half their space to the government at fixed rates. The government (especially Josiah Gorgas's Ordnance Bureau) and some southern states also bought their own blockade runners.

How effective was the blockade? There are two ways of answering this question. One way is to point out that during the war an estimated five out of six blockade runners got through (nine out of ten in 1861 scaling down to one out of two by 1865). They shipped out half a million bales of cotton and brought in a million pairs of shoes, half a million rifles, a thousand tons of gunpowder, several hundred cannon, and so on. The dollar value of Charleston's foreign trade was greater in 1863 than in the last year of peace. Confederate envoys to Britain compiled long lists of ships that had run the blockade to prove that it was a "paper blockade" entitled to no recognition by international law. In January 1863,

8. Wilmington became the principal Confederate port for blockade runners because of the tricky inlets and shoals at the mouth of the Cape Fear River guarded by Fort Fisher, whose big guns kept the blockade fleet from interfering when a runner came within their protecting range.

Jefferson Davis pronounced the "so-called blockade" a "monstrous pretension." A prominent historian of Confederate diplomacy agreed. The blockade, wrote Frank L. Owsley, was an "absurdity," "scarcely a respectable paper blockade," "old Abe's . . . practical joke on the world."[9]

But most southerners who lived through the blockade gave a different answer. "Already the blockade is beginning to shut [ammunition] out," wrote Mary Boykin Chesnut on July 16, 1861. It was "a stockade which hems us in," she added in March 1862. In July 1861 a Charleston merchant noted in his diary that the "blockade is still carried on and every article of consumption particularly in the way of groceries are getting very high." Four months later he wrote: "Business perfectly prostrated everything enormously high salt selling at 15 and 20 cents a quart hardly any shoes to be had dry goods of every kind running out." A southern naval officer conceded after the war that the blockade "shut the Confederacy out from the world, deprived it of supplies, weakened its military and naval strength."[10]

Historical opinion leans toward this latter view. While it was true that five out of six runners got through, that is not the crucial statistic. Rather, one must ask how many ships carrying how much freight *would have* entered southern ports if there had been no blockade. Eight thousand trips were made through the blockade during four years of war,[11] but

9. Rowland, *Davis*, V, 401, 403; Frank L. Owsley, *King Cotton Diplomacy: Foreign Relations of the Confederate States of America*, 2nd ed. rev. (Chicago, 1959), 229, 230.

10. Woodward, *Chesnut's Civil War*, 101, 306; Nevins, *War*, I, 289; John T. Scharf, *History of the Confederate States Navy* (New York, 1887), v.

11. These are estimates offered by Frank Owsley, *King Cotton Diplomacy*, 250–90, based on records of the Confederate State Department and the Union Navy Department. Most of the successful runs (and unsuccessful ones) were made by small coastal schooners carrying little if any cargo of military value. Indeed, a majority of the trips by these vessels were along intercoastal waterways between Confederate ports, merely redistributing freight from one part of the South to another, and could scarcely be termed "running" the blockade. From June through August 1861, for example, of 178 ships entering or clearing five major southern ports, only eighteen were involved in foreign trade. Confederate diplomats cited all this intra-southern trade as blockade running in an attempt to persuade Britain to declare the blockade an illegal "paper blockade"; the Union navy included captured vessels of this type in its statistics to pad the list of captures. Of the blockade running that really counted— fast steamers running between the South and foreign ports—there were about 1,000 successful trips out of 1,300 attempts. Stephen R. Wise, "Lifeline of the Confederacy: Blockade Running During the American Civil War," Ph.D. dissertation, University of South Carolina, 1983, pp. 44, 46, 139, 516.

more than twenty thousand vessels had cleared into or out of southern ports during the four prewar years. The blockade runners were built for speed, not capacity, and when pursued they sometimes jettisoned part of their cargo. The blockade reduced the South's seaborne trade to less than a third of normal. And of course the Confederacy's needs for all kinds of supplies were much greater than the peacetime norm. As for cotton exports, 1861 must be disregarded because the South voluntarily embargoed cotton in an attempt to influence British foreign policy (see below). After the end of this embargo in 1862 the half-million bales shipped through the blockade during the last three years of war compared rather poorly with the ten million exported in the last three antebellum years. As far as the greater dollar volume of Charleston's wartime trade is concerned, there were two reasons for this: Charleston was one of the principal ports for blockade runners because they were shut out of the other ports; and inflation so eroded the Confederate dollar that by March 1863 it required ten such dollars to buy what one had bought two years earlier. Indeed, the blockade was one of the causes of the ruinous inflation that reduced the Confederate dollar to one percent of its original value by the end of the war.

To maintain that the blockade "won the war" for the North, as naval historians are wont to do, goes entirely too far.[12] But it did play an important role in Union victory. Although naval personnel constituted only 5 percent of the Union armed forces, their contribution to the outcome of the war was much larger.

III

The question of the blockade's effectiveness became a critical foreign policy issue during the war's first year. The international law governing blockades was part of the Declaration of Paris, acceded to by European powers (but not the U. S.) in 1856 after the Crimean War: "Blockades, in order to be binding, must be effective; that is to say, maintained by

12. Howard P. Nash, Jr., A Naval History of the Civil War (New York, 1972), 300. On the other hand, the conclusion of a recent study that "the blockade did not represent a major factor in the Confederacy's economic exhaustion" and did not have a "decisive effect" on the outcome of the war may go too far in the opposite direction. It depends on one's definition of "major" and "decisive." The impact of the blockade was certainly significant, though of course it did not alone win the war. Whether the war could have been won without it must remain moot. Richard E. Beringer, Herman Hattaway, Archer Jones, and William N. Still, Jr., Why the South Lost the Civil War (Athens, Ga., 1986), 56, 63.

forces strong enough to prevent access." Southern diplomats insisted that the ease of running the blockade in 1861 proved its ineffectiveness; therefore no nation need respect it. This had been the traditional American position toward British blockades, especially during the Napoleonic wars when the United States defied the British and traded with both sides. But now the shoe was on the other foot. A major goal of Confederate diplomacy in 1861 was to persuade Britain to declare the blockade illegal as a prelude to intervention by the royal navy to protect British trade with the South.

Cotton was the principal weapon of southern foreign policy. Britain imported three-quarters of its cotton from the American South. The textile industry dominated the British economy. "What would happen if no cotton was furnished for three years?" asked James Hammond of South Carolina in his famous King Cotton speech of 1858. "England would topple headlong and carry the whole civilized world with her, save the South." The inevitability of British intervention to obtain cotton became an article of faith in the South during 1861. A Charleston merchant told the London *Times* correspondent a few days after the surrender of Fort Sumter that "if those miserable Yankees try to blockade us, and keep you from our cotton," he said, "you'll just send their ships to the bottom and acknowledge us. That will be before autumn, I think." In July 1861 Vice President Alexander Stephens expressed certainty that "in some way or other [the blockade will] be raised, or there will be revolution in Europe. . . . Our cotton is . . . the tremendous lever by which we can work our destiny." [13]

To ply this lever, southerners decided to embargo cotton exports. "The cards are in our hands," exulted the *Charleston Mercury*, "and we intend to play them out to the bankruptcy of every cotton factory in Great Britain and France or the acknowledgment of our independence." The *Memphis Argus* instructed planters to "keep every bale of cotton on the plantation. Don't send a thread to New Orleans or Memphis till England and France have recognized the Confederacy—not one thread." [14] Although the Confederate government never officially sanctioned the embargo, so powerful was public opinion that it virtually enforced itself.

---

13. *Selections from the Letters and Speeches of the Hon. James H. Hammond of South Carolina* (New York, 1866), 316–17; William Howard Russell, *My Diary North and South*, ed. Fletcher Pratt (New York, 1954), 69; Virgil Carrington Jones, *The Civil War at Sea: The Blockaders* (New York, 1960), 183.

14. Owsley, *King Cotton Diplomacy*, 24–25.

Most of the 1860 crop had been shipped before the war began. The shipping season for 1861 would normally have begun in September, but despite the looseness of the blockade little cotton went out. In the spring of 1862 southerners planted about half their usual cotton acreage and devoted the rest of the land to food production. British imports of cotton from the South in 1862 amounted to about 3 percent of the 1860 level.

King Cotton diplomacy seemed promising at first. British and French officials exchanged worried views about the probable impact of a cotton famine. Textile magnates in Lancashire and Lyons talked of shutdowns. "England must break the Blockade, or Her Millions will starve," declared a newspaper speaking for textile workers in September 1861. In October, Prime Minister Viscount Palmerston and Foreign Minister Lord Russell agreed that "the cotton question may become serious by the end of the year. . . . We cannot allow some millions of our people to perish to please the Northern States." British and French diplomats discussed the possibility of joint action to lift the blockade.[15]

But in the end several factors prevented such action. The first was Russell's and Palmerston's desire to avoid involvement in the war. "For God's sake, let us if possible keep out of it," said Russell in May 1861, while Palmerston quoted the aphorism: "They who in quarrels interpose, will often get a bloody nose." Even without Secretary of State Seward's bellicose warnings against intervention—which the British regarded as insolent blustering—Britain recognized that any action against the blockade could lead to a conflict with the United States more harmful to England's interests than the temporary loss of southern cotton. Our "true policy," Palmerston told Russell on October 18, was "to go on as we have begun, and to keep quite clear of the conflict."[16] Napoleon III of France leaned toward intervention, but was unwilling to take any action without British cooperation.

If Britain took umbrage at Seward's "bullying," many Englishmen resented even more the Confederacy's attempt at economic blackmail. If southerners "thought they could extort our cooperation by the agency of king cotton," declared the Times, they had better think again. To intervene on behalf of the South "because they keep cotton from us,"

15. Brian Jenkins, Britain and the War for the Union, 2 vols. (Montreal, 1974–80), I, 166, 170; Owsley, King Cotton Diplomacy, 73.
16. Norman B. Ferris, Desperate Diplomacy: William H. Seward's Foreign Policy, 1861 (Knoxville, 1976), 39, 36; Jenkins, Britain and the War for the Union, I, 172.

said Lord Russell in September 1861, "would be ignominious beyond measure. . . . No English Parliament could do so base a thing."[17]

Because of British (and French) sensitivity on this issue, southern diplomats could not admit the existence of a cotton embargo. But this trapped them in a paradox, for how could they proclaim the blockade ineffective if no cotton was reaching Europe? In reply to a question on this matter by the French foreign minister in February 1862, the Confederate commissioner to Paris conceded that "although a very large proportion of the vessels that attempted to run the blockade . . . had succeeded in passing, the risk of capture was sufficiently great to deter those who had not a very adventurous spirit from attempting it." Fatal admission! Eight days later Foreign Minister Russell announced Britain's position on the blockade: "The fact that various ships may have successfully escaped through it . . . will not of itself prevent the blockade from being an effective one by international law" so long as it was enforced by a number of ships "sufficient really to prevent access to [a port] *or to create an evident danger of entering or leaving it.*" By February the northern blockade certainly met this criterion. Another influence working against British acceptance of southern arguments about paper blockades was a desire not to create a precedent that would boomerang against British security in a future war. As the crown's solicitor general put it: Britain must resist "new fangled notions and interpretations of international law which might make it impossible for us effectively at some future day to institute any blockade, and so destroy our naval authority."[18]

Southern expectations of foreign intervention to break the blockade were betrayed by a double irony: first, the "success" of the cotton embargo seemed only to prove the success of the blockade; and second, the huge cotton exports of 1857–60, instead of proving the potency of King Cotton, resulted in toppling his throne. Even working overtime, British mills had not been able to turn all of this cotton into cloth. Surplus stocks of raw cotton as well as of finished cloth piled up in Lancashire warehouses. The South's embargo thus turned out to be a blessing in disguise for textile manufacturers in 1861. Although the mills went on

17. Owsley, *King Cotton Diplomacy*, 22; Jenkins, *Britain and the War for the Union*, I, 170.
18. Nevins, *War*, I, 289; D. P. Crook, *The North, the South, and the Powers 1861–1865* (New York, 1974), 177 (italics added), 178.

short time during the winter of 1861–62, the real reason for this was not the shortage of cotton but the satiated market for cloth. Inventories of raw cotton in Britain and France were higher in December 1861 than any previous December. The cotton famine from which the South expected so much did not really take hold until the summer of 1862. By then the Confederacy had scuttled its embargo and was trying desperately to export cotton through the tightening blockade to pay for imported supplies. By then, too, the stimulus of high prices had brought about an increase of cotton acreage in Egypt and India, which supplied most of Europe's cotton imports for the next three years.

The worst time of unemployment in the British textile industry occurred from the summer of 1862 to the spring of 1863. But the impact of this did not measure up to southern hopes or British fears. Even before the war, textiles had been losing their dominant role in the British economy. The war further stimulated growth in the iron, shipbuilding, armaments, and other industries. This offset much of the decline in textiles. The manufacture of woolen uniforms and blankets for American armies absorbed some of the slack in cotton manufacturing. A flourishing trade in war matériel with the North as well as blockade running to the South helped convince British merchants of the virtues of neutrality. Crop failures in western Europe from 1860 through 1862 increased British dependence on American grain and flour. During the first two years of the Civil War the Union states supplied nearly half of British grain imports, compared with less than a quarter before the war. Yankees exulted that King Corn was more powerful than King Cotton.[19] And because Confederate commerce raiders drove much of the U. S. merchant marine from the seas, most of this expanded trade with the North was carried by British ships—another economic shot in the arm that helped discourage British intervention in the war.

By the second year of the conflict, Britain was willing to tolerate extraordinary northern extensions of the blockade. In April 1862, Union warships began seizing British merchant vessels plying between England and Nassau or Bermuda, on the grounds that their cargoes were destined ultimately for the Confederacy. The first ship so captured was the *Bermuda*, which was confiscated by a U. S. prize court. The navy bought her and put her to work as a blockade ship. This added insult to the injury that had already provoked a jingoistic response in Britain. But American diplomats cited British precedents for such seizures. During

19. Crook, *The North, the South, and the Powers*, 268–72.

the Napoleonic wars the royal navy had seized American ships carrying cargoes to a neutral port with the intention of re-exporting them to France. British courts had established the doctrine of "continuous voyage" to justify confiscation of contraband destined ultimately for an enemy port even if the voyage was broken by landing at a neutral port. When this chicken came home to roost in 1862, Whitehall could hardly repudiate its own precedent.

In 1863 a northern court extended the doctrine of continuous voyage beyond any precedent in the *Peterhoff* case. In February a Union warship captured the British vessel *Peterhoff* in the Caribbean, where she was on her way to Matamoros, Mexico, with a cargo of military supplies. The Union navy had good reason to suspect that the ultimate destination of this cargo was the Confederacy. Located across the Rio Grande from Texas, Matamoros had become the *entrepôt* for trade with the South exchanging cotton for contraband. The prize court upheld the navy's extension of "continuous voyage" to include re-export of contraband across land frontiers as well as from neutral ports. This time a large portion of the British public railed against Yankee "overbearing and domineering insolence." But the Foreign Office merely recorded the precedent, which Britain cited a half-century later to justify seizure of American ships carrying contraband to neutral Holland intended for overland trans-shipment to Germany.[20]

IV

Next to obtaining British intervention against the blockade, the main goal of Confederate foreign policy was to secure diplomatic recognition of the South's nationhood. In the quest for recognition, the Confederate State Department sent to Europe a three-man commission headed by William L. Yancey. As a notorious fire-eater and an advocate of reopening the African slave trade, Yancey was not the best choice to win friends in antislavery Britain. Nevertheless, soon after the southerners arrived in London the British government announced an action that misled Americans on both sides of the Potomac to anticipate imminent diplomatic recognition of the Confederacy.

Lincoln had proclaimed the rebels to be insurrectionists. Under international law this would deny the Confederacy status as a belligerent

---

20. Quotation from Jenkins, *Britain and the War for the Union*, II, 262. For a study of the maritime legal issues involved here, see Stuart L. Bernath, *Squall Across the Atlantic: American Civil War Prize Cases and Diplomacy* (Berkeley, 1970).

power. But the North's declaration of a blockade constituted an act of war affecting neutral powers. On May 13 Britain therefore declared her neutrality in a proclamation issued by the Queen. This would seem to have been unexceptionable—except that it automatically recognized the Confederacy as a belligerent power. Other European nations followed the British lead. Status as a belligerent gave Confederates the right under international law to contract loans and purchase arms in neutral nations, and to commission cruisers on the high seas with the power of search and seizure. Northerners protested this British action with hot words; Charles Sumner later called it "the most hateful act of English history since Charles 2nd." But northern protests rested on weak legal grounds, for the blockade was a virtual recognition of southern belligerency. Moreover, in European eyes the Confederacy with its national constitution, its army, its effective control of 750,000 square miles of territory and a population of nine million people, was a belligerent power in practice no matter what it was in northern theory. As Lord Russell put it: "The question of belligerent rights is one, not of principle, but of fact."[21]

Northern bitterness stemmed in part from the context and timing of British action. The proclamation of neutrality came just after two "unofficial" conferences between Lord Russell and the Confederate envoys. And it preceded by one day the arrival in London of Charles Francis Adams, the new United States minister. The recognition of belligerency thus appeared to present Adams with a *fait accompli* to soften him up for the next step—diplomatic recognition of southern nationhood. As Seward viewed it, Russell's meetings with Yancey and his colleagues were "liable to be construed as recognition." The South did so construe them; and the *Richmond Whig* considered the proclamation of neutrality "a long and firm [step] in exactly the direction which the people of the Southern States expected."[22]

All spring Seward had been growing more agitated by British policy. When he learned of Russell's meetings with the rebel commissioners, he exploded in anger. "God damn them, I'll give them hell," he told Sumner. On May 21 Seward sent an undiplomatic dispatch to Adams instructing him to break off relations if the British government had any

---

21. Sumner quoted in Norman Graebner, "Seward's Diplomacy," unpublished ms., p. 6; Russell quoted in Robert H. Jones, *Disrupted Decades: The Civil War and Reconstruction Years* (New York, 1973), 363.

22. Jenkins, *Britain and the War for the Union*, I, 104, 109.

more dealings with southern envoys. If Britain officially recognized the Confederacy, "we from that hour, shall cease to be friends and become once more, as we have twice before been forced to be, enemies of Great Britain."[23]

Lincoln had tried with only partial success to soften Seward's language. The president did compel Seward to allow Adams discretion to present the substance of this dispatch verbally rather than handing it intact to Lord Russell. After reading Seward's bellicose words, Adams decided that in this case discretion was indeed the better part of valor. Adams had been a superb choice for the London legation. His grandfather and father had preceded him there; Charles had spent much of his youth in the St. Petersburg and London legations. His reserve and self-restraint struck an empathic chord among Englishmen, who were offended by the braggadocio they attributed to American national character. Adams and Lord Russell took each other's measure at their first meeting, and liked what they saw. Adams concealed Seward's iron fist in a velvet glove. Equally urbane, Russell assured the American minister that Britain had no present intention of granting diplomatic recognition to the Confederacy. The foreign secretary conceded that he had twice met with the southern commissioners, but "had no expectation of seeing them any more."[24]

Nor did he. It took some time for this message to sink into the minds of the southern envoys, who continued to send optimistic reports to Richmond. In September 1861, however, Yancey grew restless and he resigned. At the same time the Confederate government decided to replace the commissioners with ministers plenipotentiary in major European capitals. Richmond sent James Mason of Virginia to London and John Slidell of Louisiana to Paris.

By so doing the South unwittingly set in motion a series of events that almost brought Anglo-American relations to a rupture. The departure of Mason and Slidell from Charleston by blockade runner was scarcely a secret. The U. S. navy was embarrassed by its failure to intercept their ship before it reached Havana, where the diplomats transferred to the British steamer *Trent*. Captain Charles Wilkes decided to redeem the navy's reputation. A forty-year veteran now commanding

23. David Donald, *Charles Sumner and the Rights of Man* (New York, 1970), 21; Jenkins, *Britain and the War for the Union*, I, 104.
24. Ephraim D. Adams, *Great Britain and the American Civil War*, 2 vols. (New York, 1925), I, 106.

the thirteen-gun sloop *U. S. S. San Jacinto,* Wilkes was a headstrong, temperamental man who fancied himself an expert on maritime law. Diplomatic dispatches could be seized as contraband of war; Wilkes decided to capture Mason and Slidell as the "embodiment of despatches."[25] This novel interpretation of international law was never tested, for instead of capturing the *Trent* as a prize after stopping her on the high seas on November 8, Wilkes arrested Mason and Slidell and let the ship go on.

The northern public greeted Wilkes's act with applause; "the people," reported a journalist, "are glad to see John Bull taken by the horns." The House of Representatives passed a resolution lauding Wilkes. But after the first flush of jubilation, second thoughts began to arise. Few expected Britain to take this lying down. The risk of war sent the American stock market into a dive. Government bonds found no buyers. News from Britain confirmed fears of an ugly confrontation. The British expressed outrage at Wilkes's "impressment" of Mason and Slidell. The Union Jack had been flouted. The jingo press clamored for war. Prime Minister Palmerston told his cabinet: "You may stand for this but damned if I will."[26] The cabinet voted to send Washington an ultimatum demanding an apology and release of the Confederate diplomats. Britain ordered troops to Canada and strengthened the western Atlantic fleet. War seemed imminent.

Although the Anglophobe press in America professed to welcome this prospect, cooler heads recognized the wisdom of Lincoln's reported words: "One war at a time." The Union army's capacity to carry on even that one war was threatened by an aspect of the *Trent* crisis unknown to the public and rarely mentioned by historians. In 1861, British India was the Union's source of saltpeter, the principal ingredient of gunpowder. The war had drawn down saltpeter stockpiles to the danger point. In the fall of 1861 Seward sent a member of the du Pont company to England on a secret mission to buy all available supplies of saltpeter there and on the way from India. The agent did so, and was loading five ships with 2,300 tons of the mineral when news of the *Trent* reached London. The government clamped an embargo on all shipments to the United States until the crisis was resolved. No settlement, no saltpeter.[27]

25. Wilkes's official report, *Senate Exec. Docs.,* 37 Cong., 2 Sess., III, 123.
26. Norman B. Ferris, *The Trent Affair: A Diplomatic Crisis* (Knoxville, 1977), 29; Nevins, *War,* I, 388.
27. Alfred D. Chandler, Jr., "Du Pont, Dahlgren, and the Civil War Nitre Shortage," in *Military Analysis of the Civil War* (New York, 1977), 201–2.

This issue among others was very much on Lincoln's and Seward's minds during the tense weeks of December 1861. The problem was how to defuse the crisis without the humiliation of bowing to an ultimatum. Seward recognized that Wilkes had violated international law by failing to bring the *Trent* into port for adjudication before a prize court. In an uncharacteristic mood of moderation, Seward expressed a willingness to yield Mason and Slidell on the grounds that Wilkes had acted without instructions. Diplomatic hints had come from London that this face-saving compromise would be acceptable to the British. In a crucial Christmas day meeting, Lincoln and his cabinet concluded that they had no choice but to let Mason and Slidell go. Most of the press had reached the same conclusion, so release would not peril the administration's public support. Mason and Slidell resumed their interrupted trip to Europe, where they never again came so close to winning foreign intervention as they had done by being captured in November 1861. Their release punctured the war bubble. Du Pont's saltpeter left port and was soon turned into gunpowder for the Union army.

The afterglow of this settlement left Anglo-American relations in better shape than before the crisis. "The first effect of the release of Messrs. Mason and Slidell has been extraordinary," wrote young Henry Adams from the American legation in London, where he served as secretary to his father. "The current which ran against us with such extreme violence six weeks ago now seems to be going with equal fury in our favor." [28] This new current was strengthened by reports of the northern victories along the Atlantic coast—and even more by news of remarkable Union military successes in the West.

28. Worthington C. Ford, ed., *A Cycle of Adams Letters, 1861–1865*, 2 vols. (Boston, 1920), I, 99.

13

The River War in 1862

I

Before February 1862 there had been little fighting along the rivers south of Cairo, Illinois. But in the next four months these rivers became the scene of decisive action. The strategic value of the river network radiating from Cairo had been clear from the outset. This southernmost city in the free states grew into a large military and naval base. From there, army-navy task forces launched invasions up the Tennessee and Cumberland rivers (southward) and down the Mississippi in 1862.

One reason for the success of these offensives lay in the harmonious teamwork of the navy and army commanders at Cairo: the God-fearing, teetotaling, antislavery Connecticut Yankee Flag-Officer Andrew H. Foote; and Brigadier-General Ulysses S. Grant, who may have feared God but was indifferent toward slavery and not noted for abstinence. It was lucky for the North that Grant and Foote worked well together, because the institutional arrangements for army-navy cooperation left much to be desired. On the theory that inland operations—even on water—were the army's province, the War Department built the first gunboats for western river operations. Naval officers commanded the vessels but army officers controlled their operations. Crews for these gunboats were a mixed lot—volunteer riverboatmen, soldiers detailed from the army, civilian steamboat pilots and engineers, and a few Jack Tars recruited from the salt-water navy. Not until the autumn of 1862 did Congress rectify this anomalous arrangement by placing the river squadrons under navy control. Yet the river fleet won its greatest victories during the early, makeshift months.

The gunboats of this navy were the creation of James B. Eads, the Ericsson of the fresh-water navy. A native of Indiana who had established a boat-building business in St. Louis, Eads contracted in August 1861 to construct seven shallow-draft gunboats for river work. When completed before the end of the year, these craft looked like no other vessel in existence. They were flat-bottomed, wide-beamed, and paddle-wheeled, with their machinery and crew quarters protected by a sloping casemate sheathed in iron armor up to 2.5 inches thick. Because this casemate, designed by naval constructor Samuel Pook, reminded observers of a turtle shell, the boats were nicknamed "Pook's turtles." Although strange in appearance, these formidable craft each carried thirteen guns and were more than a match for the few converted steamboats the South could bring against them.

For defense against river-borne invasions the Confederacy relied mainly on forts. These were particularly strong on the Mississippi. At Columbus, Kentucky, only fifteen miles below Cairo, General Leonidas Polk had fortified the heights with 140 heavy guns. Well might the Confederates boast about this "Gibraltar of the West," for nothing that floated, not even Pook's turtles, seemed likely to get past those guns. Just to make sure, though, the southerners fortified several other strongpoints along the 150 miles of river down to Memphis. In strange contrast to these Gibraltars, the forts protecting the Tennessee and Cumberland rivers just south of the Kentucky border were poorly sited and unfinished at the end of 1861. Perhaps this was because the Mississippi loomed so large in southern consciousness, while the Tennessee and the Cumberland seemed less important. Yet these rivers penetrated one of the principal grain-growing, mule- and horse-breeding, and iron-producing areas of the Confederacy. The iron works at Clarksville on the Cumberland were second in the South only to Tredegar at Richmond, while Nashville on the same river was a major producer of gunpowder and the main supply depot for Confederate forces in the West.

These forces were commanded by Albert Sidney Johnston, the highest-ranking field officer in the Confederacy. A native of Kentucky who had fought for both Texas and the United States against Mexico, Johnston was commander of the Pacific Department in California when the Civil War began. Like Robert E. Lee, he declined a high commission in the Union army and made his way across the Southwest, dodging Apaches and Union patrols on his way to join the Confederacy. Tall, well-built, possessing a sense of humor and a manner of quiet authority, Johnston looked like the great soldier he was reputed to be. Jefferson Davis had admired him as a fellow student at Transylvania University and West Point in the 1820s, and had fought with him in the Black Hawk and Mexican wars. While Davis was forming a low opinion of the other Johnston—Joseph—he pronounced Albert Sidney "the greatest soldier, the ablest man, civil or military, Confederate or Federal."[1]

Johnston's Western Military Department stretched from the Appalachians to the Ozarks. By early 1862 he had about 70,000 troops on this 500-mile line facing half again as many Federals stretched along a line of similar length from eastern Kentucky to southwest Missouri. The northerners, however, were handicapped by divided authority. In November, Henry W. Halleck had replaced Frémont as commander of the Department of Missouri. Halleck's authority extended as far east as the Cumberland River. Beyond it, Don Carlos Buell headed the Department of the Ohio, with headquarters in Louisville.

The outbreak of war had found Halleck and Buell, like Johnston, in California. Their prewar careers had also produced reputations that led their countrymen to expect great things of them. Halleck had graduated near the top of his West Point class. He wrote *Elements of Military Art and Science*, essentially a paraphrase of Jomini's writings, and translated Jomini's *Life of Napoleon*. These works earned Halleck renown as a strategic theorist. Old Brains, as he was sometimes called (though not to his face), had resigned from the army in 1854 to become a businessman and lawyer in California, where he wrote two books on mining law and declined a judgeship on the state supreme court. Although balding and paunchy, with a double chin, goggle eyes, and an irritable temper, Halleck inspired confidence as a military administrator. In his early months of command he performed up to expectations, bringing order out of the chaos left by Frémont and organizing efficiently the logistical apparatus for 90,000 soldiers and the fresh-water navy in his department. Buell also proved himself an able administrator. Like McClellan, who sponsored his assignment to Louisville, Buell was a firm disciplinarian who knew how to turn raw recruits into soldiers. But unlike McClellan, he lacked charisma and was never popular with his men.

Lincoln repeatedly urged Halleck and Buell to cooperate in a joint offensive against Johnston all along the line from the Mississippi to the

1. Foote, *Civil War*, I, 169.

Appalachians. The president believed that the North would win this war only by using its superior numbers to attack "different points, at the *same* time" to prevent the enemy from shifting troops from quiet to threatened sectors. But joint action was inhibited by the divided command between Halleck and Buell, each of whom was anxious to outshine the other and both of whom feared to risk failure. Buell professed a willingness to attack the main Confederate force at Bowling Green if supported with a diversionary attack by Halleck up the Tennessee River. But Halleck demurred. "I am not ready to cooperate" with Buell, he informed Lincoln on January 1, 1862. "Too much haste will ruin everything."[2]

Lincoln was beginning to suspect that whatever merits Halleck possessed as an administrator and theorist, he was not a fighting soldier. But Halleck had a fighter under his command: Ulysses S. Grant at Cairo. While Halleck and Buell bickered by telegraph, Grant proposed to act. He urged Halleck to permit him to take his troops and Foote's new gunboats up the Tennessee to capture Fort Henry. Halleck hesitated, refused permission, then reversed himself at the end of January and ordered Grant to go ahead.

Once unleashed, Grant moved with speed and force. This was his first real opportunity to dispel doubts stemming from the drinking problems that had forced his army resignation in 1854. Since re-entering the army in June 1861, Grant had served an apprenticeship in command that had increased his self-confidence. He had discovered that his laconic, informal, commonsense manner inspired respect and obedience from his men. Unlike so many other commanders, Grant rarely clamored for reinforcements, rarely complained, rarely quarreled with associates, but went ahead and did the job with the resources at hand.

Grant's first assignment as colonel of the 21st Illinois had been to attack the camp of a rebel regiment in Missouri. Grant had proved his personal courage as a junior officer in the Mexican War. But now he was in command; he was *responsible*. As his men approached the enemy camp, Grant recalled, "my heart kept getting higher and higher until it felt to me as though it were in my throat. I would have given anything then to have been back in Illinois, but I had not the moral courage to know what to do; I kept right on." It turned out that the Missouri regiment, learning of the Yankee approach, had decamped. Grant suddenly realized that the enemy colonel "had been as much afraid of me as I

2. *CWL*, V, 98; *O.R.*, Ser. I, Vol. 7, p. 526.

had been of him. This was a view of the question I had never taken before; but it was one I never forgot. . . . The lesson was valuable." It was a lesson that McClellan and many other Union commanders, especially in the East, never learned.

A few months after this incident, Grant had taken five regiments from Cairo down the Mississippi to create a diversion in aid of another Union operation in Missouri by attacking a Confederate camp at Belmont, across the river from the southern Gibraltar at Columbus. On November 7, Grant's troops routed a rebel force of equal size but were in turn counterattacked and surrounded by reinforcements from Columbus. Some of Grant's officers panicked and advised surrender; Grant merely said that "we had cut our way in and could cut our way out just as well." So they did, and returned to their transports—not without loss, but having inflicted greater losses on the enemy. Although the battle of Belmont accomplished little in the larger scheme of war and could hardly be called a Union victory, it taught Grant more valuable lessons and demonstrated his coolness under pressure. Lincoln did not know it yet, but here was the general he had been looking for these past six months.[3]

Grant and Foote proposed to attack Fort Henry because they considered it the weak point in Albert Sidney Johnston's line. They were right. Built on a low bank dominated by surrounding hills and threatened with flooding by every rise in the river, the fort did no credit to southern engineering. Preoccupied with the need to defend Columbus and Bowling Green, where he believed the main Union attacks would come, Johnston neglected to strengthen Fort Henry until too late. On February 5, transports protected by four of Foote's ironclads and three wooden gunboats landed Grant's 15,000 troops several miles below Fort Henry. The plan was for the foot-soldiers to attack the fort from the rear while the gunboats shelled it from the river. Roads turned into quagmires by the heavy rain slowed down the troops, however, while the same rain caused the river to flood the fort's lower level. When the Union flotilla hove into sight on February 6, only nine of the fort's guns bore on the enemy, while the boats could fire twice as many guns in return from their bows-on position. Recognizing the odds as hopeless, the fort's commander sent its 2,500-man garrison cross-country to Fort Donelson, twelve miles away on the Cumberland, remaining be-

3. Quotations in these two paragraphs from *Personal Memoirs of U. S. Grant*, 2 vols. (New York, 1885), I, 250, 276.

hind with one artillery company to fight a delaying action against the gunboats.

Under the circumstances the rebel cannoneers performed well. For two hours they slugged it out with the fleet, hitting the boats some eighty times and putting one ironclad out of commission with a shot into the boiler that scalded twenty men to death. But finally the defenders, with half their men killed or wounded and most of their guns disabled, surrendered to the gunboats before Grant's soldiers, slogging through the mud, arrived on the scene. The three wooden gunboats steamed upriver to knock out a railroad bridge on the line linking Johnston's forces at Columbus with those at Bowling Green. The gunboats continued another 150 miles all the way to Muscle Shoals in Alabama, destroying or capturing nine Confederate vessels including one powerful steamboat the rebels had been turning into an ironclad to fight the Yankees on their own terms. Instead it became a part of the invader's fleet, which made of the Tennessee a Union highway into the Deep South.

Grant and Foote wasted no time celebrating their victory. "Fort Henry is ours," Grant telegraphed Halleck on February 6. "I shall take and destroy Fort Donelson on the 8th."[4] But bad weather delayed the supplying and marching of his troops overland, while Foote had to repair his battered gunboats before they could steam back down the Tennessee and up the Cumberland to Donelson. The delay allowed Johnston time to ponder his next move, but this gave him small comfort. The one-two punch of capturing Fort Henry and cutting the railroad south of it had put Grant between Johnston's two main forces. The Yankees could now attack Columbus from the rear, or overwhelm the 5,000 Confederates at Fort Donelson and then steam upriver to take Nashville, or come up behind Johnston's 25,000 at Bowling Green while Buell's 50,000 attacked them from the front. Johnston's only options seemed to be the concentration of all available men (about 35,000) to defend Donelson and perhaps counterattack to regain Fort Henry, or to give up Kentucky and concentrate his whole army to defend the vital factories and depots at Nashville.

An emergency meeting of Confederate brass at Bowling Green on February 7 canvassed these disagreeable choices. Beauregard was there, having just arrived from Virginia, where Jefferson Davis had breathed a sigh of relief at his departure. Ebullient as ever, Beauregard wanted to

4. O.R., Ser. I, Vol. 7, p. 125.

smash Grant and Buell in turn. Johnston demurred. Instead of being able to fight the two enemy forces separately, he feared that his entire army would be flattened between Grant's hammer and Buell's anvil. Johnston preferred retreat to the Nashville-Memphis line, leaving a to- ken force at Donelson to delay Grant and saving the bulk of the army to fight another day under more favorable conditions. In effect, John- ston proposed to abandon the strategy of dispersed defensive in favor of concentration for a possible offensive-defensive stroke. It was a good plan. But unaccountably Johnston changed his mind and decided to make a real fight at Fort Donelson. Instead of taking his whole available force there, however, he sent 12,000 men and retreated with the rest to Nashville. To command at Donelson, Johnston assigned none other than John Floyd, who had been transferred to Kentucky after helping to lose West Virginia. Floyd's presence made Donelson an even bigger plum for Federal picking, since he was a wanted man in the North for fraud and alleged transfer of arms to southern arsenals as Buchanan's secretary of war.

But picking that plum would give Grant and Foote more trouble than they anticipated. And in the end they did not get Floyd. "Fort" Donel- son was not really a fort; rather, it was a stockade enclosing fifteen acres of soldiers' huts and camp equipment. The business end of the defenses were two batteries of twelve heavy guns dug into the side of a hundred- foot bluff on the Cumberland to repel attack by water, and three semi- circular miles of trenches to repel it by land. Southern soldiers were strengthening these trenches as Grant's confident 15,000 Yankees ap- proached on February 12. Probing attacks next day were repulsed, con- vincing Grant that Donelson would not topple without a fight. Ten thousand Union reinforcements arrived on February 14 along with four of Foote's ironclads and two wooden gunboats. Hoping to repeat the Fort Henry experience, Grant ordered the navy to shell the fort while his troops closed the ring to prevent the garrison's escape. But this time the navy met more than its match. Foote brought his ironclads too close, causing them to overshoot their targets and giving the shorter- range Confederate guns a chance to rake them with plunging shots that riddled smokestacks, shot away tiller ropes, cracked armor, and smashed through pilot houses and decks into the bowels of the gunboats. One by one these crippled monsters drifted downstream out of the fight. Each had taken some forty or more hits; fifty-four sailors were dead or wounded while not a gun or man in the rebel batteries had been lost. The morale of the southerners, who had believed the gunboats invincible, soared.

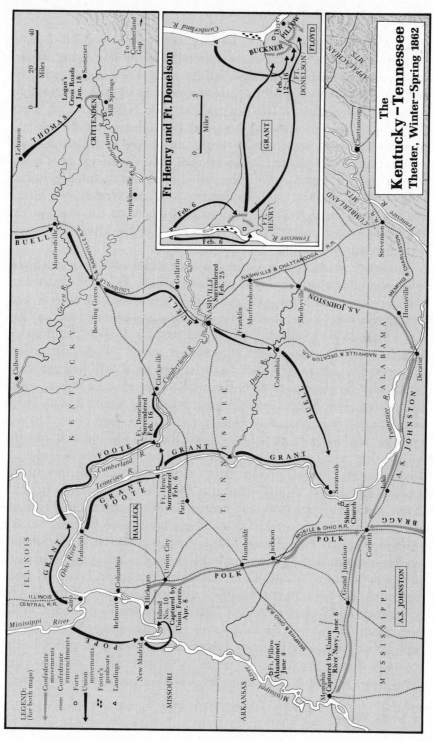

The Kentucky–Tennessee Theater, Winter–Spring 1862

Ft. Henry and Ft. Donelson

LEGEND:
(for both maps)
— Confederate movements
mmmm Confederate entrenchments
□ Forts
— Union movements
♦♦♦ Foote's gunboats
▲ Landings

Miles
0   20   40

Miles
0   3

Lebanon

THOMAS

CRITTENDEN
Somerset
Logan's Cross Roads
Jan. 18
Mill Springs
Cumberland R.
To Cumberland Gap

Tompkinsville

Munfordville

BUELL

Green R.

Calhoun

KENTUCKY

Bowling Green

LOUISVILLE & NASHVILLE R.R.

Gallatin

ILLINOIS

ILLINOIS CENTRAL R.R.

Cairo
Paducah
Ohio River

Columbus
Belmont

Hickman

Union City

POLK

New Madrid
Island No. 10
Captured by Union Forces, Apr. 8

Mississippi River

MISSOURI

ARKANSAS

GRANT

FOOTE

GRANT

HALLECK

Cumberland R.
Tennessee R.

Ft. Donelson Surrendered Feb. 16

Ft. Henry Surrendered Feb. 6

Clarksville

Paris

TENNESSEE

NASHVILLE, Surrendered Feb. 25

BUELL

Franklin
Murfreesboro

Cumberland R.

Duck R.

Columbia

Shelbyville

NASHVILLE & CHATTANOOGA

A. S. JOHNSTON

NASHVILLE & DECATUR R.R.

GRANT

Savannah
Iuka

Shiloh Church

Corinth

Jackson
Humboldt

MOBILE & OHIO R.R.

POLK

Grand Junction

MEMPHIS & OHIO R.R.

MEMPHIS & CHARLESTON R.R.

Ft. Pillow Abandoned, June 4

Memphis Captured by Union River Navy, June 6

MISSISSIPPI

A.S. JOHNSTON

BRAGG

ALABAMA

Tennessee R.

Huntsville
Stevenson

Decatur

CUMBERLAND MTS.

APPALACHIAN MTS.

Chattanooga

Cumberland R.

BUCKNER

Feb. 12–16
FT. DONELSON

PILLOW
FLOYD
Dover

GRANT

Feb. 6

FT. HENRY

Tennessee R.

Feb. 6

POPE

399

Their elation was premature, for they were still surrounded on three sides by better-armed foot soldiers and on the fourth by floating artillery which, though bruised, yet controlled the river. The besieged defenders had three apparent choices: to surrender now; to sit tight and hope for a miracle; or to cut their way out and escape to Nashville. That night, while Union soldiers who had thrown away blankets and overcoats on a previous balmy day shivered and caught pneumonia in driving sleet and snow, Confederate generals held a council of war to decide what to do. Floyd's division commanders, the self-important Tennessee politician Gideon Pillow and the darkly handsome, saturnine West Pointer Simon Bolivar Buckner, agreed to try a breakout attack on the morrow. All night they shifted troops to Pillow's sector on the left. These movements were masked by the snow and howling winds.

As chance would have it, Grant was downstream conferring with Foote when the rebel attack exploded soon after dawn. The north wind blew the sound of battle away and kept him in ignorance of what was happening five miles to the south. Not expecting any fighting that day "unless I brought it on myself," Grant had told his division commanders merely to hold their positions until further notice.[5] These instructions anticipated a pattern in Grant's generalship: he always thought more about what he planned to do to the enemy than what his enemy might do to him. This offensive-mindedness eventually won the war, but it also brought near disaster to Grant's forces more than once. On this occasion his orders to sit tight inhibited the two division commanders on the left and center from doing much to help General John A. McClernand's division on the right, which bore the full fury of the Confederate assault. McClernand was an ambitious Democrat from Illinois whose thirst for glory had earned Grant's mistrust. On this frosty morning of February 15 McClernand got his chance to fight, but the odds were against him. Many of his regiments performed well, but after several hours of hard fighting five brigades on the Union right had been driven back nearly a mile. Demoralized and out of ammunition, they were in no condition to stop the rebels from escaping through the breach.

Couriers had dashed off to find Grant, who returned post-haste to the battlefield. Meanwhile his adversaries had suffered a strange lapse of will. As he rode along his lines, General Pillow was taken aback by the exhaustion and disorganization of his victorious soldiers, who had suffered heavy casualties. He concluded that they could not march cross-

5. Grant, *Memoirs*, I, 305.

country and fight off a possible flank attack by the Union reinforcements that his scouts reported were gathering. Pillow persuaded Floyd, over Buckner's agonized protest, to call off the breakout attempt and order the troops back to the relative safety of their trenches.

During this lull of Confederate indecision, Grant arrived on the scene. As at Belmont, he refused to panic. "The position on the right must be retaken," he told his officers. "Some of our men are pretty badly demoralized, but the enemy must be more so, for he has attempted to force his way out, but has fallen back: the one who attacks first now will be victorious and the enemy will have to be in a hurry if he gets ahead of me."[6] Grant asked Foote to have the gunboats lob a few shells at the rebels to give the infantry moral support. While this request was being carried out, Union officers reorganized their brigades, counterattacked, and regained the ground lost in the morning.

Night fell on a dismal scene. Nearly a thousand Yankees and rebels had been killed and three thousand wounded, many of the latter suffering and dying in the thickening cold. A chill also fell on southern headquarters, where mutual recriminations hung heavy in the air. A planned night-time escape of the garrison was aborted when scouts reported Union regiments camped near the only practicable road. Pillow still wanted the garrison to fight its way out, but Floyd and Buckner, convinced that such false heroics would sacrifice three-fourths of their men, considered surrender the only alternative. As political generals, however, Floyd and Pillow did not want to surrender their own persons. Remembering his prewar record, Floyd anticipated little mercy from his captors. He commandeered two steamboats docked near Donelson and escaped downriver with 1,500 of his Virginia troops in the darkness before dawn. The disputatious Pillow was no more eager than Floyd to become a prisoner of war. Having proclaimed "liberty or death" as his slogan, he chose liberty—and escaped with his staff across the Cumberland in a skiff. Before leaving, Floyd had turned the command of Fort Donelson over to Pillow who in turn passed it to West Pointer Buckner. Disgusted by this opéra bouffe, Buckner intended to share the fate of his men.

Before surrendering, however, Buckner permitted another disgusted commander to escape with his men—Nathan Bedford Forrest, head of a cavalry battalion that had fought with distinction that day. A self-made man who had grown rich from slave trading and planting, Forrest en-

6. Lew Wallace, "The Capture of Fort Donelson," Battles and Leaders, I, 422; Grant, Memoirs, I, 307.

listed as a private in June 1861 and rose to lieutenant-colonel of the battalion he raised and equipped at his own expense. Self-educated, with no previous military experience, Forrest became one of the South's most innovative and hard-driving commanders. He developed combined mounted and dismounted tactics not mentioned in military textbooks—which he had never read—but ideal for the wooded terrain of western Tennessee and northern Mississippi. A large, powerful, and fearless man, Forrest possessed a killer instinct toward Yankees and toward blacks in any capacity other than slave. Before daybreak on February 16 he led 700 troopers out of Fort Donelson across an icy stream too deep for infantry to ford, and escaped without encountering a single Union picket.

Soon after dawn on February 16, Buckner sent a proposal to Grant for discussion of surrender terms. Back came a blunt reply: "No terms except an unconditional and immediate surrender can be accepted. I propose to move immediately on your works." Buckner was nettled by these "ungenerous and unchivalrous" words. After all, he had lent the down-and-out Grant money to help him get home after his resignation from the army in 1854. Nevertheless, Buckner now had no choice but to surrender his twelve or thirteen thousand men.[7] When this news reached the North, church bells rang and cannons fired salutes to celebrate the great victory. Lincoln promoted Grant to major general, making him second in command only to Halleck in the West. Eight months earlier Grant had been an obscure ex-captain of dubious reputation; now his name was celebrated by every newspaper in the land.

The strategic consequences of this campaign were the most important of the war so far. Nearly a third of Johnston's forces in the Tennessee-Kentucky theater were *hors de combat*. Half of the remainder were at Nashville and half at Columbus, 200 miles apart with a victorious enemy between them in control of the rivers and railroads. Buell's unbloodied Army of the Ohio was bearing down on Nashville from the north, while a newly organized Union Army of the Mississippi commanded by John Pope threatened Columbus from across the Mississippi River. Johnston had to evacuate Nashville on February 23, making it

7. O.R., Ser. I, Vol. 7, p. 161. No official record of the number of Confederates surrendered at Donelson was ever made. Of the 17,000 or more men in the garrison, some 500 had been killed. At least 1,000 of the wounded had been evacuated before the surrender. Another 2,000 or more men escaped with Floyd and Forrest, or made their way through the loose Union cordon after the surrender.

the first Confederate state capital and important industrial center to fall. A few days later the garrison at Columbus also pulled out. All of Kentucky and most of Tennessee came under Union military control—save for guerrilla activity and periodic rebel cavalry raids, which thenceforth became endemic in this theater. Confederate forts still guarded the Mississippi along Tennessee's western border, but they seemed doomed as well. The *New York Tribune*, a good barometer of northern opinion, rose as high as it had fallen low after Bull Run: "The cause of the Union now marches on in every section of the country," declared the *Tribune*. "Every blow tells fearfully against the rebellion. The rebels themselves are panic-stricken, or despondent. It now requires no very far-reaching prophet to predict the end of the struggle."[8]

Many rebels were indeed despondent. Southern newspapers and diarists lamented the "disgraceful . . . shameful . . . catalogue of disasters." Mary Boykin Chesnut suffered "nervous chills every day. Bad news is killing me."[9] From London, James Mason reported that "the late reverses at Fort Henry and Fort Donelson have had an unfortunate effect upon the minds of our friends here." In the midst of these gloomy tidings, Jefferson Davis was inaugurated for his six-year presidential term on February 22. Davis and his Negro footmen in the inaugural procession wore black suits. When asked why, the coachman replied dryly: "This, ma'am, is the way we always does in Richmond at funerals and sichlike." The rain that poured down during the ceremony added to the funereal atmosphere. In his inaugural address, Davis conceded that "after a series of successes and victories, we have recently met with serious disasters."[10]

Like their northern counterparts after Bull Run, however, southern spokesmen urged renewed dedication to the task. Though "the tide for the moment is against us," Davis continued, "the final result in our favor is never doubtful. . . . It was, perhaps, in the ordination of Prov-

8. *New York Tribune*, February 12, 1862, quoted in Kenneth P. Williams, *Lincoln Finds a General*, 5 vols. (1949–59), III, 231.

9. Jones, *War Clerk's Diary* (Miers), 67; E. Merton Coulter, *The Confederate States of America* (Baton Rouge, 1950), 353n; Woodward, *Chesnut's Civil War*, 286.

10. Ephraim D. Adams, *Great Britain and the American Civil War*, 2 vols. (New York, 1925), I, 272–73; Hudson Strode, *Jefferson Davis: Confederate President* (New York, 1959), 201, 199. Before February 22, 1862, Davis and his fellow officers of the Confederate government were "provisional" officials. A general election took place in November 1861. Davis and Vice President Stephens were then elected without opposition and inaugurated on Washington's birthday in 1862.

idence that we were taught the value of our liberties by the price we pay for them." The losses of Forts Henry and Donelson "were for our own good!" according to Richmond newspapers. "Days of adversity prove the worth of men and of nations. . . . We must go to the work with greater earnestness than we have yet shown."[11]

But southerners were fated to endure several more defeats before they could next celebrate a victory. Johnston's defensive line east of the Mississippi having collapsed in February, his line west of the river caved in the following month. A new general had taken command of the rebel forces in Arkansas—Earl Van Dorn, a diminutive but hard-bitten Mississippian who had been wounded five times in the Mexican War and in frontier Indian fighting. Van Dorn had dazzled Johnston with visions of an invasion through Missouri to capture St. Louis and then to descend on Grant's forces from the north. To do this, however, he first had to defeat a Union army of 11,000 men that had pushed Sterling Price's Missourians out of their home state during the winter. Van Dorn put together a motley force numbering 16,000, consisting of the divisions under Price and Ben McCulloch that had won at Wilson's Creek the previous August plus three regiments of Indians from the Five Civilized Nations in Indian Territory. The latter, mostly Cherokees, served under chiefs who had made treaties of alliance with the Confederacy in the hope of achieving greater independence within a southern nation than they enjoyed in the United States—an ironic hope, since it was mostly southerners who had driven them from their ancestral homeland a generation earlier. In any event, with Indian help the old Indian fighter Van Dorn intended to "make a reputation and serve my country. . . . I must have St. Louis—then Huzza!"[12]

The small Union army standing in Van Dorn's way just south of Pea Ridge on the Arkansas-Missouri border was commanded by Samuel R. Curtis, a colorless but competent West Pointer who had fought in Mexico and subsequently served three terms as an Iowa congressman. Rather than attack Curtis's entrenched troops frontally, Van Dorn led his army on a long flanking march to cut Union supply lines and attack them from the rear. Alert northern scouts, including "Wild Bill" Hickok, detected the move. When Van Dorn attacked what he expected to be the

11. Strode, *Davis*, 202; *Richmond Enquirer*, Feb. 18, 1862; *Richmond Examiner*, Feb. 19, 1862.
12. Robert G. Hartje, *Van Dorn: The Life and Times of a Confederate General* (Nashville, 1967), 105.

enemy rear on the bleak, overcast morning of March 7, he found that Curtis had faced his troops about and was ready for him. On the Union left, artillery fire scattered the Indian regiments while Yankee riflemen killed McCulloch and his second in command and captured the third-ranking southern officer on that part of the field, taking all the steam out of the rebel attack. Meanwhile, Union infantry on the right three miles to the east, outnumbered by more than two to one, had grudgingly given ground in fierce fighting around Elkhorn Tavern at a critical road junction.

Next morning Van Dorn discovered that when you get in the enemy's rear, he is also in yours. Confederate troops had run short of ammunition but the Union army now stood between them and their ammunition wagons. Both armies concentrated near Elkhorn Tavern, where a Federal artillery barrage knocked out southern batteries that did not have enough shells for effective counterfire. Seven thousand Union infantrymen swept forward in a picture-book charge led by Franz Sigel's division of German-American regiments from Missouri and Illinois. The rebels turned tail and ran. It was as inglorious a rout in reverse as Bull Run. Although each side suffered about 1,300 casualties, the battle of Pea Ridge was the most one-sided victory won by an outnumbered Union army during the war. Van Dorn's forces scattered in every direction. It took nearly two weeks to reassemble them. Johnston then ordered Van Dorn to bring his 15,000 men across the Mississippi to Corinth, a rail junction in northern Mississippi. But they did not arrive in time to take part in the ensuing battle near a small log church named Shiloh.

II

Criticism of Sidney Johnston rose to a crescendo after the losses in Tennessee, almost as if in mockery of the earlier praise for him. Newspapers charged him with incompetence, drunkenness, even treason. Tennessee congressmen petitioned Davis for his removal from command. But Davis was not stampeded by this "senseless clamor." "If Sidney Johnston is not a general," said the president, "we had better give up the war, for we have no general."[13] Johnston refused to reply to his critics. "The

13. James Lee McDonough, *Shiloh—In Hell before Night* (Knoxville, 1977), 60; Charles P. Roland, *Albert Sidney Johnston: Soldier of Three Republics* (Austin, Texas, 1964), 299. Davis's charity did not extend to Floyd and Pillow, who had abandoned their post at Fort Donelson. Both were suspended from duty and never again given a field command. Floyd died in 1863.

test of merit, in my profession . . . is success," he wrote privately. "It is a hard rule, but I think it right. . . . What the people want is a battle and a victory."[14]

Depressed in spirit, Johnston seemed to have little hope of achieving that victory. Beauregard stepped into the breach and helped Johnston concentrate 42,000 men at Corinth, Mississippi—27,000 from the reunited wings of Johnston's army plus 15,000 brought up from New Orleans and Mobile. Commander of the latter was Braxton Bragg, a quick-tempered martinet whose arrival injected some discipline into an army dispirited by defeat. Bragg's departure from the Gulf Coast left that region denuded of infantry and vulnerable to an amphibious attack, but southern strategists considered it essential to defend Corinth, the junction of the Confederacy's main north-south and east-west railroads in the Mississippi Valley. Beauregard wanted to do more than that; he hoped to march north and sweep the Yankees out of Tennessee. "We must do something," said Beauregard, "or die in the attempt, otherwise, all will be shortly lost."[15] Johnston caught Beauregard's vision and energy. Together they planned an offensive to regain Tennessee.

Having taken credit (as department commander) for Grant's and Foote's victories at Forts Henry and Donelson, Halleck had been promoted to the command of all Union troops west of the Appalachians. He sent Grant forward to Pittsburg Landing on the Tennessee River, twenty miles north of Corinth, and ordered Buell to join him there with 35,000 additional troops. When the two armies were united, Halleck intended to take field command of their 75,000 men and lead them against Corinth. But the rebels meant to hit Grant before Buell arrived. Beauregard drew up plans for a march by four different corps on converging roads to deploy for battle on April 4. The plans were better suited for veterans than for green troops and inexperienced staff officers. Few of these southern soldiers had made a one-day march of twenty miles, and fewer still had been in combat. In these respects Johnston's troops resembled the Federals that McDowell had led to Bull Run nine months earlier. Their experiences during the next few days also replicated those of McDowell's men. The march turned into a nightmare of confusion and delays as the divisions of one corps blocked the road where divisions of

14. Foote, *Civil War*, I, 234; Johnston to Davis, March 18, 1862, printed in Wallace, "The Capture of Fort Donelson," *Battles and Leaders*, I, 399n.
15. T. Harry Williams, *P.T.G. Beauregard: Napoleon in Gray* (Baton Rouge, 1955), 121.

another were supposed to pass, units took wrong turns and got lost, and drenching showers bogged down wagons and artillery. April 4 came and went with almost no Confederates arriving at the designated point; April 5 came and was almost gone before the army had deployed in position.

By this time Beauregard was in despair and wanted to call off the attack. The two-day delay, he said, would mean that Buell had reinforced Grant. Beauregard was also certain that the noise made by rebel soldiers firing off their guns to see if rain-dampened powder still worked had eliminated all chance of surprise.[16] But at a council of war on the afternoon of April 5, Johnston overruled his objections. Having finally gotten the army into position to fight, Johnston was not about to back down. Confederate colonels had already read out to their regiments Johnston's address pledging to lead them to "a decisive victory over agrarian mercenaries, sent to subjugate and despoil you of your liberties, property, and honor. . . . Remember the dependence of your mothers, your wives, your sisters, and your children on the result. . . . With such incentives to brave deeds . . . your generals will lead you confidently to the combat." No matter if Buell had reinforced Grant, said Johnston, "I would fight them if they were a million." He ordered his corps commanders to finish their preparations: "Gentlemen, we shall attack at daylight tomorrow."[17]

The facts on which Beauregard based his counsel of caution should have been true—but they were not. Buell's lead division had indeed arrived at Savannah, Grant's headquarters nine miles downriver from Pittsburg Landing. But neither Grant nor Buell felt a sense of urgency, so they did not send this division forward or hurry the arrival of the others. Five of Grant's six divisions were camped on the tableland west of Pittsburg Landing. The sixth, under General Lew Wallace (future author of *Ben-Hur*), was stationed five miles to the north guarding the army's supply depots at another river landing. Grant had evidently forgotten the lesson of Fort Donelson, for once again he focused his mind so intently on plans for attacking the rebels that he could spare no thoughts for what the rebels might be planning to do to him. Grant's whole army was equally offensive-minded. They shared their commander's conviction that defeat had so demoralized Johnston's army that "Corinth will fall much more easily than Donelson did when we do move. All ac-

16. Since northern soldiers were doing the same, however, the noise of such shots would not necessarily have aroused suspicions among Union officers.

17. O.R., Ser. I, Vol. 10, pt. 1, pp. 396–97; McDonough, *Shiloh*, 81.

counts agree in saying that the great mass of the rank and file are heartily tired."[18]

Grant did not entrench his men at Pittsburg Landing because he did not expect to fight there and did not want to rob them of their aggressive spirit. Regiments laid out their camps with no idea of forming a defensive line. Their picket posts and patrols were inadequate to detect enemy movements more than a few hundred yards away. The two divisions nearest Corinth, which would receive the first thrust of any attack, were composed of new troops untried by combat. Commanding one of these divisions was William Tecumseh Sherman, recently restored to command. Like Grant, Sherman was overconfident. Five months earlier the press had labeled him insane because he had exaggerated the rebel threat in Kentucky. Now, perhaps to prove that he had recovered from his attack of nerves, Sherman underestimated the enemy threat. Some of his front-line colonels thought that the increased noise and activity off to the south on April 4 and 5 indicated the buildup of something big. But Sherman dismissed this activity as nothing more "than some picket firing. . . . I do not apprehend anything like an attack on our position." To one colonel who chattered nervously about thousands of rebels out there in the woods, Sherman reportedly said: "Take your damned regiment back to Ohio. Beauregard is not such a fool as to leave his base of operations and attack us in ours."[19] For his part, Grant interpreted the signs of rebel movements as a possible threat to Wallace's isolated division downriver, and warned Wallace to be alert. Grant wrote to Halleck on April 5 that he had "scarcely the faintest idea of an attack (general one) being made upon us, but will be prepared should such a thing take place."[20]

But he was not prepared for the thousands of screaming rebels who burst out of the woods near Shiloh church next morning. They hit first the two green divisions of Sherman and of Benjamin M. Prentiss, an Illinois political general with Mexican War experience. Against all odds, Johnston had achieved a surprise—but not a total one, despite later sensationalist stories in northern newspapers that Union camps were overrun while soldiers were still asleep. Long before dawn one of Prentiss's brigade commanders had sent out a patrol that discovered advance

18. Grant to Halleck, March 21, 1862, O.R., Ser. I, Vol. 10, pt. 2, p. 55.
19. O.R., Ser. I, Vol. 10, pt. 2, p. 94; John K. Duke, *History of the 53rd Ohio Volunteer Infantry* (Portsmouth, Ohio, 1900), 41.
20. O.R., Ser. I, Vol. 10, pt. 1, p. 89.

units of the Confederate battle line. The patrol fell back slowly, skirmishing noisily to warn Prentiss's division, which scrambled into formation. Sherman's men also jumped up from breakfast and grabbed their muskets. As their commander rode forward to see what was happening, a volley rang out and Sherman's orderly fell dead at his side. "My God, we're attacked!" cried the general, finally convinced. After the initial shock, Sherman performed this day with coolness and courage. The next twelve hours proved to be the turning point of his life. What he learned that day at Shiloh—about war and about himself— helped to make him one of the North's premier generals. Sherman was everywhere along his lines at Shiloh, shoring up his raw troops and inspiring them to hurl back the initial assaults—with staggering losses on both sides. Sherman himself was wounded slightly (twice) and had three horses shot under him. On his left Prentiss's men also stood fast at first, while up from the rear came reinforcements from the other three divisions, two of which had fought at Donelson.

Waiting for Buell's arrival at army headquarters nine miles downriver, Grant heard the firing as he sat down to breakfast. Commandeering a dispatch boat, he steamed up to Pittsburg Landing and arrived on the battlefield about 9:00 a.m. The fighting by this time had reached a level unprecedented in the war. Johnston and Beauregard committed all six of their divisions early in the day; all of Grant's soldiers in the vicinity also double-timed to the front, which stretched six miles between the Tennessee River on the Union left and Owl Creek on the right. Grant sent a courier to summon Lew Wallace's division to the battlefield. But Wallace took the wrong road and had to countermarch, arriving too late to participate in the battle on April 6. For better or worse, Grant's five divisions on the field had to do all the fighting that first day at Shiloh.

For thousands of them the shock of "seeing the elephant" (the contemporary expression for experiencing combat) was too much. They fled to the rear and cowered under the bluffs at the landing. Fortunately for the Union side, thousands of southern boys also ran from the front with terror in their eyes. One of the main tasks of commanders on both sides was to reorganize their shattered brigades and plug holes caused by this leakage to the rear and mounting casualties. Grant visited each of his division commanders during the day and established a line of reorganized stragglers and of artillery along the ridge west of Pittsburg Landing to make a last-ditch stand if the rebels got that far. Johnston went personally to the front on the Confederate right to rally exhausted troops by his presence. There in midafternoon he was hit in the leg by a bullet that severed an artery and caused him to bleed to death almost before he realized he had been wounded.

Beauregard took command and tried to keep up the momentum of the attack. By this time the plucky southerners had driven back the Union right and left two miles from their starting point. In the center, though, Prentiss with the remaining fragments of his division and parts of two others had formed a hard knot of resistance along a country lane that northern soldiers called the sunken road and rebels called the hornets' nest. Grant had ordered Prentiss to "maintain that position at all hazards."[21] Prentiss obeyed the order literally. Instead of containing and bypassing this position (a tactical maneuver not yet developed), southern commanders launched a dozen separate assaults against it. Although 18,000 Confederates closed in on Prentiss's 4,500 men, the uncoordinated nature of rebel attacks enabled the Yankees to repel each of them. The southerners finally pounded the hornets' nest with sixty-two field guns and surrounded it with infantry. Prentiss surrendered his 2,200 survivors at 5:30, an hour before sunset. Their gritty stand had bought time for Grant to post the remainder of his army along the Pittsburg Landing ridge.

By then, Lew Wallace's lost division was arriving and Buell's lead brigade was crossing the river. Beauregard did not know this yet, but he sensed that his own army was disorganized and fought out. He therefore refused to authorize a final assault in the gathering twilight. Although partisans in the endless postwar postmortems in the South condemned this decision, it was a sensible one. The Union defenders had the advantages of terrain (many of the troops in a Confederate assault would have had to cross a steep backwater ravine) and of a large concentration of artillery—including the eight-inch shells of two gunboats. With the arrival of reinforcements, Yankees also gained the advantage of numbers. On the morrow Buell and Grant would be able to put 25,000 fresh troops into action alongside 15,000 battered but willing survivors who had fought the first day. Casualties and straggling had reduced the number of Beauregard's effectives to about 25,000. Sensing this, Grant never wavered in his determination to counterattack on April 7. When some of his officers advised retreat before the rebels could renew their assault in the morning, Grant replied: "Retreat? No. I propose to attack at daylight and whip them."[22]

21. *Ibid.*, p. 279.
22. Bruce Catton, *Grant Moves South* (Boston, 1960), 241.

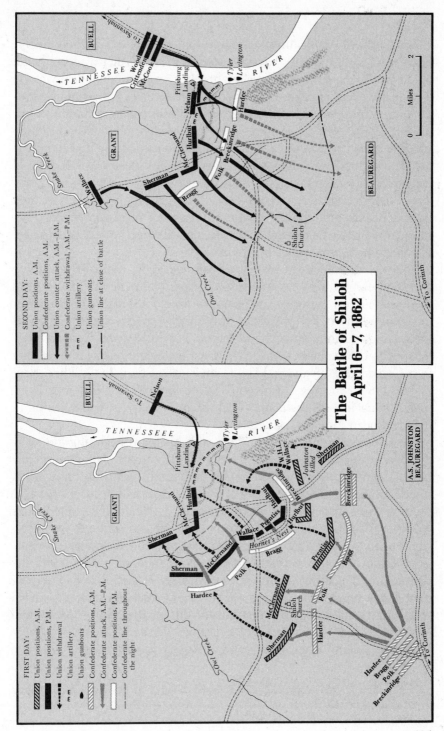

SECOND DAY:

Union positions, A.M.
Confederate positions, A.M.
Confederate counter attack, A.M.–P.M.
Confederate withdrawal, A.M.–P.M.
Union artillery
Union gunboats
Union line at close of battle

**The Battle of Shiloh
April 6–7, 1862**

BUELL

Wood
Crittenden
McCook

TENNESSEE RIVER

Pittsburg
Landing
Nelson

Tyler
Lexington

Hardee

GRANT

McClernand
Hurlbut

Polk Breckinridge

L. Wallace

Sherman

Bragg

Shiloh
Church

BEAUREGARD

Snake Creek

Owl Creek

To Savannah

To Corinth

0   Miles   2

FIRST DAY:

Union positions, A.M.
Union positions, P.M.
Union withdrawal
Union artillery
Union gunboats
Confederate positions, A.M.
Confederate attack, A.M.–P.M.
Confederate positions, P.M.
Confederate line throughout
the night

BUELL

Nelson

TENNESSEEE RIVER

Pittsburg
Landing

Tyler
Lexington

GRANT

W. H. L.
Wallace

Johnston
killed   Sherman

Breckinridge

McClernand
Hurlbut

Hurlbut

Sherman

Wallace Prentiss
Hornet's Nest

Breckinridge

Prentiss

Bragg

McClernand

Bragg

Polk

Sherman

Hardee

McClernand
Shiloh
Church

Polk

Sherman

Hardee

Hardee
Bragg
Polk
Breckinridge

A.S. JOHNSTON
BEAUREGARD

Snake Creek

Owl Creek

To Savannah

To Corinth

411

412   BATTLE CRY OF FREEDOM

Across the lines Beauregard and his men were equally confident. Beauregard sent a victory telegram to Richmond: "After a severe battle of ten hours, thanks be to the Almighty, [we] gained a complete victory, driving the enemy from every position." Tomorrow's task would be simply one of mopping up. If Beauregard had been aware of Grant's reinforcements he would not have been so confident. But the rebel high command had been misled by a report from cavalry in northern Alabama that Buell was heading that way. Cavalry nearer at hand could have told him differently. Nathan Bedford Forrest's scouts watched boats ferry Buell's brigades across the river all through the night. Forrest tried to find Beauregard. Failing in this, he gave up in disgust when other southern generals paid no attention to his warnings. "We'll be whipped like Hell" in the morning, he predicted.[23]

Soldiers on both sides passed a miserable night. Rain began falling and soon came down in torrents on the 95,000 living and 2,000 dead men scattered over twelve square miles from Pittsburgh Landing back to Shiloh church. Ten thousand of the living were wounded, many of them lying in agony amid the downpour. Lightning and thunder alternated with the explosions of shells lobbed by the gunboats all night long into Confederate bivouacs. Despite their exhaustion, few soldiers slept on this "night so long, so hideous." One Union officer wrote that his men, "lying in the water and mud, were as weary in the morning as they had been the evening before."[24]

Grant spent the night on the field with his men, declining the comfort of a steamboat cabin. Four miles away Beauregard slept comfortably in Sherman's captured tent near Shiloh church. Next morning he had a rude awakening. A second day at Shiloh began with a surprise attack, but now the Yankees were doing the attacking. All along the line Buell's Army of the Ohio and Grant's Army of Western Tennessee swept forward, encountering little resistance at first from the disorganized rebels. In mid-morning the southern line stiffened, and for a few hours the conflict raged as hotly as on the previous day. A particularly unnerving sight to advancing Union troops was yesterday's casualties. Some wounded men had huddled together for warmth during the night. "Many had died there, and others were in the last agonies as we passed," wrote a northern soldier. "Their groans and cries were heart-rending. . . . The

23. O.R., Ser. I, Vol. 10, pt. 1, p. 384; Robert S. Henry, "First with the Most" Forrest (Indianapolis, 1944), 79.
24. McDonough, Shiloh, 189, 188.

gory corpses lying all about us, in every imaginable attitude, and slain by an inconceivable variety of wounds, were shocking to behold."[25]

By midafternoon the relentless Union advance had pressed the rebels back to the point of their original attack. Not only did the Yankees have fresh troops and more men, but the southerners' morale had suffered a letdown when they realized they had not won a victory after all. About 2:30 Beauregard's chief of staff said to the general: "Do you not think our troops are very much in the condition of a lump of sugar thoroughly soaked with water, but yet preserving its original shape, though ready to dissolve? Would it not be judicious to get away with what we have?"[26] Beauregard agreed, and issued the order to retreat. The blue-coats, too fought out and shot up for effective pursuit over muddy roads churned into ooze by yet another downpour, flopped down in exhaustion at the recaptured camps. Next day Sherman did take two tired brigades in pursuit four miles down the Corinth road, but returned after a brief skirmish with Forrest's cavalry that accomplished little more than the wounding of Forrest. Both the blue and the gray had had enough fighting for a while.

And little wonder. Coming at the end of a year of war, Shiloh was the first battle on a scale that became commonplace during the next three years. The 20,000 killed and wounded at Shiloh (about equally distributed between the two sides) were nearly double the 12,000 battle casualties at Manassas, Wilson's Creek, Fort Donelson, and Pea Ridge *combined*. Gone was the romantic innocence of Rebs and Yanks who had marched off to war in 1861. "I never realized the 'pomp and circumstance' of the thing called glorious war until I saw this," wrote a Tennessee private after the battle. "Men . . . lying in every conceivable position; the dead . . . with their eyes wide open, the wounded begging piteously for help. . . . I seemed . . . in a sort of daze." Sherman described "piles of dead soldiers' mangled bodies . . . without heads and legs. . . . The scenes on this field would have cured anybody of war."[27]

Shiloh disabused Yankees of their notion of a quick Confederate collapse in the West. After the surrender of Donelson, a Union soldier had

25. *Ibid.*, 204.
26. Thomas Jordan, "Notes of a Confederate Staff-Officer at Shiloh," *Battles and Leaders*, I, 603.
27. McDonough, *Shiloh*, 4–5; Mark A. DeWolfe Howe, ed., *Home Letters of General Sherman* (New York, 1909), 222–23.

written: "My opinion is that this war will be closed in less than six months." After Shiloh he wrote: "If my life is spared I will continue in my country's service until this rebellion is put down, should it be ten years." Before Shiloh, Grant had believed that one more Union victory would end the rebellion; now he "gave up all idea of saving the Union except by complete conquest."[28] Shiloh launched the country onto the floodtide of total war.

III

Although Grant had snatched victory from the jaws of defeat at Pittsburg Landing, northern opinion at first focused more on those jaws than on victory. Newspapers reported Union soldiers bayoneted in their tents and Grant's army cut to pieces before being saved by the timely arrival of Buell. A hero after Donelson, Grant was now a bigger goat than Albert Sidney Johnston had been in the South after his retreat from Tennessee. What accounted for this fickleness of northern opinion? The reverses of the first day at Shiloh and the appalling casualties furnish part of the explanation. The self-serving accounts by some of Buell's officers, who talked more freely to reporters than did Grant and his subordinates, also swayed opinion. False rumors circulated that Grant was drunk at Shiloh. The disgraced captain of 1854 seemed unable to live down his reputation. Then, too, the magnitude of northern victory at Shiloh was not at first apparent. Indeed, Beauregard persevered in describing the battle as a southern triumph. Only "untoward events," he reported, had saved the Yankees from annihilation; the Confederate withdrawal to Corinth was part of a broader strategic plan![29]

When the recognition of Confederate failure at Shiloh finally sank in, many southerners turned against Beauregard. They blamed him for having snatched defeat from the jaws of victory by refusing to order a final twilight assault on the first day. About the time this shift occurred in southern opinion, Illinoisians began coming to Grant's defense. When a prominent Pennsylvania Republican went to Lincoln and said that Grant was incompetent, a drunkard, and a political liability to the administration, the president heard him out and replied: "*I can't spare this man; he fights.*" One of Grant's staff officers furnished Illinois Con-

28. Albert Dillahunty, *Shiloh National Military Park, Tennessee* (National Park Service Historical Handbook Series No. 10, Washington, 1955), 1; Grant, *Memoirs*, I, 368.
29. McDonough, *Shiloh*, 218.

gressman Elihu Washburne, Grant's original sponsor, with information that prompted Washburne to extol Grant in a House speech as a general whose "almost superhuman efforts" at Shiloh had "won one of the most brilliant victories" in American history.[30]

Washburne put the case too strongly. Grant made mistakes before the battle that all of his undoubted coolness and indomitable will during the fighting barely redeemed. But in the end the Union armies won a strategic success of great importance at Shiloh. They turned back the Confederacy's supreme bid to regain the initiative in the Mississippi Valley. From then on it was all downhill for the South in this crucial region. On the very day, April 7, that Beauregard's battered army began its weary retreat to Corinth, a Union army-navy team won another important—and almost bloodless—triumph on the Mississippi.

When the Confederates evacuated their Gibraltar at Columbus in February, they left a garrison of 7,000 men and fifty-two big guns at Island No. 10 fifty miles downriver. This strongpoint blocked northern shipping as completely as Columbus had done. Halleck ordered Andrew Foote's river fleet to shell the island batteries while John Pope's newly formed Army of the Mississippi closed in by land from the Missouri side of the river. Foote's seven ironclads and ten mortar boats (large scows, each mounting a thirteen-inch mortar) bombarded the rebel defenses at long range without much effect. Meanwhile Pope gained control of the Missouri bank below the island and brought several shallow-draft transports through a cutoff canal dug by his troops with the aid of contrabands. This penned in the Confederates from three sides, leaving open only a precarious supply line through the swamps on the Tennessee bank of the river. Pope pleaded with Foote for a gunboat to run the gauntlet of guns on the island and protect a downriver troop crossing to close this fourth side. The *Carondelet* did so during a spectacular thunderstorm on the night of April 4 and was followed by a second gunboat two nights later during another storm. Spearheaded by the gunboats, Pope's army crossed the Mississippi, surrounded the garrison, and on April 7 captured its 7,000 men along with guns and equipment the South could ill afford to lose. With only a handful of casualties, Pope achieved what Halleck considered a more brilliant success than Grant at Donelson, and the North acquired a new hero.

After this success, Halleck ordered Pope to join Grant and Buell at

30. Alexander K. McClure, *Abraham Lincoln and Men of War Times* (Philadelphia, 1892), 193–96; Catton, *Grant Moves South*, 259–60.

Pittsburg Landing, where Halleck took personal command of the combined armies numbering more than 100,000 men. Assembled there was the greatest concentration of military talent in the war, including four future generals in chief of the United States army: Halleck, Grant, Sherman, and Philip Sheridan (then a captain); and five other present or future commanders of whole armies: Buell, Pope, Rosecrans, George H. Thomas, and James B. McPherson. Halleck could scarcely find a use for all this talent, particularly for Grant. Old Brains still undervalued Grant's worth and put him on the shelf by appointing him to a meaningless post as second in command of the combined forces. An unhappy Grant requested transfer, but in the end he stayed on.

Halleck inched forward toward Corinth, entrenching the whole army at every skirmish with Confederate outposts. If Halleck's precautions made sure that Beauregard could not attack him, they made equally sure that he could not effectively attack Beauregard. Halleck waged war by the book—his book. It was an eighteenth-century Jominian war of maneuver and siege against "strategic points," not a modern war of all-out combat to destroy or cripple an enemy army. Halleck would be happy if he could maneuver Beauregard out of Corinth without a fight. Grant, for one, could not see "how the mere occupation of places was to close the war while large and effective rebel armies existed." But Halleck wanted no part of Grant's kind of war.[31]

Confederate leaders also considered Corinth a crucial strategic point. "If defeated here," wrote Beauregard two weeks after Shiloh, "we lose the whole Mississippi Valley and probably our cause."[32] The South scraped up reinforcements from eastern Tennessee and from as far away as the south Atlantic coast. Van Dorn brought 15,000 from Arkansas. By the beginning of May Beauregard had 70,000 men at Corinth. But many were still recovering from their Shiloh wounds, and thousands of others fell ill from typhoid or dysentery. With an inadequate water supply befouled by the army's refuse, Corinth was becoming an ecological trap. As many soldiers died there of disease as had been killed at Shiloh. Faced with this wastage and the prospect of being surrounded by a siege, Beauregard changed his mind about the need to hold Corinth at all costs. As Halleck was extending his lines around the city and hauling forward his siege guns, Beauregard on May 25 decided to pull out. He did so with great skill and stealth, leaving behind only a few stragglers

31. Grant, Memoirs, I, 381.
32. O.R., Ser. I, Vol. 10, pt. 2, p. 403.

and a pestilential town as spoils for Halleck. Fifty miles to the south at his new base in Tupelo, Mississippi, Beauregard pronounced the evacuation of Corinth "equivalent to a great victory."[33] But Jefferson Davis was shocked and angered by the news. Another such victory would sink the Confederacy. Although Beauregard talked of resuming the offensive, Davis had enough of his Napoleonic plans and Lilliputian execution. When Beauregard took an unauthorized leave of absence to recuperate his broken health, Davis seized the opportunity and replaced him with Braxton Bragg.

With the capture of Corinth, the Union army stood astride the railroad to Memphis. Before Halleck's bluecoats could take the Confederacy's fifth largest city, however, a hybrid fleet on the river did the job. It had not been easy. After the loss of Island No. 10, the next rebel strongpoint on the Mississippi was Fort Pillow, fifty miles above Memphis. In addition to the fort's forty guns, the southerners had a new river defense fleet of eight steamboats converted into armed rams. On May 10 this makeshift navy had surprised the Union fleet at Plum Run Bend above Fort Pillow with a hit and run attack that put two ironclads temporarily out of action with gaping holes below the waterline. The elated southern fleet captain assured Beauregard that the Yankees "will never penetrate farther down the Mississippi."[34]

But the bluejackets soon got some rams of their own. The ram concept was a revival of naval tactics from the days of galleys, before the advent of gunpowder and sailing ships (which could rarely be maneuvered to ram another ship) had converted navies to broadside firepower. But the development of steam propulsion made ramming feasible again. Several hundred tons of warship with a reinforced prow moving at even a slow speed could be far more lethal than any shot or shell then in existence. The *Virginia* had proved this at Hampton Roads, and the Confederate river fleet proved it again at Plum Run Bend. The most enthusiastic proponent of ram power was a thin, frail-looking, fifty-seven-year old civil engineer from Pennsylvania, Charles Ellet. Having failed to interest the Union navy in his ideas, Ellet took them to Secretary of War Stanton, who expressed enthusiasm. Stanton made Ellet a colonel and sent him west to develop a ram fleet for river fighting.

Ellet rebuilt nine steamboats according to his own calculations for maximum strength. Preferring riverboat men to naval personnel for his

33. Williams, *Beauregard*, 155.
34. *O.R. Navy*, Ser. I, Vol. 23, p. 57.

crews, he signed them up for special service. Ellet commanded the flag-boat himself, and placed his brother Alfred in command of the second boat. Seven other Ellets—brothers, nephews, and a son—also joined the enterprise, some as captains. This remarkable family and its even more remarkable flotilla wanted to prove their mettle by attacking the rebel fleet at Fort Pillow. Beauregard forestalled them by ordering the evacuation of the fort when his withdrawal from Corinth made it vul-nerable to land attack. But the Confederates decided to make a stand at Memphis. At sunrise on June 6 the southern river fleet steamed out to challenge five Union ironclads and four of Ellet's rams. Thousands of Memphis residents lined the bluffs to cheer on their side.

But in less than two hours the home team had lost. Charles and Alfred Ellet headed their rams downriver at fifteen knots against the rebel van. The shock of collision between Charles's boat and the leading Confederate ram could be felt on the bluffs. Charles's attack punched a huge hole in the rebel bow, while Alfred's boat squeezed between two southern rams converging on her, causing them to collide with each other. Alfred then circled back and rammed the rebel boat that had survived this crash. Meanwhile the Union gunboats had gotten into the action. Their salvos finished off two crippled Confederate boats, sank another, and captured three others after disabling them. Only one southern vessel escaped downriver. The rebel fleet existed no more. Residents of Memphis watched in sullen silence as Ellet's son Charles, Jr., led a four-man detachment to raise the stars and stripes over the post office. His doughty father, the only significant Union casualty of the conflict, died of his wound two weeks later. Charles, Jr., became the army's youngest colonel at nineteen and subsequently took com-mand of the ram fleet. A year later he too was dead.

The Yankees occupied Memphis and turned it into a base for future operations, while the fleet steamed 300 miles downriver to the Confed-eracy's next bastion at Vicksburg. Meanwhile the spectacular achieve-ments of the river fleet had been eclipsed by the salt-water navy, which captured New Orleans and pushed upriver to plant the American flag deep in the heart of Dixie.

The capture of New Orleans illustrated the strategic wisdom of Lin-coln's desire to attack several places simultaneously. Union pressure in Tennessee had forced southern leaders to strip Louisiana of an army division (which fought at Shiloh) and eight gunboats (the fleet destroyed at Memphis). Left to defend New Orleans were 3,000 short-term mili-tia, some river batteries just below the city where Andrew Jackson had beaten the British in 1815, a mosquito fleet of a dozen small gunboats, two unfinished ironclads, and two forts mounting 126 guns astride the Mississippi seventy-five miles below the city. The defenders relied mainly on these forts, which were expected to blow out of the water any wooden warships foolish enough to breast the three-knot current in an attempt to pass them. But the Union navy had already shown that enough ships with enough big guns commanded by an intrepid sailor were more than a match for brick forts. The navy was about to prove it again; the sailor this time was the most intrepid of all, Flag-Officer David Glasgow Farragut.

Sixty years old, Farragut had gone to sea at the age of nine and fought in the War of 1812 and the Mexican War. Like Grant, he possessed great force of character rather than a subtle intellect. Although born in Tennessee and married to a Virginian, Farragut's loyalty to the flag he had served for half a century was unswerving. When fellow southerners tried to persuade him to defect, he rejected their entreaties with the words: "Mind what I tell you: You fellows will catch the devil before you get through with this business." [35] They would catch much of it from Farragut himself. In February 1862 he took command of a task force comprising eight steam sloops (frigates drew too much water to get over the bars at the mouth of the Mississippi), one sailing sloop, and fourteen gunboats. Accompanying this force were nineteen mortar schooners to soften up the forts with high-angle fire before the fleet ran past them. To deal with any resistance on land, transports carried to the Gulf 15,000 soldiers commanded by the ubiquitous Benjamin Butler.

By early April, Farragut got his fleet over the bars and up to an anchorage a couple of miles below the forts. From there the mortar schooners began to pound the forts at the rate of 3,000 shells a day. Although this blitz dismounted a few guns and created a great deal of rubble, it did little to reduce enemy firepower. Farragut had never believed much in the mortar attack; after six days of it he decided to run the gauntlet without further delay. Two Union gunboats crept up under the forts one night to cut the chain holding a boom of hulks across the river; though discovered and fired upon, their crews succeeded in making an opening large enough for the fleet to squeeze through single file. At 2:00 a.m. on April 24, seventeen of Farragut's warships weighed anchor and began to steam upriver. The forts opened fire with eighty or

35. David D. Porter, "The Opening of the Lower Mississippi," *Battles and Leaders*, II, 22.

ninety guns; the ships replied with twice as many; the mortar fleet re-commenced its bombardment; the Confederate ironclad *Louisiana*, moored to the bank with her engines not yet working, cut loose with as many of her sixteen guns as would bear. Three of the rebel gunboats entered the fray and tried to ram Union warships (one of them suc-ceeded, sinking the ten-gun sloop *Varuna*) while the civilian captains of the other rebel boats fled upstream or scuttled their craft. Confederate tugs pushed fire-rafts heaped with flaming pine and pitch into the cur-rent to float down on Yankee ships. With all this happening in a space of scarcely a square mile, it was the greatest fireworks display in Amer-ican history.

Every Union ship that got through, as well as the four that did not, took a heavy pounding; the fleet lost thirty-seven men killed and 147 wounded during the hour and a half it took to pass the forts. The rebels suffered fewer casualties but their mosquito fleet was gone, the unfin-ished ironclads were destroyed by their crews to prevent capture, the garrisons in the forts later mutinied and surrendered, and the militia scampered for the hinterland. On the morning of April 25, Farragut's ships silenced the river batteries below New Orleans with a broadside or two. The fleet then steamed up to a city filled with burning cotton and cursing mobs brandishing pistols against the eleven-inch guns trained on their streets. A lad of seventeen at the time, George Washington Cable later recalled that on this bleak day "the crowds on the levee howled and screamed with rage. The swarming decks answered never a word; but one old tar on the *Hartford*, standing with lanyard in hand beside a great pivot-gun, so plain to view that you could see him smile, silently patted its big black breech and blandly grinned."[36] In a comic-opera scenario of "negotiations," the mayor declined the honor of sur-rendering the South's largest city. Tiring of this farce, Farragut on April 29 sent the marines to raise the flag over public buildings. Two days later Butler entered New Orleans at the head of his unscathed troops to begin an efficient but remorseless rule of the occupied city.

During the next two months most of Farragut's ships twice ascended the Mississippi, receiving the surrender of Baton Rouge and Natchez along the way. But Vicksburg proved another matter. Summoned to surrender, the military governor of the city replied: "Mississippians don't know, and refuse to learn, how to surrender. . . . If Commodore Far-

36. Cable, "New Orleans before the Capture," *Battles and Leaders*, II, 20.

ragut . . . can teach them, let [him] come and try."[37] He came, he tried, but he did not conquer. In the last week of June the Union fleets that had subdued New Orleans and Memphis met at Vicksburg with the plan of crushing its defenses between the combined weight of more than two hundred guns and twenty-three mortars. But the rebel batteries emplaced on the sides and top of the two hundred-foot bluff on which the city was built gave as good as they got. Farragut soon concluded that while naval bombardment might level the town and drive its inhabitants underground, the ship's guns could not alone overcome a determined defense. And the South was determined to defend this last barrier to Union control of the Mississippi. Earl Van Dorn had arrived to command ten thousand soldiers entrenched at Vicksburg by the end of June. A Union infantry assault up the bluffs from the river would be suicidal. The only way to crack the defenses was to attack with a large land force from the rear while maintaining the naval blockade on the river. How to do this was a knotty problem in strategy that the Union army would not solve for nearly a year.

Farragut had brought three thousand of Butler's soldiers up to Vicksburg. Too few in number for operations against Van Dorn, these men set to work (with the help of 1,500 contrabands) to dig a canal across an oxbowed neck of land out of range of Vicksburg's guns, in the hope that the river would cut a new channel and leave the Confederate fortress high and dry. But the Mississippi, dropping several inches every day in the summer drought, refused to cooperate. Farragut became alarmed that his deep-draft vessels would be stranded by the falling river. Three-fourths of the Union soldiers and half of the sailors fell ill with typhoid, dysentery, or malaria, with several dying each day.

The Yankees finally gave up the attempt to take Vicksburg this summer, but not before the rebels gave them a parting black eye. The weapon that delivered this blow was the C.S.S. Arkansas commanded by the South's own sea-dog counterpart of Farragut, Kentuckian Isaac Newton Brown. This thirty-year veteran of the U.S. navy had been overseeing the completion of a homemade ironclad up the Yazoo River while the Union fleet was shelling Vicksburg. Propelled by balky engines, carrying ten guns, and resembling the Virginia in appearance, the Arkansas steamed down to challenge the combined Federal fleets in mid-July. She first encountered and crippled the famed Carondelet, then swooped

37. O.R. Navy, Ser. I, Vol. 18, p. 492.

down between the two surprised Union flotillas tied up on either bank with their steam down and guns unloaded. They remedied the latter quickly and peppered the iron intruder with a hailstorm of shot. The *Arkansas* fired back "to every point of the circumference, without the fear of hitting a friend or missing an enemy."[38] Despite suffering sixty casualties and extensive damage, the *Arkansas* disabled one of the Ellet rams and finally drifted to safety under the guns of Vicksburg.

Angry as a hornet, Farragut tried in vain to destroy the rebel monster. He finally gave up in disgust and on July 26 started his fleet downstream before low water grounded it. The Union river gunboats returned to Helena, Arkansas. For the time being, Confederates controlled two hundred river miles of the Mississippi from Vicksburg to Port Hudson, Louisiana, where they built fortifications second in strength only to Vicksburg's. The South took heart at the *Arkansas*'s exploits. Van Dorn decided to attack the Union garrison at Baton Rouge, "and then, Ho! for New Orleans."[39] He ordered the *Arkansas* downriver to neutralize the Union gunboats at Baton Rouge while an army division attacked by land. But the *Arkansas*'s faltering engines kept her from arriving before the bluecoats had repulsed the rebel assault on August 5. Next day the ironclad's engines failed again as Union warships bore down on her. The crew blew her up to prevent capture.

This event served as a coda to what the *New York Tribune* had described in May as "A Deluge of Victories" in the West.[40] From February to May, Union forces conquered 50,000 square miles of territory, gained control of 1,000 miles of navigable rivers, captured two state capitals and the South's largest city, and put 30,000 enemy soldiers out of action. The decline of southern morale in consequence of these reverses can be measured in the diary entries of Mary Boykin Chesnut during April and May:

> Battle after battle—disaster after disaster. . . . How could I sleep? The power they are bringing to bear against our country is tremendous. . . . Every morning's paper enough to kill a well woman [or] age a strong and hearty one. . . . New Orleans gone—and with it the Confederacy. Are we not cut in two? . . . I have nothing to chronicle but disasters. . . . The reality is hideous.[41]

38. Isaac N. Brown, "The Confederate Gun-Boat 'Arkansas,'" *Battles and Leaders*, III, 576.
39. Foote, *Civil War*, I, 577.
40. *Ibid.*, 582.
41. Woodward, *Chesnut's Civil War*, 326, 327, 330, 333, 339.

IV

In the view from Richmond the threat of McClellan's splendidly equipped army loomed even larger than disasters in the West. After much anxious prodding from Lincoln, McClellan had finally submitted a plan for a spring offensive against Joseph E. Johnston's army defending Manassas. Instead of attacking the rebels directly, McClellan proposed to transport his army by water down the Chesapeake Bay to the mouth of the Rappahannock River, eighty miles southeast of Manassas. This would place the Federals between Johnston and Richmond, thereby forcing the Confederates to race southward to defend their capital. McClellan anticipated either the capture of Richmond before Johnston could get there or a battle on a field of McClellan's choice where his men would not have to assault enemy trenches.

Lincoln did not like this plan, for if it placed McClellan's army between Johnston and Richmond it also left Johnston's army between McClellan and Washington. While Lincoln did not yet share the suspicion that as a Democrat McClellan was "soft" on the rebels and did not really want to smash them, he was not happy with McClellan's concept of strategy. Like Grant, the president believed in attacking the enemy's *army* rather than in maneuvering to capture *places*. By "going down the Bay in search of a field, instead of fighting near Manassas," Lincoln told McClellan, "[you are] only shifting, and not surmounting, a difficulty. . . . [You] will find the same enemy, and the same, or equal, intrenchments, at either place."[42]

Before McClellan could launch his maneuver, Johnston anticipated it by withdrawing from Manassas in early March to a more defensible position behind the Rappahannock forty miles to the south. While perhaps prudent militarily, this retreat had adverse political consequences. Coming amid other Confederate reverses, it added to the depression of public morale. And it also drove deeper the wedge of distrust between Johnston and Davis. The latter was not persuaded of the necessity for pulling back; when he learned that Johnston had done so with a haste that required the destruction of huge stockpiles of supplies which could not be moved over muddy roads, Davis was mortified and angry.

He was no more mortified than Lincoln was by the discovery that the evacuated Confederate defenses were not as strong or extensive as McClellan had claimed. Newspaper correspondents found more Quaker guns at Centreville. One reporter wrote that "the fancied impregnability

42. CWL, V, 185.

of the position turns out to be a sham." There had clearly been no more than 45,000 rebels on the Mansassas-Centreville line, fewer than half the number McClellan had estimated. "Utterly dispirited, ashamed, and humiliated," wrote another northern reporter, "I return from this visit to the rebel stronghold, feeling that their retreat is *our defeat*."[43]

The question was, what to do now? Johnston's retreat ruined McClellan's plan for flanking the enemy via the Rappahannock. But the Union commander was loath to give up the idea of transporting his army by water to a point east of Richmond. He proposed a landing at Fortress Monroe on the tip of the peninsula formed by the York and James rivers. With a secure seaborne supply line, the Union army could then drive seventy miles up the peninsula, crossing only two rivers before reaching Richmond. This seemed to McClellan much better than Lincoln's idea of an overland invasion, which would have to advance one hundred miles from Washington to Richmond with a half-dozen rivers to cross and dependent on a railroad vulnerable to cavalry raids. Nevertheless, Lincoln remained skeptical. Operating on interior lines, the Confederates could shift troops to the peninsula and McClellan would still "find the same enemy, and the same, or equal intrenchments." But the president reluctantly consented to McClellan's plan, provided he left behind enough troops to defend Washington from a sudden rebel strike. McClellan promised.

Quartermaster-General Montgomery Meigs assembled 400 ships and barges to transport McClellan's army of more than 100,000 men, 300 cannon, 25,000 animals, and mountains of equipment to the Peninsula. It was an awesome demonstration of the North's logistical capacity. But from the outset an ill fate seemed to upset McClellan's plans. Having lost full confidence in his commander, Lincoln reduced McClellan's authority. On March 8 he appointed four corps commanders for the Army of the Potomac after consulting the Committee on the Conduct of the War but without consulting McClellan. Three days later he demoted McClellan from general in chief to commander only of the Army of the Potomac. Lincoln justified this on the ground that McClellan's duties as a field commander would prevent him from giving attention to other theaters. Although this made sense, it also signaled Lincoln's reservations about McClellan. On March 11 the president also created a new military department in West Virginia for General

43. *New York Tribune*, March 13, 1862, quoted in Williams, *Lincoln Finds a General*, I, 153; Foote, *Civil War*, I, 264.

Frémont. Republican pressure had compelled this move to give the antislavery Frémont an important command. Three weeks later the same pressure induced Lincoln to detach a division from McClellan's army and send it to Frémont.

The president subsequently withheld other divisions from McClellan because he discovered that the general had left behind fewer troops than promised for the defense of Washington. The confusion surrounding this matter led to a bizarre juggling of numbers by contemporaries that still bedevils the historian trying to arrive at truth. McClellan claimed to have assigned 73,000 men for the capital's defense. But Lincoln could count only 29,000. It turned out that McClellan had counted some troops twice and was including Nathaniel Banks's army of 23,000 in the Shenandoah Valley as part of the capital's defense. McClellan was correct in his belief that the rebels had no intention of launching a strike against Washington and that even if they did, Banks's divisions could be shifted in time to meet them. But in his impatience with civilian interference he failed to explain to Lincoln his arrangements for defending the capital. Lincoln's concern for the safety of Washington was excessive. Yet if by some chance the rebels did threaten the city, the president would stand convicted of criminal negligence in the eyes of the northern people.

Lincoln's concern was heightened by a clash in the Shenandoah Valley on March 23. Stonewall Jackson commanded a small Confederate army there. His mission was to harass Banks's force near Winchester and to prevent the transfer of Union troops from the Valley to McClellan. When Jackson learned that two of Banks's three divisions were about to be transferred, he attacked what he thought was the rear guard at Kernstown, just south of Winchester. Instead of swatting a small force, the 4,200 rebels ran into a full division of 9,000 men and were badly mauled. Jackson's tactical defeat at Kernstown—yet another Confederate reverse in this dismal spring—suddenly turned into an important strategic victory. Reasoning that Jackson would not have attacked unless he had a sizable force, Lincoln cancelled the transfer of Banks's divisions. Moreover, discovering at this time the discrepancy in the number of troops left in and near Washington, the president also ordered Irvin McDowell's large corps of 35,000 men to remain in northern Virginia. For the time being, McClellan was deprived of some 50,000 of the 150,000 men he had expected to become part of his army on the Peninsula.

An embittered McClellan later charged that the administration did not want him, a Democrat, to succeed. This accusation contained little if any truth; indeed, Republicans fumed at the general's apparent lack of will to succeed. During the first week of April about 55,000 of McClellan's troops approached the Confederate defenses near the old Revolutionary War battlefield at Yorktown. Dug in behind the Warwick River were fewer than 13,000 rebels commanded by John B. Magruder. McClellan hesitated to attack, believing that the strength of the southern works would make the cost in casualties too high. "Prince John" Magruder did his best to encourage this conviction. A lover of the theater, Magruder staged a pageant for McClellan. He marched his infantry in endless circles and moved his artillery noisily from place to place, to give the impression of having more men than he actually had. McClellan reacted as Magruder hoped. He concluded that he could take Yorktown only by a siege. This news distressed Lincoln. "I think you had better break the enemies' line . . . at once," the president wired McClellan. "By delay the enemy will relatively gain upon you." Lincoln tried to warn McClellan about growing Republican doubts of his loyalty. "It is indispensable to *you* that you strike a blow. . . . The country will not fail to note—is now noting—that the present hesitation to move upon an entrenched enemy, is but the story of Manassas repeated. . . . I have never written you . . . in greater kindness of feeling than now, nor with a fuller purpose to sustain you. . . . *But you must act.*"[44]

McClellan did not act; instead he wrote to his wife that if Lincoln wanted to break the rebel lines, "he had better come & do it himself." While the general complained of his difficult position with "the rebels on one side, & the abolitionists & other scoundrels on the other," he brought up his sappers and siege guns. Week after week went by as Union artillery prepared to blast the rebels from their trenches with mortars and 200-pound shells. Lincoln felt driven to distraction by this "indefinite procrastination." As he had warned, the Confederates used the delay to shift Johnston's whole army to the Peninsula.[45]

An inspection of the Yorktown defenses convinced Johnston that they were hopelessly weak: "No one but McClellan could have hesitated to attack."[46] Johnston recommended withdrawal all the way to prepared defenses just outside Richmond itself. But Jefferson Davis and Robert

44. Lincoln to McClellan, April 6, 9, 1862, CWL, V, 182, 185.
45. McClellan to Ellen Marcy McClellan, April 8, 30, 1862, McClellan Papers, Library of Congress; Lincoln to McClellan, May 1, 1862, CWL, V, 203.
46. Johnston to Robert E. Lee, April 22, 1862, O.R., Ser. I, Vol. 11, pt. 3, p. 456.

E. Lee vetoed this proposal and ordered Johnston to defend the York-town line as long as possible. Lee's role in this matter was a measure of Davis's loss of confidence in Johnston. The president had recalled Lee from Savannah in March and installed him in Richmond as a sort of assistant commander in chief. Johnston hung on at Yorktown until the beginning of May, when he knew that McClellan was about to pulver-ize the defenses with his siege guns. Rather than wait for this, Johnston evacuated the trenches on the night of May 3–4 and retreated up the Peninsula. Davis was as dismayed by this further loss as Lincoln was by the consumption of a month's time in accomplishing it. On May 5 a strong Confederate rear guard commanded by James Longstreet fought a delayed action near the old colonial capital of Williamsburg. At the cost of 1,700 casualties the rebels inflicted 2,200 and delayed the Union pursuit long enough to enable the rest of the army to get away with its artillery and wagons.

Frequent rains had impeded operations during April; even heavier rains bogged down the armies during May. The only significant action took place on the water. With Johnston's retreat, Norfolk and its navy yard were no longer tenable. The Confederates blew up everything there of military value—including the *Virginia*—and pulled out. The *Moni-tor* led a flotilla of five gunboats up the James River. Their captains dreamed of emulating Farragut by running the river batteries and steam-ing on to level their guns at Richmond. Confederate officials began packing the archives and preparing to leave the city. But they soon un-packed. On May 15 the batteries at Drewry's Bluff seven miles below Richmond stopped the gunboats. The *Monitor* proved ineffective be-cause her guns could not be elevated enough to hit the batteries on the ninety-foot bluff. Rebel cannons punished the other boats with a plung-ing fire while sharpshooters along the banks picked off Yankee sailors. The fleet gave up; Richmond breathed a collective sigh of relief.

Despite the gleam of cheer afforded by the battle of Drewry's Bluff, a sense of impending doom pervaded the South. McClellan's army ap-proached to within six miles of Richmond, while reports of defeats and retreats arrived almost daily from the West. In the crisis atmosphere created by these setbacks during the spring of 1862, the southern Con-gress enacted conscription and martial law. Internal disaffection in-creased; the Confederate dollar plummeted. During these same months a confident Union government released political prisoners, suspended recruiting, and placed northern war finances on a sound footing. In contrapuntal fashion, developments on the homefront responded to the rhythm of events on the battlefield.

14

The Sinews of War

I

So long as the South seemed to be winning the war, Jefferson Davis was an esteemed leader. But adversity clouded his reputation. The "patent and appalling evidences of inefficiency" demonstrated by the surrender of Forts Henry and Donelson had lost Davis "the confidence of the country," according to the *Richmond Whig*. Congressman William Boyce of South Carolina lamented "the incredible incompetency of our Executive" that "has brought us to the brink of ruin." George W. Bagby, editor of the *Southern Literary Messenger* and a Richmond correspondent for several newspapers, wrote during the spring of 1862: "We have reached a very dark hour. . . . Cold, haughty, peevish, narrow-minded, pig-headed, *malignant*, he [Davis] is the cause. While he lives, there is no hope."[1]

Davis resented what he considered "contemptible" attacks by men "who engage in strife for personal and party aggrandisement."[2] But he

---

1. *Richmond Whig*, Feb. 15, March 18, 1862, quoted in Harrison A. Trexler, "The Davis Administration and the Richmond Press, 1861–1865," *JSH*, 16 (1950), 187 and n.; Boyce to James Hammond, April 4, 12, 1862, in Rosser R. Taylor, "Boyce-Hammond Correspondence," *JSH*, 3 (1937), 351–52; Emory M. Thomas, *The Confederate Nation 1861–1865* (New York, 1979), 142.
2. Rowland, *Davis*, V, 209, 246.

was not free himself from the sins of excessive pride and willfulness. Austere and humorless, Davis did not suffer fools gladly. He lacked Lincoln's ability to work with partisans of a different persuasion for the common cause. Lincoln would rather win the war than an argument; Davis seemed to prefer winning the argument. Although he rarely defended himself in public, he sometimes privately lashed back at critics in a manner that only increased their hostility. Even Davis's devoted wife Varina admitted that "if anyone disagrees with Mr. Davis he resents it and ascribes the difference to the perversity of his opponent." Suffering from dyspepsia and a neuralgia that grew worse under wartime pressures and left him blind in one eye, Davis was wracked by constant pain that exacerbated his waspish temper. He recognized and regretted his thin-skinned defensiveness: "I wish I could learn just to let people alone who snap at me," Davis said to his wife in May 1862, "in forbearance and charity to turn away as well from the cats as the snakes."[3]

The cats wanted the administration to wage war with more vigor and boldness. It must become a total war, wrote a Confederate general, "in which the whole population and the whole production . . . are to be put on a war footing, where every institution is to be made auxiliary to war."[4] In the spring of 1862 the Confederate government enacted two radical measures to carry out such recommendations—conscription and martial law. But these acts provoked even more venomous attacks from the snakes.

By the winter of 1861–62 the bloom had faded from southern enthusiasm for the war. "The romance of the thing is entirely worn off," wrote a soldier with Stonewall Jackson's brigade in the Shenandoah Valley, "not only with myself but with the whole army."[5] The South still had more soldiers than it had weapons to arm them, but that state of affairs promised to come to an abrupt and disastrous end in the spring— not because of a windfall of weapons, but because the one-year enlistments of nearly half the troops would expire.[6] Few of them seemed ready to re–enlist. "If I live this twelve months out, I intend to try mighty hard to keep out of [the army]," wrote another Virginia soldier

---

3. Foote, *Civil War*, I, 65; Davis to Varina Davis, May 16, 1862, in Rowland, *Davis*, V, 246.
4. *O.R.*, Ser. III, Vol. 4, p. 883.
5. J. H. Langhorne to his mother, Jan. 12, 1862, in Robert G. Tanner, *Stonewall in the Valley: Thomas J. "Stonewall" Jackson's Shenandoah Valley Campaign Spring 1862* (Garden City, N.Y., 1976), 91.
6. The other half were three-year volunteers.

in January 1862. "I don't think I could stand it another year."[7] It looked like the army might melt away just as the Yankees began their spring offensives.

The Confederate Congress initially addressed this problem within the traditional framework of voluntarism. In December 1861 it enacted legislation granting a fifty-dollar bounty and a sixty-day furlough to one-year men who re-enlisted, with the additional proviso that they could join new regiments and elect new officers if they wished. As one analyst commented, "a worse law could hardly have been imposed on the South by the enemy."[8] The furloughs were likely to weaken the army as much at a critical time as refusals to re-enlist would have done; the election of new officers might oust efficient disciplinarians in favor of good ol' boys; the process of organizing new regiments was a sure-fire recipe for chaos, especially since many infantrymen decided to re-enlist in the more glamorous (and safer) cavalry or artillery.

A dismayed Robert E. Lee pronounced this law "highly disastrous" and urged instead a law "drafting them 'for the war.' " Although he had gone to war to prevent coercion of a state by the national government, Lee now believed the war would be lost unless the government in Richmond obtained the power to coerce men into the army. Davis agreed. On March 28, 1862, he sent to Congress a special message recommending conscription. State's righters and libertarians protested that such a measure contradicted what the South was fighting for. But the blunt, hot-tempered Senator Louis Wigfall of Texas took the floor and warned his colleagues to "cease this child's play. . . . The enemy are in some portions of almost every State in the Confederacy. . . . Virginia is enveloped by them. We need a large army. How are you going to get it? . . . No man has any individual rights, which come into conflict with the welfare of the country."[9]

More than two-thirds of the congressmen and senators concurred. On April 16 they enacted the first conscription law in American history. It declared all able-bodied white male citizens between the ages of eighteen and thirty-five liable to service for three years. One-year volunteers must remain in the army two more years. This universal obligation

---

7. G. K. Harlow to his family, Jan. 23, 1862, in Tanner, *Stonewall in the Valley*, 91.
8. Douglas Southall Freeman, *R. E. Lee: A Biography*, 4 vols. (New York, 1934–35), II, 26.
9. O. R., Ser. I, Vol. 6, p. 350; Wigfall quoted in Frank E. Vandiver, *Their Tattered Flags: The Epic of the Confederacy* (New York, 1970), 131.

turned out to have some loopholes, however. A drafted man could hire a substitute from the pool of "persons not liable for duty"—men outside the specified age group or immigrant aliens. The practice of buying substitutes had deep roots in European as well as American history. Men called into militia service in previous wars, including the Revolution, had been allowed to send substitutes. Even the *levée en masse* of the French Revolution permitted substitution. This practice was based on an assumption that the talents of men who could afford substitutes might be of more value on the homefront, organizing and producing the matériel of war, than in the army. But recognizing that substitution would not exempt all men necessary for behind-the-lines duty, Congress on April 21 passed a supplementary law specifying several exempt categories: Confederate and state civil officials, railroad and river workers, telegraph operators, miners, several categories of industrial laborers, hospital personnel, clergymen, apothecaries, and teachers. Congress resisted planter pressure to exempt overseers—but that issue would rise again.

Some of these exemptions created a potential for fraud. Many new schools sprang up as the teaching profession enjoyed a remarkable growth. Scores of apothecary shops suddenly appeared stocked with "a few empty jars, a cheap assortment of combs and brushes, a few bottles of 'hairdye' and 'wizard oil' and other Yankee nostrums." Governors who opposed conscription increased the number of exempt civil servants. Governors Joseph Brown of Georgia and Zebulon Vance of North Carolina showed special ingenuity in this regard: these two states accounted for 92 percent of all state officials exempted from the draft. Brown insisted that militia officers were included in this category, and proceeded to appoint hundreds of new officers. A Confederate general sarcastically described a Georgia or North Carolina militia regiment as containing "3 field officers, 4 staff officers, 10 captains, 30 lieutenants, and 1 private with a misery in his bowels."[10]

Hiring a substitute was the most controversial form of exemption. Rich men could buy their way out of the army whether or not their skills were needed at home. This gave rise to a bitter saying: "A rich man's war but a poor man's fight." Some poor men, however, might become rich—if they survived—by selling themselves as substitutes.

10. *Columbus [Ga.] Weekly Sun*, Sept. 2, 1862, and D. Harvey Hill, both quoted in Albert B. Moore, *Conscription and Conflict in the Confederacy* (New York, 1924), 56, 71n.

"Substitute brokers" established a thriving business. Many substitutes deserted as soon as they could, and sold themselves again—and again, and again. One man in Richmond was said to have sold himself thirty times. The price of substitutes rose by late 1863 to as high as $6,000 (the equivalent of $300 in gold, or three years' wages for a skilled workingman). The abuses of substitution became so obnoxious that Congress abolished the privilege in December 1863.

The main purpose of conscription was to stimulate volunteering by the threat of coercion rather than by its actual use. Thus the law allowed thirty days for potential draftees to avoid the stigma of the draft by volunteering. If they did so, they could join new regiments and elect their officers just as the volunteers of 1861 had done. Conscripts and substitutes, by contrast, were assigned to existing regiments. To a degree this carrot and stick method worked. During 1862 the total number of men in the Confederate army increased from about 325,000 to 450,000. Since about 75,000 men were lost from death or wounds during this period, the net gain was approximately 200,000. Fewer than half of these new men were conscripts and substitutes; the remainder were considered volunteers even though their motives for enlisting may not have been unalloyed patriotism.

Despite its success in getting more men into the army, conscription was the most unpopular act of the Confederate government. Yeoman farmers who could not buy their way out of the army voted with their feet and escaped to the woods or swamps. Enrollment officers met bitter resistance in the upcountry and in other regions of lukewarm or nonexistent commitment to the Confederacy. Armed bands of draft-dodgers and deserters ruled whole counties. Conscription represented an unprecedented extension of government power among a people on whom such power had rested lightly in the past. Even some soldiers, who might have been expected to welcome a law that forced slackers to share their hardships, instead considered it a repudiation of what they were fighting for. A Virginia private branded conscription "so gross a usurpation of authority . . . such a surrender of the right for which above all others we are now contending [that it] would go far to make me renounce my allegiance." A North Carolina soldier reflected that "when we hear men comparing the despotism of the *Confederacy* with that of the Lincoln government—*something must be wrong.*" [11]

11. Bell Irvin Wiley, *The Road to Appomattox* (Memphis, 1956), 56–57.

Conscription dramatized a fundamental paradox in the Confederate war effort: the need for Hamiltonian means to achieve Jeffersonian ends. Pure Jeffersonians could not accept this. The most outspoken of them, Joseph Brown of Georgia, denounced the draft as a "dangerous usurpation by Congress of the reserved rights of the States . . . at war with all the principles for which Georgia entered into the revolution."[12] In reply, Jefferson Davis donned the mantle of Hamilton. The Confederate Constitution, he pointed out to Brown, gave Congress the power "to raise and support armies" and to "provide for the common defence." It also contained another clause (likewise copied from the U.S. Constitution) empowering Congress to make all laws "necessary and proper for carrying into execution the foregoing powers." Brown had denied the constitutionality of conscription because the Constitution did not specifically authorize it. This was good Jeffersonian doctrine, sanctified by generations of southern strict constructionists. But in Hamiltonian language, Davis insisted that the "necessary and proper" clause legitimized conscription. No one could doubt the necessity "when our very existence is threatened by armies vastly superior in numbers." Therefore "the true and only test is to enquire whether the law is intended and calculated to carry out the object. . . . If the answer be in the affirmative, the law is constitutional."[13]

Most southerners probably agreed with Davis about this—especially if they lived in Virginia or western Tennessee or Mississippi or Louisiana, which unlike Georgia were threatened by invasion in 1862. "Our business now is to whip our enemies and save our homes," declared the *Richmond Enquirer*. "We can attend to questions of theory afterwards."[14] The draft was upheld by every court in which it was tested—including the supreme court of Georgia, which approved it unanimously.

Nevertheless, disaffection remained a serious problem. Another divisive controversy blew up over the question of martial law. This matter became an embarrassment to Davis. In his February 22 inaugural address he had contrasted the Confederacy's refusal "to impair personal liberty or the freedom of speech, of thought, or of the press" with Lin-

12. O. R., Ser. 4, Vol. 1, pp. 1156, 1116.
13. Rowland, *Davis*, V, 254–62.
14. April 18, 1862, quoted in Paul D. Escott, *After Secession: Jefferson Davis and the Failure of Confederate Nationalism* (Baton Rouge, 1978), 88.

coln's imprisonment without trial of "civil officers, peaceful citizens, and gentlewomen" in vile "Bastilles."[15] Davis overlooked the suppression of civil liberties in parts of the Confederacy, especially east Tennessee, where several hundred civilians languished in southern "Bastilles" and five had been executed. Only five days after Davis's inaugural address, Congress authorized him to suspend the writ of habeas corpus and declare martial law in areas that were in "danger of attack by the enemy."[16] Davis promptly proclaimed martial law in Richmond and other Virginia cities. He did so not only because of Union invasion but also because of rising crime and violence among the war-swollen population of the capital. General John H. Winder, provost marshal of the Richmond district, created an efficient but ruthless corps of military police. In addition to banning the sale of liquor, establishing a pass system, arresting drunken soldiers, gamblers, pickpockets, and thieves, Winder jailed without trial several "disloyal" citizens including two women and John Minor Botts, a venerable Virginia unionist and former U.S. congressman. The *Richmond Whig* branded these actions akin to Lincoln's suppression of civil liberties, whereupon Winder threatened to shut down the newspaper. He never did so, but a Richmond diarist noted in April 1862 that several editors "have confessed a fear of having their offices closed, if they dare to speak the sentiments struggling for utterance. It is, indeed, a reign of terror."[17]

Some newspapers, however, thought such a reign just what Richmond needed. "Our streets are quiet," rejoiced the *Dispatch*, because the military police had "arrested all loiterers, vagabonds, and suspicious-looking characters. . . . The consequences are peace, security, respect for life and property, and a thorough revival of patriotism." The *Examiner* believed that in an emergency "the Government must do all these things by military order. . . . To the dogs with Constitutional questions and moderation! What we want is an effectual resistance."[18]

15. Rowland, *Davis*, V, 199. "Gentlewomen" referred mainly to Rose O'Neal Greenhow, a Confederate spy in Washington whom Pinkerton's secret service had arrested and imprisoned.

16. James M. Mathews, ed., *Public Laws of the Confederate States of America* (Richmond, 1862), 1.

17. Jones, *War Clerk's Diary* (Miers), 73. For a discussion of the enforcement of martial law in Richmond, see Emory M. Thomas, *The Confederate State of Richmond* (Austin, 1971), 81–84.

18. *Richmond Dispatch*, April 4, 1862, quoted in Thomas, *Confederate State of Richmond*, 84; *Richmond Examiner*, Feb. 26, 1862.

Some commanders of military districts far from Richmond took it upon themselves to proclaim martial law. This provoked sharp protests. General Van Dorn's sweeping declaration of martial law in parts of Louisiana and Mississippi in July 1862 caused the governor of Louisiana to respond that "no free people can or ought to submit to [this] arbitrary and illegal usurpation of authority."[19] Davis forbade generals to suspend the writ or impose martial law on their own authority. But they sometimes honored his prohibition in the breach. Suspension of the writ proved an especially effective device to enforce conscription in parts of the South where state judges issued writs of habeas corpus ordering the release of draftees.

Civil libertarians linked martial law with conscription in their condemnations of Davis's "despotism." A triumvirate of Georgians emerged as leaders of an anti-administration faction on these issues: Governor Brown, Vice President Stephens, and Robert Toombs—now an ambitious but frustrated brigadier general. Even though the Confederate Constitution sanctioned suspension of the writ in case of invasion, Stephens considered such action "unconstitutional." "Away with the idea of getting independence first, and looking for liberty afterwards," he exclaimed. "Our liberties, once lost, may be lost forever." Brown agreed that "we have more to fear from military despotism than from subjugation by the enemy." Toombs denounced the "infamous schemes of Davis and his Jannissaries. . . . The road to liberty does not lie through slavery."[20] Bending to such protests, Congress in April limited the scope of martial law and specified that the authority to impose it would expire in September. In October Congress renewed Davis's power to suspend the writ—but provided for expiration of this power in February 1863. Draft resistance caused Congress to renew the power for a third time in February 1864, but once more it expired at the end of July.

Davis therefore possessed the authority to suspend the writ of habeas corpus for a total of only sixteen months. During most of that time he exercised this power more sparingly than did his counterpart in Washington. The rhetoric of southern libertarians about executive tyranny thus seems overblown. The Confederacy did not have the North's problem of administering captured territory with its hostile population. Nor

19. John B. Robbins, "The Confederacy and the Writ of Habeas Corpus," *Georgia Historical Quarterly*, 55 (1971), 86.
20. Foote, *War*, II, 951; Frank L. Owsley, *State Rights in the Confederacy* (Chicago, 1925), 162–64.

did the South have as large a disloyal population—sizable though it was—in its disaffected upland regions as the Union contained in the border states. These areas accounted for most of the Lincoln administration's suspension of civil liberties.

For a few months in the spring of 1862, however, the rise in Union military fortunes caused a relaxation of northern procedures. Since July 1861, Secretary of State Seward had been in charge of internal security—an odd arrangement resulting probably from Lincoln's distrust of Secretary of War Cameron. Seward had organized a corps of agents whose zeal to ferret out treason brooked no restraint by rules of evidence. Seward seemed enamored of his power to throw into prison anyone he suspected of aiding the rebellion. Cries of outrage arose from Republicans as well as Democrats. Perhaps it was necessary to arrest pro-Confederate legislators in Maryland, wrote Horace Greeley, but when the government imprisoned such a prominent northern Democrat as James Wall of New Jersey (soon to be elected to the Senate) "you tear the whole fabric of society."[21]

Lincoln recognized the justice of these protests. By February 1862 the detention of some two hundred political prisoners was doing more harm than good to the Union cause. The appointment of Edwin M. Stanton as secretary of war provided an opportunity for a change. On February 14 Lincoln transferred enforcement of internal security to the War Department. At the beginning of the rebellion, explained the president, harsh measures had been necessary because "every department of the Government was paralyzed by treason." Now the government had established itself and possessed armed forces sufficient to suppress rebellion. "The insurrection is believed to have culminated and to be declining. . . . In view of these facts and anxious to favor a return to the normal course of the administration," Lincoln therefore ordered the release of all political prisoners upon their taking an oath of loyalty. Stanton appointed a review board that applied liberal criteria for determining loyalty. Riding the crest of confidence in imminent victory, the North released most of its political prisoners during the spring of 1862. The New York Tribune rejoiced that "the reign of lawless despotism is ended." Stanton won praise as a humane civil libertarian—an ironic preview to his subsequent reputation as a ruthless tyrant.[22]

21. Nevins, War, II, 312.
22. O.R., Ser. 2, Vol. 2, pp. 221–23; New York Tribune, Feb. 17, 1862.

Stanton was also responsible for another optimistic policy decision in the spring of 1862. On April 3 he ordered all recruiting offices closed. The public perceived this as a sign that the armies were large enough to win the war. Stanton may have shared this belief; in any case he considered the existing system of raising troops inefficient. State governors, prominent individuals, and officers on detached service from active regiments were all beating the same bushes for recruits. Stanton closed down these operations in order to reorganize and rationalize them— if necessary. With the rebellion evidently collapsing in the West and McClellan poised for the final thrust up the Peninsula, many northerners believed it would not be necessary. By July they realized their mistake.

II

Events on the battlefields affected each side's ability to finance the war. The Confederate economy had started with two strikes against it. Most of the South's capital was tied up in the nonliquid form of land and slaves. While the Confederate states possessed 30 percent of the national wealth (in the form of real and personal property), they had only 12 percent of the circulating currency and 21 percent of the banking assets. The cotton embargo prevented the South from cashing in on its principal asset in 1861–62. Instead of possessing money to invest in Confederate bonds, most planters were in debt—mainly to factors who in turn were financed by northern merchants or banks.

The South initially hoped to turn that planter debt into a means of making Yankee bankers pay for the war. On May 21, 1861, Congress enacted a law requiring Confederate citizens to pay into the Treasury the amount of debts owed to U.S. citizens, in return for which they would receive Confederate bonds. Later legislation confiscated property owned by "alien enemies." Like so many other southern financial measures, however, these laws yielded disappointing results—no more than $12 million, a far cry from the estimated $200 million owed to northern creditors. Enforcement was difficult and concealment of debts easy. And some planters preferred to retain their credit rating with northern factors as an aid to selling cotton illegally across the lines.[23]

Of the three principal methods to finance the war—taxation, borrow-

---

23. John C. Schwab, *The Confederate States of America: A Financial and Industrial History* (New York, 1901), 110–20; Richard C. Todd, *Confederate Finance* (Athens, Ga., 1954), 157–65, 174.

ing, and fiat money—taxation is the least inflationary. But it also seemed the least desirable to southerners in 1861. Antebellum Americans had been one of the most lightly taxed peoples on earth. And the per capita burden in the South had been only half that in the free states. A rural society in which one-third of the people were slaves, the South had few public services and therefore little need for taxes. Except for tariff duties —which despite southern complaints were lower in the late 1850s than they had been for almost half a century—virtually all taxes were collected by state and local governments. The Confederate government possessed no machinery for levying internal taxes and its constituents had no tradition of paying them. Congress enacted a tiny tariff in 1861, but it brought in only $3.5 million during the entire war. In August 1861 a direct tax of one-half of one percent on real and personal property became law.[24] The Richmond government relied on states to collect this levy. Only South Carolina actually did so; Texas confiscated northern-owned property to pay its assessment; all the other states paid their quotas not by collecting the tax, but by borrowing the money or printing it in the form of state notes!

Loans seemed a better and fairer way to pay for the war. Risking their lives for liberty, southerners expected future generations to bear the financial cost of the independence won for them by the men of '61. The first bond issue of $15 million was quickly subscribed. Subsequent action by Congress in May and August of 1861 authorized the issuance of $100 million in bonds at 8 percent interest. But these sold slowly. Even those southerners with spare cash to invest had to dip deeply into their reserves of patriotism to buy bonds at 8 percent when the rate of inflation had already reached 12 percent a *month* by the end of 1861. Recognizing that willing investors might lack cash but possessed cotton, tobacco, and other crops, Congress permitted them to pledge the proceeds from such crops in return for bonds. This "produce loan," the brainchild of Treasury Secretary Christopher Memminger, was more ingenious in concept than successful in results. Some planters, having pledged part of their cotton, changed their minds and sold it instead on the open market or to agents of northern purchasers for higher prices. Only $34 million was eventually realized from the produce loan.

Investors bought most of the remainder of the $100 million bond issue with treasury notes. These notes came off the printing presses in

---

24. By exempting a head of family if his property was worth less than $500, this tax was partly progressive in nature.

ever-increasing volume. The South resorted to this method of financing the war from necessity, not choice. Memminger warned in 1862 that the printing of notes was "the most dangerous of all methods of raising money. . . . The large quantity of money in circulation today must produce depreciation and final disaster."[25] Indeed it did. But from the onset of war, bills accumulated on Memminger's desk faster than he could pay them with the proceeds of loans or taxes. He had no choice but to ask Congress to authorize treasury notes. Congress did so in amounts of $20 million in May 1861, another $100 million in August, a further $50 million in December, and yet another $50 million in April 1862. During the first year of its existence the Confederate government obtained three-quarters of its revenues from the printing press, nearly a quarter from bonds (purchased in part with these same treasury notes), and less than 2 percent from taxes. Although the proportion of loans and taxes increased slightly in later years, the Confederacy financed itself primarily with a billion and a half paper dollars that depreciated from the moment they came into existence.

These notes were to be redeemable in specie at face value within two years of the end of the war. In effect they were backed by the public's faith in the Confederacy's potential for survival. Some congressmen wanted to make the notes legal tender—to require by law all persons to accept them in payment for debts and obligations. But a majority of Congress, along with Memminger and President Davis, considered this unconstitutional, inexpedient, or both. A law to *compel* acceptance of the notes, they reasoned, would rouse suspicion, undermine confidence, hasten depreciation, and hence defeat the very purpose it sought to accomplish. The promise to redeem in specie after the war, said Memminger, was a better way to assure acceptability.

Southern states, counties, cities, even private businesses also began to issue notes and small-denomination "shinplasters." Shortages of high-quality paper and skilled engravers in the South meant that these as well as the Confederate notes were crudely printed and easily counterfeited. Some counterfeit notes could be detected because of their superior quality to the real thing. Awash in a sea of paper, the South experienced runaway inflation. At first the currency depreciated slowly, because Confederate victories in the summer of 1861 bolstered confidence. In September the price index stood only 25 percent above its January level.

25. Eugene M. Lerner, "The Monetary and Fiscal Programs of the Confederate Government, 1861–1865," *Journal of Political Economy*, 62 (1954), 509–10n.

But the issuance of new notes caused the index to jump 35 percent in the next three months. Military reverses in the spring of 1862 moved the index up 100 percent in the first half of the year; continued expansion of the currency caused it to double again in the second half. By the beginning of 1863 it took seven dollars to buy what a dollar had bought two years earlier.

This kind of inflation became, in effect, a form of confiscatory taxation whose burden fell most heavily on the poor. It exacerbated class tensions and caused a growing alienation of the white lower classes from the Confederate cause. Wage increases lagged far behind price increases. In 1862 wages for skilled and unskilled workers increased about 55 percent while prices rose 300 percent. Conditions on the small farms where most southern whites lived were little better. Although farm families grew much of what they consumed, the absence of adult males from many of the farms reduced crop yields and caused severe hardship.

The worst problem on many farms was the shortage of salt (the only means of preserving meat) and its catastrophic rise in price—from $2 a bag before the war to $60 in some places by the fall of 1862. Prior to 1861 the South, despite plentiful saline deposits, had imported most of its salt from the North or abroad. The war forced the rapid development of southern salt mines, but transportation priorities for war matériel, the deterioration of southern railroads, and shortages of labor kept supplies scarce and prices high. "There is now in this country much suffering amongst the poorer classes of Volunteers families," wrote a Mississippian in December 1862, "for want of corn and salt. . . . In the name of God, I ask is this to be tolerated? Is this war to be carried on and the Government upheld at the expense of the Starvation of the Women and children?" A rise in desertions from the army in 1862 resulted in part from the distress of the men's families. A mother of three children whose father was in the army wrote to Jefferson Davis in March 1862 that she could get no food. "If I and my little children suffer [and] die while there Father is in service I invoke God Almighty that our blood rest upon the South." A soldier from Mississippi who had overstayed his furlough wrote to the governor on December 1, 1861: "Poor men have been compelled to leave the army to come home to provide for their families. . . . We are poor men and are willing to defend our country but our families [come] first."[26]

26. The first and third letters are quoted in Charles W. Ramsdell, *Behind the Lines in*

Anguished southerners sought scapegoats to blame for their woes. They accused "speculators" and "extortioners" of cornering the market in essential items until the rise in price enabled them to sell for fantastic profits. "We have in fact two wars upon our hands," declared a Georgia newspaper in September 1862. "Whilst our brave soldiers are off battling the Abolitionists . . . a conscienceless set of vampires are at home warring upon their indigent families." This "band of harpies preying on the vitals of the Confederacy," these "contemptible wretches" who "would bottle the universal air and sell it at so much a bottle" had "caused the present high prices, and they are determined to make money even if one-half of the people starve."[27] Jefferson Davis himself stated that the "gigantic evil" of speculation had "seduced citizens of all classes from a determined prosecution of the war to a sordid effort to amass money." The *Richmond Examiner* lamented in July 1862 that "native Southern merchants have outdone Yankees and Jews. . . . The whole South stinks with the lust of extortion."[28]

Despite this condemnation of "native" merchants, the *Examiner* and many other southerners focused on Jews as the worst "extortioners." Jewish traders had "swarmed here as the locusts of Egypt," declared a congressman. "They ate up the substance of the country, they exhausted its supplies, they monopolized its trade." Jews were said to be more numerous in Charleston than in Jerusalem; the streets of Wilmington "swarmed" with "unctuous and oleaginous" Jews who bought up the cargoes of blockade runners. War Department clerk John B. Jones fulminated in his diary against "Jew extortioners" who had "injured our case more than the armies of Lincoln. Well, if we gain our independence, instead of being the vassals of the Yankees, we shall find all our wealth in the hands of the Jews."[29]

---

the *Southern Confederacy* (Baton Rouge, 1944), 28–30; the second letter is quoted in Escott, *After Secession*, 122. For the salt problem, see Ella Lonn, *Salt as a Factor in the Confederacy* (New York, 1933).

27. Quotations from Moore, *Conscription and Conflict*, 150; Eugene M. Lerner, "Money, Prices, and Wages in the Confederacy, 1861–65," in Ralph Andreano, *The Economic Impact of the American Civil War* (Cambridge, Mass., 1962), 30; Coulter, *Confederate States*, 225.

28. O.R., Ser. 4, Vol. 2, p. 810; *Richmond Examiner*, July 22, 1862.

29. Coulter, *Confederate States*, 227; W. Buck Yearns and John G. Barrett, eds., *North Carolina Civil War Documentary* (Chapel Hill, 1980), 74–75; Jones, *War Clerk's Diary* (Swiggett), I, 221.

Such diatribes were hardly unique to the Confederacy. As in other times and places, people suffering from causes beyond their comprehension fastened on an identifiable minority as scapegoats. There were Jewish merchants in the South, of course, and some of them speculated in consumer goods. So did a much larger number of southern-born Gentiles. But most merchants—Jewish and Gentile—were as much victims as perpetrators of shortages and inflation. To be sure, many of them sold goods at markups of 50 percent or more. But when inflation was running at 10 or 15 percent a month, they made little if any profit in real terms on much of what they sold.

By 1862 the Confederate economy had become unmanageable. The futility of trying to bring it under control was illustrated by the attempts of several states to curb "monopolies" or fix maximum prices. Anti-monopoly laws were aimed at speculators who tried to corner markets in any of several necessities, or to charge "exorbitant" prices for them. But these laws proved unenforceable, for they either created a black market or further exacerbated shortages. Richmond's czar of martial law, General John Winder, established maximum prices for several categories of food in April 1862. Farmers and fishermen immediately ceased to sell at these prices. After three weeks Winder admitted failure and lifted the controls, whereupon prices doubled or tripled. Under the pressures of blockade, invasion, and a flood of paper money, the South's unbalanced agrarian economy simply could not produce both guns and butter without shortages and inflation.

The northern economy proved more adaptable to the demands of war. But for a time in the winter of 1861–62, fiscal problems threatened to overwhelm the Union cause. Lincoln's administration entered the war with at least two financial advantages over the Confederacy: an established Treasury and an assured source of revenue from the tariff. But the lower rates enacted by the tariff of 1857 and the depression following the panic of that year had reduced revenues by 30 percent. From 1858 to 1861 the federal budget ran four consecutive deficits for the first time since the War of 1812. Secession produced a new panic. Specie fled the Treasury and the government's credit rating plunged. When Lincoln took office the national debt was the highest in forty years. Secretary of the Treasury Salmon P. Chase was a political appointee without prior financial experience—in contrast to the Confederacy's Memminger, who was an expert in commercial and banking law.

But Chase was an adept learner and turned out to be a good treasury secretary. His principal tutor was Jay Cooke, head of a Philadelphia banking firm, whose brother had been an ally of Chase in Ohio politics. Chase kept the Treasury afloat in the war's early months with short-term bank loans at 7.3 percent. Cooke persuaded some of his moneyed associates to buy longer-term bonds at 6 percent. Chase pioneered the concept of selling bonds to ordinary people, as well as to bankers, in denominations as small as $50 to be paid in monthly installments. Cooke undertook to market these bonds by patriotic advertising that anticipated the great war-bond drives of the twentieth century. Although this policy of financing a democratic war by democratic means got off to a slow start, Cooke eventually achieved great success in selling $400 million of "five-twenties"—6 percent bonds redeemable in not less than five or more than twenty years—and nearly $800 million of "seven-thirties"— three-year notes at 7.30 percent. Newspapers occasionally accused Cooke of getting rich from the commissions he earned on these sales. In fact his firm did earn some $4 million for marketing these bonds. But this amounted to a commission of about three-eighths of one percent, out of which Cooke paid all expenses for agents and advertising, leaving a net profit of about $700,000. This was a cheaper and more efficient means of selling bonds to the masses than the government could have achieved in any other way.[30]

Unlike the Confederacy, which relied on loans for less than two-fifths of its war finances, the Union raised two-thirds of its revenues by this means. And while the South ultimately obtained only 5 or 6 percent of its funds by actual taxation, the northern government raised 21 percent in this manner. Congress revised the tariff upward several times during the conflict, but wartime customs duties averaged only $75 million a year—scarcely more, after adjustment for inflation, than the $60 million annually in the mid-1850s. Far more important in potential, though not at first in realization, were the new internal taxes levied in the North, beginning with the first federal income tax in American history enacted on August 5, 1861. This revolutionary measure grew from a need to assure the financial community that sufficient revenue would be raised to pay interest on bonds. The Republican architects of the 1861 income tax made it modestly progressive by imposing the 3 percent tax on annual incomes over $800 only, thereby exempting most wage-earners. This was done, explained Senate Finance Committee Chairman Wil-

30. Ellis P. Oberholtzer, *Jay Cooke: Financier of the Civil War*, 2 vols. (Philadelphia, 1907); Henrietta M. Larson, *Jay Cooke: Private Banker* (Cambridge, Mass., 1936).

liam Pitt Fessenden, because the companion tariff bill was regressive in nature. "Taking both measures together, I believe the burdens will be more equalized on all classes of the community."[31]

Most of these taxes would not be collected until 1862. Meanwhile the government would have to depend on loans. But the legacy of the Jacksonian divorce of government from banking created complications. Gold for purchase of bonds had to be literally deposited in a government subtreasury. An ambiguous amendment to the war-loan act of August 5 seemed to repeal this requirement and permit the Treasury to leave the gold on deposit to the government's credit in banks, where it would form part of the legal reserves to support the banks' notes. But Chase, something of a hard-money Jacksonian in his fiscal views, chose not to proceed in this manner. Instead, he required banks and other purchasers of bonds to pay in specie, which then sometimes remained idle for weeks in government vaults while bank reserves dropped toward the danger point.[32]

Union defeat at the battle of Ball's Bluff in October 1861 and McClellan's failure to advance on Richmond eroded confidence in northern victory. Then came the threat of war with Britain over Captain Wilkes's seizure of Mason and Slidell from the *Trent*. The panic on financial exchanges caused a run on banks, whose specie reserves plummeted. The sequel was inevitable. On December 30 the banks of New York suspended specie payments. Banks elsewhere followed suit. Deprived of specie, the Treasury could no longer pay suppliers, contractors, or soldiers. The war economy of one of the world's richest nations threatened to grind to a halt. As Lincoln lamented on January 10, "the bottom is out of the tub. What shall I do?"

What indeed? Lincoln, no financial expert, played little role in congressional efforts to resolve the crisis. Chase proposed the chartering of national banks authorized to issue notes secured by government bonds. This would free the currency from direct specie requirements, pump new money into the economy, and create a market for the bonds. These ideas eventually bore fruit in the National Banking Act of 1863. But

31. CG, 37 Cong., 1 Sess., 255.
32. Bray Hammond, *Sovereignty and an Empty Purse: Banks and Politics in the Civil War* (Princeton, 1970), chaps. 3–5. For all practical purposes, "specie" meant gold, because the high price of silver in recent years had made a silver dollar worth more than a dollar for its metal, thus driving silver coins almost out of circulation.

Congressman Elbridge G. Spaulding of New York, chairman of the House subcommittee charged with responsibility for framing emergency legislation, believed that the immediate crisis demanded quicker action than the lengthy procedures necessary to establish a new banking system. A delegation of bankers tried to persuade Spaulding (himself a banker) to introduce legislation allowing banks to become depositories of public funds, thereby ending the wasteful practice of transferring gold from banks to subtreasury vaults, and to authorize a new issue of bonds to be sold "at the market" rather than for face value. Since such bonds would sell below par, investors would reap high interest rates and large profits at government expense. Spaulding rejected this proposal along with "any and every form of 'shinning' by Government through Wall or State streets . . . [and] the knocking down of Government stocks to seventy-five or sixty cents on the dollar."[33] Instead, he introduced a bill to authorize the issuance of $150 million in Treasury notes—i.e., fiat money.

This bill seemed to imitate the dubious Confederate example—but with a crucial difference. The U.S. notes were to be legal tender— receivable for all debts public or private except interest on government bonds and customs duties. The exemption of bond interest was intended as an alternative to selling the bonds below par, with the expectation that the payment of 6 percent interest in specie would make the bonds attractive to investors at face value. Customs duties were to be payable in specie to assure sufficient revenue to fund the interest on bonds. In all other transactions individuals, banks, and government itself would be required to accept U.S. notes—soon to be called greenbacks—as lawful money.

Opponents maintained that the legal tender bill was unconstitutional because when the framers empowered Congress "to coin money," they meant *coin*. Moreover, to require acceptance of paper money for debts previously contracted was a breach of contract. But the attorney general and most Republican congressmen favored a broad construction of the coinage and the "necessary and proper" clauses of the Constitution. "The bill before us is a war measure," Spaulding told the House, "a *necessary means* of carrying into execution the power granted in the Constitution 'to raise and *support* armies.' . . . These are extraordinary

33. Robert P. Sharkey, *Money, Class, and Party: An Economic Study of Civil War and Reconstruction* (Baltimore, 1959), 32.

times, and extraordinary measures must be resorted to in order to save our Government and preserve our nationality."[34]

Opponents also questioned the expediency, morality, even the theology of the legal tender bill. Such notes would depreciate, they said, as the Revolutionary continentals had done and as Confederate notes were even then depreciating. "The wit of man," said Democratic Congressman George Pendleton of Ohio, "has never discovered a means by which paper currency can be kept at par value, except by its speedy, cheap, certain convertibility into gold and silver." If this bill passed, "prices will be inflated . . . incomes will depreciate; the savings of the poor will vanish; the hoardings of the widow will melt away; bonds, mortgages, and notes—everything of fixed value—will lose their value." One banker insisted that "gold and silver are the only true measure of value. These metals were prepared by the Almighty for this very purpose."[35]

Supporters of the bill exposed the hollowness of such arguments. "Every intelligent man knows that coined money is not the currency of the country," said Republican Representative Samuel Hooper of Massachusetts. State banknotes—many of them depreciated and irredeemable— were the principal medium of exchange. The issue before Congress was whether the notes of a sovereign government had "as much virtue . . . as the notes of banks which have suspended specie payments."[36]

By early February most businessmen and bankers had become convinced of the necessity for the legal tender bill. So had Treasury Secretary Chase and Finance Committee Chairman Fessenden. "I came with reluctance to the conclusion that the legal tender clause is a necessity," Chase informed Congress on February 3, 1862. *"Immediate action is of great importance. The Treasury is nearly empty."* Fessenden considered the measure "of doubtful constitutionality. . . . It is bad faith. . . . It shocks all my notions of political, moral, and national honor." Nevertheless, "to leave the government without resources in such a crisis is not to be thought of." Fessenden voted for the bill.[37] So did three-fourths of his Republican colleagues in Congress, who readily overcame

---

34. CG, 37 Cong., 2 Sess., 523, 525.
35. *Ibid.*, 551; Hugh McCulloch, *Men and Measures of Half a Century* (New York, 1888), 201.
36. CG, 37 Cong., 2 Sess., 691; Sharkey, *Money, Class, and Party*, 32.
37. CG, 37 Cong., 2 Sess., 618; Fessenden quoted in Hammond, *Sovereignty and an Empty Purse*, 213–14.

the three-fourths of the Democrats who voted against it. With Lincoln's signature on February 25, the Legal Tender Act became law.

This act created a national currency and altered the monetary structure of the United States. It asserted national sovereignty to help win a war fought to preserve that sovereignty. It provided the Treasury with resources to pay its bills, it restored investor confidence to make possible the sale at par of the $500 million of new 6 percent bonds authorized at the same time, and unlocked the funds that had gone into hoarding during the financial crisis of December. All these good things came to pass without the ruinous inflation predicted by opponents, despite the authorization of another $150 million of greenbacks in July 1862. This brought the total to $300 million, nearly equal to the amount of Confederate Treasury notes then in circulation. But while the southern price index rose to 686 (February 1861 = 100) by the end of 1862, the northern index then stood only at 114. For the war as a whole the Union experienced inflation of only 80 percent (contrasted with 9,000 percent for the Confederacy), which compares favorably to the 84 percent of World War I (1917–20) and 70 percent in World War II (1941–49, including the postwar years after the lifting of wartime price controls). While the greenbacks' lack of a specie backing created a speculator's market in gold, the "gold premium" did not rise drastically except in periods of Union military reverses. During the four months after passage of the Legal Tender Act, the gold premium rose only to 106 (that is, 100 gold dollars would buy 106 greenback dollars).

Three main factors explain the success of the Legal Tender Act. First: the underlying strength of the northern economy. Second: the fortuitous timing of the law. It went into effect during the months of Union military success in the spring of 1862, floating the greenbacks on a buoyant mood of confidence in victory. The third reason was the enactment of a comprehensive tax law on July 1, 1862, which soaked up much of the inflationary pressure produced by the greenbacks. The Union ultimately raised half again as much war revenue from taxes as from the issuance of paper money—in sharp contrast with the Confederate experience.[38]

The Internal Revenue Act of 1862 taxed almost everything but the air northerners breathed. It imposed sin taxes on liquor, tobacco, and

38. The total value of greenbacks issued was $447 million. Taxes during the war amounted to nearly $700 million.

playing cards; luxury taxes on carriages, yachts, billiard tables, jewelry, and other expensive items; taxes on patent medicines and newspaper advertisements; license taxes on almost every conceivable profession or service except the clergy; stamp taxes, taxes on the gross receipts of corporations, banks, insurance companies, and a tax on the dividends or interest they paid to investors; value-added taxes on manufactured goods and processed meats; an inheritance tax; and an income tax. The law also created a Bureau of Internal Revenue, which remained a permanent part of the federal government even though most of these taxes (including the income tax) expired several years after the end of the war. The relationship of the American taxpayer to the government was never again the same.

The Internal Revenue Act was strikingly modern in several respects. It withheld the tax from the salaries of government employees and from dividends paid by corporations. It expanded the progressive aspects of the earlier income tax by exempting the first $600, levying 3 percent on incomes between $600 and $10,000, and 5 percent on incomes over $10,000.[39] The first $1,000 of any legacy was exempt from the inheritance tax. Businesses worth less than $600 were exempt from the value-added and receipts taxes. Excise taxes fell most heavily on products purchased by the affluent. In explanation of these progressive features, Chairman Thaddeus Stevens of the House Ways and Means Committee said: "While the rich and the thrifty will be obliged to contribute largely from the abundance of their means . . . no burdens have been imposed on the industrious laborer and mechanic. . . . The food of the poor is untaxed; and . . . no one will be affected by the provisions of this bill whose living depends solely on his manual labor."[40]

Whether northern wage-earners appreciated this solicitude is hard to tell. By the time the internal revenue act went into effect many of them were suffering the pinch of inflation. While far less serious than in the South, price increases did cause an average decline of 20 percent in real wages of northern workers by 1863 or 1864. In classical economic theory, the labor shortage caused by a wartime decline of immigration and by the enlistment of workers in the army should have enabled wages to keep up with the cost of living, if not exceed it. Three factors seem to have prevented this from happening. The first was some slack

39. Revised in 1864 to 5 percent on incomes from $600 to $5,000; 7½ percent from $5,000 to $10,000; and 10 percent on incomes over $10,000.
40. CG, 37 Cong., 2 Sess., 1576–77.

in the economy left from the aftershocks of the Panic of 1857 and a renewed panic and downturn caused by secession in 1861, which meant that a labor surplus did not become a labor shortage until 1862. Second, a wartime speedup in mechanization of certain key industries helped alleviate the tight labor market: for example, more reapers and mowers for harvesting grain and hay were produced during the war than ever before, easing the demand for agricultural labor; the sewing machine multiplied the productivity of seamstresses making army uniforms and other clothing; and the Blake-McKay machine for sewing uppers to the soles of shoes reduced the time consumed in that process one hundred-fold. Third was a great increase in the employment of women, in occupations ranging from government civil service and army nursing to agricultural field work and manufacturing. In agriculture, the increased use of farm machinery enabled women to fill much of the gap left by the enlistment of nearly a million northern farmers and farm laborers in the army. "I met more women driving teams on the road and saw more at work in the fields than men," wrote a traveler in Iowa during the fall of 1862. As evidence of "the great revolution which machinery is making in agriculture," reported another observer the following year, he saw "a stout matron whose sons are in the army, with her team cutting hay. . . . She cut seven acres with ease in a day, riding leisurely on her cutter." In northern industry women worked mainly in occupations where they were already prominent—textiles, clothing, shoemaking—but increased their proportion of the manufacturing labor force from one-fourth to one-third during the war. Because women earned much less than men for the same or similar jobs, their expanded proportion of the wartime labor force kept down the average of wage increases.[41]

The wage lag behind cost-of-living increases fueled protests and strikes, especially in 1863–64. A good many strikes succeeded in winning substantial wage gains, especially in skilled trades and heavy industries where machinery and women could do little to redress a now-acute labor shortage. By the last year of the war real wages in many of these trades

41. Quotations from Emerson D. Fite, *Social and Industrial Conditions in the North during the Civil War* (New York, 1910), 8; and George W. Smith and Charles Judah, eds., *Life in the North during the Civil War* (Albuquerque, 1966), 167. For other sources on which this and the following paragraphs are based, see Philip S. Foner, *History of the Labor Movement in the United States*, Vol. I (New York, 1947); and David Montgomery, *Beyond Equality: Labor and the Radical Republicans, 1862–1872* (New York, 1967).

had returned to prewar levels and were poised for postwar increases. For unskilled workers and women, however, low wages and inflation remained a searing grievance. "We are unable to sustain life for the prices offered by contractors, who fatten on their contracts by grinding immense profits out of the labor of their operatives," wrote a group of seamstresses—who in war as in peace were the most exploited group of workers—making army uniforms in 1864.[42]

Wartime activism and strikes, combined with labor's pride in its contribution to northern victory, caused an increase of worker militancy and organization. Several new national trade unions were organized during the war, and a number of labor newspapers sprang into existence, paving the way for the founding of the umbrella National Labor Union in 1866. The wartime impetus helped drive union membership to its highest proportion of the industrial labor force in the nineteenth century by the eve of the Panic of 1873. But that is a story for the next volume in this series.

III

The second session of the 37th Congress (1861–62) was one of the most productive in American history. Not only did the legislators revolutionize the country's tax and monetary structures and take several steps toward the abolition of slavery;[43] they also enacted laws of far-reaching importance for the disposition of public lands, the future of higher education, and the building of transcontinental railroads. These achievements were all the more remarkable because they occurred in the midst of an all-consuming preoccupation with war. Yet it was the war—or rather the absence of southerners from Congress—that made possible the passage of these Hamiltonian–Whig–Republican measures for government promotion of socioeconomic development.

Having appealed to voters in the Northwest with a homestead plank in the 1860 platform, Republicans easily overcame feeble Democratic and border-state opposition to pass a homestead act on May 20, 1862. This law granted 160 acres of public land to a settler after five years' residence and improvements on his (or her, since the law made no distinction of sex) claim. Although the Homestead Act never measured up to the starry-eyed vision of some enthusiasts who had hoped to "give

42. Montgomery, *Beyond Equality*, 97.
43. For a discussion of slavery, see Chapter 16, below.

every poor man a farm," it did become an important part of the explosive westward expansion after the war. Even before Appomattox, 25,000 settlers had staked claims to more than three million acres, forerunners of some half-million farm families who eventually settled eighty million acres of homesteaded land.

For years Vermont's Justin Morrill—the architect of Republican tariff legislation in 1861 and chairman of the House subcommittee that framed the Internal Revenue Act—had sponsored a bill to grant public lands to the states for the promotion of higher education in "agriculture and the mechanic arts." When Morrill brought his measure before Congress again in 1861, regional tensions within the Republican party delayed its passage. The bill proposed to grant every state (including southern states if and when they returned) 30,000 acres of public land for each congressman and senator. Since New York, Pennsylvania, and other populous eastern states would get the lion's share of the bounty while all of the public land they would receive was located in the West, the plan did not sit well with many westerners. Nevertheless a sufficient number of western Republicans supported the bill—partly as a *quid pro quo* for eastern support of the Homestead Act—to pass the Morrill Act on July 2, 1862. For good measure, Congress also created a Department of Agriculture. The success of the land-grant college movement was attested by the later development of first-class institutions in many states and world-famous universities at Ithaca, Urbana, Madison, Minneapolis, and Berkeley.

Sectional conflict over the route of a transcontinental railroad had prevented action on government aid to construct such a line in the 1850s. Freed of the southern incubus, Yankee legislators highballed forward in 1862. On July 1, the same day that the Internal Revenue Act became law, Lincoln signed the Pacific Railroad Act granting 6,400 acres of public land (later doubled) per mile and lending $16,000 per mile (for construction on the plains) and $48,000 per mile (in the mountains) of government bonds to corporations organized to build a railroad from Omaha to San Francisco Bay. Intended to prime the pump of private capital, this measure succeeded in spectacular fashion. The first rails were laid eastward from Sacramento in 1863; six years later the golden spike linked the Central Pacific and Union Pacific at Promontory, Utah. Other land grants to transcontinental railroads followed the first one, eventually totaling 120 million acres. Although these railroads became a source of corruption and of corporate power in politics, most Americans in 1862 viewed government aid as an investment in national unity and economic growth that would benefit all groups in society.

This was the philosophy that underlay all three of the land-grant laws of 1862. To some degree these laws functioned at cross purposes, for settlers, universities, and railroads competed for portions of the same land in subsequent years. Yet the 225 million acres that the government ultimately gave away under these laws constituted only a fraction of the two billion acres of public land. And despite waste, corruption, and exploitation, these land grants did help to people a vast domain, sprinkle it with schools, and span it with steel rails.

By its legislation to finance the war, emancipate the slaves, and invest public land in future growth, the 37th Congress did more than any other in history to change the course of national life. As one scholar has aptly written, this Congress drafted "the blueprint for modern America." It also helped shape what historians Charles and Mary Beard labeled the "Second American Revolution"—that process by which "the capitalists, laborers, and farmers of the North and West drove from power in the national government the planting aristocracy of the South . . . making vast changes in the arrangement of classes, in the accumulation and distribution of wealth, in the course of industrial development, and in the Constitution inherited from the Fathers."[44] This new America of big business, heavy industry, and capital-intensive agriculture that surpassed Britain to become the foremost industrial nation by 1880 and became the world's breadbasket for much of the twentieth century probably would have come about even if the Civil War had never occurred. But the war molded the particular configuration of this new society, and the legislation of the 37th Congress that authorized war bonds to be bought with greenbacks and repaid with gold and thereby helped concentrate investment capital, that confiscated southern property and strengthened northern industry by expanding internal markets, protecting those markets with tariffs, and improving access to them with subsidies to transportation, that settled the public domain and improved its cultivation, and rationalized the country's monetary and credit structure—this legislation did indeed help fashion a future different enough from the past to merit the label of revolution.

The revolution abounded in ironies, to be sure. Congressmen from

44. Leonard P. Curry, *Blueprint for Modern America: Nonmilitary Legislation of the First Civil War Congress* (Nashville, 1968); Charles A. Beard and Mary R. Beard, *The Rise of American Civilization*, 2 vols. (New York, 1927), II, 53–54.

western states had been the strongest proponents of the Legal Tender Act and the National Banking Act, in order to remedy the instability and regional imbalance of the monetary and credit system from which western states suffered most. Eastern congressmen and bankers, more satisfied with the existing system, had been lukewarm or opposed. Westerners had also been the prime supporters of federal aid to construct a transcontinental railroad, while easterners, already served by a good transportation system, were less enthusiastic. Yet the consequences of these acts were to *increase* the domination of the country's credit, transportation, and marketing structure by eastern bankers, merchants, and investors. By the 1890s the farmers of the West and South revolted against their "slavery" to an eastern "money power" that was allegedly squeezing their life blood from them. Back in the 1830s, Jacksonian artisans and yeomen had viewed with suspicion the transportation revolution, the growth of banks, and the evolution of wage-labor capitalism that seemed to threaten their republican independence. By the 1890s this economic system had penetrated the farthest reaches of the country. For the last time, perhaps, aggrieved Americans rose in the name of Jeffersonian republicanism in a counterrevolution against the second American revolution of free-labor capitalism. Once again the country rang with rhetoric of sectional conflict—this time the South and West against the Northeast—in a presidential election with the Populist ticket headed by a former Union general teamed with a former Confederate general as his running mate.

That also is a story for the next volume in this series. Before there could be such a story to tell, however, before the "Second American Revolution" could draft the "blueprint for modern America," the North must win the war. Its prospects for doing so took a sudden turn for the worse in the summer of 1862, when Stonewall Jackson and Robert E. Lee derailed the Union war machine.

15

Billy Yank's Chickahominy Blues

I

In May 1862, prospects for the Confederacy's survival seemed bleak. Most of the Mississippi Valley had fallen to the enemy. In Virginia, McClellan's army of 100,000 had advanced to within hearing of Richmond's church bells. Irvin McDowell's corps, which Lincoln had held near Fredericksburg to cover Washington, prepared to march south to join McClellan's right wing. This would give the Union forces closing in on Richmond some 135,000 men, about twice the total that Joseph E. Johnston could bring against them. Although McClellan's past performance suggested that he would lay siege to Richmond rather than attack Johnston's army, the fall of the Confederate capital seemed only a matter of time.

The next act in this drama took place not in front of Richmond but a hundred miles to the northwest in the Shenandoah Valley. Commanding the rebel forces in that strategic region, Stonewall Jackson had been reinforced to a strength of 17,000 men by a division from Johnston's army. Its commander was Richard S. Ewell, an eccentric, balding, forty-five-year old bachelor whose beaked nose and habit of cocking his head to one side reminded observers of a bird. Everything about Ewell seemed odd, from his ulcer-induced diet of hulled wheat boiled in milk with raisins and egg yolk to his manner of cursing with a lisp. But while Ewell was an unfailing source of jokes around soldier campfires, Jackson seemed even more peculiar. Attired in an old army coat he had worn in the Mexican War and a broken-visored V.M.I. cadet cap, Jackson constantly sucked lemons to palliate his dyspepsia and refused to season his food with pepper because (he said) it made his left leg ache. A disciplinary martinet, Jackson had tarnished some of the fame won at Manassas by an aborted winter campaign into West Virginia that provoked a near mutiny by some of his troops. A devout Presbyterian, Jackson came across to some colleagues as a religious fanatic. Taciturn, humorless, and secretive, he rarely explained to subordinates the purpose of his orders. His rule of strategy—"always mystify, mislead, and surprise the enemy"—seemed to apply to his own officers as well.[1] Before May 8, 1862, many of his soldiers considered him crazy and called him "Old Tom Fool." Events during the next month, however, showed them that he was crazy like a fox. These events made Jackson the South's premier hero for a time—until eclipsed by an even wilier fox with no tinge of fanaticism, Robert E. Lee.

It was Lee who unleashed Jackson in the Shenandoah Valley. Serving as Jefferson Davis's military adviser, Lee conceived the idea of a diversion in the Valley to prevent McDowell's Union corps from reinforcing McClellan. Once before, after the battle of Kernstown in March, the northern command had cancelled the transfer of troops from the Valley to eastern Virginia. Since then, one of Nathaniel Banks's three divisions west of the Blue Ridge had departed eastward. A second was preparing to follow. Lee hoped that an offensive by Jackson would compel them to return. This was Lee's first essay in the kind of offensive-defensive strategy that was to become his hallmark. And as long as Jackson lived, he commanded the mobile force that Lee relied on to spearhead this strategy. Jackson did so now, with a series of maneuvers that did indeed mislead, mystify, and surprise the enemy.

At the beginning of May, Jackson marched part of his army east across the Blue Ridge. Federal scouts reported that he was heading toward the Richmond front. Jackson's own troops believed the same. But when they arrived at the railroad near Charlottesville, Jackson put them on trains that carried them back west over the Blue Ridge to Staunton. From there Jackson led 9,000 men a few miles farther over mountain passes to the hamlet of McDowell, where on May 8 they fought and defeated a Union force half as large. These bluecoats were part of an army of 25,000 men that John C. Frémont was assembling in West

1. John B. Imboden, "Stonewall Jackson in the Shenandoah," *Battles and Leaders*, II, 297.

Virginia for a drive 250 miles southward to capture Knoxville. This impracticable plan was a compound of Frémont's romanticism and Lincoln's desire to liberate east Tennessee. Jackson's surprise attack disrupted the campaign before it got started.

Stonewall marched his men back into the Shenandoah Valley at Harrisonburg. Banks's sole remaining division had recently retreated northward from there to Strasburg, where they dug in. Jackson made as if to follow, but at New Market he suddenly swerved eastward across Massanutten Mountain, which at that point divided the Shenandoah into two smaller valleys. Jackson had spent many hours studying maps of the Valley drawn by his brilliant topographical engineer Jedediah Hotchkiss. Now all that study paid off. While Jackson's hell-for-leather cavalry under Turner Ashby kept up a feint along the pike toward Strasburg, deceiving Banks into thinking that the rebels were coming that way, the main Confederate thrust came in the Luray Valley east of Massanutten Mountain. Here on May 23 Jackson's and Ewell's combined force overwhelmed the small Union outpost at Front Royal. Jackson was now on Banks's flank only ten miles away with a force more than double the size of the Union division.

In all of these swift, deceptive movements Jackson was aided by local scouts and spies who knew every foot of the country. Northern commanders had no such advantage. Moreover, Valley residents such as Belle Boyd of Front Royal kept Jackson informed of Federal troop dispositions. Banks had to contend not only with Jackson's army but also with a hostile civilian population—a problem confronted by every invading Union army, and one that helped make this a war of peoples as well as of armies.

Impatient toward weaknesses of the flesh, Jackson had driven his infantry at a killing pace. "He classed all who were weak and weary, who fainted by the wayside, as men wanting in patriotism," said an officer. "If a man's face was as white as cotton and his pulse so low you could scarcely feel it, he looked upon him merely as an inefficient soldier and rode off impatiently." Ewell caught the spirit and ordered his marching columns stripped to the minimum. "We can get along without anything but food and ammunition," he stated. "The road to glory cannot be followed with much baggage."[2] Although barefoot, blistered, and broken down from marching 160 miles and fighting two battles in two

2. Foote, *Civil War*, I, 426; O.R., Ser. I, Vol. 12, pt. 3, p. 890.

weeks, Jackson's men no longer called him Tom Fool. Now he was Old Jack, and they were proud to be known as his foot cavalry.

They would need this pride to keep them going, for even harder marching and fighting lay ahead. The truth of his predicament having dawned on him, Banks retreated at top speed from Strasburg to his base at Winchester twenty miles north. Jackson's tired troops pressed after him on May 24, slicing into Banks's wagon train and capturing a cornucopia of supplies. Banks's main body won the race to Winchester, where they turned to fight. At foggy daybreak on May 25, some 15,000 rebels assaulted 6,000 Yankees on the hills south and west of town. After some sharp fighting the Federals broke and streamed northward for the safety of the Potomac thirty-five miles away. Ashby's undisciplined cavalry had disintegrated into looters, plundering Union camps or leading captured horses to the troopers' nearby homes. Without cavalry and with worn-out infantry, Jackson could not pursue the routed bluecoats. Nevertheless his victories at Front Royal and Winchester had reaped at least 2,000 prisoners, 9,000 rifles, and such a wealth of food and medical stores that Jackson's men labeled their opponent "Commissary Banks."

Jackson's campaign accomplished the relief of pressure against Richmond that Lee had hoped for. When Lincoln learned on May 24 of Jackson's capture of Front Royal, he made two swift decisions. First he ordered Frémont to push his troops eastward into the Valley at Harrisonburg, from where they could march north and attack Jackson's rear. Second, he suspended McDowell's movement from Fredericksburg toward Richmond and ordered him to send two divisions posthaste to the Valley to smash into Jackson's flank. Both McClellan and McDowell protested that this action played into the enemy's hand. It was "a crushing blow to us," McDowell wired Lincoln. "I shall gain nothing for you there, and shall lose much for you here."[3] Nevertheless, McDowell obeyed orders. Back to the Valley he sent James Shields's division, which Banks had sent to him only a few days earlier. McDowell himself followed with another division. Sitting in the War Department telegraph office in Washington, Lincoln fired off telegrams to the three separate commands of Frémont, Banks, and McDowell, hoping to move them like knights and bishops on the military chessboard. But his generals moved too slowly, or in the wrong direction. Instead of crossing into

3. CWL, V, 232–33.

the Valley at Harrisonburg, Frémont found the passes blocked by small enemy forces and marched forty miles northward to cross at a point northwest of Strasburg. This angered Lincoln, for it opened the way for Jackson's 16,000 to escape southward through Strasburg before Frémont's 15,000 and Shields's 10,000 (with another 10,000 close behind) converged on them from west and east.

That was precisely what happened. After the battle of Winchester, Jackson had marched to within a few miles of Harper's Ferry to give the impression that he intended to cross the Potomac. On May 30 his force was nearly twice as far from Strasburg as the converging forces of Frémont and Shields. Nothing but a few cavalry stood in the way of the Union pincers. But a strange lethargy seemed to paralyze the northern commanders. Jackson's foot cavalry raced southward day and night on May 30 while the bluecoats tarried. The rebels cleared Strasburg on June 1 and slogged southward while Frémont and Shields, finally aroused, nipped at their heels. For the next few days it became a stern chase, with Frémont pursuing Jackson on the Valley pike and Shields trudging southward on a parallel course east of Massanutten Mountain. Ashby's cavalry burned four bridges to delay Union pursuit. Several rear-guard cavalry fights took place, one of them resulting in the death of Ashby, who had become a romantic hero in the South. Jackson kept pushing his men to the edge of collapse. They won the race to the only undamaged bridge left on the Shenandoah River, at Port Republic near the south end of the Valley where Jackson had launched his epic campaign five weeks earlier. During those weeks Jackson's own division had marched more than 350 miles (Ewell's had marched 200 miles) and won three battles. Now they stopped to fight again.

On June 8, Frémont's troops advanced against Ewell's division stationed three miles north of Port Republic near the tiny village of Cross Keys. Frémont handled this attack poorly. Although outnumbering Ewell by 11,000 to 6,000, he committed only a fraction of his infantry to an attack on the Confederate right. After its repulse, Frémont settled down for an artillery duel that accomplished nothing. Reacting to this feeble effort, Jackson made a typically bold decision. His army of 15,000 was caught between two enemy forces whose combined strength he believed to be at least 50 percent greater than his own. The safe course was retreat to the nearest defensible pass in the Blue Ridge. But the two Federal armies under Frémont and Shields were separated by unfordable rivers, while Jackson's troops held the only bridge. On the night of June 8–9, Jackson ordered Ewell to leave a token force confronting

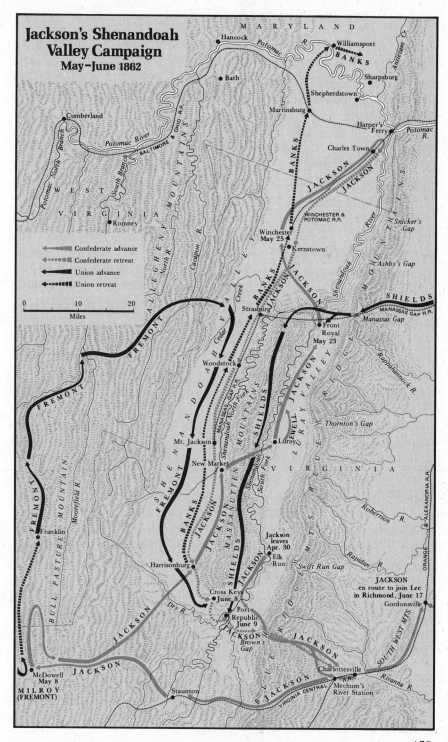

Jackson's Shenandoah Valley Campaign
May–June 1862

Legend:
- Confederate advance
- Confederate retreat
- Union advance
- Union retreat

0   10   20
Miles

MARYLAND

Hancock
Bath
Williamsport
BANKS
Sharpsburg
Shepherdstown
Martinsburg
Harper's Ferry
Potomac R.
Charles Town
Cumberland
Potomac North Branch
Potomac River
South Branch
BALTIMORE & OHIO R.R.
WINCHESTER & POTOMAC R.R.
JACKSON
JACKSON
Romney
WEST VIRGINIA
ALLEGHENY MOUNTAINS
North R.
Capon R.
Snicker's Gap
Shenandoah River
Winchester May 25
BANKS
JACKSON
Kernstown
Ashby's Gap
SHIELDS
Cedar Creek
BANKS
JACKSON
Strasburg
Front Royal May 23
MANASSAS GAP R.R.
Manassas Gap
FREMONT
Woodstock
MANASSAS GAP R.R.
Shenandoah North Fork
SHIELDS
JACKSON
LURAY VALLEY
Thornton's Gap
Rappahannock R.
EWELL
BLUE
Mt. Jackson
New Market
Luray
Shenandoah South Fork
VIRGINIA
Robertson R.
ALEXANDRIA R.R.
FREMONT
Franklin
Moorefield R.
SHENANDOAH VALLEY
FREMONT
BANKS
JACKSON
SHIELDS
MASSANUTTEN MOUNTAIN
JACKSON
RIDGE
Rapidan R.
Jackson leaves Apr. 30
Elk Run
Swift Run Gap
ORANGE
BULL PASTURE MOUNTAIN
Harrisonburg
SHIELDS
JACKSON
JACKSON en route to join Lee in Richmond, June 17
Gordonsville
Cross Keys June 8
Dry R.
Port Republic June 9
Brown's Gap
JACKSON
SOUTH WEST MTS.
McDowell May 8
MILROY (FREMONT)
Staunton
Charlottesville
Mechum's River Station
VIRGINIA CENTRAL R.R.
Rivanna R.

459

Frémont and march the rest of his division to Port Republic. Jackson intended to overwhelm Shields's advance force and then face about to attack Frémont. But the stubborn resistance of Shields's two brigades at Port Republic frustrated the plan. Three thousand bluecoats held off for three hours the seven or eight thousand men that Jackson finally got into action. The weight of numbers eventually prevailed, but by then Jackson's army was too battered to carry out the attack against Frémont, who had remained quiescent during this bloody morning of June 9. Both sides pulled back and regrouped. That night Jackson withdrew to Brown's Gap in the Blue Ridge.

Jackson's Valley campaign won renown and is still studied in military schools as an example of how speed and use of terrain can compensate for inferiority of numbers. Jackson's army of 17,000 men had outmaneuvered three separate enemy forces with a combined strength of 33,000 and had won five battles, in all but one of which (Cross Keys) Jackson had been able to bring superior numbers to the scene of combat. Most important, Jackson's campaign had diverted 60,000 Union soldiers from other tasks and had disrupted two major strategic movements—Frémont's east Tennessee campaign and McDowell's plan to link up with McClellan's right wing before Richmond. Jackson's victories in the Valley created an aura of invincibility around him and his foot cavalry. They furthered the southern tradition of victory in the Virginia theater that had begun at Manassas. Summarizing the Valley campaign, a rebel private wrote: "General Jackson 'got the drop' on them in the start, and kept it."[4] The soldier meant this in a military sense, but it was equally true in a psychological sense. Stonewall became larger than life in the eyes of many northerners; he had gotten the drop on them psychologically, and kept it until his death a year later.

Lincoln's diversion of McDowell's corps to chase Jackson was probably a strategic error—perhaps even the colossal blunder that McClellan considered it. But if Union commanders in the Valley had acted with half the energy displayed by Jackson they might well have trapped and crippled Jackson's army. And even if McDowell's corps had joined McClellan as planned, the latter's previous record offered little reason to believe that he would have moved with speed and boldness to capture Richmond.

4. Robert G. Tanner, *Stonewall in the Valley: Thomas J. "Stonewall" Jackson's Shenandoah Valley Campaign Spring 1862* (Garden City, N.Y., 1976), 259.

II

Rising a few miles north of Richmond, the Chickahominy River flows southeast until it empties into the James halfway down the Peninsula. The Chickahominy became an important factor in the defense of Richmond. Normally sluggish and shallow, the river had swollen to a raging torrent during the abnormal May rains. It bisected the ring of Union troops closing in on Richmond. McClellan had placed more than half of his army on the north side of the Chickahominy to protect his base of supplies and to hook up with McDowell's expected advance from the north. Several makeshift bridges threatened by the flooding river provided the only links between the two wings of McClellan's army.

Waiting nervously in Richmond while McClellan readied his siege artillery, Jefferson Davis prodded a reluctant Joseph Johnston to launch some kind of counterstroke. Johnston finally decided to attack the weaker Union left wing south of the river. Reinforcements from North Carolina had brought his strength to nearly 75,000 men. A torrential downpour on May 30 seemed providential to the Confederates, for it washed out most of the Chickahominy bridges and gave southern troops numerical superiority over the two isolated Union corps south of the river.

But from the beginning of Johnston's planned early-morning attack on May 31, things went wrong. A misunderstood verbal order caused James Longstreet to advance his oversize division on the wrong road where it entangled parts of two other divisions and delayed the attack until midafternoon. When the assault finally went forward it did so disjointedly, one brigade at a time, because of poor staff coordination. The Confederates managed to drive the Union left a mile through the crossroads village of Seven Pines, about seven miles east of Richmond. On the Union right, however, the leather-lunged commander of the 2nd Corps, sixty-five-year old Edwin "Bull" Sumner, got one of his divisions across the Chickahominy on swaying bridges with ankle-deep water coursing over them and brought the rebel left to a bloody halt in the dusk near the railroad station of Fair Oaks. Next day, indecisive fighting sputtered out as additional Union reinforcements from across the Chickahominy forced the Confederates to yield the ground they had won the first day.

Seven Pines (or Fair Oaks, as the Yankees called it) was a confused battle, "phenomenally mismanaged" on the Confederate side according to Johnston's chief of ordnance.[5] Most of the 42,000 men engaged on each side fought in small clusters amid thick woods and flooded clearings where wounded soldiers had to be propped against fences or stumps to prevent them from drowning in the muck. If either side gained an advantage it was the Federals, who inflicted a thousand more casualties (6,000) than they suffered. The most important southern casualty was Joe Johnston, wounded by a shell fragment and a bullet through the shoulder on the evening of May 31. To replace him Davis appointed Robert E. Lee, who recognized the futility of further fighting by breaking off the engagement on June 1.

When Lee took command of the newly designated Army of Northern Virginia, few shared Davis's high opinion of the quiet Virginian. "Evacuating Lee," sneered the *Richmond Examiner* in recollection of his West Virginia campaign, "who has never yet risked a single battle with the invader." Across the way, McClellan voiced pleasure at the change in southern command, for he considered Lee "cautious and weak under grave responsibilty . . . likely to be timid and irresolute in action."[6]

A psychiatrist trying to understand what made McClellan tick might read a great deal into these words, which described McClellan himself but could not have been more wrong about Lee. The latter ignored criticism and set about reorganizing his army for a campaign that would fit his offensive-defensive concept of strategy. Lee's first actions emphasized the defensive. He put his soldiers to work strengthening the fortifications and trenches ringing Richmond, which earned him new derision as "the king of spades." But it soon became clear that Lee's purpose was not to hunker down for a siege. On the contrary, he told Davis, "I am preparing a line that I can hold with part of our forces" while concentrating the rest for a slashing attack on McClellan's exposed right flank north of the Chickahominy.[7]

Lee knew that this flank was "in the air" (unprotected by natural or man-made obstacles such as a river, right-angle fortifications, etc.) because a remarkable reconnaissance by Jeb Stuart's cavalry had discovered the fact. Twenty-nine years old, Stuart had already won modest

---

5. Edward P. Alexander quoted in Clifford Dowdey, *The Seven Days: The Emergence of Robert E. Lee* (New York, 1964), 4.

6. *Examiner* quoted in Hudson Strode, *Jefferson Davis: Confederate President* (New York, 1959), 220; McClellan quoted in Foote, *Civil War*, I, 465.

7. Dowdey, *The Seven Days*, 132.

fame in the war but had an insatiable appetite for more. Dressed in knee-high cavalry boots, elbow-length gauntlets, red-lined cape with a yellow sash, and a felt hat with pinned-up brim and ostrich-feather plume, Stuart looked the dashing cavalier he aspired to be. He was also a superb leader of cavalry, especially in gathering information about enemy positions and movements. In this as in other tasks assigned to the cavalry—screening the army from enemy horsemen, patrolling front and flanks to prevent surprise attacks, raiding enemy supply lines, and pursuing defeated enemy infantry—the rebel troopers were superior to their adversaries at this stage of the war. Having grown up in the saddle, sons of the Virginia gentry quite literally rode circles around the neophyte Yankee horsemen. When Lee told Stuart on June 10 that he wanted a reconnaissance to discover the strength and location of the Union right, Stuart was ready.

With 1,200 picked men he rode north from Richmond on June 12 and swung east across the headwaters of the Chickahominy, brushing aside the small enemy patrols he encountered. Stuart's progress was helped by the fragmented organization of Union cavalry, which was sprinkled by companies and regiments throughout the army instead of consolidated into a separate division as the southern cavalry was. Stuart's troopers discovered the location of Fitz-John Porter's 5th Corps, which McClellan had kept north of the Chickahominy while transferring the rest of the army to the other side. Stuart had accomplished his mission. But he knew that by now the enemy was swarming in his rear. To return the way he had come would invite trouble. To continue on, to make a complete circuit around McClellan's army, might foil the pursuit. Besides, it would be a glorious achievement. In his mind Stuart could already see the headlines. He pushed on, winning skirmishes, capturing 170 enemy soldiers and nearly twice as many horses and mules, destroying wagonloads of Union supplies, traveling day and night over byways guided by troopers who had grown up in these parts, and crossed the swollen Chickahominy on an improvised bridge which the rebels burned behind themselves minutes before pursuing Union cavalry reined up impotently on the north bank. Stuart's horsemen evaded further clashes and completed the circuit to Richmond by June 16, four days and a hundred miles after setting out. This exploit won Stuart all the acclaim he could have desired. He also gained great personal satisfaction from the enterprise, for one of the opposing cavalry commanders was his father-in-law, Philip St. George Cooke, a Virginian whose decision to remain loyal to the Union had vexed Stuart. "He will regret it but once," Jeb had vowed, "and that will be continuously."[8]

Lee had the information he needed. And he knew whom he wanted to lead the attack: Jackson. He would bring Jackson's army secretly from the Valley to hit Porter's corps on the flank while three divisions of the Richmond army crossed the Chickahominy and simultaneously attacked its front. The danger in this, of course, was that while Lee concentrated 60,000 men against Porter's 30,000 north of the Chickahominy, the 75,000 bluecoats south of the river might smash through the 27,000 Confederates on their front and walk into Richmond. But Lee had already taken McClellan's measure. The Union commander, as usual, believed himself outnumbered south as well as north of the Chickahominy.

All this time McClellan was sending a steady stream of telegrams to Washington explaining why he was not quite ready to launch his own offensive: the roads were too wet; his artillery was not all up; it took time to reorganize the divisions crippled in the Seven Pines/Fair Oaks fighting, and to incorporate the one division of reinforcements finally received from McDowell; and when, asked McClellan, was the rest of McDowell's corps going to join him? By June 24, McClellan had penetrated the rebel smokescreen to learn of Jackson's approach; on June 25 he wired Stanton: "The rebel force is stated at 200,000, including Jackson [it was actually less than 90,000] . . . I shall have to contend against vastly superior odds. . . . If [the army] is destroyed by overwhelming numbers . . . the responsibility cannot be thrown on my shoulders; it must rest where it belongs."[9]

Lee attacked next day, June 26, the second day of what became known as the Seven Days' battles.[10] The fighting began inauspiciously for the rebels. Lee's plan called for Jackson to hit Porter's flank early in the morning. The sun passed the meridian while the silence continued and Lee fretted in frustration. Where was Jackson? Unable to wait longer, the impulsive A. P. Hill sent his division forward in a late-afternoon assault against an equal number of Federals (16,000) entrenched behind

8. Foote, *Civil War*, I, 472.
9. *O.R.*, Ser. I, Vol. 11, pt. 1, p. 51.
10. On June 25, Union forces reconnoitering near Seven Pines had clashed with Confederates in a large skirmish that produced about 500 casualties on each side. This action at Oak Grove was subsequently recorded as the first day of the Seven Days' battles.

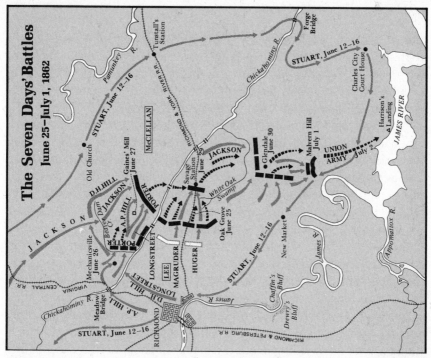

The Seven Days' Battles
June 25–July 1, 1862

STUART, June 12–16

Pamunkey R.

Tunstall's Station

RICHMOND & YORK RIVER R.R.

Forge Bridge

Chickahominy R.

STUART, June 12–16

Charles City Court House

Harrison's Landing

JAMES RIVER

Appomattox R.

Old Church

McCLELLAN

JACKSON

D.H. HILL

Gaines' Mill June 27

A.P. HILL

PORTER

Savage Station June 29

JACKSON

White Oak Swamp

Glendale June 30

Malvern Hill July 1

UNION ARMY July 2

Mechanicsville June 26

Beaver Dam Cr.

PORTER

Oak Grove June 25

STUART, June 12–16

New Market

James R.

VIRGINIA CENTRAL R.R.

Chickahominy R.

Meadow Bridge

A.P. HILL

D.H. HILL

LONGSTREET

LEE

LONGSTREET

MAGRUDER

HUGER

Chaffin's Bluff

Drewry's Bluff

James R.

STUART, June 12–16

RICHMOND

RICHMOND & PETERSBURG R.R.

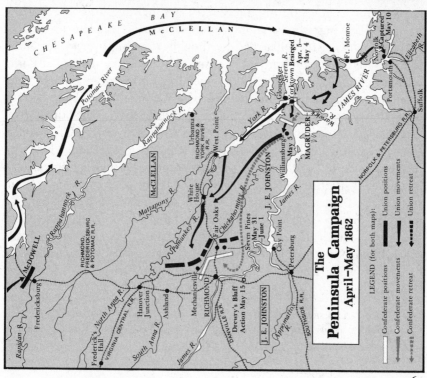

CHESAPEAKE BAY

McCLELLAN

Ft. Monroe

Norfolk Captured May 10

Elizabeth R.

Portsmouth

Suffolk

NORFOLK & PETERSBURG R.R.

Potomac River

Gloucester

Severn R.

Yorktown Besieged Apr. 5–May 4

JAMES RIVER

York R.

Warwick R.

MAGRUDER

Rappahannock R.

Urbanna

RICHMOND & YORK RIVER R.R.

West Point

Williamsburg May 5

J.E. JOHNSTON

McDOWELL

Rappahannock R.

McCLELLAN

Mattapony R.

White House

Pamunkey R.

Fair Oaks

Chickahominy R.

Seven Pines May 31 June 1

J.E. JOHNSTON

City Point

Petersburg

RICHMOND, FREDERICKSBURG & POTOMAC R.R.

Rapidan R.

Fredericksburg

Frederick's Hall

VIRGINIA CENTRAL R.R.

Hanover Junction

Ashland

North Anna R.

South Anna R.

Mechanicsville

RICHMOND

Drewry's Bluff Action May 15

DANVILLE R.R.

J.E. JOHNSTON

Appomattox R.

SOUTHSIDE R.R.

James R.

The Peninsula Campaign
April–May 1862

LEGEND (for both maps):

Confederate positions | Union positions

Confederate movements | Union movements

Confederate retreat | Union retreat

Beaver Dam Creek near Mechanicsville, about six miles northeast of Richmond. The result was a slaughter: nearly 1,500 rebels killed and wounded by Yankees who suffered only 360 casualties. All this time Jackson's three divisions were only a few miles to the north, but their commander made no effort to hasten to Hill's aid.

No single explanation for Jackson's lethargy is satisfactory. Union cavalry had harassed his advance. Northern axemen had felled trees across the road and burned bridges across creeks. But Jackson's foot cavalry had brushed this sort of thing aside in the Valley; why did it slow them now? The best answer seems to be exhaustion: the weariness of men who had endured the bone-jarring start-and-stop travel on southern railroads followed by marching in unaccustomed lowland heat before they had recovered from the exertions of their Valley campaign; and more significantly the weariness of Jackson, a man who seemed to need more than an average amount of sleep but had enjoyed only a few hours of rest during the past several days after six weeks of strain in the Valley. Jackson was probably suffering from what today would be called stress fatigue. Intolerant of weakness in others, he refused to recognize it in himself or to do anything about it—except to collapse into unscheduled naps at crucial times during the Seven Days' fighting.[11]

Despite having won what he described as a "complete victory" at Mechanicsville, McClellan had no thought of going over to the offensive. Aware of Jackson's arrival near his right flank, he instructed Porter on the night of June 26–27 to fall back four miles to an even stronger position on the high ground behind Boatswain's Swamp, near Gaines' Mill. Believing that his rail supply line north of the Chickahominy was threatened by the Confederate drive against his right, McClellan also decided to shift his base and all of his supplies to the James River on the south side of the Peninsula. This meant giving up his original plan of capturing Richmond by a siege and artillery bombardment, for his siege guns could travel overland only by rail and there was no railroad from the James. McClellan thenceforth fought only to protect his retreat, euphemistically called a "change of base." Thus while the battle of Mechanicsville had been a tactical defeat for the South, it turned out to be a strategic victory. It accomplished Lee's first goal of dislodging

11. For good discussions of this matter see Douglas Southall Freeman, *R. E. Lee: A Biography*, 4 vols. (New York, 1934–35), II, 578–82; Douglas Southall Freeman, *Lee's Lieutenants: A Study in Command* (New York, 1942–44), I, 656–59; Dowdey, *The Seven Days*, 193–202; Tanner, *Stonewall in the Valley*, 358–60.

McClellan's siege operations. It gave the Confederate commander a psychological edge over his adversary—which Lee never yielded. Even though Jackson had failed to attack on June 26, his appearance near the battlefield and his reputation from the Valley gave him the drop on the Yankees once again.

Before Lee could reap the harvest of this advantage, however, he must drive Porter's corps from its rifle pits behind Boatswain's Swamp. This proved costly. The rebel attack on June 27 again suffered from poor coordination between Lee and his division commanders. Lee's plan called for A. P. Hill to attack Porter's center while Longstreet made a feint against the left and Jackson with four divisions assaulted the Union right. If Porter shifted troops to meet Jackson's threat, Longstreet was to convert his feint into an attack and all 55,000 rebels would go forward together against Porter's 35,000. But once more Jackson was slow getting into position and lethargic in attacking. Once again A. P. Hill's division fought almost alone for several hours on a hot afternoon, attacking across a deep ravine and through entangling woods against well-placed Union defenders who punished Hill's brigades.[12] Disjointed assaults by Longstreet and by portions of Jackson's command relieved some of the pressure on Hill. Finally, near sundown, Lee got all his divisions to go forward in concert. In the middle of the line a brigade of Texans commanded by a tall, tawny-bearded, gladiatorial brigadier named John Bell Hood achieved a breakthrough. Pierced in the center, Porter's line collapsed. Fresh Union brigades from across the Chickahominy formed a rear guard and prevented a rout, enabling Porter to get most of his men and guns across the river during the night. Nevertheless, 2,800 bluecoats were captured and 4,000 were killed or wounded. But the Confederate triumph cost Lee close to 9,000 casualties—nearly as many, in six hours of fighting, as the South had lost in two days at Shiloh.

McClellan had sent Porter 6,000 men from the south side of the Chickahominy. The remaining 69,000 Federals on that side had remained quiet during the two days of bloody conflict north of the river. Their officers were transfixed by a repeat performance of Prince John Magruder's theatrics. Left by Lee in charge of 27,000 men holding the line east of Richmond, Magruder had ordered his troops to bristle with aggressive intent. These gray-costumed thespians responded enthusiast-

---

12. In all of the Seven Days', Hill's large division, containing about 15 percent of Lee's army, suffered 21 percent of the southern casualties while Jackson's three divisions, constituting 21 percent of the army, suffered 14 percent of the casualties.

ically. Artillery fired salvos; infantry lined up in attack formations and probed Union defenses; officers with stentorian voices called out orders to imaginary regiments in the woods. Several Union generals took the bait and informed McClellan that the rebels were strong and threatening on their front. The Federals thus missed an opportunity to counterattack with their overwhelming superiority south of the Chickahominy on June 27. Indeed, at 8:00 p.m. McClellan telegraphed Stanton that he had been "attacked by greatly superior numbers" on *both* sides of the Chickahominy![13]

In reality the Army of the Potomac was still in good shape despite the defeat at Gaines' Mill. But McClellan was a whipped man mentally. After midnight he again wired Stanton: "I have lost this battle because my force was too small. . . . The Government has not sustained this army. . . . If I save this army now, I tell you plainly that I owe no thanks to you or to any other persons in Washington. You have done your best to sacrifice this army." That McClellan escaped removal from command after sending such a dispatch was owing to an astonished colonel in the telegraph office, who excised the last two sentences before sending the message to Stanton.[14]

As McClellan pulled his army back toward the James River, Lee hoped to hit them in the flank while they were on the move. He improvised a new plan that called for nine Confederate divisions to converge by six different roads against the retreating bluecoats. But poor staff work, faulty maps, geographical obstacles, timid division commanders (especially Magruder and Benjamin Huger), stout Yankee resistance, and—yet again—Jackson's slowness frustrated Lee's efforts. The first failure occurred on June 29 at Savage's Station just three miles south of the Chickahominy. Three Union divisions formed a rear guard there to protect a field hospital and the southward passage of a huge wagon train. Lee ordered Magruder to attack this position from the west while Jackson came down on its right from the north. But Jackson dawdled all day rebuilding a bridge instead of fording the river. Magruder finally went forward alone with less than half of his division. The Yankees repulsed this feeble attack, then withdrew during the night leaving behind 2,500 sick and wounded men (from earlier fighting) and several surgeons who volunteered to share their captivity.

13. O.R., Ser. I, Vol. 11, pt. 3, p. 266.
14. *Ibid.*, pt. 1, p. 61.

Next day another of Lee's complicated plans for a concentric assault by seven divisions near the village of Glendale came to grief. Only Longstreet and Hill managed to get their men into action, fighting a fierce stand-up battle against parts of five Union divisions in late afternoon. The rebels gained a little ground and took a thousand prisoners but lost 3,500 killed and wounded, twice as many as the Yankees. With 25,000 men, Jackson made no contribution to the outcome except a negative one of failing to do his part. Approaching White Oak Swamp from the north, he sent a crew to rebuild the bridge over the creek. When Union artillery and sharpshooters prevented this, Jackson lay down and took a nap. Meanwhile his officers found fords practicable for infantry, but Jackson, seemingly in a trance, did nothing while Longstreet's and Hill's men bled and died two miles to the south. Jackson's failure, in the words of one historian, was "complete, disastrous and unredeemable."[15]

Yet Lee still hoped to redeem something from his attempt to destroy "those people" (his term for the enemy). Lee's temper on the morning of July 1 was frayed. If those people got away, he snapped to one unwary brigadier, it would happen "because I cannot have my orders carried out!"[16] The Federals had taken up another defensive position—the strongest one yet—three miles south of Glendale, on Malvern Hill near the James River. One hundred and fifty feet high and flanked by deep ravines a mile apart, Malvern Hill would have to be attacked frontally and uphill across open fields. Four Union divisions and 100 guns covered this front with four additional divisions and 150 guns in reserve. Unless these troops were utterly demoralized, it seemed suicidal to attack them. But Lee perceived many apparent signs of demoralization. The route of Union retreat was littered with abandoned equipment and arms. Confederate quartermasters and ordnance officers had reaped a rich harvest of captured material—including 30,000 small arms and fifty cannon. The rebels had also captured 6,000 Yankees in the previous six days, and continued to pick up scores of stragglers on the morning of July 1. In the end it turned out that the Army of the Potomac, with a resilience in the face of adversity that became its hallmark, was not demoralized after all. But its commander was. McClellan wired Washington that he had been "overpowered" by "superior numbers" and that

15. Dowdey, *The Seven Days*, 308.
16. Freeman, *Lee*, II, 202.

"I fear I shall be forced to abandon my material to save my men under cover of the gunboats."[17] With his uncanny ability to read the opposing commander's mind, Lee sensed McClellan's unnerved state but mistakenly projected it upon the men in the ranks as well.

In any event, Lee's frustration made him ready to grasp at any opportunity to strike "those people" once more. Longstreet—who had emerged as Lee's most reliable subordinate in this campaign—untypically shared this aggressive mood. On the morning of July 1 Longstreet found two elevated positions north of Malvern Hill from which he thought artillery might soften up Union defenses for an infantry assault. Lee ordered the artillery to concentrate on the two knolls. But staff work broke down again; only some of the cannoneers got the message, and their weak fire was soon silenced by Union batteries. Lee nevertheless ordered the assault to go forward. Confusion in the delivery of these orders meant that the attack was disjointed, with brigades advancing individually rather than together. This enabled Union artillery to pulverize nearly every attacking unit, allowing only a few enemy regiments to get close enough for infantry to cut them down. For perhaps the only time in the war, artillery fire caused more enemy casualties than rifle fire.[18] D. H. Hill's division was one of the most severely mauled; Hill later wrote that the battle of Malvern Hill "was not war—it was murder."[19] The 5,500 Confederates killed and wounded in this battle were more than double the Union total.

Aware that the rebels had been hurt, some Union generals wanted to mount a counterattack next day. Even McClellan's protégé Fitz-John Porter favored such a move. When McClellan instead ordered a continuation of the retreat to Harrison's Landing on the James, one of his most pugnacious brigadiers—Philip Kearny of New Jersey, who had lost an arm in the Mexican War—burst out to fellow officers: "Such an order can only be prompted by cowardice or treason. . . . We ought instead of retreating to follow up the enemy and take Richmond."[20]

For his part Lee recognized the futility of any more attacks. Twenty thousand southerners—nearly a quarter of his army—had fallen dead and wounded during the previous week, twice the Union total. Rebels

17. O.R., Ser. I, Vol. 11, pt. 3, pp. 280, 282.
18. For the war as a whole, small-arms fire caused almost 90 percent of the casualties.
19. Hill, "McClellan's Change of Base and Malvern Hill," *Battles and Leaders*, II, 394.
20. Bruce Catton, *Mr. Lincoln's Army* (Garden City, N.Y., 1956), 149.

and Yankees paused to lick their wounds. While the bluecoats had suffered only one tactical defeat in the Seven Days'—at Gaines' Mill—
they had constantly retreated and the campaign had resulted in a strategic Confederate victory, with all that meant for morale in the respective armies and on the home fronts. Nonetheless, Lee was dissatisfied.
"Our success has not been as great or as complete as I could have desired," he wrote. "Under ordinary circumstances the Federal Army should
have been destroyed."[21] Destroyed! This Napoleonic vision would continue to govern Lee's strategic thinking until that moment a year later
when the vision was itself destroyed on the gentle slope of Cemetery
Ridge near a small Pennsylvania town.

In the immediate aftermath of the Seven Days', Lee took several steps
to remedy the defects in his command structure revealed by the campaign. Because Jackson's divisions and several other brigades had joined
Lee's force only on the eve of these battles, the Army of Northern Virginia had never before fought as a unit and Lee had not time to forge
its chain of command into an extension of his will. To do so now he
shuffled several officers, exiled the weaker division commanders to Texas
and Arkansas, and promoted abler subordinates to their places. Because
the problem of communicating directly with eight or nine division commanders had proven insuperable during the Seven Days', Lee reorganized the army into two corps (though they were not officially designated as such until later) under Longstreet and Jackson. No evidence
exists that Lee reproached Jackson for his dismal performance during
the Seven Days', though the assignment of the larger corps to Longstreet
may have implied a rebuke. In any case, Jackson soon recovered from
his stress fatigue and went on to justify the confidence expressed by
Lee's giving him corps command.

III

The thirty thousand men killed and wounded in the Seven Days' equaled
the number of casualties in *all* the battles in the western theater—including Shiloh—during the first half of 1862. The Seven Days' established a pattern for harder fighting and greater casualties in battles between the Army of Northern Virginia and Army of the Potomac than
between any other armies. Most soldiers in the Army of the Potomac
were from northeastern states, while most men in the western Union

21. Dowdey, *The Seven Days*, 358.

armies hailed from the Old Northwest. The western farm boys and out-doorsmen regarded themselves as tougher soldiers than the effete "paper-collar" soldiers from the Northeast. But in truth the "pasty-faced" clerks and mechanics of the East proved to be more immune to the diseases of camp life and more capable in combat of absorbing and inflicting punishment than western Union soldiers. For the war as a whole the death rate from disease was 43 percent higher among Union soldiers from states west of the Appalachians than among the effete easterners, while the latter experienced combat mortality rates 23 percent higher than the westerners. The number of combat deaths in the Army of the Potomac was greater than in all the other Union armies combined. Forty-one of the fifty Union regiments with the highest percentage of combat casualties fought in this army. In the South, forty of the fifty highest-casualty regiments served in the Army of Northern Virginia. Of all the army commanders on both sides, Lee had the highest casualty rate.[22]

One reason for this was Lee's concept of the offensive-defensive, which he applied to tactics as well as to strategy. Lee probably deserves his reputation as the war's best tactician, but his success came at great cost. In every one of the Seven Days' battles the Confederates attacked and consequently lost a higher proportion of killed and wounded than the defenders. The same was true in several of Lee's subsequent battles. Even in 1864–65, when their backs were to the wall and they had barely strength enough to parry their adversary's heavier blows, the Army of Northern Virginia essayed several offensive counterstrokes. The in-congruity between Lee's private character as a humane, courteous, re-served, kindly man, the very model of a Christian gentleman, and his daring, aggressive, but costly tactics as a general is one of the most striking contrasts in the history of the war.

Several battles in the western theater, of course, also produced a ghastly harvest of death. One reason for the high casualties of Civil War battles was the disparity between traditional tactics and modern weapons. The

---

22. Data compiled from William F. Fox, *Regimental Losses in the American Civil War* (Albany, 1889). Reliable data on disease and combat deaths by states for the Con-federate army are not available. For army commanders, see the tables on pp. 18–23 of Grady McWhiney and Perry D. Jamieson, *Attack and Die: Civil War Mili-tary Tactics and the Southern Heritage* (University, Ala., 1982). The casualty rate in Lee's army was 20 percent in its major battles and campaigns. By way of com-parison, the figure for Ulysses S. Grant's troops was 16 percent.

tactical legacy of eighteenth-century and Napoleonic warfare had emphasized close-order formations of soldiers trained to maneuver in concert and fire by volleys. To be sure, some of the citizen-soldiers of the American Revolution fought Indian-style from behind trees or rocks, and the half-trained *levée en masse* of the French Revolution advanced in loose order like "clouds of skirmishers." But they did so mainly because they lacked training and discipline; the ideal for Washington's Continentals and Napoleon's veterans as well as Frederick's Prussians and Wellington's redcoats remained the compact, cohesive columns and lines of automatons who moved and fired with machine-like efficiency.

These tactics also stressed the offensive. Assault troops advanced with cadenced step, firing volleys on command and then double-timing the last few yards to pierce the enemy line with a bayonet charge. Napoleon used his artillery in conjunction with infantry assaults, moving the field guns forward with the foot soldiers to blast holes in enemy ranks and soften them up for the final charge. Americans used these tactics with great success in the Mexican War. West Point teaching stressed the tactical offensive. Most of the top Civil War officers had fought in Mexico and/or had attended West Point; from both experiences they had absorbed the message that the tactical offensive based on close-order infantry assaults supported by artillery won battles.[23]

In Mexico this happened without high casualties because the basic infantry weapon was the single-shot muzzle-loading smoothbore musket. The maximum range of this weapon was about 250 yards; its effective range (the distance at which a good marksman could hit a target with any regularity) was about eighty yards on a still day. The close-order formation was therefore necessary to concentrate the firepower of these inaccurate weapons; artillery could accompany charging infantry because cannoneers were relatively safe from enemy musket fire until they came within a couple of hundred yards or less; bayonet charges

23. The observations in the preceding and subsequent paragraphs are based on a general reading of military history and particularly on John Keegan, *The Face of Battle* (New York, 1977); John K. Mahon, "Civil War Infantry Assault Tactics," *Military Affairs*, 25 (1961), 57–68; McWhiney and Jamieson, *Attack and Die*; and Herman Hattaway and Archer Jones, *How the North Won: A Military History of the Civil War* (Urbana, 1983). Hattaway and Jones argue unconvincingly that West Point graduates carried into the Civil War a stronger stress on the entrenched defensive than on the offensive. It seems clear, however, that this hard-learned lesson was taught mainly by the experience of the war itself.

could succeed because double-timing infantry could cover the last eighty yards during the twenty-five seconds it took defending infantrymen to reload their muskets after firing a volley.

Rifling a musket increased its range fourfold by imparting a spin to a conical bullet that enabled it literally to bore through the air. This fact had been known for centuries, but before the 1850s only special regiments or one or two companies per regiment were equipped with rifles. These companies were used as skirmishers—that is, they operated in front and on the flanks of the main body, advancing or withdrawing in loose order and shooting at will from long range at enemy targets of opportunity. Given the rifle's greater range and accuracy, why were not all infantrymen equipped with it? Because a bullet large enough to "take" the rifling was difficult to ram down the barrel. Riflemen sometimes had to pound the ramrod down with a mallet. After a rifle had been fired a few times a residue of powder built up in the grooves and had to be cleaned out before it could be fired again. Since rapid and reliable firing was essential in a battle, the rifle was not practicable for the mass of infantrymen.

Until the 1850s, that is. Although several people contributed to the development of a practicable military rifle, the main credit belongs to French army Captain Claude E. Minié and to the American James H. Burton, an armorer at the Harper's Ferry Armory. In 1848 Minié perfected a bullet small enough to be easily rammed down a rifled barrel, with a wooden plug in the base of the bullet to expand it upon firing to take the rifling. Such bullets were expensive; Burton developed a cheaper and better bullet with a deep cavity in the base that filled with gas and expanded the rim upon firing. This was the famous "minié ball" of Civil War rifles. The superiority of the rifle was demonstrated by British and French soldiers who carried them in the Crimean War. As Secretary of War in 1855, Jefferson Davis converted the United States army to the .58 caliber Springfield rifled musket. Along with the similar British Enfield rifle (caliber .577, which would take the same bullet as the Springfield), the Springfield became the main infantry arm of the Civil War.

Because they were single-shot weapons loaded from the muzzle, these rifles were still awkward to load. Even the most dextrous soldier could fire no more than three shots per minute. Several inventors had developed breechloading rifles by 1861, but with the paper-wrapped cartridges (containing bullet and powder) then in use, gas and sometimes flame escaped from the breech and made the weapon unreliable and even dangerous to the user. Progress in solving this problem made the single-shot Sharps carbine and rifle popular with the Union cavalry and sharpshooter units that managed to obtain them. The development of metal cartridges enabled the northern army to equip its cavalry and some infantry units with repeaters by 1863, of which the seven-shot Spencer carbine was most successful. These weapons had a smaller powder charge and therefore a shorter range than the paper-cartridged Springfield and Enfield, and were more prone to malfunction. The muzzle-loaders thus remained the principal infantry weapons throughout the war.

Northern industry geared up to manufacture more than two million rifles during the war; unable to produce more than a fraction of this total, the South relied mainly on imports through the blockade and on capture of Union rifles. In 1861 neither side had many rifles, so most soldiers carried old smoothbores taken from storage in arsenals. During 1862 most Union regiments received new Springfields or Enfields, while many Confederate units still had to rely on smoothbores. This was one reason for the two-to-one excess of Confederate casualties in the Seven Days'. By 1863 nearly all infantrymen on both sides carried rifles.

The transition from smoothbore to rifle had two main effects: it multiplied casualties; and it strengthened the tactical defensive. Officers trained and experienced in the old tactics were slow to recognize these changes. Time and again generals on both sides ordered close-order assaults in the traditional formation. With an effective range of three or four hundred yards, defenders firing rifles decimated these attacks. Artillery declined in importance as an offensive weapon, because its accuracy and the reliability of shells at long range were poor, and the guns could no longer advance with the infantry toward enemy lines, for marksmen could pick off the cannoneers and especially the horses at distances up to half a mile. Sharpshooters also singled out enemy officers, which helps to explain why officers and especially generals had higher casualty rates than privates. Officers on both sides soon began to stay off horseback when possible and to wear a private's uniform with only a sewn-on shoulder patch to designate their rank. The old-fashioned cavalry charge against infantry, already obsolescent, became obsolete in the face of rifles that could knock down horses long before their riders got within saber or pistol range. The Civil War hastened the evolution of dismounted cavalry tactics in which the horse was mainly a means of transportation rather than a weapon in its own right.

As time went on experience taught soldiers new tactics adapted to the rifle. Infantry formations loosened up and became a sort of large-scale skirmish line in which men advanced by rushes, taking advantage of cover offered by the ground to reload before dashing forward another few yards, working in groups of two or three to load and shoot alternately in order to keep up a continuous rather than a volley fire. But officers had difficulty maintaining control over large units employing such tactics in that pre-radio age. This limited the employment of loose-order tactics and compelled the retention of close-order assaults in some instances to the end of the war.

And while loose-order tactics occasionally succeeded in carrying enemy lines, they did not restore dominance to the tactical offensive, especially when defenders began digging trenches and throwing up breastworks at every position, as they did by 1863 and 1864. It became a rule of thumb that attacking forces must have a numerical superiority of at least three to one to succeed in carrying trenches defended by alert troops. Robbed by the rifle of some of its potency as an offensive weapon, the artillery functioned best on the defensive by firing at attacking infantry with grapeshot and canister (as at Malvern Hill) in the manner of a huge sawed-off shotgun. Despite the occasional success of head-on tactical assaults such as the Confederate victories at Gaines' Mill, Chancellorsville, and Chickamauga or Union triumphs at Missionary Ridge and Cedar Creek, the defense usually prevailed against frontal attacks. Even when an assault succeeded, it did so at high cost in killed and wounded. Steeped in romantic martial traditions, glorying in the "charge" and in "valor," southern soldiers in the Seven Days' suffered grievously from their assaults. Well might D. H. Hill reflect in later years on the bodies piled in front of Union lines at Gaines' Mill: "It was thought to be a great thing to charge a battery of artillery or an earthwork lined with infantry. . . . We were very lavish of blood in those days."[24]

During 1862 and 1863, Confederate armies went on the tactical offensive in six of the nine battles in which the killed and wounded of both sides together exceeded fifteen thousand. Although they won two of these six battles (Chancellorsville and Chickamauga) and achieved a strategic success in a third (the Seven Days'), their total casualties in these six contests exceeded Union casualties by 20,000 men (89,000 to 69,000). In the spring of 1864 the situation was reversed as Grant's men suffered nearly twice the casualties of Lee's army when the Yankees took the offensive from the Wilderness to Petersburg. The quest of both sides for victory through tactical assaults in the old manner proved a chimera

24. Hill, "Lee's Attacks North of the Chickahominy," *Battles and Leaders*, II, 352.

in the new age of the rifle. The tactical predominance of the defense helps explain why the Civil War was so long and bloody. The rifle and trench ruled Civil War battlefields as thoroughly as the machine-gun and trench ruled those of World War I.

IV

In the fog-enshrouded gloom at Malvern Hill on the morning of July 2, 1862, a Union cavalry officer looked over the field of the previous day's conflict. "Our ears had been filled with agonizing cries from thousands before the fog was lifted," he wrote two decades later with the sight still imprinted in his mind, "but now our eyes saw an appalling spectacle upon the slopes down to the woodlands half a mile away. Over five thousand dead and wounded men were on the ground . . . enough were alive and moving to give to the field a singular crawling effect."[25] Soon the two armies agreed on a truce to bury the dead and succor the wounded. These tasks etched the horrors of war even more indelibly than the actual fighting. "The sights and smells that assailed us were simply indescribable," wrote a southern soldier on burial detail, "corpses swollen to twice their original size, some of them actually burst asunder with the pressure of foul gases. . . . The odors were nauseating and so deadly that in a short time we all sickened and were lying with our mouths close to the ground, most of us vomiting profusely." Writing home after another battle, a Yank described a field hospital established in farm buildings. "About the building you could see the Hogs belonging to the Farm eating [amputated] arms and other portions of the body."[26]

Many civilians on both sides, especially in the South, experienced these sights and smells of war directly as well as through soldiers' letters. Much of the fighting in May and June 1862 occurred almost on Richmond's doorstep. Many of the 21,000 wounded Confederates from Seven Pines and the Seven Days' were brought into the city. "We lived in one immense hospital, and breathed the vapors of the charnel house," wrote a Richmond woman.[27] Churches, hotels, warehouses, shops, barns, even private homes were pressed into service as temporary hospitals. White women volunteered by the hundreds as nurses; slaves were mobilized as orderlies and gravediggers.

25. William W. Averell, "With the Cavalry on the Peninsula," *Battles and Leaders*, II, 432.
26. Wiley, *Johnny Reb*, 75; Wiley, *Billy Yank*, 83.
27. Emory M. Thomas, *The Confederate State of Richmond* (Austin, Tex., 1971), 100.

Like the Union army, the Confederates gave first aid and emergency treatment of wounded in field hospitals near or on the battlefield. The South was slow to establish general hospitals for the treatment and convalescence of the badly wounded and of soldiers with long-term illnesses. At first such hospitals were maintained primarily by local or private initiative. By late 1861 the Confederate Medical Department had taken over this function. The army established several general hospitals in Richmond, the principal one on an east-side hill, Chimborazo Hospital, which became the largest such facility in the world with 250 pavilion buildings each housing forty to sixty patients and 100 tents with space for eight to ten convalescents each. But only a fraction of these structures had been completed by June 1862, when thousands of wounded poured into the city and many died in the streets because there was nowhere else to put them. The shock of the Seven Days' and of subsequent battles in Virginia compelled the expansion and modernization of southern general hospitals.

This shock plus the vital example of women volunteers in Richmond and at Corinth, Mississippi, also forced a reversal of the Medical Department's initial hostility to female nurses.

On the eve of the Civil War Florence Nightingale was as much a heroine to American women as she was in England. Nightingale had revolutionized the inadequate British army medical services in the Crimea. She had also dignified nursing as a profession and in 1860 had established the world's first school of nursing at St. Thomas's Hospital in London. When war came to America, several southern white women volunteered their services as nurses or founded small hospitals for soldiers. One of the best such hospitals was established in Richmond by Sally Louisa Tompkins, whom Jefferson Davis eventually commissioned as a captain so that her infirmary could qualify as an army hospital.

These examples defied a prejudice against "refined ladies" working in military hospitals. It was permissible for white women to nurse the sick at home or even in the slave quarters, but they had no business in the masculine milieu of an army hospital which presented sights that no lady should see. Women should stay at home and make bandages, knit socks for soldiers, and comfort the menfolk when they returned from the rigors of battle. Despite the initial wartime prevalence of this view, numerous southern women of good families braved the frowns of father or brother to volunteer as nurses. One of them was twenty-seven-year old Kate Cumming of Mobile, who in April 1862 went to Corinth where Beauregard's battered army was trying to recover after Shiloh. "As to the

plea of its being no place for a refined lady," Cumming wrote, "I wondered what Miss Nightingale and the hundreds of refined ladies of Great
Britain who went to the Crimea, would say to that!"[28]

When Cumming arrived at a Corinth hotel that had been turned into
a hospital, she blanched at the sight. "Nothing that I had ever heard or
read had given me the faintest idea of the horrors witnessed here." But
she and her sisters in mercy fought down the desire to run away, and
went immediately to work. "I sat up all night, bathing the men's wounds,
and giving them water," she wrote in her diary. "The men are lying all
over the house, on their blankets, just as they were brought in from the
battlefield. . . . The foul air from this mass of human beings at first
made me giddy and sick, but I soon got over it. We have to walk, and
when we give the men anything kneel, in blood and water; but we think
nothing of it."[29]

Cumming and other white women who nursed in military hospitals
during the summer of 1862 were volunteers. The official army nurses
were soldiers detailed for the purpose (many of them convalescents
themselves) and slave "attendants" impressed as cooks, laundresses, and
cleanup workers. Some of the white women volunteers were Lady
Bountiful types who played at nursing for a few days and then departed.
But most rendered valuable service, and thereby overcame the prejudices of many army surgeons who had initially opposed the presence of
white women. The medical director of the army hospital at Danville,
Virginia, came to prefer women rather than his soldier nurses whom he
described as "rough country crackers" who did not "know castor oil
from a gun rod nor laudanum from a hole in the ground." In September 1862 the Confederate Congress enacted a law providing for civilian
matrons and nurses in army general hospitals, "giving preference in all
cases to females where their services may best subserve the purpose."[30]
A good many white women became part of the official army medical
service under this law. They and their volunteer sisters earned the plau-
dits that, after the war, enshrined their contribution with a halo of lost-
cause glory equal to that of Confederate soldiers.[31] Many other women

28. Richard B. Harwell, ed., *Kate: The Journal of a Confederate Nurse* (Baton Rouge,
    1959), xii.
29. *Ibid.*, 14, 15.
30. Horace H. Cunningham, *Doctors in Gray: The Confederate Medical Service* (Baton
    Rouge, 1958), 72, 73.
31. Two of the most famous Confederate nurses were Kate Cumming and Phoebe

who did not go into the hospitals also contributed in a crucial way by organizing soldiers' aid or hospital relief societies throughout the South to provide supplies, services, and money to aid sick and wounded soldiers or their families. These efforts were part of the mobilization of resources for total war in 1862. They projected southern women into public activities on an unprecedented scale and did much to emancipate them from the pedestal of ethereal femininity that had constricted their lives.

Similar experiences befell their northern sisters who, already more emancipated when the war began, threw themselves into the fray with equal energy and in greater numbers. The principal vehicle for their activity was the United States Sanitary Commission. This powerful organization, the largest voluntary association yet formed in a country noted for such enterprises, grew from a fusion of local soldiers' aid societies that had sprung up within days of the firing on Sumter. Women took the lead in forming these associations, drawing upon their sense of commitment and previous experience in societies advocating the abolition of slavery, women's rights, temperance, education, missions, and the like. Elizabeth Blackwell, the first American woman to brave male derision to earn an M.D. (1849), took the lead in organizing a meeting of three thousand women at Cooper Institute in New York on April 29, 1861. Several prominent men also participated in this meeting, which formed the Women's Central Association for Relief to coordinate the work of numerous smaller associations. The initial task of the W.C.A.R. was to establish a training program for nurses—the first such venture in the United States. The W.C.A.R. also became the nucleus of the United States Sanitary Commission.

The "Sanitary," as it came to be called, was inspired by the example of the British Sanitary Commission in the Crimean War. Filth and primitive sanitation had bred disease and infections that had decimated

---

Pember. Cumming became matron of an army hospital in Chattanooga after Beauregard evacuated Corinth, and subsequently served as matron at various places in Georgia when Sherman's advance forced Confederate hospitals to retreat further and further south. Pember, a native of Charleston who migrated to Richmond in 1862, became the first matron at Chimborazo Hospital. Cummings' journal and Pember's autobiography, published after the war and available today in reprint editions, are valuable sources for the history of Confederate medical services. See Harwell, ed., *Kate*; and Phoebe Yates Pember, *A Southern Woman's Story: Life in Confederate Richmond*, ed. Bell Irvin Wiley (Jackson, Tenn., 1959).

the Allied armies in the Crimea and provoked a reformist response in Britain. A number of American medical men and women wanted to organize a similar commission to alleviate such problems in the Union army. On May 15 a delegation of distinguished physicians (all men) headed by Henry Bellows, a prominent Unitarian clergyman interested in medical problems, traveled to Washington as representatives of the W.C.A.R. and affiliated organizations. This delegation encountered opposition at first from the Army Medical Bureau, whose head (the surgeon general) was an aging veteran of forty-three years in the regular army who wanted no interference by busybody civilians. He also looked with skepticism upon the prospect of female nurses. The delegation went over his head to talk with Secretary of War Cameron and with the president. At first Lincoln could see little use for a civilian auxiliary to the Medical Bureau, referring to such as a "fifth wheel to the coach." But he acquiesced nevertheless, and on June 13 signed the order creating the U.S. Sanitary Commission.[32]

The Commission's official powers were investigatory and advisory only. But the decentralized, do-it-yourself nature of northern mobilization in 1861 offered an opportunity for a voluntary association to create its own powers. With Bellows as president and the talented Frederick Law Olmsted as executive secretary, the Sanitary did precisely that. It enlisted physicians and other prominent citizens as officers of local affiliates. Seven thousand locals dotted the North by 1863. The national officers and most of the five hundred paid agents of the Commission were men; most of the tens of thousands of volunteer workers were women. They held bazaars and "Sanitary Fairs" to raise money. They sent bandages, medicine, clothing, food, and volunteer nurses to army camps and hospitals. They provided meals and lodging to furloughed soldiers going and coming from the front. Because of the close ties between Commission leaders and the citizen volunteers who became officers of regiments, the Sanitary helped shape the hygienic conditions of army camps despite the continuing coldness of the Army Medical Bureau. "Sanitary inspectors" from the Commission instructed soldiers in proper camp drainage, placement of latrines, water supply, and cooking. Many soldiers paid little attention, and suffered the consequences. Others benefited by improved health from following this advice.

The Sanitary won popularity with soldiers and influence with con-

---

32. William Quentin Maxwell, *Lincoln's Fifth Wheel: The Political History of the United States Sanitary Commission* (New York, 1928), chap. 1.

gressmen. By the winter of 1861–62 it had become a power in national politics. It decided to use this power to attack the Medical Bureau's seniority system which kept young, progressive surgeons down and left the Bureau in charge of men like Surgeon-General Clement A. Finley whose thinking was geared to the somnolent bureaucracy of a 16,000-man peacetime army. "It is criminal weakness to intrust such responsibilities as those resting on the surgeon-general to a self-satisfied, supercilious, bigoted blockhead, merely because he is the oldest of the old mess-room doctors of the frontier-guard of the country," wrote Commission secretary Olmsted in a private letter. "He knows nothing, and does nothing, and is capable of knowing nothing and doing nothing but quibble about matters of form and precedent." Commission president Bellows drafted a bill to enable Lincoln to bypass the seniority system and promote younger men to top positions in the Medical Bureau. Such legislation, said Bellows, "would lay on the shelf all the venerable do-nothings and senile obstructives that now vex the health and embarrass the safety of our troops." [33]

The army medical establishment fought back against "sensation preachers, village doctors, and strong-minded women" of the Commission. [34] But the bill passed on April 18, 1862. It not only suspended the seniority system but also gave the surgeon general authority to appoint eight medical inspectors with power to institute reforms in army procedures. Lincoln immediately appointed the Sanitary's candidate as the new surgeon general: thirty-three-year old William Hammond, a progressive, energetic, strong-willed army surgeon. Hammond's appointment marked the end of an adversarial relationship between the army and the Commission, and the beginning of an extraordinarily productive partnership between public and private medical enterprise. The army turned over several passenger steamers to the Commission, which fitted them up as hospital ships staffed with volunteer nurses for evacuation of wounded from the Peninsula to general hospitals in Washington and New York. The Commission had already proved the value of such a policy by chartering its own hospital boats to evacuate wounded men

---

33. Olmsted to John Murray Forbes, Dec. 15, 1861, Bellows to Forbes, Dec. 19, 1861, quoted in A. Howard Meneely, *The War Department, 1861: A Study in Mobilization and Administration* (New York, 1928), 228.

34. George Worthington Adams, *Doctors in Blue: The Medical History of the Union Army in the Civil War* (Collier Books ed., New York, 1961 [1952], 68.

from Shiloh. The Sanitary also pioneered in the development of hospital trains with specially fitted cars for rail transport of wounded.

Surgeon-General Hammond was so impressed by the Sanitary Commission nurses who staffed the hospital ships that he issued an order in July 1862 requiring at least one-third of the army nurses in general hospitals to be women. As early as April 1861 the venerable reformer of insane asylums, Dorothea Dix, had been named "Superintendent of Female Nurses" with rather vaguely defined powers. An assertive individualist whose long suit was not administrative ability, Dix worked in uneasy cooperation with the Sanitary Commission to recruit nurses. By the end of the war more than three thousand northern women had served as paid army nurses. In addition, several thousand women continued to work as volunteers and as salaried agents of the Sanitary Commission.

These were not the only means by which northern women and men performed medical services in the war. Some worked for other volunteer agencies such as the Western Sanitary Commission (separate from the U.S.S.C.) in the trans-Mississippi theater, or the Christian Commission, founded by YMCA leaders in November 1861 to provide blankets, clothing, books, and physical as well as spiritual nurture to Union soldiers. And some northern women who earned fame as nurses operated pretty much on their own. One of these was Clara Barton, a forty-year old spinster working as a clerk in the patent office when the war broke out. She became a one-woman soldiers' aid society, gathering medicines and supplies and turning up on several battlefields or at field hospitals to comfort the wounded and goad careless or indifferent surgeons. Barton's friendship with influential congressmen helped bring political pressure to bear for reforms in army medicine. Her wartime experiences motivated her postwar crusade for American affiliation with the international Red Cross. Another remarkable woman was Mary Ann Bickerdyke, a forty-five-year old widow from Illinois who began her service in 1861 at the fever-ridden army base at Cairo. A large, strong, indomitable yet maternal woman, she swept through the camp like an avenging angel. She became the gadfly of obtuse officers and the special champion of enlisted men, who fondly named her Mother Bickerdyke. She cleaned up the camps and continued on with Grant's and then Sherman's armies from Fort Donelson to Atlanta. Bickerdyke earned the respect of both of these Union generals; she was the only woman that Sherman allowed in his advanced base hospitals.

Not all the female army nurses belonged to that category known in the nineteenth century as "respectable." Some regiments on both sides sheltered the ancient army institution of "camp followers"—female laundresses or cooks who sometimes doubled as prostitutes and as nurses. Nonetheless, "respectable" women nurses had overcome by 1862 many of the prejudices that had prevailed against them at the war's beginning. They had achieved—with soldiers and the public if not always with surgeons—the status and esteem that Florence Nightingale and her cohorts had earned in Britain. The courage and energy demonstrated by many women chipped away at the weaker-sex image. This may even have improved the quality of some marriages. The wife of George Templeton Strong (treasurer of the Sanitary Commission) insisted on going to the Virginia Peninsula as a volunteer nurse in June 1862. There she performed capably, found new purpose in her life, and transformed her husband's view of her. "The little woman has come out amazingly strong during these two months," wrote Strong in his diary. "Have never given her credit for a tithe of the enterprise, pluck, discretion, and force of character that she has shown. God bless her."[35]

The Civil War marked a milestone in the transformation of nursing from a menial service to a genuine profession. The war also produced important innovations in army medical practice. One such innovation was the creation of a special ambulance corps for first-aid treatment of the wounded and their evacuation to field hospitals. Traditional practice in both armies assigned regimental musicians and soldiers "least effective under arms" as stretcher-bearers to carry the wounded from the field and assist the surgeons in field hospitals. Civilian teamsters were expected to double as ambulance drivers. The large-scale fighting in 1862 quickly revealed the defects of this system. Lacking training and *esprit*, the men and boys (many of the bandsmen were under eighteen) assigned to these tasks all too often fled in terror when the shooting started. Even when ambulance drivers remained on duty, there were not enough ambulances. Fighting men often defied orders and dropped out of line to carry wounded friends to the rear because they knew no one else would.

This wretched situation became a scandal in the Union army during the summer of 1862 and caused Surgeon-General Hammond to appoint Jonathan K. Letterman as the new medical director of the Army of the

35. Strong, *Diary*, 239.

Potomac after the Seven Days'. This appointment brought improvement. The Sanitary Commission had long advocated the creation of a trained ambulance corps. Letterman instituted such a unit in the Army of the Potomac, from where it spread to other Union armies and was formally mandated by law in 1864. Wearing special uniforms and imbued with high morale, these noncombatant medics risked their lives to reach the wounded in the midst of battle and evacuate them as quickly as possible to surgeons' stations and field hospitals. The ambulance corps became a model for European armies down to World War I; both the Germans and French adopted the system in the Franco-Prussian War.[36] The South evolved a similar "infirmary corps" in 1862 but did not institute it on the same scale. The Confederate medical service, like everything else in the southern war effort, did wonders with the resources available but did not have enough men, medicines, or ambulances to match the Union effort. This was one reason why about 18 percent of the wounded rebels died of their wounds compared with 14 percent of the wounded Yankees.[37]

The record of both armies in this respect, of course, was abysmal by twentieth-century standards. In the Korean War only one of every fifty wounded Americans died of his wounds; in Vietnam the proportion was one in four hundred. The Civil War soldier was eight times more likely to die of a wound and ten times more likely to die of disease than an American soldier in World War I. Indeed, twice as many Civil War soldiers died of disease as were killed and mortally wounded in combat.

36. Adams, *Doctors in Blue*, 88.
37. The percentage cited here for the mortality of Union wounded is based on the official report of the surgeon general used as the basis for the compilations in Fox, *Regimental Losses*, 24 and passim. No comparable data exist for the Confederacy. My estimate of 18 percent is based on fragmentary data in Fox; in Thomas L. Livermore, *Numbers and Losses in the Civil War* (Boston, 1901); in Cunningham, *Doctors in Gray*; and in Courtney R. Hall, "Confederate Medicine," *Medical Life*, 42 (1935), 473. In addition to a less efficient stretcher and ambulance service after 1862, there were other possible reasons for the slightly higher Confederate mortality rate from battle wounds: shortages of medicine in the South; and the inadequate diet of southern soldiers, which left them less able than their Union counterparts to survive the trauma caused by wounds or surgery. To some extent the difference in death rates from wounds may have been a statistical artifact, for Confederate officers were less likely than Union officers to report minor wounds in their units, and this probably meant that a somewhat higher proportion of reported wounds in the Confederate army were serious and therefore potentially fatal.

Such a record seems at first glance to justify the conclusion shared by several historians that "the medical services represent one of the Civil War's most dismal failures."[38]

This appraisal echoes a good deal of opinion at the time. Newspapers and Sanitary Commission reports published horror stories about fetid hospitals, drunken surgeons, untended sick or wounded soldiers dying in agony, and the like. The reputation of many army doctors as "quacks" or "butchers" reflected the generally low repute of the medical profession. Soldiers dreaded hospitals and sometimes went to great lengths to conceal wounds or illnesses in order to avoid them. "I beleave the Doctors kills more than they cour," wrote an Alabama soldier in 1862. "Doctors haint Got half Sence." Yanks were inclined to agree. An Illinois private wrote that "our doctor knows about as much as a ten year old boy," while a Massachusetts officer pronounced his regimental surgeon "a jackass."[39]

Soldiers who believed they were more likely to get well outside a hospital than inside it may have been right. But this was owing more to the state of medical knowledge in general than to the particular incompetence of army doctors. The Civil War was fought at the end of the medical Middle Ages. The 1860s witnessed the dawn of a new era with the research in Europe of Louis Pasteur, Joseph Lister, and others who discovered those microscopic culprits that infected water and food and entered the bloodstream through open wounds. Within a generation the new science of bacteriology had revolutionized medicine. The discovery of the link between mosquitoes and yellow fever and malaria made possible the control of these killer diseases. Civil War doctors knew none of these things. The medical revolution came too late to benefit them. They were not aware of the exact relationship between water and typhoid, between unsterilized instruments and infection, between mosquitoes and malaria. The concept of asepsis and antisepsis in surgery had not been developed. Doctors could not conceive of antibiotics because they scarcely had a notion of biotics. Moreover, the large caliber and low muzzle velocity of Civil War rifles caused horrible wounds with the bullet usually remaining in the body rather than going through it. Surgeons knew of few ways except amputation to stop gangrene or osteomyelitis or pyemia. Stomach wounds were generally fatal because there was no known prevention of peritonitis. Chloroform and ether

38. Peter J. Parish, *The American Civil War* (New York, 1975), 147.
39. Wiley, *Johnny Reb*, 267; Wiley, *Billy Yank*, 131.

were used as anesthetics, but shortages especially in the South some-times required soldiers to be dosed with whiskey and literally to bite the bullet during an operation.[40] This was the "heroic age" of medicine in which soldiers who suffered anything from dysentery to constipation to malaria to a cold were dosed with calomel or tartar emetic or quinine or morphine or laudanum. Little wonder that many soldiers preferred to remain out of the clutches of doctors. Little wonder, also, that some became narcotics addicts.

Disease was a greater threat to the health of Civil War soldiers than enemy weapons. This had been true of every army in history. Civil War armies actually suffered comparatively less disease mortality than any previous army. While two Union or Confederate soldiers died of disease for each one killed in combat, the ratio for British soldiers in the Na-poleonic and Crimean wars had been eight to one and four to one. For the American army in the Mexican War it had been seven to one. Only by twentieth-century standards was Civil War disease mortality high. Nevertheless, despite improvement over previous wars in this respect, disease was a crippling factor in Civil War military operations. At any given time a substantial proportion of men in a regiment might be on the sicklist. Disease reduced the size of most regiments from their initial complement of a thousand men to about half that number before the regiment ever went into battle.

Sickness hit soldiers hardest in their first year. The crowding together of thousands of men from various backgrounds into a new and highly contagious disease environment had predictable results. Men (especially those from rural areas) who had never before been exposed to measles, mumps, or tonsilitis promptly came down with these childhood mala-dies. Though rarely fatal, these illnesses could cripple units for weeks at a time. More deadly were smallpox and erysipelas, which went through some rural regiments like a scythe. If soldiers recovered from these dis-eases and remained for some time at the training or base camp—where by poor sanitary practices and exposure to changeable weather they fouled their water supply, created fertile breeding grounds for bacteria, and became susceptible to deadly viruses—many of them contracted one of the three principal killer diseases of the war: diarrhea/dysentery, typhoid,

40. The number of times when surgeons had to perform an operation without anes-thetics, however, was relatively small even in the Confederacy. Stonewall Jackson's troops had captured 15,000 cases of chloroform in the Valley campaign, which helped Confederate surgeons greatly in this respect.

or pneumonia. As they marched southward in summer campaigns, many of them caught the fourth most prevalent mortal disease: malaria. A good many Union occupation troops in southern cities as well as Confederate soldiers camped near other cities—especially Richmond—experienced another soldiers' malady, venereal disease, of which there were about as many reported cases as of measles, mumps, and tonsilitis combined.[41]

Disease disrupted several military operations. Lee's West Virginia campaigns of 1861 failed in part because illness incapacitated so many of his men. One reason for the abandonment of the first effort to capture Vicksburg in July 1862 was the sickness of more than half of the Union soldiers and sailors there. Beauregard's decision to abandon Corinth was influenced by illness of epidemic proportions that put more than a third of his army on the sicklist. By the time Halleck's Union army had established its occupation of Corinth in early June, a third or more of the Yankee soldiers were also ill. Nearly half of the twenty-nine Union generals came down sick during the Corinth campaign and its aftermath, including Halleck himself and John Pope with what they ruefully called the "Evacuation of Corinth" (diarrhea) and Sherman with malaria. Halleck's failure after Corinth to continue his invasion into Mississippi resulted in part from fears of even greater disease morbidity among unacclimated northern soldiers in a Deep-South summer campaign.

Illness also influenced the denouement of the Peninsula campaign in Virginia. The health of McClellan's army, already affected by the heavy rains and humid heat among the Chickahominy swamps in May and June, deteriorated further after the army's arrival at Harrison's Landing in July. Nearly a fourth of the unwounded men were sick. Scores of new cases of malaria, dysentery, and typhoid were reported every day. McClellan himself had not fully recovered from an earlier bout with dysentery. With the sickliest season of the year (August–September) coming on, the administration decided over McClellan's protest to withdraw his army from the Peninsula.

Strategic and political questions also played a part in this decision. Recognizing the drawbacks of trying to function as his own general in chief, Lincoln had called Halleck out of the West to take this post. The president had also formed a new army out of Banks's, Frémont's, and

41. See the tabulation of diseases in the Union army in Paul E. Steiner, *Disease in the Civil War* (Springfield, Ill., 1968), 10–11.

McDowell's corps in northern Virginia and had brought John Pope east to command it. While this was going on, Congress was passing a bill to confiscate the property (including slaves) of Confederates, and Lincoln was making up his mind to issue an emancipation proclamation. The failure of McClellan's Peninsula campaign was not alone a military failure; it represented also the downfall of the limited war for limited ends that McClellan favored. From now on the North would fight not to preserve the old Union but to destroy it and build a new one on the ashes.

16

We Must Free the Slaves
or Be Ourselves Subdued

I

If Robert E. Lee was unhappy with the escape of McClellan's army from destruction in the Seven Days', the southern people did not share his discontent. "The fatal blow has been dealt this 'grand army' of the North," wrote a Richmond diarist. "Lee has turned the tide, and I shall not be surprised if we have a long career of successes." Lee became the hero of the hour. No more was heard of the King of Spades or Evacuating Lee. The *Richmond Whig* proclaimed that the quiet Virginian had "amazed and confounded his detractors by the brilliancy of his genius . . . his energy and daring. He has established his reputation forever, and has entitled himself to the lasting gratitude of his country."[1]

These commentators, of course, could not foresee the profound irony of Lee's achievement. If McClellan's campaign had succeeded, the war might have ended. The Union probably would have been restored with minimal destruction in the South. Slavery would have survived in only slightly modified form, at least for a time. By defeating McClellan, Lee assured a prolongation of the war until it destroyed slavery, the Old South, and nearly everything the Confederacy was fighting for.

After the Seven Days', Union policy took a decisive turn toward total war. Northern morale initially plunged downward as far as southern

1. Jones, *War Clerk's Diary* (Miers), 88–89; Douglas Southall Freeman, *R. E. Lee: A Biography*, 4 vols. (New York, 1934–35), II, 244–45.

morale ascended skyward. "The feeling of despondency here is very great," wrote a prominent Democrat from New York, while a Republican diarist recorded "the darkest day we have seen since Bull Run. . . . Things look disastrous. . . . I find it hard to maintain my lively faith in the triumph of the nation and the law." Although equally depressed, Lincoln did not falter. "I expect to maintain this contest," he informed state governors, "until successful, or till I die, or am conquered . . . or Congress or the country forsakes me."[2]

Lincoln now recognized that the cessation of recruiting in April had been a mistake. But he feared that if he issued a new appeal for recruits in the wake of the Seven Days', "a general panic and stampede would follow." Seward solved this dilemma with a clever tactic. He hastened to New York and conferred with northern governors. They agreed to issue an address (written by Seward) to the president urging him to call on the states for new volunteers to "follow up" the "recent successes of the Federal arms" and "speedily crush the rebellion." Seward backdated this document to June 28 in order to avoid the appearance of a panicked response to McClellan's retreat. In pretended compliance with the governors' appeal, Lincoln on July 2 called for 300,000 new volunteers to bring the war "to a speedy and satisfactory conclusion."[3]

Once again recruiting committees in the North geared up their machinery. Governors called on men to join up to fight for "the old flag, for our country, Union, and Liberty." James S. Gibbons, a Quaker abolitionist with "a reasonable leaning toward wrath in cases of emergency," wrote a popular recruiting poem that was set to music by Stephen Foster, Luther O. Emerson, and others, "We are Coming, Father Abraham, Three Hundred Thousand More." But the three hundred thousand came forward with painful slowness. The parades and rallies of 1862 were a pale imitation of the stirring demonstrations of 1861. The lengthening casualty lists had taught people that war was not a glorious game. Although the North had mobilized only a third of its potential military manpower, a booming war economy and the busy summer season on farms had left few young men at loose ends and ready to volunteer. Moreover, the new recruits, like those already in the army, had to enlist for three years. Governors informed the War De-

---

2. Samuel L. M. Barlow to Henry D. Bacon, July 15, 1862, Barlow Papers, Henry E. Huntington Library; Strong, *Diary*, 234, 236, 239, 241; CWL, V, 292.

3. CWL, V, 292–97. The War Department established state quotas for these 300,000 volunteers apportioned on the basis of population.

partment that they could easily raise enough short-term men to fill their quotas, but getting three-year recruits would be difficult.

In response the government adopted an ingenious carrot and stick approach. The carrot was bounties. The War Department authorized payment in advance of $25 of the traditional $100 bounty normally paid in full upon honorable discharge. In addition, some states or cities offered bounties to three-year recruits. Intended as a compensation for the economic sacrifice made by a volunteer and his family, these initially modest bounties were the forerunner of what later became a mercenary bidding contest for warm bodies to fill district quotas. The stick was a militia law enacted by Congress on July 17, 1862. This law defined the militia as comprising all able-bodied men between ages eighteen and forty-five and empowered the president to call state militia into federal service for a period of up to nine months. Since the militia in several states had fallen into a comatose condition, a key provision of the act authorized the president to "make all necessary rules and regulations . . . to provide for enrolling the militia and otherwise putting this act into execution."[4] Here was a potential for an enormous expansion of federal power at the expense of the states. The government did not hesitate to use this power to reach across state boundaries and institute a quasi-draft. On August 4 the War Department imposed on the states a levy of 300,000 nine-month militia *in addition to* the 300,000 three-year volunteers called for a month earlier.[5] Moreover, any deficiency in meeting quotas under the earlier call must be made up by levying an equivalent number of additional nine-month men. And if the states did not mobilize these militia, the War Department would step in and do it for them. Secretary of War Stanton softened the blow of this big stick, however, with a regulation stipulating that every three-year volunteer enlisted above quota would be counted as four men against the nine-month militia quota.

Although of dubious legality and confusing arithmetic, this regulation achieved its purpose. With the help of several postponed deadlines, most states enrolled a sufficient combination of three-year and nine-month recruits to avoid a draft of nine-month men. Before the end of 1862 this procedure had produced 421,000 three-year volunteers and 88,000 militiamen, which according to Stanton's arithmetic exceeded the com-

4. U.S. *Statutes at Large*, XII, 597.
5. Men employed in several occupations vital to the war effort were exempted from militia service.

bined quotas by 45 percent. Most of the volunteers were recruited by the time-honored method of organizing new regiments with their complement each of thirty-odd officers' commissions as political plums. Some of these new regiments became crack units by 1863, but in the process they had to go through the same high-casualty trial-and-error experiences as their 1861 predecessors.

In several states a militia draft became necessary to fill the quotas. This draft met violent resistance in some areas, especially Irish Catholic neighborhoods in the coalfields of eastern Pennsylvania, Butternut districts in Ohio and Indiana, and German Catholic townships in Wisconsin. Mobs murdered two enrollment officers in Indiana and wounded a commissioner in Wisconsin. The army had to send troops into all four states to keep order and carry out the draft. On September 24, Lincoln issued a proclamation suspending the writ of habeas corpus and subjecting to martial law "all persons discouraging volunteer enlistments, resisting militia drafts, or guilty of any disloyal practice affording aid and comfort to the rebels." The War Department took off the gloves to enforce this decree. Stanton created a network of provost marshals who arrested and imprisoned without trial several hundred draft resisters and antiwar activists, including five newspaper editors, three judges, and several minor political leaders.[6]

Most of the men arrested were Democrats. This did not signify a determination by the Republican administration to get rid of its political adversaries—as Democrats charged. Rather it reflected the reality that virtually all those who denounced and resisted the militia draft were Democrats. They represented the most conservative wing of the party on such issues as emancipation, the draft, and the financial legislation passed by the Republican Congress in 1862. Opposition to these measures was strongest among Irish and German Catholics and among Butternuts of the southern Midwest whose wealth and income were significantly below the northern median. These groups rioted against the draft while carrying banners proclaiming "The Constitution As It Is, The Union As It Was" and "We won't fight to free the nigger."[7]

Such slogans offer a key to understanding both the motives of anti-

6. CWL, V, 436–37; Robert E. Sterling, "Civil War Draft Resistance in the Middle West," Ph.D. dissertation, Northern Illinois University, 1974, chaps. 3–4.
7. Sterling, "Draft Resistance in the Middle West," 96–97. This study contains valuable data correlating draft resistance with political, ethnocultural, geographic, and economic variables. See especially 129, 248, and 535.

draft resisters and the Republican response to them. The "copperhead" faction of the northern Democratic party opposed the transformation of the Civil War into a total war—a war to destroy the old South instead of to restore the old Union.[8] In Republican eyes, opposition to Republican war aims became opposition to the war itself. Opponents therefore became abettors of the rebellion and liable to military arrest. Most such arrests in 1861 had occurred in border states where pro-Confederate sentiment was rife. In 1862, many of the men arrested were northern Democrats whose disaffection from the war had been sparked by Republican adoption that year of emancipation as a war policy.

II

By the beginning of 1862 the impetus of war had evolved three shifting and overlapping Republican factions on the slavery question. The most dynamic and clearcut faction were the radicals, who accepted the abolitionist argument that emancipation could be achieved by exercise of the belligerent power to confiscate enemy property. On the other wing of the party a smaller number of conservatives hoped for the ultimate demise of bondage but preferred to see this happen by the voluntary action of slave states coupled with colonization abroad of the freed slaves. In the middle were the moderates, led by Lincoln, who shared the radicals' moral aversion to slavery but feared the racial consequences of wholesale emancipation. Events during the first half of 1862 pushed moderates toward the radical position.

One sign of this development was the growing influence of abolitionists. "Never has there been a time when Abolitionists were as much respected, as at present," rejoiced one of them in December 1861. "It is hard to realize the wondrous change which has befallen us," mused

8. Like most political labels, "copperhead" was originally an epithet invented by opponents. Ohio Republicans seem to have used it as early as the fall of 1861 to liken antiwar Democrats to the venomous snake of that name. By the fall of 1862 the term had gained wide usage and was often applied by Republicans to the whole Democratic party. By 1863 some Peace Democrats proudly accepted the label and began wearing badges bearing likenesses of the Goddess of Liberty from the copper penny to symbolize their opposition to Republican "tyranny." Albert Matthews, "Origin of Butternut and Copperhead," *Proceedings of the Colonial Society of Massachusetts* (1918), 205–37; Charles H. Coleman, "The Use of the Term 'Copperhead' during the Civil War," *MVHR*, 25 (1938), 263–64.

another.[9] The most radical of them all, Wendell Phillips, lectured to packed houses all over the North in the winter and spring of 1862. In March he came to Washington—which he could scarcely have entered without danger to his life a year earlier—and spoke on three occasions to large audiences that included the president and many members of Congress. Phillips also had the rare privilege of a formal introduction on the floor of the Senate. "The Vice-President left his seat and greeted him with marked respect," wrote a reporter for the *New York Tribune*. "The attentions of Senators to the apostle of Abolition were of the most flattering character." Noting the change from the previous winter when mobs had attacked abolitionists as troublemakers who had provoked the South to secession, the *Tribune* observed: "It is not often that history presents such violent contrasts in such rapid succession. . . . The deference and respect now paid to him by men in the highest places of the nation, are tributes to the idea of which he, more than any other one man, is a popular exponent." Even the *New York Times* gave abolitionists its imprimatur in January 1862 by sending a reporter to the convention of the Massachusetts Anti-Slavery Society. "In years heretofore a great deal has been said and much fun has been made . . . of these gatherings," said the *Times*. "The facts that black and white met socially here, and that with equal freedom men and women addressed the conglomerate audience, have furnished themes for humorous reporters and facetious editors; but no such motives have drawn here the representatives of fifteen of the most widely circulated journals of the North. Peculiar circumstances have given to [abolitionist meetings] an importance that has hitherto not been theirs."[10]

These peculiar circumstances were the growing Republican conviction that the fate of the nation could not be separated from the fate of slavery. In an important House speech on January 14, 1862, radical leader George W. Julian of Indiana set the tone for Republican congressional policy. "When I say that this rebellion has its source and life in slavery, I only repeat a simple truism," declared Julian. The four million slaves "cannot be neutral. As laborers, if not as soldiers, they will be the allies of the rebels, or of the Union." By freeing them the North would convert their labor power from support of treason to support of

9. *Principia*, Dec. 21, 1861; Mary Grew to Wendell P. Garrison, Jan. 9, 1862, Garrison Family Papers, Rush Rhees Library, University of Rochester.
10. *New York Tribune*, March 15, 18, 1862; *New York Times*, Jan. 25, 1862.

Union and liberty. This would hasten the day of national triumph, but even if the nation should triumph without such action "the mere suppression of the rebellion will be an empty mockery of our sufferings and sacrifices, if slavery shall be spared to canker the heart of the nation anew, and repeat its diabolical deeds."[11]

By midsummer 1862 all but the most conservative of Republicans had come to a similar conclusion. "You can form no conception of the change of opinion here as to the Negro question," wrote Senator John Sherman in August to his brother the general. "I am prepared for one to meet the broad issue of universal emancipation." A conservative Boston newspaper conceded that "the great phenomenon of the year is the terrible intensity which this [emancipation] resolution has acquired. A year ago men might have faltered at the thought of proceeding to this extremity, [but now] they are in great measure prepared for it."[12]

Given this mood, antislavery bills poured into the congressional hopper like leaves dropping from trees in autumn. Referred to committees, they met a friendly reception. A unique combination of history and geography had given New England-born radicals extraordinary power in Congress, especially the Senate. New England and the upper tier of states west of the Hudson settled by Yankee emigrants had been the birthplace of abolitionism and free soil politics. From these regions had come to Washington the earliest and most radical Republicans. Eleven of the twelve New England senators chaired committees, and men born in New England but now representing other states held five of the eleven remaining chairmanships. Five of the ten most prominent radicals in the House, including the speaker and the chairman of the ways and means committee (Galusha Grow and Thaddeus Stevens, both of Pennsylvania) had been born and raised in New England. Little wonder, then, that seven emancipation or confiscation bills were favorably reported out of congressional committees by mid-January and became law during the next six months.[13]

Some of these laws fulfilled longstanding free-soil goals: prohibition

11. CG, 37 Cong., 2 Sess., 327–32.
12. John Sherman to William T. Sherman, Aug. 24, 1862, in Rachel S. Thorndike, ed., *The Sherman Letters: Correspondence between General and Senator Sherman from 1837 to 1891* (London, 1894), 156–57; *Boston Advertiser*, Aug. 20, 1862.
13. Leonard P. Curry, *Blueprint for Modern America: Nonmilitary Legislation of the First Civil War Congress* (Nashville, 1968), esp. chaps. 1–4; Allan G. Bogue, *The Earnest Men: Republicans of the Civil War Senate* (Ithaca, N.Y., 1981), esp. chaps. 1–6.

of slavery in the territories; ratification of a new treaty with Britain for more effective suppression of the slave trade; and abolition of slavery in the District of Columbia. But while these would have been heralded as great antislavery achievements in peacetime, they scarcely touched the real war issues concerning slavery in 1862. More important was a new article of war passed on March 13 forbidding army officers to return fugitive slaves to their masters. This grappled with the question first raised by Benjamin Butler's "contraband" policy in 1861. Union conquests along the south Atlantic coast and in the lower Mississippi Valley had brought large numbers of slaves into proximity to the Yankees. Many of them escaped their owners and sought refuge—and freedom—in Union camps.

Sometimes their welcome was less than friendly. While northern soldiers had no love for slavery, most of them had no love for slaves either. They fought for Union and against treason; only a minority in 1862 felt any interest in fighting for black freedom. Rare was the soldier who shared the sentiments of a Wisconsin private: "I have no heart in this war if the slaves cannot be free." More common was the conviction of a New York soldier that "we must first conquer & then its time enough to talk about the *dam'd niggers*." While some Yanks treated contrabands with a degree of equity or benevolence, the more typical response was indifference, contempt, or cruelty. Soon after Union forces captured Port Royal, South Carolina, in November 1861, a private described an incident there that made him "ashamed of America": "About 8–10 soldiers from the New York 47th chased some Negro women but they escaped, so they took a Negro girl about 7–9 years old, and raped her." From Virginia a Connecticut soldier wrote that some men of his regiment had taken "two niger wenches . . . turned them upon their heads, & put tobacco, chips, sticks, lighted cigars & sand into their behinds."[14] Even when Billy Yank welcomed the contrabands, he often did so from utilitarian rather than humanitarian motives. "Officers & men are having an easy time," wrote a Maine soldier from occupied Louisiana in 1862. "We have Negroes to do all fatigue work, cooking and washing clothes."[15]

Before March 1862, Union commanders had no legislative guidelines for dealing with contrabands. Some officers followed Butler's precedent

14. Wiley, *Billy Yank*, 40, 44, 114.
15. Bell I. Wiley, "The Boys of 1861," in William C. Davis, ed., *Shadows of the Storm*, Vol. I of *The Image of War: 1861–1865* (Garden City, N.Y., 1981), 127.

of sheltering them and turning away white men who claimed to be their owners. The Treasury Department sent agents to the conquered South Carolina sea islands to supervise contraband labor in completing the harvest of cotton for sale to New England mills. Abolitionists organized freedmen's aid societies which sent teachers and labor superintendents to these islands to launch a well-publicized experiment in free labor and black education. But in other areas, commanding officers refused to admit slaves to Union camps and returned them to owners. In his Western Department, General Halleck ordered contrabands excluded from Union lines on grounds of military security. Though many of Halleck's field commanders honored this order in the breach, its existence produced an outcry from radicals who insisted that the army had no business enforcing the fugitive slave law. Thus Congress enacted the new article of war prohibiting, under penalty of court-martial, the return of fugitives from army camps even to masters who claimed to be loyal.

Here was a measure with large potential for breaking down slavery in the Union as well as the Confederate slave states. This circumstance gave added force to Lincoln's first step in the direction of an emancipation policy. As a gradualist who hoped to end slavery without social dislocation and with the voluntary cooperation of slaveowners, Lincoln in 1862 thought he saw an opening in the mounting pressures against the institution. Border-state unionists could scarcely fail to recognize the portent of these pressures, he reasoned. Therefore they might respond positively to an offer of federal compensation for voluntary emancipation of their slaves. On March 6, Lincoln asked Congress to pass a resolution offering "pecuniary aid" to "any state which may adopt gradual abolishment of slavery." This was not merely a humanitarian measure, said the president; it was a means of shortening the war, for if the border states became free the Confederacy would no longer be sustained by the hope of winning their allegiance. To those who might deplore the cost of compensation, Lincoln pointed out that three months of war expenditures would buy all the slaves in the four border states. To slaveholders the president uttered a thinly veiled warning: if they refused this offer "it is impossible to foresee all the incidents which may attend and all the ruin which may follow" a continuation of the war.[16]

Congress adopted Lincoln's resolution on April 10. All Republicans supported it; 85 percent of the Democrats and border-state unionists voted against it. The latter's opposition was a discouraging sign. Lincoln

16. CWL, V, 144–46.

had already held one unsuccessful meeting with border-state congress-men, on March 10, when they questioned the constitutionality of his proposal, bristled at its hint of federal coercion, and deplored the potential race problem that would emerge with a large free black population.[17]

In the months following this meeting the scale of the war and of emancipation sentiment increased. Congress moved toward passage of an act confiscating Confederate property. Tens of thousands more contrabands came under Union army control. On May 9, General David Hunter, commander of Union forces occupying the islands off the South Carolina and Georgia coast, issued a sweeping declaration of martial law abolishing slavery in all three states constituting his "Department of the South" (South Carolina, Georgia, and Florida). Hunter, like Frémont and Cameron before him, had taken this action without informing Lincoln, who first learned of it from the newspapers. "No commanding general shall do such a thing, on *my* responsibility, without consulting me," Lincoln told Treasury Secretary Chase, who had urged approval of Hunter's edict. Lincoln revoked it and rebuked the general. While conservatives applauded this action, they should have noticed the antislavery sting in the tail of Lincoln's revocation. The *substance* of Hunter's order might "become a necessity indispensable to the maintenance of the government," hinted the president, but this was a decision which "I reserve to myself." Lincoln then appealed to border-state unionists to reconsider his offer of compensated, gradual emancipation. The changes produced by such a plan "would come gently as the dews of heaven, not rending or wrecking anything. Will you not embrace it? . . . You can not if you would, be blind to the signs of the times."[18]

Lincoln's estimate of the border-state representatives' vision was too generous. In May 1862 these men shared the northern expectation of imminent military victory. If McClellan could capture Richmond the rebellion might be ended with slavery still intact. The Seven Days' should

---

17. Memorandum of the meeting written by Representative John W. Crisfield of Maryland, printed in Charles M. Segal, ed., *Conversations with Lincoln* (New York, 1961), 164–68.

18. *CWL*, V, 219, 222–23. By gradual emancipation Lincoln had in mind the example after the Revolution of northern states that had provided for the future emancipation of slaves when they reached a certain age. He had also suggested to a Delaware senator the setting of a date (for example, 1882) by which the institution of slavery would be legally terminated. Lincoln to James A. McDougal, March 14, 1862 (*ibid.*, 160).

have destroyed this hope. The new measures of recruitment and mobilization undertaken in response to McClellan's defeat indicated a turn toward total war in which preservation of "the Union as it was" became an impossible dream—but still most border-state politicians remained blind to the signs.

In July 1862 the 37th Congress climaxed its second session with passage of two laws that signaled the turn toward a harsher war policy. The first was the militia act under which the government subsequently called for a draft of nine-month men. This bill also empowered the president to enroll "persons of African descent" for "any war service for which they may be found competent"—including service as soldiers, a step that would horrify conservatives and that the adminstration was not yet prepared to take. But the law gave the government revolutionary leverage. As even moderate Republican senators observed, "the time has arrived when . . . military authorities should be compelled to use all the physical force of this country to put down the rebellion." The war must be fought on "different principles"; the time for "white kid-glove warfare" was past.[19]

This theme was underlined by the confiscation act of July 1862 which punished "traitors" by confiscating their property, including slaves who "shall be deemed captives of war and shall be forever free." But the law was so confusing and poorly drawn that a good lawyer probably could have "driven through it with a two horse team." The confusion resulted mainly from the dual character of the Civil War as a domestic insurrection and as a war. The confiscation act seized the property of rebels as a punishment for treason but also freed their slaves as "captives of war." Chairman Lyman Trumbull of the Senate Judiciary Committee saw no inconsistency in this. "We may treat them as traitors," he said, "and we may treat them as enemies, and we have the right of both, belligerent and sovereign."[20] But the law's provisions for enforcing the sovereign right were vague, consisting of *in rem* proceedings by district courts that were of course not functioning in the rebellious states. Yet the confiscation act was important as a symbol of what the war was becoming—a war to overturn the southern social order as a means of reconstructing the Union.

19. *U.S. Statutes at Large*, XII, 597; Senators John Sherman and William Pitt Fessenden quoted in Bogue, *Earnest Men*, 162.
20. *U.S. Statutes at Large*, XII, 589–92; *New York Herald*, July 18, 1862; Trumbull quoted in Bogue, *Earnest Men*, 220.

The agency for accomplishing this was the executive working through the enforcing power of the army. July 1862 brought a significant hardening of attitude in both army and executive. John Pope arrived from the West to take command of the newly designated Army of Virginia, formed from the divisions of Banks, Frémont, and McDowell that had chased Stonewall Jackson so futilely in the Shenandoah Valley. Irked by this promotion of a junior general over his head, Frémont offered his resignation, which Lincoln gratefully accepted. Although the radical Republicans thereby lost one of their favorite commanders, they soon discovered in Pope a kindred spirit. One of his first acts in Virginia was a series of general orders authorizing his officers to seize rebel property without compensation, to shoot captured guerrillas who had fired on Union troops, to expel from occupied territory any civilians who refused to take the oath of allegiance, and to treat them as spies if they returned.

Southerners erupted in anger toward Pope, whom they execrated with a fury felt toward no other Yankee "vandal" except Butler and, later, Sherman. Robert E. Lee declared that this "miscreant Pope" must be "suppressed." Jefferson Davis threatened retaliation on Union prisoners if captured guerrillas were executed. Pope's orders were undoubtedly ill-advised, but not groundless. Southern civilians behind Union lines did form partisan bands to pick off Yankee stragglers, teamsters, and other rear-area personnel. Captured papers of Confederate Colonel John D. Imboden, commander of the First Partisan Rangers in Virginia, included orders "to wage the most active war against our brutal invaders . . . to hang about their camps and shoot down every sentinel, picket, courier, and wagon driver we can find."[21]

Although Pope did not shoot any guerrillas or expel any civilians, his policy concerning southern property was carried out, in Virginia as in other theaters, by privates as well as officers, with or without orders. Large portions of the South were becoming a wasteland. Much of this was the inevitable destruction of war, as both armies cut down trees and tore up fences for firewood, wrecked bridges and culverts and railroads or cannibalized whatever structures they could find to rebuild wrecked bridges and railroads, or seized crops, livestock, and poultry for food. Soldiers have pillaged civilian property since the beginning of time. But by midsummer 1862 some of the destruction of southern property had acquired a purposeful, even an ideological dimension. More and more Union soldiers were writing that it was time to take off the "kid gloves"

21. Nevins, *War*, II, 155–56.

in dealing with "traitors." "The iron gauntlet," wrote one officer, "must be used more than the silken glove to crush this serpent." It seemed only logical to destroy the property of men who were doing their best to destroy the Union—to "spoil the Egyptians," as Yankee soldiers put it. "This thing of guarding rebel property when the owner is in the field fighting us is played out," wrote the chaplain of an Ohio regiment. "That is the sentiment of every private soldier in the army."[22] It was a sentiment sanctioned from the top. In July, Lincoln called Halleck to Washington to become general in chief. One of Halleck's first orders to Grant, now commander of occupation forces in western Tennessee and Mississippi, was to "take up all active [rebel] sympathizers, and either hold them as prisoners or put them beyond our lines. Handle that class without gloves, and take their property for public use. . . . It is time that they should begin to feel the presence of the war."[23]

Take their property. Here was abolition in action. As one of Grant's subordinates explained, "the policy is to be terrible on the enemy. I am using Negroes all the time for my work as teamsters, and have 1,000 employed." Emancipation was a *means* to victory, not yet an end in itself. Grant informed his family that his only desire was "to put down the rebellion. I have no hobby of my own with regard to the Negro, either to effect his freedom or to continue his bondage. . . . I am using them as teamsters, hospital attendants, company cooks and so forth, thus saving soldiers to carry the musket. I don't know what is to become of these poor people in the end, but it weakens the enemy to take them from them."[24]

One prominent northerner who deplored this new turn in the war was McClellan. When Lincoln came down to Harrison's Landing on July 8 to see for himself the condition of McClellan's army, the general handed him a memorandum on the proper conduct of the war. "It should not be a war looking to the subjugation of the [southern] people," McClellan instructed the president. "Neither confiscation of property . . . [n]or forcible abolition of slavery should be contemplated for a moment. . . . It should not be a war upon population, but against armed forces. . . . Military power should not be allowed to interfere with the relations of servitude. . . . A declaration of radical views, especially upon slavery, will rapidly disintegrate our present armies."[25]

22. Bruce Catton, *Grant Moves South* (Boston, 1960), 294, 296.
23. O.R., Ser. I, Vol. 17, pt. 1, p. 150.
24. Grenville Dodge and Grant quoted in Catton, *Grant Moves South*, 294, 297.
25. George B. McClellan, *McClellan's Own Story* (New York, 1887), 487–89.

Lincoln read these words in McClellan's presence without comment. But the president's thoughts can be reconstructed. Three or four months earlier he would have agreed with McClellan. But now he had become convinced of the necessity for "forcible abolition of slavery" and had begun to draft a proclamation of emancipation. To a southern unionist and a northern Democrat who several days later made the same points as McClellan, the president replied with asperity that the war could no longer be fought "with elder-stalk squirts, charged with rose water. . . . This government cannot much longer play a game in which it stakes all, and its enemies stake nothing. Those enemies must understand that they cannot experiment for ten years trying to destroy the government, and if they fail still come back into the Union unhurt." The demand by border-state slaveowners "that the government shall not strike its open enemies, lest they be struck by accident" had become "the paralysis— the dead palsy—of the government in this whole struggle."[26]

In this mood Lincoln called border-state congressmen to the White House on July 12. Once more he urged favorable action on his plan for compensated emancipation. "The unprecedentedly stern facts of our case," said the president, could no longer be ignored. In revoking General Hunter's emancipation edict two months earlier "I gave dissatisfaction, if not offense, to many whose support the country cannot afford to lose. And this is not the end of it. The pressure, in this direction, is still upon me, and is increasing." If the border states did not make "a *decision* at once to emancipate *gradually* . . . the institution in your states will be extinguished by mere friction and abrasion—by the mere incidents of the war . . . and you will have nothing valuable in lieu of it." But even this blunt warning fell on mostly deaf ears. Two-thirds of the border-state representatives signed a manifesto rejecting Lincoln's proposal because it would produce too "radical [a] change in our social system"; it was "interference" by the government with a state matter; it would cost too much (a curious objection from men whose states would benefit from a tax that would fall mainly on the free states); and finally, instead of shortening the conflict by depriving the Confederacy of hope for border-state support, it would lengthen the war and jeopardize victory by driving many unionist slaveholders into rebellion.[27]

This response caused Lincoln to give up trying to conciliate conser-

---

26. Lincoln to Cuthbert Bullitt, July 28, 1862, Lincoln to August Belmont, July 31, 1862, in CWL, V, 344–46, 350–51.
27. CWL, V, 317–19, for Lincoln's address; *New York Tribune*, July 19, 1862, for border-state replies.

vatives. From then on the president tilted toward the radical position, though this would not become publicly apparent for more than two months. On July 13, the day he received the border-state manifesto, Lincoln privately told Seward and Welles of his intention to issue an emancipation proclamation. As Welles recorded the conversation, Lincoln said that this question had "occupied his mind and thoughts day and night" for several weeks. He had decided that emancipation was "a military necessity, absolutely essential to the preservation of the Union. We must free the slaves or be ourselves subdued. The slaves were undeniably an element of strength to those who had their service, and we must decide whether that element should be with us or against us." Lincoln brushed aside the argument of unconstitutionality. This was a *war*, and as commander in chief he could order seizure of enemy slaves just as surely as he could order destruction of enemy railroads. "The rebels . . . could not at the same time throw off the Constitution and invoke its aid. Having made war on the Government, they were subject to the incidents and calamities of war." The border states "would do nothing" on their own; indeed, perhaps it was not fair to ask them to give up slavery while the rebels retained it. Therefore "the blow must fall first and foremost on [the rebels]. . . . Decisive and extensive measures must be adopted. . . . We wanted the army to strike more vigorous blows. The Administration must set an example, and strike at the heart of the rebellion."[28]

McClellan had made it clear that he was not the general to strike this sort of vigorous blow. After giving the president his memorandum on noninterference with slavery, McClellan followed it with a letter to Stanton warning that "the nation will support no other policy. . . . For none other will our armies continue to fight." This was too much for Stanton and Chase. They joined a growing chorus of Republicans who were urging Lincoln to remove McClellan from command.[29] But Lincoln demurred. He may have known that McClellan was privately denouncing the administration as fools and villains for failing to sustain his Peninsula campaign. The general's Democratic partisans were broadcasting such sentiments loudly. Lincoln also knew that prominent New

28. Gideon Welles, "The History of Emancipation," *The Galaxy*, 14 (Dec. 1872), 842–43.
29. McClellan to Stanton, July 8, 1862, in *McClellan's Own Story*, 478; Richard B. Irwin, "The Administration in the Peninsular Campaign," *Battles and Leaders*, II, 438.

York Democrats including copperhead Fernando Wood had visited McClellan at Harrison's Landing to court him as the party's next presidential nominee. But Lincoln also recognized that soldiers in the Army of the Potomac revered McClellan as the leader who had molded them into a proud army. The enlisted men did not subscribe to Republican criticisms of McClellan, and many of their officers did not share the Republican vision of an antislavery war. Because of this, Lincoln believed that he could not remove McClellan from command without risking demoralization in the army and a lethal Democratic backlash on the homefront.

This threat of a Democratic fire in the rear helped delay announcement of an emancipation policy. On July 22 Lincoln informed the cabinet of his intention to issue a proclamation of freedom, and invited comment. Only Montgomery Blair dissented, on the ground that such an edict would cost the Republicans control of Congress in the fall elections. Secretary of State Seward approved the proclamation but counseled its postponement "until you can give it to the country supported by military success." Otherwise the world might view it "as the last measure of an exhausted government, a cry for help . . . our last *shriek*, on the retreat." The wisdom of this suggestion "struck me with very great force," said the president later. He put his proclamation in a drawer to wait for a victory.[30]

It would prove to be a long wait. Meanwhile the polarization of opinion on the slavery issue reached new extremes. On the left, abolitionists and radicals grew abusive of a president who remained publicly uncommitted to emancipation. Lincoln was "nothing better than a wet rag," wrote William Lloyd Garrison, and his war policies were "stumbling, halting, prevaricating, irresolute." Frederick Douglass believed that Lincoln was "allowing himself to be . . . the miserable tool of traitors and rebels." In a letter to Charles Sumner on August 7, Horace Greeley asked: "Do you remember that old theological book containing this: 'Chapter One—Hell; Chapter Two—Hell Continued.' Well, that gives a hint of the way Old Abe *ought to be* talked to in this crisis." Greeley proceeded to give Lincoln hell in the columns of the *New York Tribune*.[31]

---

30. *CWL*, V, 336–37; Francis B. Carpenter, *Six Months at the White House* (New York, 1866), 22.

31. Garrison to Oliver Johnson, Sept. 9, 1862, Garrison Papers, Boston Public Library; *Liberator*, July 25, 1862; *Douglass' Monthly*, V (Aug. 1862), 694; William H.

Hard words, these, but Lincoln could stand them better than the sticks and stones hurled by Democrats. The emergence of slavery as the most salient war issue in 1862 threatened to turn a large element of the Democrats into an antiwar party. This was no small matter. The Democrats had received 44 percent of the popular votes in the free states in 1860. If the votes of the border states are added, Lincoln was a minority president of the Union states. By 1862 some "War Democrats" were becoming Republicans, even radicals—General Butler and Secretary of War Stanton are outstanding examples. Other War Democrats such as McClellan remained in their party and supported the goal of Union through military victory, but opposed emancipation. In 1862 a third element began to emerge: the Peace Democrats, or copperheads, who would come to stand for reunion through negotiations rather than victory—an impossible dream, and therefore in Republican eyes tantamount to treason because it played into Confederate hands. Southerners pinned great hopes on the copperhead faction, which they considered "large & strong enough, if left to operate constitutionally, to paralyze the war & majority party."[32]

War and Peace Democrats would maintain a shifting, uneasy, and sometimes divided coalition, but on one issue they remained united: opposition to emancipation. On four crucial congressional roll-call votes concerning slavery in 1862—the war article prohibiting return of fugitives, emancipation in the District of Columbia, prohibition of slavery in the territories, and the confiscation act—96 percent of the Democrats were united in opposition, while 99 percent of the Republicans voted aye. Seldom if ever in American politics has an issue so polarized the major parties. Because of secession the Republicans had a huge majority in Congress and could easily pass these measures, but an anti-emancipation backlash could undo that majority in the fall elections. This explains Montgomery Blair's concern and Lincoln's caution.

As they had done in every election since the birth of the Republican party, northern Democrats exploited the race issue for all they thought it was worth in 1862. The Black Republican "party of fanaticism" intended to free "two or three million semi-savages" to "overrun the North

Hale, *Horace Greeley, Voice of the People* (Collier Books ed., New York, 1961), 268–69.

32. William K. Scarborough, ed., *The Diary of Edmund Ruffin*, Vol. II, *The Years of Hope April, 1862–June, 1863* (Baton Rouge, 1976), 34.

and enter into competition with the white laboring masses" and mix with "their sons and daughters." "Shall the Working Classes be Equalized with Negroes?" screamed Democratic newspaper headlines.[33] Ohio's soldiers, warned that state's congressman and Democratic leader Samuel S. Cox, would no longer fight for the Union "if the result shall be the flight and movement of the black race by millions northward." And Archbishop John Hughes added his admonition that "we Catholics, and a vast majority of our brave troops in the field, have not the slightest idea of carrying on a war that costs so much blood and treasure just to gratify a clique of Abolitionists."[34]

With this kind of rhetoric from their leaders, it was little wonder that some white workingmen took their prejudices into the streets. In a half-dozen or more cities, anti-black riots broke out during the summer of 1862. Some of the worst violence occurred in Cincinnati, where the replacement of striking Irish dockworkers by Negroes set off a wave of attacks on black neighborhoods. In Brooklyn a mob of Irish-Americans tried to burn down a tobacco factory where two dozen black women and children were working. The nightmare vision of blacks invading the North seemed to be coming true in southern Illinois, where the War Department transported several carloads of contrabands to help with the harvest. Despite the desperate need for hands to gather crops, riots forced the government to return most of the blacks to contraband camps south of the Ohio River.

Anti-black sentiments were not a Democratic monopoly. The antebellum Negro exclusion laws of several midwestern states had commanded the support of a good many Whigs. In 1862 about two-fifths of the Republican voters joined Democrats to reaffirm Illinois's exclusion law in a referendum. Senator Lyman Trumbull of Illinois, architect of the confiscation act, conceded that "there is a very great aversion in the

33. Resolution of the Pennsylvania Democratic convention, July 4, 1862, quoted in Williston Lofton, Jr., "Northern Labor and the Negro during the Civil War," *Journal of Negro History*, 34 (1949), 254; *Columbus Crisis* and *Chicago Times*, quoted in V. Jacque Voegeli, *Free But Not Equal: The Midwest and the Negro during the Civil War* (Chicago, 1967), 6; *New York Day Book* quoted in Forrest G. Wood, *Black Scare: The Racist Response to Emancipation and Reconstruction* (Berkeley, 1968), 35.
34. *CG*, 37 Cong., 2 Sess., *Appendix*, 242–49; Hughes quoted in Foote, *Civil War*, I, 538. For another and similar pronouncement by Hughes, see Benjamin J. Blied, *Catholics and the Civil War* (Milwaukee, 1945), 44–45.

West—I know it to be so in my State—against having free negroes come among us. Our people want nothing to do with the negro."[35] To placate this aversion, some Republicans maintained that it was *slavery* which forced blacks to flee North toward freedom; emancipation would keep this tropical race in the South by giving them freedom in a congenial clime. This thesis encountered considerable skepticism, however. To meet the racial fears that constituted the party's Achilles' heel, many Republicans turned to colonization.

This solution of the race problem was stated crudely but effectively by an Illinois soldier: "I am not in favor of freeing the negroes and leaving them to run free among us nether is Sutch the intention of Old Abe but we will Send them off and colonize them."[36] Old Abe did indeed advocate colonization in 1862. From his experience in Illinois politics he had developed sensitive fingers for the pulse of public opinion on this issue. He believed that support for colonization was the best way to defuse much of the anti-emancipation sentiment that might otherwise sink the Republicans in the 1862 elections. This conviction underlay Lincoln's remarks to a group of black leaders in the District of Columbia whom he invited to the White House on August 14, 1862. Slavery was "the greatest wrong inflicted on any people," Lincoln told the delegation in words reported by a newspaper correspondent who was present. But even if slavery were abolished, racial differences and prejudices would remain. "Your race suffer very greatly, many of them, by living among us, while ours suffer from your presence." Blacks had little chance to achieve equality in the United States. "There is an unwillingness on the part of our people, harsh as it may be, for you free colored people to remain among us. . . . I do not mean to discuss this, but to propose it as a fact with which we have to deal. I cannot alter it if I would." This fact, said Lincoln, made it necessary for black people to emigrate to another land where they would have better opportunities. The president asked the black leaders to recruit volunteers for a government-financed pilot colonization project in Central America. If this worked, it could pave the way for the emigration of thousands more who might be freed by the war.[37]

Most black spokesmen in the North ridiculed Lincoln's proposal and

35. CG, 37 Cong., 2 Sess., 1780.
36. Wiley, *Billy Yank*, 112.
37. CWL, V, 370–75, from *New York Tribune*, Aug. 15, 1861. The *Tribune's* reporter submitted this account as the "substance of the President's remarks."

denounced its author. "This is our country as much as it is yours," a Philadelphia Negro told the president, "and we will not leave it." Frederick Douglass accused Lincoln of "contempt for negroes" and "canting hypocrisy." The president's remarks, said Douglass, would encourage "ignorant and base" white men "to commit all kinds of violence and outrage upon the colored people." Abolitionists and many radical Republicans continued to oppose colonization as racist and inhumane. "How much better," wrote Salmon P. Chase, "would be a manly protest against prejudice against color!—and a wise effort to give free[d] men homes in America!"[38]

But conservatives chided their radical colleagues for ignoring the immutability of racial differences. Abolitionists "may prattle as they wish about the end of slavery being the end of strife," wrote one conservative, but "the great difficulty will then but begin! The question is the profound and awful one of race." Two-thirds of the Republicans in Congress became sufficiently convinced of the need to conciliate this sentiment that they voted for amendments to the District of Columbia emancipation bill and the confiscation act appropriating $600,000 for colonization. As a practical matter, said one Republican, colonization "is a damn humbug. But it will take with the people."[39]

The government managed to recruit several hundred prospective black emigrants. But colonization did turn out to be a damn humbug in practice. The Central American project collapsed in the face of opposition from Honduras and Nicaragua. In 1863 the U.S. government sponsored the settlement of 453 colonists on an island near Haiti, but this enterprise also foundered when starvation and smallpox decimated the colony. The administration finally sent a naval vessel to return the 368 survivors to the United States in 1864. This ended official efforts to colonize blacks. By then the accelerating momentum of war had carried most northerners beyond the postulates of 1862.

Lincoln's colonization activities in August 1862 represented one part of his indirect effort to prepare public opinion for emancipation. Although he had decided to withhold his proclamation until Union arms

38. *New York Tribune*, Sept. 20, 1862; *Douglass' Monthly*, V (Sept. 1862), 707–8; David Donald, ed., *Inside Lincoln's Cabinet: The Civil War Diaries of Salmon P. Chase* (New York, 1954), 112.
39. *Boston Post*, quoted in *Boston Commonwealth*, Oct. 18, 1862; Robert F. Durden, *James Shepherd Pike: Republicanism and the American Negro, 1850–1882* (Durham, N.C., 1957), 37.

won a victory, he did drop hints of what might be coming. On August 22 he replied to Horace Greeley's emancipation editorial, "The Prayer of Twenty Millions," with an open letter to the editor. "My paramount object in the struggle *is* to save the Union, and is *not* either to save or to destroy slavery," wrote Lincoln in a masterpiece of concise expression. "If I could save the Union without freeing *any* slave I would do it, and if I could save it by freeing *all* the slaves I would do it; and if I could save it by freeing some and leaving others alone, I would also do that."[40] Here was something for all viewpoints: a reiteration that preservation of the Union remained the purpose of the war, but a hint that partial or even total emancipation might become necessary to accomplish that purpose.

The same intentional ambiguity characterized Lincoln's reply on September 13 to a group of clergymen who presented him a petition for freedom. The president agreed that "slavery is the root of the rebellion," that emancipation would "weaken the rebels by drawing off their laborers" and "would help us in Europe, and convince them that we are incited by something more than ambition." But in present circumstances, "when I cannot even enforce the Constitution in the rebel states . . . what *good* would a proclamation of emancipation from me do? . . . I do not want to issue a document that the whole world will necessarily see must be inoperative, like the Pope's bull against the comet!"[41] Here too was something for everybody: an assertion that emancipation was desirable though at present futile but perhaps imminent if the military situation took a turn for the better.

Military matters preoccupied Lincoln as he uttered these words. For two months, events in both the western and eastern theaters had been deteriorating to the point where by mid-September three southern armies were on the march northward in a bold bid for victory. But within the next few weeks the Confederate tide receded southward again without prevailing, thus ending the chance for European recognition and giving Lincoln the victory he needed to issue the emancipation proclamation.

40. *CWL*, V, 388–89.
41. *Ibid.*, 419–21.

17

Carry Me Back to Old Virginny

I

While Lee was driving McClellan away from Richmond, prospects also began to turn sour for Union forces in the West. The conquest of the Mississippi bogged down before Vicksburg. Triumphs on land came to a halt at Corinth. Why did this happen? The usual answer is to blame Halleck for dispersing his army and missing a grand opportunity to cripple the rebellion in the Mississippi Valley. The true answer is more complex.

Four tasks faced Halleck after his army of 110,000 occupied Corinth at the end of May. 1) Push on south after the retreating rebels and try to capture Vicksburg from the rear. 2) Send a force against Chattanooga to "liberate" east Tennessee. 3) Repair and defend the network of railroads that supplied Federal armies in this theater. 4) Organize occupation forces to preserve order, administer the contraband camps where black refugees had gathered, protect unionists trying to reconstruct Tennessee under military governor Andrew Johnson whom Lincoln had sent to Nashville, and oversee the revival of trade with the North in occupied areas. In the best of all possible worlds, Halleck would have done all four tasks simultaneously. But he did not have the resources to do so. Secretary of War Stanton and General Grant thought his first priority ought to be the capture of Vicksburg. Halleck's decision to defer this effort in favor of the other three has been the subject of much critical appraisal. An all-out campaign against Vicksburg, according to the critics, might have severed this Confederate artery and shortened the war.[1]

This thesis overlooks some physical, logistical, and political realities. The disease problem for unacclimated northern soldiers has already been mentioned. An unusually wet spring had turned into a disastrously dry summer. The streams and springs that supplied water for men and horses were rapidly drying up in northern Mississippi. Several cavalry and infantry brigades did pursue the Confederates twenty miles south of Corinth but could go no farther by July for lack of water.[2] Halleck's detachment of several brigades for railroad repair and guard duty was not so obtuse as it is sometimes portrayed, for as the rivers dropped below navigable stage the armies became wholly dependent on rail supply. Any overland campaign against Vicksburg would have been vulnerable to rebel raids on railroads and supply depots, as Grant learned six months later when such raids compelled him to abandon his first campaign against Vicksburg. Other brigades had to be detached from combat forces for the politically necessary tasks of policing and administering occupied territory. Finally, Lincoln's cherished aim of restoring east Tennessee made this political goal into a top military priority.[3]

Halleck therefore divided the Army of the Tennessee[4] under Grant into several fragments for occupation and railroad-repair duties, detached a division to reinforce Union troops confronting a new threat in Arkansas, and ordered the 40,000 men in the Army of the Ohio under Buell to move against Chattanooga. Buell's campaign—the major Union effort in the West during the summer of 1862—turned out as badly as McClellan's drive against Richmond. As old army friends, Buell and McClellan had much in common. Buell's idea of strategy was similar to McClellan's: "The object is," wrote Buell, "not to fight great battles,

1. *Personal Memoirs of U. S. Grant*, 2 vols. (New York, 1886), I, 381–84; Bruce Catton, *Grant Moves South* (Boston, 1960), 278–79; Foote, *Civil War*, I, 542–45; Nevins, *War*, II, 112.
2. Col. Edward Hatch of the 2nd Iowa Cavalry to Thomas Smith, July 10, 1862, Civil War Collection, Henry E. Huntington Library.
3. For defenses of Halleck, see Stephen E. Ambrose, *Halleck: Lincoln's Chief of Staff* (Baton Rouge, 1962), 55–57; and Herman Hattaway and Archer Jones, *How the North Won: A Military History of the Civil War* (Urbana, Ill., 1983), 205–6.
4. Sometimes called the Army of West Tennessee in 1862. The Army of the Tennessee was formally designated in October 1862 and known by that name for the rest of the war. When Halleck went to Washington as general in chief in July 1862, command of the two principal Union armies in the West was divided between Grant and Buell.

and storm impregnable fortifications, but by demonstrations and ma-neuvering to prevent the enemy from concentrating his scattered forces."[5]

A political conservative, Buell also believed in limited war for limited goals. This slowed his drive toward Chattanooga along the railroad from Corinth through northern Alabama. Guerrillas cut his supply lines fre-quently. "We are attacked nightly at bridges and outposts," reported one division commander. Buell's belief in a "soft" war precluded a ruthless treatment of the civilian population that sheltered guerrillas or a levy upon this population for supplies. Buell therefore could move only as fast as repair crews could rebuild bridges and re-lay rails. Three weeks after leaving Corinth he had advanced only ninety miles and was still less than halfway to Chattanooga. On July 8, Halleck informed the harassed Buell: "The President telegraphs that your progress is not sat-isfactory and that you should move more rapidly."[6]

By this time the Army of the Ohio was approaching Stevenson, Ala-bama, where it opened a new rail supply line from Nashville. But Buell's troubles had barely begun. Just as the first trainload of supplies started south from Nashville on July 13, Nathan Bedford Forrest's cavalry struck the Union garrison at Murfreesboro. Forrest captured the garrison, wrecked the railroad, and escaped eastward through the Cumberland Mountains before a division sent by Buell could catch him. When the repair crews finished mending the damage, Forrest struck again, de-stroying three bridges just south of Nashville and once more escaping the pursuing Federals. Forrest's attacks stalled Buell's creeping advance for more than two weeks. From Washington came further word of "great dissatisfaction." When Buell tried to explain, back came a threat of removal if he did not remedy his "apparent want of energy and activ-ity."[7]

As Buell finally prepared to cross the Tennessee River twenty miles from Chattanooga, disaster struck again in the form of yet another rebel cavalry raid. This time the enemy commander was John Hunt Morgan, a thirty-six-year-old Kentuckian whose style combined elements of Stuart's dash and Forrest's ferocity. Soft-spoken, a fastidious dresser, Morgan had raised a brigade of lean and hard Kentucky horsemen who first achieved fame in July 1862 with a thousand-mile raid through Ken-

5. Buell to "My Dear Friend," Dec. 18, 1861, Civil War Collection, Henry E. Hun-tingon Library.
6. O.R., Ser. I, Vol. 10, pt. 2, p. 180, Vol. 16, pt. 2, p. 104.
7. Ibid., Vol. 16, pt. 2, p. 360.

tucky and middle Tennessee that captured 1,200 prisoners and tons of supplies at the cost of fewer than ninety Confederate casualties. In mid-August, Morgan's merry men suddenly reappeared in middle Tennessee and blocked the railroad north of Nashville by pushing flaming boxcars into an 800-foot tunnel, causing the timbers to burn and the tunnel to cave in. This exploit cut Buell off from his main supply base at Louisville.

These cavalry raids illustrated the South's advantage in fighting on the defensive in their own territory. With 2,500 men Forrest and Morgan had immobilized an invading army of forty thousand. Living off the friendly countryside and fading into the hills like guerrillas, rebel horsemen could strike at times and places of their own choosing. To defend all the bridges, tunnels, and depots along hundreds of miles of railroad was virtually impossible, for guerrillas and cavalry could carry out hit-and-run raids against isolated garrisons or undefended stretches almost with impunity. The only effective counterforce would be Union cavalry equally well mounted and led, with troopers who knew the country and could ride and shoot as well as the southerners. Such a force could track and intercept rebel cavalry, could fight on equal terms, and could carry out its own raids deep into the Confederate rear. Union commanders learned these things the hard way in 1862. The Yankees did not catch up with the rebels in this respect until 1863, when they finally began to give as good as they got in the war of cavalry raids.

Buell's campaign also illustrated the strengths and weaknesses of railroad logistics. The iron horse could transport more men and supplies farther and faster than the four-legged variety. As an invading force operating on exterior lines over greater distances, Union armies depended more on rail transport than did the Confederates. In January 1862 the northern Congress authorized the president to take over any railroad "when in his judgment the public safety may require it." The government rarely exercised this power in northern states, though Stanton used it as a prod to induce railroads to give priority and fair rates to military traffic. But in the occupied South the government went into the railroad business on a large scale. In February 1862 Stanton established the U.S. Military Rail Roads and appointed Daniel McCallum superintendent. A former Erie Railroad executive and an efficient administrator, McCallum eventually presided over more than 2,000 miles of lines acquired, built, and maintained by the U.S.M.R.R. in conquered portions of the South.

The War Department in Richmond did not achieve similar control over southern railroads until May 1863, and thereafter rarely exercised this power. There was no southern counterpart of the U.S.M.R.R. The Confederate government was never able to coax the fragmented, run-down, multi-gauged network of southern railroads into the same degree of efficiency exhibited by northern roads. This contrast illustrated another dimension of Union logistical superiority that helped the North eventually to prevail.[8]

But in 1862 the dependence of Union armies on railroads proved as much curse as blessing. "Railroads are the weakest things in war," declared Sherman; "a single man with a match can destroy and cut off communications." Although "our armies pass across and through the land, the war closes in behind and leaves the same enemy behind," Sherman continued. It was the fate of any "railroad running through a country where every house is a nest of secret, bitter enemies" to suffer "bridges and water-tanks burned, trains fired into, track torn up" and "engines run off and badly damaged."[9] These experiences would ultimately teach Union generals the same lesson that Napoleon had put into practice a half-century earlier. The huge armies of the French emperor could not have been supplied by the wagon transport of that era, so they simply lived off the country they swarmed through like locusts.

Buell was unwilling to fight this kind of war, and that led to his downfall. Braxton Bragg, the new commander of the Confederate Army of Mississippi (soon to be known as the Army of Tennessee), saw the opening created by Morgan's and Forrest's raids against Buell's supply lines. "Our cavalry is paving the way for me in Middle Tennessee and Kentucky," he wrote in late July.[10] Bragg decided to leave 32,000 men in Mississippi under Van Dorn and Price to defend Vicksburg and central Mississippi. He planned to take the remaining 34,000 to Chattanooga, from where he would launch an invasion of Kentucky. Bragg hoped to repeat the Morgan and Forrest strategy on a larger scale. Buell would be forced to follow him and might present Bragg an opportunity to hit the Federals in the flank. If Grant moved to Buell's aid, Van Dorn and Price could strike northward to recover western Tennessee.

8. Robert C. Black, *The Railroads of the Confederacy* (Chapel Hill, 1952); Thomas Weber, *The Northern Railroads in the Civil War, 1861–1865* (New York, 1952); George E. Turner, *Victory Rode the Rails* (Indianapolis, 1953). At the beginning of the war there were 113 railroad companies in the Confederacy operating 9,000 miles of track of three different gauges.
9. Quoted in Hattaway and Jones, *How the North Won,* 250.
10. Foote, *Civil War,* I, 571.

Forrest's and Morgan's cavalry would continue to harass the Union rear, while Bragg was also assured of cooperation from Edmund Kirby Smith's East Tennessee army of 18,000 men, who had been warily watching Buell's snail-paced advance toward Chattanooga. The Confederates believed Kentuckians to be chafing at the bit to join the southern cause. Bragg requisitioned 15,000 extra rifles to arm the men of the bluegrass he expected to join his army.

Since taking over from the dismissed Beauregard in June, Bragg had been reorganizing and disciplining the army for a new campaign. A sufferer from ulcers and migraine, the short-tempered and quarrelsome Bragg was a hard driver. He sent several soldiers before a firing squad for desertion, and he executed one private who had disobeyed orders and shot at a chicken but hit a Negro instead. These measures seemed to work; desertion decreased and discipline improved. The boys in the ranks had learned, as one of them put it, that Bragg was a "man who would do what he said and whose orders were to be obeyed." But another Reb added that "not a single soldier in the whole army ever loved or respected him."[11]

This hardly bothered Bragg; his main problem just now was to get his invasion force from Mississippi to Chattanooga. He came up with an ironic solution: he would send them by rail—not the direct 200-mile route along which Buell had been crawling for six weeks, but a 776-mile roundabout journey south to Mobile, northeast to Atlanta, and thence north to Chattanooga. He sent the infantry a division at a time beginning July 23; two weeks later they were all in Chattanooga. It was the largest Confederate railroad movement of the war.[12] By mid-August, Bragg and Smith were ready to march forth on the great invasion. "Van Dorn and Price will advance simultaneously with us from Mississippi on West Tennessee," wrote an enthusiastic Bragg, "and I trust we may all unite in Ohio." In what he intended as an inspirational address to his troops, Bragg declared: "The enemy is before us, devastating our fair country . . . insulting our women, and desecrating our altars. . . . It is for you to decide whether our brothers and sisters of Tennessee and

---

11. Bruce Catton, *Terrible Swift Sword* (Garden City, N.Y., 1963), 380; Foote, *Civil War*, I, 569.
12. Bragg's supply wagons and artillery traveled by road and arrived later than the rail-borne foot soldiers. A year later Longstreet took two divisions with their artillery by rail from Virginia to Chickamauga, a greater distance than Bragg's troops traveled. But Longstreet's transfer involved 12,000 men compared with Bragg's 30,000.

Kentucky shall remain bondmen and bondwomen of the Abolition tyrant or be restored to the freedom inherited from their fathers."[13]

Kirby Smith started first and moved fastest. With 21,000 men (including one of Bragg's divisions) he left Knoxville on August 14 and struck northward toward the Cumberland Gap, which had been captured by a Union force of 8,000 two months earlier. Not wishing to assault this Thermopylae, Kirby Smith bypassed it and continued northward, leaving behind a division to watch the Federals at the Gap. Smith moved with a speed that Lincoln wished his generals could emulate. In two weeks he reached Richmond, Kentucky, 150 miles from Knoxville and only 75 miles south of Cincinnati, whose residents were startled into near panic by the approach of the rebels. At Richmond, Smith encountered his first significant opposition, a division of 6,500 new recruits never before under fire. The southerners surged forward with a rebel yell on August 30 and drove the Yanks back, killing or wounding more than a thousand and capturing most of the rest at a cost of fewer than five hundred southern casualties.

Smith's army occupied Lexington and prepared to inaugurate a Confederate governor in the nearby capital at Frankfort. Meanwhile Bragg's thirty thousand had marched northward from Chattanooga on a parallel route about a hundred miles to the west of Kirby Smith. As they crossed the border into Kentucky, Bragg paused to issue a proclamation:

> Kentuckians, I have entered your State . . . to restore to you the liberties of which you have been deprived by a cruel and relentless foe. . . . If you prefer Federal rule, show it by your frowns and we shall return whence we came. If you choose rather to come within the folds of our brotherhood, then cheer us with the smiles of your women and lend your willing hands to secure you in your heritage of liberty.[14]

Kentucky women treated the ragged soldiers to plenty of smiles. But few of the men came forward to fight for the South. Most of those inclined to do so had joined the Confederate army a year earlier; the others preferred to join a winner, and Bragg had not yet proved himself that—even though his army captured a Union garrison of four thousand at Munfordville only sixty miles south of Louisville. Perhaps Kentuckians understood what Bragg did not yet realize: his "invasion" was really

13. O.R., Ser. I, Vol. 16, pt. 1, p. 749; Foote, *Civil War*, I, 584.
14. O.R., Ser. I, Vol. 16, pt. 2, p. 822.

a large-scale raid. The rebels had neither the manpower nor the resources to convert a raid into an occupation and defense of the state against aroused Federal countermeasures. Already Buell had been reinforced to a strength of 55,000 by two divisions from Grant, with another on the way, while 60,000 new Union recruits were organizing in Louisville and Cincinnati.

Bragg's apparent military success and political failure caused his mood to fluctuate from elation to despondency. On September 18 he wrote to his wife: "We have made the most extraordinary campaign in military history." But a few days later he expressed himself "sadly disappointed in the want of action by our friends in Kentucky. We have so far received no accession to this army. . . . Enthusiasm runs high but exhausts itself in words. . . . The people here have too many fat cattle and are too well off to fight. . . . Unless a change occurs soon we must abandon the garden spot of Kentucky to its own cupidity."[15]

As Buell's army backtracked toward Louisville, Bragg was in a position to attack its flank. But knowing himself outnumbered he was eager to unite with Kirby Smith, who was still in the Lexington-Frankfort area a hundred miles to the east. Bragg asked Smith to link up with him at Bardstown, a point halfway between the two Confederate armies and only thirty-five miles south of Louisville. There the combined forces could fight the decisive battle for Kentucky. Meanwhile the two commanders took time out to witness the inauguration of Kentucky's Confederate governor. They hoped that this symbolic action might encourage timid Kentuckians to jump off the fence onto the southern side.

But the ceremony was rudely interrupted by the booming of advancing Union artillery. Goaded by a disgusted Lincoln and an angry northern press, Buell had finally turned to strike his rebel tormentors. For the past month his larger, better-equipped army had seemed to do nothing to stop the Confederate invasion. All through September, Halleck had kept the wires humming with messages prodding Buell to action: "Here as elsewhere you move too slowly. . . . The immobility of your army is most surprising. Bragg in the last two months has marched four times the distance you have." If Buell did not get moving he would be removed. Speaking figuratively (one hopes), Halleck warned that "the

---

15. Catton, *Terrible Swift Sword*, 413; O.R., Ser. I, Vol. 16, pt. 2, p. 876; David Urquhart, "Bragg's Advance and Retreat," *Battles and Leaders*, III, 602; Grady McWhiney, "Controversy in Kentucky: Braxton Bragg's Campaign of 1862," CWH, 6 (1960), 23.

Government seems determined to apply the guillotine to all unsuccessful generals. . . . Perhaps with us now, as in the French Revolution, some harsh measures are required."[16]

Buell got the point, and in the first week of October he got moving. He had organized his army into a striking force of 60,000 men—fully a third of whom, however, were raw recruits who had not yet fired a shot in anger. Bragg and Smith had 40,000 veterans in the vicinity, but they were scattered across a front of sixty miles from Lexington to Bardstown. Buell sent one division on a feint toward Frankfort (this was the force that disrupted the inauguration) while marching the remainder in three mutually supporting columns toward Bragg's main army at Bardstown. Bragg was deceived by the feint, which pinned nearly half of the Confederate force in the Frankfort area while Buell's three main columns bore down on the rest, commanded in Bragg's absence by Bishop Leonidas Polk. Outnumbered two to one, the bishop retreated and sent appeals to Bragg for reinforcements.

The sequel was much influenced by both armies' search for water in the drought-parched countryside. With only 16,000 men, Polk took up a defensive position just west of the Chaplin River at Perryville on October 7. That evening one Union corps arrived and attacked unsuccessfully to gain control of the few stagnant pools in a tributary of the river. Commanding the most aggressive division in this corps was Philip Sheridan, a small, bandy-legged man whose only distinctions in the prewar army had been pugnacity and a handlebar mustache. The pugnacity served him well once the war gave him a chance. Languishing as a quartermaster captain during the conflict's first year, he obtained field command of a cavalry regiment by a fluke in May 1862 and within weeks had proved himself so able ("he is worth his weight in gold," wrote one superior) that he had been promoted to brigade command and in September to division command. At dawn on October 8, Sheridan's thirsty division attacked again and gained control of the creek as well as the hills beyond. During the day the rest of Buell's main force filed into line on the left and right of Sheridan.

But thereafter Buell lost the initiative in a battle that set a new record for confusion among top brass on both sides. Still believing that the main part of Buell's army was at Frankfort, Bragg ordered Polk's 16,000 to attack the fragment (as he thought) at Perryville. In early afternoon a reluctant Polk sent two of his three divisions against the two divisions

16. O.R., Ser. I, Vol. 16, pt. 2, pp. 530, 421.

holding the Union left. The rebels were in luck, for one of these blue divisions was composed of new troops. In an attempt to calm their fears the previous evening, two generals and a colonel had pointed out the high odds against any given man being killed in a particular battle. In the first wave of the Confederate assault next day all three officers were killed.[17] The green troops broke, sweeping the other Union division back with them a mile or more before reinforcements halted the rout. Meanwhile in the center, Sheridan attacked the remaining southern division and drove it back through the streets of Perryville. Less than half of the Union army was engaged in this fighting, while a freak combination of wind and topography (known as acoustic shadow) prevented the right wing and Buell himself from hearing the battle a couple of miles away. Not until a courier came pounding back to headquarters on a sweat-lathered horse did the Union commander know that a battle was raging. By then the approaching darkness prevented an attack by the Union right against the lone rebel brigade in its front. Buell ordered an assault all along the line at dawn, but when the Yanks went forward next morning they found the rebels gone. Finally recognizing that he faced three times his numbers at Perryville, Bragg had retreated during the night to link up with Kirby Smith—several days too late.

For both sides this climactic battle of a long campaign turned out to be anticlimactic. Casualties were relatively high in proportion to the numbers engaged—4,200 Federals and 3,400 Confederates—but neither side really "won." Buell missed a chance to wipe out one-third of the rebels who had invaded Kentucky; Bragg and Smith failed to clinch their invasion with a smashing blow that might have won Kentuckians to their side. After Perryville the contending armies maneuvered warily for a few days without fighting. With supplies short, the sicklist lengthening, and a larger army in his front, Bragg succumbed to pessimism once again and decided to abandon the campaign. To the accompaniment of mutual recrimination among some of his generals and a growing chorus of criticism from the southern press, Bragg ordered his weary men to retrace their steps to Knoxville and Chattanooga. Summoned later to Richmond to explain the failure of his campaign, Bragg apparently satisfied Davis, who kept him in command and expressed a confidence in the general shared by a decreasing number of southerners.

Buell followed the retreating rebels gingerly. From Washington came a string of telegrams urging him to attack, or at least to drive Bragg out

17. Charles C. Gilbert, "On the Field of Perryville," *Battles and Leaders*, III, 57n.

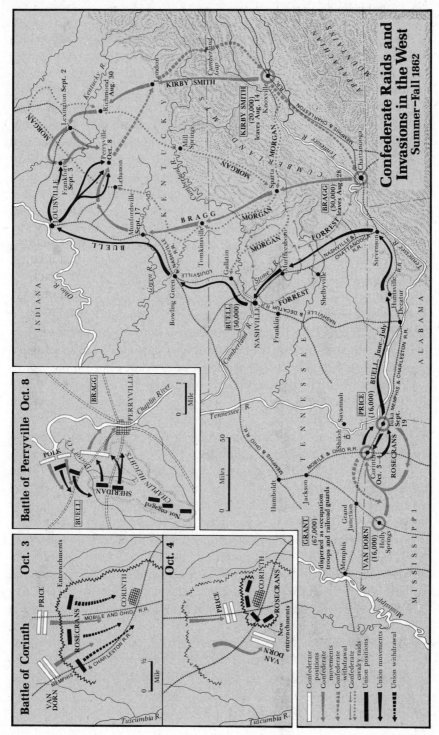

Confederate Raids and Invasions in the West
Summer–Fall 1862

Battle of Perryville Oct. 8

BRAGG

PERRYVILLE

Chaplin River

POLK

Doctor C.

CHAPLIN HEIGHTS

SHERIDAN

Not engaged

BUELL

0 1 Mile

Battle of Corinth

Oct. 3

PRICE

Entrenchments

CORINTH

VAN DORN

MEMPHIS & CHARLESTON R.R.

ROSECRANS

MOBILE AND OHIO R.R.

Oct. 4

PRICE

CORINTH

New entrenchments

ROSECRANS

VAN DORN

Tuscumbia R.

Tuscumbia R.

0 ½ Mile

KIRBY SMITH

MORGAN

Lexington Sept. 2

Kentucky R.

Richmond Aug. 30

London

Cumberland Gap

KIRBY SMITH (20,000) leaves Aug. 14

Knoxville

APPALACHIAN MOUNTAINS

MEMPHIS & CHARLESTON R.R.

Tennessee R.

CUMBERLAND MTS.

MORGAN

Hill Springs

Perryville Oct. 8

LOUISVILLE

Frankfort Sept. 3

Lebanon

Munfordsville Sept. 17

BRAGG

MORGAN

Sparta Aug. 28

Chattanooga

BRAGG (30,000) leaves Aug. 28

BUELL

INDIANA

Ohio R.

Green R.

Bowling Green

NASHVILLE & DECATUR R.R.

Tomkinsville

Gallatin

LOUISVILLE

Stone R.

Murfreesboro

NASHVILLE & CHATTANOOGA R.R.

FORREST

FORREST

MORGAN

Stevenson

Tennessee R.

BUELL (50,000)

NASHVILLE

Cumberland R.

Franklin

Shelbyville

NASHVILLE & DECATUR R.R.

Huntsville

Decatur

MEMPHIS & CHARLESTON R.R.

ALABAMA

BUELL, June–July

TENNESSEE

Tennessee R.

Savannah

Shiloh

PRICE (16,000)

Iuka Sept. 19

MEMPHIS & CHARLESTON R.R.

Corinth Oct. 3–4

ROSECRANS

Jackson

MEMPHIS & OHIO R.R.

MOBILE & OHIO R.R.

Humboldt

GRANT (67,000) dispersed as occupation troops and railroad guards

Grand Junction

Memphis

VAN DORN (16,000)

Holly Springs

MISSISSIPPI

Mississippi R.

0 50 Miles

Confederate positions
Confederate movements
Confederate withdrawal
Confederate cavalry raids
Union positions
Union movements
Union withdrawal

of east Tennessee and accomplish Lincoln's cherished goal of recovering that unionist region. "Neither the Government nor the country can endure these repeated delays," Halleck wired Buell. Back to Washington went telegrams from Buell explaining that he could not pursue faster lest his army outmarch its supplies. Halleck replied in words that reflected Lincoln's impatience with this general who, like McClellan, seemed more adept at framing excuses than taking action. "You say that [east Tennessee] is the heart of the enemy's resources; make it the heart of yours. Your army can live there if the enemy's can. . . . [The president] does not understand why we cannot march as the enemy marches, live as he lives, and fight as he fights."[18] It was no good. Buell was not the general to march and fight while living off the country. When he made clear his intent to re-establish a base at Nashville instead of going after the rebels, Lincoln removed him and named William S. Rosecrans to command the renamed Army of the Cumberland.

Events 300 miles away in Mississippi had influenced both Bragg's decision to retreat and Lincoln's decision to appoint Rosecrans. Just after the battle of Perryville, Bragg received word of the defeat of Van Dorn and Price in the battle of Corinth four days earlier. Since Bragg's hope for a successful invasion had been contingent on a similar northward thrust by the troops he had left behind in Mississippi, this defeat compounded his discouragement. The Union commander at Corinth was Rosecrans. While Buell had failed to keep the rebels out of central Tennessee and Kentucky, Rosecrans had earned credit in Lincoln's eyes by keeping them out of west Tennessee.

On September 14, Price's 15,000 troops had driven a small Union force from the railroad town of Iuka in northern Mississippi. This was a first step in the contemplated invasion of Tennessee. Grant thought he saw an opening for a counterattack. He devised a plan to trap Price in Iuka between converging Union forces. Grant sent two divisions under General Edward Ord eastward along the railroad from Corinth and ordered two others under Rosecrans to circle up on Iuka from the south for an assault on Price's flank while Ord attacked his front. But this pincers movement went awry, as such maneuvers often did in an era when communications depended on couriers. Smelling the trap, Price attacked Rosecrans's advance units south of town on September 19 while Ord (accompanied by Grant) was still three miles to the west. Here too an acoustic shadow masked all sound of the fighting from Ord, whose

18. O.R., Ser. I, Vol. 16, pt. 2, pp. 638, 626–27.

troops remained in blissful ignorance of Rosecrans's battle a few miles away. In a short, sharp contest the outnumbered Yankees gave a good account of themselves and inflicted more casualties than they received. But after nightfall Price got away to the south on a road that Rosecrans had neglected to block. When the Union pincers finally closed next morning, they grasped an empty town.

Grant had at least stopped Price's thrust northward. But the enterprising Missouri rebel marched his little army to join Van Dorn for another try. With a combined mobile force of 22,000 they attacked the main Union position at Corinth. The Confederates ran into more than they bargained for—21,000 men commanded by Rosecrans, a tough and skillful fighter. On October 3 the southerners assaulted the outer defenses north of Corinth with the screaming élan and willingness to take high casualties that had become their trademark. During a long, hot day they drove the Yankees back two miles to the inner defenses. Next morning the rebels attacked again, but after early success they succumbed to exhaustion and thirst in the ninety-degree heat. By noon a Union counterattack had put Van Dorn and Price to flight.

Having expressed disappointment after Iuka at "not capturing [Price's] entire army or in destroying it, as I hoped to do," Grant tried again after Corinth.[19] He ordered a division from west Tennessee to intercept the escaping Confederates in front while Rosecrans pitched into their rear. But Old Rosy, as his men had begun to call him, was slow in pursuit. Van Dorn's force got away after a sharp fight at a bridge with Grant's intercepting column in which the southerners lost another 600 men. Despite his admiration for Rosecrans's tenacity as a fighter, Grant was thereafter cool toward the general who he believed had twice let the rebels escape from a trap. Nevertheless, what turned out to be the last Confederate offensive in the Mississippi theater had been thwarted. The initiative went over to Grant, who launched his first (and unsuccessful) campaign against Vicksburg a month later. Rosecrans earned promotion to a new army command. The rebel reverses in Mississippi, coupled with Bragg's retreat from Kentucky, produced discouragement in Richmond and relief in Washington.

Despite their importance in the overall strategic picture, these events in the western theater from June to October faded into the background of public perception, which focused primarily on military developments

19. John Y. Simon, ed., *The Papers of Ulysses S. Grant*, 14 vols. to date (Carbondale, Ill., 1967–85), VI, 97.

in the East. The eastern campaigns seemed more crucial because they took place closer to the two capitals and to the major newspapers that dominated the reporting of war news. At the same time that Kirby Smith and Bragg moved north from Knoxville and Chattanooga, Jackson and Lee moved north from Richmond. Although the western invasions covered more territory, the eastern fighting as usual produced more casualties. These simultaneous Confederate northward thrusts represented the South's boldest bid for victory.

II

When Lincoln appointed Henry Halleck general in chief in July 1862, he hoped that Old Brains would coordinate an offensive by McClellan's 100,000 on the Peninsula with Pope's 50,000 north of Richmond. But three men blighted this hope; their names were Pope, McClellan, and Jackson.

Pope's first act as commander of the newly designated Army of Virginia was to issue an address to his troops. He did nothing to diminish his reputation for braggadocio in this singularly inept document. "I come to you out of the West, where we have always seen the backs of our enemies," he declared. "I am sorry to find so much in vogue amongst you . . . certain phrases [like] . . . 'lines of retreat,' and 'bases of supplies.' . . . Let us study the probable lines of retreat of our opponents, and leave our own to take care of themselves. Let us look before us and not behind. Success and glory are in the advance, disaster and shame lurk in the rear."[20]

This snide denigration of eastern troops won Pope few friends. Fitz-John Porter declared that Pope had "written himself down, what the military world has long known, an Ass." This expressed McClellan's opinion as well. At the same time, Pope believed that McClellan's "incompetency and indisposition to active movements were so great" that little help could be expected from the Army of the Potomac.[21] Lee could hardly have hoped for a more mutually antagonistic pair of opponents had he chosen them himself.

After the Seven Days', McClellan expressed readiness to renew the offensive if Lincoln would send him another 50,000 men. Privately,

20. O.R., Ser. I, Vol. 12, pt. 3, pp. 473–74.
21. Porter quoted in Catton, *Terrible Swift Sword*, 387; Pope quoted by Salmon P. Chase in David Donald, ed., *Inside Lincoln's Cabinet: The Civil War Diaries of Salmon P. Chase* (New York, 1954), 97.

however, the general was telling a New York Democratic leader that he had "lost all regard and respect" for the administration and doubted "the propriety of my brave men's blood being shed to further the designs of such a set of heartless villains." When Halleck became general in chief, McClellan vented his anger at serving under an officer "whom I know to be my inferior." As for Stanton, he was a "deformed hypocrite & villain." If he "had lived in the time of the Savior, Judas Iscariot would have remained a respected member of the fraternity of Apostles." [22] For his part, Lincoln had lost faith in McClellan's willingness to fight Lee. The president did not have 50,000 men to spare, but even if he could have sent 100,000, he told a senator, McClellan would suddenly discover that Lee had 400,000. [23] At the end of July, Lincoln and Halleck decided to withdraw the Army of the Potomac from the Peninsula to unite it with Pope's force.

Confederate actions had influenced this decision. To counter Pope's threat to the rail junction at Gordonsville northwest of Richmond, Lee had sent Jackson with 12,000 men to that point on July 13. When McClellan remained quiet on the Richmond front, Lee detached A. P. Hill with another 13,000 to join Jackson on July 27. Rumor magnified this force—for in spite of Jackson's failures on the Peninsula his name was worth several divisions—and helped persuade Lincoln of the need to reinforce Pope. As Lee pieced together information about McClellan's withdrawal, he used his interior lines to shift most of his troops by rail sixty miles to Gordonsville. The Army of the Potomac had to travel several times that far by water down the James, along the Chesapeake Bay, and up the Potomac before arriving within marching distance of Pope. The efficiency of this Union movement was not helped by McClellan's bitter protests against it or by his subordinates' distaste for coming under Pope's command. "Pope will be thrashed . . . & be disposed of" by Lee, wrote McClellan to his wife with relish at the prospect. "Such a villain as he is ought to bring defeat upon any cause that employs him." [24]

While McClellan sulked in his tent, Jackson moved against Pope's

22. McClellan to Samuel L. M. Barlow, July 15, 23, 1862, Barlow Papers, Henry E. Huntington Library; McClellan to Ellen McClellan, July 13, 22, 1862, McClellan Papers, Library of Congress.

23. Theodore C. Pease and James G. Randall, eds., *The Diary of Orville Hickman Browning*, 2 vols. (Springfield, Ill., 1927–33), I, 563.

24. McClellan to Ellen McClellan, Aug. 10, 1862, McClellan Papers.

two advance divisions near Cedar Mountain twenty miles north of Gordonsville. Commanding this Union force was none other than Jackson's old adversary Nathaniel P. Banks. Eager to redeem his reputation, Banks attacked on August 9 even though he knew that Jackson outnumbered him at least two to one. Expecting imminent reinforcements, the Union general sent his two undersize divisions forward in a headlong assault that drove back the surprised rebels and put Jackson's old Stonewall Brigade to flight. Having mishandled the first stage of the fight, Jackson went to the front himself to rally his troops and then watched approvingly as A. P. Hill's division punished the Yankees with a slashing counterattack. Banks fell back several miles to the support of late-arriving reinforcements after losing 30 percent of his force. Within the next two days the rest of Pope's army came up and forced Jackson to pull back to Gordonsville.

The chief result of this battle of Cedar Mountain was to confirm the transfer of operations from the Peninsula to the Rappahannock River halfway between Richmond and Washington. Here for ten days Lee's reunited force of 55,000 (he had left 20,000 around Richmond) carried on a campaign of thrust and parry with Pope's army of equal size. Lee probed for an opening to isolate and attack a portion of the enemy, while Pope maneuvered to hold his position while awaiting the arrival of reinforcements from the Peninsula that would enable him to go over to the offensive. Since that was just what Lee wanted to prevent, he determined on what was becoming a typical Lee stratagem: he divided his army and sent Jackson's corps on a long clockwise flanking march to cut Union rail communications deep in Pope's rear. This maneuver defied military maxims about keeping an army concentrated in the presence of an enemy of equal or greater size. But Lee believed that the South could never win by following maxims. His well-bred Episcopalian demeanor concealed the audacity of a skillful gambler ready to stake all on the turn of a card. The dour Presbyterian who similarly concealed the heart of a gambler was the man to carry out Lee's strategy.

For Jackson had reverted from the sluggard of the Chickahominy to the gladiator of the Valley. Indeed, the Valley was where Pope thought the rebels were heading when his scouts detected Jackson's march northwestward along the Rappahannock on August 25. But Pope's understrength cavalry failed to detect Jackson's turn to the east on August 26, when he marched unopposed along the railroad to Manassas, the main

Union supply base twenty-five miles behind Pope. In one of the war's great marches, Jackson's whole corps—24,000 men—had covered more than fifty miles in two days. The hungry, threadbare rebels swooped down on the mountain of supplies at Manassas like a plague of grasshoppers. After eating their fill and taking everything they could carry away, they put the torch to the rest.

The accumulation of supplies at Manassas and the maintenance of the vulnerable single-track line that linked Pope to his base had been the work of Herman Haupt, the war's wizard of railroading. The brusque, no-nonsense Haupt was chief of construction and transportation for the U.S. Military Rail Roads in Virginia. He had brought order out of chaos in train movements. He had rebuilt destroyed bridges in record time. His greatest achievement had been the construction from green logs and saplings of a trestle 80 feet high and 400 feet long with unskilled soldier labor in less than two weeks. After looking at this bridge, Lincoln said: "I have seen the most remarkable structure that human eyes ever rested upon. That man, Haupt, has built a bridge . . . over which loaded trains are running every hour, and upon my word, gentlemen, there is nothing in it but beanpoles and cornstalks."[25] Haupt developed prefabricated parts for bridges and organized the first of the Union construction corps that performed prodigies of railroad and bridge building in the next three years. Their motto, like that of their Seabee descendants in World War II, might have been: "The difficult we can do immediately; the impossible will take a little longer." As an awed contraband put it, "the Yankees can build bridges quicker than the Rebs can burn them down."[26]

Within four days Haupt had trains running over the line Jackson had cut. But unfortunately for the North, Pope's military abilities did not match Haupt's engineering genius. Still confident and aggressive, Pope saw Jackson's raid as an opportunity to "bag" Jackson before the other half of Lee's army could join him. The only problem was to find the slippery Stonewall. After burning the supply depot at Manassas, Jackson's troops disappeared. Pope's overworked cavalry reported the rebels to be at various places. This produced a stream of orders and countermanding orders to the fragmented corps of three commands: his own,

25. Francis A. Lord, *Lincoln's Railroad Man: Herman Haupt* (Rutherford, N.J., 1969), 77.
26. Turner, *Victory Rode the Rails*, Frontispiece.

two corps of the Army of the Potomac sent to reinforce him, and part of Burnside's 9th Corps which had been transferred from the North Carolina coast.

One of the Army of the Potomac units moving up to support Pope was Fitz-John Porter's corps, whose commander had called Pope an Ass and who had recently written in another private letter: "Would that this army was in Washington to rid us of incumbents ruining our country."[27] During this fateful August 28, Porter's friend McClellan was at Alexandria resisting Halleck's orders to hurry forward another Army of the Potomac corps to Pope's aid. McClellan shocked the president with a suggestion that all available troops be held under his command to defend Washington, leaving Pope "to get out of his scrape by himself." If "Pope is beaten," wrote McClellan to his wife, "they may want me to save Washington again. Nothing but their fears will induce them to give me any command of importance."[28] Almost broken down by worry, Halleck failed to assert his authority over McClellan. Thus two of the best corps in the Army of the Potomac remained within marching distance of Pope but took no part in the ensuing battle.

Meanwhile Jackson's troops had gone to ground on a wooded ridge a couple of miles west of the old Manassas battlefield. Lee and Longstreet with the rest of the army were only a few miles away, having broken through a gap in the Bull Run Mountains which Pope had neglected to defend with a sufficient force. Stuart's cavalry had maintained liaison between Lee and Jackson, so the latter knew that Longstreet's advance units would join him on the morning of August 29.

The previous evening one of Pope's divisions had stumbled onto Jackson's hiding place. In a fierce firefight at dusk the outnumbered bluecoats had inflicted considerable damage before withdrawing in a battered condition themselves. Conspicuous in this action was an all-western brigade (one Indiana and three Wisconsin regiments) that soon earned a reputation as one of the best units in the army and became known as the Iron Brigade. By the war's end it suffered a higher percentage of casualties than any other brigade in the Union armies—a distinction matched by one of the units it fought against on this and other battle-

---

27. Porter to Manton Marble, Aug. 10, 1862, quoted in T. Harry Williams, *Lincoln and His Generals* (New York, 1952), 148.
28. *CWL*, V, 399; Dennett, *Lincoln/Hay*, 45; McClellan to Ellen McClellan, Aug. 22, 1862, McClellan Papers.

fields, the all-Virginia Stonewall Brigade, which experienced more casualties than any other Confederate brigade.

Having found Jackson, Pope brought his scattered corps together by forced marches during the night and morning of August 28–29. Because he thought that Jackson was preparing to retreat toward Longstreet (when in fact Longstreet was advancing toward Jackson), Pope committed an error. Instead of waiting until he had concentrated a large force in front of Jackson, he hurled his divisions one after another in piecemeal assaults against troops who instead of retreating were ensconced in ready-made trenches formed by the cuts and fills of an unfinished railroad. The Yankees came on with fatalistic fury and almost broke Jackson's line several times. But the rebels hung on grimly and threw them back.

Pope managed to get no more than 32,000 men into action against Jackson's 22,000 on August 29. The fault was not entirely his. Coming up on the Union left during the morning were another 30,000 in McDowell's large corps and Porter's smaller one. McDowell maneuvered ineffectually during the entire day; only after dark did a few of his regiments get into a moonlight skirmish with the enemy. As for Porter, his state of mind this day is hard to fathom. He believed that Longstreet's entire corps was in his front—as indeed it was by noon—and therefore with 10,000 men Porter did nothing while thousands of other northern soldiers were fighting and dying two miles away. Not realizing that Longstreet's corps had arrived, Pope ordered Porter in late afternoon to attack Jackson's right flank. Porter could not obey because Longstreet connected with Jackson's flank; besides, Porter had no respect for Pope and resented taking orders from him, so he continued to do nothing. For this he was later court-martialed and cashiered from the service.[29]

29. Porter remained in command of the 5th Corps until November, when he was ordered before the court-martial, which convicted him. After the war the cashiered general repeatedly sought a new trial and finally won reversal of the verdict in 1886, when testimony by Confederate officers and the evidence provided by captured southern records demonstrated that Longstreet had indeed been in Porter's front and that the Union general therefore could not have obeyed Pope's order. To some degree Porter was the victim of Republican attacks on McClellan and his associates, of whom Porter was the closest. But Porter's failure to do *anything* with his corps on August 29 deserved at least mild censure. For a study of this affair that is sympathetic to Porter, see Otto Eisenschiml, *The Celebrated Case of Fitz-John Porter*

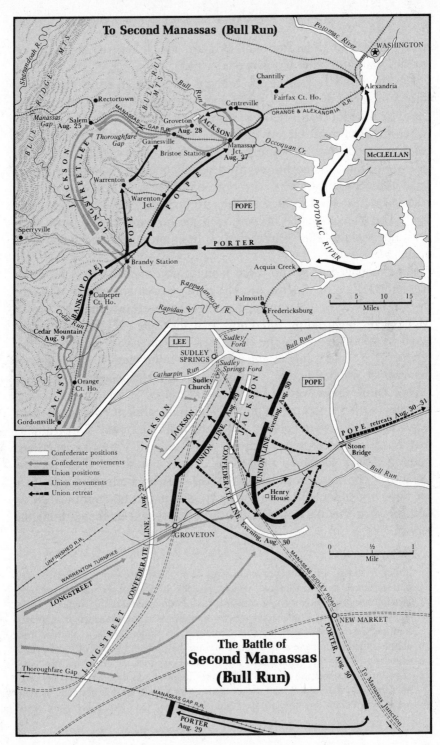

To Second Manassas (Bull Run)

WASHINGTON

Potomac River

Chantilly

Fairfax Ct. Ho.

Alexandria

ORANGE & ALEXANDRIA R.R.

Centreville

Groveton
Aug. 28

JACKSON

Manassas
Jct.
Aug. 27

Occoquan Cr.

McCLELLAN

Rectortown

BULL RUN MTS.

Bull Run

Salem
Aug. 25

MANASSAS GAP R.R.

Manassas
Gap

Thoroughfare
Gap

Gainesville

Bristoe Station

POTOMAC RIVER

POPE

Warrenton

BLUE RIDGE MTS.

Shenandoah R.

LONGSTREET, LEE

Warenton
Jct.

JACKSON

POPE

PORTER

Sperryville

Brandy Station

Acquia Creek

0   5   10   15
Miles

BANKS (POPE)

Culpeper
Ct. Ho.

Cedar Run

Rappahannock R.

Rapidan R.

Rappahannock R.

Falmouth

Fredericksburg

Cedar Mountain
Aug. 9

Orange
Ct. Ho.

JACKSON

Gordonsville

LEE

Sudley
Ford

Bull Run

SUDLEY
SPRINGS

Sudley
Springs Ford

POPE

Catharpin Run

Sudley
Church

JACKSON
Aug. 29

JACKSON

UNION LINE, Aug. 29

CONFEDERATE LINE

UNION LINE, Evening, Aug. 30

JACKSON

POPE retreats Aug. 30–31

Confederate positions
Confederate movements
Union positions
Union movements
Union retreat

Stone
Bridge

Bull Run

Henry
House

UNFINISHED R.R.

CONFEDERATE LINE, Aug. 29

UNION LINE, Evening, Aug. 30

GROVETON

WARRENTON TURNPIKE

LONGSTREET

CONFEDERATE LINE, Aug. 29

MANASSAS SUDLEY ROAD

NEW MARKET

PORTER, Aug. 30

To Manassas Junction

Thoroughfare Gap

LONGSTREET

MANASSAS GAP R.R.

0   ½
Mile

The Battle of
Second Manassas
(Bull Run)

PORTER
Aug. 29

While Pope fought only with his right hand on August 29, Lee parried only with his left. When Longstreet got his 30,000 men in line during the early afternoon, Lee asked him to go forward in an attack to relieve the pressure on Jackson. But Longstreet demurred, pointing out that a Union force of unknown strength (Porter and McDowell) was out there somewhere in the woods. Unlike Lee and Jackson, Longstreet preferred to fight on the defensive and hoped to induce these Federals to attack *him*. Lee deferred to his subordinate's judgment. Thus while Longstreet's presence neutralized 30,000 Federals, they also neutralized Longstreet.

That night a few Confederate brigades pulled back from advanced positions to readjust their line. Having made several wrong guesses about the enemy's intentions during the past few days, Pope guessed wrong again when he assumed this movement to be preliminary to a retreat. He wanted so much to "see the backs of our enemies"—as he had professed always to have done in the West—that he believed it about to happen. He sent a victory dispatch to Washington and prepared to pursue the supposedly retreating rebels.

But when Pope's pursuit began next day the bluecoats went no more than a few hundred yards before being stopped in their tracks by bullets from Jackson's infantry still holding their roadbed trenches. The Federals hesitated only momentarily before attacking in even heavier force than the previous day. The exhausted southerners bent and almost broke. Some units ran out of ammunition and resorted to throwing rocks at the Yankees. Jackson was forced to swallow his pride and call on Longstreet for reinforcements. Longstreet had a better idea. He brought up artillery to enfilade the Union attackers and then hurled all five of his divisions in a screaming counterattack against the Union left, which had been weakened by Pope's shift of troops to his right for the assaults on Jackson. Once Longstreet's men went into action they hit the surprised northerners like a giant hammer. Until sunset a furious contest raged all along the line. The bluecoats fell back doggedly to Henry House Hill, scene of the hardest fighting in that first battle in these parts thirteen months earlier. Here they made a twilight stand that brought the rebel juggernaut to a halt.

That night Pope—all boastfulness gone—decided to pull back toward

(Indianapolis, 1950); for brief critical appraisals, see Kenneth P. Williams, *Lincoln Finds a General*, 5 vols. (New York, 1949–59), I, 324–30, II, 785–89; and Catton, *Terrible Swift Sword*, 522–23.

Washington. On September 1 two blue divisions fought a vicious rear-guard action at Chantilly, only twenty miles from Washington, against Jackson's weary corps which Lee had sent on another clockwise march for one final attempt to hit the retreating Union flank. After warding off this thrust in a drenching thunderstorm, the beaten-down bluecoats trudged into the capital's defenses. During the previous five days they had suffered 16,000 casualties out of a total force of 65,000, while Lee's 55,000 had lost fewer than 10,000 men. Lee's achievement in his second strategic offensive was even more remarkable than in his first. Less than a month earlier the main Union army had been only twenty miles from Richmond. With half as many troops as his two opponents (Pope and McClellan), Lee had shifted the scene to twenty miles from Washington, where the rebels seemed poised for the kill.

Behind Union lines all was confusion. When news of the fighting reached Washington, Secretary of War Stanton appealed for volunteer nurses to go out to help with the wounded. Many government clerks and other civilians responded, but a portion of them—a male portion—turned out to be worse than useless. Some were drunk by the time they reached the front, where they bribed a few ambulance drivers with whiskey to take *them* back to Washington instead of the wounded. To this shameful episode should be contrasted the herculean labors of Herman Haupt, who sent trains through the chaos to bring back wounded men, and the sleepless work of numerous women nurses headed by Clara Barton. "The men were brot down from the field and laid on the ground beside the train and so back up the hill 'till they covered acres," wrote Barton a few days later. The nurses opened hay bales and spread the hay on the ground to provide bedding. "By midnight there must have been *three thousand* helpless men lying in that hay. . . . All night we made compresses and slings—and bound up and wet wounds, when we could get water, fed what we could, travelled miles in that dark over these poor helpless wretches, in terror lest some one's candle fall *into the hay* and consume them all."[30]

The despair of that dark night spread through the North during the first half of September. "The nation is rapidly sinking just now," wrote a New York diarist. "Stonewall Jackson (our national bugaboo) about to invade Maryland, 40,000 strong. General advance of the rebel line threatening our hold on Missouri and Kentucky. Cincinnati in danger.

---

30. Barton to Mrs. Shaver, Sept. 4, 1862, Civil War Collection, Henry E. Huntington Library.

. . . Disgust with our present government is certainly universal."[31] Army morale also plunged. Although the men had fought well, they knew they had been mishandled. And they knew whom to blame: Pope and McDowell. Baseless rumors of treason rose against McDowell—for no other reason, perhaps, than that this luckless general had commanded the army at first Bull Run and commanded its largest corps in the reprise. Pope and McDowell in turn blamed McClellan and Porter for lack of cooperation and refusal to obey orders.

The administration was inclined to agree with Pope. Lincoln considered McClellan's behavior "unpardonable." He "wanted Pope to fail," the president told his private secretary. The cabinet almost unanimously favored McClellan's dismissal. But the president instead merged Pope's army into the Army of the Potomac, put McClellan in charge of the defense of Washington, sent Pope to Minnesota to pacify Indians, and relieved McDowell of command and ultimately exiled him to California. Stanton and Chase remonstrated against the retention of McClellan. Lincoln himself was "greatly distressed" by having to do it. But while McClellan "had acted badly in this matter," said the president, he "has the Army with him. . . . We must use what tools we have. There is no man in the Army who can lick these troops of ours into shape half as well as he. . . . If he can't fight himself, he excels in making others ready to fight."[32]

Lincoln's judgment was confirmed by an extraordinary incident that occurred during the dispirited retreat of Pope's troops toward Washington on September 2. The weather was "cold and rainy," recalled a veteran years later. "Everything bore a look of sadness in unison with our feelings. . . . Here were stragglers plodding through the mud . . . wagons wrecked and forlorn; half-formed regiments, part of the men with guns and part without . . . while everyone you met . . . looked as if he would like to hide his head somewhere from all the world." Suddenly an officer with a lone escort rode by and a captain came running back to the bivouac. "Colonel! Colonel! General McClellan is here!" he shouted. " 'Little Mac' is back here on the road."

> Enlisted men caught the sound! . . . From extreme sadness we passed in a twinkling to a delirium of delight. A Deliverer had come. . . .

31. Strong, *Diary*, 253, 252, 256.
32. Dennett, *Lincoln/Hay*, 47; Howard K. Beale, ed., *The Diary of Gideon Welles*, 3 vols. (New York, 1960), I, 113; Donald, ed., *Inside Lincoln's Cabinet: Diaries of Chase*, 116–21.

Men threw their caps high into the air, and danced and frolicked like school-boys. . . . Shout upon shout went out into the stillness of the night; and as it was taken up along the road and repeated by regiment, brigade, division, and corps, we could hear the roar dying away in the distance. . . . The effect of this man's presence upon the Army of the Potomac . . . was electrical, and too wonderful to make it worth while attempting to give a reason for it.[33]

Within days McClellan had the army ready for field service again. And they had to take the field immediately, for with scarcely a pause Lee was leading his ragged but confident veterans across the Potomac for an invasion of the North. Most northerners saw this as a calamity. But Lincoln viewed it as an opportunity to cripple Lee's army far from its home base. He told McClellan to go after Lee, and "destroy the rebel army, if possible."[34]

Lee and Davis recognized that this could happen, but after weighing the alternatives they had decided that the possible gains outweighed the risk. The Army of Northern Virginia could not attack the formidable Washington defenses. It could not stay where it was, in a fought-over region denuded of supplies at the end of a long and precarious rail line. Men and horses were worn down by the relentless marching and fighting of the past ten weeks; their "uniforms" were rags; some of them lacked shoes. The safe course was to pull back toward Richmond to rest and refit. But Lee was not the man to choose the safe course. Though weary, his army was flushed with victory and the enemy was unnerved by defeat. Lee sensed that this was the North's low-water mark. Kirby Smith and Bragg were marching into Kentucky. Van Dorn and Price were preparing to invade Tennessee. This was no time for the Army of Northern Virginia to rest on its laurels. It must take the war into the North and force the Lincoln government to sue for peace. Maryland like Kentucky beckoned with the prospect of joining her sister slave states. Lee's hungry warriors could feed themselves from the fat farms of Maryland and Pennsylvania while drawing the enemy out of war-ravaged Virginia during the harvest season. At the very least, Lee could cut the B & O and—if things went well—burn the Pennsylvania Railroad bridge over the Susquehanna at Harrisburg, thereby severing Washington's main links with the West. A successful invasion might induce European pow-

33. William H. Powell and George Kimball quoted in *Battles and Leaders*, II, 490n. and 550–51n.
34. Lincoln to McClellan, Sept. 15, 1862, in *CWL*, V, 426.

ers to recognize Confederate nationhood. It might encourage Peace Democrats in the upcoming northern elections. A "proposal of peace" backed by southern armies on northern soil, wrote Lee to Davis on September 8, "would enable the people of the United States to determine at their coming elections whether they will support those who favor a prolongation of the war, or those who wish to bring it to a termination."[35]

For political as well as military reasons, therefore, Lee started his army splashing across the Potomac fords thirty-five miles above Washington on September 4. Reinforced by three divisions called from Richmond, the army numbered some 55,000 men before it crossed the river. But from a variety of causes—exhaustion, hunger, sickness from subsisting on green corn, torn feet from marching barefoot on stony roads—stragglers fell out by the thousands during the next few days. A Virginia woman who lived in a Potomac River town described these stragglers:

> When I say that they were hungry, I convey no impression of the gaunt starvation that looked from their cavernous eyes. All day they crowded to the doors of our houses, with always the same drawling complaint: "I've been a-marchin' and a-fightin' for six weeks stiddy, and I ain't had n-a-r-thin' to eat 'cept green apples an' green cawn, an' I wish you'd please to gimme a bite to eat." . . . I saw the troops march past us every summer for four years, and I know something of the appearance of a marching army, both Union and Southern. There are always stragglers, of course, but never before or after did I see anything comparable to [this]. . . . That they could march or fight at all seemed incredible.[36]

Most of the soldiers, however, were in high spirits as they entered Frederick on September 6 singing "Maryland, My Maryland." But like Bragg's army in Kentucky, they received a less enthusiastic welcome than they had hoped. This was the unionist part of Maryland. And these rebels did not inspire confidence. One resident of Frederick described them as "the filthiest set of men and officers I ever saw; with clothing that . . . had not been changed for weeks. They could be

---

35. Clifford Dowdey, ed., *The Wartime Papers of R. E. Lee* (Boston, 1961), 301. For an analysis of Lee's motives and goals for the invasion, see Douglas Southall Freeman, *R. E. Lee: A Biography*, 4 vols. (New York, 1934–35), II, 350–53.

36. Mary Bedinger Mitchell, "A Woman's Recollections of Antietam," *Battles and Leaders*, II, 687–88.

smelt all over the entire inclosure."[37] Although the men behaved with more restraint toward civilian property than Union soldiers were wont to do, their purchases of supplies with Confederate scrip did not win popularity. Despite the cool reception, Lee doggedly followed President Davis's instructions and issued an address "To the People of Maryland." We have come, he said, "with the deepest sympathy [for] the wrongs that have been inflicted upon the citizens of a commonwealth allied to the States of the South by the strongest social, political, and commercial ties . . . to aid you in throwing off this foreign yoke, to enable you again to enjoy the inalienable rights of freemen."[38] The silent response of Marylanders was eloquent. It constituted the first failure of the invasion.

The second was caused by a stroke of fate which proved that truth can indeed be stranger than fiction. Although Lee expected his army to live largely off the land, he needed to open a minimal supply line through the Shenandoah Valley, especially for ammunition. But the Union garrison at Harper's Ferry blocked this route. Known as the "railroad brigade," this unit had the duty of protecting the B & O and the Chesapeake and Ohio Canal. When the Confederate invasion cut these arteries east of Harper's Ferry, McClellan urged Halleck to transfer the garrison to the Army of the Potomac, which was marching from Washington to intercept Lee. But Halleck refused—an unsound strategic decision that unwittingly baited a trap for Lee.

To eliminate this garrison in his rear, Lee detached almost two-thirds of his army and sent them in three columns (the largest under Jackson) to converge on the heights overlooking Harper's Ferry. Planning to net the 12,000 bluecoats there like fish in a barrel, Lee intended to reunite his army for a move on Harrisburg before McClellan could cross the South Mountain range that protected the rebel flank. For the third time in three campaigns Lee was dividing his army in the presence of a larger enemy. To an officer who expressed concern about this, Lee replied: "Are you acquainted with General McClellan? He is an able general but a very cautious one. . . . His army is in a very demoralized and chaotic condition, and will not be prepared for offensive operations—or he will not think it so—for three or four weeks. Before that time I hope to be on the Susquehanna."[39]

37. James F. Murfin, *The Gleam of Bayonets: The Battle of Antietam and Robert E. Lee's Maryland Campaign, September 1862* (New York, 1965), 108.
38. *O.R.*, Ser. I, Vol. 19, pt. 2, 601–2.
39. John G. Walker, "Jackson's Capture of Harper's Ferry," *Battles and Leaders*, II, 605–6.

But instead of three of four weeks, Lee had only that many days before the enemy would be upon him. To be sure, McClellan with 70,000 men (soon reinforced to 80,000) was moving cautiously in search of Lee's 50,000 (which he estimated at 110,000). But the bluecoats were no longer demoralized, and on September 13 their non-gambling commander hit the all-time military jackpot. In a field near Frederick two Union soldiers found a copy of Lee's orders, wrapped around three cigars lost by a careless southern officer, detailing the objectives for the four separate parts of his army. This fantastic luck revealed to McClellan that each part of the enemy army was several miles from any of the others and that the two largest units were twenty or twenty-five miles apart with the Potomac between them. With his whole force McClellan could push through the South Mountain passes and gobble up the pieces of Lee's army before they could reunite. McClellan recognized his opportunity; to one of his generals he exulted, "Here is a paper with which if I cannot whip 'Bobbie Lee,' I will be willing to go home."[40]

Although animated by this vision, McClellan did not want to move rashly—after all, those rebels still outnumbered him. Instead of setting his troops in motion immediately, McClellan made careful plans and did not order the men forward until daylight on September 14, eighteen hours after he had learned of Lee's dispositions. As things turned out, this delay enabled Lee to concentrate and save his army. A pro-Confederate citizen of Maryland had witnessed McClellan's response to the finding of the lost orders and had ridden hard to inform Stuart, who passed the information along to Lee on the night of September 13. Lee ordered troops to block the passes through South Mountain. Next day two Union corps fought up-hill against D. H. Hill's Confederate division defending Turner's Gap. Taking heavy losses, Hill's hardy band hung on behind stone walls and trees until Longstreet came up with reinforcements and held off the Federals until nightfall. Withdrawing after dark, these outnumbered rebels had given Lee an extra day. Meanwhile another Union corps under William B. Franklin had smashed through Crampton's Gap six miles to the south after a sharp firefight with three Confederate brigades. Despite great numerical superiority, Franklin advanced timidly southward toward the forces besieging Harper's Ferry and failed to arrive in time to save the Union garrison at the Ferry.

40. John Gibbon, *Personal Recollections of the Civil War* (New York, 1928), 73.

Although the half of Lee's army north of the Potomac had warded off disaster, the invasion of Maryland appeared doomed. The whole Union army would be across South Mountain next day. The only apparent Confederate option seemed to be retreat into the Shenandoah Valley. But when Lee received word that Jackson expected to capture Harper's Ferry on September 15, he changed his mind about retreating. He ordered the whole army to concentrate at Sharpsburg, a Maryland village about a mile from the Potomac. Lee had decided to offer battle. To return to Virginia without fighting would mean loss of face. It might endanger diplomatic efforts to win foreign recognition. It would depress southern morale. Having beaten the Federals twice before, Lee thought he could do it again—for he still believed the Army of the Potomac to be demoralized.

Lee's estimate of northern morale seemed to be confirmed by Jackson's easy capture of Harper's Ferry. The Union garrison was composed mostly of new troops under a second-rate commander—Colonel Dixon Miles, a Marylander who had been reprimanded for drunkenness at First Bull Run and whose defense of Harper's Ferry was so inept as to arouse suspicions of treason. Killed in the last exchange of fire before the surrender, Miles did not have to defend himself against such a charge. As Jackson rode into town dressed as usual in a nondescript uniform and battered fatigue cap, one of the disarmed Union soldiers said, "Boys, he's not much for looks, but if we'd had him we wouldn't have been caught in this trap!"[41]

The various Confederate units that had besieged Harper's Ferry marched as fast as possible for Sharpsburg fifteen miles away. Until they arrived on September 16 and 17, Lee had only three divisions in line with their backs to the Potomac over which only one ford offered an escape in case of defeat. During September 15 the Army of the Potomac began arriving at Antietam Creek a mile or two east of Lee's position. Still acting with the caution befitting his estimate of Lee's superior force, McClellan launched no probing attacks and sent no cavalry reconnaissance across the creek to determine Confederate strength. On September

41. Henry Kyd Douglas, "Stonewall Jackson in Maryland," *Battles and Leaders*, II, 627. Paul R. Teetor, *A Matter of Hours: Treason at Harper's Ferry* (Rutherford, N.J., 1982), argues from circumstantial evidence that Miles deliberately sabotaged the defense of the garrison. A retired judge who presents his argument in the manner of a brief against Miles, Teetor cannot be said to have "proved" his case though he has raised several disturbing questions.

16 the northern commander had 60,000 men on hand and another 15,000 within six miles to confront Lee's 25,000 or 30,000. Having informed Washington that he would crush Lee's army in detail while it was separated, McClellan missed his second chance to do so on the 16th while he matured plans for an attack on the morrow. Late that afternoon—as two more Confederate divisions slogged northward from Harper's Ferry—McClellan sent two corps across the Antietam north of the Confederate left, precipitating a sharp little fight that alerted Lee to the point of the initial Union attack at dawn next day.

Antietam (called Sharpsburg by the South) was one of the few battles of the war in which both commanders deliberately chose the field and planned their tactics beforehand. Instead of entrenching, the Confederates utilized the cover of small groves, rock outcroppings, stone walls, dips and swells in the rolling farmland, and a sunken road in the center of their line. Only the southernmost of three bridges over the Antietam was within rebel rifle range; this bridge would become one of the keys to the battle. McClellan massed three corps on the Union right to deliver the initial attack and placed Burnside's large 9th Corps on the left with orders to create a diversion to prevent Lee from transferring troops from this sector to reinforce his left. McClellan held four Union divisions and the cavalry in reserve behind the right and center to exploit any breakthrough. He also expected Burnside to cross the creek and roll up the Confederate right if opportunity offered. It was a good battle plan and if well executed it might have accomplished Lincoln's wish to "destroy the rebel army."

But it was not well executed. On the Union side the responsibility for this lay mainly on the shoulders of McClellan and Burnside. McClellan failed to coordinate the attacks on the right, which therefore went forward in three stages instead of simultaneously. This allowed Lee time to shift troops from quiet sectors to meet the attacks. The Union commander also failed to send in the reserves when the bluecoats did manage to achieve a breakthrough in the center. Burnside wasted the morning and part of the afternoon crossing the stubbornly defended bridge when his men could have waded the nearby fords against little opposition. As a result of Burnside's tardiness, Lee was able to shift a division in the morning from the Confederate right to the hard-pressed left where it arrived just in time to break the third wave of the Union attack. On the Confederate side the credit for averting disaster belonged to the skillful generalship of Lee and his subordinates but above all to the desperate courage of men in the ranks. "It is beyond all wonder," wrote a

Union officer after the battle, "how such men as the rebel troops can fight on as they do; that, filthy, sick, hungry, and miserable, they should prove such heroes in fight, is past explanation."[42]

The fighting at Antietam was among the hardest of the war. The Army of the Potomac battled with grim determination to expunge the dishonor of previous defeats. Yankee soldiers were not impelled by fearless bravery or driven by iron discipline. Few men ever experience the former and Civil War soldiers scarcely knew the latter. Rather, they were motivated in the mass by the potential shame of another defeat and in small groups by the potential shame of cowardice in the eyes of comrades. A northern soldier who fought at Antietam gave as good an explanation of behavior in battle as one is likely to find anywhere. "We heard all through the war that the army 'was eager to be led against the enemy,' " he wrote with a nice sense of irony. "It must have been so, for truthful correspondents said so, and editors confirmed it. But when you came to hunt for this particular itch, it was always the next regiment that had it. The truth is, when bullets are whacking against treetrunks and solid shot are cracking skulls like egg-shells, the consuming passion in the breast of the average man is to get out of the way. Between the physical fear of going forward and the moral fear of turning back, there is a predicament of exceptional awkwardness." But when the order came to go forward, his regiment did not falter. "In a second the air was full of the hiss of bullets and the hurtle of grape-shot. The mental strain was so great that I saw at that moment the singular effect mentioned, I think, in the life of Goethe on a similar occasion—the whole landscape for an instant turned slightly red." This psychological state produced a sort of fighting madness in many men, a superadrenalized fury that turned them into mindless killing machines heedless of the normal instinct of self-preservation. This frenzy seems to have prevailed at Antietam on a greater scale than in any previous Civil War battle. "The men are loading and firing with demoniacal fury and shouting and laughing hysterically," wrote a Union officer in the present tense a quarter-century later as if that moment of red-sky madness lived in him yet.[43]

42. Murfin, The Gleam of Bayonets, 250.
43. David L. Thompson, "With Burnside at Antietam," Battles and Leaders, II, 661–62; Rufus R. Dawes of the 6th Wisconsin, quoted in Murfin, The Gleam of Bayonets, 218. The 6th Wisconsin, a regiment in the Iron Brigade, lost 40 men killed and 112 wounded out of about 300 engaged at Antietam.

Joseph Hooker's Union 1st Corps led the attack at dawn by sweeping down the Hagerstown Pike from the north. Rebels waited for them in what came to be known as the West Woods and The Cornfield just north of a whitewashed church of the pacifist Dunkard sect. "Fighting Joe" Hooker—an aggressive, egotistical general who aspired to command the Army of the Potomac—had earned his sobriquet on the Peninsula. He confirmed it here. His men drove back Jackson's corps from the cornfield and pike, dealing out such punishment that Lee sent reinforcements from D. H. Hill's division in the center and Longstreet's corps on the right. These units counterpunched with a blow that shattered Hooker's corps before the Union 12th Corps launched the second wave of the northern assault. This attack also penetrated the Confederate lines around the Dunkard Church before being hurled back with heavy losses, whereupon a third wave led by a crack division of "Bull" Sumner's 2nd Corps broke through the rebel line in the West Woods. Before these bluecoats could roll up the flank, however, one Confederate division that had arrived that morning from Harper's Ferry and another that Lee had shifted from the inactive right near Burnside's bridge suddenly popped out in front, flank, and rear of Sumner's division and all but wiped it out with a surprise counterattack. Severely wounded and left for dead in this action was a young captain in the 20th Massachusetts, Oliver Wendell Holmes, Jr.

For five hours a dreadful slaughter raged on the Confederate left. Twelve thousand men lay dead and wounded. Five Union and five Confederate divisions had been so cut up that they backed off as if by mutual consent and did no more serious fighting this day. In the meantime Sumner's other two divisions had obliqued left to deal with a threat to their flank from Confederates in a sunken farm road southeast of the Dunkard Church. This brought on the midday phase of the battle in which blue and gray slugged it out for this key to the rebel center, known ever after as Bloody Lane. The weight of numbers and firepower finally enabled the blue to prevail. Broken southern brigades fell back to regroup in the outskirts of Sharpsburg itself. A northern war correspondent who came up to Bloody Lane minutes after the Federals captured it could scarcely find words to describe this "ghastly spectacle" where "Confederates had gone down as the grass falls before the scythe."[44]

Now was the time for McClellan to send in his reserves. The enemy center was wide open. "There was no body of Confederate infantry in

44. Charles Carleton Coffin, "Antietam Scenes," *Battles and Leaders*, II, 684.

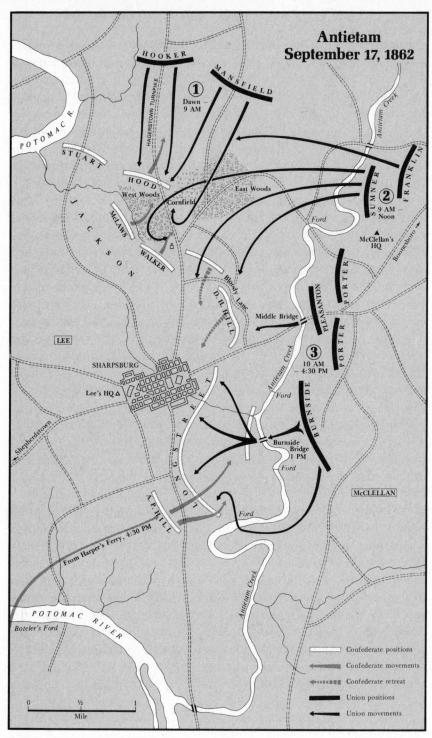

**Antietam
September 17, 1862**

HOOKER

MANSFIELD

① Dawn – 9 AM

HAGERSTOWN TURNPIKE

POTOMAC R.

STUART

HOOD

West Woods

Cornfield

East Woods

JACKSON

McLAWS

WALKER

Bloody Lane

D. H. HILL

Antietam Creek

SUMNER

② 9 AM – Noon

FRANKLIN

Ford

McClellan's HQ

Boonesboro

Ford

PLEASANTON

PORTER

Middle Bridge

PORTER

LEE

③ 10 AM – 4:30 PM

SHARPSBURG

Antietam Creek

Ford

Lee's HQ △

LONGSTREET

Burnside Bridge 1 PM

BURNSIDE

Ford

McCLELLAN

Shepherdstown

Ford

A. P. HILL

From Harper's Ferry, 4:30 PM

Antietam Creek

POTOMAC RIVER

Boteler's Ford

0   ½   1
Mile

Confederate positions

Confederate movements

Confederate retreat

Union positions

Union movements

542

this part of the field that could have resisted a serious advance," wrote a southern officer. "Lee's army was ruined, and the end of the Confederacy was in sight," added another.[45] But the carnage suffered by three Union corps during the morning had shaken McClellan. He decided not to send in the fresh 6th Corps commanded by Franklin, who was eager to go forward. Believing that Lee must be massing his supposedly enormous reserves for a counterattack, McClellan told Franklin that "it would not be prudent to make the attack."[46] So the center of the battlefield fell silent as events on the Confederate right moved toward a new climax.

All morning a thin brigade of Georgians hidden behind trees and a stone wall had carried on target practice against Yankee regiments trying to cross Burnside's bridge. The southern brigade commander was Robert A. Toombs, who enjoyed here his finest hour as a soldier. Disappointed by his failure to become president of the Confederacy, bored by his job as secretary of state, Toombs had taken a brigadier's commission to seek the fame and glory to which he felt destined. Reprimanded more than once by superiors for inefficiency and insubordination, Toombs spent many of his leisure hours denouncing Jefferson Davis and the "West Point clique" who were ruining army and country. For his achievement in holding Burnside's whole corps for several hours at Antietam—and being wounded in the process—Toombs expected promotion, but did not get it and subsequently resigned to go public with his antiadministration exhortations.

In the early afternoon of September 17 two of Burnside's crack regiments finally charged across the bridge at a run, taking heavy losses to establish a bridgehead on the rebel side. Other units found fords about the same time, and by mid-afternoon three of Burnside's divisions were driving the rebels in that sector back toward Sharpsburg and threatening to cut the road to the only ford over the Potomac. Here was another crisis for Lee and an opportunity for McClellan. Fitz-John Porter's 5th Corps stood available as a reserve to support Burnside's advance. One of Porter's division commanders urged McClellan to send him in to bolster Burnside. McClellan hesitated and seemed about to give the order when he looked at Porter, who shook his head. "Remember, General," Porter was heard to say, "I command the last reserve of the last

45. Frederick Tilbert, *Antietam* (Washington, 1961), 39; E. P. Alexander, *Military Memoirs of a Confederate*, ed. T. Harry Williams (Bloomington, 1962), 262.
46. *O.R.*, Ser. I, Vol. 19, pt. 1, p. 377.

army of the Republic."[47] This warning reminded McClellan of the danger from those phantom reserves on the other side, so he refused to give the order.

Meanwhile Lee looked anxiously to the south where his right flank seemed to be disintegrating. Suddenly he saw a cloud of dust in the distance that soon materialized as marching men. "Whose troops are those?" Lee asked a nearby lieutenant with a telescope. The lieutenant peered intently for what seemed an eternity, then said: "They are flying the Virginia and Confederate flags, sir." Sighing with relief, Lee observed: "It is A. P. Hill from Harper's Ferry."[48] Indeed it was. Having remained behind to complete the surrender arrangements, Hill had driven his hard-fighting division up the road at a killing pace in response to an urgent summons from Lee. These troops crashed into Burnside's flank in late afternoon just as the Yankees seemed about to crumple Lee's right. Surprised and confused, the Union attackers milled around, stopped, and retreated. The surprise was compounded by the captured blue uniforms many of Hill's men were wearing, which caused four Union flank regiments to hold their fire for fatal minutes.

Night fell on a scene of horror beyond imagining. Nearly 6,000 men lay dead or dying, and another 17,000 wounded groaned in agony or endured in silence. The casualties at Antietam numbered four times the total suffered by American soldiers at the Normandy beaches on June 6, 1944. More than twice as many Americans lost their lives in one day at Sharpsburg as fell in combat in the War of 1812, the Mexican War, and the Spanish-American war *combined*. After dark on September 17 the weary southern corps and division commanders gathered at Lee's headquarters to report losses of 50 percent or more in several brigades. Scarcely 30,000 Confederates remained alive and unwounded. Lee nevertheless stayed in position next day almost as if to dare McClellan to renew the assault. McClellan refused the dare. Although two more fresh Union divisions arrived in the morning, he was still hypnotized by a vision of Lee's limitless legions. The armies remained quiet during the 18th, and that night Lee yielded to necessity and ordered his troops back to Virginia. McClellan mounted a feeble pursuit, which A. P. Hill brushed off on September 20, and the Confederates got clean away into the Valley.

47. Thomas M. Anderson, in *Battles and Leaders*, II, 656n. Porter later denied the occurrence of this incident, but his testimony is suspect.
48. Murfin, *The Gleam of Bayonets*, 282.

McClellan wired news of a great victory to Washington. "Maryland is entirely freed from the presence of the enemy, who has been driven across the Potomac. No fears need now be entertained for the safety of Pennsylvania." Forgotten were Lincoln's instructions to "destroy the rebel army." Secretary of the Navy Welles may have echoed the president's opinion when he wrote two days after the battle: "Nothing from the army, except that, instead of following up the victory, attacking and capturing the Rebels, they . . . are rapidly escaping across the river. . . . Oh dear!" In letters to his wife, McClellan expressed pride in his achievement and pique at such fault-finding. "Those in whose judgment I rely tell me that I fought the battle splendidly & that it was a masterpiece of art. . . . I feel that I have done all that can be asked in twice saving the country. . . . I feel some little pride in having, with a beaten & demoralized army, defeated Lee so utterly. . . . Well, one of these days history will I trust do me justice."[49]

History can at least record Antietam as a strategic Union success. Lee's invasion of Maryland recoiled more quickly than Bragg's invasion of Kentucky. Nearly one-third of the rebels who marched into Maryland became casualties. When an unwary regimental band struck up "Maryland, My Maryland" after the retreat across the Potomac, men in the ranks hissed and groaned. Seeing the point, the musicians switched to "Carry Me Back to Old Virginny." At Whitehall and the White House the battle of Antietam also went down as a northern victory. It frustrated Confederate hopes for British recognition and precipitated the Emancipation Proclamation. The slaughter at Sharpsburg therefore proved to have been one of the war's great turning points.

49. Beale, ed., *Diary of Welles*, I, 140; McClellan to Halleck, Sept. 19, 1862, in *McClellan's Own Story* (New York, 1887), 621; McClellan to Ellen McClellan, Sept. 18, 20, 1862, McClellan Papers.

18

John Bull's Virginia Reel

I

The course of the war in the summer of 1862 revived Confederate hopes for European diplomatic recognition. Lee's offensives convinced British and French leaders that northern armies could never restore the Union. These powers contemplated an offer of mediation, which would have constituted de facto recognition of Confederate independence. Influential elements of British public opinion grew more sympathetic to the southern cause. The Palmerston government seemed to shut its eyes to violations of British neutrality by Liverpool shipbuilders who constructed rebel cruisers to prey on the American merchant marine. The long-awaited cotton famine finally took hold in the summer of 1862. Louis Napoleon toyed with the idea of offering recognition and aid to the Confederacy in return for southern cotton and southern support for French suzerainty in Mexico.

Of all these occurrences, the building of commerce raiders was the only one that generated tangible benefits for the Confederacy. Liverpool was a center of pro-southern sentiment. The city "was made by the slave trade," observed a caustic American diplomat, "and the sons of those who acquired fortunes in the traffic, now instinctively side with the rebelling slave-drivers."[1] Liverpool shipyards built numerous blockade

1. Sarah A. Wallace and Frances E. Gillespie, eds., *The Journal of Benjamin Moran, 1857–1865*, 2 vols. (Chicago, 1948–49), II, 984.

runners. In March 1862 the first warship that the southern agent James D. Bulloch had ordered was also nearing completion. The ship's purpose as a commerce raider was an open secret, owing to the tenacious detective work of the U.S. consul at Liverpool, Thomas H. Dudley.

This combative Quaker was a match for Bulloch. Dudley hired spies and informers who assembled evidence to prove the ship's Confederate destination; Bulloch countered with forged papers showing that the vessel, named the *Oreto*, was owned by a merchant of Palermo. At issue was the meaning of Britain's Foreign Enlistment Act, which forbade the construction *and* arming of warships in British territory for a belligerent power. Remaining within the letter of the law while violating its spirit, Bulloch took delivery of the ship without arms, sent it to the Bahamas, and transported the guns from England in another vessel. The sleek warship took on her guns at a deserted Bahamian Cay and began her fearsome career as the *Florida*. She destroyed thirty-eight American merchant vessels before the Union navy captured her by a subterfuge in the harbor of Bahia, Brazil, in October 1864.

The willingness of British officials to apply a narrow interpretation of the Foreign Enlistment Act encouraged Bulloch's efforts to get his second and larger cruiser out of Liverpool in the summer of 1862. In a contest of lawyers, spies, and double agents that would furnish material for an espionage thriller, Dudley amassed evidence of the ship's illegal purpose and Bulloch struggled to slip through the legal net closing around him by July. Once again bureaucratic negligence, legal pettifoggery, and the Confederate sympathies of the British customs collector at Liverpool gave Bulloch time to ready his ship for sea. When an agent informed him of the government's belated intention to detain the ship, Bulloch sent her out on a "trial cruise" from which she never returned. Instead she rendezvoused at the Azores with a tender carrying guns and ammunition sent separately from Britain. Named the *Alabama*, this cruiser had as her captain Raphael Semmes, who had already proved his prowess as a salt-water guerrilla on the now-defunct C.S.S. *Sumter*. For the next two years Semmes and the *Alabama* roamed the seas and destroyed or captured sixty-four American merchant ships before being sunk by the U.S.S. *Kearsarge* off Cherbourg in June 1864. The *Alabama* and *Florida* were the most successful and celebrated rebel cruisers. Although their exploits did not alter the outcome of the war, they diverted numerous Union navy ships from the blockade, drove insurance rates for American vessels to astronomical heights, forced these vessels to remain in port or convert to foreign registry, and helped topple the American merchant marine from its once-dominant position, which it never regained.

In addition to the escape of the *Alabama* from Liverpool, another straw in the wind seemed to preview a southern tilt in British foreign policy. Henry Hotze, a Swiss-born Alabamian who arrived in London early in 1862, was an effective propagandist for the South. Twenty-seven years old and boyish in appearance, Hotze nevertheless possessed a suavity of manner and a style of witty understatement that appealed to the British upper classes. He gained entry to high circles on Fleet Street and was soon writing pro-Confederate editorials for several newspapers. Hotze also recruited English journalists to write for the *Index*, a small newspaper he established in May 1862 to present the southern viewpoint. Hotze did a good job in stirring up British prejudices against the bumptious Yankees. To liberals he insisted that the South was fighting not for slavery but for self-determination. To conservatives he presented an image of a rural gentry defending its liberties against a rapacious northern government. To businessmen he promised that an independent Confederacy would open its ports to free trade, in contrast with the Union government which had recently raised tariffs yet again. To the textile industry he pledged a resumption of cotton exports.

This last prospect had a powerful appeal, for the cotton famine was beginning to pinch. In July 1862 the supply of raw cotton in Britain stood at one-third the normal level. Three-quarters of the cotton-mill workers were unemployed or on short time. Charity and the dole could not ward off hardship and restiveness in Lancashire working-class districts. Young Henry Adams, son and secretary of the American minister in London, conceded as early as May 1862 that "the suffering among the people in Lancashire and in France is already very great and is increasing enormously." Chancellor of the Exchequer William E. Gladstone feared an outbreak of rioting unless something was done to relieve the distress. Gladstone favored British intervention to stop the war and start the flow of cotton across the Atlantic. A British diplomat predicted that "so great a pressure may be put upon the government [that] they will find it difficult to resist."[2]

2. Henry Adams to Charles Francis Adams, Jr., May 8, 1862, in Worthington C. Ford, ed., *A Cycle of Adams Letters 1861–1865*, 2 vols. (Boston, 1920), I, 139; Frank L. Owsley, *King Cotton Diplomacy*, 2nd ed. rev. by Harriet C. Owsley (Chicago, 1959), 137, 337, 340. Similar pressures were building in France, whose foreign minister told the American minister to Belgium that "we are nearly out of

The attitude of textile workers toward the American war has been something of a puzzle to historians as well as to contemporaries. Henry Hotze confessed frustration at his failure to win support from this class whose economic self-interest would seem to have favored the South. "The Lancashire operatives," wrote Hotze, are the only "class which as a class continues actively inimical to us. . . . With them the unreasoning . . . aversion to our institutions is as firmly rooted as in any part of New England. . . . They look upon us, and . . . upon slavery as the author and source of their present miseries." The American Minister Charles Francis Adams echoed this appraisal. "The great body of the aristocracy and the commercial classes are anxious to see the United States go to pieces," wrote Adams in December 1862, while "the middle and lower class sympathise with us" because they "see in the convulsion in America an era in the history of the world, out of which must come in the end a general recognition of the right of mankind to the produce of their labor and the pursuit of happiness."[3]

In this view, the issues of the American Civil War mirrored the issues of class conflict in Britain. The Union stood for popular government, equal rights, and the dignity of labor; the Confederacy stood for aristocracy, privilege, and slavery. Lincoln expressed this theme in his speeches portraying the war as "essentially a People's contest . . . a struggle for maintaining in the world that form and substance of government whose leading object is to elevate the condition of men . . . to afford all an unfettered start, and a fair chance in the race of life."[4] British radicals expounded numerous variations on the theme. For a generation they had fought for democratization of British politics and improved conditions for the working class. For them, America was a "beacon of freedom" lighting the path to reform. The leading British radical, John Bright, passionately embraced the Union cause. "There is no country in which men have been so free and prosperous" as the Union states, declared Bright. "The existence of that free country and that free government has a prodigious influence upon freedom in Europe." Confederates were "the worst foes of freedom that the world has ever seen,"

cotton, and cotton we *must have*." Lynn M. Case and Warren F. Spencer, *The United States and France: Civil War Diplomacy* (Philadelphia, 1970), 290.

3. Frank J. Merli, *Great Britain and the Confederate Navy 1861–1865* (Boomington, 1965), 23; Charles Francis Adams to C. F. Adams, Jr., Dec. 25, 1862, Ford, *Cycle of Adams Letters*, I, 220–21.

4. CWL, IV, 438.

Bright told workingmen. That was why "Privilege thinks it has a great interest in this contest, and every morning, with blatant voice, it comes into your streets and curses the American Republic." Liberal intellectuals shared this belief that a southern victory, in the words of John Stuart Mill, "would be a victory of the powers of evil which would give courage to the enemies of progress and damp the spirits of its friends all over the civilized world."[5] A German revolutionary living in exile in England also viewed the American war against the "slave oligarchy" as a "world-transforming . . . revolutionary movement." "The workingmen of Europe," continued Karl Marx, felt a kinship with Abraham Lincoln, "the single-minded son of the working class. . . . As the American War of Independence initiated a new era of ascendancy for the middle class, so the American anti-slavery war will do for the working classes."[6]

But a number of historians have discovered cracks in the apparent pro-Union unity of working men. Indeed, some have gone so far as to maintain that most Lancashire textile workers favored British intervention on behalf of the South to obtain cotton. The rhetoric favoring the cause of the Union, according to these historians, was the work of radical intellectuals like Bright or Marx and did not represent the real sentiments of the unemployed operatives. The mass meetings of workers that passed pro-Union resolutions are said to have been engineered by these middle-class outsiders. One historian has found twice as many meetings in Lancashire supporting the Confederacy as favoring the Union.[7]

This revisionist interpretation overcorrects the traditional view. Cotton manufacturing was not the only industry in Britain or even in Lancashire. Workers in wool, flax, armaments, shipping, and other industries prospered from increased wartime trade. And in any case, a good deal of truth still clings to the old notion of democratic principle tran-

5. Bright quoted in G. D. Lillibridge, *Beacon of Freedom: The Impact of American Democracy upon Great Britain 1830–1870* (Philadelphia, 1955), 121, and in Ephraim D. Adams, *Great Britain and the American Civil War*, 2 vols. (New York, 1925), II, 132; Mill quoted in Belle B. Sideman and Lillian Friedman, eds., *Europe Looks at the Civil War* (New York, 1960), 117–18.
6. Saul K. Padover, ed. and trans., *Karl Marx on America and the Civil War* (New York, 1972), 237, 263, 264.
7. Mary Ellison, *Support for Seccession: Lancashire and the American Civil War* (Chicago, 1972), 226–27 and passim. For a review of the historiography on this question see Peter d'A. Jones's "Epilogue" to this book, pp. 199–219.

scending economic self-interest in Lancashire. As a veteran Chartist leader put it in February 1863: "The people had said there was something higher than work, more precious than cotton . . . it was right, and liberty, and doing justice, and bidding defiance to all wrong."[8]

Much truth also adheres to the notion of British upper-class support for the South—or at least hostility to the North, which amounted to almost the same thing. Well-born Englishmen professed to dislike Yankees as much for their manners as for their dangerous democratic example to the lower orders. Many of the gentry expressed delight at the "immortal smash" of 1861 which demonstrated "the failure of republican institutions in time of pressure." The Earl of Shrewsbury looked upon "the trial of Democracy and its failure" with pleasure. "The dissolution of the Union [means] that men now before me will live to see an aristocracy established in America."[9] Similar statements found their way into prominent newspapers, including the London *Morning Post* and the magisterial *Times*, both with close ties to the Palmerston government. The *Times* considered the destruction of "the American Colossus" a good "riddance of a nightmare. . . . Excepting a few gentlemen of republican tendencies, we all expect, we nearly all wish, success to the Confederate cause." If by some remote and hateful chance the North did manage to win, said the *Morning Post*, "who can doubt that Democracy will be more arrogant, more aggressive, more levelling and vulgarizing, if that be possible, than ever before."[10] This war of words against the Yankees contributed to an embitterment of Anglo-American relations for a generation after the *Alabama* had sunk below the waves and the Enfield rifles shipped through the blockade had fallen silent.

In 1862 an incident in New Orleans intensified British upper-class alienation from the North. Benjamin Butler's heavy hand as commander of occupation troops caused many complaints, but no act occasioned more uproar than his order of May 15 that any woman who persisted in the practice of insulting northern soldiers "shall be regarded

8. Quoted in Philip S. Foner, *British Labor and the American Civil War* (New York, 1981), 52. This study vigorously reasserts and documents strong working-class support for the Union.
9. William H. Russell to John Bigelow, April 14, 1861, quoted in Norman Ferris, *Desperate Diplomacy: William H. Seward's Foreign Policy, 1861* (Knoxville, 1976), 210n.; Shrewsbury quoted in Adams, *Britain and the Civil War*, II, 282.
10. *Morning Post*, Feb. 22, 1861, quoted in Adams, *Britain and the Civil War*, II, 284; *Times*, Aug. 15, 1862, March 27, 1863, quoted in Owsley, *King Cotton Diplomacy*, 186.

and held liable to be treated as a woman of the town plying her avocation." Butler had issued this maladroit order after considerable provocation, climaxed by a woman who dumped the contents of a chamber pot from a French-Quarter balcony on Fleet Captain David Farragut's head. Butler conceived of his order as a means of humiliating southern civilians into decent behavior; southerners and Europeans chose to interpret it as a barbarous license for northern soldiers to treat refined ladies as prostitutes. In an extraordinary statement to the House of Commons, Palmerston branded Butler's conduct "infamous. Sir, an Englishman must blush to think that such an act has been committed by one belonging to the Anglo-Saxon race." This was more than Charles Francis Adams could stand. For months he had silently endured the gibes of Englishmen. But this self-righteous condemnation of Butler, with its implied approval of a people who held two million women in slavery, evoked an official protest by Adams. Palmerston's huffy reply caused an estrangement between the two men at a time when Anglo-American relations were entering a critical stage.[11]

The correlation between class and British attitudes toward the American conflict should not be exaggerated. The Union had few warmer friends than the Duke of Argyll, and the same could be said of others whose blood matched the color of northern uniforms. At the same time, several liberals and even radicals were attracted to the South's fight for self-determination. Many Englishmen had cheered the Greek fight for independence or the struggle of Hungary and Italian states to throw off Hapsburg rule. Some viewed the South's revolution against Yankee overlordship in a similar light. Such convictions motivated Russell and Gladstone, the most important members of the Palmerston ministry next to Old Pam himself. "Jefferson Davis and other leaders of the South," said Gladstone in a celebrated speech at Newcastle in October 1862, "have made an army; they are making, it appears, a navy; and they have made what is more than either; they have made a nation."[12]

The canker in this image of southerners as freedom-loving nationalists, of course, was slavery. One thing upon which Englishmen prided themselves was their role in suppressing the transatlantic slave trade and abolishing slavery in the West Indies. To support a rebellion in behalf of slavery would be un-British. To accept the notion that the South fought

11. Brian Jenkins, *Britain and the War for the Union* (Montreal, 1980), II, 50–59.
12. D. P. Crook, *The North, the South, and the Powers 1861–1865* (New York, 1974), 227–29.

for independence rather than slavery required considerable mental leg-erdemain. But so long as the North did *not* fight for freedom, many Britons could see no moral superiority in the Union cause. If the North wanted to succeed in "their struggle [for] the sympathies of English-men," warned a radical newspaper, "they must abolish slavery."[13]

But these issues of ideology and sentiment played a secondary role in determining Britain's foreign policy. A veteran of a half-century in Brit-ish politics, Palmerston was an exponent of *Realpolitik*. When pro-southern members of Parliament launched a drive in the summer of 1862 for British recognition of the Confederacy, Palmerston professed not to see the point. The South, he wrote, would not be "a bit more independent for our saying so unless we followed up our Declaration by taking Part with them in the war." Few in Britain were ready for that. Palmerston would like more cotton, but it remained unclear just how diplomatic recognition would get it. Southerners believed that recogni-tion would help the Confederacy by boosting its credibility abroad and strengthening the peace party in the North. They may have been right. But so far as Palmerston was concerned, the South could earn recogni-tion only by winning the war: Britain must "know that their separate independence is a truth and a fact" before declaring it to be so.[14]

Across the Channel, Louis Napoleon felt fewer inhibitions against expressing his partisanship for the South. To the extent that the French people thought about it, they disliked slavery. But the French press paid less attention to the American war than did British newspapers, and except for distress caused by shortages of cotton, most Frenchmen cared little about what happened in America. Napoleon cared, however, and he thought he saw a way to get cotton and to enhance his imperial designs at the same time. By the summer of 1862 thousands of French soldiers were fighting in Mexico to overthrow the liberal regime of Ben-ito Juarez and turn the country into a French colony. Napoleon had sent these troops on the pretext of enforcing the collection of Mexican debts. But his real purpose was the creation of an empire in the new world to replace the one that his uncle had sold to Thomas Jefferson. The Union government supported Juarez, but was in no position to help him in 1862; the Confederacy decided to support Napoleon, and believed they *could* help him—for a price. In July 1862, John Slidell offered Napoleon several hundred thousand bales of cotton and an alli-

13. *Reynolds Weekly*, quoted in Lillibridge, *Beacon of Freedom*, 115.
14. Jenkins, *Britain and the War for the Union*, II, 66, 95–100.

ance against Juarez in return for French diplomatic recognition and possible naval assistance in breaking the blockade.

Napoleon was intrigued by the offer but reluctant to court hostilities with the United States. He told Slidell he would think about it. In truth, Napoleon dared not act unilaterally. Although he hoped to surpass Britain as the world's leading power, he recognized that a confrontation with the Union navy without Britain at his side might scuttle his plans. From his summer palace, Napoleon therefore instructed his foreign secretary: "Demandez au government anglais s'il ne croit pas le moment venu de reconnaitre le Sud."[15] But les anglais were not ready to cooperate. The ancient hostility between Britain and France had not vanished. Palmerston was suspicious of Napoleon's global designs. The British prime minister warded off a parliamentary motion for Confederate recognition in mid-July even though a majority in Commons clearly favored such a step.

But as the summer wore on, Confederate victories seemed likely to fulfill Palmerston's criterion for recognition: establishment of southern nationhood as truth and fact. During 1861 most British observers had assumed as a matter of course that the North could never conquer so large an area and so militant a people. After all, if the Redcoats could not prevail over a much weaker nation in 1776, how could the Yankees expect to win? Union victories in the first half of 1862 had threatened this smug assumption, but Jackson and Lee—who became instant legends in Britain—revived and made it stronger than ever. Even some of the Union's staunchest friends came to share the *Times*'s conviction that "North and South must now choose between separation and ruin." The "useless butchery and carnage" had proved only that "nine millions of people, inhabiting a territory of 900,000 square miles, and animated by one spirit of resistance, can never be subdued." By September, according to the French foreign secretary, "not a reasonable statesman in Europe" believed that the North could win.[16]

In both Whitehall and on the Quai d'Orsay a sentiment favoring an offer of mediation grew stronger as reports of new Confederate victories filtered across the Atlantic. By bringing the war to an end, mediation might prove the quickest and safest way to get cotton. A joint offer by

---

15. Adams, *Britain and the Civil War*, II, 19.
16. The *Times* quoted in Owsley, *King Cotton Diplomacy*, 297, in Crook, *The North, the South, and the Powers*, 245, and in Nevins, *War*, II, 246; Eduard Thouvenel quoted in Crook, *The North, the South, and the Powers*, 247.

several powers—Britain, France, Russia, and perhaps Austria and Prussia—would be most effective, for the North could not ignore the united opinion of Europe and even the bellicose Seward could scarcely declare war on all of them. A mediation proposal would be tantamount to recognition of Confederate independence. Rumors that such a move was afoot caused euphoria among southern diplomats and plunged the American legation into gloom. "I am more hopeful," wrote Slidell from Paris, "than I have been at any moment since my arrival." In London, James Mason "look[ed] now for intervention speedily in some form." [17] Henry Adams reported "the current . . . rising every hour and running harder against us than at any time since the Trent affair." Consul Thomas Dudley in Liverpool, depressed by his failure to apprehend the *Alabama*, reported that "we are more in danger of intervention than we have been at any previous period. . . . They are all against us and would rejoice at our downfall." [18]

The European belief that defeat might induce Lincoln to accept mediation misjudged his determination to fight through to victory. "I expect to maintain this contest until successful, or till I die," Lincoln had said, and he meant it. Even after the setback at Second Bull Run, Seward told the French minister that "we will not admit the division of the Union . . . at any price. . . . There is no possible compromise." Such obstinacy compelled the proponents of mediation to pin their hopes on a Democratic triumph in the northern elections. Betraying a typical British misunderstanding of the American constitutional system, Foreign Minister Russell expected that Democratic control of the House would force Lincoln to change his foreign policy. "The Democratic party may by that time [November] have got the ascendancy," wrote Russell in October. "I heartily wish them success." [19]

So did Robert E. Lee, as he invaded Maryland to conquer a peace. The fate of diplomacy rode with Lee in this campaign. The Federals "got a very complete smashing" at Bull Run, wrote Palmerston to Russell on September 14, "and it seems not altogether unlikely that still greater disasters await them, and that even Washington or Baltimore

17. Slidell to Jefferson Davis, July 25, 1862, Mason to Mrs. Mason, July 20, 1862, quoted in Hudson Strode, *Jefferson Davis: Confederate President* (New York, 1959), 294, 292.
18. Henry Adams to Charles Francis Adams, Jr., July 19, 1861, in Ford, *Cycle of Adams Letters*, I, 166; Dudley quoted in Strode, *Davis*, 294.
19. Seward and Russell quoted in Owsley, *King Cotton Diplomacy*, 330, 353.

may fall into the hands of the Confederates. If this should happen, would it not be time for us to consider whether . . . England and France might not address the contending parties and recommend an arrangement upon the basis of separation?" Russell was ready and willing. On September 17—the very day of the fighting at Sharpsburg—he concurred in the plan to offer mediation, adding that if the North refused, "we ought ourselves to recognise the Southern States as an independent State." But even before reports of Antietam reached England (news required ten days or more to cross the Atlantic), Palmerston turned cautious. On September 23 he told Russell that the outcome of the campaign in Maryland "must have a great effect on the state of affairs. If the Federals sustain a great defeat, they may be at once ready for mediation, and the iron should be struck while it is hot. If, on the other hand, they should have the best of it, we may wait awhile and see what may follow."[20] Having learned of Lee's retreat to Virginia, Palmerston backed off. "These last battles in Maryland have rather set the North up again," he wrote to Russell early in October. "The whole matter is full of difficulty, and can only be cleared up by some more decided events between the contending armies."[21]

But Antietam did not cool the ardor of Russell and Gladstone for recognition. They persisted in bringing the matter before the cabinet on October 28, despite Palmerston's repeated insistence that matters had changed since mid-September, "when the Confederates seemed to be carrying all before them. . . . I am very much come back to our original view that we must continue merely to be lookers-on till the war shall have taken a more decided turn."[22] The cabinet voted Russell and Gladstone down. The French weighed in at this point with a suggestion that Britain, France, and Russia propose a six months' armistice—during which the blockade would be suspended. This so blatantly favored the South that pro-Union Russia quickly rejected it. The British cabinet, after two days of discussion, also turned it down.

Thus ended the South's best chance for European intervention. It did not end irrevocably, for the military situation remained fluid and most

20. This correspondence is conveniently published in James V. Murfin, *The Gleam of Bayonets: The Battle of Antietam and Robert E. Lee's Maryland Campaign, September 1862* (New York, 1965), 394, 396–97, 399–400.
21. Jenkins, *Britain and the War for the Union*, II, 170; Murfin, *Gleam of Bayonets*, 400–401.
22. Palmerston to Russell, Oct. 22, 1862, in Owsley, *King Cotton Diplomacy*, 351.

Britons remained certain that the North could never win. But at least they had avoided losing. Antietam had, in Charles Francis Adams's understatement, "done a good deal to restore our drooping credit here."[23] It had done more; by enabling Lincoln to issue the Emancipation Proclamation the battle also ensured that Britain would think twice about intervening against a government fighting for freedom as well as Union.

II

On September 22, five days after the battle of Antietam, Lincoln called his cabinet into session. He had made a covenant with God, said the president, that if the army drove the enemy from Maryland he would issue his Emancipation Proclamation. "I think the time has come," he continued. "I wish it were a better time. I wish that we were in a better condition. The action of the army against the rebels has not been quite what I should have best liked." Nevertheless, Antietam was a victory and Lincoln intended to warn the rebel states that unless they returned to the Union by January 1 their slaves "shall be then, thenceforward, and forever free." The cabinet approved, though Montgomery Blair repeated his warning that this action might drive border-state elements to the South and give Democrats "a club . . . to beat the Administration" in the elections. Lincoln replied that he had exhausted every effort to bring the border states along. Now "we must make the forward movement" without them. "They [will] acquiesce, if not immediately, soon." As for the Democrats, "their clubs would be used against us take what course we might."[24]

The Proclamation would apply only to states in rebellion on January 1. This produced some confusion, because the edict thus appeared to "liberate" only those slaves beyond Union authority while retaining in bondage all those within the government's reach. A few disappointed radicals and abolitionists looked upon it this way. So did tories and some liberals in England. The conservative British press affected both to abhor and to ridicule the measure: to abhor it because it might en-

23. Adams to C. F. Adams, Jr., Oct. 17, 1862, in Ford, *Cycle of Adams Letters*, I, 192.
24. David Donald, ed., *Inside Lincoln's Cabinet: The Civil War Diaries of Salmon P. Chase* (New York, 1954), 149–52; Howard K. Beale, ed., *Diary of Gideon Welles*, 3 vols. (New York, 1960), I, 142–45; John G. Nicolay and John Hay, *Abraham Lincoln: A History*, 10 vols. (New York, 1890), VI, 158–63; the text of the Proclamation is in *CWL*, V, 433–36.

courage a servile rebellion that would eclipse the horrors of the 1857 Sepoy uprising in India; to ridicule it because of its hypocritical impotence. "Where he has no power Mr. Lincoln will set the negroes free; where he retains power he will consider them as slaves," declared the London *Times*. "This is more like a Chinaman beating his two swords together to frighten his enemy than like an earnest man pressing forward his cause."[25]

But such remarks missed the point and misunderstood the president's prerogatives under the Constitution. Lincoln acted under his war powers to seize enemy resources; he had no constitutional power to act against slavery in areas loyal to the United States. The Proclamation would turn Union forces into armies of liberation after January 1—if they could win the war. And it also invited the slaves to help them win it. Most antislavery Americans and Britons recognized this. "We shout for joy that we live to record this righteous decree," wrote Frederick Douglass, while William Lloyd Garrison considered it "an act of immense historic consequence."[26] A British abolitionist pronounced September 22 "a memorable day in the annals of the great struggle for the freedom of an oppressed and despised race"; a radical London newspaper believed it "a gigantic stride in the paths of Christian and civilized progress."[27] Lincoln's own off-the-record analysis showed how much his conception of the war had changed since ten months earlier, when he had deprecated a "remorseless revolutionary struggle." After January 1, Lincoln told an official of the Interior Department, "the character of the war will be changed. It will be one of subjugation. . . . The [old] South is to be destroyed and replaced by new propositions and ideas."[28]

Would the army fight for freedom? From an Indiana colonel came words that could have answered for most soldiers. Few of them were abolitionists, he wrote, but they nevertheless wanted "to destroy everything that in *aught* gives the rebels strength," including slavery, so "this army will sustain the emancipation proclamation and enforce it with

25. *Times*, Oct. 7, 1862.
26. *Douglass' Monthly*, Oct. 1862, p. 721; *Liberator*, Sept. 26, 1862.
27. Quoted in Jenkins, *Britain and the War for the Union*, II, 153, and Nevins, *War*, II, 270.
28. T. J. Barnett to Samuel L. M. Barlow, Sept. 25, 1862, Barlow Papers, Henry E. Huntington Library. These words were Barnett's paraphrase of Lincoln's comments, but the president's sentiments were "indicated plainly enough," according to Barnett.

the bayonet." A Democratic private in the Army of the Potomac whose previous letters had railed against abolitionists and blacks now expressed support for "putting away any institution if by so doing it will help put down the rebellion, for I hold that nothing should stand in the way of the Union—niggers, nor anything else." General-in-Chief Halleck explained his position to Grant: "The character of the war has very much changed within the last year. There is now no possible hope of reconciliation. . . . We must conquer the rebels or be conquered by them. . . . Every slave withdrawn from the enemy is the equivalent of a white man put *hors de combat*."[29]

But would McClellan and officers of the Army of the Potomac go along with this? Much Republican opposition to McClellan stemmed from the belief that he would not. And indeed, the general's first response to the Proclamation indicated indecision. He considered it "infamous" and told his wife that he "could not make up my mind to fight for such an accursed doctrine as that of a servile insurrection." McClellan consulted Democratic friends in New York, who advised him "to submit to the Presdt's proclamation & quietly continue doing [your] duty as a soldier."[30] But some of McClellan's associates stirred up opposition to the new policy. Fitz-John Porter denounced this "absurd proclamation of a political coward." A staff officer confided to a colleague that Lee's army had not been "bagged" at Sharpsburg because "that is not the game. The object is that neither army shall get much advantage of the other; that both shall be kept in the field till they are exhausted, when we will make a compromise and save slavery." When word of this conversation reached Lincoln he cashiered the officer to "make an example" and put a stop to such "silly, treasonable expressions."[31] Belatedly awakening to the danger of such loose talk among his officers, McClellan on October 7 issued a general order reminding them of the necessity for military subordination to civil authority. "The

---

29. Indiana colonel quoted in Nevins, *War*, II, 239; John H. Burrill to his parents, Jan. 1, 1863, Civil War Times Illustrated Collection, United States Military History Institute; O.R., Ser. I, Vol. 24, pt. 3, p. 157.
30. McClellan to Ellen McClellan, Sept. 25, Oct. 5, 1862, McClellan Papers, Library of Congress; McClellan to William H. Aspinwall, Sept. 26, 1862, Civil War Collection, Henry E. Huntington Library.
31. Porter to Manton Marble, Sept. 30, 1862, quoted in Nevins, *War*, II, 238–39; the case of the cashiered major can be followed in CWL, V, 442–43, 508–9, and in Nicolay and Hay, *Lincoln*, VI, 186–88.

remedy for political errors, if any are committed," concluded Mc-
Clellan with an artful reference to the imminent elections, "is to be
found only in the action of the people at the polls."[32]

Democrats scarcely needed this hint. They had already made emancipation the main issue in their quest for control of Congress. The New
York Democratic platform denounced the Emancipation Proclamation
as "a proposal for the butchery of women and children, for scenes of
lust and rapine, and of arson and murder." The party nominated for
governor the suave, conservative veteran of thirty years in New York
politics Horatio Seymour, who declared: "If it be true that slavery must
be abolished to save this Union, then the people of the South should
be allowed to withdraw themselves from the government which cannot
give them the protection guaranteed by its terms."[33] Democrats in Ohio
and Illinois took similar ground. Branding the Emancipation Proclamation "another advance in the Robespierrian highway of tyranny and
anarchy," they asserted that if abolition was "the avowed purpose of the
war, the South cannot be subdued and ought not to be subdued. . . .
In the name of God, no more bloodshed to gratify a religious fanaticism." An Ohio Democrat amended the party's slogan to proclaim "the
Constitution as it is, the Union as it was, *and the Niggers where they
are.*"[34]

Lincoln's suspension of habeas corpus to enforce the militia draft also
hurt the Republicans. "A large majority," declared an Ohio editor, "can
see no reason why *they* should be shot for the benefit of niggers and
Abolitionists." If "the *despot* Lincoln" tried to ram abolition and conscription down the throats of white men, "he would meet with the fate
he deserves: hung, shot, or burned."[35] The arrests of Democrats for
antiwar activities and the indictment of forty-seven members of the Knights
of the Golden Circle in Indiana probably backfired against Republicans
by enabling Democrats to portray themselves as martyrs to civil liberty.

Subsuming all these issues was the war itself. "After a year and a half
of trial," admitted one Republican, "and a pouring out of blood and
treasure, and the maiming and death of thousands, we have made no

32. O.R., Ser. I, Vol. 19, pt. 2, pp. 295–96.
33. Nevins, War, II, 302, 303.
34. Wood Gray, The Hidden Civil War: The Story of the Copperheads (New York,
    1942), 115; Frank L. Klement, The Limits of Dissent: Clement L. Vallandigham
    and the Civil War (Lexington, Ky., 1970), 106, 107.
35. Gray, Hidden Civil War, 112.

sensible progress in putting down the rebellion. . . . The people are desirous of some change, they scarcely know what." [36] This remained true even after northern armies turned back Confederate invasions at Antietam, Perryville, and Corinth. None of these battles was a clear-cut Union victory; the failure to follow them with a blow to the retreating rebels produced a feeling of letdown. In October, enemy forces stood in a more favorable position than five months earlier: Bragg's army occupied Murfreesboro in central Tennessee only thirty miles from Nashville, and Lee's army remained only a few miles from Harper's Ferry. Jeb Stuart's cavalry had thumbed their noses at the Yankees again by riding around the entire Army of the Potomac (October 10–12), raiding as far north as Chambersburg, Pennsylvania, and returning to their own lines with 1,200 horses while losing only two men. If anything seemed to underscore northern military futility, this was it.

Democrats scored significant gains in the 1862 elections: the governorship of New York, the governorship and a majority of the legislature in New Jersey, a legislative majority in Illinois and Indiana, and a net increase of thirty-four congressmen. Only the fortuitous circumstance that legislative and gubernatorial elections in Ohio and Pennsylvania were held in odd-numbered years and that the Republican governors of Illinois and Indiana had been elected in 1860 to four-year terms prevented the probable loss of these posts to the Democrats in 1862. Panicky Republicans interpreted the elections as "a great, sweeping revolution of public sentiment," *"a most serious and severe reproof."* Gleeful Democrats pronounced "Abolition Slaughtered." [37] Nearly all historians have agreed: the elections were "a near disaster for the Republicans"; "a great triumph for the Democrats"; "the verdict of the polls showed clearly that the people of the North were opposed to the Emancipation Proclamation." [38]

But a closer look at the results challenges this conclusion. Republicans retained control of seventeen of the nineteen free-state governorships and sixteen of the legislatures. They elected several congressmen in

36. *Ibid.*, 110.
37. Strong, *Diary*, 271; Carl Schurz to Lincoln, Nov. 20, 1861, in *CWL*, V, 511; *Indianapolis State Sentinel*, Oct. 5, 1861, quoted in V. Jacque Voegeli, *Free But Not Equal: The Midwest and the Negro during the Civil War* (Chicago, 1967), 64.
38. Peter J. Parish, *The American Civil War* (New York, 1975), 208–9; Joel H. Silbey, *A Respectable Minority: The Democratic Party in the Civil War Era, 1860–1868* (New York, 1977), 144; William B. Hesseltine, *Lincoln and the War Governors* (New York, 1948), 165.

Missouri for the first time, made a net *gain* of five seats in the Senate, and retained a twenty-five-vote majority in the House after experiencing the *smallest* net loss of congressional seats in an off-year election in twenty years. It is true that the congressional delegations of the six lower-North states from New York to Illinois would have a Democratic majority for the next two years. But elsewhere the Republicans more than held their own. And the Democratic margins in most of those six states were exceedingly thin: 4,000 votes in Pennsylvania, 6,000 in Ohio, 10,000 each in New York and Indiana. These majorities could be explained, as Lincoln noted, by the absence of soldiers at the front, for scattered evidence already hinted at a large Republican edge among enlisted men, a hint that would be confirmed in future elections when absentee soldier voting was permitted.[39]

Although disappointed by the elections, Lincoln and the Republicans did not allow it to influence their actions. Indeed, the pace of radicalism increased during the next few months. On November 7, Lincoln removed McClellan from command of the Army of the Potomac. Although military factors prompted this action, it had important political overtones. In December the House decisively rejected a Democratic resolution branding emancipation "a high crime against the Constitution," and endorsed the Emancipation Proclamation by a party-line vote. Congress also passed an enabling act requiring the abolition of slavery as a condition of West Virginia's admission to statehood.[40]

During December the Democratic press speculated that Lincoln, having been rebuked by the voters, would not issue the final Emancipation Proclamation. The president's message to Congress on December 1 fed this speculation. Lincoln again recommended his favorite plan for gradual, compensated emancipation in every state "wherein slavery now exists." Worried abolitionists asked each other: "If the President means to carry out his edict of freedom on the New Year, what is all this stuff about gradual emancipation?" But both the friends and enemies of freedom misunderstood Lincoln's admittedly ambiguous message. Some failed to notice his promise that all slaves freed "by the chances of war"—

39. *The Tribune Almanac for 1863* (New York, 1863), 50–64; Lincoln to Carl Schurz, Nov. 10, 1862, in *CWL*, V, 494; Daniel Wallace Adams, "Illinois Soldiers and the Emancipation Proclamation," *Journal of the Illinois State Historical Society*, 67 (1974), 408–10; Oscar O. Winther, "The Soldier Vote in the Election of 1864," *New York History*, 25 (1944), 440–58.

40. *CG*, 37 Cong., 3 Sess., 15, 52; *U.S. Statutes at Large*, XII, 633.

including his Proclamation—would remain forever free. The Proclamation was a war measure applicable only against states in rebellion; Lincoln's gradual emancipation proposal was a peace measure to *abolish the institution* everywhere by constitutional means. The president's peroration should have left no doubt of his position: "Fellow citizens, *we* cannot escape history. . . . The fiery trial through which we pass, will light us down, in honor or dishonor, to the latest generation. . . . The dogmas of the quiet past, are inadequate to the stormy present. . . . In *giving* freedom to the *slave*, we *assure* freedom to the *free*. . . . We must disenthrall ourselves, and then we shall save our country."[41]

On New Year's Day Lincoln ended all speculation. The Proclamation he signed that day exempted the border states along with Tennessee and Union-controlled portions of Louisiana and Virginia. To meet the criticism that the preliminary Proclamation had invited slaves to revolt, the final edict enjoined them to "abstain from all violence." But in other respects this Proclamation went beyond the first one. Not only did it justify emancipation as an "act of justice" as well as a military necessity, but it also sanctioned the enlistment of black soldiers and sailors in Union forces.[42]

Here was revolution in earnest. Armed blacks were truly the *bête noire* of southern nightmares. The idea of black soldiers did not, of course, spring full-blown from Lincoln's head at the time of the Emancipation Proclamation. The notion had been around since the beginning of the war, when northern blacks in several cities had volunteered for the Union army. But on the principle that it was "a white man's war," the War Department had refused to accept them. Despite the service of black soldiers in the Revolution and the War of 1812, Negroes had been barred from state militias since 1792 and the regular army had never enrolled black soldiers. The prejudices of the old order died hard. Lincoln had squelched Secretary of War Cameron's reference to arming slaves in December 1861, and the administration refused at first to accept the organization of black regiments in Kansas, occupied Louisiana, and the South Carolina sea islands during the summer of 1862.

The Union navy, however, had taken men of all colors and conditions from the outset. Blacks at sea served mainly as firemen, coal heavers, cooks, and stewards. But as early as August 1861 a group of contra-

41. *Boston Commonwealth*, Dec. 6, 1862; CWL, V, 529–37.
42. CWL, VI, 28–30.

bands served as a gun crew on the *U.S.S. Minnesota*. In May 1862 a South Carolina slave, Robert Smalls, commandeered a dispatch boat in Charleston harbor and ran it out to the blockading fleet. Smalls became a pilot in the U. S. navy.

Meanwhile black leaders, abolitionists, and radical Republicans continued to push for enlistment of black soldiers. This would not only help the North win the war, they said; it would also help free the slaves and earn equal rights for the whole race. Frederick Douglass made the point succinctly: "Once let the black man get upon his person the brass letters, U.S.; let him get an eagle on his button, and a musket on his shoulder and bullets in his pocket, and there is no power on earth which can deny that he has earned the right to citizenship."[43]

Helping blacks to earn citizenship was not the main motive for a congressional mandate (in the militia act of July 17, 1862) to enroll Negroes in "any military or naval service for which they may be found competent." Rather, the need for labor battalions to free white soldiers for combat prompted this legislation. The Emancipation Proclamation envisaged a limited role for black soldiers "to garrison forts, positions, stations, and other places" instead of to fight as front-line troops. But reality had a way of surpassing policy. Just as Lincoln, nine days before issuing the preliminary Proclamation, had told a delegation that such an edict would be like the Pope's bull against the comet, so on August 4, three weeks before the War Department authorized enlistment of contrabands as soldiers in occupied South Carolina, he told a delegation that "to arm the negroes would turn 50,000 bayonets against us that were for us."[44] But even as Lincoln uttered these words, a regiment of free Negroes was completing its organization in Louisiana and a regiment of free and contraband blacks was forming in Kansas. Two more Louisiana regiments along with the authorized South Carolina regiment quietly completed their organization during the fall. In October the Kansans saw action in a Missouri skirmish that left ten of them dead— the first black combat casualties of the war.

By the year's end the government was ready to acknowledge the existence of these regiments. It could hardly help but do so, for Massachusetts had gotten into the act. The colonel of the 1st South Carolina Volunteers was the Bay State's Thomas Wentworth Higginson, whose pen was at least as mighty as his sword. After taking part of his regiment

43. *Douglass' Monthly*, Aug. 1863.
44. *O.R.*, Ser. I, Vol. 14, pp. 377–78; *CWL*, V, 357.

on a minor raid along a South Carolina river in January 1863, Higginson wrote an enthusiastic report to the War Department which, as intended, found its way into the newspapers. "Nobody knows anything about these men who has not seen them in battle," wrote Higginson. "No officer in this regiment now doubts that the key to the successful prosecution of the war lies in the unlimited employment of black troops." The *New York Tribune* commented that such reports were sure "to shake our inveterate Saxon prejudice against the capacity and courage of negro troops."[45] About the time of Higginson's raid, Governor Andrew of Massachusetts squeezed permission from the War Department to raise a black regiment. Commissioning prominent abolitionists as recruiters and officers, Andrew enlisted enough men from northern states for two regiments, the 54th and 55th Massachusetts, the first of which became the most famous black regiment of the war.

The recruitment of black soldiers did not produce an instantaneous change in northern racial attitudes. Indeed, to some degree it intensified the Democratic backlash against emancipation and exacerbated racial tensions in the army. The black regiments reflected the Jim Crow mores of the society that reluctantly accepted them: they were segregated, given less pay then white soldiers, commanded by white officers some of whom regarded their men as "niggers," and intended for use mainly as garrison and labor battalions. One of the first battles these black troops had to fight was for a chance to prove themselves in combat.

Even so, the organization of black regiments marked the transformation of a war to preserve the Union into a revolution to overthrow the old order. Lincoln's conversion from reluctance to enthusiasm about black soldiers signified the progress of this revolution. By March 1863 the president was writing to Andrew Johnson, military governor of Tennessee: "The bare sight of fifty thousand armed, and drilled black soldiers on the banks of the Mississippi, would end the rebellion at once. And who doubts that we can present that sight, if we but take hold in earnest?"[46]

The southern response to emancipation and the enlistment of black troops was ferocious—at least on paper and, regrettably, sometimes in fact as well. Upon learning of the preliminary Emancipation Proclamation, General Beauregard called for "execution of abolition prisoners [i.e., captured Union soldiers] after 1st of January. . . . Let the exe-

45. O.R., Ser. I, Vol. 14, pp. 195–98; *New York Tribune*, Feb. 11, 1863.
46. Lincoln to Johnson, Mar. 26, 1863, CWL, VI, 149–50.

cution be with the garrote." Jefferson Davis's message to Congress on January 12, 1863, pronounced the Emancipation Proclamation "the most execrable measure in the history of guilty man." Davis promised to turn over captured Union officers to state governments for punishment as "criminals engaged in inciting servile insurrection." The punishment for this crime, of course, was death.[47]

Sober second thoughts prevented the enforcement of such a policy. But the South did sometimes execute captured black soldiers and their officers. Even before official adoption of black enlistment by the Union government, southerners got wind of the premature efforts along this line in occupied Louisiana and South Carolina. From Confederate army headquarters on August 21, 1862, came a general order that such "crimes and outrages" required "retaliation" in the form of "execution as a felon" of any officer of black troops who was captured. When a rebel commando raid seized four blacks in Union uniforms on a South Carolina island in November, Secretary of War James A. Seddon and President Davis approved their "summary execution" as an "example" to discourage the arming of slaves.[48] A month later, on Christmas Eve, Davis issued a general order requiring all former slaves and their officers captured in arms to be delivered up to state officials for trial. On May 30, 1863, the Confederate Congress sanctioned this policy but stipulated that captured officers were to be tried and punished by military courts rather than by the states.[49]

Though the South did not actually do this, considerable evidence indicates that captured officers were sometimes "dealt with red-handed on the field or immediately thereafter," as Secretary of War Seddon suggested to General Kirby Smith in 1863. Black prisoners of war were sometimes shot "while attempting to escape." A Confederate colonel whose regiment captured a squad of black soldiers in Louisiana reported that when some of them tried to escape, "I then ordered every one shot, and with my Six Shooter I assisted in the execution of the order." A North Carolina soldier wrote to his mother that after a skirmish with a black regiment "several [were] taken prisoner & afterwards either bayoneted or burnt. The men were perfectly exasperated at the idea of negroes opposed to them & rushed at them like so many devils."[50]

47. Beauregard to W. Porcher Miles, Oct. 13, 1862, in O.R., Ser. II, Vol. 4, p. 916; Rowland, *Davis*, V, 409.
48. O.R., Ser. II, Vol. 4, pp. 857, 945–46, 954.
49. *Ibid.*, Vol. 5, pp. 797, 940–41.
50. Seddon to Kirby Smith, Aug. 12, 1863, in O.R., Ser. I, Vol. 22, pt. 1, p. 965;

Rumors and reports of several such massacres vexed Union authorities through the rest of the war and forced them more than once to threaten retaliation. This was one reason for the hesitation to use black troops in combat, where they ran a heightened risk of capture. The Confederate refusal to treat captured black soldiers as legitimate prisoners of war contributed to the eventual breakdown in prisoner of war exchanges that had tragic consequences for both sides.

III

Northern diplomats were disappointed by the initial skeptical response of many Englishmen to the Emancipation Proclamation. But as the real import of the edict sank in, and as Lincoln made clear on January 1 that he really meant it, British antislavery sentiment mobilized for the Union. Mass meetings took place throughout the kingdom. Confederate sympathizers were forced to lie low for a time. The effect of "this development of sentiment," noted Charles Francis Adams happily, "is to annihilate all agitation for recognition." Young Henry Adams, whose mood tended to swing from despair to euphoria, was thrilled by the outpouring of British pro-Union expressions. "The Emancipation Proclamation has done more for us here than all our former victories and all our diplomacy," wrote Henry with hyperbole to his brother Charles Francis, Jr., a cavalry captain in the Army of the Potomac. "If only you at home don't have disasters, we will give such a checkmate to the foreign hopes of the rebels as they never yet have had."[51]

But the Union armies did have more disasters. The foreign hopes as well as domestic prospects of the rebels rose again during this northern winter of discontent.

Col. Frank Powers to Col. Jonathan L. Logan, Sept. 2, 1863, in Ira Berlin et al., ed., *Freedom: A Documentary History of Emancipation*, Series II, *The Black Military Experience* (Cambridge, 1982), 585; Thomas R. Roulhac to his mother, March 13, 1864, in Randall Clair Jimerson, "A People Divided: The Civil War Interpreted by Participants," Ph.D. dissertation, University of Michigan, 1977, p. 146.
51. Ford, *Cycle of Adams Letters*, I, 243.

19

Three Rivers in Winter, 1862–1863

I

Although disappointed by McClellan's failure to thrash Lee at Antietam, Lincoln expected the Army of the Potomac to push after the rebels and fight them again while they were far from home. Lincoln visited the army in early October and urged McClellan to get moving before the Confederates could be reinforced and refitted. Upon returning to Washington, the president had Halleck send McClellan an order: "Cross the Potomac and give battle. . . . Your army must move now while the roads are good."[1]

But McClellan as usual protested that he could not act until his supply wagons were full and his soldiers reorganized. Halleck threw up his hands in despair. He knew that the Army of Northern Virginia was in worse shape than the Army of the Potomac. "I am sick, tired, and disgusted" with McClellan's inactivity, wrote Halleck in October. "There is an immobility here that exceeds all that any man can conceive of. It requires the lever of Archimedes to move this inert mass." Republicans shared Halleck's impatience. "What devil is it that prevents the Potomac Army from advancing?" asked the editor of the *Chicago Tribune* on October 13. "What malign influence palsies our army and wastes these glorious days for fighting? If it is McClellan, does not the President see that he is a traitor?"[2]

1. Halleck to McClellan, Oct. 6, 1862, *O.R.*, Ser. I, Vol. 19, pt. 1, p. 72.
2. Halleck to Hamilton R. Gamble, Oct. 30, 1862, *ibid.*, Ser. III, Vol. 2, pp. 703–4;

Lincoln too was becoming exasperated. But instead of removing McClellan he decided to try some fatherly advice. "You remember my speaking to you of what I called your over-cautiousness," Lincoln wrote the general on October 13. "Are you not over-cautious when you assume that you can not do what the enemy is constantly doing?" McClellan had argued that his men could not march twenty miles a day and fight without full stomachs and new shoes. Yet the rebels marched and fought with little food and no shoes. To wait for a full supply pipeline "ignores the question of *time*, which can not and must not be ignored." If McClellan crossed the Potomac quickly and got between the enemy and Richmond he could force Lee into the open for a fight to the finish. "We should not so operate as to merely drive him away. If we can not beat the enemy where he now is [west of Harper's Ferry], we never can. . . . If we never try, we shall never succeed."[3]

But this appeal failed to move McClellan. When little happened for another two weeks except telegrams citing broken-down horses, Lincoln lost patience: "Will you pardon me for asking what the horses of your army have done since the battle of Antietam that fatigues anything?" Such goading made McClellan waspish. "The good of the country," he wrote to his wife, "requires me to submit to all this from men whom I know to be my inferior! . . . There never was a truer epithet applied to a certain individual than that of the 'Gorilla.' "[4] In truth, McClellan had again lost sight of reality. Considering himself the hero of Antietam, he believed he could dictate to the government. "I have insisted that Stanton shall be removed, & that Halleck shall give way to me as Comdr. in Chief," McClellan informed his wife. "The only safety for the country & for me is to get rid of the lot of them."[5]

The Army of the Potomac finally began to cross its namesake river on October 26, but moved so slowly that Lee was able to interpose Longstreet's corps between Richmond and the bluecoats while Jackson remained in the Shenandoah Valley on McClellan's flank. For Lincoln this was the last straw; he was tired of trying to "bore with an auger too dull to take hold." On November 7 he replaced McClellan with Burn-

---

Joseph Medill to O. M. Hatch, Oct. 13, quoted in James V. Murfin, *The Gleam of Bayonets* (New York, 1965), 300.

3. *CWL*, V, 460–61.
4. Lincoln to McClellan, Oct. 25, 1862, *ibid.*, 474; McClellan to Ellen Marcy McClellan, undated but probably Oct. 30, 1862, McClellan Papers, Library of Congress.
5. McClellan to Ellen McClellan, Sept. 20, Oct. 31, 1862, McClellan Papers.

side.[6] To his private secretary Lincoln explained that when McClellan kept "delaying on little pretexts of wanting this and that I began to fear that he was playing false—that he did not want to hurt the enemy." If he let Lee block an advance toward Richmond "I determined to . . . remove him. He did so & I relieved him."[7]

McClellan's farewell to the army was emotional. A few officers muttered darkly about "changing front on Washington" and "throwing the infernal scoundrels into the Potomac." Nothing came of this, however, and nothing in McClellan's tenure of command became him like his leaving of it. "Stand by General Burnside as you have stood by me, and all will be well," he told the men as they yelled their affection for the leader who had created them as an army. Among those who most regretted McClellan's removal was Burnside himself. Although he was one of the few Union generals in the East with marked successes to his credit—along the coast of North Carolina—Burnside considered himself unqualified to command the Army of the Potomac. This conviction would all too soon be confirmed.

Burnside started well, however. Instead of continuing straight south, using the vulnerable railroad through Manassas as his supply line, he moved the ponderous army of 110,000 men with unwonted speed to Falmouth, across the Rappahannock from Fredericksburg. From there he hoped to cross the river and drive toward Richmond, with his supply line secured by naval control of the rivers flowing into the Chesapeake Bay. The drawback to this strategy was the number of rivers the army would have to cross, beginning with the Rappahannock. By moving quickly, though, Burnside had gotten two advance corps to Falmouth on November 17, before Lee could shift troops to block a crossing. But the pontoons Burnside needed to bridge the river did not show up for more than a week—a delay caused by Burnside's unfortunate knack for issuing unclear instructions and Halleck's misunderstanding of where and when Burnside intended to cross the river. As a result, Lee had most of his 75,000 men dug in along the hills south of the Rappahannock by the time the pontoons arrived.

Lee was willing to sit there all winter, but Burnside could not afford to do so. Lincoln and the public expected an offensive. After thinking

6. Quotation from Foote, *Civil War*, I, 752. The order removing McClellan from command was dated November 5 but delivered on November 7; the order is in *CWL*, V, 485.
7. Dennett, *Lincoln/Hay*, 218–19.

it over and concluding that Lee would expect him to cross the river above or below Fredericksburg, Burnside decided that "the enemy will be more surprised by a crossing immediately in our front." Lee was surprised only by the folly of this move. He had Longstreet's corps posted along four miles of high ground overlooking Fredericksburg with a sweeping field of fire over the half-mile of open fields that attacking troops would have to cross. As one of Longstreet's artillery officers put it, "a chicken could not live on that field when we open on it."[8] Hoping that the Federals would assault this position, Lee decided to offer just enough resistance to their river crossing to give Jackson's corps time to move upstream and connect with Longstreet to extend the Confederate line another three miles.

In the pre-dawn darkness of December 11, Union engineers began laying three pontoon bridges at Fredericksburg and three more a couple of miles downstream. Covered by artillery, the downstream bridge-builders did their job without trouble. But in Fredericksburg a brigade of Mississippians firing from buildings and rifle-pits picked off the engineers as soon as it became light enough to see. Federal artillery shelled the buildings (most civilians had been evacuated) but the rebel snipers continued to fire from the rubble. Three blue regiments finally crossed in boats and drove them away in house-to-house fighting. After the rest of the army crossed, northern soldiers looted the town, smashing "rebel" furniture, pianos, glassware, and anything else they could find in the abandoned houses.

For many of the looters it was the last night of their lives. The battle of Fredericksburg on December 13 once again pitted great valor in the Union ranks and mismanagement by their commanders against stout fighting and effective generalship on the Confederate side. Burnside's tactics called for the left wing under General William B. Franklin to assault the Confederate right commanded by Jackson while the Union right tapped Longstreet's defenses on Marye's Heights behind the town. If Franklin managed to roll up Jackson's flank, the Union probe on the right could be converted into a real attack. Whatever slim prospects this plan had were marred by Burnside's confusing written orders to Franklin and the latter's failure to push ahead with his 50,000 infantrymen when opportunity offered.

The fog lifted at mid-morning on December 13 to reveal the panoply of Franklin's men advancing across the plain south of Lee's hilltop

8. James Longstreet, "The Battle of Fredericksburg," *Battles and Leaders*, III, 79.

headquarters. These Federals soon assaulted Jackson's position on Prospect Hill. A division of Pennsylvanians commanded by George Gordon Meade found a seam in Jackson's line along a wooded ravine and penetrated the Confederate defenses. Here was a potential breakthrough if supporting troops were thrown in—but Franklin failed to throw them in. Southern reserves double-timed forward and counterattacked, driving the Pennsylvanians out of the woods and into the open until halted by Union artillery. Watching anxiously from his command post, Lee sighed with relief as his men repaired the breach, and said to Longstreet: "It is well that war is so terrible—we should grow too fond of it!"[9]

Franklin never got more than half of his men into action and did not renew the attack despite orders from Burnside to do so. Meanwhile the initial probe by the Union right had turned into a series of brigade-size attacks as courageous and hopeless as anything in the war. Wave after wave of blue soldiers poured out of the town toward Marye's Heights. Channeled by ravines, a marsh, and a drainage ditch toward a sunken road fronted by a half-mile long stone fence at the base of the hill, these waves broke fifty yards short of the fence, each one leaving hundreds of dead and dying men as it receded. Behind the fence stood four ranks of Georgians and North Carolinians loading and shooting so fast that their firing achieved the effect of machine guns. Still the Yankees surged forward through the short but endless December afternoon, fourteen brigades in all. "It can hardly be in human nature for men to show more valor," wrote a newspaper reporter, "or generals to manifest less judgment."[10]

When the early twilight finally turned to darkness the Union army had suffered one of its worst defeats of the war. Nearly 13,000 Federals were casualties—about the same number as at Antietam—most of them in front of the stone wall at the base of Marye's Heights. Fighting on the defensive behind good cover, the Confederates suffered fewer than 5,000 casualties. Distraught by the disaster, Burnside wanted personally to lead a desperation charge by his old 9th Corps next day but came to his senses and withdrew the army unmolested across the river on the stormy night of December 15.

Yet another drive "on to Richmond" had come to grief. Fredericksburg brought home the horrors of war to northerners more vividly, per-

9. Douglas Southall Freeman, R. E. Lee: A Biography, 4 vols. (New York, 1934–35), II, 462.
10. Foote, Civil War, II, 44.

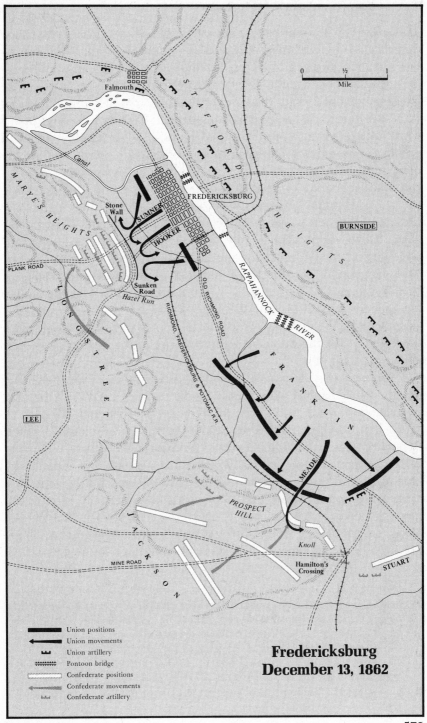

Falmouth

STAFFORD

Canal

MARYE'S HEIGHTS

Stone Wall

SUMNER

FREDERICKSBURG

HEIGHTS

BURNSIDE

HOOKER

PLANK ROAD

Sunken Road

Hazel Run

L O N G S T R E E T

OLD RICHMOND ROAD

RICHMOND, FREDERICKSBURG & POTOMAC R.R.

RAPPAHANNOCK

RIVER

F R A N K L I N

LEE

M E A D E

J A C K S O N

PROSPECT HILL

Knoll

STUART

MINE ROAD

Hamilton's Crossing

0   ½   1
Mile

Union positions
Union movements
Union artillery
Pontoon bridge
Confederate positions
Confederate movements
Confederate artillery

Fredericksburg
December 13, 1862

573

574   BATTLE CRY OF FREEDOM

haps, than any previous battle. The carpet of bodies in front of the stone wall left an indelible mark in the memory of one soldier who helped bury the dead during a truce on December 15. The corpses were "swollen to twice their natural size, black as Negroes in most cases." Here lay "one without a head, there one without legs, yonder a head and legs without a trunk . . . with fragments of shell sticking in oozing brain, with bullet holes all over the puffed limbs." [11] This terrible cost with nothing accomplished created a morale crisis in the army and on the homefront. Soldiers wrote home that "my loyalty is growing weak. . . . I am sick and tired of disaster and the fools that bring disaster upon us. . . . All think Virginia is not worth such a loss of life. . . . Why not confess we are worsted, and come to an agreement?" The people "have borne, silently and grimly, imbecility, treachery, failure, privation, loss of friends," declared the normally staunch *Harper's Weekly*, "but they cannot be expected to suffer that such massacres as this at Fredericksburg shall be repeated." [12] Burnside manfully took the blame, but Lincoln himself became the target for much of the criticism: "He is ignorant, self-willed . . . incompetent." "If there is a worse place than Hell," said the president upon learning of the disaster at Fredericksburg, "I am in it." [13]

These were dark days in Washington. Strange rumors swept the capital: the whole cabinet would resign, to be replaced by War Democrats; or Lincoln himself would resign in favor of Hannibal Hamlin; or McClellan would be recalled to head a military government; or radical Republicans were plotting a coup to reorganize the cabinet. This last rumor contained some truth. On December 16 and 17, Republican senators met in caucus and with but one dissenting vote decided to urge a reorganization of the cabinet. Seward was the intended victim of this move, which reflected the conflict between conservative and radical Republicans symbolized by a cabinet rivalry between Seward and Chase. Playing a deep game that he hoped might land him a future presidential

11. *Ibid.*, 43.
12. Soldiers quoted in Bruce Catton, *Glory Road: The Bloody Route from Fredericksburg to Gettysburg* (Garden City, N.Y., 1952), 95, and in Randall Clair Jimerson, "A People Divided: The Civil War Interpreted by Participants," Ph.D. dissertation, University of Michigan, 1977, p. 339; *Harper's Weekly*, Dec. 27, 1862.
13. George Bancroft quoted in Bruce Catton, *Never Call Retreat: Centennial History of the Civil War*, vol. 3 (Pocket Books ed., New York, 1967), 24; Lincoln quoted in William H. Wadsworth to Samuel L. M. Barlow, Dec. 16, 1862, Barlow Papers, Henry E. Huntington Library.

nomination, Chase had helped create an impression that Seward exercised undue influence over the president. This influence was said to have inhibited the prosecution of vigorous war measures including emancipation, black soldiers, and the appointment of antislavery generals.

Lincoln was "more distressed" by news of the senatorial caucus "than by any event of my life." "What do these men want?" he asked a friend. "They wish to get rid of me, and sometimes I am more than half disposed to gratify them. . . . We are now on the brink of destruction. It appears to me that the Almighty is against us."[14] But the president pulled himself together and handled the affair in a manner that ultimately strengthened his leadership. On December 19 he met with a delegation of Republican senators and listened to speeches "attributing to Mr. Seward a lukewarmness in the conduct of the war." Seward had already offered to resign, but Lincoln did not reveal this. Instead he invited the delegation back next day, when they were surprised to find the whole cabinet (except Seward) on hand. Lincoln defended the absent secretary of state and asserted that all members of the cabinet had supported major policy decisions, for which he as president was solely responsible. Lincoln turned to the cabinet for confirmation. Put on the spot, Chase could only mumble assent. Deflated and embarrassed, the senators departed. Next day a chagrined Chase offered his resignation. Lincoln was now master of the situation. The senators could not get rid of Seward without losing Chase as well. The president refused both resignations. The stormy political atmosphere in Washington began to clear. Though military prospects remained bleak, Lincoln had warded off a threat to his political right flank—for the time being.[15]

II

Jefferson Davis also encountered vexing problems during the winter of 1862–63. While Lincoln faced down senators in Washington, Davis traveled to Tennessee and Mississippi to confront generals about military contretemps in those theaters. In November, Joseph E. Johnston

14. Theodore C. Pease and James G. Randall, eds., *The Diary of Orville Hickman Browning*, 2 vols. (Springfield, Ill., 1927–33), I, 600–601.

15. For contemporary accounts of this crisis, see *ibid.*, 596–604, and Howard K. Beale, ed., *The Diary of Gideon Welles*, 3 vols. (New York, 1960), I, 194–204. For secondary accounts, see Nevins, *War*, II, 350–65, and James G. Randall, *Lincoln the President*, 4 vols. (New York, 1945–55), II, 241–49.

had reported himself ready for duty after recovering from his Seven Pines wounds. Because of his earlier differences with Davis, Johnston had become a rallying point for some of the president's critics. Perhaps to confound these critics, Davis on November 24 named Johnston "plenary commander" of a newly formed Department of the West embracing everything between the Mississippi and the Appalachians. Although this new department appeared impressive on paper, Johnston glumly appraised the appointment as an attempt to put him on the shelf with a "nominal and useless" command.[16] This was unfair, because Davis really did want someone to take charge of the strategic problem in the West. Johnston regarded the task as thankless, in part because the Army of Tennessee at Murfreesboro was still riven by dissension between Bragg and his corps commanders, while the new head of the Army of Mississippi at Vicksburg was unpopular because of his nativity. He was John C. Pemberton, an artillery expert whom Davis had transferred in October from command of the defenses of Charleston to those of Vicksburg. A native of Philadelphia who had become an adoptive southerner by marrying a Virginian, the curt and crusty Pemberton had compiled no combat record that justified to Mississippians the assignment of this "Yankee" to defend their state. Indeed, it is hard to understand why Davis appointed him (instead, for example, of sending Johnston to Vicksburg) except as a way of making room for another problem general, Beauregard. The colorful Creole took Pemberton's place at Charleston, where he had become a hero by firing on Fort Sumter and starting the war.

This kettle of catfish in the West prompted Davis to rise from a sickbed to make a December journey to the afflicted theaters. Instead of straightening matters out, however, this trip in some respects made them worse. Without consulting Johnston, Davis ordered a 7,500-man division in Bragg's army transferred to Pemberton. When Bragg and Johnston protested that this would encourage Rosecrans's army at Nashville to attack the weakened Army of Tennessee, Davis responded that Pemberton faced even longer odds and that holding Vicksburg was more vital than defending middle Tennessee. Accompanying Davis to Vicksburg, Johnston disapproved of Pemberton's defensive arrangements and urged a

16. Joseph E. Johnston, "Jefferson Davis and the Mississippi Campaign," *Battles and Leaders*, II, 475. See also James Lee McDonough, *Stones River: Bloody Winter in Tennessee* (Knoxville, 1980), 33–38.

shorter fortified line that could be held by a skeleton force to free most of the army for mobile operations. Johnston also believed that the main Confederate army in Mississippi was too small for success, and urged its reinforcement from across the river even if this meant the temporary loss of Arkansas. Though Davis suggested that the Arkansas commander send troops to Vicksburg, he did not *order* it—and it was not done. Johnston tried to resign his nugatory post. The president persuaded him to stay on, but their lack of mutual confidence and their differing concepts of strategy boded ill for the future.

For the short term, however, Confederate prospects in the West suddenly took a turn for the better. Applying the previous summer's successful formula, rebel cavalry raids on Union supply lines disrupted Grant's first Vicksburg campaign and came close to wrecking Rosecrans's drive against Bragg.

After the battle of Corinth in October, Grant had launched an invasion southward along the Mississippi Central Railroad to capture Vicksburg. Establishing a forward base at Holly Springs, Grant with 40,000 men had advanced to Oxford by early December. But one enemy in front and two in the rear threatened his further progress. In front, Pemberton entrenched 20,000 men along the Yalabusha River at Grenada. Behind Grant, 150 miles of railroad offered a tempting target to enemy cavalry. Deep in his rear—all the way back to Illinois, in fact—Grant faced a potential threat from his former subordinate John A. McClernand, a political general who was organizing a separate army to proceed down the Mississippi for its own attack on Vicksburg. A War Democrat from Lincoln's home state, McClernand had managed to persuade the president that he could rekindle the patriotism of Democrats in the Old Northwest if given an independent command. Without informing Grant, Lincoln told McClernand to go ahead. With great energy fueled by dreams of military glory, McClernand recruited and forwarded to Memphis dozens of new regiments during the fall. Grant got wind of this activity and requested clarification of his authority. General-in-Chief Halleck, who shared Grant's reservations about McClernand, wired Grant that he had full control of all troops in his department. Halleck also ordered the divisions organized by McClernand formed into two corps to be commanded by McClernand and Sherman. When McClernand learned of this, he protested bitterly to Lincoln that a West Point conspiracy had defrauded him of his army. Lincoln upheld Grant and Halleck, however, and advised McClernand for his own good and the good of the country to obey orders and get on with the war.[17]

McClernand's greatest humiliation occurred when he arrived at Memphis on December 28 to find his troops gone. Grant had again outwitted the political general in the game of army politics, with an unwitting assist from none other than Nathan Bedford Forrest. When Grant learned of the new troops arriving at Memphis he sent Sherman to prepare them for a downriver expedition against Vicksburg in tandem with Grant's overland invasion. This two-pronged drive, if successful, would force Pemberton to divide his outnumbered forces and enable the Federal pincers to close on Vicksburg by land and by river. If McClernand reached Memphis before the river expedition left, he would take command by reason of seniority. Sherman therefore sped his preparations and got off on December 20. Meanwhile Grant's telegram to Illinois informing McClernand of the expedition's imminent departure was delayed because a raid by Forrest had cut Grant's communications.

Grant had little reason to feel thankful to Forrest, however, because this action and another simultaneous cavalry raid by Van Dorn brought Grant's first Vicksburg campaign to grief. Forrest rode westward from central Tennessee in mid-December with 2,000 men. Picking up local guerrillas along the way, Forrest outfought, outmaneuvered, or outbluffed several Union garrisons and cavalry detachments while tearing up fifty miles of railroad and telegraph line, capturing or destroying great quantities of equipment, and inflicting 2,000 Union casualties. The rebels lost only 500 men, who were more than replaced with new recruits attracted by Forrest's hell-for-leather tactics and inspiring leadership. While this was going on, Earl Van Dorn with another cavalry force of 3,500 rode northward from Grenada, circled behind Grant's army, and wrecked the poorly-defended supply depot at Holly Springs on December 20. For good measure Van Dorn tore up several sections of the railroad and returned to Confederate lines before Union horsemen could catch up with him.

Dangling deep in enemy territory without a supply line, Grant called off his advance on Vicksburg. During the retreat to Tennessee the army lived off food and forage seized along the way. Grant was "amazed at the quantity of supplies the country afforded. It showed that we could have subsisted off the country for two months. . . . This taught me a

17. CWL, VI, 70–71; Bruce Catton, *Grant Moves South* (Boston, 1960), 323–340.

lesson."[18] Grant and Sherman would apply the lesson with spectacular results in the future, but just now Grant's retreat left Sherman out on a limb. The latter had taken his (and McClernand's) corps up the Yazoo River a few miles north of Vicksburg for an assault on the Confederate defenses overlooking Chickasaw Bayou. This morass of swamps and waterways offered the only route to high and dry ground for an attack on the northside land defenses of Vicksburg itself. Sherman's plans were based on the assumption that Grant's simultaneous advance would oc-cupy most of Pemberton's troops. The downed telegraph lines prevented Grant from informing Sherman of his withdrawal. On December 29 Sherman managed to get two-thirds of his 32,000 men across the nar-row causeways and through the sloughs for an assault on the bluffs. The 14,000 dug-in defenders knocked them down like tenpins. After losing nearly 1,800 men (to the Confederates' 200), Sherman called it quits. The battered and water-logged bluecoats pulled back to the Mississippi a dozen miles above Vicksburg. News of this repulse added to the gloomy mood in the North.

But tidings soon arrived from Tennessee that relieved some of Lin-coln's distress. Since taking over the Union Army of the Cumberland in late October, William S. Rosecrans had built up supplies and reor-ganized his troops for an advance. Rosecrans was a study in paradox: a man of bulldog courage, he seemed reluctant to get into a fight; slow and methodical in preparation, he moved quickly once he started; a convivial drinking man, he was a devout Catholic who loved to argue theology with his staff officers. Rosecrans had gotten his job because Buell was too cautious; Lincoln prodded Old Rosy to march against the rebels at Murfreesboro forthwith if he wanted to keep the job. After exasperating delays, Rosecrans's 42,000 men finally moved out from Nashville the day after Christmas for the showdown with Bragg's Army of Tennessee.

Bragg had 8,000 fewer infantrymen than Rosecrans. But the rebel cavalry evened the odds. Forrest and Morgan raided deep behind Union lines while Bragg's remaining cavalry under twenty-six-year-old Joseph Wheeler slowed the northern infantry with hit-and-run skirmishes. On December 29, Wheeler took off on a ride completely around the enemy rear where he wreaked havoc on supply wagons and captured part of Rosecrans's reserve ammunition. But the Yankees came on relentlessly. On December 30 they moved into line two miles northwest of Mur-

18. *Personal Memoirs of U. S. Grant*, 2 vols. (New York, 1885–86), I, 435.

freesboro to confront Bragg's divisions drawn up astride Stones River. Both commanders formed similar plans for the morrow: to turn the enemy's right, get into his rear, and cut him off from his base. As the two armies bedded down a few hundred yards from each other, their bands commenced a musical battle as prelude to the real thing next day. Northern musicians blared out "Yankee Doodle" and "Hail Columbia," and were answered across the way by "Dixie" and "The Bonnie Blue Flag." One band finally swung into the sentimental strains of "Home Sweet Home"; others picked it up and soon thousands of Yanks and Rebs who tomorrow would kill each other were singing the familiar words together.

At dawn on December 31 the southerners struck first, catching the bluecoats at breakfast as they had done twice before, at Donelson and Shiloh. This time their initial success was even greater, as 13,000 rebels massed on the left "swooped down on those Yankees like a whirl-a-gust of woodpeckers in a hail storm," in the words of a Tennessee private.[19] In several hours of ferocious fighting the graybacks drove back the Union flank three miles, but were stopped short of the railroad and turnpike in the Union rear. Rosecrans cancelled his attack on the Confederate right and rushed reinforcements to shore up his own crumpled right. Old Rosy was at his bulldog best in this crisis, riding from one part of the line to another, his uniform spattered with blood from a staff officer beheaded by a cannonball while riding alongside Rosecrans.

The Union army was saved from disaster during the morning by the fierce resistance of Philip Sheridan's division in the right center. Anticipating Bragg's tactics, Sheridan had his division awake and under arms by 4:00 A.M.; when the rebels swept down on them after wrecking two other Union divisions, Sheridan's men were ready. They shredded and slowed the rebel attack at heavy cost to themselves as well as to the enemy: all three of Sheridan's brigade commanders were killed and more than one-third of his men became casualties in four hours of fighting. By noon the Union line had been forced into the shape of a bent jack-knife. The hinge was located in a patch of woods along the railroad and turnpike known locally as the Round Forest. Believing this position the key to the Union defense, Bragg ordered the division commanded by John C. Breckinridge—Buchanan's vice president and the southern Democratic presidential candidate in 1860—to go forward in a do or die attack on the Round Forest. They went, many died, but the Yan-

19. Foote, *Civil War*, II, 87.

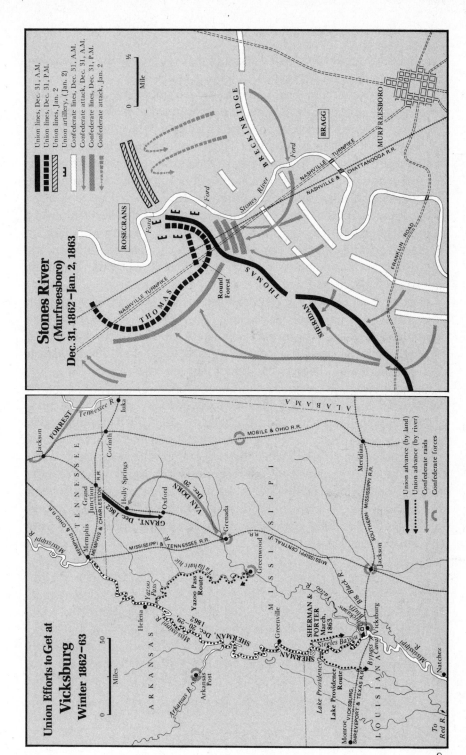

Stones River (Murfreesboro)
Dec. 31, 1862 – Jan. 2, 1863

Union lines, Dec. 31, A.M.
Union lines, Dec. 31, P.M.
Union lines, Jan. 2
Union artillery, (Jan. 2)
Confederate lines, Dec. 31, A.M.
Confederate attack, Dec. 31, A.M.
Confederate lines, Dec. 31, P.M.
Confederate attack, Jan. 2

0   ½
Mile

ROSECRANS

BRECKINRIDGE

BRAGG

THOMAS

SHERIDAN

THOMAS

Round
Forest

NASHVILLE TURNPIKE

NASHVILLE TURNPIKE

NASHVILLE & CHATTANOOGA R.R.

FRANKLIN ROAD

MURFREESBORO

Stones River

Ford

Ford

Ford

Ford

Ford

Union Efforts to Get at Vicksburg
Winter 1862–63

0   50
Miles

Union advance (by land)
Union advance (by river)
Confederate raids
Confederate forces

TENNESSEE

ALABAMA

MISSISSIPPI

ARKANSAS

LOUISIANA

Tennessee R.

Jackson

FORREST

Iuka

Corinth

MOBILE & OHIO R.R.

Meridian

Memphis

Grand
Junction

MEMPHIS & CHARLESTON R.R.

Holly Springs

Oxford

GRANT, Dec. 1862

VAN DORN
Dec. 20

Grenada

MISSISSIPPI & TENNESSEE R.R.

Greenwood

MISSISSIPPI CENTRAL R.R.

SOUTHERN MISSISSIPPI R.R.

Jackson

MEMPHIS & OHIO R.R.

Mississippi R.

Helena

Yazoo
Pass

Yazoo Pass
Route

To Tallahatchie R.

SHERMAN, Dec. 20–29

Greenville

Yazoo R.

Big Black R.

SHERMAN &
PORTER
March, 1863

SHERMAN

Steeles Bayou

Haines
Bluff

Vicksburg

Lake Providence
Route

Lake Providence

Monroe

VICKSBURG,
SHREVEPORT & TEXAS R.R.

Biggs
Canal

Natchez

To
Red R.

Arkansas R.

Arkansas
Post

581

kees held firm amid firing so deafening that many soldiers stuffed their ears with cotton plucked from the fields.

The darkness of New Year's Eve descended on a scene filled not with the sound of music but with the cries of wounded men calling for help. Bragg believed that he had won a great victory and wired the good news to Richmond, where it produced "great exaltation." Bragg's dispatch added that the enemy "is falling back."[20] But this was wishful thinking. During the night Rosecrans held a council of war with his commanders and decided to hold tight. Skirmishes on New Year's Day took a few more lives, but the main action on January 1 was the occupation of a hill east of Stones River by a Union division. On January 2 Bragg ordered Breckinridge to clear this force off the hill. The Kentuckian protested that such an attack would fail with great loss because Union artillery on high ground across the river would enfilade his line. Bragg insisted, Breckinridge's men swept forward with a yell and routed the bluecoats, but then were indeed cut down by fifty-eight Union guns across the river and driven back to their starting point by an infantry counterattack, having lost 1,500 men in an hour. This affair added to the growing tension between Bragg and his generals.

Nonplussed by Rosecrans's refusal to retreat, Bragg seemed not to know what to do. But in truth there was little he could do, for more than a third of his troops had been killed, wounded, or captured. The Yankees had suffered 31 percent casualties, making Stones River the most deadly battle of the war in proportion to numbers engaged. When Bragg awoke on January 3 to find the enemy still in place and receiving reinforcements from Nashville, he knew the game was up. That night the rebels pulled back to a new position behind the Duck River, twenty-five miles to the south. For the second time in three months, the Army of Tennessee had retreated after its commander claimed to have won a victory.

The outcome at Stones River brought a thin gleam of cheer to the North. It blunted, temporarily, the mounting copperhead offensive against the administration's war policy. "God bless you, and all with you," Lincoln wired Rosecrans. "I can never forget, whilst I remember anything," the president wrote later, that "you gave us a hard earned victory which, had there been a defeat instead, the nation could hardly have lived

20. O.R., Ser. I, Vol. 20, pt. 1, p. 662, Vol. 52, pt. 2, p. 402; Jones, *War Clerk's Diary* (Miers), 145.

over."[21] The Army of the Cumberland was so crippled by this "victory," however, that Rosecrans felt unable to renew the offensive for several months.

While Washington breathed a sigh of relief after Stones River, dissension came to a head in the Army of Tennessee. All of Bragg's corps and division commanders expressed a lack of confidence in their chief. Senior Generals William J. Hardee and Leonidas Polk asked Davis to put Johnston in command of the army. Division commander B. Franklin Cheatham vowed he would never again serve under Bragg. Breckinridge wanted to challenge Bragg to a duel. Bragg struck back, court-martialing one division commander for disobeying orders, accusing another (Cheatham) of drunkenness during the battle, and blaming Breckinridge for inept leadership. This internecine donnybrook threatened to do more damage to the army than the Yankees had done. Disheartened, Bragg told a friend that it might "be better for the President to send someone to relieve me," and wrote Davis to the same effect.[22]

Davis passed the buck to Johnston by asking him to look into the situation and recommend a solution. Johnston passed it back. He found many officers hostile to Bragg but reported the enlisted men to be in good condition with high morale. This dubious discovery prompted him to advise Bragg's retention in command. Davis had apparently wanted and expected Johnston to take command himself. But what Johnston wanted, it appeared from his letters to friends, was to return to his old post as head of the Army of Northern Virginia! If the government desired to replace Bragg, he said, let them send Longstreet to Tennessee. And if they thought that Johnston's supervisory role over the whole Western Department was so important, let them put Lee in charge of it and give Johnston his old job in Virginia. In March the War Department virtually ordered Johnston to take command of the Army of Tennessee. But he demurred on the grounds that to remove Bragg while his wife was critically ill would be inhumane. Johnston himself then fell ill. So Bragg stayed on and continued to feud with his leading subordinates.[23]

21. CWL, VI, 39, 424.
22. Bragg to Clement C. Clay, Jan. 10, 1863, Bragg to Davis, Jan. 17, quoted in Catton, *Never Call Retreat*, 49.
23. Johnston to Louis T. Wigfall, March 4, 8, 1863, quoted in *ibid.*, 52; Thomas L.

Lincoln handled similar disaffection in the Army of the Potomac with more deftness and firmness than Davis had shown. Demoralization reached epidemic proportions in this army after Fredericksburg. Four generals in the 6th Corps headed by William B. Franklin went directly to Lincoln with complaints about Burnside's leadership. McClellan's friends were declaring that "we *must* have McClellan back with unlimited and unfettered powers." [24] Joe Hooker was intriguing to obtain the command for himself. Hooker also told a reporter that what the country needed was a dictator. Men in the ranks were deserting at the rate of a hundred or more every day during January. Thousands of others went on the sicklist because slack discipline in regimental camps and corruption in the commissary had produced sanitary and dietary deficiencies. Recognizing that he had lost the army's confidence, Burnside offered to resign—suggesting to Lincoln at the same time that he fire Stanton, Halleck, and several disgruntled generals.

Discord in the Army of the Potomac climaxed with the inglorious "Mud March." Unusually dry January weather encouraged Burnside to plan a crossing of the Rappahannock at fords several miles above Fredericksburg. Success would put the Federals on Lee's flank and force the rebels out of their trenches for a fair fight. Some of Burnside's subordinates openly criticized the move. Franklin "has talked so much and so loudly to this effect," wrote an artillery colonel, "that he has completely demoralized his whole command." [25] Even God seemed to be against Burnside. As soon as the general got his army in motion on January 20 the heavens opened, rain fell in torrents, and the Virginia roads turned into swamps. Artillery carriages sank to their axles, men sank to their knees, mules sank to their ears. Confederate pickets across the river watched this with amusement and held up signs pointing "This Way to Richmond." With his army bogged down in the mud, Burnside on January 22 called the whole thing off.

The mortified and furious commander hastened to Washington and told the president that either Hooker, Franklin, and a half-dozen other generals must go, or he would. Lincoln decided to remove Burnside— probably to the latter's relief. The president also transferred a few other

---

Connelly, *Autumn of Glory: The Army of Tennessee, 1862–1865* (Baton Rouge, 1971), 70–92.

24. Catton, *Never Call Retreat*, 63.

25. Charles S. Wainwright, *A Diary of Battle*, ed. Allan Nevins (New York, 1962), 157–58.

malcontents to distant posts. But Lincoln astonished Burnside by appointing Hooker as his successor. Fighting Joe was hardly an exemplary character. Not only had he schemed against Burnside, but his moral reputation stood none too high. Hooker's headquarters, wrote Charles Francis Adams, Jr., archly, was "a place which no self-respecting man liked to go, and no decent woman could go. It was a combination of barroom and brothel."[26]

But Hooker proved a popular choice with the men. He took immediate steps to cashier corrupt quartermasters, improve the food, clean up the camps and hospitals, grant furloughs, and instill unit pride by creating insignia badges for each corps. Hooker reorganized the cavalry into a separate corps, a much-needed reform based on the Confederate model. Morale rose in all branches of the army. Sickness declined, desertions dropped, and a grant of amnesty brought many AWOLs back to the ranks. "Under Hooker, we began to *live*," wrote a soldier. An officer who disliked Hooker admitted that "I have never known men to change from a condition of the lowest depression to that of a healthy fighting state in so short a time."[27]

When Lincoln appointed Hooker he handed him a letter which the general later described as the kind of missive that a wise father might write to his son. Hooker should know, wrote the president, "that there are some things in regard to which, I am not quite satisfied with you." In running down Burnside "you have taken counsel of your ambition . . . in which you did a great wrong to the country, and to a most meritorious and honorable brother officer. I have heard, in such way as to believe it, of your recently saying that both the Army and the Government needed a Dictator. Of course it was not *for* this, but in spite of it, that I have given you the command. Only those generals who gain successes, can set up dictators. What I now ask of you is military success, and I will risk the dictatorship."[28] Two months after appointing Hooker, Lincoln visited the Army of the Potomac on the Rappahannock. The president was pleased by what he saw, and agreed with Hooker's proud description of it as "the finest army on the planet." Lincoln was less enthusiastic about the general's cockiness. The question, said Hooker, was not *whether* he would take Richmond, but *when*. "The

26. Quoted in Foote, *Civil War*, II, 233–34.
27. Catton, *Glory Road*, 161; Darius N. Couch, "Sumner's 'Right Grand Division,' " *Battles and Leaders*, III, 119.
28. CWL, VI, 78–79.

hen is the wisest of all the animal creation," Lincoln remarked pointedly, "because she never cackles until the egg is laid."[29]

III

While the armies in Virginia sat out the rest of the winter and the
armies in Tennessee licked their wounds after Stones River, plenty of
action but little fighting took place around Vicksburg. After the failure
of his first campaign to capture this river citadel, Grant went down the
Mississippi to Milliken's Bend to take personal command of a renewed
army-navy campaign. Nature presented greater obstacles to this enterprise than the rebels. Although Union forces controlled the endless rivers and swamps north and west of Vicksburg, continual rains during the
winter made army movements almost impossible and many of Grant's
45,000 men were felled by lethal diseases. High and dry ground east of
the city offered the only suitable terrain for military operations. Grant's
problem was to get his army to this terrain with enough artillery and
supplies for a campaign. Since he had the assistance of the gunboat
fleet commanded by David Dixon Porter, Grant hoped to use the high
water as an asset. During the winter he launched four separate efforts
to flank Vicksburg by water and transport his army to the east bank
above or below the city.

The first project was completion of the cutoff canal that Union soldiers and contrabands had begun digging the previous summer. Sherman's corps went to work on this with much energy but no success.
The river refused to cooperate in the plan to cut a new channel out of
range of Vicksburg's guns, and even if it had done so the rebels could
have planted new batteries to dominate the mouth of the canal four
miles downstream. Although work on this canal continued until rising
waters in February threatened Sherman's men with drowning, Grant
soon pinned his hopes on a second enterprise known as the Lake Providence route. This project became the task of soldiers in the corps of
General James B. McPherson, formerly Grant's chief engineer and now
next to Sherman his favorite combat officer.[30] This route followed a
meandering course from an oxbow lake fifty miles above Vicksburg
through Louisiana swamps and bayous to the Mississippi again 400 river-

29. T. Harry Williams, *Lincoln and His Generals* (New York, 1952), 232–34; Foote,
   Civil War, II, 235–37.
30. To answer a question frequently asked the author, he will state here that he is no
   relation to General McPherson.

miles below. Midwestern farm boys who had joined the army to fight rebels found themselves dredging tons of mud and sawing off trees eight feet under water to clear a channel for gunboats and transports. After a great deal of labor, however, this effort was called off because it looked as if it would go on until doomsday.

More promising—or so it appeared at first—were two water routes through the jungle-like Yazoo Delta north of Vicksburg. If gunboats and transports could ferry the army through this maze for a dry-ground landing north of the fortified bluffs, Grant's troops could go to work as soldiers instead of ditch-diggers. Several gunboats and part of Mc-Clernand's corps went to Helena, 400 river-miles above Vicksburg, and blew up a levee to float the gunboats into the flooded Delta rivers. But the fleet soon ran into trouble. Overhanging cypress and cottonwood branches smashed smokestacks, lifeboats, and everything else above deck. Rushing logs carried by the flood crashed into the boats while they maneuvered through channels scarcely wider than their beams. Confederates felled trees across the rivers in front of them. The naval commander in charge of the expedition began to show signs of a nervous breakdown. When his boats came under fire from a hastily built Confederate fort near Greenwood, Mississippi, he collapsed—and so did the expedition.

Meanwhile another flotilla commanded by Porter himself and carrying a division of Sherman's troops was working its way through a 200-mile tangle of bayous and tributaries just north of Vicksburg. These boats also encountered obstacles of tree branches, logs, snags, and rebel axemen. Snakes, coons, and wildcats dropped from the trees and had to be swept overboard by sailors with brooms. Immobilized by the jungle's tentacles, Porter's gunboats were in a bad spot by March 20, with Confederate infantry converging on them hopeful of capturing the whole lot. Porter swallowed his naval pride and called on the army for help. He sent a contraband with a note to Sherman a few miles back with the transports:

> Dear Sherman,
> Hurry up, for Heaven's sake. I never knew how helpless an ironclad could be steaming around through the woods without an army to back her.[31]

Sherman disembarked his men to march through waist-deep swamps and drive off the rebels. Porter's paddlewheeled monsters backed ignom-

---

31. Samuel Carter III, *The Final Fortress: The Campaign for Vicksburg 1862–1863* (New York, 1980), 147.

iniously up the choked channels, and another effort to flank Vicksburg came to an end.

For two months Grant's army had been floundering in the mud. Many of them rested permanently below the mud, victims of pneumonia or typhoid or dysentery or any of a dozen other maladies. Vicksburg stood defiant as ever. Republican editors began to join Democrats in branding Grant an incompetent failure—and a drunkard to boot. "Grant has no plans for taking Vicksburg," wrote General Cadwallader Washburn to his brother Elihu, Grant's chief sponsor in Congress. "He is frittering away time and strength to no purpose. The truth must be told even if it hurts. You cannot make a silk purse out of a sow's ear." Although many such complaints came to Lincoln, he refused to throw Grant to the wolves. "I think Grant has hardly a friend left, except myself," said the president. But "what I want . . . is generals who will fight battles and win victories. Grant has done this, and I propose to stand by him."[32]

A prevalent theme in complaints about Grant concerned his drinking. According to one story, Lincoln deflected such charges with humor, telling a delegation of congressmen that he would like to know Grant's brand of whiskey so he could send some to his other generals.[33] It is hard to separate fact from fiction in this matter. Many wartime stories of Grant's drunkenness are false; others are at best dubious. Grant's meteoric rise to fame provoked jealousy in the hearts of men who indulged in gossip to denigrate him. Subject to sick headaches brought on by strain and loss of sleep, Grant sometimes acted unwell in a manner to give observers the impression that he had been drinking. But even when the myths have been stripped away, a hard substratum of truth about Grant's drinking remains. He may have been an alcoholic in the medical meaning of that term. He was a binge drinker. For months he could go without liquor, but if he once imbibed it was hard for him to stop. His wife and his chief of staff John A. Rawlins were his best protectors. With their help, Grant stayed on the wagon nearly all the time during the war. If he did get drunk (and this is much disputed by his-

32. Cadwallader Washburn to Elihu B. Washburne (the brothers spelled their surname differently), March 28, 1863, in Nevins, *War*, II, 388; Foote, *Civil War*, II, 217. See also T. Harry Williams, *Lincoln and His Generals*, 225–26.

33. John Eaton, *Grant, Lincoln and the Freedmen* (New York, 1907), 64. Although some historians regard this story as apocryphal, and in any case it appears not to have been original with Lincoln—having been told about other generals in earlier wars—Bruce Catton considers Eaton a reliable source and accepts the story as true. Catton, *Grant Moves South* (Boston, 1960), 396–97.

torians) it never happened at a time crucial to military operations. Recognized today as an illness, alcoholism in Grant's time was considered a moral weakness. Grant himself believed it so and battled to overcome the shame and guilt of his weakness. In the end, as a recent scholar has suggested, his predisposition to alcoholism may have made him a better general. His struggle for self-discipline enabled him to understand and discipline others; the humiliation of prewar failures gave him a quiet humility that was conspicuously absent from so many generals with a reputation to protect; because Grant had nowhere to go but up, he could act with more boldness and decision than commanders who dared not risk failure.[34]

Despite Lincoln's continuing faith in Grant, he permitted Secretary of War Stanton to send a special agent in March 1863 to investigate matters in the Army of the Tennessee. The agent was Charles A. Dana, former managing editor of the New York Tribune and now an assistant secretary of war. Dana went to the Mississippi ostensibly to straighten out the paymaster service in western armies, but Grant was aware of his real mission. Instead of giving Dana the cold shoulder—as some of his staff advised—Grant welcomed him. It was a wise action. Dana sized up the general favorably and began sending a stream of commendatory dispatches to Washington. Grant was "the most modest, the most disinterested and the most honest man I ever knew, with a temper that nothing could disturb," wrote Dana later in summary of his impressions

34. The best analysis of Grant's drinking, informed by modern studies of alcoholism, is Lyle W. Dorsett, "The Problem of Grant's Drinking During the Civil War," *Hayes Historical Journal*, 4 (1983). Among historians, Bruce Catton and Kenneth P. Williams question or deny Grant's weakness for liquor, while Benjamin Thomas, William McFeely, Shelby Foote, and Lyle Dorsett tend to accept its truth. The only detailed eye-witness account of a Grant binge during the war was written thirty years later by Sylvanus Cadwallader, a Chicago newspaper correspondent who spent more than two years with Grant's armies during the war: see Cadwallader, *Three Years with Grant*, ed. Benjamin P. Thomas (New York, 1955), 102–21. Catton and Williams and John Y. Simon challenge the authenticity of this particular story, though other historians accept it. For additional discussions of the issue of Grant's drinking, including the Cadwallader story, see Catton, *Grant Moves South*, 95–97, 462–65, 535–36; Kenneth P. Williams, *Lincoln Finds a General*, 5 vols. (New York, 1949–59), IV, 439–51, 577–82; exchange between Kenneth Williams and Benjamin Thomas in *American Heritage*, 7 (1956), 106–11; Foote, *Civil War*, II, 416–21; William S. McFeely, *Grant: A Biography* (New York, 1981), esp. 132–35, 148; John Y. Simon, ed., *The Papers of Ulysses S. Grant*, 14 vols. (Carbondale, Ill., 1967–85), VIII, 322–25n.

at the time. "Not a great man except morally; not an original or brilliant man, but sincere, thoughtful, deep and gifted with courage that never faltered."[35]

Men in the ranks shared Dana's opinion. They appreciated Grant's lack of "superfluous flummery," his tendency to wear a plain uniform "without scarf, sword, or trappings of any sort save the double-starred shoulder straps." A private reported that the men "seem to look upon him as a friendly partner of theirs, not as an arbitrary commander." Instead of cheering him when he rode by, they were likely to "greet him as they would address one of their neighbors at home. 'Good morning, General,' 'Pleasant day, General,' and like expressions are the greetings he meets everywhere. . . . There was no nonsense, no sentiment; only a plain business man of the republic, there for the one single purpose of getting that command over the river in the shortest time possible."[36]

Get them over the river Grant would soon do, with spectacular results. But at the end of March 1863 the northern public could see only the failures of the past four months—on the Mississippi as well as in Virginia. "This winter is, indeed, the Valley Forge of the war," wrote a Wisconsin officer. Such a remark at least implied a hope for ultimate success. But many other Yankees had given up hope. Captain Oliver Wendell Holmes, Jr., recovering from his Antietam wound, wrote dispiritedly that "the army is tired with its hard and terrible experience. . . . I've pretty much made up my mind that the South have achieved their independence." The staunchly loyal Joseph Medill, editor of the *Chicago Tribune*, believed that "an armistice is bound to come during the year '63. The rebs can't be conquered by the present machinery."[37] Into this crisis of confidence strode the copperheads with their program for peace without victory.

---

35. Charles A. Dana, *Recollections of the Civil War* (New York, 1902), 61–62.
36. Quotations from Catton, *Grant Moves South*, 390–91, and Foote, *Civil War*, II, 218–19.
37. Wisconsin officer quoted in Catton, *Glory Road*, 95; Mark DeWolfe Howe, ed., *Touched with Fire: Civil War Letters and Diary of Oliver Wendell Holmes, Jr., 1861–1864* (Cambridge, Mass., 1946), 73; Medill to Elihu Washburne, Jan. 16, 1863, in Catton, *Grant Moves South*, 369–70.

20

Fire in the Rear

I

Despite his preoccupation with military matters, Lincoln told Charles Sumner in January 1863 that he feared " 'the fire in the rear'—meaning the Democracy, especially at the Northwest—more than our military chances."[1] The president had ample grounds for concern. The peace faction of the Democratic party grew stronger with each setback of Union armies. And the enactment of a conscription law in March 1863 gave the antiwar movement additional stimulus.

By 1863 Clement L. Vallandigham had emerged as leader of the Peace Democrats. Only forty-two years old, the handsome Ohio congressman had cut his political eyeteeth on the Jeffersonian philosophy of limited government. "It is the desire of my heart," he declared soon after the outbreak of war, "to restore the Union, the Federal Union as it was forty years ago." To this desire Vallandigham added sympathy for the South produced by descent from a Virginia family and marriage to the daughter of a Maryland planter. Although Ohio Republicans had gerrymandered him into defeat in the 1862 election, Vallandigham went out with a bang rather than a whimper. In a farewell speech to the House on January 14, 1863, and a subsequent tour from New Jersey

1. Sumner to Francis Lieber, Jan. 17, 1863, in Edward L. Pierce, *Memoir and Letters of Charles Sumner*, 4 vols. (Boston, 1877–93), IV, 114.

to Ohio, he set forth his indictment of the war and his proposals for peace.[2]

Vallandigham professed himself a better unionist than the Republicans whose fanaticism had provoked this ruinous war. These same Republicans, he continued, were now fighting not for Union but for abolition. And what had they accomplished? "Let the dead at Fredericksburg and Vicksburg answer." The South could never be conquered; the only trophies of this war were "defeat, debt, taxation, sepulchres . . . the suspension of *habeas corpus*, the violation . . . of freedom of the press and of speech . . . which have made this country one of the worst despotisms on earth for the past twenty months." What was the solution? "Stop fighting. Make an armistice. . . . Withdraw your army from the seceded States." Start negotiations for reunion. Vallandigham had no use for the "fanaticism and hypocrisy" of the objection that an armistice would preserve slavery. "I see more of barbarism and sin, a thousand times, in the continuance of this war . . . and the enslavement of the white race by debt and taxes and arbitrary power" than in Negro slavery. "In considering terms of settlement we [should] look only to the welfare, peace, and safety of the white race, without reference to the effect that settlement may have on the African."[3]

This became the platform of Peace Democrats for the next two years. During the early months of 1863 this faction commanded the support of a large minority of the party—perhaps even a majority. A mass meeting of New York Democrats resolved that the war "against the South is illegal, being unconstitutional, and should not be sustained." And while Governor Horatio Seymour of New York promised "to make every sacrifice . . . for the preservation of this Union," he also denounced emancipation as "bloody, barbarous, revolutionary" and pledged to "maintain and defend the sovereignty" of New York against unconstitutional violations by the federal government.[4]

2. Frank L. Klement, *The Limits of Dissent: Clement L. Vallandigham and the Civil War* (Lexington, Ky., 1970), chaps. 1–6; quotation from p. 79.
3. Vallandigham, *The Great Civil War in America* (New York, 1863), a pamphlet publication of his January speech in the House, reprinted in Frank Freidel, ed., *Union Pamphlets of the Civil War*, 2 vols. (Cambridge, Mass., 1967), II, 697–738. Quotations from pp. 706, 707, 711, 719, 732.
4. New York meeting quoted in Wood Gray, *The Hidden Civil War: The Story of the Copperheads* (New York, 1964 [1942]), 147; Seymour quoted in Nevins, *War*, II, 394, and in William B. Hesseltine, *Lincoln and the War Governors* (New York, 1948), 282.

In Butternut regions of the Midwest, economic grievances reinforced the cultural attitudes of people descended from southern settlers. The war had cut off their normal trade routes along the Mississippi and its tributaries, forcing them into dependence on Yankee railroads and canals feeding an east-west pattern of trade. Real and imaginary grievances against high rates and poor service on these routes exacerbated the hostility of Butternuts toward New Englanders whom they charged with controlling their destiny through manipulation of Congress as well as of the economy. *"Shall we sink down as serfs to the heartless, speculative Yankees,"* asked an Ohio editor, *"swindled by his tariffs, robbed by his taxes, skinned by his railroad monopolies?"* [5]

This sense of Butternut identity with the South and hostility to the Northeast gave rise to talk among western Democrats of a "Northwest Confederacy" that would reconstruct a Union with the South, leaving New England out in the cold until she confessed the error of her ways and humbly petitioned for readmission. However bizarre such a scheme appears in retrospect, it commanded much rhetorical support during the war. "The people of the West demand peace, and they begin to more than suspect that New England is in the way," warned Vallandigham in January 1863. "If you of the East, who have found this war against the South, and for the negro, gratifying to your hate or profitable to your purse, will continue it . . . [be prepared for] *eternal divorce between the West and the East."* Though less extreme than Vallandigham, Congressman Samuel S. Cox of Ohio agreed that "the erection of the states watered by the Mississippi and its tributaries into an independent Republic is the talk of every other western man." [6] This threat to reopen the Mississippi by a separate peace generated General McClernand's proposal to reopen it with his separate campaign against Vicksburg. The whole issue lent an urgency to Grant's efforts to capture Vicksburg and a bitter edge to criticisms of his initial failures to do so.

An important law passed by Congress in February 1863 intensified the alienation of western Democrats: the National Banking Act. This measure owed much to Secretary of the Treasury Chase's desire to aug-

---

5. *Columbus Crisis*, Jan. 21, 1863, quoted in Gray, *Hidden Civil War*, 125. For the regional economic bases of copperheadism, see Frank L. Klement, "Economic Aspects of Middle Western Copperheadism," *Historian*, 14 (1951), 27–44, and Klement, *The Copperheads in the Middle West* (Chicago, 1960).
6. Vallandigham, *The Great Civil War*, in Freidel, ed., *Union Pamphlets*, 724, 729–30; Cox, "Puritanism in Politics," in Cox, *Eight Years in Congress* (New York, 1865), 283.

ment the market for war bonds; it owed even more to the Whiggish Republican desire to rationalize the decentralized, unstable structure of state banks and to create a uniform banknote currency. Treasury notes (greenbacks) provided a national currency, but they circulated alongside several hundred types of banknotes of varying degrees of soundness. No effective national regulation of banking had existed since the Jacksonian era. A nation "which leaves the power to regulate its currency to the legislation of thirty-four different states abandons one of the essential attributes of sovereignty," said Representative Samuel Hooper of Massachusetts. "The policy of this country," added Senate Finance Committee Chairman John Sherman, "ought to be to make everything national as far as possible; to nationalize our country so that we shall love our country."[7]

On February 25, 1863, the National Banking Act became law with the affirmative votes of 78 percent of the Republicans overcoming the negative votes of 91 percent of the Democrats. As supplemented by additional legislation the next year, this law authorized the granting of federal charters to banks that met certain standards, required them to purchase U. S. bonds in an amount equal to one-third of their capital, and permitted them to issue banknotes equal to 90 percent of the value of such bonds. Not until Congress drove state banknotes out of circulation with a 10 percent tax levied on them in 1865 did most state banks convert to federal charters. But the 1863 law laid the groundwork for the banking system that prevailed for a half-century after the war. Not surprisingly, Jacksonian Democrats in the Old Northwest denounced "this monstrous Bank Bill" as new evidence of the wartime conspiracy by "the money monopoly of New England" to "destroy the fixed institutions of the States, and to build up a central moneyed despotism."[8]

The years of real passion on the bank issue, however, belonged to the 1830s and 1890s. In 1863, hostility to emancipation was the principal fuel that fired antiwar Democrats. On this issue, also, New England was the main enemy. The "Constitution-breaking, law-defying, negroloving Phariseeism of New England" had caused the war, said Samuel S. Cox. "In the name of God," cried a former governor of Illinois in December 1862, "no more bloodshed to gratify a religious fanaticism." An Ohio editor branded Lincoln a "half-witted usurper" and his Eman-

---

7. Quotations from Bray Hammond, *Sovereignty and an Empty Purse: Banks and Politics in the Civil War* (Princeton, 1970), 314, 326–27.
8. Klement, "Economic Aspects of Middle Western Copperheadism," *loc. cit.*, 39–40.

cipation Proclamation "monstrous, impudent, and heinous . . . insulting to God as to man, for it declares those 'equal' whom God created unequal."[9]

Did such rhetoric fall within the rights of free speech and a free press? A case can be made that it stimulated desertion from the army and resistance to the war effort. Democratic newspapers that circulated among soldiers contained many editorials proclaiming the illegality of an anti-slavery war. "You perceive that it is to emancipate slaves . . . that you are used as soldiers," declared the *Dubuque Herald*. "Are you, as soldiers, bound by patriotism, duty or loyalty to fight in such a cause?" Newspapers printed many alleged letters written by family members at home to soldiers in the army. "I am sorry you are engaged in this . . . unholy, unconstitutional and hellish war," a father supposedly wrote to his son, "which has no other purpose but to free the negroes and enslave the whites." Another letter advised an Illinois soldier "to come home, if you have to desert, you will be protected—the people are so enraged that you need not be alarmed if you hear of the whole of our Northwest killing off the abolitionists."[10] Such propaganda had its intended effect. So many members of two southern Illinois regiments deserted "rather than help free the slaves" that General Grant had to disband the regiments. Soldiers from several other regiments allowed themselves to be captured so they could be paroled and sent home.[11]

Equally serious were the actions of the newly elected Democratic legislatures of Indiana and Illinois. The lower houses in both states passed resolutions calling for an armistice and a peace conference. Both lower houses also demanded retraction of the "wicked, inhuman and unholy" Emancipation Proclamation as the price for continued state support of the war. When the two legislatures began work on bills to take control of state troops away from the Republican governors (elected in 1860), these governors decided to act. With the acquiescence of the Lincoln administration, Richard Yates of Illinois used an obscure clause of the state constitution to prorogue the legislature in June 1863. Though a

9. Cox, "Puritanism in Politics," *Eight Years in Congress*, 283; John Reynolds quoted in Gray, *Hidden Civil War*, 115; Samuel Medary quoted in V. Jacque Voegeli, *Free But Not Equal: The Midwest and the Negro during the Civil War* (Chicago, 1967), 77.

10. Quotations from Gray, *Hidden Civil War*, 122, 133.

11. Nevins, *War*, II, 290; Bruce Catton, *Glory Road: The Bloody Route from Fredericksburg to Gettysburg* (Garden City, N.Y., 1952), 246; *O.R.*, Ser. II, Vol. 5, p. 216.

state court found that he had exceeded his authority, the court could not itself order the legislature back into session. Indiana's iron-willed Oliver P. Morton simply persuaded Republican legislators to absent themselves, thereby forcing the legislature into adjournment for lack of a quorum. For the next two years Morton ran the state without a legislature—and without the usual appropriations. He borrowed from banks and businesses, levied contributions on Republican counties, and drew $250,000 from a special service fund in the War Department—all quite extralegal, if not illegal. But Republicans everywhere endorsed the principle of Morton's action: the Constitution must be stretched in order to save constitutional government from destruction by rebellion.[12]

This reasoning buttressed Lincoln's policy in the most celebrated civil liberties case of the war—the military arrest and conviction of Vallandigham for disloyalty. Vallandigham was hardly a selfless martyr in this case; on the contrary, he courted arrest in order to advance his languishing candidacy for the Democratic gubernatorial nomination in Ohio. He found an unwitting ally in General Burnside, whose political judgment proved no more subtle than his military judgment at Fredericksburg. Appointed commander of the Department of the Ohio (embracing states bordering that river) after transfer from the Army of the Potomac, Burnside decided to come down hard on the copperheads. In April 1863 he issued a general order declaring that any person committing "expressed or implied" treason would be subject to trial by a military court and punishment by death or banishment.[13] What constituted implied treason Burnside did not say, but the country would soon find out.

Vallandigham recognized this order as his opportunity. With plenty of advance publicity to ensure that Burnside's agents would be on hand, he spoke at a rally in Mount Vernon, Ohio, on May 1. His address was a rehash of standard antiwar themes. As recorded by Burnside's staff officer, Vallandigham denounced this "wicked, cruel and unnecessary war" waged "for the purpose of crushing out liberty and erecting a despotism . . . a war for the freedom of the blacks and the enslavement of the whites." This was enough for Burnside. He sent a squad of soldiers to arrest Vallandigham at his home in Dayton. In a manner that lent credence to accusations of despotism, soldiers broke down the door in the middle of the night and hustled Vallandigham away leaving behind his hysterical wife and a terrified sister-in-law. While his support-

12. Hesseltine, *Lincoln and the War Governors*, 311–18; Nevins, *War*, II, 391–93.
13. O.R., Ser. I, Vol. 23, pt. 2, p. 237.

ers rioted and burned down the office of Dayton's Republican newspaper, a military commission met in Cincinnati on May 6 and convicted Vallandigham "of having expressed sympathy" for the enemy and having uttered "disloyal sentiments and opinions, with the object and purpose of weakening the power of the Government [to suppress] an unlawful rebellion."[14] Unwilling to go so far as to put Vallandigham before a firing squad, the commission recommended his imprisonment for the war's duration, and Burnside so ordered. Vallandigham filed for a writ of habeas corpus, which was denied by a federal judge who pointed out that Lincoln had suspended the writ in such cases.

These proceedings produced cries of outrage from Democrats and murmurings of anxiety from many Republicans. The most important protest came from a meeting of War Democrats in Albany, who pointedly asked whether the government was trying to suppress rebellion in the South or "to destroy free institutions in the North." The Vallandigham case did indeed raise troubling constitutional questions. Could a speech be treason? Could a military court try a civilian? Did a general, or for that matter a president, have the power to impose martial law or suspend habeas corpus in an area distant from military operations where the civil courts were functioning?[15]

These questions went to the heart of the administration's policy for dealing with the fire in the rear. Lincoln would have preferred not to have had the issue raised in this particular manner. He was embarrassed by Burnside's arrest of Vallandigham, about which the president learned from the newspapers. Presented with a *fait accompli*, Lincoln decided that more damage would be done by repudiating Burnside than by upholding him. But in an attempt to minimize the political consequences, Lincoln commuted Vallandigham's sentence from imprisonment to banishment. On May 25 Union cavalry escorted the Ohioan under flag of truce to General Bragg's lines south of Murfreesboro, where the reluctant rebels accepted this uninvited guest.

Lincoln's shrewd move failed in one respect: while in exile, Vallandigham rode to the gubernatorial nomination on a wave of sympathy from Ohio Democrats. After traveling through the Confederacy to Wilmington, he boarded a blockade-runner for Canada and made his way to the border city of Windsor, from which he conducted his campaign

14. *Ibid.*, Ser. II, Vol. 5, pp. 633–46.
15. The Albany resolutions are published in Freidel, ed., *Union Pamphlets*, II, 740–45.

for governor. Before leaving the South, he spoke with several Confederate congressmen and army officers. He made clear to them his commitment to reunion through an armistice and negotiations. Southerners replied that they would accept peace only on the basis of independence. If Vallandigham thought the Union could be restored by compromise, they declared, he was "badly deluded." In a confidential interview with a Confederate agent, Vallandigham said that if the South *can only hold out* this year . . . the peace party of the North would sweep the Lincoln dynasty out of existence." Vallandigham clung to his hope for eventual reunion, but left this agent with the impression that if the South refused to come back "then possibly he is in favor of recognizing our independence."[16]

It was on these principles—minus the "possible" recognition of southern independence—that Vallandigham conducted his strange campaign-in-exile for governor. Long before voters went to the Ohio polls in October, however, an upturn of Union military fortunes would undermine his peace platform. In the meantime Lincoln sought to defuse the civil liberties issue with two public replies to Democratic critics. He rejected the charge that Vallandigham had been arrested "for no other reason than words addressed to a public meeting." Rather it was "because he was laboring, with some effect, to prevent the raising of troops [and] to encourage desertions. . . . He was damaging the army, upon the existence and vigor of which the life of the nation depends." The president than asked a rhetorical question that turned out to be the most powerful—and famous—part of his argument. "Must I shoot a simple-minded soldier boy who deserts, while I must not touch a hair of a wily agitator who induces him to desert? . . . I think that in such a case to silence the agitator and save the boy is not only constitutional, but withal a great mercy." This "giant rebellion" reached into the North itself, Lincoln continued, where "under cover of 'liberty of speech,' 'liberty of the press,' and *Habeas corpus*,' [the rebels] hoped to keep on foot amongst us a most efficient corps of spies, informers, suppliers, and aiders and abettors of their cause." Thus the whole country was a war zone and military arrests in areas far from the fighting front were justified. Civil courts were "utterly incompetent" to deal with such a massive threat to the nation's life. This was precisely the contingency that framers of the

16. Klement, *The Limits of Dissent*, 209–11; Jones, *War Clerk's Diary* (Miers), 229–30, summarizing a memorandum of the interview written by agent Robert Ould. The memorandum itself has been lost.

Constitution foresaw when they authorized suspension of the writ of habeas corpus in cases of rebellion or invasion. With a homely but effective metaphor, Lincoln affirmed that he could no more believe that the necessary curtailment of civil liberties in wartime would establish precedents fatal to liberty in peacetime "than I am able to believe that a man could contract so strong an appetite for emetics during temporary illness, as to persist in feeding upon them through the remainder of his healthful life." [17]

Lincoln's two letters on civil liberties were published far and wide by the newly established Union League and Loyal Publication Society. Believing that the copperheads were organized in vast secret societies such as the Knights of the Golden Circle and Order of American Knights, unionists felt impelled to fight back with their own societies. Founded by businessmen and professional men of substance and influence, the Union Leagues, Loyal Leagues and their publication boards achieved much greater power than the Democratic secret societies, whose supposed legions existed more in the fevered imaginations of Republicans than in fact. The Union Leagues became in effect an auxiliary of the Republican party, which began to call itself the Union party in several states—thereby implying that the opposition was a *dis*-union party. [18]

The first successes of this counterattack against Democratic defeatism came in New Hampshire and Connecticut. These states held gubernatorial elections in the spring. The results in 1863 were closely watched elsewhere as a portent. In both states the Democrats nominated peace men of the Vallandigham stripe, hoping to cash in on voter disillusionment with the war. Republicans and Union Leagues mobilized to stem the apparent Democratic tide. The War Department helped by granting well-timed furloughs to soldiers who were expected to go home and vote

17. CWL, VI, 260–69, 300–06. Vallandigham's attorneys appealed his conviction to the Supreme Court, arguing that the military trial of a civilian in a non-war zone where civil courts were functioning was unconstitutional. The Court ducked this issue in 1864, claiming no appellate jurisdiction over the proceedings of a military court. But in 1866, after the wartime emergency was over, the Supreme Court ruled that a similar military trial in 1864 of an Indiana copperhead named Lambdin Milligan was unconstitutional.

18. For a brief history of the Union Leagues and similar societies, and a broad sample of their publications, see Freidel, *Union Pamphlets*. Frank L. Klement, *Dark Lanterns: Secret Political Societies, Conspiracies, and Treason Trials in the Civil War* (Baton Rouge, 1984), compares the membership and purposes of these various organizations.

Republican. These efforts succeeded—but just barely. The Republican candidate in Connecticut won with 52 percent of the vote. In New Hampshire the presence of a War Democratic third party prevented any candidate from winning a majority and threw the election into the Republican legislature, which elected their man.[19]

A prime issue in both elections was the draft, enacted by Congress on March 3, 1863. Democrats added conscription to emancipation and military arrests in their catalogue of Republican sins. The Enrollment Act of 1863 was designed mainly as a device to stimulate volunteering by the threat of a draft. As such it worked, but with such inefficiency, corruption, and perceived injustice that it became one of the most divisive issues of the war and served as a model of how *not* to conduct a draft in future wars.

By the beginning of 1863 recruitment in the North arrived at the same impasse it had reached in the South a year earlier. The men likely to enlist for patriotic reasons or adventure or peer-group pressure were already in the army. War weariness and the grim realities of army life discouraged further volunteering. The booming war economy had shrunk the number of unemployed men to the vanishing point. The still tentative enlistment of black soldiers could scarcely begin to replace losses from disease and combat and desertion during the previous six months. Like the Confederacy in early 1862, the Union army in 1863 faced a serious manpower loss through expiration of enlistments: 38 two-year regiments raised in 1861, and 92 nine-month militia regiments organized in 1862 were due to go home during the spring and summer of 1863. This prompted Congress to act.

In its nationalizing tendencies the resulting law was similar to the recently passed Banking Act. State governors had taken the lead in the organization of volunteer regiments in 1861–62. The draft was a national process. Congress authorized a Provost Marshals Bureau in the War Department to enforce conscription. This Bureau sent to each congressional district a number of provost marshals whose first task was to enroll every male citizen and immigrant who had filed for citizenship aged twenty to forty-five.[20] This became the basis for each district's quota

19. Christopher Dell, *Lincoln and the War Democrats* (Rutherford, N.J., 1975), 231–36; John Niven, *Connecticut for the Union: The Role of the State in the Civil War* (New Haven, 1965), 305–8.
20. Men eligible for the draft were divided into two classes. Class 1 included all single men and married men aged 20 to 35. Class 2 included married men over 35. Men

in the four calls for new troops that Lincoln issued after passage of the conscription act in March 1863. In the first draft (July 1863), provost marshals called up 20 percent of the enrollees, chosen by lot in each district. In the three drafts of 1864, the War Department assigned each district a quota determined by its pro rata share of the number of soldiers called for by the president, after adjustment for men who had already enlisted from the district. Each district had fifty days to fill its quota with volunteers. Those that failed to do so then held a lottery draft to obtain a sufficient number of men to meet the quota.

If a man's name was drawn in this lottery, one of several things would happen to him next—the least likely of which was induction into the army. Of the men chosen in the four drafts, more than one-fifth (161,000 of 776,000) "failed to report"—fleeing instead to the West, to Canada, or to the woods. Of those who did report to the provost marshal's office, one-eighth were sent home because of already filled quotas. Three-fifths of the remaining 522,000 were exempted for physical or mental disability or because they convinced the inducting officer that they were the sole means of support for a widow, an orphan sibling, a motherless child, or an indigent parent. Unlike the Confederate Congress, Union lawmakers allowed no occupational exemptions. But a draftee who passed the physical exam and could not claim any dependent relatives still had two options: he could hire a substitute, which exempted him from this and any future draft; or he could pay a commutation fee of $300, which exempted him from this draft but not necessarily the next one.[21] Of the 207,000 men who were drafted, 87,000 paid the commutation fee and 74,000 furnished substitutes, leaving only 46,000 who went personally into the army. The pool of substitutes was furnished by eighteen- and nineteen-year olds and by immigrants who had not filed for citizenship, who were not liable to conscription.[22]

---

from class 2 would not be drafted until class 1 had been exhausted. In practice, that meant virtually never.

21. Criticisms of commutation led to its repeal in 1864—except for conscientious objectors—so that with this minor exception the commutation option did not apply to the last two drafts of July and December 1864.

22. This and the following paragraphs are based on several studies, especially Fred A. Shannon, *The Organization and Administration of the Union Army, 1861–1865,* 2 vols. (Cleveland, 1928), I, 195–323, II, 11–260; Eugene C. Murdock, *Patriotism Limited 1862–1865: The Civil War Draft and the Bounty System* (Kent, Ohio, 1967); Murdock, *One Million Men: The Civil War Draft in the North* (Madison, 1971); and Peter Levine, "Draft Evasion in the North during the Civil War, 1863–

There were numerous opportunities for fraud, error, and injustice in this cumbersome and confusing process. The enrollment of men eligible for the draft was only as good as the officials who carried it out— and some of them were venal or incompetent. Enrollers probably missed even more of the floating population than census takers missed. On the other hand, some officials padded their rolls with fictitious names in order to draw their pay without doing the hard work of canvassing door to door. Timid enrollers feared to venture into Butternut counties of the Midwest, coal-mining districts of Pennsylvania, tough neighborhoods in New York, and other areas hostile to the draft and to the war. Many men "skedaddled" to avoid enrollment. Consequently some districts were under-enrolled while others had padded lists, with resulting inequities in quotas. Governors and congressmen brought pressure for adjustment of quotas, and some districts had to be re-enrolled. Governor Seymour of New York (a Democrat) accused the administration of padding the enrollment in Democratic districts to increase their quotas. Although discrepancies between Democratic and Republican districts did sometimes occur, the usual reason was not a Republican plot but rather a smaller previous enlistment from Democratic districts, leaving a larger quota to be conscripted.

Numerous openings for fraud also existed after enrollment was completed and men whose names had been drawn were called for examination. Surgeons could be bribed, false affidavits claiming dependent support could be filed, and other kinds of under-the-table influence could be exerted. Some potential draftees feigned insanity or disease. Others practiced self-mutilation. Some naturalized citizens claimed to be aliens.

In the South, the privilege of hiring a substitute had produced the bitter slogan of "rich man's war and poor man's fight." In the North, commutation was even more unpopular than substitution. "Three Hundred Dollars or Your Life" blazoned the headlines in Democratic newspapers. A parody of a popular recruiting song made the rounds: "We Are Coming, Father Abraham, Three Hundred Dollars More."[23] The price of commutation amounted to almost a year's wages for an unskilled laborer. *"The rich are exempt!"* proclaimed an Iowa editor.

1865," *JAH*, 67 (1981), 816–34. Nearly all draftees were under 30 years of age, for older men generally were able to claim exemption for cause or to pay for commutation or a substitute.

23. Basil L. Lee, *Discontent in New York City 1861–1865* (Washington, 1943), 90; Foote, *Civil War*, II, 151.

"Did you ever know aristocratic legislation to so directly point out the poor man as inferior to the rich?" On the face of it, the privileges of commutation and substitution did seem to make the conscription act, in the words of a modern historian, "one of the worst pieces of class legislation ever passed by the United States Congress."[24]

But a closer examination challenges this conclusion. Substitution was hallowed by tradition, having existed in European countries (even in France during the *levée en masse*), in American states during the Revolution, in the militia, and in the Confederacy. The Republican architects of the draft law inserted commutation as a means of putting a cap on the price of substitutes. In the South the cost of a substitute had already soared above $1,000. The commutation alternative in the North would prevent the price of a substitute going much higher than $300. Republicans saw this as a way of bringing exemption within reach of the working class instead of discriminating against them.

Of course a draft without either substitution or commutation would have been more equitable. But substitution was so deeply rooted in precedent as to be viewed as a right. Civil War experience changed this perception, and after twenty months of such experience the Confederacy repealed substitution in December 1863. But the North retained it through all four of its draft calls (also a period of about twenty months). Commutation remained an alternative in the first two Union drafts (summer 1863 and spring 1864). In these drafts it worked as Republicans said it would. Studies of conscription in New York and Ohio have found virtually no correlation between wealth and commutation. Districts in New York with low per capita wealth had about the same percentage of men who paid commutation (or hired substitutes) as those with higher wealth. In four Ohio districts—two rural and two urban—the proportion of unskilled laborers who commuted was 18 percent, compared with 22 percent for skilled laborers, 21 percent for merchants, bankers, manufacturers, doctors, lawyers, and clerks, and 47 percent for farmers and farm laborers. Since skilled and unskilled laborers had the highest percentage of "failure to report" when their names were drawn, it appears that at least in Ohio the laborers and farmers were *more* likely than men in white-collar jobs to avoid the draft. In this respect it does not seem to have been especially a poor man's fight.[25]

24. Robert E. Sterling, "Civil War Draft Resistance in the Middle West," Ph.D. dissertation, Northern Illinois University, 1974, pp. 167, 150.
25. James W. Geary, "Civil War Conscription in the North: A Historiographical Re-

Yet the outcry against "blood money" prompted Congress to repeal commutation in July 1864, despite warnings by some Republicans that this would drive the price of substitutes beyond the reach of the poor. The warning proved to be only partly true. The proportion of laborers and farmers who bought their way out of the last two drafts declined by half after the abolition of commutation. But the percentage of exemptions purchased by white-collar and professional classes also declined by almost half. And in the four drafts taken together the poor seem to have suffered little comparative disadvantage. In New York City districts with the highest concentration of Irish immigrants, 98 percent of the men not otherwise exempted paid commutation or hired substitutes. The following table provides a detailed occupational breakdown of men whose names were drawn in four sample Ohio districts:[26]

Occupation	Failed to Report	Exempted for Cause	Commuted or Hired Substitute	Held to Service
Unskilled Laborer	24.9%	45.1%	24.2%	5.8%
Skilled Laborer	25.7%	43.8%	21.9%	8.6%
Farmer & Farm Laborer	16.1%	34.1%	30.9%	18.9%
Merchant, Manufacturer, Banker, Broker	22.6%	46.3%	29.1%	2.0%
Clerk	26.2%	47.7%	24.3%	1.8%
Professional	16.3%	48.5%	28.9%	6.3%

How could laborers come up with the price of commutation or a substitute? Few of them did, out of their own pockets. But numerous cities and counties appropriated funds raised by property taxes to pay the $300 for those who could not afford it. Tammany Hall ward committees collected money to hire substitutes for draftees, and political machines elsewhere followed suit. Several factories and businesses and railroads bought exemptions for drafted workers with funds contributed by employers and by a 10 percent levy on wages. Draft insurance societies sprang up everywhere to offer a $300 policy for premiums of a few dollars a month. In this manner more than three-quarters of all draftees

---

view, *CWH* (1986), 208–28; Eugene C. Murdock, "Was It a 'Poor Man's Fight'?" *CWH*, 10 (1964), 241–45; Murdock, *Patriotism Limited*, 211–15; Hugh C. Earnhart, "Commutation: Democratic or Undemocratic?" *CWH*, 12 (1966), 132–42; Levine, "Draft Evasion," *loc. cit.*, 820–29.

26. Calculated from the raw data presented in Earnhart, "Commutation," *loc. cit.*, 138–42.

who reported to the provost marshal's office and were not exempted for cause were able to buy their way out of serving.

What kind of conscription was this, in which only 7 percent of the men whose names were drawn actually served? The answer: it was not conscription at all, but a clumsy carrot and stick device to stimulate volunteering. The stick was the threat of being drafted and the carrot was a bounty for volunteering. In the end this method worked, for while only 46,000 drafted men served and another 74,000 provided substitutes, some 800,000 men enlisted or re-enlisted voluntarily during the two years after passage of the conscription act. While the social and economic cost of this process was high, Americans seemed willing to pay the price because compulsory service was contrary to the country's values and traditions. Alexis de Tocqueville's words a generation earlier were still relevant in 1863: "In America conscription is unknown and men are induced to enlist by bounties. The notions and habits of the people . . . are so opposed to compulsory recruitment that I do not think it can ever be sanctioned by their laws."[27]

Yet in the end, bounty-stimulated volunteering came to seem an even greater evil than the draft. Implicit bounties began in the first days of the war, when soldiers' aid societies raised money to help support the families of men who gave up their jobs to go off to war. States, counties, and municipalities also appropriated funds for this purpose. These patriotic subsidies aroused no controversy. In the summer of 1862, however, several northern localities found it necessary to pay explicit bounties in order to fill quotas under Lincoln's two calls for troops. A year later the shock of the first draft enrollment and lottery, which provoked bitter resistance in many areas, caused communities to resolve to fill future quotas by any means possible to avoid a draft. Lincoln's three calls for troops in 1864 produced a bidding war to buy volunteers. Private associations raised money for bounties. Cities and counties competed for recruits. The federal government got into the act in October 1863 with a $300 bounty (financed by the $300 commutation fee) for volunteers and re-enlistees.

The half-billion dollars paid in bounties by the North represented something of a transfer of wealth from rich to poor—an ironic counterpoint to the theme of rich man's war/poor man's fight. By 1864 a canny recruit could pyramid local, regional, and national bounties into grants

27. Quoted in Adrian Cook, *The Armies of the Streets: The New York City Draft Riots of 1863* (Lexington, Ky., 1974), 48.

of $1,000 or more. Some men could not resist the temptation to take this money, desert, assume a different name, travel to another town, and repeat the process. Several of these "bounty jumpers" got away with the practice several times. "Bounty brokers" went into business to seek the best deals for their clients—with a cut of the bounty as payment. They competed with "substitute brokers" for a share of this lucrative trade in cannon fodder. Relatively few of the bounty men or substitutes actually became cannon fodder, however, for many deserted before they ever got into action and others allowed themselves to be captured at the first contact with the enemy. Thus while the conscription-substitute-bounty system produced three-quarters of a million new men,[28] they did little to help win the war. This task fell mainly on the pre-bounty veterans of 1861 and 1862—who with exaggerated contempt viewed many of the bounty men and substitutes of 1864 as "off-scourings of northern slums . . . dregs of every nation . . . branded felons . . . thieves, burglars, and vagabonds."[29]

One notorious facet of the bounty and substitute business was the crimping of immigrants. Immigration had declined sharply during the first half of the war, but picked up again in 1863 because of wartime labor shortages. Some of these immigrants came with the intention of joining the army to cash in on bounties or substitute fees. Others were virtually kidnapped into the service by unscrupulous "runners." The substantial number of immigrants in the Union army gave rise to long-standing southern myth that "the majority of Yankee soldiers were foreign hirelings."[30] But in fact quite the opposite was true. Immigrants were proportionally under-represented in the Union's armed services. Of some two million white soldiers and sailors, half a million had been born abroad. While immigrants therefore constituted 25 percent of the servicemen, 30 percent of the males of military age in the Union states were foreign-born. Despite the fighting reputation of the Irish Brigade, the Irish were the most under-represented group in proportion to population, followed by German Catholics. Other immigrant groups enlisted in rough proportion to their share of the population.[31]

28. More than 150,000 re-enlisting veterans also received bounties.
29. Wiley, *Billy Yank*, 343–44; Bruce Catton, *A Stillness at Appomattox* (Garden City, N.Y., 1957), 25–29.
30. Wiley, *Billy Yank*, 428n. 51, quoting an unnamed southern historian who made this assertion in 1951.
31. Data on the number of foreign-born soldiers in the Union army are contained in

The under-representation of Catholic immigrants can be explained in part by the Democratic allegiance of these groups and their opposition to Republican war aims, especially emancipation. Some of them had not yet filed for citizenship—or claimed not to have done so—and were therefore exempt from the draft. Although this group furnished a large number of substitutes and bounty men during the final year of war— thereby achieving an inglorious visibility—they also furnished a large number of deserters and bounty jumpers. Together with Butternuts from the Ohio River valley, they likewise provided many of those who "skedaddled" to escape the draft.[32] This ethnocultural pattern reinforced economic class, for Butternuts and Catholic immigrants were concentrated in the lower end of the wealth and income scale. Perhaps this confirms the theme of a "rich man's war"—for many of these people wanted no part of the war—but it modifies the "poor man's fight" notion. This modification is borne out by the following table comparing previous occupations of white Union soldiers with the occupational distribution of males in the states from which they came.[33]

Benjamin A. Gould, *Investigations in Military and Anthropological Statistics of American Soldiers* (New York, 1869); in Ella Lonn, *Foreigners in the Union Army and Navy* (Baton Rouge, 1951), esp. 581–82; in Wiley, *Billy Yank*, 306–15; in William F. Fox, *Regimental Losses in the American Civil War 1861–1865* (Albany, 1889), 62–63; and in Edward Channing, *The War for Southern Independence* (Vol. 6 of his *History of the United States*, New York, 1925), 426n. An excellent analysis of this matter in the state with the highest proportion of foreign-born men, Wisconsin, finds that while more than half of the males of military age had been born abroad, only 40 percent of the Wisconsin soldiers were foreign-born. Richard N. Current, *The History of Wisconsin: The Civil War Era 1848–1873* (Madison, 1976), 306, 335.

32. Levine, "Draft Evasion," *loc. cit.*, 820–34; Sterling, "Midwest Draft Resistance," 251–62.

33. The data for occupations of all males in 1860 are drawn from the occupational tables in the 1860 printed census. The samples of the previous occupations of Union soldiers are from: 1) a U. S. Sanitary Commission survey of the occupations of 666,530 Union soldiers from all Union states except Maryland and Delaware; 2) Bell Wiley's sample of 13,392 white Union soldiers in 114 companies from all the free states plus Missouri. (California, Oregon, and the territories are not included in these data.) The Sanitary Commission and Wiley samples were drawn from company muster rolls and are representative of the proportion of soldiers from the various states. The Sanitary Commission data were reported in Gould, *Investigations in Military and Anthropological Statistics*, and the Wiley data were kindly supplied to the author by Wiley before his death. I am indebted to his generosity and to the painstaking labor of Patricia McPherson, who compiled the occupational data from the 1860 census.

Occupational Categories	Union Soldiers (U.S. Sanitary Commission Sample)	Union Soldiers (Bell Wiley Sample)	All Males (From 1860 Census)
Farmers and farm laborers	47.5%	47.8%	42.9%
Skilled laborers	25.1	25.2	24.9
Unskilled laborers	15.9	15.1	16.7
White-collar and commercial	5.1	7.8	10.0
Professional	3.2	2.9	3.5
Miscellaneous and unknown	3.2	1.2	2.0

From this table it might appear that the white-collar class was the most under-represented group in the army. But this appearance is deceptive, for the median age of soldiers at enlistment was 23.5 years while the occupational data from the census were for all adult males. Two-fifths of the soldiers were twenty-one or younger. Studies of nineteenth-century occupational mobility have shown that 10 percent or more of young men who started out as laborers subsequently moved up the occupational ladder.[34] If one could control for the age of soldiers, it seems likely that the only category significantly under-represented would be unskilled workers.

Even if the dichotomy rich man's war/poor man's fight lacked objective reality, it remained a powerful symbol to be manipulated by Democrats who made conscription a partisan and class issue. While 100 percent of the congressional Republicans supported the draft bill, 88 percent of the Democrats voted against it.[35] Scarcely any other issue except emancipation evoked such clearcut partisan division. Indeed, Democrats linked these two issues in their condemnation of the draft as

34. Stephan Thernstrom, *The Other Bostonians: Poverty and Progress in the American Metropolis* (Cambridge, Mass., 1973), esp. table on p. 234. This table summarizes the results of studies of occupational mobility in several cities. These studies show that an average of 15 to 20 percent of the young blue-collar workers eventually moved into white-collar jobs, while 5 to 10 percent of the young white-collar workers eventually dropped to blue-collar positions. These studies do not measure the occupational mobility of farm boys, who may have experienced a higher rate of movement into white-collar jobs.

35. CG, 37 Cong., 3 Sess., pp. 1293, 1389.

an unconstitutional means to achieve the unconstitutional end of freeing the slaves. A democratic convention in the Midwest pledged that "we will not render support to the present Administration in its wicked Abolition crusade [and] we will *resist* to the *death* all attempts to draft any of our citizens into the army." Democratic newspapers hammered at the theme that the draft would force white working men to fight for the freedom of blacks who would come north and take away their jobs. The editor of New York's leading Catholic weekly told a mass meeting that "when the President called upon them to go and carry on a war for the nigger, he would be d____d if he believed they would go." In a Fourth of July 1863 speech to Democrats in the city, Governor Seymour warned Republicans who pleaded military necessity for emancipation and conscription: "Remember this—that the bloody and treasonable doctrine of public necessity can be proclaimed by a mob as well as by a government."[36]

Such rhetoric inflamed smoldering tensions. Draft dodgers and mobs killed several enrollment officers during the spring and summer. Anti-Negro violence erupted in a number of cities. Nowhere was the tinder more flammable than in New York City, with its large Irish population and powerful Democratic machine. Crowded into noisome tenements in a city with the worst disease mortality and highest crime rate in the Western world, working in low-skill jobs for marginal wages, fearful of competition from black workers, hostile toward the Protestant middle and upper classes who often disdained or exploited them, the Irish were ripe for revolt against this war waged by Yankee Protestants for black freedom. Wage increases had lagged 20 percent or more behind price increases since 1861. Numerous strikes had left a bitter legacy, none more than a longshoremen's walkout in June 1863 when black stevedores under police protection took the place of striking Irishmen.

Into this setting came draft officers to begin the drawing of names on Saturday, July 11. Most of the militia and federal troops normally stationed in the city were absent in Pennsylvania pursuing Lee's army after the battle of Gettysburg. The first day's drawing went quietly enough, but on Sunday hundreds of angry men congregated in bars and vowed to attack the draft offices next morning. They made good their threat, setting off four days of escalating mob violence that terrorized the city

36. Convention quoted in Gray, *Hidden Civil War*, 123; Editor James McMaster of *Freeman's Journal* quoted in Lee, *Discontent in New York City*, 239; Seymour quoted in Cook, *Armies of the Streets*, 53.

and left at least 105 people dead. It was the worst riot in American history.[37]

Many of the men (and women) in the mobs indulged in indiscriminate looting and destruction. But as in most riots, the mobs singled out certain targets that were related to the underlying causes of the outbreak. Draft offices and other federal property went up in flames early in the rioting. No black person was safe. Rioters beat several, lynched a half-dozen, smashed the homes and property of scores, and burned the Colored Orphan Asylum to the ground. Mobs also fell upon several business establishments that employed blacks. Rioters tried to attack the offices of Republican newspapers and managed to burn out the ground floor of the *Tribune* while howling for Horace Greeley's blood. Several editors warded off the mob by arming their employees with rifles; Henry Raymond of the *Times* borrowed three recently invented Gatling guns from the army to defend his building. Rioters sacked the homes of several prominent Republicans and abolitionists. With shouts of "Down with the rich" and "There goes a $300 man" they attacked well-dressed men who were incautious enough to show themselves on the streets. These hints of class warfare were amplified by assaults on the property of reputed anti-labor employers and the destruction of street-sweeping machines and grain-loading elevators that had automated the jobs of some of the unskilled workers who made up the bulk of the rioters. Several Protestant churches and missions were burned by the mobs whose membership was at least two-thirds Irish.[38]

Untrained in riot control, New York's police fought the mobs courageously but with only partial success on July 13 and 14. Army officers desperately scraped together a few hundred troops to help. The War Department rushed several regiments from Pennsylvania to New York, where on July 15 and 16 they poured volleys into the ranks of rioters with the same deadly effect they had produced against rebels at Gettysburg two weeks earlier. By July 17 an uneasy peace returned to the shattered city. Determined to carry out the draft in New York lest successful resistance there spawn imitation elsewhere, the government built

37. Exaggerated contemporary estimates of more than a thousand persons killed found their way into popular histories of the riot. But the careful research of Adrian Cook has established that only 105 people were definitely killed, and another dozen or so deaths may have been linked to the rioting. Eleven of those killed were black victims of the mob, eight were soldiers, and two were policemen; the rest were rioters. Cook, *Armies of the Streets*, 193–94, 310n.

38. *Ibid.*, passim, esp. 117, 195–96.

up troop strength in Manhattan to 20,000 men who enforced calm during the resumption of drafting on August 19. By then the city council had appropriated funds to pay the commutation fees of drafted men—including, no doubt, some of the rioters.

II

The specter of class conflict also haunted the South. As in the North, conscription worsened the friction. Manpower needs had forced the Confederate Congress in September 1862 to raise the upper age limit from thirty-five to forty-five. This made the heads of many poor families suddenly subject to the draft at a time when that summer's drought had devastated food crops. And Congress added insult to injury by a provision to exempt one white man on every plantation with twenty or more slaves.

This controversial exemption was the result of pressure from planter families. The South had gone to war, among other reasons, to defend slavery. But if all white men on plantations went into the army, discipline would erode, slaves would continue to run off to the swamps or to the Yankees, and slavery itself would crumble away. The South was also fighting to preserve a certain vision of womanhood. To leave white women alone on plantations to cope with large numbers of slaves was hardly compatible with this vision. A letter from an Alabama woman to the governor in September 1862 bespoke a situation that seemed to call for action. "I have no brother *no one* on whom I can call for aid," she wrote. "I am living *alone* now, with only my child a little girl of 2 years old. I am now surrounded on all sides by plantations of negroes—many of them have not a white [man] on them. I am now begging you will not you in kindness to a poor unprotected woman and child give me the power of having my overseer recalled." The Confederacy also needed the food and fiber raised on plantations, and southerners believed that without overseers the slaves would raise nothing. Planters insisted that the exemption of overseers was at least as important to the war effort as the exemption of teachers or apothecaries. In October 1862 Congress concurred, though not without objections by some senators against this legislation "in favour of slave labour against white labour." [39]

By granting a special privilege to a class constituting only 5 percent

---

39. Quotations from Armstead Robinson, "Bitter Fruits of Bondage: Slavery's Demise and the Collapse of the Confederacy, 1861–1865," unpublished ms, chap. 5, pp. 15, 27.

of the white population, the "Twenty-Negro Law" became as unpopular in the South as commutation in the North. Although only four or five thousand planters or overseers obtained exemptions under the law—representing about 15 percent of the eligible plantations and 3 percent of the men exempted for all causes—the symbolism of the law was powerful. Many of the men who deserted from Confederate armies during the winter of 1862-63 agreed with a Mississippi farmer who went AWOL because he "did not propose to fight for the rich men while they were at home having a good time." Alarmed by what he heard on a trip home from Richmond, Mississippi's Senator James Phelan wrote to his friend Jefferson Davis on December 9: "Never did a law meet with more universal odium. . . . Its influence upon the poor is calamitous. . . . It has aroused a spirit of rebellion in some places, I am informed, and bodies of men have banded together to resist; whilst in the army it is said it only needs some daring men to raise the standard to develop a revolt."[40]

Such protests made limited headway against planter influence. Congress modified but never repealed the twenty-Negro exemption, which remained a divisive issue for the rest of the war. One modification in May 1863 required planters to pay $500 for the privilege; another in February 1864 reduced the number of slaves to fifteen but specified that exempted plantations must sell to the government at fixed cost 200 pounds of meat per slave, part of it for the families of needy soldiers. As this requirement suggests, hunger was a serious factor in the disaffection of yeoman and laboring classes. Despite the conversion of much acreage from cotton to food crops in 1862, the drought and the breakdown of southern transportation—not to mention Union conquest of prime agricultural regions—led to severe food shortages the following winter. The quickening pace of inflation also drove the price of food, even when available, beyond the reach of many. Having doubled in the latter half of 1862, the price index doubled again in the first half of 1863. In Richmond, War Department clerk John Jones saw his salary fall farther and farther behind the cost of living until in March 1863 "the shadow of the gaunt form of famine is upon us." Jones had lost twenty pounds

40. Quotations from Bell Irvin Wiley, *Southern Negroes 1861–1865* (New Haven, 1938), 49n., and O.R., Ser. I, Vol. 17, pt. 2, p. 790. For statistics on draft exemptions, see Albert B. Moore, *Conscription and Conflict in the Confederacy* (New York, 1924), 107–08.

"and my wife and children are emaciated." Even the rats in his kitchen were so hungry that they ate bread crumbs from his daughter's hand "as tame as kittens. Perhaps we shall have to eat them!"[41]

Women and children on farms suffered as much as those in cities. A farm woman in North Carolina wrote to Governor Zebulon Vance in April 1863 describing how "a crowd of we Poor wemen went to Greenesborough yesterday for something to eat as we had not a mouthful of meet nor bread in my house what did they do but put us in gail in plase of giveing us aney thing to eat. . . . I have 6 little children and my husband in the armey and what am I to do?" What indeed? Some women wrote to Confederate officials pleading for the discharge of their husbands. One letter to the secretary of war insisted that the writer's husband "is not able to do your government much good and he might do his children some good and thare is no use in keeping a man thare to kill him and leave widows and poore little orphen children to suffer while the rich has aplenty to work for them."[42]

Such appeals availed little, so thousands of husbands discharged themselves. "There is already a heap of men gone home," wrote a Mississippi private to his wife in November 1862, "and a heap says if their familys get to suffering that they will go [too]." A month later a distressed officer in Bragg's Army of Tennessee declared that "desertions are multiplying so fast in this army that almost one-third of it is gone."[43]

Many of these deserters joined with draft-evaders in backcountry regions to form guerrilla bands that resisted Confederate authority and virtually ruled whole counties. Some of these "regulators" formed ties with the antiwar or unionist secret societies that sprang up in 1862 and 1863: the Peace and Constitution Society in Arkansas; the Peace Society in northern Alabama and northern Georgia; and the Heroes of America in western North Carolina and east Tennessee. The rich man's war/poor man's fight theme stimulated the growth of these societies just as it strengthened copperheads in the North. Although the southern peace societies did not achieve the visibility or influence that an established political party gave northern copperheads, they drained vitality from the

41. Jones, *War Clerk's Diary* (Miers), 170, 243, 164.
42. W. Buck Yearns and John G. Barrett, eds., *North Carolina Civil War Documentary* (Chapel Hill, 1980), 221; Paul D. Escott, *After Secession: Jefferson Davis and the Failure of Confederate Nationalism* (Baton Rouge, 1978), 108.
43. Robinson, "Bitter Fruits of Bondage," chap. 5, pp. 38, 40.

Confederate war effort in certain regions and formed the nucleus for a significant peace movement if the war should take a turn for the worse.[44]

Was it especially a poor man's fight in the South? Probably no more than it was in the North, according to the following table based on data from seven Confederate states.[45]

Occupational Categories	Confederate Soldiers	White Males (From 1860 Census)
Planters, farmers, and farm laborers	61.5%	57.5%
Skilled laborers	14.1	15.7
Unskilled laborers	8.5	12.7
White-collar and commercial	7.0	8.3
Professional	5.2	5.0
Miscellaneous and unknown	3.7	.8

From this sample it appears that, adjusted for age, both skilled and unskilled laborers were under-represented in the Confederate army while business and professional classes may have been over-represented. The most important categories in this rural society, however, were farmers and planters. Unfortunately, neither the census nor the regimental muster rolls consistently distinguished between these two classes, so it is impossible to tell whether "planters" were under-represented. The only study of this question found that in three piedmont counties of Georgia the average wealth of men who did not serve in the army was about 20 percent greater than those who did.[46] The pattern indicated by this lim-

44. Georgia Lee Tatum, *Disloyalty in the Confederacy* (Chapel Hill, 1944).

45. The data on Confederate soldiers are drawn from a sample of 9,057 men listed in the company rolls of regiments from Alabama, Arkansas, Georgia, Louisiana, Mississippi, North Carolina, and Virginia. I am indebted to the late Bell Irvin Wiley for his generosity in supplying me these data from his research files.

46. J. William Harris, *Plain Folk and Gentry in a Slave Society: White Liberty and Black Slavery in Augusta's Hinterlands* (Middletown, Conn., 1986), 152. Harris compiled a sample of men of military age from three Georgia counties, determined their wealth and slaveholding (or that of their families) from the manuscript returns of the 1860 census, and searched the roster of Georgia soldiers in the Confederate army to determine which men in his sample served in the army and which did not.

ited sample may have been counterbalanced for the Confederacy as a whole by the greater tendency of men from its poorest upcountry regions to skedaddle, desert, or otherwise avoid Confederate service.

In any case, the symbolic power of the twenty-Negro law and the actual suffering of poor families gave greater credence to the poor man's fight theme in the South than in the North. After all, "men cannot be expected to fight for the Government that permits their wives & children to starve," wrote a southern leader in November 1862. The government—more particularly state and county governments—recognized this. Most southern states and many counties appropriated funds for assistance to the families of poor soldiers. These expenditures were financed by taxes on slaves and large landholdings, thus representing an attempt to alleviate class discontent by transferring resources from the rich to the poor. The two states that did most in this line were Georgia and North Carolina—the very states whose governors, Joseph Brown and Zebulon Vance, interposed state's-rights roadblocks to the southern war effort. The common people tended to applaud Brown or Vance and to criticize Davis, not necessarily because they favored state's rights at the expense of the Confederacy but because the state helped them while the Richmond government took away their husbands and sons and their livelihood.[47]

The Confederate government's taxes and impressments to sustain the army also caused it to appear as an oppressor. By the spring of 1863, runaway inflation finally compelled Richmond's lawmakers to seek alternatives to the printing press to finance the war. In April they followed the Union example and enacted a comprehensive tax law that included a progressive income tax, an 8 percent levy on certain goods held for sale, excise and license duties, and a 10 percent profits tax on whole-

His findings must be used with caution, however, for he found fewer than half of the men in his sample in the roster of Georgia regiments, while we know that 70 to 80 percent of southern white men of military age served in the Confederate armed forces. The wealth and slaveholding of men missing from the incomplete army records might have modified Harris's findings if they could have been identified.

47. Quotation from Robinson, "Bitter Fruits of Bondage," chap. 6, p. 12. For progressive taxation and public welfare policies in Georgia and North Carolina, see Peter Wallenstein, "Rich Man's War, Rich Man's Fight: Civil War and the Transformation of Public Finance in Georgia," *JSH*, 50 (1984), 15–42; and Paul D. Escott, "Poverty and Government Aid for the Poor in Confederate North Carolina," *North Carolina Historical Review*, 61 (1984), 462–80.

salers intended to take back some of the money that "speculators" had "extorted" from the people. But the notion that these taxes would make the rich pay their share was neutralized by an additional category of items that were taxed and one that was not. Because money had so little value, Congress imposed a 10 percent "tax in kind" on agricultural produce. After reserving a subsistence for his family, each farmer had to turn over 10 percent of the surplus to one of the three thousand agents who fanned out through the South to collect it. Yeoman farmers bitterly resented this levy. Why should the poor husbandman—or rather husbandwoman, since so many men were at the front—have to pay 10 percent, they asked, when a clerk or teacher with a salary of $1,500 paid only 2 percent of his income? More pointedly, why was the chief property of the rich—slaves—*not* taxed? The answer: a tax on slaves was considered a direct tax, constitutionally permissible only after an apportionment on the basis of population. No census could be taken in wartime, hence no direct tax was possible. The relevance of this constitutional inhibition escaped most dirt farmers, who saw only that the revenue agents took their produce while the rich man's slaves escaped taxation.

In practice the tax in kind seemed little different from "impressment" of supplies by the army. Desperate for provisions, commissary and quartermaster officers scoured the countryside for food, fodder, and work animals. They paid whatever price *they* (not the farmer) considered fair with promissory notes that deteriorated in value still further before the farmer could cash them. By the end of the war an estimated half-billion dollars of these worthless IOUs were outstanding. Some army units, especially the cavalry, took what they wanted without even pretending to pay. "If God Almighty," wrote an angry Governor Vance to the War Department in 1863, "had yet in store another plague worse than all others which he intended to have let loose on the Egyptians in case Pharoah still hardened his heart, I am sure it must have been a regiment or so of half-armed, half-disciplined Confederate cavalry." Despite the notorious reputation of northern invaders in this regard, many southerners believed that "the Yankees cannot do us any more harm than our own soldiers have done."[48] Impressment fell with impartial injustice on the rich and the poor who happened to live near active military operations. But because the family farmer could scarcely afford to lose what little he had, impressment became another source of his alienation from the government and the cause it represented.

48. Quotations from Escott, *After Secession*, 111.

Responding to the outcries against impressment, Congress in March 1863 passed a law to regulate it by creating commissions to fix and arbitrate "fair" prices. This law was honored most often in the breach, however, and abuses continued. More successful were revisions of the tax law in February 1864. Suspending the requirement for a census-based apportionment of direct taxes, Congress imposed a 5 percent levy on land and slaves. Families with property worth less than $500 were exempted from the tax in kind. At the same time the revision of the twenty-Negro law that impressed 200 pounds of meat per slave got the Confederate government into the food-welfare business.

But these measures came too late to avert the most shocking revelation of internal stress—the bread riots in the spring of 1863. In a dozen or more cities and hamlets from Richmond to Mobile, desperate women raided shops or supply depots for food. Many of the riots followed a similar pattern. Groups of women, many of them wives of soldiers and some armed with knives or revolvers, marched in a body to shops owned by "speculators" and asked the price of bacon or flour. When informed, they denounced such "extortion," took what they wanted, and marched away.[49]

By far the largest and most momentous riot occurred in Richmond. Special circumstances made the Confederate capital particularly volatile. Its population had more than doubled since 1861. Military operations had desolated many food-producing areas of Virginia. Lee's army on the Rappahannock, reduced to half-rations by March 1863, competed with the civilian population for dwindling stocks of the previous year's drought-curtailed crops. In late March a freak nine-inch snowfall made roads impassable for several days. Prices for the few goods left on merchants' shelves skyrocketed to famine levels. On April 2 several hundred women—many of them wives of employees at the Tredegar Iron Works—met at a Baptist church and proceeded to the governor's mansion to make known their distress. The governor offered little comfort, and as the delegation moved on it turned into a mob. A middle-class bystander talked to one of the members, an emaciated girl of eighteen. "As she raised her hand to remove her sunbonnet, her loose calico sleeve slipped up, and revealed a mere skeleton of an arm. She perceived my expression as I looked at it, and hastily pulled down her sleeve with a short laugh. 'This is all that's left of me!' she said. 'It seems

49. E. Merton Coulter, *The Confederate States of America 1861–1865* (Baton Rouge, 1950), 422–23.

real funny don't it?' " The bystander asked what was going on. "We are starving," said the girl. "We are going to the bakeries and each of us will take a loaf of bread. That is little enough for the government to give us after it has taken all our men." Grown to more than a thousand persons, including some men and boys, the mob broke into shops and warehouses. "Bread! Bread!" they shouted. "Our children are starving while the rich roll in wealth." Emboldened by success, some women began to seize clothing, shoes, even jewelry as well as food. The governor and mayor confronted the rioters and called on them to disperse. A hastily mobilized company of militia marched up and loaded their muskets. A few timid souls left but the majority remained, confident that the militia—which contained friends and perhaps even a few husbands of the rioters—would not obey orders to fire on the crowd.[50]

At this juncture Jefferson Davis himself arrived and climbed onto a cart to address the mob. He commanded their attention by taking several coins from his pocket and throwing them into the crowd. He then told them to go home so that the muskets leveled against them could be turned against the common enemy—the Yankees. The crowd was unmoved, and a few boys hissed the president. Taking out his watch, Davis gave the rioters five minutes to disperse before he ordered the troops to fire. Four minutes passed in tense silence. Holding up his watch, the president said firmly: "My friends, you have one minute more." This succeeded. The rioters melted away. Davis pocketed his watch and ordered the police to arrest the ringleaders. Several of these were later convicted and briefly imprisoned. Military officials ordered newspapers to make no mention of the riot in order not "to embarrass our cause [or] to encourage our enemies."[51] The lead editorial in the *Richmond Dispatch* next day was entitled "Sufferings in the North."

But the rioters had made their point. The government distributed some of its stock of rice to needy citizens. Apprehensive merchants brought out reserve stocks of food, and prices dropped by half. The Richmond city council expanded its welfare food aid. Other localities did likewise. More acreage than the previous year went over from cotton to corn. But

50. Mrs. Roger A. Pryor, *Reminiscences of Peace and War* (New York, 1905), 238; Hudson Strode, *Jefferson Davis: Confederate President* (New York, 1959), 381. Two good descriptions of the riot can be found in Emory M. Thomas, *The Confederate State of Richmond* (Austin, 1971), 117–22; and Emory M. Thomas, *The Confederate Nation: 1861–1865* (New York, 1979), 201–6.
51. O.R., Ser. I, Vol. 18, p. 958.

serious problems persisted, and the South was never able to solve them. Priorities for military traffic on deteriorating railroads caused food to rot at sidings while thousands went hungry a hundred miles away. Union advances further constricted the food-producing areas of the Confederacy. In July 1863 the commissary general warned of a subsistence crisis for southern armies. In September a mob at Mobile, crying "bread or blood," looted stores on Dauphine Street. In October the *Richmond Examiner* declared that civilians were being reduced "to a point of starvation." A government clerk told of the following exchange between a woman and a shopkeeper in Richmond who asked $70 for a barrel of flour. "My God!" she exclaimed. "How can I pay such prices? I have seven children; what shall I do?" "I don't know, madam," the merchant replied, "unless you eat your children."[52]

Refugees exacerbated the South's food crisis. Tens of thousands of civilians fled their homes as the Yankee juggernaut bore down on them. Thousands of others were exiled by Confederate officers who turned their cities into a battle zone (Corinth and Fredericksburg, for example) or by commanders of Union occupation forces who insisted that they take the oath of allegiance or leave. All wars produce refugees; these homeless people generally suffer more than the rest of the civilian population; in the American Civil War this suffering was confined almost entirely to the South. As these fugitives packed the roads and crowded in with friends and relatives or endured cheerless boardinghouses in towns and cities, they taxed the South's ever-decreasing resources and added to the uncounted deaths of white and black civilians from disease and malnutrition—deaths that must be included in any reckoning of the war's human cost.[53]

52. Thomas, *Confederate Nation*, 204–5; Jones, *War Clerk's Diary* (Miers), 296.
53. Mary Elizabeth Massey, *Refugee Life in the Confederacy* (Baton Rouge, 1964), chronicles the hardships of the refugees but makes no attempt to estimate their numbers or their mortality. Civilians in a fought-over country often suffer a higher number of war-related deaths than soldiers, because there are so many more civilians than soldiers. Probably twice as many civilians as soldiers in Europe died as a direct or indirect result of the Napoleonic wars. The shorter duration and smaller geographical scope of the fighting in the Civil War surely kept the civilian death rate far below this level. And with the exception of a yellow fever outbreak in Wilmington during 1862, there appear to have been no serious epidemics during the American Civil War. Suffering and death were widespread, nevertheless, and a fair estimate of war-related civilian deaths might total 50,000, which should be added to the 260,000 Confederate soldier deaths to measure the human cost of the war to the South.

Most civilians in conquered areas, of course, stayed home to live under their new rulers. And in the material if not the spiritual realm, they lived better than their compatriots who fled southward. The Yankee occupation, indeed, presented lucrative opportunities to interested parties on both sides of the line. Flourishing trade, both licit and illicit, grew up between former and sometimes continuing enemies.

Clandestine commerce between enemies is as old as war itself. Americans had proved themselves skilled at this enterprise in the Revolution and the War of 1812. The Civil War offered vastly greater scope for such activities. Free and slave states had lived in economic symbiosis before 1861; their mutual dependence became even more urgent in some respects during the war. "Physically speaking, we cannot separate," Lincoln had said in his first inaugural address. "We cannot remove our respective sections from each other . . . and intercourse, either amicable or hostile, must continue between them."[54] Intercourse both hostile *and* amicable continued for the next four years in ways that neither Lincoln nor anyone else had anticipated. The South needed salt, shoes, clothing, bacon, flour, medicine, gunpowder, lead, and other necessities of war from the outside world. Since the blockade restricted the flow of these supplies from abroad, canny Confederates sought to flank the blockade by direct trade with the North. Enterprising Yankees were willing to exchange such goods for cotton. Both governments officially banned trade with the enemy. But when the price of a pound of cotton leapt from ten cents to a dollar in the North while the price of a sack of salt jumped from $1.25 to $60 in parts of the South, venturesome men would find a way to trade cotton for salt. An English resident of the Confederacy observed that "a Chinese wall from the Atlantic to the Pacific" could not stop this commerce.[55]

The war's first year witnessed a considerable amount of smuggling between the lines in Kentucky and through southern counties of Maryland. The real bonanza, however, began with the Union conquests in the Mississippi Valley during 1862. First Nashville, then New Orleans and Memphis became centers of a flourishing trade in this region. Some of this exchange was legitimate. Eager to restore commercial activities in occupied areas and to win their inhabitants back to unionism, the Treasury Department issued trade permits to merchants and planters who took an oath of allegiance. Having taken the oath a merchant in

54. CWL, IV, 269.
55. Coulter, *Confederate States*, 287.

Memphis, for example, could sell cotton for cash or credit which he could then use to purchase a cargo of salt, flour, and shoes from Cincinnati for sale within Union-occupied territory. The Treasury hoped that trade would follow the flag as northern armies moved south until the whole South was commercially "reconstructed."

The problem was that trade had a tendency to get ahead of the flag. Some southerners within Union lines swore the oath with mental reservations. Others bribed Treasury agents to obtain a trading permit. Having sold cotton and bought salt or shoes, these men in turn smuggled the latter to southern armies or to merchants serving the civilian market behind Confederate lines. Some northern traders paid for cotton with gold, which eventually found its way to Nassau in the Bahamas to pay for rifles shipped through the blockade. Traders sometimes bribed Union soldiers to look the other way when cotton or salt was going through the lines. A good many soldiers could not resist the temptation to get in on the profits directly. The "mania for sudden fortunes made in cotton," wrote Charles A. Dana from Memphis in January 1863, "has to an alarming extent corrupted and demoralized the army. Every colonel, captain, or quartermaster is in secret partnership with some operator in cotton; every soldier dreams of adding a bale of cotton to his monthly pay. I had no conception of the extent of this evil until I came and saw for myself." [56]

On the other side of the line a Confederate officer complained that the cotton trade had also "corrupted and demoralized" southerners who were subtly enticed into the Union web instead of burning their cotton to keep it out of Yankee hands. The *Richmond Examiner* spoke bitterly in July 1863 of "those rampant cotton and sugar planters, who were so early and furiously in the field for secession" but "having taken the oath of allegiance to the Yankees, are now raising cotton in partnership with their Yankee *protectors*, and shipping it to Yankee markets." This "shameless moral turpitude . . . inflicts a heavy injury upon the general cause of the South, which is forsaken by these apostates." [57]

In theory the Confederate War Department agreed that "all trade with the enemy" was indeed "demoralizing and illegal and should, of course, be discountenanced, but [and this was a big but] situated as the people to a serious extent are . . . some barter or trading for the supply of their necessities is almost inevitable." Even Jefferson Davis, incorrupti-

56. O.R., Ser. I, Vol. 52, pt. 1, p. 331.
57. *Ibid.*, Ser. IV, Vol. 3, pp. 646–48; *Richmond Examiner*, July 21, 1863.

ble to a fault, conceded that "as a last resort we might be justified in departing from the declared policy" against trade with the enemy, "but the necessity should be absolute."[58] For the Confederacy the necessity was usually absolute. Trade with the Yankees prevented famine in some areas and kept Van Dorn's Army of Mississippi in the field during the fall of 1862. "The alternative," stated the secretary of war starkly, "is thus presented of violating our established policy of withholding cotton from the enemy or of risking the starvation of our armies."[59]

Believing that "we cannot carry on war and trade with a people at the same time," Sherman and Grant did their best to stop the illicit cotton trade through Memphis and western Tennessee in 1862.[60] The two generals issued a stream of regulations to tighten the granting of permits for legal trade, banished southerners who refused to take the oath and imprisoned some who violated it, required that all payments for cotton be made in U.S. greenbacks (instead of gold that could be converted into guns at Nassau), and tried to prevent the access of unscrupulous northern traders to Memphis. But much of this was like Canute trying to hold back the waves. The order banning gold payments was overruled in Washington. And one of Grant's restrictive regulations was also rescinded after achieving an unhappy notoriety.

Several highly visible traders who defied Grant's orders were Jews. Grant and other Union generals had frequently complained about Jewish "speculators whose love of gain is greater than their love of country."[61] When Grant's own father brought three Jewish merchants to Memphis seeking special permits, his son the general lost his temper and on December 17, 1862, issued this order: "The Jews, as a class, violating every regulation of trade established by the Treasury Department, and also Department orders, are hereby expelled from the Department." Jewish spokesmen denounced this "enormous outrage" that punished a whole group for the alleged sins of a few. Sensing an issue, House Democrats introduced a resolution, but Republicans tabled it. Lincoln rescinded Grant's order, explaining through Halleck that while

58. O.R., Ser. IV, Vol. 2, pp. 334–35, 175.

59. Ludwell H. Johnson, "Trading with the Union: The Evolution of Confederate Policy," The Virginia Magazine of History and Biography, 78 (1970), 314.

60. O. R., Ser. I, Vol. 17, pt. 2, p. 141.

61. Ibid., 123. Although most traders were not in fact Jewish, harassed Union officers had come to use the word "Jew" in the same way many southerners used "Yankee"—as a shorthand way of describing anyone they considered shrewd, acquisitive, aggressive, and possibly dishonest.

he had no objection to expelling dishonest traders, the order "proscribed a whole class, some of whom are fighting in our ranks."[62] Grant said no more about Jews, but six months later he summed up the frustrations of his efforts to regulate a trade that "is weakening us of at least 33 percent of our force. . . . I will venture that no honest man has made money in West Tennessee in the last year, whilst many fortunes have been made there during that time."[63]

Fortunes were made in New Orleans, too, where Benjamin Butler ruled a restive city with a sharp two-edged sword. Cynical, clever, and apparently unscrupulous, Butler in New Orleans presented a paradox. On the one hand his Woman Order, his hanging of a southern gambler who had torn down the U. S. flag at the beginning of the occupation, and his imprisonment of several citizens who defied or displeased him earned everlasting southern hatred of "Beast" Butler. In December 1862, Jefferson Davis even issued a proclamation declaring Butler an outlaw and ordering any Confederate officer so lucky as to capture him to hang him straightway. On the other hand, Butler's martial law gave New Orleans the most efficient and healthy administration it had ever had. Rigorous enforcement of sanitary and quarantine measures cleaned the normally filthy streets and helped ward off the annual scourge of yellow fever. Butler was "the best scavenger we ever had," wryly commented a native. Before the war, conceded a local newspaper, New Orleans had been ruled by plug-ugly street gangs—"the most godless, brutal, ignorant, and ruthless ruffianism the world has ever heard of." After three months of martial law even the pro-Confederate *Picayune* had to confess that the city had never been "so free from burglars and cutthroats."[64]

The paradox extended to Butler's economic policies. The Union blockade by sea and the Confederate blockade of river commerce with the North had strangled the city's economy. Most workers were unemployed when Farragut captured the city. Butler distributed Union rations to the poor and inaugurated an extensive public works program financed in part by high taxes on the rich and confiscation of the prop-

---

62. Documentation and details of this matter can be found in John Y. Simon, ed., *The Papers of Ulysses S. Grant*, 14 vols. (Carbondale, Ill., 1967–85), VII, 50–56. See also Bruce Catton, *Grant Moves South* (Boston, 1960), 352–56.
63. Grant to Salmon P. Chase, July 31, 1863, in O.R., Ser. I, Vol. 24, pt. 3, p. 538.
64. Quotations from Gerald M. Capers, *Occupied City: New Orleans under the Federals 1862–1865* (Lexington, Ky., 1965), 89, 73, 71.

erty of some wealthy rebels who refused to take the oath of allegiance. These procedures earned the general another Confederate cognomen— "Spoons" Butler—for allegedly stealing southerners' silver for the enrichment of himself and his Yankee friends. Some truth stuck to this charge, as Union officers and other northerners who flocked to the city bought confiscated valuables at auction for nominal prices. The northerners included Butler's brother Andrew and other Yankee businessmen who helped the general with his project of obtaining cotton for northern mills. These speculators bribed their way through Treasury officials and army officers to make deals with planters and brokers beyond Union lines, trading salt and gold for cotton and sugar. Both sides sometimes used French agents as go-betweens to preserve the fiction of trading with a neutral instead of the enemy. Nothing illegal was proved against Butler himself—an unfriendly Treasury officer described him as "such a smart man, that it would, in any case, be difficult to discover what he wished to conceal"—but his brother Andrew returned home several hundred thousand dollars richer than he came.[65]

Butler's notoriety compelled Lincoln to recall him in December 1862. His successor was Nathaniel P. Banks, fresh from defeats by Stonewall Jackson in Virginia. Banks tried to ban trade with the enemy and to substitute conciliation for coercion in ruling the natives—with limited success in both efforts. Treasury regulations and congressional legislation in 1863–64 curtailed the permit system for private traders. The North also began obtaining more cotton from the cultivation of plantations in occupied territory by freed slaves. But none of this seemed to diminish the commerce between the lines. The Davis administration looked the other way out of necessity; the Lincoln administration looked the other way out of policy. The North needed the cotton for its own industry and for export to earn foreign exchange. To one angry general who could not understand this policy, Lincoln explained that the war had driven the gold price of cotton to six times its prewar level, enabling the South to earn as much foreign exchange from the export of one bale through the blockade as it would have earned from six bales in peacetime. Every bale that came North, even by means of "private interest and pecuniary greed," was one less bale for the enemy to export. "Better give him *guns* for it than let him, as now, get both guns and ammunition for it."[66]

65. *Ibid.*, 79–94, 161–67; quotation from p. 84.
66. Lincoln to Edward R. S. Canby, Dec. 12, 1864, in *CWL*, VIII, 163–64. During

Lincoln's rationalization did not satisfy the general, nor does it fully satisfy the historian. Cotton was the great corrupter of the Civil War; as a Confederate general noted, it made "more damn rascals on both sides than anything else."[67] This corrosion in the rear—like the antiwar fire in the rear—grew from a malaise of the flesh in the resource-starved South and a malaise of the spirit in the North. During the winter of 1862–63 this northern malaise, spread by military defeat, appeared more fatal than the South's malaise of the flesh. Military success was a strong antidote for hunger. Buoyed by past victories in Virginia and the apparent frustration of Grant's designs against Vicksburg, the South faced the spring military campaigns with confidence. "If we can baffle them in their various designs this year," wrote Robert E. Lee in April 1863, "next fall there will be a great change in public opinion at the North. The Republicans will be destroyed & I think the friends of peace will become so strong as that the next administration will go in on that basis. We have only therefore to resist manfully . . . [and] our success will be certain."[68]

---

the war some 900,000 bales of cotton found their way from the Confederacy to the North—nearly double the amount the South managed to export through the blockade. About one-third of this trade with the North was lawful commerce by permit in occupied territory; the remainder was illicit. Stanley Lebergott, "Why the South Lost: Commercial Purpose in the Confederacy, 1861–1865," *JAH*, 70 (1983), 72–73.

67. Capers, *Occupied City*, 164.
68. Robert E. Lee to his wife, April 19, 1863, in Clifford Dowdey and Louis H. Manarin, eds., *The Wartime Papers of R. E. Lee* (New York, 1961), 438.

21

Long Remember: The Summer of '63

I

Grant's failure during the winter of 1862–63 to get his army on dry land for a drive against Vicksburg bolstered Confederate faith in this "Gibraltar of the West." Believing that the Yankees were giving up, Pemberton on April 11 informed Joseph Johnston that "Grant's forces are being withdrawn to Memphis." Pemberton had earlier sent most of his cavalry to Bragg in Tennessee, where danger appeared more imminent, and he now prepared to dispatch an 8,000-man infantry division to Bragg. On April 16 the *Vicksburg Whig* gloated that the enemy's gunboats "are all more or less damaged, the men dissatisfied and demoralized. . . . There is no immediate danger here." Civilians and officers celebrated at a gala ball held in Vicksburg that night of April 16. As the dancers swung from a waltz into a cotillion, flashes of light and loud explosions suddenly rent the air. "Confusion and alarm" erupted in the ballroom. Yankee gunboats were running the batteries. Grant had not gone to Memphis; he had only backed up for a better start.[1]

One northerner who had never lost confidence in eventual victory at Vicksburg was Grant. All of his roundabout routes through canals, bayous, and swamps having failed, he resolved on a bold plan to march his

---

1. Samuel Carter III, *The Final Fortress: The Campaign for Vicksburg 1862–1863* (New York, 1980), 155; Peter F. Walker, *Vicksburg: A People at War, 1860–1865* (Chapel Hill, 1960), 151, 152.

626

army down the west bank of the Mississippi to a point below Vicksburg while sending the fleet straight past the batteries to rendezvous with the troops downriver. There they could carry the army across the mile-wide water for a dry-ground campaign against this Gibraltar from the south-east. Apparently simple, the plan involved large risks. The gunboat fleet might be destroyed or crippled. Even if it survived to ferry Grant's soldiers across the river, they would be virtually cut off from their base, for while the ironclads and even some supply transports might get past Vicksburg *down*river with the help of a four-knot current, they would be sitting ducks if they tried to go back up again. The army would have to operate deep in enemy territory without a supply line against a force of unknown strength which held interior lines and could be reinforced.

Grant's staff and his most trusted subordinates, Sherman and Mc-Pherson, opposed the plan. Go back to Memphis, Sherman advised Grant, and start over again with a secure supply line. Grant's reply demonstrated his true mettle. Like Lee, he believed that success could not be achieved without risk, and he was willing to lay his career on the line to prove it. As for returning to Memphis, he told Sherman,

> the country is already disheartened over the lack of success on the part of our armies. . . . If we went back so far as Memphis it would discourage the people so much that bases of supplies would be of no use: neither men to hold them nor supplies to put in them would be furnished. The problem for us was to move forward to a decisive victory, or our cause was lost. No progress was being made in any other field, and we had to go on.[2]

Grant's first gamble paid off; the gunboats got through. As they floated silently on the current toward Vicksburg on the moonless night of April 16, rebel pickets spotted them and lit bonfires along the banks to illuminate the target for Vicksburg's gunners, who fired 525 rounds and scored sixty-eight hits but sank only one of the three transports and none of the eight gunboats. A few nights later, volunteer crews ran six more transports past the batteries and got five of them through. By the end of April Grant had a powerful fleet and two of his three corps thirty miles south of Vicksburg ready to cross the river.

To divert Pemberton from challenging this crossing, Grant arranged a cavalry raid deep in the rebel rear and an infantry feint above Vicksburg. On the day after Porter's fleet had so rudely interrupted the Vicks-

---

2. *The Personal Memoirs of U. S. Grant*, 2 vols. (New York, 1885), I, 542–43n.

burg ball, a former music teacher from Illinois set forth on what would become the most spectacular cavalry adventure of the war. Benjamin Grierson had disliked horses since one kicked him in the head as a child. When the war broke out he had joined the infantry, but the governor of Illinois soon assigned this erstwhile bandmaster to the cavalry. It was a stroke of genius, for Grierson soon became one of the finest horse soldiers in the western theater, where he rose to brigade command in 1862. In the spring of 1863 Grant borrowed a leaf from the enemy's book and ordered Grierson's 1,700-man brigade on an expedition into the heart of Mississippi to tear up Pemberton's supply lines and distract Confederate attention from the Union infantry toiling down the river's west bank. Combining speed, boldness, and cunning, Grierson's troopers swept through the entire state of Mississippi during the last two weeks of April. They won several skirmishes, killed or wounded a hundred rebels, and captured five hundred at a cost of two dozen casualties. They tore up fifty miles of three different railroads supplying Pemberton's army, burned scores of freight cars and depots, and finally rode exhausted into Union lines at Baton Rouge after sixteen days and six hundred miles of marauding. They had lured most of Pemberton's depleted cavalry plus a full infantry division into futile pursuit—futile because Grierson, having detached smaller units from the main body to ride off in various false directions, was never where the rebels expected him to be. Grierson more than evened the score against Forrest and Morgan. The Yankees rode through enemy territory, while the southern horsemen raided in Tennessee and Kentucky, where friendly natives aided them. And the strategic consequences of Grierson's foray were greater, perhaps, than those of any other cavalry raid of the war, for it played a vital role in Grant's capture of Vicksburg.

Thanks to Grierson's raid, and thanks also to a feigned attack north of Vicksburg by one of Sherman's divisions, Grant's crossing on April 30 was unopposed. Sherman had landed this division near the site of his Chickasaw Bayou repulse the previous December. For two days Sherman's artillery and a few light gunboats shelled Confederate defenses while the infantry deployed as if for attack. Pemberton took the bait. In response to a panicky message from the commander confronting Sherman—"The enemy are in front of me in force such as has never before been seen at Vicksburg. Send me reinforcements"—Pemberton recalled 3,000 troops who had been on their way to challenge Grant.[3]

3. Carter, *Final Fortress*, 182.

The 23,000 bluecoats with Grant moved quickly to overwhelm the only rebels in the vicinity, 6,000 infantry at Port Gibson ten miles east of the river. The Yankees brushed them aside after a sharp fight on May 1. Having established a secure lodgement, Grant sent for Sherman and the rest of his troops, who would bring Union strength east of the river to more than 40,000 to oppose Pemberton's 30,000 scattered in various detachments. Pemberton finally recognized that Grant had crossed his whole army below Vicksburg. But what to do about it was a puzzle because Grant's purpose remained unclear. His most logical move would seem to be a drive straight northward toward Vicksburg, keeping his left flank in contact with the river where he might hope to receive additional supplies from transports that ran the batteries. But Grant knew that Joseph Johnston was trying to scrape together an army at Jackson, the state capital forty miles east of Vicksburg. If he ignored Johnston and went after Pemberton, the Yankees might suddenly find another enemy on their right flank. So Grant decided to drive eastward, eliminate the Johnston threat before it became serious and before Pemberton realized what was happening, and then turn back west to attack Vicksburg.

As for provisions, Grant remembered what he had learned after Van Dorn's destruction of his supply base the previous December. This time he intended to cut loose from his base, travel light, and live off the country. Although civilians were going hungry in Mississippi, Grant was confident that his soldiers would not. A powerful army on the move could seize supplies that penniless women and children could not afford to buy. For the next two weeks the Yankee soldiers lived well on hams, poultry, vegetables, milk and honey as they stripped bare the plantations in their path. Some of these midwestern farm boys proved to be expert foragers. When an irate planter rode up on a mule and complained to a division commander that plundering troops had robbed him of everything he owned, the general looked him in the eye and said: "Well, those men didn't belong to my division at all, because if they were my men they wouldn't have left you that mule."[4]

Divided counsels and paralysis in the face of Grant's unexpected and rapid movements crippled the Confederate response. On May 9 the War Department in Richmond ordered Johnston to take overall command of the Mississippi defenses and promised him reinforcements. But Johnston got no farther than Jackson, where he found 25,000 confident Yan-

4. Bruce Catton, *Grant Moves South* (Boston, 1960), 438.

kees bearing down on the capital after bowling over a small rebel force at Raymond a dozen miles to the west. Coming on through a rainstorm, Sherman's and McPherson's corps on May 14 launched a straight-ahead attack against the 6,000 entrenched Confederates defending Jackson and sent them flying through the streets out of town. Sherman's corps set to work at a task in which they soon became experts—wrecking railroad facilities and burning foundries, arsenals, factories, and machine shops in the capital along with a fair number of homes that got in the way of the flames, doing their work so thoroughly that Jackson became known to its conquerors as Chimneyville.

Meanwhile Johnston urged Pemberton to unite his troops with Johnston's 6,000 survivors north of Jackson, where with expected reinforcements they would be strong enough to attack Grant. This would leave Vicksburg undefended, but Johnston cared little about that. His strategy was to concentrate superior numbers against Grant and beat him, after which the Confederates could reoccupy Vicksburg at leisure. Pemberton disagreed. He had orders to hold Vicksburg and he intended to do so by shielding it with his army. Before the two southern generals could agree on a plan, the Yankees made the matter moot by slicing up Pemberton's mobile force on May 16 at Champion's Hill, midway between Jackson and Vicksburg.

This was the key battle of the campaign, involving about 29,000 Federals against 20,000 Confederates. The Union troops were McPherson's and McClernand's corps (Sherman's men were still burning Jackson), which found the rebels posted along four miles of the seventy-foot high Champion's Hill ridge. While the normally aggressive McClernand showed unwonted caution, McPherson pitched into the enemy left with blows that finally crumpled this flank after several hours of bloody fighting. If McClernand had done his part, Grant believed, the Yankees might have bagged most of Pemberton's army; as it was the bluecoats inflicted 3,800 casualties at the cost of 2,400 to themselves and cut off one whole division from the rest of Pemberton's force. The main body of Confederates fell back in demoralized fashion to the Big Black River only ten miles east of Vicksburg. Grant's cocky midwesterners came after them on May 17. The rebel position at the Big Black was strong, but an impetuous brigade in McClernand's corps, chafing at its lack of a share in the previous day's glory, swept forward without orders and routed the left of the Confederate line defending the bridge that Pemberton was trying to keep open for his lost division, which unbeknown to him was marching in the opposite direction to join Johnston. The unnerved rebels collapsed once again, losing 1,750 men (mostly prisoners) while Union casualties were only 200. Pemberton retreated to Vicksburg, where citizens were shocked by the exhausted countenances of the soldiers. "I shall never forget the woeful sight," wrote a Vicksburg woman on the evening of May 17. "Wan, hollow-eyed, ragged, footsore, bloody, the men limped along unarmed . . . humanity in the last throes of endurance."[5]

Thus had Grant wrought in a seventeen-day campaign during which his army marched 180 miles, fought and won five engagements against separate enemy forces which if combined would have been almost as large as his own, inflicted 7,200 casualties at the cost of 4,300, and cooped up an apparently demoralized enemy in the Vicksburg defenses. Of all the tributes Grant received, the one he appreciated most came from his friend Sherman. "Until this moment I never thought your expedition a success," Sherman told Grant on May 18 as he gazed down from the heights where his corps had been mangled the previous December. "I never could see the end clearly until now. But this is a campaign. This is a success if we never take the town."[6]

But Grant hoped to take the town, immediately, while its defenders were still stunned. Without stopping to rest, he ordered an attack by his whole army on May 19. With confidence bred by success, northern boys charged the maze of trenches, rifle pits, and artillery ringing the landward side of Vicksburg. But as they emerged into the open the rebel line came alive with sheets of fire that stopped the bluecoats in their tracks. Ensconced behind the most formidable works of the war, the rebels had taken heart. They proved the theory that one soldier under cover was the equal of at least three in the open.

Bloodied but still undaunted, the Union troops wanted to try again. Grant planned another assault for May 22, preceded this time by reconnaisance to find weak points in enemy lines (there were few) and an artillery bombardment by 200 guns on land and 100 in the fleet. Again the Yankees surged forward against a hail of lead, this time securing lodgement at several points only to be driven out by counterattacks. After several hours of this, McClernand on the Union left sent word of a breakthrough and a request for support to exploit it. Distrustful as ever of McClernand, Grant nevertheless ordered Sherman and McPherson to renew their attacks and send reinforcements to the left. But these

5. Quoted in Walker, *Vicksburg*, 161.
6. Quoted in Carter, *Final Fortress*, 208.

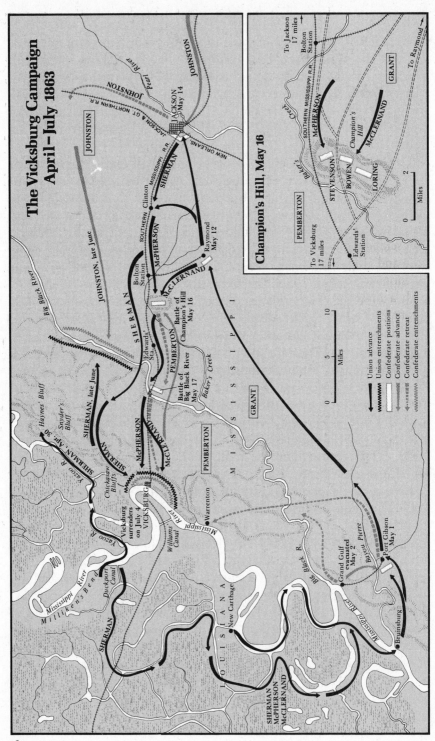

The Vicksburg Campaign
April–July 1863

JOHNSTON

JOHNSTON

Pearl River

JACKSON May 14

JACKSON & GT. NORTHERN R.R.

NEW ORLEANS

JOHNSTON

JOHNSTON, late June

SHERMAN

Clinton

SOUTHERN

MISSISSIPPI R.R.

McPHERSON

Raymond
May 12

Bolton
Station

McCLERNAND

SHERMAN

Battle of
Champion's Hill
May 16

Edwards'
Sta.

PEMBERTON

Baker's Creek

Battle of
Big Black River
May 17

Big Black River

GRANT

MISSISSIPPI

SHERMAN, late June

Haynes' Bluff

Snyder's
Bluff

Yazoo R.

SHERMAN, Apr. 30

Chickasaw
Bluffs

SHERMAN

McPHERSON

McCLERNAND

PEMBERTON

Warrenton

Vicksburg
surrenders
on July 4

VICKSBURG

Williams' Canal

Mississippi River

Duckport Canal

Mississippi River

Millikens Bend

LOUISIANA

New Carthage

SHERMAN
McPHERSON
McCLERNAND

Big Black R.

Grand Gulf
evacuated
May 2

Bayou Pierre

Port Gibson
May 1

Bruinsburg

Mississippi River

Union advance
Union entrenchments
Confederate positions
Confederate advance
Confederate retreat
Confederate entrenchments

Miles
0   5   10

Champion's Hill, May 16

To Jackson
17 miles

Bolton
Station

To Raymond

SOUTHERN MISSISSIPPI R.R.

GRANT

Baker's
Creek

McPHERSON

McCLERNAND

Champion's
Hill

PEMBERTON

STEVENSON

BOWEN

LORING

To Vicksburg
17 miles

Edwards'
Station

Miles
0   2

efforts, said Grant later, "only served to increase our casualties without giving any benefit."[7] For the second time in four days the southerners threw back an all-out attack, doing much to redeem their earlier humiliation and inflicting almost as many casualties on the enemy as in all five earlier clashes combined.

Though they failed, Grant did not consider these assaults a mistake. He had hoped to capture Vicksburg before Johnston could build up a relief force in his rear and before summer heat and disease wore down his troops. Moreover, he explained, the men "believed they could carry the works in their front, and they would not [afterwards] have worked so patiently in the trenches if they had not been allowed to try."[8] After the May repulses the bluecoats dug their own elaborate network of trenches and settled down for a siege. Grant called in reinforcements from Memphis and other points to build up his army to 70,000. He posted several divisions to watch Johnston, who was now hovering off to the northeast with a makeshift army of 30,000, some of them untrained conscripts. Grant had no doubt of ultimate success. On May 24 he informed Halleck that the enemy was "in our grasp. The fall of Vicksburg and the capture of most of the garrison can only be a question of time."[9]

Pemberton thought so too, unless help arrived. Regarding Vicksburg as "the most important point in the Confederacy," he informed Johnston in a message smuggled through Federal lines by a daring courier that he intended to hold it "as long as possible." But Pemberton could hold on only if Johnston pierced the blue cordon constricting him. "The men credit and are encouraged by a report that you are near with a large force." For the next six weeks Pemberton's soldiers and some three thousand civilians trapped in Vicksburg lived in hope of rescue by Johnston. "We certainly are in a critical situation," wrote a southern army surgeon, but "we can hold out until Johnston arrives with reinforcements and attacks Yankees in rear. . . . Davis can't intend to sacrifice us."[10]

But Davis had no more reinforcements to send. Braxton Bragg had already lent Johnston two divisions and could not spare another. Robert E. Lee insisted that he needed every soldier in Virginia for his impending invasion of Pennsylvania. In Louisiana, General Richard Taylor

7. Grant, *Memoirs*, I, 531.
8. *Ibid.*, 530–31.
9. Quoted in Foote, *Civil War*, II, 388.
10. *Ibid.*, 387; Carter, *Final Fortress*, 207, 223.

(son of Mexican War hero Zachary Taylor) reluctantly diverted three brigades from his campaign against Banks to assist Pemberton. Their only accomplishment, however, was to publicize the controversy surrounding northern employment of black troops. In a futile attempt to disrupt Grant's restored supply line, one of Taylor's brigades on June 7 attacked the Union garrison at Milliken's Bend on the Mississippi above Vicksburg. This post was defended mainly by two new regiments of contrabands. Untrained and armed with old muskets, most of the black troops nevertheless fought desperately. With the aid of two gunboats they finally drove off the enemy. For raw troops, wrote Grant, the freedmen "behaved well." Assistant Secretary of War Dana, still with Grant's army, spoke with more enthusiasm. "The bravery of the blacks," he declared, "completely revolutionized the sentiment of the army with regard to the employment of negro troops. I heard prominent officers who formerly in private had sneered at the idea of negroes fighting express themselves after that as heartily in favor of it."[11] But among the Confederates, Dana added, "the feeling was very different." Infuriated by the arming of former slaves, southern troops at Milliken's Bend shouted "no quarter!" and reportedly murdered several captured blacks. If true, such behavior undoubtedly reflected their officers' sentiment: the rebel brigade commander "consider[ed] it an unfortunate circumstance that any negroes were captured," while General Taylor reported that "a very large number of the negroes were killed and wounded, and, unfortunately, some 50, with 2 of their white officers, captured." The War Department in Washington learned that some of the captured freedmen were sold as slaves.[12]

The repulse at Milliken's Bend cut short Confederate attempts to succor Vicksburg from west of the Mississippi. All hopes for relief now focused on Johnston. The Vicksburg newspaper (reduced in size to a square foot and printed on wallpaper) buoyed up spirits with cheerful predictions: "The undaunted Johnston is at hand"; "We may look at any hour for his approach"; "Hold out a few days longer, and our lines will be opened, the enemy driven away, the siege raised."[13] During the first month of the siege, morale remained good despite around-the-clock

11. Grant, *Memoirs*, I, 545; Charles A. Dana, *Recollections of the Civil War* (New York, 1899), 86.
12. O.R., Ser. I, Vol. 24, pt. 2, pp. 466, 459.
13. Walker, *Vicksburg*, 187–88.

Union artillery and gunboat fire that drove civilians into man-made caves that dotted the hillsides.

But as the weeks passed and Johnston did not come, spirits sagged. Soldiers were subsisting on quarter rations. By the end of June nearly half of them were on the sicklist, many with scurvy. Skinned rats appeared beside mule meat in the markets. Dogs and cats disappeared mysteriously. The tensions of living under siege drove people to the edge of madness: if things went on much longer, wrote a Confederate officer, "a building will have to be arranged for the accommodation of maniacs." The tone of the newspaper changed from confidence to complaint: in the last week of June it was no longer "Johnston is coming!" but "Where is Johnston?"[14]

Johnston had never shared the belief in himself as Deliverer. "I consider saving Vicksburg hopeless," he informed the War Department on June 15. To the government this looked like a western refrain of Johnston's behavior on the Virginia Peninsula in 1862, when he had seemed reluctant to fight to defend Richmond. "Vicksburg must not be lost without a desperate struggle," the secretary of war wired back. "The interest and the honor of the Confederacy forbid it. . . . You must hazard attack. . . . The eyes and hopes of the whole Confederacy are upon you."[15] But Johnston considered his force too weak. He shifted the burden to Pemberton, urging him to try a breakout attack or to escape across the river (through the gauntlet of Union ironclads!). At the end of June, in response to frantic pressure from Richmond, Johnston began to probe feebly with his five divisions toward seven Union divisions commanded by Sherman which Grant had detached from the besiegers to guard their rear. Johnston's rescue attempt was too little and too late. By the time he was ready to take action, Pemberton had surrendered.

Inexorable circumstances forced Pemberton to this course—though many southerners then and later believed that only his Yankee birth could have produced such poltroonery. All through June, Union troops had dug approaches toward Confederate lines in a classic siege operation. They also tunneled under rebel defenses. To show what they could do, northern engineers exploded mines and blew holes in southern lines

14. Bruce Catton, *Never Call Retreat* (New York: Pocket Books ed., 1967), 195–96; Walker, *Vicksburg*, 192–96.
15. O.R., Ser. I, Vol. 24, pt. 1, pp. 227–28.

on June 25 and July 1, but Confederate infantry closed the breaches. The Yankees readied a bigger mine to be set off July 6 and followed by a full-scale assault. But before then it was all over. Literally starving, "Many Soldiers" addressed a letter to Pemberton on June 28: "If you can't feed us, you had better surrender, horrible as the idea is, than suffer this noble army to disgrace themselves by desertion. . . . This army is now ripe for mutiny, unless it can be fed."[16] Pemberton consulted his division commanders, who assured him that their sick and malnourished men could not attempt a breakout attack. On July 3, Pemberton asked Grant for terms. Living up to his Donelson reputation, Grant at first insisted on unconditional surrender. But after reflecting on the task of shipping 30,000 captives north to prison camps when he needed all his transport for further operations, Grant offered to parole the prisoners.[17] With good reason he expected that many of them, disillusioned by suffering and surrender, would scatter to their homes and carry the contagion of defeat with them.

The Fourth of July 1863 was the most memorable Independence Day in American history since that first one four score and seven years earlier. Far away in Pennsylvania the high tide of the Confederacy receded from Gettysburg. Here in Mississippi, white flags sprouted above rebel trenches, the emaciated troops marched out and stacked arms, and a Union division moved into Vicksburg to raise the stars and stripes over the courthouse. "This was the most Glorious Fourth I ever spent," wrote an Ohio private. But to many southerners the humiliation of surrendering on July 4 added insult to injury. The good behavior of the occupation troops, however, mitigated the insult. Scarcely a taunt escaped their lips as Union soldiers marched into the city; on the contrary, they paid respect to the courage of the defenders and shared rations with them. Indeed, the Yankees did what many Vicksburg citizens had wanted to do for weeks—they broke into the stores of "speculators" who had been holding food for higher prices. As described by a Louisiana sergeant, northern soldiers brought these "luxuries" into the streets "and throwing them down, would shout, 'here rebs, help yourselves, you are naked

---

16. O.R. Navy, Ser. I, Vol. 25, p. 118.
17. A parole was an oath by a captured soldier, given in return for release from captivity, not to bear arms again until formally exchanged. A year earlier, in July 1862, the Union and Confederate governments had agreed to a cartel for exchange of prisoners.

and starving and need them.' What a strange spectacle of war between those who were recently deadly foes." [18]

A Vicksburg woman who watched the entry of Union soldiers pronounced an epitaph on the campaign: "What a contrast [these] stalwart, well-fed men, so splendidly set-up and accoutered [were] to . . . the worn men in gray, who were being blindly dashed against this embodiment of modern power." But in Richmond an embittered Jefferson Davis attributed the loss of Vicksburg not to the enemy's power but to Joe Johnston's timidity. When a War Department official commented that lack of provisions had doomed the garrison, Davis responded: "Yes, from want of provisions inside and a General outside who wouldn't fight." [19]

The capture of Vicksburg was the most important northern strategic victory of the war, perhaps meriting Grant's later assertion that "the fate of the Confederacy was sealed when Vicksburg fell." [20] But the Union commander did not intend to rest on his Fourth of July laurels. Johnston still threatened his rear, and the Confederate garrison at Port Hudson 240 river miles to the south still held out against Nathaniel P. Banks's besieging army. Grant ordered Sherman with 50,000 men to go after Johnston's 31,000 "and inflict all the punishment you can." [21] Grant also prepared to send a division or two to help Banks capture Port Hudson.

In the event, however, Banks needed no more help than the news of Vicksburg's capitulation, which persuaded the southern commander at Port Hudson to surrender his now untenable position. After a two-month campaign to establish Union control of the rich sugar and cotton regions along Bayou Teche, Banks's soldiers aided by Farragut's warships had laid siege to Port Hudson in the last week of May. Outnumbering the Confederate garrison by 20,000 to 7,000, Banks nevertheless had to contend with natural and man-made defenses as rugged as those at Vicksburg. Two head-on northern assaults on May 27 and June 14 produced only a twelve to one disparity in casualties. In the attack of May 27 two Union regiments of Louisiana blacks proved that they could die

18. Quotations from Carter, *Final Fortress*, 297–98, 301.
19. Dora Miller Richards, "A Woman's Diary of the Siege of Vicksburg," *Century Magazine*, 30 (1885), 775; Frank E. Vandiver, ed., *The Civil War Diary of General Josiah Gorgas* (University, Ala., 1947), 50.
20. Grant, *Memoirs*, I, 567.
21. *O.R.*, Ser. I, Vol. 24, pt. 3, p. 473.

as bravely as white Yankees. After the failure of these assaults, Banks had to rest content with starving the garrison into submission. Port Hudson's defenders lived in the hope that Johnston would rescue them after he had disposed of Grant at Vicksburg. When news came instead that the upriver fortress had fallen, the garrison at Port Hudson—subsisting on mules and rats—did likewise on July 9. A week later an unarmed merchant ship from St. Louis arrived in New Orleans after an unmolested trip down the Mississippi. "The Father of Waters again goes unvexed to the sea," announced Lincoln. The Confederacy was cut in twain.[22]

Johnston was also soon disposed of. Retreating to his defenses at Jackson, the cautious southern commander hoped to lure Sherman into a frontal assault. Having learned the cost of such attacks at Vicksburg, Sherman refused the bait. He started to surround the city and cut its communications. Johnston evaded the trap by slipping across the Pearl River on the night of July 16. Unlike Pemberton he had saved his army— an achievement cited by his defenders—but its withdrawal halfway to Alabama abandoned central Mississippi's plantations and railroads to the none-too-tender mercies of Sherman's army. Johnston's retreat came as icing on the cake of Grant's Vicksburg campaign, which Lincoln described as "one of the most brilliant in the world"—a judgment echoed by a good many subsequent military analysts. "Grant is my man," the president declared on July 5, "and I am his the rest of the war."[23]

II

Important as they were, Grant's achievements in Mississippi took second place in public attention to events in the Virginia theater. The Union ultimately won the war mainly by victories in the West, but the Confederacy more than once came close to winning it in the East. During the spring and summer of 1863, Robert E. Lee scored his greatest success in this effort—followed by his greatest failure.

That Lee could take any initiative at all seemed unlikely in April 1863. Food and forage for his army were in such short supply that men hunted sassafras buds and wild onions to ward off scurvy while horses died for lack of grass. Longstreet had taken two divisions to confront

---

22. CWL, VI, 409. Lincoln's felicitous phrase was not entirely accurate, for Confederate guerrillas continued to vex Union traffic on the Mississippi.
23. CWL, VI, 230; T. Harry Williams, *Lincoln and His Generals* (New York, 1952), 272.

Federal thrusts from Norfolk and the North Carolina coast. These Union movements amounted to little in the end, but Longstreet remained in southeast Virginia through April to harass the enemy and gather supplies from this unscarred region. Without these two divisions, Lee had only 60,000 men along the Rappahannock to watch double that number of bluecoats under their new and dynamic commander, Joseph Hooker. The Confederate cavalry had to disperse over a wide area to find grass for the horses, further weakening southern forces at a time when Hooker had reorganized his cavalry into a single corps better armed and mounted than Jeb Stuart's troopers. The days of easy rebel cavalry superiority were over.

Nevertheless, morale remained high in Confederate ranks, the supplies sent by Longstreet improved their rations, and the elaborate network of trenches they held along twenty-five miles of the Rappahannock near Fredericksburg gave them confidence that they could hold off any number of Yankees. But Hooker had no intention of assaulting those trenches. Having reinvigorated the Army of the Potomac after the Burnside disasters, he planned a campaign of maneuver to force Lee into the open for a showdown fight. Brash and boastful, Hooker reportedly said: "May God have mercy on General Lee, for I will have none."[24]

For a few days at the end of April, Hooker seemed ready to make good his boast. He divided his large army into three parts. Ten thousand blue horsemen splashed across the Rappahannock far upstream and headed south to cut Lee's supply lines. Seventy thousand northern infantry also marched upriver to cross at fords several miles beyond Lee's left flank, while another 40,000 feigned an advance at Fredericksburg to hold Lee in place while the flanking force pitched into his left and rear. The Army of the Potomac carried out these complicated maneuvers swiftly. By the evening of April 30 Hooker had his 70,000 infantry near a crossroads mansion called Chancellorsville, nine miles west of Fredericksburg in the midst of a dense second-growth forest called locally the Wilderness. For once the Yankees had stolen a march on Lee and seemed to have the outnumbered rebels gripped in an iron pincers. "Our enemy must ingloriously fly," declared Hooker in a congratulatory order to his men, "or come out from behind his defenses and give us battle on our own ground, where certain destruction awaits him."[25]

Despite his nickname of Fighting Joe, Hooker seems to have ex-

24. Williams, *Lincoln and His Generals*, 232.
25. O.R., Ser. I, Vol. 25, pt. 1, p. 171.

pected—and hoped—that Lee would "ingloriously fly" rather than "give us battle." When Lee instead showed fight, Hooker mysteriously lost his nerve. Perhaps his resolve three months earlier to go on the wagon had been a mistake, for he seemed at this moment to need some liquid courage. Or perhaps a trait noted by a fellow officer in the old army had surfaced again: "Hooker could play the best game of poker I ever saw until it came to the point where he should go a thousand better, and then he would flunk."[26] Whatever the reason, when Lee called his bet on May 1, Hooker gave up the initiative to the boldest of gamblers in this deadliest of games.

Guessing correctly that the main threat came from the Union troops at Chancellorsville, Lee left only 10,000 infantry under feisty Jubal Early to hold the Fredericksburg defenses, and put the rest on the march westward to the Wilderness on May 1. At mid-day they clashed with Hooker's advance units a couple of miles east of Chancellorsville. Here the dense undergrowth gave way to open country where the Federals' superior weight of numbers and artillery gave them an edge. But instead of pressing the attack, Hooker ordered his troops back to a defensive position around Chancellorsville—where the thick woods evened these odds. Thunderstruck, Union corps commanders protested but obeyed. Years later General Darius Couch of the 2nd Corps wrote that when Hooker informed him "that the advantages gained by the successive marches of his lieutenants were to culminate in fighting a defensive battle in that nest of thickets . . . I retired from his presence with the belief that my commanding general was a whipped man."[27]

Sensing his psychological edge, Lee decided to take the offensive despite being outnumbered nearly two to one. On the night of May 1, Jackson and Lee sat on empty hardtack boxes and conferred by firelight. The Federals' entrenched line on high ground around Chancellorsville seemed too strong for a direct assault. The Union left was anchored on the Rappahannock and could not be turned. While the two generals discussed how to get at "those people," Stuart brought reports from his scouts that Hooker's right flank was "in the air" three miles west of Chancellorsville. Here was the opportunity Lee needed, and Jackson was the man to seize it. The only problem was to find a route through the wilderness of scrub oak and thorny undergrowth by which a force could get around to this flank unobserved. One of Jackson's staff officers

26. Alexander K. McClure, *Recollections of Half a Century* (Salem, Mass., 1902), 348.
27. Couch, "The Chancellorsville Campaign," *Battles and Leaders*, III, 161.

solved this problem by finding a local resident to guide them along a track used to haul charcoal for an iron-smelting furnace.

Screened by Stuart's cavalry, Jackson's 30,000 infantry and artillery left early May 2 for a roundabout twelve-mile march to their attack position. Lee remained with only 15,000 men to confront Hooker's main force. This was the most daring gamble Lee had yet taken. Jackson's flank march across the enemy's front—one of the most dangerous maneuvers in war—left his strung-out column vulnerable to attack. Lee's holding force was likewise in great peril if Hooker should discover its weakness. And Early still faced nearly three times his numbers at Fredericksburg (from which Hooker had called one more corps to Chancellorsville). But Lee counted on Hooker doing nothing while Jackson completed his march; the Union commander fulfilled expectations.

Hooker could not blame his cavalry for failure to detect Jackson's maneuver, for he had sent nearly all of it away on a raid that threw a scare into Richmond but otherwise accomplished little. Besides, Federal infantry units spotted Jackson's movement and reported it to Hooker— who misinterpreted it. Two of Daniel Sickles's 3rd Corps divisions moved out and attacked the tail of Jackson's column. Sickles was a character of some notoriety, the only political general among Hooker's corps commanders, a prewar Tammany Democrat with a reputation for philandering. His wife, perhaps in revenge, had taken a lover whom Sickles shot dead on a Washington street in 1859. He was acquitted of murder after the first successful plea of temporary insanity in the history of American jurisprudence. Rising from colonel to major general in Hooker's old division, Sickles was one of the army commander's favorites. His probing attack on May 2 alerted Hooker to Jackson's movement toward the southwest. Fighting Joe momentarily wondered if the slippery Stonewall was up to his old flanking tricks, but the wishful thought that the rebels must "ingloriously fly" soon convinced him that Lee's whole army was retreating! Hooker therefore failed to prepare for the blow soon to fall on his right.

Commander of the 11th Corps holding the Union right was Oliver O. Howard, the opposite in every respect of Sickles. A West Point professional whose distinguished combat record included loss of an arm at Fair Oaks, Howard was a monogamous teetotaling Congregationalist known as the Christian Soldier. He had little in common with the German-American soldiers who constituted a large part of his corps. This "Dutch" corps, only 12,000 strong, had a poor reputation, having turned in mediocre performances under Frémont in the Shenandoah

Valley and Franz Sigel at Second Bull Run. What happened at Chancellorsville did nothing to improve that reputation. All through the afternoon, alarmed pickets sent word to Howard that the rebels were building up to something off to the west. Howard assured Hooker that he was ready for an attack. Yet most of his regiments were facing south, for Howard considered the thick woods to the west impenetrable. And like Hooker he also thought that this enemy activity was designed to cover a retreat. As suppertime approached, many of Howard's troops were relaxing or cooking.

A few hundred yards to the west, Jackson's rugged veterans—their uniforms torn to worse tatters than usual by briars and brush—were deployed for attack at 5:15. Coming through the woods from the west on a front two miles wide and three divisions deep, the yelling rebels hit the south-facing Union regiments endwise and knocked them down like tenpins. Despite wild confusion, some of the 11th Corps brigades and batteries maintained discipline and fought desperately, slowing the Confederate advance but being forced in the end to join the stampede of routed regiments fleeing to the rear. By dusk Jackson had rolled up the Union right for two miles before Howard and Hooker improvised a new line out of troops from four different corps to bring the jubilant but disorganized southerners to a halt. The two divisions remaining with Lee had joined the attack on their front. For several hours, sporadic and disordered fighting flared up in the moon-shadowed woods, with some units firing on their own men in one of the rare night actions of the Civil War.

Misfortune beyond the usual tragedies of war struck the Confederates during this moonlit melee. Determined to keep the Yankees on the run, Jackson and several officers rode ahead of their lines to reconnoiter for a renewed attack. Returning at a trot, they were fired on by nervous rebels who mistook them for Union cavalry. Jackson fell with two bullets in his left arm, which had to be amputated. Stuart took command of his corps and led it well for the rest of the battle. But the loss of Jackson proved to be permanent and irreparable. Pneumonia set in, and the inimitable Stonewall died eight days later.

The morning after Jackson's wounding, May 3, saw the crisis of the battle. Some of the war's hardest fighting took place on two fronts separated by nine miles. During the night Hooker had ordered "Uncle" John Sedgwick (so named by his men for his avuncular manner), commander of the 6th Corps at Fredericksburg, to carry the heights back of the town and push on toward Lee's rear at Chancellorsville. At daybreak

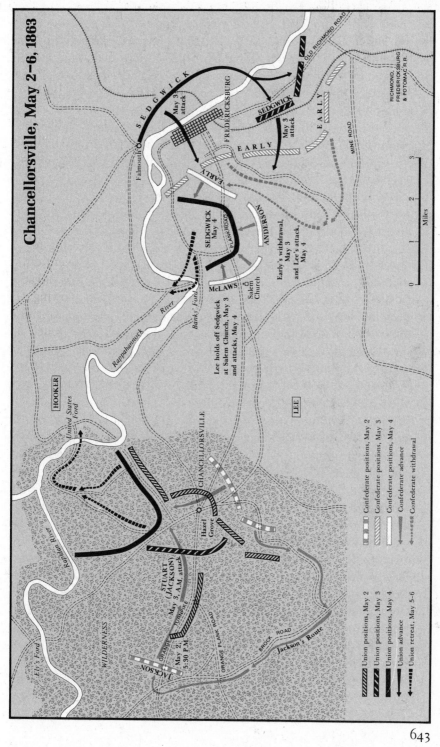

Chancellorsville, May 2–6, 1863

United States Ford

HOOKER

Rappahannock

River

Banks' Ford

Falmouth

SEDGWICK

May 3 attack

FREDERICKSBURG

SEDGWICK

May 3 attack

RICHMOND, FREDERICKSBURG & POTOMAC R.R.

OLD RICHMOND ROAD

EARLY

EARLY

MINE ROAD

EARLY

SEDGWICK May 4

PLANK ROAD

ANDERSON

McLAWS

Salem Church

Early's withdrawal, May 3 and Lee's attack, May 4

Lee holds off Sedgwick at Salem Church, May 3 and attacks, May 4

Ely's Ford

Rapidan River

CHANCELLORSVILLE

Hazel Grove

LEE

STUART (JACKSON) May 3 A.M. attack

TURNPIKE

ORANGE PLANK ROAD

BROCK ROAD

JACKSON May 2, 5:30 P.M. attack

Jackson's Route

WILDERNESS

Union positions, May 2
Union positions, May 3
Union positions, May 4
Union advance
Union retreat, May 5–6

Confederate positions, May 2
Confederate positions, May 3
Confederate positions, May 4
Confederate advance
Confederate withdrawal

0   1   2   3
Miles

Uncle John hurled his three divisions against the trenches and the stone wall below Marye's Heights where Burnside's troops had come to grief the previous December. History appeared to repeat itself as Jubal Early's division threw them back twice. But on the third try, in one of the war's few genuine bayonet charges, the first wave of blue attackers carried the heights, captured a thousand prisoners, and sent the rebels flying.

Meanwhile Hooker at Chancellorsville had remained strangely passive, seeming to expect Sedgwick to do all the army's offensive fighting. Hooker had even ordered Sickles's corps to fall back at dawn from a salient on high ground at Hazel Grove, a mile west of the Chancellorsville crossroads. This allowed Lee and Stuart to reunite the two wings of their army and to mass their artillery at Hazel Grove, one of the few places in the Wilderness where it could be used effectively. The Confederates pressed an all-out attack on the three corps holding the immediate area around Chancellorsville. Hooker kept three other Union corps idle despite openings for them to fall on Lee's flanks. Hooker seemed in a daze even before a cannonball hit his headquarters and knocked him unconscious in mid-morning. He recovered in time to retain command—a pity, in the eyes of several subordinates, who had hoped that the ranking corps commander would take charge and launch a counterattack. Instead, Hooker ordered withdrawal a mile or two northward to a contracted defensive line.

The exhausted but exultant rebels, who had fought with an élan unprecedented even in this victorious army, cheered wildly as Lee rode into the clearing around the burning Chancellor mansion. It was the Virginian's greatest triumph—but the battle was not yet over. While the two armies around Chancellorsville broke off fighting as if by mutual consent to rescue hundreds of wounded men threatened by brush fires started by exploding shells, Lee received word of Sedgwick's breakthrough at Fredericksburg. Here was a serious threat to his rear even though Hooker seemed cowed in his front. Without hesitation Lee dispatched a division which blunted Sedgwick's advance near a country church midway between Fredericksburg and Chancellorsville. Next day Lee took yet another division from his front to attack Sedgwick. This left only 25,000 Confederates under Stuart to face Hooker's 75,000, but Lee seemed to know that his benumbed adversary would remain passive. In the late afternoon of May 4 a disjointed attack by 21,000 rebels against Sedgwick's equal force was repulsed. Aware that Hooker had given up, however, Sedgwick pulled his troops back over the Rappahannock during the night.

At a council of war that same night, a majority of the Union corps commanders with Hooker voted to counterattack. True to form, Hooker disregarded this vote and decided to retreat across the river. The Army of the Potomac accomplished this difficult task during a rainstorm the next night. Aggressive as ever, Lee had planned another assault on the morning of May 6 and expressed regret, as he had done the previous summer, that the Federals escaped destruction. But by any standard he had won an astounding victory, recognized as such in both North and South. Without Longstreet and with little more than half as many men as an enemy that had initially outmaneuvered him, Lee had grasped the initiative, gone over to the attack, and had repeatedly divided and maneuvered his forces in such a way as to give them superiority or equality of numbers at the point of attack. Like a rabbit mesmerized by the gray fox, Hooker was frozen into immobility and did not use half his power at any time in the battle.

The triumph at Chancellorsville, however, came at great cost. The Confederates suffered 13,000 casualties, 22 percent of their force (the Union figures were 17,000 and 15 percent). The most grievous loss was Jackson, who had done so much to make the victory possible. And the boost that the battle gave to southern morale proved in the end harmful, for it bred an overconfidence in their own prowess and a contempt for the enemy that led to disaster. Believing his troops invincible, Lee was about to ask them to do the impossible.

During the battle Lincoln haunted the War Department telegraph office. For several days he received only fragmentary and contradictory reports. When the truth became clear on May 6, the president's face turned "ashen," according to a newspaperman who was present. "My God! my God!" exclaimed Lincoln. "What will the country say?" It said plenty, all of it bad. Copperheads saw in the outcome further proof, if any was necessary, that the North could never cobble the Union together by force. Republicans expressed despair. "Lost, lost, all is lost!" cried Charles Sumner when he heard the news.[28]

Northern morale descended into the slough of despond in the spring of 1863. Reports of Grant's advances in Mississippi were slow in coming and uncertain in meaning, especially after the failure of assaults at Vicksburg on May 19 and 22. Rosecrans had done nothing in middle Tennessee since his bloody and ambiguous New Year's victory at Stones

---

28. Noah Brooks, *Washington in Lincoln's Time* (New York, 1896), 57–58; *Diary of Gideon Welles*, ed. Howard K. Beale, 3 vols. (New York, 1960), I, 293.

River. On April 7 an attack on Fort Sumter by eight supposedly irresistible Monitors had been repulsed in a manner that gave the Union navy a black eye. The attack had been the first step in an effort to capture Charleston, whose symbolic significance was greater than its strategic importance. The failure of the Monitors proved again that these ironclads could take an enormous amount of punishment but that their offensive punch was limited. Rebel artillery got off more than 2,200 shots, scoring some 440 hits on the eight ships and sinking only one. But most of the Monitors suffered damage to their gun turrets that limited their firing capacity, and the fleet was able to get off only 140 shots and inflict limited damage with about forty hits. The high hopes for naval conquest of the citadel of secession were dashed. Union army troops began a slow, frustrating, and ultimately unsuccessful advance along the coastal islands and through the swamps in an attempt to starve or pound Charleston into submission.

III

The Confederacy could not rest on Lee's laurels in Virginia or Beauregard's at Charleston. Although beaten, Hooker's army still bristled 90,000 strong along the Rappahannock. Grant was on the move in Mississippi. Rosecrans showed signs of motion in middle Tennessee. Pressed on all sides by invading forces, the South needed an offensive-defensive stroke to relieve the pressure. Longstreet thought he saw a way to accomplish this. Returning with his two detached divisions to rejoin Lee on the Rappahannock, Longstreet stopped in Richmond on May 6 for a meeting with Secretary of War James Seddon. Longstreet proposed that he take these two divisions to reinforce Bragg in Tennessee. With additional help from Johnston, they would drive Rosecrans back to the Ohio. This would compel Grant to break off his campaign against Vicksburg and go to the rescue of the shattered Army of the Cumberland. Seddon liked the idea, but suggested that Longstreet go instead to Mississippi to help Johnston and Pemberton smash Grant, after which they could turn their attention to Rosecrans. Jefferson Davis favored this proposal, for he was concerned about his home state and convinced that the retention of Vicksburg was crucial.

But Lee dashed cold water on the enterprise. It would take weeks for Longstreet's divisions to travel nearly a thousand miles to Mississippi over the Confederacy's mangled railroads. If Vicksburg could hold out that long, said Lee, it would be safe without reinforcements, for "the climate in June will force the enemy to retire." In the meantime a reinforced Army of the Potomac might return to the offensive against

Lee's depleted forces. Although he had held off Hooker before without these two divisions, Lee now believed that he needed them—and additional troops as well. In sum, he concluded, "it becomes a question between Virginia and Mississippi."[29]

Lee's opinion carried so much weight that Davis felt compelled to concur. The president remained disquieted by news from Mississippi, however, and called Lee to Richmond for a strategy conference on May 15. This time the Virginian dazzled Davis and Seddon with a proposal to invade Pennsylvania with a reinforced army and inflict a crushing defeat on the Yankees in their own backyard. This would remove the enemy threat on the Rappahannock, take the armies out of war-ravaged Virginia, and enable Lee to feed his troops in the enemy's country. It would also strengthen Peace Democrats, discredit Republicans, reopen the question of foreign recognition, and perhaps even conquer peace and recognition from the Union government itself.

The cabinet was awed by this vision. Postmaster-General John Reagan was the sole dissenter. The only member of the cabinet from west of the Mississippi (Texas), Reagan still thought that preservation of Vicksburg as a link between the Confederacy's two halves should have top priority.[30] But Lee convinced the others that even if the climate failed to drive the Yankees out of Mississippi, a successful invasion of Pennsylvania would draw them out. In the post-Chancellorsville aura of invincibility, anything seemed possible. "There never were such men in an army before," said Lee of his soldiers. "They will go anywhere and do anything if properly led." So great was the prestige of Lee, "whose fame," said a cabinet member, "now filled the world," that he carried the day. Even Longstreet came around. "When I agreed with [Seddon] and yourself about sending troops west," he wrote to Senator Wigfall of Texas, "it was under the impression that we would be obliged to remain on the defensive here. But the prospect of an advance changes the aspect of affairs."[31]

29. Lee to Seddon, telegram and letter both dated May 10, 1863, O.R., Ser. I, Vol. 25, pt. 2, p. 790. For an analysis of this issue, see Archer Jones, *Confederate Strategy from Shiloh to Vicksburg* (Baton Rouge, 1961), 206–14.

30. John H. Reagan, *Memoirs, with Special Reference to Secession and the Civil War* (Austin, 1906), 120–22, 150–53.

31. Lee to John Bell Hood, May 21, 1863, in Clifford Dowdey and Louis H. Manarin, eds., *The Wartime Papers of R. E. Lee* (Boston, 1961), 490; cabinet member quoted in Foote, *Civil War*, II, 432; Longstreet to Louis Wigfall, May 13, quoted in Jones, *Confederate Strategy*, 208. After the war a controversy arose between Longstreet and several Virginia generals concerning responsibility for the defeat at Gettysburg.

So Lee set about reorganizing his augmented army into an invasion force of three infantry corps and six cavalry brigades—a total of 75,000 men. A. P. Hill became commander of the new 3rd Corps while Jackson's old 2nd Corps went to Richard Ewell, now sporting a wooden leg as souvenir of Second Manassas. Having used the month after Chancellorsville to rest and refit, the Army of Northern Virginia was much better prepared for this invasion than it had been for the previous one in September 1862. Morale was high, most men had shoes, and few stragglers fell out as Lee edged westward in the first week of June to launch his invasion through the Shenandoah Valley. Ewell's corps led the way, adding to its laurels won in the Valley under Jackson the previous year by capturing 3,500 men in the Union garrisons at Winchester and Martinsburg.

This success and the apparently unimpeded advance of the fearsome rebels into Pennsylvania set off panic in the North and heightened southern euphoria. "From the very beginning the true policy of the South has been invasion," declared the *Richmond Examiner* as first reports arrived of a great victory in Pennsylvania:

> The present movement of General Lee . . . will be of infinite value as disclosing the . . . easy susceptibility of the North to invasion. . . . Not even the Chinese are less prepared by previous habits of life and education for martial resistance than the Yankees. . . . We can . . . carry our armies far into the enemy's country, exacting peace by blows leveled at his vitals.

The date of this editorial was July 7, 1863.[32]

Only one untoward event had marred the invasion's success so far.

The Virginians criticized Longstreet for his half-hearted participation in an invasion he had opposed and especially for his alleged tardiness and inept leadership of the attacks on July 2 and 3. Such allegations were at worst false and at best distorted. Longstreet did support the invasion, as this letter indicates, though he later claimed that while endorsing a strategic offensive he had recommended defensive tactics once the Confederates reached northern soil. Longstreet asserted that Lee had concurred in this policy. No contemporary evidence supports such an unlikely commitment to defensive tactics by Lee. For a review of the controversy see Glenn Tucker, *Lee and Longstreet at Gettysburg* (Indianapolis, 1968), and Thomas L. Connelly, *The Marble Man: Robert E. Lee and His Image in American Society* (New York, 1977), chap. 3.

32. The irony of the date of this editorial will not escape the reader, for it came four days after the Confederate defeat at Gettysburg. Word of that outcome did not reach Richmond until July 9, and it took a day or two longer for this inversion of initially optimistic reports from Pennsylvania to sink in.

On June 9 the Union cavalry crossed the Rappahannock in force twenty-five miles above Fredericksburg to find out what Lee was up to. Catching Stuart napping, the blue troopers learned that the enemy had begun to move north. The rebel horsemen rallied and finally pushed the Yankees back after the biggest cavalry battle of the war at Brandy Station. The southern press criticized Stuart for the initial surprise of his "puffed up cavalry."[33] His ego bruised, Stuart hoped to regain glory by some spectacular achievement in the invasion. His troopers efficiently screened the infantry's advance. But the improved northern cavalry also kept Stuart from learning of Hooker's movements. To break this stalemate, Stuart on June 25 took his three best brigades for another raid around the rear of the Union infantry slogging northward after Lee. In its initial stages this foray caused alarm in Washington and added to the scare in Pennsylvania. But Stuart became separated from the Army of Northern Virginia for a full week. This deprived Lee of intelligence about enemy movements at a crucial time.

Nevertheless these halcyon June days seemed to mark a pinnacle of Confederate success. Lee forbade pillaging of private property in Pennsylvania, to show the world that southern soldiers were superior to the Yankee vandals who had ravaged the South. But not all rebels refrained from plunder and arson. The army destroyed Thaddeus Stevens's ironworks near Chambersburg, wrecked a good deal of railroad property, levied forced requisitions of money from merchants and banks ($28,000 in York, for example), and seized all the shoes, clothing, horses, cattle, and food they could find—giving Confederate IOUs in return. Lee's invasion became a gigantic raid for supplies that stripped clean a large area of south-central Pennsylvania. In Chambersburg, Longstreet's quartermaster began to break open shops with axes until local merchants gave him the keys. To a farm woman who protested the seizure of all her hogs and cattle, Longstreet replied: "Yes, madam, it's very sad—very sad; and this sort of thing has been going on in Virginia more than two years—very sad." Southern soldiers also seized scores of black people in Pennsylvania and sent them south into slavery.[34]

33. Douglas Southall Freeman, *Lee's Lieutenants: A Study in Command*, 3 vols. (New York, 1942–44), III, 19.
34. Quotation from Walter Lord, ed., *The Fremantle Diary: Being the Journal of Lieutenant Colonel James Arthur Lyon Fremantle, Coldstream Guards, on his Three Months in the Southern States* (Boston, 1954), 224. See also Edwin B. Coddington, *The Gettysburg Campaign: A Study in Command* (New York, 1968), 153–79.

One of Lee's purposes in ordering restraint toward (white) civilians was to cultivate the copperheads. He placed great faith in "the rising peace party of the North" as a "means of dividing and weakening our enemies." It was true, Lee wrote to Davis on June 10, that the copperheads professed to favor reunion as the object of peace negotiations while the South regarded independence as the goal. But it would do no harm, Lee advised Davis, to play along with this reunion sentiment to weaken northern support for the war, which "after all is what we are interested in bringing about. When peace is proposed to us it will be time enough to discuss its terms, and it is not the part of prudence to spurn the proposition in advance, merely because those who made it believe, or affect to believe, that it will result in bringing us back to the Union." If Davis agreed with these views, Lee concluded, "you will best know how to give effect to them."[35]

Davis did indeed think he saw a chance to carry peace proposals on the point of Lee's sword. In mid-June, Alexander Stephens suggested to Davis that in light of "the failure of Hooker and Grant," this might be the time to make peace overtures. Stephens offered to approach his old friend Lincoln under flag of truce to discuss prisoner-of-war exchanges, which had stopped because of Confederate refusal to exchange blacks. This issue could serve as an entering wedge for the introduction of peace proposals. Davis was intrigued by the idea. He gave Stephens formal instructions limiting his powers to negotiations on prisoner exchanges and other procedural matters. What additional informal powers Stephens carried with him are unknown. On July 3 the vice president boarded a flag-of-truce boat for a trip down the James to Union lines at Norfolk on the first leg of his hoped-for trip to Washington.[36]

Lee's invasion also sparked renewed Confederate hopes for diplomatic recognition. In the wake of Chancellorsville, John Slidell in Paris queried the French whether "the time had not arrived for reconsidering the question of recognition." Napoleon agreed, as usual, but would not act independently of Britain. In that country, news of Lee's success stirred

---

A Chambersburg woman described the seizure by Confederates of several black women and children in that town, who were "driven by just like we would drive cattle." James C. Mohr, ed., *The Cormany Diaries: A Northern Family in the Civil War* (Pittsburgh, 1982), 328–30.

35. Dowdey and Manarin, eds., *Wartime Papers of Lee*, 507–9.
36. Alexander H. Stephens, *A Constitutional View of the Late War Between the States*, 2 vols. (Chicago, 1868–70), II, 557–68; Rowland, *Davis*, V, 513–19.

Confederate sympathizers into vigorous action. During June a flurry of meetings among southern diplomats and their supporters on both sides of the channel worked out a plan for a motion in the British Parliament favoring joint Anglo-French steps toward recognition. Napoleon gave his blessing to the enterprise. But the M. P. who presented the motion, a diminutive firebrand named John Roebuck whom Henry Adams described as "rather more than three-quarters mad," put his foot in his mouth with a speech on June 30 that indiscreetly disclosed all details of his conversation with the French emperor. The notion of allowing the Frogs to dictate British foreign policy was like a red flag to John Bull. The motion died of anti-French backlash, but British proponents of recognition eagerly awaited reports of Lee's triumph in Pennsylvania. "Diplomatic means can now no longer prevail," wrote Confederate publicist Henry Hotze from London on July 11, "and everybody looks to Lee to conquer recognition."[37]

Northerners abroad understood only too well the stakes involved in military operations during June 1863. "The truth is," wrote Henry Adams, "all depends on the progress of our armies." In Washington, Lincoln was not pleased with the progress of Hooker's army. When Hooker first detected Lee's movement in early June, he wanted to cross the Rappahannock and pitch into the rebel rear. Lincoln disapproved and urged Hooker to fight the enemy's main force north of the river instead of crossing it at the risk of becoming "entangled upon the river, like an ox jumped half over a fence and liable to be torn by dogs front and rear without a fair chance to gore one way or kick the other." Hooker seemed unimpressed by this advice, for a few days later he proposed that since the Army of Northern Virginia was moving north, the Army of the Potomac should move south and march into Richmond! Lincoln began to suspect that Hooker was afraid to fight Lee again. "I think *Lee's* Army, and not *Richmond*, is your true objective point," he wired Hooker. "If he comes toward the Upper Potomac, follow on his flank, and on the inside track. . . . Fight him when opportunity offers." With the head of the enemy force at Winchester and the tail still back at Fredericks-

37. Slidell quoted in Frank Lawrence Owsley, *King Cotton Diplomacy* (Chicago, 1931), 465; Henry Adams to Charles Francis Adams, Jr., June 25, 1863, in Worthington, C. Ford, ed., *A Cycle of Adams Letters 1861–1865*, 2 vols. (Boston, 1920), II, 40; Hotze quoted in Brian Jenkins, *Britain and the War for the Union*, 2 vols. (Montreal, 1974–80), II, 313.

burg, "the animal must be very slim somewhere. Could you not break him?"[38]

Although Hooker finally lurched the Army of the Potomac into motion, he moved too late to prevent Lee's whole force from crossing the Potomac. But this actually encouraged Lincoln. To Hooker he sent word that this "gives you back the chance [to destroy the enemy far from his base] that I thought McClellan lost last fall." To Secretary of the Navy Welles, Lincoln said that "we cannot help beating them, if we have the man." But Lincoln became convinced that Hooker was not the man. The general began to fret that Lee outnumbered him, that he needed more troops, that the government was not supporting him. Looking "sad and careworn," the president told his cabinet that Hooker had turned out to be another McClellan. On June 28 he relieved Hooker from command and named George Gordon Meade in his place.[39]

If the men in the ranks had been consulted, most of them probably would have preferred the return of McClellan. Although Meade had worked his way up from brigade to corps command with a good combat record, he was an unknown quantity to men outside his corps. By now, though, their training in the school of hard knocks under fumbling leaders had toughened the soldiers to a flinty self-reliance that left many of them indifferent to the identity of their commander. The men "have something of the English bull-dog in them," wrote one officer. "You can whip them time and again, but the next fight they go into, they are . . . as full of pluck as ever. They are used to being whipped, and no longer mind it. Some day or other we shall have our turn."[40] As the army headed north into Pennsylvania, civilians along the way began to cheer them as friends instead of reviling them as foes. Their morale rose with the latitude. "Our men are three times as Enthusiastic as they have been in Virginia," wrote a Union surgeon. "The idea that Pennsylvania is invaded and that we are fighting on our own soil proper, influences them strongly. They are more determined than I have ever before seen them."[41]

---

38. Henry Adams to Charles Francis Adams, Jr., June 25, 1863, in Ford, *Cycle of Adams Letters*, II, 40–41; CWL, VI, 249, 257, 273.
39. CWL, VI, 281; Beale, ed., *Diary of Gideon Welles*, I, 340, 344, 348.
40. Stephen M. Weld to his mother, June 10, 1863, in *War Diary and Letters of Stephen Minot Weld 1861–1865* (Boston, 1912), 213. Weld was a captain in the 18th Massachusetts Infantry.
41. Wiley, *Billy Yank*, 283.

When Meade took over the army, its 90,000 effectives were concentrated in the vicinity of Frederick, Maryland. Longstreet's and Hill's Confederate corps were forty miles to the north near Chambersburg, Pennsylvania. Part of Ewell's corps was at York, threatening a railroad bridge over the Susquehanna, while the remainder was at Carlisle preparing to move on Harrisburg to sever the main line of the Pennsylvania Railroad and capture the state capital. Lee had cut himself off from his faraway Virginia base, as Lincoln had hoped, but he had done so purposely. Like Grant's army in Mississippi, Lee's invaders took enough ammunition for their needs and lived off the country as they moved. Lee's greatest worry was not supplies, but rather the absence of Stuart with information about the whereabouts of the enemy. By contrast, Meade obtained accurate intelligence of the rebels' location and moved quickly to confront them.

On the night of June 28, one of Longstreet's scouts brought word that the Army of the Potomac was north of its namesake river. Alarmed by the proximity of a concentrated enemy while his own forces remained scattered, Lee sent couriers to recall Ewell's divisions from York and Carlisle. Meanwhile one of A.P. Hill's divisions learned of a reported supply of shoes at Gettysburg, a prosperous town served by a dozen roads that converged from every point on the compass. Since Lee intended to reunite his army near Gettysburg, Hill authorized this division to go there on July 1 to "get those shoes."

When Hill's would-be Crispins approached Gettysburg that morning, however, they found something more than the pickets and militia they had expected. Two brigades of Union cavalry had arrived in town the previous day. Their commander was weather-beaten, battle-wise John Buford, who like Lincoln had been born in Kentucky and raised in Illinois. Buford had noted the strategic importance of this crossroads village flanked by defensible ridges and hills. Expecting the rebels to come this way, he had posted his brigades with their breech-loading carbines on high ground northwest of town. Buford sent word to John Reynolds, a Pennsylvanian who commanded the nearest infantry corps, to hurry forward to Gettysburg. If there was to be a battle, he said, this was the place to fight it. When A.P. Hill's lead division came marching out of the west next morning, Buford's horse soldiers were ready for them. Fighting dismounted behind fences and trees, they held off three times their number for two hours while couriers on both sides galloped up the roads to summon reinforcements. Lee had told his subordinates not to bring on a general engagement until the army was concentrated. But the engagement became general of its own accord as the infantry of both armies marched toward the sound of guns at Gettysburg.

As Buford's tired troopers were beginning to give way in mid-morning, the lead division of Reynolds's 1st Corps double-timed across the fields and brought the rebel assault to a standstill. One unit in this division was the Iron Brigade, five midwestern regiments with distinctive black hats who confirmed here their reputation as the hardest-fighting outfit in the Army of the Potomac. They also lost two-thirds of the men they took into the battle. The most crucial Union casualty on this first morning of July was John Reynolds—considered by many the best general in the army—drilled through the head by a sharpshooter. About noon, General Howard's "Dutch" 11th Corps arrived and deployed north of town to meet the advance units of Ewell's Confederate 2nd Corps coming fast after a brisk march from the Susquehanna. By early afternoon some 24,000 Confederates confronted 19,000 bluecoats along a three-mile semicircle west and north of Gettysburg. Neither commanding general had yet reached the field; neither had intended to fight there; but independently of their intentions a battle destined to become the largest and most important of the war had already started.

As Ewell's leading divisions swept forward against Howard, Lee rode in from the west. Quickly grasping the situation, he changed his mind about waiting for Longstreet's corps, still miles away, and authorized Hill and Ewell to send in everything they had. With a yell, four southern divisions went forward with the irresistible power that seemed to have become routine. The right flank of Howard's corps collapsed here as it had done at Chancellorsville. When the 11th Corps retreated in disorder through town to Cemetery Hill a half-mile to the south, the right flank of the Union 1st Corps was uncovered and these tough fighters, too, were forced back yard by yard to the hill, where Union artillery and a reserve division that Howard had posted there caused the rebel onslaught to hesitate in late afternoon. The battle so far appeared to be another great Confederate victory.

But Lee could see that so long as the enemy held the high ground south of town, the battle was not over. He knew that the rest of the Army of the Potomac must be hurrying toward Gettysburg; his best chance to clinch the victory was to seize those hills and ridges before they arrived. So Lee gave Ewell discretionary orders to attack Cemetery Hill "if practicable." Had Jackson still lived, he undoubtedly would have found it practicable. But Ewell was not Jackson. Thinking the enemy position too strong, he did not attack—thereby creating one of the controversial "ifs" of Gettysburg that have echoed down the years. By the time dusk approached, General Winfield Scott Hancock of the 2nd Corps had arrived and laid out a defense line curling around Culps and Cemetery hills and extending two miles south along Cemetery Ridge to a hill called Little Round Top. As three more Union corps arrived during the night—along with Meade himself—the bluecoats turned this line into a formidable position. Not only did it command high ground, but its convex interior lines also allowed troops to be shifted quickly from one point to another while forcing the enemy into concave exterior lines that made communication between right and left wings slow and difficult.

Studying the Union defenses through his field glasses on the evening of July 1 and again next morning, Longstreet concluded that this line was too strong for an attack to succeed. He urged Lee to turn its south flank and get between the Union army and Washington. This would compel Meade to attack the Army of Northern Virginia in *its* chosen position. Longstreet liked best the tactical defensive; the model he had in mind was Fredericksburg where Yankee divisions had battered themselves to pieces while the Confederates had suffered minimal casualties. Longstreet had not been present at Chancellorsville nor had he arrived at Gettysburg on July 1 until after the whooping rebels had driven the enemy pell-mell through the town. These were the models that Lee had in mind. He had not accomplished the hoped-for "destruction" of the enemy in the Seven Days' or at Chancellorsville. Gettysburg presented him with a third chance.[42] The morale of his veteran troops had never been higher; they would regard such a maneuver as Longstreet suggested as a retreat, Lee thought, and lose their fighting edge. According to a British military observer accompanying the Confederates, the men were eager to attack an enemy "they had beaten so constantly" and for whose fighting capacity they felt "profound contempt." Lee intended to un-

---

42. Twenty years later Isaac Trimble, one of Lee's division commanders at Gettysburg, wrote from memory an "almost verbatim" account of a conversation with Lee on June 27, four days before the battle began. When the Army of the Potomac came up into Pennsylvania seeking him, Lee told Trimble, "I shall throw an overwhelming force on their advance, crush it, follow up the success, drive one corps back on another, and by successive repulses and surprises . . . create a panic and virtually destroy the army. . . . [Then] the war will be over and we shall achieve the recognition of our independence." Douglas Southall Freeman, *R. E. Lee: A Biography*, 4 vols. (New York, 1934–35), III, 58–59.

leash them. Pointing to Cemetery Hill, he said to Longstreet: "The enemy is there, and I am going to attack him there." Longstreet replied: "If he is there, it will be because he is anxious that we should attack him; a good reason, in my judgment, for not doing so." But Lee had made up his mind, and Longstreet turned away sadly with a conviction of impending disaster.[43]

Although aware of Longstreet's reluctance, Lee assigned to him the principal attack duty on July 2. Two of Hill's three divisions had suffered heavy casualties the previous day and could not fight today. Ewell still regarded the Union defenses on Cemetery and Culp's hills as too strong for a successful assault. Lee grudgingly agreed. He therefore ordered Longstreet's two fresh divisions (the third, under George Pickett, had been posted as rear guard and could not arrive in time) to attack the Union left holding the southern end of Cemetery Ridge. The assault would be supported by Hill's one fresh division, while Ewell was to demonstrate against the Union right and convert this demonstration into an attack when Meade weakened his right to reinforce his left. If this plan worked, both enemy flanks would crumble and Lee would have the war-winning Cannae that he sought.[44]

Longstreet's state of mind as he prepared for this attack is hard to fathom. The only non-Virginian holding high command in the Army of Northern Virginia (and the only prominent Confederate general to join the postwar Republican party), Longstreet became the target of withering criticism from Virginians after the war for insubordination and tardiness at Gettysburg. They held him responsible for losing the battle—and by implication the war. Some of this criticism was self-serving, intended to shield Lee and other Virginians (mainly Stuart and Ewell) from blame. But Longstreet did seem to move slowly at Gettysburg. Although Lee wanted him to attack as early in the day as possible, he did not get his troops into position until 4:00 p.m. There were ex-

---

43. Lord, ed., *The Fremantle Diary*, 205; Longstreet's account of his conversation with Lee was contained in two articles written years later: "Lee in Pennsylvania," *Annals of the War* (Philadelphia, 1879), 421; and "Lee's Right Wing at Gettysburg," *Battles and Leaders*, III, 339–40.

44. Cannae was a battle in 216 B.C. in which Hannibal of Carthage defeated and virtually annihilated a Roman army—which by coincidence almost equaled the size of the Union force at Gettysburg—with a double envelopment that crushed both flanks. Cannae became a byword in military history for a total, annihilative tactical victory.

tenuating reasons for this delay: his two divisions had made night marches to reach the vicinity of Gettysburg and were then compelled to counter-march by a circuitous route to reach the attack position because Lee's guide led them initially on a road in sight of an enemy signal post on Little Round Top, a high hill at the south end of the Union line. Yet Longstreet may have been piqued by Lee's rejection of his flanking suggestion, and he did not believe in the attack he was ordered to make. He therefore may not have put as much energy and speed into its preparation as the situation required.

To compound the problem, Longstreet did not find the Yankee left on Cemetery Ridge where Lee's scout had reported it to be. It was not there because of an unauthorized move by Dan Sickles, commander of the 3rd Corps holding the Union left. Distressed by the exposed nature of the low ground at the south end of Cemetery Ridge before it thrust upward at Little Round Top, Sickles had moved his two divisions a half-mile forward to occupy slightly higher ground along a road running southwest from Gettysburg. There his troops held a salient with its apex in a peach orchard and its left anchored in a maze of boulders locally called Devil's Den, just below Little Round Top. Although this gave Sickles high ground to defend, it left his men unconnected to the rest of the Union line and vulnerable to attack on both flanks. When Meade learned what Sickles had done, it was too late to order him back to the original line. Longstreet had launched his attack.

Sickles's unwise move may have unwittingly foiled Lee's hopes. Finding the Union left in an unexpected position, Longstreet probably should have notified Lee. Scouts reported that the Round Tops were unoccupied, opening the way for a flanking move around to the Union rear. Longstreet's division commanders urged a change of attack plans to take advantage of this opportunity. But Longstreet had already tried at least twice to change Lee's mind. He did not want to risk another rebuff. Lee had repeatedly ordered him to attack here, and here he meant to attack. At 4:00 p.m. his brigades started forward in echelon from right to left.

During the next few hours some of the war's bloodiest fighting took place in the peach orchard, in a wheat field to the east of the orchard, at Devil's Den, and on Little Round Top. Longstreet's 15,000 yelling veterans punched through the salient with attacks that shattered Sickles's leg and crushed his undersize corps. But with skillful tactics, Meade and his subordinates rushed reinforcements from three other corps to plug the breaks. Part of Hill's fresh division finally joined Longstreet's

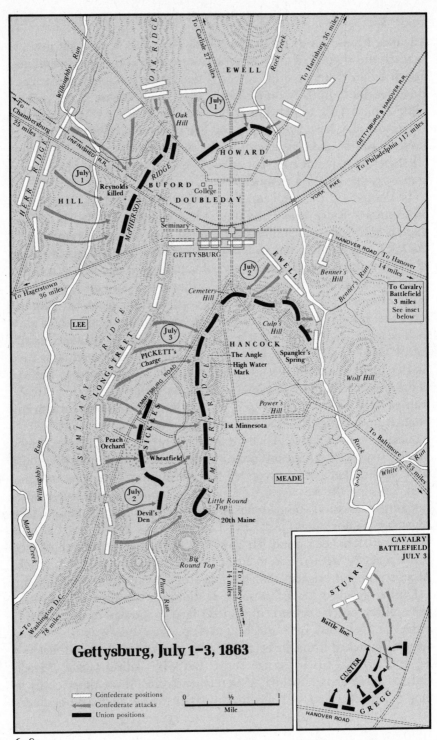

Gettysburg, July 1–3, 1863

To Carlisle 27 miles
To Harrisburg 36 miles
EWELL
Rock Creek
OAK RIDGE
July 1
Oak Hill
To Chambersburg 25 miles
UNFINISHED R.R.
HERR RIDGE
July 1
HILL
Reynolds killed
BUFORD
McPHERSON
RIDGE
College
DOUBLEDAY
HOWARD
GETTYSBURG & HANOVER R.R.
To Philadelphia 117 miles
YORK PIKE
Seminary
GETTYSBURG
HANOVER ROAD
To Hagerstown 36 miles
To Hanover 14 miles
July 2
EWELL
Benner's Hill
Benner's Run
LEE
Cemetery Hill
To Cavalry Battlefield 3 miles See inset below
July 3
SEMINARY RIDGE
LONGSTREET
PICKETT's Charge
Culp's Hill
HANCOCK
The Angle
High Water Mark
Spangler's Spring
Wolf Hill
EMMITSBURG ROAD
CEMETERY RIDGE
Power's Hill
1st Minnesota
To Baltimore 53 miles
Peach Orchard
SICKLES
Wheatfield
MEADE
Rock Creek
White's Run
July 2
Devil's Den
Little Round Top
20th Maine
Willoughby Run
Marsh Creek
Big Round Top
Plum Run
To Taneytown 14 miles
To Washington D.C. 78 miles

Confederate positions
Confederate attacks
Union positions

0   ½   1
Mile

CAVALRY BATTLEFIELD JULY 3

STUART
Battle line
CUSTER
GREGG
HANOVER ROAD

assault, while at the other end of the line Ewell's men belatedly went forward but achieved only limited gains before Union counterattacks and darkness halted them.

The most desperate struggle occurred on Longstreet's front, where two Union regiments at separated points of this combat zone, the 20th Maine and the 1st Minnesota, achieved lasting fame by throwing back Confederate attacks that came dangerously close to breakthroughs. Rising above the surrounding countryside, the two Round Tops dominated the south end of Cemetery Ridge. If the rebels had gotten artillery up there, they could have enfiladed the Union left. Sickles's advance had uncovered these hills. A brigade of Alabamians advanced to seize Little Round Top. Minutes earlier nothing but a Union signal station had stood in their way. But Meade's chief of engineers, General Gouverneur K. Warren, discovered this appalling situation as enemy troops were approaching. Galloping down the hill, Warren persuaded the 5th Corps commander to send a brigade double-timing to the crest of Little Round Top just in time to meet the charging rebels.

Posted at the far left of this brigade was the 20th Maine, commanded by Colonel Joshua L. Chamberlain. A year earlier Chamberlain had been a professor of rhetoric and modern languages at Bowdoin College. Taking a leave of absence ostensibly to study in Europe, he joined the army instead and now found himself responsible for preventing the rebels from rolling up the Union left. The fighting professor and his down-easterners proved equal to the occasion. For nearly two hours they stood off repeated assaults by portions of several Confederate regiments along the rocky, wooded slope filled with smoke, noise, and terror. But their valor seemed in vain. With more than a third of his men down and the remainder out of ammunition—and with the Johnnies forming for another assault—Chamberlain was in a tight spot. But cool and quick-witted—perhaps a legacy of dealing with fractious students—he ordered his men to fix bayonets on their empty rifles and charge. With a yell, these smoke-grimed Yanks lurched downhill against the surprised rebels. Exhausted by their uphill fighting following a twenty-five mile march that day to reach the battlefield, and shocked by the audacity of this bayonet assault, the Alabamians surrendered by scores to the jubilant boys from Maine. Little Round Top remained in northern hands. Although Sickles's corps was driven back yard by yard through the peach orchard, the wheat field, and Devil's Den, the Union left on Little Round Top was secure.

A mile to the north, however, another Alabama brigade threatened to puncture the Cemetery Ridge line near its center. Their attack hit a gap in the Union line created by the earlier advance of Sickles's corps to the peach orchard. Winfield Scott Hancock's 2nd Corps occupied this sector, but until Hancock could shift reinforcements to stop the assault he had only eight companies of one regiment on hand to meet the oncoming brigade. The regiment was the 1st Minnesota, veterans of all the army's battles since the beginning at Bull Run. Hancock ordered these 262 men to charge the 1,600 Alabamians and slow them down long enough for reinforcements to arrive. The Minnesotans did the job, but only forty-seven of them came back. Hancock plugged the gap, and the Confederate attack all along the southern half of the battlefield flickered out in the twilight.

To the north the shift of Union troops from Cemetery and Culp's hills to meet Longstreet's assault gave Ewell's corps the opportunity Lee had hoped for to convert its demonstration into an attack. But the opportunity slipped away. Several of Ewell's brigades did finally advance as dusk descended. One of them seized some trenches on Culp's Hill left unoccupied by a Federal unit sent to the other end of the battlefield, but could advance no farther against determined opposition. Two other gray brigades scored a temporary lodgement against the hapless 11th Corps at Cemetery Hill, but a 2nd Corps brigade counterattacked in the gathering darkness and drove them back.

The Confederate assaults on July 2 were uncoordinated and disjointed. The usual skill of generalship in the Army of Northern Virginia was lacking this day. On the Union side, by contrast, officers from Meade down to regimental colonels acted with initiative and coolness. They moved troops to the right spots and counterattacked at the right times. As a result, when night fell the Union line remained firm except for the loss of Sickles's salient. Each side had suffered 9,000 or more casualties, bringing the two-day totals for both armies to nearly 35,000.

It was the heaviest single-battle toll in the war thus far, but the fighting was not over. Despite stout resistance by the Yankees, Lee believed that his indomitable veterans had almost achieved victory. One more push, he thought, and "those people" would break. Lee seemed unusually excited by the supposed success of the past two days. At the same time, however, he was weakened by a bout with diarrhea and irritated by Stuart's prolonged absence (Jeb's tired troopers had finally rejoined the army during the day). In any case, Lee's judgment was not at its best. He had come to Pennsylvania in quest of a decisive victory and he was determined not to leave without it. He had attacked both enemy flanks, causing Meade (he believed) to weaken his center. With Pickett's fresh division as a spearhead, therefore, Lee would send three divisions preceded by an artillery barrage against that weakened center on July 3. Stuart would circle around the Union rear and Ewell would assail the right flank to clamp the pincers when Pickett broke through the front. With proper coordination and leadership, his invincible troops could not fail.

Across the way a midnight council of Union generals resolved to stay and fight it out. With prescience, Meade told the general commanding his center that "if Lee attacks to-morrow, it will be in *your front*."[45] At first light, however, fighting broke out at the extreme right of the Union line along the base of Culp's Hill. Units of the Federal 12th Corps, which had been shifted to the left the previous day, came back during the night and attacked at dawn to regain their abandoned trenches now occupied by the rebels. In a seven-hour firefight they succeeded, and thus dimmed Lee's chances for turning the Union right simultaneously with the planned piercing of the center.

While this was going on, Longstreet once more urged Lee to maneuver around Meade's left. Again Lee refused, and ordered Longstreet to attack the Union center with Pickett's division and two of Hill's—fewer than 15,000 men to advance three-quarters of a mile across open fields and assault dug-in infantry supported by ample artillery. "General Lee," Longstreet later reported himself to have said, "there never was a body of fifteen thousand men who could make that attack successfully." Lee impatiently replied that his magnificent army had done it before and could do it again. "My heart was heavy," wrote Longstreet subsequently. "I could see the desperate and hopeless nature of the charge and the hopeless slaughter it would cause. . . . That day at Gettysburg was one of the saddest of my life."[46]

In this mood Longstreet ordered a concentration of Confederate artillery—some 150 guns—for the largest southern bombardment of the war, to soften up the enemy at the point of attack. At 1:07 p.m. Longstreet's guns shattered the uneasy silence that had followed the morning's fight on the Union right. For almost two hours an artillery duel among nearly 300 guns filled the Pennsylvania countryside with an ear-splitting roar heard as far away as Pittsburgh. Despite this sound and fury, the Union

45. John Gibbon, "The Council of War on the Second Day," *Battles and Leaders*, III, 314.
46. Longstreet, "Lee's Right Wing at Gettysburg," *ibid.*, 343, 345.

infantry lying behind stone walls and breastworks suffered little, for the rebel aim was high.

Pickett's all-Virginia division waited with nervous impatience to go in and get it over with. Thirty-eight years old, George Pickett had graduated last in the same West Point class as George McClellan (who graduated second). Pickett did well in the Mexican War, but in the present conflict he had enjoyed few chances to distinguish himself. His division did not fight at Chancellorsville and marked time guarding supply wagons during the first two days at Gettysburg. With his long hair worn in ringlets and his face adorned by a drooping mustache and goatee, Pickett looked like a cross between a Cavalier dandy and a riverboat gambler. He affected the romantic style of Sir Walter Scott's heroes and was eager to win everlasting glory at Gettysburg.

Finally, about 3:00 p.m., Longstreet reluctantly ordered the attack. The Confederate bombardment seemed to have disabled the enemy's artillery; it was now or never. With parade-ground precision, Pickett's three brigades moved out joined by six more from Hill's division on their left and two others in reserve. It was a magnificent mile-wide spectacle, a picture-book view of war that participants on both sides remembered with awe until their dying moment—which for many came within the next hour. Pickett's charge represented the Confederate war effort in microcosm: matchless valor, apparent initial success, and ultimate disaster. As the gray infantry poured across the gently undulating farmland with seemingly irresistible force, northern artillery suddenly erupted in a savage cascade, sending shot and shell among the southern regiments and changing to canister as they kept coming. The Union guns had not been knocked out after all; their canny chief of artillery, General Henry J. Hunt, had ordered them to cease firing to lure on the rebels and conserve ammunition to welcome them. Yankee infantry behind stone walls opened up at 200 yards while Vermont, Ohio, and New York regiments on the left and right swung out to rake both flanks of the attacking force. The southern assault collapsed under this unbearable pressure from front and flanks. Two or three hundred Virginians and Tennesseeans with General Lewis A. Armistead breached the first Union line, where Armistead was mortally wounded with his hand on a Yankee cannon and his followers fell like leaves in an autumn wind. In half an hour it was all over. Of the 14,000 Confederates who had gone forward, scarcely half returned. Pickett's own division lost two-thirds of its men; his three brigadiers and all thirteen colonels were killed or wounded.

As the dazed survivors stumbled back to their starting point, they met

Lee and Longstreet working to form a defensive line against Meade's expected counterattack. "It's all my fault," said Lee as he rode among his men. "It is I who have lost this fight, and you must help me out of it the best way you can. All good men must rally."[47] Rally they did— some of them, at least. But Meade did not counterattack. For this he has been criticized down the years. Hancock, despite being wounded in the repulse of Pickett's assault, urged Meade to launch the 20,000 fresh reserves of the 5th and 6th Corps in pursuit of Lee's broken brigades. But a heavy load of responsibility weighed on Meade's shoulders. He had been in command only six days. For three of them his army had been fighting for the nation's life, as he saw the matter, and had narrowly saved it. Meade could not yet know how badly the enemy was hurt, or that their artillery was low on ammunition. He did know that Stuart was loose in his rear, but had not yet learned that a division of blue troopers had stopped the southern cavalry three miles east of Gettysburg—thus foiling the third part of Lee's three-pronged plan for Meade's undoing. Meanwhile two Union cavalry regiments on the left flank south of the Round Tops charged the rebel infantry in anticipation of orders for a counterattack, but were badly shot up by the alert enemy. In late afternoon a few units from the 5th and 6th Corps advanced over the scene of the previous day's carnage in Devil's Den and the wheat field. They flushed out the rear guard of Longstreet's two divisions, which were pulling back to a new line. Meade apparently did have some idea of attacking in this vicinity next day—the Fourth of July—but a heavy rainstorm that began shortly after noon halted the move.

Meade's lack of aggressiveness was caused by his respect for the enemy. He could scarcely believe that he had beaten the victors of Chancellorsville. Meade also explained later that he had not wanted to follow "the bad example [Lee] had set me, in ruining himself attacking a strong position." "We have done well enough," he said to a cavalry officer eager to do more. In a congratulatory telegram, a former corps commander expressed a widely felt astonishment that the long-suffering Army of the Potomac had actually won a big victory: "The glorious success of the Army of the Potomac has electrified all. I did not believe the enemy could be whipped."[48]

The news did indeed electrify the North. "VICTORY! WATERLOO

---

47. Clifford Dowdey, *Death of a Nation: The Story of Lee and His Men at Gettysburg* (New York, 1958), 341; Foote, *Civil War*, II, 567–68.

48. O.R., Ser. I, Vol. 27, pt. 3, p. 539; Foote, *Civil War*, II, 575; Freeman Cleaves, *Meade of Gettysburg* (Norman, Okla., 1960), 172.

ECLIPSED!" shouted a headline in the *Philadelphia Inquirer*. The glad tidings reached Washington the day after Pickett's repulse, making this the capital's most glorious Fourth ever. "I *never* knew such excitement in Washington," wrote one observer. When word arrived three days later of the surrender at Vicksburg, the excitement doubled. Lincoln appeared at a White House balcony to tell a crowd of serenaders that this "gigantic Rebellion" whose purpose was to "overthrow the principle that all men are created equal" had been dealt a crippling blow.[49] In New York the diarist George Templeton Strong rejoiced that

> the results of this victory are priceless. . . . The charm of Robert Lee's invincibility is broken. The Army of the Potomac has at last found a general that can handle it, and has stood nobly up to its terrible work in spite of its long disheartening list of hard-fought failures. . . . Copperheads are palsied and dumb for the moment at least. . . . Government is strengthened four-fold at home and abroad.[50]

Strong's final sentence was truer than he could know. Confederate Vice-President Stephens was on his way under flag of truce to Union lines at Norfolk as the battle of Gettysburg reached its climax. Jefferson Davis had hoped that Stephens would reach Washington from the south while Lee's victorious army was marching toward it from the north. Reports of Stephens's mission and of Gettysburg's outcome reached the White House at the same time. Lincoln thereupon sent a curt refusal to Stephens's request for a pass through the lines.[51] In London the news of Gettysburg and Vicksburg gave the *coup de grâce* to Confederate hopes for recognition. "The disasters of the rebels are unredeemed by even any hope of success," crowed Henry Adams. "It is now conceded that all idea of intervention is at an end."[52]

The victory at Gettysburg was purchased at high human cost: 23,000 Union casualties, more than one-quarter of the army's effectives. Yet the cost to the South was greater: 28,000 men killed, wounded, or missing, more than a third of Lee's army. As the survivors began their sad retreat to Virginia in the rain on July 4, thousands of wounded men suffered torture as ambulances and commandeered farm wagons bounced

49. Cleaves, *Meade of Gettysburg*, 171; CWL, VI, 319–20.
50. Strong, *Diary*, 330.
51. Beale, ed., *Diary of Gideon Welles*, I, 358–62.
52. Henry Adams to Charles Francis Adams, Jr., July 23, 1863, in Ford, ed., *Cycle of Adams Letters*, II, 59–60.

along rutted roads. Seven thousand rebel wounded were left behind to be attended by Union surgeons and volunteer nurses who flocked to Gettysburg. Lee was profoundly depressed by the outcome of his campaign to conquer a peace. A month later he offered his resignation to Jefferson Davis. "No one," wrote Lee, "is more aware than myself of my inability for the duties of my position. I cannot even accomplish what I myself desire. How can I fulfill the expectations of others?"[53] Thus said a man whose stunning achievements during the year before Gettysburg had won the admiration of the Western world. Of course Davis refused to accept his resignation. Lee and his men would go on to earn further laurels. But they never again possessed the power and reputation they carried into Pennsylvania those palmy midsummer days of 1863. Though the war was destined to continue for almost two more bloody years, Gettysburg and Vicksburg proved to have been its crucial turning point.

Perceptive southerners sadly recognized this. The fall of Vicksburg "is a terrible blow, and has produced much despondency," wrote War Department clerk John Jones when he heard the news on July 8. Next day his spirits sank lower, for "the news from Lee's army is appalling. . . . This [is] the darkest day of the war." The fire-eater Edmund Ruffin "never before felt so despondent as to our struggle." And the usually indefatigable Josiah Gorgas, chief of Confederate ordnance, sat down on July 28 and wrote a diary entry whose anguish echoes across the years:

> Events have succeeded one another with disastrous rapidity. One brief month ago we were apparently at the point of success. Lee was in Pennsylvania, threatening Harrisburgh, and even Philadelphia. Vicksburgh seemed to laugh all Grant's efforts to scorn. . . . Port Hudson had beaten off Banks' force. . . . Now the picture is just as sombre as it was bright then. . . . It seems incredible that human power could effect such a change in so brief a space. Yesterday we rode on the pinnacle of success—today absolute ruin seems to be our portion. The Confederacy totters to its destruction.[54]

53. Lee to Davis, Aug. 8, 1863, in Dowdey and Manarin, eds., *Wartime Papers of R. E. Lee*, 589–90.
54. Jones, *War Clerk's Diary* (Miers), 238, 239; Betty L. Mitchell, *Edmund Ruffin: A Biography* (Bloomington, 1981), 231; Vandiver, ed., *Diary of Gorgas*, 55.

22

Johnny Reb's Chattanooga Blues

I

Lincoln also believed that the victories at Gettysburg and Vicksburg had set the Confederacy tottering. One more push might topple it. "If General Meade can complete his work . . . by the literal or substantial destruction of Lee's army," said the president on July 7, "the rebellion will be over."[1] But Lincoln was doomed to disappointment. Although Lee was in a tight spot after Gettysburg, the old Gray Fox once again gave the blue hounds the slip.

It was a near thing, however. A Union cavalry raid wrecked the Confederate pontoon bridge across the Potomac, and days of heavy rain that began July 4 made the swollen river unfordable. The rebels were compelled to stand at bay with their backs to the Potomac while engineers tore down warehouses to build a new bridge. The tired soldiers fortified a defensive perimeter at Williamsport and awaited Yankee attack. But no attack came. Having given Lee a two-day head start from Gettysburg, Meade did not get his reinforced army into line facing the Confederates at Williamsport until July 12. In Washington an "anxious and impatient" Lincoln awaited word of Lee's destruction. As the days passed and no word arrived, the president grew angry. When Meade finally telegraphed on July 12 that he intended "to attack them tomorrow, unless

1. *CWL*, VI, 319.

something intervenes," Lincoln commented acidly: "They will be ready to fight a magnificent battle when there is no enemy there to fight."[2] Events proved him right. A pretended deserter (a favorite southern ruse) had entered Union lines and reported Lee's army in fine fettle, eager for another fight. This reinforced Meade's wariness. He allowed a majority of his corps commanders to talk him out of attacking on the 13th. When the Army of the Potomac finally groped forward on July 14, it found nothing but a rear guard. The slippery rebels had vanished across a patched-together bridge during the night.

"Great God!" cried Lincoln when he heard this news. "What does it mean? . . . There is bad faith somewhere. . . . Our Army held the war in the hollow of their hand & they would not close it." Lincoln's estimate of the situation at Williamsport was not quite accurate. An attack on the strong Confederate position might have succeeded—with heavy casualties—or it might not. In either case, the destruction of Lee's veteran army was scarcely a sure thing. When word of Lincoln's dissatisfaction reached Meade, the testy general offered his resignation. But Lincoln could hardly afford to sack the victor of Gettysburg, so he refused to accept it. On July 14 he sat down to write Meade a soothing letter. "I am very—*very*— grateful to you for the magnificent success you gave the cause of the country at Gettysburg," said the president. But as his pen scratched on, Lincoln's distress at the presumed lost opportunity took over. "My dear general, I do not believe you appreciate the magnitude of the misfortune involved in Lee's escape. He was within your easy grasp, and to have closed upon him would, in connection with our other late successes, have ended the war. As it is, the war will be prolonged indefinitely." Upon reflection, Lincoln concluded that this letter was unlikely to mollify Meade, so he did not send it. And the war continued.[3]

Lincoln's temper soon recovered. In early August his secretary John Hay wrote that "the Tycoon is in fine whack. I have seldom seen him more serene."[4] The president's spirits had been buoyed by the "other late successes" he noted in the unsent letter to Meade. These successes included victories west of the Mississippi and Rosecrans's expulsion of

2. Dennett, *Lincoln/Hay*, 66; *O.R.*, Ser. I, Vol. 22, pt. 1, p. 91; David Homer Bates, *Lincoln in the Telegraph Office* (New York, 1907), 157.
3. *The Diary of Gideon Welles*, ed. Howard K. Beale, 3 vols. (New York, 1960), I, 370; Dennett, *Lincoln/Hay*, 69, 67; CWL, VI, 327–28.
4. Dennett, *Lincoln/Hay*, 76.

Bragg's army from middle Tennessee as well as the capture of Vicksburg and Port Hudson.

The transfer of Van Dorn's Confederate army to Mississippi in the spring of 1862 had left northern Arkansas shorn of defenders. Samuel R. Curtis's small Union force began advancing toward Little Rock, slowed only by skittish militia and harassing guerrillas. Into the Confederate breach stepped Thomas C. Hindman, a political general five feet tall who made up in energy what he lacked in size. Hindman enforced conscription with a will that created a 20,000-man army of lukewarm Arkansans, hardened Texans, and Missouri guerrillas. This force deflected the enemy campaign against Little Rock and went over to the offensive in the fall, driving the Federals northward almost to Missouri. But then the initiative went over to the Yankees. Their leader was General James G. Blunt, a Maine-born Kansas abolitionist who had learned his fighting with John Brown. While Blunt and Hindman were sparring in northwest Arkansas during the first week of December, two small Union divisions marched 110 miles in three days from Missouri to help Blunt. Turning to attack this force at Prairie Grove on December 7, Hindman suddenly found himself attacked in front and flank by three converging Yankee divisions. Forced to retreat in freezing weather, the diminutive Arkansan watched helplessly as his conscript army melted away.

In the spring of 1863 Jefferson Davis reorganized the trans-Mississippi Department by assigning overall command to Edmund Kirby Smith and sending Sterling Price to Little Rock. Both generals did well with their small resources. Kirby Smith turned the trans-Mississippi into a virtually autonomous region after it was cut off from the rest of the Confederacy by the loss of Vicksburg. But Price could not stop the blue invaders who advanced toward Little Rock from two directions in midsummer. Blunt led a multiracial force of white, black, and Indian regiments down the Arkansas River from Honey Springs in Indian Territory, where they had defeated a Confederate army of white and Indian regiments on July 17. In early September Blunt occupied Fort Smith, while another Union army approached Little Rock from the east and captured it on September 10. The rebels fled to the southwest corner of the state, yielding three-quarters of Arkansas to Union control—though southern guerrillas and the small number of occupation troops made that control tenuous in large areas.

Gratifying to Lincoln as these results were, they took second place to events in Tennessee. Northern progress in that theater had been exasperatingly slow. All through the spring of 1863 the administration had been urging Rosecrans to advance in concert with Grant's movements in Mississippi and Hooker's in Virginia. This would achieve Lincoln's strategy of concurrent pressure on all main Confederate armies to prevent one of them from reinforcing another. But Rosecrans balked like a sulky mule. The memory of the New Year's Eve bloodbath at Stones River convinced him that he must not attack without sufficient resources to insure success. His delays enabled Bragg to send reinforcements to Mississippi, an action that increased Lincoln's exasperation. But when Rosecrans finally made his move on June 24, his careful planning produced a swift and almost bloodless success. Each of the four northern infantry corps and one cavalry corps burst through a different gap in the Cumberland foothills south of Murfreesboro. Having confused Bragg with feints, Rosecrans got strong forces on both Confederate flanks in the Duck River Valley. Despite constant rain that turned roads to gluten, the Yankees kept moving. One blue brigade of mounted infantry armed with seven-shot Spencer carbines got in the rebel rear and threatened to cut their rail lifeline. At the beginning of July, Bragg decided to fall back all the way to Chattanooga rather than risk a battle.

In little more than a week of marching and maneuvering, the Army of the Cumberland had driven its adversary eighty miles at the cost of only 570 casualties. Rosecrans was annoyed by Washington's apparent lack of appreciation. On July 7 Secretary of War Stanton sent Rosecrans a message informing him of "Lee's army overthrown; Grant victorious. You and your noble army now have the chance to give the finishing blow to the rebellion. Will you neglect the chance?" Rosecrans shot back: "You do not appear to observe the fact that this noble army has driven the rebels from Middle Tennessee. . . . I beg in behalf of this army that the War Department may not overlook so great an event because it is not written in letters of blood."[5]

Southern newspapers agreed that Rosecrans's brief campaign was "masterful." Bragg confessed it "a great disaster" for the Confederates.[6] His retreat offered two rich prizes to the Federals if they could keep up the momentum: Knoxville and Chattanooga. The former was the center

5. O.R., Ser. I, Vol. 23, pt. 2, p. 518.
6. Foote, Civil War, II, 674, 675.

of east Tennessee unionism, which Lincoln had been trying to redeem for two years. Chattanooga had great strategic value, for the only railroads linking the eastern and western parts of the Confederacy converged there in the gap carved through the Cumberlands by the Tennessee River. Having already cut the Confederacy in two by the capture of Vicksburg, Union forces could slice up the eastern portion by penetrating into Georgia via Chattanooga.

For these reasons Lincoln urged Rosecrans to push on to Chattanooga while he had the enemy off balance. From Kentucky General Burnside, now commanding the small Army of the Ohio, would move forward on Rosecrans's left flank against the 10,000 Confederate troops defending Knoxville. But once again Rosecrans dug in his heels. He could not advance until he had repaired the railroad and bridges in his rear, established a forward base, and accumulated supplies. July passed as General-in-Chief Halleck sent repeated messages asking and finally ordering Rosecrans to get moving. On August 16, after more delays, he did.

Rosecrans repeated the deceptive strategy of his earlier advance, feinting a crossing of the Tennessee above Chattanooga (where Bragg expected it) but sending most of his army across the river at three virtually undefended points below the city. Rosecrans's objective was the railroad from Atlanta. His 60,000 men struck toward it in three columns through gaps in the mountain ranges south of Chattanooga. At the same time, a hundred miles to the north Burnside's army of 24,000 also moved through mountain passes in four columns like the fingers of a hand reaching to grasp Knoxville. The outnumbered defenders, confronted by Yankees soldiers in front and unionist partisans in the rear, abandoned the city without firing a shot. Burnside rode into town on September 3 to the cheers of most citizens. His troops pushed patrols toward the North Carolina and Virginia borders to consolidate their hold on east Tennessee, while the rebel division that had evacuated Knoxville moved south to join Bragg just in time to participate in the evacuation of Chattanooga on September 8. With Rosecrans on his southern flank, Bragg had decided to pull back to northern Georgia before he could be trapped in this city enfolded by river and mountains.

"When will this year's calamities end?" asked a despairing Confederate official on September 13. Desertions from southern armies rose alarmingly. "There is no use fighting any longer no how," wrote a Georgia deserter after the evacuation of Chattanooga, "for we are done gon up the Spout." Jefferson Davis confessed himself to be "in the depths of

gloom. . . . We are now in the darkest hour of our political existence."[7]

But it had been almost as dark after Union victories in early 1862,
until Jackson and Lee had rekindled southern hopes. Davis was determined to make history repeat itself. Lee had turned the war around by
attacking McClellan; Davis instructed Bragg to try the same strategy against
Rosecrans. To aid that effort, two divisions had already joined Bragg
from Joseph Johnston's idle army in Mississippi. This brought Bragg's
numbers almost equal to Rosecrans's. In view of the low morale in the
Army of Tennessee, though, Davis knew this was not enough. Having
once before called on Lee to command at the point of greatest crisis,
the president tried to do so again. But Lee demurred at Davis's request
that he go south in person to take over Bragg's augmented army. The
Virginian also objected at first to Longstreet's renewed proposal to reinforce Bragg with his corps. Instead, Lee wanted to take the offensive
against Meade on the Rappahannock, where the Army of Northern Virginia and the Army of the Potomac had been shadow-boxing warily
since Gettysburg. But this time Davis overruled Lee and ordered Longstreet to Georgia with two of his divisions (the third, Pickett's, had not
yet recovered from Gettysburg). The first of Longstreet's 12,000 veterans
entrained on September 9. Because of Burnside's occupation of east
Tennessee, the direct route of 550 miles was closed off. Instead, the
soldiers had to make a roundabout 900-mile excursion through both
Carolinas and Georgia over eight or ten different lines. Only half of
Longstreet's men got to Chickamauga Creek in time for the ensuing
battle—but they helped win a stunning victory over Longstreet's old
West Point roommate Rosecrans.

With help on the way, Bragg went over to the offensive. To lure
Rosecrans's three separated columns through the mountains where he
could pounce on them individually in the valley south of Chattanooga,
Bragg sent sham deserters into Union lines bearing tales of Confederate
retreat. Rosecrans took the bait and pushed forward too eagerly. But
Bragg's subordinates failed to spring the traps. Three times from September 10 to 13 Bragg ordered attacks by two or more divisions against
outnumbered and isolated fragments of the enemy. But each time the
general assigned to make the attack, considering his orders discretionary,
found reasons for not doing so. Warned by these maneuvers, Rosecrans

---

7. Jones, *War Clerk's Diary* (Swiggett), II, 43; Wiley, *Johnny Reb*, 131; Rowland, *Davis*,
V, 548, 554.

concentrated his army in the valley of West Chickamauga Creek during the third week of September.

Angered by the intractability of his generals—who in turn distrusted his judgment—Bragg nevertheless devised a new plan to turn Rosecrans's left, cut him off from Chattanooga, and drive him southward up a dead-end valley. With the arrival on September 18 of the first of Longstreet's troops under the fighting Texan John Bell Hood with his arm in a sling from a Gettysburg wound, Bragg was assured of numerical superiority. If he had been able to launch his attack that day, he might have succeeded in rolling up Rosecrans's flank, for only one Union corps stood in his way. But Yankee cavalry with repeating carbines blunted the rebels' sluggish advance. That night Virginia-born George Thomas's large Union corps made a forced march to strengthen the Union left. Soon after dawn on September 19, enemy patrols bumped into each other just west of Chickamauga Creek, setting off what became the bloodiest battle in the western theater.

Bragg persisted in trying to turn the Union left. All through the day the rebels made savage division-size attacks mostly against Thomas's corps through woods and undergrowth so thick that units could not see or cooperate with each other. Rosecrans fed reinforcements to Thomas who held the enemy to minimal gains, at harsh cost to both sides. That evening Longstreet arrived personally with two more of his brigades. Bragg organized his army into two wings, gave Longstreet command of the left and Leonidas Polk of the right, and ordered them to make an echelon attack next morning from right to left. Polk's assault started several hours late—a failing that had become a habit—and made little headway against Thomas's stubborn defenders fighting behind breastworks they had built overnight. Exasperated, Bragg canceled the echelon order of attack and told Longstreet to go forward with everything he had. At 11:30 a.m. Longstreet complied, and charged into one of the greatest pieces of luck in the war.

Over on the Union side, Rosecrans had been shifting reinforcements to his hard-pressed left. During this confusing process a staff officer, failing to see a blue division concealed in the woods on the right, reported a quarter-mile gap in the line at that point. To fill this supposedly dangerous hole, Rosecrans ordered another division to move over, thus creating a real gap in an effort to remedy a nonexistent one. Into this breach unwittingly marched Longstreet's veterans from the Army of Northern Virginia, catching the Yankees on either side in the flank and spreading a growing panic. More gray soldiers poured into the break,

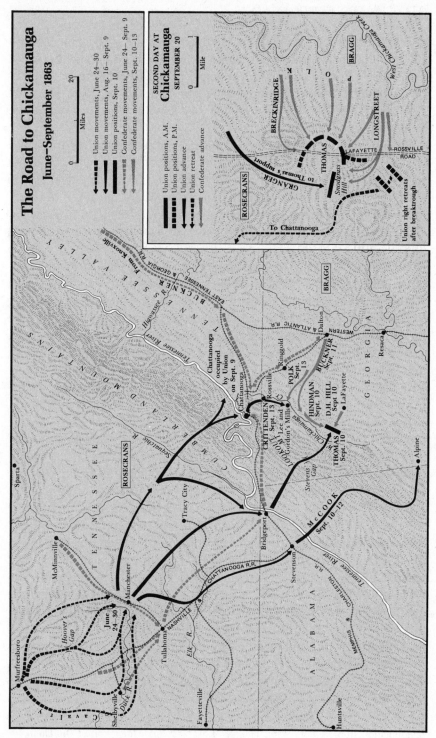

The Road to Chickamauga
June–September 1863

Union movements, June 24–30
Union movements, Aug. 16– Sept. 9
Union positions, Sept. 10
Confederate movements, June 24– Sept. 9
Confederate movements, Sept. 10–13

Miles
0   20

SECOND DAY AT
Chickamauga
SEPTEMBER 20

Union positions, A.M.
Union positions, P.M.
Union advance
Union retreat
Confederate advance

0   1
Mile

BRAGG

West Chickamauga Creek

BRECKINRIDGE

POLK

THOMAS

LONGSTREET

to Thomas's support

GRANGER

Snodgrass Hill

LAFAYETTE

ROSSVILLE
ROAD

ROSECRANS

Union right retreats
after breakthrough

To Chattanooga

TENNESSEE VALLEY

BUCKNER from Knoxville

EAST TENNESSEE & GEORGIA R.R.

Sequatchie River

Tennessee River

CUMBERLAND MOUNTAINS

Chattanooga
occupied by Union
on Sept. 9

Chattanooga

Sparta

ROSECRANS

Tracy City

Manchester

McMinnville

Hoover's
Gap

June
24–30

Murfreesboro

Shelbyville

Tullahoma NASHVILLE

Duck R.

Elk R.

CHATTANOOGA R.R.

Bridgeport

Fayetteville

Huntsville

Stevenson

CHARLESTON R.R.

MEMPHIS

Tennessee River

ALABAMA

McCOOK
Sept. 10–12

Stevens Gap

THOMAS
Sept. 10

CRITTENDEN
Sept. 13

Rossville

Lee and
Gordon's Mills

Chickamauga Cr.

LOOKOUT

Ringgold

POLK
Sept. 13

HINDMAN
Sept. 10

D.H. HILL
Sept. 10

LaFayette

BUCKNER
Sept. 11

WESTERN & ATLANTIC R.R.

Dalton

Resaca

GEORGIA

BRAGG

Alpine

CAVALRY

CUMBERLAND

673

rolling up Rosecrans's right and sending one-third of the blue army—along with four division commanders, two corps commanders, and a traumatized Rosecrans whose headquarters had been overrun—streaming northward toward Chattanooga eight miles away. Here were the makings of the decisive victory that had eluded western Confederate armies for more than two years.

Recognizing the opportunity, Longstreet sent in his reserves and called on Bragg for reinforcements. But the commander said he could not spare a man from his fought-out right, so a disgusted Longstreet had to make the final push with what he had. By this time, however, the Federals had formed a new line along a ridge at right angles to their old one. George Thomas took charge of what was left of the army and organized it for a last-ditch stand. For his leadership this day he won fame as the Rock of Chickamauga. Thomas got timely help from another northern battle hero, Gordon Granger, commander of the Union reserve division posted several miles to the rear. On his own initiative Granger marched toward the sound of the guns and arrived just in time for his men to help stem Longstreet's repeated onslaughts. As the sun went down, Thomas finally disengaged his exhausted troops for a nighttime retreat to Chattanooga. There the two parts of the army—those who had fled and those who had stood—were reunited to face an experience unique for Union forces, the defense of a besieged city.

Longstreet and Forrest wanted to push on next morning to complete the destruction of Rosecrans's army before it could reorganize behind the Chattanooga fortifications. But Bragg was more appalled by the wastage of his own army than impressed by the magnitude of its victory. In two days he had lost 20,000 killed, wounded, and missing—more than 30 percent of his effectives. Ten Confederate generals had been killed or wounded, including Hood who narrowly survived amputation of a leg. Although the rebels had made a rich haul in captured guns and equipment, Bragg's immediate concern was the ghastly spectacle of dead and wounded lying thick on the ground. Half of his artillery horses had also been killed. Thus he refused to heed the pleas of his lieutenants for a rapid pursuit—a refusal that laid the groundwork for bitter recriminations that swelled into an uproar during the coming weeks. "What does he fight battles for?" asked an angry Forrest, and soon many others in the South were asking the same question. The tactical triumph at Chickamauga seemed barren of strategic results so long as the enemy held Chattanooga.[8]

8. Quotation from Robert Selph Henry, *"First with the Most" Forrest* (Indianapolis,

Bragg hoped to starve the Yankees out. By mid-October he seemed likely to succeed. The Confederates planted artillery on the commanding height of Lookout Mountain south of Chattanooga, infantry along Missionary Ridge to the east, and infantry on river roads to the west. This enabled them to interdict all of Rosecrans's supply routes into the city except a tortuous wagon road over the forbidding Cumberlands to the north. Mules consumed almost as much forage as they could haul over these heights, while rebel cavalry raids picked off hundreds of wagons. Union horses starved to death in Chattanooga while men were reduced to half rations or less.

Rosecrans seemed unequal to the crisis. The disaster at Chickamauga and the shame of having fled the field while Thomas stayed and fought unnerved him. Lincoln considered Rosecrans "confused and stunned like a duck hit on the head."[9] The Army of the Cumberland clearly needed help. Even before Chickamauga, Halleck had ordered Sherman to bring four divisions from Vicksburg to Chattanooga, rebuilding the railroad as he went. But the latter task would take weeks. So, on September 23, Stanton pressed a reluctant Lincoln to transfer the understrength 11th and 12th Corps by rail from the Army of the Potomac to Rosecrans. This would handicap Meade's operations on the Rappahannock, protested the president. Meade could not be prodded into an offensive anyhow, replied Stanton, so these corps should be put to work where they could do some good. Lincoln finally consented, and activated Joe Hooker to command the expeditionary force. Stanton summoned railroad presidents to his office. Orders flew around the country; dozens of trains were assembled; and forty hours after the decision, the first troops rolled out of Culpeper for a 1,233-mile trip through Union-held territory over the Appalachians and across the unbridged Ohio River twice. Eleven days later more than 20,000 men had arrived at the railhead near Chattanooga with their artillery, horses, and equipment. It was an extraordinary feat of logistics—the longest and fastest movement of such a large body of troops before the twentieth century.[10]

But there was no point putting these men into Chattanooga when the

---

1944), 193. Union casualties at Chickamauga were about 16,000. Glen Tucker, *Chickamauga: Bloody Battle in the West* (Indianapolis, 1961), 388–89.

9. Dennett, *Lincoln/Hay*, 106.

10. George Edgar Turner, *Victory Rode the Rails* (Indianapolis, 1953), 288–94; Thomas Weber, *The Northern Railroads in the Civil War* (New York, 1952), 181–86. From first to last, the transfer of Longstreet's 12,000 infantry about 900 miles had required twelve days and the transportation of their artillery and horses an additional four days. Longstreet left his supply wagons and their horses behind in Virginia.

soldiers already there could not be fed. And there seemed to be no remedy for that problem without new leadership. In mid-October, Lincoln took the matter in hand. He created the Division of the Mississippi embracing the whole region between that river and the Appalachians, and put Grant in command "with his headquarters in the field."[11] The field just now was Chattanooga, so there Grant went. On the way he authorized the replacement of Rosecrans with Thomas as commander of the Army of the Cumberland. Within a week of Grant's arrival on October 23, Union forces had broken the rebel stranglehold on the road and river west of Chattanooga and opened a new supply route dubbed the "cracker line" by hungry bluecoats. Although Rosecrans's staff had planned the operation that accomplished this, it was Grant who ordered it done. A Union officer later recalled that when Grant came on the scene "we began to see things move. We felt that everything came from a plan."[12] The inspiration of Grant's presence seemed to extend even to the 11th Corps, which had suffered disgrace at Chancellorsville and Gettysburg but fought well during a night action October 28–29 to open the cracker line. By mid-November, Sherman had arrived with 17,000 troops from the Army of the Tennessee to supplement the 20,000 men Hooker had brought from the Army of the Potomac to reinforce the 35,000 infantry of Thomas's Army of the Cumberland. Though Bragg still held Lookout Mountain and Missionary Ridge, his immediate future began to look cloudy.

This cloudiness stemmed in part from continuing internecine warfare within Bragg's command. Soon after Chickamauga, Bragg suspended Polk and two other generals for slowness or refusal to obey crucial orders before and during the battle. The hot-blooded Forrest, bitter about failure to follow up the victory, refused to serve any longer under Bragg and returned to an independent command in Mississippi after telling Bragg to his face: "I have stood your meanness as long as I intend to. You have played the part of a damned scoundrel. . . . If you ever again try to interfere with me or cross my path it will be at the peril of your life." Several generals signed a petition to Davis asking for Bragg's removal. Longstreet wrote to the secretary of war with a lugubrious prediction that "nothing but the hand of God can save us or help us as long as we have our present commander."[13]

Twice before—after Perryville and Stones River—similar dissensions

---

11. O.R., Ser. I, Vol. 30, pt. 4, p. 404.

12. Bruce Catton, *Grant Takes Command* (Boston, 1969), 56.

13. Henry, *"First with the Most" Forrest*, 199; O.R., Ser. I, Vol. 30, pt. 4, p. 706.

had erupted in the Army of Tennessee. On October 6 a weary Jefferson Davis boarded a special train for the long trip to Bragg's headquarters where he hoped to straighten out the mess. In Bragg's presence all four corps commanders told Davis that the general must go. After this embarrassing meeting, Davis talked alone with Longstreet and may have sounded him out on the possibility of taking the command. But as a sojourner from Lee's army, Longstreet professed unwillingness and recommended Joseph Johnston. At this the president bridled, for he had no confidence in Johnston and considered him responsible for the loss of Vicksburg. Beauregard was another possibility for the post. Although he was then doing a good job holding off Union attacks on Charleston, Davis had tried Beauregard once before as commander of the Army of Tennessee and found him wanting. In the end there seemed no alternative but to retain Bragg. In an attempt to reduce friction within the army, Davis authorized the transfer of several generals to other theaters. He also counseled Bragg to detach Longstreet with 15,000 men for a campaign to recapture Knoxville—an ill-fated venture that accomplished nothing while depriving Bragg of more than a quarter of his strength. Indeed, none of Davis's decisions during this maladroit visit had a happy result. The president left behind a sullen army as he returned to Richmond.

With Longstreet's departure in early November the Confederates yielded the initiative to Grant. As soon as Sherman's reinforcements arrived, Grant set in motion a plan to drive the rebels away from Chattanooga and open the gate to Georgia. As usual the taciturn general's offensive succeeded, but this time not in quite the way he had planned. Grant rejected the idea of a frontal assault against the triple line of trenches on Missionary Ridge as suicidal. He intended to attack both ends of Bragg's line to get on the enemy's flanks. Believing that Thomas's Army of the Cumberland was still demoralized from their shock at Chickamauga and "could not be got out of their trenches to assume the offensive," Grant assigned them the secondary role of merely threatening the Confederate center on Missionary Ridge while Sherman's and Hooker's interlopers from the Armies of the Tennessee and the Potomac did the real fighting on the flanks.[14] By this plan Grant unwittingly applied a goad to Thomas's troops that would produce a spectacular though serendipitous success.

Hooker carried out the first part of his job with a flair. On November

14. *Memoirs of General William T. Sherman*, 2 vols. (2nd ed., New York, 1886), I, 390.

24 he sent the better part of three divisions against three Confederate brigades holding the northern slope of Lookout Mountain. The Yankee infantry scrambled uphill over boulders and fallen trees through an intermittent fog that in later years became romanticized as the "Battle Above the Clouds." With surprisingly light casualties (fewer than 500), Hooker's troops drove the rebels down the reverse slope, forcing Bragg that night to evacuate his defenses on Lookout and pull the survivors back to Missionary Ridge.

During the night the skies cleared to reveal a total eclipse of the moon; next morning a Kentucky Union regiment clawed its way to Lookout's highest point and raised a huge American flag in sunlit view of both armies below. For the South these were ill omens, though at first it did not appear so. On the other end of the line Sherman had found the going hard. When his four divisions pressed forward on November 24 they quickly took their assigned hill at the north end of Missionary Ridge—but found that it was not part of the ridge at all, but a detached spur separated by a rock-strewn ravine from the main spine. The latter they attacked with a will on the morning of November 25 but were repeatedly repulsed by Irish-born Patrick Cleburne's oversize division, the best in Bragg's army. Meanwhile Hooker's advance toward the opposite end of Missionary Ridge was delayed by obstructed roads and a wrecked bridge.

His plan not working, Grant in mid-afternoon ordered Thomas to launch a limited assault against the first line of Confederate trenches in the center to prevent Bragg from sending reinforcements to Cleburne. Thomas made the most of this opportunity to redeem his army's reputation. He sent four divisions, 23,000 men covering a two-mile front, across an open plain straight at the Confederate line. It looked like a reprise of Pickett's charge at Gettysburg, with blue and gray having switched roles. And this assault seemed even more hopeless than Pickett's, for the rebels had had two months to dig in and Missionary Ridge was much higher and more rugged than Cemetery Ridge. Yet the Yankees swept over the first line of trenches with astonishing ease, driving the demoralized defenders pell-mell up the hill to the second and third lines at the middle and top of the crest.

Having accomplished their assignment, Thomas's soldiers did not stop and await orders. For one thing, they were now sitting ducks for the enemy firing at them from above. For another, these men had something to prove to the rebels in front of them and to the Yankees on their flanks. So they started up the steep ridge, first by platoons and compa-

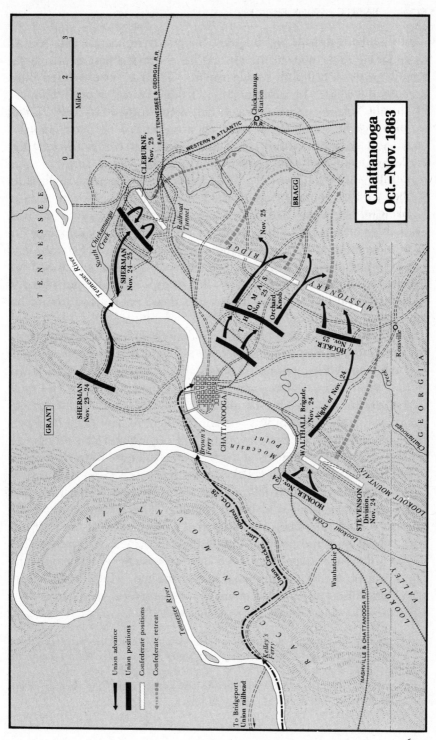

**Chattanooga
Oct.–Nov. 1863**

TENNESSEE

Tennessee River

South Chickamauga Creek

CLEBURNE,
Nov. 25

EAST TENNESSEE & GEORGIA R.R.

WESTERN & ATLANTIC

Chickamauga
Station

BRAGG

Railroad
Tunnel

SHERMAN
Nov. 24–25

MISSIONARY RIDGE

THOMAS
Nov. 25

Orchard
Knob

Nov. 25

GRANT

SHERMAN
Nov. 23–24

SHERMAN
Nov. 23–24

HOOKER,
Nov. 25

Rossville

CHATTANOOGA

Brown's Ferry

Moccasin Point

WALTHALL Brigade,
Night of Nov. 24

Night of Nov. 24

GEORGIA

Creek

Chattanooga

HOOKER, Nov. 24

Union Cracker Line, opened Oct. 28

RACCOON MOUNTAIN

Tennessee River

STEVENSON
Division,
Nov. 24

LOOKOUT MOUNTAIN

Lookout Creek

Wauhatchie

LOOKOUT VALLEY

Kelley's Ferry

To Bridgeport
Union railroad

NASHVILLE & CHATTANOOGA R.R.

0 1 2 3
Miles

Union advance
Union positions
Confederate positions
Confederate retreat

nies, then by regiments and brigades. Soon sixty regimental flags seemed to be racing each other to the top. At his command post a mile in the rear, Grant watched with bewilderment. "Thomas, who ordered those men up the ridge?" he asked angrily. "I don't know," replied Thomas. "I did not." Someone would catch hell if this turned out badly, Grant muttered as he clamped his teeth on a cigar. But he need not have worried. Things turned out better than anyone at Union headquarters could have expected—the miracle at Missionary Ridge, some of them were calling it by sundown. To the Confederates it seemed a nightmare. As the Yankees kept coming up the hill the rebels gaped with amazement, panicked, broke, and fled. "Completely and frantically drunk with excitement," blueclad soldiers yelled "Chickamauga! Chickamauga!" in derisive triumph at the backs of the disappearing enemy. Darkness and a determined rear-guard defense by Cleburne's division, which had not broken, prevented effective pursuit. But Bragg's army did not stop and regroup until it had retreated thirty miles down the railroad toward Atlanta.[15]

Union soldiers could hardly believe their stunning success. When a student of the battle later commented to Grant that southern generals had considered their position impregnable, Grant replied with a wry smile: "Well, it *was* impregnable." Bragg himself wrote that "no satisfactory excuse can possibly be given for the shameful conduct of our troops. . . . The position was one which ought to have been held by a line of skirmishers."[16] But explanations if not excuses can be offered. Some Confederate regiments at the base of Missionary Ridge had orders to fall back after firing two volleys; others had received no such orders. When the latter saw their fellows apparently breaking to the rear, they were infected by panic and began running. The Union attackers followed the retreating rebels so closely that Confederates in the next line had to hold their fire to avoid hitting their own men. As northern soldiers climbed the slope, they used dips and swells in the ground for cover against enemy fire from the line at the top, which Bragg's engineers had mistakenly located along the *topographical* crest rather than

15. Quotations from Joseph S. Fullerton, "The Army of the Cumberland at Chattanooga," *Battles and Leaders*, III, 725, and James A. Connolly, *Three Years in the Army of the Cumberland*, ed. Paul M. Angle (Bloomington, 1959), 158.

16. Ulysses S. Grant, "Chattanooga," *Battles and Leaders*, III, 693n; Bragg's official report in *O.R.*, Ser. I, Vol. 31, pt. 2, p. 666.

the *military* crest where the line of fire would not be blocked by such dips and swells. Perhaps the ultimate explanation, however, was the Army of Tennessee's dispirited morale which had spread downward from backbiting generals to the ranks. Bragg conceded as much in a private letter to Jefferson Davis tendering his resignation. "The disaster admits of no palliation," he wrote. "I fear we both erred in the conclusion for me to retain command here after the clamor raised against me."[17] As the army went into winter quarters, Davis grasped the nettle and grudgingly appointed Johnston to the command.

Meanwhile the repulse on November 29 of Longstreet's attack against Knoxville deepened Confederate woes. In Virginia a campaign of maneuver by Lee after the 11th and 12th Corps left the Army of the Potomac also turned out badly. During October, Lee tried to turn the Union right and get between Meade and Washington. Having foiled that move, Meade in November attempted to turn Lee's right on the Rapidan. Though unsuccessful, the Federals inflicted twice as many casualties as they suffered during these maneuvers, subtracting another 4,000 men from the Army of Northern Virginia it could ill afford to lose.

The glimmer of southern optimism that had flared after Chickamauga died in November. When he heard the news of Chickamauga, War Department clerk John B. Jones had written: "The effects of this great victory will be electrical. The whole South will be filled again with patriotic fervor, and in the North there will be a corresponding depression. . . . [They] must now see the impossibility of subjugating the Southern people." But two months later Jones confessed despair at Bragg's "incalculable disaster." Another southern official wrote of "calamity . . . defeat . . . utter ruin. Unless something is done . . . we are irretrievably gone." And at the end of 1863 diarist Mary Chesnut found "gloom and unspoken despondency hang[ing] like a pall everywhere."[18]

17. Bragg to Jefferson Davis, Dec. 1, 1863, in *O.R.*, Ser. I, Vol 52, pt. 2, p. 745. The best accounts of the internal strife in the Army of Tennessee can be found in Thomas Lawrence Connelly, *Autumn of Glory: The Army of Tennessee, 1862–1865* (Baton Rouge, 1971), chap. 10, and James Lee McDonough, *Chattanooga— A Death Grip on the Confederacy* (Knoxville, 1984), passim.
18. Jones, *War Clerk's Diary* (Swiggett), II, 50, 106; Hugh Lawson Clay quoted in Bell Irvin Wiley, *The Road to Appomattox* (Atheneum ed., New York, 1973), 65; Woodward, *Chesnut's Civil War*, 501.

II

In foreign policy, too, the second half of 1863 brought cruel disappointment to the South. Not only had dreams of British recognition gone glimmering after Vicksburg and Gettysburg, but hopes for a new super-weapon to break the blockade were also dashed.

British laxity in allowing the commerce raiders *Florida* and *Alabama* to escape from Liverpool encouraged Confederate naval envoy James Bulloch to aim even higher. In the summer of 1862 he had contracted with the Laird firm for construction of two armor-plated vessels carrying turrets for nine-inch guns and a seven-foot iron spike attached to the prow to pierce wooden ships below the waterline. These fearsome "Laird rams" were expected to raise havoc with the blockade fleet, perhaps even to steam into New York harbor and hold the city for ransom.

While such extravagant hopes were doubtless unrealistic, the diplomatic crisis generated by the rams was real enough. Charles Francis Adams bombarded the Foreign Office with protests and warnings. Bulloch countered by transferring ownership of the vessels to a French firm which was ostensibly buying them for His Serene Highness the Pasha of Egypt. This subterfuge deceived only those who wished to be deceived. The diplomatic tension escalated as the ships neared completion in midsummer 1863.

A British court decision in an unrelated case buoyed Bulloch's prospects. In April the Palmerston government had seized the commerce raider *Alexandra* being built for the Confederacy, on the grounds that its warlike intent could be inferred from its structure despite the absence of guns. But in June the Court of Exchequer ruled against the government in this case. The way seemed clear for Bulloch to sail his unarmed rams out of Liverpool through a loophole in British law. Adams sent Foreign Secretary Russell increasingly acerbic protests culminating in a declaration on September 5: "It would be superfluous in me to point out to your Lordship that this is war." Unknown to Adams, the Palmerston ministry had decided to detain the ships even before receiving this note. But when the diplomatic correspondence was later published, Adams became a hero at home for apparently forcing John Bull to give in. Despite Palmerston's resentment of Adams's tone ("We ought," the prime minister told Russell, "to say to him in civil Terms 'you be damned' "), Union diplomacy had won a victory that Henry Adams described as "a second Vicksburg."[19]

19. Quotations from D. P. Crook, *The North, the South, and the Powers 1861–1865*

A disheartened James Bulloch transferred his efforts to France, where during 1863 the Confederates contracted for four commerce raiders and two double-turreted ironclad rams. Louis Napoleon continued to nurture southern hopes for recognition. He was still trying to restore a French empire in the new world. In June 1863 a French army of 35,000 men captured Mexico City and overthrew the republican government of Benito Juarez. Meanwhile the Confederates had formed alliances with anti-Juarez chieftains in provinces bordering Texas to foster the contraband trade across the Rio Grande. Perceiving a similarity of interests with the clerical monarchists and hacienda owners whose laborers were peons, southern leaders welcomed French intervention in behalf of this group. When Napoleon made clear his intent to set up the Hapsburg Archduke Ferdinand Maximilian as Emperor of Mexico, Confederate envoys made contact with Maximilian and offered to recognize him if he would help obtain French recognition of the South. Maximilian was willing, but by January 1864 Napoleon seemed to have lost interest in the scheme.

A combination of Union diplomacy and European great-power politics had produced this outcome. The United States was friendly to the Juarez government. When it was overthrown, the Lincoln administration called home the American minister and refused to recognize the French-installed provisional government. Lincoln also modified Union military strategy in order to show the flag in Texas as a warning to the French. After the capture of Vicksburg and Port Hudson, Grant and Banks wanted to mount a campaign against Mobile. But for purposes of diplomacy, the government ordered Banks to move against Texas instead. The first Union effort in this direction, at Sabine Pass on the Texas-Louisiana border, turned into a fiasco in September 1863 when a single Confederate battery drove off the gunboats trying to protect an infantry landing. Banks did better in November, capturing Brownsville and making a token lodgement near the Mexican border for Napoleon to ponder.

Ponder it he did, for he wanted no trouble with the United States at a time when his intricate house of cards in European diplomacy seemed about to collapse. Part of Napoleon's purpose in setting Maximilian on the Mexican throne was to extract favors from Austria in the delicate but deadly game of diplomacy and war among the Continental powers as each sought to protect its flanks while trying to defend or gobble up

<hr />

(New York, 1974), 325, 326; and Worthington C. Ford, ed., *A Cycle of Adams Letters 1861–1865*, 2 vols. (Boston, 1920), II, 82.

parts of Poland, Italy, and Denmark. Austria's alliance with Prussia in a war against Denmark by which Prussia gained Schleswig-Holstein cooled Napoleon's ardor for the Hapsburg connection. In early 1864 he scaled down the French commitment to Maximilian and spurned Confederate attempts to use Mexico as bait for French recognition. Napoleon's foreign ministry also shut down Confederate efforts to build a navy in France. The six ships contracted for by the South were sold instead to Peru, Prussia, and Denmark. But Bulloch went down fighting. Through legal legerdemain at which he had become expert, he eventually obtained transfer of one ironclad from Denmark to the Confederacy. Christened C.S.S. Stonewall, it crossed the Atlantic and arrived one month after Lee had surrendered at Appomattox. The Stonewall ultimately found its way into the Japanese navy. [20]

III

For the Lincoln administration, victories on the battlefield translated into political success at home as well as abroad in 1863. Several state elections occurred during the fall, of which the most important were the gubernatorial contests in Ohio and Pennsylvania. A year earlier the Republicans had suffered a setback in congressional elections. The issues in 1863 remained the same: the conduct of the war; emancipation; civil liberties; and conscription. On the war issue Republicans seemed in good shape, for Chickamauga only barely dimmed the luster of Gettysburg, Vicksburg, and other triumphs. Nevertheless Lincoln was nervous about the Ohio and Pennsylvania elections—indeed, he told Gideon Welles that "he had more anxiety in regard to [them] than he had in 1860 when he was chosen"—because the Democrats in both states had nominated copperheads for governor. The election of either would revive sagging Confederate morale and might depress the northern will to win. [21]

Clement Vallandigham conducted his campaign for the Ohio governorship from exile in Windsor, Canada. George W. Woodward remained in dignified silence on his bench as a state supreme court judge in Pennsylvania while the party ran his campaign for governor. But a

20. Frank L. Owsley, *King Cotton Diplomacy* (Chicago, 1931), 88–145, 438–42, 447–49, 527–49; Crook, *The North, the South, and the Powers*, 333–43; Lynn M. Case and Warren F. Spencer, *The United States and France: Civil War Diplomacy* (Philadelphia, 1970), 427–80.
21. Beale, ed., *Diary of Gideon Welles*, I, 470.

Blue and Gray lie together in peace at the foot of Little Round Top

Library of Congress

Unwounded survivors of the original eighty-six men in Co. I of the 57th Massachusetts after six weeks of fighting from the Wilderness to Petersburg in 1864

U.S. Army Military History Institute

Port and rail facilities at City Point, Virginia, on the James River, Union supply base in the Petersburg campaign

Library of Congress

Sherman's soldiers tearing up the railroad in Atlanta before setting forth on their march to the sea

Library of Congress

Confederate soldiers captured at Gettysburg

U.S. Army Military History Institute

Andersonville prison, with Confederate guards along the fence in the background and the prisoners' sinks (latrines) in the foreground

Library of Congress

Ulysses S. Grant

Library of Congress

David G. Farragut

Library of Congress

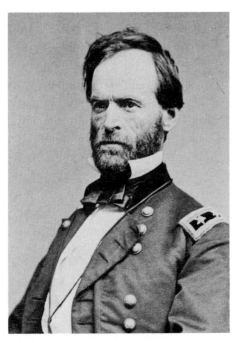

William Tecumseh Sherman

Louis A. Warren Lincoln Library and Museum

Joseph E. Johnston

Louis A. Warren Lincoln Library and Museum

On deck of the *U.S.S. Hartford*, Admiral Farragut's flagship, with the wheel manned by John McFarland, who won a Congressional Medal of Honor for his helmsmanship in the battle of Mobile Bay

U.S. Naval Historical Center

Battery A, 2nd U.S. Colored Artillery, which fought at the battle of Nashville

Chicago Historical Society

Union trenches at Petersburg
Library of Congress

Confederate trenches at Petersburg, with chevaux-de-frise (pointed stakes)
and dead soldier, after the successful Union assault on April 2, 1865
U.S. Army Military History Institute

Confederate soldier killed in the Petersburg trenches
Library of Congress

An end of fighting: Confederate trenches at Petersburg after the
Union assault on April 2, 1865

Minnesota Historical Society

The fruits of war: remains of a plantation house near Fredericksburg

Library of Congress

Richmond on April 4, 1865, as viewed from the Confederate Treasury building, with Yankee cavalry horses tied in the foreground as their owners finish putting out the fires set by departing rebels

U.S. Army Military History Institute

little investigative reporting by Republicans dug up information about his views on the war, which were similar to Vallandigham's. "Slavery was intended as a special blessing to the people of the United States," believed Woodward. "Secession is not disloyalty," he had written in 1860, for the election of Lincoln had destroyed the old Union of consent and comity. "I cannot in justice condemn the South for withdrawing. . . . I wish Pennsylvania could go with them." Although two of his sons fought in the Army of the Potomac, Woodward did not think reunion could be achieved by military victory. As a state judge, he wrote an opinion that the national conscription act was unconstitutional and inoperative in Pennsylvania. A prominent Democrat campaigning for Woodward declared that when elected he would unite with Governors Vallandigham of Ohio and Seymour of New York (representing together nearly half of the North's population) "in calling from the army troops from their respective States for the purpose of compelling the Administration to invite a convention of the States to adjust our difficulties."[22]

Both Woodward and Vallandigham had been nominated before the Union triumphs at Gettysburg and Vicksburg. These battles undercut their theme of the war's failure. Though neither candidate changed his personal views, the party recognized that excessive antiwar statements would alienate War Democrats whose votes were necessary for victory. It came hard for War Democrats to swallow Vallandigham, but Woodward proved more digestible. He published a statement condemning the rebellion. And on election eve the party achieved a coup by persuading McClellan (who resided in neighboring New Jersey) to write a letter stating that if he could vote in Pennsylvania he would "give to Judge Woodward my voice and my vote."[23]

Because of Republican advantages on the war question, however, Democrats concentrated mainly on such tried and true issues as emancipation. In Ohio the party portrayed the contest as an " 'irrepressible conflict' between white and black laborers. . . . Let every vote count in favor of the *white* man, and against the Abolition hordes, who would place negro children in your schools, negro jurors in your jury boxes,

---

22. Arnold Shankman, "For the Union as It Was and the Constitution as It Is: A Copperhead Views the Civil War," in James I. Robertson, Jr., and Richard M. McMurry, eds., *Rank and File: Civil War Essays in Honor of Bell Irvin Wiley* (San Rafael, Cal., 1976), 97–98, 104.
23. Arnold M. Shankman, *The Pennsylvania Antiwar Movement, 1861–1865* (Cranbury, N.J., 1980), 133, 139.

and negro votes in your ballot boxes!" Party orators lampooned the portly Republican gubernatorial candidate John Brough as a "fat Knight of the corps d'Afrique." Similar though less strident outcries against "political and social equality" also typified the Pennsylvania campaign.[24]

But anti-abolitionism and racism seemed to have lost potency as Democratic shibboleths. Two almost simultaneous events in July 1863 were largely responsible for this phenomenon. The first was the New York draft riot, which shocked many northerners into a backlash against the consequences of virulent racism. The second was a minor battle in the campaign against Charleston. At dusk on July 18 two Union brigades assaulted Fort Wagner, a Confederate earthwork defending the entrance to Charleston harbor. Leading the attack was the 54th Massachusetts Infantry. This was not unusual in itself: Bay State regiments fought in the hottest part of many battles, and the combat casualties of Massachusetts were among the highest for Union states. But the 54th was the North's showcase black regiment. Its colonel and lieutenant colonel were sons of prominent abolitionist families. More was riding on the 54th's first big action than the capture of a fort, important as that might be. Colonel Robert Gould Shaw had implored his brigade commander to give the regiment a chance to prove its mettle. The general responded by assigning Shaw to lead the frontal assault across a narrow spit of sand against this strong earthwork. The result was predictable; the rebels drove back the attacking brigades and inflicted heavy losses.

The 54th took the largest casualties, losing nearly half of its men including Colonel Shaw with a bullet through his heart. Black soldiers gained Wagner's parapet and held it for an hour in the flame-stabbed darkness before falling back. The achievements and losses of this elite black regiment, much publicized by the abolitionist press, wrought a change in northern perceptions of black soldiers. "Through the cannon smoke of that dark night," declared the *Atlantic Monthly*, "the manhood of the colored race shines before many eyes that would not see." The *New York Tribune* believed that this battle "made Fort Wagner such a name to the colored race as Bunker Hill had been for ninety years to the white Yankees." When a Confederate officer reportedly re-

---

24. Frank L. Klement, *The Limits of Dissent: Clement L. Vallandigham and the Civil War* (Lexington, Ky., 1970), 245, 243; Wood Gray, *The Hidden Civil War: The Story of the Copperheads* (New York, 1964 [1942]), 150; Shankman, *Pennsylvania Antiwar Movement*, 103–4.

plied to a request for the return of Shaw's body with the words "we have buried him with his niggers," Shaw's father quelled a northern effort to recover his son's body with these words: "We hold that a soldier's most appropriate burial-place is on the field where he has fallen." [25]

This apotheosis of Shaw and his men took place just after Democratic rioters in New York had lynched black people and burned the Colored Orphan Asylum. Few Republican newspapers failed to point the moral: black men who fought for the Union deserved more respect than white men who fought against it. Lincoln expressed this theme in a public letter of August 26 addressed to Democrats. "You are dissatisfied with me about the negro," wrote the president. But "some of the commanders of our armies in the field who have given us our most important successes, believe the emancipation policy, and the use of colored troops, constitute the heaviest blow yet dealt to the rebellion." [26] "You say you will not fight to free negroes," continued Lincoln. "Some of them seem willing to fight for you; but, no matter. Fight you, then, exclusively to save the Union. I issued the proclamation on purpose to aid you in saving the Union." When this war was won, concluded the president, "there will be some black men who can remember that, with silent tongue, and clenched teeth, and steady eye, and well-poised bayonet, they have helped mankind on to this great consummation; while, I fear, there will be some white ones, unable to forget that, with malignant heart, and deceitful speech, they have strove to hinder it." [27]

Lincoln's letter set the tone for Republicans in the 1863 campaign. Many of them had previously felt defensive about emancipation; now they could put Democrats on the defensive. Opposition to emancipation became opposition to northern victory. Linking abolition and Union, Republicans managed to blunt the edge of Democratic racism in Ohio, Pennsylvania, and New York (where legislative elections were held in 1863). The party carried two-thirds of the legislative districts in New

25. *Atlantic Monthly*, quoted in Lawrence Lader, *The Bold Brahmins* (New York, 1961), 290; *New York Tribune*, Sept. 8, 1865; Luis F. Emilio, *A Brave Black Regiment: History of the Fifty-Fourth Regiment of Massachusetts Volunteer Infantry 1863–1865* (Boston, 1894), 102–3.

26. This was a reference to Grant, who had written to Lincoln on August 23 that "by arming the negro we have added a powerful ally. . . . This, with the emancipation of the negro, is the heaviest blow yet given the Confederacy. . . . They will make good soldiers and taking them from the enemy weakens him in the same proportion they strengthen us." Lincoln Papers, Library of Congress.

27. CWL, VI, 401–10.

York. In Ohio it buried Vallandigham under a victory margin of 100,000 votes, winning an unprecedented 61 percent of the ballots. Especially gratifying to Republicans was their 94 percent share of the absentee soldier vote. Efforts to persuade soldiers to "vote as they shot" paid off in a big way. Significantly, in an opinion written by none other than George Woodward, the Pennsylvania Supreme Court had ruled a year earlier that soldiers could not vote outside their home districts. Since only a few thousand Pennsylvania soldiers could be furloughed home for the election, their votes contributed only a small part of the Republians' 15,000-vote victory (51.5 percent) over Woodward.

Republicans additionally scored significant gains in state and local elections elsewhere. They interpreted these results as signs of a transformation of public opinion toward emancipation. The Republican newspaper in Lincoln's hometown of Springfield commented that if a referendum had been held on the Emancipation Proclamation a year earlier, "there is little doubt that the voice of a majority would have been against it. And yet not a year has passed before it is approved by an overwhelming majority." A New York Republican observed that "the change of opinion on this slavery question . . . is a great and historic fact. . . . Who could have predicted . . . this great and blessed revolution? . . . God pardon our blindness of three years ago." The Emancipation Proclamation had been "followed by dark and doubtful days," admitted Lincoln in his annual message to Congress on December 8, 1863. But now "the crisis which threatened the friends of the Union is past."[28] If Lincoln's optimism proved premature, it nevertheless mirrored the despair that threatened to undermine the southern will to continue fighting.

28. *Illinois State Journal*, Dec. 1, 1863, quoted in V. Jacque Voegeli, *Free But Not Equal: The Midwest and the Negro during the Civil War* (Chicago, 1967), 131; Strong, *Diary*, 408; CWL, VII, 49–50.

23

When This Cruel War Is Over

I

Unhappily for Jefferson Davis, elections for the Confederate Congress took place in the fall of 1863 when southern morale was at low ebb. The Davis administration suffered a more severe rebuke from voters than the Lincoln administration had sustained the previous year in a similar situation. The difference resulted not only from the greater calamity to Confederate arms but also from the different political structures in North and South.

Formal political parties did not exist in the Confederacy. This state of affairs arose from two main causes: the erosion of the two-party system in the 1850s and the perceived need for a united front during the emergencies of secession and war. Although the Whig party had experienced a brief reincarnation as the Constitutional Union party in 1860, it seemed to disappear again in the crisis of 1861. Below the surface of southern politics Whiggery persisted in the form of memory and sentiment, but the most assiduous researchers employing the tools of roll-call analysis have been unable to identify party organizations or significant partisan patterns of voting in the Confederate Congress from 1861 through 1863.[1]

---

1. Thomas B. Alexander, "Persistent Whiggery in the Confederate South, 1860–1877," *JSH*, 27 (1961), 305–10; Richard E. Beringer, "The Unconscious 'Spirit of Party' in the Confederate Congress," *CWH*, 18 (1972), 312–16; Thomas B. Alexander and

Southerners considered this circumstance a source of strength. The president pro tem of the first Congress congratulated its members that "the spirit of party has never shown itself for an instant in your deliberations."[2] But in fact, as historians now recognize, the absence of parties was actually a source of weakness. In the North the two-party system disciplined and channeled political activity. The Republican party became the means for mobilizing war resources, raising taxes, creating a new financial system, initiating emancipation, and enacting conscription. Democrats opposed most of these measures; the existence of this well-defined opposition caused Republicans to close ranks when the chips were down. Because measures were supported or opposed by *parties*, voters could identify those responsible for them and register their approval or disapproval at the polls by voting a party ticket. Both parties, of course, used their well-oiled machinery to rally voters to their side. In the Confederacy, by contrast, the Davis administration had no such means to mobilize support. No parties meant no institutionalized discipline over congressmen or governors. Davis could not invoke party loyalty and patronage in behalf of his policies, as Lincoln could. Opposition to the Davis administration became personal or factional and therefore difficult to deal with.

In the North, where nearly all state governors were Republicans, the ties of party bound them to the war effort. In the South the obstructionist activities of several governors hindered the centralized war effort because the centrifugal tendencies of state's rights were not restrained by the centripetal force of party. The Confederate Constitution limited the president to a single six-year term, so Davis had no reason to create a party organization for re-election. Such government policies as conscription, impressment, the tax in kind, and management of finances were the main issues in the congressional elections of 1863. Opposition candidates ran on an individual rather than a party basis, and the government could not muster political artillery to shoot at all these scattered targets.[3]

Richard E. Beringer, *The Anatomy of the Confederate Congress* (Nashville, 1972), 35–57.

2. *Journal of the Congress of the Confederate States of America, 1861–1865* (Washington, 1904–05), I, 846.

3. For many of the ideas in these two paragraphs I am indebted to Eric L. McKitrick's stimulating essay, "Party Politics and the Union and Confederate War Efforts," in William Nisbet Chambers and Walter Dean Burnham, *The American Party Systems* (New York, 1967), 117–51.

Historians have identified "proto-parties" emerging in the Confederacy by 1863. Former Whigs were most prominent in the crystallizing
opposition, but the lack of a definite pattern was illustrated by the prominence of Louis Wigfall and the private influence of General Joseph E.
Johnston among Davis's adversaries. A fire-eating Democrat who had
served briefly under Johnston as a general in Virginia before being elected
by Texas to the Senate in 1862, Wigfall became a bitter critic of Davis's
"pigheadiness and perverseness" in 1863. While Davis blamed Johnston
for the loss of Vicksburg, Johnston and Wigfall blamed Davis for the
ambiguous command structure in the West that had led to disaster.
Although Johnston did not speak out publicly, his letters to friends made
no secret of his opinions. By the fall of 1863 Johnston had become, in
the words of another Confederate general, a "shield" behind which critics of the administration "gathered themselves . . . and shot arrows at
President Davis."[4]

Worsening inflation and shortages heaped fuel on the fires of political
opposition. In the four months after Gettysburg, prices jumped nearly
70 percent. "Yesterday flour sold at auction at $100 per barrel; to-day it
sells for $120," wrote a resident of Richmond in November. "A genteel
suit of clothes cannot be had now for less than $700. . . . We are a
shabby-looking people now—gaunt, and many in rags. . . . Every night
robberies of poultry, salt meats, and even of cows and hogs are occurring. . . . There must be an explosion of some sort soon." The head
of the War Department's administrative bureau, a loyal Davis man,
confessed in November that "the irretrievable bankruptcy of the national
finances, the tenacity with which the President holds to men in whom
the country has lost all confidence, the scarcity of means of support
. . . are producing deep disgust. . . . I have never actually despaired
of the cause, priceless, holy as it is, but my faith . . . is yielding to a
sense of hopelessness."[5]

In this atmosphere the congressional elections took place. They produced an increase of openly anti-administration representatives from 26
to 41 (of 106). Twelve of the twenty-six senators in the next Congress
were identified with the opposition. The proportion of former Whigs

4. Richard M. McMurry, " 'The Enemy at Richmond': Joseph E. Johnston and the
   Confederate Government," CWH, 27 (1981), 15–16.
5. Jones, War Clerk's Diary (Miers), 302, 303, 304, 309; Edward Younger, ed., Inside
   the Confederate Government: The Diary of Robert Garlick Hill Kean (New York,
   1957), 119.

and conditional unionists in Congress grew from one-third to half. Erstwhile Whigs won several governorships in 1863, including those of Alabama and Mississippi for the first time ever. Although the administration did preserve a narrow majority in Congress, this margin rested on an ironic anomaly. Support for the Davis government was strongest among congressmen from areas under Union occupation: Kentucky, Missouri (both considered part of the Confederacy and represented in its Congress), Tennessee, and substantial portions of Louisiana, Arkansas, Mississippi, and Virginia. Regular elections were impossible in these areas, of course, so the incumbents merely continued themselves in office or were "elected" by a handful of refugees from their districts. These irredentist congressmen had the strongest of motives for supporting "war to the last ditch." They constituted the closest thing to an administration party that existed in the Confederacy. They provided the votes for higher taxes that would not be levied on their constituents and for tougher conscription laws that would take no men from their districts. The areas of the South still under Confederate control, by contrast, sent an anti-administration majority to Congress. From the two largest such constituencies, North Carolina and Georgia, sixteen of the nineteen new congressmen opposed the government.[6]

As in the North, the opposition took two forms. Most anti-administration southerners backed the government's war aims but dissented from some of the total-war measures intended to achieve those aims. Other opponents, however, branded the war a failure and demanded peace through negotiations even if this risked the country's war aims. In the North such men were called copperheads; in the South they were known as reconstructionists or tories. In both North and South the peace faction grew stronger when the war went badly.

The pro-war but anti-administration faction was most outspoken in Georgia. There the triumvirate of Vice-President Alexander Stephens, ex-General Robert Toombs, and Governor Joseph Brown turned their opposition into a personal vendetta against Davis. Stephens likened the president to "my poor old blind and deaf dog." Resentful of the "West Point clique" that had blocked his rise to military glory, Toombs in 1863 lashed out at Davis as a "false and hypocritical . . . wretch" who

6. Wilfred B. Yearns, *The Confederate Congress* (Athens, Ga., 1960), 49–59; Beringer, "The Unconscious 'Spirit of Party' in the Confederate Congress," *loc. cit.*, 314–23; Alexander, "Persistent Whiggery in the Confederate South," *loc. cit.*, 308–9; Alexander and Beringer, *Anatomy of the Confederate Congress*, passim.

had "neither the ability nor the honesty to manage the revolution." The government's financial policy, said Toombs, was "pernicious," "ruinous," "insupportable"; the impressment of farm products was "force and fraud"; conscription had "outraged justice and the constitution." "The road to liberty for the white man does not lie through slavery," thundered Toombs in November 1863. "Mr. Davis's present policy will overthrow the revolution in six months." Governor Brown did more than speak against the draft. He appointed several thousand new constables, militia officers, justices of the peace, coroners, and county surveyors to exempt them from conscription.[7]

A Georgia crisis erupted in February 1864 when the lame-duck session of the old Confederate Congress authorized the president to suspend the writ of habeas corpus to suppress disloyalty and enforce the draft.[8] Both of Georgia's senators voted against the bill. Vice-President Stephens condemned it as a "blow at the very 'vitals of liberty' " by a president "aiming at absolute power. . . . Far better that our country should be overrun by the enemy, our cities sacked and burned, and our land laid desolate, than that the people should thus suffer the citadel of their liberties to be entered and taken by professed friends." Stephens also helped write an address by Brown to the legislature denouncing the law as a step toward "military despotism." "What will we have gained when we have achieved our independence of the Northern States," asked Brown rhetorically, "if in our efforts to do so, we have . . . lost *Constitutional Liberty* at home?" The legislature passed resolutions written by Stephens' brother condemning suspension of the writ of habeas corpus as unconstitutional.[9]

From Richmond's viewpoint all this was bad enough, but worse was a proposal by Brown for peace negotiations. Alexander Stephens seemed

---

7. Stephens to Herschel V. Johnson, April 8, 1864, in O.R., Ser. IV, Vol. 3, pp. 278–80; Ulrich B. Phillips, ed., *The Correspondence of Robert Toombs, Alexander H. Stephens, and Howell Cobb* (Washington, 1913), 608, 611, 619, 623, 627, 628, 629; Albert B. Moore, *Conscription and Conflict in the Confederacy* (New York, 1924), 256–70.

8. A few judges in North Carolina, Georgia, and elsewhere had been granting writs to petitioners to restrain conscription officers from enrolling these petitioners in the army.

9. James Z. Rabun, "Alexander H. Stephens and Jefferson Davis," AHR, 58 (1953), 308; Moore, *Conscription and Conflict in the Confederacy*, 270–71; John B. Robbins, "The Confederacy and the Writ of Habeas Corpus," *Georgia Historical Quarterly*, 55 (1971), 93–94.

to support this suggestion in a three-hour speech to the legislature, and his brother introduced additional resolutions urging the people "through their state organizations and popular assemblies" to bring pressure on the government to end the war. This had an ominous ring. It smacked of treason. In reality, Brown and Stephens wanted to begin negotiations *after* the next Confederate victory, with independence as a precondition of peace. No one, Stephens included, expected Lincoln to negotiate on such conditions. The resolutions were intended to divide northern opinion and strengthen the Peace Democrats for the 1864 election by giving the impression of a southern willingness to negotiate. But this subtlety escaped most southerners, who regarded Brown and Stephens as reconstructionists advocating peace at any price. Instead of dividing and conquering the North, their peace gambit seemed likely to play into the hands of Yankees hoping to divide and conquer the South.

Most of the southern press, even in Georgia, reprimanded the vice president. Georgia regiments at the front passed resolutions condemning Brown and the legislature. Georgia's senators privately slapped Stephens's wrist. "You have allowed your antipathy to Davis to mislead your judgment," Senator Herschel Johnson told the vice president. "You are wrong in view of your official position; you are wrong because the whole movement originated in a mad purpose to make war on Davis & Congress;—You are wrong because the movement is joyous to the enemy, and they are already using it in their press." The legislature hastily passed a resolution pledging Georgia's continuing support for the war.[10]

While the dissidents in Georgia hoped for peace through victory, in North Carolina a part of the opposition seemed to want peace through reconstruction. The last state to secede, North Carolina's commitment to the Confederacy had remained shaky despite her contribution of more soldiers than any other state save Virginia. North Carolina also contributed more deserters than any other state.[11] The western part of the

10. Rabun, "Alexander H. Stephens and Jefferson Davis," *loc. cit.*, 311. See also John R. Brumgardt, "The Confederate Career of Alexander H. Stephens: The Case Reopened," *CWH*, 27 (1981), 64–81; and Moore, *Conscription and Conflict in the Confederacy*, 272–73.

11. Most studies of this question list 23,000 deserters from North Carolina. This was more than a fifth of all Confederate deserters and nearly twice as many as from any other state. But working from samples of North Carolina regimental rosters, Richard Reid concluded that the total number of deserters from the state should be reduced to about 14,000. While still higher than any other state, this total would give North Carolina a desertion rate not appreciably greater than the average for all

state resembled east Tennessee and West Virginia in socio-economic structure and unionist leanings. The inaccessibility of this region to northern armies, however, inhibited the development there of a significant unionist political movement before 1863. In that year the Order of the Heroes of America, a secret peace society, attained a large following in piedmont and upcountry North Carolina as war weariness and defeatism grew after Gettysburg. Thousands of deserters returned to the state, where in alliance with "tories" and draft-dodgers they gained virtual control of whole counties.[12]

North Carolina's most powerful political leaders were Zebulon B. Vance and William W. Holden. An antebellum Whig and in 1861 a conditional unionist, Vance commanded a regiment in the Army of Northern Virginia before winning the governorship in 1862. Though he feuded with Davis over matters of state versus Confederate authority, Vance backed the war effort and continued to "fight the Yankees and fuss with the Confederacy" until the end.[13] Holden was of another stripe. Beginning his career as a Whig, he became a Democratic secessionist in the 1850s but broke with the party and resisted secession until the last moment in 1861. As editor of the Raleigh *North Carolina Standard* he championed civil liberties and attacked administration policies during the war. Emphasizing the rich man's war/poor man's fight theme, Holden won a large following among yeoman farmers and workingmen. His "Conservative party," composed mainly of old Whigs and conditional unionists, had supported Vance for governor on a platform of state sovereignty within the Confederacy. By the summer of 1863, however, Holden became convinced that the South could not win the war

---

Confederate states. Reid, "A Test Case of the 'Crying Evil': Desertion among North Carolina Troops during the Civil War," *North Carolina Historical Review*, 58 (1981), 234–62. But Reid's data are based primarily on the regiments enlisted during the first year of the war, and the records for many of these regiments are complete only through late 1864. Since desertion from later-organized regiments tended to be higher than from those formed early in the war, and since desertions increased disastrously in the last months of the conflict when it became clear that the war was lost, Reid's estimate of 14,000 deserters appears to be too low.

12. Georgia Lee Tatum, *Disloyalty in the Confederacy* (Chapel Hill, 1934), 107–35; William T. Auman and David D. Scarboro, "The Heroes of America in Civil War North Carolina," *North Carolina Historical Review*, 58 (1981), 327–63; William T. Auman, "Neighbor against Neighbor: The Inner Civil War in the Randolph County Area of Confederate North Carolina," *North Carolina Historical Review*, 61 (1984), 59–92.

13. John G. Barrett, *The Civil War in North Carolina* (Chapel Hill, 1963), 242.

and that conscription, impressment, "military despotism," and economic ruin represented a greater threat to North Carolinians than reunion with the United States.

Aided by the Heroes of America, Holden and his associates organized
more than a hundred antiwar meetings which adopted resolutions lifted
from *Standard* editorials urging negotiations for an "honorable peace."
What this meant was anybody's guess; to committed Confederates it
looked like treason. One observer unsympathetic to Holden reported in
August 1863 that at several peace meetings in the western part of the
state "the most treasonable language was uttered, and Union flags raised."
In September 1863 a War Department official noted that Holden's followers "are throwing off all disguises and have begun to hold 'Union'
meetings in some of the western counties. . . . Reconstruction is openly
advocated."[14] A brigade in Longstreet's corps en route to Bragg's army
stopped in Raleigh on September 9 and plundered Holden's newspaper
office, whereupon a mob of Holden's supporters next day demolished
the office of Raleigh's pro-administration newspaper.

Against this background at least five and perhaps eight of the congressmen elected from North Carolina in 1863 were "reported to be in
favor of peace." The meaning of this remained unclear, but after the
elections Holden began to call for North Carolina to invoke its sovereignty and open separate negotiations with the North. He insisted that
such a course would produce Confederate independence, but few took
that seriously. As one of Holden's backers put it in a letter to Governor
Vance, "we want this war stopped, we will take peace on *any terms* that
are *honorable*. We would prefer our independence, if that were possible,
but let us prefer *reconstruction* infinitely to *subjugation*."[15]

Vance had earlier vouched for Holden's loyalty, but by the end of
1863 he became convinced that the editor wanted to take North Carolina out of the Confederacy. This he could not tolerate. "I will see the
Conservative party blown into a thousand atoms and Holden and his
understrappers in hell," exclaimed the governor, "before I will consent
to a course which I think would bring dishonor and ruin upon both
state and Confederacy." Yet Vance could not move precipitately, for he

14. J. C. McRae to Peter Mallett, Aug. 21, 1863, in *O.R.*, Ser. I, Vol. 29, pt. 2, p.
660; Younger, ed., *Inside the Confederate Government*, 103–4.
15. Tatum, *Disloyalty*, 125 and n.; "An Old Friend" to Vance, Jan. 2, 1864, in W.
Buck Yearns and John G. Barrett, eds., *North Carolina Civil War Documentary*
(Chapel Hill, 1980), 296.

believed that a majority of North Carolinians supported Holden. So the governor sought Jefferson Davis's help to outflank the peace movement. In a letter to the president on December 30, Vance urged "some effort at negotiation with the enemy" to allay "the sources of discontent in North Carolina." Of course, added Vance hastily, the South could negotiate only on the basis of independence. If these "fair terms are rejected," as he expected them to be, "it will tend greatly to strengthen and intensify the war feeling, and will rally all classes to more cordial support of the government."[16]

The Machiavellian subtlety of Vance's suggestion eluded Davis.[17] What possible good could an offer of peace achieve? he replied. It would merely be treated as a confession of weakness. "That despot" Lincoln had already made clear that the South could have peace only by "emancipating all our slaves, swearing allegiance and obedience to him and his proclamations, and becoming in point of fact the slaves of our own negroes." The true path to peace, Davis lectured Vance, was to continue the war "until the enemy is beaten out of his vain confidence in our subjugation." North Carolina must do her part in this struggle; instead of dallying with traitors, Vance must "abandon a policy of conciliation and set them at defiance."[18]

Davis took his own advice. In a message to Congress on February 3, 1864, urging passage of the law to suspend the writ of habeas corpus, he said that such legislation was needed to deal with "citizens of well-known disloyalty" who were seeking to "accomplish treason under the form of the law." Holden knew this meant him. On February 24 he announced that he was suspending publication of the *Standard* because, he later explained, "if I could not continue to print as a free man I would not print at all."[19] But this did not stop the peace movement;

16. Vance to W. A. Graham, Jan. 1, 1864, quoted in Richard E. Yates, *The Confederacy and Zeb Vance* (Tuscaloosa, Ala., 1958), 95; Vance to Davis, Dec. 30, 1863, in Rowland, *Davis*, VI, 141–42.

17. It also eluded the astute Mary Boykin Chesnut and her husband James, who was Davis's aide de camp. They interpreted Vance's letter as a suggestion for accepting peace without victory, a death knell for the Confederacy. Woodward, *Chesnut's Civil War*, 527.

18. Davis to Vance, Jan. 8, 1864, in Rowland, *Davis*, VI, 143–46.

19. *Ibid.*, 165; Horace W. Raper, "William W. Holden and the Peace Movement in North Carolina," *North Carolina Historical Review*, 31 (1954), 509–10. Holden resumed publication of the *Standard* in May.

on the contrary, a week later Holden announced his intention to run against Vance for governor in the midsummer election.

This was the most serious internal threat to the Confederacy so far. Most observers expected Holden to win. But Vance went on the offensive and in a clever campaign captured much of the peace vote on a war platform. "We all want peace," the spell-binding governor told audiences. The question was how to get it. Holden's plan for a separate state convention would lead North Carolina back into the Union. "Instead of getting your sons back to the plow and fireside, they would be drafted . . . to fight alongside of [Lincoln's] negro troops in exterminating the white men, women, and children of the South." The only way to obtain a real peace was "to fight it out *now*" and win the war despite its mismanagement by Richmond.[20]

Vance succeeded in pinning the reconstructionist label on Holden. A timely exposure late in the campaign of the Heroes of America as a treasonable organization secretly aiding Holden gave the editor's candidacy the *coup de grâce*. Few believed Holden's denial of any connection with the society. North Carolina soldiers at the front damned Holden for disgracing the state. "There has been a good many N. Carolinians shot in this army for desertion," wrote a private. "Old traitor Holden is Responsible for the most of it. . . . I think the N C soldiers passing through Raleigh on Furlough ought to stop and hang the old son of a bitch." On election day Vance smothered Holden, winning 88 percent of the soldier vote and 77 percent of the civilian vote. North Carolina remained safe for the Confederacy.[21]

II

The signs of southern disaffection in the fall of 1863 encouraged Lincoln to announce a policy for the reconstruction of recanting Confederates. "Whereas it is now desired by some persons heretofore engaged in said rebellion to resume their allegiance to the United States, and to reinaugurate loyal State governments," declared the president in a proclamation on December 8, he offered pardon and amnesty to such persons

20. Yearns and Barrett, eds., *North Carolina Civil War Documentary*, 302–4.
21. Richard Bardolph, "Inconstant Rebels: Desertion of North Carolina Troops in the Civil War," *North Carolina Historical Review*, 41 (1964), 184. See also Marc W. Kruman, *Parties and Politics in North Carolina, 1836–1865* (Baton Rouge, 1983), 249–65.

who took an oath of allegiance to the United States and to all of its laws and proclamations concerning slavery. (Confederate government officials and high-ranking military officers were exempted from this blanket offer of amnesty.) Whenever the number of persons in any state taking the oath reached 10 percent of the number of voters in 1860, this loyal nucleus could form a state government which would be recognized by the president. To Congress, of course, belonged the right to decide whether to seat the senators and representatives elected from such states.[22]

This deceptively simple document grew from multiple layers of experience and debate during the previous two years. By the end of 1863 a consensus existed among Republicans that the pieces of the old Union could not be cobbled together. One piece lost but not lamented was slavery; another that must go was the prominent role played in southern politics by the old state's-rights secessionists. Beyond this, however, a spectrum of opinions could be found in the Republican party concerning both the process and substance of reconstruction.

Lincoln never deviated from the theory that secession was illegal and southern states therefore remained in the Union. Rebels had temporarily taken over their governments; the task of reconstruction was to return "loyal" officials to power. At one level all Republicans subscribed to this theory of indestructible states in an indissoluble Union; to believe otherwise would stultify their war aims. But at another level, no one could deny that the southern states had gone *out* of the Union and had formed a new government with all the attributes of a nation. A few radical Republicans led by Thaddeus Stevens boldly insisted that they had therefore ceased to exist as legal states. When invaded and controlled by the Union army they became "conquered provinces" subject to the conqueror's will. But most Republicans were unwilling to go this far. Instead, many of them subscribed to one variant or another of a theory that by attempting the treasonable act of secession, southern states had committed "state suicide" (Charles Sumner's phrase) or had "forfeited" their rights as states and reverted to the condition of territories.[23]

Discussion of these theories consumed much time and energy in

22. CWL, VII, 53–56.
23. For summaries of these theories see Charles H. McCarthy, *Lincoln's Plan of Reconstruction* (New York, 1901), 190–217; Eric L. McKitrick, *Andrew Johnson and Reconstruction* (Chicago, 1960), 96–119; and Herman Belz, *Reconstructing the Union: Theory and Policy during the Civil War* (Ithaca, 1969), 7–13.

Congress. Disliking "pernicious abstraction," Lincoln expressed impatience with this "merely metaphysical question" whether "the seceded States, so called, are in the Union or out of it." Everyone agreed, he said, that they were "out of their proper practical relation with the Union; and that the sole object of the government . . . is to again get them into that proper practical relation."[24] What Lincoln well understood, but did not acknowledge, was that the "metaphysical question" of reconstruction theories concealed a power struggle between Congress and the Executive over control of the process. If the southern states had reverted to the status of territories, Congress had the right to frame the terms of their readmission under its constitutional authority to govern territories and admit new states. If, on the other hand, the states were indestructible and secession was the act of individuals, the president had the power to prescribe the terms of restoration under his constitutional authority to suppress insurrection and to grant pardons and amnesty.

Underlying this conflict over procedure was a significant difference of opinion about substance. Of Kentucky birth and moderate antislavery persuasion, Lincoln had been a Whig and had maintained cordial relations with southern Whigs and unionists almost to the end in 1861. He believed that these men had been swept into secession against their better judgment and were ready by 1863 to return like prodigal sons. By offering them pardons on the conditions of Union and emancipation, Lincoln hoped to set in motion a snowballing defection from the Confederacy and a state-by-state reconstruction of the Union.

Despite the exclusion of top Confederate leaders from Lincoln's blanket offer of amnesty, his policy would preserve much of the South's old ruling class in power. To most abolitionists and radical Republicans this was unacceptable. They insisted that simply to abolish slavery without also destroying the economic and political structure of the old order would merely convert black people from slaves to landless serfs and leave the political power of the planter class untouched. By restoring property and the franchise to Confederates, said Wendell Phillips, the president's amnesty program "leaves the large landed proprietors of the South still to domineer over its politics, and makes the negro's freedom a mere sham." When these pardoned Confederates gained control of their states, Phillips continued, "the Revolution may be easily checked with the aid of the Administration, which is willing that the negro should be free

24. CWL, VIII, 402-3.

but seeks nothing else for him. . . . What McClellan was on the battle-field—'Do as little hurt as possible!'—Lincoln is in civil affairs—'Make as little change as possible!' "[25]

Phillips and other radicals envisaged reconstruction as a revolution. "The whole system of the Gulf States [must] be taken to pieces," said Phillips. "The war can be ended only by annihilating that Oligarchy which formed and rules the South and makes the war—by annihilating a state of society." Similar rhetoric came from Chairman Thaddeus Stevens of the House Ways and Means Committee, whom a foreign observer described as "the Robespierre, Danton, and Marat" of this second American Revolution. Reconstruction must "revolutionize Southern institutions, habits, and manners," said Stevens. "The foundation of their institutions . . . must be broken up and relaid, or all our blood and treasure have been spent in vain."[26]

Although Stevens and Lincoln had different visions of the South's future, Congress and Executive had not yet become polarized on this issue. For his part, Lincoln remained flexible toward reconstruction as he had done earlier toward emancipation. While his plan of amnesty and restoration "is the best the Executive can present, with his present impressions," he said, "it must not be understood that no other mode would be acceptable." For their part, most congressional Republicans also entertained a range of shifting and flexible opinions less radical than those of Phillips and Stevens. But many moderates as well as radicals believed that some way must be found to ensure political domination by genuine unionists in the South. They distrusted the sincerity of some of those repentant rebels. And a growing number of Republicans favored at least partial enfranchisement of freed slaves to offset the voting power of former Confederates. "I find," wrote Salmon P. Chase at the end of 1863, "that almost all who are willing to have colored men fight are willing to have them vote."[27] Believing that Lincoln lagged

25. Phillips to Benjamin Butler, Dec. 13, 1863, Benjamin Butler Papers, Library of Congress; Phillips to George W. Julian, March 27, 1864, Giddings-Julian Papers, Library of Congress; *Liberator*, May 20, 1864.

26. *Liberator*, Aug. 8, 1862; *New York Tribune*, Jan. 23, 1863; Eric Foner, "Thaddeus Stevens, Confiscation, and Reconstruction," in Stanley Elkins and Eric McKitrick, eds., *The Hofstadter Aegis: A Memorial* (New York, 1974), 154; Fawn M. Brodie, *Thaddeus Stevens: Scourge of the South* (New York, 1959), 231–32.

27. CWL, VII, 56; Chase to Horace Greeley, Dec. 29, 1863, quoted in Hans L. Trefousse, *The Radical Republicans: Lincoln's Vanguard for Racial Justice* (New York, 1969), 285.

behind them by only a few months on this matter as on emancipation, most Republicans responded favorably at first to his amnesty and reconstruction proclamation. And indeed, about a month later Lincoln did write privately to a New York Republican that, having offered amnesty to whites, he also favored suffrage for blacks, "at least, suffrage on the basis of intelligence and military service."[28] Both Lincoln and congressional moderates stepped warily around this issue in public, however. Black men could vote in only six northern states, and the possibility of them doing so elsewhere was no more popular among many northern voters than the prospect of emancipation had been a year or two earlier.

On theoretical and procedural questions, Lincoln and congressional Republicans had also moved closer together by 1863. Several bills to provide territorial governments for rebellious states had come before the previous Congress. More than two-thirds of House Republicans favored this concept. But the remainder along with Democrats and border-state unionists produced enough votes to defeat the one measure that came to a vote. Sobered by this experience, a majority of Republicans turned to a new approach that combined the view of indestructible states with a notion of congressional power to intervene in the affairs of these states under extraordinary circumstances. Article IV, Section 4, of the Constitution stipulates that "the United States shall guarantee to every state in this Union a republican form of government." Here was a concept of sufficient ambiguity to attract supporters of various viewpoints. A "republican form of government" might mean Negro suffrage; it could be construed to prohibit slavery; it certainly discountenanced rebellion. And best of all, the Constitution did not state whether Congress or the Executive had the principal responsibility in this matter, and earlier Supreme Court interpretations had suggested dual responsibility. Although the theories of conquered provinces, state suicide, and the like did not disappear, the "republican form of government" clause became by 1863

28. Lincoln to James S. Wadsworth, probably in January 1864, in CWL, VII, 101. Some controversy surrounds the authenticity of this letter, but the doubt focuses on two probably spurious paragraphs that are not quoted here. Even the doubters accept the probable genuineness of the letter's first two paragraphs, including the quotation above. See Ludwell H. Johnson, "Lincoln and Equal Rights: The Authenticity of the Wadsworth Letter," JSH, 32 (1966), 83–87; and Harold M. Hyman, "Lincoln and Equal Rights for Negroes: The Irrelevancy of the 'Wadsworth Letter,'" CWH, 12 (1966), 258–66. Wadsworth was a major general in the Army of the Potomac as well as a leading New York Republican who had been defeated for governor in 1862. He was killed in action on May 6, 1864.

the basis for both presidential and congressional approaches to reconstruction.

In the matter of intervening in the affairs of states the president as commander in chief had an inherent advantage over Congress in time of war. While Congress had debated in 1862, Lincoln had acted. He appointed military governors for the portions of Tennessee, Louisiana, and Arkansas that came under Union control, and he authorized them to prepare for the restoration of civil government. The continuation of active fighting in all three states postponed this prospect for a year or more. But with the capture of Port Hudson, the expulsion of Bragg from Tennessee, and the occupation of Little Rock in the latter part of 1863, Lincoln urged his military governors to begin the process of reconstruction. He intended his amnesty proclamation and 10 percent proposal to serve as "a rallying point—a plan of action."[29]

Louisiana seemed to offer the best prospect for an early test of Lincoln's policy. Union forces had controlled two of the state's four congressional districts since the spring of 1862. New Orleans contained a cosmopolitan and politically active population which had voted overwhelmingly for Bell or Douglas in 1860. Many wealthy sugar and cotton planters along the bayous had been Whigs and conditional unionists. They readily took the oath of allegiance—if only to obtain trade permits to sell cotton. The light-skinned free black community in New Orleans was well-educated and prosperous, supported a bilingual Republican newspaper during the Union occupation, and furnished two regiments that fought at Port Hudson. In Nathaniel Banks, veteran Republican who commanded the occupation forces, and George F. Shepley, prewar Maine Democrat who became a radical Republican and military governor of occupied Louisiana, Lincoln had political generals eager to aid the reconstruction process.

But the process was slowed by Banks's military campaign to plant the flag in Texas as a warning to France and by the division of unionists into two factions. The first and smaller faction was the planters, many of whom accepted with reluctance the quasi-emancipation imposed by the army (occupied Louisiana had been exempted from the Emancipation Proclamation). This faction sent a delegation to Lincoln in June 1863 urging the election of a new state government under the existing Louisiana constitution. Suspecting that their purpose was to preserve the

29. CWL, VII, 52.

framework of slavery, Lincoln rebuffed them. But these conservatives did not stop trying; the idea of reconstructing the state under the old constitution remained alive.

The second and more dynamic faction was led by lawyers, doctors, and entrepreneurs most of whom had been born in the North or abroad but had resided in New Orleans for many years before the war. They had opposed secession, and some had gone into exile rather than support the Confederacy. They organized a Union Association and proposed to hold a state convention to adopt a new constitution abolishing slavery and ridding the old constitution of other conservative features. Once this was accomplished, an election of state officials and congressmen could be held and a purified Louisiana could rejoin the Union.

In the summer of 1863 Lincoln approved this procedure. But the registration of voters lagged because neither Banks nor Shepley took the matter in hand. "This disappoints me bitterly," Lincoln wrote Banks in November. Though less than half the state was under Union military control, the president did not consider that a reason for delay. "Without waiting for more territory," he told Banks, "go to work and give me a tangible nucleus which the rest of the State may rally around as fast as it can, and which I can at once recognize and sustain as the true State government."[30] It was this desire for a prompt beginning that caused Lincoln to fix the "tangible nucleus" at 10 percent of a state's 1860 voters.

Stung by Lincoln's censure, Banks decided to move quickly by military fiat. Instead of organizing an election first of delegates to a constitutional convention, as the Union Association wished, he ordered the election of state officials in February 1864 under the existing constitution, to be followed in April by a convention. To take care of the problem of slavery, Banks simply issued an order declaring the institution "inoperative and void." The planters, he explained in a letter to Lincoln, would accept emancipation by ukase in preference to being compelled to enact it themselves in a new constitution. As for holding a convention first, Banks feared that delegates would debate "every theory connected with human legislation," occasioning "dangerous if not fatal delay." If Lincoln wanted prompt restoration, assured emancipation, and participation by at least 10 percent of the voters, insisted Banks, the election of state officials must be held first and the convention later.

30. Lincoln to Banks, Nov. 5, 1863, *ibid.*, 1–2.

Convinced by these arguments, Lincoln told the general to "proceed with all possible despatch."[31]

The radical unionists in New Orleans were dismayed by this decision. They believed that it cut the ground from under their efforts to create a genuine new order in Louisiana. Indeed, that had been part of Banks's purpose, for he considered the Free State General Committee, recently organized by these unionists, too radical. It advocated a limited Negro suffrage, and one of its conventions had seated delegates from the city's free black community. This went farther than most Louisiana whites were willing to go—and for that matter, farther than many northern whites would accept. The rhetoric of revolution abounded at Free State meetings. The leader of the movement, a Philadelphia-born lawyer named Thomas J. Durant who had lived in New Orleans most of his life, rivaled Wendell Phillips in his enthusiasm for the "great principle of equality and fraternity" on which the new order must be founded. "There could be no middle ground in a revolution. It must work a radical change in society; such had been the history of every great revolution." But Banks also professed to be a student of revolutions, and he drew different lessons from the past. "The *history* of the world shows that Revolutions which are not controlled, and held within reasonable limits, produce counter Revolutions," he wrote to Lincoln. "We are not likely to prove an exception. . . . If the policy proposed [in Louisiana] is . . . too Radical it will bring a Counter Revolution."[32]

Banks's program split the Free State Committee into radical and moderate factions. Each faction plus the conservative planters nominated candidates for governor and other state offices in the February 22 election. Banks and most federal officials in New Orleans supported the moderates, who won with a vote greater than the combined total of the radicals and conservatives. The number of votes cast in this election amounted to nearly a quarter of the total recorded for the entire state in 1860.

It seemed a triumph for Lincoln's 10 percent policy. Meanwhile in Arkansas a convention of unionists representing half the state's counties adopted a new constitution repudiating secession and abolishing slavery.

31. Banks to Lincoln, Dec. 30, 1863, Lincoln Papers, Library of Congress; Lincoln to Banks, Jan. 13, 1864, CWL, VII, 123–24.
32. Quotations from Peyton McCrary, *Abraham Lincoln and Reconstruction: The Louisiana Experiment* (Princeton, 1978), 197, 228; Banks to Lincoln, Dec. 30, 1863, Lincoln Papers.

A vote equal to almost one-quarter of the 1860 total ratified the constitution and elected a state government in March. But this success remained almost unnoticed in the shadow cast by events in Louisiana—and in Tennessee, where quarrels between iron-clad unionists and recanting Confederates delayed action through most of 1864. This problem plus continuing controversy over affairs in Louisiana drove a wedge into the Republican party that threatened a serious split between the president and Congress. Four related issues emerged in this conflict: the fate of slavery; the political role of blacks in reconstruction; the definition of loyalty; and the status of free black labor in the new order. As each issue generated heat in Louisiana, the temperature also rose in Congress where Republican lawmakers sought to frame their own approach to reconstruction.

The doom of slavery was their first concern. As military measures, both Lincoln's Emancipation Proclamation and Banks's edict declaring slavery "void" in Louisiana would have precarious legal force when the war was over. That was why Louisiana radicals considered a new constitution abolishing slavery a necessary prerequisite to the election of a new state government. Many congressional Republicans also feared a revival of slavery if conservatives should gain control of a reconstructed Louisiana. The best solution for this problem was a national constitutional amendment abolishing slavery. All Republicans including Lincoln united in favor of this in 1864. But the problem persisted. The Senate quickly mustered the necessary two-thirds majority for a Thirteenth Amendment abolishing slavery, but Democratic gains in the 1862 congressional elections prevented similar success in the House, where a 93–65 vote for the Amendment on June 15 fell thirteen votes short of success. In an attempt to ensure that emancipation became part of reconstruction, therefore, the Wade-Davis bill[33] passed by Congress on July 2 included a provision outlawing slavery in Confederate states as a condition of their return to the Union.

Fears that moderates and conservatives in Louisiana might make a deal to preserve slavery proved groundless. Despite the refusal of many radicals to participate in the election of a convention in March 1864,

33. Named for Benjamin Wade, chairman of the Senate Committee on Territories, and Henry Winter Davis, chairman of a special House reconstruction committee. Both were radicals. Davis was from Maryland—a significant sign of how the war had revolutionized that border state. On June 24, 1864, a state constitutional convention in Maryland adopted an amendment abolishing slavery, which voters narrowly ratified on October 13.

that body, meeting from April to July, wrote a prohibition of slavery into Louisiana's fundamental law. It also mandated public schools for all children, opened the militia to blacks, and provided equal access to the courts for both races. In the context of Louisiana's previous history, these were indeed revolutionary achievements. Lincoln described the constitution as "excellent . . . better for the poor black man than we have in Illinois."[34]

But on the matter that would emerge as the central issue of postwar reconstruction, Negro suffrage, the convention balked. A Louisiana moderate probably spoke with accuracy when he said that scarcely one in twenty white men favored suffrage even for literate, cultured Creoles—much less for newly freed field hands. Nevertheless, pressures for enfranchisement of blacks continued to grow. Abolitionists and radicals won converts among congressional Republicans with their argument that it was not only immoral but also fatuous to grant the ballot to former rebels and withhold it from loyal blacks. In January 1864 the "free people of color" in New Orleans drew up a petition asking for the right to vote. This memorial bore the signatures of more than a thousand men. Twenty-seven of them had fought with Andrew Jackson to defend New Orleans against the British in 1815; many others had sons or brothers in the Union army. Two delegates carried the petition to Washington, where radical congressmen praised them and Lincoln welcomed them to the White House. Impressed by their demeanor, the president wrote to the newly elected governor of Louisiana, Michael Hahn, a letter whose diffident wording conveyed a plain directive. When the forthcoming convention took up the question of voter qualifications, said Lincoln, "I barely suggest for your private consideration, whether some of the colored people may not be let in—as, for instance, the very intelligent, and especially those who have fought gallantly in our ranks. They would probably help, in some trying time to come, to keep the jewel of liberty in the family of freedom." Hahn and Banks got the message. But persuading a convention of Louisiana whites, even unionists who had swallowed emancipation, to confer political equality on blacks was uphill work. The best that the governor and general could do by cajolery, threats, and patronage was to reverse an initial vote for a clause *forbidding* Negro suffrage and secure instead a clause authorizing the legislature to enfranchise blacks if it saw fit.[35]

34. CWL, VIII, 107.
35. Lincoln to Hahn, March 13, 1864, CWL, VII, 243. See also McCrary, *Lincoln*

Unaware of these efforts by Banks and Hahn, several radicals denounced the Louisiana constitution for its "spirit of caste." Regarding
Louisiana as "Mr. Lincoln's model of reconstruction . . . which puts
all power in the hands of an unchanged white race," a number of
congressional Republicans turned against Lincoln's policy in the spring
of 1864.[36] Yet in the matter of Negro suffrage, Congress could do no
better. The initial version of the House reconstruction bill included a
requirement for the registration of "all loyal male citizens." This phrase
had become a Republican code for black enfranchisement. But moderates were not ready for such a step, so they modified the bill by adding
the word "white." When the measure came to the Senate, Benjamin
Wade's Committee on Territories deleted "white." But after counting
heads, Wade added it again before passage on July 2 "because, in my
judgment, [black suffrage] will sacrifice the bill."[37] Some radicals expressed outrage at such a surrender to expediency. "And this is called
'guaranteeing to the States a Republican form of Government,' is it?"
said one abolitionist sarcastically, while a radical newspaper in Boston
commented that "until Congress has sense enough and decency enough
to pass bills without the color qualification, we care not how quickly
they are killed."[38]

The Negro suffrage issue was part of a larger debate over who constituted the "loyal" population of a state for purposes of reconstruction.
Radicals considered blacks and unionist whites who had never supported
the Confederacy to be the only true loyalists. Some moderates went
along with Lincoln in wishing to include whites who repudiated their
allegiance to the Confederacy and took an oath of future loyalty to the
Union. But the unionism of these "galvanized" rebels was suspect in
the eyes of many Republicans, who therefore wanted to enfranchise
blacks to ensure a unionist majority. If blacks could not vote, then neither should recanting whites—at least not until the war was won and all
danger of their relapse into rebellion was over. Moreover, congressional
Republicans considered 10 or even 25 percent of a state's *white* voters

and Reconstruction, 256–63; LaWanda Cox, *Lincoln and Black Freedom: A Study
in Presidential Leadership* (Columbia, S.C., 1981), 92; and Ted Tunnell, *Crucible
of Reconstruction: War, Radicalism and Race in Louisiana 1862–1877* (Baton Rouge,
1984), 36–65.

36. Cox, *Lincoln and Black Freedom*, 104; McCrary, *Lincoln and Reconstruction*, 271–
72.

37. CG, 38 Cong., 1 Sess., p. 3449. See also Belz, *Reconstructing the Union*, 183,
201–2, 217.

38. *Principia*, May 12, 1864; *Boston Commonwealth*, July 15, 1864.

too slender a basis for reconstruction—especially when, as they saw it, that process in Louisiana had been "imposed on the people by military orders under the form of elections." In the words of Henry Winter Davis, chairman of the House reconstruction committee, the new government in New Orleans was a "hermaphrodite government, half military and half republican, representing the alligators and frogs of Louisiana." [39]

The fourth area of contention concerned the degree of freedom in the free-labor system to replace slavery. "Any provision which may be adopted . . . in relation to the freed people" by new state governments, declared Lincoln in his proclamation of amnesty and reconstruction, "which shall recognize and declare their permanent freedom, provide for their education, and which may yet be consistent, as a temporary arrangement, with their present condition as a laboring, landless, and homeless class, will not be objected to by the national Executive." [40] Here in a nutshell was the problem that would preoccupy the South for generations after the war. How "temporary" would this suggested system of apprenticeship turn out to be? What kind of education would freed slaves receive? How long would their status as a "laboring, landless, and homeless class" persist? These were questions that could not be fully resolved until after the war—if then. But they had already emerged in nascent form in the army's administration of contraband affairs in the occupied South.

From Maryland to Louisiana several hundred thousand contrabands came under Union army control during the war. Many of them had uprooted themselves—or had been uprooted—from their homes. The first task was to provide them food and shelter. The army was ill-equipped to function as a welfare agency. Its main task was to fight the rebels; few soldiers wanted to have anything to do with contrabands except perhaps to exploit them or vent their dislike of them. Thousands of blacks huddled in fetid "contraband camps" where disease, exposure, malnutrition, and poor sanitation took an appalling toll that accounted for a large share of the civilian casualties suffered by the South.

A degree of order gradually emerged from this chaos. Northern philanthropy stepped into the breach and sent clothing, medicine, emergency economic aid, and teachers to the contrabands. Supported by the American Missionary Association, the National Freedmen's Relief Association, the New England Freedmen's Aid Society, the Western

39. *New York Tribune*, Aug. 5, 1864; CG, 38 Cong., 1 Sess., 682.
40. CWL, VII, 55.

Freedmen's Aid Commission, and many other such organizations both religious and secular, hundreds of missionaries and schoolma'ams followed Union armies into the South to bring material aid, spiritual comfort, and the three Rs to freed slaves. Forerunners of a larger invasion that occurred after the war, these emissaries of Yankee culture—most of them women—saw themselves as a peaceful army come to elevate the freedmen and help them accomplish the transition from slavery to a prosperous freedom.

Of predominantly New England heritage and abolitionist conviction, these reformers exerted considerable influence in certain quarters of the Union government. In 1863 they persuaded the War Department to create a Freedmen's Inquiry Commission, whose recommendations eventually led to establishment of the Freedmen's Bureau in the last days of the war. They also managed to secure the appointment of sympathetic army officers to administer freedmen's affairs in several parts of the occupied South—particularly General Rufus Saxton on the South Carolina sea islands and Colonel John Eaton, whom Grant named superintendent of contrabands for the Mississippi Valley in November 1862. By 1863 the army had gotten many of the freedmen out of the contraband camps and put them to work on "home farms" to provide some of their own support. The army also hired many able-bodied freedmen as laborers and recruited others into black regiments, one of whose functions was to protect contraband villages and plantations from raids by rebel guerrillas or harassment by white Union soldiers.

The need of northern and British textile mills for cotton also caused the army to put many freed people to work growing cotton—often on the same plantations where they had done the same work as slaves. Some of these plantations remained in government hands and were administered by "labor superintendents" sent by northern freedmen's aid societies. Others were leased to Yankee entrepreneurs who hoped to make big money raising cotton with free labor. Still others remained in the hands of their owners, who took the oath of allegiance and promised to pay wages to workers who had recently been their slaves. Some land was leased by the freedmen themselves, who farmed it without direct white supervision and in some cases cleared a handsome profit that enabled them subsequently to buy land of their own. The outstanding example of a self-governing black colony occurred at Davis Bend, Mississippi, where former slaves of the Confederate president and his brother leased their plantations (from the Union army, which had seized them) and made good crops.

The quality of supervision of contraband labor by northern superintendents, Yankee lessees, and southern planters ranged from a benign to a brutal paternalism, prefiguring the spectrum of labor relations after the war. Part of the freedmen's wages was often withheld until the end of the season to ensure that they stayed on the job, and most of the rest was deducted for food and shelter. Many contrabands, understandably, could see little difference between this system of "free" labor and the bondage they had endured all their lives. Nowhere was the apparent similarity greater than in occupied Louisiana, where many planters took the oath of allegiance and continued to raise cotton or sugar under regulations issued by General Banks. Because of the national political focus on the reconstruction process in Louisiana, these regulations became another irritant between radical and moderate Republicans and another issue in the controversy between Congress and president. By military fiat Banks fixed the wages for plantation laborers and promised that the army would enforce "just treatment, healthy rations, comfortable clothing, quarters, fuel, medical attendance, and instruction for children." But further regulations ensured that some of these promises were likely to be honored in the breach. A worker could not leave the plantation without a pass and must sign a contract to remain for the entire year with his employer, who could call on provost marshals to enforce "continuous and faithful service, respectful deportment, correct discipline and perfect subordination." This system amounted to a virtual "reestablishment of slavery," charged abolitionists. It "makes the [Emancipation] Proclamation of 1863 a mockery and delusion," said Frederick Douglass. "Any white man," declared the black newspaper in New Orleans, "subjected to such restrictive and humiliating prohibitions, would certainly call himself a slave." If "this is the definition [of freedom] which the administration and people prefer," observed a radical newspaper in Boston, "we have got to go through a longer and severer struggle than ever."[41]

41. Banks's regulations are printed in O.R., Ser. I, Vol. 15, pp. 666–67, and Vol. 34, pt. 2, pp. 227–31; the abolitionist and black responses are quoted from James M. McPherson, *The Struggle for Equality: Abolitionists and the Negro in the Civil War and Reconstruction* (Princeton, 1964), 290, 293; and McPherson, *The Negro's Civil War* (New York, 1965), 129–30. The account in the preceding paragraphs of wartime policies toward the freedmen is based on the author's own research and on a number of studies by other scholars, especially Bell Irvin Wiley, *Southern Negroes 1861–1865* (New Haven, 1938); Willie Lee Rose, *Rehearsal for Reconstruction: The Port Royal Experiment* (Indianapolis, 1964); Louis S. Gerteis, *From Contraband to*

Indeed they did, but most of that struggle lay in the post-war future. In 1864 the controversy over freedmen's policy in Louisiana added its force to the process by which Congress hammered out a reconstruction bill. As finally passed after seemingly endless debate, the Wade-Davis bill reached Lincoln's desk on the 4th of July. By limiting suffrage to whites it did not differ from the president's policy. In another important respect—the abolition of slavery—it only appeared to differ. While the bill mandated emancipation and Lincoln's policy did not, the president's offer of amnesty required recipients of pardon to swear their support for all government actions on slavery. The two states thus far "reconstructed," Louisiana and Arkansas, had abolished the institution. Nevertheless a fear persisted among some Republicans that a residue of slavery might survive in any peace settlement negotiated by Lincoln, so they considered abolition by statute vital.

More significant were other differences between presidential and congressional policy: the Wade-Davis bill required 50 percent instead of 10 percent of the voters to swear an oath of allegiance, specified that a constitutional convention must take place *before* election of state officers, and restricted the right to vote for convention delegates to men who could take the "ironclad oath" that they had never voluntarily supported the rebellion. No Confederate state (except perhaps Tennessee) could meet these conditions; the real purpose of the Wade-Davis bill was to postpone reconstruction until the war was won. Lincoln by contrast wanted to initiate reconstruction immediately in order to convert lukewarm Confederates into unionists as a means of winning the war.[42]

Lincoln decided to veto the bill. Since Congress had passed it at the end of the session, he needed only to withhold his signature to prevent it from becoming law (the so-called pocket veto). This he did, but he also issued a statement explaining why he had done so. Lincoln denied the right of Congress to abolish slavery by statute. To assert such a right would "make the fatal admission" that these states were out of the Union and that secession was therefore legitimate. The pending Thirteenth Amendment, said the president, was the only constitutional way to abolish

---

Freedman: Federal Policy Toward Southern Blacks 1861–1865 (Westport, Conn., 1973); Lawrence N. Powell, *New Masters: Northern Planters During the Civil War and Reconstruction* (New Haven, 1980); C. Peter Ripley, *Slaves and Freedmen in Civil War Louisiana* (Baton Rouge, 1976); McCrary, *Abraham Lincoln and Reconstruction*; and Cox, *Lincoln and the Freedmen*.

42. CG, 38 Cong., 1 Sess., 2107–8, 3518; Belz, *Reconstructing the Union*, 241–42.

slavery. Lincoln also refused "to be inflexibly committed to any single plan of restoration" as required by the bill, since this would destroy "the free-state constitutions and governments, already adopted and installed in Arkansas and Louisiana."[43]

Because Congress had no official way to respond to this quasi-veto message, Wade and Davis decided to publish their own statement in the press. As they drafted it, their pent-up bitterness toward "Executive usurpation" carried them into rhetorical excess. "This rash and fatal act of the President," they declared, was "a blow at the friends of his Administration, at the rights of humanity, and at the principles of Republican Government." The congressional bill, unlike Lincoln's policy, protects "the loyal men of the nation" against the "great dangers" of a "return to power of the guilty leaders of the rebellion" and "the continuance of slavery." The president's cool defiance of this measure was "a studied outrage on the legislative authority." If Lincoln wanted Republican support for his re-election, "he must confine himself to his Executive duties—to obey and execute, not make the laws—to suppress by arms armed rebellion, and leave political reorganization to Congress."[44]

That final sentence provides a key to understanding this astonishing attack on a president by leaders of his own party. The reconstruction issue had become tangled with intraparty political struggles in the Republican presidential campaign of 1864. The Wade-Davis manifesto was part of a movement to replace Lincoln with a candidate more satisfactory to the radical wing of the party.

III

Lincoln's renomination and re-election were by no means assured, despite folk wisdom about the danger of swapping horses in midstream. No incumbent president had been renominated since 1840, and none had been re-elected since 1832. Even the war did not necessarily change the rules of this game. If matters were going badly at the front, voters would punish the man in charge. And if the man in charge was not conducting affairs to the satisfaction of his party, he might fail of renomination. The Republican party contained several men who in 1860 had considered themselves better qualified for the presidency than the man who won it. In 1864 at least one of them had not changed his opinion: Salmon P. Chase.

43. *CWL*, VII, 433.
44. *New York Tribune*, Aug. 5, 1864.

"I think a man of different qualities from those the President has will be needed for the next four years," wrote Chase at the end of 1863. "I am not anxious to be that man; and I am quite willing to leave that question to the decision of those who agree in thinking that some such man should be chosen." This was the usual double-talk of a politician declaring his candidacy. Chase was an ambitious as well as an able man. The republic rewarded him with many high offices: governor, senator, secretary of the treasury, chief justice. But the highest office eluded him despite a most assiduous pursuit of it. Chase had no doubts about his qualifications for the job; as his friend Benjamin Wade said of him, "Chase is a good man, but his theology is unsound. He thinks there is a fourth person in the Trinity."[45]

Chase used Treasury Department patronage to build a political machine for his nomination in 1864. The emergence of dissatisfaction with Lincoln's reconstruction policy strengthened his cause. In December 1863 a Chase committee took shape in Washington headed by Senator Samuel C. Pomeroy of Kansas. Misreading congressional grumbling for an anti-Lincoln groundswell, the committee decided to bring its movement into the open in February 1864. Pomeroy issued a "circular" declaring that Lincoln's "manifest tendency toward temporary expedients" made "the 'one-term principle' absolutely essential" to ensure a victorious war and a just peace. Chase was the man to achieve these goals.[46]

This attempt to promote a Chase boom backfired. Once again, as in the cabinet crisis of December 1862, the secretary proved no match for the president in the game of politics. While Chase had filled the Treasury Department with his partisans, Lincoln had not neglected the patronage. Postmaster-General Montgomery Blair did yeoman service for the president in this respect. And his brother Frank Blair, on leave from corps command in Sherman's army to take a seat in Congress, functioned in a capacity that a later generation would describe as "hatchet man" for the administration. A week after the Pomeroy Circular appeared, Frank Blair caused an uproar with a blistering anti-Chase speech in the House that among other things charged widespread Treasury corruption in the issuance of cotton-trading permits. Many radical Repub-

---

45. Chase to William Sprague, Nov. 26, 1863, in J. W. Schuckers, *Life and Public Services of Salmon Portland Chase* (New York, 1874), 494; Wade quoted in Dennett, *Lincoln/Hay*, 53.
46. James G. Randall and Richard N. Current, *Lincoln the President: Last Full Measure* (New York, 1955), 99.

licans never forgave the Blair family for this climactic event in a series of intraparty dogfights which found the Blairs leading the conservative faction. Meanwhile Republican state committees, legislatures, newspapers, and Union Leagues throughout the North—including Chase's home state of Ohio—passed resolutions endorsing Lincoln's renomination. Embarrassed by this boomerang destruction of his aspirations, Chase disingenuously disavowed any connection with the Pomeroy Circular, withdrew his name from consideration for the presidency, and offered to resign from the cabinet. For his part the president—perhaps with equal disingenuousness—disavowed any connection with Blair's attack and refused to accept Chase's resignation. Describing Chase's ambition for the presidency as a form of "mild insanity," Lincoln considered him less dangerous inside the government than out of it.[47]

Although most Republicans climbed aboard the Lincoln bandwagon, some of them did so with reluctance. As the reconstruction issue drove its wedge deeper into party unity, several radicals continued to hope that the bandwagon could be stopped. Horace Greeley futilely urged postponement of the national convention from June until September in a Micawber-like hope that something might turn up. Others launched trial balloons for an unlikely series of candidates including Grant, Butler, and Frémont. Of these only Frémont's balloon became airborne, carrying as strange a group of passengers as American politics ever produced.

Bitter toward a president who did not assign him to an important military command, Frémont like McClellan had been "awaiting orders" since 1862. Indeed, these two disgruntled generals represented the foremost political dangers to Lincoln. Of the two, McClellan posed the greater threat because he seemed likely to become the Democratic nominee later in the summer. In the meantime Frémont attracted a coalition of abolitionists and radical German-Americans into a third party. A few Republicans lent behind-the-scenes support to this movement, hoping to use it as a cat's-paw to scratch Lincoln from the main party ticket and bring Chase back to life. But the sparsely attended convention that met in Cleveland on May 31 to nominate Frémont contained not a single influential Republican. The most prominent supporter of this

---

47. Chase to Lincoln, Feb. 22, 1864, Lincoln to Chase, Feb. 29, 1864, in *CWL*, VII, 200–201, 212–13; Thomas Graham Belden, *So Fell the Angels* (Boston, 1956), 108–17; Randall and Current, *Lincoln the President*, 95–110; William Frank Zornow, *Lincoln & the Party Divided* (Norman, Okla., 1954), 23–56.

nomination was Wendell Phillips, whose letter to the convention proclaimed that Lincoln's reconstruction policy "makes the freedom of the negro a sham, and perpetuates slavery under a softer name." The convention adopted an apparently radical platform that called for a constitutional amendment to abolish slavery and "secure to all men absolute equality before the law." The platform also asserted that Congress rather than the president must control reconstruction, and urged confiscation of land owned by "rebels" for redistribution "among the soldiers and actual settlers." At the same time, however, the platform denounced Lincoln's suspension of habeas corpus and suppression of free speech. This of course was the main Democratic indictment of the administration. The convention also nominated a Democrat for vice president, and the new party called itself the Radical *Democratic* party.[48]

Thereby hung a tale—and a tail that soon began to wag the dog. Shrewd Democrats had not overlooked this opportunity to stir up trouble among the opposition. They infiltrated the convention and held out to the naive Frémont the prospect of a coalition with Democrats to beat Lincoln. The unemployed general took the bait. His acceptance letter repudiated the confiscation plank, ignored the "equality before the law" plank, but dwelt at length on Lincoln's misconduct of the war and violation of civil liberties. As the Democratic game of using Frémont to divert a few thousand Republican votes to a third party in close states became evident, most radicals (but not Phillips) renounced the venture and concluded that they had no alternative but Lincoln.

The Republican convention in Baltimore during the second week of June exhibited the usual hoopla and love-feast unity of a party renominating an incumbent. The assemblage called itself the National Union convention to attract War Democrats and southern unionists who might flinch at the name Republican. But it nevertheless adopted a down-the-line Republican platform, including endorsement of unremitting war to force the "unconditional surrender" of Confederate armies and the passage of a constitutional amendment to abolish slavery. When this latter plank was presented, "the whole body of delegates sprang to their feet . . . in prolonged cheering," according to William Lloyd Garrison, who was present as a reporter for his newspaper *The Liberator*. "Was not a spectacle like that rich compensation for more than thirty years of personal opprobrium?"[49]

48. *New York Tribune*, June 1, 1864; Zornow, *Lincoln & the Party Divided*, 72–86; McPherson, *The Struggle for Equality*, 267–78.
49. *Liberator*, June 24, 1864.

The platform dealt with the divisive reconstruction issue by ignoring it. Delegations from the Lincoln-reconstructed states of Louisiana, Arkansas, and Tennessee were admitted, while with the president's covert sanction the convention made a gesture of conciliation to radicals by seating an anti-Blair delegation from Missouri which cast a token ballot for Grant before changing its vote to make Lincoln's nomination unanimous. The only real contest at the convention was generated by the vice-presidential nomination. The colorless incumbent Hannibal Hamlin would add no strength to the ticket. The attempt to project a Union party image seemed to require the nomination of a War Democrat from a southern state. Andrew Johnson of Tennessee best fitted this bill. After backstairs maneuvers whose details still remain obscure, Johnson received the nomination on the first ballot.[50] This nomination had a mixed impact on radical-moderate tensions in the party. On the one hand, Johnson had dealt severely with "rebels" in Tennessee. On the other, he embodied Lincoln's executive approach to reconstruction.

The unanimity at Baltimore only temporarily papered over cracks in the party. By the time of Benjamin Wade's and Henry Winter Davis's angry manifesto against the president's reconstruction policy two months later, those cracks had become so wide that a serious move was on foot to replace Lincoln with another candidate. But the pressures that produced this astounding development arose less from controversy over what to do with the South when the war was won than from despair about whether it could be won at all. A Confederacy that had seemed on the ropes at the end of 1863 had come back fighting and appeared likely to survive after a season of slaughter whose toll eclipsed even that of the terrible summers of '62 and '63.

50. A postwar controversy arose over whether Lincoln remained neutral in this matter or played a role in engineering Johnson's nomination. Two of the most thorough students of this matter concluded that Lincoln's role was decisive: see Randall and Current, *Lincoln the President*, 13–34; and Zornow, *Lincoln & the Party Divided*, 99–103.

24

If It Takes All Summer

I

"Upon the progress of our arms," said Lincoln late in the war, "all else chiefly depends."[1] Never was this more true than in 1864, when "all else" included Lincoln's own re-election as well as the fate of emancipation and of the Union.

In the spring of 1864 the progress of Union arms seemed assured. Congress had revived the rank of lieutenant general (last held by George Washington), and Lincoln had promoted Grant to this rank with the title of general in chief. Henry W. Halleck stepped down to the post of chief of staff. Grant designated Sherman as his successor to command western armies and came east to make his headquarters with the Army of the Potomac. Though Meade remained in charge of this army subject to Grant's strategic orders, Phil Sheridan also came east to take over its cavalry. With the Union's three best generals—Grant, Sherman, Sheridan—in top commands, the days of the Confederacy appeared numbered.

After their setbacks during the latter half of 1863, rebel armies had suffered through a hard winter of short rations. The South was scraping the bottom of the manpower barrel. The Confederate Congress abolished the privilege of substitution (making those who had previously bought substitutes liable to conscription) and required soldiers whose

1. *CWL*, VIII, 332.

three-year enlistments were about to expire to remain in the army. Congress also stretched the upper and lower age limits of the draft to fifty and seventeen. Despite these efforts to maintain the army's strength, southern forces numbered fewer than half the enemy's as spring sunshine began to dry the red clay roads of Virginia and Georgia.

But there were flaws in the Union sword and hidden strengths in the Confederate shield. Northern success paradoxically created military weakness. Union armies had to detach many divisions as occupation forces to police 100,000 square miles of conquered territory. Other divisions had similar responsibilities in the border slave states. Invading armies also had to drop off large numbers of troops to guard their supply lines against cavalry and guerrilla raids. In Sherman's campaign for Atlanta in 1864 the number of men protecting his rail communications 450 miles back to Louisville nearly equaled the number of front-line soldiers he could bring against the enemy.

These subtractions from Union forces reduced the odds against the Confederacy. In spite of defeat at Gettysburg and the hardships that followed, the morale of the Army of Northern Virginia remained high. Many of these lean, tough veterans had re-enlisted even before Congress on February 17 required them to do so. They had become a band of brothers fighting from motives of pride in themselves, comradeship with each other, and devotion to Marse Robert. Many of them also shared Lee's sentiments, expressed on the eve of the 1864 military campaign, that "if victorious, we have everything to hope for in the future. If defeated, nothing will be left for us to live for."[2] Joseph Johnston had not been able to instill the same *esprit* in the army he inherited from Braxton Bragg. But he had done more in that direction by May 1864 than anyone who watched these troops flee from Missionary Ridge the previous November would have thought possible.

Most of the Confederate soldiers were veterans. Many of the veterans in the Union army were due to go home in 1864 when their three-year enlistments were up. If this happened, the South might well seize victory from the jaws of defeat. The Union Congress did not emulate its southern counterpart and require these veterans to re-enlist. Regarding their three-year term as a contract that could not be abrogated, the Washington lawmakers relied instead on persuasion and inducements. Three-year veterans who re-enlisted would receive a special chevron to

2. Clifford Dowdey, *Lee's Last Campaign: The Story of Lee and His Men against Grant— 1864* (Boston, 1960), 60.

wear on their sleeves, a thirty-day furlough, a $400 federal bounty plus local and state bounties, and the spread-eagle praise of politicians back home. If three-quarters of the men in a regiment re-enlisted, that regiment would retain its identity and thus its unit pride. This provision created effective peer pressure on holdouts to re-enlist. "They use a man here," wrote a weary Massachusetts veteran, "just the same as they do a turkey at a shooting match, fire at it all day and if they don't kill it raffle it off in the evening; so with us, if they can't kill you in three years they want you for three more—but I will stay."[3]

Some 136,000 veterans re-enlisted. Another hundred thousand or so decided not to. This latter group experienced the usual aversion to risk-taking during their final weeks in the army, thus limiting their combat capacity and damaging the morale of their re-enlisted comrades at crucial times during the summer of 1864. To replace wounded, killed, and discharged soldiers the Union armies mustered conscripts, substitutes, and bounty men who had been obtained by the first draft in 1863. This procedure affected most the Army of the Potomac, which had suffered higher casualties than any other army and had a re-enlistment rate of only 50 percent. Veteran officers and men regarded most of these new recruits with contempt. "Such another depraved, vice-hardened and desperate set of human beings never before disgraced an army," wrote a disgusted New Hampshire veteran. A Connecticut soldier described the new men in his regiment as "bounty jumpers, thieves, and cutthroats"; a Massachusetts officer reported that forty of the 186 "substitutes, bounty-jumpers . . . thieves and roughs" who had been assigned to his regiment disappeared the first night after they arrived. This he considered a blessing, as did a Pennsylvania officer who wrote that the "gamblers, thieves, pickpockets and blacklegs" given to his charge "would have disgraced the regiment beyond all recovery had they remained . . . but thanks to a kind Providence . . . they kept deserting, a dozen at a time, until they were nearly all gone."[4] Much of the North's apparent superiority in numbers thus dissolved during 1864. "The men we have been getting in this way nearly all desert," Grant complained in September, "and out of five reported North as having enlisted we don't get more than one effective soldier."[5]

Southern leaders discerned these flaws in their foe's sword. They hoped

3. Bruce Catton, *A Stillness at Appomattox* (Garden City, N.Y., 1957), 36.

4. *Ibid.*, 25, 26; Wiley, *Billy Yank*, 343–44; John J. Pullen, *The Twentieth Maine: A Volunteer Regiment in the Civil War* (Philadelphia, 1957), 154.

5. *O.R.*, Ser. I, Vol. 42, pt. 2, p. 783.

to exploit them in such a manner as to influence the 1864 presidential election in the North. The Prussian military theorist Carl von Clausewitz had defined war as the pursuit of political goals by other means. Confederate strategy in 1864 certainly conformed to this definition. If southern armies could hold out until the election, war weariness in the North might cause the voters to elect a Peace Democrat who would negotiate Confederate independence. Whether Lincoln "shall ever be elected or not depends upon . . . the battle-fields of 1864," predicted a Georgia newspaper. "If the tyrant at Washington be defeated, his infamous policy will be defeated with him." In Richmond a War Department official believed that "if we can only *subsist*" until the northern election, "giving an opportunity for the Democrats to elect a President . . . we may have peace."[6] Recognizing "the importance of this [military] campaign to the administration of Mr. Lincoln," Lee intended to "resist manfully" in order to undermine the northern war party. "If we can break up the enemy's arrangements early, and throw him back," explained Longstreet, "he will not be able to recover his position or his morale until the Presidential election is over, and then we shall have a new President to treat with."[7]

Grant was well aware of these southern hopes. But he intended to crush rebel armies and end the war before November. Eastern Yankees curious about the secret of this western general's success thought they saw the answer in his unpretentious but resolute demeanor. This "short, round-shouldered man" with "a slightly seedy look," according to observers in Washington who saw Grant for the first time, nevertheless possessed "a clear blue eye" and "an expression as if he had determined to drive his head through a brick wall, and was about to do it." Even a jaded New Yorker who had watched the reputations of a half-dozen Union generals perish "because their owners did not know how to march through Virginia to Richmond" believed that "Grant may possess the talisman."[8]

6. Larry E. Nelson, *Bullets, Ballots, and Rhetoric: Confederate Policy for the United States Presidential Contest of 1864* (University, Ala., 1980), 14, 51; Jones, *War Clerk's Diary* (Swiggett), II, 229.

7. Douglas Southall Freeman, ed., *Lee's Dispatches: Unpublished Letters of General Robert E. Lee . . . to Jefferson Davis* (New York, 1915), 185; Herman Hattaway and Archer Jones, *How the North Won: A Military History of the Civil War* (Urbana, Ill., 1983), 532; O.R., Ser. I, Vol. 32, pt. 3, p. 588.

8. Foote, *Civil War*, III, 4, 5; Strong, *Diary*, 416.

Grant did not confine his attention solely to Virginia. Instead, believing that the various northern armies in the past had "acted independently and without concert, like a balky team, no two ever pulling together," he worked out plans for coordinated advances on several fronts to prevent any one of the Confederate armies from reinforcing another. "Lee's Army will be your objective point," Grant instructed Meade. "Wherever Lee goes, there will you go also." Sherman received orders "to move against Johnston's army, to break it up, and to get into the interior of the enemy's country as far as you can, inflicting all the damage you can against their war resources."[9] These two main Union armies would have a numerical advantage of nearly two to one over their adversaries, but Grant issued additional orders to increase the odds. On the periphery of the main theaters stood three northern armies commanded by political generals whose influence prevented even Grant from getting rid of them: Benjamin Butler's Army of the James on the Peninsula; Franz Sigel's scattered forces in West Virginia and the Shenandoah Valley; and Nathaniel Banks's Army of the Gulf in Louisiana. Grant directed Banks to plan a campaign to capture Mobile, after which he was to push northward and prevent rebel forces in Alabama from reinforcing Johnston. At the same time Butler was to advance up the James to cut the railroad between Petersburg and Richmond and threaten the Confederate capital from the south, while Sigel moved up the Valley to pin down its defenders and cut Lee's communications to that region. Lincoln was delighted with Grant's strategic design. With a typical backwoods metaphor, he described the auxiliary role of Banks, Butler, and Sigel: "Those not skinning can hold a leg."[10]

But the leg-holders bungled their jobs. The first to fail was Banks. The administration shared responsibility for this outcome, for it diverted Banks from the attack on Mobile to a drive up the Red River in Louisiana to seize cotton and expand the area of Union political control in the state. Only after achieving these objectives was he to turn eastward against Mobile. As it turned out, Banks achieved none of the goals except the seizure of a little cotton—along with the wanton destruction of much civilian property, an outcome that hardly won the hearts and minds of Louisianians for the Union.

Banks's nemesis was Richard Taylor (the son of Zachary Taylor), who had learned his fighting trade as a brigade commander under Stonewall Jackson in 1862. Taking command of some 15,000 men after the loss

9. O.R., Ser. I, Vol. 46, pt. 1, p. 11, Vol. 33, pp. 827–28, Vol. 32, pt. 3, p. 246.
10. Dennett, *Lincoln/Hay*, 178–79.

of southern Louisiana to the Union, Taylor prepared to defend what was left of the state in which he had gained wealth as a planter. Banks had been humiliated in Virginia by Jackson; he suffered the same fate a thousand miles away at the hands of Stonewall's protégé. On April 8, Taylor struck the vanguard of Banks's army at Sabine Crossroads thirty-five miles south of the Union objective of Shreveport. Driving the routed Yankees pell-mell back to their supports, Taylor came on and attacked again next day at Pleasant Hill. This time the bluecoats held, forcing the rebels in turn to recoil after taking sharp punishment.

Despite this success, Banks was unnerved by the nonarrival of a co-operating Union force pushing south from Little Rock (it had been deflected by guerrillas and cavalry harassment) and by the abnormally low Red River, which threatened to strand the already damaged Union gunboat fleet above the rapids at Alexandria. Banks decided to retreat. Disaster to the gunboats was averted by the ingenuity of a Wisconsin colonel who used his lumbering experience to construct a series of wing dams that floated the fleet through the rapids. The dispirited army did not get back to southern Louisiana until May 26, a month too late to begin the aborted Mobile campaign. As a consequence Joseph Johnston received 15,000 reinforcements from Alabama. Moreover, 10,000 soldiers that Banks had borrowed from Sherman for the Red River campaign never rejoined the Union army in Georgia. Instead they remained in the Tennessee-Mississippi theater to cope with threats by Forrest against Sherman's rail communications. Banks was superseded as department commander and returned to his controversial role as military administrator of Louisiana's reconstruction.[11]

Butler and Sigel fared no better than Banks in their assignments to hold rebel legs. Butler had a real chance to achieve the glory that had eluded him since the war's early days. With 30,000 men drawn from coastal operations in the Carolinas he steamed up the James River and landed midway between Richmond and Petersburg on May 5. The two cities were defended by only 5,000 troops plus hastily mobilized government clerks serving as militia. Their commander—none other than P. G. T. Beauregard, who was transferred from Charleston to southside Virginia—had not yet arrived on the scene. If Bulter had moved quickly to cut the railroad between Petersburg and Richmond he might have smashed into the capital against little opposition. Lee could have done nothing to prevent this, for he was otherwise engaged with the Army of

11. Ludwell H. Johnson, *Red River Campaign: Politics and Cotton in the Civil War* (Baltimore, 1958).

the Potomac sixty miles to the north. But the squint-eyed Union commander fumbled his chance. Instead of striking fast with overwhelming force, he advanced cautiously with detached units, which managed to tear up only a few miles of track while fending off rebel skirmishers. Not until May 12, a week after landing, did Butler get his main force on the march for Richmond. By then Beauregard had brought reinforcements from the Carolinas and was ready to meet Bulter on almost even terms. On May 16 the Confederates attacked near Drewry's Bluff, eight miles south of Richmond. After severe casualites on both sides, the rebels drove Bulter's men back to their trenches across a neck between the James and Appomattox rivers. There the southerners entrenched their own line and sealed off Butler's army, in Grant's caustic words, "as if it had been in a bottle strongly corked." [12]

Grant received the news of Butler's corking about the same time he learned of a similar setback to Franz Sigel in that vale of Union sorrows, the Shenandoah Valley. With 6,500 men Sigel had advanced up the Valley to capture Staunton, whence Lee's army received some of its meager supplies. Before Sigel could get there, however, former U.S. Vice President John C. Breckinridge, now commanding a scraped-together rebel force of 5,000, attacked Sigel at New Market on May 15 and drove him back. This small battle was marked on one side by Sigel's skill at retreating and on the other by a spirited charge of 247 V.M.I. cadets aged fifteen to seventeen, who were ever after immortalized in southern legend. Convinced that Sigel "will do nothing but run; he never did anything else," Halleck and Grant prevailed upon Lincoln to remove him from command. [13]

The failure of Grant's leg-holders in Virginia complicated the task of skinning Lee. The Armies of the Potomac and of Northern Virginia had wintered a few miles apart on opposite sides of the Rapidan. As the dogwood bloomed, Grant prepared to cross the river and turn Lee's right. He hoped to bring the rebels out of their trenches for a showdown battle somewhere south of the Wilderness, that gloomy expanse of scrub oaks and pines where Lee had mousetrapped Joe Hooker exactly a year earlier. Remembering that occasion, Lee decided not to contest the river crossing but instead to hit the bluecoats in the flank as they marched through the Wilderness, where their superiority in numbers—115,000 to 64,000—would count for less than in the open.

12. O.R., Ser. I, Vol. 46, pt. 1, p. 20.
13. Ibid., Vol. 36, pt. 2, p. 840.

Accordingly on May 5 two of Lee's corps coming from the west ran into three Union corps moving south from the Rapidan. For Lee this collision proved a bit premature, for Longstreet's corps had only recently returned from Tennessee and could not come up in time for this first day of the battle of the Wilderness. The Federals thus managed to get more than 70,000 men into action against fewer than 40,000 rebels. But the southerners knew the terrain and the Yankees' preponderance of troops produced only immobility in these dense, smoke-filled woods where soldiers could rarely see the enemy, units blundered the wrong way in the directionless jungle, friendly troops fired on each other by mistake, gaps in the opposing line went unexploited because unseen, while muzzle flashes and exploding shells set the underbrush on fire to threaten wounded men with a fiery death. Savage fighting surged back and forth near two road intersections that the bluecoats needed to hold in order to continue their passage southward. They held on and by dusk had gained a position to attack Lee's right.

Grant ordered this done at dawn next day. Lee likewise planned a dawn assault in the same sector to be spearheaded by Longstreet's corps, which was on the march and expected to arrive before light. The Yankees attacked first and nearly achieved a spectacular success. After driving the rebels almost a mile through the woods they emerged into a small clearing where Lee had his field headquarters. Agitated, the gray commander tried personally to lead a counterattack at the head of one of Longstreet's arriving units, a Texas brigade. "Go back, General Lee, go back!" shouted the Texans as they swept forward. Lee finally did fall back as more of Longstreet's troops double-timed into the clearing and brought the Union advance to a halt.

The initiative now shifted to the Confederates. By mid-morning Longstreet's fresh brigades drove the bluecoats in confusion almost back to their starting point. The southerners' local knowledge now came into play. Unmarked on any map, the roadbed of an unfinished railroad ran past the Union left. Vines and underbrush had so choked the cut that an unwary observer saw nothing until he stumbled into it. One of Longstreet's brigadiers knew of this roadbed and suggested using it as a concealed route for an attack against the Union flank. Longstreet sent four brigades on this mission. Shortly before noon they burst out of thickets and rolled up the surprised northern regiments. Then tragedy struck the Confederates as it had done a year earlier only three miles away in this same Wilderness. As the whooping rebels drove in from the flank they converged at right angles with Longstreet's other units attacking straight ahead. In the smoke-filled woods Longstreet went down with a bullet in his shoulder fired by a Confederate. Unlike Jackson he recovered, but he was out of the war for five months.

With Longstreet's wounding the steam went out of this southern assault. Lee straightened out the lines and renewed the attack in late afternoon. Combat raged near the road intersection amid a forest fire that ignited Union breastworks. The Federals held their ground and the fighting gradually died toward evening as survivors sought to rescue the wounded from cremation. At the other end of the line General John B. Gordon, a rising brigadier from Georgia, discovered that Grant's right flank was also exposed. After trying for hours to get his corps commander Richard Ewell to authorize an attack, Gordon went to the top and finally obtained Lee's permission to pitch in. The evening assault achieved initial success and drove the Federal flank back a mile while capturing two northern generals. Panic spread all the way to Grant's headquarters, where a distraught brigadier galloped up on a lathered horse to tell the Union commander that all was lost—that Lee was repeating Jackson's tactics of a year earlier in these same woods. But Grant did not share the belief in Lee's superhuman qualities that seemed to paralyze so many eastern officers. "I am heartily tired of hearing what Lee is going to do," Grant told the brigadier. "Some of you always seem to think he is suddenly going to turn a double somersault, and land on our rear and on both our flanks at the same time. Go back to your command, and try to think what we are going to do ourselves, instead of what Lee is going to do."[14]

Grant soon showed that he meant what he said. Both flanks had been badly bruised, and his 17,500 casualties in two days exceeded the Confederate total by at least 7,000. Under such circumstances previous Union commanders in Virginia had withdrawn behind the nearest river. Men in the ranks expected the same thing to happen again. But Grant had told Lincoln that "whatever happens, there will be no turning back."[15] While the armies skirmished warily on May 7, Grant prepared to march around Lee's right during the night to seize the crossroads village of Spotsylvania a dozen miles to the south. If successful, this move would place the Union army closer to Richmond than the enemy and force Lee to fight or retreat. All day Union supply wagons and the reserve artillery moved to the rear, confirming the soldiers' weary expectation of retreat. After dark the blue divisions pulled out one by one. But

14. Horace Porter, *Campaigning with Grant* (New York, 1897), 69–70.
15. Foote, *Civil War*, III, 186.

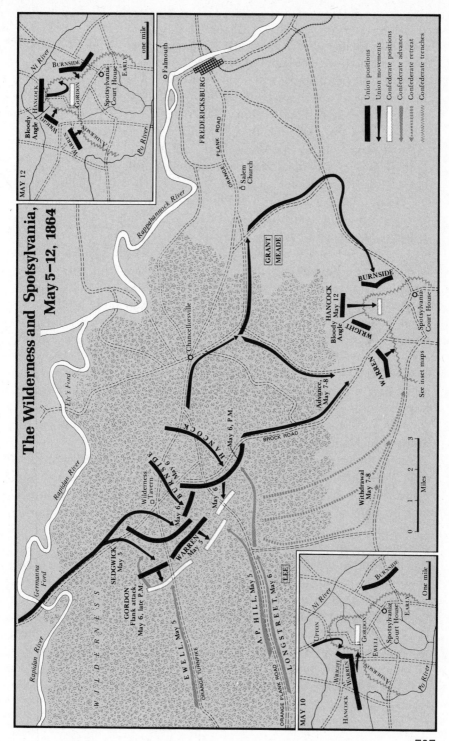

The Wilderness and Spotsylvania, May 5–12, 1864

Legend:
- Union positions
- Union movements
- Confederate positions
- Confederate advance
- Confederate retreat
- Confederate trenches

MAY 12 (inset map, top left)

Ni River · BURNSIDE · EARLY · Spotsylvania Court House · GORDON · HANCOCK · Bloody Angle · WRIGHT · WARREN · ANDERSON · Po River · one mile

Falmouth · FREDERICKSBURG · ORANGE PLANK ROAD · Salem Church · Rappahannock River · GRANT · MEADE · BURNSIDE · Spotsylvania Court House · HANCOCK May 12 · Bloody Angle · WRIGHT · WARREN · Advance May 7–8 · See inset maps · BROCK ROAD · May 6, P.M. · Withdrawal May 7–8

Chancellorsville · Ely's Ford · Rapidan River · Germanna Ford · Rapidan River · WILDERNESS · HANCOCK · BURNSIDE May 6 · May 6 · May 6, P.M. · Wilderness Tavern · SEDGWICK May 5 · GORDON Flank attack, May 6, late P.M. · WARREN May 5 · EWELL May 5 · A. P. HILL May 5 · LONGSTREET, May 6 · ORANGE TURNPIKE · ORANGE PLANK ROAD · LEE

Miles 0 1 2 3

MAY 10 (inset map, bottom right)

Ni River · BURNSIDE · UPTON · GORDON · EARLY · Spotsylvania Court House · EWELL · WRIGHT · WARREN · HANCOCK · ANDERSON · Po River · One mile

727

instead of heading north they turned *south*. A mental sunburst brightened their minds. It was not "another Chancellorsville . . . another skedaddle" after all. "Our spirits rose," recalled one veteran who remembered this moment as a turning point in the war. Despite the terrors of the past three days and those to come, "we marched free. The men began to sing." For the first time in a Virginia campaign the Army of the Potomac stayed on the offensive after its initial battle.[16]

Sheridan's cavalry had thus far contributed little to the campaign. Their bandy-legged leader was eager to take on Jeb Stuart's fabled troopers. Grant obliged Sheridan by sending him on a raid to cut Lee's communications in the rear while Grant tried to pry him out of his defenses in front. Aggressive as always, Sheridan took 10,000 horsemen at a deliberate pace southward with no attempt at deception, challenging Stuart to attack. The plumed cavalier chased the Yankees with only half his men (leaving the others to patrol Lee's flanks at Spotsylvania), nipping at Sheridan's heels but failing to prevent the destruction of twenty miles of railroad, a quantity of rolling stock, and three weeks' supply of rations for Lee's army. On May 11, Stuart made a stand at Yellow Tavern, only six miles north of Richmond. Outnumbering the rebels by two to one and outgunning them with rapid-fire carbines, the blue troopers rolled over the once-invincible southern cavalry and dispersed them in two directions. A grim bonus of this Union victory was the mortal wounding of Stuart—a blow to Confederate leadership next only to the death of Jackson a year and a day earlier.

While the cavalry played its deadly game of cut and thrust near Richmond, the infantry back at Spotsylvania grappled like muscle-bound giants. By this stage of the war the spade had become almost as important for defense as the rifle. Wherever they stopped, soldiers quickly constructed elaborate networks of trenches, breastworks, artillery emplacements, traverses, a second line in the rear, and a cleared field of fire in front with the branches of felled trees (abatis) placed at point-blank range to entangle attackers. At Spotsylvania the rebels built the strongest such fieldworks in the war so far. Grant's two options were to flank these defenses or smash through them; he tried both. On May 9 he sent Winfield Scott Hancock's 2nd Corps to turn the Confederate left. But this maneuver required the crossing of a meandering river twice, giving Lee time to shift two divisions on May 10 to counter it. Believing that this weakening of the Confederate line made it vulnerable to as-

16. *Ibid.*, 189–91; Catton, *A Stillness at Appomattox*, 91–92.

sault, Grant ordered five divisions to attack the enemy's left-center on a mile-wide front during the afternoon of May 10. But they found no weakness, for Lee had shifted those reinforcements from his right.

Farther along toward the center of the line, however, on the west face of a salient jutting out a half-mile along high ground and dubbed the Mule Shoe because of its shape, a Union assault achieved a potentially decisive breakthrough. Here Colonel Emory Upton, a young and intensely professional West Pointer who rarely restrained his impatience with the incompetence he found among fellow officers, made a practical demonstration of his theory on how to attack trenches. With twelve picked regiments formed in four lines, Upton took them across 200 yards of open ground and through the abatis at a run. Not stopping to fire until they reached the trenches, screaming like madmen and fighting like wild animals, the first line breached the defenses and fanned left and right to widen the breach while the following line kept going to attack the second network of trenches a hundred yards farther on. The third and fourth lines came on and rounded up a thousand dazed prisoners. The road to Richmond never seemed more open. But the division assigned to support Upton's penetration came forward halfheartedly and retreated wholeheartedly when it ran into massed artillery fire. Stranded without support a half-mile from their own lines, Upton's regiments could not withstand a withering counterattack by rebel reinforcements. The Yankees fell back in the gathering darkness after losing a quarter of their numbers.

Their temporary success, however, won Upton a battlefield promotion and persuaded Grant to try the same tactics with a whole corps backed by follow-up attacks all along the line. As a cold, sullen rain set in next day (May 11) to end two weeks of hot weather, reports by rebel patrols of Union supply wagons moving to the rear caused Lee to make a wrong guess about Grant's intentions. Believing that the wagon traffic presaged another flanking maneuver, Lee ordered the removal of twenty-two guns in preparation for a quick countermove. The apex of the salient defended by these guns was exactly the point that Hancock's corps planned to hit at dawn on May 12. Too late the guns were ordered back—just in time to be captured by yelling bluecoats as fifteen thousand of them swarmed out of the mist and burst through the Confederate trenches. Advancing another half-mile and capturing most of the famed Stonewall division, Hancock's corps split Lee's army in two. At this crisis the southern commander came forward with a reserve division. As he had done six days previously in the Wilderness, Lee started to lead them himself in a desperate counterattack. Again the soldiers—Virginians and Georgians this time—shouted "General Lee to the rear!" and vowed to drive back "those people" if Marse Robert would only stay safely behind. Lee acceded, and the division swept forward. Their counterattack benefited from the very success of the Yankees, whose rapid advance in rain and fog had jumbled units together in a disorganized mass beyond control of their officers. Forced back to the toe of the Mule Shoe, bluecoats rallied in the trenches they had originally captured and there turned to lock horns with the enemy in endless hours of combat across a no-man's land at some places but a few yards wide.

While this was going on the Union 5th and 9th Corps attacked the left and right of the Confederate line with little success, while the 6th Corps came in on Hancock's right to add weight to a renewed attempt to crush the salient. Here was the famous Bloody Angle of Spotsylvania. For eighteen hours in the rain, from early morning to midnight, some of the war's most horrific fighting raged along a few hundred yards of rebel trenches. "The flags of both armies waved at the same moment over the same breastworks," recalled a 6th Corps veteran, "while beneath them Federal and Confederate endeavored to drive home the bayonet through the interstices of the logs."[17] Impelled by a sort of frenzy, soldiers on both sides leaped on the parapet and fired down at enemy troops with bayoneted rifles handed up from comrades, hurling each empty gun like a spear before firing the next one until shot down or bayoneted themselves. So intense was the firing that at one point just behind the southern lines an oak tree nearly two feet thick was cut down by minié balls.[18]

Hand-to-hand fighting like this usually ended quickly when one side broke and ran; but today neither line broke and few men ran. It became an atavistic territorial battle. Blood flowed as copiously as the rain, turning trench floors into a slimy ooze where dead and wounded were tram-

17. Joseph P. Cullen, *Where a Hundred Thousand Fell: The Battles of Fredericksburg, Chancellorsville, the Wilderness, and Spotsylvania Court House* (Washington, 1966), 52–53.
18. In postwar reminiscences several northern regiments claimed to have accomplished this feat. The stump was later exhibited at the Centennial Exposition in Philadelphia and preserved in the Smithsonian Institution. Splinters from the tree seemed to become as ubiquitous as relics of the true Cross. G. Norton Galloway, "Hand-to-Hand Fighting at Spotsylvania," Robert McAllister, "McAllister's Brigade at the Bloody Angle," and James L. Bowen, "General Edwards's Brigade at the Bloody Angle," in *Battles and Leaders*, IV, 173, 176, 177.

pled down by men fighting for their lives. "I never expect to be fully believed when I tell what I saw of the horrors of Spotsylvania," wrote a Union officer, "because I should be loath to believe it myself were the case reversed." Long after nightfall Lee finally sent word to exhausted Confederate survivors to fall back to a new line a half-mile in the rear which his engineers had worked feverishly to fortify. Next morning the Bloody Angle contained only corpses; Union soldiers on a burial detail found 150 dead southerners piled several deep in one area of trench measuring 200 square feet, and buried them by simply pushing in the parapet on top of them.[19]

As the armies battered each other in Virginia, citizens back home crowded newspaper and telegraph offices in a mood of "painful suspense [that] unfits the mind for mental activity." These were "fearfully critical, anxious days," wrote a New Yorker, in which "the destines of the continent for centuries" would be decided. In Richmond, elation at the first reports of Lee's victories in the Wilderness turned to "grave apprehension" and "feverish anxiety" as his army fell back to Spotsylvania while Butler and Sheridan approached Richmond.[20] The day before the Bloody Angle, Grant had sent a dispatch to Washington declaring that "I propose to fight it out on this line if it takes all summer." Newspapers picked up this phrase and made it as famous as Grant's unconditional surrender note at Fort Donelson. Coupled with reports describing the Union advance southward from the Wilderness, Grant's dispatch produced jubilant headlines in northern newspapers: "Glorious Successes"; "Lee Terribly Beaten"; "The End Draws Near." A veteran newspaper reporter recalled that "everybody seemed to think that Grant would close the war and enter Richmond before the autumn leaves began to fall."[21]

Lincoln feared that such high expectations would boomerang if they turned out to be overly optimistic—as indeed they did. "The people are too sanguine," he told a reporter. "They expect too much at once." To a group of serenaders who appeared at the White House, Lincoln said that "I am very glad at what has happened; but there is a great deal still to be done." When it became clear by May 17 that Grant had not

19. Catton, A *Stillness at Appomattox*, 127; Bruce Catton, *Grant Takes Command* (Boston, 1968), 235; Galloway, "Hand-to-Hand Fighting at Spotsylvania," *Battles and Leaders*, IV, 174.
20. Howard K. Beale, ed., *Diary of Gideon Welles*, 3 vols. (New York, 1960), II, 33; Strong, *Diary*, 449; Jones, *War Clerk's Diary* (Swiggett), 213, 219.
21. *O.R.*, Ser. I, Vol. 36, pt. 2, p. 672; Nevins, *War*, IV, 35; Noah Brooks, *Washington in Lincoln's Time* (New York, 1895), 148–49.

broken Lee's lines at Spotsylvania and that Butler had been "bottled up" south of Richmond, the northern mood turned "despondent and bad."[22] The price of gold, an inverse barometer of public opinion, rose from 171 to 191 during the last two weeks of May.[23] The appalling casualty reports that began to filter up from Virginia did not help morale. From May 5 through May 12 the Army of the Potomac lost some 32,000 men killed, wounded, and missing—a total greater than for all Union armies *combined* in any previous week of the war. As anxious relatives scanned the casualty lists, a pall of gloom settled over hundreds of northern communities.

Lee's casualties had been proportionately as great—about 18,000— and his loss of twenty of fifty-seven commanders of infantry corps, divisions, and brigades was devastating. Yet it could truly be said that both sides had just begun to fight. Each army made good about half of its losses by calling in reinforcements. Six brigades from the Richmond front and two from the Shenandoah Valley joined Lee. Grant received a few thousand new recruits and combed several heavy artillery regiments out of the Washington defenses and converted them to infantry. Lee's replacements were higher in quality though lower in number than Grant's, for the southerners were combat veterans, while the "heavies" from Washington had seen no real fighting during their two or three years of garrison duty. And even as the Union reinforcements came forward, the first of the thirty-six regiments whose time would expire in the next six weeks began to leave the army.[24] While the available manpower pool in the North was much larger, therefore, Lee could more readily replace his losses with veterans than Grant could during these crucial weeks of May and June.

After the Bloody Angle Grant wasted no time licking his wounds. During the next week he tried several maneuvers on Lee's flanks and another assault up the middle. Aided by rains that slowed Union movements, the rebels countered all these moves. All that the Yankees could

22. Brooks, *Washington in Lincoln's Time*, 149; CWL, VII, 334; Strong, *Diary*, 447.
23. The price of gold measured the value of the dollar in relation to the value of gold. A price of 191 meant that this many greenback dollars were required to purchase 100 gold dollars. The value of the greenback dollar rose and fell in proportion to confidence in northern military prospects; the higher the price of gold, the lower the value of the dollar.
24. Not all the soldiers in these regiments went home. Some had re-enlisted as individuals; the enlistments of others had not yet expired. Men in these categories were incorporated into other regiments from the same states.

show for these six days of maneuvering and fighting were three thousand more casualties. Recognizing the impossibility of loosening the Confederate hold on Spotsylvania by head-on attacks or short-range flanking efforts, Grant decided to lure Lee out by another race twenty-five miles south toward a rail junction just beyond the North Anna River. Lee detected the move by a reconnaissance in force on May 19 that cost him a thousand men and blooded one of Grant's converted heavy artillery divisions.

Holding the inside track, Lee got his army behind the North Anna River before the Union vanguard arrived. Entrenching a strong position on the south bank, the Confederates fought several small actions against probing bluecoats. Grant decided to move twenty miles downriver for another attempt to get around Lee's right. The Federals crossed the Pamunkey River unscathed, only to find the rebels, who again moved on shorter interior lines, entrenched behind Totopotomy Creek nine miles northeast of Richmond. Although half-starved from lack of rations, the southerners were still full of fight. After two days of skirmishing at the end of May the Yankees sidled southward once more—moving to their left as always, to maintain a short, secure supply line via the tidal rivers controlled by the navy.

Grant's objective was a dusty crossroads named Cold Harbor near the Gaines' Mill battlefield of 1862. Sheridan's cavalry seized the junction after an intense fight on May 31 with southern horsemen commanded by Lee's nephew Fitzhugh Lee. Next day Sheridan's troopers held on against an infantry counterattack until Union infantry came up and pushed the rebels back. During the night of June 1–2 the remainder of both armies arrived and entrenched lines facing each other for seven miles from the Totopotomy to the Chickahominy. To match additional southern reinforcements from south of the James, Grant pried one of Butler's corps from the same sector. At Cold Harbor, 59,000 Confederates confronted 109,000 Federals. Both armies had thus built themselves back up almost to the numbers with which they started the campaign four long weeks earlier.

These four weeks had been exhausting as well as bloody beyond all precedent. The Federals had suffered some 44,000 casualties, the Confederates about 25,000.[25] This was a new kind of relentless, ceaseless warfare. These two armies had previously fought several big set-piece

25. Since no records exist for overall Confederate losses during this campaign, casualty figures for Lee's army are at best an estimate.

battles followed by the retreat of one or the other behind the nearest river, after which both sides rested and recuperated before going at it again. Since the beginning of this campaign, however, the armies had never been out of contact with each other. Some kind of fighting along with a great deal of marching and digging took place almost every day and a good many nights as well. Mental and physical exhaustion began to take a toll; officers and men suffered what in later wars would be called shell shock. Two of Lee's unwounded corps commanders, A. P. Hill and Richard Ewell, broke down for a time during the campaign, and Ewell had to be replaced by Jubal Early. Lee fell sick for a week. On the Union side an officer noted that in three weeks men "had grown thin and haggard. The experience of those twenty days seemed to have added twenty years to their age." "Many a man," wrote Captain Oliver Wendell Holmes, Jr., "has gone crazy since this campaign began from the terrible pressure on mind & body." [26]

All of this was on Grant's mind as he pondered his next move. Another flanking maneuver to the left would entangle his army in the Chickahominy bottomlands where McClellan had come to grief. And it would only drive Lee back into the Richmond defenses, which had been so strengthened during the past two years that the usual defensive advantage of fieldworks would be doubled. Another dozen Union regiments were scheduled to leave the army when their time expired in July; this factor also argued against postponement of a showdown battle. Grant's purpose was not a war of attrition—though numerous historians have mislabeled it thus. From the outset he had tried to maneuver Lee into open-field combat, where Union superiority in numbers and firepower could cripple the enemy. It was Lee who turned it into a war of attrition by skillfully matching Grant's moves and confronting him with an entrenched defense at every turn. Although it galled Lee to yield the initiative to an opponent, his defensive strategy exacted two enemy casualties for every one of his own. This was a rate of attrition that might stun northern voters into denying Lincoln re-election and ending the war. To avoid such a consequence Grant had vowed to fight it out on this line if it took all summer. "This line" had now become Cold Harbor, and the results of a successful attack there might win the war. If beaten, the Confederates would be driven back on the Chickahominy

26. Catton, *A Stillness at Appomattox*, 138; Mark DeWolfe Howe, ed., *Touched with Fire; Civil War Letters and Diary of Oliver Wendell Holmes, Jr.*, 1861–1864 (Cambridge, Mass., 1946), 149–50.

and perhaps annihilated. Grant knew that the rebels were tired and hungry; so were his own men, but he believed that they had the edge in morale. "Lee's army is really whipped," he had written to Halleck a few days earlier. "The prisoners we now take show it, and the action of his army shows it unmistakably. A battle with them outside of intrenchments cannot be had. Our men feel that they have gained the morale over the enemy and attack with confidence." [27] So Grant ordered an assault at dawn on June 3.

The outcome revealed his mistake in two crucial respects. Lee's army was not whipped, nor did Grant's men attack with confidence. Indeed, hundreds of them pinned slips of paper with name and address on their uniforms so their bodies could be identified after the battle. At dawn came the straight-ahead assault delivered primarily by three corps on the left and center of the Union line. A sheet of flame greeted the blue uniforms with names pinned on them. The rebels fought from trenches described by a newspaper reporter as "intricate, zig-zagged lines within lines, lines protecting flanks of lines, lines built to enfilade opposing lines . . . works within works and works without works." [28] Although a few regiments in Hancock's 2nd Corps—the same that had breached the Angle at Spotsylvania—managed to penetrate the first line of trenches, they were quickly driven out at the cost of eight colonels and 2,500 other casualties. Elsewhere along the front the result was worse—indeed it was the most shattering Union repulse since the stone wall below Marye's Heights at Fredericksburg. The Yankees suffered 7,000 casualties this day; the Confederates fewer than 1,500. By early afternoon Grant admitted defeat and called off further efforts. "I regret this assault more than any one I have ever ordered," he said that evening. "I think Grant has had his eyes opened," Meade wrote dryly to his wife, "and is willing to admit now that Virginia and Lee's army is not Tennessee and Bragg's army." [29]

The horrors of this day, added to those of Spotsylvania, created something of a Cold Harbor syndrome in the Army of the Potomac. Men in the ranks had learned what European armies on the Western Front a half-century later would have to learn all over again about trench warfare. "The men feel at present a great horror and dread of attacking

27. O.R., Ser. I, Vol. 36, pt. 3, p. 206.
28. Catton, A Stillness at Appomattox, 159.
29. Porter, Campaigning with Grant, 179; George Meade, Life and Letters of George Gordon Meade, 2 vols. (New York, 1913), II, 201.

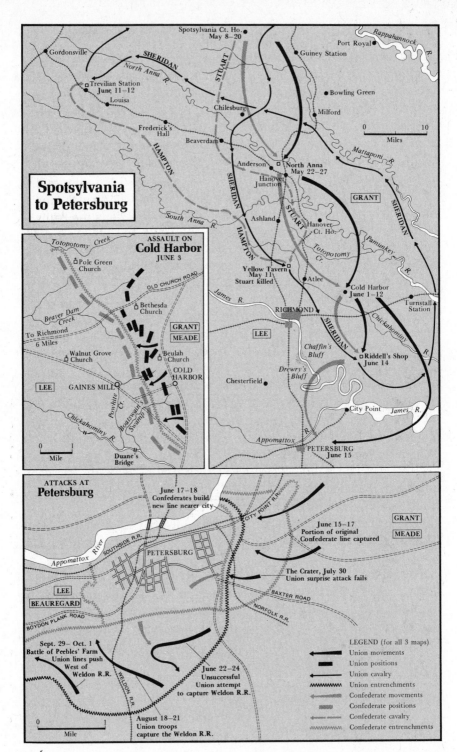

Spotsylvania to Petersburg

Gordonsville

SHERIDAN

North Anna R.

Trevilian Station
June 11–12

Louisa

Frederick's
Hall

HAMPTON

Beaverdam

South Anna R.

Spotsylvania Ct. Ho.
May 8–20

STUART

Guiney Station

Chilesburg

Anderson

North Anna
May 22–27

Hanover
Junction

SHERIDAN

HAMPTON

Ashland

Hanover
Ct. Ho.

Totopotomy
Cr.

STUART

Yellow Tavern
May 11
Stuart killed

Atlee

Port Royal

Rappahannock R.

Bowling Green

Milford

0   10
Miles

GRANT

Pamunkey R.

SHERIDAN

Cold Harbor
June 1–12

Turnstall
Station

Chickahominy R.

ASSAULT ON
Cold Harbor
JUNE 3

Totopotomy Creek

Pole Green
Church

OLD CHURCH ROAD

Bethesda
Church

Beaver Dam Creek

To Richmond
6 Miles

GRANT
MEADE

Walnut Grove
Church

Beulah
Church

COLD
HARBOR

LEE

GAINES MILL

COLD
HARBOR

Powhite Cr.

Boatswain's Swamp

Chickahominy R.

0   1
Mile

Duane's
Bridge

James R.

RICHMOND

LEE

SHERIDAN

Chaffin's
Bluff

Drewry's
Bluff

Chesterfield

Riddell's Shop
June 14

City Point   James R.

Appomattox R.

PETERSBURG
June 15

ATTACKS AT
Petersburg

June 17–18
Confederates build
new line nearer city

CITY POINT R.R.

June 15–17
Portion of original
Confederate line captured

GRANT

MEADE

Appomattox River

SOUTHSIDE R.R.

PETERSBURG

The Crater, July 30
Union surprise attack fails

BAXTER ROAD

LEE

BEAUREGARD

NORFOLK R.R.

BOYDON PLANK ROAD

Sept. 29– Oct. 1
Battle of Peebles' Farm
Union lines push
West of
Weldon R.R.

WELDON R.R.

June 22–24
Unsuccessful
Union attempt
to capture Weldon R.R.

August 18–21
Union troops
capture the Weldon R.R.

0   1
Mile

LEGEND (for all 3 maps)

Union movements

Union positions

Union cavalry

Union entrenchments

Confederate movements

Confederate positions

Confederate cavalry

Confederate entrenchments

earthworks again," was how one officer put it.[30] So Grant devised a new three-part plan to cut Lee's supply lines and flank him out of his trenches. He ordered the army in the Shenandoah Valley, now led by David Hunter, to renew Sigel's aborted effort to move up the Valley (southward) and destroy its railroads, cross the Blue Ridge to smash the Confederate supply depot at Lynchburg, and continue east toward Richmond, wrecking the railroads and the James River Canal. At the same time Sheridan was to take two cavalry divisions westward on a raid to lay waste the same railroads from the other end and link up with Hunter midway for a grand climax of demolition before rejoining the Army of the Potomac somewhere south of Richmond. While all this was going on, Grant planned to disengage from Cold Harbor, march swiftly to cross the James, seize Petersburg with its hub of railroads linking Richmond to the South, and force Lee into the open.

Federal units carried out handsomely the first step in each part of this intricate plan. But thereafter the vigorous Confederate responses plus failures of nerve by subordinate Union commanders brought all three efforts to a halt. Out in the Valley, Hunter's 15,000 men constituted his first field command since he had been wounded at Bull Run in 1861. His main distinction in the war stemmed from his abortive attempt in 1862 to abolish slavery along the south Atlantic coast and to raise the first black regiment there. He was eager to achieve a military success. On June 5 at Piedmont, Virginia—halfway between Harrisonburg and Staunton—his men got him off on the right foot by overrunning a smaller rebel force, killing its commander, and capturing more than a thousand prisoners. Hunter moved on through Staunton to Lexington, home of the Virginia Military Institute.

Along the way his soldiers destroyed a good deal more than military property. Many of them had spent the war fighting guerrillas in western Virginia. The foremost of such enemies was John Singleton Mosby. A diminutive but fearless man who a decade earlier had been expelled from the University of Virginia and jailed for shooting a fellow student, Mosby studied law in prison, received a pardon from the governor, and became a lawyer. After serving as a cavalry scout for Jeb Stuart, Mosby raised a guerrilla company under the Partisan Ranger Act of April 1862. His fame spread with such exploits as the capture of a northern general in bed ten miles from Washington in March 1863. Never totaling more than 800 men, Mosby's partisans operated in squads of twenty to eighty

30. Catton, A Stillness at Appomattox, 159.

and attacked Union outposts, wagon trains, and stragglers with such fury and efficiency that whole counties in northern Virginia became known as Mosby's Confederacy. No Union supplies could move in this area except under heavy guard.

Southerners lionized Mosby's partisans and numerous other guerrilla bands in Virginia for their boldness and dash. Northern soldiers expressed a different view. To one bitter bluecoat, Mosby's raiders were " 'honest farmers' who have taken the oath of allegiance [to the Union] a few times" and then

> arm[ed] themselves with anything that comes handy—pistols, sabres, carbines, shotguns, etc. and being mounted and in citizen clothes proceed to lay in wait for some poor devil of a blue jacket. If they can catch a few after berries, without arms, their valor shines—they take 'em and kill them on the spot. . . . But if a body of troops come upon them they plunge into a piece of woods, hide their arms, and "dig" for some house. . . . The gallant Chevalier of Southern Maidens, Mosby, continues to dash out on sutlers, where he can find them unguarded or broken down, and he generally takes them without loss of a man. Now and then an ambulance or two, full of sick men, is taken by him without loss.[31]

Union soldiers were not likely to treat with kid gloves any guerrillas they caught or the civilian population among whom—in Mao Tse-tung's phrase—the partisans swam like fish in the sea. During Hunter's advance up the Valley, guerrillas swarmed over his supply wagons. The farther from his base he marched, the more vulnerable became his communications. For a month after May 20 only one wagon train got through. Getting angrier as they grew hungrier, Hunter's men foraged savagely from civilians and burned what they did not take. By the time they reached Lexington on June 12 the soldiers were in a foul mood. Looting escalated to terrorizing of citizens; destruction of military property escalated to the burning of V.M.I. and the home of the current governor—who had recently called on civilians to take up arms as guerrillas. Justifying their behavior, one Union soldier wrote: "Many of the women look sad and do much weeping over the destruction that is going

---

31. Letters from a soldier of the 122nd New York in the *Syracuse Daily Journal*, Aug. 10, 1863, Sept. 19, 1864, quoted in David B. Swinfen, *Ruggles' Regiment: The 122nd New York Volunteers in the American Civil War* (Hanover, N.H., 1982), 91.

on. We feel that the South brought on the war and the State of Virginia is paying dear for her part." [32]

Short of ammunition because none could get through, Hunter left Lexington in flames and moved on toward Lynchburg. Lee regarded this threat to his rear as most serious. To meet it he sent Jubal Early with Jackson's old corps back to the vicinity of their great achievements two years earlier. Though reduced by casualties to 10,000 men, Early's veterans brought Confederate strength at Lynchburg equal to Hunter's 15,000. Hunter tapped at the Lynchburg defenses on June 17–18, learned of Early's arrival, pondered his shortage of ammunition, and decided to retreat. And he did so *westward*, into West Virginia, rather than risk a movement back down the Valley with guerrillas on his flanks and Early in his rear. This path of retreat left the Valley open to the Confederates. Believing that Early would draw more strength away from Grant by staying there than by returning to the Richmond front, Lee authorized him to emulate Jackson by using the Valley as an avenue to threaten Maryland and Washington. Hunter spent the rest of the war rationalizing his decision to retreat into West Virginia, but he soon lost his command as well as his reputation.

Sheridan's raid fared only slightly better than Hunter's expedition. Lee sent 5,000 of his cavalry to head off Sheridan's 7,000. The rebel horsemen were now commanded by Wade Hampton, a South Carolina planter reputed to be the richest man in the South, who had already been wounded three times in this war. Catching up with the Federals sixty miles northwest of Richmond, the gray troopers slugged it out with Sheridan's men for two days near Trevilian Station on June 11–12. With casualties of 20 percent on each side, this was the bloodiest cavalry action of the war. On the Union side a Michigan brigade commanded by George Armstrong Custer did the hardest fighting. Sheridan managed to keep the graybacks at bay while he tore up the railroad, but he abandoned the plan to link up with Hunter, and the southerners soon repaired the railroad.

While all this was going on, the whole Army of the Potomac withdrew from Cold Harbor on the night of June 12–13. While one corps went around to the James by water, the other four marched overland, screened by the one cavalry division that Sheridan had left behind. So smoothly was the operation carried out, with feints toward Richmond

32. Virgil Carrington Jones, *Gray Ghosts and Rebel Raiders*, 2 vols. (Mockingird Books ed., Atlanta, 1973), II, 73.

to confuse Lee, that the Confederate commander remained puzzled for several days about Grant's intentions. Meanwhile Union engineers built perhaps the longest pontoon bridge in military history, 2,100 feet, anchored to hold against strong tidal currents and a four-foot tidal rise and fall. Bluecoats began crossing the James on June 14 and next day two corps approached Petersburg, which was held by Beauregard with a scratch force of 2,500. Grant had borrowed a leaf from his Vicksburg campaign and gotten in the enemy's rear before his opponent realized what was happening.

But the denouement was different from Vicksburg, because Grant's corps commanders failed him here and because Beauregard and Lee were not Pemberton and Johnston. The first Union troops to reach Petersburg were the 18th Corps, which Grant had borrowed from Butler two weeks earlier for the Cold Harbor assault. Their commander was William F. "Baldy" Smith, who had quarreled with Butler and had not distinguished himself in this theater. With a chance to retrieve his reputation, Smith became cautious as he approached Petersburg and surveyed the formidable defensive line: ten miles of twenty-foot thick breastworks and trenches fronted by fifteen-foot ditches and linking fifty-five artillery redans bristling with cannon. Having seen at Cold Harbor what happened to soldiers attacking much less imposing works, Smith paused, not realizing that Beauregard had only a handful of men to hold them. The Union forces finally went forward near sundown and easily captured more than a mile of line and sixteen guns. One of Smith's three divisions was composed of black troops who tasted here their first combat and performed well. As a bright moon lighted the captured trenches, Smith took counsel of rumors that reinforcements from Lee had arrived and failed to push on. "Petersburg at that hour," wrote Beauregard after the war, "was clearly at the mercy of the Federal commander, who had all but captured it."[33]

More such missed opportunities crowded the next three days. On the night of June 15–16, Beauregard's survivors desperately entrenched a new line while two rebel divisions from north of the James came to bolster it. Next day another two Union corps arrived and in late afternoon 48,000 bluecoats seized more of Beauregard's lines but did not achieve a breakthrough. By June 17, Lee recognized that Grant was bringing almost his whole army south of the James. Although the Union

33. P. G. T. Beauregard, "Four Days of Battle at Petersburg," *Battles and Leaders*, IV, 541.

forces that day missed a chance to turn the Confederate right, their disjointed attacks did force Beauregard to pull his whole line back at night almost to the outskirts of Petersburg while proclaiming, melodramatically, that "the last hour of the Confederacy had arrived."[34] At dawn on June 18 some 70,000 Federals stumbled forward but overran nothing but empty trenches. By the time they got into position again for an attack on the new rebel line, Lee with most of his troops had arrived to defend it.

The Cold Harbor syndrome inhibited Union soldiers from pressing home their assaults. Corps commanders executed orders sluggishly, waiting in Alphonse-Gaston fashion for other units on their left or right to move, so nobody moved at all. General Meade's famous temper snapped on the afternoon of June 18. "What additional orders to attack you require I cannot imagine," he railed at one hapless commander by field telegraph. To another: "Finding it impossible to effect cooperation by appointing an hour for attack, I have sent an order to each corps commander to attack at all hazards and without reference to each other."[35] But men who had survived previous assaults on trenches were not eager to try it again. In one 2nd Corps brigade, veterans wriggled forward under cover but refused to get up and charge across bullet-swept open ground. Next to them one of the converted heavy artillery regiments, the 1st Maine, prepared to sweep ahead in 1861 picture-book style. "Lie down, you damn fools," called the veterans. "You can't take them forts!" But the heavies went in anyway and were shot to pieces, losing 632 of 850 men in this one action. Meade finally called off the futile assaults because "our men are tired and the attacks have not been made with the vigor and force which characterized our fighting in the Wilderness; if they had been, I think we should have been more successful." Grant concurred: "We will rest the men and use the spade for their protection until a new vein has been struck."[36]

Thus ended a seven-week campaign of movement and battle whose brutal intensity was unmatched in the war. Little wonder that the Army of the Potomac did not fight at Petersburg with "the vigor and force" it had shown in the Wilderness—it was no longer the same army. Many of its best and bravest had been killed or wounded; thousands of others,

34. Catton, A Stillness at Appomattox, 196.
35. O.R., Ser. I, Vol. 40, pt. 2, pp. 179, 205.
36. Catton, A Stillness at Appomattox, 198, 199; O.R., Ser. I, Vol. 40, pt. 2, pp. 156–57.

their enlistments expired or about to expire, had left the war or were unwilling to risk their lives during the few days before leaving. Some 65,000 northern boys were killed, wounded, or missing since May 4. This figure amounted to three-fifths of the total number of combat casualties suffered by the Army of the Potomac during the *previous three years*. No army could take such punishment and retain its fighting edge. "For thirty days it has been one funeral procession past me," cried General Gouverneur K. Warren, commanding the 5th Corps, "and it has been too much!"[37]

Could the northern people absorb such losses and continue to support the war? Financial markets were pessimistic; gold shot up to the ruinous height of 230. A Union general home on sick leave found "great discouragement over the North, great reluctance to recruiting, strong disposition for peace."[38] Democrats began denouncing Grant as a "butcher," a "bull-headed Suvarov" who was sacrificing the flower of American manhood to the malign god of abolition. "Patriotism is played out," proclaimed a Democratic newspaper. "Each hour is but sinking us deeper into bankruptcy and desolation." Even Benjamin Butler's wife wondered "what is all this struggling and fighting for? This ruin and death to thousands of families? : . . What advancement of mankind to compensate for the present horrible calamities?"[39]

Lincoln tried to answer such anguished queries in a speech to a fundraising fair of the Sanitary Commission in Philadelphia on June 16. He conceded that this "terrible war" had "carried mourning to almost every home, until it can almost be said that 'the heavens are hung in black.' " To the universal question, "when is the war to end?" Lincoln replied: "We accepted this war for [the] worthy object . . . of restoring the national authority over the whole national domain . . . and the war will end when that object is attained. Under God, I hope it never will until that time. [Great Cheering] . . . General Grant is reported to have said, I am going through on this line if it takes all summer. [Cheers] . . . I say we are going through on this line if it takes three years more.

37. George R. Agassiz, ed., *Meade's Headquarters, 1863–1865; Letters of Colonel Theodore Lyman* (Boston, 1922), 147.
38. John H. Martindale to Benjamin Butler, Aug. 5, 1864, in Jesse A. Marshall, ed., *Private and Official Correspondence of General Benjamin F. Butler during the Period of the Civil War*, 5 vols. (Norwood, Mass., 1917), V, 5.
39. Frank L. Klement, *The Copperheads in the Middle West* (Chicago, 1960), 233; Mrs. Sarah Butler to Benjamin Butler, June 19, 1864, in Marshall, ed., *Correspondence of Benjamin Butler*, IV, 418.

[Cheers]" This Spartan call for a fight to the finish must have offered cold comfort to many listeners, despite the cheers.[40]

In his speech Lincoln praised Grant for having gained "a position from whence he will never be dislodged until Richmond is taken." And indeed, despite its horrendous losses the Army of the Potomac had inflicted a similar percentage of casualties (at least 35,000) on Lee's smaller army, had driven them south eighty miles, cut part of Lee's communications with the rest of the South, pinned him down in defense of Richmond and Petersburg, and smothered the famed mobility of the Army of Northern Virginia. Lee recognized the importance of these enemy achievements. At the end of May he had told Jubal Early: "We must destroy this army of Grant's before it gets to the James River. If he gets there it will become a siege, and then it will be a mere question of time."[41]

II

In the long run, to be sure, Lee and the South could not withstand a siege. But in the short run—three or four months—time was on the Confederacy's side, for the northern presidential election was approaching. In Georgia as well as Virginia the rebels were holding out for time. At the end of June, Joe Johnston and Atlanta still stood against Sherman despite an eighty-mile penetration by the Yankees in Georgia to match their advance in Virginia.

While Grant and Lee sought to destroy or cripple each other's army, Sherman and Johnston engaged in a war of maneuver seeking an advantage that neither found. While Grant continually moved around Lee's right after hard fighting, Sherman continually moved around Johnston's left without as much fighting. Differences in terrain as well as in the personalities of commanders determined these contrasting strategies. Unlike Lee, whom necessity compelled to adopt a defensive strategy, Johnston by temperament preferred the defensive. He seemed to share with his prewar friend George McClellan a reluctance to commit troops to all-out combat; perhaps for that reason Johnston was idolized by his men as McClellan had been. In Virginia in 1862, Johnston had retreated from Manassas without a battle and from Yorktown almost to Richmond with little fighting. In Mississippi he never did come to grips

40. *CWL*, VII, 394–95.
41. *Ibid.*, 396; Foote, *Civil War*, III, 442.

with Grant at Vicksburg. This unwillingness to fight until everything was just right may have been rooted in Johnston's character. A wartime story made the rounds about an antebellum visit by Johnston to a plantation for duck hunting. Though he had a reputation as a crack shot, he never pulled the trigger. "The bird flew too high or too low—the dogs were too far or too near—things never did suit exactly. He was . . . afraid to miss and risk his fine reputation."[42] In the spring of 1864 Jefferson Davis prodded Johnston to make some move against Sherman before Sherman attacked him. But Johnston preferred to wait in his prepared defenses until Sherman came so close that he could not miss.

Sherman refused to oblige him. Despite his ferocious reputation, "Uncle Billy" (as his men called him) had little taste for slam-bang combat: "Its glory is all moonshine; even success the most brilliant is over dead and mangled bodies, with the anguish and lamentation of distant families."[43] Sherman's invasion force consisted of three "armies" under his single overall command: George Thomas's Army of the Cumberland, now 60,000 strong including the old 11th and 12th Corps of the Army of the Potomac reorganized as the 20th Corps; 25,000 men in the Army of the Tennessee, which had been Grant's first army and then Sherman's and was now commanded by their young protégé James B. McPherson; and John M. Schofield's 13,000-man corps, called the Army of the Ohio, which had participated in the liberation of east Tennessee the previous autumn. This composite army was tied to a vulnerable single-track railroad for its supplies. The topography of northern Georgia favored the defense even more than in Virginia. Steep, rugged mountains interlaced by swift rivers dominated the landscape between Chattanooga and Atlanta. Johnston's army of 50,000 (soon to be reinforced to 65,000 by troops from Alabama) took position on Rocky Face Ridge flanking the railroad twenty-five miles south of Chattanooga and dared the Yankees to come on.

Sherman declined to enter this "terrible door of death." Instead, like a boxer he jabbed with his left—Thomas and Schofield—to fix Johnston's attention on the ridge, and sent McPherson on a wide swing to the right through mountain gaps to hit the railroad at Resaca, fifteen miles in the Confederate rear. Through an oversight by Johnston's cavalry, Snake Creek Gap was almost unguarded when McPherson's fast-marching infantry poured through on May 9. Finding Resaca protected

42. Woodward, Chesnut's Civil War, 268.
43. Basil H. Liddell Hart, Sherman: Soldier, Realist, American (New York, 1929), 402.

by strong earthworks, however, McPherson skirmished cautiously, over-estimated the force opposing him (there were only two brigades), and pulled back without reaching the railroad. Alerted to this threat in his rear, Johnston sent additional troops to Resaca and then retreated with his whole army to this point on the night of May 12–13. Sherman's knockout punch never landed. "Well, Mac," he told the chagrined McPherson, "you missed the opportunity of your life."[44]

For three days Sherman's whole force probed the Resaca defenses without finding a weak spot. Once again part of McPherson's army swung southward by the right flank, crossed the Oostanaula River, and threatened Johnston's railroad lifeline. Disengaging skillfully, the southerners withdrew down the tracks, paused briefly fifteen miles to the south for an aborted counterpunch against the pursuing Yankees, then continued another ten miles to Cassville, where they turned at bay. The rebels wrecked the railroad as they retreated, but Uncle Billy's repair crews had it running again in hours and his troops remained well supplied. In twelve days of marching and fighting, Sherman had advanced half-way to Atlanta at a cost of only four or five thousand casualties on each side. The southern government and press grew restive at Johnston's retreats without fighting. So did some soldiers. "The truth is," wrote a private in the 29th Georgia to his wife, "we have run until I am getting out of heart & we must make a Stand soon or the army will be demoralized, but all is in good spirits now & beleave Gen. Johnston will make a stand & whip the yankees badley."[45]

Johnston's most impatient subordinate was John Bell Hood. The crippling of Hood's left arm at Gettysburg and the loss of his right leg at Chickamauga had done nothing to abate his aggressiveness. Schooled in offensive tactics under Lee, Hood had remained with the Army of Tennessee as a corps commander after recovering from his wound at Chickamauga, where his division had driven home the charge that ruined Rosecrans. Eager to give Sherman the same treatment, Hood complained behind his commander's back to Richmond of Johnston's Fabian strategy.

At Cassville, Johnston finally thought the time had come to fight. But ironically it was Hood who turned cautious and let down the side. Sherman's pursuing troops were spread over a front a dozen miles wide, marching on several roads for better speed. Johnston concentrated most

44. Lloyd Lewis, *Sherman: Fighting Prophet* (New York, 1932), 357.
45. Samuel Carter III, *The Siege of Atlanta, 1864* (New York, 1973), 125.

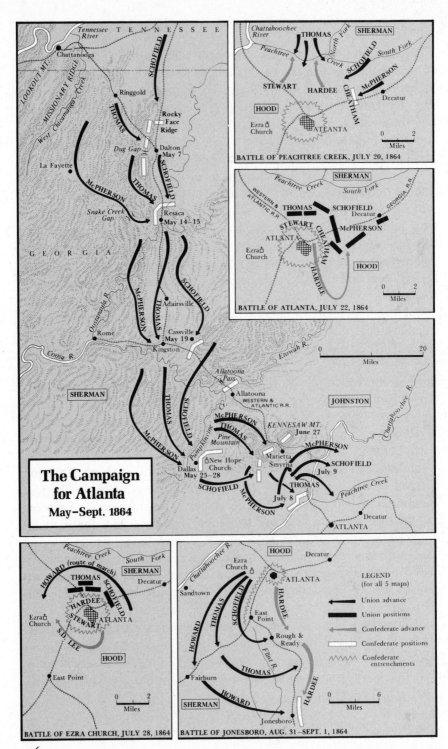

The Campaign for Atlanta
May–Sept. 1864

BATTLE OF PEACHTREE CREEK, JULY 20, 1864

BATTLE OF ATLANTA, JULY 22, 1864

BATTLE OF EZRA CHURCH, JULY 28, 1864

BATTLE OF JONESBORO, AUG. 31–SEPT. 1, 1864

LEGEND
(for all 5 maps)

→ Union advance

▬ Union positions

→ Confederate advance

▭ Confederate positions

〰 Confederate entrenchments

746

of his army on the right under Hood and Leonidas Polk to strike two of Sherman's corps isolated seven miles from any of the others. On May 19, Johnston issued an inspirational order to the troops: "You will now turn and march to meet his advancing columns. . . . Soldiers, I lead you to battle." This seemed to produce the desired effect. "The soldiers were jubilant," recalled a private in the 1st Tennessee. "We were going to whip and rout the Yankees."[46] But confidence soon gave way to dismay. Alarmed by reports that the enemy had worked around to *his* flank, Hood pulled back and called off the attack. The Union threat turned out to have been only a cavalry detachment. But the opportunity was gone; the rebels took up a defensive position and that night pulled back another ten miles to a line (constructed in advance by slaves) overlooking the railroad and the Etowah River through Allatoona pass.

This latest retreat proved a serious blow to morale. Blaming Hood, Johnston's chief of staff wrote that "I could not restrain my tears when I found we could not strike." Mutual recrimination among Johnston and his corps commanders began to plague the army with the same factionalism that had nearly wrecked it under Bragg. Opinion in the government and press was similarly divided: Davis's supporters criticized Johnston, while the anti-Davis faction censured the government for fostering intrigue against the general. In northern Georgia people voted with their feet and took to the roads as refugees. "Nearly the whole Population is moving off, taking their negroes south," wrote one Georgian. "There will scarcely be any provisions raised about here this year, which will seriously effect us another year whether the war continues or not."[47] In Atlanta a note of apprehension began to creep into the newspapers, though most of them continued to praise Johnston as a "masterful" strategist who was luring Sherman ever deeper into a trap to make his destruction more certain.

But Johnston could not spring the trap at Allatoona, for Sherman never came near the place. Instead he paused to rest his men, repair the railroad, bring up twenty days of supplies, and cut loose from the railroad for another flanking move around Johnston's left. Sherman's objective was a road junction in the piney woods at Dallas, twenty miles

46. Gilbert E. Govan and James W. Livingood, A *Different Valor: The Story of General Joseph E. Johnston, C.S.A.* (Indianapolis, 1956), 274; Sam R. Watkins, "Co. Aytch": A Side Show of the Big Show (Collier Books ed., New York, 1962), 169.

47. Govan and Livingood, A *Different Valor*, 277; Carter, *Siege of Atlanta*, 130.

in Johnston's rear and not much farther from Atlanta itself. But Johnston's cavalry detected the move in time for the rebels to fall back on the inside track and entrench another line before the Yankees got there. Sharp fighting took place on May 25 and 27 near New Hope Church before both armies settled in for weeks of skirmishing and sniping (in which Leonidas Polk was killed) as each vainly sought an opening for attack or maneuver. "A big Indian war," the frustrated Sherman called it as continual rains turned red clay roads to soft grease. The two armies gradually moved their lines eastward until both were astride the railroad just north of Marietta, where the Confederates entrenched a formidable position along Kennesaw Mountain and its spurs.

Sherman chafed during this impasse. His concern focused not only on the rebels in his front but also on others 300 miles to the rear. Any significant interference with his rail supply line through Tennessee would cripple Sherman's campaign as decisively as a defeat here in Georgia. And with Bedford Forrest loose in Mississippi, anything might happen. This hard-bitten cavalryman had mauled the Yankees so often that—as Forrest himself would have said—he had "put the skeer on 'em." Forrest's most recent exploit had been the destruction on April 12 of the Union garrison at Fort Pillow on the Mississippi River, where some of his men had murdered black soldiers after they surrendered.[48] When Sherman began his campaign in Georgia, Johnston urged "the immediate movement of Forrest into Middle Tennessee" to cut the railroad. To prevent this, Sherman ordered the garrison commander at Memphis to send out 8,000 men to chase Forrest down. The Federals marched into Mississippi, found Forrest, fought him, and were routed at Brice's Crossroads on June 10 by a force little more than half their size. It was the most humiliating Union defeat in the western theater, but it did divert Forrest from the railroad in Tennessee. Nevertheless, an angry Sherman ordered another and larger expedition out of Memphis to "fol-

---

48. Although formerly disputed by southerners, the truth of a massacre of several dozen black prisoners and some whites—along with their commander Major William F. Bradford, who was captured and subsequently shot "while attempting to escape"— is now well established and generally accepted. For summaries and analyses of the evidence, see Robert Selph Henry, "First with the Most" Forrest (Indianapolis, 1944), 248–69; Albert Castel, "The Fort Pillow Massacre: A Fresh Examination of the Evidence," CWH, 4 (1958), 37–50; and John Cimprich and Robert C. Mainfort, Jr., "Fort Pillow Revisited: New Evidence about an Old Controversy," CWH, 28 (1982), 293–306.

low Forrest to the death, if it cost 10,000 lives and breaks the Treasury. There never will be peace in Tennessee till Forrest is dead."[49] This time 14,000 Federals lured half as many rebels into an attack at Tupelo, Mississippi, on July 14 and repulsed them at a high cost in southern casualties, including Forrest himself who was wounded.

This enabled Sherman to breathe easier about Tennessee—for the time being. The guards he had dropped off along the railroad between Chattanooga and Marietta also managed to keep Johnston's cavalry under Joe Wheeler from doing much damage. But the main rebel force at Kennesaw Mountain appeared to have him stymied as Lee had stalled Grant at Petersburg. Another flanking move on the glutinous roads seemed impossible—it was hard enough to move supplies only six miles from the railhead to the Union right wing. Sherman also feared that constant maneuver and entrenchment without battle was dulling his army's fighting edge. "A fresh furrow in a plowed field will stop the whole column, and all begin to entrench," he grumbled. "We are on the offensive, and . . . must assail and not defend." Reasoning that Johnston expected another turning movement, Sherman decided to "feign on both flanks and assault the center. It may cost us dear but in results would surpass an attempt to pass around."[50]

It cost him dear, but the results were nil. On June 27 several Union divisions assaulted the southern spurs of Kennesaw Mountain near the points where small streams divided Johnston's center from his two wings. As the temperature rose toward a hundred in the shade, Yankees recoiled from breastworks that rivaled those at Petersburg. After the attacks had been beaten back, a Confederate soldier looked around at his fellows. "I never saw so many broken down and exhausted men in my life," he wrote years later. "I was as sick as a horse, and as wet with blood and sweat as I could be, and many of our men were vomiting with excessive fatigue, over-exhaustion, and sunstroke; our tongues were parched and cracked for water, and our faces blackened with powder and smoke, and our dead and wounded were piled indiscriminately in the trenches."[51] By early afternoon Sherman recognized failure and called off the operation. He had lost 3,000 killed and wounded—small numbers compared with battles in Virginia, but the largest for any engage-

49. Henry, *Forrest*, 277; O.R., Ser. I, Vol. 39, pt. 2, p. 121.
50. O.R., Ser. I, Vol. 38, pt. 4, pp. 507, 492.
51. Watkins, "Co. Aytch," 160.

ment so far in Georgia—while inflicting only a fifth as many on the enemy.

Perhaps worse, from the Union viewpoint, the battle of Kennesaw Mountain bolstered southern morale and increased northern frustration. "Everyone feels unbounded confidence in General Johnston," wrote an Atlanta woman, while one of the city's newspapers declared Sherman's army "whipped" and soon to be "cut to pieces."[52] Admittedly the invaders had suffered altogether fewer than 17,000 casualties in the campaign while driving to within twenty miles of Atlanta. But Johnston had lost only 14,000 men compared with Lee's 35,000, and morale in the Army of Tennessee was reported to be "as good as could be desired." After two months of fighting and 90,000 casualties on all fronts, Union armies seemed little if any closer to winning the war than when they started. "Who shall revive the withered hopes that bloomed at the opening of Grant's campaign?" asked the Democratic New York World. Even Republicans seemed "discouraged, weary, and faint-hearted," reported a New York diarist. "They ask plaintively, 'Why don't Grant and Sherman do something?'"[53]

52. Mary Mallard quoted in Carter, Siege of Atlanta, 141; Atlanta Daily Intelligencer, July 3, 1864, quoted in A. A. Hoehling, Last Train from Atlanta (New York, 1958), 23.
53. Carter, Siege of Atlanta, 141; New York World, July 12, 1864; Strong, Diary, 467.

25

After Four Years of Failure

I

Grant and Sherman certainly intended to "do something." But for two more long, weary months their doing seemed to accomplish little except more bloodshed. To be sure, during July Sherman made apparent progress toward the capture of Atlanta, a goal that had come to overshadow the destruction of Johnston's army. Atlanta was indeed a great prize. Its population had doubled to 20,000 during the war as foundries, factories, munitions plants, and supply depots sprang up at this strategic railroad hub. The fall of Atlanta, said Jefferson Davis, would "open the way for the Federal Army to the Gulf on the one hand, and to Charleston on the other, and close up those rich granaries from which Lee's armies are supplied. It would give them control of our network of railways and thus paralyze our efforts."[1] Because the South invested so much effort in defending the city, Atlanta also became a symbol of resistance and nationality second only to Richmond. As the Petersburg front stabilized to trench warfare, concern in the Confederate capital shifted to Georgia, where mobile warfare resumed as the rains ceased.

Slaves had prepared two more defensive positions between Kennesaw Mountain and the Chattahoochee River, which flowed from northeast to southwest only eight miles from Atlanta. Johnston had told a senator who visited his headquarters on July 1 that he could hold Sherman

1. A. A. Hoehling, ed., *Last Train from Atlanta* (New York, 1958), 17.

751

north of the Chattahoochee for two months. By the time Davis received word of this assurance on July 10, the Yankees had crossed the river. Once again Sherman had sent McPherson swinging around Johnston's left, forcing the rebels to fall back six miles on July 3 and another six to the river on the 4th. Sherman now reached deeper into his bag of tricks. Having always moved around the enemy's left, he instructed McPherson and a cavalry division to make a feint in that direction while another cavalry division and Schofield's infantry corps moved secretly upriver several miles above Johnston's right for a surprise crossing against a handful of cavalry pickets. At one point Yankee troopers swam the river naked except for their cartridge belts and captured the bemused pickets. At another ford, blue horsemen waded dismounted through neck-deep water with their Spencer carbines. "As the rebel bullets began to splash around pretty thick," recalled a Union officer, northern soldiers discovered that they could pump the waterproof metal cartridges into the Spencer's chamber underwater; "hence, all along the line you could see the men bring their guns up, let the water run from the muzzle a moment, then take quick aim, fire his piece and pop down again." The astonished rebels called to each other: "Look at them Yankee sons of bitches, loading their guns under water! What sort of critters be they, anyhow?"[2] The pickets surrendered to this submarine assault; Sherman had part of his army across the river on Johnston's flank by July 9. The Confederates pulled back to yet another fortified position behind Peach-tree Creek, only four miles from downtown Atlanta. Civilians scrambled for space on southbound trains. Newspapers in the city still uttered defiance, but they packed their presses for a quick departure.

In Richmond, consternation grew. Emergency meetings of the cabinet produced nothing but "a gloomy view of affairs in Georgia." Davis cast about for some way of "averting calamity."[3] In an unwise move he sent Braxton Bragg—whom he had appointed as his military adviser after the general's resignation as commander of the Army of Tennessee—to Georgia on a fact-finding mission. Bragg was no more popular now than he had been earlier. As a troubleshooter he seemed to cause more trouble than he resolved. He consulted mainly with Hood, who was clearly angling for the command. "We should attack," Hood de-

---

2. Ibid., 58–59.
3. Edward Younger, ed., Inside the Confederate Government: The Diary of Robert Garlick Hill Kean (New York, 1957), 165; Jefferson Davis to Joseph E. Johnston, July 7, 1864, in Rowland, Davis, VI, 283.

clared. "I regard it as a great misfortune to our country that we failed to give battle to the enemy many miles north of our present position. Please say to the President that I shall continue to do my duty cheerfully . . . and strive to do what is best for our country." Bragg urged Davis to appoint Hood in Johnston's place. Davis had already pretty much made up his mind to do so, even though Lee advised against it on the grounds that while aggressive, Hood was too reckless. "All lion," said Lee of him, "none of the fox."[4] Davis decided to give Johnston one last chance: on July 16 he telegraphed the general a request for "your plan of operations." Johnston replied that his plan "must depend upon that of the enemy. . . . We are trying to put Atlanta in condition to be held by the Georgia militia, that army movements may be freer and wider."[5] This hint of an intention to give up Atlanta was the final straw. Next day the thirty-three-year-old Hood replaced Johnston.

This action stirred up a controversy that has echoed down the years. Like Lincoln's removal of McClellan, the removal of Johnston was supported by the cabinet and by the pro-administration faction in Congress but condemned by the opposition and deplored in the army.[6] For his part, Sherman professed to be "pleased at this change." He wrote after the war that "the Confederate Government rendered us a most valuable service" by replacing a cautious defensive strategist with a bold fighter. "This was just what we wanted," declared Sherman, "to fight on open

4. Hood to Bragg, July 14, 1864, in O.R., Ser. I, Vol. 38, pt. 5, pp. 879–80; Clifford Dowdey, ed., The Wartime Papers of R. E. Lee (New York, 1961), 821–22; Herman Hattaway and Archer Jones, How the North Won: A Military History of the Civil War (Urbana, 1983), 607.
5. O.R., Ser. I, Vol. 38, pt. 5, pp. 882–83.
6. Anti-administration newspapers attributed Johnston's removal to Davis's "cold snaky hate" for the general. One army veteran remembered that several soldiers deserted when they learned of Johnston's removal. But some soldiers agreed with an artillery lieutenant who wrote that no one "ever dreamed of Johnston falling back this far. . . . I don't believe Johnston ever did or ever will fight." Richmond Whig, quoted in Thomas L. Connelly, Autumn of Glory: The Army of Tennessee, 1862–1865 (Baton Rouge, 1971), 405; Sam R. Watkins, "Co. Aytch": A Side Show of the Big Show (Collier Books ed., New York, 1962), 172; Hoehling, Last Train from Atlanta, 49, 77. For appraisals of the controversy by historians, see Connelly, Autumn of Glory, 391–426; Gilbert E. Govan and James W. Livingood, A Different Valor: The Story of General Joseph E. Johnston (Indianapolis, 1956), 308–36; and Richard M. McMurry, John Bell Hood and the War for Southern Independence (Lexington, Ky., 1982), 116–24.

ground, on any thing like equal terms, instead of being forced to run up against prepared intrenchments."[7] So he said, with benefit of hindsight. But Davis, like Lincoln, preferred generals who would fight. To have lost Atlanta without a battle would have demoralized the South. And whatever else Hood's appointment meant, it meant fight.

Sure enough, two days after taking command Hood tried to squash the Yankees. As events turned out, however, it was the rebels who got squashed. After crossing the Chattahoochee, Sherman had again sent McPherson on a wide swing—this time to the left—to cut Atlanta's last rail link with the upper South. Schofield followed on a shorter arc, while Thomas's Army of the Cumberland, separated from Schofield by a gap of two miles, prepared to cross Peachtree Creek directly north of Atlanta. Hood saw his chance to hit Thomas separately, but the attack on July 20 started several hours too late to catch the bluecoats in the act of crossing the stream. Five Union divisions drove an equal number of rebels back after the bloodiest combat in the campaign thus far.

Not succeeding at first, Hood tried again. On July 21 he pulled the army back into elaborate defenses ringing the city. After dark Hood sent one corps on an exhausting all-night march to attack the exposed south flank of McPherson's Army of the Tennessee on July 22. They did, but found the flank less exposed than expected. After recovering from their initial surprise the bluecoats fought with ferocity and inflicted half as many casualties on Hood's army in one afternoon as it had suffered in ten weeks under Johnston. But the Confederates exacted a price in return: the death of McPherson, shot from his saddle when he refused to surrender after riding blindly into Confederate lines while trying to restore his own.

Though grieved by the loss of his favorite subordinate, Sherman wasted no time getting on with the job. He gave command of the Army of the Tennessee to Oliver O. Howard, a transplant from the Army of the Potomac. The one-armed Christian general from Maine took his profane midwesterners on another wide swing around the Confederate left and headed south to tear up the one remaining open railroad out of Atlanta. Hood sent a corps to stop them and readied another to follow up with a counterattack. But the Federals handled them so roughly at the Ezra Church crossroads two miles west of the city on July 28 that

7. William T. Sherman, "The Grand Strategy of the Last Year of the War," *Battles and Leaders*, IV, 253; *Memoirs of General William T. Sherman*, 2nd ed., 2 vols. (New York, 1886), II, 72.

the rebels had to entrench instead of continuing the attack. Neverthe-less, they kept the bluecoats off the railroad.

In three battles during the past eight days Hood's 15,000 casualties were two and one-half times Sherman's 6,000. But southern valor did seem to have stopped the inexorable Yankee advance on Atlanta. Union infantry and artillery settled down for a siege, while Sherman sent his cavalry on raids to wreck the railroad far south of the city. One division of northern horsemen headed for Andersonville to liberate Union cap-tives at the notorious prison, but rebel cavalry headed them off halfway. Six hundred of these Yankee troopers did reach Andersonville—as pris-oners. Confederate cavalry and militia prevented other Union detach-ments from doing more than minimal damage to the railroad, while southern raids in turn on Sherman's supply line fared little better.

Civilians continued to flee the city; some of those who remained were killed by northern shells that rained down on their streets. "War is war, and not popularity-seeking," wrote Sherman in pursuance of his career as Georgia's most unpopular visitor.[8] The defiant courage of Atlantans who stayed raised the spirits of southerners everywhere. Much of the Confederate press viewed Hood's attacks as victories. The *Atlanta Intel-ligencer* (published in Macon) predicted that "Sherman will suffer the greatest defeat that any Yankee General has suffered during the war. . . . The Yankee forces will disappear before Atlanta before the end of August." The "cheering" news from Georgia convinced a War Depart-ment clerk in Richmond that "Sherman's army is *doomed.*"[9] Richmond newspapers exulted that "Atlanta is now felt to be safe, and Georgia will soon be free from the foe. . . . Everything seems to have changed in that State from the deepest despondency."[10]

Opinion north of the Potomac reflected the other side of this coin of southern euphoria. As Sherman closed in on Atlanta during July, northern newspapers had daily predicted the city's capture before the next edition. By early August the forecast had moderated to "a question of a few days," and one reporter confessed himself "somewhat puzzled at the

---

8. *Memoirs of Sherman*, II, 111. It should be noted that factories, rail facilities, ware-houses, and other military targets—including artillery emplacements—were scat-tered among residential areas of Atlanta.
9. *Intelligencer* quoted in Hoehling, *Last Train from Atlanta*, 325, and in Samuel Carter III, *The Siege of Atlanta, 1864* (New York, 1973), 275; Jones, *War Clerk's Diary* (Swiggett), II, 259.
10. Quoted in Hoehling, *Last Train from Atlanta*, 167, 251.

stubborn front presented by the enemy." By the middle of the month a Boston newspaper expressed "much apprehension" while the *New York Times* warned against "these terrible fits of despondency, into which we plunge after each of our reverses and disappointments." A Wisconsin soldier, formerly confident, wrote home on August 11 that "we make but little progress toward Atlanta, and it may be some time before we take the place." In New York a prominent member of the Sanitary Commission feared that "both Grant and Sherman are on the eve of disaster."[11]

II

Indeed, Grant's siege of Petersburg seemed even less successful during those dog days of summer than Sherman's operations against Atlanta. Soldiers on both sides burrowed ever deeper in the trenches at Petersburg to escape the daily toll exacted by sharpshooters and mortars. Grant did not cease his efforts to interdict Lee's supply lines and break through the defenses. During the latter half of June the rebels turned back an infantry drive and a cavalry raid that tried to cut Richmond's remaining three railroads, though the Yankees managed to break all three temporarily. In these actions many of the exhausted veterans and inexperienced new troops in the Army of the Potomac performed poorly. The vaunted 2nd Corps, bled to a shadow of its former self, made an especially bad showing. And soon afterward Grant had to send away his best remaining unit, the 6th Corps.

This happened because Jubal Early's 15,000 rebels, after driving David Hunter away from Lynchburg in June, had marched down the Shenandoah Valley and crossed the Potomac on July 6. They bowled over a scratch force of Federals at the Monocacy River east of Frederick on July 9 and marched unopposed toward Washington. This seemed a stunning reversal of the fortunes of war. Northern hopes of capturing Richmond were suddenly replaced by fears for the safety of their own capital. The rebels appeared in front of the Washington defenses five miles north of the White House on July 11. Except for convalescents, militia, and a few odds and ends of army units there were no troops to man them, for Grant had pulled the garrison out for service in Virginia. But the fortifications ringing the capital were immensely strong, and Grant, in re-

11. Northern newspapers quoted in *ibid.*, 92, 99, 107, 126, 221, 278, 330; Wisconsin soldier quoted in *ibid.*, 290; Strong, *Diary*, 474.

sponse to frantic appeals from the War Department, quickly sent the 6th Corps to Washington. These hardened veterans filed into the works just in time to discourage Early from assaulting them.

During the skirmishing on July 12 a distinguished visitor complete with stovepipe hat appeared at Fort Stevens to witness for the first time the sort of combat into which he had sent a million men over the past three years. Despite warnings, President Lincoln repeatedly stood to peer over the parapet as sharpshooters' bullets whizzed nearby. Out of the corner of his eye a 6th Corps captain—Oliver Wendell Holmes, Jr.— noticed this ungainly civilian popping up. Without recognizing him, Holmes shouted "get down, you damn fool, before you get shot!" Amused by this irreverent command, Lincoln got down and stayed down.[12] With the 6th Corps in his front and other Union troops gathering in his rear, Early wisely decided that it was time to return to Virginia. He did so with only a few scratches, much to Grant's and Lincoln's disgust, because the forces chasing him were divided among four command jurisdictions that could never quite coordinate their efforts.

During their raid some of Early's soldiers made as little distinction between military and private property as did many northern soldiers in the South. Indeed, they went the Union invaders one better, for while the latter often seized or burned whatever tangible goods they could find they rarely took Confederate money, which was almost worthless. But northern greenbacks were another matter; the rebels levied $20,000 on Hagerstown and $200,000 on Frederick, besides drinking up the contents of Francis Preston Blair's wine cellar, burning down the Silver Spring home of his son Montgomery the postmaster-general, and putting the torch to the private residence of Maryland's governor. To add further injury to insult, on July 30 two of Early's cavalry brigades rode into Pennsylvania, demanded $500,000 from the citizens of Chambersburg as restitution for Hunter's pillaging in Virginia, and burned the town when they refused to pay.

Early's foray to the outskirts of Washington caused the London *Times* to comment that "the Confederacy is more formidable than ever." Many discouraged Yankees agreed. Gold soared to 285. "I see no bright spot anywhere," wrote New York diarist George Templeton Strong, only "humiliation and disaster. . . . The blood and treasure spent on this

---

12. James G. Randall and Richard N. Current, *Lincoln the President: Last Full Measure* (New York, 1955), 200; Benjamin P. Thomas, *Abraham Lincoln: A Biography* (New York, 1952), 434.

summer's campaign have done little for the country."[13] On July 18, Lincoln issued a new call for 500,000 men, with quota deficiencies to be filled by a draft just before the fall elections. "Lincoln is deader than dead," chortled a Democratic editor.[14]

Angered by the inability of fragmented Union forces to run Early down, Grant cut through the Washington red tape and put Phil Sheridan in charge of a newly created Army of the Shenandoah consisting of the 6th Corps, several brigades from David Hunter's former Army of West Virginia, two divisions recently transferred from Louisiana, and two divisions of Sheridan's own cavalry. Grant ordered Sheridan to go after Early "and follow him to the death."[15] Sheridan was just the man for the job, but it would take him time to organize this composite army. Meanwhile Grant suffered another frustration in his attempt to break Lee's lines at Petersburg.

This was the famous battle of the Crater. In conception it bid fair to become the most brilliant stroke of the war; in execution it became a tragic fiasco. A section in the center of the Union line at Petersburg held by Burnside's 9th Corps lay within 150 yards of an enemy salient on high ground where the rebels had built a strong redoubt. One day in June, Colonel Henry Pleasants of the 48th Pennsylvania, a Schuylkill County regiment containing many coal miners, overheard one of his men growl: "We could blow that damn fort out of existence if we could run a mine shaft under it." A prewar mining engineer, Pleasants liked the idea, proposed it to his division commander, who submitted it to Burnside, who approved it. Pleasants put his regiment to work excavating a tunnel more than 500 feet long. They did so with no help from the army's engineers, who scoffed at the project as "claptrap and nonsense" because ventilation problems had limited all previous military tunnels in history to less than 400 feet.[16] Meade consequently put no faith in the enterprise. Nevertheless, the 48th Pennsylvania improvised its own tools and found its own lumber to timber the shaft. Burnside borrowed an old-fashioned theodolite from a civilian so Pleasants could triangulate for distance and direction. Pleasants also rigged a coal-

13. *Times* quoted in Foote, *Civil War*, III, 461; Strong, *Diary*, 467, 474.
14. *CWL*, VII, 448–49; Frank L. Klement, *The Copperheads in the Middle West* (Chicago, 1960), 233.
15. O.R., Ser. I, Vol. 37, pt. 2, p. 558.
16. Henry Pleasants, Jr., *The Tragedy of the Crater* (Washington, 1938), 32; William H. Powell, "The Battle of the Petersburg Crater," *Battles and Leaders*, IV, 545.

mining ventilation shaft with a fire at the base to create a draft and pull in fresh air through a tube. In this manner the colonel confounded the skeptics. His men dug a shaft 511 feet long with lateral galleries at the end each nearly forty feet long under the Confederate line in which they placed four tons of gunpowder. Reluctantly converted, Meade and Grant authorized Burnside to spring the mine and attack with his corps through the resulting gap.

The sidewhiskered general's enthusiasm for the project had grown steadily from the time it began on June 25. Here was a chance to redeem his failure at Fredericksburg by capturing Petersburg and winning the war. Burnside's corps contained four divisions. Three had been worn down by combat since the Wilderness; the fourth was fresh, having seen no action except guarding rear-area supply lines. It was a black division, and few officers in the Army of the Potomac from Meade down yet believed in the fighting capacity of black troops. Burnside was an exception, so he designated this fresh division to lead the assault. The black soldiers received special tactical training for this task. Their morale was high; they were eager "to show the white troops what the colored division could do," said one of their officers.[17] Grant arranged a diversion by Hancock's corps north of the James which pulled several of Lee's divisions away from the Petersburg front. Everything seemed set for success when the mine was scheduled to explode at dawn on July 30.

Only hours before this happened, however, Meade—with Grant's approval—ordered Burnside to send in his white divisions first. Meade's motive seems to have been lack of confidence in the inexperienced black troops, though in later testimony before the Committee on the Conduct of the War Grant mentioned another reason as well: If things went wrong, "it would then be said . . . that we were shoving these people ahead to get killed because we did not care anything about them. But that could not be said if we put white troops in front."[18]

Apparently demoralized by the last-minute change of his battle plan, Burnside lost all control over the operation. The commander of the division designated to lead the assault (chosen by drawing straws!), James H. Ledlie, had a mediocre record and an alcohol problem. During the assault he stayed behind in the trenches drinking rum cadged from the surgeon. With no preparation and without leadership, his men attacked

17. Henry Goddard Thomas, "The Colored Troops at Petersburg," *Battles and Leaders*, IV, 563.
18. Powell, "The Battle of the Petersburg Crater," *ibid.*, 548.

in disordered fashion. The explosion blew a hole 170 feet long, 60 feet wide, and 30 feet deep. One entire rebel regiment and an artillery battery were buried in the debris. Confederate troops for a couple of hundred yards on either side of the crater fled in terror. When Ledlie's division went forward, its men stopped to gawk at the awesome spectacle. Mesmerized by this vision of what they supposed Hell must be like, many of them went *into* the crater instead of fanning out left and right to roll up the torn enemy flanks. The two following white divisions did little better, degenerating into a disorganized mob as rebel artillery and mortars found the range and began shooting at the packed bluecoats in the crater as at fish in a barrel. Frantic officers, with no help from Burnside or from division commanders, managed to form fragments of brigades for a further penetration. But by mid-morning a southern division commanded by William Mahone was ready for a counterattack. The black troops who had finally pushed their way through the milling or retreating white Yankees caught the brunt of Mahone's assault. As on other fields, rebel soldiers enraged by the sight of black men in uniform murdered several of them who tried to surrender. When it was all over, the 9th Corps had nothing to show for its big bang except 4,000 casualties (against fewer than half as many for the enemy), a huge hole in the ground, bitter mutual recriminations, and new generals commanding the corps and one of its divisions. Grant pronounced the epitaph in a message to Halleck: "It was the saddest affair I have witnessed in the war. Such opportunity for carrying fortifications I have never seen and do not expect again to have." [19]

III

The months of July and August 1864 brought a greater crisis of northern morale than the same months in 1862. The theme of homefront war songs (which enjoyed an extraordinary popularity during the conflict, with sheet music selling millions of copies) took a sudden turn from ebullient patriotism to a longing for peace. *When This Cruel War Is Over*, with its haunting refrain "Weeping, sad and lonely" became the best-seller of 1864, while the chorus of *Tenting on the Old Camp Ground* seemed more than ever to echo northern sentiment: "Many are the hearts that are weary tonight, Wishing for the war to cease." From the presses poured new songs whose titles hardly encouraged martial enthusiasm:

19. O.R., Ser. I, Vol. 40, pt. 1, p. 17.

Bear This Gently to My Mother; Yes, I Would the War Were Over;
Brother, Will You Come Back? Tell Me, Is My Father Coming Back?

Even the spectacular achievement of David Farragut's fleet in Mobile
Bay did little at first to dispel northern depression. As the fog lifted on
the morning of August 5, Farragut took his fourteen wooden ships and
four Monitors past the largest of the three forts guarding the entrance to
Mobile Bay. During a terrific duel between fort and fleet, Farragut
climbed the mainmast to see what was going on above the smoke from
the guns of his flagship *U.S.S. Hartford*. A quartermaster lashed the
admiral to the mast and thereby created an unforgettable image in the
rich traditions of the U.S. Navy. Farragut soon added a memorable
phrase as well. The rebels had scattered mines across the channel. One
of them blew up the leading Monitor and sent her to the bottom with
more than ninety of her crew. This halted the whole fleet under the
punishing guns of the fort. Refusing to countenance retreat, Farragut
shouted "Damn the torpedoes! Full speed ahead." He took his flagship
through the minefield safely, followed by the rest of the fleet. When
they reached the bay they pounded into submission a rebel flotilla led
by the giant ironclad *C.S.S. Tennessee*, the most redoubtable but also
one of the most unwieldly ships afloat. During the next three weeks,
combined operations by the navy and one army division captured the
three forts. Though the city of Mobile thirty miles to the north at the
head of the bay remained in Confederate hands, this last blockade-
running port in the Gulf east of Texas was out of business.

The dimensions of Farragut's victory were more apparent to the North
in retrospect than in August, when so much dismal attention was focused on the apparent lack of progress in Virginia and Georgia. Defeatism and a desire for peace spread from the copperheads like widening
rings from a stone thrown in the water. "Stop the War!" declared editorials in Democratic newspapers. "If nothing else would impress upon
the people the absolute necessity of stopping this war, its utter failure to
accomplish any results would be sufficient." By the beginning of August
the veteran Republican leader Thurlow Weed was convinced that "Lincoln's reelection [is] an impossibility. . . . The people are wild for
peace."[20]

Clement L. Vallandigham had returned from his Canadian exile in

20. Wood Gray, *The Hidden Civil War: The Story of the Copperheads* (New York,
    1942), 174; Edward Chase Kirkland, *The Peacemakers of 1864* (New York, 1927),
    108.

June to attend an Ohio Democratic convention which denounced this "unnecessary war" and adopted resolutions calling for an "immediate cessation of hostilities" to negotiate "a just and lasting peace." Not wishing to revive Vallandigham's martyrdom, Lincoln decided to leave him alone. Aware that the Ohio copperhead had been elected "Grand Commander" of a shadowy organization known as the Sons of Liberty—which Republican propaganda pumped up to a vast pro-Confederate conspiracy—the administration probably hoped that if given enough rope he would hang himself. Instead, Vallandigham's return seemed to kindle a forest fire of peace resolutions in Democratic district conventions throughout the North. It appeared that the peace faction would control the party's national convention beginning in Chicago on August 29.[21]

Believing that all was lost, the mercurial Horace Greeley wrote to the president in July. "Our bleeding, bankrupt, almost dying country," he declaimed, "longs for peace—shudders at the prospect of fresh conscriptions, of further wholesale devastations, and of new rivers of human blood." Greeley had learned that two Confederate envoys were at Niagara Falls, Canada, supposedly bearing peace proposals from Jefferson Davis. "I entreat you," Greeley wrote Lincoln, "to submit overtures for pacification to the Southern insurgents." The president responded immediately, authorizing Greeley to bring to Washington under safe conduct "any person anywhere professing to have any proposition of Jefferson Davis in writing, for peace, embracing the restoration of the Union and abandonment of slavery."[22]

Lincoln knew perfectly well that Davis had not authorized negotiations on such conditions. He also knew that the rebel agents had come to Canada not to negotiate peace but to stir up antiwar opposition in the North. Union detectives had infiltrated copperhead groups that were in contact with these agents in Canada. The detectives had uncovered a series of bizarre plots linked to the Richmond government. Confederate leaders shared with Republicans the conviction that a potent fifth column of southern sympathizers in the Midwest stood poised for an uprising to take their states out of the Union and establish a separate peace with the Confederacy. That this "Northwest Conspiracy" existed only in the dreams of fringe elements among the Peace Democrats did

21. Frank L. Klement, *The Limits of Dissent: Clement L. Vallandigham and the Civil War* (Lexington, Ky., 1970), 262–78; Gray, *Hidden Civil War*, 172–74.
22. Greeley to Lincoln, July 7, 1864, Lincoln to Greeley, July 9, 1864, CWL, VII, 435.

not prevent it from becoming a crucial factor in the calculations of both governments in 1864.

To the War and State departments in Richmond came reports from Confederate spies of "a perfect organisation . . . of formidable character" in the lower Midwest variously known as the Knights of the Golden Circle, the Order of American Knights, or the Sons of Liberty and containing half a million members "for the purpose of revolution and the expulsion or death of the abolitionists and free negroes."[23] Perhaps the most influential such report came from Captain Thomas C. Hines, a Kentuckian and a scout with John Hunt Morgan's cavalry division which had done so much damage behind Union lines in Kentucky during 1862–63. In July 1863 Morgan had led a raid across the Ohio River into the North. After a long chase through southern Indiana and Ohio, Union cavalry had finally captured Morgan and most of his men, including Hines. Imprisoned in the Ohio penitentiary, Morgan and Hines along with several other officers made a spectacular tunnel escape in November 1863. They returned to the Confederacy after thrilling adventures of derring-do. These credentials helped Hines persuade southern leaders of the potential for Canadian-based sabotage operations against the North. In a secret session on February 15, 1864, the Confederate Congress appropriated $5 million for this purpose. Jefferson Davis dispatched Hines to Canada with instructions to take charge of other escaped rebel prisoners there and to carry out "appropriate enterprises of war against our enemies." On his way through the North, Hines was to "confer with the leading persons friendly or attached to the cause of the Confederacy, or who may be advocates of peace, and do all in your power to induce our friends to organize and prepare themselves to render such aid as circumstances may allow."[24]

The Confederate government also sent a number of civilian agents by blockade-runner to Canada. Leaders of this group were Jacob Thompson, a former U.S. secretary of the interior in the Buchanan administration, and Clement C. Clay, former U.S. senator from Alabama. Both men had many friends among northern Democrats. During

23. Oscar A. Kinchen, *Confederate Operations in Canada and the North* (North Quincy, Mass., 1970), 29–30; Larry E. Nelson, *Bullets, Ballots, and Rhetoric: Confederate Policy for the United States Presidential Contest of 1864* (University, Ala., 1980), 19–20; Jones, *War Clerk's Diary* (Swiggett), II, 155.
24. *Journal of the Confederate Congress* (Washington, 1905), VI, 845; Secretary of War James A. Seddon to Hines, March 16, 1864, in James D. Horan, *Confederate Agent: A Discovery in History* (New York, 1954), 72–73.

the summer of 1864 these rebel agents conferred with dozens of Peace Democrats (including Vallandigham before he returned to the United States) at various cities in Canada, especially St. Catherines near Niagara Falls. They plotted a fantastic variety of activities ranging from Confederate subsidies of Democratic newspapers and of peace candidates for state offices to the capture of a Union gunboat on Lake Erie and the liberation of Confederate prisoners at Johnson's Island on that lake and at Camp Douglas near Chicago. Some of these operations actually occurred. Thompson channelled funds to newspapers, to organizers of peace rallies, and to the Democratic candidate for governor in Illinois. Rebel agents distributed weapons and canisters of "Greek fire" to copperheads. Hines's arson squad of southern soldiers who had escaped from Union prisons filtered back into the states and managed to destroy or damage a half-dozen military steamboats at St. Louis, an army warehouse at Mattoon, Illinois, and several hotels in New York City. They also carried out a daring raid across the border to rob the banks of St. Albans, Vermont. In an official report on his mission, Jacob Thompson claimed that subsidized copperheads had burned "a great amount of property" in northern cities. "[We must continue] to burn whenever it is practicable, and thus make the men of property feel their insecurity and tire them out with the war."[25]

The success of Canadian-based rebel operations, however, was inhibited by two contradictions. First, Hines and his colleagues were trying to prod *peace* Democrats into *war* against their own government. A few bellicose copperheads did hide caches of arms in anticipation of the glorious day of insurrection against Union arsenals and POW camps. But that day never came, for these "leaders" could not mobilize their followers. The vast army of Sons of Liberty ready to rise and overthrow

25. Thompson to Judah P. Benjamin, Dec. 3, 1864, in *O.R.*, Ser. I, Vol. 43, pt. 2, pp. 930–36. Much of the information in this paragraph is drawn from Kinchen, *Confederate Operations in Canada*, and Nelson, *Bullets, Ballots, and Rhetoric*, which are scholarly studies based on captured Confederate documents and on the papers of Confederate officials; and from Horan, *Confederate Agent*, a somewhat sensationalized account heavily dependent on the memoirs of Hines and other Confederate agents. Even Frank Klement, the leading historian of the copperheads who considers most evidence of their conniving with rebels to be a tissue of "rumors, conjecture, and fancy" woven by Republicans for political purposes, admits that Confederate agents turned over money and arms to several Peace Democrats in 1864. Klement, *Dark Lanterns: Secret Political Societies, Conspiracies, and Treason Trials in the Civil War* (Baton Rouge, 1984), 33, 154–77.

Lincoln's tyranny turned out to be a phantom. No fewer than five planned "uprisings" died a-borning.

The first was intended to coincide with Vallandigham's return to Ohio in June. His expected arrest was to be the signal. But the administration left Vallandigham alone. Hopes next turned to the Democratic convention scheduled to open in Chicago on July 4. Anticipating an attempt by the government or by Republican vigilantes to interfere with the gathering, the Canadian plotters intended to fan the ensuing riot into a rebellion. But the uncertain military situation caused the Democratic National Committee to postpone the convention until August 29. Impatient Confederate agents now demanded action on July 20, after Lincoln announced his expected draft call. Hines and his ex-soldiers would "start the ball" and the legions of copperheads would take their arms out of hiding to "join in the play." Thompson was confident of success; a Chicago Democrat had promised two regiments "eager, ready, organized, and armed"; Indiana Sons of Liberty were prepared "to seize and hold Indianapolis and release the prisoners there." Lincoln did issue a draft call on July 18, but copperhead leaders were getting cold feet. One of them confessed himself "overwhelmed with the responsibility of speedy action on so momentous a subject."[26] Others echoed this sentiment; with a groan of exasperation, the rebel agents called off the operation and summoned a half-dozen Sons of Liberty to St. Catherines for a meeting.

The southerners insisted on an irrevocable date of August 16 for an uprising. Again the copperheads demurred, fearing that Federal troops would easily crush them unless a Confederate invasion of Kentucky or Missouri took place at the same time. Unable to promise such an undertaking, the agents agreed to a final postponement until August 29, when the throngs at the Democratic convention would provide a cover for Hines's commandos and Sons of Liberty to gather for an attack on Camp Douglas to release the prisoners. Hines brought seventy men armed with revolvers to Chicago, where they mixed with the crowds and hunted in vain for their allies. They found only a few, who explained that infiltration by Union agents had led to the arrest of several leaders and the strengthening of the guard at Camp Douglas. The plot collapsed. One disappointed copperhead declared angrily that there were "too many political soldiers in the Sons of Liberty. It is as hard to make a real

26. Thompson to Benjamin, July 7, 1864, James P. Holcombe to Clement C. Clay, July 10, 1864, quoted in Kinchen, *Confederate Operations in Canada*, 55.

soldier out of a politician as it is to make a silk purse out of a sow's ear."[27]

In truth, the mainstream Peace Democrats shrank from violent counter-revolution in part because their chances of overthrowing Lincoln by legitimate political means seemed ever brighter as the weeks passed. The civilian Confederate agents in Canada recognized this and encouraged the process with rebel gold. But here a second contradiction arose. For Confederates the goal of peace was independence. But most northern Democrats viewed an armistice as the first step toward negotiations for reunion. Thompson and his fellow agents tried to resolve this contradiction with vague doubletalk. They focused on the need for an armistice now, to be followed by a cooling-off period which, they assured Peace Democrats, could lead to "a treaty of amity and commerce . . . and possibly to an alliance defensive, or even, for some purposes, both defensive and offensive." If Peace Democrats wanted to believe that such a process would eventually produce reunion, the Confederates were careful not to dispel this "fond delusion." They well understood that any cessation of the fighting, in the context of midsummer 1864, would be tantamount to a Confederate victory.[28]

Lincoln understood this too; that was why he insisted in his letter to Greeley on reunion and emancipation as *prior conditions* of peace negotiations. Knowing full well that Jefferson Davis insisted on independence and slavery as prior conditions, Lincoln hoped to provoke the southern agents into saying so and thereby demonstrate to the northern people that peace with Union was possible only through military victory. But on this occasion the rebels outmaneuvered Lincoln.

On July 18, Greeley and John Hay, the president's private secretary, met in Niagara Falls, Canada, with Confederate agents Clement Clay and James Holcombe. Hay handed them a letter from Lincoln offering them safe conduct to Washington to discuss "any proposition which embraces the restoration of peace, the integrity of the whole Union, and the abandonment of slavery." Clay and Holcombe had no authority to negotiate *any* peace terms—that was not their purpose in Canada—much less these terms, which amounted to Confederate surrender. So the Niagara Falls conference came to nothing. But the southerners saw a chance to score a propaganda triumph by "throw[ing] upon the Fed-

27. Quoted in *ibid.*, 72.
28. Clement C. Clay to Judah P. Benjamin, Aug. 11, 1864, in *O.R.*, Ser. IV, Vol. 3, p. 585; Nelson, *Bullets, Ballots, and Rhetoric*, 82–85.

eral Government the odium of putting an end to all negotiation." They sent a report of the conference to the Associated Press. Saying nothing of southern conditions for peace, they accused Lincoln of deliberately sabotaging the negotiations by prescribing conditions he knew to be unacceptable. "If there be any citizen of the Confederate States who has clung to the hope that peace is possible," wrote Clay and Holcombe, Lincoln's terms "will strip from their eyes the last film of such delusion." And if there were "any patriots or Christians" in the North "who shrink appalled from the illimitable vistas of private misery and public calamity" presented by Lincoln's policy of perpetual war, let them "recall the abused authority and vindicate the outraged civilization of their country."[29]

The response was all the Confederates could have hoped for. Zebulon Vance exploited the affair in his gubernatorial campaign against peace candidate William Holden in North Carolina. Southern newspapers used it to paint lurid new strokes in their portrait of Lincoln the monster. In the North, reported Clay with delight, "all the Democratic presses denounce Mr. Lincoln's manifesto in strong terms, and many Republican presses (among them the New York Tribune) admit it was a blunder. . . . From all that I can see or hear, I am satisfied that this correspondence has tended strongly toward consolidating the Democracy and dividing the Republicans." Greeley did indeed scold Lincoln for giving "to the general eye" the impression that the rebels were "anxious to negotiate, and that we repulse their advances." If nothing was done to correct this impression, "we shall be beaten out of sight next November."[30]

Jefferson Davis did something to neutralize the southern propaganda victory by his response to a simultaneous but less publicized peace overture. This one was borne to Richmond by two northerners: James R. Gilmore, a free-lance journalist, and James Jaquess, colonel of an Illinois regiment and a Methodist clergyman who carried a sword in one hand and an olive branch in the other. Although conferring on them no official status, Lincoln permitted them to pass through the lines with the renewed hope that they could smoke out Davis's intransigent peace terms. This time it worked. The Confederate president agreed reluc-

29. CWL, VII, 451; Clay and Holcombe to Jefferson Davis, July 25, 1864, in Nelson, Bullets, Ballots, and Rhetoric, 67; New York Tribune, July 22, 1864.
30. Clay to Judah P. Benjamin, Aug. 11, 1864, in O.R., Ser. IV, Vol. 3, pp. 585–86; Greeley to Lincoln, Aug. 9, 1864, Lincoln Papers, Library of Congress.

tantly to meet with the Yankees; he expected no substantive results, but he had his own peace movement to contend with and could not appear to spurn an opportunity for negotiations. Davis and Secretary of State Judah Benjamin talked with Gilmore and Jaquess on July 17. The northerners informally reiterated the same terms Lincoln had stated in his reconstruction proclamation the previous December: reunion, abolition, and amnesty. Davis scorned these terms. "Amnesty, Sir, applies to criminals," he declared. "We have committed no crime. . . . At your door lies all the misery and crime of this war. . . . We are fighting for INDEPENDENCE and that, or extermination, we will have. . . . You may 'emancipate' every negro in the Confederacy, but *we will be free*. We will govern ourselves . . . if we have to see every Southern plantation sacked, and every Southern city in flames."[31]

With Lincoln's agreement, Gilmore published a brief report of this meeting in northern newspapers. His account appeared at the same time as the story of Greeley's meeting with rebel agents at Niagara Falls. After all the publicity, no one could doubt that Davis's irreducible condition of peace was disunion while Lincoln's was Union. This served Lincoln's purpose of discrediting copperhead notions of peace *and* reunion through negotiations. As the president later put it in a message to Congress, Davis "does not attempt to deceive us. He affords us no excuse to deceive ourselves. He cannot voluntarily reaccept the Union; we cannot voluntarily yield it. Between him and us the issue is distinct, simple, and inflexible. It is an issue which can only be tried by war, and decided by victory."[32]

But in the dejected state of northern morale during August, Democratic newspapers were able to slide around the awkward problem of Davis's conditions by pointing to Lincoln's second condition—emancipation—as the real stumbling block to peace. "Tens of thousands of white men must yet bite the dust to allay the negro mania of the Presi-

31. Several versions of Davis's exact words appeared subsequently in print—three of them by Gilmore in the *Boston Transcript*, July 22, 1864, in the *Atlantic Monthly*, 14 (Sept. 1864), 378–83, and in James R. Gilmore, *Personal Recollections of Abraham Lincoln and the Civil War* (Boston, 1898), 261–73; and one by Judah P. Benjamin in a circular to James M. Mason, "Commissioner to the Continent," Aug. 25, 1864, in *O. R. Navy*, Ser. II, vol. 3, pp. 1190–95. Although these versions varied in wording, they agreed in substance. The quotations here are mainly from the version accepted by Hudson Strode, *Jefferson Davis, Tragic Hero: 1864–1889* (New York, 1964), 76–81. See also Kirkland, *Peacemakers of 1864*, 85–96.
32. CWL, VIII, 151.

dent," according to a typical Democratic editorial. "Is there any man that wants to be shot down for a niger?" asked a Connecticut soldier. "That is what we are fighting for now and nothing else." Even staunch Republicans condemned Lincoln's "blunder" of making emancipation "a fundamental article," for it "has given the disaffected and discontented a weapon that doubles their power of mischief."[33] Henry J. Raymond, editor of the *New York Times* and chairman of the Republican National Committee, told Lincoln on August 22 that "the tide is setting strongly against us." If the election were held now, party leaders in crucial states believed they would lose. "Two special causes are assigned to this great reaction in public sentiment,—the want of military success, and the impression . . . that we *can* have peace with Union if we would . . . [but that you are] fighting not for Union but for the abolition of slavery."[34]

These reports filled Lincoln with dismay. He denied that he was "now carrying on this war for the sole purpose of abolition. It is & will be carried on so long as I am President for the sole purpose of restoring the Union. But no human power can subdue this rebellion without using the Emancipation lever as I have done." Lincoln pointed out to War Democrats that some 130,000 black soldiers and sailors were fighting for the Union: "If they stake their lives for us they must be prompted by the strongest motive—even the promise of freedom. And the promise being made, must be kept." To abandon emancipation "would ruin the Union cause itself. All recruiting of colored men would instantly cease, and all colored men now in our service would instantly desert us. And rightfully too. Why should they give their lives for us, with full notice of our purpose to betray them? . . . Abandon all the posts now possessed by black men, surrender all these advantages to the enemy, & we would be compelled to abandon the war in 3 weeks." Besides, there was the moral question: "There have been men who have proposed to me to return to slavery the black warriors of Port Hudson & Olustee [a battle in Florida in which black soldiers fought]. I should be damned in time & in eternity for so doing. The world shall know that I will keep my faith to friends & enemies, come what will."[35]

33. *Columbus Crisis*, Aug. 3, 1864; Henry Thompson to his wife, Aug. 17, 1864, quoted in Randall C. Jimerson, "A People Divided: The Civil War Interpreted by Participants," Ph.D. dissertation, University of Michigan, 1977, p. 131; Strong, *Diary*, 474.
34. Raymond to Lincoln, Aug. 22, 1864, in *CWL*, VII, 517–18.
35. These quotations are from the draft of a letter to a Wisconsin War Democrat dated

This seemed clear enough. But the pressure to back away from a public commitment to abolition as a condition for negotiations grew almost irresistible. At the same time Lincoln was well aware of a move among some Republicans to call a new convention and nominate another candidate. The motive force of this drive was a belief that Lincoln was a sure loser; but many of its participants were radicals who considered his reconstruction and amnesty policy too *soft* toward rebels. These crosscutting pressures during August made Lincoln's life a hell; no wonder his photographs from this time show an increasing sadness of countenance; no wonder he could never escape that "tired spot" at the center of his being.

Lincoln almost succumbed to demands for the sacrifice of abolition as a stated condition of peace. To a War Democrat on August 17 he drafted a letter which concluded: "If Jefferson Davis . . . wishes to know what I would do if he were to offer peace and re-union, saying nothing about slavery, let him try me." While he pondered whether to send this letter, the Republican National Committee met in New York on August 22. Speaking through Henry Raymond, they urged Lincoln to send a commissioner *"to make distinct proffers of peace of Davis . . . on the sole condition of acknowledging the supremacy of the constitution,—all* the other questions to be settled in a convention of the people of all the States." This would be a public relations gesture, said Raymond, not a real abandonment of emancipation. For "if it should be rejected, (as it would be,) it would plant seeds of disaffection in the south, dispel all the delusions about peace that prevail in the North . . . reconcile public sentiment to the War, the draft, & the tax as inevitable *necessities*." Lincoln authorized Raymond himself to go to Richmond and "propose, on behalf [of] this government, that upon the restoration of the Union and the national authority, the war shall cease at once, all remaining questions to be left for adjustment by peaceful modes."[36]

Having gone this far, Lincoln pulled back. On August 25 he met with Raymond and convinced him that "to follow his plan of sending a commission to Richmond would be worse than losing the Presidential contest—it would be ignominiously surrendering it in advance." Whatever the purport of this ambiguous statement, recorded by one of Lincoln's private secretaries, Raymond did not go to Richmond nor did

August 17 and from notes taken by one of two Wisconsin Republicans who talked with Lincoln on August 19. A modified version of these notes was published in the *New York Tribune*, Sept. 10, 1864. CWL, VII, 499–501, 506–7.

36. CWL, VII, 501, 518n., 517.

Lincoln send his "let Jefferson Davis try me" letter. His peace terms remained Union *and* emancipation. The president fully anticipated defeat in November on this platform. "I am going to be beaten," he told an army officer, "and unless some great change takes place *badly* beaten." On August 23 he wrote his famous "blind memorandum" and asked cabinet members to endorse it sight unseen: "This morning, as for some days past, it seems exceedingly probable that this Administration will not be re-elected. Then it will be my duty to so co-operate with the President elect, as to save the Union between the election and the inauguration; as he will have secured his election on such ground that he can not possibly save it afterwards."[37]

Lincoln expected George B. McClellan to be the next president. McClellan was the most popular Democrat and the most powerful symbol of opposition to Lincoln's war policies. The only uncertainty concerned his position on the peace plank to be submitted by Vallandigham, chairman of the resolutions subcommittee of the platform committee. Although McClellan had endorsed a copperhead candidate for governor of Pennsylvania the previous year, he was widely known as a War Democrat and in a recent address at West Point he had seemed to sanction the cause of Union through military victory. This caused the Peace Democrats to look elsewhere, though they could apparently find no one except Thomas Seymour of Connecticut, who had lost the gubernatorial election in 1863, or Governor Horatio Seymour of New York—who refused to be a candidate. Nevertheless, the peace faction would command close to half of the delegates and might jeopardize McClellan's chances by bolting the party if the convention nominated him. Behind the scenes, McClellan's principal adviser assured doubters that "the General is for peace, not war. . . . If he is nominated, he would prefer to restore the Union by peaceful means, rather than by war." McClellan himself reportedly told a St. Louis businessman on August 24: "If I am elected, I will recommend an immediate armistice and a call for a convention of all the states and insist upon exhausting all and every means to secure peace without further bloodshed."[38]

37. John G. Nicolay and John Hay, *Abraham Lincoln: A History*, 10 vols. (New York, 1890), IX, 221; William Frank Zornow, *Lincoln and the Party Divided* (Norman, Okla., 1954), 112; CWL, VII, 514.
38. Samuel L. M. Barlow to Manton Marble, Aug. 24, 1864, S. L. M. Barlow Papers, Henry E. Huntington Library; James Harrison to Louis V. Bogy, Aug. 24, 1864,

Doubts about McClellan's peace credentials persisted, however, so the party "bridged the crack" between its peace and war factions by nominating the general on a peace platform and giving him as a running mate Congressman George Pendleton of Ohio, a close ally of Vallandigham. Scion of an old Virginia family, Pendleton had opposed the war from the start, had voted against supplies, and expressed sympathy with the South. The platform condemned the government's "arbitrary military arrests" and "suppression of freedom of speech and of the press." It pledged to preserve "the rights of the States unimpaired" (a code phrase for slavery). On these matters all Democrats could agree. More divisive (but adopted almost unanimously) was the plank drafted by Vallandigham: "After four years of failure to restore the Union by the experiment of war . . . [we] demand that immediate efforts be made for a cessation of hostilities, with a view to an ultimate convention of the states, or other peaceable means, to the end that, at the earliest practicable moment, peace may be restored on the basis of the Federal Union."[39]

This crucial resolution made peace the first priority and Union a distant second. Republicans and Confederates alike interpreted it thus, and responded accordingly. "It contemplates surrender and abasement," wrote a New York Republican. "Jefferson Davis might have drawn it." Alexander Stephens declared joyfully that "it presents . . . the first ray of real light I have seen since the war began." The Charleston Mercury proclaimed that McClellan's election on this platform "must lead to peace and our independence . . . [provided] that for the next two months we hold our own and prevent military success by our foes."[40]

BUT . . . From the diary of George Templeton Strong, September 3, 1864:

Clement C. Clay Papers, National Archives, quoted in Kinchen, Confederate Operations in Canada, 93. If McClellan really did say this, it represented a reversal of his position from two weeks earlier, when he rejected advice that he should write a letter suggesting an armistice, and commented: "These fools will ruin the country." McClellan to W. C. Prime, Aug. 10, 1864, McClellan Papers, Library of Congress.

39. Edward McPherson, The Political History of the United States During the Great Rebellion, 2nd ed. (Washington, 1865), 419–20.

40. Strong, Diary, 479; Stephens to Herschel V. Johnson, Sept. 5, 1864, and Charleston Mercury, Sept. 5, 1864, both quoted in Nelson, Bullets, Ballots, and Rhetoric, 115, 113. Neither Stephens nor the editor of the Mercury had learned of the fall of Atlanta when they penned these remarks.

"Glorious news this morning—Atlanta taken at last!!! . . . It is (coming at this political crisis) the greatest event of the war."

Or as a Republican newspaper headlined the news:

VICTORY
Is the War a Failure?
Old Abe's Reply to the Chicago Convention
Consternation and Despair Among the Copperheads[41]

41. Strong, *Diary*, 480–81; *St. Paul Press*, Sept. 4, 1864, quoted in Gray, *Hidden Civil War*, 189.

26

We Are Going To Be
Wiped Off the Earth

I

It happened this way. While Sherman's and Hood's cavalry had gone off on futile raids into each other's rear during the first half of August, the Union infantry had continued to probe unsuccessfully toward the railroad south of Atlanta. When all but one blue corps suddenly disappeared on August 26, Hood jubilantly concluded that Sherman had retreated. But celebrations by Atlantans proved premature. Sherman had withdrawn nearly all of his army from the trenches, all right, but they were marching *south* to slice across the roads and railroads far beyond Confederate defenses. As the Democrats met in Chicago to declare the war a failure, northern soldiers 700 miles away were making "Sherman neckties" out of the last open railroad into Atlanta by heating the rails over a bonfire of ties and twisting the iron around trees.

Hood woke up to the truth a day too late. On August 30 he sent two corps against the enemy at Jonesborough twenty miles south of Atlanta. They found the Yankees too strong and were repulsed with heavy loss. Next day Sherman counterattacked and mauled the rebels. To avoid being cut off and trapped, Hood evacuated Atlanta on September 1 after destroying everything of military value in it. Next day the bluecoats marched in with bands blaring Union songs and raised the American flag over city hall. Sherman sent a jaunty wire to Washington: "Atlanta is ours, and fairly won."

The impact of this event cannot be exaggerated. Cannons boomed

774

100-gun salutes in northern cities. Newspapers that had bedeviled Sherman for years now praised him as the greatest general since Napoleon. In retrospect the victory at Mobile Bay suddenly took on new importance as the first blow of a lethal one-two punch. "Sherman and Farragut," exulted Secretary of State Seward, "have knocked the bottom out of the Chicago platform." The *Richmond Examiner* reflected glumly that "the disaster at Atlanta" came "in the very nick of time" to "save the party of Lincoln from irretrievable ruin. . . . [It] obscures the prospect of peace, late so bright. It will also diffuse gloom over the South."[1] Gloom became a plentiful commodity indeed. "Never until now did I feel hopeless," wrote a North Carolinian," but since God seems to have forsaken us I despair." The South Carolina diarist Mary Boykin Chesnut saw doom approaching. "Since Atlanta I have felt as if all were dead within me, forever," she wrote. "We are going to be wiped off the earth."[2]

Far to the north George B. McClellan digested the news of Atlanta as he wrote his letter accepting the Democratic nomination. If he endorsed the platform, or said nothing about it, he would by implication commit himself to an armistice and negotiations. McClellan felt great pressure from the party's peace faction to do just that. "Do not listen to your Eastern friends," Vallandigham implored him, "who, in an evil hour, may advise you to *insinuate* even a little war into your letter of acceptance. . . . If anything implying war is presented, two hundred thousand men in the West will withhold their support."[3] Early drafts of McClellan's letter would have satisfied Vallandigham: they endorsed an armistice qualified only by a proviso calling for renewal of the war if negotiations failed to produce reunion.

But McClellan's "Eastern friends"—War Democrats including the banker August Belmont, chairman of the Democratic National Committee—convinced him that if once stopped, the war could not be started again; an armistice without conditions would mean surrender of the Union. After Atlanta such a proposal would stultify his candidacy. So

1. Seward quoted in Lloyd Lewis, *Sherman: Fighting Prophet* (New York, 1932), 409; *Richmond Examiner*, Sept. 5, 1864.
2. Larry E. Nelson, *Bullets, Ballots, and Rhetoric: Confederate Policy for the United States Presidential Contest of 1864* (University, Ala., 1980), 119; Woodward, *Chesnut's Civil War*, 648, 645.
3. Vallandigham to McClellan, Sept. 4, 1864, McClellan Papers, Library of Congress.

McClellan's letter released on September 8 repudiated the "four years of failure" plank. "I could not look in the faces of gallant comrades of the army and navy . . . and tell them that their labor and the sacrifice of our slain and wounded brethren had been in vain," he wrote. No, when "our present adversaries are ready for peace, on the basis of the Union," negotiations could begin in "a spirit of conciliation and compromise. . . . The Union is the one condition of peace—we ask no more."[4]

Peace Democrats fumed that McClellan had betrayed them. They held hurried meetings to consider nominating another candidate. But nobody seemed to want this dubious honor, and the revolt subsided. Most Peace Democrats including Vallandigham eventually returned to the fold—though they campaigned mainly for the party and its platform rather than for McClellan.

A similar process occurred in the Republican party. The news from Atlanta dissolved the movement for a new convention to replace Lincoln. The president was now a victorious leader instead of a discredited loser. Only John C. Frémont's splinter candidacy stood in the way of a united party. Behind the scenes, radicals negotiated Frémont's withdrawal on September 22 in return for Montgomery Blair's resignation from the cabinet. Though some radicals remained less than enthusiastic about Lincoln, they went to work with a will. The Democrats' Janus face toward the war presented Republicans with an easy target. "Neither you nor I," said a party orator, "nor the Democrats themselves, can tell whether they have a peace platform or a war platform. . . . Upon the whole it is both peace and war, that is peace with the rebels but war against their own government."[5]

---

4. For an analysis of the successive drafts of McClellan's acceptance letter, see Charles R. Wilson, "McClellan's Changing Views on the Peace Plank of 1864," AHR, 38 (1933), 498–505. Drafts of McClellan's letter are in the McClellan Papers, Library of Congress, and in the Samuel L. M. Barlow Papers, Henry E. Huntington Library. The first three drafts expressed "cordial concurrence" with the platform's call for a "cessation of hostilities" and declared that "we have fought enough to satisfy the military honor of the two sections." Two letters from powerful War Democrats that helped persuade McClellan to drop such phrases from the final version are August Belmont to McClellan, Sept. 3, 1864, and S. L. M. Barlow to McClellan, Sept. 3, McClellan Papers.
5. Robert Schenck, quoted in William Frank Zornow, Lincoln & the Party Divided (Norman, Okla., 1954), 139.

After a slow start in the Shenandoah Valley, Phil Sheridan soon gave Republicans more cheering news. Mindful of Grant's injunction to follow Jubal Early "to the death," Sheridan was also aware of the long record of Union disasters in the Valley. Therefore his Army of the Shenandoah sparred carefully with Early's rebels for six weeks without driving them any farther south than Winchester. Intelligence reports of the reinforcement of Early by four divisions from Lee (in fact he had received only two) added to Sheridan's unwonted caution. Taking advantage of this weakening of the Petersburg defenses, Grant in late August had cut the railroad linking the city to the blockade-running port of Wilmington. Forced to lengthen his lines and protect wagon trains hauling supplies around this break, Lee recalled one division from the Valley. Learning of this from Rebecca Wright, a Quaker schoolteacher and Union sympathizer in Winchester, Sheridan decided to strike. On September 19 his 37,000 bluecoats attacked the 15,000 Confederates at Winchester. The wagon train of one Union corps tangled up the troops of another and almost halted the assault before it began. But with much energy and profanity Sheridan straightened out the jam, got his troops into line, and led them forward in an irresistible wave. Northern cavalry with their rapid-firing carbines played a conspicuous role; two divisions of horsemen even thundered down on Early's left in an old-fashioned saber charge and captured the bulk of the 2,000 rebels who surrendered. "We have just sent them whirling through Winchester," wired Sheridan's chief of staff in a phrase that looked good in the newspapers, "and we are after them to-morrow."[6]

Having lost one-fourth of his army, Early retreated twenty miles to a strong defensive position on Fisher's Hill just south of Strasburg. Sheridan indeed came "after them tomorrow." On September 22 two corps made a feint against Early's entrenched line while a third—mostly West Virginians and Ohioans who had fought through this rugged terrain for three years—worked their way up mountain paths to hit the Confederate left end-on. Bursting out of thick woods with the setting sun at their backs, they crumbled the surprised southern flank like a dry leaf. The Federals again sent Early "whirling" southward some sixty miles to a pass in the Blue Ridge where the rebels holed up to lick their wounds.

"Sheridan has knocked down gold and G. B. McClellan together," wrote a New York Republican. "The former is below 200 [for the first

6. O.R., Ser. I, Vol. 43, pt. 2, p. 124.

time since May], and the latter is nowhere."[7] Grant weighed in with renewed attacks on both ends of Lee's line south and north of the James River. Though failing to score a breakthrough, Union forces advanced another two miles southwest of Petersburg and captured an important fort only six miles from Richmond. Panic gripped the Confederate capital as provost guards rounded up every able-bodied male under fifty they could find—including two indignant cabinet members—to put them into the trenches.[8] But Lee's veterans stopped the Yankees before they reached these inner defenses. Northern newspapers nevertheless puffed this action into a great victory—pale though it was in comparison with Sheridan's triumphs.

Having followed Early almost to the death, Sheridan proceeded to carry out the second part of Grant's instructions: to turn "the Shenandoah Valley [into] a barren waste . . . so that crows flying over it for the balance of this season will have to carry their provender with them."[9] Besides serving as an avenue for invasion of the North, the Valley had supplied much of the food for Confederate armies in Virginia. Destroying its crops would put an end to both functions. Sheridan was the man for this job. "The people must be left nothing," he said, "but their eyes to weep with over the war." Union horsemen swept up the Valley like a plague of locusts. By October 7, Sheridan could report that they had "destroyed over 2,000 barns filled with wheat, hay, and farming implements; over seventy mills filled with flour and wheat; have driven in front of the army over 4,000 head of stock, and have killed and issued to the troops not less than 3,000 sheep." But this was just the beginning. By the time he was through, Sheridan promised, "the Valley, from Winchester up to Staunton, ninety-two miles, will have little in it for man or beast."[10]

This was playing for keeps. Northern barnburners made little distinction between rebel farmers and those who claimed to be loyal to the Union. The grain and fodder of both would go to the Confederates if not seized or destroyed, or it would be consumed by the guerrillas who swarmed around the army's flanks and rear and tried to sting it to death.

7. Strong, *Diary*, 494. At the same time gold rose to 3,000 against the Confederate dollar.
8. Jones, *War Clerk's Diary* (Swiggett), II, 295–96.
9. *O.R.*, Ser. I, Vol. 43, pt. 2, p. 202; Vol. 40, pt. 3, p. 223.
10. Thomas C. Leonard, *Above the Battle: War-Making in America from Appomattox to Versailles* (New York, 1978), 18; *O.R.*, Ser. I, Vol. 43, pt. 1, pp. 30–31.

Partisans cut the throat of one of Sheridan's aides, shot his medical inspector, and murdered another popular officer after he had surrendered. Enraged by these incidents, bluecoated arsonists took it out on civilians whom they believed to be sheltering these "bushwhackers." One Union officer claimed that Sheridan's swath of destruction had finally "purified" the Valley of partisan bands: "As our boys expressed it, 'we burned out the hornets.' "[11]

It was a hard war and would soon become even harder, down in Georgia and South Carolina. Meanwhile the rebels decided that they could not give up the Shenandoah Valley without another fight. Lee reinforced Early with an infantry division and a cavalry brigade, which caused Sheridan to postpone the planned return of the 6th Corps to the Petersburg front. Leaving his army camped near Cedar Creek fifteen miles south of Winchester, Sheridan entrained for Washington on October 16 for a strategy conference to decide what to do next. While he was gone, Early borrowed a leaf from the book of his mentor Stonewall Jackson and decided to make a surprise attack. On the night of October 18–19 four Confederate divisions silently moved into position for a dawn assault on the two left-flank Union divisions. The surprise was complete. The rudely awakened bluecoats fell back on the next two divisions, communicating their panic and causing the whole Army of the Shenandoah to retreat in a rout four miles down the Valley after losing 1,300 prisoners and eighteen guns.

Early believed he had won a great victory. So did his hungry soldiers, who broke ranks to forage in the Union camps. But it was only ten o'clock in the morning. The Union cavalry and the 6th Corps, which had not been routed, remained intact with remnants of four broken divisions scattered behind them. And Sheridan was coming. He had returned to Winchester the previous evening. Puzzled at breakfast by the ominous rumbling of artillery off to the south, he saddled up and began his ride into legend. As Sheridan approached the battlefield, stragglers recognized him and began to cheer. "God *damn* you, don't cheer me!" he shouted at them. "If you love your country, come up to the front! . . . There's lots of fight in you men yet! Come up, God damn you! Come up!" By dozens and then hundreds they followed him. Sheridan's performance this day was the most notable example of personal battlefield leadership in the war. A veteran of the 6th Corps

11. Bruce Catton, *A Stillness at Appomattox* (Garden City, N.Y., 1953), 286.

recalled: "Such a scene as his presence and such emotion as it awoke cannot be realized but once in a century."[12]

While across the way Early seemed mesmerized by his victory, Sheridan reorganized his army during the hazy autumn afternoon and sent it forward in a counterattack. With cavalry slashing in from the flanks and infantry rolling ahead like ocean surf, the Yankees sent Early's graybacks reeling back over the morning's battleground. Driving the rebels across Cedar Creek, bluecoats captured a thousand prisoners along with the eighteen guns they lost in the morning and twenty-three more for good measure. Early's army virtually disintegrated as it fled southward in the gathering darkness with blue cavalry picking off most of its wagon train. Within a few hours Sheridan had converted the battle of Cedar Creek from a humiliating defeat into one of the more decisive Union victories of the war.

To follow it up, Grant tried another double swipe at both ends of Lee's line at Petersburg and Richmond. Though unsuccessful, this forced Lee to lengthen his defenses further, until they now stretched 35 miles from a point east of Richmond to another one southwest of Petersburg. This line was so thin, Lee informed Davis, that, unless he could get more troops, "I fear a great calamity will befall us."[13]

Northerners were beginning to think so too. Scenting victory and wanting to be part of it, many three-year veterans who had mustered out in the spring re-enlisted in the fall. They helped fill enlistment quotas and relieved the pressure of the draft, which proceeded with unexpected smoothness. They also helped restore the Army of the Potomac's tone, which had all but disappeared during the summer under the weight of conscripts, substitutes, and bounty-jumpers.

Republican politicians knew how to use this scent of victory to their advantage. One of their best campaign documents was a poem, "Sheridan's Ride," written by Thomas B. Read after the battle of Cedar Creek. Recited aloud in the meter of a galloping horse (from Winchester to the battlefield), it seldom failed to rouse crowds at political rallies to roars of patriotic fervor:

> Up from the South, at break of day,
> Bringing to Winchester fresh dismay . . .

---

12. Bruce Catton, *Never Call Retreat* (Pocket Books ed., New York, 1967), 374; Catton, *Stillness at Appomattox*, 314.
13. Clifford Dowdey, ed., *The Wartime Papers of R. E. Lee* (New York, 1961), 868.

But there is a road from Winchester town,
A good, broad highway leading down. . . .

Still sprang from these swift hoofs, thundering south,
The dust like smoke from the cannon's mouth,
Or the trail of a comet, sweeping faster and faster,
Foreboding to traitors the doom of disaster. . . .

II

Republicans also knew how to make the best use of evidence, real and imagined, of continued Democratic involvement with rebel schemes hatched in Canada. The aborted uprising at the Chicago Democratic convention did not put an end to such enterprises. The most bizarre was an attempt to capture the *U.S.S. Michigan*, the sole navy gunboat on Lake Erie, where it guarded the prisoner of war camp at Johnson's Island near Sandusky, and to liberate Confederate prisoners there. On September 19 some twenty rebel agents from Canada seized a steamboat near Sandusky with the idea of boarding the *Michigan* whose officers were to have been drugged by northern sympathizers. But a War Department detective had infiltrated the group. The northern sympathizers were arrested and the *Michigan* put on alert. Forestalled, the Confederates steamed back to Windsor empty-handed and scuttled their captured boat.[14]

More ambitious but equally abortive was a plot for an uprising by copperheads in Chicago and New York on election day. Having apparently learned nothing from the fiasco at the time of the Chicago convention, southern agents listened with pathetic eagerness to a few Democratic desperadoes who promised that this time their army of peace men would surely go into action—if enough rebel gold was forthcoming. Once again dozens of Confederate ex-soldiers turned up in Chicago as well as New York and other cities a few days before the scheduled rising. Once again nothing happened—except that Federal authorities, forewarned by secret service operatives who had penetrated the loose security of the Sons of Liberty, arrested more than a hundred copperheads and rebels in Chicago and seized a cache of arms. In New York, Benjamin Butler arrived with 3,500 soldiers to prevent trouble on election day. Whatever his deficiencies as a battlefield commander, Butler

14. Oscar A. Kinchen, *Confederate Operations in Canada and the North* (North Quincy, Mass., 1970), 104–16.

demonstrated anew—as he had done in Baltimore and New Orleans—his ability to cow potential civilian rioters. "This election has been quiet beyond precedent," wrote a surprised resident of New York.[15]

From the supposed hotbed of copperhead sentiment in southern Indiana came spectacular revelations—some of them probably true—of skullduggery and treason. Provost marshals uncovered hiding places containing weapons and arrested several prominent members of the Sons of Liberty. In October these men went on trial before a military court for "conspiracy, affording aid and comfort to the rebels, inciting insurrection, [and] disloyal practices." Testimony by Union agents who had infiltrated the order implicated prominent Democrats including Vallandigham. Republican newspapers fed voters a daily diet of sensational headlines: "REBELLION IN THE NORTH!! Extraordinary Disclosure! Val's Plan to Overthrow the Government! Peace Party Plot!"[16] The military court condemned four defendants to death. Delays and appeals kept them in prison until after the war, when the Supreme Court invalidated the conviction of one of them—Lambdin P. Milligan—on the ground that civilians could not be tried by military courts in non-war zones where civil courts were functioning. The alleged conspirators—along with several others convicted by military courts—went free.

But in October 1864 all that lay in the future. Simultaneously with the Indiana treason trials, U.S. Judge-Advocate General Joseph Holt released a report on the Sons of Liberty that portrayed them as a disciplined, powerful organization armed to the teeth and in the pay of Jefferson Davis to help him destroy the Union. "Judea produced but one Judas Iscariot," Holt perorated, but "there has arisen together in our land an entire brood of such traitors . . . all struggling with the same relentless malignity for the dismemberment of our Union."[17] This report became grist for Republican mills. The party and the Union Leagues

---

15. Strong, *Diary*, 510. Kinchen, *Confederate Operations in Canada*, 148–63, is a sober, matter-of-fact account of the Chicago and New York conspiracies. James D. Horan, *Confederate Agent: A Discovery in History* (New York, 1954), 181–98, 208–10, is a more romanticized story of the same events. Nat Brandt, *The Man Who Tried to Burn New York* (Syracuse, 1986), combines elements of sobriety and romance. Frank L. Klement, *Dark Lanterns: Secret Political Societies, Conspiracies, and Treason Trials in the Civil War* (Baton Rouge, 1984), dismisses these conspiracies as mostly figments of Republican propaganda, but a close reading of this book reveals a considerable core of truth to them in Klement's own evidence.

16. Frank L. Klement, *The Copperheads in the Middle West* (Chicago, 1960), 190.

17. O.R., Ser. II, Vol. 7, pp. 930–53; quotation from p. 953.

printed thousands of copies; Republican campaign speakers quoted Holt freely, equating the Democratic party with copperheadism and copperheadism with treason.

Democrats condemned Holt's report and the testimony of government detectives as "absolute falsehoods and fabrications . . . too ridiculous to be given a moment's credit." Lincoln himself did not take the conspiracy threat seriously, regarding the Sons of Liberty as "a mere political organization, with about as much of malice [as of] puerility."[18] A number of modern scholars take a similar view. The leading historian of midwestern copperheads brands "the great Civil War myth of conspiracies and subversive secret societies" as a "fairy tale," a "figment of Republican imagination" compounded of "lies, conjecture and political malignancy."[19]

This carries revisionism a bit too far. There was some real fire under that smokescreen of Republican propaganda. The Sons of Liberty and similar organizations did exist. A few of their leaders—perhaps only a lunatic fringe—did conspire with rebel agents in Canada, receive arms for treasonable purposes, and plot insurrections against the government. Although Vallandigham and other prominent Democrats probably did not participate actively in these plots, some of them did confer with Jacob Thompson in Canada. Vallandigham was "Supreme Grand Commander" of the Sons of Liberty, and he lied under oath when he denied all knowledge of conspiracies at the treason trials of the Chicago conspirators in early 1865. As Thompson wrote in the final report on his Canadian mission, "I have so many papers in my possession, which would utterly ruin and destroy very many of the prominent men in the North."[20]

Whatever the true extent of pro-Confederate activity in the Old Northwest may have been, no one could deny its potency and danger in Missouri. There the shadowy "Order of American Knights" estab-

18. Klement, Copperheads in the Middle West, 205, 201; Dennett, Lincoln/Hay, 192.
19. Klement, Copperheads in the Middle West, 202; Frank L. Klement, The Limits of Dissent: Clement L. Vallandigham & the Civil War (Lexington, Ky., 1970), 293, 294. See also Frank L. Klement, "Civil War Politics, Nationalism, and Postwar Myths," Historian, 38 (1976), 419–38, and Klement, Dark Lanterns, passim.
20. Thompson to Judah P. Benjamin, Dec. 3, 1864, in O.R., Ser. I, Vol. 43, pt. 1, p. 935. For balanced appraisals of this matter, see Stephen Z. Starr, "Was There a Northwest Conspiracy?" The Filson Club Historical Quarterly, 38 (1964), 323–41, and William G. Carleton, "Civil War Dissidence in the North: The Perspective of a Century," South Atlantic Quarterly, 65 (1966), 390–402.

lished connections with various guerrilla bands that ravaged the state. Confederate General Sterling Price was designated "military commander" of the O.A.K.[21] In September 1864, Price coordinated an invasion of Missouri with guerrilla attacks behind northern lines that represented a greater threat to Union control there than all the cloudy conspiracies in other parts of the Midwest.

Partisan warfare along the Kansas-Missouri border continued the violence that had begun in 1854. The vicious conflicts between Border Ruffians and Jayhawkers expanded a hundredfold after 1861 as they gained sanction from Confederate and Union governments. The guerrilla fighting in Missouri produced a form of terrorism that exceeded anything else in the war. Jayhawking Kansans and bushwhacking Missourians took no prisoners, killed in cold blood, plundered and pillaged and burned (but almost never raped) without stint. Jayhawkers initiated a scorched-earth policy against rebel sympathizers three years before Sheridan practiced it in the Shenandoah Valley. Guerrilla chieftains, especially the infamous William Clarke Quantrill, initiated the slaughter of unarmed soldiers as well as civilians, whites as well as blacks, long before Confederate troops began murdering captured black soldiers elsewhere. Guerrilla bands in Missouri provided a training ground for outlaw gangs that emerged after the war—most notably the James and Younger brothers.

The war of raid and ambush in Missouri seemed often to have little relation to the larger conflict of which it was a part. But the hit-and-run tactics of the guerrillas, who numbered only a few thousand, tied down tens of thousands of Union soldiers and militia who might otherwise have fought elsewhere. The guerrillas' need for sanctuary in the countryside and the army's search and destroy missions forced civilians to choose sides or else suffer the consequences—usually both. Confederate generals frequently attached guerrilla bands to their commands or requested these bands to destroy Union supply lines and bases in conjunction with orthodox operations against northern forces. In August

21. When the O.A.K. changed its name to the Sons of Liberty elsewhere in early 1864, it appears to have retained the old name in Missouri. Frank L. Klement, "Phineas C. Wright, the Order of the American Knights, and the Sanderson Exposé," *CWH*, 18 (1972), 5–23, maintains that Sterling Price's alleged role in the Knights was invented by Union detectives and perjured witnesses. But Albert Castel, *General Sterling Price and the Civil War in the West* (Baton Rouge, 1968), 193–96, while conceding that the O.A.K. amounted to little, asserts that Price was indeed its military commander.

1862, Quantrill's band captured Independence, Missouri, as part of a raid by rebel cavalry from Arkansas. As a reward Quantrill received a captain's commission in the Confederate army—and thereafter claimed to be a colonel.

The motives of guerrillas and Jayhawkers alike sometimes seemed nothing more than robbery, revenge, or nihilistic love of violence. But ideology also played a part. Having battled proslavery Missourians for nearly a decade, many Jayhawkers were hardened abolitionists intent on destroying slavery and the social structure that it sustained. The notorious 7th Kansas Cavalry—"Jennison's Jayhawkers"—that plundered and killed their way across western Missouri were commanded by an abolitionist colonel with Susan B. Anthony's brother as lieutenant colonel and John Brown, Jr., as captain of a company. To a man the soldiers were determined to exterminate rebellion and slaveholders in the most literal manner possible. On the other side, guerrilla outlaws such as the James brothers have been celebrated in myth, by Hollywood films, and by some scholars as Robin-Hood types or "primitive rebels" who defended small farmers by attacking the agencies of Yankee capitalism— the Union army during the war, banks and railroads afterwards. But in reality, as a recent study has shown, the guerrillas tended to be the sons of farmers and planters of southern heritage who were three times more likely to own slaves and possessed twice as much wealth as the average Missourian. To the extent that ideology motivated their depredations, they fought for slavery and Confederate independence.[22]

The most notorious of their leaders was William Clarke Quantrill. The son of an Ohio schoolteacher, Quantrill had drifted around the West until the war came along to give full rein to his particular talents. Without any ties to the South or to slavery, he chose the Confederacy apparently because in Missouri this allowed him to attack all symbols of authority. He attracted to his gang some of the most psychopathic killers in American history. In kaleidoscopic fashion, groups of these men would split off to form their own bands and then come together again for larger raids. An eruption of such activities along Missouri's western border in the spring of 1863 infuriated the Union commander there, Thomas Ewing. A brother-in-law of William T. Sherman, Ew-

22. Don Bowen, "Guerrilla Warfare in Western Missouri, 1862–1865: Historical Extensions of the Relative Deprivation Hypothesis," *Comparative Studies in Society and History* (1977), 30–51. I am indebted to my colleague Richard D. Challener for calling this article to my attention.

ing had learned what Sherman was learning—that this was a war between peoples, not simply between armies. The wives and sisters of Quantrill's men fed and sheltered the guerrillas. Ewing arrested these women and lodged them under guard in Kansas City. There on August 14 a building containing many of them collapsed, killing five of the women.

This tragedy set in motion a greater one. Inflamed by a passion for revenge, the raiders combined in one large band of 450 men under Quantrill (including the Younger brothers and Frank James) and headed for Lawrence, Kansas, the hated center of free soilism since Bleeding Kansas days. After crossing the Kansas line they kidnapped ten farmers to guide them toward Lawrence and murdered each one after his usefulness was over. Approaching the town at dawn on August 21, Quantrill ordered his followers: "Kill every male and burn every house." They almost did. The first to die was a United Brethren clergyman, shot through the head while he sat milking his cow. During the next three hours Quantrill's band murdered another 182 men and boys and burned 185 buildings in Lawrence. They rode out of town ahead of pursuing Union cavalry and after a harrowing chase made it back to their Missouri sanctuary, where they scattered to the woods.[23]

This shocking act roused the whole country. A manhunt for Quantrill's outlaws netted a few of them, who were promptly hanged or shot. An enraged General Ewing issued his famous Order No. 11 for the forcible removal of civilians from large parts of four Missouri counties bordering Kansas. Union soldiers ruthlessly enforced this banishment of ten thousand people, leaving these counties a wasteland for years. None of this stopped the guerrillas, however. Quite the contrary, their raids became more daring and destructive during the following year.

General Sterling Price, who longed to redeem Missouri from the Yankees, was impressed by Quantrill's prowess. In November 1863 Price sent him words of "high appreciation of the hardships you . . . and your gallant command . . . have so nobly endured and the gallant struggle you have made against despotism and the oppression of our

---

23. Jay Monaghan, *Civil War on the Western Border 1854–1865* (New York, 1955), 274–89; Richard S. Brownlee, *Gray Ghosts of the Confederacy: Guerrilla Warfare in the West, 1861–1865* (Baton Rouge, 1958), 110–57; Albert E. Castel, *A Frontier State at War: Kansas, 1861–1865* (Ithaca, 1950), 124–41. The best study of Quantrill is Albert E. Castel, *William Clarke Quantrill: His Life and Times* (New York, 1962).

State, with the confident hope that success will soon crown our efforts."[24] Guerrilla chieftains convinced Price that Missourians would rise *en masse* if a Confederate army invaded the state, which had been denuded of first-line Union troops to deal with Forrest in Tennessee. Scraping together 12,000 cavalry from the trans-Mississippi, Price moved northward through Arkansas and entered Missouri in September 1864. He instructed partisan bands to spread chaos in the Union rear, while the O.A.K. mobilized civilians to welcome the invaders. The latter enterprise came to nothing, for when Union officers arrested the Order's leaders the organization proved to be an empty shell. The guerrillas were another matter. Raiding in small bands all over central Missouri they brought railroad and wagon transportation to a standstill and even halted boat traffic on the Missouri.

The most effective partisan was "Bloody Bill" Anderson, who had split from Quantrill with about fifty followers—all of them pathological killers like their leader. Through August and September, Anderson's band struck isolated garrisons and posts, murdering and scalping teamsters, cooks, and other unarmed personnel as well as soldiers. The climax of this saturnalia came at Centralia on September 27. With thirty men including Frank and Jesse James, Bloody Bill rode into town, burned a train and robbed its passengers, and murdered twenty-four unarmed northern soldiers traveling home on furlough. Chased out of town by three companies of militia, the guerrillas picked up 175 allies from other bands, turned on their pursuers, and slaughtered 124 of the 147 men, including the wounded, whom they shot in the head.

That same day, September 27, Price's invasion met its first setback 140 miles to the south at Pilot Knob, Missouri. There a Union force of 1,000 men under Thomas Ewing held a fort against assaults by 7,000 rebels and inflicted on them 1,500 casualties at the cost of only 200. Deflected by this action from his initial objective of St. Louis—which was filling up with Union reinforcements—Price turned westward toward the capital at Jefferson City. Here he expected to inaugurate a Confederate governor who had accompanied him. But the Federals had strengthened its defenses, so the rebels continued to plunder their way westward along the south bank of the Missouri. Recruits and guerrilla bands swelled Price's ranks—he welcomed Bloody Bill Anderson to Boonville on October 11—but now they were beginning to think of flight rather than attack. Missouri and Kansas militia were swarming in

24. *O.R.*, Ser. I, Vol. 53, p. 908.

their front; Union cavalry were coming up from behind; and a veteran infantry division was marching fast to cut off escape to the south. In skirmishes and battles east and south of Kansas City from October 20 to 28, these Union forces pummelled Price and drove him south along the border all the way back to Arkansas via the Indian Territory and Texas. Although Price put the best possible face on his invasion—boasting that he had marched 1,400 miles from beginning to end, far more than any other Confederate army—it was a greater disaster than any other southern foray into Union territory. Though he had started with 12,000 men and picked up thousands of recruits along the way, he returned to Arkansas with fewer than 6,000. Organized Confederate resistance in Missouri came to an end.

Best of all from a Union standpoint, the fighting had wrecked most of the guerrilla bands and killed many of their leaders, including Bloody Bill Anderson. Quantrill left Missouri and headed east with the avowed intent of assassinating Lincoln. But he ran afoul of a Union patrol in Kentucky and was killed. In the presidential election, meanwhile, Lincoln had carried Missouri with 70 percent of the vote (most southern sympathizers, of course, were excluded from the polls by refusal or inability to take the loyalty oath). The radical Republican faction triumphed over the conservatives and called a constitutional convention which abolished slavery in Missouri in January 1865. The state's troubles were not over, however, for when the war ended the James and Younger brothers along with other surviving guerrillas were allowed to surrender as soldiers and go free.

III

Sensational revelations of copperhead activities in Missouri helped the Republican effort to discredit the opposition as disloyal. Democrats fought back with their tried and true weapon—racism. On this issue the party remained united and consistent. Sixty-five of sixty-eight Democratic congressmen had voted against the 13th Amendment, denying it the necessary two-thirds majority in the House. These congressmen also published a manifesto denouncing the enlistment of black soldiers as a vile Republican scheme to establish "the equality of the black and white races."[25] Democratic opposition forced compromises in a Republican bill to equalize the pay of black and white soldiers. Under the terms of

25. CG, 38 Cong., 1 Sess., 1995; Forrest G. Wood, *Black Scare: The Racist Response to Emancipation and Reconstruction* (Berkeley, 1968), 42.

the militia act passed in July 1862, blacks enrolled in the army were regarded as laborers and paid several dollars a month less than white soldiers. A concession to prejudice, this provision was blatantly inconsistent with the combat status of 100,000 black soldiers by 1864. In response to bitter protests by abolitionists and incipient mutiny among black troops, Republicans sponsored a law for retroactive equalization of pay. But a coalition of Democrats who opposed any equalization and conservative Republicans who questioned the retroactive clause prevented passage. To satisfy the latter and enact the bill, Congress made equal pay retroactive only to January 1, 1864—except for blacks who had been free before the war, who received equal pay from date of enlistment.[26]

Having gained votes in 1862 by tarring Republicans with the brush of racial equality, Democrats expected to do the same in 1864. The vulgarity of their tactics almost surpasses belief. An editor and a reporter for the *New York World*, McClellan's most powerful newspaper, coined a new word with their anonymous pamphlet *Miscegenation: The Theory of the Blending of the Races*. Pretending to be Republicans, the authors recommended "miscegenation" as a solution of the race problem. This fusion, the pamphlet declared, would particularly "be of infinite service to the Irish." If the Republicans were re-elected they would prosecute the war to "its final fruit, to the blending of the white and the black." Although the Democratic press tried to pump up this hoax into a serious Republican program, few readers except confirmed copperheads seemed to take it seriously.

Democrats nevertheless exploited the miscegenation issue *ad nauseam*. The Emancipation Proclamation became the Miscegenation Proclamation. A pamphlet entitled *Miscegenation Indorsed by the Republican Party* circulated far and wide. Numerous cartoons showed thick-lipped, grinning, coarse black men kissing apple-cheeked girls "with snow-white bosoms" or dancing with them at the "Miscegenation Ball" to follow Lincoln's re-election. The "Benediction" of a leaflet entitled "Black Republican Prayer" invoked "the blessings of Emancipation throughout our unhappy land" so that "illustrious, sweet-scented Sambo [may] nestle in the bosom of every Abolition woman, that she may be quickened by the pure blood of the majestic African."[27] Campaign pamphlets and

26. Ira Berlin et al., eds., *Freedom: A Documentary History of Emancipation 1861–1867*, Series II: *The Black Military Experience* (Cambridge, 1982), 362–405.
27. Sidney Kaplan, "The Miscegenation Issue in the Election of 1864," *Journal of*

newspapers reported that "a great many squint-eyed yellow babies" had been born in New Orleans since Benjamin Butler was there; that New England schoolmarms teaching freedpeople on the South Carolina sea islands had produced numerous mulatto children; and that five thousand mulatto babies had been born in Washington since 1861. This, declared a Democratic pamphlet, was "what the President means by 'Rising to the Occasion.' "[28]

"Abraham Africanus the First" was of course the chief target of the tar brush. "Passing the question as to his taint of negro blood," commented a Catholic weekly, "Abe Lincoln . . . is brutal in all his habits. . . . He is obscene. . . . He is an animal. . . . Filthy black niggers, greasy, sweaty, and disgusting, now jostle white people and even ladies everywhere, even at the President's levees."[29] Lincoln was "Abe the Widowmaker" who had sent half a million white men to their graves in this insane war to free the slaves because he "loves his country less, and the negro more." Commenting on petitions to suspend the draft, a Pennsylvania newspaper urged citizens to "go a step further, brethren, and suspend Old Abe—by the neck if necessary to stop the accursed slaughter of our citizens."[30] And a copperhead editor in Wisconsin published a parody of the song "When Johnny Comes Marching Home":

> The widow-maker soon must cave,
> Hurrah, Hurrah,
> We'll plant him in some nigger's grave,
> Hurrah, Hurrah.
>
> Torn from your farm, your ship, your raft,
> Conscript. How do you like the draft,
> And we'll stop that too,
> When little Mac takes the helm.[31]

For all their stridency, Democrats appear to have profited little from the race issue in this election. For most undecided voters, the success

Negro History, 34 (1949), 274–343; Wood, Black Scare, 53–76, and reproductions of campaign broadsides between pp. 92 and 93.

28. Arnold M. Shankman, The Pennsylvania Antiwar Movement, 1861–1865 (Rutherford, N.J., 1980), 165; "The Lincoln Catechism," in Frank Freidel, ed., Union Pamphlets of the Civil War (Cambridge, Mass., 1967), 1000–1001.
29. New-York Freeman's Journal & Catholic Register, Aug. 24, April 23, 1864.
30. Freidel, ed., Union Pamphlets, 983; Shankman, Pennsylvania Antiwar Movement, 192.
31. Jean H. Baker, Affairs of Party: The Political Culture of Northern Democrats in the Mid-Nineteenth Century (Ithaca, 1983), 40.

or failure of the war was more salient than the possibility of blacks marrying their sisters. Republicans were far more successful in pinning the label of traitor on Democrats than the latter were in pinning the label of miscegenationist on Republicans. If anything, racism may have boomeranged against the Democrats this time, for after Sherman's and Sheridan's victories many northern voters began to congratulate themselves on the selflessness of their sacrifices in this glorious war for Union *and* freedom.

On one issue tangentially linked to racial policy—the prisoners of war issue—the Democrats undoubtedly suffered a backlash, for northerners embittered by the condition of Union soldiers in southern prisons were not likely to favor a party stereotyped as pro-southern. The Democratic platform contained a plank condemning the administration's "shameful disregard" of "our fellow-citizens who now are, and long have been, prisoners of war in a suffering condition."[32] When this plank was written, the overcrowding and shocking circumstances at Andersonville in particular had already become notorious. The anger evoked by this situation opens a window on one of the most emotional issues of the war.

The relatively few prisoners captured in 1861 imposed no great strain on either side. Obsolete forts, converted warehouses, county jails, and other existing buildings proved sufficient to hold prisoners while they awaited the informal exchanges that occasionally took place. Field commanders sometimes paroled captives or worked out local exchanges on the spot after a skirmish. Not wishing the burden of feeding prisoners, the Confederacy pressed for a formal exchange cartel. The Lincoln administration was reluctant to grant the official recognition that such a cartel might imply. After the fighting from Fort Donelson to the Seven Days' poured thousands of prisoners into inadequate facilities, however, the administration succumbed to growing northern pressure for regularized exchanges. Taking care to negotiate with a belligerent *army*, not government, the Union army accepted an exchange cartel on July 22, 1862. Specifying a rank weighting whereby a non-commissioned officer was equal to two privates, a lieutenant to four, and so on up to a commanding general who was worth sixty privates, this cartel specified a man-for-man exchange of all prisoners. The excess held by one side or another were to be released on parole (that is, they promised not to take up arms until formally exchanged). For ten months this arrangement

32. Edward McPherson, *The Political History of the United States during the Great Rebellion*, 2nd ed. (Washington, 1865), 420.

worked well enough to empty the prisons except for captives too sick or wounded to travel.[33]

But two matters brought exchanges to a halt during 1863. First was the northern response to the southern threat to reenslave or execute captured black soldiers and their officers. When the Confederate Congress in May 1863 authorized this policy, which Jefferson Davis had announced four months earlier, the Union War Department suspended the cartel in order to hold southern prisoners as hostages against fulfillment of the threat. A trickle of informal exchanges continued, but the big battles in the second half of 1863 soon filled makeshift prisons with thousands of men. Grant averted an even greater problem by paroling the 30,000 Vicksburg captives; Banks followed suit with the 7,000 captured at Port Hudson. But the South's handling of these parolees provoked a second and clinching breakdown in exchange negotiations. Alleging technical irregularities in their paroles, the Confederacy arbitrarily declared many of them exchanged (without any real exchange taking place) and returned them to duty. Grant was outraged when the Union army recaptured some of these men at Chattanooga.[34]

Attempts to renew the cartel foundered on the southern refusal to treat freedmen soldiers as prisoners of war or to admit culpability in the case of the Vicksburg parolees. "The enlistment of our slaves is a barbarity," declared the head of the Confederate Bureau of War. "No people . . . could tolerate . . . the use of savages [against them]. . . . We cannot on any principle allow that *our property* can acquire adverse rights by virtue of a theft of it." By the end of 1863 the Confederacy expressed a willingness to exchange black captives whom it considered to have been legally free when they enlisted.[35] But the South would "die in the last ditch," said the Confederate exchange commissioner, before "giving up the right to send slaves back to slavery as property recaptured." Very well, responded Union Secretary of War Stanton. The 26,000 rebel captives in northern prisons could stay there. For the Union government to accede to Confederate conditions would be "a

---

33. William B. Hesseltine, *Civil War Prisons: A Study in War Psychology* (Columbus, Ohio, 1930), chaps. 1–5.

34. *Ibid.*, 99–113; *O.R.*, Ser. II, Vols. 5 and 6.

35. Edward Younger, ed., *Inside the Confederate Government: The Diary of Robert Garlick Hill Kean* (New York, 1957), 92–93; Benjamin F. Butler to Kellogg Carter, Nov. 29, 1863, Civil War Collection, Henry E. Huntington Library; Dudley Taylor Cornish, *The Sable Arm: Negro Troops in the Union Army, 1861–1865* (New York, 1956), 171.

shameful dishonor. . . . When [the rebels] agree to exchange all alike there will be no difficulty."[36] After becoming general in chief, Grant confirmed this hard line. "No distinction whatever will be made in the exchange between white and colored prisoners," he ordered on April 17, 1864. And there must be "released to us a sufficient number of officers and men as were captured and paroled at Vicksburg and Port Hudson. . . . Non-acquiescence by the Confederate authorities in both or either of these propositions will be regarded as a refusal on their part to agree to the further exchange of prisoners."[37] Confederate authorities did not acquiesce.

The South's actual treatment of black prisoners is hard to ascertain. Even the number of Negro captives is unknown, for in refusing to acknowledge them as legitimate prisoners the Confederates kept few records. Many black captives never made it to prison camp. In the spirit of Secretary of War Seddon's early directive that "we ought never to be inconvenienced with such prisoners . . . summary execution must therefore be inflicted on those taken," hundreds were massacred at Fort Pillow, Poison Spring, the Crater, and elsewhere.[38] An affidavit by a Union sergeant described what happened after Confederates recaptured Plymouth on the North Carolina coast in April 1864:

> All the negroes found in blue uniform or with any outward marks of a Union soldier upon him was killed—I saw some taken into the woods and hung—Others I saw stripped of all their clothing, and they stood upon the bank of the river with their faces riverwards and then they were shot—Still others were killed by having their brains beaten out by the butt end of the muskets in the hands of the Rebels—
>
> All were not killed the day of the capture—Those that were not, were placed in a room with their officers, they (the Officers) having previously been dragged through the town with ropes around their necks, where they were kept confined until the following morning when the remainder of the black soldiers were killed.[39]

36. O.R., Ser. II, Vol. 6, pp. 441–42, 647–49, 226.
37. Ibid., Vol. 7, pp. 62–63.
38. Ibid., Vol. 4, p. 954, Vol. 7, p. 204.
39. Benjamin Butler to Ulysses S. Grant, July 12, 1864, enclosing affidavit of Samuel Johnson, Letters Received by General Grant, Records of the Headquarters of the Army, RG 108, National Archives, printed in Berlin, ed., The Black Military Experience, 588–89; also published with standard punctuation in O.R., Ser. I, Vol. 7, pp. 459–60.

Black prisoners who survived the initial rage of their captors sometimes found themselves returned as slaves to their old masters or, occasionally, sold to a new one. While awaiting this fate they were often
placed at hard labor on Confederate fortifications. The *Mobile Advertiser and Register* of October 15, 1864, published a list of 575 black
prisoners in that city working as laborers until owners claimed them.[40]

What to do about the murder or enslavement of black captives presented the Union government with a dilemma. At first Lincoln threatened an eye-for-an-eye retaliation. "For every soldier of the United States
killed in violation of the laws of war," he ordered on July 30, 1863, "a
rebel soldier shall be executed; and for every one enslaved by the enemy
or sold into slavery, a rebel soldier shall be placed at hard labor on the
public works." But this was easier said than done; as Lincoln himself
put it, "the difficulty is not in stating the principle, but in practically
applying it."[41] After the Fort Pillow massacre the cabinet spent two
meetings trying to determine a response. To execute an equal number
of rebel prisoners would punish the innocent for the crimes of the guilty.
The government must not undertake such a "barbarous . . . inhuman
policy," declared Secretary of the Navy Welles. Lincoln agreed that
"blood can not restore blood, and government should not act for revenge." The cabinet decided to retaliate against actual offenders from
Forrest's command, if any were captured, and to warn Richmond that
a certain number of southern officers in northern prisons would be set
apart as hostages against such occurrences in the future.[42]

But no record exists that either recommendation was carried out. As
Lincoln sadly told Frederick Douglass, "if once begun, there was no
telling where [retaliation] would end." Execution of innocent southern
prisoners—or even guilty ones—would produce Confederate retaliation
against northern prisoners in a never-ending vicious cycle. In the final
analysis, concluded the Union exchange commissioner, these cases "can

40. Walter L. Williams, "Again in Chains: Black Soldiers Suffering in Captivity," *Civil
War Times Illustrated*, 20 (May 1981), 40–43; Cornish, *Sable Arm*, 177–78. For
two directives from Secretary of War Seddon concerning the return of captured
blacks to slavery, dated June 3, 1863, and Aug. 31, 1864, see O.R., Ser. II, Vol.
5, pp. 966–67, Vol. 7, 703–4.
41. CWL, VI, 357, VII, 382.
42. Howard K. Beale, ed., *Diary of Gideon Welles*, 3 vols. (New York, 1960), II, 24;
CWL, VII, 329, 345–46; John G. Nicolay and John Hay, *Abraham Lincoln: A
History*, 10 vols. (New York, 1890), VI, 478–84.

only be effectually reached by a successful prosecution of the war." After all, "the rebellion exists on a question connected with the right or power of the South to hold the colored race in slavery; and the South will only yield this right under military compulsion." Thus "the loyal people of the United States [must] prosecute this war with all the energy that God has given them."[43]

Union field commanders in South Carolina and Virginia carried out the only official retaliation for southern treatment of black prisoners. When Confederates at Charleston and near Richmond put captured Negroes to work on fortifications under enemy fire in 1864, northern generals promptly placed an equal number of rebel prisoners at work on Union facilities under fire. This ended the Confederate practice. Some black soldiers did their own retaliating. After Fort Pillow several Negro units vowed to take no prisoners and yelled "Remember Fort Pillow" when they went into action. "The darkies fought ferociously," wrote Captain Charles Francis Adams, Jr., of an attack by a black division against the Petersburg defenses on June 15, 1864. "If they murder prisoners, as I hear they did . . . they can hardly be blamed."[44]

Although Union threats of retaliation did little to help ex-slaves captured by Confederates, they appear to have forced southern officials to make a distinction between former slaves and free blacks. "The serious consequences," wrote Secretary of War Seddon to South Carolina's governor, "which might ensue from a rigid enforcement of the act of Congress" (which required *all* captured blacks to be turned over to states for punishment as insurrectionists) compel us "to make a distinction between negroes so taken who can be recognized or identified as slaves and those who were free inhabitants of the Federal States."[45] The South generally treated the latter—along with white officers of black regiments—as prisoners of war. This did not necessarily mean equal treatment. Prison guards singled out black captives for latrine and burial details or other onerous labor. At Libby Prison in Richmond ten white officers and four enlisted men of a black regiment were confined to a small cell next to the kitchen where they subsisted on bread and water

43. *Life and Times of Frederick Douglass*, rev. ed. (1892; Collier Books reprint, 1962), 348–49; *O.R.*, Ser. II, Vol. 6, p. 171.
44. Charles Francis Adams, Jr., to Charles Francis Adams, June 19, 1864, in Worthington Chauncey Ford, ed., *A Cycle of Adams Letters 1861–1865*, 2 vols. (Boston, 1920), II, 154.
45. *O.R.*, Ser. II, Vol. 7, pp. 703–4. See also Howard C. Westwood, "Captive Black Union Soldiers in Charleston—What to Do?" *CWH*, 28 (1982), 30–31, 38, 41.

and almost suffocated from cooking smoke. "An open tub," wrote anther prisoner, "was placed in the room for the reception of their excrement, where it was permitted to remain for days before removal." In South Carolina captured black soldiers from the 54th Massachusetts and other northern units were kept in the Charleston jail rather than in a POW camp.[46]

They probably fared as well in jail—if not better—as their white fellows in war prisons. The principal issue that aroused northern emotions was not the treatment of black prisoners but of all Union prisoners. As the heavy fighting of 1864 piled up captives in jerry-built prisons, grim stories of disease, starvation, and brutality began to filter northward. The camp at Andersonville in southwest Georgia became representative in northern eyes of southern barbarity. Andersonville prison was built in early 1864 to accommodate captives previously held at Belle Isle on the James River near Richmond, because the proximity of Union forces threatened liberation of these prisoners and the overworked transport system of Virginia could barely feed southern citizens and soldiers, let alone Yankees. A stockade camp of sixteen acres designed for 10,000 prisoners, Andersonville soon became overcrowded with captives from Sherman's army as well from the eastern theater. It was enlarged to twenty-six acres, in which 33,000 men were packed by August 1864— an average of thirty-four square feet per man—without shade in a Deep South summer and with no shelter except what they could rig from sticks, tent flies, blankets, and odd bits of cloth. (By way of comparison, the Union prison camp at Elmira, New York, generally considered the worst northern prison, provided barracks for the maximum of 9,600 captives living inside a forty-acre enclosure—an average of 180 square feet per man.) During some weeks in the summer of 1864 more than a hundred prisoners died every day in Andersonville. Altogether 13,000 of the 45,000 men imprisoned there died of disease, exposure, or malnutrition.[47]

Andersonville was the most extreme example of what many northerners regarded as a fiendish plot to murder Yankee prisoners.[48] After the

46. Frank L. Byrne, ed., "A General Behind Bars: Neal Dow in Libby Prison," in William B. Hesseltine, ed., *Civil War Prisons* (Kent, Ohio, 1962), 77; Williams, "Again in Chains," *loc. cit.*, 41; Westwood, "Captive Black Union Soldiers," *loc. cit.*, 39.

47. Hesseltine, *Civil War Prisons*, chap. 7; Ovid L. Futch, *History of Andersonville Prison* (Gainesville, Fla., 1968); *Andersonville* (Eastern Acorn Press, n.p., 1983).

48. No other southern prison ever held more than one-quarter as many men as Ander-

war a Union military commission tried and executed its commandant, Henry Wirz, for war crimes—the only such trial to result from the Civil War. Whether Wirz was actually guilty of anything worse than bad temper and inefficiency remains controversial today. In any case, he served as a scapegoat for the purported sins of the South. The large genre of prisoner memoirs, which lost nothing in melodramatics with passage of time, kept alive the bitterness for decades after the war. On this matter, at least, the victors wrote the history, for at least five-sixths of the memoirs were written by northerners.[49]

During 1864 a crescendo rose in the northern press demanding retribution against rebel prisoners to coerce better treatment of Union captives. "Retaliation is a terrible thing," conceded the New York Times, "but the miseries and pains and the slowly wasting life of our brethren and friends in those horrible prisons is a worse thing. No people or government ought to allow its soldiers to be treated for one day as our men have been treated for the last three years." When a special exchange of sick prisoners in April returned to the North several living skeletons, woodcut copies of their photographs appeared in illustrated papers and produced a tidal wave of rage. What else could one expect of slaveholders "born to tyranny and reared to cruelty?" asked the normally moderate Times.[50] The Committee on the Conduct of the War and the U.S. Sanitary Commission each published an account of Confederate prison conditions based on intelligence reports and on interviews with exchanged or escaped prisoners. "The enormity of the crime committed by the rebels," commented Secretary of War Stanton, "cannot but fill with horror the civilized world. . . . There appears to have been a deliberate system of savage and barbarous treatment." An editorial in an Atlanta newspaper during August made its way across the lines and was picked up by the northern press: "During one of the intensely hot days of last week more than 300 sick and wounded Yankees died at

---

sonville's maximum of 33,000 in August 1864. The largest northern prison was at Point Lookout in southern Maryland, which held 20,000 men at one time. Measured by mortality statistics, Andersonville was not the worst southern prison. That dubious distinction belonged to Salisbury, North Carolina, where 34 percent (compared with Andersonville's 29 percent) of the total of 10,321 men incarcerated there died. The highest death rate in a northern prison was 24 percent at Elmira.

49. Based on a count of the 250 prisoner memoirs listed in the bibliography of Hesseltine, Civil War Prisons.

50. New York Times, Mar. 31, April 22, 1864, quoted in Hesseltine, Civil War Prisons, 194, 195.

Andersonville. We thank Heaven for such blessings." This was the sort of thing that convinced otherwise sensible northerners that "Jefferson Davis's policy is to starve and freeze and kill off by inches all the prisoners he dares not butcher outright. . . . We *cannot* retaliate, it is said; but why can we not?"[51]

The Union War Department did institute a limited retaliation. In May 1864, Stanton reduced prisoner rations to the same level that the Confederate army issued to its own soldiers. In theory this placed rebel prisoners on the same footing as Yankee prisoners in the South, who in theory received the same rations as Confederate soldiers. But in practice few southern soldiers ever got the official ration by 1864—and Union prisoners inevitably got even less—so most rebel captives in the North probably ate better than they had in their own army. Nevertheless, the reduction of prisoner rations was indicative of a hardening northern attitude. Combined with the huge increase in the number of prisoners during 1864, this produced a deterioration of conditions in northern prisons until the suffering, sickness, and death in some of them rivaled that in southern prisons—except Andersonville, which was in a class by itself.[52]

This state of affairs produced enormous pressures for a renewal of exchanges. Many inmates at Andersonville and other southern prisons signed petitions to Lincoln asking for renewal, and the Confederates allowed delegations of prisoners to bear these petitions to Washington. Nothing came of them. Entries in prison diaries at Andersonville became increasingly bitter as the summer wore on: "What can the Government be thinking of to let soldiers die in this filthy place?" "Can a government exist and let their men die inch by inch here?" "I do not think that our rulers can be so base to their men." "We are losing all trust in old Abe."[53] A spokesman for a group of clergymen and physicians implored Lincoln in September 1864: "For God's sake, interpose! . . . We know you can have them exchanged if you give your attention to it. It is simple murder to neglect it longer." From local Republican leaders came warnings that many good Union men "will work and vote

---

51. O.R., Ser. II, Vol. 7, p. 110; *Atlanta Intelligencer* (published at Macon), Aug. 19, 1864, quoted in A. A. Hoehling, ed., *Last Train from Atlanta* (New York, 1958), 330; and in Samuel Carter III, *The Siege of Atlanta, 1864* (New York, 1973), 296; Strong, *Diary*, 494.
52. O.R., Ser. II, Vol. 7, pp. 150–51; Hesseltine, *Civil War Prisons*, 172–209.
53. Futch, *Andersonville Prison*, 43.

against the President, because they think sympathy with a few negroes, also captured, is the cause of a refusal" to exchange.[54]

Lincoln could indeed have renewed the exchange if he had been willing to forget about ex-slave soldiers. But he no more wanted to concede this principle than to renounce emancipation as a condition of peace. On August 27, Benjamin Butler, who had been appointed a special exchange agent, made the administration's position clear in a long letter to the Confederate exchange commissioner—a letter that was published widely in the newspapers. The United States government would renew exchanges, said Butler, whenever the Confederacy was ready to exchange *all* classes of prisoners. "The wrongs, indignities, and privations suffered by our soldiers," wrote Butler who was a master of rhetoric, "would move me to consent to anything to procure their exchange, except to barter away the honor and the faith of the Government of the United States, which has been so solemnly pledged to the colored soldiers in its ranks. Consistently with national faith and justice we cannot relinquish that position."[55]

General Grant had privately enunciated another argument against exchange: it would strengthen enemy armies more than Union armies. "It is hard on our men held in Southern prisons not to exchange them," Grant said in August 1864, "but it is humanity to those left in our ranks to fight our battles." Most exchanged rebels—"hale, hearty, and well-fed" as northerners believed them to be—would "become active soldier[s] against us at once" while "the half-starved, sick, emaciated" Union prisoners could never fight again. "We have got to fight until the military power of the South is exhausted, and if we release or exchange prisoners captured it simply becomes a war of extermination."[56]

A good many historians—especially those of southern birth—have pointed to Grant's remarks as the real reason for the North's refusal to exchange. Concern for the rights of black soldiers, in this view, was just for show. The northern strategy of a war of attrition, therefore, was responsible for the horrors of Andersonville and the suffering of pris-

54. D. C. Anderson and J. H. Brown to Lincoln, Sept. 4, 1864, H. Brewster to Stanton, Sept. 8, 1864, in O.R., Ser. II, Vol. 7, pp. 767–68, 787. See also Samuel White to Lincoln, Sept. 12, *ibid.*, 816.

55. Butler to Robert Ould, Aug. 27, 1864, in O.R., Ser. II, Vol. 7, pp. 687–91; quotation from p. 691. The letter was published in the *New York Times*, Sept. 6, 1864, and printed as a leaflet by the government for general circulation.

56. O.R., Ser. II, Vol. 7, pp. 607, 615, 691.

oners on both sides.[57] This position is untenable. Grant expressed his opinion more than a year after the exchange cartel had broken down over the Negro prisoner question. And an opinion was precisely what it was; Grant did not *order* exchanges prohibited for purposes of attrition, and the evidence indicates that if the Confederates had conceded on the issue of ex-slaves the exchanges would have resumed. In October 1864, General Lee proposed an informal exchange of prisoners captured in recent fighting on the Richmond-Petersburg front. Grant agreed, on condition that blacks be exchanged "the same as white soldiers." If this had been done, it might have provided a precedent to break the impasse that had by then penned up more than a hundred thousand men in POW camps. But Lee replied that "negroes belonging to our citizens are not considered subjects of exchange and were not included in my proposition." Grant thereupon closed the correspondence with the words that because his "Government is bound to secure to all persons received into her armies the rights due to soldiers," Lee's refusal to grant such rights to former slaves "induces me to decline making the exchanges you ask."[58]

In January 1865 the rebels finally gave in and offered to exchange "all" prisoners. Hoping soon to begin recruiting black soldiers for their own armies, Davis and Lee suddenly found the Yankee policy less barbaric. The cartel began functioning again and several thousand captives a week were exchanged over the next three months, until Appomattox liberated everyone.[59]

Few if any historians would now contend that the Confederacy deliberately mistreated prisoners. Rather, they would concur with contemporary opinions—held by some northerners as well as southerners—that a deficiency of resources and the deterioration of the southern economy were mainly responsible for the sufferings of Union prisoners. The South could not feed its own soldiers and civilians; how could it feed enemy prisoners? The Confederacy could not supply its own troops with enough tents; how could it provide tents for captives? A certain makeshift quality in southern prison administration, a lack of planning and efficiency,

57. See especially Hesseltine, *Civil War Prisons*, and Foote, *Civil War*, III, 131. This view was not confined to southerners; James Ford Rhodes, for example, shared it. See Rhodes, *History of the United States from the Compromise of 1850 . . .* 7 vols. (New York, 1920), V, 499.

58. *O.R.*, Ser. II, Vol. 7, pp. 906–7, 909, 914.

59. *Ibid.*, Vol. 8, pp. 98, 123, 504; Hesseltine, *Civil War Prisons*, 229–32.

also contributed to the plight of prisoners. Because Confederates kept
expecting exchanges to be resumed, they made no long-range plans.
The matter of shelter at Andersonville affords an example of shortages
and lack of foresight. Although the South had plenty of cotton, it did
not have the industrial capacity to turn enough of that cotton into tent
canvas. The South had plenty of wood to build barracks, but there was
a shortage of nails at Andersonville and no one thought to order them
far enough in advance. Not enough sawmills existed in that part of
Georgia to make boards, and the sawmills that did exist were working
day and night for railroads whose ties and rolling stock the Yankees kept
burning. Prisoners could have hewn log huts from the pine forests that
surrounded Andersonville, but no one thought to supply axes, and the
young boys and old men who guarded the prisoners were too inexperienced to prevent escapes from work details outside the stockade.

So the prisoners broiled in the sun and shivered in the rain. Union
captives at other enlisted men's prison camps endured a similar lack of
shelter—in contrast to northern prisons, all of which provided barracks
except Point Lookout in Maryland, where prisoners lived in tents. During the war numerous southerners criticized their own prisons. After
describing conditions at the Florence camp, a South Carolina woman
told the governor: "If such things are allowed to continue they will most
surely draw down some awful judgment upon our country. . . . Don't
think that I have any liking for the Yankee; I have none. . . . But I
have not yet become quite brute enough to know of such suffering without trying to do something, even for a Yankee." A young Georgia woman
expressed similar sentiments after a visit to Andersonville. "I am afraid
God will suffer some terrible retribution to fall upon us for letting such
things happen. If the Yankees ever should come to South-West Georgia
. . . and see the graves there, God have mercy on the land!"[60]

"And yet, what can we do?" she asked herself. "The Yankees themselves are really more to blame than we, for they won't exchange these
prisoners, and our poor, hard-pressed Confederacy has not the means
to provide for them, when our own soldiers are starving in the field."
This defensive tone became dominant in southern rhetoric after the
war. "Whose fault was it that there was no exchange of prisoners?"
asked a former Andersonville guard. In any case, he continued, "An-

60. O.R., Ser. II, Vol. 7, p. 976; Eliza Frances Andrews, The War-Time Journal of a
    Georgia Girl, 1864–1865 (New York, 1908), 78–79.

dersonville was no worse than northern prisons. There was suffering at Andersonville; there was also suffering at Johnson's Island; there were hardships in all prisons." In their memoirs Jefferson Davis and Alexander Stephens maintained that the death rate at southern prisons was actually lower than at northern prisons. And the responsibility for "all this sacrifice of human life," asserted Stephens, "rests *entirely* on the Authorities at Washington" who refused to exchange prisoners.[61] The state of Georgia has placed two historical markers near Andersonville declaring that wartime shortages caused the suffering there, which thus cannot be blamed on anybody, and that "deaths among the prison guards were as high as among the prisoners." In 1909 the United Daughters of the Confederacy erected a monument to Henry Wirz (which still stands in the village of Andersonville) proclaiming that this "hero-martyr" was "judicially murdered" by Yankees whose general in chief prevented the exchange of prisoners.

These defenders of the South doth protest too much. Readers of this book will form their own conclusions about responsibility for the breakdown in prisoner exchanges. As for the comparison of Andersonville with Johnson's Island, the mortality of southern prisoners at the latter was 2 percent—and at Andersonville, 29 percent. This percentage of deaths among inmates at Andersonville was in fact five or six times higher than among guards.[62] Davis and Stephens were also wide of the mark. Because of the loss or destruction of many Confederate records, the actual number of Union dead in all southern prisons can never be known. The best estimate based on existing records finds that 30,218 (15.5 percent) of the 194,743 northern inmates of southern prisons died there, compared with 25,976 (12 percent) of 214,865 southerners who died in northern prisons. The figure for Union prisoners is undoubtedly too low.[63] In any event, the treatment of prisoners during the Civil War was something that neither side could be proud of.

61. James Dunwoody Jones, "Recollections of a Young Confederate Officer," in *Andersonville*, p. 1; Jefferson Davis, *The Rise and Fall of the Confederate Government*, 2 vols. (New York, 1881), II, 607; Alexander H. Stephens, A *Constitutional View of the Late War Between the States*, 2 vols. (Chicago, 1868–70), II, 507–9.
62. Edward T. Downer, "Johnson's Island," in Hesseltine, ed., *Civil War Prisons*, 105; Futch, *Andersonville Prison*, 106–7.
63. General F. C. Ainsworth, Chief of the Record and Pension Office, to James Ford Rhodes, June 29, 1903, in Rhodes, *History*, V, 507–8. In April and again in the fall of 1864 the Confederates exchanged several thousand sick prisoners in excess of the number of ill prisoners received from the North in return. Several hundred

IV

In the end the POW issue played a minor role in the presidential election. The principal issue was the war itself, and how it should be ended. In this matter the Republicans managed to get a patent on the policy of peace through victory. Even McClellan could not escape the copper taint of peace without victory. Most Confederates saw McClellan's candidacy that way, after some initial hesitation caused by the general's warlike letter of acceptance. Southern agent Clement C. Clay in Canada expressed disappointment with that letter. Yet "the platform means peace, unconditionally," Clay reasoned. "McClellan will be under the control of the true peace men. . . . At all events, he is committed by the platform to cease hostilities and to try negotiations. . . . An armistice will inevitably result in peace. The war cannot be renewed if once stopped, even for a short time." If McClellan was elected, predicted a War Department clerk in Richmond, "we shall have peace and independence."[64]

War-weary rebel soldiers hoped fervently for McClellan and peace. "The enemy are exceedingly anxious to hold out until after the Presidential election," reported Grant from the Petersburg front. "Deserters come into our lines daily who tell us that the men are nearly universally tired of the war, and that desertions would be much more frequent, but they believe peace will be negotiated after the fall elections."[65] Such sentiments provoked opposite feelings among Union soldiers. Although "many leading officers" in the Army of the Potomac were still "McClellanized," according to a general in another Union army, most men in the ranks no longer favored their former commander. "Not that the soldiers dislike the man so much as the company he keeps," wrote one enlisted man. "There are a good many soldiers who would vote for McClellan but they cannot go Vallandigham." A Democratic triumph would mean "inglorious peace and shame, the old truckling subserviency to Southern domination," declared an officer in the Iron Brigade. "I had rather stay out here a lifetime (much as I dislike it)," wrote

---

of these Union prisoners died soon after they were exchanged, but their deaths have not been included in the mortality toll of prisoners.

64. Clay to Judah P. Benjamin, Sept. 12, 1864, in O.R., Ser. IV, Vol. 3, pp. 637–38; Jones, *War Clerk's Diary* (Swiggett), II, 285.

65. Grant to Elihu Washburne, Aug. 16, 1864, quoted in Bruce Catton, *Grant Takes Command* (Boston, 1969), 355; Grant to Stanton, Sept. 13, 1864, in O.R., Ser. III, Vol. 4, p. 713.

another soldier, a former Democrat, "than consent to a division of our country. . . . We all want peace, but none *any* but an *honorable* one."[66]

Many Union soldiers had a chance to register their opinions at the ballot box. Here was a bold experiment in democracy: allowing fighting men to vote in what amounted to a referendum on whether they should continue fighting. But as Grant put it, "they are American citizens, [and] they have as much right to [vote] as those citizens who remain at home. Nay, more, for they have sacrificed more for their country."[67] By 1864 nineteen states had enacted provisions for soldiers to vote in the field. Of the states that had not, the three most important were Indiana, Illinois, and New Jersey where Democratic legislatures had blocked the measure. Although much rhetoric about "proconsular rule" and "Caesarism" had accompanied this opposition, the true reason was the recognition by Democrats that the army had become overwhelmingly Republican—or at least "Union," as the Republican party styled itself in 1864.

Twelve of the states allowing absentee voting provided for the separate tabulation of soldier ballots. Lincoln received 119,754 of them to McClellan's 34,291, a majority of 78 percent for the president compared with 53 percent of the civilian vote in those states. The absentee soldier-vote majority for Republicans in the other seven states was probably at least as great. Of the states that did not permit absentee voting, the contest was particularly close and important in Indiana. As commander in chief, the president could help along his cause there and did not shrink from doing so. "The loss of [Indiana] to the friends of the Government," Lincoln wrote to General Sherman in Atlanta, "would go far towards losing the whole Union cause," so the president would be pleased if the general could furlough as many Indiana soldiers as possible to go home and vote.[68] Several thousand soldiers did get to Indiana to vote; the War Department also combed military hospitals for convalescent Indiana soldiers well enough to travel. Some members of a Massachusetts regiment temporarily stationed in Indiana may have added their votes to the Republican total there.[69]

In none of the states with separately tabulated soldier ballots did this

66. Catton, *Stillness at Appomattox*, 303, 324, 323; John Berry to Samuel L. M. Barlow, Aug. 24, 1864, Barlow Papers, Henry E. Huntington Library.
67. O.R., Ser. I, Vol. 42, pt. 2, pp. 1045–46.
68. CWL, VIII, 11.
69. Democrats charged fraud and intimidation in connection with the soldier vote in

vote change the outcome of the presidential contest—Lincoln would have carried all of them except Kentucky in any case. But in two close states where soldier votes were lumped with the rest, New York and Connecticut, these votes may have provided the margin of Lincoln's victory. The men in blue also decided the outcome in several congressional districts, and the votes of Maryland soldiers for a state constitutional amendment abolishing slavery more than offset the slight majority of the home vote against it.

Lincoln's popular-vote majority of half a million translated into an electoral count of 212 to 21. The president won all the states but Kentucky, Delaware, and New Jersey; his party also captured control of the governorships and legislatures of all but those states. The next Congress would have a Republican majority of three-fourths. The similarity between the "Union" vote of 1864 and the Republican vote of 1860 in the northern states was remarkable. Lincoln received virtually the same 55 percent from the same regions and constituencies within these states that he had received four years earlier. Republicans continued to draw their greatest support from native-born and British Protestant farmers, skilled workers, and white-collar voters especially in New England and the greater New England of the upper North. Democrats remained strongest among unskilled workers, immigrant Catholics, and Butternuts in the southern Midwest. As the "Union" party, Republicans expanded their base beyond 1860 in the border states (including West Virginia) where they won 54 percent of the vote (compared with about 9 percent in 1860) and drew most of their support from the urban middle class and prosperous non-slaveholding farmers. Democrats retained the slaveholders, immigrants, and poorer farmers.

---

several places. Although there were undoubtedly some irregularities, their partisan benefits tended to cancel each other out. Indeed, the worst frauds were committed by Democratic commissioners sent to receive the vote of New York soldiers. Two of the commissioners were subsequently convicted (one of them having confessed) of forging McClellan votes. The voting of soldiers in 1864 was about as fair and honest as 19th-century elections generally were, and Lincoln's majority was probably an accurate reflection of soldier sentiment. The War Department did all it could to expedite the furloughing of soldiers likely to vote Republican, however, and in other ways lent its considerable weight to the Republican side in the gathering of the soldier vote. The best studies of this matter are Oscar O. Winther, "The Soldier Vote in the Election of 1864," *New York History*, 25 (1944), 440–58, and Josiah Henry Benton, *Voting in the Field: A Forgotten Chapter of the Civil War* (Boston, 1915).

Contemporaries interpreted the election of 1864 as a triumph for Lincoln's policy of compelling the unconditional surrender of the Confederacy. "I am astonished," wrote the American correspondent of the *London Daily News*, at "the extent and depth of [this] determination . . . to fight to the last. . . . [The northern people] are in earnest in a way the like of which the world never saw before, silently, calmly, but desperately in earnest."[70]

But Jefferson Davis was also in earnest. He had never shared southern hopes for the election of McClellan and a negotiated peace. "We are fighting for existence; and by fighting alone can independence be gained," Davis had told audiences during a morale-building tour of the lower South after the fall of Atlanta. The Confederacy remained "as erect and defiant as ever," he informed Congress in November. "Nothing has changed in the purpose of its Government, in the indomitable valor of its troops, or in the unquenchable spirit of its people."[71] It was to quench this spirit that Sherman set forth on his march from Atlanta to the sea.

70. *London Daily News*, Sept. 27, 1864, quoted in Nevins, *War*, IV, 141.
71. Nelson, *Bullets, Ballots, and Rhetoric*, 132; Rowland, *Davis*, VI, 386.

27

South Carolina Must Be Destroyed

I

John B. Hood's Army of Tennessee did not crawl into the woods and die after losing Atlanta. Quite the contrary; inspired by a visit from Jefferson Davis, the aggressive Hood planned to circle around to Sherman's rear, cut his rail lifeline from Chattanooga, and pounce at leisure on the fragments of the stricken and starving Yankee army. Meanwhile Forrest had returned to his wonted occupation of smashing up Union railroads and supply depots in Tennessee. President Davis told cheering crowds in Georgia and South Carolina what to expect next. "I see no chance for Sherman to escape from a defeat or a disgraceful retreat," he declared a month after Atlanta's fall. "The fate that befell the army of the French Empire in its retreat from Moscow will be re-enacted. Our cavalry and our people will harass and destroy his army, as did the Cossacks that of Napoleon, and the Yankee general, like him, will escape with only a bodyguard." That accomplished, "we must march into Tennessee" where "we will draw from twenty thousand to thirty thousand to our standard, and . . . push the enemy back to the banks of the Ohio and thus give the peace party of the North an accretion no puny editorial can give."[1]

This glorious prospect may have pumped new life into flagging southern spirits. But when Grant read of Davis's speeches he snorted: "Who

1. Rowland, *Davis*, VI, 341–42, 353, 358.

is to furnish the snow for this Moscow retreat?"[2] A clever riposte; but in truth Sherman was vulnerable to enemy harassment. Having attained one of his objectives—the capture of Atlanta—he had not achieved the other—the destruction of Hood's army. Forty thousand strong, these tired but game rebels moved along the railroad to Chattanooga during October attacking targets of opportunity. Sherman left a corps to hold Atlanta and pursued Hood with the rest of his army. Skirmishing and fighting northward over the terrain they had conquered while marching southward four months earlier, the Yankees finally drove Hood's graybacks into Alabama and repaired the railroad.

Sherman grew exasperated with this kind of warfare. To continue chasing Hood would play the rebel game. "It will be a physical impossibility to protect the [rail]roads," Sherman told Grant, "now that Hood, Forrest, and Wheeler, and the whole batch of devils, are turned loose, without home or habitation. By attempting to hold the roads, we will lose a thousand men monthly and will gain no result." Instead, Sherman wanted to ignore Hood and march through the heart of Georgia to the coast. "I could cut a swath through to the sea," he assured Grant, "divide the Confederacy in two, and come up on the rear of Lee."[3] Lincoln, Halleck, and even Grant resisted this idea at first. To leave Hood loose in his rear while the Union army abandoned its supply lines in the midst of enemy territory seemed doubly dangerous. But Sherman intended to station George Thomas in Tennessee with 60,000 men, more than enough to cope with anything the rebels might try. Sherman's own army of 62,000 hardened campaigners could find plenty to eat in the interior of Georgia. "If I turn back now, the whole effect of my campaign will be lost," Sherman insisted. But if I "move through Georgia, smashing things to the sea . . . instead of being on the defensive, I would be on the offensive." And the psychological effect of such a campaign might be greater even than its material impact. "If we can march a well-appointed army right through [Jefferson Davis's] territory, it is a demonstration to the world, foreign and domestic, that we have a power which Davis cannot resist. . . . I can make the march, and make Georgia howl!"[4]

Sherman persuaded Grant, who in turn persuaded a still skeptical Lincoln. Sherman returned to Atlanta and prepared to move out a week

2. Horace Porter, *Campaigning with Grant* (New York, 1897), 313.
3. *O.R.*, Ser. I, Vol. 39, pt. 3, p. 162; Porter, *Campaigning with Grant*, 292–93.
4. Foote, *Civil War*, III, 613; *O.R.*, Ser. I, Vol. 39, pt. 3, pp. 161, 202, 595, 660.

after the presidential election. Like Lincoln, he believed in a hard war and a soft peace. "War is cruelty and you cannot refine it," Sherman had told Atlanta's mayor after ordering the civilian population expelled from the occupied city. But "when peace does come, you may call on me for anything. Then will I share with you the last cracker." Until then, though, "we are not only fighting hostile armies, but a hostile people, and must make old and young, rich and poor, feel the hard hand of war." Union armies must destroy the capacity of the southern people to sustain the war. Their factories, railroads, farms—indeed their will to resist—must be devastated. "We cannot change the hearts of those people of the South, but we can make war so terrible . . . [and] make them so sick of war that generations would pass away before they would again appeal to it."[5]

Sherman's soldiers shared their leader's total-war philosophy. Acting on it, they put the torch to everything of military value (by a broad definition) that Hood had left standing in Atlanta and marched out on November 15. As Sherman started south, Hood prepared to move north from Alabama into Tennessee, creating the odd spectacle of two contending armies turning their backs on each other and marching off in opposite directions. As it turned out, there was more method in Sherman's madness than in Hood's.

No enemy stood between Sherman's army and Savannah 285 miles away except several thousand Georgia militia and 3,500 rebel cavalry commanded by Joseph Wheeler. Union cavalry kept the gray horsemen at bay while weaving back and forth across the flanks of four infantry corps spread over a front varying from twenty-five to sixty miles wide. The militia attacked a rear-guard Union infantry brigade on November 22, but after suffering 600 casualties to the Yankees' sixty they made no more such efforts. Southerners wrecked bridges, burned provisions, toppled trees and planted mines on the roads ahead of the Yankees, but this accomplished little except to make them more vengeful. In truth, nothing could stop the bluecoats' relentless pace of a dozen miles a day. For most northern soldiers the march became a frolic, a moving feast in which they "foraged liberally on the country" and destroyed everything of conceivable military value—along with much else—that they did not consume. "This is probably the most gigantic pleasure excursion

5. William T. Sherman, *Memoirs*, 2nd ed. rev., 2 vols. (New York, 1886), II, 126–27; Burke Davis, *Sherman's March* (New York, 1980), 109; John Bennett Walters, "General William T. Sherman and Total War," *JSH*, 14 (1948), 463, 470.

ever planned," wrote one officer on the second day out of Atlanta. "It already beats everything I ever saw soldiering, and promises to prove much richer yet."[6]

Indeed it did. Groups of foraging soldiers, soon called "bummers," roamed through the countryside and found more than enough food for their regiments. Under slack discipline, they helped themselves to anything they wanted from farms, plantations, even slave cabins. The pillage of Sherman's bummers has become legendary; like most legends it has some basis in fact. Not all the bummers were Yankees, however. Georgia unionists and liberated slaves hung on the flanks and rear of the army and lost few chances to despoil their rebel neighbors and former masters. Confederate deserters and stragglers from Wheeler's cavalry were perhaps even worse. Southern newspapers complained of "the destructive lawlessness" of Wheeler's troopers. "I do not think the Yankees are any worse than our own army," said a southern soldier. They "steal and plunder indiscriminately regardless of sex."[7]

The worst havoc, nevertheless, was caused by Sherman's soldiers who, in the words of one of them, "destroyed all we could not eat, stole their niggers, burned their cotton & gins, spilled their sorghum, burned & twisted their R. Roads and raised Hell generally." The hell-raising became grimmer after an incident at Milledgeville, the state capital. The soldiers' Thanksgiving Day feast there was interrupted by the arrival of several prisoners who had escaped from Andersonville. Hollow-cheeked, emaciated, with nothing but rags on their backs, these men wept uncontrollably at the sight of food and the American flag. This experience "sickened and infuriated" Sherman's soldiers who thought "of the tens of thousands of their imprisoned comrades, slowly perishing with hunger in the midst of . . . barns bursting with grain and food to feed a dozen armies."[8]

An Alabama-born major on Sherman's staff censured the vandalism committed by bummers. But he recognized that only a thin line separated such plundering from the destruction of enemy resources and morale necessary to win the war. "It is a terrible thing to consume and

6. Davis, *Sherman's March*, 42.
7. *Charleston Courier*, Jan. 10, 1865; William M. Cash and Lucy Somerville Howard, ed., *My Dear Nellie: The Civil War Letters of William L. Nugent to Eleanor Smith Nugent* (Jackson, Miss., 1977), 211.
8. Bruce Catton, *Never Call Retreat* (Pocket Books ed., New York, 1967), 395; Lloyd Lewis, *Sherman: Fighting Prophet* (New York, 1932), 448.

destroy the sustenance of thousands of people," the major wrote in his diary. But

> while I deplore this necessity daily and cannot bear to see the soldiers swarm as they do through fields and yards . . . nothing *can* end this war but some demonstration of their helplessness. . . . This Union and its Government must be sustained, at any and every cost; to sustain it, we must war upon and destroy the organized rebel forces,—must cut off their supplies, destroy their communications . . . [and] produce among the *people of Georgia* a thorough conviction of the personal misery which attends war, and the utter helplessness and inability of their "rulers," State or Confederate, to protect them. . . . If that terror and grief and even want shall help to paralyze their husbands and fathers who are fighting us . . . it is mercy in the end.[9]

As the Yankees closed in on Savannah in mid-December the 10,000 rebel soldiers defending it decided that discretion was the better part of valor and escaped before they could be trapped in the city. Sherman sent one of his sportive telegrams to Lincoln: "I beg to present you, as a Christmas gift, the city of Savannah, with 150 heavy guns and . . . about 25,000 bales of cotton." The president responded with "many, many thanks" to Sherman and his army for their "great success," especially when "taking the work of Gen. Thomas into the count," which had brought "those who sat in darkness, to see a great light."[10]

Thomas had indeed weighed in with an achievement equalling Sherman's—the virtual destruction of Hood's Army of Tennessee. Hood's activities after Sherman left Atlanta seemed to have been scripted in never-never land. Although he faced Union forces under Thomas totaling more than 60,000 men with only 40,000 of his own—one-fourth of them wearing shoes so rotten that by December they would march barefoot—Hood hoped to drive through Tennessee into Kentucky, where he expected to pick up 20,000 recruits and smash Thomas. Then, Hood fantasized, he would move eastward to Virginia, combine with Lee, and defeat Grant and Sherman in turn.

This enterprise started well. Moving into Tenneessee during the last week of November, Hood tried to get between Thomas's advance force of 30,000 commanded by John Schofield at Pulaski and the 30,000

9. Mark A. DeWolfe Howe, ed., *Marching with Sherman: Passages from the Letters and Campaign Diaries of Henry Hitchcock* (New Haven, 1927), 82, 125, 168.
10. *O.R.*, Ser. I, Vol. 44, p. 783; *CWL*, VIII, 181–82.

at Nashville seventy-five miles to the North. Schofield detected this effort in time to fall back to the Duck River at Columbia, where Hood skirmished with the Federals, November 24–27. Not wishing to risk a frontal assault, Hood sent Forrest's cavalry and two infantry corps on a deep flanking march to get into Schofield's rear, hoping to emulate "the grand results achieved by the immortal Jackson in similar maneuvers."[11] But Union horsemen spotted this move and Schofield rushed two divisions to hold the turnpike in his rear at the crossroads village of Spring Hill. Uncoordinated rebel attacks failed to dislodge these Yankees—and nothing went right for Hood's army ever again.

During the night of November 29–30 Schofield pulled his whole force back and entrenched a line covering the crossings of the Harpeth River at Franklin, fifteen miles south of Nashville. An angry Hood blamed his subordinates and even his predecessor Joe Johnston for the failure at Spring Hill. Since taking over the army four months earlier, Hood had frequently complained of its defensive mentality instilled, he believed, by Johnston. On November 30 he followed Schofield to Franklin and ordered his infantry to make a head-on assault, almost as if by such punishment to purge them of their supposed timidity. Hood's corps commanders protested this order to attack equal numbers who were dug in with strong artillery support, while nearly all the Confederate artillery and part of the infantry were far in the rear and could not arrive in time for action on this short November afternoon. Their protests only confirmed Hood's suspicions of the army's élan and his determination to force it to fight. He had broken the enemy line at Gaines' Mill and at Chickamauga; he would do it again here.

Twenty-two thousand southern soldiers swept forward in the slanted sunlight of an Indian summer afternoon. Parts of Patrick Cleburne's hard-hitting division and another gray division temporarily broke the Union line but were driven out with heavy losses in hand to hand combat as fierce as anything at the Bloody Angle of Spotsylvania. For hours after dark the firing raged until toward midnight the bluecoats broke off and headed north to Nashville. Hood could hardly claim a victory, however, for his 7,000 casualties were three times the enemy total. Hood lost more men killed at Franklin than Grant at Cold Harbor or McClellan in all of the Seven Days. A dozen Confederate generals fell at Franklin, six of them killed including Cleburne and a fire-eating South

11. John B. Hood, *Advance and Retreat: Personal Experiences in the United States and Confederate States Armies* (New Orleans, 1880), 283.

Carolinian by the name of States Rights Gist. No fewer than fifty-four southern regimental commanders, half of the total, were casualties. Having proved even to Hood's satisfaction that they would assault breastworks, the Army of Tennessee had shattered itself beyond the possibility of ever doing so again. Southerners were appalled by the news from Franklin of "fearful loss and no results."[12]

The lack of results galled Hood too as he prodded his battered troops northward toward Nashville, where they entrenched a defensive line along the hills four miles south of Tennessee's capital. Like Micawber, Hood seemed to be waiting for something to turn up—specifically, reinforcements from across the Mississippi. But Union gunboats prevented that. Afraid that a retreat to Alabama would trigger wholesale desertions by Tennessee soldiers, Hood hunkered down and waited for Thomas to attack. So did an impatient General Grant. Unaware of the crippled condition of Hood's army, northern leaders far from the scene feared that this rebel raid, like Jubal Early's the previous summer, might undo all the results of recent Union successes. While Thomas methodically prepared to attack, Stanton fumed that "this looks like the McClellan and Rosecrans strategy of do nothing and let the rebels raid the country."[13] Grant bombarded Thomas with telegraphic exhortations to action, and he started for Nashville himself to relieve the ponderous general from command when news came that Thomas had finally made his move.

When he did, it turned out like Joe Louis's second fight with Max Schmeling—a devastating knockout that almost annihilated the adversary. The analogy is appropriate, for Thomas's battle plan called for one division (including two brigades of black soldiers) to pin down Hood's right with a left jab while three Union infantry corps and the cavalry smashed the other flank with a roundhouse right. All worked as planned, though it took two winter days to finish the job. On December 15 the lifting fog at midmorning revealed 50,000 bluecoats coming on against Hood's 25,000 (most of Forrest's cavalry was thirty miles away watching a small Union force at Murfreesboro). All day the rebels hung on by their fingernails against the feinting jabs at their right and sledgeham-

12. Quotation from Edward Younger, ed., *Inside the Confederate Government: The Diary of Robert Garlick Hill Kean* (New York, 1957), 181. For a recent and thorough study of the battle of Franklin, see James Lee McDonough and Thomas L. Connelly, *Five Tragic Hours: The Battle of Franklin* (Knoxville, 1983).

13. O.R., Ser. I, Vol. 45, pt. 2, pp. 15–16.

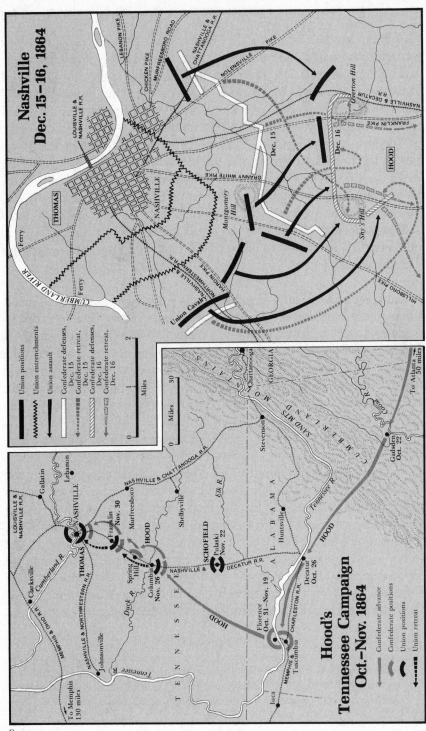

Nashville
Dec. 15–16, 1864

Union positions
Union entrenchments
Union assault
Confederate defenses, Dec. 15
Confederate retreat, Dec. 15
Confederate defenses, Dec. 16
Confederate retreat, Dec. 16

Miles
0   1   2

THOMAS

CUMBERLAND RIVER

Ferry
Ferry

NASHVILLE

LOUISVILLE & NASHVILLE R.R.

LEBANON PIKE
CHICKEN PIKE
MURFREESBORO ROAD
NASHVILLE & CHATTANOOGA R.R.
NOLENSVILLE PIKE
GRANNY WHITE PIKE
Montgomery Hill
FRANKLIN PIKE
NASHVILLE & NORTHWESTERN R.R.
HARDIN PIKE
NASHVILLE & DECATUR R.R.
Overton Hill
Shy's Hill
HILLSBORO PIKE

Dec. 15
Dec. 16

HOOD

Union Cavalry

Hood's
Tennessee Campaign
Oct.–Nov. 1864

Confederate advance
Confederate positions
Union positions
Union retreat

Miles
0   30

LOUISVILLE & NASHVILLE R.R.
Gallatin
Lebanon
NASHVILLE
THOMAS
Clarksville
Cumberland R.
MEMPHIS & OHIO R.R.
NASHVILLE & NORTHWESTERN R.R.
Johnsonville
To Memphis 130 miles
Tennessee R.

Franklin Nov. 30
Murfreesboro
NASHVILLE & CHATTANOOGA R.R.
Shelbyville
Spring Hill
HOOD
Columbia Nov. 26
Duck R.
NASHVILLE & DECATUR R.R.
SCHOFIELD
Pulaski Nov. 22
Elk R.
Stevenson
Chattanooga

ALABAMA
GEORGIA
CUMBERLAND MTS.
SAND MTS.
Huntsville

Decatur Oct. 26
MEMPHIS & CHARLESTON R.R.
CHARLESTON R.R.
Tuscumbia
Florence Oct. 31–Nov. 19
HOOD
Iuca
TENNESSEE

Gadsden Oct. 22
To Atlanta 50 miles
Coosa R.
Tennessee R.
HOOD

814

mer blows at their left. As darkness began to fall the fingernails on the left let go, and during the night Hood pulled his army back two miles to a new and shorter line anchored by hills on both ends.

The Federals moved forward with titanic inexorability next day and repeated the tactics of left jab and right uppercut. Again the Confederates parried groggily until late afternoon. But dismounted Union cavalrymen with rapid-firing carbines had worked around to the rear of Hood's left while two infantry corps hit this flank head-on. When the collapse finally came during a drenching rain and gathering darkness, it came with calamitous suddenness. From left to right, southern brigades toppled like dominoes. Thousands of rebels surrendered, and others streamed southward throwing away their arms and equipment to make better time. Officers tried to rally them, "but the line they formed," a private recalled, "was like trying to stop the current of the Duck River with a fish net."[14]

Yankee cavalrymen scrambled to find their horses and take up the pursuit over roads shin-deep in mud. For nearly two weeks the chase continued from one river to the next through Tennessee into Alabama and Mississippi. At each river or creek Forrest's cavalry would make a stand and fall back, while the exhausted infantry—half of them now without shoes—leaked stragglers and deserters by the hundreds. By the beginning of 1865 the remnants of Hood's army had fetched up at Tupelo, Mississippi, where a head count found barely half of the 40,000 who had marched northward seven weeks earlier. Heartsick and broken, Hood resigned his command on January 13—a Friday.

The news of Hood's "irretrievable disaster" and of Savannah's surrender to Sherman spread dejection through the South. This was "one of the gloomiest [days] in our struggle," wrote Ordnance Chief Josiah Gorgas on December 19. "The darkest and most dismal day . . . a crisis such as not been experienced before," moaned War Department clerk John B. Jones on the same date. "The deep waters are closing over us," wrote diarist Mary Chesnut—also on December 19.[15]

As the full extent of Hood's defeat became known and as shortages exacerbated by Sherman's and Sheridan's ravages became more serious,

14. Sam R. Watkins, "Co. Aytch": A Side Show of the Big Show (Collier Books ed., New York, 1962), 241.
15. Frank E. Vandiver, ed., The Civil War Diary of General Josiah Gorgas (University, Ala., 1947), 156; Jones, War Clerk's Diary (Swiggett), II, 357, 359; Woodward, Chesnut's Civil War, 694.

the head of the Confederate War Bureau conceded that "things are getting worse very rapidly. . . . Ten days ago the last meat ration was issued [to Lee's army] and not a pound remained in Richmond. . . . The truth is we are prostrated in all our energies and resources." The price of gold rose to 5,000, and the value of the Confederate dollar slipped to less than 2 percent of its 1861 level. The heretofore resolute General Gorgas, who had performed miracles to keep rebel armies supplied with arms and ammunition, wondered in January 1865: "Where is this to end? No money in the Treasury—no food to feed Gen. Lee's army—no troops to oppose Gen. Sherman. . . . Is the cause really hopeless? Is it to be lost and abandoned in this way? . . . Wife and I sit talking of going to Mexico to live out there the remnant of our days."[16]

The upbeat tone of Lincoln's annual message to Congress on December 6 provided a northern counterpoint to southern gloom. "The purpose of the people . . . to maintain the integrity of the Union, was never more firm, nor more nearly unanimous, than now," said Lincoln. And the resources to do the job "are unexhausted, and, as we believe, inexhaustible." With 671 warships the navy was the largest in the world. With a million men in uniform the army was larger and better equipped than ever. And despite the deaths of over 300,000 soldiers, immigration and natural increase had more than made up the loss. Thus while "material resources are now more complete and abundant than ever," we also "have *more* men *now* than we had when the war *began*. . . . We are *gaining* strength, and may, if need be, maintain the contest indefinitely."[17]

These were chilling words to the South. Josiah Gorgas noted in his diary that "Lincoln's message *spawns* nothing but subjugation."[18] Nor was the president's talk of abundant and inexhaustible resources mere gasconade. On the contrary, the demands of war had boosted the northern economy to new heights of productivity following the temporary setback of 1861–62 caused by departure of the South with its markets and raw materials. Coal and iron production declined in the first year or so of the war, but increased by 1864 to higher levels than ever before. Iron production in the Union states was 29 percent higher in 1864 than for the whole country in the previous record year of 1856; coal produc-

16. Younger, ed., *Inside the Confederate Government*, 181, 184; Vandiver, ed., *Civil War Diary of Josiah Gorgas*, 163–64, 166.
17. CWL, VIII, 144, 149–51.
18. Vandiver, ed., *Civil War Diary of Josiah Gorgas*, 155.

tion in the North during the four war years was 21 percent greater than in the highest four peacetime years for both North and South. The North built more merchant ship tonnage during the war than the whole country had built in any comparable peacetime period despite the crippling of the transatlantic merchant marine by southern commerce raiders and the competing demands of the navy on shipbuilding capacity. Although new railroad construction slowed during the war, the amount of traffic over existing lines increased by 50 percent or more, absorbing the excess capacity created by the railroad-building boom of the 1850s. Traffic on the Erie Canal also increased by more than 50 percent during the war. Despite a drastic decline of 72 percent in the North's leading industry, cotton textiles, the overall manufacturing index stood 13 percent higher in 1864 for the Union states alone than for the entire country in 1860. The North had to import hundreds of thousands of rifles in the first year or two of the war; by 1864 the firearms industry was turning out more than enough rifles and artillery for the large Union army.

And the northern economy churned out plenty of butter as well as guns. Despite the secession of southern states, war in the border states, and the absence of a half-million farmers in the army, Union states grew more wheat in both 1862 and 1863 than the entire country had grown in the previous record year of 1859. Despite the food needs of the army and the civilian population, the United States actually doubled its exports of wheat, corn, pork, and beef during the war to help fill the void created by crop failures in western Europe during the early 1860s. In 1864 the president of the Illinois Agricultural Society boasted of "railroads pressed beyond their capacity with the freights of our people . . . more acres of fertile land under culture . . . and more prolific crops than ever before . . . whitening the Northern lakes with the sails of its commerce . . . and then realize, if you can, that all this has occurred and is occurring in the midst of a war the most stupendous ever prosecuted among men." It was an impressive achievement, all right, made possible by the stimulus of war production, by mechanization of agriculture, and by the expanded employment of women as well as machines in northern industry. In the contrasting impact of the war on the northern and southern economies could be read not only the final outcome of the war but also the future economic health of those regions.[19]

19. Quotation from Emerson D. Fite, *Social and Industrial Conditions in the North*

The North had enough manpower and energy left over from the war effort to continue the process of westward expansion. As Lincoln noted in his 1864 message, a hundred miles of the eastern end of the transcontinental railroad had been surveyed and twenty miles of tracks already laid on the other end in California. Gold production held steady during the war, copper increased by 50 percent, and silver quadrupled as new mines were opened, especially in Nevada, which entered the Union as a state in 1864. Western growth had its dark side, of course: many of the new settlers were draft dodgers from states east of the Mississippi; the politics of federal aid to railroad construction were none too scrupulous; and worst of all, the extinguishment of Indian titles to the land proceeded ruthlessly, accompanied by bloody fighting in Minnesota, Colorado, and elsewhere during the war.[20]

New industries also blossomed in the hothouse climate of the southern wartime economy. Gunpowder mills, ordnance plants, machine shops, and the like sprang up at Augusta, Selma, Atlanta, and numerous other places, while the Tredegar Works in Richmond turned out iron for every conceivable military use. But Yankee invasions and raids sooner or later destroyed most of this new industry, along with anything else of economic value within reach, so that by war's end much of the South was an economic desert. The war not only killed one-quarter of the Confederacy's white men of military age. It also killed two-fifths of southern livestock, wrecked half of the farm machinery, ruined thousands of miles of railroad, left scores of thousands of farms and plantations in weeds and disrepair, and destroyed the principal labor system on which southern productivity had been based. Two-thirds of assessed southern wealth vanished in the war. The wreckage of the southern economy caused the 1860s to become the decade of least economic growth in American history before the 1930s. It also produced a wrenching redistribution of wealth and income between North and South. As measured by the census, southern agricultural and manufacturing capital declined by 46 percent between 1860 and 1870, while northern capital

---

during the Civil War (New York, 1910), 23. Statistical data in these two paragraphs were obtained from *ibid.*, passim; and from the relevant tables of *Historical Statistics of the United States* (Washington, 1975) and Ralph Adreano, ed., *The Economic Impact of the American Civil War* (Cambridge, Mass., 1962).

20. For a succinct recent account of Indian affairs during the war, see Robert M. Utley, *The Indian Frontier of the American West 1846–1890* (Albuquerque, 1984), chap. 3.

increased by 50 percent.[21] In 1860 the southern states had contained 30 percent of the national wealth; in 1870, only 12 percent. Per capita commodity output (including agriculture) was almost equal in North and South in 1860; by 1870 the North's per capita output was 56 percent greater. In 1860 the average per capita income of southerners including slaves was about two-thirds of the northern average; after the war southern income dropped to less than two-fifths of the northern average and did not rise above that level for the rest of the nineteenth century. Such were the economic consequences of the South's bid for independence.[22]

II

Despite Confederate disasters in the last months of 1864, the war was not yet over—at least Jefferson Davis and his colleagues refused to admit that it was over. To persuade them, the Yankees put the finishing touches on Winfield Scott's Anaconda Plan, conceived nearly four years earlier, by capturing Fort Fisher in January 1865. By then Robert E. Lee's Army of Northern Virginia was the only substantial military force left in the Confederacy, and the Carolinas were just about the only region from which it could draw supplies. Many of these came on blockade runners that were still getting into Wilmington, twenty miles up the Cape Fear River from Fort Fisher. This massive L-shaped fort, almost a mile long on its seaward face, represented a new version of an ancient idea in fortifications. Instead of masonry, it was built of sand and dirt over a log framework. Twenty-five feet thick and ten to thirty feet high, sodded with tough marsh grass, it absorbed shot and shell as a pillow absorbs punches—unlike, for example, Fort Sumter which had been blasted to rubble by the Union fleet. Fort Fisher's forty-seven big guns threatened dire punishment to any Union warship that tried to close in on blockade runners weaving their way through the treacherous shoals and channels at the mouth of the Cape Fear River.

21. If slaves are counted as capital, the southern decline was 74 percent.
22. Data compiled from Donald B. Dodd and Wynelle S. Dodd, *Historical Statistics of the South 1790–1970* (University, Ala., 1973); Lee Soltow, *Men and Wealth in the United States 1850–1870* (New Haven, 1975); Stanley Engerman, "Some Economic Factors in Southern Backwardness in the Nineteenth Century," in John F. Kain and John R. Meyers, eds., *Essays in Regional Economics* (Cambridge, Mass., 1971), 291, 300–302; and James L. Sellers, "The Economic Incidence of the Civil War in the South," *MVHR*, 14 (1927), 179–91.

Union strategists were slow to make the capture of Fort Fisher a top priority. In 1863 the wasteful diversion of resources to the futile attempt to seize Charleston delayed the project. Finally in the fall of 1864 Admiral David D. Porter assembled the largest fleet of the war—nearly sixty warships plus troop transports to carry 6,500 soldiers—for an all-out effort against Fort Fisher. Commander of the infantry was Benjamin Butler, who by virtue of his early, politically motivated promotion to major general outranked everyone in the eastern theater except Grant. Butler conceived the idea of loading an old ship with 215 tons of gunpowder, running it into the shallows near the fort, and exploding it with the expectation that the blast would damage the fort and stun its garrison. Storms delayed the project until Christmas Eve day. The exploding ship did virtually no damage, the open air having absorbed the shock wave. The fleet then pummelled the fort with the heaviest bombardment of the war but managed to damage only a few of its guns. Butler got part of his infantry onto the beach but called off the attack when he found the parapet bristling with artillery and the approaches mined with "torpedoes."

This fiasco provided Grant with the excuse he had been looking for to get rid of Butler. With the election safely over, Lincoln could disregard the political influence that had kept Butler in the army so long; on January 8, 1865, the Massachusetts general was relieved of his command. Grant ordered a second attempt against Fort Fisher, this time with the bright young General Alfred Terry in command of a beefed-up infantry force of 8,000. On January 13 they waded ashore through the surf and worked their way down the narrow peninsula toward the fort's north face while the fleet opened a barrage that rained 800 tons of shot and shell on the defenders. This time the navy's big guns disabled nearly all of those in the fort and cut the detonating wires for the mines, preparing the way for an assault on January 15 by 4,500 infantrymen against the north face while 2,000 sailors and marines stormed the bastion from the seaward side. Although the attackers took more than a thousand casualties, the army troops finally broke through and captured the fort along with its garrison of 2,000 men. Wilmington was cut off from the sea, and Lee's soldiers in the trenches at Petersburg would have to tighten further their belts whose buckles were already scraping their backbones.

Wilmington itself soon fell, and most of coastal North Carolina was in Yankee hands. Desertions from Lee's army, especially of North Carolina troops, rose to disastrous levels. "Hundreds of men are deserting nightly," reported Lee in February. In a single month the army lost 8 percent of its strength by desertion. Most of these men went home to protect and sustain their families; some went over to the enemy, where they knew they could find food and shelter. A Massachusetts soldier on the Petersburg line wrote to his parents: "The boys talk about Johnnies as at home we talk about suckers and eels. The boys will look around in the evening and guess that there will be a good run of Johnnies."[23] Confederate officers recognized that "the depressed and destitute conditions of the soldiers' families was one of the prime causes of desertion," but that "the chief and prevailing reason was a conviction among them that our cause was hopeless and that further sacrifices were useless." Whatever the reasons for this "epidemic" of desertions, wrote Lee, "unless it can be changed, [it] will bring us calamity."[24]

Confederate officials regarded the loss of Fort Fisher as a "stunning" blow. Alexander Stephens pronounced it "one of the greatest disasters that had befallen our Cause from the beginning of the war."[25] The southern Congress, then in session, stepped up its attacks on the administration. Secretary of War Seddon succumbed to the pressure and resigned. Some congressmen even called on Davis to step down in favor of Robert E. Lee as dictator. Congress did pass a law creating the post of general in chief. Although Davis recognized this as a gesture of nonconfidence in his own leadership, he appointed Lee to the position. Davis and Lee maintained their cordial relationship, and both vowed to fight on until victory. But the fall of Fort Fisher had convinced many congressmen that "we cannot carry on the war any longer" and should "make terms with the enemy, on the basis of the old Union."[26]

In this climate of opinion another movement for peace negotiations flared up and then fizzled out. This time it was the old Jacksonian Francis Preston Blair—as quixotic in his own way as Horace Greeley— who set up a meeting between Lincoln and Confederate commissioners. Convinced that he could reunite North and South by proposing a joint

23. O.R., Ser. I, Vol. 46, pt. 2, p. 1258; Bruce Catton, A Stillness at Appomattox (Garden City, N.Y., 1957), 330–31.

24. Catton, Never Call Retreat, 414; Ella Lonn, Desertion During the Civil War (New York, 1928), 28.

25. Jones, War Clerk's Diary (Swiggett), II, 389; Alexander H. Stephens, A Constitutional View of the War between the States, 2 vols. (Philadelphia, 1868–70), II, 619.

26. Vandiver, ed., Civil War Diary of Josiah Gorgas, 166. See also Younger, ed., Inside the Confederate Government, 187–88.

campaign to throw the French out of Mexico, Blair badgered Lincoln to give him a pass through the lines to present this proposal to Jefferson Davis. Lincoln wanted nothing to do with Blair's hare-brained Mexican scheme, but he allowed him to go to Richmond to see what might develop. For his part, Davis anticipated nothing better from negotiations than the previous demands for "unconditional submission." But he saw an opportunity to fire up the waning southern heart by eliciting such demands publicly. Davis thus authorized Blair to inform Lincoln that he was ready to "enter into conference with a view to secure peace to the two countries." Lincoln responded promptly that he too was ready to receive overtures "with the view of securing peace to the people of our one common country."[27]

Hoping to discredit the peace movement by identifying it with humiliating surrender terms, Davis appointed a three-man commission consisting of prominent advocates of negotiations: Vice-President Stephens, President *pro tem* of the Senate Robert M. T. Hunter, and Assistant Secretary of War John A. Campbell, a former U.S. Supreme Court justice. Their proposed conference with William H. Seward, whom Lincoln had sent to Hampton Roads to meet with them, almost aborted because of the irreconcilable differences between the agendas for "two countries" and "our one common country." But after talking with Stephens and Hunter and becoming convinced of their sincere desire for peace, General Grant telegraphed Washington that to send them home without a meeting would leave a bad impression. On the spur of the moment Lincoln decided to journey to Hampton Roads and join Seward for a face-to-face meeting with the Confederate commissioners.

This dramatic confrontation took place February 3 on the Union steamer *River Queen*. Lincoln's earlier instructions to Seward formed the inflexible Union position during four hours of talks: "1) The restoration of the National authority throughout all the States. 2) No receding by the Executive of the United States on the Slavery question. 3) No cessation of hostilities short of an end of the war, and the disbanding of all forces hostile to the government." In vain did Stephens try to divert Lincoln by bringing up Blair's Mexican project. Equally unprofitable was Hunter's proposal for an armistice and a convention of states. No armistice, said Lincoln; surrender was the only means of stopping the war. But even Charles I, said Hunter, had entered into agreements with rebels in arms against his government during the English Civil

27. *CWL*, VIII, 275–76.

War. "I do not profess to be posted in history," replied Lincoln. "All I distinctly recollect about the case of Charles I, is, that he lost his head."[28]

On questions of punishing rebel leaders and confiscating their property Lincoln promised generous treatment based on his power of pardon. On slavery he even suggested the possibility of compensating owners to the amount of $400 million (about 15 percent of the slaves' 1860 value).[29] Some uncertainty exists about exactly what Lincoln meant in these discussions by "no receding . . . on the Slavery question." At a minimum he meant no going back on the Emancipation Proclamation or on other wartime executive and congressional actions against slavery. No slaves freed by these acts could ever be re-enslaved. But how many *had* been freed by them? asked the southerners. All of the slaves in the Confederacy, or only those who had come under Union military control after the Proclamation was issued? As a war measure would it cease to operate with peace? That would be up to the courts, said Lincoln. And Seward informed the commissioners that the House of Representatives had just passed the Thirteenth Amendment. Its ratification would make all other legal questions moot. If southern states returned to the Union and voted against ratification, thereby defeating it, would such action be valid? That remained to be seen, said Seward.[30] In any case,

28. *Ibid.*, 279; Stephens, *Constitutional View*, II, 613.
29. Upon his return to Washington, Lincoln actually drafted a message to Congress asking for an appropriation of this amount to compensate slaveowners after the Confederacy had surrendered and ratified the 13th Amendment. The cabinet unanimously disapproved, however, so Lincoln never sent the message to Congress—which in any case would have been unlikely to appropriate funds for such a purpose. *CWL*, VIII, 260–61.
30. Some historians have interpreted this exchange as evidence that Seward and Lincoln were willing to consider a peace settlement that did not necessarily include universal emancipation. See especially Richard N. Current, *The Lincoln Nobody Knows* (New York, 1958), 243–47, and Ludwell H. Johnson, "Lincoln's Solution to the Problem of Peace Terms, 1864–1865," *JSH*, 34 (1968), 581–86. But since these discussions were informal and no contemporary record of them was kept, the evidence for this interpretation rests almost entirely on Alexander Stephens's postwar memoirs. See Stephens, *Constitutional View*, II, 611–12. It is probable that Stephens was reading his own viewpoint into Seward's remarks. Stephens also recalled that Lincoln had urged him to go home to Georgia and persuade the legislature to take the state out of the war and to ratify the 13th Amendment *prospectively*, to take effect in five years, thereby mitigating the evils of immediate emancipation. *Ibid.*, 614. This too seems highly unlikely. Lincoln was too good a lawyer to suggest an impossibility like "prospective" ratification. Both Lincoln and Seward were committed to the ratification of the 13th Amendment as soon as pos-

remarked Lincoln, slavery as well as the rebellion was doomed. Southern leaders should cut their losses, return to the old allegiance, and save the blood of thousands of young men that would be shed if the war continued. Whatever their personal preferences, the commissioners had no power to negotiate such terms. They returned dejectedly to Richmond.[31]

Southern professions of shock and betrayal at the North's demand for "unconditional surrender" were disingenuous, for Lincoln had never given them reason to expect otherwise. The three commissioners drafted a brief, matter-of-fact report on their mission. When Davis tried to get them to add phrases expressing resentment of "degrading submission" and "humiliating surrender" they refused, knowing that the president wished to use them to discredit the whole idea of negotiations. So Davis added the phrases himself in a message to Congress on February 6 accompanying the commissioners' report. The South must fight on, said Davis that evening in a public speech which breathed "unconquerable defiance," according to press reports. We will never submit to the "disgrace of surrender," declared the Confederate leader. Denouncing the northern president as "His Majesty Abraham the First," Davis predicted that Lincoln and Seward would find that "they had been speaking to their masters," for southern armies would yet "compel the Yankees, in less than twelve months, to petition us for peace on our own terms.[32]

The press and public—in Richmond at least—took their cue from Davis. "To talk now of any other arbitrament than that of the sword is to betray cowardice or treachery," proclaimed the *Whig*. Ordnance Chief

---

sible. The president expressed pride that his own state of Illinois was the first to ratify it, and he backed the successful drives for immediate abolition in Maryland, Missouri, and Tennessee. Seward had stopped off at Annapolis on his way to Hampton Roads and had successfully lobbied the Maryland legislature for ratification.

31. Stephens, *Constitutional View*, II, 584–619, provides the fullest account of the conference by a participant. Lincoln laid all of the correspondence concerning it before Congress; see *CWL*, VIII, 274–86. The most detailed secondary accounts can be found in John G. Nicolay and John Hay, *Abraham Lincoln: A History*, 10 vols. (New York, 1890), X, 91–129; Edward Chase Kirkland, *The Peacemakers of 1864* (New York, 1927), 197–251; and James G. Randall and Richard N. Current, *Lincoln the President: Last Full Measure* (New York, 1955), 326–40.

32. Younger, ed., *Inside the Confederate Government*, 196; Hudson Strode, *Jefferson Davis: Tragic Hero* (New York, 1964), 140–43; Randall and Current, *Lincoln the President: Last Full Measure*, 336–37; Rowland, *Davis*, VI, 465–67; Jones, *War Clerk's Diary* (Swiggett), II, 411; *Richmond Dispatch*, Feb. 7, 1865, quoted in Nicolay and Hay, *Lincoln*, X, 130.

Josiah Gorgas reported that "the war feeling has blazed out afresh in Richmond," while war clerk John B. Jones recorded similar "cheerful" tidings. "Valor alone is relied upon now for our salvation," wrote Jones. "Every one thinks the Confederacy will at once gather up its military strength and strike such blows as will astonish the world."[33]

III

If William Tecumseh Sherman had read these words he would have uttered a sigh of exasperation. Having bent but apparently not broken the South's "unconquerable defiance," his army was now smashing and burning its way through South Carolina to finish the job.

At the beginning of 1865 the only sizable portions of the Confederate heartland still untouched by invading Yankees were the interior of the Carolinas and most of Alabama. Grant and Thomas planned a two-pronged campaign to deal with the latter. Using troops drawn from the Army of the Gulf and from Thomas's force in Tennessee, General E. R. S. Canby was to invade southern Alabama through Mobile. At the same time twenty-seven-year-old James H. Wilson, who had risen to command of Thomas's cavalry, was to take 13,000 troopers armed with repeating carbines on a strike from Tennessee into Alabama to destroy the munitions complex at Selma and seize the original Confederate capital of Montgomery. Both operations got under way in March; both were complete successes, especially Wilson's raid. Brushing aside Forrest's outmanned and outgunned horsemen, the blue cavalry burned or smashed or blew up great quantities of cotton, railroads, bridges, rolling stock, factories, niter works, rolling mills, arsenals, a navy yard, and captured Montgomery, while Mobile fell to Canby's infantry in April.

Destructive as these enterprises were, they became a sideshow to Sherman's march through South Carolina. As his army had approached Savannah in December 1864, Georgians said to Sherman: "Why don't you go over to South Carolina and serve them this way? They started it." Sherman had intended to do so all along. He converted Grant to the idea, and on February 1, Sherman's 60,000 blue avengers left Savannah for their second march through the heart of enemy territory.

33. *Richmond Whig*, Feb. 6, 1865, quoted in Kirkland, *Peacemakers*, 254; Vandiver, ed., *Civil War Diary of Josiah Gorgas*, 168; Jones, *War Clerk's Diary* (Swiggett), II, 411.

This one had two strategic purposes: to destroy all war resources in Sherman's path; and to come up on Lee's rear to crush the Army of Northern Virginia in a vise between two larger Union armies and "wipe out Lee," in Grant's succinct phrase.[34]

Sherman's soldiers had a third purpose in mind as well: to punish the state that had hatched this unholy rebellion. "The truth is," Sherman informed Halleck, "the whole army is burning with an insatiable desire to wreak vengeance upon South Carolina. I almost tremble at her fate, but feel that she deserves all that seems to be in store for her." The soldiers' temper was not improved by the taunts of southern newspapers against this "grand army of Mudsills." One of the mudsills, an Ohio private, vowed to make South Carolina "suffer worse than she did at the time of the Revolutionary War. We will let her know that it isn't so sweet to secede as she thought it would be."[35] Another soldier declared: "Here is where treason began and, by God, here is where it shall end!" A South Carolina woman whose house was plundered recalled that the soldiers "would sometimes stop to tell me they were sorry for the women and children, but South Carolina must be *destroyed*."[36]

Destroyed it was, through a corridor from south to north narrower than in Georgia but more intensely pillaged and burned. Not many buildings remained standing in some villages after the army marched through. The same was true of the countryside. "In Georgia few houses were burned," wrote an officer; "here few escaped." A soldier felt confident that South Carolina "will never want to seceed again. . . . I think she has her 'rights' now." When the army entered North Carolina the destruction of civilian property stopped. "Not a single column of the fire or smoke which a few days ago marked the positions of heads of column, can be seen on the horizon," noted an officer after two days in North Carolina. "Not a house was burned, and the army gave to the people more than it took from them."[37]

34. Lewis, *Sherman*, 446; Herman Hattaway and Archer Jones, *How the North Won: A Military History of the Civil War* (Urbana, Ill., 1983), 656–57; Foote, *Civil War*, III, 737–38.

35. O.R., Ser. I, Vol. 44, p. 799; John G. Barrett, *Sherman's March Through the Carolinas* (Chapel Hill, 1956), 44; Davis, *Sherman's March*, 142.

36. Soldier quoted in Lewis, *Sherman*, 489; Mrs. St. Julien Ravenel quoted in James G. Randall and David Donald, *The Civil War and Reconstruction* (Boston, 1969), 432.

37. Lewis, *Sherman*, 493; Joseph T. Glatthaar, *The March to the Sea and Beyond:*

The war of plunder and arson in South Carolina was not pretty, and hardly glorious, but Sherman considered it effective. The terror his bummers inspired "was a power, and I intended to utilize it. . . . My aim then was to whip the rebels, to humble their pride, to follow them to their inmost recesses, and make them fear and dread us." It seemed to work: "All is gloom, despondency, and inactivity," wrote a South Carolinian on February 28. "Our army is demoralized and the people panic stricken. . . . The power to do has left us. . . . to fight longer seems to be madness."[38]

Even more important, perhaps, than the destructive vengeance of Sherman's army in spreading this demoralization was its stunning logistical achievements. Sherman himself later rated the march through the Carolinas as ten times more important in winning the war than the march from Atlanta to the sea. It was also ten times more difficult. "The march to the sea seems to have captured everybody," said Sherman after the war, "whereas it was child's play compared with the other."[39] Terrain and weather posed much greater problems in South Carolina than in Georgia. The march from Atlanta to Savannah proceeded 285 miles parallel to major rivers in dry autumn weather against token opposition. The march northward from Savannah was aimed at Goldsboro, North Carolina, 425 miles away, where Sherman expected to be resupplied by Union forces moving inland from Wilmington. Sherman's soldiers would have to cross nine substantial rivers and scores of their tributaries during what turned out to be the wettest winter in twenty years.

Confederate defenders expected the swamps in tidewater South Carolina to stop Sherman before he got fairly started. "My engineers," wrote Joseph E. Johnston, "reported that it was absolutely impossible for an army to march across the lower portions of the State in winter." Indeed, so far under water were the roads in this region that Union scouts had to reconnoiter some of them in canoes. But Sherman organized "pioneer battalions" of soldiers and freedmen (some of the latter recruited from the thousands of contrabands who had trailed the army to Savan-

Sherman's Troops in the Savannah and Carolinas Campaigns (New York, 1985), 146; John Bennett Walters, Merchant of Terror: General Sherman and Total War (Indianapolis, 1973), 203.

38. Foote, Civil War, II, 753; Sherman, Memoirs, II, 249; South Carolinian quoted in Barrett, Sherman's March Through the Carolinas, 95.
39. Barrett, Sherman's March Through the Carolinas, vii.

nah) to cut saplings and trees to corduroy the roads, build bridges, and construct causeways. Meeting resistance from Wheeler's cavalry at some rain-swollen streams and rivers, the bluecoats sent out flanking columns that waded through water up to their armpits, brushing aside alligators and snakes, and drove the rebels away. The worst obstacle was the many-channeled Salkehatchie River fifty miles north of Savannah. "The Salk is impassable," declared southern General William Hardee. The Yankees built miles of bridges and crossed it. "I wouldn't have believed it if I hadn't seen it," commented Hardee. Northward lapped the blue wave at a rate of nearly ten miles a day for forty-five days including skirmishing and fighting. Rain fell during twenty-eight of those days, but this seemed to benefit South Carolina only by slightly damping the style of Sherman's arsonists. "When I learned that Sherman's army was marching through the Salk swamps, making its own corduroy roads at the rate of a dozen miles a day," said Joseph Johnston, "I made up my mind that there had been no such army in existence since the days of Julius Caesar."[40]

Johnston soon acquired the dubious honor of trying to stop these latter-day legions. One of Lee's first acts as general in chief was to persuade Davis to appoint Johnston on February 22 to command all Confederate troops in the Carolinas. There were not many of them, and they had already been flanked out of South Carolina by Sherman's feints and fast marching. The four Union corps moved northward on separate roads in a Y formation with the forward units pointing toward Augusta and Charleston and the inner corps in a position to reinforce them quickly in case of trouble. The rebels had scraped together about 20,000 troops plus Wheeler's cavalry to resist Sherman. They consisted of the demoralized remnants of Hood's Army of Tennessee, the Charleston garrison reinforced by Hardee's troops that had evacuated Savannah, and a brigade of South Carolina cavalry that Lee sent from Virginia along with Wade Hampton to rally faltering morale in his home state. Some ten thousand of these troops were stationed in Augusta and about the same number in Charleston with the expectation that Sherman would attack one or both cities—Augusta because of its gunpowder and munitions plants, Charleston because of its symbolic value. Sherman kept up the feint toward both but went near neither. Instead he sliced through the center of the state destroying the railroad between them and heading

40. Quotations of Johnston and Hardee in Lewis, *Sherman*, 484, and Jacob D. Cox, *Military Reminiscences of the Civil War*, 2 vols. (New York, 1900), II, 531–32.

for the capital at Columbia. With their communications cut and an enemy army of 60,000 in their rear, the defenders of Charleston evacuated the city on February 18. The rebel troops at Augusta also slogged northward to combine with Hardee's divisions now under Johnston's overall command to offer some resistance when Sherman reached North Carolina.

Charleston was fortunate that it was occupied by troops from the Department of the South (including black regiments), who put out fires started when departing rebels blew up military supplies, instead of by Sherman's bummers, who probably would have started new fires of their own. Columbia was not so fortunate. Units from two of Sherman's corps occupied the capital on February 17; by next morning almost half of the city was rubble and ashes. The greatest atrocity charged against Sherman, the burning of Columbia, also provoked an ongoing controversy about responsibility for the tragedy. Sherman and other Union officers maintained that the fire spread in a high wind from smoldering cotton bales set afire by rebel cavalry as they evacuated the town. Southerners believed that drunken Union soldiers torched the city. Other contemporaries and historians have pointed the finger of guilt at vengeful Union prisoners who had escaped from a nearby prison camp, at local criminals who had escaped from jail, or at Negroes drunk with freedom or liquor or both. The fullest and most dispassionate study of this controversy blames all parties in varying proportions. It also blames Confederate authorities for the disorder that characterized the evacuation of Columbia, leaving thousands of cotton bales in the streets (some of them burning) and huge quantities of liquor undestroyed, much of it having been shipped from Charleston by merchants and wealthy citizens who had believed Columbia safe from the enemy. Black and white residents of Columbia distributed some of this liquor by the dipperful to the first troops entering town in an effort to curry their favor; instead it turned some of them into inebriated incendiaries. Sherman did not burn Columbia, but some of his men unquestionably helped to do so, and their officers' attempts to restrain them were too little and too late. On the other hand, far more Union soldiers including Sherman worked through the night to put out the fires than to set them. Only the abatement of gale-force winds after 3:00 a.m. prevented more of the city from going up. In any event, the fate of Columbia was not inconsistent with the scorched-earth policy experienced by other parts of South Carolina.[41]

41. Marion Brunson Lucas, *Sherman and the Burning of Columbia* (College Station,

Sherman kept the enemy guessing about his ultimate objective until mid-March, when it became clear that he was headed for Goldsboro and a junction with 30,000 additional bluecoats moving in from the coast. In the forlorn-hope style that had become southern strategy, Johnston planned to attack one wing of Sherman's army and try to cripple it before the remainder could come up in support. On March 16 two of Johnston's divisions fought a delaying action against four of Sherman's at Averasborough, thirty-odd miles south of Raleigh. From this affair the rebels learned that the two wings of Sherman's army were separated by a dozen or more miles. Johnston concentrated his infantry (17,000 men) to ambush about the same number of Federals strung out on the road in the advance of the left wing near Bentonville on March 19. The attackers achieved some initial success, but the Yankees dug in and repulsed several assaults during the afternoon. That night and next day the rest of Sherman's army was hard on the march to reinforce the left wing. On March 21 a Union division drove in the Confederate left, but Sherman called off the attack and let Johnston slip away during the night.

What prompted this reluctance to finish off an opponent he outnumbered by three to one? Sherman wanted to get his road-weary troops to Goldsboro to replenish equipment and supplies after seven weeks of the most strenuous campaigning of the war. Beyond that, despite his ferocious reputation Sherman was careful with the lives of his soldiers. "I don't want to lose men in a direct attack when it can be avoided," he said.[42] He would rather win by strategy and maneuver than by battle. He was confident that the war was nearly over and that his destruction of enemy resources had done much to win it. Johnston's small and demoralized force, in Sherman's view, hardly mattered any more. The important thing was to rest and refit his army for the move up to Virginia to help Grant "wipe out Lee."

Tex., 1976). This fine study reduces the estimated extent of the damage to about one-third of the buildings in Columbia, including most of the business district but relatively few homes in residential districts. Lucas also deflates the number of drunken Union soldiers and the amount of plundering from the wholesale orgy of rapine into which it had ballooned in southern mythology.

42. O.R., Ser. I, Vol. 47, pt. 2, p. 910.

28

We Are All Americans

I

The Confederacy had one last string to its bow—a black string. Early in the war a few voices had urged the arming of slaves to fight for their masters. But to most southerners such a proposal seemed at best ludicrous and at worst treasonable. With a president who denounced the North's emancipation and recruitment of slaves as "the most execrable measure recorded in the history of guilty man," it required rash courage to suggest that the Confederacy itself put arms in the hands of slaves.[1]

After the fall of Vicksburg and the defeat at Gettysburg, however, the voices suggesting such a thing had become less lonely. Several newspaper editors in Mississippi and Alabama began speaking out in extraordinary fashion. "We are forced by the necessity of our condition," they declared, "to take a step which is revolting to every sentiment of pride, and to every principle that governed our institutions before the war." The enemy was "stealing our slaves and converting them into soldiers. . . . It is better for us to use the negroes for our defense than that the Yankees should use them against us." Indeed, "we can make them fight better than the Yankees are able to do. Masters and overseers can marshal them for battle by the same authority and habit of obedience with which they are marshalled to labor." It was true, admitted the *Jackson*

---

1. Davis quoted in Robert F. Durden, ed., *The Gray and the Black: The Confederate Debate on Emancipation* (Baton Rouge, 1972), 24.

Mississippian, that "such a step would revolutionize our whole industrial system" and perhaps lead to universal emancipation, "a dire calamity to both the negro and the white race." But if we lose the war we lose slavery anyway, for "Yankee success is death to the institution . . . so that it is a question of necessity—a question of a choice of evils. . . . We must . . . save ourselves from the rapacious North, WHATEVER THE COST."[2]

General Patrick Cleburne had been thinking along similar lines. He wrote down his ideas and presented them to division and corps commanders in the Army of Tennessee in January 1864. The South was losing the war, said Cleburne, because it lacked the North's manpower and because "slavery, from being one of our chief sources of strength at the commencement of the war, has now become, in a military point of view, one of our chief sources of weakness." The Emancipation Proclamation had given the enemy a moral cause to justify his drive for conquest, Cleburne continued, had made the slaves his allies, undermined the South's domestic security, and turned European nations against the Confederacy. Hence we are threatened with "the loss of all we now hold most sacred—slaves and all other personal property, lands, homesteads, liberty, justice, safety, pride, manhood." To save the rest of these cherished possessions we must sacrifice the first. Let us recruit an army of slaves, concluded Cleburne, and "guarantee freedom within a reasonable time to every slave in the South who shall remain true to the Confederacy."[3]

Twelve brigade and regimental commanders in Cleburne's division endorsed his proposal. This was a potentially explosive matter, for these were not just editors expressing an opinion, but fighting men on whom the hopes for Confederate survival rested. Cleburne's arguments cut to the heart of a fundamental ambiguity in the Confederacy's *raison d'être.* Had secession been a means to the end of preserving slavery? Or was slavery one of the means for preserving the Confederacy, to be sacrificed if it no longer served that purpose? Few southerners in 1861 would have recognized any dilemma: slavery and independence were each a means as well as an end in symbiotic relationship with the other, each essential

2. These quotations are from editorials in the *Jackson Mississippian* reprinted in *Montgomery Mail,* Sept. 9, 1863; *Montgomery Weekly Mail,* Sept. 2, 1863; and *Mobile Register,* Nov. 26, 1863, all reprinted in Durden, *The Gray and the Black,* 30–35, 42–44.

3. *O.R.,* Ser. I, Vol, 52, pt. 2, pp. 586–92.

for the survival of both. By 1864, however, southerners in growing numbers were beginning to wonder if they might have to make a choice between them. "Let not slavery prove a barrier to our independence," intoned the *Jackson Mississippian*. "Although slavery is one of the principles that we started to fight for . . . if it proves an insurmountable obstacle to the achievement of our liberty and separate nationality, away with it!"[4]

At the time of Cleburne's proposal, however, such opinions still seemed dangerous. Most generals in the Army of Tennessee disapproved of Cleburne's action, some of them vehemently. This "monstrous proposition," wrote a division commander, was "revolting to Southern sentiment, Southern pride, and Southern honor." A corps commander abhorred it as "at war with my social, moral, and political principles." A shocked and angry brigadier insisted that "we are not whipped, & cannot be whipped. Our situation requires resort to no such remedy. . . . Its propositions contravene the principles upon which we fight."[5]

Convinced that the "promulgation of such opinions" would cause "discouragements, distraction, and dissension" in the army, Jefferson Davis ordered the generals to stop discussing the matter.[6] So complete was their compliance that the affair remained unknown outside this small circle of southern officers until the U. S. government published the war's *Official Records* a generation later. The only consequence of Cleburne's action seemed to be denial of promotion to this ablest of the army's division commanders, who was killed ten months later at the battle of Franklin.

By then the South's dire prospects had revived the notion of arming blacks. In September 1864 the governor of Louisiana declared that "the time has come for us to put into the army every able-bodied negro man as a soldier." A month later the governors of six more states, meeting in conference, enigmatically urged the impressment of slaves for "the public service as may be required." When challenged, all but two of the governors (those of Virginia and Louisiana) hastened to deny that they meant the *arming* of slaves. On November 7, Jefferson Davis urged

4. As reprinted in *Montgomery Weekly Mail*, Sept. 9, 1863, in Durden, *The Gray and the Black*, 31–32.
5. Patton Anderson in *O.R.*, Ser. I, Vol. 52, pt. 2, pp. 598–99; Alexander P. Stewart to William H. T. Walker, Jan. 9, 1864, William B. Bate to Walker, Jan. 9, 1864, Civil War Collection, Henry E. Huntington Library.
6. *O.R.*, Ser. I, Vol. 52, pt. 2, p. 608.

Congress to purchase 40,000 slaves for work as teamsters, pioneers, and laborers with the promise of freedom after "service faithfully rendered." But this cautious proposal proved much too radical for most of the press and Congress. It would crack the door of Abolition, declared the *Richmond Whig*. The idea of freeing slaves who performed faithfully was based on the false assumption "that the condition of freedom is so much better for the slave than servitude, that it may be bestowed upon him as a reward." This was "a repudiation of the opinion held by the whole South . . . that servitude is a divinely appointed condition for the highest good of the slave."[7]

Congress did not act on the president's request. But the issue would not go away. Although Davis in his November 7 message had opposed the notion of arming blacks *at that time*, he added ominously: "Should the alternative ever be presented of subjugation or the employment of the slave as a soldier, there seems no reason to doubt what should then be our decision." Within three months the alternative stared the South starkly in the face. The president and his cabinet made their choice. "We are reduced," said Davis in February 1865, "to choosing whether the negroes shall fight for or against us."[8] And if they fought for us, echoed some newspapers, this would not necessarily produce wholesale abolition. Perhaps those who fought must be offered freedom, but that would only "affect units of the race and not the whole institution." By enabling the South to whip the Yankees, it was the only way to *save* slavery. "If the emancipation of a part is the means of saving the rest, then this partial emancipation is eminently a pro-slavery measure." Some advocates went even further and said that discipline rather than the motive of freedom was sufficient to make slaves fight. "It is not true," declared General Francis Shoup, "that to make good soldiers of these people, we must either give or promise them freedom. . . . As well might one promise to free one's cook . . . with the expectation of thereby securing good dinners."[9]

Such talk prompted one exasperated editor to comment that "our Southern people have not gotten over the vicious habit of not believing

7. O.R., Ser. I, Vol. 41, pt. 3, p. 774; Rowland, *Davis*, VI, 394–97; *Richmond Whig*, Nov. 9, 1864, in Durden, *The Gray and the Black*, 110.
8. Rowland, *Davis*, VI, 396; O.R., Ser. IV, Vol. 3, p. 1110.
9. *Lynchburg Virginian*, Nov. 3, 1864; *Richmond Sentinel*, Nov. 24, 1864; article by Shoup in *Richmond Whig*, Feb. 20, 1865, all in Durden, *The Gray and the Black*, 79, 121, 214.

what they don't wish to believe."[10] Most participants in this debate recognized that if slaves became soldiers, they and probably their families must be promised freedom or they might desert to the enemy at first opportunity. If one or two hundred thousand slaves were armed (the figures most often mentioned), this would free at least half a million. Added to the million or so already liberated by the Yankees, how could the institution survive? asked opponents of the proposal.

These opponents remained in the majority until February 1865. Yet with the Yankees thundering at the gates, their arguments took flight into an aura of unreality. We can win without black help, they said, if only the absentees and stragglers return to the ranks and the whole people rededicate themselves to the Cause. "The freemen of the Confederate States must work out their own redemption, or they must be the slaves of their own slaves," proclaimed the *Charleston Mercury* edited by those original secessionists the Robert Barnwell Rhetts, father and son. "The day that the army of Virginia allows a negro regiment to enter their lines as soldiers they will be degraded, ruined, and disgraced," roared Robert Toombs. His fellow Georgian Howell Cobb agreed that "the moment you resort to negro soldiers your white soldiers will be lost to you. . . . The day you make soldiers of them is the beginning of the end of the revolution. If slaves will make good soldiers our whole theory of slavery is wrong."[11]

And was not that the theory the South fought for? "It would be the most extraordinary instance of self-stultification the world ever saw" to arm and emancipate slaves, declared the Rhetts. "It is abolition doctrine . . . the very doctrine which the war was commenced to put down," maintained a North Carolina newspaper. It would "surrender the essential and distinctive principle of Southern civilization," agreed the *Richmond Examiner*.[12] Many southerners apparently preferred to lose the war than to win it with the help of black men. "Victory itself would be robbed of its glory if shared with slaves," said a Mississippi congressman.

10. *Charlottesville Chronicle*, reprinted in *Richmond Sentinel*, Dec. 21, 1864, in Durden, *The Gray and the Black*, 147.
11. *Charleston Mercury*, Nov. 3, 1864, in Durden, *The Gray and the Black*, 99; Toombs quoted in Foote, *Civil War*, III, 860; Cobb in O.R., Ser. IV, Vol. 3, pp. 1009–10.
12. *Charleston Mercury*, Nov. 3, 19, 1864, *North Carolina Standard*, Jan. 17, 1865, in Durden, *The Gray and the Black*, 99, 114, 177; *Richmond Examiner*, Jan. 14, 1865, quoted in Paul D. Escott, *After Secession: Jefferson Davis and the Failure of Confederate Nationalism* (Baton Rouge, 1978), 154.

It would mean "the poor man . . . reduced to the level of a nigger," insisted the *Charleston Mercury*. "His wife and daughter are to be hustled on the street by black wenches, their equals. Swaggering buck niggers are to ogle them and elbow them." Senator Louis Wigfall of Texas "wanted to live in no country in which the man who blacked his boots and curried his horse was his equal." "If such a terrible calamity is to befall us," declared the *Lynchburg Republican*, "we infinitely prefer that Lincoln shall be the instrument of our disaster and degradation, than that we ourselves should strike the cowardly and suicidal blow." [13]

But the shock effect of Lincoln's insistence at Hampton Roads on unconditional surrender helped the Davis administration make headway against these arguments. During February many petitions and letters from soldiers in the Petersburg trenches poured into Richmond to challenge the belief that white soldiers would refuse to fight alongside blacks. While "slavery is the normal condition of the negro . . . as indispensable to [his] prosperity and happiness . . . as is liberty to the whites," declared the 56th Virginia, nevertheless "if the public exigencies require that any number of our male slaves be enlisted in the military service in order to [maintain] our Government, we are willing to make concessions to their false and unenlightened notions of the blessings of liberty." [14]

Robert E. Lee's opinion would have a decisive influence. For months rumors had circulated that he favored arming the slaves. Lee had indeed expressed his private opinion that "we should employ them without delay [even] at the risk which may be produced upon our social institutions." On February 18 he broke his public silence with a letter to the congressional sponsor of a Negro soldier bill. This measure was "not only expedient but necessary," wrote Lee. "The negroes, under proper circumstances, will make efficient soldiers. I think we could at least do as well with them as the enemy. . . . Those who are employed should be freed. It would be neither just nor wise . . . to require them to serve as slaves." [15]

13. Mississippi congressman quoted in Durden, *The Gray and the Black*, 140; *Charleston Mercury*, Jan. 26, 1865, quoted in Bell Irvin Wiley, *Southern Negroes 1861–1865* (New Haven, 1938), 156–57; Louis Wigfall quoted in E. Merton Coulter, *The Confederate States of America 1861–1865* (Baton Rouge, 1950), 268; *Lynchburg Republican*, Nov. 2, 1864, in Durden, *The Gray and the Black*, 94.

14. Published in *Richmond Whig*, Feb. 23, 1865, reprinted in Durden, *The Gray and the Black*, 222–23.

15. Lee to Andrew Hunter, Jan. 11, 1865, in O.R., Ser. IV, Vol. 3, pp. 1012–13;

Lee's great prestige carried the day—but just barely. Although the powerful *Richmond Examiner* dared to express a doubt whether Lee was "a 'good Southerner'; that is, whether he is thoroughly satisfied of the justice and beneficence of negro slavery," even this anti-administration newspaper recognized that "the country will not venture to deny to General Lee . . . *anything* he may ask for."[16] By a vote of 40 to 37 the House passed a bill authorizing the president to requisition a quota of black soldiers from each state. In deference to state's rights, the bill did not mandate freedom for slave soldiers. The Senate nevertheless defeated the measure by a single vote, with both senators from Lee's own state voting No. The Virginia legislature meanwhile enacted its own law for the enlistment of black soldiers—without, however, requiring the emancipation of those who were slaves—and instructed its senators to vote for the congressional bill. They did so, enabling it to pass by 9 to 8 (with several abstentions) and become law on March 13. In the few weeks of life left to the Confederacy no other state followed Virginia's lead. The two companies of black soldiers hastily organized in Richmond never saw action. Nor did most of these men obtain freedom until the Yankees—headed by a black cavalry regiment—marched into the Confederate capital on April 3.[17]

A last-minute diplomatic initiative to secure British and French recognition in return for emancipation also proved barren of results. The impetus for this effort came from Duncan F. Kenner of Louisiana, a prominent member of the Confederate Congress and one of the South's largest slaveholders. Convinced since 1862 that slavery was a foreign-policy millstone around the Confederacy's neck, Kenner had long urged an emancipationist diplomacy. His proposals got nowhere until December 1864, when Jefferson Davis called Kenner in and conceded that the time had come to play this last card. Kenner traveled to Paris and Lon-

---

Lee to Ethelbert Barksdale, Feb. 18, 1865, in Durden, *The Gray and the Black*, 206.

16. *Richmond Examiner*, Feb. 16, 25, in Durden, *The Gray and the Black*, 199, 226.

17. War Department regulations governing the recruitment of slave soldiers bootlegged a quasi-freedom into the process by stipulating that a slave could be enlisted only with his own consent and that of his master, who was required to grant the slave in writing, "as far as he may, the rights of a freedman." Whether this ambiguous language actually conferred freedom, as several historians maintain, must remain forever moot. See Durden, *The Gray and the Black*, 268–70; Escott, *After Secession*, 252; and Emory Thomas, *The Confederate Nation 1861–1865* (New York, 1979), 296–97.

don as a special envoy to offer abolition for recognition. Davis of course could not commit his Congress on this matter, and these lawmakers could not in turn commit the states, which had constitutional authority over the institution. But perhaps European governments would overlook these complications.

Kenner's difficulties in getting out of the Confederacy foretokened the fate of his mission. The fall of Fort Fisher prevented his departure on a blockade-runner. He had to travel in disguise to New York and take ship from this Yankee port for France. Louis Napoleon as usual refused to act without Britain. So James Mason accompanied Kenner to London, where on March 14 they presented the proposition to Palmerston. Once again the Confederates learned the hard lesson of diplomacy: nothing succeeds like military success. "On the question of recognition," Mason reported to Secretary of State Benjamin, "the British Government had not been satisfied at any period of the war that our independence was achieved beyond peradventure, and did not feel authorized so to declare [now] when the events of a few weeks might prove it a failure. . . . As affairs now stood, our seaports given up, the comparatively unobstructed march of Sherman, etc., rather increased than diminished previous objections."[18]

II

While the South debated the relationship of slavery to its Cause, the North acted. Lincoln interpreted his re-election as a mandate for passage of the 13th Amendment to end slavery forever. The voters had retired a large number of Democratic congressmen. But until the 38th Congress expired on March 4, 1865, they retained their seats and could block House passage of the Amendment by the necessary two-thirds majority. In the next Congress the Republicans would have a three-quarters House majority and could easily pass it. Lincoln intended to call a special session in March if necessary to do the job. But he preferred to accomplish it sooner, by a bipartisan majority, as a gesture of wartime unity in favor of this measure that Lincoln considered essential to Union victory. "In a great national crisis, like ours," he told Congress in his message of December 6, 1864, "unanimity of action among those seeking a common end is very desirable—almost indispensable." This was

18. Frank Lawrence Owsley, *King Cotton Diplomacy: Foreign Relations of the Confederate States of America* (Chicago, 1931), 550–61; quotation from 560.

an expression of an ideal rather than reality, since most war measures, especially those concerning slavery, had been passed by a strictly Republican vote. For the historic achievement of terminating the institution, however, Lincoln appealed to Democrats to recognize the "will of the majority" as expressed by the election.[19]

But most Democrats preferred to stand on principle in defense of the past. Even if the war had killed slavery, they refused to help bury it. The party remained officially opposed to the 13th Amendment as "unwise, impolitic, cruel, and unworthy of the support of civilized people." A few Democratic congressmen believed otherwise, however. The party had suffered disaster in the 1864 election, said one, "because we [would] not venture to cut loose from the dead carcass of negro slavery." Another declared that to persist in opposition to the Amendment "will be to simply announce ourselves a set of impracticables no more fit to deal with practical affairs than the old gentleman in Copperfield."[20] Encouraged by such sentiments, the Lincoln administration targeted a dozen or so lame-duck Democratic congressmen and subjected them to a barrage of blandishments. Secretary of State Seward oversaw this lobbying effort. Some congressmen were promised government jobs for themselves or relatives; others received administration favors of one sort or another.[21]

This arm-twisting and log-rolling paid off, though until the House voted on January 31, 1865, no one could predict which way it would go. As a few Democrats early in the roll call voted Aye, Republican faces brightened. Sixteen of the eighty Democrats finally voted for the Amendment; fourteen of them were lame ducks. Eight other Democrats had absented themselves. This enabled the Amendment to pass with two votes to spare, 119 to 56. When the result was announced, Republicans on the floor and spectators in the gallery broke into prolonged— and unprecedented—cheering, while in the streets of Washington cannons boomed a hundred-gun salute. The scene "beggared description,"

19. *CWL*, VIII, 149.
20. Christopher Dell, *Lincoln and the War Democrats* (Rutherford, N.J., 1975), 290; Anson Herrick of New York in *CG*, 38 Cong., 2 Sess., 525–25; Samuel S. Cox quoted in Joel H. Silbey, *A Respectable Minority: The Democratic Party in the Civil War Era, 1860–1868* (New York, 1977), 183.
21. James G. Randall and Richard N. Current, *Lincoln the President: Last Full Measure* (New York, 1955), 307–13; LaWanda Cox and John H. Cox, *Politics, Principle, and Prejudice 1865–1866: Dilemma of Reconstruction America* (New York, 1963), 1–30.

wrote a Republican congressman in his diary. "Members joined in the shouting and kept it up for some minutes. Some embraced one another, others wept like children. I have felt, ever since the vote, as if I were in a new country." By acclamation the House voted to adjourn for the rest of the day "in honor of this immortal and sublime event."[22]

The Thirteenth Amendment sped quickly through Republican state legislatures that were in session; within a week eight states had ratified it and during the next two months another eleven did so. Ratification by five additional northern states was certain as soon as their legislatures met. Of the Union states only those carried by McClellan in the presidential election—New Jersey, Kentucky, and Delaware—held out.[23] The "reconstructed" states of Louisiana, Arkansas, and Tennessee ratified readily. Since the Lincoln administration had fought the war on the theory that states could not secede, it considered ratification by three-quarters of *all* the states including those in the Confederacy to be necessary. One of the first tasks of reconstruction would be to obtain the ratification of at least three more ex-Confederate states to place the Amendment in the Constitution.

Among the spectators who cheered and wept for joy when the House passed the 13th Amendment were many black people. Their presence was a visible symbol of the revolutionary changes signified by the Amendment, for until 1864 Negroes had not been allowed in congressional galleries. Blacks were also admitted to White House social functions for the first time in 1865, and Lincoln went out of his way to welcome Frederick Douglass to the inaugural reception on March 4. Congress and northern states enacted legislation that began to break down the pattern of second-class citizenship for northern Negroes: admission of black witnesses to federal courts; repeal of an old law that barred blacks from carrying mail; prohibition of segregation on streetcars in the District of Columbia; repeal of black laws in several northern states that had imposed certain kinds of discrimination against Negroes or barred their entry into the state; and steps to submit referendums to the voters of several states to grant the ballot to blacks (none of these referendums passed until 1868).

Perhaps the most dramatic symbol of change occurred on February

22. "George W. Julian's Journal," *Indiana Magazine of History*, 11 (1915), 327; CG, 38 Cong., 2 Sess., 531.
23. New Jersey ratified the Amendment in 1866 after Republicans gained control of the legislature.

1, the day after House passage of the 13th Amendment. On that day Senator Charles Sumner presented Boston lawyer John Rock for admission to practice before the Supreme Court, and Chief Justice Salmon P. Chase swore him in. There was nothing unusual in this except that Rock was a black man, the first Negro accredited to the highest Court which eight years earlier had denied U.S. citizenship to his race. The Court had been virtually reconstructed by Lincoln's appointment of five new justices including Chase. The transition from Roger Taney to Chase as leader of the Court was itself the most sweeping judicial metamorphosis in American history.[24]

Important questions concerning emancipation and reconstruction were sure to come before this new Court. Two such questions might well grow out of actions taken in the area of freedmen's affairs during the winter of 1864–65. Thousands of contrabands had attached themselves to Sherman's army on its march from Atlanta to the sea. Reports filtered northward of Sherman's indifference to their welfare and ill-treatment of them by some officers and men. To sort out the rumors and problems, Secretary of War Stanton journeyed to Savannah in January for a talk with Sherman and an interview with black leaders, most of them former slaves. Among the questions Stanton asked these men was how best they could support their families in freedom. "The way we can best take care of ourselves," they answered, "is to have land, and turn in and till it by our labor. . . . We want to be placed on land until we are able to buy it, and make it our own."[25]

Stanton and Sherman thought this a good idea, so the conservative general prepared the most radical field order of the war. Issued January 16, Sherman's "Special Field Orders, No. 15" designated the sea islands and the rich plantation areas bordering rivers for thirty miles inland from Charleston down to Jacksonville for settlement by freedmen. Each head of family could be granted forty acres of land, to which he would be given a "possessory title" until Congress "shall regulate their title."[26] This land had of course belonged to slaveholders. Their dispossession of it by Sherman's order, like Lincoln's dispossession of their slaves by

24. In June 1864, Lincoln had finally accepted Chase's third offer to resign from the cabinet. In October, Taney died, and two months later the president appointed Chase chief justice in part as a gesture of conciliation to the radical wing of his party.
25. *Liberator*, Feb. 24, 1865.
26. O.R., Ser. IV, Vol. 47, pt. 2, pp. 60–62.

the Emancipation Proclamation, was a military measure carried out under "war powers." The 13th Amendment confirmed Lincoln's action; it remained to be seen how Court, Congress, and Executive would deal with the consequences of Sherman's Order No. 15. The army did not wait, however. During the next several months General Rufus Saxton, an abolitionist who commanded the Union occupation forces on the South Carolina sea islands, supervised the settlement of 40,000 freedmen on land designated in Sherman's order.

The wartime experience of Union army officers who governed occupied territory, of Treasury agents who had charge of abandoned plantations, and of freedmen's aid societies that sent missionaries and teachers to the freed slaves made clear the need for a government agency to coordinate their efforts. All too often these various groups pulled in different directions—and the freedmen themselves in still another direction. In 1863 Congress first considered legislation to create a Freedmen's Bureau. Disagreement whether this agency should be part of the War or the Treasury Department prevented final enactment of a bill until March 3, 1865. By then Chase was no longer secretary of the treasury, so radical Republicans who had wanted him in charge of the Bureau were now willing to place it in the War Department. The function of the Bureau (formally called the Bureau of Refugees, Freedmen, and Abandoned Lands) would be to dispense rations and relief to the hundreds of thousands of white as well as black refugees uprooted by the war and to assist the freedmen during the difficult transition from slavery to freedom. Congress also gave the Bureau control of "abandoned" land with the provision that individual freedmen "shall be assigned not more than forty acres" of such land at rental for three years and an option to buy at the end of that time with "such title thereto as the United States can convey."[27] Here was Sherman's Order No. 15 writ large. Whether Congress would be able to convey any title was a troublesome question, given the constitutional ban on bills of attainder and the presidential power of pardon and restoration of property. In any event, the Freedmen's Bureau represented an unprecedented extension of the federal government into matters of social welfare and labor relations—to meet unprecedented problems produced by the emancipation of four million slaves and the building of a new society on the ashes of the old.

The success or failure of the Freedmen's Bureau would be partly de-

27. U. S. *Statutes at Large*, XIII, 507–9.

termined by the political terms of reconstruction. This matter occupied much of Congress's time during the winter of 1864–65. Prospects seemed good for a compromise with the president. The afterglow of a Republican electoral sweep had dissolved the bitterness that had crested with Lincoln's pocket veto of the Wade-Davis bill. Chase's elevation to the Court was another step toward rapprochement between Lincoln and radical Republicans. The president's reference to reconstruction in his message to Congress on December 6 hinted at the likelihood of "more rigorous measures than heretofore."[28] This willingness to meet Congress halfway set the stage for an attempt to enact a new reconstruction bill. The outlines of such legislation soon emerged in negotiations between Lincoln and congressional leaders: Congress would accept the already reconstructed regimes of Louisiana and Arkansas (soon to be joined by Tennessee) in return for a presidential promise to sign legislation similar to the Wade-Davis bill for the other Confederate states.

As first introduced in the House this new bill enfranchised "all male citizens"—including blacks. Lincoln persuaded the committee chairman in charge of the bill to modify it to limit this provision to black soldiers. During the next two months the measure went through a bewildering series of revisions and amendments in committee and on the House floor. At one stage it enfranchised literate blacks as well as soldiers; at another it removed racial qualifications altogether; at still another it applied these provisions to Louisiana and Arkansas as well as to the other states. Democrats voted with moderate Republicans to defeat the more radical versions of the bill and joined radicals to defeat the more conservative versions. Consequently no bill could be passed. Not wishing to create a precedent for Executive reconstruction by seating Louisiana's senators and representatives in Congress, radicals teamed with Democrats to deny them admission. Thus the 38th Congress expired without any further action on reconstruction. Radical Republicans thought this just as well. The next Congress would have more radicals and fewer Democrats, noted one of them, and "in the meantime I hope the nation may be educated up to our demand for universal suffrage."[29]

The prospect of "educating" Lincoln up to this demand seemed

28. *CWL*, VIII, 152.
29. Congressman James M. Ashley in *Boston Commonwealth*, March 4, 1865. For a skillful analysis of these confusing debates and votes on reconstruction see Herman Belz, *Reconstructing the Union: Theory and Policy during the Civil War* (Ithaca, 1969), 244–76.

promising. He had moved steadily leftward during the war, from no emancipation to limited emancipation with colonization and then to universal emancipation with limited suffrage. This trajectory might well carry him to a broader platform of equal suffrage by the time the war ended. The entreaty in Lincoln's second inaugural address for "malice toward none" and "charity for all" provided few clues on this question, though it seemed to endorse generous treatment of ex-rebels. At the same time this address left no doubt of Lincoln's intention to fight on until slavery was crushed forever. "Fondly do we hope—fervently do we pray—that this mighty scourge of war may speedily pass away," said the nation's sixteenth president at the beginning of his second term. "Yet if God wills that it continue, until all the wealth piled up by the bond-man's two hundred and fifty years of unrequited toil shall be sunk, and until every drop of blood drawn with the lash, shall be paid by another drawn with the sword, as was said three thousand years ago, so it must be said 'the judgments of the Lord, are true and righteous alto-gether.' "[30]

III

Ulysses S. Grant was determined that it should not take that long. During the winter, Union forces at Petersburg had fought their way west-ward to cut off the last road into town from the south and threaten the last open railroad. With Lee's army of 55,000 melting away by deser-tions while the oncoming spring dried roads after an exceptionally raw, wet winter, the final success of Grant's 120,000 seemed only a matter of time. Sherman could be expected on Lee's rear by late April, but Grant wanted the Army of the Potomac to "vanquish their old enemy" without help that might produce future gloating by Sherman's veterans. "I mean to end the business here," the general in chief told Phil Sher-idan. Grant's main concern now was that he might wake one morning to find Lee gone to join Johnston's 20,000 for an attack on Sherman.[31] Lee had precisely that in mind. In his effort to accomplish it, however, he gave Grant a long-sought opportunity to drive the ragged rebels from their trenches into the open.

By March, Lee had become convinced that he must soon abandon the Petersburg lines to save his army from encirclement. This would

30. CWL, VIII, 333.
31. Bruce Catton, *Grant Takes Command* (Boston, 1969), 437; *Personal Memoirs of U. S. Grant*, 2 vols. (New York, 1886), II, 424–25, 430–31, 459–61.

mean the fall of Richmond, but better that than loss of the army which was the only thread holding the Confederacy together. To force Grant to contract his lines and loosen the stranglehold blocking a rebel escape, Lee planned a surprise attack on the enemy position just east of Petersburg. Southern corps commander John B. Gordon sent false deserters to fraternize with Yankee pickets in front of Fort Stedman on the night of March 24–25. The "deserters" suddenly seized the dumbfounded pickets, and Gordon's divisions swarmed into sleepy Fort Stedman. Capturing several batteries and a half-mile of trenches, the Confederates seemed to have achieved a smashing breakthrough. But a northern counterattack recaptured all lost ground plus the forward trenches of the Confederate line, trapping many of the rebels and forcing them to surrender. Lee lost nearly 5,000 men; Grant only 2,000. Instead of compelling Grant to shorten his lines, Lee had to thin his own to the breaking point. And Grant lost little time in breaking them.

On March 29 he ordered an infantry corps and Sheridan's cavalry, recently returned from the Shenandoah Valley, to turn the Confederate right ten miles southwest of Petersburg. Lee sent George Pickett with two divisions of infantry through a drenching downpour to help the worn-down rebel cavalry counter this move. Hard fighting across a sodden landscape on the last day of March stopped the Federals temporarily. But next afternoon they launched an enveloping attack against Pickett's isolated force at the road junction of Five Forks. Sheridan's rapid-firing troopers, fighting on foot, attacked head-on, while Gouverneur K. Warren's 5th Corps moved sluggishly against Pickett's flank. Storming up and down the line cajoling and god-damning the infantry to move faster and hit harder, Sheridan finally coordinated an assault that achieved the most one-sided Union victory since the long campaign began eleven months earlier in the Wilderness. Pickett's divisions collapsed, half of their men surrendering to the whooping Yankees and the other half running rearward in rout. When the news reached Grant that evening, he ordered an assault all along the line next morning, April 2.

At dawn it came, with more élan and power than the Army of the Potomac had shown for a long time. And the Army of Northern Virginia—weary, hungry, shorn of more than one-fifth of its strength by the fighting on March 25 and April 1—could no longer hold the Yankees off. Sheridan got astride the last railroad into Petersburg, and the blue infantry punched through Confederate lines at several places southwest of the city. The rebels fought desperately as they fell back, but it was only to hold on to the inner defenses until dark in order to get away.

For Lee knew that he must pull out. As Jefferson Davis worshipped at St. Paul's Church in Richmond this balmy Sunday, a messenger tiptoed down the aisle and gave him a telegram. It was from Lee: Richmond must be given up. Turning pale, the president left the church without a word. But parishioners read the message on his face, and the news spread quickly through the city. Everyone who could beg, borrow, or steal a conveyance left town. Government officials crowded aboard ramshackle trains headed for Danville with the Treasury's remaining gold and as much of the archives as they could carry, the rest being put to the torch. So was everything of military and industrial value in Richmond. As night came and the army departed, mobs took over and the flames spread. Southerners burned more of their own capital than the enemy had burned of Atlanta or Columbia. When the Yankees arrived next morning, their first tasks were to restore order and put out the flames. Among the troops who marched into Richmond as firemen and policemen were units from the all-black 25th Corps.

Following the northern soldiers into Richmond came a civilian—the number one civilian, in fact, Abraham Lincoln. The president had taken a short vacation from Washington to visit the Army of the Potomac, arriving just before it broke up the Confederate attack on Fort Stedman. Wanting to be there for the end, which now seemed imminent, Lincoln had stayed on as Grant's guest. Commander in chief and general in chief entered Petersburg on April 3 only hours after the Army of Northern Virginia had left. Grant soon rode west on the chase to head off Lee. Lincoln returned to the Union base on the James River and told Admiral David D. Porter: "Thank God I have lived to see this. It seems to me that I have been dreaming a horrid dream for four years, and now the nightmare is gone. I want to see Richmond."[32] Porter took Lincoln upriver to the enemy capital where the President of the United States sat down in the study of the President of the Confederate States forty hours after Davis had left it.

Lincoln's visit to Richmond produced the most unforgettable scenes of this unforgettable war. With an escort of only ten sailors, the president walked the streets while Porter peered nervously at every window for would-be assassins. But the Emancipator was soon surrounded by an impenetrable cordon of black people shouting "Glory to God! Glory!

32. Foote, *Civil War*, III, 896.

Glory! Glory!" "Bless the Lord! The great Messiah! I knowed him as soon as I seed him. He's been in my heart four long years. Come to free his children from bondage. Glory, Hallelujah!" Several freed slaves touched Lincoln to make sure he was real. "I know I am free," shouted an old woman, "for I have seen Father Abraham and felt him." Overwhelmed by rare emotions, Lincoln said to one black man who fell on his knees in front of him: "Don't kneel to me. That is not right. You must kneel to God only, and thank Him for the liberty you will enjoy hereafter."[33] Among the reporters from northern newspapers who described these events was one whose presence was a potent symbol of the revolution. He was T. Morris Chester, who sat at a desk in the Confederate Capitol drafting his dispatch to the *Philadelphia Press*. "Richmond has never before presented such a spectacle of jubilee," he wrote. "What a wonderful change has come over the spirit of Southern dreams."[34] Chester was a black man.

For Robert E. Lee and his army the dreams had turned into a nightmare. Reduced to 35,000 men, the scattered divisions from Petersburg and Richmond rendezvoused at Amelia Courthouse thirty-five miles to the west, where the starving men expected to find a trainload of rations. Because of a mixup they found ammunition instead, the last thing they needed since the worn-out horses could scarcely pull the ordnance the army was carrying. A delay to forage the countryside for food proved fatal. Lee had intended to follow the railroad down to Danville, where he could link up with Johnston and where Jefferson Davis on April 4 issued a rallying cry to his people: "Relieved from the necessity of guarding cities . . . with our army free to move from point to point . . . and where the foe will be far removed from his own base . . . nothing is now needed to render our triumph certain, but . . . our own unquenchable resolve."[35] But the foe was closer to Danville than Lee's army was. Racing alongside the retreating rebels a few miles to the south were Sheridan's cavalry and three infantry corps. On April 5 they cut the Danville railroad, forcing Lee to change direction toward Lynchburg and the Blue Ridge passes beyond.

But this goal too was frustrated by the weariness of Lee's despondent

33. Burke Davis, *To Appomattox: Nine April Days, 1865* (New York, 1959), 184; Foote, *Civil War*, III, 897; Charles Carleton Coffin, *The Boys of '61* (Boston, 1896), 538–42.
34. *Philadelphia Press*, April 11, 12, 1865.
35. Rowland, *Davis*, VI, 529–31.

men and the speed of Union pursuers who sniffed victory and the end of the war. Stabbing attacks by blue cavalry garnered scores of prisoners, while hundreds of other southerners collapsed in exhaustion by the roadside and waited for the Yankees to pick them up. Along an obscure stream named Sayler's Creek on April 6, three Union corps cut off a quarter of Lee's army, captured 6,000 of them, and destroyed much of their wagon train. "My God!" exclaimed Lee when he learned of this action. "Has the army been dissolved?"[36]

Not yet, but it soon would be. As the remaining rebels trudged westward on April 7, Grant sent Lee a note under flag of truce calling on him to surrender. Lee responded with a feeler about Grant's terms. The northern commander offered the same terms as at Vicksburg: parole until exchanged. Since Lee's surrender would virtually end the war, the part about exchange was a mere formality. As the tension mounted on April 8—Grant had a splitting headache and Meade suffered from nausea—Lee parried with a vague proposal to discuss a general "restoration of peace," a political matter on which Grant had no authority to negotiate. Grant shook his aching head and commented: "It looks as if Lee meant to fight."[37]

Lee did have that notion, intending to try a breakout attack against Sheridan's troopers blocking the road near Appomattox Courthouse on the morning of April 9. For the last time rebel yells shattered the Palm Sunday stillness as the gray scarecrows drove back Union horsemen— only to reveal two Yankee infantry corps coming into line behind them. Two other Union corps were closing in on Lee's rear. Almost surrounded, outnumbered by five or six to one in effective troops, Lee faced up to the inevitable. One of his subordinates suggested an alternative to surrender: the men could take to the woods and become guerrillas. No, said Lee, who did not want all of Virginia devastated as the Shenandoah Valley had been; the guerrillas "would become mere bands of marauders, and the enemy's cavalry would pursue them and overrun many sections they may never [otherwise] have occasion to visit. We would bring on a state of affairs it would take the country years to recover from." With a heavy heart Lee decided that "there is nothing left for me to do but go and see General Grant, and I would rather die a thousand deaths."[38]

36. Douglas Southall Freeman, R. E. Lee: A Biography, 4 vols. (New York, 1934–35), IV, 84.
37. Catton, Grant Takes Command, 460.
38. Freeman, Lee, IV, 120–23.

Lee sent a note through the lines offering to surrender. Grant's headache and Meade's illness vanished. The bleeding and dying were over; they had won. To the home of Wilmer McLean went Lee and Grant for the surrender formalities. In 1861, McLean had lived near Manassas, where his house was a Confederate headquarters and a Yankee shell had crashed into his dining room. He moved to this remote village in southside Virginia to escape the contending armies only to find the final drama of the war played out in his living room. The vanquished commander, six feet tall and erect in bearing, arrived in full-dress uniform with sash and jeweled sword; the victor, five feet eight with stooped shoulders, appeared in his usual private's blouse with mud-spattered trousers tucked into muddy boots—because his headquarters wagon had fallen behind in the race to cut off the enemy. There in McLean's parlor the son of an Ohio tanner dictated surrender terms to the scion of a First Family of Virginia.

The terms were generous: officers and men could go home "not to be disturbed by U.S. authority so long as they observe their paroles and the laws in force where they may reside." This clause had great significance. Serving as a model for the subsequent surrender of other Confederate armies, it guaranteed southern soldiers immunity from prosecution for treason. Lee asked another favor. In the Confederate army, he explained, enlisted men in the cavalry and artillery owned their horses; could they keep them? Yes, said Grant; privates as well as officers who claimed to own horses could take them home "to put in a crop to carry themselves and their families through the next winter." "This will have the best possible effect upon the men," said Lee, and "will do much toward conciliating our people." After signing the papers, Grant introduced Lee to his staff. As he shook hands with Grant's military secretary Ely Parker, a Seneca Indian, Lee stared a moment at Parker's dark features and said, "I am glad to see one real American here." Parker responded, "We are all Americans." [39]

The surrender completed, the two generals saluted somberly and parted. "This will live in history," said one of Grant's aides. But the Union commander seemed distracted. Having given birth to a reunited nation, he experienced a post-partum melancholy. "I felt . . . sad and depressed," Grant wrote, "at the downfall of a foe who had fought so long

---

39. O.R., Ser. I, Vol. 46, pt. 1, pp. 57–58; Horace Porter, "The Surrender at Appomattox Courthouse," *Battles and Leaders*, IV, 739–40; Davis, *To Appomattox*, 386.

and valiantly, and had suffered so much for a cause, though that cause was, I believe, one of the worst for which a people ever fought." As news of the surrender spread through Union camps, batteries began firing joyful salutes until Grant ordered them stopped. "The war is over," he said; "the rebels are our countrymen again, and the best sign of rejoicing after the victory will be to abstain from all demonstrations."[40] To help bring those former rebels back into the Union, Grant sent three days' rations for 25,000 men across the lines. This perhaps did something to ease the psychological as well as physical pain of Lee's soldiers.

So did an important symbolic gesture at a formal ceremony three days later when Confederate troops marched up to stack arms and surrender their flags. As they came, many among them shared the sentiments of one officer: "Was this to be the end of all our marching and fighting for the past four years? I could not keep back the tears." The Union officer in charge of the surrender ceremony was Joshua L. Chamberlain, the fighting professor from Bowdoin who won a medal of honor for Little Round Top, had been twice wounded since then, and was now a major general. Leading the southerners as they marched toward two of Chamberlain's brigades standing at attention was John B. Gordon, one of Lee's hardest fighters who now commanded Stonewall Jackson's old corps. First in line of march behind him was the Stonewall Brigade, five regiments containing 210 ragged survivors of four years of war. As Gordon approached at the head of these men with "his chin drooped to his breast, downhearted and dejected in appearance," Chamberlain gave a brief order, and a bugle call rang out. Instantly the Union soldiers shifted from order arms to carry arms, the salute of honor. Hearing the sound General Gordon looked up in surprise, and with sudden realization turned smartly to Chamberlain, dipped his sword in salute, and ordered his own men to carry arms. These enemies in many a bloody battle ended the war not with shame on one side and exultation on the other but with a soldier's "mutual salutation and farewell."[41]

The news of Lee's surrender traveled through a North barely recovered from boisterous celebrations of Richmond's capture. The fall of the rebel capital had merited a *nine-hundred* gun salute in Washington;

40. Davis, *To Appomattox*, 387; *Personal Memoirs of Grant*, II, 489; Porter, "The Surrender at Appomattox Courthouse," 743.
41. Davis, *To Appomattox*, 362; Joshua L. Chamberlain, "The Last Salute of the Army of Northern Virginia," in *Southern Historical Society Papers*, 32 (1904), 362.

the surrender of Lee produced another five hundred. "From one end of Pennsylvania Avenue to the other," wrote a reporter, "the air seemed to burn with the bright hues of the flag. . . . Almost by magic the streets were crowded with hosts of people, talking, laughing, hurrahing and shouting in the fullness of their joy. Men embraced one another, 'treated' one another, made up old quarrels, renewed old friendships, marched arm-in-arm singing." The scene was the same on Wall Street in New York, where "men embraced and hugged each other, *kissed* each other, retreated into doorways to dry their eyes and came out again to flourish their hats and hurrah," according to an eyewitness. "They sang 'Old Hundred,' the Doxology, 'John Brown,' and 'The Star-Spangled Banner' . . . over and over, with a massive roar from the crowd and a unanimous wave of hats at the end of each repetition." "My only experience of a people stirred up to like intensity of feeling," wrote a diarist, "was the great Union meeting at Union Square in April 1861." But this time the feeling was even more intense because "founded on memories of years of failure, all but hopeless, and the consciousness that national victory was at last secured."[42]

Lincoln shared this joyous release of pent-up tension, but he was already thinking more of the future than of the past. While in Richmond he had met with John A. Campbell, one of the Confederate commissioners at the earlier Hampton Roads conference. Campbell was now ready to return to the Union on Lincoln's terms. He suggested an apparent way to undermine what was left of the southern war effort: allow the Virginia legislature to meet so it could withdraw the state's troops from the Confederacy. The president thought this a good idea and on April 6 gave the necessary permission. But Campbell misconstrued Lincoln's position to be one that recognized the legislature as the legitimate government of the state. Lincoln had no such purpose. He had authorized a meeting of "the gentlemen who had *acted* as the Legislature of Virginia . . . having power *de facto* to do a specific thing," but did not intend to recognize them as "the rightful Legislature." Lee's surrender which included nearly all of Virginia's soldiers made the whole matter academic, so Lincoln revoked his permission for the legislature to meet. And on April 11 he delivered from a White House balcony a carefully prepared speech on peace and reconstruction to a crowd celebrating Union victory. "There is no authorized organ for us to treat with," he said—thereby disposing of state governments as well as Jeffer-

---

42. Foote, *Civil War*, III, 900; Strong, *Diary*, 574–75.

son Davis's fugitive government. "We must simply begin with, and mould from, disorganized and discordant elements." This he had done in Louisiana, Arkansas, and Tennessee. Defending the government of Louisiana, Lincoln conceded that he would prefer it to have enfranchised literate Negroes and black veterans. He hoped that it would soon do so; as for the unreconstructed states, Lincoln promised an announcement soon of a new policy for their restoration to the Union.[43]

At least one listener interpreted this speech as moving Lincoln closer to the radical Republicans. "That means nigger citizenship," snarled John Wilkes Booth to a companion. "Now, by God, I'll put him through. That is the last speech he will ever make."[44]

43. CWL, VIII, 406–7, 399–405.
44. William Hanchett, *The Lincoln Murder Conspiracies* (Urbana, Ill., 1983), 37.

Epilogue
To the Shoals of Victory

The weeks after Booth fulfilled his vow on Good Friday passed in a dizzying sequence of events. Jarring images dissolved and reformed in kaleidoscopic patterns that left the senses traumatized or elated: Lincoln lying in state at the White House on April 19 as General Grant wept unabashedly at his catafalque; Confederate armies surrendering one after another as Jefferson Davis fled southward hoping to re-establish his government in Texas and carry on the war to victory; Booth killed in a burning barn in Virginia; seven million somber men, women, and children lining the tracks to view Lincoln's funeral train on its way back home to Springfield; the steamboat *Sultana* returning northward on the Mississippi with liberated Union prisoners of war blowing up on April 27 with a loss of life equal to that of the *Titanic* a half-century later; Jefferson Davis captured in Georgia on May 10, accused (falsely) of complicity in Lincoln's assassination, imprisoned and temporarily shackled at Fortress Monroe, Virginia, where he remained for two years until released without trial to live on until his eighty-first year and become part of the ex-Confederate literary corps who wrote weighty tomes to justify their Cause; the Army of the Potomac and Sherman's Army of Georgia marching 200,000 strong in a Grand Review down Pennsylvania Avenue on May 23–24 in a pageantry of power and catharsis before being demobilized from more than one million soldiers to fewer than 80,000 a year later and an eventual peacetime total of 27,000; weary, ragged Confederate soldiers straggling homeward begging or stealing food from dispirited civilians who often did not know where their own next meal was coming from; joyous black people celebrating the jubilee of a freedom whose boundaries they did not yet discern; gangs of southern deserters, guerrillas, and outlaws ravaging a region that would not know real peace for many years to come.

The terms of that peace and the dimensions of black freedom would preoccupy the country for a decade or more. Meanwhile the process of chronicling the war and reckoning its consequences began immediately and has never ceased. More than 620,000 soldiers lost their lives in four years of conflict—360,000 Yankees and at least 260,000 rebels. The number of southern civilians who died as a direct or indirect result of the war cannot be known; what *can* be said is that the Civil War's cost in American lives was as great as in all of the nation's other wars combined through Vietnam. Was the liberation of four million slaves and the preservation of the Union worth the cost? That question too will probably never cease to be debated—but in 1865 few black people and not many northerners doubted the answer.

In time even a good many southerners came to agree with the sentiments of Woodrow Wilson (a native of Virginia who lived four years of his childhood in wartime Georgia) expressed in 1880 when he was a law student at the University of Virginia: "*Because* I love the South, I rejoice in the failure of the Confederacy. . . . Conceive of this Union divided into two separate and independent sovereignties! . . . Slavery was enervating our Southern society. . . . [Nevertheless] I recognize and pay loving tribute to the virtues of the leaders of secession . . . the righteousness of the cause which they thought they were promoting— and to the immortal courage of the soldiers of the Confederacy."[1] Wilson's words embodied themes that would help reconcile generations of southerners to defeat: their glorious forebears had fought courageously for what they believed was right; perhaps they deserved to win; but in the long run it was a good thing they lost. This Lost Cause mentality took on the proportions of a heroic legend, a southern *Götterdämmerung* with Robert E. Lee as a latter-day Siegfried.

But a persistent question has nagged historians and mythologists alike: if Marse Robert was such a genius and his legions so invincible, why did they lose? The answers, though almost as legion as Lee's soldiers, tend to group themselves into a few main categories. One popular an-

1. Quoted in Thomas J. Pressly, *Americans Interpret Their Civil War* (Princeton, 1962), 199–200.

swer has been phrased, from the northern perspective, by quoting Napoleon's aphorism that God was on the side of the heaviest battalions. For southerners this explanation usually took some such form as these words of a Virginian: "They never whipped us, Sir, unless they were four to one. If we had had anything like a fair chance, or less disparity of numbers, we should have won our cause and established our independence."[2] The North had a potential manpower superiority of more than three to one (counting only white men) and Union armed forces had an actual superiority of two to one during most of the war. In economic resources and logistical capacity the northern advantage was even greater. Thus, in this explanation, the Confederacy fought against overwhelming odds; its defeat was inevitable.

But this explanation has not satisfied a good many analysts. History is replete with examples of peoples who have won or defended their independence against greater odds: the Netherlands against the Spain of Philip II; Switzerland against the Hapsburg Empire; the American rebels of 1776 against mighty Britain; North Vietnam against the United States of 1970. Given the advantages of fighting on the defensive in its own territory with interior lines in which stalemate would be victory against a foe who must invade, conquer, occupy, and destroy the capacity to resist, the odds faced by the South were not formidable. Rather, as another category of interpretations has it, internal divisions fatally weakened the Confederacy: the state-rights conflict between certain governors and the Richmond government; the disaffection of non-slaveholders from a rich man's war and poor man's fight; libertarian opposition to necessary measures such as conscription and the suspension of habeas corpus; the lukewarm commitment to the Confederacy by quondam Whigs and unionists; the disloyalty of slaves who defected to the enemy whenever they had a chance; growing doubts among slaveowners themselves about the justice of their peculiar institution and their cause. "So the Confederacy succumbed to internal rather than external causes," according to numerous historians. The South suffered from a "weakness in morale," a "loss of the will to fight." The Confederacy did not lack "the means to continue the struggle," but "the will to do so."[3]

2. Quoted in David Donald, ed., *Why the North Won the Civil War* (Baton Rouge, 1960), ix.
3. Richard E. Beringer, Herman Hattaway, Archer Jones, and William N. Still, Jr., *Why the South Lost the Civil War* (Athens, Ga., 1986), 439, 55; Kenneth M. Stampp, *The Imperiled Union: Essays on the Background of the Civil War* (New York, 1980),

To illustrate their argument that the South could have kept fighting for years longer if it had tried harder, four historians have cited the instructive example of Paraguay. That tiny country carried on a war for six years (1865–71) against an alliance of Brazil, Argentina, and Uruguay whose combined population outnumbered Paraguay's by nearly thirty to one. Almost every male from twelve to sixty fought in the Paraguayan army; the country lost 56 percent of its total population and 80 percent of its men of military age in the war. Indeed, "the Confederate war effort seems feeble by comparison," for a mere 5 percent of the South's white people and 25 percent of the white males of military age were killed. To be sure, Paraguay lost the war, but its "tenacity . . . does exhibit how a people can fight when possessed of total conviction."[4]

It is not quite clear whether these four historians think the South should have emulated Paraguay's example. In any case the "internal division" and "lack of will" explanations for Confederate defeat, while not implausible, are not very convincing either. The problem is that the North experienced similar internal divisions, and if the war had come out differently the Yankees' lack of unity and will to win could be cited with equal plausibility to explain that outcome. The North had its large minority alienated by the rich man's war/poor man's fight theme; its outspoken opposition to conscription, taxation, suspension of habeas corpus, and other war measures; its state governors and legislatures and congressmen who tried to thwart administration policies. If important elements of the southern population, white as well as black, grew disaffected with a war to preserve slavery, equally significant groups in the North dissented from a war to abolish slavery. One critical distinction between Union and Confederacy was the institutionalization of obstruction in the Democratic party in the North, compelling the Republicans to close ranks in support of war policies to overcome and ultimately to discredit the opposition, while the South had no such institutionalized political structure to mobilize support and vanquish resistance.

Nevertheless, the existence of internal divisions on both sides seemed to neutralize this factor as an explanation for Union victory, so a number of historians have looked instead at the quality of leadership both military and civilian. There are several variants of an interpretation that

---

255; Clement Eaton, A *History of the Southern Confederacy* (Collier Books ed., New York, 1961), 250.

4. Beringer et al., *Why the South Lost*, 440–42.

emphasizes a gradual development of superior northern leadership. In Beauregard, Lee, the two Johnstons, and Jackson the South enjoyed abler military commanders during the first year or two of the war, while Jefferson Davis was better qualified by training and experience than Lincoln to lead a nation at war. But Lee's strategic vision was limited to the Virginia theater, and the Confederate government neglected the West, where Union armies developed a strategic design and the generals to carry it out, while southern forces floundered under incompetent commanders who lost the war in the West. By 1863, Lincoln's remarkable abilities gave him a wide edge over Davis as a war leader, while in Grant and Sherman the North acquired commanders with a concept of total war and the necessary determination to make it succeed. At the same time, in Edwin M. Stanton and Montgomery Meigs, aided by the entrepreneurial talent of northern businessmen, the Union developed superior managerial talent to mobilize and organize the North's greater resources for victory in the modern industrialized conflict that the Civil War became.[5]

This interpretation comes closer than others to credibility. Yet it also commits the fallacy of reversibility—that is, if the outcome had been reversed some of the same factors could be cited to explain Confederate victory. If the South had its bumblers like Bragg and Pemberton and Hood who lost the West, and Joseph Johnston who fought too little and too late, the North had its McClellan and Meade who threw away chances in the East and its Pope and Burnside and Hooker who nearly lost the war in that theater where the genius of Lee and his lieutenants nearly won it, despite all the South's disadvantages. If the Union had its Stanton and Meigs, the Confederacy had its Josiah Gorgas and other unsung heroes who performed miracles of organization and improvisation. If Lincoln had been defeated for re-election in 1864, as he anticipated in August, history might record Davis as the great war leader and Lincoln as an also-ran.

Most attempts to explain southern defeat or northern victory lack the

5. See especially T. Harry Williams, "The Military Leadership of North and South," and David M. Potter, "Jefferson Davis and the Political Factors in Confederate Defeat," in Donald, ed., Why the North Won, 23–48, 91–114; Thomas L. Connelly, "Robert E. Lee and the Western Confederacy: A Criticism of Lee's Strategic Ability," in John T. Hubbell, ed., Battles Lost and Won: Essays from Civil War History (Westport, Conn., 1975), 197–214; Allan Nevins, The War for the Union, 4 vols. (New York, 1959–71); Herman Hattaway and Archer Jones, How the North Won: A Military History of the Civil War (Urbana, 1983).

dimension of *contingency*—the recognition that at numerous critical points during the war things might have gone altogether differently. Four major turning points defined the eventual outcome. The first came in the summer of 1862, when the counter-offensives of Jackson and Lee in Virginia and Bragg and Kirby Smith in the West arrested the momentum of a seemingly imminent Union victory. This assured a prolongation and intensification of the conflict and created the potential for Confederate success, which appeared imminent before each of the next three turning points.

The first of these occurred in the fall of 1862, when battles at Antietam and Perryville threw back Confederate invasions, forestalled European mediation and recognition of the Confederacy, perhaps prevented a Democratic victory in the northern elections of 1862 that might have inhibited the government's ability to carry on the war, and set the stage for the Emancipation Proclamation which enlarged the scope and purpose of the conflict. The third critical point came in the summer and fall of 1863 when Gettysburg, Vicksburg, and Chattanooga turned the tide toward ultimate northern victory.

One more reversal of that tide seemed possible in the summer of 1864 when appalling Union casualties and apparent lack of progress especially in Virginia brought the North to the brink of peace negotiations and the election of a Democratic president. But the capture of Atlanta and Sheridan's destruction of Early's army in the Shenandoah Valley clinched matters for the North. Only then did it become possible to speak of the inevitability of Union victory. Only then did the South experience an irretrievable "loss of the will to fight."

Of all the explanations for Confederate defeat, the loss of will thesis suffers most from its own particular fallacy of reversibility—that of putting the cart before the horse. Defeat causes demoralization and loss of will; victory pumps up morale and the will to win. Nothing illustrates this better than the radical transformation of *northern* will from defeatism in August 1864 to a "depth of determination . . . to fight to the last" that "astonished" a British journalist a month later. The southern loss of will was a mirror image of this northern determination. These changes of mood were caused mainly by events on the battlefield. Northern victory and southern defeat in the war cannot be understood apart from the contingency that hung over every campaign, every battle, every election, every decision during the war. This phenomenon of contingency can best be presented in a narrative format—a format this book has tried to provide.

Arguments about the causes and consequences of the Civil War, as well as the reasons for northern victory, will continue as long as there are historians to wield the pen—which is, perhaps even for this bloody conflict, mightier than the sword. But certain large consequences of the war seem clear. Secession and slavery were killed, never to be revived during the century and a quarter since Appomattox. These results signified a broader transformation of American society and polity punctuated if not alone achieved by the war. Before 1861 the two words "United States" were generally rendered as a plural noun: "the United States *are* a republic." The war marked a transition of the United States to a singular noun. The "Union" also became the nation, and Americans now rarely speak of their Union except in an historical sense. Lincoln's wartime speeches betokened this transition. In his first inaugural address he used the word "Union" twenty times and the word "nation" not once. In his first message to Congress, on July 4, 1861, he used "Union" thirty-two times and "nation" three times. In his letter to Horace Greeley of August 22, 1862, on the relationship of slavery to the war, Lincoln spoke of the Union eight times and of the nation not at all. Little more than a year later, in his address at Gettysburg, the president did not refer to the "Union" at all but used the word "nation" five times to invoke a new birth of freedom and nationalism for the United States. And in his second inaugural address, looking back over the events of the past four years, Lincoln spoke of one side seeking to dissolve the *Union* in 1861 and the other accepting the challenge of war to preserve the *nation*.

The old federal republic in which the national government had rarely touched the average citizen except through the post-office gave way to a more centralized polity that taxed the people directly and created an internal revenue bureau to collect these taxes, drafted men into the army, expanded the jurisdiction of federal courts, created a national currency and a national banking system, and established the first national agency for social welfare—the Freedmen's Bureau. Eleven of the first twelve amendments to the Constitution had limited the powers of the national government; six of the next seven, beginning with the Thirteenth Amendment in 1865, vastly expanded those powers at the expense of the states.

This change in the federal balance paralleled a radical shift of political power from South to North. During the first seventy-two years of the republic down to 1861 a slaveholding resident of one of the states that joined the Confederacy had been President of the United States for forty-nine of those years—more than two-thirds of the time. In Congress, twenty-three of the thirty-six speakers of the House and twenty-four of the presidents pro tem of the Senate had been southerners. The Supreme Court always had a southern majority; twenty of the thirty-five justices to 1861 had been appointed from slave states. After the war a century passed before a resident of an ex-Confederate state was elected president. For half a century *none* of the speakers of the House or presidents pro tem of the Senate came from the South, and only five of the twenty-six Supreme Court justices appointed during that half-century were southerners.

These figures symbolize a sharp and permanent change in the direction of American development. Through most of American history the South has seemed different from the rest of the United States, with "a separate and unique identity . . . which appeared to be out of the mainstream of American experience."[6] But when did the northern stream become the mainstream? From a broader perspective it may have been the *North* that was exceptional and unique before the Civil War. The South more closely resembled a majority of the societies in the world than did the rapidly changing North during the antebellum generation. Despite the abolition of legal slavery or serfdom throughout much of the western hemisphere and western Europe, most of the world—like the South—had an unfree or quasi-free labor force. Most societies in the world remained predominantly rural, agricultural, and labor-intensive; most, including even several European countries, had illiteracy rates as high or higher than the South's 45 percent; most like the South remained bound by traditional values and networks of family, kinship, hierarchy, and patriarchy. The North—along with a few countries of northwestern Europe—hurtled forward eagerly toward a future of industrial capitalism that many southerners found distasteful if not frightening; the South remained proudly and even defiantly rooted in the past before 1861.

Thus when secessionists protested that they were acting to preserve traditional rights and values, they were correct. They fought to protect their constitutional liberties against the perceived northern threat to overthrow them. The South's concept of republicanism had not changed in three-quarters of a century; the North's had. With complete sincerity the South fought to preserve its version of the republic of the founding

6. Monroe L. Billington, ed., *The South: A Central Theme?* (Huntington, N.Y. 1976), 1.

fathers—a government of limited powers that protected the rights of property and whose constituency comprised an independent gentry and yeomanry of the white race undisturbed by large cities, heartless factories, restless free workers, and class conflict. The accession to power of the Republican party, with its ideology of competitive, egalitarian, free-labor capitalism, was a signal to the South that the northern majority had turned irrevocably toward this frightening, revolutionary future. Indeed, the Black Republican party appeared to the eyes of many southerners as "essentially a revolutionary party" composed of "a motley throng of Sans culottes . . . Infidels and freelovers, interspersed by Bloomer women, fugitive slaves, and amalgamationists."[7] Therefore secession was a pre-emptive counterrevolution to prevent the Black Republican revolution from engulfing the South. "We are not revolutionists," insisted James B. D. DeBow and Jefferson Davis during the Civil War, "We are resisting revolution. . . . We are conservative."[8]

Union victory in the war destroyed the southern vision of America and ensured that the northern vision would become the American vision. Until 1861, however, it was the North that was out of the mainstream, not the South. Of course the northern states, along with Britain and a few countries in northwestern Europe, were cutting a new channel in world history that would doubtless have become the mainstream even if the American Civil War had not happened. Russia had abolished serfdom in 1861 to complete the dissolution of this ancient institution of bound labor in Europe. But for Americans the Civil War marked the turning point. A Louisiana planter who returned home sadly after the war wrote in 1865: "Society has been completely changed by the war. The [French] revolution of '89 did not produce a greater change in the 'Ancien Régime' than this has in our social life." And four years later George Ticknor, a retired Harvard professor, concluded that the Civil War had created a "great gulf between what happened before in our century and what has happened since, or what is likely to happen hereafter. It does not seem to me as if I were living in the country in which I was born."[9] From the war sprang the great flood that caused

---

7. *New Orleans Daily Delta*, Nov. 3, 1860; Steven A. Channing, *Crisis of Fear: Secession in South Carolina* (New York, 1970), 287.
8. *DeBow's Review*, 33 (1862), 44; Rowland, *Davis*, VI, 357.
9. Richard Taylor to Samuel L. M. Barlow, Dec. 13, 1865, Barlow Papers, Henry E. Huntington Library; Ticknor quoted in Morton Keller, *Affairs of State: Public Life in Late Nineteenth Century America* (Cambridge, Mass., 1977), 2.

the stream of American history to surge into a new channel and transferred the burden of exceptionalism from North to South.

What would be the place of freed slaves and their descendants in this new order? In 1865 a black soldier who recognized his former master among a group of Confederate prisoners he was guarding called out a greeting: "Hello, massa; bottom rail on top dis time!"[10] Would this new arrangement of rails last? That is a question for subsequent volumes in this series to ponder.

10. Leon F. Litwack, *Been in the Storm So Long: The Aftermath of Slavery* (New York, 1979), 102.

Afterword

Re-reading a book that I wrote more than fifteen years ago is a humbling experience. I see small things that could have been improved at the time and more substantial elements that I could make better if I were writing it now. The large quantity and high quality of Civil War scholarship during the past fifteen years has deepened and broadened our knowledge of many of the era's events. If I were writing the book today I could incorporate the findings of this scholarship to enrich my own narrative and interpretation.

But as the novelist Thomas Wolfe said, "you can't go home again." A book is the unique product of the time and circumstances in which an author wrote it. To revisit the book two decades later and attempt to revise the product of a particular cultural environment would be a mistake. Besides, my ego continues to be flattered by letters and other communications from strangers who tell me that *Battle Cry* has stimulated in them an insatiable interest in the Civil War era and is the best single volume on the subject they have read. The book continues to be assigned in many college and advanced placement high school courses.

A year after the initial publication of *Battle Cry*, the historian Maris Vinovskis published an article with the double-entendre title "Have Social Historians Lost the Civil War?"[1] Social history had been the

1. "Have Social Historians Lost the Civil War? Some Preliminary Demographic Speculations," *Journal of American History* 76 (June 1989), 34–58.

most active and innovative field of American historiography since the 1960s, but so far, said Vinovskis, social historians had given little attention to the Civil War, which remained the province of military and political historians. Since 1989, social historians have found the Civil War and they may even wind up winning it.

Because the number of books and articles published on Civil War social history as well as other themes in the past fifteen years is so large, to cite only the few titles for which there is room here would be invidious.[2] What I can say is that work on the experiences of civilians on the home front, especially women and even children, has been a rich field of inquiry. Gender history has become an important field of Civil War scholarship, and this includes a new emphasis on ideas of masculinity among soldiers. The social backgrounds and ideologies of soldiers have also been the subjects of numerous books. The several hundred women who dressed as men and managed to enlist as soldiers have received a great deal of attention. Even the narratives of military campaigns and battles, which still constitute a large proportion of Civil War studies, now focus much more on the backgrounds and experiences of men in the ranks than earlier studies. Civil War prisons and prisoners have finally begun to get the attention they have so long needed. Historians are finally beginning to investigate the importance of religion to the Civil War generation. The experiences of slaves during a war that enabled them to win freedom had been the subject of many studies before1988, but have become the focus of even more scholarship since then.

Nor have traditional subjects been neglected during the past decade and a half. New books about Abraham Lincoln appear virtually every year, and three major biographies of Jefferson Davis have been published. Several new biographies of Ulysses S. Grant have offered a long-overdue positive reappraisal of his generalship and even his presidency. By contrast, several books critical of the once-untouchable icon Robert E. Lee have come out since 1988 and have been answered by a legion of Lee defenders. New books on William Tecumseh Sherman have almost equaled the number of Grant or Lee biographies during that period, while books and articles about Joshua Lawrence Chamberlain have become something of a cottage industry.

2. For summaries of scholarship through 1998, see James M. McPherson and William J. Cooper, eds., *Writing the Civil War: The Quest to Understand* (Columbia, S.C., 1998).

If I were writing *Battle Cry* today, I would benefit richly from this scholarship. But I have been pleasantly surprised to discover that *Battle Cry* anticipated some of the newer findings and that many of my own interpretations stand up quite well in the light of subsequent scholarship. In re-reading my own words, however, I discovered that I left one of my principle themes unfinished. The book's title, the song that furnished that title, and the preface set forth the varied and contrasting themes of Freedom as the goals for which both Union and Confederacy fought in 1861 and the expanded goal of abolishing slavery that emerged as the slaves'—and ultimately the North's—war aim. But there is more to be said about this complicated question of Freedom, or Liberty.

As usual, Abraham Lincoln said it best. In April 1864 he returned to Baltimore for the first time since he had passed through the city secretly in the middle of the night three years earlier to foil a plot to assassinate him. This time he came in the full light of day and gave one of his few public speeches during the war. "The world has never had a good definition of the word liberty, and the American people, just now, are much in want of one," said Lincoln on that occasion. "We all declare for liberty; but in using the same *word* we not all mean the same *thing*. With some the word liberty may mean for each man to do as he pleases with himself, and the product of his labor; while with others the same may mean for some men to do as they please with other men, and the product of other men's labor. Here are two, not only different, but incompatible things, called by the same name—liberty." Lincoln went on to illustrate his point with a parable about animals. "The shepherd drives the wolf from the sheep's throat," he said, "for which the sheep thanks the shepherd as a *liberator*, while the wolf denounces him for the same act as the destroyer of liberty, especially as the sheep is a black one. Plainly the sheep and the wolf are not agreed upon a definition of the word liberty; and precisely the same difference prevails to-day among us human creatures, even in the North, and all professing to love liberty. Hence we behold the processes by which thousands are daily passing from under the yoke of bondage, hailed by some as the advance of liberty, and bewailed by others as the destruction of all liberty."[3]

The shepherd in this remarkable fable was, of course, Lincoln himself; the black sheep was a slave and the wolf was his owner. Lincoln

3. CWL, VII, 301–2.

here prophesied the impending victory of the shepherd's and black sheep's version of liberty. But he did more than that—he signified a deeper transformation in the meaning of liberty accomplished by the Civil War. This was a transformation from what the late Isaiah Berlin described as "Negative Liberty" to "Positive Liberty."[4] The idea of negative liberty is perhaps more familiar. It can be defined as the absence of restraint, a freedom from interference by outside authority with individual thought or behavior. A law requiring motorcyclists to wear a helmet would be, under this definition, to prevent them from enjoying the freedom to go bareheaded if they wish. Negative liberty, therefore, can be described as freedom *from*. Positive liberty can best be understood as freedom *to*. It is not necessarily incompatible with negative liberty, but has a different focus or emphasis. Freedom of the press is generally viewed as a negative liberty—freedom from interference with what a writer writes or a reader reads. But an illiterate person suffers from a denial of positive liberty; he is unable to enjoy the freedom to write or read whatever he chooses, not because some authority prevents him from doings so but because he cannot read or write anything. He suffers not the absence of a negative liberty—freedom from—but of a positive liberty—freedom *to* read and write. The remedy lies not in removal of restraint but in achievement of the capacity to read and write.

Another way of defining the distinction between these two concepts of liberty is to describe their relation to power. Negative liberty and power are at opposite poles; power is the enemy of liberty, especially power concentrated in the hands of a central government. That is the kind of power that many of the founding fathers feared most; that is why they fragmented power in the Constitution and the federal system; that is why they wrote a bill of rights to restrain the power of the national government to interfere with individual liberty. In the first ten amendments to the Constitution, usually called the Bill of Rights, the phrase "shall not" recurs again and again as a restraint on the power of the national government.

Throughout the antebellum era, southern defenders of slavery relied on this concept of negative liberty to deny the power of the national government to interfere with their right to own slaves and take them into the territories. "That *perfect* liberty they sigh for," said

4. Isaiah Berlin, *Four Essays on Liberty* (New York, 1970), 118–72.
5. CWL, II, 250.

Lincoln in 1854, is "the liberty of making slaves of other people."[5] Secession was the most extreme form of negative liberty, which therefore became treason in the eyes of most northerners, including Lincoln.

Positive liberty in the form of the *power* of Union armies became the newly dominant American understanding of liberty. Liberty and power were no longer in conflict. As commander in chief of an army of a million men in 1864, Lincoln the shepherd needed every bit of that power to protect the freedom of the black sheep from the slaveholding wolf. This new concept of positive liberty permanently transformed the U.S. Constitution, starting with the 13th, 14th, and 15th Amendments, which abolished slavery and granted equal civil and political rights to the freed slaves. Instead of the "shall nots" of earlier constitutional amendments, these three contained the sentence: "Congress *shall have the power* to enforce this article." (Italics added) So did three of the next four constitutional amendments adopted after the 15th.

Even though for three generations after 1877 the nation reneged on its pledge of civil and political equality contained in the 14th and 15th Amendments, Supreme Court decisions and the civil rights movement in the second half of the twentieth century breathed new life into Lincoln's concept of positive liberty. The libertarians and southern conservatives of the 1980s and 1990s who wanted to revive the exclusively negative form of liberty that prevailed before the Civil War were right to make Lincoln a target of their intellectual artillery.[6] Unlike these one-dimensional philosophers of negative liberty, however, Lincoln understood that secession and war had launched a revolution that changed America forever. Eternal vigilance against the tyrannical power of government remains the price of our negative liberties, to be sure. But it is equally true that the instruments of government power remain necessary to defend the equal justice under law of positive liberty.

James M. McPherson
Princeton, April 23, 2003

6. See Jeffrey Rogers Hummel, *Emancipating Slaves, Enslaving Free Men: A History of the American Civil War* (Chicago, 1996); Thomas J. DiLorenzo, *The Real Lincoln: A New Look at Abraham Lincoln, His Agenda, and an Unnecessary War* (New York, 2002); M. E. Bradford, *Remembering Who We Are: Observations of a Southern Conservative* (Athens, Ga., 1985) and *The Reactionary Imperative: Essays Literary and Political* (Peru, Ill., 1990).

Abbreviated Titles

AHR	*American Historical Review*
Battles and Leaders	Clarence C. Buel and Robert U. Johnson, eds., *Battles and Leaders of the Civil War*, 4 vols. (New York, 1888)
CG	*Congressional Globe*
CWH	*Civil War History*
CWL	Roy C. Basler, ed., *The Collected Works of Abraham Lincoln*, 9 vols. (New Brunswick, N.J., 1952–55)
Dennett, *Lincoln/Hay*	Tyler Dennett, ed., *Lincoln and the Civil War in the Diaries and Letters of John Hay* (New York, 1939)
Foote, *Civil War*	Shelby Foote, *The Civil War: A Narrative*, 3 vols. (New York, 1958, 1963, 1974)
Jones, *War Clerk's Diary* (Miers)	John B. Jones, *A Rebel War Clerk's Diary*, ed. Earl Schenck Miers (New York, 1958)
Jones, *War Clerk's Diary* (Swiggett)	John B. Jones, *A Rebel War Clerk's Diary at the Confederate States Capitol*, ed. Henry Swiggett (New York, 1935)
JAH	*Journal of American History*
JSH	*Journal of Southern History*
MVHR	*Mississippi Valley Historical Review*
Nevins, *Ordeal*	Allan Nevins, *Ordeal of the Union*, 2 vols. (New York, 1947). Vol. I: *Fruits of Manifest Destiny, 1847–1852*. Vol. II: *A House Dividing, 1852–1857*

Nevins, *Emergence*   Allan Nevins, *The Emergence of Lincoln*, 2 vols. (New York, 1950). Vol. I: *Douglas, Buchanan, and Party Chaos 1857–1859*. *Vol. II: Prologue to Civil War, 1859–1861*

Nevins, *War*   Allan Nevins, *The War for the Union*, 4 vols. (New York, 1959, 1960, 1971). Vol. I: *The Improvised War, 1861–1862*. Vol. II: *War Becomes Revolution*. Vol. III: *The Organized War, 1863–1864*. Vol. IV: *The Organized War to Victory, 1864–1865*

O.R.   *War of the Rebellion . . . Official Records of the Union and Confederate Armies*, 128 vols. (Washington, 1880–1901)

O.R. Navy   *Official Records of the Union and Confederate Navies in the War of the Rebellion*, 30 vols. (Washington, 1894–1922)

Potter, *Impending Crisis*   David M. Potter, *The Impending Crisis 1848–1861* (New York, 1976)

Rowland, *Davis*   Dunbar Rowland, ed., *Jefferson Davis, Constitutionalist: His Letters, Papers, and Speeches*, 10 vols. (Jackson, Miss., 1923)

Strong, *Diary*   *The Diary of George Templeton Strong*, vol. 3: *The Civil War 1860–1865*, ed. Allan Nevins and Milton Halsey Thomas (New York, 1952)

Wiley, *Johnny Reb*   Bell Irvin Wiley, *The Life of Johnny Reb: The Common Soldier of the Confederacy* (Indianapolis, 1943)

Wiley, *Billy Yank*   Bell Irvin Wiley, *The Life of Billy Yank: The Common Soldier of the Union* (Indianapolis, 1952)

Woodward, *Chesnut's Civil War*   C. Vann Woodward, ed., *Mary Chesnut's Civil War* (New Haven, 1981)

Bibliographical Note

This guide to books about the Civil War and its causes includes only a fraction of the studies cited in the footnotes, which in turn constitute but a portion of the sources consulted in the research for this book. And that research merely sampled the huge corpus of literature on the Civil War era, which totals more than 50,000 books and pamphlets on the war years alone—not to mention a boundless number of articles, doctoral dissertations, and manuscript collections. Indeed, there are said to be more works in English on Abraham Lincoln than on any other persons except Jesus of Nazareth and William Shakespeare.

The best introduction to this era can be found in two multi-volume studies, published a half-century apart, which have become classics in American historiography: James Ford Rhodes, *History of the United States from the Compromise of 1850 to the Restoration of Home Rule at the South*, 7 vols. (New York, 1892–1906); and Allan Nevins, *Ordeal of the Union*, 4 vols., and *The War for the Union*, 4 vols. (New York, 1947–71). These magisterial volumes present a strong nationalist interpretation of the crisis of the Union, as do nearly all biographies of Lincoln, of which the fullest are John G. Nicolay and John Hay, *Abraham Lincoln: A History*, 10 vols. (New York, 1890), by the wartime president's private secretaries; and James G. Randall, *Lincoln the President*, 4 vols. (New York, 1945–55; Vol. IV completed by Richard N. Current), a scholarly *tour de force* marred only by Randall's attempt to squeeze

Lincoln into a conservative mold that he did not quite fit. For an overcorrection of that viewpoint, consult the most readable one-volume biography, Stephen B. Oates, *With Malice Toward None: The Life of Abraham Lincoln* (New York, 1977). Reflecting a southern viewpoint toward this divisive era is Hudson Strode's biography *Jefferson Davis*, 3 vols. (New York, 1955–64). The papers of these two leading actors in the ordeal of American and Confederate nationalism have been published in Roy P. Basler, ed., *The Collected Works of Abraham Lincoln*, 9 vols. (New Brunswick, 1953–55) and *The Collected Works of Abraham Lincoln—Supplement, 1832–1865* (New Brunswick, 1974); and Dunbar Rowland, ed., *Jefferson Davis, Constitutionalist: His Letters, Papers, and Speeches*, 10 vols. (Jackson, Miss., 1923). Rowland's edition has been superseded for the years through 1855 by Haskell M. Monroe, Jr., James T. McIntosh, Lynda L. Crist, and Mary S. Dix, eds., *The Papers of Jefferson Davis*, 5 vols. to date (Baton Rouge, 1971–85). Mark E. Neely, Jr., *The Abraham Lincoln Encyclopedia* (New York, 1982) contains an extraordinary amount of useful information about the sectional conflict and war; as does David C. Roller and Robert W. Twyman, eds., *The Encyclopedia of Southern History* (Baton Rouge, 1979). Two other reference works, while focusing mainly on military events and personnel, also include some political developments of the antebellum as well as war years: Mark M. Boatner III, *The Civil War Dictionary* (New York, 1959); and Patricia L. Faust, ed., *Historical Times Illustrated Encyclopedia of the Civil War* (New York, 1986).

A study of antebellum economic developments that has achieved the status of a classic well worth reading is George Rogers Taylor, *The Transportation Revolution, 1815–1860* (New York, 1951). A more recent study by the dean of American economic historians, Thomas C. Cochran, *Frontiers of Change: Early Industrialism in America* (New York, 1981), also focuses on the antebellum era. The rise of the "American System of Manufactures" is chronicled in Nathan Rosenberg, ed., *The American System of Manufactures* (Edinburgh, 1969); and Otto Mayr and Robert C. Post, eds., *Yankee Enterprise: The Rise of the American System of Manufactures* (Washington, 1981). Paul Wallace Gates, *The Farmers' Age: Agriculture 1815–1860* (New York, 1962), chronicles changes in agriculture during this era; while Gavin Wright, *The Political Economy of the Cotton South* (New York, 1978), and Harold D. Woodman, *King Cotton and His Retainers* (Lexington, 1968), analyze the production and marketing of the South's leading crop. Daniel J. Boorstin, *The Americans: The National Experience* (New York, 1965), provides fascinating vignettes on how Americans in all walks of life interacted with each other and with their environment.

The most succinct and sensible study of education during this era is Carl F. Kaestle, *Pillars of the Republic: Common Schooling and American Society, 1780–1860* (New York, 1983), which synthesizes a large body of scholarship in a readable, informative fashion. On immigration and nativism, three classic studies are still the best places to begin: Marcus Lee Hansen, *The Atlantic Migration 1607–1860* (Cambridge, Mass., 1940); Oscar Handlin, *Boston's Immigrants 1790–1880: A Study in Acculturation* (rev. ed., Cambridge, Mass., 1959); and Ray Allen Billington, *The Protestant Crusade 1800–1860* (New York, 1938). The image of Irish-Americans is analyzed in Dale T. Knobel, *Paddy and the Republic: Ethnicity and Nationality in Antebellum America* (Middletown, Conn., 1986). For the antebellum temperance movement, see Ian R. Tyrell, *Sobering Up: From Temperance to Prohibition in Antebellum America 1800–1860* (Westport, Conn., 1979); and Jed Dannenbaum, *Drink and Disorder: Temperance Reform in Cincinnati from the Washingtonian Revival to the WCTU* (Urbana, 1984). Perhaps the best introductions to the large literature on the abolitionist movement are James Brewer Stewart, *Holy Warriors: The Abolitionists and American Slavery* (New York, 1976); and Ronald G. Walters, *The Antislavery Appeal: American Abolitionism after 1830* (Baltimore, 1976).

The impact of the antebellum economic transformation on the American working class has been the subject of numerous excellent studies in recent years, including: Thomas Dublin, *Women at Work: The Transformation of Work and Community in Lowell, Massachusetts, 1826–1860* (New York, 1979); Jonathan Prude, *The Coming of Industrial Order: Town and Factory Life in Rural Massachusetts, 1810–1860* (Cambridge, 1983); Sean Wilentz, *Chants Democratic: New York City and the Rise of the American Working Class, 1788–1850* (New York, 1984); and Steven J. Ross, *Workers on the Edge: Work, Leisure, and Politics in Industrializing Cincinnati, 1788–1890* (New York, 1985). Changes in the roles of women and the family during this era have also generated a rich and growing body of literature, including: Nancy F. Cott, *The Bonds of Womanhood: "Woman's Sphere" in New England, 1780–1835* (New Haven, 1977); Carl N. Degler, *At Odds: Women and the Family in America from the Revolution to the Present* (New York, 1980); Mary P. Ryan, *Cradle of the Middle Class: The Family in Oneida County, New York, 1790–1865* (Cambridge, Mass., 1981); Catherine Clinton, *The Plantation Mistress: Woman's World in the Old South* (New York,

1982); and Ellen Carol DuBois, *Feminism and Suffrage: The Emergence of an Independent Women's Movement in America 1848–1869* (Ithaca, 1978).

The "Second Party System" of Jacksonian Democrats and Clay Whigs that formed around economic issues associated with banking, the transportation revolution, and industrialization in the 1830s is analyzed in Richard P. McCormick, *The Second American Party System: Party Formation in the Jacksonian Era* (Chapel Hill, 1966); Arthur M. Schlesinger, Jr., *The Age of Jackson* (Boston, 1945); Jean Baker, *Affairs of Party: The Political Culture of Northern Democrats in the Mid-Nineteenth Century* (Ithaca, 1983); Daniel Walker Howe, *The Political Culture of the American Whigs* (Chicago, 1979); John Ashworth, "*Agrarians & Aristocrats": Party Political Ideology in the United States, 1837–1846* (London, 1983); Bray Hammond, *Banks and Politics in America from the Revolution to the Civil War* (Princeton, 1957); James Roger Sharp, *The Jacksonians versus the Banks: Politics in the States after the Panic of 1837* (New York, 1970); and William G. Shade, *Banks or No Banks: The Money Issue in Western Politics, 1832–1865* (Detroit, 1972). The strongest advocates of an "ethnocultural" interpretation of northern politics are: Lee Benson, *The Concept of Jacksonian Democracy: New York as a Test Case* (Princeton, 1961); and Ronald P. Formisano, *The Birth of Mass Political Parties: Michigan, 1827–1861* (Princeton, 1971). The shape of the relationship between economy, society, and political culture in the South, with particular emphasis on non-slaveholding whites, is outlined by: J. Mills Thornton III, *Politics and Power in a Slave Society: Alabama, 1800–1860* (Baton Rouge, 1978); Steven Hahn, *The Roots of Southern Populism: Yeoman Farmers and the Transformation of the Georgia Upcountry, 1850–1890* (New York, 1983); Marc W. Kruman, *Parties and Politics in North Carolina 1836–1865* (Baton Rouge, 1983); Harry L. Watson, *Jacksonian Politics and Community Conflict: The Emergence of the Second American Party System in Cumberland County, North Carolina* (Baton Rouge, 1981); Paul D. Escott, *Many Excellent People: Power and Privilege in North Carolina, 1850–1900* (Chapel Hill, 1985); and J. William Harris, *Plain Folk and Gentry in a Slave Society: White Liberty and Black Slavery in Augusta's Hinterlands* (Middletown, Conn., 1986).

No aspect of southern history—indeed, of American history—has attracted more attention than slavery. Among the scores of challenging and important books on slaves and masters, the following constitute a starting point for understanding the peculiar institution: Ulrich B. Phillips, *American Negro Slavery* ([1918]; reissued edition with Foreword by Eugene Genovese, Baton Rouge, 1966); Kenneth M. Stampp, *The Peculiar Institution: Slavery in The Ante-Bellum South* (New York, 1956); Stanley M. Elkins, *Slavery: A Problem in American Institutional and Intellectual Life* (1st ed., 1959; 3rd ed., rev., Chicago, 1976); Eugene D. Genovese, *The Political Economy of Slavery* (New York, 1965) and *Roll, Jordan, Roll: The World the Slaves Made* (New York, 1974); John W. Blassingame, *The Slave Community: Plantation Life in the Antebellum South* (1st ed., 1972, rev. and enlarged ed., New York, 1979); Robert W. Fogel and Stanley L. Engerman, *Time on the Cross: The Economics of American Negro Slavery* (Boston, 1974); an anthology of some of the numerous criticisms and challenges of this work is *Reckoning with Slavery: A Critical Study in the Quantitative History of American Negro Slavery* by Paul A. David and others (New York, 1976); also see Herbert G. Gutman, *The Black Family in Slavery and Freedom* (New York, 1976); Willie Lee Rose, *Slavery and Freedom* (New York, 1982); and James Oakes, *The Ruling Race: A History of American Slaveholders* (New York, 1982). The unhappy lot of free blacks in both North and South has been chronicled by Leon F. Litwack, *North of Slavery: The Negro in the Free States* (Chicago, 1961); and Ira Berlin, *Slaves without Masters: The Free Negro in the Antebellum South* (New York, 1974). For the success story of a free black family that owned slaves, see Michael P. Johnson and James L. Roark, *Black Masters: A Free Family of Color in the Old South* (New York, 1984).

Only a tiny sampling of the rich literature on the frontier and the westward movement can be listed here. Malcolm J. Rohrbaugh's *The Trans-Appalachian Frontier* (New York, 1978) narrates the settlement of the inland empire between the Appalachians and the Mississippi, while Ray Allen Billington's *The Far Western Frontier 1830–1860* (New York, 1956) does the same for the vast region west of the Mississippi. The expansionism of the Polk administration that led to war with Mexico is treated in: Frederick Merk, *Manifest Destiny and Mission in American History* (New York, 1963); Norman A. Graebner, *Empire on the Pacific: A Study in Continental Expansion* (New York, 1955); and David Pletcher, *The Diplomacy of Annexation: Texas, Mexico, and the Mexican War* (Columbia, Mo., 1973). The popular enthusiasm generated by the victorious war of conquest is documented by Robert W. Johannsen, *To the Halls of the Montezumas: The War with Mexico in the American Imagination* (New York, 1985); but for the strong opposition to the war among Whigs and antislavery people, see John H.

Schroeder, *Mr. Polk's War: American Opposition and Dissent, 1846–1848* (Madison, 1973).

The fateful consequences of the controversy over expansion of slavery into the territories acquired from Mexico are the starting point for the best single book on the sectional conflict leading to Civil War, David M. Potter, *The Impending Crisis 1848–1861* (New York, 1976). A briefer study that emphasizes the breakdown of the second party system as a causal factor of secession rather than as a result of sectional conflict is Michael F. Holt, *The Political Crisis of the 1850s* (New York, 1978). The emergence of the Free Soil party is discussed in: Richard H. Sewell, *Ballots for Freedom: Antislavery Politics in the United States 1837–1860* (New York, 1976); Joseph G. Rayback, *Free Soil: The Election of 1848* (Lexington, Ky., 1970); and Frederick J. Blue, *The Free Soilers: Third Party Politics 1848–1854* (Urbana, 1973). The most concise account of the complex process that produced the Compromise of 1850 is Holman Hamilton, *Prologue to Conflict: The Crisis and Compromise of 1850* (Lexington, Ky., 1964).

The hostility and violence generated by the fugitive slave law can be followed in: Stanley W. Campbell, *The Slave Catchers: Enforcement of the Fugitive Slave Law 1850–1860* (Chapel Hill, 1970); and Thomas D. Morris, *Free Men All: The Personal Liberty Laws of the North 1780–1861* (Baltimore, 1974). The South's failed quest for economic independence in the 1850s is the subject of: Robert Royal Russel, *Economic Aspects of Southern Sectionalism, 1840–1861* (Urbana, 1923); Herbert Wender, *Southern Commercial Conventions 1837–1859* (Baltimore, 1930); and Fred Bateman and Thomas Weiss, *A Deplorable Scarcity: The Failure of Industrialization in the Slave Economy* (Chapel Hill, 1981). For southern efforts to acquire new slave territory by both legal and illegal means, see Robert E. May, *The Southern Dream of a Caribbean Empire, 1854–1862* (Baton Rouge, 1973); Charles H. Brown, *Agents of Manifest Destiny: The Lives and Times of the Filibusters* (Chapel Hill, 1980); and William O. Scroggs, *Filibusters and Financiers: The Story of William Walker and His Associates* (New York, 1916). Southern support for reopening the slave trade is documented in Ronald T. Takaki, *A Pro-Slavery Crusade: The Agitation to Reopen the Slave Trade* (New York, 1971). All these developments and other manifestations of southern nationalism are discussed in John McCardell, *The Idea of a Southern Nation . . . 1830–1860* (New York, 1979). The preoccupation of southern politicians with the defense of slavery is the theme of William J. Cooper, Jr., *The South and the Politics of Slavery 1828–*

1856 (Baton Rouge, 1978); while Clement Eaton, *The Freedom-of-Thought Struggle in the Old South* (rev. and enlarged ed., New York, 1964), discusses the southern closing of ranks against outside criticism; Avery Craven's *The Coming of the Civil War* (rev. ed., Chicago, 1957) and *The Growth of Southern Nationalism 1848–1861* (Baton Rouge, 1953) tend to justify southern sectionalism as a natural response to northern aggression. Bertram Wyatt-Brown, *Southern Honor: Ethics and Behavior in the Old South* (New York, 1982), analyzes that quality in southern culture that made southrons so touchy about affronts to their "rights."

The best introduction to the free-labor ideology of the Republican party that underlay its opposition to the expansion of slavery is Eric Foner, *Free Soil, Free Labor, Free Men: The Ideology of the Republican Party before the Civil War* (New York, 1970); while the fullest account of the matrix of politics, ideology, and nativism out of which the party was born is William E. Gienapp, *The Origins of the Republican Party, 1852–1856* (New York, 1987). For the tangled web of Democratic politics that produced the Kansas-Nebraska Act, consult George Fort Milton, *The Eve of Conflict: Stephen A. Douglas and the Needless War* (Boston, 1934); and Robert W. Johannsen, *Stephen A. Douglas* (New York, 1973). For a sensitive rendering of the response by Lincoln in the context of the emerging Republican opposition, see Don E. Fehrenbacher, *Prelude to Greatness: Lincoln in the 1850's* (Stanford, 1962). For the consequences of the Kansas-Nebraska Act in Kansas as well as Washington, see James A. Rawley, *Race and Politics: "Bleeding Kansas" and the Coming of the Civil War* (Philadelphia, 1969); and Alice Nichols, *Bleeding Kansas* (New York, 1954). The transformation of politics in two important states is analyzed by Stephen E. Maizlish, *The Triumph of Sectionalism: The Transformation of Ohio Politics, 1844–1856* (Kent, 1983); and Dale Baum, *The Civil War Party System: The Case of Massachusetts, 1848–1876* (Chapel Hill, 1984).

The development of a sectional schism in the Democratic party during the Buchanan administration is the subject of Roy F. Nichols, *The Disruption of the American Democracy* (New York, 1948). Every conceivable facet of the Dred Scott case is examined by Don E. Fehrenbacher, *The Dred Scott Case: Its Significance in American Law and Politics* (New York, 1978). The most systematic analysis of the Lincoln-Douglas debates is Harry V. Jaffa, *An Interpretation of the Issues in the Lincoln-Douglas Debates* (New York, 1959). Of the large literature on John Brown and the Harper's Ferry raid, the most detailed study is Oswald Garrison Villard, *John Brown, 1800–1859* (Boston, 1910); and the most recent biography is Stephen B. Oates, *To Purge This Land with Blood: A Biography of John Brown* (New York, 1970). Some new information and insights can be found in Jeffery S. Rossbach, *Ambivalent Conspirators: John Brown, the Secret Six, and a Theory of Slave Violence* (Philadelphia, 1982). Four older monographs on the election of 1860 that emphasize the emergence of Lincoln and the South's behavior in light of his probable election are still of value: Emerson D. Fite, *The Presidential Campaign of 1860* (New York, 1911); William E. Baringer, *Lincoln's Rise to Power* (Boston, 1937); Reinhard H. Luthin, *The First Lincoln Campaign* (Cambridge, Mass., 1944); and Ollinger Crenshaw, *The Slave States in the Presidential Election of 1860* (Baltimore, 1945).

An older monograph on the secession movement is also still of value: Dwight L. Dumond, *The Secession Movement 1860–1861* (New York, 1931). Ralph Wooster, *The Secession Conventions of the South* (Princeton, 1962), presents basic factual data on the conventions and their delegates; while Donald E. Reynolds, *Editors Make War: Southern Newspapers in the Secession Crisis* (Nashville, 1970), documents the important role of the press in whipping up sentiment for secession. Among the best and most recent studies of the lower-South states that went out first are: Steven A. Channing, *A Crisis of Fear: Secession in South Carolina* (New York, 1970); William L. Barney, *The Secessionist Impulse: Alabama and Mississippi in 1860* (Princeton, 1974); and Michael P. Johnson, *Toward a Patriarchal Republic: The Secession of Georgia* (Baton Rouge, 1977). Several older studies chronicle the initial unionism and post-Sumter secession of the upper South: Henry T. Shanks, *The Secession Movement in Virginia, 1847–1861* (Richmond, 1934); J. Carlyle Sitterson, *The Secession Movement in North Carolina* (Chapel Hill, 1939); and Mary E. R. Campbell, *The Attitude of Tennesseans toward the Union* (New York, 1961). For the border states, see William J. Evitts, *A Matter of Allegiances: Maryland from 1850 to 1861* (Baltimore, 1974); E. Merton Coulter, *The Civil War and Readjustment in Kentucky* (Chapel Hill, 1926); and William E. Parrish, *Turbulent Partnership: Missouri and the Union, 1861–1865* (Columbia, Mo., 1963). Among several one-volume histories of the Confederacy, the most detailed and the most recent both contain good accounts of secession and the establishment of a new Confederate government: E. Merton Coulter, *The Confederate States of America 1861–1865* (Baton Rouge, 1950); and

Emory M. Thomas, *The Confederate Nation, 1861–1865* (New York, 1979).

Essential for understanding the response of the North and especially of Republicans to southern secession are books by two of the foremost historians of this era: David M. Potter, *Lincoln and His Party in the Secession Crisis* (New Haven, 1942, reissued with new preface, 1962); and Kenneth M. Stampp, *And the War Came: The North and the Secession Crisis, 1860–61* (Baton Rouge, 1950). For the failure of the Washington peace conference to resolve the secession crisis, see Robert G. Gunderson, *Old Gentleman's Convention: The Washington Peace Conference of 1861* (Madison, 1961). The issues and the action at Fort Sumter are dramatically laid out by Richard N. Current, *Lincoln and the First Shot* (Philadelphia, 1963); and William A. Swanberg, *First Blood: The Story of Fort Sumter* (New York, 1957).

The military campaigns of the Civil War have evoked some of the most vivid writing in American historical literature, only a tiny sample of which can be included here. The most graphic epic, nearly three thousand pages by a novelist who is also a fine historian, is Shelby Foote, *The Civil War: A Narrative*, 3 vols. (New York, 1958–74), which leans slightly South in its sympathies. Leaning slightly the other way and written in a similarly readable style is Bruce Catton, *The Centennial History of the Civil War*: Vol. I: *The Coming Fury*; Vol. II: *Terrible Swift Sword*; Vol. III: *Never Call Retreat* (Garden City, 1961–65). Another trilogy by a prolific historian of the Civil War is in progress, with two volumes having thus far appeared: William C. Davis, *The Imperiled Union: 1861–1865*: Vol. I: *The Deep Waters of the Proud* and Vol. II: *Stand in the Day of Battle* (Garden City, N.Y. 1982–83). Two marvelous volumes on Civil War soldiers, by one of the giants of Civil War historiography, are based on research in hundreds of collections of letters, diaries, and memoirs, published and unpublished: Bell Irvin Wiley's *The Life of Johnny Reb* (Indianapolis, 1943) and *The Life of Billy Yank* (Indianapolis, 1952). Ella Lonn, *Desertion During the Civil War* (New York, 1928), provides data on that melancholy subject. For the war at sea and on the rivers, see especially Virgil Carrington Jones, *The Civil War at Sea*, 3 vols. (New York, 1960–62).

Retrospective accounts of campaigns and battles by participants, first published in *Scribner's Magazine* two decades after the war and then gathered in four large volumes (available today in an inexpensive reprint edition) are Clarence C. Buel and Robert U. Johnson, eds., *Battles and*

Leaders of the Civil War (New York, 1888, reprint ed. Secaucus, N.J., 1982). The official records of military operations, published a generation or more after the war by the U. S. government, are also accessible today in libraries, second-hand bookstores, and reprint editions: *War of the Rebellion . . . Official Records of the Union and Confederate Armies*, 128 vols. (Washington, 1880–1901) and *Official Records of the Union and Confederate Navies in the War of the Rebellion*, 30 vols. (Washington, 1894–1922). The Civil War took place at the dawn of the age of photography, and many thousand wet-plate photographs of soldiers, battlefields, political leaders, and other images of the war have survived and can be viewed in modern publications, most of which also include a fine narrative text to accompany the pictures. See especially Francis T. Miller, ed., *The Photographic History of the Civil War*, 10 vols. (New York, 1911, reprint ed., 1957); and William C. Davis, ed., *The Image of War 1861–1865*, 6 vols. (Garden City, N.Y., 1981–84). Another visual aid to understanding Civil War campaigns and battles is maps; the best, with accompanying text, can be found in Vol. I of Vincent J. Esposito, ed., *The West Point Atlas of American Wars* (New York, 1959). An indispensable reference guide to military operations is E. B. Long, *The Civil War Day by Day: An Almanac 1861–1865* (Garden City, N.Y., 1971). Two essential compilations of the strength, organization, and casualties of Civil War armies are: William F. Fox, *Regimental Losses in the American Civil War, 1861–1865* (Albany, 1880); and Thomas L. Livermore, *Numbers and Losses in the Civil War in America, 1861–1865* (Boston, 1901).

Of the many hundreds of excellent narratives of campaigns and battles, biographies of generals and of other military leaders, and studies of particular armies, space allows a listing here of only a few outstanding titles in the latter two categories. Brief biographies of all generals on both sides can be found in Ezra J. Warner, *Generals in Gray* (Baton Rouge, 1959) and *Generals in Blue* (Baton Rouge, 1964). One of the true classics of Civil War literature is Douglas Southall Freeman, *R. E. Lee: A Biography*, 4 vols. (New York, 1934–35) which, along with Freeman's *Lee's Lieutenants: A Study in Command*, 3 vols. (New York, 1942–44), constitute an exhaustive history of the Army of Northern Virginia. Historian Thomas L. Connelly has been the chief critic of Lee for the limitation of his strategic vision to the Virginia theater and the chief chronicler of the Confederacy's principal western army; see Connelly's *The Marble Man: Robert E. Lee and His Image in American Society* (New York, 1977), *Army of the Heartland: The Army of Tennes-*

see, 1861–1862 (Baton Rouge, 1967), *Autumn of Glory: The Army of Tennessee, 1862–1865* (Baton Rouge, 1971), and, with Archer Jones, *The Politics of Command: Factions and Ideas in Confederate Strategy* (Baton Rouge, 1973). A British army officer and historian, G. F. R. Henderson, has contributed an appreciative biography of Stonewall Jackson that is also a fine analysis of Confederate operations in Virginia until Jackson's death: *Stonewall Jackson and the American Civil War*, 2 vols. (New York, 1898).

On the Union side both T. Harry Williams, *Lincoln and His Generals* (New York, 1952), and Kenneth P. Williams, *Lincoln Finds a General: A Military Study of the Civil War*, 5 vols. (New York, 1949–59), are critical of McClellan and appreciative of Grant as strategic leaders. Bruce Catton's superb trilogy on the Army of the Potomac, *Mr. Lincoln's Army; Glory Road;* and *A Stillness at Appomattox* (Garden City, N.Y., 1951–53), demonstrates the resilience of these Yankee soldiers despite incompetent leadership and defeat. Two books by a British military expert and historian also offer important insights on Grant's strategic prowess: J. F. C. Fuller, *The Generalship of Ulysses S. Grant* (London, 1929), and *Grant and Lee: A Study in Personality and Generalship* (London, 1923). The best military biography of Grant is Bruce Catton's two volumes: *Grant Moves South* (Boston, 1960) and *Grant Takes Command* (Boston, 1969). William S. McFeely, *Grant: A Biography* (New York, 1981), is less enlightening on Grant's Civil War leadership. The general's activities can be followed in his own words in his superb *Personal Memoirs of U. S. Grant*, 2 vols. (New York, 1885); and in John Y. Simon, ed., *The Papers of Ulysses S. Grant*, 14 vols. (Carbondale, Ill., 1967–85). For important insights on Sherman, the best place to start is Basil H. Liddell Hart, *Sherman: Soldier, Realist, American* (New York, 1929), a shrewd analysis by a British army officer; and Sherman's own *Memoirs of W. T. Sherman*, 2 vols. (2nd ed., New York, 1887). For a fascinating modern analysis of Sherman's philosophy and practice of total war, see James Reston, Jr., *Sherman and Vietnam* (New York, 1985). Other memoirs by Civil War generals of interest for their intrinsic literary merits or their stance on controversial issues include: George B. McClellan, *McClellan's Own Story* (New York, 1886); Philip H. Sheridan, *Personal Memoirs of P. H. Sheridan*, 2 vols. (New York, 1888); Joseph E. Johnston, *Narrative of Military Operations . . . during the Late War between the States* (New York, 1874); James Longstreet, *From Manassas to Appomattox: Memoirs of the Civil War in America* (rev. ed., 1903); and Richard Taylor, *Destruction and Recon-*

struction: Personal Experiences of the Late War (New York, 1879).

Numerous historians have implicitly or explicitly addressed the question of why the North won the war—or alternatively, why the South lost. Five different answers were forthcoming in an anthology edited by David Donald, *Why the North Won the Civil War* (Baton Rouge, 1960). Herman Hattaway and Archer Jones cite superior northern management of logistical and other resources to explain in *How the North Won* (Urbana, Ill., 1983); a thesis anticipated by Benjamin P. Thomas and Harold M. Hyman, *Stanton: The Life and Times of Lincoln's Secretary of War* (New York, 1962). Grady McWhiney and Perry D. Jamieson, *Attack and Die: Civil War Military Tactics and the Southern Heritage* (University, Ala., 1982), attribute the South's offensive tactics, which bled Confederate armies to death, to cultural factors, while Michael C. C. Adams, *Our Masters the Rebels: A Speculation on Union Military Failure in the East, 1861–1865* (Cambridge, Mass., 1978), cites cultural factors to explain why Union armies almost lost the war in the Virginia theater before importing successful western commanders to apply their strategy in the East. Richard E. Beringer, Herman Hattaway, Archer Jones, and William N. Still, Jr., *Why the South Lost the Civil War* (Athens, Ga., 1986), are the most recent exponents of the loss of will thesis to explain Confederate defeat.

Although the existing scholarship on conscription in both South and North is not adequate, good places to begin to study this subject are: Albert B. Moore, *Conscription and Conflict in the Confederacy* (New York, 1924); and Eugene C. Murdock, *One Million Men: The Civil War Draft in the North* (Madison, 1971). There is a large literature on black soldiers in the war. The pioneering work is Dudley T. Cornish, *The Sable Arm: Negro Troops in the Union Army* (New York, 1956). Mary Frances Berry, *Military Necessity and Civil Rights Policy: Black Citizenship and the Constitution, 1861–1868* (Port Washington, N.Y., 1977), measures the impact of black military service on the enactment of postwar equal rights legislation. Robert Durden interweaves an account of the Confederate decision to arm blacks with illustrative documents, in *The Gray and the Black: The Confederate Debate on Emancipation* (Baton Rouge, 1972); while Ira Berlin et al., eds., *The Black Military Experience*, Series II of *Freedom: A Documentary History of Emancipation* (Cambridge, 1982) publishes a large number of documents from army records and provides excellent headnotes and introductions. Civil War prisons and the prisoner exchange question badly need a modern historian; William B. Hesseltine's *Civil War Prisons: A Study in War Psychology* (Columbus, Ohio, 1930) is the only comprehensive monograph, while Ovid L. Futch's *History of Andersonville Prison* (Gainesville, Fla., 1968) is the most dispassionate study of that impassioned subject.

Technological innovations produced to meet military needs during the war are the subjects of two studies full of fascinating information: Robert V. Bruce, *Lincoln and the Tools of War* (Indianapolis, 1956); and Milton F. Perry, *Infernal Machines: The Story of Confederate Submarine and Mine Warfare* (Baton Rouge, 1965). The role of railroads is the subject of: George E. Turner, *Victory Rode the Rails* (Indianapolis, 1953); Thomas Weber, *The Northern Railroads in the Civil War* (New York, 1952); and Robert C. Black, *The Railroads of the Confederacy* (Chapel Hill, 1952). Civil War medicine is treated by: Paul E. Steiner, *Disease in the Civil War* (Springfield, Ill., 1968); George W. Adams, *Doctors in Blue: The Medical History of the Union Army in the Civil War* (New York, 1952); and Horace H. Cunningham, *Doctors in Gray: The Confederate Medical Service* (Baton Rouge, 1958). For a basic history of the U. S. Sanitary Commission, see William Q. Maxwell, *Lincoln's Fifth Wheel: The Political History of the United States Sanitary Commission* (New York, 1956). Readers interested in a stimulating interpretation of the Sanitary Commission in the context of wartime transformations in northern attitudes toward other social and cultural issues should consult George M. Frederickson, *The Inner Civil War: Northern Intellectuals and the Crisis of the Union* (New York, 1965).

The foreign relations of both Union and Confederacy have attracted a great deal of scholarly attention; among the most useful studies are: David P. Crook, *The North, the South, and the Powers 1861–1865* (New York, 1974); Frank L. Owsley and Harriet C. Owsley, *King Cotton Diplomacy: Foreign Relations of the Confederate States of America* (2nd ed., Chicago, 1959); Ephraim D. Adams, *Great Britain and the American Civil War*, 2 vols. (New York, 1925); Brian Jenkins, *Britain and the War for the Union*, 2 vols. (Montreal, 1974–80); and Lynn M. Case and Warren F. Spencer, *The United States and France: Civil War Diplomacy* (Philadelphia, 1970).

A long-influential study of northern politics during the war was T. Harry Williams, *Lincoln and the Radicals*, (Madison, 1941), which stressed ideological conflict within the Republican party. For the now-accepted modification of this view, see Hans L. Trefousse, *The Radical*

Republicans: Lincoln's Vanguard for Racial Justice (New York, 1969), which emphasizes essential Republican agreement in the face of sharp differences with the Democrats. William B. Hesseltine, *Lincoln and the War Governors* (New York, 1948), shows the shift of power from states to the national government to meet the demands of war. Leonard P. Curry's *Blueprint for Modern America: Non-Military Legislation of the First Civil War Congress* (Nashville, 1968) is a careful study of legislation that supplemented the war's revolutionary impact in transforming the United States from a decentralized agrarian republic to an industrial nation. For a study of some of the leaders who helped accomplish this result, see Allan G. Bogue, *The Earnest Men: Republicans of the Civil War Senate* (Ithaca, 1981).

The opposition, loyal and otherwise, is analyzed by: Joel Silbey, *A Respectable Minority: The Democratic Party in the Civil War Era* (New York, 1977); Christopher Dell, *Lincoln and the War Democrats* (Madison, N.J., 1975); Wood Gray, *The Hidden Civil War: The Story of the Copperheads* (New York, 1942), which tends to indict the Peace Democrats as disloyal; and in three books by Frank L. Klement, who sometimes protests too much in his attempt to exonerate the copperheads from all such calumnies: *The Copperheads in the Middle West* (Chicago, 1960); *The Limits of Dissent: Clement L. Vallandigham and the Civil War* (Lexington, Ky., 1970); and *Dark Lanterns: Secret Political Societies, Conspiracies, and Treason Trials in the Civil War* (Baton Rouge, 1984). For military arrests and the suspension of the writ of habeas corpus to squelch anti-war opposition in the North, see: Dean Sprague, *Freedom under Lincoln* (Boston, 1965); James G. Randall, *Constitutional Problems under Lincoln* (rev. ed., Urbana, Ill., 1951); and Harold M. Hyman, *A More Perfect Union: The Impact of the Civil War and Reconstruction on the Constitution* (New York, 1973). The peace issue in 1864 is treated by Edward C. Kirkland, *The Peacemakers of 1864* (New York, 1927); while the in-fighting within the Republican party during the initial stages of the election campaign that year is chronicled by William F. Zornow, *Lincoln and the Party Divided* (Norman, Okla., 1954). The best single place to go for the history and historiography of Lincoln's assassination is William Hanchett, *The Lincoln Murder Conspiracies* (Urbana, 1983).

For the northern homefront, Emerson D. Fite's *Social and Economic Conditions in the North* (New York, 1910) is still valuable. It should be supplemented by George W. Smith and Charles Judah, eds., *Life in the North During the Civil War* (Albuquerque, 1966), which reprints numerous contemporary documents. Paul W. Gates, *Agriculture and the Civil War* (New York, 1965), deals with both North and South; while the essays in Ralph Andreano, ed., *The Economic Impact of the Civil War* (2nd ed., Cambridge, Mass., 1967) and in David Gilchrist and W. David Lewis, eds., *Economic Change in the Civil War Era* (Greenville, Del. 1965), focus mainly on the North; and Bray Hammond, *Sovereignty and an Empty Purse: Banks and Politics in the Civil War* (Princeton, 1970), covers only the North.

Two enlightening books on northern religion during the war are: James H. Moorhead, *American Apocalypse: Yankee Protestants and the Civil War* (New Haven, 1978); and Benjamin Blied, *Catholics and the Civil War* (Milwaukee, 1945). For the role of northern women both on the homefront and in military hospitals, see Mary Elizabeth Massey, *Bonnett Brigades* (New York, 1966); and Agatha Young, *Women and the Crisis: Women of the North in the Civil War* (New York, 1959). For northern labor, see David Montgomery, *Beyond Equality: Labor and the Radical Republicans, 1862–1872* (New York, 1967). The class and ethnic tensions that flared into the New York draft riots are analyzed in: Basil L. Lee, *Discontent in New York City, 1861–1865* (Washington, 1943); and Adrian Cook, *The Armies of the Streets: The New York City Draft Riots of 1863* (Lexington, Ky., 1974).

Southern politics during the war have received a great deal of attention. For general histories of the Confederacy, see the volumes by E. Merton Coulter and Emory Thomas cited earlier. Wilfred B. Yearns, *The Confederate Congress* (Athens, Ga., 1960), provides a narrative history of that institution; while Thomas B. Alexander and Richard E. Beringer's *The Anatomy of the Confederate Congress* (Nashville, 1972) offers a quantitative analysis. For the Confederate cabinet, see Rembert Patrick, *Jefferson Davis and His Cabinet* (Baton Rouge, 1944). Bell Irvin Wiley's *The Road to Appomattox* (Memphis, 1956) contains a caustic analysis of Jefferson Davis's leadership. Larry E. Nelson, *Bullets, Bayonets, and Rhetoric: Confederate Policy for the United States Presidential Contest of 1864* (University, Ala., 1980), documents Davis's attempt to undermine the Lincoln administration. Frank L. Owsley, *State Rights in the Confederacy* (Chicago, 1925), expresses the theme that the Confederacy died of state's rights; but May S. Ringold, *The Role of State Legislatures in the Confederacy* (Athens, Ga., 1966) and W. Buck Yearns, ed., *The Confederate Governors* (Athens, 1984), emphasize the positive role that most legislatures and governors played in the war effort. For the two states in which opposition to the Davis administration was strongest, see John G. Barrett, *The Civil War in North Carolina* (Chapel Hill, 1963); and T. Conn Bryan, *Confederate Georgia* (Athens, 1953). Robert L. Kerby, *Kirby Smith's Confederacy: The Trans-Mississippi, 1863–1865* (New York, 1972), studies a region that became semi-autonomous after the fall of Vicksburg.

Georgia Lee Tatum, *Disloyalty in the Confederacy* (New York, 1972), documents anti-war activity and unionism among disaffected whites, especially in the upcountry. Paul D. Escott, *After Secession: Jefferson Davis and the Failure of Southern Nationalism* (Baton Rouge, 1978), maintains that the greatest failure of Confederate leadership was its inability to sustain the support of non-slaveholders who increasingly saw the southern cause as a rich man's war and a poor man's fight. The theme of yeoman alienation and class tensions is also developed in: Philip S. Paludan, *Victims: A True History of the Civil War* (Knoxville, 1981); in several good articles published in recent years in the *North Carolina Historical Review* and the *Journal of Southern History*; and in many of the books on southern politics cited on pp. 868. A special category of unhappy southerners is treated in Mary Elizabeth Massey, *Refugee Life in the Confederacy* (Baton Rouge, 1964). Another group of "outsiders" is the subject of Ella Lonn, *Foreigners in the Confederacy* (Chapel Hill, 1940). The contribution of women to the southern war effort is documented by Francis B. Simkins and James W. Patton, *The Women of the Confederacy* (Richmond, 1936).

The basic study of the Confederate homefront is Charles W. Ramsdell, *Behind the Lines in the Southern Confederacy* (Baton Rouge, 1944). John C. Schwab, *The Confederate States . . . A Financial and Industrial History of the South during the Civil War* (New York, 1901), is the encyclopedic treatment of this subject, while Richard C. Todd, *Confederate Finance* (Athens, Ga., 1954), is more readable. Emory M. Thomas, *The Confederacy as a Revolutionary Experience* (Englewood Cliffs, 1971), treats the hot-house industrialization forced on the South by the war, while Louise B. Hill, *State Socialism in the Confederate States of America* (Charlottesville, 1936), documents the role of state and Confederate governments in this process. Ella Lonn, *Salt as a Factor in the Confederacy* (New York, 1933), and Mary Elizabeth Massey, *Ersatz in the Confederacy* (Columbia, S.C., 1952), document the efforts to cope with wartime shortages.

The drive to make emancipation a northern war aim is chronicled by James M. McPherson, *The Struggle for Equality: Abolitionists and the Negro in the Civil War and Reconstruction* (Princeton, 1964), which also focuses on abolitionist hopes for racial equality as a result of the war. The role of northern blacks in this effort is the subject of: Benjamin Quarles, *The Negro in the Civil War* (Boston, 1953); and James M. McPherson, *The Negro's Civil War* (New York, 1965), a collection of primary sources woven together by a narrative. The hostile responses of many northerners to emancipation are chronicled by: V. Jacque Voegeli, *Free But Not Equal: The Midwest and the Negro in the Civil War* (Chicago, 1967); and Forrest G. Wood, *Black Scare: The Racist Response to Emancipation and Reconstruction* (Berkeley, 1968). The attempts by Republicans to hammer out a reconstruction policy during the war are analyzed in three books by Herman Belz: *Reconstructing the Union: Theory and Policy during the Civil War* (Ithaca, 1969); *A New Birth of Freedom: The Republican Party and Freedmen's Rights, 1861–1866* (Westport, Conn., 1976); and *Emancipation and Equal Rights: Politics and Constitutionalism in the Civil War Era* (New York, 1978). Louisiana became a showcase of wartime reconstruction efforts and also a historiographical focus on that subject; see especially Peyton McCrary, *Abraham Lincoln and Reconstruction: The Louisiana Experiment* (Princeton, 1978); and LaWanda Cox, *Lincoln and Black Freedom: A Study in Presidential Leadership* (Columbia, S.C., 1981).

The pioneering study of the hard but exhilarating experiences of slaves and freedmen during the war is Bell Irvin Wiley, *Southern Negroes 1861–1865* (New Haven, 1938); the richest recent study is Leon F. Litwack, *Been in the Storm So Long: The Aftermath of Slavery* (New York, 1979). Ira Berlin and his team of editors have masterfully blended narrative and interpretation with illustrative documents in *The Destruction of Slavery*, Ser. I, Vol. I of *Freedom: A Documentary History of Emancipation* (Cambridge, Mass., 1985), which portrays vividly the process by which many slaves emancipated themselves by coming into Union lines and thereby forcing this issue on the army and government. The role of blacks and the process of emancipation have been the subject of monographs for several southern states: James H. Brewer, *The Confederate Negro: Virginia's Craftsmen and Military Laborers 1861–1865* (Durham, 1969); C. Peter Ripley, *Slaves and Freedmen in Civil War Louisiana* (Baton Rouge, 1978); William F. Messner, *Freedmen and the Ideology of Free Labor: Louisiana, 1862–1865* (Lafayette, La., 1978); John Cimprich, *Slavery's End in Tennessee, 1861–1865* (University, Ala., 1985); Clarence L. Mohr, *On the Threshold of Freedom: Masters and Slaves in Civil War Georgia* (Athens, 1986); Victor B. Howard, *Black Liberation in Kentucky: Emancipation and Freedom, 1862–1884* (Lexington, 1983); Charles L. Wagandt, *The Mighty Revolution: Negro Emancipation in Maryland, 1862–1864* (Baltimore, 1964), and Barbara Jeanne Fields, *Slavery and Freedom on the Middle Ground: Maryland during the Nineteenth Century* (New Haven, 1985). A superb local study with broad national implications is Willie Lee Rose, *Rehearsal for Reconstruction: The Port Royal Experiment* (Indianapolis, 1964). Many of the foregoing books include accounts of the Union army's and government's flawed administration of freedmen's affairs, which is the explicit focus of Louis S. Gerteis, *From Contraband to Freedman: Federal Policy Toward Southern Blacks 1861–1865* (Westport, Conn., 1973). The slaveholders' response to their loss of mastery is the theme of James L. Roark, *Masters without Slaves: Southern Planters in the Civil War and Reconstruction* (New York, 1977); while Lawrence N. Powell writes wryly of *New Masters: Northern Planters during the Civil War and Reconstruction* (New Haven, 1980).

Index

Abolition of slavery, *see* Emancipation of slaves; Thirteenth Amendment

Abolitionists, 54; and Second Great Awakening, 8, 31; women and, 35-36; on breakup of slave families, 37-39; resist fugitive slave law, 81-86; and issue of nonviolence, 202-4; and 1860 election, 221, 227-28; on slavery and the war, 312, 354-55, 358; growing influence of, 494-95; oppose colonization, 509. *See also* Antislavery movement

Adams, Charles Francis: and Free Soil party, 62; on Compromise of 1850, 76; and Know Nothings, 139; and 1860 election, 226, 233; in secession crisis, 256; minister to Britain, 388-89; on British attitudes toward war, 549; rebukes Palmerston, 552; on consequences of Antietam, 557; on consequences of Emancipation Proclamation, 567; Laird rams, 682

Adams, Charles Francis, Jr., 567, 585, 795

Adams, Henry: on settlement of *Trent* crisis, 391; on cotton famine, 548; fears British intervention, 555; on Emancipation Proclamation, 567; on Roebuck motion, 651; on Gettysburg and Vicksburg, 664; on Laird rams, 682

Adams, John Quincy, 62

African Labor Supply Association, 103

Alabama, C.S.S., 5, 315, 316, 547-48, 551, 682

American Missionary Association, 709

American party, 140; splits on slavery issue, 141; and Republicans, 143-44; in 1856, 153-54, 156-57, 162n; disappearance of, 188

"American system of manufactures," 15-19

"Anaconda Plan," 333-34, 335, 819

Anderson, "Bloody Bill," 292, 787, 788

Anderson, Robert: and Fort Sumter, 264-74; recruits Kentucky unionists, 295

Andersonville prison: notoriety of, 755, 791; conditions at, 796; mortality at, 796, 796-97n, 802; controversies about, 797-98, 801-2, 810

Andrew, John: and 1860 election, 227; sends regiments to Washington, 274, 286; and General Stone, 363; raises black regiments, 565

Anthony, Susan B., 785

Antietam, battle of, 538-44, 559, 569, 572; consequences of, 545, 556-57, 561, 858

Antislavery movement: origins of, 8, 88; and free soil sentiment in 1840s, 54-55; and Whig party, 86-87; and nativism, 137-38. *See also* Abolitionists; Free Soil party; Republican party

Appomattox Courthouse: Lee's surrender at, 684, 848-50; northern celebration of, 850-51

Arkansas, C.S.S., 421-22

Armistead, Lewis A., 662

Army, Confederate: number of men in, 306-7n; organization and mobilization of, 316-21, 330-31n; election of officers, 327-28; political generals, 328; discipline and training, 329-31; strategy, 336-38; tactics, 472-

888

Grant, Ulysses (*continued*)
  718; on substitutes and bounty men, 720;
  strategic plans for 1864, 721-22, 724; battle
  of the Wilderness, 725-26; of Spotsylvania,
  728-33; Cold Harbor asault, 734-37, 812;
  move to Petersburg, 739-41; criticism of for
  heavy casualties, 742, 759; defended by Lincoln, 743; Petersburg siege, 751, 756, 777,
  778, 811, 826, 830; and Early's Washington
  raid, 757; sends Sheridan to the Valley, 758;
  battle of the Crater, 759-60; anger at southern violations of prisoner paroles, 792; and
  breakdown of prisoner exchanges, 793, 799-
  80; on McClellan's candidacy, 803; on soldier vote, 804; on Sherman's march to the
  sea, 807-8; prods Thomas at Nashville, 813;
  and Benjamin Butler, 820; and Hampton
  Roads peace conference, 822; plans Alabama campaigns, 825; breakthrough at Petersburg, 844-45, 846; and Lee's surrender,
  848-50; weeps for Lincoln, 853
Greeley, Horace, 13, 42, 138, 224, 821; on
  territorial aquisition, 49; on slavery, 96; and
  temperance, 135; and Lecompton, 167; on
  tariff, 192; on John Brown, 210; and 1860
  election, 217, 227; on secession, 251-52;
  "Forward to Richmond" editorials, 334; on
  1st Bull Run, 347, 348; on military arrests,
  436; and emancipation, 505; Lincoln's letter
  to, 510, 859; target of draft rioters, 610;
  "peace negotiations" in 1864, 762, 766-68
Greenhow, Rose O'Neal, 340, 434n
Gregg, William, 94, 96, 97
Grier, Robert, 172, 173, 179
Grierson, Benjamin, and Grierson's raid, 628
Grow, Galusha, 168, 496
Guadalupe Hidalgo, Treaty of, 3-4, 50
Guerrillas and guerrilla warfare, 307; in Mis-
  souri, 292, 783-88; in West Virginia, 303;
  in Virginia, 501; in Tennessee, 513, 515;
  Mosby and, 737-38; and Sheridan's Valley
  campaign, 778-79

Habeas corpus, writ of: in Union: Lincoln's
  suspension of, 287-90, 433-34, 436, 560; in
  Confederacy, suspended, 429, 433-35, 697,
  693; and military arrests in 1862, 493-94;
  issue exploited by Democrats, 592, 597,
  598-99, 716
Hahn, Michael, 707-8
Hale, John P., 67n
Halleck, Henry W., 826; commander of western
  department, 313, 367, 394, 498; on political
  generals, 328; military scholar, 331, 394;
  and attack on Fort Henry, 395; and Fort
  Donelson, 397, 402, 406; Corinth campaign, 415-17, 488; named general in chief,

488, 502, 524; western strategy after Corinth, 511-13; prods Buell, 518-19, 522; and
  McClellan, 525; and 2nd Bull Run, 528;
  Antietam campaign, 536; on emancipation,
  559; prods McClellan, 568; McClellan wants
  removed, 569; and pontoons at Fredericks-
  burg, 570; and McClernand, 577; and Grant's
  "Jew order," 622-23; and Vicksburg cam-
  paign, 633; prods and reinforces Rosecrans,
  670, 675; becomes chief of staff, 718; and
  removal of Sigel, 724; and the Crater, 760;
  Sherman's march to the sea, 808
Halstead, Murat, 214
Hamilton, Alexander, 433
Hamlin, Hannibal, 220, 574, 717
Hammond, James H.: sectional champion, 57;
  and rural values, 98; on Lecompton, 166;
  King Cotton and mudsill speech, 196, 383
Hammond, William, 482, 483, 484
Hampton, Wade, 318, 341-42, 739, 828
Hampton Roads peace conference, 822-24, 838,
  851
Hancock, Winfield Scott: in Mexican War, 5;
  at Gettysburg, 655, 660, 663; at Spotsyl-
  vania, 728-30; at Cold Harbor, 735; on Pe-
  tersburg front, 759
Hardee, William J., 583, 828, 829
Harper's Ferry: John Brown raid, 201-6; Virginia
  militia seizes, 279, 319; capture of by Jack-
  son in 1862, 536-38, 544
Harrison, William Henry, 218
Hartford, U.S.S., Farragut's flagship, 420; at
  Mobile Bay, 761
Hatteras Inlet, Union capture of, 370, 372, 376
Haupt, Herman, 527, 532
Hawthorne, Nathaniel, 36
Hay, John, 675, 766
Helper, Hinton Rowan, 199-200, 242
Henry, Judith, 341
Heroes of America,, 613, 695-96, 698
Hickok, "Wild Bill," 404
Hicks, Thomas, 285, 287
Higginson, Thomas Wentworth: attempted res-
  cue of Burns, 119-20; and John Brown, 204,
  207-8; commands black regiment, 564-65
Hill, Ambrose Powell, 276; and Seven Days'
  battles, 464, 466-67, 469; Cedar Mountain,
  525-26; at Antietam, 544; gains corps com-
  mand, 648; at Gettysburg, 653-54, 656-57,
  661; breaks down in Wilderness campaign,
  734
Hill, Benjamin H., 229
Hill, Daniel Harvey, 276; and Malvern Hill,
  470; on Gaines' Mill, 476; battle of South
  Mountain, 537; and Antietam, 541
Hindman, Thomas C., 668
Hines, Thomas C., 763-64, 765
Holcome, James, 766-67